GENDER, RACE, AND CLASS IN MEDIA

EDITION

3

GENDER, RACE, AND CLASS IN MEDIA

A CRITICAL READER

EDITION

3

EDITORS

GAIL DINES
Wheelock College

JEAN M. HUMEZ
University of Massachusetts, Boston

$SAGE

Los Angeles | London | New Delhi
Singapore | Washington DC

For information:

 SAGE Publications, Inc.
2455 Teller Road
Thousand Oaks, California 91320
E-mail: order@sagepub.com

SAGE Publications Ltd.
1 Oliver's Yard
55 City Road
London EC1Y 1SP
United Kingdom

SAGE Publications India Pvt. Ltd.
B 1/I 1 Mohan Cooperative Industrial Area
Mathura Road, New Delhi 110 044
India

SAGE Publications Asia-Pacific Pte. Ltd.
33 Pekin Street #02-01
Far East Square
Singapore 048763

Printed in the United States of America

Library of Congress Cataloging-in-Publication Data

Dines, Gail.
Gender, race, and class in media: a critical reader/Editors, Gail Dines, Jean M. Humez. — 3rd ed.
     p. cm.
Includes bibliographical references and index.
ISBN 978-1-4129-7441-7 (pbk.)
    1. Mass media and culture—United States. 2. Mass media and sex—United States. 3. Mass media and race relations—United States. 4. Social classes in mass media. 5. Mass media—Social aspects—United States. 6. Popular culture—United States. 7. United States—Social conditions—1980- I. Humez, Jean McMahon, 1944- II. Title.

P94.65.U6G46 2011
302.230973—dc22   2010037257

This book is printed on acid-free paper.

10   11   12   13   14   10   9   8   7   6   5   4   3   2   1

Executive Editor:	Diane McDaniel
Associate Editor:	Leah Mori
Editorial Assistant:	Nathan Davidson
Production Editor:	Astrid Virding
Copy Editor:	Gillian Dickens
Permissions Editor:	Karen Ehrmann
Typesetter:	C&M Digitals (P) Ltd.
Proofreaders:	Scott Oney, Dennis Webb
Indexer:	Jean Casalegno
Cover Designer:	Janet Kiesel
Marketing Manager:	Helen Salmon

CONTENTS

PREFACE TO THE THIRD EDITION

In this new edition of *Gender, Race, and Class in Media*, our overall goal remains the same as in previous editions: to introduce undergraduate students to some of the richness, sophistication, and diversity that characterize contemporary media scholarship, in a way that is accessible and builds on students' own media experiences and interests. We intend to help demystify the nature of mass media entertainment culture and new media by examining their production, analyzing the texts of some of the most pervasive forms or genres, and exploring the processes by which audiences make meaning out of media imagery or texts—meaning that helps shape our personal, social, and political worlds. We start from the position that as social beings, we construct our realities out of the cultural norms and values that are dominant in our society, and the mass media are among the most important reproducers of such norms and values.

We have designed this as a volume to help teachers (a) introduce the most powerful theoretical concepts in contemporary media studies, (b) explore some of the most influential and interesting forms of contemporary media culture, and (c) focus on issues of gender and sexuality, race and class from a critical perspective. Most of the readings in this book take an explicitly critical or progressive political perspective. We have chosen readings that make the following assumptions, as we do: (a) that industrialized and high-tech societies are stratified along lines of gender and sexuality, race and class; (b) that everyone living in such a society "has" gender and sexuality, race and class, and other aspects of social identity that help structure our experience; and (c) that economic and other resources, advantages, and privileges are distributed inequitably in part because of power dynamics involving these categories of experience (as well as others such as age, ethnicity, ability, or disability). Our selection of material has been guided by our belief that an important goal of a critical education is to enable people to conceptualize social justice clearly and to work toward it more effectively. For us, greater social justice would mean beginning with a fairer distribution of our society's cultural and economic resources.

Our book is situated within both media studies and **cultural studies.** When we started working on the first edition of *Gender, Race, and Class in Media* in the early 1990s, cultural studies was a relatively new academic field in the United States, although it had been popular for some time in England (where it originated at Birmingham University). The cultural studies approach has now been dominant in U.S. media studies for almost a generation. Several other interdisciplinary fields concerned with social issues and representation, such as American studies and women's studies, have been heavily influenced by cultural studies.

Cultural studies is actually a **multidisciplinary** field, drawing from history, literary studies, philosophy, sociology, and psychology. Because of its progressive politics and because it offers a much broader and apparently more democratic definition of culture than was used in humanistic studies such as literary criticism in the past, many scholars and students who are particularly interested in race, gender, and class have been attracted under its umbrella. (For a more extended discussion of the development of multiculturalism and cultural studies in the last decades of the 20th century, see Douglas Kellner's lead chapter in Part I.)

In this third edition, we continue to emphasize, with Kellner, three separable but interconnected areas of analysis: political economy, textual analysis, and audience reception. For Kellner, it is crucial to link all three in order to provide a full understanding of the entire media culture communication process, from production through consumption. Indeed, one of the initial goals of cultural studies was to contextualize the media text within the wider society that informs its production, construction, and consumption.

Traditionally, **political economy** looks at the ways in which texts are produced within a society marked by class, gender, and racial inequality. Questions such as who owns and controls the media, who makes the decisions about content, how financing affects the range of texts produced, and the ways in which the profit motive drives production are central to an understanding of what eventually gets produced and circulated in the mainstream commercial mass media industries. With the advent of new media technologies that enable consumers to produce and widely distribute their own content, however, we must broaden our view of production, as do many of the chapters chosen for this edition of our book.

Textual analysis provides us with strong insights into how cultural texts—from TV sitcoms, dramas, or reality shows to fan-produced music videos—are structured and how to analyze their ideological significance since media representations are never just simple mirrors or "reflections of reality." (And despite the name, so-called reality TV is, of course, still a highly artificial construct.) Traditional audience research in media studies focuses on exploring ethnographically how actual audiences—as opposed to critics—interpret, make sense of, understand, and use media texts. Clearly, gender, race, ethnicity, class, sexuality, political beliefs, and age are important factors to take into account when exploring what particular audiences may take away from an advertisement, movie, sitcom, and so on. In more recent scholarship on audiences, the focus is increasingly on how fans both consume and produce meanings, in ways often quite different from those intended by the original text producers. However we conceptualize the audience, it is still important to study all three components of media representations, production, text, and consumption to understand how such texts can and do strengthen—or perhaps undermine in some ways—our dominant systems of gender, race, and class inequality.

In this third edition, we have maintained our thematic focus on gender (including sexuality), race, and class since we believe that media studies need to address the issues of social inequality that continue to plague our society and undermine its democratic potential. Some of the chapters in this book employ an *intersectional analysis*, that is, one that complicates each of these social categories by examining how they interact with one another. Whenever possible, we have selected chapters that give voice to the multiple levels of analysis needed to make media studies a truly **multicultural** endeavor. We acknowledge the ever-intensifying interrelationships among media cultures globally, while continuing to focus primarily on the North American examples of media texts that we see as most likely to be familiar to instructors and students working with this book.

For teachers who may have used an earlier edition, it will be obvious that we have replaced many older selections with newer chapters that better reflect the shifts in media content, production, distribution, and consumption that have been seen over the first decade of the 21st century. Chief among these shifts is the seismic impact of Internet and new digital media technologies on the media landscape. It is hard to overstate how radical has been the change brought about by the sudden and massive adoption of these technologies to the ways vast numbers of people communicate, do business, buy products, entertain themselves, form and sustain virtual communities, link with like-minded people, and potentially organize politically.

For the third edition, we again located, read, and discussed many new journal articles and book chapters. We consulted with colleagues who teach media courses and spoke to students to see what they found compelling. More than three quarters of the readings (49 chapters) in this edition are new. This reflects both the rapid evolution of the field and our desire to provide analysis of relatively recent current and media texts that would be familiar to students. The eight "classic" articles we reprint from earlier editions of this book were key to highly significant developments in the field, and they still offer important and clearly articulated historical and theoretical insights into media analysis. We also include two new and six updated original commissioned essays.

We've grouped our selections into thematic sections that both highlight some of the important changes that have taken place in the worlds of entertainment mass media and new media over the past several years and also reflect our experience of student interest. In this edition, we have added an index of chapter topics, which will allow instructors to create alternative groupings of readings to suit their own course design. We hope that instructors and students will find the themes and genres represented in this collection provocative, stimulating, and an invitation to further thinking, research, and perhaps even media activism.

In condensing longer journal articles and book chapters, we have aimed at preserving the central arguments and retaining challenging ideas, while making the often difficult analytical language of cultural studies scholarship as accessible as possible for undergraduates. (Please see the "Glossary" [pp. 623–631] for fuller explanations of specialized media studies vocabulary.)[1] Our brief introductory essays to each section highlight key concepts and interesting connections among the readings in that section.

Finally, we have provided some suggestions of supplementary resources for the teacher, as well as a selective list of the many media activist organizations easily located on the Internet for those who, inspired by the egalitarian ideals espoused by many of the writers in this collection, would like to explore this kind of grassroots consumer and citizens' activism on behalf of a more democratic media culture in the future.

---

[1]Bold terms in text are defined in the Glossary section.

ANCILLARY MATERIAL

www.sagepub.com/dines3estudy

The web-based study site includes the following 13 chapters that were included in the Second Edition of *Gender, Race, and Class in Media: A Critical Reader*:

- "The New Media Giants: Changing Industry Structure" by David Croteau and William Hoynes
- "Popular Culture and Queer Representation: A Critical Perspective" by Diane Raymond
- "Who(se) Am I? The Identity and Image of Women in Hip-Hop" by Imani Perry
- "Space Jam: Media Conglomerates Build the Entertainment City" by Susan G. Davis
- " 'Con-fusing' Exotica: Producing India in U.S. Advertising" by Sanjukta Ghosh
- "Advertising and People of Color" by Clint C. Wilson II and Félix Gutiérrez
- "Television Violence: At a Time of Turmoil and Terror" by George Gerbner
- "Pornography and the Limits of Experimental Research" by Robert Jensen
- "King Kong and the White Women: Hustler Magazine and the Demonization of Black Masculinity" by Gail Dines
- " 'I Think of Them as Friends': Interpersonal Relationships in the Online Community" by Nancy K. Baym
- "In Their Prime: Women in Nighttime Drama" by Karen Lindsey
- "Ling Woo in Historical Context: The New Face of Asian American Stereotypes on Television" by Chyng Feng Sun
- "Dating on the Net: Teens and the Rise of 'Pure' Relationships" by Lynn Schofield Clark

ACKNOWLEDGMENTS

W e would like to thank the many colleagues and students who have contributed over the years to our thinking about the questions raised in this book. They are too many to be mentioned individually, but they include faculty and students at the University of Massachusetts Boston and Wheelock College, as well as colleagues and associates with whom we have worked in multiple other locations.

We appreciate all of the writers whose essays and articles have been included in the three editions, for their original insights and willingness to allow us to shorten their texts.

We heartily thank the reference librarians at our home institutions for all of their professional help as we did the literature searches for all three editions.

We gratefully acknowledge the acquisitions and production staff at Sage Publications for their belief in the book and their careful work in bringing it into print.

We are indebted to the external reviewers of all three editions of the book, and most recently to the reviewers of this edition: Akil Houston (Ohio University), Christine Scodari (Florida Atlantic University), Amy Nyberg (Seton Hall University), Laura Hahn (Humboldt State University), Barbara Gottfried (Boston University), Eleanor Hubbard (University of Colorado at Boulder), and Joe Rumbo (James Madison University).

And we salute the members of our families who provided much-needed moral support as we pursued our editorial labors.

PART I

A CULTURAL STUDIES APPROACH TO MEDIA

Theory

In this book, we offer a selection of critical discussions of mass media entertainment culture and **new media** to exemplify a powerful method of analysis that you will be able to apply on your own to other examples. In this way, we hope to promote and support *critical media literacy.* While there are many ways to think about media literacy, for the purposes of this book, we argue that in a postindustrial society in which public regulation of a for-profit media system is very weak, media literacy can be one tool to help limit the discursive power of media in our lives. While a high level of media literacy cannot replace other efforts to democratize our society's economic and cultural resources, in our view, it does give audiences the skills necessary for analyzing and questioning the ideologies that often work at a subtextual level within media texts.

We begin with media theory because we think students will find it useful to have a good grasp of several central concepts illustrated in an introductory way here, before going on to tackle later readings in which an understanding of these concepts is often presumed. In the media theory section, we highlight especially the central concepts and terms of the field of cultural studies as applied to mass media. As in all the other sections in this book, there are many ways in which the collected articles and essays in this section are in dialogue with one another. In these opening comments, we give only one possible reading of the ways in which their main themes connect.

We open with "Cultural Studies, Multiculturalism, and Media Culture," by Douglas Kellner (I.1). This sets out the three-part approach to cultural studies (political economy/production, textual analysis, and audience reception/consumption) that characterizes this field. With Professor Kellner, we believe that to understand fully a media product such as a TV show or advertising image or online digital game, one ideally needs to be able to understand the socioeconomic context in which it is created (political economy/production), analyze its constructed meaning(s) through careful attention to its particular visual/verbal/auditory languages or **codes** (textual analysis), and determine through ethnographic research what its real-world audiences contribute to the meaning-making process and even to the production and distribution of cultural products (audience consumption/production). In addition, Kellner points to the importance of better integrating considerations of **gender, race,** and **class** as categories of social analysis in cultural studies work in the future.

We begin with political economy because, above all, commercial entertainment is a profit-oriented business, largely controlled by giant corporations. According to media scholars David Croteau and William Hoynes (2006), media industries have changed dramatically along four dimensions over the past three decades:

1. *Growth.* Mergers and buyouts have made media corporations bigger than ever.

2. *Integration.* The new media giants have integrated either horizontally by moving into multiple forms of media, such as film, publishing, and radio, or vertically by owning different stages of production and distribution or both.

3. *Globalization.* To varying degrees, the major media conglomerates have become global entities, marketing their wares worldwide.

4. *Concentration of ownership.* As major players acquire more media holdings, the ownership of mainstream media has become increasingly concentrated (Croteau & Hoynes, 2006, 77).

This section of the book appropriately includes a chapter on media ownership by Dwayne Winseck (I.2), which can draw our attention at the outset to what is at stake when our national and international cultural production is so largely controlled by a few profit-oriented corporations. As he shows, even though in recent decades, new media outlets such as cable and satellite TV channels as well as the growth of the Internet have allowed for "a wider range of media available to a greater number of people than in the past" (p. 19), there is still ample cause to be concerned about media concentration, especially if we are concerned about increasing limitation on the number of voices and opinions we may be exposed to. Mega-media conglomerates still dominate much of the media culture produced for mass audiences, and Winseck's analysis shows that "source diversity is shrinking." He offers a list of reasons why, as citizens as well as media culture consumers, we need to be concerned with media ownership and concentration, concluding that the issue is "critical . . . with not only concerns of bias and the abuse of personalized power at stake, but the future of media evolution and potential of democracy itself" (p. 23).

In "The Meaning of Memory" (I.3), an important historical background piece that sheds light on how and why corporations came to so heavily dominate media culture in the United States, George Lipsitz shows how the needs of the national economy in the post–World War II period facilitated the development of mass television production. He explores how the increase in the sale of televisions and the development of a group of situation comedies were used to transform a traditional, ethnic immigrant ideology that stressed values of community, thrift, and commitment to labor unions into an American Dream ideology that stressed individualism, consumerism, and suburban domesticity—values consistent with the needs of the expanding postwar capitalist economy.

James Lull (I.4) also focuses on the relationship between **capitalism** and **ideology** by discussing the neo-**Marxist** theory of **hegemony** developed by theorists such as Antonio Gramsci, Louis Althusser, and Stuart Hall, three thinkers who helped lay the foundation for critical cultural studies. Drawing on these theorists, Lull defines *hegemony* as "the power or dominance that one social group holds over others." As Lull points out,

> Owners and managers of media industries can produce and reproduce the content, inflections, and tones of ideas favorable to them far more easily than other social groups because they manage key socializing institutions, thereby guaranteeing that their points of view are constantly and attractively cast into the public arena. (p. 34)

This point is made explicit in Gareth Palmer's chapter (I.5) on the reality show *Extreme Makeover: Home Edition*. Palmer argues that this is one of a number of TV programs that are "becoming active elements, working practically and ideologically to change the world." This show, in which individual homeowners are assisted in their quest for a dream home by neighbors and businesses, is likened to a fairy tale with a happily-ever-after ending. According to Palmer's analysis, this television text tries to render invisible what he calls "the massive cracks in the American Dream." It does this by encoding the idea that government assistance no longer has any significant role to play in improving the lives of its citizens, a neoliberal theme that is also apparent in other media entertainment discussed in this book.

Although the hegemonic ideology of **neoliberalism** is expressed in a large number of contemporary texts, it is important to remind ourselves that it is not a completely dominant perspective throughout mass media. As cultural studies scholars often emphasize, drawing upon the complex concept of power famously articulated by Michel Foucault, competing voices and alternative perspectives always arise to contest the hegemonic formulations in an ongoing and decentralized struggle for superiority. Thus, even in a socially conservative time and place, there is always some space for more progressive (democratic) ideologies to be expressed.

Textual analysis of the ideological dimension in media entertainment, such as that provided by Palmer, is an important dimension of understanding how the text works, especially when linked with background knowledge about the producers' political and economic interests. However, there is still another element that students of media culture need to take into account. Irrespective of whether the media text appears to encode dominant or subversive cultural ideas, Kellner reminds us that as students of media culture, we cannot simply assume that we know how consumers of media texts actually read or **decode** them (constructing meaning from texts for themselves). For that piece of the equation, we must turn to studies of *reception*—how audiences consume media texts.

There is wide agreement among scholars that consumers of the media should not be conceptualized as mere passive pawns of media imagery, completely controlled by the dominant culture, but there are several different ways of understanding the activity of the audience. First, according to the influential concept of **oppositional readings,** initiated by Stuart Hall (also discussed by Kellner in I.1), the meaning of media texts cannot simply be established by one critic's decoding of the text—no matter how subtle and full—because all texts are to some degree "open" (**polysemic,** or capable of multiple meanings). Therefore, we must also seek to know how audiences, both as individuals and as members of various communities, bring different experiences and complex identities to the processes of reading/viewing by which they actually feel, think about, and come to understand these texts. According to Hall's paradigm, readers or audience members may do one of three things in relation to the intended or **preferred** meanings encoded in the text: (1) accept them uncritically and read the text as its producers intended, (2) produce a **negotiated reading** (partially resisting the encoded meaning), or (3) create an oppositional reading of their own, completely rejecting the preferred meaning of the text.

Janice Radway's classic ethnographic research into the audience reception of romance novels was an early and influential study of how specific readers actually engage with a mass media text. In "Women Read the Romance" (I.6), Radway looked closely at how a group of White lower income women in the 1970s and 1980s negotiated with the genre of the romance novel, in terms of both the books they selected and the ways they actually read the text and appropriated and changed its meanings. Radway acknowledges that "romance reading . . . can function as a kind of training for the all-too-common task of reinterpreting a spouse's unsettling actions as the signs of passion, devotion, and love" (p. 52). Yet she sees, in these women's selection of certain books as favorites and their rejection of others, an active tendency to critique certain **patriarchal** masculine behaviors, substituting an ideal of the "nurturing" male that might have been missing in their own family lives. Through the act of reading itself, she argued, this group of women romance readers escaped temporarily from familial demands on their time, and Radway interprets this action as potential **resistance** to or refusal to accept completely the patriarchal restrictions of their lives. While encouraging respect for women's own experiences as cultural consumers, however, Radway warns that we should not confuse modes of resistance that reside in textual consumption (and therefore consciousness

alone) with more practical, real-world modes of resistance (such as organized protest against the patriarchal abuses women like these met in real life).

Radway's work helped establish the field of audience studies, which has since developed into a rich body of research and interpretation. At the same time, over the past two decades or so, a distinct subfield of audience study has emerged, devoted to one particularly active kind of text consumer, the **fan**. In an early and very influential essay, "*Star Trek* Rerun, Reread, Rewritten: Fan Writing as Textual Poaching" (I.7), Henry Jenkins drew our attention to "a largely unexplored terrain of cultural activity, a subterranean network of readers and writers who remake [media texts] in their own image." For Jenkins and many who have been influenced by his work,

> "Fandom" is a vehicle for marginalized subterranean groups (women, the young, gays, etc.) to pry open space for their cultural concerns within dominant representations; it is a way of appropriating media texts and rereading them in a fashion that serves different interests, a way of transforming mass culture into a popular culture. (p. 58)

Drawing on his studies of fans organized around their mutual appreciation of the long-running television series centered on space exploration by a team of diverse characters, Jenkins brought to light a fascinating body of fan fiction written for the most part by female fans, whom he conceptualized as

> reluctant poachers who steal only those things that they truly love, who seize televisual property only to protect it against abuse by those who have created it and who have claimed ownership over it. In embracing popular texts, the fans claim those works as their own, remaking them in their own image. . . . Consumption becomes production; reading becomes writing; spectator culture becomes participatory culture. (p. 64)

Following Jenkins's lead, contemporary fandom studies foreground the **agency** and creativity of culture consumers who go on to produce their own cultural materials, often through such "poaching" of ideas and materials from the original mass-produced texts. New digital technologies have clearly added to the opportunities available to do-it-yourself cultural producers outside the commercial world of the media industries, including fans. Moreover, some fans have taken advantage of social networking programs on the Internet to facilitate not only their own fan networking but also a more politicized fan activism to protect favorite mass media culture texts from fates such as cancellation. (See Part VIII for examples of these kinds of fan activity and fan activism.)

Some critical media theorists have warned (as Kellner does) of the dangers of overemphasizing the power of media audiences to resist or effectively challenge the dominant ideologies that normalize social and economic inequities, simply through their activities as consumers—even if they become activist fans. We would agree that broader political efforts are still necessary to pressure mainstream producers and owners to create and distribute different kinds of representations. Certainly, achieving a more democratic system of media ownership and access will require a very high and sustained level of citizen activism—including working to change public media policies favoring corporate control, such as the deregulation of broadcast media. Still, for those interested in the relationship of media to cultural democracy, active audiences and media activism are welcome exercises of media consumer power.

Reference

Croteau, D., & Hoynes, W. (2006). *The business of media: Corporate media and the public interest*. Thousand Oaks, CA: Sage.

Cultural Studies, Multiculturalism, and Media Culture

Douglas Kellner

Radio, television, film, and the other products of media culture provide materials out of which we forge our very identities; our sense of selfhood; our notion of what it means to be male or female; our sense of class, of ethnicity and race, of nationality, of sexuality; and of "us" and "them." Media images help shape our view of the world and our deepest values: what we consider good or bad, positive or negative, moral or evil. Media stories provide the symbols, myths, and resources through which we constitute a common culture and through the appropriation of which we insert ourselves into this culture. Media spectacles demonstrate who has power and who is powerless, who is allowed to exercise force and violence, and who is not. They dramatize and legitimate the power of the forces that be and show the powerless that they must stay in their places or be oppressed.

We are immersed from cradle to grave in a media and consumer society, and thus it is important to learn how to understand, interpret, and criticize its meanings and messages. The media are a profound and often misperceived source of cultural pedagogy: They contribute to educating us how to behave and what to think, feel, believe, fear, and desire—and what not to. The media are forms of pedagogy that teach us how to be men and women. They show us how to dress, look, and consume; how to react to members of different social groups; how to be popular and successful and how to avoid failure; and how to conform to the dominant system of norms, values, practices, and institutions. Consequently, the gaining of critical media literacy is an important resource for individuals and citizens in learning how to cope with a seductive cultural environment. Learning how to read, criticize, and resist sociocultural manipulation can help one empower oneself in relation to dominant forms of media and culture. It can enhance individual sovereignty vis-à-vis media culture and give people more power over their cultural environment.

In this chapter, I will discuss the potential contributions of a cultural studies perspective to media critique and literacy. In recent years, cultural studies has emerged as a set of approaches to the study of culture and society. The project was inaugurated by the University of Birmingham Centre for Contemporary Cultural Studies, which developed a variety of critical methods for the analysis, interpretation, and criticism of cultural artifacts. Through a set of internal debates, and responding to social struggles and movements of the 1960s and the

1970s, the Birmingham group came to focus on the interplay of representations and ideologies of class, gender, race, ethnicity, and nationality in cultural texts, including media culture. They were among the first to study the effects of newspapers, radio, television, film, and other popular cultural forms on audiences. They also focused on how various audiences interpreted and used media culture differently, analyzing the factors that made different audiences respond in contrasting ways to various media texts.[1]

Through studies of youth subcultures, British cultural studies demonstrated how culture came to constitute distinct forms of identity and group membership. For cultural studies, media culture provides the materials for constructing views of the world, behavior, and even identities. Those who uncritically follow the dictates of media culture tend to "mainstream" themselves, conforming to the dominant fashion, values, and behavior. Yet cultural studies is also interested in how subcultural groups and individuals resist dominant forms of culture and identity, creating their own style and identities. Those who obey ruling dress and fashion codes, behavior, and political ideologies thus produce their identities within the mainstream group, as members of specific social groupings (such as White, middle-class conservative Americans). Persons who identify with subcultures, like punk culture or Black nationalist subcultures, look and act differently from those in the mainstream and thus create oppositional identities, defining themselves against standard models.

Cultural studies insists that culture must be studied within the social relations and system through which culture is produced and consumed and that thus study of culture is intimately bound up with the study of society, politics, and economics. Cultural studies shows how media culture articulates the dominant values, political ideologies, and social developments and novelties of the era. It conceives of U.S. culture and society as a contested terrain with various groups and ideologies struggling for dominance (Kellner, 1995, 2010). Television,

film, music, and other popular cultural forms are thus often liberal or conservative or occasionally express more radical or oppositional views.

Cultural studies is valuable because it provides some tools that enable one to read and interpret one's culture critically. It also subverts distinctions between "high" and "low" culture by considering a wide continuum of cultural artifacts ranging from novels to television and by refusing to erect any specific cultural hierarchies or canons. Previous approaches to culture tended to be primarily literary and elitist, dismissing media culture as banal, trashy, and not worthy of serious attention. The project of cultural studies, by contrast, avoids cutting the field of culture into high and low, or popular against elite. Such distinctions are difficult to maintain and generally serve as a front for normative aesthetic valuations and, often, a political program (i.e., either dismissing mass culture for high culture or celebrating what is deemed "popular" while scorning "elitist" high culture).

Cultural studies allows us to examine and critically scrutinize the whole range of culture without prior prejudices toward one or another sort of cultural text, institution, or practice. It also opens the way toward more differentiated political, rather than aesthetic, valuations of cultural artifacts in which one attempts to distinguish critical and oppositional from conformist and conservative moments in a cultural artifact. For instance, studies of Hollywood film show how key 1960s films promoted the views of radicals and the counterculture and how film in the 1970s was a battleground between liberal and conservative positions; late 1970s films, however, tended toward conservative positions that helped elect Ronald Reagan as president (see Kellner & Ryan, 1988). During the Bush-Cheney era, there were many oppositional films such as the work of Michael Moore and liberal films that anticipated the election of Barack Obama (Kellner, 2010).

There is an intrinsically critical and political dimension to the project of cultural studies that distinguishes it from objectivist and apolitical academic approaches to the study of culture and society. British cultural studies, for example, analyzed culture historically in the context of its societal origins and effects. It situated culture within a theory of social production and reproduction, specifying the ways that cultural forms served either to further social domination or to enable people to resist and struggle against domination. It analyzed society as a hierarchical and antagonistic set of social relations characterized by the oppression of subordinate class, gender, race, ethnic, and national strata. Employing Gramsci's model of hegemony and counterhegemony, it sought to analyze "hegemonic," or ruling, social and cultural forces of domination and to seek "counterhegemonic" forces of resistance and struggle. The project was aimed at social transformation and attempted to specify forces of domination and resistance in order to aid the process of political struggle and emancipation from oppression and domination.

For cultural studies, the concept of ideology is of central importance, for dominant ideologies serve to reproduce social relations of domination and subordination.[2] Ideologies of class, for instance, celebrate upper-class life and denigrate the working class. Ideologies of gender promote sexist representations of women, oppressive ideologies of sexuality promote homophobia, and ideologies of race use racist representations of people of color and various minority groups. Ideologies make inequalities and subordination appear natural and just and thus induce consent to relations of domination. Contemporary societies are structured by opposing groups who have different political ideologies (liberal, conservative, radical, etc.), and cultural studies specifies what, if any, ideologies are operative in a given cultural artifact (which could involve, of course, the specification of ambiguities and ideological contradictions). In the course of this study, I will provide some examples of how different ideologies are operative in media cultural texts and will accordingly provide examples of ideological analysis and critique.

Because of its focus on representations of race, gender, sexuality, and class and its critique of ideologies that promote various forms of oppression, cultural studies lends itself to a multiculturalist program that demonstrates how culture reproduces certain forms of racism, sexism, and biases against members of subordinate classes, social groups, or alternative lifestyles. Multiculturalism affirms the worth of different types of culture and cultural groups, claiming, for instance, that Black, Latino, Asian, Native American, gay and lesbian, and other oppressed and marginal voices have their own validity and importance. An insurgent multiculturalism attempts to show how various people's voices and experiences are silenced and omitted from mainstream culture, and struggles to aid in the articulation of diverse views, experiences, and cultural forms from groups excluded from the mainstream. This makes it a target of conservative forces that wish to preserve the existing canons of White male, Eurocentric privilege and have thus attack multiculturalism in cultural wars raging from the 1960s to the present over education, the arts, and the limits of free expression.

Cultural studies thus promotes a critical multiculturalist politics and media pedagogy that aims to make people sensitive to how relations of power and domination are "encoded" in cultural texts, such as those of television or film. But it also specifies how people can resist the dominant encoded meanings and produce their own critical and alternative readings. Cultural studies can show how media culture manipulates and indoctrinates us and thus can empower individuals to resist the dominant meanings in media cultural products and to produce their own meanings. It can also point to moments of resistance and criticism within media culture and thus help promote development of more critical consciousness.

A critical cultural studies—embodied in many of the chapters collected in this reader—thus develops concepts and analyses that will enable readers to analytically dissect the artifacts of contemporary media culture and to gain power over their cultural environment. By exposing the entire field of culture to knowledgeable scrutiny, cultural studies provides a broad, comprehensive framework to undertake studies of culture, politics, and society for the purposes of individual empowerment and social and political struggle and transformation. In the following pages, I will therefore indicate some of the chief components of the type of cultural studies that I find most useful.

Components of a Critical Cultural Studies

As a theoretical apparatus, cultural studies contains a threefold project of analyzing the production and political economy of culture, cultural texts, and the audience reception of those texts and their effects. This comprehensive approach avoids too narrowly focusing on one dimension of the project to the exclusion of others. To avoid such limitations, I propose a multiperspectival approach that (a) discusses production and political economy, (b) engages in textual analysis, and (c) studies the reception and use of cultural texts.[3]

Production and Political Economy

Because it has been neglected in many modes of recent cultural studies, it is important to stress the importance of analyzing cultural texts within their system of production and distribution, often referred to as the political economy of culture.[4] Inserting texts into the system of culture within which they are produced and distributed can help elucidate features and effects of the texts that textual analysis alone might miss or downplay. Rather than being an antithetical approach to culture, political economy can actually contribute

to textual analysis and critique. The system of production often determines what sort of artifacts will be produced, what structural limits there will be as to what can and cannot be said and shown, and what sort of audience effects the text may generate.

Study of the codes of television, film, or popular music, for instance, is enhanced by studying the formulas and conventions of production. These cultural forms are structured by well-defined rules and conventions, and the study of the production of culture can help elucidate the codes actually in play. Because of the demands of the format of radio or music television, for instance, most popular songs are 3 to 5 minutes, fitting into the format of the distribution system. Because of their control by giant corporations oriented primarily toward profit, film and television production in the United States is dominated by specific genres such as talk and game shows, soap operas, situation comedies, action/adventure series, reality TV, and so on. This economic factor explains why there are cycles of certain genres and subgenres, sequelmania in the film industry, crossovers of popular films into television series, and a certain homogeneity in products constituted within systems of production marked by rigid generic codes, formulaic conventions, and well-defined ideological boundaries.

Likewise, study of political economy can help determine the limits and range of political and ideological discourses and effects. My study of television in the United States, for instance, disclosed that the takeover of the television networks by major transnational corporations and communications conglomerates in the 1980s was part of a "right turn" within U.S. society whereby powerful corporate groups won control of the state and the mainstream media (Kellner, 1990). For example, during the 1980s, all three networks were taken over by major corporate conglomerates: ABC was taken over in 1985 by Capital Cities, NBC was taken over by GE, and CBS was taken over by the Tisch Financial Group. Both ABC and NBC sought corporate mergers, and this motivation, along with other benefits derived from Reaganism, might well have influenced them to downplay criticisms of Reagan and to generally support his conservative programs, military adventures, and simulated presidency.

Corporate conglomeratization has intensified further, and today AOL and Time Warner, Disney, and other global media conglomerates control ever more domains of the production and distribution of culture (McChesney, 2000, 2007). In this global context, one cannot really analyze the role of the media in the Gulf War, for instance, without analyzing the production and political economy of news and information, as well as the actual text of the Gulf War and its reception by its audience (see Kellner, 1992). Likewise, the ownership by conservative corporations of dominant media corporations helps explain mainstream media support of the Bush-Cheney administration and their policies, such as the wars in Afghanistan and Iraq (Kellner, 2003, 2005).

Looking toward entertainment, one cannot fully grasp the Madonna phenomenon without analyzing her marketing strategies, her political environment, her cultural artifacts, and their effects (Kellner, 1995). In a similar fashion, younger female pop music stars, such as Britney Spears, Beyoncé, or Lady Gaga, also deploy the tools of the glamour industry and media spectacle to become icons of fashion, beauty, style, and sexuality, as well as purveyors of music. And in appraising the full social impact of pornography, one needs to be aware of the sex industry and the production process of, say, pornographic films and videos and not just dwell on the texts themselves and their effects on audiences.

Furthermore, in an era of globalization, one must be aware of the global networks that produce and distribute culture in the interests of profit and corporate hegemony. Yet political economy alone does not hold the key to cultural studies, and important as it is, it has limitations as a single approach. Some political economy analyses reduce the meanings and effects of texts to rather circumscribed and reductive ideological functions, arguing that media culture merely reflects the ideology of the ruling economic elite that controls the culture industries and is nothing more than a vehicle for capitalist ideology. It is true that media culture overwhelmingly supports capitalist values, but it is also a site of intense struggle between different races, classes, and gender and social groups. Thus, to fully grasp the nature and effects of media culture, one needs to develop methods to analyze the full range of its meanings and effects.

Textual Analysis

The products of media culture require multidimensional close textual readings to analyze their various forms of discourses, ideological positions, narrative strategies, image construction, and effects. There have been a wide range of types of textual criticism of media culture, ranging from quantitative content analysis that dissects the number of, say, episodes of violence in a text to qualitative study that examines images of women, Blacks, or other groups or that applies various critical theories to unpack the meanings of the texts or to explicate how texts function to produce meaning. Traditionally, the qualitative analysis of texts was the task of formalist literary criticism, which explicates the central meanings, values, symbols, and ideologies in cultural artifacts by attending to the formal properties of imaginative literature texts—such as style, verbal imagery, characterization, narrative structure and point of view, and other formal elements of the artifact. From the 1960s on, however, literary-formalist textual analysis has been enhanced by methods derived from semiotics, a system for investigating the creation of meaning not only in written languages but also in other, nonverbal codes, such as the visual and auditory languages of film and TV.

Semiotics analyzes how linguistic and nonlinguistic cultural "signs" form systems of meanings, as when giving someone a rose is interpreted as a sign of love or getting an A on a college paper is a sign of mastery of the rules of the specific assignment. Semiotic analysis can be connected with genre criticism (the study of conventions governing established types of cultural forms, such as soap operas) to reveal how the codes and forms of particular genres follow certain meanings. Situation comedies, for instance, classically follow a conflict/resolution model that demonstrates how to solve certain social problems by correct actions and values and thus provide morality tales of proper and improper behavior. Soap operas, by contrast, proliferate problems and provide messages concerning the endurance and suffering needed to get through life's endless miseries, while generating positive and negative models of social behavior. And advertising shows how commodity solutions solve problems of popularity, acceptance, success, and the like.

A semiotic and genre analysis of the film *Rambo* (1982), for instance, would show how it follows the conventions of the Hollywood genre of the war film that dramatizes conflicts between the United States and its "enemies" (see Kellner, 1995). Semiotics describes how the images of the villains are constructed according to the codes of World War II movies and how the resolution of the conflict and happy ending follows the traditional Hollywood classical cinema, which portrays the victory of good over evil. Semiotic analysis would also include study of the strictly cinematic and formal elements of a film like *Rambo,* dissecting the ways that camera angles present Rambo as a god or slow-motion images of him gliding through the jungle code him as a force of nature. Using a more recent example, semiotic analysis of James Cameron's *Avatar* (2009) would reveal how the images in the film present an anti-militarist and pro-ecological agenda. Although the narrative form celebrates a White male savior, replicating more conservative ideologies,

Avatar also demonstrates how fantasy artifacts can project a wealth of political and ideological meanings, often ambiguous or contradictory. Discussions of *Avatar* have also generated heated debates in the politics of representation, concerning how it has represented gender, sexuality, race, the military, and the environment, as well as other dimensions of the film.

The textual analysis of cultural studies thus combines formalist analysis with critique of how cultural meanings convey specific ideologies of gender, race, class, sexuality, nation, and other ideological dimensions. Ideological textual analysis should deploy a wide range of methods to fully explicate each dimension and to show how they fit into textual systems. Each critical method focuses on certain features of a text from a specific perspective: The perspective spotlights, or illuminates, some features of a text while ignoring others. Marxist methods tend to focus on class, for instance, while feminist approaches will highlight gender, critical race theory spotlights race and ethnicity, and gay and lesbian theories explicate sexuality.

Various critical methods have their own strengths and limitations, their optics and blind spots. Traditionally, Marxian ideology critiques have been strong on class and historical contextualization and weak on formal analysis, while some versions are highly "reductionist," reducing textual analysis to denunciation of ruling class ideology. Feminism excels in gender analysis and in some versions is formally sophisticated, drawing on such methods as psychoanalysis and semiotics, although some versions are reductive, and early feminism often limited itself to analysis of images of gender. Psychoanalysis in turn calls for the interpretation of unconscious contents and meaning, which can articulate latent meanings in a text, as when Alfred Hitchcock's dream sequences project cinematic symbols that illuminate his characters' dilemmas or when the image of the female character in *Bonnie and Clyde* (1967), framed against the bar of her bed, suggests her sexual frustration, imprisonment in middle-class family life, and need for revolt.

Of course, each reading of a text is only one possible reading from one critic's subject position, no matter how multiperspectival, and may or may not be the reading preferred by audiences (which themselves will be significantly different according to their class, race, gender, ethnicity, ideologies, and so on). Because there is a split between textual encoding and audience decoding, there is always the possibility of a multiplicity of readings of any text of media culture (Hall, 1980b). There are limits to the openness or polysemic nature of any text, of course, and textual analysis can explicate the parameters of possible readings and delineate perspectives that aim at illuminating the text and its cultural and ideological effects. Such analysis also provides the materials for criticizing misreadings, or readings that are one-sided and incomplete. Yet to further carry through a cultural studies analysis, one must also examine how diverse audiences actually read media texts and attempt to determine what effects they have on audience thought and behavior.

Audience Reception and Use of Media Culture

All texts are subject to multiple readings depending on the perspectives and subject positions of the reader. Members of distinct genders, classes, races, nations, regions, sexual preferences, and political ideologies are going to read texts differently, and cultural studies can illuminate why diverse audiences interpret texts in various, sometimes conflicting, ways. Media culture provides materials for individuals and communities to create identities and meanings, and cultural studies work on audiences detects a variety of potentially empowering uses of cultural forms. It is one of the merits of cultural studies to have focused on

audience reception in recent years, and this focus provides one of its major contributions, although there are also some limitations and problems with the standard cultural studies approaches to the audience.[5]

Ethnographic research is frequently used in an attempt to determine how texts affect audiences and shape their beliefs and behavior. Ethnographic cultural studies have indicated some of the various ways that audiences use and appropriate texts, often to empower themselves. For example, teenagers use video games and music television as an escape from the demands of a disciplinary society. Males use sports as a terrain of fantasy identification, in which they feel empowered as "their" team or star triumphs. Such sports events also generate a form of community, currently being lost in the privatized media and consumer culture of our time. Indeed, fandoms of all sorts, ranging from *Star Trek* fans ("Trekkies") to devotees of Buffy the Vampire Slayer or various soap operas, also form communities that enable people to relate to others who share their interests and hobbies. Some fans, in fact, actively re-create their favorite cultural forms (see examples in Jenkins, 1992; Lewis, 1992). Other studies have shown that audiences can subvert the intentions of the producers or managers of the cultural industries that supply them, as when astute young media users laugh at obvious attempts to hype certain characters, shows, or products (see de Certeau, 1984, for more examples of audiences constructing meaning and engaging in practices in critical and subversive ways).

The emphasis on active audience reception and appropriation, then, has helped cultural studies overcome the previous one-sided textualist orientations to culture and also has directed focus on the actual political effects that texts may have. By combining quantitative and qualitative research, audience reception studies, including some of the chapters in this reader, are providing important contributions to how people actually interact with cultural texts.

Yet there are several problems that I see with reception studies as they have been constituted within cultural studies, particularly in the United States. First, there is a danger that class will be downplayed as a significant variable that structures audience decoding and use of cultural texts. Cultural studies in England were particularly sensitive to class differences—as well as subcultural differences—in the use and reception of cultural texts, but I have noted many dissertations, books, and articles in cultural studies in the United States where attention to class has been downplayed or is missing altogether. This is not surprising, as a neglect of class as a constitutive feature of culture and society is an endemic deficiency in the American academy in most disciplines.

There is also the reverse danger, however, of exaggerating the constitutive force of class and downplaying, or ignoring, such other variables as gender or ethnicity. Staiger (1992) notes that Fiske, building on Hartley, lists seven "subjectivity positions" that are important in cultural reception— "self, gender, age-group, family, class, nation, ethnicity"—and proposes adding sexual orientation. All of these factors, and no doubt more, interact in shaping how audiences receive and use texts and must be taken into account in studying cultural reception, for audiences decode and use texts according to the specific constituents of their class, race or ethnicity, gender, sexual preferences, and so on.

Furthermore, I would warn against a tendency to romanticize the "active audience," by claiming that all audiences produce their own meanings and denying that media culture may have powerful manipulative effects. There is a tendency within the cultural studies tradition of reception research to dichotomize between dominant and oppositional readings (Hall, 1980b, a dichotomy that structures much of Fiske's work). "Dominant" readings are those in which audiences appropriate texts in line with the interests of the dominant culture and the ideological intentions of a text, as

when audiences feel pleasure in the restoration of male power, law and order, and social stability at the end of a film such as Die Hard, after the hero and representatives of authority eliminate the terrorists who had taken over a high-rise corporate headquarters. An "oppositional" reading, by contrast, celebrates the resistance to this reading in audience appropriation of a text; for example, Fiske (1993) observes resistance to dominant readings when homeless individuals in a shelter cheered the destruction of police and authority figures during repeated viewings of a videotape of Die Hard.

Although this can be a useful distinction, there is a tendency in cultural studies to celebrate resistance per se without distinguishing between types and forms of resistance (a similar problem resides with indiscriminate celebration of audience pleasure in certain reception studies). For example, resistance to social authority by the homeless evidenced in their viewing of Die Hard could serve to strengthen brutal masculist behavior and encourage manifestations of physical violence to solve social problems. Jean-Paul Sartre, Frantz Fanon, and Herbert Marcuse, among others, have argued that violence can be either emancipatory, when directed at forces of oppression, or reactionary, when directed at popular forces struggling against oppression. Many feminists, by contrast, or those in the Gandhian tradition see all violence as forms of brute masculist behavior, and many people see it as a problematical form of conflict resolution. Resistance and pleasure cannot therefore be valorized per se as progressive elements of the appropriation of cultural texts, but difficult discriminations must be made as to whether the resistance, oppositional reading, or pleasure in a given experience is progressive or reactionary, emancipatory or destructive.

Thus, while emphasis on the audience and reception was an excellent correction to the one-sidedness of purely textual analysis, I believe that in recent years, cultural studies has overemphasized reception and textual analysis while underemphasizing the production of culture and its political economy. This type of cultural studies fetishizes audience reception studies and neglects both production and textual analysis, thus producing populist celebrations of the text and audience pleasure in its use of cultural artifacts. This approach, taken to an extreme, would lose its critical perspective and would lead to a positive gloss on audience experience of whatever is being studied. Such studies also might lose sight of the manipulative and conservative effects of certain types of media culture and thus serve the interests of the cultural industries as they are presently constituted.

A new way, in fact, to research media effects is to use the databases that collect media texts, such as Dialogue or Nexis/Lexis, and to trace the effects of media artifacts such as *The X-Files, Buffy the Vampire Slayer, American Idol,* and *24* or advertisements for corporations such as Nike and McDonalds, through analysis of references to them in the media. Likewise, there is a new terrain of Internet audience research that studies how fans act in chat rooms devoted to their favorite artifacts of media culture, create their own fansites, or construct artifacts that disclose how they are living out the fantasies and scripts of the culture industries. Previous studies of the audience and the reception of media privileged ethnographic studies that selected slices of the vast media audiences, usually from the site where researchers themselves lived. Such studies are invariably limited, and broader effects research can indicate how the most popular artifacts of media culture have a wide range of effects. In my book *Media Culture* (Kellner, 1995), I studied some examples of popular cultural artifacts that clearly influenced behavior in audiences throughout the globe. Examples include groups of kids and adults who imitated Rambo in various forms of asocial behavior or fans of Beavis and Butt-Head who started fires or tortured animals in the modes practiced by the popular MTV cartoon characters. Media effects are complex and controversial, and it is the merit of cultural studies to make their study an important part of its agenda.

Finally, new media such as Facebook, YouTube, and other social networking sites produce forums for more active audiences, as well as new sites for audience research. As audiences critically discuss or celebrate their preferred artifacts of media culture and, in some cases, produce their own versions, disseminated to audiences throughout the Internet and new technologies, media culture expands its reach and power while audiences can feel that they are part of their preferred cultural sites and phenomena.

Toward a Cultural Studies That Is Critical, Multicultural, and Multiperspectival

To avoid the one-sidedness of textual analysis approaches or audience and reception studies, I propose that cultural studies itself be multiperspectival, getting at culture from the perspectives of political economy, text analysis, and audience reception, as outlined above. Textual analysis should use a multiplicity of perspectives and critical methods, and audience reception studies should delineate the wide range of subject positions, or perspectives, through which audiences appropriate culture. This requires a multicultural approach that sees the importance of analyzing the dimensions of class, race and ethnicity, and gender and sexual preference within the texts of media culture, while studying as well their impact on how audiences read and interpret media culture.

In addition, a critical cultural studies attacks sexism, racism, or bias against specific social groups (i.e., gays, intellectuals, seniors, etc.) and criticizes texts that promote any kind of domination or oppression. As an example of how considerations of production, textual analysis, and audience readings can fruitfully intersect in cultural studies, let us reflect on the Madonna phenomenon. Madonna first appeared in the moment of Reaganism and embodied the materialistic and consumer-oriented ethos of the 1980s ("Material Girl"). She also appeared in a time of dramatic image proliferation, associated with MTV, fashion fever, and intense marketing of products. Madonna was one of the first MTV music video superstars who consciously crafted images to attract a mass audience. Her early music videos were aimed at teenage girls (the Madonna wannabes), but she soon incorporated Black, Hispanic, and minority audiences with her images of interracial sex and multicultural "family" in her concerts. She also appealed to gay and lesbian audiences, as well as to feminist and academic audiences, as her videos became more complex and political (i.e., "Like a Prayer," "Express Yourself," "Vogue," etc.).

Thus, Madonna's popularity was in large part a function of her marketing strategies and her production of music videos and images that appealed to diverse audiences. To conceptualize the meanings and effects in her music, films, concerts, and public relations stunts requires that her artifacts be interpreted within the context of their production and reception, which involves discussion of MTV, the music industry, concerts, marketing, and the production of images (see Kellner, 1995). Understanding Madonna's popularity also requires focus on audiences, not just as individuals but as members of specific groups, such as teenage girls, who were empowered in their struggles for individual identity by Madonna, or gays, who were also empowered by her incorporation of alternative images of sexuality within popular mainstream cultural artifacts. Yet appraising the politics and effects of Madonna also requires analysis of how her work might merely reproduce a consumer culture that defines identity in terms of images and consumption. It would make an interesting project to examine how former Madonna fans view the evolution and recent incarnations of the superstar, such as her marriages and recent world tours, as

well as to examine how contemporary fans view Madonna in an age that embraces younger teen pop singers such as Britney Spears or Beyoncé.

Likewise, Michael Jackson's initial popularity derived from carefully managed media spectacles, first with the Jackson Five and then with his own career. Michael Jackson achieved his superstar status, as did Madonna, from his MTV-disseminated music videos and spectacular concert performances, in which promotion, image management, and his publicity apparatus made him the King of Pop. While, like Madonna, his frequent tabloid and media presence helped promote his career, media spectacle and tabloids also derailed it, as he was charged with child abuse in well-publicized cases. After his death in 2009, however, he had a remarkable surge of popularity as his works were disseminated through the media, including new media and social networking sites.

In short, a cultural studies that is critical and multicultural provides comprehensive approaches to culture that can be applied to a wide variety of artifacts, from pornography to Madonna and Michael Jackson, from MTV to TV news, or to specific events such as the 2000 or 2008 U.S. presidential election (Kellner, 2001, 2009) or media representations of the 2001 terrorist attacks on the United States and the U.S. response (Kellner, 2003). Its comprehensive perspectives encompass political economy, textual analysis, and audience research and provide critical and political perspectives that enable individuals to dissect the meanings, messages, and effects of dominant cultural forms. Cultural studies is thus part of a critical media pedagogy that enables individuals to resist media manipulation and to increase their freedom and individuality. It can empower people to gain sovereignty over their culture and to be able to struggle for alternative cultures and political change. Cultural studies is thus not just another academic fad but can be part of a struggle for a better society and a better life.

Notes

1. For more information on British cultural studies, see Hall (1980b), Johnson (1986–1987), Fiske (1986), O'Connor (1989), Turner (1990), Grossberg (1989), Agger (1992), and the articles collected in Grossberg, Nelson, and Treichler (1992); During (1998); Durham and Kellner (2006); and Hammer and Kellner (2009). The Frankfurt school also provided much material for a critical cultural studies in their works on mass culture from the 1930s through the present; on the relation between the Frankfurt school and British cultural studies, see Kellner (1997).

2. On the concept of ideology, see Kellner (1978, 1979), the Centre for Contemporary Cultural Studies (1980), Kellner and Ryan (1988), and Thompson (1990).

3. This model was adumbrated in Hall (1980a) and Johnson (1986–1987) and guided much of the early Birmingham work. Around the mid-1980s, however, the Birmingham group began to increasingly neglect the production and political economy of culture (some believe that this was always a problem with their work), and many of their studies became more academic, cut off from political struggle. I am thus trying to recapture the spirit of the early Birmingham project, reconstructed for our contemporary moment. For a fuller development of my conception of cultural studies, see Kellner (1992, 1995, 2001).

4. The term *political economy* calls attention to the fact that the production and distribution of culture take place within a specific economic system, constituted by relations between the state and economy. For instance, in the United States, a capitalist economy dictates that cultural production is governed by laws of the market, but the democratic imperatives of the system mean that there is some regulation of culture by the state. There are often tensions within a given society concerning how many activities should be governed by the imperatives of the market, or economics, alone and how much state regulation or intervention is desirable, to ensure a wider diversity of broadcast programming, for instance, or the prohibition of

phenomena agreed to be harmful, such as cigarette advertising or pornography (see Kellner, 1990; McChesney, 2007).

5. Cultural studies that have focused on audience reception include Brunsdon and Morley (1978), Radway (1983), Ang (1985, 1996), Morley (1986), Fiske (1989a, 1989b), Jenkins (1992), and Lewis (1992).

References

Agger, B. (1992). *Cultural studies*. London: Falmer.

Ang, I. (1985) *Watching* Dallas. New York: Metheun.

Ang, I. (1996). *Living room wars: Rethinking media audiences for a postmodern world.* London: Routledge.

Brunsdon, C., & Morley, D. (1978). *Everyday television: "Nationwide."* London: British Film Institute.

Centre for Contemporary Cultural Studies. (1980). *On ideology.* London: Hutchinson.

de Certeau, M. (1984). *The practice of everyday life.* Berkeley: University of California Press.

Durham, M. G., & Kellner, D. (Eds.). (2006). *Media and cultural studies: Key works* (Rev. 2nd ed.). Malden, MA: Blackwell.

During, S. (1998). *Cultural studies.* London: Routledge.

Fiske, J. (1986). British cultural studies and television. In R. C. Allen (Ed.), *Channels of discourse* (pp. 254–289). Chapel Hill: University of North Carolina Press.

Fiske, J. (1989a). *Reading the popular.* Boston: Unwin Hyman.

Fiske, J. (1989b). *Understanding popular culture.* Boston: Unwin Hyman.

Fiske, J. (1993). *Power plays, power works.* London: Verso.

Grossberg, L. (1989). The formations of cultural studies: An American in Birmingham. *Strategies, 22,* 114–149.

Grossberg, L., Nelson, C., & Treichler, P. (1992). *Cultural studies.* New York: Routledge.

Hall, S. (1980a). Cultural studies and the Centre: Some problematics and problems. In S. Hall, D. Hobson, A. Lowe, & P. Willis (Eds.),

Culture, media, language: Working papers in cultural studies, 1972–79 (pp. 15–47). London: Hutchinson.

Hall, S. (1980b). Encoding/decoding. In S. Hall, D. Hobson, A. Lowe, & P. Willis (Eds.), *Culture, media, language: Working papers in cultural studies, 1972–79* (pp. 128–138). London: Hutchinson.

Hammer, R., & Kellner, D. (2009). *Media/cultural studies: Critical approaches*. New York: Peter Lang.

Jenkins, H. (1992). *Textual poachers*. New York: Routledge.

Johnson, R. (1986–1987). What is cultural studies anyway? *Social Text, 16*, 38–80.

Kellner, D. (1978, November–December). Ideology, Marxism, and advanced capitalism. *Socialist Review, 42*, 37–65.

Kellner, D. (1979, May–June). TV, ideology, and emancipatory popular culture. *Socialist Review, 45*, 13–53.

Kellner, D. (1990). *Television and the crisis of democracy*. Boulder, CO: Westview.

Kellner, D. (1992). *The Persian Gulf TV war*. Boulder, CO: Westview.

Kellner, D. (1995). *Media culture: Cultural studies, identity, and politics between the modern and the postmodern*. London: Routledge.

Kellner, D. (1997). Critical theory and British cultural studies: The missed articulation. In J. McGuigan (Ed.), *Cultural methodologies* (pp. 12–41). London: Sage.

Kellner, D. (2001). *Grand Theft 2000*. Lanham, MD: Rowman & Littlefield.

Kellner, D. (2003). *From September 11 to terror war: The dangers of the Bush legacy*. Lanham, MD: Rowman & Littlefield.

Kellner, D. (2005). *Media spectacle and the crisis of democracy*. Boulder, CO: Paradigm.

Kellner, D. (2009). Barack Obama and celebrity spectacle. *International Journal of Communication, 3*, 1–20. http://ijoc.org/ojs/index.php/ijoc/article/view/559/350

Kellner, D. (2010). *Cinema wars: Hollywood film and politics in the Bush/Cheney era*. Malden, MA: Blackwell.

Kellner, D., & Ryan, M. (1988). *Camera politica: The politics and ideology of contemporary Hollywood film*. Bloomington: Indiana University Press.

Lewis, L. A. (1992). *Adoring audience: Fan culture and popular media*. New York: Routledge.

McChesney, R. (2000). *Rich media, poor democracy: Communications politics in dubious times*. New York: New Press.

McChesney, R. (2007). *Communication revolution: Critical junctures and the future of media*. New York: New Press.

Morley, D. (1986). *Family television*. London: Comedia.

O'Connor, A. (1989, December). The problem of American cultural studies. *Critical Studies in Mass Communication*, pp. 405–413.

Radway, J. (1983). *Reading the romance*. Chapel Hill: University of North Carolina Press.

Staiger, J. (1992). Film, reception, and cultural studies. *Centennial Review, 26*(1), 89–104.

Thompson, J. (1990). *Ideology and modern culture*. Cambridge, UK: Polity Press and Stanford University Press.

Turner, G. (1990). *British cultural studies: An introduction*. New York: Unwin Hyman.

The State of Media Ownership and Media Markets

Competition or Concentration and Why Should We Care?

Dwayne Winseck

The 500-Channel Universe and Marketplace Democracy

In the eyes of many, the emergence of new television networks and the explosive growth of cable and satellite channels—MTV, HBO, ESPN, CNN, Fox News and Canal1, A&E, Al-Jazeera, to name just a few—offers an unprecedented abundance of choice. The 500-channel universe is, if not already here, just around the corner. Even the half-dozen major Hollywood Studios—Columbia, Disney, Paramount, Twentieth Century Fox, Universal Pictures and Warner Bros—appear to be losing their iron-clad grip over American and international film audiences, with their share of the US market tumbling from 85% in 1994 to just over 66% in 2004. Throw into this mix the explosive growth of the Internet, with its endless well of web pages, news sources, music and video downloading services, and the free-wheeling commentary of innumerable blogs, and the idea of concentrated media markets sounds anachronistic. Many believe that new technologies have rendered limits on media concentration obsolete. . . . As media economist Compaine (2001) states, 'the democracy of the marketplace may be flawed but it is . . . getting better, not worse.'

Most scholars agree that there is a wider range of media available to a greater number of people than in the past. However, some also claim that media markets are becoming more concentrated. . . .

While the size of the global media market in 2005 was a staggering $258 billion and consists of hundreds of firms, the 'big 10' global media firms account for just over 80% of all revenues. The 'big 10,' ranked by revenues, are listed in Table 1.

From Winseck, D. (2008). The state of media ownership and media markets: Competition or concentration and why should we care? *Sociology Compass*, 2(1), 34–47. Reproduced with permission of Blackwell Publishing Ltd.

Table 1	Top 10 Global Media Companies (by Revenue)			
	Firm	Revenue (billion USD)	Ownership	National Base
1.	Time Warner	$43.7	Diversified	USA
2.	Disney	$31.9	Diversified	USA
3.	Bertelsmann	$28.9	Bertelsmann/Mohn	Germany
4.	News Corp	$25.3	Murdoch and others	USA
5.	Viacom	$24.1	Redstone family	USA
6.	Comcast	$22.7	Roberts family	USA
7.	NBC/Universal	$14.0	Diversified	USA
8.	Pearson	$7.5	Diversified	UK
9.	Fuji TV Network	$5.0	Unclear	Japan
10.	ITV	$3.9	Diversified	UK

This evidence suggests that markets are becoming more consolidated. The top 10 global media companies are also among the largest corporations in the world, with 7 of the top 10 listed on *Fortune* (2006) magazine's list of the global 500. They are also all media conglomerates, meaning that they operate across many different media markets, including television, film, newspapers, publishing and the Internet, where their websites are now among some of the most visited sites worldwide. There is also a surprising number of 'owner-controlled' companies among the big 10: Bertelsmann, News Corp, Viacom and Comcast. In terms of revenue, these multimedia firms dwarf their smaller regional and national counterparts, many of whom operate in only one or two media sectors. The big 10 are also solidly based in the USA (6), Britain (2), Germany (1) and Japan (1). In addition, while boasting of reaching hundreds of millions of homes across the world through channels such as MTV, A&E, Showtime, FoxNews, CNN, Canal+ and so forth, these firms derive the lion's share of their revenues from their home markets and then from Europe, North America and Japan. Only a fraction of their revenues comes from the rest of the world.[1]

Mediasaurus: Mapping the Terrain

Recent media mergers and acquisitions are notable in terms of their *sheer size*. This is perhaps best illustrated by the unprecedented, but ill-fated, AOL and Time Warner deal, initially valued at $166 billion in 2000 but that fell to $106 billion a year later, and even less since. A few transactions have also been *transnational in scope,* such as the purchase of Universal Studios by the French diversified conglomerate, Vivendi, in 2000 ($35 billion), although the failure of that deal spawned yet another round of consolidation when GE/NBC acquired Universal Studios in 2004. The current wave of consolidation has also resulted in unprecedented common ownership and *vertical integration* between the major US television networks and Hollywood studios: Twentieth Century Fox and the Fox Network (1985), Disney with ABC (1995), Time Warner and the WB Network (1995), CBS and Viacom (1999) and NBC/Universal (2004). These alignments fundamentally distinguish the state of the US media today from any other time in US media history (Kunz 2007). The *acquisition of independent firms,* such as Disney and Viacom's purchase of Miramax and DreamWorks, respectively, in 2005 also undercut the influence of independents that had been seriously chipping away at Hollywood's dominance of USA and international film markets over the past two decades.

Vertical integration across the supply and distribution of film and television programs has three effects. First, it gives Hollywood studios secure access to more distribution outlets, through conventional and satellite and cable television channels. Television networks, in return, gain access to a steady source of film and television programs. Whereas the big three networks obtained most of their programming from outside sources and the rest 'in-house' in the 1980s, today nearly 80% of new series are acquired in-house. Second, locking up access to both of these critical resources—content and distribution— helps media firms manage the inherently risky nature of the media business. Third, however, this hold over content and distribution creates a significant barrier for independents and rivals, and, thus, limits creativity and the diversity of the marketplace for cultural commodities (Croteau and Hoynes 2006, 91).

Media firms . . . have a history of using deep pockets and litigation to reduce the threat of new technologies, from the buying up of competing patents in the early days of radio and film to recent lawsuits

against new music and video downloading services. While this continues to be the case, they are also using acquisitions and alliances to ensure that new technologies offer more opportunities than threats. The annual reports of the major global media conglomerates reveals the shift, notably with News Corp's purchase of the social networking site MySpace ($580 billion), gaming and entertainment site IGN.com ($620 million) and the top sports site in the USA, Scout Media ($60 million) in 2005. Similarly, ITV acquired the eighth-ranked site in Britain, Friends Reunited ($200 million) in 2005, while Viacom bought Neopets ($160 million), a children's website in the USA, and IFilm.com in 2004 and 2005, respectively. The global media firms have also forged alliances with cellular telephone companies and computer firms such as Apple and Microsoft to stake out a key role in new mobile television, music and film download services. While the largest such deal in the post-dot.com bubble era occurred in 2006 when Google took over the video-sharing site, YouTube ($1.65 billion), that transaction was preceded by agreements with NBC Universal, Sony BMG, Time Warner, Viacom and News Corp that aimed to achieve three goals: first, to implement content identification technology that helps these companies maximize control over their content; second, to share traffic and advertising revenue; and third, to share access to Google's technology among these groups.[2]

These agreements will not allow these firms to obtain 'perfect control' over their content. However, they will help to insure that Google and emerging services do not dislodge the largest global media conglomerates from their dominant position in the media economy. These arrangements also give 'old' media firms a strong hand in shaping the evolution of new technologies. Those who believe that new technologies are inherently antagonistic to concentrations of economic, political and cultural power ignore these points. The Internet is not immune from these tendencies and this can be seen in Google's overwhelming dominance of the search engine market (56%), with the next three companies— Yahoo!, MSN and Time Warner/AOL— accounting for roughly 35%, yielding a concentration ratio of over 91%.... It is this reality that has allowed Google to become such a powerful nexus in the unfolding relationship between the 'old' and 'new' media, a phenomenon that we might call a 'Googlopoly.'

The staying power of the global media giants can be seen in the fact that Time Warner, Disney and NBC possess four out of the top 10 Internet news sites in the USA, while the *New York Times, Tribune* newspapers, *Knight Ridder* and *USA Today* take up another four. The fact that the remaining leading news sites rely on these sources as well as a few global news agencies for most of their news content further magnifies this influence. Indeed, producing almost no original news of their own, Yahoo! and Google do little to diversify the range of available news sources. These patterns are also true globally, where the same firms dominate, with the exception of the BBC and three Chinese sites, the latter of which all rely solely on reports from the state-controlled Chinese media (Comscore 2006; Paterson 2005, 157–60).

Explaining the Consequences of Media Concentration

What are the consequences of this growing consolidation? Many critics argue that the most significant consequence lies in the ability of a handful of media owners to exert influence on media content and, thus, people's view of the world. This is a crucial issue, but it is also one that is fraught with difficulties and also, I believe, rather like trying to draw a camel through the eye of a needle. One of the difficulties with measuring

the impact of media ownership on content stems from the changing organizational structure of large media conglomerates. Demers and Merskin (2000) make this point when they argue that the potential for media owners to influence content has been sharply diminished by the rise of the modern corporation. Under these conditions, ownership is usually widely dispersed, with actual control resting in the hands of expert managers, with media workers relatively free to do as they please within the limits of professional standards and good business practice. In general, this claim has merit and mirrors trends in the growth of publicly traded media conglomerates. . . . Nonetheless, it is important to note that four of the top-10 global media firms— News Corp (Rupert Murdoch), Bertelsmann (heirs to founder, Carl Bertelsmann), Viacom (Sumner Redstone) and Comcast (Roberts family)—are still owner controlled. In Canada, 11 of the top 12 firms are still owner controlled. The phenomenon is also prominent . . . throughout Latin America and Australia, among other places. In short, it is far too early to sound the death knell of media moguls who have the potential to use their outlets to pursue political and ideological objectives. However, discovering the direct links between owners, content and people's beliefs is fraught with difficulties, including the anecdotal nature of the evidence and the well-known limits of media effects research.

A larger view of the issues considers the consequences of consolidation on the allocation of resources within media firms. While some believe that the deeper pockets of media conglomerates allows them to commit more resources to production, news gathering and so forth, a counterargument is that resources are being diverted from these goals to meet the high cost of financing mergers and acquisitions. . . . As an example of this, NBC recently announced that it is cutting its workforce by 700 people, eliminating news bureaus in favour of a centralized operation in New York to feed the NBC network, MSNBC,

CNBC and its Spanish-language network, Telemundo, and replacing high-cost dramatic programs in early prime time with cheaper 'reality-TV' series and game shows. Overall, the number of television network journalists has fallen by over one third since 1985 in the USA, while international news bureaus have been slashed (Project for Excellence in Journalism 2006). . . .

The magnitude of such changes differs between media firms, but the trend is toward fully integrated news operations that serve multiple channels, budget cuts, smaller journalistic staffs, fewer foreign bureaus and the replacement of high-cost dramatic programs with a smaller number of 'blockbusters' and more low-budget shows.

Media Concentration: Some Concluding Thoughts

These trends are bound by audience tastes and the complexity of the media business, but several points remain to be made in any final assessment of the consolidation of media markets. First, audiences now have more media channels than ever, but source diversity is shrinking. Second, media professionals are experiencing vast changes in the quantity and quality of work available to them and this has created deep rifts within the media. Media workers in the USA, Canada, Britain and many other countries report that bottom-line pressures now have a greater impact on their work than in the past, that the influence of owners, managers and advertisers is increasing and that their trust in media executives is declining (Project for Excellence in Journalism 2006). Lastly, the structure and feel of the media is being subtly altered as media organizations strive to maximize control over their content through aggressive litigation, pressuring legislatures to expand the scope and duration of copyright

laws and implement digital rights management technologies that increase audience surveillance and set limits around what people can and cannot do with the new media. The upshot of these changes is a subtle shift in the architecture of the media in favour of closure and control versus the values of openness and real diversity that are the *sine qua non* of democratic societies. For all these reasons, media ownership and concentration remains an absolutely critical issue, with not only concerns of bias and the abuse of personalized power at stake, but the future of media evolution and potential of democracy itself.

Notes

1. These observations are based on data from the *Annual Reports* published by each of the media companies referred to here.

2. The following paragraph is drawn from information contained in each of the 'big 10' global media firms' annual reports for 2005 and 2006.

References

Compaine, Benjamin 2001. *The Myth of Encroaching Global Media Ownership.* www.opendemocracy.net/media-globalmedia ownership/article_87.jsp (last accessed May 23, 2007).

Comscore 2006. Half of All U.S. Internet Users Visited News Sites in June 2006. August 7. www.comscore.com/press/release.asp?press= 971 (last accessed May 23, 2007).

Croteau, David and William Hoynes 2006. *The Business of Media: Corporate Media and the Public Interest.* Thousand Oaks, CA: Pine Forge Press.

Demers, David and Donna Merskin 2000. 'Corporate News Structure and the Managerial Revolution.' *Journal of Media Economics* 13: 103–21.

Kunz, William 2007. *Culture Conglomerates: Consolidation in the Motion Picture and Television Industries*. Lanham, MD: Rowman and Littlefield Publishers.

Paterson, Christopher 2005. "News Agency Dominance in International News on the Internet." Pp. 145–64 in *Converging Media, Diverging Politics*, edited by David Skinner, James Compton and Michael Gasher. Lanham, MD: Rowman & Littlefield.

Project for Excellence in Journalism 2006. *The State of the News Media*. www.stateofthe newsmedia.org/2006/ (last accessed May 23, 2007).

The Meaning of Memory

Family, Class, and Ethnicity in Early Network Television Programs

George Lipsitz

The Meaning of Memory

The Meaning of Memory

. . . In the midst of extraordinary social change, television became the most important dis-cursive medium in American culture. As such, it was charged with special responsibilities for making new economic and social relations credible and legitimate to audiences haunted by ghosts from the past. Urban ethnic working-class situation comedies provided one means of addressing the anxieties and contradictions emanating from the clash between the con-sumer present of the 1950s and collective social memory about the 1930s and 1940s.

The consumer consciousness emerging from economic and social change in postwar America conflicted with the lessons of historical experience for many middle- and work-ing-class American families. The Great Depression of the 1930s had not only damaged the economy, it also undercut the political and cultural legitimacy of American capital-ism. Herbert Hoover had been a national hero in the 1920s, with his credo of "rugged individualism" forming the basis for a widely shared cultural ideal. But the depression discredited Hoover's philosophy and made him a symbol of yesterday's blasted hopes to millions of Americans. In the 1930s, cultural ideals based on mutuality and collectivity eclipsed the previous decade's "rugged individualism" and helped propel massive union organizing drives, anti-eviction movements, and general strikes. President Roosevelt's New Deal attempted to harness and co-opt that grass roots mass activity in an attempt to restore social order and recapture credibility and legitimacy for the capitalist system (Romasco 1965). The social welfare legislation of the "Second New Deal" in 1935 went far beyond any measures previously favored by Roosevelt and most of his advisors, but radical action proved necessary for the Administration to contain the upsurge of

Reproduced by permission of the American Anthropological Association from *Cultural Anthropology,* Volume 1, Issue 4, pp. 355–387, 1986. Not for sale or further reproduction.

activism that characterized the decade. Even in the private sector, industrial corporations made more concessions to workers than naked power realities necessitated because they feared the political consequences of mass disillusionment with the system (Berger 1982).

World War II ended the depression and brought prosperity, but it did so on a basis even more collective than the New Deal of the 1930s. Government intervention in the wartime economy reached unprecedented levels, bringing material reward and shared purpose to a generation raised on the deprivation and sacrifice of the depression. In the postwar years, the largest and most disruptive strike wave in American history won major improvements in the standard of living for the average worker, both through wage increases and through government commitments to insure full employment, decent housing, and expanded educational opportunities. Grass roots militancy and working-class direct action wrested concessions from a reluctant government and business elite—mostly because the public at large viewed workers' demands as more legitimate than the desires of capital (Lipsitz 1981).

Yet the collective nature of working-class mass activity in the postwar era posed severe problems for capital. In sympathy strikes and secondary boycotts, workers placed the interests of their class ahead of their own individual material aspirations. Strikes over safety and job control far outnumbered wage strikes, revealing aspirations to control the process of production that conflicted with capitalist labor-management relations. Mass demonstrations demanding government employment and housing programs indicated a collective political response to problems previously adjudicated on a personal level. Radical challenges to the authority of capital (like the 1946 United Auto Workers' strike demand that wage increases come out of corporate profits rather than from price hikes passed on to consumers), demonstrated a social responsibility and a commitment toward redistributing wealth, rare in the history of American labor (Lipsitz 1981:47–50).

Capital attempted to regain the initiative in the postwar years by making qualified concessions to working-class pressures for redistribution of wealth and power. Rather than paying wage increases out of corporate profits, business leaders instead worked to expand the economy through increases in government spending, foreign trade, and consumer debt. Such expansion could meet the demands of workers and consumers without undermining capital's dominant role in the economy. On the presumption that "a rising tide lifts all boats," business leaders sought to connect working-class aspirations for a better life to policies that insured a commensurate rise in corporate profits, thereby leaving the distribution of wealth unaffected. Federal defense spending, highway construction programs, and home loan policies expanded the economy at home in a manner conducive to the interests of capital, while the Truman Doctrine and Marshall Plan provided models for enhanced access to foreign markets and raw materials for American corporations. The Taft-Hartley Act of 1947 banned the class-conscious collective activities most threatening to capital (mass strikes, sympathy strikes, secondary boycotts); the leaders of labor, government, and business accepted as necessity the practice of paying wage hikes for organized workers out of the pockets of consumers and unorganized workers, in the form of higher prices (Lipsitz 1981).

Commercial network television played an important role in this emerging economy, functioning as a significant object of consumer purchasers as well as an important marketing medium. Sales of sets jumped from three million during the entire decade of the 1940s to over five million a *year* during the 1950s (*TV Facts* 1980:141). But television's most important economic function came from its role as an instrument of legitimation for transformations in values initiated by the new economic imperatives of postwar America. For Americans to accept the new world of 1950s' consumerism, they had to make a break with the past. The depression years had helped generate fears about installment buying and excessive materialism, while the New Deal and wartime mobilization had provoked suspicions about individual acquisitiveness and upward mobility. Depression era and war time scarcities of consumer goods had led workers to internalize discipline and frugality while nurturing networks of mutual support through family, ethnic, and class associations. Government policies after the war encouraged an atomized acquisitive consumerism at odds with the lessons of the past. At the same time, federal home loan policies stimulated migrations to the suburbs from traditional, urban ethnic working-class neighborhoods. The entry of television into the American home disrupted previous patterns of family life and encouraged fragmentation of the family into separate segments of the consumer market.[1] The priority of consumerism in the economy at large and on television may have seemed organic and unplanned, but conscious policy decisions by officials from both private and public sectors shaped the contours of the consumer economy and television's role within it.

Commercial Television and Economic Change

Government policies during and after World War II shaped the basic contours of home television as an advertising medium. Government-sponsored research and development during the war perfected the technology of home television while federal tax policies solidified its economic base. The government allowed corporations to deduct the cost of advertising from their taxable incomes during the war, despite the fact that rationing and defense production left business with few products to market. Consequently, manufacturers kept the names of their products before the public

while lowering their tax obligations on high wartime profits. Their advertising expenditures supplied radio networks and advertising agencies with the capital reserves and business infrastructure that enabled them to dominate the television industry in the postwar era. After the war, federal antitrust action against the motion picture studios broke up the "network" system in movies, while the FCC sanctioned the network system in television. In addition, FCC decisions to allocate stations on the narrow VHF band, to grant the networks ownership and operation rights over stations in prime markets, and to place a freeze on the licensing of new stations during the important years between 1948 and 1952 all combined to guarantee that advertising-oriented programming based on the model of radio would triumph over theater TV, educational TV, or any other form (Boddy 1985; Allen 1983). Government decisions, not market forces, established the dominance of commercial television, but these decisions reflected a view of the American economy and its needs which had become so well accepted at the top levels of business and government that it had virtually become the official state economic policy.

Fearing both renewed depression and awakened militancy among workers, influential corporate and business leaders considered increases in consumer spending—increases of 30% to 50%—to be necessary to perpetuate prosperity in the postwar era (Lipsitz 1981:46, 120–121). Defense spending for the Cold War and Korean Conflict had complemented an aggressive trade policy to improve the state of the economy, but it appeared that the key to an expanding economy rested in increased consumer spending fueled by an expansion of credit (Moore and Klein 1967; Jezer 1982). Here too, government policies led the way, especially with regard to stimulating credit purchases of homes and automobiles. During World War II, the marginal tax rate for most wage earners jumped from 4% to 25%, making the home ownership deduction more desirable. Federal housing loan policies favored construction of new single family detached suburban housing over renovation or construction of central city multifamily units. Debt-encumbered home ownership in accord with these policies stimulated construction of 30 million new housing units in just twenty years, bringing the percentage of home-owning Americans from below 40% in 1940 to more than 60% by 1960. Mortgage policies encouraging long term debt and low down payments freed capital for other consumer purchases, while government highway building policies undermined mass transit systems and contributed to increased demand for automobiles (Hartman 1982:165–168). Partly as a result of these policies, consumer spending on private cars averaged $7.5 billion per year in the 1930s and 1940s, but grew to $22 billion per year in 1950 and almost $30 billion by 1955 (Mollenkopf 1983:111).

For the first time in U.S. history, middle-class and working-class families could routinely expect to own homes or buy new cars every few years. Between 1946 and 1965 residential mortgage debt rose three times as fast as the gross national product and disposable income. Mortgage debt accounted for just under 18% of disposable income in 1946, but it grew to almost 55% by 1965 (Stone 1983:122). In order to insure eventual payment of current debts, the economy had to generate tremendous expansion and growth, further stimulating the need to increase consumer spending. Manufacturers had to find new ways of motivating consumers to buy ever increasing amounts of commodities, and television provided an important means of accomplishing that end.

Television advertised individual products, but it also provided a relentless flow of information and persuasion that placed acts of consumption at the core of everyday life. The physical fragmentation of suburban growth and declines in motion picture attendance created an audience more likely to stay at home and receive entertainment there than ever before. But television also provided a locus redefining American ethnic, class, and family identities into consumer

identities. In order to accomplish this task effectively, television programs had to address some of the psychic, moral, and political obstacles to consumption among the public at large.

The television and advertising industries knew that they had to overcome these obstacles. Marketing expert and motivational specialist Ernest Dichter stated that "one of the basic problems of this prosperity is to give people that sanction and justification to enjoy it and to demonstrate that the hedonistic approach to life is a moral one, not an immoral one" (Jezer 1982:127). Dichter went on to note the many barriers that inhibited consumer acceptance of unrestrained hedonism, and he called on advertisers "to train the average citizen to accept growth of his country and its economy as *his* growth rather than as a strange and frightening event" (Dichter 1960:210). One method of encouraging that acceptance, according to Dichter, consisted of identifying new products and styles of consumption with traditional, historically sanctioned practices and behavior. He noted that such an approach held particular relevance in addressing consumers who had only recently acquired the means to spend freely and who might harbor a lingering conservatism based on their previous experiences (Dichter 1960:209). . . .

Family Formation and the Economy—The Television View

Advertisers incorporated their messages into urban ethnic working-class comedies through indirect and direct means. Tensions developed in the programs often found indirect resolution in commercials. Thus Jeannie MacClennan's search for an American sweetheart in one episode of *Hey Jeannie* set up commercials proclaiming the abilities of Drene shampoo to keep one prepared to accept last minute dates and of Crest toothpaste to produce an attractive smile (*Hey Jeannie:* "The Rock and Roll Kid"). Conversations about shopping for new furniture in an episode of *The Goldbergs* directed viewers' attention to furnishings in the Goldberg home provided for the show by Macy's department store in exchange for a commercial acknowledgment (*The Goldbergs:* "The In-laws").

But the content of the shows themselves offered even more direct emphasis on consumer spending. In one episode of *The Goldbergs,* Molly expresses disapproval of her future daughter-in-law's plan to buy a washing machine on the installment plan. "I know Papa and me never bought anything unless we had the money to pay for it," she intones with logic familiar to a generation with memories of the Great Depression. Her son, Sammy, confronts this "deviance" by saying, "Listen, Ma, almost everybody in this country lives above their means—and everybody enjoys it." Doubtful at first, Molly eventually learns from her children and announces her conversion to the legitimacy of installment buying by proposing that the family buy two cars so as to "live above our means—the American way" (*The Goldbergs:* "The In-laws"). In a subsequent episode, Molly's daughter, Rosalie, assumes the role of ideological tutor to her mother. When planning a move out of their Bronx apartment to a new house in the suburbs, Molly ruminates about where to place her furniture in the new home. "You don't mean we're going to take all this junk with us into a brand new house?" asks an exasperated Rosalie. With traditionalist sentiment Molly answers, "Junk? My furniture's junk? My furniture that I lived with and loved for twenty years is junk?" But in the end she accepts Rosalie's argument—even selling off all her old furniture to help meet the down payment on the new house, and deciding to buy new furniture on the installment plan (*The Goldbergs:* "Moving Day").

Chester A. Riley confronts similar choices about family and commodities in *The Life of Riley.* His wife complains that

he only takes her out to the neighborhood bowling alley and restaurant, not to "interesting places." Riley searches for ways to impress her and discovers from a friend that a waiter at the fancy Club Morambo will let them eat first and pay later, at a dollar a week plus ten percent interest. "Ain't that dishonest?" asks Riley. "No, it's usury," his friend replies. Riley does not borrow the money, but he impresses his wife anyway by taking the family out to dinner on the proceeds of a prize that he received for being the one-thousandth customer in a local flower shop. Though we eventually learn that Peg Riley only wanted attention, not an expensive meal, the happy ending of the episode hinges totally on Riley's prestige, restored when he demonstrates his ability to provide a luxury outing for the family (*Life of Riley:* R228).

The same episode of *The Life of Riley* reveals another consumerist element common to this subgenre. When Riley protests that he lacks the money needed to fulfill Peg's desires, she answers that he would have plenty if he didn't spend so much on "needless gadgets." His shortage of cash becomes a personal failing caused by incompetent behavior as a consumer. Nowhere do we hear about the size of his paycheck, relations between his union and his employer, or, for that matter, the relationship between the value of his labor and the wages paid to him by the Stevenson Aircraft Company. Like Uncle David in *The Goldbergs*—who buys a statue of Hamlet shaking hands with Shakespeare and an elk's tooth with the Gettysburg address carved on it—Riley's comic character stems in part from a flaw which in theory could be attributed to the entire consumer economy: a preoccupation with "needless gadgets." By contrast, Peg Riley's desire for an evening out is portrayed as reasonable and modest—as reparation due her for the inevitable tedium of housework. The solution to her unhappiness, of course, comes from an evening out rather than from a change in her own work circumstances. Even within the home, television elevates consumption over production; production is assumed to be a constant—only consumption can be varied. But more than enjoyment is at stake: unless Riley can provide her with the desired night on the town, he will fail in his obligations as a husband (*Life of Riley:* R228; *The Goldbergs:* "Bad Companions"). . . .

"Mama's Birthday," broadcast in 1954, delineated the tensions between family loyalty and consumer desire endemic to modern capitalist society. The show begins with Mama teaching Katrin to make Norwegian potato balls, the kind she used long ago to "catch" Papa. Unimpressed by this accomplishment, Katrin changes the subject and asks Mama what she wants for her upcoming birthday. In an answer that locates Mama within the gender roles of the 1950s, she replies, "Well, I think a fine new job for your Papa. You and Dagmar to marry nice young men and have a lot of wonderful children—just like I have. And Nels, well, Nels to become president of the United States" (Meehan and Ropes 1954). In one sentence Mama has summed up the dominant culture's version of legitimate female expectations: success at work for her husband, marriage and childrearing for her daughters, the presidency for her son—and nothing for herself.

But we learn that Mama does have some needs, although we do not hear it from her lips. Her sister, Jenny, asks Mama to attend a fashion show, but Mama cannot leave the house because she has to cook a roast for a guest whom Papa has invited to dinner. Jenny comments that Mama never seems to get out of the kitchen, adding that "it's a disgrace when a woman can't call her soul her own," and "it's a shame that a married woman can't have some time to herself." The complaint is a valid one, and we can imagine how it might have resonated for women in the 1950s. The increased availability of household appliances and the use of synthetic fibers and commercially processed food should have decreased the amount of time women spent in housework,

but surveys showed that home-makers spent the same number of hours per week (51 to 56) doing housework as they had done in the 1920s. Advertising and marketing strategies undermined the potential of technological changes by upgrading standards for cleanliness in the home and expanding desires for more varied wardrobes and menus for the average family (Hartmann 1982:168). In that context, Aunt Jenny would have been justified in launching into a tirade about the division of labor within the Hansen household or about the possibilities for cooperative housework, but network television specializes in a less social and more commodified dialogue about problems like housework: Aunt Jenny suggests that her sister's family buy her a "fireless cooker"—a cast iron stove—for her birthday. "They're wonderful," she tells them in language borrowed from the rhetoric of advertising. "You just put your dinner inside them, close 'em up, and go where you please. When you come back your dinner is all cooked" (Meehan and Ropes 1954). Papa protests that Mama likes to cook on her woodburning stove, but Jenny dismisses that objection with an insinuation about his motive, when she replies, "Well, I suppose it *would* cost a little more than you could afford, Hansen" (Meehan and Ropes 1954). By identifying a commodity as the solution to Mama's problem, Aunt Jenny unites the inner voice of Mama with the outer voice of the sponsors of television programs. . . .

Prodded by their aunt, the Hansen children go shopping and purchase the fireless cooker from a storekeeper who calls the product "the new Emancipation Proclamation—setting housewives free from their old kitchen range" (Meehan and Ropes 1954). Our exposure to advertising hyperbole should not lead us to miss the analogy here: housework is compared to slavery, and the commercial product takes on the aura of Abraham Lincoln. The shopkeeper's appeal convinces the children to pool their resources and buy the stove for Mama. But we soon learn that Papa plans to make a fireless cooker for Mama with his tools. When Mama discovers Papa's intentions she persuades the children to buy her another gift. Even Papa admits that his stove will not be as efficient as the one made in a factory, but Mama nobly affirms that she will like his better because he made it himself. The children use their money to buy dishes for Mama, and Katrin remembers the episode as Mama's happiest birthday ever (Meehan and Ropes 1954).

The stated resolution of "Mama's Birthday" favors traditional values. Mama prefers to protect Papa's feelings rather than having a better stove, and the product built by a family member has more value than one sold as a commodity. Yet the entire development of the plot leads in the opposite direction. The "fireless cooker" is the star of the episode, setting in motion all the other characters, and it has unquestioned value even in the face of Jenny's meddlesome brashness, Papa's insensitivity, and Mama's old-fashioned ideals. Buying a product is unchallenged as the true means of changing the unpleasant realities or low status of women's work in the home.

This resolution of the conflict between consumer desires and family roles reflected television's social role as mediator between the family and the economy. Surveys of set ownership showed no pronounced stratification by class, but a clear correlation between family size and television purchases: households with three to five people were most likely to own television sets, while those with only one person were least likely to own them (Swanson and Jones 1951). The television industry recognized and promoted its privileged place within families in advertisements like the one in the *New York Times* in 1950 that proclaimed, "Youngsters today need television for their morale as much as they need fresh air and sunshine for their health" (Wolfenstein 1951). Like previous communications media,

television sets occupied honored places in family living rooms, and helped structure family time; unlike other previous communications media, they displayed available commodities in a way that transformed all their entertainment into a glorified shopping catalogue. . . .

Note

1. Nielsen ratings demonstrate television's view of the family as separate market segments to be addressed independently. For an analysis of the industry's view of children as a special market, see Patricia J. Bence (1985), "Analysis and History of Typology and Forms of Children's Network Programming from 1950 to 1980."

References

Allen, Jeanne. 1983. The Social Matrix of Television: Invention in the United States. In *Regarding Television*. E. Ann Kaplan, ed. Pp. 109–119. Los Angeles: University Publications of America.

Berger, Henry. 1982. Social Protest in St. Louis. Paper presented at a Committee for the Humanities Forum. St. Louis, Missouri. March 12.

Boddy, William. 1985. The Studios Move Into Prime Time: Hollywood and the Television Industry in the 1950s. *Cinema Journal* 12(4):23–37.

Dichter, Ernest. 1960. *The Strategy of Desire*. Garden City: Doubleday.

Goldbergs, The. 1955. Moving Day. Academy of Television Arts Collection. 35F34I. University of California, Los Angeles.

———. 1955. The In-laws. Academy of Television Arts Collection. F32I8. University of California, Los Angeles.

———. 1955. Bad Companions. Academy of Television Arts Collection. F32I9. University of California, Los Angeles.

Hartmann, Susan. 1982. *The Home Front and Beyond*. Boston: Twayne.

Hey Jeannie. 1956. The Rock and Roll Kid. Academy of Television Arts Collection. University of California, Los Angeles.

Jezer, Marty. 1982. *The Dark Ages*. Boston: South End.

Life of Riley. 1953. Academy of Television Arts Collection. R228. University of California, Los Angeles.

Lipsitz, George. 1981. *Class and Culture in Cold War America: A Rainbow at Midnight*. New York: Praeger.

Meehan, Elizabeth, and Bradford Ropes. 1954. *Mama's Birthday*. Theater Arts Collection. University Research Library. University of California, Los Angeles.

Mollenkopf, John. 1983. *The Contested City*. Princeton: Princeton University Press.

Moore, Geoffrey, and Phillip Klein. 1967. *The Quality of Consumer Installment Credit*. Washington, D.C.: National Bureau of Economic Research.

Romasco, Albert U. 1965. *The Poverty of Abundance*. New York: Oxford University Press.

Stone, Michael. 1983. Housing and the Economic Crisis. In *America's Housing Crisis: What Is to be Done?* Chester Hartman, ed. Pp. 99–150. London and New York: Routledge and Kegan Paul.

Swanson, Charles E. and Robert L. Jones (1951). Television Ownership and Its Correlates. *Journal of Applied Psychology* 35:352–357.

TV Facts. 1980. New York: Facts on File.

Wolfenstein, Martha. 1951. The Emergence of Fun Morality. *Journal of Social Issues* 7(4):15–25.

Hegemony

James Lull

Hegemony is the power or dominance that one social group holds over others. This can refer to the "asymmetrical interdependence" of political-economic-cultural relations between and among nation-states (Straubhaar, 1991) or differences between and among social classes within a nation. Hegemony is "dominance and subordination in the field of relations structured by power" (Hall, 1985). But hegemony is more than social power itself; it is a method for gaining and maintaining power.

Classical Marxist theory, of course, stresses economic position as the strongest predictor of social differences. Today, more than a century after Karl Marx and Friedrich Engels wrote their treatises about capitalist exploitation of the working class, economic disparities still underlie and help reproduce social inequalities in industrialized societies. . . . Technological developments in the twentieth century, however, have made the manner of social domination much more complex than before. Social class differences in today's world are not determined solely or directly by economic factors. Ideological influence is crucial now in the exercise of social power.

The Italian intellectual Antonio Gramsci—to whom the term hegemony is attributed—broadened materialist Marxist theory into the realm of ideology. Persecuted by his country's then fascist government (and writing from prison), Gramsci emphasized society's "super structure," its ideology-producing institutions, in struggles over meaning and power (1971; 1973; 1978; see also Boggs, 1976; Sassoon, 1980; and Simon, 1982). A shift in critical theory thus was made away from a preoccupation with capitalist society's "base" (its economic foundation) and towards its dominant dispensaries of ideas. Attention was given to the structuring of authority and dependence in symbolic environments that correspond to, but are not the same as, economically determined class-based structures and processes of industrial production. Such a theoretical turn seems a natural and necessary development in an era when communications technology is such a pervasive and potent ideological medium. According to Gramsci's theory of ideological hegemony, mass media are tools that ruling elites use to "perpetuate their power, wealth, and status [by popularizing] their own philosophy, culture and morality" (Boggs, 1976: 39). The mass media uniquely "introduce elements into individual consciousness that would not otherwise appear there, but will not be rejected by consciousness because they are so commonly shared in the cultural community" (Nordenstreng, 1977: 276). Owners and managers of media industries can produce and reproduce the content, inflections, and tones of ideas favorable to them far more easily than other social groups because they manage key socializing institutions, thereby guaranteeing that their points of view are constantly and attractively cast into the public arena.

Mass-mediated ideologies are corroborated and strengthened by an interlocking system of efficacious information-distributing agencies and taken-for-granted social practices that permeate every aspect of social and cultural reality. Messages supportive of the status quo emanating from schools, businesses, political organizations, trade unions, religious groups, the military and the mass media all dovetail together ideologically. This inter-articulating, mutually reinforcing process of ideological influence is the essence of hegemony. Society's most entrenched and powerful institutions—which all depend in one way or another on the same sources for economic support—fundamentally agree with each other ideologically.

Hegemony is not a *direct* stimulation of thought or action, but, according to Stuart Hall, is a "framing [of] all competing definitions of reality within [the dominant class's] range bringing all alternatives within their horizons of thought. [The dominant class] sets the limits—mental and structural—within which subordinate classes 'live' and make sense of their subordination in such a way as to sustain the dominance of those ruling over them" (1977: 333). British social theorist Philip Elliott suggested similarly that the most potent effect of mass media is how they subtly influence their audiences to perceive social roles and routine personal activities. The controlling economic forces in society use the mass media to provide a "rhetoric [through] which these [concepts]

are labeled, evaluated, and explained" (1974: 262). Television commercials, for example, encourage audiences to think of themselves as "markets rather than as a public, as consumers rather than citizens" (Gitlin, 1979: 255).

But hegemony does not mature strictly from ideological articulation. Dominant ideological streams must be subsequently reproduced in the activities of our most basic social units—families, workplace networks, and friendship groups in the many sites and undertakings of everyday life. Gramsci's theory of hegemony, therefore, connects ideological representation to culture. Hegemony requires that ideological assertions become self-evident cultural assumptions. Its effectiveness depends on subordinated peoples accepting the dominant ideology as "normal reality or common sense . . . in active forms of experience and consciousness" (Williams, 1976: 145). Because information and entertainment technology is so thoroughly integrated into the everyday realities of modern societies, mass media's social influence is not always recognized, discussed, or criticized, particularly in societies where the overall standard of living is relatively high. Hegemony, therefore, can easily go undetected (Bausinger, 1984).

Hegemony implies a willing agreement by people to be governed by principles, rules, and laws they believe operate in their best interests, even though in actual practice they may not. Social consent can be a more effective means of control than coercion or force. Again, Raymond Williams: "The idea of hegemony, in its wide sense, is . . . especially important in societies [where] electoral politics and public opinion are significant factors, and in which social practice is seen to depend on consent to certain dominant ideas which in fact express the needs of a dominant class" (1976: 145). Thus, in the words of Colombian communication theorist Jesús Martín-Barbero, "one class exercises hegemony to the extent that the dominating class has interests which the subaltern classes recognize as being in some degree their interests too" (1993: 74).

Relationships between and among the major information-diffusing, socializing agencies of a society and the interacting, cumulative, socially accepted ideological orientations they create and sustain is the essence of hegemony. The American television industry, for instance, connects with other large industries, especially advertising companies but also national and multinational corporations that produce, distribute, and market a wide range of commodities. So, for example, commercial TV networks no longer buy original children's television shows. Network executives only want new program ideas associated with successful retail products already marketed to children. By late 1990 more than 20 toy-based TV shows appeared on American commercial TV weekly. Television also has the ability to absorb other major social institutions— organized religion, for instance—and turn them into popular culture. The TV industry also connects with government institutions, including especially the federal agencies that are supposed to regulate telecommunications. The development of American commercial broadcasting is a vivid example of how capitalist economic forces assert their power. Evacuation of the legislatively mandated public service ideal could only have taken place because the Federal Communications Commission stepped aside while commercial interests amassed power and expanded their influence. Symptomatic of the problem is the fact that government regulators typically are recruited from, and return to, the very industries they are supposed to monitor. . . .

Hegemony as an Incomplete Process

Two of our leading critical theorists, Raymond Williams and Stuart Hall, remind us that hegemony in any political context is indeed fragile. It requires renewal and modification through the assertion and reassertion of power. Hall suggests that "it is crucial to the concept that hegemony is not a 'given' and permanent state of affairs, but it has to be actively won and secured; it can also be lost" (1977: 333). Ideological work is the winning and securing of hegemony over time. . . . Ideology is composed of "texts that are not closed" according to Hall, who also notes that ideological "counter-tendencies" regularly appear in the seams and cracks of dominant forms (Hall, 1985). Mediated communications ranging from popular television shows to rap and rock music, even graffiti scrawled over surfaces of public spaces, all inscribe messages that challenge central political positions and cultural assumptions.

Counter-hegemonic tendencies do not inhere solely in texts. They are formulated in processes of communication—in the interpretations, social circulation, and uses of media content. As with the American soldiers' use of military gas masks as inhaling devices to heighten the effect of marijuana smoke, or the homeless's transformation of supermarket shopping carts into personal storage vehicles, ideological resistance and appropriation frequently involve reinventing institutional messages for purposes that differ greatly from their creators' intentions. Expressions of the dominant ideology are sometimes reformulated to assert alternative, often completely resistant or contradictory messages. . . .

Furthermore, resistance to hegemony is not initiated solely by media consumers. Texts themselves are implicated. Ideology can never be stated purely and simply. Ways of thinking are always reflexive and embedded in a complex, sometimes contradictory, ideological regress. . . .

Audience interpretations and uses of media imagery also eat away at hegemony. Hegemony fails when dominant ideology is weaker than social resistance. Gay subcultures, feminist organizations, environmental groups, radical political parties, music-based forma- tions such as punks, B-boys, Rastafarians, and metal heads all use media and their social networks to endorse counter-hegemonic values and lifestyles. Indeed, we have only just begun to examine the complex relation- ship between ideological representation and social action.

References

Bausinger, H. (1984). Media, technology, and everyday life. *Media, Culture & Society*, 6, 340–52.

Boggs, C. (1976). *Gramsci's Marxism*. London: Pluto.

Elliott, P. (1974). Uses and gratifications research: A critique and a sociological alter- native. In J. G. Blumler and E. Katz (eds.), *The Uses of Mass Communications: Current Perspectives on Gratifications Research*. Beverly Hills, CA: Sage.

Gitlin, T. (1979). Prime-time ideology: The hege- monic process in television entertainment. *Social Problems*, 26, 251–66.

Gramsci, A. (1971). *Selections from the Prison Notebooks*. New York: International.

Gramsci, A. (1973). *Letters from Prison*. New York: Harper and Row.

Gramsci, A. (1978). *Selections from Cultural Writings*. Cambridge, MA: Harvard University Press.

Hall, S. (1977). Culture, media, and the "ideolog- ical effect." In J. Curran, M. Gurevitch, and J. Woollacott (eds.), *Mass Communication and Society*. London: Edward Arnold.

Hall, S. (1985). Master's session. International Communication Association. Honolulu, Hawaii.

Martín-Barbero, J. (1993). *Communication, Culture and Hegemony*. Newbury Park, CA: Sage.

Nordenstreng, K. (1977). From mass media to mass consciousness. In G. Gerbner (ed.), *Mass Media Policies in Changing Cultures*. New York: Wiley.

Sassoon, A. S. (1980). *Gramsci's Politics*. New York: St. Martin's.

Simon, R. (1982). *Gramsci's Political Thought*. London: Lawrence and Wishart.

Straubhaar, J. (1991). Beyond media imperial- ism: Asymmetrical interdependence and cultural proximity. *Critical Studies in Mass Communication*, 8, 39–59.

Williams, R. (1976). *Key Words: A Vocabulary of Culture and Society*. New York: Oxford University Press.

Extreme Makeover: Home Edition

An American Fairy Tale

Gareth Palmer

It's a fairy tale. It's a guaranteed happy ending (Forman 2005).

ABC's *Extreme Makeover: Home Edition* (hereafter *EMHE*) was one of the top ten programmes of the 2004/05 season in America and winner of the 2005 Emmy for Outstanding Reality TV Programme. *EMHE* tells a fascinating story about modern day America where the return of a strong right-wing ideology privileges the traditional family and the interests of business, yet also affords a glimpse of the crises affecting ordinary Americans. In the model of community proposed by the programme, the state has no role to play: in its place are people coming together out of fellow-feeling for their neighbours. But the repair work is so extreme it throws into relief the mundane quality of most American homes. In promoting such a perspective both in the programme and through its various affiliated enterprises with Sears etc., ABC are championing an America which resonates with its mythical past but which is utterly unrepresentative of family life for most Americans. The programme is, in short, a fairy tale where magic is represented by selfless communities, free goods, labour, and dreams coming true.

The Family

> . . . Representations have become a critical battleground in the conflicts over family and family values leading to the spectacularization of the family as the platform on which society's profound debates about sexual and personal morality are performed. (Chambers 2001: 176)

From Palmer, G. (2007). *Extreme Makeover: Home Edition:* An American fairy tale. In D. Heller (Ed.), *Makeover TV: Realities remodelled* (pp. 165–176). London: I. B. Taurus.

EMHE starts every week with a sequence in which the assorted designers who will lead the re-design of the house are situated in a van watching the targeted family's videotape. Team Leader Ty Pennington gives the background to this family and the rest of this sequence involves reaction shots of all involved. What is remarkable about this sequence, at least for this British viewer, is that these video-diary sequences sent in by the family are all extraordinarily revealing about the state of America.

In many cases the desperation of families is a direct result of the fact that agencies of the state have abandoned them. For example, in one case a family had to watch their son die because ambulances and police refused to go into their neighbourhood for fear of their lives. In another video we see a family whose son is dying because he is ineligible for medical aid. In yet another typical episode, an Iraq War veteran has materials provided for him, as the state does not support veterans very generously. Week after week we see first hand video testimony that the state is in retreat and only those lucky enough to have many friends, family and neighbours are able to survive. . . .

After watching their tape for a few moments the crew arrive, and the family to be chosen is woken very early in the morning, on the doorstep of their home. This magical moment is only the first of many such other-worldly touches in the narrative. After meeting the team and crying tears of gratitude, the family is then whisked away for a week-long holiday while crew, enlisted community, and contractors go about the business of changing their home.

What follows is a monumental effort to effect the transformation. But why has all this energy been devoted to making the home so central? In the last ten years, makeover shows have become a mainspring of TV schedules in Britain and America. In each case a person with limited resources is assisted into a new look and given the confidence he or she needs to progress. However, at the centre of these 'reveals' is

the family. In examples ranging from *This Old House* to *The Swan* it is the family that has inspired the change and the family who are focused on in their reaction to it. In this way the home is remade as a machine for keeping families together, the place to retreat to. It need hardly be said that such an approach brings to mind long and powerful myths about the centrality of the family. In Anthony Giddens' formulation, 'The site for the democratisation of intimate relationships, the family becomes a major platform on which debates about moralities and ethics get staged' (Giddens 1999: 165).

The makeover show turns individuals into family members, foregrounds the family and makes it a part of the wider community. It is hard to imagine a clearer message about the centrality of the home and the importance of keeping the family together come what may. . . .

It might be argued that there are two families at work in *EMHE*—the subject of the makeover and the extended family of the design team. It is, after all, this latter family that we get to know every week through their work and their relationships with one another. It is they who represent a modern family with no fixed relationships and no permanent 'home' they can call their own. (We might also note that the five men exhibit some of the camp characteristics that are now a trademark of the makeover genre: only in this sense can the hint of homosexuality be tolerated, in a space marked off from ordinary life.) In a sense, the *EMHE* team represent the fluid upwardly mobile petit bourgeoisie against the time-worn virtues of the proletariat. This divide between the classes ensures that the working class are always receptive and thankful for the 'good taste' bestowed upon them by the middle class. But while it is the role of the working class to be properly grateful, the designers are all seen to be humbled by their experience, which extends beyond the show and is maintained through letters and notes pinned to a message board.

The coming together of these two family groupings is about 'learning'—a theme that dominates so much American television. While the working class learn taste, the petit bourgeoisie learn about 'real people' (i.e. the sort of people they would not normally ever encounter in their lives as designers for the rich and famous). This learning is a means of bringing groups together, the wider theme that animates the series and which keys it into the classic picture of an America constituted of families connected to communities making one nation (Morley and Robins 1995: 109).

At the end of the show the ramshackle house, held together by the depth of the bonds between the family members, is replaced by a magnificent home. . . . As we are led through the magically transformed home at the same time as the family, we, too, can be awestruck by the changes wrought by the designers and of course the wider community. In one sense, we marvel at the high quality of the work achieved, but perhaps more significant is the fact that we are reminded that this transformation is also a reward—it is because people have held the family together in very difficult situations that they deserve this home. In clips and segments that remind us of the past, we are moved to see that these people have got what they deserve. The home is an extension of the love that the family members hold for one another. By undergoing this transformation as a reward for their dedication to the family, the individuals go from being objects of our pity to ones of our envy. . . .

Community

'A better community—get involved and help—click here.' (ABC website)

Makeover programmes are the most overt sign of the ways television perceives itself to be engaged in a project of advising ordinary viewers about their transformation into happier, more satisfied, up-to-date versions of their selves. (Bonner 2003: 136)

The community plays a central role in *EMHE*. It is made clear throughout the programme and in all accompanying materials that it is the community that are responsible for making the whole thing come together. While it may be designers who provide the creative impetus, it is the community that are seen doing all the unglamorous heavy work. Unlike the virtual shadow-communities inspired to 'call the cops' in response to televised police appeals, which dissolve once their contribution is made, *EMHE* features real communities showing us all how to work together.

To begin with, the community has often been the sponsor of the families who are featured. As Forman has said: 'Most of the families we end up doing are nominations. The kind of families we're looking for don't say "Gee, I need help". They are quietly trying to solve their problems themselves and it's a neighbor or co-worker who submits and application on their behalf.' (Forman 2005)

We see the community, shortly after the programme begins, giving testimony to the deserving family, then later throughout the show at work in various jobs. They play small but significant roles in the drama as the glue in the cracks of the community holding everything together. And yet they are also there in the reveal. They 'star' here because of what they have done to bring about these changes. Whether as contractors, friends, tradesmen or simply labourers, all have a role to play and are defined not so much as individuals but as part of a greater whole. No individual pulls focus: it is always about the larger community. But what actually constitutes this community?

It is important to see the entire series in context as a trigger for activating a wide variety of communities. For example, the local press are often keen to highlight the series if a local family is involved. In Salt Lake City we learn of the '1,500 workers and volunteers working 24 hours a day to build a bigger home for the Johnson family.' In the *Boston Globe* we read about how residents had 'been rooting for more than a year for a family to be picked up by the show.' Once they had been selected, the community were all too keen to get involved.

Two allied supporters of this community effort are local businesses and the Church. John McMurria has pointed out how Sears has benefited from the programme (McMurria 2005). But plenty of other local services are represented in *EMHE,* not as profit-led businesses but as benevolent organizations. The value of PR here can be enormous as big cardboard cheques are presented to tearful local residents. As one business said of a veteran—'He has such a sweet and humble spirit and we wanted to thank him for the way he loves for his country and his family.'

It is important also to note that American Christian groups have been generous in praising the show. As Evangelical journalist Holly Vincente Robaina wrote, 'It's a rare phenomenon. Believers of every age, ethnicity and denomination are embracing the primetime television show ABC's *Extreme Makeover: Home Edition*' (Robaina 2006).

Executive producer Tom Forman was specifically asked whether any plan was made to 'include elements that would connect specifically with Christian values.' Forman responded that the show appealed because 'good things happen to good people. That's possibly why it resonates with the Christian community and all of our viewers' (Forman, ABC interview).

Church leaders are quoted by the local press, such as Mr A. Wigston in the *Cass County Democrat of Missouri.* 'It was really neat to see God working through the hearts of the designers for people with disabilities.' Some other churches have set out on 'copy-cat' schemes in which members decorate or attempt mini-makeovers of

their own in just the way that producer Forman had hoped they would. Not only does this imitative practice privilege the role of the Church in the community, but the reporting and celebration of this role presents a clear ideological message on the centrality of helping heterosexual families. But is this at the expense of other communities?

These timeless myths of the American 'heartland', featuring the happy smiling community working for nothing but love, bring to mind classic American TV fictions such as *Little House on the Prairie* and *The Waltons.* These idealized versions of perfect family life may be instructive about nostalgia in the 1970s and 1980s, and for settled family life in a time of great upheaval. But of course these fictions were located in the past when such a myth may have been feasible. But what are we to make of *EMHE*'s portrait of American life, which suggests such ideals are here with us now? . . .

The Magical Market

. . . One of the most unusual factors about the programme for British viewers is the complete absence of cost. In contrast to many UK makeover shows, costs are never mentioned in *EMHE.* Why is this? The instinctual answer has to be that costs have no place in a fairy tale. Do we know where the Prince bought the glass slippers? Of course not—these are crass questions. It is our role simply to be enchanted by the transformations wrought. But, at the risk of breaking the spell, there are various economic elements that I think merit discussion, for they speak to the real and entirely non-magical base of the programme.

In the first place, we might consider the costs of labour. What would it cost to hire such designers or to employ upwards of 150 people for 24 hours a day, seven days a week? Secondly, we might look at the cost of the furnishings, the materials and the many other artful purchases that go into the ideal home. It is only at the end of the show that we have any sort of opportunity to calculate the cost of this transformation, but by then we are too emotionally involved to make such calculations. The point is that all of these costs are hidden in the service of repairing families. But not mentioning costs makes these repairs appear free or even magical. As most communities know, the economic is determining and not at all magical. The fact is that there are many who profit enormously from the show.

While it is clearly the case that one family will benefit from the makeover, the public relations benefits to others involved are extraordinary. The most obvious recipient of good PR is the Sears corporation. The programme's website makes it clear that the company is a major partner in the production of the show. It is worth noting that Sears also sponsor *EMHE* host Ty Pennington. Pennington's 'can-do' attitude represents something that Sears wants—as long as the 'can-do' he recommends is connected to Sears products. Pennington legitimates Sears as a caring company through his leadership of such obvious good works.

But Sears is only the most high profile of sponsors. Every week we hear of many other local organizations that have devoted their goods and services to the families in need. At this point we are encouraged to think of local businesses not as profit driven but as charitable organizations. The PR benefit of this publicity is enhanced when favourable coverage appears in the local papers about the *EMHE* projects in their town. This would be a good time for local businesses to place adverts reminding consumers of their modest role in the transformation.

Thirdly, and perhaps most obviously, the benefits to ABC will be very considerable. Firstly, there are the benefits in revenue that accrue to shows that are doing well. This factor is particularly important when competition from other stations and other media is more intensive than ever before. During the show the families often thank

ABC while the presenters and others also make subtle mention of how the programme has only been possible through the good offices of the station. Again, this will represent an invaluable opportunity for the station to define itself as family-driven in contrast to its more ruthless rivals CBS, Fox and NBC. This benefit sometimes informs the company's well-advertised outreach programmes and also helps to inspire other shows. The praise heaped on the programme by churches and other religious groups helps ABC reposition itself in the family market. (The station's owner, The Disney channel, has used gay-friendly corporate policies and has sponsored broadcast gay-themed sitcoms such as *Ellen*, resulting in criticism from Christian groups. *EMHE* redefines ABC as a wholesome family station.)

Finally, is it not also the case that the programme is of enormous benefit to the eight designers who appear on the show? The 'good works' they do here will drive business to their companies as well as raise their price in the celebrity market as guest speakers, seminar leaders, etc.

But what is crucial to all of this is that the market appears to be driven not by the hunt for profit but by the simple desire to do 'good works'. In this way, capitalism is sold to audiences as a warm and responsive mechanism reacting to community needs rather than a system for maximizing profits. It is not money that pulls people together, but a sort of magic. . . .

Television That Works

An ethics of care as presented in lifestyle programmes is primarily about care and responsibility . . . good and bad way[s] to live their lives. (Hill 2005: 184)

EMHE is part of a growing number of television programmes that are not simply recording or reflecting on society but becoming active elements, working practically and ideologically to change the world. . . .

In one sense, television has always done this. Magical solutions to practical problems for everyday people have been the staple of quiz and games shows for decades. But the past twenty years have seen a distinct rise in the number of programmes that focus on intervening in the lives of the public. In a curious historical quirk, commercial television is engaging with the public in a way that PBS, public television, can no longer afford to do. But commercial interests inspire all these interventions. *Wife Swap*, *Big Brother* and *Temptation Island* are not there to help the public (despite the rhetoric) but to offer mutual exploitation opportunities. They work, however, and this fact is proved night after night in reality TV shows, makeover shows, talk shows, cosmetic surgery shows, and many other programmes made at the behest of commercial institutions. Like any other product maker, the apparatus of ABC has a vested interest in producing 'good' (i.e. repeatable) results. Furthermore, if it does this in a way which makes it look socially responsible, then it gets a double-whammy. Not only does this help to keep the profile of the medium high but it also foregrounds television as a site for the validation of the person. To be on television is now one of the highest honours that can be accorded someone.

There is another significant point underscoring and helping to guarantee the effects of *EMHE* and others in the lifestyle genre, and it is in the craft of performance. *EMHE* is a very polished production that pulls together emotionally moving performances with the use of music, lighting and photography. Not only does the styling of the show borrow creatively from drama, it also emphasizes a theatrical transformation that will impress children—the next generation whose devotion to the medium all stations need to cherish. . . .

It would be comforting to think that our own responses to the transformations,

led by the families and designers, heralded some sort of emotional literacy, but even if we try to gain comfort from this we cannot escape the fact that this is all wrought for commercial profit (Littler 2004: 20). It is sad to reflect upon, but the radical changes to one family's life that we see in *EMHE* would simply not happen if it were not for television. Despite the powerful and manipulative devices that bring forth our involvement, at base the programme is a device for selling audiences to advertisers. It is not an engine for social change. . . .

Conclusion

Commercial culture does not manufacture ideology, it relays and reproduces and processes and packages and focuses ideology that is constantly arising set forth both from social elites and from active social groups and movements throughout the society. (Gitlin 1994: 518)

We have seen that *EMHE* produces a vision of America that has powerful emotional resonances. Its view of the world articulates connections with families, the Christian right and the neo-conservative policies of the Bush era. Yet the programme also provides gaps and fissures through which we can see massive cracks appearing in the American Dream. Although *EMHE* might seem like an unadulterated paean of praise to Capitalism, it fails to completely convince because of what it reveals as the inspirations to the makeover: things have got to be so bad because of the retreat of the state, that radical, even magical, consumer surgery is necessary. . . .

The fact is that in modern-day America many families and communities have been wrecked by policies that force them to uproot and look for work elsewhere. While the statistics attest to the breakdown of the family unit, ABC is doing the massive ideological labour of shoring it up. In the face of this breakdown *EMHE* deploys its excesses. The revamped houses look like sets because they are there to provide ideal templates for the performance of family roles.

As capitalism continues to deepen divisions between rich and poor, ABC offers the cold comfort of the *EMHE* fairy tale, the belief that if the family holds together despite everything that can be thrown against it, then the reward will eventually come.

Hope may be all they have.

References

Bonner, Frances. *Ordinary Television: Analyzing Popular TV.* London: Sage, 2003.

Chambers, D. *Representing the Family.* London: Sage, 2001.

Forman, T. Interview at official ABC website. (2005) www.abc.go.com/primetime/xtreme home/index.html

Giddens, Anthony. *Runaway World: How Globalisation Is Reshaping Our Lives.* London: Profile Books, 1999.

Gitlin, T. "Prime Time Ideology: The Hegemonic Process in Television Entertainment." In Horace Newcomb, ed., *Television: The Critical View.* Oxford: Oxford University Press, 1994.

Hill, Annette. *Reality TV: Audiences and Popular Factual Television.* London: Routledge, 2005.

Littler, J. "Making Fame Ordinary: Intimacy, Reflexitivity, Keeping It Real." *Mediactive.* 2 (2004): 8–25.

McMurria, John. "Desperate Citizens." Flow. 3.3 (2005). http://jot.communication.utexas .edu/flow/?jot=view&id+1047

Morley, D. and K. Robins. *Spaces of Identity: Global Media, Electronic Landscapes and Cultural Boundaries.* London: Routledge, 1995.

Robaina, Holly Vincente. "A Foundation of Faith." Christianity Today. www.christianity today.com. *Salt Lake City Tribune.* (2006) www.sltrib.com

Women Read the Romance

The Interaction of Text and Context

Janice Radway

. . . The interpretation of the romance's cultural significance offered here has been developed from a series of extensive ethnographic-like interviews with a group of compulsive romance readers in a predominantly urban, central midwestern state among the nation's top twenty in total population.[1] I discovered my principal informant and her customers with the aid of a senior editor at Doubleday whom I had been interviewing about the publication of romances. Sally Arteseros told me of a bookstore employee who had developed a regular clientele of fifty to seventy-five regular romance readers who relied on her for advice about the best romances to buy and those to avoid. When I wrote to Dot Evans, as I will now call her, to ask whether I might question her about how she interpreted, categorized, and evaluated romantic fiction, I had no idea that she had also begun to write a newsletter designed to enable bookstores to advise their customers about the quality of the romances published monthly. She has since copyrighted this newsletter and incorporated it as a business. Dot is so successful at serving the women who patronize her chain outlet that the central office of this major chain occasionally relies on her sales predictions to gauge romance distribution throughout the system. Her success has also brought her to the attention of both editors and writers for whom she now reads manuscripts and galleys.

My knowledge of Dot and her readers is based on roughly sixty hours of interviews conducted in June 1980 and February 1981. I have talked extensively with Dot about romances, reading, and her advising activities as well as observed her interactions with her customers at the bookstore. I have also conducted both group and individual interviews with sixteen of her regular customers and administered a lengthy questionnaire to forty-two of these women. Although not representative of all women who read romances, the group appears to be demographically similar to a sizable segment of that audience as it has been mapped by several rather secretive publishing houses.

From Janice A. Radway, "Women Read the Romance: The Interaction of Text and Context," originally published in *Feminist Studies*, Volume 9, Number 1 (Spring 1983): 56–68, is used by permission of the publisher, *Feminist Studies*, Inc.

Dorothy Evans lives and works in the community of Smithton, as do most of her regular customers. A city of about 112,000 inhabitants, Smithton is located five miles due east of the state's second largest city, in a metropolitan area with a total population of over 1 million. Dot was forty-eight years old at the time of the survey, the wife of a journeyman plumber, and the mother of three children in their twenties. She is extremely bright and articulate and, while not a proclaimed feminist, holds some beliefs about women that might be labeled as such. Although she did not work outside the home when her children were young and does not now believe that a woman needs a career to be fulfilled, she feels women should have the opportunity to work and be paid equally with men. Dot also believes that women should have the right to abortion, though she admits that her deep religious convictions would prevent her from seeking one herself. She is not disturbed by the Equal Rights Amendment and can and does converse eloquently about the oppression women have endured for years at the hands of men. Despite her opinions, however, she believes implicitly in the value of true romance and thoroughly enjoys discovering again and again that women can find men who will love them as they wish to be loved. Although most of her regular customers are more conservative than Dot in the sense that they do not advocate political measures to redress past grievances, they are quite aware that men commonly think themselves superior to women and often mistreat them as a result.

In general, Dot's customers are married, middle-class mothers with at least a high school education.[2] More than 60 percent of the women were between the ages of twenty-five and forty-four at the time of the study, a fact that duplicates fairly closely Harlequin's finding that the majority of its readers is between twenty-five and forty-nine.[3] Silhouette Books has also recently reported that 65 percent of the romance market is below the age of 40.[4]

Exactly 50 percent of the Smithton women have high school diplomas, while 32 percent report completing at least some college work. Again, this seems to suggest that the interview group is fairly representative, for Silhouette also indicates that 45 percent of the romance market has attended at least some college. The employment status and family income of Dot's customers also seem to duplicate those of the audience mapped by the publishing houses. Forty-two percent of the Smithton women, for instance, work part-time outside the home. Harlequin claims that 49 percent of its audience is similarly employed. The Smithton women report slightly higher incomes than those of the average Harlequin reader (43 percent of the Smithton women have incomes of $15,000 to $24,999, 33 percent have incomes of $25,000 to $49,999—the average income of the Harlequin reader is $15,000 to $20,000), but the difference is not enough to change the general sociological status of the group. . . .

When asked why they read romances, the Smithton women overwhelmingly cite escape or relaxation as their goal. They use the word "escape," however, both literally and figuratively. On the one hand, they value their romances highly because the act of reading them literally draws the women away from their present surroundings. Because they must produce the meaning of the story by attending closely to the words on the page, they find that their attention is withdrawn from concerns that plague them in reality. One woman remarked with a note of triumph in her voice: "My body may be in that room, but I'm not!" She and her sister readers see their romance reading as a legitimate way of denying a present reality that occasionally becomes too onerous to bear. This particular means of escape is better than television viewing for these women, because the cultural value attached to books permits them to overcome the guilt they feel about avoiding their responsibilities.

They believe that reading of any kind is, by nature, educational.[5] They insist accordingly that they also read to learn.[6]

On the other hand, the Smithton readers are quite willing to acknowledge that the romances which so preoccupy them are little more than fantasies or fairy tales that always end happily. They readily admit in fact that the characters and events discovered in the pages of the typical romance do not resemble the people and occurrences they must deal with in their daily lives. On the basis of the following comments, made in response to a question about what romances "do" better than other novels available today, one can conclude that it is precisely the unreal, fantastic shape of the story that makes their literal escape even more complete and gratifying. Although these are only a few of the remarks given in response to the undirected question, they are representative of the group's general sentiment.

> Romances hold my interest and do not leave me depressed or up in the air at the end like many modern day books tend to do. Romances also just make me feel good reading them as I identify with the heroines.

> The kind of books I mainly read are very different from everyday living. That's why I read them. Newspapers, etc., I find boring because all you read is sad news. I can get enough of that on TV news. I like stories that take your mind off everyday matters.

> Different than everyday life.

> Everyone is always under so much pressure. They like books that let them escape.

> Because it is an escape, and we can dream. And pretend that it is our life. I'm able to escape the harsh world a few hours a day.

> It is a way of escaping from everyday living.

> They always seem an escape and they usually turn out the way you wish life really was.

> I enjoy reading because it offers me a small vacation from everyday life and an interesting and amusing way to pass the time.

These few comments all hint at a certain sadness that many of the Smithton women seem to share because life has not given them all that it once promised. A deep-seated sense of betrayal also lurks behind their deceptively simple expressions of a need to believe in a fairy tale. Although they have not elaborated in these comments, many of the women explained in the interviews that despite their disappointments, they feel refreshed and strengthened by their vicarious participation in a fantasy relationship where the heroine is frequently treated as they themselves would most like to be loved.

This conception of romance reading as an escape that is both literal and figurative implies flight from some situation in the real world which is either stifling or overwhelming, as well as a metaphoric transfer to another, more desirable universe where events are happily resolved. Unashamed to admit that they like to indulge in temporary escape, the Smithton women are also surprisingly candid about the circumstances that necessitate their desire. When asked to specify what they are fleeing from, they invariably mention the "pressures" and "tensions" they experience as wives and mothers. Although none of the women can cite the voluminous feminist literature about the psychological toll exacted by the constant demand to physically and emotionally nurture others, they are nonetheless eloquent about how draining and unrewarding their duties can be.[7] When first asked why women find it necessary to escape, Dot gave the following answer without once pausing to rest:

> As a mother, I have run 'em to the orthodontist. I have run 'em to the swimming

pool. I have run 'em to baton twirling lessons. I have run up to school because they forgot their lunch. You know, I mean really. And you do it. And it isn't that you begrudge it. That isn't it. Then my husband would walk in the door and he'd say, "Well, what did you do today?" You know, it was like, "Well, tell me how you spent the last eight hours, because I've been out working." And I finally got to the point where I would say, "Well, I read four books, and I did the wash and got the meal on the table and the beds are all made and the house is tidy." And I would get defensive like, "So what do you call all this? Why should I have to tell you because I certainly don't ask you what you did for eight hours, step by step."

But their husbands do that. We've compared notes. They hit the house and it's like "Well, all right. I've been out earning a living. Now what have you been doin' with your time?" And you begin to be feeling, "Now, really, why is he questioning me?"

Romance reading, as Dot herself puts it, constitutes a temporary "declaration of independence" from the social roles of wife and mother. By placing the barrier of the book between themselves and their families, these women reserve a special space and time for themselves alone. As a consequence, they momentarily allow themselves to abandon the attitude of total self-abnegation in the interest of family welfare which they have so dutifully learned is the proper stance for a good wife and mother. Romance reading is both an assertion of deeply felt psychological needs and a means for satisfying those needs. Simply put, these needs arise because no other member of the family, as it is presently constituted in this still-patriarchal society, is yet charged with the affective and emotional reconstitution of a wife and mother. If she is depleted by her efforts to care for others, she is nonetheless expected to restore and sustain herself as well. As one of Dot's customers put it,

"You always have to be a Mary Poppins. You can't be sad, you can't be mad, you have to keep everything bottled up inside."

Nancy Chodorow has recently discussed this structural peculiarity of the modern family and its impact on the emotional lives of women in her influential book, *The Reproduction of Mothering*,[8] a complex reformulation of the Freudian theory of female personality development. Chodorow maintains that women often continue to experience a desire for intense affective nurturance and relationality well into adulthood as a result of an unresolved separation from their primary caretaker. It is highly significant, she argues, that in patriarchal society this caretaker is almost inevitably a woman. The felt similarity between mother and daughter creates an unusually intimate connection between them which later makes it exceedingly difficult for the daughter to establish autonomy and independence. Chodorow maintains, on the other hand, that because male children are also reared by women, they tend to separate more completely from their mothers by suppressing their own emotionality and capacities for tenderness which they associate with mothers and femininity. The resulting asymmetry in human personality, she concludes, leads to a situation where men typically cannot fulfill all of a woman's emotional needs. As a consequence, women turn to the act of mothering as a way of vicariously recovering that lost relationality and intensity.

My findings about Dot Evans and her customers suggest that the vicarious pleasure a woman receives through the nurturance of others may not be completely satisfying, because the act of caring for them also makes tremendous demands on a woman and can deplete her sense of self. In that case, she may well turn to romance reading in an effort to construct a fantasy-world where she is attended, as the heroine is, by a man who reassures her of her special status and unique identity.

The value of the romance may have something to do, then, with the fact that women find it especially difficult to indulge in the restorative experience of visceral regression to an infantile state where the self is cared for perfectly by another. This regression is so difficult precisely because women have been taught to believe that men must be their sole source of pleasure. Although there is nothing biologically lacking in men to make this ideal pleasure unattainable, as Chodorow's theories tell us, their engendering and socialization by the patriarchal family traditionally masks the very traits that would permit them to nurture women in this way. Because they are encouraged to be aggressive, competitive, self-sufficient, and unemotional, men often find sustained attention to the emotional needs of others both unfamiliar and difficult. While the Smithton women only minimally discussed their husbands' abilities to take care of them as they would like, when they commented on their favorite romantic heroes they made it clear that they enjoy imagining themselves being tenderly cared for and solicitously protected by a fictive character who inevitably proves to be spectacularly masculine and unusually nurturant as well.[9]

Indeed, this theme of pleasure recurred constantly in the discussions with the Smithton women. They insisted repeatedly that when they are reading a romance, they feel happy and content. Several commented that they particularly relish moments when they are home alone and can relax in a hot tub or in a favorite chair with a good book. Others admitted that they most like to read in a warm bed late at night. Their association of romances with contentment, pleasure, and good feelings is apparently not unique, for in conducting a market research study, Fawcett discovered that when asked to draw a woman reading a romance, romance readers inevitably depict someone who is exaggeratedly happy.[10]

The Smithton group's insistence that they turn to romances because the experience of reading the novels gives them hope, provides pleasure, and causes contentment raises the

unavoidable question of what aspects of the romantic narrative itself could possibly give rise to feelings such as these. How are we to explain, furthermore, the obvious contradiction between this reader emphasis on pleasure and hope, achieved through vicarious appreciation of the ministrations of a tender hero, and the observations of the earlier critics of romances that such books are dominated by men who at least temporarily abuse and hurt the women they purportedly love? In large part, the contradiction arises because the two groups are not reading according to the same interpretive strategies, neither are they reading nor commenting on the same books. Textual analyses like those offered by Douglas, Modleski, and Snitow are based on the common assumption that because romances are formulaic and therefore essentially identical, analysis of a randomly chosen sample will reveal the meaning unfailingly communicated by every example of the genre. This methodological procedure is based on the further assumption that category readers do not themselves perceive variations within the genre, nor do they select their books in a manner significantly different from the random choice of the analyst.

In fact, the Smithton readers do not believe the books are identical, nor do they approve of all the romances they read. They have elaborated a complex distinction between "good" and "bad" romances and they have accordingly experimented with various techniques that they hoped would enable them to identify bad romances before they paid for a book that would only offend them. Some tried to decode titles and cover blurbs by looking for key words serving as clues to the book's tone; others refused to buy romances by authors they didn't recognize; still others read several pages *including the ending* before they bought the book. Now, however, most of the people in the Smithton group have been freed from the need to rely on these inexact predictions because Dot Evans shares their perceptions and evaluations of the category and can alert them to unusually successful romantic fantasies while steering them away from those they call "disgusting perversions."

When the Smithton readers' comments about good and bad romances are combined with the conclusions drawn from an analysis of twenty of their favorite books and an equal number of those they classify as particularly inadequate, an illuminating picture of the fantasy fueling the romance-reading experience develops.[11] To begin with, Dot and her readers will not tolerate any story in which the heroine is seriously abused by men. They find multiple rapes especially distressing and dislike books in which a woman is brutally hurt by a man only to fall desperately in love with him in the last four pages. The Smithton women are also offended by explicit sexual description and scrupulously avoid the work of authors like Rosemary Rogers and Judith Krantz who deal in what they call "perversions" and "promiscuity." They also do not like romances that overtly perpetuate the double standard by excusing the hero's simultaneous involvement with several women. They insist, one reader commented, on "one women—one man." They also seem to dislike any kind of detailed description of male genitalia, although the women enjoy suggestive descriptions of how the hero is emotionally aroused to an overpowering desire for the heroine. . . .

According to Dot and her customers, the quality of the ideal romantic fantasy is directly dependent on the character of the heroine and the manner in which the hero treats her. The plot, of course, must always focus on a series of obstacles to the final declaration of love between the two principals. However, a good romance involves an unusually bright and determined woman and a man who is spectacularly masculine, but at the same time capable of remarkable empathy and tenderness. Although they enjoy the usual chronicle of misunderstandings and mistakes which inevitably leads to the heroine's belief that the hero intends to harm her, the Smithton readers prefer

stories that combine a much-understated version of this continuing antagonism with a picture of a gradually developing love. They most wish to participate in the slow process by which two people become acquainted, explore each other's foibles, wonder about the other's feelings, and eventually "discover" that they are loved by the other.

In conducting an analysis of the plots of the twenty romances listed as "ideal" by the Smithton readers, I was struck by their remarkable similarities in narrative structure. In fact, all twenty of these romances are very tightly organized around the evolving relationship between a single couple composed of a beautiful, defiant, and sexually immature woman and a brooding, handsome man who is also curiously capable of soft, gentle gestures. Although minor foil figures are used in these romances, none of the ideal stories seriously involves either hero or heroine with one of the rival characters.[12] They are employed mainly as contrasts to the more likable and proper central pair or as purely temporary obstacles to the pair's delayed union because one or the other mistakenly suspects the partner of having an affair with the rival. However, because the reader is never permitted to share this mistaken assumption in the ideal romance, she knows all along that the relationship is not as precarious as its participants think it to be. The rest of the narrative in the twenty romances chronicles the gradual crumbling of barriers between these two individuals who are fearful of being used by the other. As their defenses against emotional response fall away and their sexual passion rises inexorably, the typical narrative plunges on until the climactic point at which the hero treats the heroine to some supreme act of tenderness, and she realizes that his apparent emotional indifference was only the mark of his hesitancy about revealing the extent of his love for and dependence upon her.

The Smithton women especially like romances that commence with the early marriage of the hero and heroine for reasons of convenience. Apparently, they do so because they delight in the subsequent, necessary chronicle of the pair's growing awareness that what each took to be indifference or hate is, in reality, unexpressed love and suppressed passion. In such favorite romances as *The Flame and the Flower, The Black Lyon, Shanna,* and *Made For Each Other,* the heroine begins marriage thinking that she detests and is detested by her spouse. She is thrown into a quandary, however, because her partner's behavior vacillates from indifference, occasional brusqueness, and even cruelty to tenderness and passion. Consequently, the heroine spends most of her time in these romances, as well as in the others comprising this sample, trying to read the hero's behavior as a set of signs expressing his true feelings toward her. The final outcome of the story turns upon a fundamental process of reinterpretation, whereby she suddenly and clearly sees that the behavior she feared was actually the product of deeply felt passion and a previous hurt. Once she learns to reread his past behavior and thus to excuse him for the suffering he has caused her, she is free to respond warmly to his occasional acts of tenderness. Her response inevitably encourages him to believe in her and finally to treat her as she wishes to be treated. When this reinterpretation process is completed in the twenty ideal romances, the heroine is always tenderly enfolded in the hero's embrace and the reader is permitted to identify with her as she is gently caressed, carefully protected, and verbally praised [with] words of love.[13] At the climactic moment (pp. 201–2) of *The Sea Treasure,* for example, when the hero tells the heroine to put her arms around him, the reader is informed of his gentleness in the following way:

She put her cold face against his in an attitude of surrender that moved him to unutterable tenderness. He swung her clear of the encroaching water and eased his way up to the next level, with painful slowness. . . . When at last he

had finished, he pulled her into his arms and held her against his heart for a moment. . . . Tenderly he lifted her. Carefully he negotiated the last of the treacherous slippery rungs to the mine entrance. Once there, he swung her up into his arms and walked out into the starlit night.

The cold air revived her, and she stirred in his arms.

"Dominic?" she whispered.

He bent his head and kissed her.

"Sea Treasure," he whispered.

Passivity, it seems, is at the heart of the romance-reading experience in the sense that the final goal of the most valued romances is the creation of perfect union in which the ideal male, who is masculine and strong, yet nurturant, finally admits his recognition of the intrinsic worth of the heroine. Thereafter, she is required to do nothing more than exist as the center of this paragon's attention. Romantic escape is a temporary but literal denial of the demands these women recognize as an integral part of their roles as nurturing wives and mothers. But it is also a figurative journey to a utopian state of total receptiveness in which the reader, as a consequence of her identification with the heroine, feels herself the passive *object* of someone else's attention and solicitude. The romance reader in effect is permitted the experience of feeling cared for, the sense of having been affectively reconstituted, even if both are lived only vicariously.

Although the ideal romance may thus enable a woman to satisfy vicariously those psychological needs created in her by a patriarchal culture unable to fulfill them, the very centrality of the rhetoric of reinterpretation to the romance suggests also that the reading experience may indeed have some of the unfortunate consequences pointed to by earlier romance critics.[14] Not only is the dynamic of reinterpretation an essential component of the plot of the ideal romance, but it also characterizes the very process of constructing its meaning because the reader is inevitably given more information about the hero's motives than is the heroine herself. Hence, when Ranulf temporarily abuses his young bride in *The Black Lyon,* the reader understands that what appears as inexplicable cruelty to Lyonene, the heroine, is an irrational desire to hurt her because of what his first wife did to him.[15] It is possible that in reinterpreting the hero's behavior before Lyonene does, the Smithton women may be practicing a procedure which is valuable to them precisely because it enables them to reinterpret their own spouse's similar emotional coldness and likely preoccupation with work or sports. In rereading this category of behavior, they reassure themselves that it does not necessarily mean that a woman is not loved. Romance reading, it would seem, can function as a kind of training for the all-too-common task of reinterpreting a spouse's unsettling actions as the signs of passion, devotion, and love.

If the Smithton women are indeed learning reading behaviors that help them to dismiss or justify their husbands' affective distance, this procedure is probably carried out on an unconscious level. In any form of cultural or anthropological analysis in which the subjects of the study cannot reveal all the complexity or covert significance of their behavior, a certain amount of speculation is necessary. The analyst, however, can and should take account of any other observable evidence that might reveal the motives and meanings she is seeking. In this case, the Smithton readers' comments about bad romances are particularly helpful.

In general, bad romances are characterized by one of two things: an unusually cruel hero who subjects the heroine to various kinds of verbal and physical abuse, or a diffuse plot that permits the hero to become involved with other women before he settles upon the heroine. Since the Smithton readers will tolerate complicated subplots in some romances if the hero and heroine continue to function as a pair, clearly it is the involvement with others rather than the plot complexity that distresses them. When asked why they disliked these books despite the fact that they all ended happily with the hero converted into the heroine's attentive lover, Dot and her customers replied again and again that they rejected the books precisely because they found them unbelievable. In elaborating, they insisted indignantly that they could never forgive the hero's early transgressions and they see no reason why they should be asked to believe that the heroine can. What they are suggesting, then, is that certain kinds of male behavior associated with the stereotype of male machismo can never be forgiven or reread as the signs of love. They are thus not interested only in the romance's happy ending. They want to involve themselves in a story that will permit them to enjoy the hero's tenderness *and* reinterpret his momentary blindness and cool indifference as the marks of a love so intense that he is wary of admitting it. Their delight in both these aspects of the process of romance reading and their deliberate attempt to select books that will include "a gentle hero" and "a slight misunderstanding" suggest that deeply felt needs are the source of their interest in both components of the genre. On the one hand, they long for emotional attention and tender care; on the other, they wish to rehearse the discovery that a man's distance can be explained and excused as his way of expressing love.

It is easy to condemn this latter aspect of romance reading as a reactionary force that reconciles women to a social situation which denies them full development, even as it refuses to accord them the emotional sustenance they require. Yet to identify romances with this conservative moment alone is to miss those other benefits associated with the act of reading as a restorative pastime whose impact on a beleaguered woman is not so simply dismissed. If we are serious about feminist politics and committed to reformulating not only our own lives but those of others, we would do well not to condescend to romance readers as hopeless traditionalists who are recalcitrant in their refusal to acknowledge the emotional costs of patriarchy. We must begin to recognize that romance reading is fueled by dissatisfaction and disaffection, not by perfect contentment with woman's lot. Moreover, we must also understand that some romance readers' experiences are not strictly congruent with the set of ideological propositions that typically legitimate patriarchal marriage. They are characterized, rather, by a sense of longing caused by patriarchal marriage's failure to address all their needs.

In recognizing both the yearning and the fact that its resolution is only a vicarious one not so easily achieved in a real situation, we may find it possible to identify more precisely the very limits of patriarchal ideology's success. Endowed thus with a better understanding of what women want, but often fail to get from the traditional arrangements they consciously support, we may provide ourselves with that very issue

whose discussion would reach many more women and potentially raise their consciousnesses about the particular dangers and failures of patriarchal institutions. By helping romance readers to see why they long for relationality and tenderness and are unlikely to get either in the form they desire if current gender arrangements are continued, we may help to convert their amorphous longing into a focused desire for specific change. . . .

Notes

1. All information about the community has been taken from the 1970 U.S. Census of the Population *Characteristics of the Population*, U.S. Department of Commerce, Social and Economic Statistics Administration, Bureau of the Census, May 1972. I have rounded off some of the statistics to disguise the identity of the town.

2. See Table 1.

Table 1 Select Demographic Data: Customers of Dorothy Evans			
Category	**Responses**	**Number**	**%**
Age	(42) Less than 25	2	5
	25–44	26	62
	45–54	12	28
	55 and older	2	5
Marital Status	(40) Single	3	8
	Married	33	82
	Widowed/Separated	4	10
Parental Status	(40) Children	35	88
	No children	4	12

(Continued)

Table 1 (Continued)			
Category	**Responses**	**Number**	**%**
Age at Marriage	Mean 19.9		
	Median 19.2		
Educational Level	(40) High school diploma	21	53
	1–3 Years of college	10	25
	College degree	8	20
Work Status	(40) Full or part time	18	45
	Child or home care	17	43
Family Income	(38) $14,999 or below	2	5
	15,000–24,999	18	47
	25,000–49,999	14	37
	50,000+	4	11
Church Attendance	(40) Once or more a week	15	38
	1–3 times per month	8	20
	A few times per year	9	22
	Not in two(2) years	8	20

Note: (40) indicates the number of responses per questionnaire category. A total of 42 responses per category is the maximum possible. Percent calculations are all rounded to the nearest whole number.

3. Quoted by Barbara Brotman, "Ah, Romance! Harlequin Has an Affair for Its Readers." *Chicago Tribune*, 2 June 1980. All other details about the Harlequin audience have been taken from this article. . . .

4. See Brotman (1980), cited above. All other details about the Silhouette audience have been drawn from Brotman's article. . . .

5. The Smithton readers are not avid television watchers. . . .

6. The Smithton readers' constant emphasis on the educational value of romances was one of the most interesting aspects of our conversations, and chapter 3 of *Reading the Romance* discusses it in depth. Although their citation of the instructional value of romances

to a college professor interviewer may well be a form of self-justification, the women also provided ample evidence that they do in fact learn and remember facts about geography, historical customs, and dress from the books they read. Their emphasis on this aspect of their reading, I might add, seems to betoken a profound curiosity and longing to know more about the exciting world beyond their suburban homes.

7. For material on housewives' attitudes toward domestic work and their duties as family counselors, see Ann Oakley, *The Sociology of Housework* (New York: Pantheon, 1975) and *Woman's Work: The Housewife, Past and Present* (New York: Pantheon. 1975); see also

Mirra Komorovsky, *Blue Collar Marriage* (New York: Vintage, 1967) and Helena Znaniecki Lopata, *Occupation:* Housewife (New York: Oxford University Press, 1971).

8. Nancy Chodorow, *The Reproduction of Mothering: Psychoanalysis and the Sociology of Gender* (Berkeley: University of California Press, 1978). I would like to express my thanks to Sharon O'Brien for first bringing Chodorow's work to my attention and for all those innumerable discussions in which we debated the merits of her theory and its applicability to women's lives, including our own.

9. After developing my argument that the Smithton women are seeking ideal romances which depict the generally tender treatment of the heroine, I discovered Beatrice Faust's *Women, Sex, and Pornography: A Controversial Study* (New York: MacMillan, 1981) in which Faust points out that certain kinds of historical romances tend to portray their heroes as masculine, but emotionally expressive. . . .

10. Daisy Maryles, "Fawcett Launches Romance Imprint with Brand Marketing Techniques," *Publishers Weekly* 216 (3 Sept. 1979), 69.

11. Ten of the twenty books in the sample for the ideal romance were drawn from the Smithton group's answers to requests that they list their three favorite romances and authors. . . . I also added *Summer of the Dragon* (1979) by Elizabeth Peters because she was heavily cited as a favorite author although none of her titles were specifically singled out. Three more titles were added because they were each voluntarily cited in the oral interviews more than five times. . . . Seven were added because Dot gave them very high ratings in her newsletter. Because I did not include a formal query in the questionnaire about particularly bad romances, I drew the twenty titles from oral interviews and from Dot's newsletter reviews.

12. There are two exceptions to this assertion. Both *The Proud Breed* by Celeste DeBlasis and *The Fulfillment* by LaVyrle Spencer detail the involvement of the principal characters with other individuals. Their treatment of the subject, however, is decidedly different from that typically found in the bad romances. Both of these

books are highly unusual in that they begin by detailing the extraordinary depth of the love shared by hero and heroine, who marry early in the story. The rest of each book chronicles the misunderstandings that arise between heroine and hero. In both books the third person narrative always indicates very clearly to the reader that the two are still deeply in love with each other and are acting out of anger, distrust, and insecurity.

13. In the romances considered awful by the Smithton readers, this reinterpretation takes place much later in the story than in the ideal romances. In addition, the behavior that is explained away is more violent, aggressively cruel, and obviously vicious. Although the hero is suddenly transformed by the heroine's reinterpretation of his motives, his tenderness, gentleness, and care are not emphasized in the "failed romances" as they are in their ideal counterparts.

14. Modleski has also argued that "the mystery of male motives" is a crucial concern in all romantic fiction (p. 439). Although she suggests, as I will here, that the process through which male misbehavior is reinterpreted in a more favorable light is a justification or legitimation of such action, she does not specifically connect its centrality in the plot to a reader's need to use such a strategy in her own marriage. While there are similarities between Modleski's analysis and that presented here, she emphasizes the negative, disturbing effects of romance reading on readers. In fact, she claims the novels "end up actually intensifying conflicts for the reader" (p. 445) and cause women to "reemerge feeling . . . more guilty than ever" (p. 447). While I would admit that romance reading might create unconscious guilt, I think it absolutely essential that any explanation of such behavior take into account the substantial amount of evidence indicating that women not only enjoy romance reading, but feel replenished and reconstituted by it as well. See Tania Modleski, "The Disappearing Act: A Study of Harlequin Romances," *Signs* 5 (Spring 1980), 435–48.

15. Jude Deveraux, *The Black Lyon* (New York: Avon, 1980), 66.

Star Trek Rerun, Reread, Rewritten

Fan Writing as Textual Poaching

Henry Jenkins III

In late December 1986, *Newsweek* (Leerhsen, 1986, p. 66) marked the 20th anniversary of *Star Trek* with a cover story on the program's fans, "the Trekkies, who love nothing more than to watch the same 79 episodes over and over." The *Newsweek* article, with its relentless focus on conspicuous consumption and "infantile" behavior and its patronizing language and smug superiority to all fan activity, is a textbook example of the stereotyped representation of fans found in both popular writing and academic criticism, "Hang on: You are being beamed to one of those *Star Trek* conventions, where grown-ups greet each other with the Vulcan salute and offer in reverent tones to pay $100 for the autobiography of Leonard Nimoy" (p. 66). Fans are characterized as "kooks" obsessed with trivia, celebrities, and collectibles; as misfits and crazies; as "a lot of overweight women, a lot of divorced and single women" (p. 68). . . .

Fans appear to be frighteningly out of control, undisciplined and unrepentant, rogue readers. Rejecting aesthetic distance, fans passionately embrace favored texts and attempt to integrate media representations within their own social experience. Like cultural scavengers, fans reclaim works that others regard as worthless and trash, finding them a rewarding source of popular capital. Like rebellious children, fans refuse to read by the rules imposed upon them by the schoolmasters. For fans, reading becomes a type of play, responsive only to its own loosely structured rules and generating its own types of pleasure.

Michel de Certeau (1984) has characterized this type of reading as "poaching," an impertinent raid on the literary preserve that takes away only those things that seem useful or pleasurable to the reader. "Far from being writers . . . readers are travelers; they move across lands belonging to someone else, like nomads poaching their way across fields they did not write, despoiling the wealth of Egypt to enjoy it themselves" (p. 174). De Certeau perceives popular reading as a series of "advances and retreats, tactics and games played with the text" (p. 175), as a type of cultural bricolage through which readers fragment texts and reassemble the broken shards according to their own blueprint, salvaging bits and pieces of found material in making sense of their own social experience. Far from viewing consumption as imposing meanings upon the public, de Certeau suggests, consumption involves reclaiming textual material, "making it one's own, appropriating or reappropriating it" (p. 166). . . .

In this chapter, I propose an alternative approach to fan experience, one that perceives "Trekkers" (as they prefer to be called) not as cultural dupes, social misfits, or mindless consumers but rather as, in de Certeau's term, "poachers" of textual meanings. Behind the exotic stereotypes fostered by the media lies a largely unexplored terrain of cultural activity, a subterranean network of readers and writers who remake programs in their own image. "Fandom" is a vehicle for marginalized subterranean groups (women, the young, gays, etc.) to pry open space for their cultural concerns within dominant representations; it is a way of appropriating media texts and rereading them in a fashion that serves different interests, a way of transforming mass culture into a popular culture.

I do not believe this essay represents the last word on *Star Trek* fans, a cultural community that is far too multivocal to be open to easy description. Rather, I explore some aspects of current fan activity that seem particularly relevant to cultural studies. My primary concern is with what happens when these fans produce their own texts, texts that inflect program content with their own social experience and displace commercially produced commodities for a kind of popular economy. For these fans, *Star Trek* is not simply something that can be reread; it is something that can and must be rewritten in order to make it more responsive to their needs, in order to make it a better producer of personal meanings and pleasures.

No legalistic notion of literary property can adequately constrain the rapid proliferation of meanings surrounding a popular text. Yet, there are other constraints, ethical constraints and self-imposed rules, that are enacted by the fans, either individually or as part of a larger community, in response to their felt need to legitimate their unorthodox appropriation of mass media texts. E. P. Thompson (1971) suggests that eighteenth and nineteenth century peasant leaders, the historical poachers behind de Certeau's apt metaphor, responded to a kind of "moral economy," an informal set of consensual norms that justified their uprisings against the landowners and tax collectors in order to restore a preexisting order being corrupted by its avowed protectors. Similarly, the fans often cast themselves not as poachers but as loyalists, rescuing essential elements of the primary text misused by those who maintain copyright control over the program materials. Respecting literary property even as they seek to appropriate it for their own uses, these fans become reluctant poachers, hesitant about their relationship to the program text, uneasy about the degree of manipulation they can legitimately perform on its materials, and policing each other for abuses of their interpretive license. . . .

Fans: From Reading to Writing

The popularity of *Star Trek* has motivated a wide range of cultural productions and creative reworkings of program materials: from children's backyard play to adult interaction games, from needlework to elaborate costumes, from private fantasies to computer programming. This ability to transform personal reaction into social interaction, spectator culture into participatory culture, is one of the central characteristics of fandom. One becomes a fan not by being a regular viewer of a particular program but by translating that viewing into some type of cultural activity, by sharing feelings and thoughts about the program content with friends, by joining a community of other fans who share common interests. For fans, consumption sparks production, reading generates writing, until the terms seem logically inseparable. In fan writer Jean Lorrah's words (1984, p. 1):

> Trekfandom . . . is friends and letters and crafts and fanzines and trivia and costumes and artwork and filksongs [fan parodies] and buttons and film clips and conventions—something for everybody who has in common the inspiration of a television show which grew far beyond its TV and film incarnations to become a living part of world culture.

Lorrah's description blurs all boundaries between producers and consumers, spectators and participants, the commercial and the home crafted, to construct an image of fandom as a cultural and social network that spans the globe.

Many fans characterize their entry into fandom in terms of a movement from social and cultural isolation, doubly imposed upon them as women within a patriarchal society and as seekers after alternative pleasures within dominant media representations, toward more and more active participation in a community receptive to their cultural productions, a community where they may feel a sense of belonging. . . .

For some women, trapped within low paying jobs or within the socially isolated sphere of the homemaker, participation within a national, or international, network of fans grants a degree of dignity and respect otherwise lacking. For others, fandom offers a training ground for the development of professional skills and an outlet for creative impulses constrained by their workday lives. Fan slang draws a sharp contrast between the mundane, the realm of everyday experience and those who dwell exclusively within that space, and fandom, an alternative sphere of cultural

experience that restores the excitement and freedom that must be repressed to function in ordinary life. One fan writes, "Not only does 'mundane' mean 'everyday life,' it is also a term used to describe narrow-minded, pettiness, judgmental, conformity, and a shallow and silly nature. It is used by people who feel very alienated from society" (Osborne, 1987, p. 4). To enter fandom is to escape from the mundane into the marvelous.

The need to maintain contact with these new friends, often scattered over a broad geographic area, can require that speculations and fantasies about the program content take written form, first as personal letters and later as more public newsletters, "letterzines" or fan fiction magazines. Fan viewers become fan writers. . . .

Although fanzines may take a variety of forms, fans generally divide them into two major categories: "letterzines" that publish short articles and letters from fans on issues surrounding their favorite shows and "fictionzines" that publish short stories, poems, and novels concerning the program characters and concepts.[1] Some fan-produced novels, notably the works of Jean Lorrah (1976, 1978) and Jacqueline Lichtenberg (1976), have achieved a canonized status in the fan community, remaining more or less in constant demand for more than a decade.[2]

It is important to be careful in distinguishing between these fan-generated materials and commercially produced works, such as the series of *Star Trek* novels released by Pocket Books under the official supervision of Paramount, the studio that owns the rights to the *Star Trek* characters. Fanzines are totally unauthorized by the program producers and face the constant threat of legal action for their open violation of the producer's copyright authority over the show's characters and concepts. Paramount has tended to treat fan magazines with benign neglect as long as they are handled on an exclusively nonprofit basis. Producer Gene Roddenberry and many of the cast members have contributed to such magazines. Bantam Books even released several anthologies showcasing the work of *Star Trek* fan writers (Marshak & Culbreath, 1978).

Other producers have not been as kind. Lucasfilm initially sought to control *Star Wars* fan publications, seeing them as a rival to its officially sponsored fan organization, and later threatened to prosecute editors who published works that violated the "family values" associated with the original films. Such a scheme has met considerable resistance from the fan community that generally regards Lucas' actions as unwarranted interference in its own creative activity. Several fanzine editors have continued to distribute adult-oriented *Star Wars* stories through an underground network of special friends, even though such works are no longer publicly advertised through *Datazine* or sold openly at conventions. A heated editorial in *Slaysu*, a fanzine that routinely published feminist-inflected erotica set in various media universes, reflects these writers' opinions:

> Lucasfilm is saying, "you must enjoy the characters of the *Star Wars* universe for male reasons. Your sexuality must be correct and proper by my (male) definition." I am not male. I do not want to be. I refuse to be a poor imitation, or worse, someone's idiotic ideal of femininity. Lucasfilm has said, in essence, "this is what we see in the *Star Wars* films and we are telling you that this is what you will see." (Siebert, 1982, p. 44)

C. A. Siebert's editorial asserts the rights of fanzine writers to consciously revise the character of the original texts, to draw elements from dominant culture in order to produce underground art that explicitly challenges patriarchal assumptions. Siebert and the other editors deny the traditional property rights of textual producers in favor of a right of free play with the program materials, a right of readers to use

media texts in their own ways and of writers to reconstruct characters in their own terms. Once characters are inserted into popular discourse, regardless of their source of origin, they become the property of the fans who fantasize about them, not the copyright holders who merchandise them. Yet the relationship between fan texts and primary texts is often more complex than Siebert's defiant stance might suggest, and some fans do feel bound by a degree of fidelity to the original series' conceptions of those characters and their interactions.

Gender and Writing

Fan writing is an almost exclusively feminine response to mass media texts. Men actively participate in a wide range of fan-related activities, notably interactive games and conference planning committees, roles consistent with patriarchal norms that typically relegate combat—even combat fantasies—and organizational authority to the masculine sphere. Fan writers and fanzine readers, however, are almost always female. Camille Bacon-Smith (1986) has estimated that more than 90% of all fan writers are female. The greatest percentage of male participation is found in the "letter-lines," like *Comlink* and *Treklink*, and in "nonfiction" magazines, like *Trek* that publish speculative essays on aspects of the program universe. Men may feel comfortable joining discussions of future technologies or military lifestyle but not in pondering Vulcan sexuality, McCoy's childhood, or Kirk's love life.

Why this predominance of women within the fan writing community? . . .

A particular fascination of *Star Trek* for these women appears to be rooted in the way that the program seems to hold out a suggestion of nontraditional feminine pleasures, of greater and more active involvement for women within the adventure of professional space travel, while finally reneging on those promises. Sexual equality was an essential component of producer Roddenberry's optimistic vision of the future; a woman, Number One (Majel Barrett), was originally slated to be the Enterprise's second in command. Network executives, however, consistently fought efforts to break with traditional feminine stereotypes, fearing the alienation of more conservative audience members (Whitfield & Roddenberry, 1968). Number One was scratched after the program pilot, but throughout the run of the series women were often cast in nontraditional jobs, everything from Romulan commanders to weapon specialists. The networks, however reluctantly, were offering women a future, a "final frontier" that included them.

Fan writers, though, frequently express dissatisfaction with these women's characterizations within the episodes. In the words of fan writer Pamela Rose (1977, p. 48), "When a woman is a guest star on *Star Trek,* nine out of ten times there is something wrong with her." Rose notes that these female characters have been granted positions of power within the program, only to demonstrate through their erratic emotion-driven conduct that women are unfit to fill such roles. Another fan writer, Toni Lay (1986, p. 15), expresses mixed feelings about *Star Trek*'s social vision:

> It was ahead of its time in some ways, like showing that a Caucasian, all-American, all-male crew was not the only possibility for space travel. Still, the show was sadly deficient in other ways, in particular, its treatment of women. Most of the time, women were referred to as "girls." And women were never shown in a position of authority unless they were aliens, i.e., Deela, T'Pau, Natira, Sylvia, etc. It was like the show was saying "equal opportunity is OK for their women but not for our girls."

. . . Indeed, many fan writers characterize themselves as "repairing the damage" caused by the program's inconsistent and often demeaning treatment of its female characters. Jane Land (1986, p. 1), for instance, characterizes her fan novel, *Kista,* as "an attempt to rescue one of *Star Trek*'s female characters [Christine Chapel] from an artificially imposed case of foolishness." Promising to show "the way the future never was," *The Woman's List,* a recently established fanzine with an explicitly feminist orientation, has called for "material dealing with all range of possibilities for women, including: women of color, lesbians, women of alien cultures, and women of all ages and backgrounds." Its editors acknowledge that their publication's project necessarily involves telling the types of stories that network policy blocked from airing when the series was originally produced. A recent flier for that publication explains:

> We hope to raise and explore those questions which the network censors, the television genre, and the prevailing norms of the time made it difficult to address. We believe that both the nature of human interaction and sexual mores and the structure of both families and relationships will have changed by the 23rd century and we are interested in exploring those changes.

Telling such stories requires the stripping away of stereotypically feminine traits. The series characters must be reconceptualized in ways that suggest hidden motivations and interests heretofore unsuspected. They must be reshaped into full-blooded feminist role models. While, in the series, Chapel is defined almost exclusively in terms of her unrequited passion for Spock and her professional subservience to Dr. McCoy, Land represents her as a fiercely independent woman, capable of accepting love only on her own terms, ready to pursue her own ambitions wherever they take her, and outspoken in response to the patronizing attitudes of the command crew. Siebert (1980, p. 33) has performed a similar operation on the character of Lieutenant Uhura, as this passage from one of her stories suggests:

> There were too few men like Spock who saw her as a person. Even Captain Kirk, she smiled, especially Captain Kirk, saw her as a woman first. He let her do certain things but only because military discipline required it. Whenever there was any danger, he tried to protect her. . . . Uhura smiled sadly, she would go on as she had been, outwardly a feminine toy, inwardly a woman who was capable and human.

Here, Siebert attempts to resolve the apparent contradiction created within the series text by Uhura's official status as a command officer and her constant displays of "feminine frailty." Uhura's situation, Siebert suggests, is characteristic of the way that women must mask their actual competency behind traditionally feminine mannerisms within a world dominated by patriarchal assumptions and masculine authority. By rehabilitating Uhura's character in this fashion, Siebert has constructed a vehicle through which she can document the overt and subtle forms of sexual discrimination that an ambitious and determined woman faces as she struggles for a command post in Star Fleet (or for that matter, within a twentieth century corporate board room).

Fan writers like Siebert, Land, and Karen Bates (1982; 1983; 1984), whose novels explore the progression of a Chapel-Spock marriage through many of the problems encountered by contemporary couples trying to juggle the conflicting demands of career and family, speak directly to the concerns of professional women in a way that more traditionally feminine works fail to do. These writers create situations where Chapel and Uhura must heroically overcome the same types of obstacles that challenge their male counterparts within the primary texts and often discuss directly the types of personal and professional problems particular to working women. . . .

The fan community continually debates what constitutes a legitimate reworking of program materials and what represents a violation of the special reader-text relationship that the fans hope to foster. The earliest *Star Trek* fan writers were careful to work within the framework of the information explicitly included within the broadcast episodes and to minimize their breaks with series conventions. In fan writer Jean Lorrah's words (1976, p. 1), "Anyone creating a *Star Trek* universe is bound by what was seen in the aired episodes; however, he is free to extrapolate from those episodes to explain what was seen in them." Leslie Thompson (1974, p. 208) explains, "If the reasoning [of fan speculations] doesn't fit into the framework of the events as given [on the program], then it cannot apply no matter how logical or detailed it may be." As *Star Trek* fan writing has come to assume an institutional status in its own right and therefore to require less legitimization through appeals to textual fidelity, a new conception of fan fiction has emerged, one that perceives the stories not as a necessary expansion of the original series text but rather as chronicles of alternate universes, similar to the program world in some ways and different in others:

> The "alternate universe" is a handy concept wherein you take the basic *Star Trek* concept and spin it off into all kinds of ideas that could never be aired. One reason Paramount may be so liberal about fanzines is that by their very nature most fanzine stories could never be sold professionally. (L. Slusher, personal communication, August 1987)

Such an approach frees the writers to engage in much broader play with the program concepts and characterizations, to produce stories that reflect more diverse visions of human interrelationships and future worlds, to rewrite elements within the primary texts that hinder fan interests. Yet, even alternate universe stories struggle to maintain some consistency with the original broadcast material and to establish some point of contact with existing fan interests, just as more faithful fan writers feel compelled to rewrite and revise the program material in order to keep it alive in a new cultural context.

Borrowed Terms: Kirk/Spock Stories

The debate in fan circles surrounding Kirk/Spock (K/S) fiction, stories that posit a homo-erotic relationship between the show's two primary characters and frequently offer detailed accounts of their sexual couplings, illustrates these differing conceptions of the relationship between fan fiction and the primary series text.[3] Over the past decade, K/S stories have emerged from the margins of fandom toward numerical dominance over *Star Trek* fan fiction, a movement that has been met with considerable opposition from more traditional fans. For many, such stories constitute the worst form of character rape, a total violation of the established characterizations. Kendra Hunter (1977, p. 81) argues that "it is out of character for both men, and as such comes across in the stories as bad writing. . . . A relationship as complex and deep as Kirk/Spock does not climax with a sexual relationship." Other fans agree but for other reasons. "I do not accept the K/S homosexual precept as plausible," writes one fan. "The notion that two men that are as close as Kirk and Spock are cannot be 'just friends' is indefensible to me" (Landers, 1986, p. 10). Others struggle to reconcile the information provided on the show with their own assumptions about the nature of human sexuality: "It is just as possible for their friendship to progress into a love-affair, for that is what it is, than to remain status quo. . . . Most of us see Kirk and Spock simply as two people who love each other

and just happen to be of the same gender" (Snaider, 1987, p. 10). . . .

What K/S does openly, all fans do covertly. In constructing the feminine countertext that lurks in the margins of the primary text, these readers necessarily redefine the text in the process of rereading and rewriting it. As one fan acknowledges, "If K/S has 'created new characters and called them by old names,' then all of fandom is guilty of the same" (Moore, 1986, p. 7). Jane Land (1987, p. ii) agrees: "All writers alter and transform the basic *Trek* universe to some extent, choosing some things to emphasize and others to play down, filtering the characters and the concepts through their own perceptions."

If these fans have rewritten *Star Trek* in their own terms, however, many of them are reluctant to break all ties to the primary text that sparked their creative activity and, hence, feel the necessity to legitimate their activity through appeals to textual fidelity. The fans are uncertain how far they can push against the limitations of the original material without violating and finally destroying a relationship that has given them great pleasure. Some feel stifled by those constraints; others find comfort within them. Some claim the program as their personal property, "treating the series episodes like silly putty," as one fan put it (Blaes, 1987, p. 6). Others seek compromises with the textual producers, treating the original program as something shared between them.

What should be remembered is that whether they cast themselves as rebels or loyalists, it is the fans themselves who are determining what aspects of the original series concept are binding on their play with the program material and to what degree. The fans have embraced *Star Trek* because they found its vision somehow compatible with their own, and they have assimilated only those textual materials that feel comfortable to them. Whenever a choice must be made between fidelity to their program and fidelity to their own social norms, it is almost inevitably made in favor of lived experience. The women's conception of the *Star Trek* realm as inhabited by psychologically rounded and realistic characters insures that no characterization that violated their own social perceptions could be satisfactory. The reason some fans reject K/S fiction has, in the end, less to do with the stated reason that it violates established characterization than with unstated beliefs about the nature of human sexuality that determine what types of character conduct can be viewed as plausible. When push comes to shove, as Hodge and Tripp (1986, p. 144) recently suggested, "Non-televisual meanings can swamp televisual meanings" and usually do.

Conclusion

The fans are reluctant poachers who steal only those things that they truly love, who seize televisual property only to protect it against abuse by those who created it and who have claimed ownership over it. In embracing popular texts, the fans claim those works as their own, remaking them in their own image, forcing them to respond to their needs and to gratify their desires. Female fans transform *Star Trek* into women's culture, shifting it from space opera into feminist romance, bringing to the surface the unwritten feminine countertext that hides in the margins of the written masculine text. Kirk's story becomes Uhura's story and Chapel's and Amanda's as well as the story of the women who weave their own personal experiences into the lives of the characters. Consumption becomes production; reading becomes writing; spectator culture becomes participatory culture. . . .

Notes

1. Both Lorrah and Lichtenberg have achieved some success as professional science

fiction writers. For an interesting discussion of the relationship between fan writing and professional science fiction writing, see Randall (1985).

2. Although a wide range of fanzines were considered in researching this essay, I have decided, for the purposes of clarity, to draw my examples largely from the work of a limited number of fan writers. While no selection could accurately reflect the full range of fan writing, I felt that Bates, Land, Lorrah, and Siebert had all achieved some success within the fan community, suggesting that they exemplified, at least to some fans, the types of writing that were desirable and reflected basic tendencies within the form. . . .

3. The area of Kirk/Spock fiction falls beyond the project of this particular paper. My reason for discussing it here is because of the light its controversial reception sheds on the norms of fan fiction and the various ways fan writers situate themselves toward the primary text. For a more detailed discussion of this particular type of fan writing, see Lamb and Veith (1986), who argue that K/S stories, far from representing a cultural expression of the gay community, constitute another way of feminizing the concerns of the original series text and of addressing feminist concern within the domain of a popular culture that offers little space for heroic action by women.

References

Bacon-Smith, C. (1986, November 16). Spock among the women. *The New York Times Book Review*, pp. 1, 26, 28.

Bates, K. A. (1982). *Starweaver two*. Missouri Valley, IA: Ankar Press.

Bates, K. A. (1983). *Nuages one*. Tucson, AZ: Checkmate Press.

Bates, K. A. (1984). *Nuages two*. Tucson, AZ: Checkmate Press.

Blaes, T. (1987). Letter. *Treklink, 9*, 6–7.

de Certeau, M. (1984). *The practice of everyday life*. Berkeley: University of California Press.

Hodge, R., & Tripp, D. (1986). *Children and television: A semiotic approach.* Cambridge: Polity Press.

Hunter, K. (1977). Characterization rape. In W. Irwin & G. B. Love (Eds.), *The best of Trek 2* (pp. 74–85). New York: New American Library.

Lamb, P. F., & Veith, D. L. (1986). Romantic myth, transcendence, and *Star Trek* zines. In D. Palumbo (Ed.), *Erotic universe: Sexuality and fantastic literature* (pp. 235–256). New York: Greenwood Press.

Land, J. (1986). *Kista.* Larchmont, NY: Author.

Land, J. (1987). *Demeter.* Larchmont, NY: Author.

Landers, R. (1986). Letter. *Treklink, 7,* 10.

Lay, T. (1986). Letter. *Comlink, 28,* 14–16.

Leerhsen, C. (1986, December 22). *Star Trek's* nine lives. *Newsweek,* pp. 66–73.

Lichtenberg, J. (1976). *Kraith collected.* Grosse Point Park, MI: Ceiling Press.

Lorrah, J. (1976). *The night of twin moons.* Murray, KY: Author.

Lorrah, J. (1978). The Vulcan character in the NTM universe. In J. Lorrah (Ed.), *NTM collected* (Vol. 1, pp. 1–3). Murray, KY: Author.

Lorrah, J. (1984). *The Vulcan academy murders.* New York: Pocket.

Marshak, S., & Culbreath, M. (1978). *Star Trek: The new voyages.* New York: Bantam Books.

Moore, R. (1986). Letter. *Treklink, 4,* 7–8.

Osborne, E. (1987). Letter. *Treklink, 9,* 3–4.

Randall, M. (1985). Conquering the galaxy for fun and profit. In C. West (Ed.), *Words in our pockets* (pp. 233–241). Paradise, CA: Dustbooks.

Rose, P. (1977). Women in the federation. In W. Irwin & G. B. Love (Eds.), *The best of Trek 2* (pp. 46–52). New York: New American Library.

Siebert, C. A. (1980). Journey's end at lover's meeting. *Slaysu, 1,* 28–34.

Siebert, C. A. (1982). By any other name. *Slaysu, 4,* 44–45.

Snaider, T. (1987). Letter. *Treklink, 8,* 10.

Thompson, E. P. (1971). The moral economy of the English crowd in the 18th century. *Past and Present, 50,* 76–136.

Thompson, L. (1974). *Star Trek* mysteries—Solved! In W. Irwin & G. B. Love (Eds.), *The best of Trek* (pp. 207–214). New York: New American Library.

Whitfield, S. E., & Roddenberry, G. (1968). *The making of Star Trek.* New York: Ballantine Books.

PART II

REPRESENTATIONS OF GENDER, RACE, AND CLASS

The chapters in this section apply many of the theoretical concepts we isolated above to the analysis of *gender and sexuality, race and class* in media production, text construction, and consumption. This book insists on the need to develop and ground theory within an understanding of how **media** texts may either contribute to or undermine the inequalities that exist in postindustrialized societies like our own. The linkage of media theory and politics is particularly important within critical cultural studies, which is concerned with the lived experience of socially subordinate groups and with making visible the ways in which media industries contribute to the continuation of inequalities.

What do we mean when we say that we view gender (and sexuality), race, and class as "social constructs"? To take this approach means to reduce the explanatory role of biology or "nature" in all our social arrangements and power imbalances. Instead, we shift our attention to the social, economic, and political forces that shape and reshape these conceptual categories over time and place. Many examples can be offered of the "instability" (changeable or shifting nature) of these concepts—some from recent history.

To speak first of **gender,** one of the major accomplishments of **feminism**(s) has been the widespread recognition that women are "not born but made." It is now common wisdom that the process of taking on gender attributes begins at birth and requires intensive socialization. We also recognize that a given **culture**'s idea of the "perfect woman" or "real man" (its gender norms) can shift dramatically in response to changing economic and social conditions. The "Rosie the Riveter" propaganda campaign to bring women into defense industry work during World War II—quickly succeeded by the "just a housewife" propaganda pushing women back into the home in the postwar period and the 1950s—is one well-known historical example.

The artificiality or "constructedness" of femininity is the focus of Mary Rogers's provocative brief chapter, "Hetero Barbie?" (II.8). As Rogers writes, Barbie's femininity "entails a lot of artifice, a lot of clothes, a lot of props such as cuddly poodles and shopping bags, and a lot of effort." Indeed, Rogers playfully raises the possibility

> that Barbie may not be heterosexual. Indeed she may not even be a woman. Barbie may be a drag queen. Much in the tradition made widely visible by stars like RuPaul, Barbie may be the ultrafeminine presence that drag queens personify. (p. 71)

As Rogers's chapter suggests, the term *gender* has acquired a whole new range of associations in light of the **queer theory** that has grown out of both activist politics and postmodern scholarship over recent years. The influential feminist philosopher and queer theorist Judith Butler has likened gender to a theatrical performance—a matter of gradually learned role-playing, with no necessary correlation to one's biological sex (Butler, 2006).

Queer theory draws upon the work of historians of gender and sexuality, who have pointed out that the very idea of fixed and opposite sexual orientations,

"heterosexuality" and "homosexuality," and certainly the words that describe them, are only about a century old. These terms were produced within a late 19th-century medical **discourse** developed by the emerging professional health fields of psychology and sexology. Through the cultural dominance of the new medical discourse in the 20th century, heterosexuality came into being as a norm against which same-sex attraction and love (as well as many other desires and sexual behaviors) could be defined as threateningly deviant or "other." A queer theory approach questions traditional ideas of "normal" and "deviant" in the realms of both gender and sexuality by arguing against the commonsense notion that there are only two genders (masculine and feminine) and two kinds of desire or attraction (straight and gay). In queer theory, gender, sexuality, and desire are all seen as ambiguous, shifting, unstable, and too complex to fit neatly into **binary** (either/or) systems. Drag performance, cross-dressing, and a myriad of other types of gender-bending activities, behavior, and identities now highly visible in 21st-century urban culture certainly suggest the futility of attempts to maintain that the once traditional categories are fixed by nature.

Queer theory has thus given us a new, certainly unsettling, but also exciting and potentially liberating way of thinking about **representations** of gender and sexuality in popular culture. For example, from a "queer theory" perspective, the recently completed popular HBO dramatic serial *Sex and the City,* which followed the heterosexual adventures of four single women living in New York City in the first decade of the 21st century, can also be read as subversive, to a degree, of *normative* heterosexuality and femininity. As media text analyst Jane Gerhard (II.9) writes,

> The challenge the friendships pose to the women's heterosexual identities is not that such friendships mark them as gay. Rather, the connections they have with each other create an alternative to their

boyfriends, an alternative that, by its very existence, grants the women options different from those traditionally signified as "heterosexual" (where women satisfy their desires with one man, serially or monogamously). (p. 77)

Gerhard finds *Sex and the City* both conventional and safely "postfeminist" in its narrative insistence on the women's "search for the right man." At the same time, she acknowledges that the show's emphasis on heterosexual women's frank discussions of sex and its depiction of their ability to enjoy sex without romance was truly innovative.

As we turn to the concept of "race," we need to begin with a brief overview of the ideas of **critical race theory.** In the 1960s, 1970s, and 1980s, the civil rights movement and subsequent antiracist organizing and institutions mobilized many vigorous campaigns focusing public attention on denigrating racial representations that buttressed an inequitable economic and political status quo. Academic fields such as Black studies, Africana studies, Asian American studies, and Native American studies developed important critiques of taken-for-granted but demeaning imagery originating from the "White imaginary" (the culturally dominant store of ideas and feelings about "race"). Building on this base, the 1990s saw the development of sophisticated studies in critical race theory and postcolonial theory that critiqued Western European and U.S. historical narratives of "progress" and "civilization" and assimilation. In such narratives, the politically and culturally dominant (White, Eurocentric) group defined the terms and projected simplicity, closeness to nature, and a host of other less desirable characteristics upon the racial "Other"—whether African, Arab, East or South Asian, Pacific Islander, or indigenous (Native American). Such studies help us understand the role of concepts of race both within U.S. culture and globally, in relation to international politics.

Thanks to the political work done by the civil rights movement, as a society we have developed some sensitivity to the more overt racist images of the past. But as Stuart Hall points out in the classic piece "The Whites of Their Eyes" (II.10), we still need to educate ourselves about inferential racism, which he defines as

those apparently naturalized representations of events and situations referring to race, whether "factual" or "fictional," which have racist premises and propositions inscribed in them as a set of unquestioned assumptions. (p. 83)

One assumption about race that has historical resonance in U.S. media representations is that African Americans in particular are hypersexual. This imputed hypersexuality has played a part in the creation of "otherness" and has historically legitimized acts of violence such as the rape of Black women and the lynching of Black men.

Drawing on sports media coverage of tennis athletic stars Serena and Venus Williams, McKay and Johnson (II.11) help contextualize the "sexual grotesquerie" they identify in these recent media texts by placing them within a larger context of historic denigration of Black bodies by Europeans and Euro-Americans. Acknowledging that "the exceptional performances of the Williams sisters have provoked complex and ambivalent narratives of qualified praise and grudging approval, as well as subtle and overt racism and sexism" (p. 87), these scholars argue that the socially constructed images of Black women need to be understood as linked to ideologies of Blacks as embodying a deviant sexuality.

Most of us wish mightily for a postracist society—that is, one in which race is no longer the basis for discrimination in our economic, political, and social lives. However, the idea that we have already arrived in a "postracial" world of equity and harmony is seductive but highly problematic. Jennifer Esposito's study of the television workplace comedy *Ugly Betty* (II.12) shows how "race still structures our lives." This show features a highly nontraditional heroine: "a brown-skinned girl wearing braces and glasses" working for a boss who is "an irresponsible sex addict." In Esposito's reading, "while the show does try to satirize stereotypes of race, gender, class and sexuality, it nonetheless contributes to the reinscription of some stereotypes" (p. 96). Closely analyzing an episode in which Betty, a Latina, wins a contest with a White gay male colleague for a coveted job opportunity, Esposito points out that an unquestioned discourse of *meritocracy* is encoded in the episode.

A similar case can be made for the ways in which television representations of *social class* contribute to maintaining the social and political status quo, again by failing to question the hegemonic discourse of meritocracy. While the category of social class is less well represented in media scholarship than gender and race, it is still very important to recognize its interactive relationship with the two other more discussed categories of social analysis.

As Richard Butsch shows in his study on television representations of the male working-class buffoon (II.13), viewers are offered the idea that the lower class (working low-income people) is not succeeding in becoming rich because they are laughably stupid, rather than because they confront an economic and educational structure that limits class mobility. Butsch's study is also of particular interest from a political economy perspective in showing how the business of

television program production can create a kind of inertia that makes changing such long-lasting **stereotypes** difficult. His interviews with producers, writers, and directors of pilot sitcom episodes indicated that they were aware of the stereotyping but justified it as necessary "on the basis of time and dramatic constraints."

They also argue that to diverge from widely held stereotypes would draw attention away from the action, the storyline, or other characters and destroy dramatic effect. In addition, stereotyped stock characters are familiar to audiences, requiring less dramatic explanation. Thus, unless the contradiction of the stereotype is the basic story idea . . . there is a very strong pressure to reproduce existing stereotypes. (p. 107)

The issues related to gender, sexuality, race, and class ideology in media culture that have been highlighted here will be important to bear in mind throughout subsequent chapters, where a wide array of media cultural forms are examined in more depth, through our organization into thematic chapters that we hope will be of lively interest to you.

Reference

Butler, J. (2006). *Gender trouble: Feminism and the subversion of identity.* New York: Routledge.

Hetero Barbie?

Mary F. Rogers

As they enter their teenage years, if not before, most heterosexual females begin putting a boy or young man at the center of their lives. Moving through puberty toward adulthood, girls and young women find that their popularity at school, their feminine credibility, and much else hinge on their attractiveness to boys and their relationship with one particular boy.[1] As they get heterosexualized, then, girls and young women face pressures to give boys and dating a lot of priority. In turn, they pay increasing attention to the size and shape of their bodies, the range and contents of their wardrobes, the styling of their hair, and the making up of their faces. Barbie epitomizes, even exaggerates, these families mandates. She gives girls endless opportunities to costume her, brush and style her hair, and position her in settings like aerobics class, a school dance, or the shopping mall.

Yet Barbie escapes the typical outcomes of such activities. In the end she seems not to have her heart in her relationship with Ken, who in no way monopolizes her attention. Barbie exudes an independence that deviates from the codes of mainstream femininity. That she is insistently single and perpetually childless means that hers is no "normal" femininity. Again, one comes up short by looking for an explanation in Barbie's teenage status, for she is no teenager when it comes to occupations, travel, and other aspects of her lifestyle. The facts of Barbie's having neither a husband nor a child do not speak for themselves, then. Instead, these circumstances leave Barbie open to multiple, conflicting interpretations. They enlarge this icon's field of meanings and thus the range of consumers she can attract.

Within that field of cultural meanings stands the possibility that Barbie may not be heterosexual. Indeed, she may not even be a woman. Barbie may be a drag queen. Much in the tradition made widely visible by stars like RuPaul, Barbie may be the ultrafeminine presence that drag queens personify. Her long, long legs and flat hips suggest this possibility. So does her wardrobe, especially her shimmering evening gowns, high heels, heavy-handed makeup, and brilliant tiaras and other headpieces. Barbie's is a bright, glittery femininity never visibly defiled by a Lady Schick or Kotex. This exceptionally, emphatically feminine icon has some appeal among gay men.

That appeal shows up in diverse ways. I have no interest in whether or not this designer or that, this collector or that, this event or that is gay, however. My concern is with the *gay-themed* character of what one comes across in some corners of Barbie's far-reaching world. In many cultural worlds heterocentrism and heterosexism prevail in no uncertain terms. In the world of "Father Knows Best" or the feminine mystique, attention to gender and family center on heterosexuality strongly enough to snuff out alternative readings whereby "transgressive" sexualities such as lesbianism or bisexuality can enter the picture. Commonly intertwined with such heterocentrism are values celebrating heterosexuality as normal and natural while condemning or at least rejecting lesbigay sexualities. The world of Barbie is *relatively* free of such heterocentrism and heterosexism and thus holds *relative* appeal for nonheterosexual people, especially gay men. Lesbians, particularly those inclined toward feminism, are more likely to reject some of the central features of Barbie's world, as are bisexuals who might find her apparent monosexuality unappealing. In any case, Barbie's world allows for nonstraight readings, just as many other "straight" cultural products do.[2] I tap such possibilities here by treating Barbie's sexual identity as less than certain while arguing that her sweeping appeal revolves around such ambiguities.

As an icon of drag, Barbie illustrates what feminists and culture critics have been saying for some years. In no uncertain terms Barbie demonstrates that femininity is a manufactured reality. It entails a lot of artifice, a lot of clothes, a lot of props such as cuddly poodles and shopping bags, and a lot of effort, however satisfying at times.[3] If Barbie can join drag queens as an exemplar of the constructed character of femininity, she can also be an icon of nonheterosexual femininity. In the extreme Barbie might be a lipstick lesbian, a lesbian fem, or a lesbian closeted more tightly than most who choose not to "come out." She might be a bisexual woman who once cared about and pursued a relationship with Ken but now prefers her "best friend" Midge. Most radically of all, Barbie might be asexual. She might be sexy without being sexual, attractive without being attracted. . . .

Not surprisingly, RuPaul sometimes shows up in Barbie's world. Scott Arend (1995) reports that Ivan Burton, who designs artist dolls, has done a "one-of-a-kind RuPaul." Jim Washburn (1994) says that Michael Osborne, a Barbie doll collector, wants to be buried with what he calls his "RuPaul Barbie, or Ru-Barbie for short." Osborne's favorite doll is made from a My Size Barbie, the 18-inch version of the doll, and has "brown skin, blue eyes and platinum hair."

The feature story on Osborne, which appeared in the *Los Angeles Times,* illustrates how a gay-themed text fits into a mainstream publication, that is, how a gay reading of a supposedly straight text involves little stretch of the nonheterosexual imagination. Twenty-four-year-old Osborne, who has been collecting Barbie dolls since he was thirteen, has nearly 300 of them and makes no attempt to hide his "love" for them. Osborne says he has friends employed by Mattel who help him acquire some of his more unusual dolls, such as a hairless Skipper, Barbie's little sister. Like other collectors, Osborne keeps a lot of his dolls in their original packaging. (NRFB, or Never Removed From Box, enhances the market value of a doll.) Osborne, however, has "play-with dolls, whose outfits he changes monthly." He also shampoos his dolls' hair and gives them permanents. Also, Osborne once dressed as Barbie at Halloween and claims to have "looked pretty darn snappy." Asked about the possibility that his sizable Barbie collection could be an obstacle to "finding a mate," Osborne responds in terms of "friends who have had rocky relationships with *people* because they did not really like Barbie." Washburn poses the more difficult question: What "if it came down to a choice between giving up the Barbies or the *person?*" Osborne answers, "It depends on the *person,* but probably the *person.*"

Where a heterocentrist text would talk about finding a wife or a woman, this one refers only to mates and people and persons. In view of its subject matter this text readily passes as gay-themed. Along those lines Osborne reports, "I had always liked fashion, always liked doing hair. When people asked what I wanted to be when I grew up, I said I wanted to be a hairdresser and president of Mattel." Osborne's interest in being a hairdresser expresses an interest in what queer theorists, who theorize about nonheterosexual or "transgressive" sexualities, call *non-normative occupations.* Such lines of work are those that attract disproportionate numbers of lesbigay people and are widely considered inappropriate for people of a given gender. The ballet and hairdressing for men and the military and auto mechanics for women are examples. In any event Osborne's interest in a non-normative occupation bespeaks a gay-themed text, as does his claim that "the best times of his life have been Barbie times." . . .

More generally, *Barbie Bazaar* often offers gay-themed fare for those attuned to it. Like most such material, it does not leap out to most readers as lesbigay even while leaving room for "queer" interpretations. . . . Often, too, gay-themed material shows up in comments about or articles on doll artists, most of whom appear to be men often working in conjunction with male "partners" to refashion Barbie in designs of their own. In one *Barbie Bazaar* article Pattie Jones (1995), for instance, mentions Jim Faraone, who once designed jewelry for Anne Klein but now "designs hand-beaded Barbie doll outfits." Faraone began collecting in 1986 and now has a thousand Barbie dolls. Two of his artist dolls are pictured in Janine Fennick's *The Collectible Barbie Doll* (1996). One is AIDS Awareness Barbie where the AIDS-awareness red ribbon runs around the

back of Barbie's neck, across her breasts, and then crosses at her waist. Also showing up in *Barbie Bazaar* are references to Mattel's participation with collectors and other Barbie fans in AIDS fundraisers, often targeting children with AIDS as beneficiaries. . . .

Barbie thus points to what Jesse Berrett (1996) sees as "mass culture's power to define, commodify, and mutate sexual identity." Put more queerly in terms used in *Out* magazine:

> RuPaul's larger-than-life, gayer-than-gay presence on runways, VH1, and New York radio and everywhere else . . . suggests that the mall of America has embraced him not as a novelty but as a genuine homo star. But it doesn't take a drag queen to have an impact. (1997: 96)

Mattel can unintentionally sponsor the same impact, it seems. . . .

Notes

1. For insights into this state of affairs, see Eder with Evans and Parker (1995), Fine (1992), and Walkerdine (1990).

2. See, for example, Valerie Traub, "The Ambiguities of 'Lesbian' Viewing Pleasure: The (Dis)Articulation of *Black Widow,*" in Julia Epstein and Kristina Straub (eds.), *Body Guards: The Cultural Politics of Gender Ambiguity* (New York, Routledge, 1991), pp. 304–9; Bonnie Zimmerman, "Seeing, Reading, Knowing: The Lesbian Appropriation of Literature," in Joan E. Hartman and Ellen Messer-Davidow (eds.), *(En)Gendering Knowledge: Feminists in Academe* (Knoxville, University of Tennessee Press, 1991), pp. 92–7.

3. Dorothy E. Smith is one of the best commentators on how pleasurable some of the projects of femininity can be. She talks, for example, about the pleasures of female community built up around such feminine pastimes as clothes shopping. See *Texts, Facts,*

and Femininity: Exploring the Relations of Ruling (London and New York: Routledge, 1990), p. 199.

References

Arend, S. (1994). Review of mondo Barbie. *Barbie Bazaar, 6,* 51.

Berrett, J. (1996). The sex revolts: Reading gender and identity in mass culture. *Radical History Review, 66,* 210–219.

Eder, D., with Evans, C., & Parker, P. (1995). *School talk: Gender and adolescent culture.* New Brunswick, NJ: Rutgers University Press.

Fennick, J. (1996). *The collectible Barbie doll: An illustrated guide to her dreamy world.* Philadelphia: Courage Books.

Fine, M. (1992). *Disruptive voices: The possibilities of feminist research.* Ann Arbor: University of Michigan Press.

Jones, P. (1995). Viva la Barbie. *Barbie Bazaar, 7,* 63–67.

Walkerdine, V. (1990). *Schoolgirl fictions.* London and New York: Verso.

Washburn, J. (1994). The man who would be Ken. *Los Angeles Times,* 2 August: 1: Life & Style Section.

Sex and the City

Carrie Bradshaw's Queer Postfeminism

Jane Gerhard

Endings

In February 2004, the final credits of HBO's *Sex and the City* (*SATC*) rolled and a near-total media frenzy of goodbyes, tributes, commentary, and post mortems on the show ensued, testifying to the importance of the show to many viewers. Decidedly not innovative in its format, the show chronicled the life and loves of Carrie Bradshaw, a thirty-something single writer living in New York City. Where it was innovative, however, was its placement of Carrie in a tight-knit group of female friends with whom she could talk. In its combination of frank sex talk and best girlfriends, *SATC* became one of the most watched and discussed television series in recent memory.

The popularity of *SATC,* I believe, is due in part to its place at the juncture of two related trends in recent popular culture: postfeminism and queerness. The show is postfeminist . . . in the ways in which the women of *SATC* enjoy the fruits of women's post 70s equality. In many ways obvious and subtle, the series explores the meaning of women's sexual equality in the wake of the social and cultural achievements of second wave feminism. For postfeminists like Carrie and her friends, gender differences, such as wanting to look sexy and flirt are playful, stylistic, and unrelated to the operations of social power and authority. Women, if they so chose, can work, talk, and have sex "like men" while still maintaining all the privileges associated with being an attractive woman. At the same time and despite its insistent heterosexuality, *SATC* is a series that has taken advantage of the narrative possibilities afforded by queerness. By "queerness" I mean narratives, images, and plot structures that can be read as queer, whether or not the characters, actors or writers involved identified themselves as queer. As queer involves attempts to weaken the naturalized and normalizing binaries of sexuality (straight vs. gay) and of gender (masculine vs. feminine), it offers important insights into the show's approach to the women's desires. . . .

From Gerhard, J. (2005). *Sex and the City:* Carrie Bradshaw's queer postfeminism. *Feminist Media Studies,* 5(1), 37–49.

Carrie's World of Love and Ritual

SATC is structured by two major and over-lapping themes, both of which testify to the entanglement of postfeminism and queerness. The first, which is potentially the most disruptive to heterosexual allegiances, is that of the committed friendships between the women. The second is the bawdy talk the women engage in about their sexual partners. Explicit sex talk is the feature of the show most celebrated by critics, but also the feature of the series that does the most work towards expelling any potential for heterosexual instability. Together, both the female friendships and the frank sex talk demonstrate the incoherence that Janet Halley describes as a key feature of heterosexuality. In many ways, weekly episodes of *SATC* can be read as short lessons in the ways in which Carrie manages her incoherent desires. She manages her heterosexual identity not by "leaving" it and taking up a new one, like "becoming" bisexual or gay. Carrie finds satisfactions beyond those offered by men through her committed relationships with her girlfriends—Miranda, Charlotte, and Samantha—without whom she would be adrift in a sea of orgasms, shoes, and inadequate boyfriends.

When one tunes into the show, one quickly gathers that these women's girlfriends are the most valued people in their lives. And indeed, the show insists that these relationships are more lasting and trustworthy than those with men or potential husbands. The friends enjoy an intimacy that nostalgically returns female viewers to college dorms, boarding school, or sleep away camp. The friends have their own apartments, jobs and lives, yet thanks to modern communications are in constant contact with each other. If they are not talking on their cell phones with each other, they are walking the streets deep in conversation, or riding in cabs together. Their conversations are as intimate as the sex with men they enjoy. In many episodes, the heterosexual sex is akin to jogging or clubbing, but the talk is the true subject, the process by which the show's narrative, its knowledge and its pleasures, are generated. The pleasures of talking are challenged by the competing ones of eating and stylish self-presentation. The episodes unfold around the friends' shared breakfasts, lunches, dinners, and cocktails. At each gathering, the friends appear in different outfits and are ready to discuss the latest chapter in the chronicle of their sexual and romantic problems. Eating heartily, even if salad or saltwater taffy, literally and metaphorically stands in for other bodily pleasures, pleasures given to oneself yet amplified when done with others. Such eating moments literally structure the show far more than do the women's sexual encounters. Shared meals, in conjunction with the never-ending conversations, function as the pauses where the women make sense of their lives, where they try to sort out what matters and what does not. They measure themselves against each other, listening in sympathy or outrage to how one of their friends might handle the same situation.

These conversations, on cell phones or face to face, become the bedrock of their collective life and of Carrie's sex column. For not only does she get a regular supply of dating stories from her friends, Carrie also gets the discussion and debate about sex and its significance. Through these conversations, in fact, Carrie gets access to a more discursive and imaginary place where sexual pleasure is not confined only to the bodies of those involved, but to those who get to listen to the stories about pleasure. For example, in season four, when Carrie has a gigantic orgasm with a guy who has an Attention Deficit Disorder, part of the pleasure of that orgasm comes from talking about it to her friends. The friends' collective marveling at a night of pleasure, at a forbidden practice, or at specific orgasms, secures the pleasure in time and place, makes it more real, and importantly makes it possible for the speaker (and the audience) to savor it all the more. The connections that are not genital, but are pleasurable, that make sex more real than when one had it, complicate the series' representation of heterosexuality. For what the friends come to want are not only the good nights of sex, but also the pleasures they get from sharing it, through conversation, with that someone special who cares.

Crucially, these friendships, with their problems and jealousies, offer the women an emotional alternative to the compromising world of boyfriends and potential husbands. The bonds that they forge, and upon which they rely, provide the women with the support that the endless stream of men cannot give them. The friends rely on each other to pay attention to their worries, to care about their latest $400 shoes, to be there when their mother dies, when a boyfriend dumps them, or when they dump a boyfriend. Ultimately, in function if not in name, they provide each other with an alternative family. This elective family structure is one that gay men and lesbians have relied on for generations—a self-selected family that willingly meets its members' needs.

The challenge the friendships pose to the women's heterosexual identities is not that such friendships mark them as gay. Rather, the connections they have with each other create an alternative to their boyfriends, an alternative that, by its very existence, grants the women options different from those traditionally signified as "heterosexual" (where women satisfy their desires with one man, serially or monogamously). Carrie, Miranda, Charlotte, and Samantha have created a world within a world or, to borrow historian Carroll Smith Rosenberg's term, a "female world of love and ritual" that supplements the heterosexual world of men in which they also live (Carroll Smith Rosenberg 1975). . . .

One of the projects of feminist historians in the late 1970s was to reclaim women's friendships from the shadows of the nineteenth-century private sphere. For slave women, as documented by Deborah Gray White and Angela Davis, or for white middle-class women, as documented by Carroll Smith Rosenberg, the culture of separateness forged deep bonds with other women over birth, death, marriage, baptism, and care-taking.[1] Women's historians have argued that these private bonds were passionate, that they involved psychological and physical intimacy, and provided support and love that women living in racial/ gender hierarchies could not get from men, who like women, lived largely in homosocial worlds. . . .

If *Sex and the City*'s raison d'être is the detailing of how hard it is to find a man worth committing to in modern Gotham, the show is nevertheless structured around the women's non-heterosexual desires. Its clever innovation was to build the narrative around the very familiar and under-theorized alternative that women do have to men, to boyfriends and to the institutions of heterosexuality. The world of love and ritual that the four friends create for themselves allows the series' exploration of female heterosexuality to go forward without marking the women as homosexuals.

Female friendship, then, is the first thematic of *SATC*. The second is female sexuality itself. Sexual explicitness occurs in two related arenas in the show: showing the women having sex with multiple partners over the course of the series, and the characters' use of explicit language to describe to their friends the sex they have had with men. The sex talk, which makes up the bulk of the friends' discussions, is one site of the series' postfeminist sensibility. The tactic of show-and-tell around the women's sex demonstrates that "heterosexual sex" refers to many things besides the missionary position or female sexual subservence. Many critics and viewers initially believed that the sex talk was the aspect of the show that was most innovative and had the most potential to disrupt confining gender constructions.

The women's frank talk about the explicit sex achieves a number of important effects. First, the sex talk takes place in the context of the friends' conversations, conversations that constitute what is knowable by the show. This knowledge works in the same way that consciousness-raising sessions did for second wave feminists. The women's talk provides an account of the "dissonance" the characters experience between ideas about heterosexual romance and their experience of straight sex. The talk explains what's not comfortable in sex, what they don't like about what this or that lover does, what they would like more of in pleasures of heterosexual sex for women. These women are shown enjoying intercourse in an array of positions with numerous partners. The characters love penises and the men who bear them. They love feeling desirable. The pleasure they take in sex, which they narrate to each other in conversation, both binds them to each other and erotically to heterosexual pleasures. This must be seen as an important contribution the show makes—these women are the subjects of heterosexual sex, not its object.

That said, the series' postfeminist sensibility undoes some of its potentially liberating aspects. At the same time the talk focuses on the pleasures of heterosexual sex, it also centers on their search for "the right man." While the show celebrates the friends' pleasurable sexual encounters, these moments of sex are narrated (on multiple levels of the show) in and through the quest for romantic love. The search for lasting romance reproduces the enduring message that woman's ultimate personal and sexual liberation lies with men. While the show demonstrates that it is good to find a hard man, for Carrie and her friends, a good man remains so hard to find.

Paradoxically, the search for the right man, which up until the last season had inevitably failed, underscores the centrality of the women to each other. In episode forty, "All or Nothing," Samantha gets sick and none of her lovers come to nurse her. In her hour of need, when all the desirability is gone, when there is no makeup, no lacy underwear, and no fancy cocktails, it is Carrie who comes to give her medicine and wipe her nose. Carrie reassures her lonely and despairing friend that they are not alone, that they have each other. A moment of postfeminist angst—being liberated is not all we were told it would be—is mitigated by the show's queer perspective. Having each other becomes the way these women manage what is often represented as their lonely heterosexuality.

The show returns viewers back to this meta-narrative of queer families and even insists on ritualizing those self-chosen bonds. At the end of season four (episode sixty-four, "Ring a Ding Ding") Carrie asks Charlotte for a loan with which to buy her literal home and to preserve her symbolic autonomy. At lunch with wine, a now separated Charlotte slides her engagement ring, encased in its original soft velvet box, the symbol of what straight women are said to desire, across the table to Carrie as a down payment for a new home. Carrie inhales sharply, looks up and searches Charlotte's eyes for her meaning. "Will you take it?" Charlotte asks. Carrie takes Charlotte's hand, and whispers, in a voice full of love, "Are you sure?" The penultimate scene that haunts Carrie and her friends' inner closet of romantic desire is enacted, but not with the "proper" person that straight women imagine themselves sitting across from. Instead of the boyfriend, it is the girlfriend. Not the lesbian girlfriend, but the straight girlfriend. And for this show, at least, and in this literary Gotham, this is indeed the "proper" person, the friend who will always be there.

Similarly, in the final season (episode eighty-eight, "The Ick Factor"), Carrie demands that her new boyfriend acknowledge the centrality of her relationship with Samantha. Samantha, recently diagnosed with breast cancer, is the character that is at once the most sexually adventurous and the most vulnerable to fears of growing old alone. During Miranda's wedding, Carrie and Samantha hold hands. Underscoring the family that already exists, the camera turns to Carrie and Samantha as we hear Miranda promise to her husband "to have and to hold, in sickness and health, as long as we both shall live." Boys on the side, indeed. Call the boyfriend to dispose of rodents, and girlfriends to dispel fears of growing old alone. What made *SATC* different was that it regularly suggested that this family of four could be enough to make up a life, a life still worth living without the husband and baby, a life led outside the historic feminine and feminist script.

Yet throughout its tenure, the show walked the fine line between exploring the potential enough-ness of same sex families while never tipping the women into outright gayness. This unstable project—at once insisting on the women's autonomy from men through their relationships with each other and their heterosexuality— reflects the convergence of postfeminism and queerness in the series as it struggled to conceptualize women's freedom, sexually and psychologically. Rather than insisting that Carrie is not straight, we must note the multiple ways in which *SATC* demonstrates, inadvertently and episodically, that heterosexuals have desires that sometimes defy the simple equation between genital contact and sexuality, that sometimes disrupt the lines we draw between homosexuality

and heterosexuality, and that sometimes crack the false divides between emotional and sexual pleasures. Gender similarity continues to provide the ground of psychological and emotional pleasures so rich as to be closeted. In its postfeminism, *SATC*'s solution to the historic problem of sexuality for women simultaneously reaches backward to nineteenth-century bonds of womanhood and forward to female independence based on those same bonds.

Note

1. Carroll Smith Rosenberg (1975), Deborah Gray White (1985), and Angela Davis (1989) are three of many examples.

References

Davis, Angela (1989) *Women, Culture and Politics,* Random House, New York.

Rosenberg, Carroll Smith (1975) 'The female world of love and ritual: relations between women in 19th century America,' *Signs,* vol. 1, pp. 1–29.

White, Deborah Gray (1985) *Ar'nt I a Woman? Female Slaves in the Plantation South,* Norton, New York.

The Whites of Their Eyes

Racist Ideologies and the Media

Stuart Hall

We begin by defining some of the terms of the argument. 'Racism and the media' touches directly the problem of *ideology*, since the media's main sphere of operations is the production and transformation of ideologies. . . .

I am using the term ideology to refer to those images, concepts and premises which provide the frameworks through which we represent, interpret, understand and 'make sense' of some aspect of social existence. Language and ideology are not the same—since the same linguistic term ('democracy' for example, or 'freedom') can be deployed within different ideological discourses. But language, broadly conceived, is by definition the principal medium in which we find different ideological discourses elaborated.

Three important things need to be said about ideology in order to make what follows intelligible. First, ideologies do not consist of isolated and separate concepts, but in the articulation of different elements into a distinctive set or chain of meanings. In liberal ideology, 'freedom' is connected (articulated) with individualism and the free market; in socialist ideology, 'freedom' is a collective condition, dependent on, not counterposed to, 'equality of condition,' as it is in liberal ideology. The same concept is differently positioned within the logic of different ideological discourses. One of the ways in which ideological struggle takes place and ideologies are transformed is by articulating the elements differently, thereby producing a different meaning: breaking the chain in which they are currently fixed (e.g. 'democratic' = the 'Free' West) and establishing a new articulation (e.g. 'democratic' = deepening the democratic content of political life). This 'breaking of the chain' is not, of course, confined to the head: it takes place through social practice and political struggle.

Second, ideological statements are made by individuals: but ideologies are not the product of individual consciousness or intention. Rather we formulate our intentions *within ideology*. They pre-date individuals, and form part of the determinate social formations and

Extract from *Silver Linings: Some Strategies for the Eighties* (George Bridges and Ros Brunt, eds.), Lawrence & Wishart, 1981, "The Whites of Their Eyes: Racist Ideologies and the Media," by Stuart Hall, pp. 31–32, 34–35, 36–37, and 29–41.

conditions into which individuals are born. We have to 'speak through' the ideologies which are active in our society and which provide us with the means of 'making sense' of social relations and our place in them. The transformation of ideologies is thus a collective process and practice, not an individual one. Largely, the processes work *unconsciously*, rather than by conscious intention. Ideologies produce different forms of social consciousness, rather than being produced by them. They work most effectively when we are not aware that how we formulate and construct a statement about the world is underpinned by ideological premises; when our formations seem to be simply descriptive statements about how things are (i.e. must be), or of what we can 'take-for-granted.' 'Little boys like playing rough games; little girls, however, are full of sugar and spice' is predicated on a whole set of ideological premises, though it seems to be an aphorism which is grounded, not in how masculinity and femininity have been historically and culturally constructed in society, but in Nature itself. Ideologies tend to disappear from view into the taken-for-granted 'naturalized' world of common sense. Since (like gender) race appears to be 'given' by Nature, racism is one of the most profoundly 'naturalized' of existing ideologies.

Third, ideologies 'work' by constructing for their subjects (individual and collective) positions of identification and knowledge which allow them to 'utter' ideological truths as if they were their authentic authors. This is not because they emanate from our innermost, authentic and unified experience, but because we find ourselves mirrored in the positions at the centre of the discourses from which the statements we formulate 'make sense.' Thus the same 'subjects' (e.g. economic classes or ethnic groups) can be differently constructed in different ideologies. . . .

Let us look, then, a little more closely at the apparatuses which generate and circulate ideologies. In modern societies, the different media are especially important sites for the production, reproduction and transformation of ideologies. Ideologies are of course, worked on in many places in society, and not only in the head. The fact of unemployment is, among other things, an extremely effective ideological instrument for converting or constraining workers to moderate their wage claims. But institutions like the media are peculiarly central to the matter since they are, by definition, part of the dominant means of *ideological* production. What they 'produce' is, precisely, representations of the social world, images, descriptions, explanations and frames for understanding how the world is and why it works as it is said and shown to work. And, amongst other kinds of ideological labour, the media construct for us a definition of what *race* is, what meaning the imagery of race carries, and what the 'problem of race' is understood to be. They help to classify out the world in terms of the categories of race.

The media are not only a powerful source of ideas about race. They are also one place where these ideas are articulated, worked on, transformed and elaborated. We have said 'ideas' and 'ideologies' in the plural. For it would be wrong and misleading to see the media as uniformly and conspiratorially harnessed to a single, racist conception of the world. Liberal and humane ideas about 'good relations' between the races, based on open-mindedness and tolerance, operate inside the world of the media. . . .

It would be simple and convenient if all the media were simply the ventriloquists of a unified and racist 'ruling class' conception of the world. But neither a unifiedly conspiratorial media nor indeed a unified racist 'ruling class' exists in anything like that simple way. I don't insist on complexity for its own sake. But if critics of the media subscribe to too simple or reductive a view of their operations, this inevitably lacks credibility and weakens the case they are making because the theories and critiques don't square with reality. . . .

Another important distinction is between what we might call 'overt' racism and 'inferential' racism. By *overt* racism, I mean those many occasions when open and favourable coverage is given to arguments, positions and spokespersons who are in the business of elaborating an openly racist argument or advancing a racist policy or view.

By *inferential* racism I mean those apparently naturalized representations of events and situations relating to race, whether 'factual' or 'fictional,' which have racist premises and propositions inscribed in them as a set of *unquestioned assumptions*. These enable racist statements to be formulated without ever bringing into awareness the racist predicates on which the statements are grounded. . . .

An example of *inferential* racist ideology is the sort of television programme which deals with some 'problem' in race relations. It is probably made by a good and honest liberal broadcaster, who hopes to do some good in the world for 'race relations' and who maintains a scrupulous balance and neutrality when questioning people interviewed for the programme. The programme will end with a homily on how, if only the 'extremists' on *either side* would go away, 'normal blacks and whites' would be better able to get on with learning to live in harmony together. Yet every word and image of such programmes are impregnated with unconscious racism because they are all predicated on the unstated and unrecognized assumption that the *blacks* are the *source of the problem*. Yet virtually the whole of 'social problem' television about race and immigration—often made, no doubt, by well intentioned and liberal minded broadcasters—is precisely predicated on racist premises of this kind. . . .

Recent critics of imperialism have argued that, if we simply extend our definition of nineteenth century fiction from one branch of 'serious fiction' to embrace popular literature, we will find a second, powerful strand of the English literary imagination to set beside the *domestic* novel: the male-dominated world of imperial adventure which takes *empire*, rather than *Middlemarch* as its microcosm.

I remember a graduate student, working on the construction of race in popular literature and culture at the end of the Nineteenth Century, coming to me in despair—racism was so *ubiquitous,* and at the same time, so *unconscious*—simply assumed to be the case—that it was impossible to get any critical purchase on it. In this period, the very idea of *adventure* became synonymous with the demonstration of the moral, social and physical mastery of the colonizers over the colonized.

Later, this concept of 'adventure'—one of the principal categories of modern *entertainment*—moved straight off the printed page into the literature of crime and espionage, children's books, the great Hollywood extravaganzas and comics. There, with recurring persistence, they still remain. Many of these older versions have had their edge somewhat blunted by time. They have been distanced from us, apparently, by our superior wisdom and liberalism. But they still reappear on the television screen, especially in the form of 'old movies' (some 'old movies,' of course, continue to be made). But we can grasp their recurring resonance better if we identify some of the base image of the 'grammar of race.'

There is, for example, the familiar *slave-figure*: dependable, loving in a simple, childlike way—the devoted 'Mammy' with the rolling eyes, or the faithful field-hand or retainer, attached and devoted to 'his' Master. The best known extravaganza of all—*Gone With The Wind*—contains rich variants of both. The 'slave-figure' is by no means limited to films and programmes *about* slavery. Some 'Injuns' and many Asians have come on to the screen in this disguise. A deep and unconscious ambivalence pervades this stereotype. Devoted and childlike, the 'slave' is also unreliable, unpredictable and undependable—capable of 'turning nasty,' or of plotting in a treacherous way, secretive, cunning, cut-throat once his or her Master's or Mistress's back is turned: and inexplicably given to running away into the bush at the slightest opportunity. The whites can never be sure that this childish simpleton—'Sambo'—is not mocking his master's white manners behind his hand, even when giving an exaggerated caricature of white refinement.

Another base-image is that of the 'native.' The good side of this figure is portrayed in a certain primitive nobility and simple dignity. The bad side is portrayed in terms of cheating and cunning, and, further out, savagery and barbarism. Popular culture is still full today of countless savage and restless 'natives,' and sound-tracks constantly repeat the threatening sound of drumming in the night, the hint of primitive rites and cults. Cannibals, whirling dervishes, Indian tribesmen, garishly got up, are constantly threatening to overrun the screen. They are likely to appear at any moment out of the darkness to decapitate the beautiful heroine, kidnap the children, burn the encampment or threaten to boil, cook and eat the innocent explorer or colonial administrator and his lady-wife. These 'natives' always move as an anonymous collective mass—in tribes or hordes. And against them is always counterposed the isolated white figure, alone 'out there,' confronting his Destiny or shouldering his Burden in the 'heart of darkness,' displaying coolness under fire and an unshakeable authority—exerting mastery over the rebellious natives or quelling the threatened uprising with a single glance of his steel-blue eyes.

A third variant is that of the 'clown' or 'entertainer.' This captures the 'innate' humour, as well as the physical grace of the licensed entertainer—putting on a show for The Others. It is never quite clear whether we are laughing with or at this figure: admiring the physical and rhythmic grace, the open expressivity and emotionality of the 'entertainer,' or put off by the 'clown's' stupidity.

One noticeable fact about all these images is their deep *ambivalence*—the double vision of the white eye through which they are seen. The primitive nobility of the ageing tribesman or chief, and the native's rhythmic grace always contain both a nostalgia for an innocence lost forever to the civilized, and the threat of civilization being over-run or undermined by the recurrence of savagery, which is always lurking just below the surface; or by an untutored sexuality, threatening to 'break out.' Both are aspects—the good and the bad sides—of *primitivism*. In these images, 'primitivism' is defined by the fixed proximity of such people to Nature.

Is all this so far away as we sometimes suppose from the representations of race which fill the screens today? These *particular* versions may have faded. But their *traces* are still to be observed, reworked in many of the modern and up-dated images. And though they may appear to carry a different meaning, they are often still constructed on a very ancient grammar.

Pornographic Eroticism and Sexual Grotesquerie in Representations of African American Sportswomen

James McKay and Helen Johnson

Go Back To The Cotten [sic] Plantation Nigger. (Banner in the stands when Althea Gibson walked on court to defend her US Open title in 1958)

That's the way to do it! Hit the net like any Negro would! (Racist male heckling Serena Williams before she served at the 2007 Sony Ericsson Championships in Miami)

In this paper we use sport to encourage 'white' people to deconstruct the privileged lens through which they construct and view 'black' people. More specifically, we analyse how sections of the media have framed tennis champions Serena and Venus Williams as threats to sport's racist and sexist regime. Like other sportswomen of colour, the Williams sisters have challenged racist and sexist stereotypes and inspired millions of females around the world (Hargreaves, 2000, 2007). However, given that Althea Gibson and Serena Williams were subjected to blatant racism at tennis tournaments nearly 50 years apart, we should not be sanguine about the social constraints that African American sportswomen still encounter. . . .

From McKay, J., & Johnson, H. (2008). Pornographic eroticism and sexual grotesquerie in representations of African American sportswomen. *Social Identities, 14*(4), 491–504.

African American Sportswomen as Threats to Gender and Racial Hierarchies

Rowe (1990, p. 409) argues that gender hierarchies are threatened whenever women's bodies are deemed to be excessive: 'too fat, too mouthy, too old, too dirty, too pregnant, too sexual (or not sexual enough) for the norms of conventional gender representation.' Following Schulze (1990, p. 198), we can add muscularity to this list of corporeal transgressions: '[t]he deliberately muscular woman disturbs dominant notions of sex, gender, and sexuality, and any discursive field that includes her risks opening up a site of contest and conflict, anxiety and ambiguity.' While muscularity in women and men is becoming an increasingly desirable body type, it is, in the twenty-first century, hyper-muscularity in women that threatens heteronormative gender relations (Heywood & Dworkin, 2003). . . .

Hyper-muscularity as both a new social phenomenon and a denigrating stereotype is especially evident in sport, which has embodied in the past the 'natural' superiority of men in contrast to the 'otherness' of female athletes as objects of ridicule, weakness, inferiority, decoration, passivity and as erotically desirable yet transgressive, but which is now searching for new ways to disparage the powerful and therefore 'uppity' African American sportswomen. . . .

A common strategy of reasserting masculine hegemony in sport is via 'pornographic eroticism,' in which sexuality is constructed as the 'primary characteristic of the person represented' (Heywood, 1998). Heywood distinguishes 'pornographic eroticism' from 'athletic eroticism,' in which sexuality is 'one dimension of human experience, as a quality that emerges from the self-possession, autonomy, and strength so evident in the body of a female athlete.' Although Heywood refers to bodybuilding, examples of 'pornographic eroticism' are prevalent in most sports (Glenny, 2006;

Messner, Dunbar & Hunt, 2002; Messner, Duncan & Cooky, 2003).

While Heywood's concept of 'pornographic eroticism' is useful for explaining how female athletes in general are recuperated by the media, the negative coverage of the Williams sisters that we analyse below demonstrates that African American sportswomen also threaten racial hierarchies. Hence, we propose that the racialized anxieties that drive censorious responses to African American sportswomen are most effectively understood when situated within the historical context of black women's enslavement, colonial conquest, and exhibition as ethnographic 'grotesquerie.' The categorization of black women's bodies as hyper-muscular and their targeting for lascivious comment mirrors the public and pseudo-scientific response to nineteenth century exhibits of Saartjie Baartman, the South African woman labeled the 'Hottentot Venus' (Hobson, 2003, p. 87). Thus, we also use Hobson's concept of 'sexual grotesquerie,' which, in turn, was suggested by Morgan's (1997) analysis of European explorers' writings about Africa that depicted African women's bodies as mythic and monstrous. . . .

The 'Ghetto Cinderellas'

On Tuesday the story was Maria Sharapova's Swan Lake dress. On Wednesday it was Tatiana Golovin's red knickers. Yesterday it was Venus Williams' hot pants . . . [C]overage of men's tennis tends to focus on tennis. Not so the women's game, especially in the first week of a Grand Slam event when the lack of depth in the field means the opening rounds serve as a glorified warm-up for the 'big beasts.' (Moore 2007)

'Pornographic eroticism' is particularly prominent in media coverage of women's tennis, where many players' physiques and performances are the objects of a constant gaze and are monitored for 'excess' (Harris & Clayton, 2002; Kennedy, 2001; Miller, McKay & Martin, 1999; Stevenson, 2002). Anna Kournikova has been criticized for trading on her looks and displaying more style than substance; Amelie Mauresmo was reproached for being openly lesbian and having a strong body and powerful topspin backhand; former world number 1 Justine Henin is belittled for having a drab image, while Maria Sharapova has been nicknamed 'The Glamazon,' to describe her combination of conventional good looks, statuesque physique, and powerful forehand (she also has been dubbed 'Shriekapova' and 'Belle of the Decibel' and censured for having a 'banshee-like grunt'); Daniela Hantuchova has been accused of being an anorexic, while Casey Dellacqua and Marion Bartoli have been condemned for allegedly being overweight. For instance, journalist Sue Mott (2007) described 2007 Wimbledon singles finalist Bartoli as 'more Friar Tuck than Maid Marion.'

Matthew Syed (2008) contends that

there has always been a soft-porn dimension to women's tennis, but with the progression of Maria Sharapova, Ana Ivanovic, Jelena Jankovic and Daniela Hantuchova to the semi-finals of the Australian Open, this has been into the realms of adolescent (and non-adolescent) male fantasy.

He complains that Western society has not 'reached a place where heterosexual men can acknowledge the occasionally erotic dimension of watching women's sport without being dismissed as deviant' thus articulating the unreflective, heterosexual, white male-centred viewpoint that is normative in mainstream media.

The Williams sisters also have been subjected to the carping critical gaze that both structures and is a key discursive theme of 'pornographic eroticism.' Of great significance, however, is that they also have been constructed by derogatory racial, sexual and class stereotypes associated with African Americans. . . .

Since 1999 the Williams sisters have dominated international women's tennis by winning 14 Grand Slam singles titles (Serena eight, Venus six), five women's doubles and four mixed doubles Grand Slam titles, and gold medals in singles (Venus) and women's doubles at the Olympics. The Williams sisters began playing sport early while living in Compton, an economically impoverished area of Los Angeles, before moving to Florida while young. Whereas many tennis prodigies attend private tennis academies, the Williams sisters trained under the unorthodox regime of their father, Richard, a sharecropper's son from Louisiana. Serena and Venus have become wealthy international sporting superstars and celebrities, with incomes estimated at over $US100 million from endorsement contracts with firms such as McDonald's, Nike, Wilson, Estée Lauder, and Reebok. Thus, they have been constructed within a 'ghetto-to-glory' narrative: a journalist referred to their ascent as a 'fairy tale, that astonishing narrative of the "ghetto Cinderella"' (Adams, 2005); one described Venus as a former 'teenage curio from a Los Angeles ghetto' (Muscat, 2007); and another stated that, 'Only in America would Venus have risen from her cradle of crack dealers and grunge courts to contest the women's singles final at Wimbledon' (Mott, 2000). Patton (2001, p. 122) refers to these sorts of narratives as 'an Africanized version of the Horatio Alger story in which athletics provides a route out of the ghetto.'

The exceptional performances of the Williams sisters have provoked complex and ambivalent narratives of qualified praise and grudging approval, as well as subtle and overt racism and sexism (Douglas, 2002, 2005; Schultz, 2002; Spencer, 2001, 2004). Media coverage of the Williams sisters is not always negative, because their performances are too extraordinary to be completely denigrated. For instance, in the lead-up to the 2003 French Open, Serena appeared in an action shot on the cover of *Sports Illustrated* with the caption 'Awesome.' Journalist Will Buckley (2007, p. 15) compared the Williams sisters to male legends like Pele, Muhammad Ali, Roger Federer, Tiger Woods, and Jack Nicklaus, rating them as the 'greatest duo' in sporting history. However, such praise co-exists with both subtle and overt racism and sexism. The Williams sisters have been criticized for lacking 'commitment' by refusing to conform to the Spartan training regime of professional tennis, restricting their playing schedules, having too many 'off-court interests' in acting, music, product endorsements, fashion and interior design, and their Jehovah's Witness religion. They have been accused of fixing matches against one another, cheating, and engaging in unsporting behaviour. They have been called arrogant, aloof, and self-absorbed; indicted for putatively ostentatious lifestyles and wearing expensive jewelry while not assisting African Americans affected by Hurricane Katrina; and disparaged for competing while wearing beaded cornrows and/or tinted hairstyles and 'tacky' outfits. At the 2002 US Open Serena was condemned for wearing a black 'catsuit,' and in 2003 her appearance at a public function was disparaged as a 'hooker look' by *The Washington Post*'s fashion writer:

> She wore an orange crochet hussy dress modeled after something that Wilma Flintstone might choose. The low-cut dress, with its embroidered bodice, had a hemline that looked like it had been gnawed by Dino. . . . Her admirers paint a picture of poise and exuberance, talent and physical grace. One only wishes that Williams would use her wealth and notoriety to paint herself in equally flattering terms. (PostWatch, 2002)

In an article about the 2007 Wimbledon tournament, entitled 'Street style gives Venus her deadly cutting edge,' Venus was compared poorly to her vanquished opponent Akiko Morigami:

Williams the elder is urban hip-hop, a swirling, whirling, street babe who believes tennis is a sport best played at full volume. . . . With Williams wearing an ill-fitting vest and hot-pants outfit that might have been plucked off the *Primark* bargain rail, Morigami, the ultimate in femininity, won the consolation fashion stakes in her broderie anglaise skirt and scalloped sleeved top. (Philip, 2007)

The title of another article about Wimbledon condensed many of the above points. Although Venus was portrayed in an 'action shot,' the title was, 'Williams has designs on title despite host of outside distractions.' Much of the material was devoted to suggesting that Venus had played in her underwear, to her preoccupation with her interior design company, to the gold handbag she brings courtside, and to her guitar-playing skill (Smith, 2007). While Serena and Venus have been described as the 'Sisters Sledgehammer' (Bierley, 2004) and as having an 'Amazonian physique and piranha mentality' (Mott, 2000), Daniela Hantuchova, in contrast, was portrayed as playing tennis 'with grace and artistry, words that appeared to have been all but crushed by the blitzkrieg that was Venus and Serena Williams' (Viner, 2007).

Such commentary has often been anchored by the stereotypes to which we have alluded of black people being constructed as animalistic and closer to nature. Following Venus' victory at Wimbledon in 2000, a journalist hailed her as a 'role model for blacks' and lamented that black people had not been given more opportunities to participate in sport, because 'there is a natural physical superiority about those of African origin . . . only centuries of repression has prevented them becoming masters of so many sports' (Miller, 2000). Serena was described as a 'cat woman' at the 2002 US Open (Schutz, 2002), and Venus' quarterfinal victory over Sharapova at Wimbledon in 2007 was headlined 'Dying swan devoured as giant bird of prey returns to SW19,' with Barnes (2007) writing that,

'The dying swan [Maria Sharapova] slunk out in her tutu, savaged to death by a giant bird of prey—a Californian condor, if you like.' Marion Bartoli's loss to Venus in the final was attributed to the 'immense hard luck that Venus can chase from side to side like a cheetah on the run' (Mott, 2007), and Venus was also depicted as 'a panther, sensing a wounded animal' (White, 2007).

The Williams sisters arrived at the 2006 Australian Open in the unusual situation of being ranked lowly due to injuries and long lay-offs. Their commitment, fitness, and weight were targeted even before competition began. In 'Aussie defeat is the bottom line for overweight Serena,' British journalist Alix Ramsay (2006) claimed that

Both Venus and Serena were unfit, unprepared and under-done as the Open began. . . . Swanning into Melbourne as only they can, the sisters were seen shopping and posing around town. They certainly acted the part of superstar athletes but they certainly did not look it. Serena, in particular, was patently overweight and pictures of her larger-than-life figure were splashed across every newspaper in the land. . . . Clearly the sisters, 'crossover celebrities' both, are too busy to devote their time exclusively to tennis.

Journalists' fixation with Serena's diet, weight, fitness, and appearance then shifted into categories of 'pornographic eroticism' and 'sexual grotesquerie.' Her breasts and bottom were fetishized via headlines such as, 'Size up Serena Williams at your own risk' (Stevens, 2006), 'Serena out to kick butt' (Epstein, 2006), and 'Easybeat? Fat chance' (Crawford, 2006a), and photographs of her allegedly abnormal gluteal muscles and weight. When asked about her physical status, Serena commented that: 'Honestly, I've never read any comments about my fitness. I don't read the papers. I saw (a picture) of me running. And I was like, "Wow, my hamstring muscle is that big?" I had no idea my muscle was like that. But that's about it' (Epstein, 2006). One newspaper used the

headline 'Serena Shocked by Pictures,' but selectively printed Serena's comment about her hamstring being large, thereby suggesting she was alarmed (Crawford, 2006b). In one of Australia's 'quality' newspapers, journalist Stephen Gibbs (2006) compared Serena with Maria Sharapova in his article 'Big bum rap for Serena.'

Serena Williams has this great big arse. Some tennis commentators seem able to ignore the urge to record that for posterity and instead have concentrated on her career . . .

Righto. This is the spot for a sentence that starts: 'Before the letters of complaint come flooding in from the hairy-armpit brigade . . . ' This may or may not be interesting but, in fact, they never do. Those sentences are written for female colleagues and partners rather than letter-writing lesbians.

[But] Sharapova is a Russian glamour girl and can apparently play a bit, too. She is tanned, teenaged, firm of bottom and pert of breast. She has for some time been ranked No. 1 by the tennis world as the female player heterosexual males most want to up-end.

But that is not how they put it in the media, just as we don't say Serena Williams has a big arse.

. . . The authoritative discourse of 'science' was . . . used by a journalist, who consulted a sports medicine specialist about Serena's physique, and was advised that, 'It is the African-American race. They just have this huge gluteal strength. With Serena, that's her physique and genetics' (Stevens, 2006). The media attributed early upset losses by both Serena and Venus to excess weight, lack of commitment, and interest in 'frivolous' pursuits outside tennis, while an Australian journalist 'joked' that the quick exit of local hero Lleyton Hewitt was due to his dislike for the Rebound Ace courts, which were 'more dangerous than trying to steal Serena Williams's lunch box' (Hinds, 2006).

While Serena publicly stated during the 2007 Australian Open that her critics were haters who simply served to motivate her, such defiance intensified media attention. For instance, Hinds (2007a) wrote that Serena's game has always been about as subtle as a 'kick in the groin,' she had 'bludgeoned her way to seven grand slam titles with the swing of her executioner's blade,' and she had a 'chip on her shoulder.' He also alluded to her displeasure over losing a challenge to the electronic officiating system, Hawk-Eye, by posing the rhetorical question: 'Is she a Hawk-Eye hater, too?' (Hinds, 2007a). Despite struggling in the preliminary rounds, Serena reached the final, only to receive ongoing criticism that her progress highlighted the inferior status of women's tennis:

> That she has reached the final speaks volumes for her competitive spirit and determination, while once again underlining the general lack of intelligence and creative ability of the other leading players. . . . Williams has played so few tournaments in the last 13 months that her success here rather makes a mockery of the circuit. Why play at all if you can get to a grand slam final with virtually no previous match-play? . . . Williams should not have been able to get to the final with such ease. The fact that she has must be deeply embarrassing. (Bierley, 2007)

Serena easily defeated top-seeded Maria Sharapova in the final, an outcome that could have been embedded in several stock heroic sporting narratives: 'Champion rises to the occasion,' 'Comeback Queen,' or 'Serena battles through adversity.' Instead, her triumph was narrativized in recurrent deprecating and sexualized scripts: 'Champ focused on retail therapy after responding to critics' (Scott, 2007); 'Serena ignores the knockers' (Pearce, 2007); 'Cyclone Serena slams Maria and her knockers' (in which Serena was described as 'the game's Alpha female'—Niall, 2007a); and 'Sharapova

and the critics dealt a blow by Williams' sledgehammer' (in which Serena was said to resemble a 'wrecking ball' and to have an 'Exocet return'—Niall, 2007b). Hinds (2007b) reported her success via a mock attack on the behaviour of the highly respectable and respected men's champion, Roger Federer, with the sarcastic conclusion: 'See, Serena, you were right. We can hate anyone. It's just that you make it so much easier.' Serena's post-match response to the barrage of criticism was as powerful and as eloquent as her tennis:

> I have a large arse and it always just looks like I'm bigger than the rest of the girls, but I have been the same weight for I don't know how long. If I lost 20 pounds, I'm still going to have these knockers, forgive me, and I'm still going to have this arse.

While the narratives of 'pornographic eroticism' were used to portray Griffith-Joyner nearly 20 years earlier, a journalist described a match by Serena at Wimbledon in 2007 in terms that had hardened into those of 'sexual grotesquerie':

> Cartoonists would have been hard pressed to create Serena. First there was the body—all bosom, bottom and muscle. In her skintight faux leather bodysuit she gave Lara Croft a run for her money. (The great kinkster cartoonist Robert Crumb told me that she was his ideal woman; his idea of heaven was to be given a piggyback by Serena.) (Hattenstone, 2007)

At the 2008 Australian Open, the fixation turned to Venus with one newspaper article using the title, 'Venus Williams with a superior posterior' (Johnson, 2008). Jessica Halloran (2000), in a story entitled 'Venus win helps keep focus on bottom line,' reported that television commentator Roger Rasheed practically started salivating when admiring Venus's rear end during her first-round win. Venus then fielded questions about Rasheed's comment with grace and humor in the post-game interview.

Conclusion

Our study shows that despite their outstanding sporting achievements, the Williams sisters have been subjected to the 'gender-specific images that deem black bodies as less desirable if not downright ugly' (Collins, 2004, p. 284); that is, their bodies have been positioned by the 'sexually grotesque.' The complex and ambivalent ways in which the Williams sisters have been constructed—exotic/erotic yet deviant and repulsive, athletic yet animalistic and primitive, unfeminine yet hyperfeminine, muscular yet threateningly hyper-muscular—is a reinscription of the 'Hottentot Venus' genealogy. . . .

However, the very contradictions of their lived experiences as sportswomen provide some African-American sportswomen with the discursive tools to re-imagine and re-work their experiences in new ways, as the Williams sisters' responses to the media demonstrate. Paying attention to the multifaceted discourses and symbolic expressions through which African American people construct new forms of social identities has contributed to sociological understandings of marginalized people's responses to racism. Listening to the positive responses of African American women to negative readings of their corporeality could enable the sports industry to cultivate what Hobson (2003, p. 98) calls a black feminist aesthetic that recognizes the black female body as 'beautiful and desirable' in its distinction from stereotypes of white beauty.[1]

Of greater significance, however, is the need for 'white' people to deconstruct their privileged perspectives and the powerful lenses through which they construct and view 'black' people, to develop a new critical race consciousness that can inform sporting commentary and media narratives. Since sport both reinforces and reproduces the 'persistent,' 'resurgent,' and 'veiled' forms of white power that permeate society (King, Leonard & Kusz, 2007, p. 4), a systematic targeting and 'outing' of racist and sexist narratives in sport has the potential to enable African American women and men to envision and achieve equality within a broader framework of social justice.[2]

Notes

1. Creef (1993) and Fabos (2001) have shown how Asian and Asian-American women figure skaters have also been inscribed by racist and sexist narratives.

2. For alternatives to the prevailing able-bodied, racist, sexist, and commodified representations of sportswomen, see the book, exhibition, and educational outreach programs based on Jane Gottesman's collection of photographs, which emphasize diversity and inclusion (Gottesman, 2003; *Game Face: What Does a Female Athlete Look Like?*).

References

Adams, T. (2005, January 9). Selling the sisters. *The Observer.* Retrieved July 1, 2005 from http://observer.guardian.co.uk/osm/story/0,,1 383632.00.html

Barnes, S. (2007, July 5). Dying swan devoured as giant bird of prey returns to SW19. *Timesonline.* Retrieved July 5, 2007 from http://www.timesonline.co.uk/tol/sport/columnists/simon_barnes/article2028764.ece

Bennett, M., & Dickerson, V. (2001). Introduction. In M. Bennett & V. Dickerson (Eds.), *Recovering the black female body: Self-representations by African American women* (pp. 1–12). New Brunswick, NJ: Rutgers University Press.

Bierley, S. (2004, January 14). Sisters sledgehammer lured towards siren song of celebrity. *The Guardian.* Retrieved June 1, 2007 from http://sport.guardian.co.uk/columnists/story/ 0,,1122498,00.html

Bierley, S. (2007, January 26). Fighting Williams sets up Sharapova showdown. *The Guardian.* Retrieved January- 28. 2007 from http:// sport.guardian.co.Uk/australianopen2007/st ory/0,, 1998879, 00.html

Buckley, W. (2007, September 16). Ali? Laver? Best? No, the Williams sisters. *The Observer,* p. 15.

Collins, P. H. (2004). *Black sexual politics: African Americans, gender, and the new racism.* New York: Routledge.

Crawford, C. (2006a, January 15). Easybeat? Fat chance. *The Sun-Herald,* p. 34.

Crawford, C. (2006b, January 15). Serena shocked by pictures. *The Sunday Mail,* p. 23.

Creef, E. T. (1993). Model minorities and monstrous selves: The winter Olympic showdown of Kristi Yamaguchi and Midori Ito; or: 'How to tell your friends apart from the Japs.' *Visual Anthropology Review, 9*(1), 141–146.

Douglas, D. D. (2002). To be young, gifted, black and female: A meditation on the cultural politics at play in representations of Venus and Serena Williams. *Sociology of Sport Online, 5*(2). Retrieved July I, 2006 from http:// physed.otago.ac.nz/sosol/v5i2/v5i2_3.html

Douglas, D. D. (2005). Venus, Serena, and the Women's Tennis Association (WTA): When and where 'race' enters. *Sociology of Sport Journal, 22*(3), 256–282.

Epstein, J. (2006, January 15). Serena out to kick butt. *MensTennisForums.com.* Retrieved January 16, 2006 from http://www.menstenn isforums.com/archive/index.php/t-63698.html

Fabos, B. (2001). Forcing the fairy tale: Narrative strategies in figure skating competition coverage. *Sport in Society,* 4 (2), 185–212.

Game Face: What does a female athlete look like? Retrieved January 28, 2007 from http:// www.gamefaceonline.org/4_5_press.html

Gibbs, S. (2006, January 21). Big bum rap for Serena. *The Age,* p. 63.

Gilman, S. (1985). *Difference and pathology.* Ithaca, NY: Cornell University Press.

Glenny, G. H. (2006). Visual culture and the world of sport. *The Scholar & Feminist Online.* Retrieved January 30, 2007 from http://

www.barnard.edu/sfonline/sport/glenny_ 01.htm

Gottesman, J. (2003). *Game face: What does a female athlete look like?* New York, NY: Random House.

Hadfield, W. (1988, September 30). Fast as a cheetah but Flo-Jo no cheater. *The Australian,* p. 33.

Hadley Freydberg, E. (1995). Sapphires, spitfires, sluts, and superbitches: Aframericans and Latinas in contemporary American film. In K. M. Vaz (Ed.), *Black women in America* (pp. 222–243). Thousand Oaks, CA: Sage.

Halloran, J. (2008, January 18). Venus win helps keep focus on bottom line. *The Sydney Morning Herald.* Retrieved January 18, 2008 from http://www.smh.com.au/news/ tennis/venus-win-helps-keep-focus-on-bottom-line/2008/01/17/1200419971695.html

Hargreaves, J. (2000). *Heroines of sport: The politics of difference and identity.* London: Routledge.

Hargreaves, J. (2007). Sport, exercise, and the female Muslim body: Negotiating Islam, politics, and male power. In J. Hargreaves & P. Vertinsky (Eds.), *Physical culture, power and the body* (pp. 74–100). London: Routledge.

Harris, J., & Clayton, B. (2002). Femininity, masculinity, physicality and the English tabloid press: The case of Anna Kournikova. *International Review for the Sociology of Sport, 37*(3/4), 397–413.

Hattenstone, S. (2007, January 31). Serena's triumph over tragedy a weepy classic. *The Guardian.* Retrieved January 31, 2007 from http://sport.guardian.co.uk/columnists/ story/0,,2002277,00.html

Heywood, L. (1998). Athletic vs pornographic eroticism: How muscle magazines compromise female athletes and delegitimize the sport of bodybuilding in the public eye. *Mesomorphosis Interactive, 1*(1). Retrieved July 1, 2007 from http://www.mesomorphosis .com/exclusive/heywood/eroticism01.htm

Heywood, L., & Dworkin, S. L. (2003). *Built to win: The female athlete as cultural icon.* Minneapolis, MN: University of Minnesota Press.

Hinds, R. (2006, January 30). Crocks, shocks and 'nots' did the Open proud. *The Sydney Morning Herald,* p. 54.

Hinds, R. (2007a, January 26). Surrounded by 'haters,' rampaging American plays angry. *The Age*, p. 62.

Hinds, R. (2007b, January 28). I hate to admit it, Serena, but we can even dislike Federer. *The Sun-Herald*, p. 59.

Hobson, J. (2003). The 'batty' politic: Toward an aesthetic of the black female body. *Hypatia, 18*(4), 87–105.

Johnson, M. (2008, January 18). Venus Williams with a superior posterior. *The Telegraph*. Retrieved January 18, 2008, from http://www.telegraph.co.uk/sport/main.jhtml?xml=/sport/2008/01/18/stjohn118.xml

Kennedy, E. (2001). She wants to be a sledgehammer: Tennis femininities in British television. *Journal of Sport & Social Issues, 25*(1), 56–72.

King, C. R., Leonard, D. J., & Kusz, K. W. (2007). White power and sport: An introduction. *Journal of Sport & Social Issues, 31*, 3–10.

Messner, M. A., Dunbar, M., & Hunt, D. (2002). The televised sports manhood formula. *Journal of Sport & Social Issues, 24*, 380–394.

Messner, M. A., Duncan, C. M., & Cooky, C. (2003). Silence, sports bras, and wrestling porn: Women in televised sports news and highlights shows. *Journal of Sport & Social Issues, 27*, 38–51.

Miller, D. (2000, July 10). Victor deserves role model status. *The Sunday Telegraph*. Retrieved June 15, 2005 from www.telegraph.co.uk:80/et?ac=003087666203340&rtmo=aq4CWX4J&atmo=99999999&pg -/et/00/7/9/strole09.html

Miller, T., McKay, J., & Martin, R. (1999). Courting lesbianism. *Women and Performance: A Journal of Feminist Theory, 11*(1), 211–234.

Moore, G. (2007, June 29). Williams' fashion statement the hot topic. *The Independent*. Retrieved June 29, 2007 from http://sport.independent.co.uk/tennis/article2720027.ecc

Moore, K. (1988, July 25). Get up and go. *Sports Illustrated*. Retrieved June 12, 2005 from sportsillustrated.cnn.com/olympics/features/joyner/flashback2.html

Morgan, J. L. (1997). 'Some could suckle over their shoulder': Male travelers, female bodies, and the gendering of racial ideology, 1500–1770. *William and Mary Quarterly, 54*, 167–92.

Morton, P. (1991). Introduction. *Disfigured images: The historical assault on Afro-American women*. Westport, CT: Greenwood Press.

Mott, S. (2000, December 14). Wimbledon: Triumph of American values. *The Daily Telegraph*. Retrieved June 30, 2006 from http://www.telegraph.co.uk/sport/main.jhtml;jsessionid=TP5GNFRXV0LFLQ-FIQMFSFFWAVCB00IV()?xml=/sport/tennis/stmott08.xml

Mott, S. (2007, July 9). Star quality is no match for Venus. *The Daily Telegraph*. Retrieved July 9, 2007 from http://www.telegraph.co.uk/sport/main.jhtml?xml=/sport/2007/07/09/stmott109.xml

Muscat, J. (2007, June 28). Molik stirs the lighting character in Williams. *Timesonline*. Retrieved June 29, 2007 from http://www.timesonline.co.uk/tol/sport/tennis/article1996666.ece

Niall, J. (2007a, January 28). Cyclone Serena slams Maria and her knockers. *The Sydney Morning Herald*, p. 54.

Niall, J. (2007b, January 28). Sharapova and the critics dealt a blow by Williams' sledgehammer. *The Age*, p. 54.

Patton, C. (2001). 'Rock hard': Judging the female physique. *Journal of Sport & Social Issues, 25*(2), 118–140.

Pearce, L. (2007, January 24). Serena ignores the knockers. *The Sydney Morning Herald*. Retrieved January 25, 2007 from http://www.smh.com.au/ncws/tennis/serena-ignores-the-knockers/2007/01/23/1169518709298.html

Peterson, C. (2001). Foreword: Eccentric bodies. In M. Bennett & V. Dickerson (Eds.), *Recovering the black female body: Self-representations by African American women* (pp. ix–xvi). New Brunswick, NJ: Rutgers University Press.

Philip, R. (2007, July 3). Street style gives Venus her deadly cutting edge. *The Daily Telegraph*. Retrieved July 3, 2007 from http://vvww.telegraph.co.uk/sport/main.jht ml?xml=/sport/2007/07/03/Stphil 103.xml

PostWatch. (2002). *Defending the trashy.* Retrieved July 1, 2006 from http://post watch.blogspot.com/2002_08_25_post watch_archive.html

Ramsay, A. (2006, January 22). Aussie defeat is the bottom line for overweight Serena. *News.scotsman.com.* Retrieved August 14, 2006 from http://sport.scotsman.com/tennis .cfm?id=105902006

Rowe, K. (1990). Roseanne: Unruly woman as domestic goddess. *Screen, 31*(4), 408–419.

Schultz, L. (2002). Reading the catsuit: Serena Williams and the production of blackness at the 2002 US Open. *Journal of Sport & Social Issues, 29*(3), 338–357.

Schulze, L. (1990). On the muscle. In J. Gaines & C. Herzog (Eds.), *Fabrications: Costume and the female body* (pp. 59–78). London: Routledge.

Scott, B. (2007, January 28). Champ focused on retail therapy after responding to critics. *The Sun-Herald,* p. 57.

Sharpley-Whiting, T. D. (1999). *Black Venus: Sexualized savages, primal fears, and primitive narratives in French.* Durham, NC: Duke University Press.

Smith, G. (2007, June 29). Williams has designs on title despite host of outside distractions. *The Times,* p. 104.

Spencer, N. E. (2001). From 'child's play' to 'party crasher': Venus Williams, racism and professional Women's tennis. In

D. L. Andrews & S. J. Jackson (Eds.), *Sport stars: The cultural politics of sporting celebrity* (pp. 87–101). London: Routledge.

Spencer, N. E. (2004). Sister Act VI: Venus and Serena Williams at Indian Wells: 'Sincere fictions' and white racism. *Journal of Sport & Social Issues, 28*(2), 115–135.

Stevens, M. (2006, January 12). Size up Serena Williams at your own risk. *The Sun-Herald,* p. 57.

Stevenson, D. (2002). Women, sport and globalization: Competing discourses of sexuality and nation. *Journal of Sport & Social Issues, 26,* 209–225.

Syed, M. (2008, January 24). They play great. They look great. So what, exactly, is the problem? *The Times.* Retrieved January 24, 2008 from http://www.timesonline.co.uk/ tol/sport/tennis/article3241414.ece

Vertinsky, P., & Captain, G. (1998). More myth than history: American culture and representations of the black female's athletic ability. *Journal of Sport History, 25,* 532–561.

Viner, B. (2007, June 15). There is way too much emphasis on how we look. Focus on my game. *The Independent.* Retrieved June 15, 2007 from http://sport.independent.co.uk/ tennis/article2659628.ece

White, C. (2007, January 28). Williams silences critics. *The Telegraph.* Retrieved January 28, 2007 from http://www.telegraph.co.uk/ sport/main.jhtml?xml=/sport/2007/OI/28/ stlina28.xml

What Does Race Have to Do With *Ugly Betty*?

An Analysis of Privilege and Postracial(?) Representations on a Television Sitcom

Jennifer Esposito

The term "postracial" has been utilized in increasing amounts in the media to denote some people's perceptions that the election of Barack Obama marks a new era in our society—one in which race no longer matters. This notion, while perhaps well-meaning, contradicts the very ways our society is structured. Race is an organizing principle (Henry 1995) in institutions such as government, schools, and popular culture. We cannot think or even act without racial categories becoming prominent. . . .

One place where racial discourse is especially powerful is within the institution of popular culture. We must continually critique and examine representations of racialized bodies, especially those bodies already marginalized within the system of racial hierarchies. In the spirit of continuing the examination of racial discourse, this chapter examines ABC's television comedy *Ugly Betty*, in particular one episode that explores race-based affirmative action decisions and quotas ("When Betty Met YETI"). This episode of *Ugly Betty* aired two weeks after the 2008 election of Barack Obama. . . .

Ugly Betty, Privilege, and Affirmative Action

Betty Suarez, the fashion-challenged heroine of ABC's sitcom *Ugly Betty*, works as an assistant to the editor of *Mode*, a high-fashion magazine. Part of her job entails meeting the multiple personal and professional needs of her boss, Daniel Meade, an irresponsible sex addict.

From Esposito, J. (2009). What does race have to do with *Ugly Betty*? An analysis of privilege and postracial(?) representations on a television sitcom. *Television and New Media*, 10(6), 521–535.

Betty was hired by Daniel's father, Mr. Meade, precisely because Mr. Meade realized Daniel would not be attracted to a brown-skinned girl wearing braces and glasses. *Mode Magazine* is the context in which the series comedically explores issues of race, class, gender, and sexuality. The show offers lessons about making it in a competitive environment where beauty is everything and it is no secret that "beauty" is defined as "white, thin, upper-class, straight femininity"—a narrow conception of beauty. Those characters, including Betty, who fall outside of the definition of beauty learn to utilize other means to negotiate the environment. While the show does try to satirize stereotypes of race, gender, class, and sexuality, it nonetheless contributes to the reinscription of some stereotypes. Of course, as Stephen Neale and Frank Krutnik (1990, 93) suggest, "It is hardly surprising that comedy often perpetuates prejudice, or draws uncritically on racist and sexist stereotypes, since they provide a ready-made set of images of deviation from social and cultural norms." In addition, utilizing comedy to explore complex issues allows for the topics to be taken less seriously.

The regular characters of the show include Betty Suarez (played by America Ferrera), a twenty-two-year-old Mexican girl who works as an assistant to the editor, Daniel Meade (Eric Mabius). Other assistants include Marc (Michael Urie), who is white, gay, and knowledgeable about high fashion; and Amanda (Becki Newton), who is a blonde-haired, white, very thin woman who has sex with Daniel. . . .

Betty and Marc are both assistants: Betty works directly for Daniel while Marc works directly for Wilhelmina. Both their jobs include completing rather personal tasks for their bosses that would not seem part of their job descriptions. For example, Betty had to track down a watch Daniel left at a woman's house. He, however, could not remember which woman he slept with the night he left the watch. Betty had to send flowers and then make personal visits to seven women's apartments to retrieve the watch. Marc, on the other hand, must flatter Wilhelmina on her beauty, brains, and accomplishments. He also injects her with botox, a chemical to help her retain a "youthful" appearance. Both Betty and Marc understand how they are used and not appreciated and, thus, have dreams of being much more than mere assistants and strive to be editors.

In the third season, Betty and Marc both apply to YETI (Young Editors Training Institute). The program is highly competitive and accepts one assistant per magazine for training and apprenticeship as editor. As part of the interview, each applicant must create and market a magazine. Applicants must also be sponsored by an "insider" to the business. Marc worked on his magazine presentation for three months and created a complete magazine. He also chose celebrity sponsors who happened to know one of the judges. Betty only found out about the program forty-eight hours before the interview, so she rushed to put a magazine presentation together. She also asked Daniel to sponsor her, and although he said yes, he never finished her letter of recommendation.

As viewers, we see Betty's interview. She is her usual self—not very confident but charming nonetheless. In fact, one of the judges, a caramel-complexioned woman (her race is not evident but she appears white or Latina, based on hair and skin color), tries to give Betty personal encouragement by smiling and nodding during her presentation. Betty's idea, a magazine about women who are intelligent, beautiful, and independent, seemed to be liked by the judges. We are not, as viewers, privy to Marc's presentation. We do know that Marc shows up with a "team" and his sponsors, and we are led to believe he also completed a very good interview. It is Betty, however, who is accepted into the program. Marc is denied entry because he and Betty both work at the same magazine and YETI only accepts one intern per magazine.

Betty walks over to apologize to Marc when she finds out she was accepted and he was not. Marc, acting bitter about his loss, tells Betty his presentation was one thousand times better than hers. Betty says to him, "Maybe they just liked my concept better . . . who knows why they picked me?" Marc laughs and says, "Yeah, OK. Whatever." Betty suggests that perhaps she "wanted it" more than he did and, therefore, she was offered the internship. It is in this way Betty relies on the ideology of meritocracy as she believes that she wanted it more and, therefore, worked harder for it. She understands that she and Marc were evaluated as individuals and her presentation obviously conveyed more passion than Marc's. Marc does not believe this and implies (via tone of voice and a knowing look) that he knows the "real" reasons she was picked and he was not. Betty asks him why he thinks they picked her over him. Marc refuses to tell her, so Betty continues to ask him. Finally he says, "Do you really think that what you did in two days is better than what I spent three months working on? Are you really gonna make me say it?" Betty incredulously asks, "Say what?" Marc fires at her, "You help them meet their quota." Betty looks shocked and says, "What are you talking about?" Marc yells, "I mean they picked you, Betty Suarez of Queens, because you are Latina." Betty pulls back, shaking her head no. Marc continues, "Because you are a token ethnic girl." Betty gets upset and says "What? They picked me . . . that doesn't even make sense. Wow, Marc you have said a lot of ugly things to me in the past but that is by far and away the ugliest." Marc refuses to back down from his position and says, "Well, I'm sorry Betty. It may be ugly, but it's the truth." At this moment, we have no idea how Marc has even acquired this knowledge or if it is just his assumption. But the anger the issue raises between them is palpable.

Marc does not utilize the term "affirmative action." Instead, he refers to quotas, a word indelibly linked in popular discourse with race-based affirmative action policies. Affirmative action became policy in the 1960s under President Johnson. The policy was initially launched to help improve the employment and educational access of "minorities," including people of color, and white women. Affirmative action now has a long history of contestation by whites and has been charged with creating "reverse discrimination." At issue is the notion of whiteness as property and the questions surrounding who owns it, who has access to it, and who fights to protect it. Claims about reverse discrimination belie the very ways white privilege has been made invisible. Affirmative action is perceived as a threat to whiteness as property because it enables people of color access to education and employment previously reserved as the "property" of whites (Harris 1993). Although much of Marc's disdain for a race-based affirmative action policy is communicated through his facial expressions, he is portrayed as angry and ready to claim the status of "victim."

In the next scene, Betty's family comes in to the office to celebrate her acceptance into YETI. They speak and sing, partially in Spanish and partially in English, while making lots of celebratory noise. Betty's Mexicanness becomes hypervisible at this moment. Although she is regularly positioned as Other because of her looks and her status as a working-class Latina from Queens, she has never before apologized for her identity and, in fact, seems oblivious that her status within race, class, and beauty hierarchies could even affect her. Betty, up until this point, has been the poster child for the belief in meritocracy: that as long she works hard enough, she will achieve. The text generally seems to support this notion as well. Although Betty faces obstacles related to her looks, class, and race, she always manages to overcome. As the loveable heroine, Betty always finds a way to get the job done without ever claiming she was discriminated against or without any recognition that hierarchies exist in the fashion and business worlds.

In this episode, however, Betty seems embarrassed, as white coworkers look at her and her family in disgust. Betty seems to recognize the ways her family has been positioned due to racialized hierarchies.

The usually quiet office had been interrupted with difference (loud colors and Spanish words/songs). Betty pulls her father and sister into a separate room and explains what happened. She says she was nothing more than a quota to YETI. She says, "Well, I called and they didn't exactly deny it." Her sister says, "Who cares *why* you got in? You got in. Look, you got to take every advantage you can in this life." Hilda shares with Betty that when she goes to the butcher shop, "I put on my tightest tank top and say thank you to the pointer sisters" (she points to her breasts); she says that is what gets her to the front of the line and she does not care if it is unfair to other people.

Ignacio, Betty's father, also helps lift her spirits. He starts to remind her of the struggles he and her mother faced as immigrants to the country. Hilda complains while rolling her eyes, "Oh, here goes the young immigrant story." Although Betty seems equally annoyed about the story, she bows her head and sits. Her father tells her, "If being Mexican helped this time, take it." Betty replies, "No, Papi. I wanted to be accepted because I earned it." He touches her head and says, "You did."

The scene ends with that tender moment, but we are left wondering what Ignacio meant. In what ways did Ignacio believe Betty earned it? As viewers we are left to weigh the evidence. Marc had spent three months on his magazine to Betty's one night. Marc had two important sponsors and a slight advantage with nepotism (although not directly related to each other, Marc and his sponsors share the same race and sexual orientation). Betty's sponsor did not even submit a letter of reference for her. Marc had worked as an assistant for four years to Betty's two years. Marc had a team who helped him prepare while Betty only had herself. Did Ignacio really believe that Betty earned the acceptance into the program of her own accord?

In this episode, as in many affirmative action debates, a race-based affirmative action decision is portrayed as being made without regard to qualifications and talent. . . . A binary has clearly been created between talent and race. Perhaps Betty's talent was similar to Marc's, but we do not know this. We only know that Marc assumes Betty was given the opportunity because she satisfied a quota, and that when Betty called YETI to ask if this was true, "They didn't exactly deny it." How do we, as viewers, make sense of this?

In the next relevant scene, Betty walks up to Marc, hands him an envelope, and says, "You're in. You were right. Your presentation was better than mine. I dropped out and you're in." Marc responds in disbelief, "Are you crazy? I have been discriminated against my whole life. If I was given an advantage like you I would take it and run with it." Betty does not buy Marc's claims of oppression, and she replies, "Marc, you are a gay man in the fashion industry. You have plenty of advantages." Marc says to her, "That gets me nothing." Of course, in the guise of comedy, it is then that a stereotypical gay man comes up to Marc and hands him backstage Madonna tickets. Recognizing the irony of this, Marc tilts his head and clarifies that it is *outside of the fashion world* he gets nothing. Betty tells him, "Marc, at the end of the day you deserved it more." Marc pauses, and Betty tells him to take it before she changes her mind. He takes it.

This exchange does not force Marc to examine his white privilege. Marc, as a white gay man working in the fashion world, is relationally privileged and oppressed. Gay men are relatively prominent in the fashion world (see Lewis [2007] for a recent critique of *Queer Eye for the Straight Guy*, a television show where five gay men are positioned as fashion and lifestyle experts). Betty tries to make Marc's gay privilege within the realm of *Mode* visible, but he gets defensive and will not truly recognize it. Claiming a victim stance, Marc shrugs off the example of the concert ticket as an individual privilege. Betty sees the irony of this, but Marc silences the rest of the conversation by claiming that he is oppressed as a gay man outside of the fashion world. . . .

As in all lighthearted comedies, by the end of the episode, all is well. Daniel makes a call and tells YETI that Betty also worked at *Players Magazine* that year. She and Marc, therefore, could be listed as assistants at separate magazines. Daniel also provides Betty a copy of the recommendation letter he sent to YETI. It is a six-page document, and we are led to believe that Daniel, although he often falls through on promises to Betty, genuinely cares for her despite his many faults. This move on his part—making one phone call to solve Betty's current problem—constructs him as the "great white hope" (see Giroux [1993] for a discussion of the role of whites as saviors in the lives of young adults of color). He becomes Betty's savior by swooping down at the last minute and exercising his power and privilege.

While Betty certainly gains from this move, the real issues of race-based affirmative action and quotas are never fully explored. Marc's resentment is still there. Betty's doubts about her abilities in relation to Marc's still remain. And viewers are left with reified notions of difference. . . .

Betty's refusal to accept the internship (once she realized being Mexican assisted her) reifies the notion that one must succeed on her or his own without anyone's assistance. What is ironic about the episode is that, while Betty believed morally and ethically that she wanted to be accepted into the program on her own merits, Marc's standpoint was different, although it was not articulated as such. Marc brought a "team" with him, including his two famous sponsors (thereby promoting nepotism) and friends/coworkers who helped him with his presentation. While Betty sat at her kitchen table alone and constructed her presentation, it is presumed Marc had his team help him construct his.

Yet Marc feels powerless against race-based affirmative action policies. He believes he was the better candidate and that

Betty, the "Latina from Queens," did not fully earn her acceptance into the internship. As Applebaum (2005) articulates,

> The ability to deny the presence and power of current everyday racism and the undeserved benefits that some groups accrue at the expense of others, is premised on the ability to see oneself "as an individual" and not to see oneself "as white." To see oneself "as white" and to interrogate what that means would undermine the appeal of the innocent victim upon which arguments about reverse discrimination are based. (p. 286)

Based on this reading of *Ugly Betty* as a text about race, one can surmise that we, as a nation, are not postracial. On the contrary, race still structures our lives. . . . In lieu of ignoring race, we need, instead, to start examining the ways race, history, popular culture and the political economy continue to work in tangent to sustain racialized hierarchies.

References

Applebaum, B. 2005. In the name of morality: Moral responsibility, whiteness and social justice education. *Journal of Moral Education* 34 (3): 277–90.

Giroux, H. A. 1993. *Living dangerously: Multiculturalism and the politics of difference.* New York: Peter Lang.

Harris, C. I. 1993. Whiteness as property. *Harvard Law Review* 106: 1707–91.

Henry, A. 1995. Growing up black, female, and working class: A teacher's narrative. *Anthropology & Education Quarterly* 26 (3): 279–305.

Lewis, T. 2007. "He needs to face his fears with these five queers!" *Queer Eye for the Straight Guy*, makeover TV, and the lifestyle expert. *Television and New Media* 8 (4): 285–311.

Neale, S., and F. Krutnik. 1990. *Popular film and television comedy.* New York: Routledge.

Ralph, Fred, Archie, Homer, and the King of Queens

Why Television Keeps Re-Creating the Male Working-Class Buffoon

Richard Butsch

Strewn across our mass media are portrayals that justify class relations of modern capitalism. Studies of comic strips, radio serials, television series, movies, and popular fiction reveal a very persistent pattern, underrepresenting working-class occupations and overrepresenting professional and managerial occupations, minimizing the visibility of the working class. Similar patterns are evident for other subordinate statuses on race, gender, and regional lines.

My own studies of class in prime-time network television family series from 1946 to 2004 (Butsch, 1992, 2005; Butsch & Glennon, 1983; Glennon & Butsch, 1982) indicate that this pattern persists over six decades of television and roughly 400 domestic situation comedies, including such icons as *I Love Lucy, The Brady Bunch, All in the Family,* and *The Simpsons.* In only about 10% of the series were heads of house portrayed as working class (i.e., holding occupations as blue-collar, clerical, or unskilled or semi-skilled service workers). Widespread affluence was exaggerated as well. More lucrative, glamorous, or prestigious professions predominated over more mundane ones. Working wives were almost exclusively middle class and pursuing a career. Working-class wives, like *Roseanne,* who have to work to help support the family, were rare.

Throughout these decades, the few working-class men were portrayed as buffoons. They were dumb, immature, irresponsible, and lacking in common sense. This is the character of the husbands in almost every sitcom depicting a blue-collar head of house, *The Honeymooners, The Flintstones, All in the Family, The Simpsons,* and *The King of Queens* being the most famous examples. The man was typically well intentioned, even lovable, but no one to respect or emulate. These men were played against more sensible wives, such as Alice in *The Honeymooners* or Carrie in *King of Queens.*

For most of this history, there were few buffoons in middle-class series. More typically, both parents were wise and worked cooperatively to raise their children in practically perfect families like those in *Father Knows Best, The Brady Bunch,* and *The Bill Cosby Show.* The humor came from the innocent foibles and fumbles of the children. The few middle-class buffoons were usually the dizzy wife, like Lucy, while the professional/managerial husband was the sensible, mature partner. Inverting gender status in working-class but not middle-class sitcoms makes this a statement about class more than gender.

The 1990s brought a shift in parts of this pattern. There was a significant increase in the number and percentage of working-class families represented in domestic sitcoms: Of 42 new domestic sitcoms from 1991 to 1999, 16 featured working-class families, and 9 were Black. Reverting to form, in the 2000s, only 3 more new working-class and 4 African American sitcoms were added. By 2008, working-class sitcoms again disappeared ("TV's Class Struggle," 2008). The depictions of middle-class males became more diverse in these two decades, with males in shows such as *Home Improvement* and *Two and a Half Men,* who succeeded at work but at home exhibited an insistent adolescent macho maleness—not buffoons, but not super-parents either.

Still, the portrayals of working-class men remained relatively unchanged. The successful *King of the Hill* (1997), *King of Queens* (1998), and *Family Guy* (1999), as well as several shorter lived series throughout the decade, reproduced the traditional stereotyped working-class man cast opposite capable women. *Plus ça change, plus c'est la même chose.*

Why does television keep re-producing these caricatures across six decades, despite major changes in the television industry? How does it happen? Seldom have studies of television industries pinpointed how specific content arises. Studies of production have not been linked to studies of content any more than audience studies have. What follows is an effort to explain the link between sitcom production and the persistent images produced. In the words of

Connell (1977), "No evil-minded capitalistic plotters need be assumed because the production of ideology is seen as the more or less automatic outcome of the normal, regular processes by which commercial mass communications work in a capitalist system" (p. 195). It is the outcome of a complex of structural and cultural factors that shaped and continues to shape the representation of working-class men, even as the television industry underwent remarkable changes from the 1980s on.

I will describe the factors as they worked from the beginnings of TV sitcoms in the late 1940s into the 1980s, then examine what effects on representation were wrought by the growth of cable TV and VCR in the 1980s, computers and the Internet in the 1990s, and the concomitant restructuring of the industry into a new oligopoly of global multimedia corporations. I will look at three levels of organization: (1) network domination of the industry, (2) the organization of decisions within the networks and on the production line, and (3) the work community and culture of the "creative personnel." I will trace how these may explain the consistency and persistence of the portrayals, the underrepresentation of the working class, and the specific negative stereotypes of working-class men in prime-time domestic sitcoms.

Network Domination and Persistent Images

For four decades, ABC, CBS, and NBC dominated the television industry. Ninety percent of television audiences watched these networks. They accounted for more than half of all television advertising revenues in the 1960s and 1970s, and just under half by the late 1980s (Owen & Wildman, 1992). They therefore had the money and the audience to dominate the market as the only buyers of series programming from Hollywood producers and studies. The television series market was thus an oligopsony—the buyer equivalent to an oligopoly—with only three buyers of sitcoms and several sellers (Federal Communications Commission [FCC], 1980; Owen & Wildman, 1992).

Through the 1980s, cable networks and multistation owners (companies that own several local broadcast stations) began to challenge the dominance of the big three. The big networks' combined rating shrank from 56.5% in 1980 to 39.7% in 1990—the latter number even including the new Fox Broadcasting network that debuted in 1986 (Butsch, 2000, p. 269; Hindman & Wiegand, 2008). By 1999, the four-network rating had slipped to 28.6% ("Upscale Auds Ease B'casters," 1999), while advertising-supported cable had grown to 23.9% ("Young Auds Seek Web, Not Webs," 1999). Still, only five cable networks had sufficient funds in the 1990s to qualify as buyers of drama programming (Blumler & Spicer, 1990). In 2000, cable networks were beginning to become a factor in the market for new drama and comedy series ("B'cast, Cable: Trading Places," 2000), yet ABC, CBS, and NBC still accounted for the development of the overwhelming majority of new series. However, by 2008, cable networks had become major buyers of new scripted series ("TV Role Reversal," 2009).

Dominance by the broadcast networks may have slipped, but many of the same factors that shaped their programming decisions shape the decisions of their cable competitors as well. The increased number of buyers has not resulted in the innovation and diversity in program development once expected (FCC, 1980). Jay Blumler and Carolyn Spicer (1990) and Robert Kubey (2004) interviewed writers, directors, and producers and found that the promise of more openness to innovation and creativity was short-lived. The cost of drama programming limits buyers to only a handful of large corporations and dictates that programs must attract a large audience and avoid risk. Moreover, even when cable networks

became viable buyers, they did not increase significantly the number of buyers because they seek niche markets, and a given new series idea can be sold only to a cable network seeking that niche. In other words, sitcoms tend to be custom-made for a particular network.

Using their market power, networks have maintained sweeping control over production decisions of even highly successful producers, from the initial idea for a new program to a final film or tape (Bryant, 1969, pp. 624–626; Gitlin, 1983; Pekurny, 1977, p. 1982; Winick, 1961). In the 1990s, the FCC freed the broadcast networks from rules established in 1970 to reduce their power. This allowed them to increase ownership of programs and in-house production and re-create the vertical integration of television production of the 1950s and 1960s ("TV's Little Guys Stayin' Alive," 2001).

Both broadcast and cable networks' first concern affecting program decisions is risk avoidance. Popular culture success is notoriously unpredictable. The music recording industry spreads risk over many albums so that any single decision is less significant (Peterson & Berger, 1971; Rossman, 2005). Spreading risk is not a strategy available to networks (neither broadcast nor cable) since only a few programming decisions fill the prime-time hours that account for most income. Networks are constrained further from expanding the number of their decisions by their use of the series as the basic unit of programming. The benefit of the series format is that it increases ratings predictability from week to week, but it reduces the number of prime-time programming decisions to less than 50 for the whole season. So each decision represents a considerable financial risk, not simply in production costs but in advertising income as well. Success may produce a windfall. For example, ABC multiplied its profits fivefold from 1975 to 1978 by raising its average prime-time ratings from 16.6 to 20.7 (W. Behanna, personal communication, 1980). But mistakes can cause severe losses.

Since programming decisions were and continue to be risky and costly, and network executives' careers rest on their ability to make the right decisions, they are constrained, in their own interest, to avoid innovation and novelty. They stick to tried and true formulas, a common complaint among successful television writers and producers (Brown, 1971; Kubey, 2004; Wakshlag & Adams, 1985). They also prefer those who have a track record of success. The result is a small, closed community of proven creative personnel (roughly 500 producers, writers, and directors) closely tied to and dependent on the networks (Gitlin, 1983, pp. 115, 135; Kubey, 2004; Pekurny, 1982; Tunstall & Walker, 1981, pp. 77–79). These proven talents then self-censor their work on the basis of a product image their previous experience tells them the networks will tolerate (Cantor, 1971; Pekurny, 1982; Ravage, 1978), creating an "imaginary feedback loop" (DiMaggio & Hirsch, 1976) between producers and network executives. These same conditions characterized program development in the 1980s, 1990s, and 2000s, since the new buyers of programming, cable networks, operate under the same constraints as broadcast networks.

To avoid risk, network executives have chosen programs that repeat the same images of class, decade after decade. More diverse programming appeared only in the early days of the industry when there were no past successes to copy—broadcast television in the early 1950s and cable in the early 1980s—or when declining ratings made it clear that past successes no longer worked (Blumler & Spicer, 1990; Turow, 1982b, p. 124). Dominick (1976) found that the lower the profits of the networks, the more variation in program types could be discerned from season to season and the less network schedules resembled each other. For example, in the late 1950s, ABC introduced hour-long western series to prime time in order to become competitive with NBC and CBS (FCC, 1965). Again, in

1970, CBS purchased Norman Lear's then controversial *All in the Family*—other networks turned it down—to counteract a drift to an audience with demographics (rural and over 50) not desired by advertisers. Increased numbers of working-class and African American sitcoms occurred in the 1990s when television executives feared that the white middle class was turning to other entertainments ("Genre-ation Gap Hits Sitcoms," 1999).

Acceptance by networks of innovative programs takes much longer than conventional programs and requires backing by the most successful producers (Turow, 1982b, p. 126). For example, *Roseanne* was introduced by Carsey-Werner, producers of the top-rated *Cosby Show*, when ABC was trying to counter ratings losses (Reeves, 1990, pp. 153–154). Hugh Wilson, the creator of *WKRP* and *Frank's Place*, described CBS in 1987 as desperate about slipping ratings: "Consequently they were the best people to work for from a creative standpoint" (Campbell & Reeves, 1990, p. 8). Even as declining ratings spurred networks to try innovative programs in the 1990s, they still tended to hire proven talent within the existing production community. The new ideas that were accepted came from (or through) established figures in the industry. As cable networks began to buy series, they contributed to this pattern by supporting programming that satisfied their niche audience but would offend some portion of the broadcast networks' mass market.

Network Decision Making— Program Development

The second factor affecting network decisions on content is the need to produce programming suited to advertising. What the audience wants—or what network executives imagine they want—is secondary to ad revenue. Pay-cable networks, not bound by this constraint, have been freer to explore sexual and violent content, as in the

Sopranos, that may have scared off advertisers but attracts an audience. In matters of content, advertising-supported networks avoid content that will offend or dissatisfy advertisers (Bryant, 1969). For example, ABC contracts with producers in 1977 stipulated that

> no program or pilot shall contain . . . anything . . . which does not conform with the then current business or advertising policies of any such sponsor; or which is detrimental to the good will or the products or services of . . . any such sponsor. (FCC, 1980, Appendix C, p. A-2)

Gary Marshall, producer of several highly successful series in the 1970s, stated that ABC rejected a storyline for *Mork & Mindy,* the top-rated show for 1978, in which Mork takes TV ads literally, buys everything, and creates havoc. Despite the series' and Marshall's proven success, the network feared advertisers' reactions to such a storyline.

An advertiser's preferred program is one that allows full use of the products being advertised. The program should be a complementary context for the ad. In the 1950s, an ad agency rejecting a play about working-class life stated, "It is the general policy of advertisers to glamorize their products, the people who buy them, and the whole American social and economic scene" (Barnouw, 1970, p. 32). Advertisers in 1961 considered it "of key importance" to avoid "irritating, controversial, depressive, or 'downbeat' material" (FCC, 1965, p. 373). This requires dramas built around affluent characters for whom consuming is not problematic. Thus, affluent characters predominate and occupational groups with higher levels of consumer expenditure are overrepresented. Even in a working-class domestic sitcom, it is unusual for financial strain to be a regular theme of the show—*The Honeymooners* and *Roseanne* are two exceptions to this.

A third factor in program decisions is whether it will attract the right audience.

Network executives construct a product image of what they *imagine* the audience wants—which surprisingly often is not based on actual market research on audiences (Blumler & Spicer, 1990; Pekurny, 1982). Michael Dann, a CBS executive, was "concerned the public might not accept a program about a blue collar worker" when offered the pilot script for *Arnie* in 1969 (before *All in the Family* proved that wrong and after a decade in which the only working-class family appearing in prime time was *The Flinstones*). On the other hand, in 1979, an NBC executive expressed the concern that a couple in a pilot was too wealthy to appeal to most viewers (Turow, 1982b, p. 123). Sitcom producer Lee Rich said, "A television series, to be truly successful, has got to have people you can identify with or dream about being" (Kubey, 2004, p. 102). For the sought after middle-class audience, then, advertisers prefer affluent middle-class characters.

Aside from anecdotes such as I have mentioned, almost no research has examined program development or production decisions about class content of programs. My own research found no significant differences between characters in sitcom pilots and series from 1973 to 1982, indicating that class biases in content begin very early in the decision-making process, when the first pilot episode is being developed (Butsch, 1984). I therefore conducted a mail survey of the producers, writers, or directors of the pilots from 1973 to 1982. I specifically asked how the decisions were made about the occupation of the characters in their pilot. I was able to contact 40 persons concerning 50 pilots. I received responses from 6 persons concerning 12 pilots.

Although this represents only a small portion of the original sample, their responses are strikingly similar. Decisions on occupations of main characters were made by the creators and made early in program development, as part of the program idea. In no case did the occupation become a matter of debate or disagreement with the networks. Moreover, the choice of occupation was incidental to the situation or other aspect of the program idea; thus, it was embedded in the creators' conception of the situation. For example, according to one writer, a character was conceived of as an architect "to take advantage of the Century City" location for shooting the series; the father in another pilot was cast as owner of a bakery after the decision to do a series about an extended Italian family; in another pilot, the creator thought the actor "looked like your average businessman." The particular occupations and even the classes are not necessitated by the situations that creators offered as explanations. But they do not seem to be hiding the truth; their responses were open and unguarded. It appears they did not consciously consider whether they wished to portray this *particular* class or occupation; rather, to them, the occupations were derivative of the situation or location or actors they chose. They didn't think of characters explicitly in terms of a class but rather as a personality type that may conjure up a particular occupation. This absence of any awareness of decisions about class is confirmed by Gitlin's (1983) and Kubey's (2004) interviews with industry personnel. Thus, the process of class construction seems difficult to document given the unspoken guidelines, the indirect manner in which they suggest class, and the absence of overt decisions about class. Class or occupation is not typically an issue for discussion, as obscenity and race are. The choice of class is thus diffuse and indirect, drawn from a culture that provides no vocabulary to think explicitly and speak directly about class. To examine this further, we need to look at the organization of the production process and the culture of creative personnel.

The Hollywood Input— Television Series Production

Within the production process in Hollywood studios and associated organizations, as well as in the work culture of creative personnel, we find factors that contribute to the use of simple and repetitious stereotypes of working-class men.

An important factor in television drama production is the severe time constraints of production (Kubey, 2004; Lynch, 1973; Ravage, 1978; Reeves, 1990). The production schedule for a series requires that a finished program be delivered to the networks each week. Even if the production company had the entire year over which to complete the season's 22 to 24 episodes, an episode would have to be produced on the average every 2 weeks, including script writing, casting, staging, filming, and editing. This is achieved through an assembly line process where several episodes are in various stages of production and being worked on simultaneously by the same team of producer, writers, director, and actors.

Such a schedule puts great pressures on the production team to simplify the amount of work necessary and decisions to be made, as much as possible. The series format is advantageous for this reason: When the general storyline and main characters are set, the script can be written following a simple formula. For situation comedy, even the sets and the cast do not change from episode to episode.

The time pressures contribute in several ways to dependence on stereotypes for characterization. First, sitcoms are based on central characters rather than plot and development. These characters are coming into the living rooms of people who have to like to watch the characters and find them believable (Kubey, 2004). All this means that, to sell a new series, writers should offer stock characters (i.e., stereotypes). Writing for the same stock character, week after week, also greatly reduces the task of producing a script.

Also, time pressure encourages typecasting for the minor characters who are new in each episode. The script is sent to a "breakdown" agency, which reads the script and extracts the description of characters for that episode. These brief character descriptions, not the script, are used by the casting agency to recommend actors (Turow, 1978). Occupation and, by inference, class are an important part of these descriptions, being identified for 84% of male characters. Not surprisingly, the descriptions are highly stereotyped (Turow, 1980).

Producers, casting directors, and casting agencies freely admit the stereotyping but argue its necessity on the basis of time and dramatic constraints. Typecasting is easier and much quicker. They also argue that to diverge from widely held stereotypes would draw attention away from the action, the storyline, or other characters and destroy dramatic effect. In addition, stereotyped stock characters are familiar to audiences, requiring less dramatic explanation. Thus, unless the contradiction of the stereotype is the basic story idea—as in *Arnie,* a blue-collar worker suddenly appointed corporate executive—there is a very strong pressure to reproduce existing stereotypes.

The time pressures also make it more likely that the creators will stick to what is familiar to them as well. Two of the most frequent occupations of main characters in family series were in entertainment and writing (i.e., modeled on the creators' own lives; Butsch & Glennon, 1983). The vast majority of writers and producers come from upper-middle-class families, with little direct experience of working-class life (Cantor, 1971; Gitlin, 1983; Kubey, 2004; Stein, 1979; Thompson & Burns, 1990). Moreover, the tight schedules and deadlines of series production leave no time for becoming familiar enough with working-class lifestyle to be able to capture it realistically. Those who have done so (e.g., Jackie Gleason, Norman Lear) had childhood memories of working-class neighborhoods to draw upon.

Thus, the time pressure encourages creative personnel to rely heavily on a shared and consistent product image—including diffuse and undifferentiated images of class—embedded in what Elliott (1972) called the media culture. The small, closed community of those engaged in television production, including Hollywood creators and network executives (Blumler & Spicer, 1990; Gitlin, 1983; Stein, 1979; Tunstall & Walker, 1981; Turow, 1982a), shares a culture that includes certain conceptions of what life is like and what the audience finds interesting. The closeness of this community is both reflected in and reinforced by the hiring preference for proven talent already in the community, lack of any apprenticeship system to train new talent, and the importance of social networking or, as one director phrased it, "nepotism," in obtaining work (Kubey, 2004). According to Norman Lear, the production community draws its ideas from what filters into it from the mass media, which is then interpreted through the lens of their own class experience and culture, to guess what "the public" would like and formulate images of class they think are compatible (Gitlin, 1983, pp. 204, 225–226).

While the consistency of image, the underrepresentation of the working class, and the use of stereotypes can be explained by structural constraints, the particular stereotypes grow from a rather diffuse set of cultural images, constrained and framed by the structure of the industry.

Reaching the vast majority of the population for over a half century and seeping into everyday conversation, sitcoms have made a significant contribution to our culture's attitude toward the man who makes his living with his hands. It is an attitude based on the presumption that these sitcoms repeated again and again—that this man is dumb, immature, irresponsible, lacking common sense, often frustrated, and sometimes angry. This legitimates his low pay and close supervision at work. Furthermore, it is an attitude of disrespect for him everywhere else in the public realm. It is that disrespect that is the ultimate "hidden injury" that working-class interviewees expressed to Richard Sennett and Jonathan Cobb (1972) in the early 1970s, just about the time Archie Bunker first appeared on network television.

The continuing stereotype in sitcoms tells us *plus ça change,* the injury remains the same.

References

Barnouw, E. (1970). *The image empire: A history of broadcasting in the U.S. from 1953.* New York: Oxford University Press.

B'cast, cable: Trading places. (2000, April 24). *Variety,* p. 61.

Blumler, J., & Spicer, C. (1990). Prospects for creativity in the new television marketplace. *Journal of Communication, 40*(4), 78–101.

Brown, L. (1971). *Television: The business behind the box.* New York: Harcourt, Brace.

Bryant, A. (1969). Historical and social aspects of concentration of program control in television. *Law and Contemporary Problems, 34,* 610–635.

Butsch, R. (1984, August). *Minorities from pilot to series: Network selection of character statuses and traits.* Paper presented at the annual meeting of the Society for the Study of Social Problems, Washington, DC.

Butsch, R. (1992). Class and gender in four decades of television situation comedy. *Critical Studies in Mass Communication, 9,* 387–399.

Butsch, R. (2000). *The making of American audiences.* Cambridge, UK: Cambridge University Press.

Butsch, R. (2005). Five decades and three hundred sitcoms about class and gender. In G. Edgerton & B. Rose (Eds.), *Thinking outside the box: A contemporary television genre reader* (pp. 111–135). Lexington: University Press of Kentucky.

Butsch, R., & Glennon, L. M. (1983). Social class: Frequency trends in domestic situation comedy, 1946–1978. *Journal of Broadcasting, 27,* 77–81.

Campbell, R., & Reeves, J. (1990). Television authors: The case of Hugh Wilson. In R. Thompson & G. Burns (Eds.), *Making television: Authorship and the production process* (pp. 3–18). New York: Praeger.

Cantor, M. (1971). *The Hollywood TV producer.* New York: Basic Books.

Connell, B. (1977). *Ruling class, ruling culture.* Cambridge, UK: Cambridge University Press.

DiMaggio, P., & Hirsch, P. (1976). Production organization in the arts. *American Behavioral Scientist, 19,* 735–752.

Dominick, J. (1976, Winter). Trends in network prime time, 1953–74. *Journal of Broadcasting, 26,* 70–80.

Elliott, P. (1972). *The making of a television series: A case study in the sociology of culture.* New York: Hastings.

Federal Communications Commission, Network Inquiry Special Staff. (1980). *Preliminary reports.* Washington, DC: Government Printing Office.

Federal Communications Commission, Office of Network Study. (1965). *Second interim report: Television network program procurement* (Part II). Washington, DC: Government Printing Office.

Genre-ation gap hits sitcoms. (1999, April 26). *Variety,* p. 25.

Gitlin, T. (1983). *Inside prime time.* New York: Pantheon.

Glennon, L. M., & Butsch, R. (1982). The family as portrayed on television, 1946–78. In National Institute of Mental Health (Ed.), *Television and social behavior: Ten years of scientific progress and implications for the eighties* (Vol. 2, Technical Review, pp. 264–271). Washington, DC: Government Printing Office.

Hindman, D., & Wiegand, K. (2008). The big three's prime-time decline. *Journal of Broadcasting and Electronic Media, 52*(1), 119–135.

Kubey, R. (2004). *Creating television: Conversations with the people behind 50 years of American TV.* Mahwah, NJ: Lawrence Erlbaum.

Lynch, J. (1973). Seven days with *All in the Family:* A case study of the taped TV drama. *Journal of Broadcasting, 17*(3), 259–274.

Owen, B., & Wildman, S. (1992). *Video economics.* Cambridge, MA: Harvard University Press.

Pekurny, R. (1977). *Broadcast self-regulation: A participant observation study of NBC's broadcast standards department.* Ph.D. diss., University of Minnesota, Minneapolis.

Pekurny, R. (1982). Coping with television production. In J. S. Ettema & D. C. Whitney (Eds.), *Individuals in mass media organizations: Creativity and constraint* (pp. 131–144). Beverly Hills: Sage.

Peterson, R. A., & Berger, D. (1971). Entrepreneurship in organizations: Evidence from the popular music industry. *Administrative Science Quarterly, 16,* 97–107.

Ravage, J. (1978). *Television: The director's viewpoint.* New York: Praeger.

Reeves, J. (1990). Rewriting culture: A dialogic view of television authorship. In R. Thompson & G. Burns (Eds.), *Making television: Authorship and the production process* (pp. 147–160). New York: Praeger.

Rossman, G. (2005). *The effects of ownership concentration on media content.* Ph.D. diss., Princeton University, Princeton, NJ.

Sennett, R., & Cobb, J. (1972). *The hidden injuries of class.* New York: W. W. Norton.

Stein, B. (1979). *The view from Sunset Boulevard.* New York: Basic Books.

Thompson, R., & Burns, G. (Eds.). (1990). *Making television: Authorship and the production process.* New York: Praeger.

Tunstall, J., & Walker, D. (1981). *Media made in California.* New York: Oxford University Press.

Turow, J. (1978). Casting for TV parts: The anatomy of social typing. *Journal of Communication, 28*(4), 18–24.

Turow, J. (1980). Occupation and personality in television dramas. *Communication Research, 7*(3), 295–318.

Turow, J. (1982a). Producing TV's world: How important is community? *Journal of Communication, 32*(2), 186–193.

Turow, J. (1982b). Unconventional programs on commercial television. In J. S. Ettema & D. C. Whitney (Eds.), *Individuals in mass media organizations.* Beverly Hills: Sage.

TV's class struggle. (2008, September 22). *Variety,* p. 1.

TV's little guys stayin' alive. (2001, February 19). *Variety,* p. 1.

TV role reversal. (2009, January 12). *Variety,* p. 1.

Upscale auds ease b'casters. (1999, August 23). *Variety,* p. 34.

Wakshlag, J., & Adams, W. J. (1985). Trends in program variety and prime time access rules. *Journal of Broadcasting and Electronic Media, 29,* 23–34.

Winick, C. (1961). Censor and sensibility: A content analysis of the television censor's comments. *Journal of Broadcasting, 5,* 117–135.

Young auds seek Web, not webs. (1999, January 4). *Variety,* p. 65.

Zook, K. B. (1999). *Color by Fox: The Fox network and the revolution in Black television.* New York: Oxford University Press.

PART III

READING MEDIA TEXTS CRITICALLY

Media scholars have recognized that media texts are never simple, however obvious they may seem. According to the view of media texts as "open" or polysemic (discussed in the introduction to Part I), there is frequently room to make readings that go at least partially against dominant ideologies (**counterhegemonic** readings). However, in our everyday media text consumption, we don't always attend closely to the mechanisms and techniques that are helping to influence the way we make meanings out of these texts. This inattention makes us more likely to internalize the messages encoded in the texts, to become passive consumers.

In this section, we have assembled a group of chapters that provide a variety of models for how to "deconstruct" or get underneath the surface of media texts, in order to understand better how they are encoding ideologies of gender, sexuality, race, and class. We acknowledge that some students may find that doing close analysis interferes with the pleasure they get from media texts. But if you are in this situation, we would invite you to join media scholars in finding the special pleasure (and power) available to those who become critical readers of texts. As audiences build media literacy skills, a dual consciousness can develop, enabling us both to enjoy reading the text at face value and simultaneously to take pleasure in decoding its more subtle and nuanced meanings.

This section begins with one of the most popular television dramas of the past two decades: *Law & Order: Special Victims Unit,* a show that began broadcasting in 1999 as a spin-off of the widely acclaimed earlier series *Law & Order.* At first reading, as Cuklanz and Moorti (III.14) point out, this show appears politically progressive, in that it has encoded a feminist understanding of sexual assault. In addition, it is notable among police dramas in that one of its main characters is a woman who is not afraid to stand up to the men in her team and who repeatedly advocates for rape victims. Moreover, as these writers point out, "by showcasing women who survive their sexual assaults *SVU* asserts a key feminist idea: There is life after rape—that is, the raped woman is a survivor with agency" (p. 117).

However, as these scholars look more deeply into patterns of character and plot in the text of this series, they make a more critical reading and assessment. Noting that on the show, "numerous storylines depicted families that produce criminal children," in many cases casting mothers as "either criminals in their own right" or responsible for the criminality of their children, Cuklanz and Moorti assess the show's political content as problematic for feminists:

> The monstrous maternal storylines show *SVU* grappling with the limits of the detective-cop show genre. In this genre, traditionally associated with masculinity, the vilification of feminine qualities and the association of women with horrific crimes within the family counterbalances the feminist perspective presented in many episode narratives in relation to rape and rape reform. (p. 124)

Mothers are also constructed as monsters within the world of mass-mediated celebrity gossip, according to Shelley Cobb, whose study of "bad celebrity motherhood" (III.15) treats the mothers of Paris Hilton, Britney Spears, and Lindsay Lohan as media texts. Cobb shows that these mothers "have been strongly criticized in the media for not raising their daughters 'well' and for not taking immediate corrective measures when their troubles began." Cobb goes on to point out the tendency in gossip media both to idealize protective White middle-class motherhood and to condemn the "stage mother" figure as "white trash"—whatever the actual financial resources she might have. As she writes,

> Class snobbery toward the stage mother remains because of the conflation of middle-class family values with perceptions of appropriate femininity. . . . The perception is that these mothers have pushed, if not forced, their daughters into show business careers in order to make money off them, and the gossip blog users suggest that they do so to relive the youths that they gave up to be mothers, making an inappropriate spectacle of themselves and their daughters. (pp. 132–133)

Motherhood is also on the mind of hip-hop feminist and critic Marlo David Azikwe (III.16), who highlights African American women's perspectives, both as cultural producers and as critics of the genre. Azikwe first points to the complexity and urgency of the task of learning to read hip-hop culture in more nuanced ways than most people do:

> Reading hip-hop culture is a messy business. While we must resist simplistic readings that force us to assess what is good or bad, positive or negative for the black community, it is also possible and desirable to understand how hip-hop disrupts racist, sexist, [and] classist culture. . . . Hip-hop feminist critique makes space for the gray areas, the ironies, and contradictions that are part of hip-hop and life, but it should also provide a way out of the mire of postmodern detachment to invite women and men to get down to the business of "bringing wreck" against the social forces that control their lives. (p. 139)

From her own perspective as a hip-hop feminist, Azikwe explores the problematic theme of motherhood in hip hop, even within Black female rappers' lyrics. Motherhood is a particularly fraught concept for the African American community, given the history of public blaming of Black mothers as the "matriarchs" whose excessive power in the traditional Black family was said in the infamous Moynihan Report of 1965 to have "emasculated" Black men, which in turn led to the endemic poverty of single-parent families. From Azikwe's perspective, in the "body politics" articulated by much of masculinist hip hop and even by some female rappers "talking back," the female body is represented as strong only through heterosexual sexiness. The Black mothering body, by contrast, is associated with weakness and vulnerability. Azikwe's goal is to show that "there is room at the table for black feminists, womanists and hip-hop feminists to address the representations of black motherhood and their importance to our communities" (p. 141).

Azikwe's chapter reminds us that there is no one completely dominant perspective encoded throughout mass media. As cultural studies scholars often emphasize, drawing upon the complex concept of power famously articulated by Michel Foucault, competing voices and alternative perspectives always arise to contest the hegemonic formulations, in an ongoing and decentralized struggle for superiority. Thus, even in a socially conservative time and place, there is always some space for more progressive (democratic) ideologies to be expressed.

In the early 21st century, one place within mass media production where arguably counterhegemonic views can be found is in the more narrowly targeted commercial entertainment media such as cable TV channels. For example, the Comedy Channel's *The Daily Show with Jon Stewart,* featuring comedian Jon Stewart, slyly conveys dissident political views through parodying the conventions of the mainstream television news format. Jamie Warner (III.17) compares Stewart's show's tactics to those

practiced by activist "culture jammers," who are "rebelling against the hegemony of the messages promoting global capitalism." In Stewart's case, the target is frequently the "branding techniques" used by politicians and political parties "to drown out dissident messages," and the method for subverting these "brand" messages is "dissident humor":

> Like other culture jammers, *The Daily Show* subversively employs emotional and aesthetic modalities similar to those employed by political branding itself, thus interrupting it from within. Unlike many culture jammers, however, *The Daily Show*'s reliance on a humorous version of parody means that they can add their voices to the conversation in a seemingly innocuous way. (After all, it is *just* a joke.) (p. 146)

Another example of a potentially subversive TV show is *The Simpsons,* the long-running edgy satirical animation series on the Fox Network that has been very popular with young people. Gilad Padva (III.18) situates *The Simpsons* within "the popular subgenre of animated TV sitcoms in the late 1990s and 2000s," which "integrates semi-anarchistic humor and spectacular imagery that often challenge conventional ethnic, social, gender and sexual patterns of representation." Using an episode from *The Simpsons* called "Homer Phobia," which lampoons the leading character Homer Simpson for knee-jerk antigay attitudes, Padva deconstructs the text, showing how it can be understood to encode a celebration of "queer counter-culture" and to be susceptible of different readings for those "in the know."

> Although straight audiences too enjoy this episode, its hyperbolic scenes particularly empower gay viewers, who likely identify the linguistic maneuvers and decode the queer meanings. (p. 160)

Gay masculinity is also discussed by Chong-suk Han (III.19), who critiques

Asian gay male representation within mainstream gay print media. In his view,

> While "gay" masculinity can never be hegemonic, it can, nonetheless, position itself closer to the hegemonic ideal by pitting the more feminized masculinity of Asian men as a counter balance. (p. 168)

Reading the gay journals closely to document both gay Asian invisibility and the presence of race-related stereotypes, Han provides evidence for his argument that gay masculinity in mainstream gay media has reflected the traditional hegemony of White masculinity by marginalizing men of color.

On a more hopeful note, another study suggests cracks opening up in the wall of hegemonic heterosexist masculinity as represented and reproduced in sports media. David Nylund (III.20) reminds us that sports have been crucial to the social construction of hegemonic masculinity in the United States. Yet, interestingly, Nylund found that well-known sports radio talk show host Jim Rome unexpectedly critiqued the use of homophobic slurs by callers, thus opening up space through his show for questioning dominant social ideas. Nylund is careful to point out, however, that "Rome's location of the problem of **homophobia** in a few bigoted, intolerant individuals leaves unchallenged the larger societal structures that perpetuate **heterosexism**" (p. 178).

Like Nylund, Kathleen LeBesco (III.21) points to both hegemonic and counterhegemonic elements in the media text she examines. In the case of *The Sopranos*, the HBO serial drama that broke with convention in many ways and was highly successful with audiences and critics alike, LeBesco offers a reading of its representations of gendered disability that is on balance highly laudatory. She writes,

> As I logged *Sopranos* episodes for this project, I notice[d] that a transformation began to take place in my own perceptions. . . . Characters exist with cancer, stroke, Borderline Personality Disorder, food poisoning, developmental disabilities, depression, panic attacks, Epstein-Barr disease, Carpal Tunnel Syndrome, sore backs, gunshot wounds to the spleen, Attention Deficit Disorder, low vision, heroin addiction, learning disabilities, obesity, amputated legs, and other conditions that are feared or reviled to different degrees in everyday life. On the show, they're mostly just another fact of life. . . . With its sharp writing and masterful acting, *The Sopranos* makes physical limitation, loss of ability, distance from body ideals, and pain comprehensible to its audience. (p. 191)

While LeBesco points to some problems in the representation of female fatness, she applauds the show in particular for its progressive image of a female amputee, Svetlana Kirilenko, who has a brief sexual affair with the mobster protagonist, Tony Soprano. In LeBesco's reading, Svetlana is "a passionate disabled woman capable of enjoying a quick affair, but recognizing the nondisabled partner (Tony) as an emotional drain she's unwilling to take on. . . . Svetlana's sex scene flies in the face of the tradition of disabled women rarely being portrayed as sexual beings. . . . As both a paid worker and a sexual subject, Svetlana is accorded full personhood, even as a minor character" (pp. 186–187).

Television's "New" Feminism

Prime-Time Representations of Women and Victimization

Lisa M. Cuklanz and Sujata Moorti

In the fall of 1999, NBC debuted its second program in the *Law & Order* franchise, *Law & Order: Special Victims Unit* (hereafter *SVU*), a scripted series devoted to crimes of sexual assault and rape. Although the runaway success of the original *Law & Order* helped assure an eager audience for the new venture, the seemingly narrow focus on a subject as emotionally and politically charged as rape took the television crime genre in an unexpected direction. *SVU*'s popularity over the last five years raises questions about the series' ability to introduce the topic of sexual violence into the prime-time arena and sustain viewership. How does a prime-time fictional chronicling of sexual violence, trauma, and victimization operate within the confines of the traditionally masculine genre of detective fiction? What forms of feminism, if any, does such a prime-time focus on sexual violence enable?

With its "ripped from the headlines" storylines *SVU* centers on cases undertaken by a police unit modeled after the New York Police Department's Special Victims Unit.[1] In the tradition of television crime dramas, the series spotlights the detective duo of Olivia Benson (Mariska Hargitay) and Elliot Stabler (Christopher Meloni), and an ensemble cast of characters that include Odafin Tutuola (Ice-T) and John Munch (Richard Belzer), Captain Donald Cragen (Dann Florek), Assistant D. A. Casey Novak (Diane Neal), medical examiner Melinda Warner (Tamara Tunie), and police psychologist George Huang (B. D. Wong).[2] *SVU* is both similar to and different from the original title series, *Law & Order*, which combines the genres of the cop show and the legal drama. *SVU* episodes rarely include a trial and although most of its narratives end with the positive identification of the perpetrator,

From Cuklanz, L. M., & Moorti, S. (2006). Television's "new" feminism: Prime-time representations of women and victimization. *Critical Studies in Media Communications, 23*(4), 302–321. Copyright © National Communication Association, reprinted by permission of Taylor & Francis Ltd. (http://www.tandf.co.uk/journals) on behalf of the National Communication Association.

some conclude with the criminal still at large.[3] Producer Dick Wolf characterizes it as a "compelling" cop drama that tracks the emotional effects of the crimes on its two protagonist detectives and on victims. Like the original title series, *SVU* begins with a voice-over that provides the program with a sense of verisimilitude:

> In the criminal justice system, sexually-based offenses are considered especially heinous. In New York City, the dedicated detectives who investigate these vicious felonies are members of an elite squad known as the Special Victims Unit. These are their stories. (http://www .tvtome.com/lawandorder/svu)

Shot on location in New York City, *SVU* shares several of the signature elements of the title series: scene-setting labeling, staccato music, edgy camerawork, sudden shifts in scenes, and use of street argot. Airing originally on NBC, episodes are shown nine days later on the cable channel USA, following a unique syndication policy termed "repurposing."

SVU is distinguished by its subject matter, which reprises decades-long feminist discussions of violence against women. If rape provides a foundational feminist allegory for women's subordinated status in society (Sielke, 2002), *SVU*'s decision to base an entire prime-time series on this topic locates it within the limited body of programming that can be characterized as feminist television. However, *SVU*'s depictions mark a new stage in the trajectory of televisual feminism. Analysis of the first five seasons of *SVU* suggests that its representations of rape facilitate a feminism that is markedly different both from the lifestyle feminism that dominated 1970s and 1980s prime-time entertainment and the postfeminism of the 1990s. We will show that, in a seemingly contradictory move, *SVU* storylines couple feminist premises and assumptions with an indictment of so-called female traits.

The storylines on *SVU* thematize and elaborate key elements of feminist understandings of sexual violence. However, paradoxically, this feminist take on the subject of rape is not carried through in *SVU*'s treatment of women. Some of the storylines condemn aspects of feminine behavior and character, including empathy and intuition. Female characters seldom can or do form bonds with each other. Female criminals are manipulative and use relationships to harm others; numerous storylines explore narratives of moral depravity and extreme violence on the part of women. While criminal women are nothing new in popular cultural products, *SVU*'s particular construction of the dangerous woman takes an unusual turn. The criminal women on *SVU* use their power in the domestic realm to harm those closest to them, particularly their own children. Their criminality is often linked with misguided maternalism. We contend that the feminist elements of the storylines appear primarily in the depiction of sexual assault; at the level of the deep structure the narratives articulate an anxiety about feminine characteristics and the power women possess within the private sphere. Thus, in *SVU* narratives the home—the primary arena of women's activities and the site of the feminine qualities of nurturing, caregiving, and affect—is presented repeatedly as the site within which a dangerous maternal instinct motivates women to commit heinous crimes. . . .

SVU's claims of feminism are encouraged by press quotes given by the show's cast. After completing two months of victim advocate training with the Sexual Assault and Violence Intervention Program at Mount Sinai Hospital, New York City, Mariska Hargitay told reporters she hoped to incorporate the perspectives of the police and of victim advocates (Beck & Smith, 2003). Hargitay is known for her work with rape survivors and for her "Joyful Heart" foundation, which Hargitay's website indicates is "committed to helping victims of rape and sexual assault heal—mind, body, and spirit" (http://www.joyfulheartfoundation .org/). Like other cast members, Hargitay emphasizes the show's commitment to realistic representations of sexual assault and to presenting victim/survivor perspectives. One news article noted her assertion that *SVU* writers "don't try to sensationalize the stories," and quoted her comment that "rape . . . is not about sex, it's about anger and violence towards women, and we really go into what that's all about" (Fidgeon, 2003). Her character is often regarded as a feminist heroine. For example, a *New York Times* television review noted that her character is one of just a few who "mirror the feminist ethos of the past—dedicated, seasoned, and tough" (Stanley, 2005). Reporters also cite Hargitay's volunteer work outside the show to emphasize the commitment of both *SVU* the program and Benson the character to victims' perspectives and experiences. . . .

Demystifying Rape Myths

SVU's feminist depiction of rape is clearest when the episodes are viewed cumulatively. Following a trend since the late 1980s, *SVU* does not objectify sexual assault victims. The series rarely depicts the sexual assault itself, thus omitting titillating and objectifying details common in previous media representations. The majority of storylines track events after a rape so the sexual assault itself remains beyond the diegetic space of the series. This "post-rape" narrative strategy permits *SVU* to sidestep the problematic of rape's resistance to representation (Bal, 1992). Simultaneously, by showcasing women who survive their sexual assaults *SVU* asserts a key feminist idea: There is life after rape—that is, the raped woman is a survivor with agency (Rajan, 1993).

While the series, in title and content, pays silent homage to the achievements of the women's movement of the 1970s, storylines are more overt in highlighting the rape law reforms initiated by feminists. *SVU* also underscores the continuing shortcomings of the judicial system. *SVU* episodes often are limited to investigation of the crime and apprehension of the criminal. That said,

storylines that include a trial segment often underscore the juridical hurdles that preclude more systematic prosecution of criminals. For example, some episodes exploring the legal definition of consent emphasized how slippery the term becomes during trial. The episode "Consent" featured a female college student who was raped while under the influence of a date rape drug. The rapists were exonerated after the lawyer exploited the murky definition of consent. Other episodes highlighted definitions of statutory rape as well as more complicated ethical dimensions of consent. In "Waste," detectives pondered the possibility of filing a rape charge when a comatose patient was suddenly discovered to be six weeks pregnant. The episode parsed the meaning of consent in a complex manner by introducing a subplot where the fetus was aborted, but the patient's mother filed charges since she did not consent to the termination of the pregnancy. Some storylines showcased the troubling questions of who can press charges and who can offer evidence in rape cases, while other episodes highlighted how often rapists invoke the spousal confidentiality clause to halt the disclosure of crucial evidence. In each of these instances, *SVU* episodes revealed some of the rape law reforms such as rape shield laws, but also gave voice to feminist concerns about the lacunae that remain.

The absence of on-screen depictions of sexual assault and the critique of existing legal practices are the two predominant axes along which *SVU* introduces feminist understandings of sexual assault into the arena of prime-time entertainment. Even as these feminist insights are introduced unproblematically as a meta-discourse, individual episodes spell out more carefully the numerous rape demystification strategies that have been central to the women's movement. Most significantly, storylines highlight myths and misunderstandings that continue to surround the topic of sexual assault.

Feminists have insisted on dismantling the categories of "good" and "bad" victims that have dominated common sense (and media) definitions of the crime (Benedict, 1992). Unequivocally asserting that consent—rather than the conduct of the victim—is central to definitions of rape, *SVU* narratives repeatedly showcase assaults on prostitutes. In "Hysteria," an African-American teenager's rape and murder was treated lightly by police officers who assumed she was a prostitute. *SVU* detectives, however, managed to set the record straight, tracking down her murderer, a policeman, and unraveling the unsolved murders of at least 18 prostitutes. Storylines have presented the rape of police officers. While most victim-survivors are depicted as "normal" everyday people, some episodes have centered on "sexually adventurous" women. The detectives might make awkward jokes about these women's kinky sexual habits, but they do not discount the possibility of sexual violation. *SVU* narratives repeatedly declare that a person's sexual practices must not be used to undermine the person's credibility. The series rejects the assumption that only virtuous and sexually chaste women can be violated.

Apart from showcasing a range of survivor-victims including gay men and an MTF transsexual, storylines have contested the myth that women are assaulted when they are alone in "unsafe" public places. *SVU* narratives have depicted the sexual assault of women in public and private spaces with equal levels of complexity. "Remorse" depicted an attractive reporter who was raped by two strangers in an abandoned swimming pool. "Contact" provided a different valence to the term "public space" with the rapist assaulting women in crowded subway cars. Other *SVU* episodes featured assaults in "safe spaces" such as the home. "Limitations" tracked a serial rapist who attacked women in their beds and used a hair dryer as a "fake" gun, while "Disappearing Acts" featured an executive raped in her office. Thus the series does not categorize public and private spaces as safe or unsafe. By insistently inscribing the presence of sexual assault in all spaces, perpetrated by strangers and acquaintances, the series helps forward a pivotal feature of feminist definitions of rape.

As the key female protagonist, Benson is a singular figure through which the show espouses identifiably feminist attitudes toward rape and police work. When a reporter Benson dates said he would like to "playfully" re-enact the subway rapes they had been discussing, Benson's reaction was swift and categorical. After telling the reporter his suggestion was disgusting, she locked herself in the bathroom with the instruction that he'd better be gone when she returned. The scene provided an unambiguous model for dealing with unwanted sexual behavior. Likewise, when a vice cop remarked that prostitutes cannot really be raped, Benson made clear that she did not mind offending him to make explicit her belief that the definition of rape does not depend on a victim's identity or profession. In "Limitations," she was angered by a retired SVU detective whose failure to document and take seriously a rape claimant's information resulted in multiple repeat offenses by a perpetrator at large for years. When the retired detective said it was "clear" that the alleged victim was just fantasizing about the rape, Benson confronted him with his sexism and incompetence and stomped away in disgust. The scene clearly differentiated between the traditional police view of rape and Benson's more feminist understanding, clearly taking a side in her favor.

The storylines also work to demystify the black male rapist myth. Walk-on characters often include interracial couples, heterosexual and gay; but rarely are people of color depicted as assailants (and often these are foreigners). Several narratives raised the prospect of the black male rapist. Inevitably, though, once arrested, the black male was found innocent, thus highlighting how racist assumptions of criminality shape policing practices. For instance, a black athlete was initially assumed to be the rapist in "Sophomore Jinx," but the narrative instead offered an eloquent assessment of the stereo-types and racist assumptions that shape the everyday lives of African Americans. People of color are rarely depicted as criminals in interracial crimes. This, too, is a departure from the history of popular culture representations. The series also manages to render visible the victimization of women of color. In storylines featuring interracial couples the victim-survivor is always a woman of color. Perhaps these racialized depictions of criminality and victimization might be shaped by the network's standards department (Gitlin, 1983). In any case they help articulate concerns of feminists regarding the ways in which fears of black male sexuality have shaped cultural definitions of sexual assault (Brownmiller, 1975; Davis, 1978) and of critical race theorists, who highlighted the historical silencing of black female victimization. *SVU*'s depiction of racialized victims thus helps correct the dominant tropes of black femininity in popular culture (Collins, 2005; Crenshaw, 1995).

SVU offers an unequivocally feminist understanding of sexual assault in its depiction of power imbalances as causing rape. Thus, while the majority of the episodes in the first season focused on the victimization of "classic" powerless subjects—women and children—storylines have increasingly drawn attention to other violated bodies, those gendered subjects who occupy the space of the female body in "rape scripts" (Marcus, 1992). Several *SVU* narratives featured the rape of men—heterosexual and gay—in a manner akin to that of their female counterparts, highlighting how the broader social climate of homophobia helps render this particular brand of sexual assault either invisible or sensational. In effect, the series does not prioritize the victimization of one sex over the other. Rather, it asserts that sexual violence pivots on power imbalances.

Portrayals of perpetrators of sexual assaults are as heterogeneous as the victim-survivors. They include authority figures (judges, doctors, and police officers),

working-class men, those that are "mentally retarded," and felons. *SVU* storylines have depicted men and women as child molesters, but only once were women presented as rapists. In "Ridicule," three women raped a male stripper; they were not prosecuted for this crime, although one of them was convicted of murder. This ecumenical presentation of sexual assault criminals echoes the feminist slogan that rape is not sex but is the assertion of power.

SVU storylines often go beyond offering an individual-centered explanation for sexual assault. They reiterate feminists' claim that violent masculinity is facilitated by society at large. Dworkin (1976), Griffin (1986), MacKinnon (1987), and other scholars have identified an interlocking web of social factors—such as the prevalence of pornographic representations that perpetuate the sexual objectification of women—as constituting a climate that makes possible men's assault of women. Storylines point out factors such as pornography, beauty pageants, and an overall "sexual objectification of women" that promote a rape culture. Thus, for instance, "Care" explored how young boys might learn and replicate the misogyny depicted in video games. "Appearances," featuring a 10-year-old beauty pageant participant, indicted the broader social milieu that normalizes the sexual objectification of all females, young and adult. Several *SVU* storylines evocatively described the complicated manner in which female college students are victimized by fraternity culture and institutional practices that facilitate the expression of male violence.

The New Televisual Feminism

Within these feminist elements, however, is enfolded a demonization of feminine characteristics. We do not assume that televisual representations should follow or develop only one perspective on controversial issues related to rape and sexual assault, or even of women. *SVU*'s depictions of violent and criminal women are not necessarily unrealistic or inherently anti-feminist. We recognize that competing elements and themes, as well as a range of reading positions, characterize televisual detective fiction. Nonetheless, we find that *SVU*'s representations of violent women present female power in the domestic sphere as not only dangerous, but as a cause of crime in general. Having analyzed the specific ways that *SVU* tells the stories of criminal women, we offer below some instances that highlight how the narratives castigate feminine characteristics even as the episodes adhere to a feminist understanding of sexual violence.

SVU's strategy of granting legitimacy to some feminist ideas about rape while subtly condemning feminine characteristics is exemplified in the character development of Detective Elliot Stabler. A proto-feminist family man, Stabler has from the first season been seen as encountering the limits of his male-centered understanding of sexual assault. With the assistance of his female partner he realizes a key feminist insight that sexual crimes often defy rationality. This process of coming into consciousness was demonstrated in *SVU*'s debut episode, "Payback." This storyline drew Stabler and Benson into a gruesome investigation of a cab driver who was posthumously castrated. The forensic trail allowed the detectives to identify the taxi driver as a Serbian war criminal who had committed numerous atrocities, including participation in rape camps.[4] The detectives eventually located three survivors of the rape camps who now resided in New York City, two of whom collaborated to murder the taxi driver/war criminal. Stabler pursued the rule of law; he insisted that the two women be prosecuted for murder. However, Benson used the women's narratives to make the case that such acts of violence are the only recourse available to women victims of civil war atrocities, in the absence of viable international institutions of justice. While

Stabler never abandoned his faith in U.S. law and order institutions, by the narrative's end he showed remorse because one of the accused women committed suicide and the other was imprisoned.

Through similar narrative strategies, Stabler became the vehicle for the enunciation of a nuanced feminist idea. He often understands the cases he is investigating through a connected mode of reasoning reminiscent of Gilligan's (1982) understanding of female knowledge acquisition patterns. Stabler's professional successes do not always stem from a rule-orientation. Rather, the male detective arrives at a better and more accurate sense of sexual crimes when he imagines one of his four children in the place of the actual victims. For instance, in "Or Just Look Like One," a storyline about the rape and murder of teenage models, Stabler understood, with Benson's prompting, that they were not investigating a "simple" crime. Rather, he better understood the rape culture engendered by the beauty business in coming to terms with his older daughter's struggles with her body image. In particular, Benson instructed Stabler on the stakes women have in their looks, and the anger and insecurities that follow the loss of one's looks. Armed with this knowledge the detectives tracked down the criminal, a former female supermodel.

While the main storyline in this episode elaborated on the unrealistic body image promoted by the fashion industry, a secondary storyline depicted Stabler comprehending his daughter's battles with anorexia only after he recognized the physical, psychological, and material price the cult of thinness exacts from women. *SVU* storylines repeatedly present Stabler as blurring the public and domestic realms in the sense that his professional conduct is informed by insights from the domestic realm. This narrative choice underscores a key feminist idea that separating the public and private arenas is an untenable ideological device. Notably, *SVU* enacts a gender role reversal in articulating this idea. Stabler is presented repeatedly as a concerned father who is successful in his detective work when he projects his children as victims of the crimes he is asked to pursue. While other television shows deprecated female characters who cannot separate their public conduct from the domestic realm, *SVU* has normalized Stabler as a concerned father who brings his domestic life and concerns into the workplace. Benson, meanwhile, maintains a rigid separation of the two arenas. She is rarely shown outside the professional realm; often she is depicted as having no private life.

The proto-feminist gestures enacted by Stabler's character, however, also impede his work. Understanding cases by imagining his children in the place of the victims makes Stabler too emotionally invested in his cases. For instance, in "Wanderlust," Stabler was convinced that a teenage girl must be a victim of sexual crime. Picturing his teenage daughter at the crime scene, he refused to follow Benson's hunch that the teenager was the murderer. It was left to Benson to explain that young teenagers can fall in love with father figures and commit crimes of passion. Benson finally convinced Stabler that all adolescent girls are not innocent and always-already victimized. Thus, Stabler's tendency to see his job through the prism of his family often hinders his work. Stabler is blinded by his concern for his family and his identification with women. Stabler's feminine characteristics of empathy and emotionality prevent him from apprehending female criminality.

Since the 1970s, feminists have worked actively with the police to alter the ways in which rapes are investigated, including by forming special victims' units, and ensuring that detectives are less skeptical and cynical about women's rape claims. So, it is striking that *SVU* has featured a number of storylines with false rape charges. We do not question the possibility of false rape claims but draw attention to the cultural work accomplished by the many storylines that focus on women who fabricate rape charges. In the series as a whole, survivors are relatively rare, since most victims die during or after their attacks; this narrative strategy enables *SVU* to avoid titillating representations of rape and to concentrate on the aftermath. Nevertheless, the fact that *SVU* storylines position several survivors as false claimants of rape makes this a provocative and weighted strategy, one that cannot be dismissed as a twist intended to produce a "fresh" angle.[5] Often the most eloquent survivors, those who can coherently and poignantly reconstruct their assault and the trauma they have experienced, turn out to be dissemblers. The false rape episodes are never depicted as "imagined" assaults; rather, the women are portrayed as maliciously and willfully fabricating the false charge. The female claimant's manipulative staging of false crimes, her ability to wield dangerously controlling interpersonal power over accomplices, and efforts to fool detectives become the focus of these storylines. . . .

Women as Victimizers

We have identified an archetypal "family" scenario where anti-women sentiments are present in the deep structure of the narrative. These stories center on the recurrent manifestation of what we call the monstrous maternal. Since these scenarios draw attention to the family as a site of violence, at first glance these storylines appear to articulate feminist concerns about a patriarchal space where male power is exercised and sometimes abused. Yet the limits of the detective genre come into visibility in these narratives, which tend to reflect an anxiety about feminine qualities and women's power.

During the first five seasons, numerous storylines depicted families that produce criminal children, or couples without children who are the source of crimes. When all of the "damaged families" narratives are totaled, over 40 episodes (approximately one third of the episodes aired in the first five seasons) focused largely on family problems that result in crime. With a few notable exceptions that featured innocent victims who cannot ultimately be helped by law and order institutions ("Wrong is Right" centered on a young boy adopted by a pedophile; in "Disrobed" a judge abused domestic violence survivors and then extorted them), the direction of cause and effect in nearly all of these suggests that damaged families create damaged individuals who become criminals. The episodes reiterate a simple causal logic—that individual "sick" families cause social problems, and that "the system" fails some families that it should help. The dysfunctional family is a cause of crime, rather than the symptom or result of larger institutions and social problems. In *SVU* narratives, mothers often are either criminals in their own right or they cause the criminal behavior of their children. *SVU* women misuse their domestic power in the commission of crime as often as men do. Women's abuse of their power in the domestic realm is presented as more dangerous in its physical immediacy as well as more psychologically damaging than that of men. Bad mothering is much more frequently depicted as the cause of criminal behavior by adult children than is bad fathering.

The Monstrous Maternal

In *Motherhood and Representation* (1992) Kaplan identified two primary—and predominating—types of "bad" or "evil" mothers in popular culture. The so-called "fusional" mother is the "possessive and destructive all-devouring one," while the second is over-indulgent and vicariously satisfies her own needs through the child (p. 47). These mothers "project on to the child [their] resentments, disappointments and failures for which the child is also to suffer" (p. 47). Kaplan explained that much

less attention has been given to abusive fathers than to abusive mothers because of prevailing mother-constructs dictating that mothers be gentle and self-sacrificing. "Their deviation is then all the more reprehensible" (p. 193). Men's/father's abuse is "more socially acceptable" (p. 193), because they are not held up to the same standard of gentleness and self-sacrifice. Kaplan added that mothers are usually "blamed as individuals, rather than blame being placed on social structures and governmental priorities" (p. 192). Although Kaplan is primarily referring to news coverage, her description of popular representations of abusive mothers is borne out in *SVU*'s ripped-from-the-headlines fictional world as well. Here, mothers commit a range of horrific crimes related to their maternal role (such as withholding food, failing to nurture, or psychologically manipulating their children). They are also implicated much more often than are fathers in the crimes of rapists, sociopaths, pedophiles, and a range of extreme criminals who are their children.

The numbers of abusive mothers and abusive fathers in the first five seasons of *SVU* are almost identical. We analyzed more than two dozen episodes featuring criminally insane, violent, or otherwise dangerous mothers, referred to here as monstrous maternal figures. The monstrous maternal involves women who fail in their parental roles so grievously as to cause serious harm or even death to their children or others. The monstrous maternal storylines contend that violent women are often more dangerous and harmful than male victimizers; mothers are implicated in crimes committed by their children, whereas fathers are implicated almost exclusively in psychological damage that harms the children.

Our concept of the monstrous maternal differs somewhat from Creed's (1993) "monstrous feminine." Creed focused on the horror film genre. For example, her discussion of "Alien" treated non-human elements such as the Alien monster and its mode of attack as cases of the "monstrous feminine." Often, women's sexuality is depicted as the underlying problem in horror films, revealing male fears of women's sexual power. Working from a psychoanalytic model in order to understand the relationships between the human and non-human in horror film, Creed focused on women as victims. Our "monstrous maternal," while she may pose as victim, is always the aggressor. However, with both concepts, the texts emphasize the threat posed to men by women, particularly mothers, and suggest that it is women who pose the real threat to the social order. In *SVU,* the monstrous mother particularly focuses on children or others under her care as her victims, but her crimes may also represent a misdirection of the maternal role.

In many episodes about dysfunctional families, mothers' crimes were violent and immediate. Three episodes centered on mothers who had murdered their own children, and two others involved mothers who either accidentally or sympathetically killed their own children. No episodes featured fathers who murder their own children (although in "Monogamy," a man attacked his wife and killed the fetus they conceived). In three episodes maternal figures (two mothers and a grandmother with full guardianship) murdered their children through some variation of Munchausen by Proxy syndrome, physically abusing or poisoning them secretly in order to gain sympathy as caretakers of sick children.

Mothers are frequently the perpetrators of ongoing violence, whereas fathers' abuse is usually located in the distant past. Significantly, female perpetrators often utilize the domestic sphere as their means of committing crime. In addition to committing straightforward physical abuse (in "Careless," a foster mother murdered a child in her care), women poison their children's food, commit psychological abuse by seducing or dominating their sons, fail to nurture and love their children, abandon sick children, and murder (others) to

assure their children's happiness. Women's crimes are thus associated with misdirections of caregiving (poisoning not nourishing, murdering to protect, abusing rather than loving). Women's crimes are generally motivated by greed, jealousy, competition, and materialism, while men's serious crimes are committed for simple pleasure and covering up sexual wrongdoing. The worst female criminals are nearly always mothers of some kind. . . .

Repeatedly, *SVU*'s dysfunctional families present the monstrous maternal as resulting from a misguided sense of caring and nurturing or a pathological selfishness. The mother-child bond itself is presented as profoundly dangerous. Often the episodes do not feature women as mothers but surrogates who within the domestic sphere occupy the role of caregivers and nurturers. *SVU* episodes feature women criminals as loving grandmother, devoted wife, sister ("Painless" depicted a woman whose resentment against her own mother turned to sociopathy; she murdered dozens of elderly nursing home patients who, she recalled, "were all called mother"), or long-suffering mother. In "Sacrifice" a porn star mother played the part of rape victim while she framed her husband for murder and abandoned her daughter to pursue an acting career. In "Shaken," a single mother was overwhelmed by her infant daughter's crying and suffocated her. . . .

Feminism in a New Era

SVU departs from most other prime-time fare in several important ways. It fits solidly within the historically masculine detective genre while deliberately focusing on a subject of primary interest to women. It positions itself as a dramatic series with feminist sympathies, addressing a subject that was long a focus of feminist activism. It is uniquely issue-oriented, building its emotional and dramatic appeal from a political issue rather than focusing on an eponymous protagonist (such as *Cagney and Lacey*). *SVU* highlights power in gender relations, including within the family, and provides evidence of "rape culture" as a potential factor in the commission of the crime. Yet in many instances the real victims are men and patriarchal institutions. Enfolded in the feminist perspectives on sexual assault are problematic depictions of feminine characteristics. . . .

We argue that *SVU*'s co-dependent linkage of a critical view of feminine qualities with a feminist understanding of sexual assault and rape reform constitutes a new brand of televisual feminism, distinct from the lifestyle feminism of the 1970s and 1980s and the postfeminism of the 1990s. *SVU*'s misogynist feminism includes false claims of rape; negative portrayals of feminine characteristics such as intuition, emotion, and manipulation; criminal use of interpersonal power by women; and the figure of the monstrous mother. Feminine characteristics such as empathy, intuition, passion, and nurturance are deployed in the conduct of crimes, but even in these episodes that "criminalize" feminine characteristics, *SVU* maintains a feminist understanding of sexual assaults. This self-contradictory double-movement comes to the forefront in episodes dealing with female criminality within the family. Episodes with female criminals not only inveigh against feminine characteristics such as nurturance, but also give voice to anxieties about women's power within the domestic sphere. The monstrous maternal storylines show *SVU* grappling with the limits of the detective-cop show genre. In this genre, traditionally associated with masculinity, the vilification of feminine qualities and the association of women with horrific crimes within the family counterbalances the feminist perspective presented in many episode narratives in relation to rape and rape reform. We contend that the cumulative effect of the anti-feminine traits makes the series appear more misogynist rather than feminist.

This new brand of televisual feminism may be spreading to other television genres, particularly those that have not traditionally been understood as "women's" genres (such as the soap opera) and those that have not historically been on the cutting edge of progressive politics (such as the situation comedy). Meanwhile, the new brand of televisual feminism emerging in crime dramas shows a retrenchment of a traditional gendered split between public and private spheres. Crime drama has drifted toward realism, including the inclusion of more and more powerful professional women in the public sphere. *SVU* is no exception. However, its construction of crime and criminals maintains a gender division between public and private spheres. Male criminality is portrayed primarily as an ambiguous, lurking threat from unknown strangers who attack from outside the family. Female criminality is primarily depicted as an insidious interpersonal dysfunction that destroys the family and society from within.

Notes

1. The *Law & Order* franchise pivots on storywriters' ability to cull news stories for ideas about crime and criminality. This "ripped-from-the-headlines" technique provides an aura of newness and contemporaneity. Simultaneously, the news origins of these storylines replicate journalism's reliance on the unique and the exceptional. Special victims units were added to real-world police forces starting in the late 1970s in response to feminist activists who vehemently decried the severe mishandling of all stages of rape investigation. See Fairstein (1993) for an insider's view on these units' functioning.

2. Several characters reprise roles from other series, such as Detective Munch from *Homicide* and Captain Cragen from the original *Law & Order* series. *SVU* relies on and plays on audiences' television archives—memories of past programs and surrounding discourses that frame

their interpretations of programming (Deming, 1992). While the criminals may appear monochromatic, the officers themselves are cast to present an appropriately multicultural rainbow. Ice-T's character had a walk-on role in several episodes of the first season but in the second season Odafin Tutuola became an integral part of the ensemble cast. During an interview with Tavis Smiley, Ice-T exclaimed that only in America can someone who raps about being a cop killer become a police officer in another media outlet. Similarly, B. D. Wong's character began as a recurring figure but was formally included in the fourth season's cast. Monique Jeffries, Alexandra Cabot, Dr. Audrey Jackson, and Dr. Emil Skoda were replaced after the first season by new cast members.

3. Television representations of sexual violence sometimes involve a trial, such as in *L.A. Law;* the crime drama genre generally does not include trials.

4. "Rape camps" refers to specially-designated areas where women are raped systematically during wars by military personnel. While estimates vary, most human rights organizations estimate that at least 20,000 women were raped and tortured during the Bosnia-Herzegovina war. Rape camps are not unique to the former Yugoslavia but have been established in various conflict zones. See Salzman (1998).

5. Feminists say that false rape claims, about two percent of filed charges, are similar to false claims in other crimes.

References

Bal, M. (2001). *Looking in: The art of viewing.* Amsterdam: G & B Arts International.

Beck, M., & Smith, S. J. (2003, May 26). *Lifestyle* (p. D4). Chattanooga Times Free Press.

Benedict, H. (1992). *Virgin or vamp: How the press covers sex crimes.* New York: Oxford University Press.

Brownmiller, S. (1975). *Against our will: Men, women, and rape.* New York: Simon & Schuster.

Collins, P. H. (2005). *Black sexual politics: African Americans, gender, and the new racism.* New York: Routledge.

Creed, B. (1993). *The monstrous-feminine: Film, feminism, psychoanalysis.* New York: Routledge.

Crenshaw, K. W. (1995). Mapping the margins: Intersectionality, identity politics, and violence against women of color. In C. Crenshaw, N. Gotanda, G. Peller, & K. Thomas (Eds.), *Critical race theory: The key writings that formed the movement* (pp. 357–383). New York: The New Press.

Cuklanz, L. M. (1998). The masculine ideal: Prime time representations of rape, 1976–1978. *Critical Studies in Mass Communication, 15,* 423–448.

Cuklanz, L. M. (2000). *Rape on prime time: Television, masculinity, and sexual violence.* Philadelphia: University of Pennsylvania Press.

Davis, A. (1978). Rape, racism, and the capitalist setting. *Black Scholar, 9*(7), 24–30.

Deming, R. (1992). Kate and Allie: New women and audiences' television archives. In L. Spigel & D. Mann (eds.), *Private screenings: Television and the female consumer* (pp. 203–214). Minneapolis, MN: University of Minnesota Press.

Dworkin, A. (1974). *Woman hating.* New York: Dutton.

Fairstein, L. (1993). *Sexual violence: Our war against rape.* New York: William Morrow & Company.

Fidgeon, R. (2003, July 16). Boom or Bust. *Herald Sun,* p. H08.

Gilligan, C. (1982). *In a different voice: Psychological theory and women's development.* Cambridge, MA: Harvard University Press.

Gitlin, T. (1983). *Inside prime time.* New York: Pantheon Books.

Griffin, S. (1986). *Rape, the power of consciousness* (3rd ed.). San Francisco: Harper & Row.

Kaplan, E. A. (1992). *Motherhood and representation: The mother in popular culture and melodrama.* London: Routledge.

MacKinnon, C. (1987). *Feminism unmodified: Discourses on life and law.* Cambridge, MA: Harvard University Press.

Marcus, S. (1992). Fighting bodies, fighting words: A theory and politics of rape prevention. In J. Butler & J. Scott (Eds.), *Feminists theorize the political* (pp. 385–403). New York: Routledge.

Moorti, S. (2002). *Color of rape: Gender and race in television's public spheres.* Albany, NY: State University of New York Press.

Projansky, S. (2001). *Watching rape: Film and television in postfeminist culture.* New York: New York University Press.

Rajan, R. S. (1993). *Real and imagined women: Gender, culture, and postcolonialism.* New York: Routledge.

Salzman, T. (1998). Rape camps as a means of ethnic cleansing: Religious, cultural, and ethical responses to rape victims in the former Yugoslavia. *Human Rights Quarterly, 20,* 348–378.

Sielke, S. (2002). *Reading rape: The rhetoric of sexual violence in American literature and culture, 1790–1990.* Princeton, NJ: Princeton University Press.

Stanley, A. (2005, June 13). Cracking cases (and superiors) with more than good looks. *New York Times,* p. E9.

http://www.joyfulheartfoundation.org

http://www.tvtome.com/lawandorder/svu

Mother of the Year

Kathy Hilton, Lynne Spears, Dina Lohan, and Bad Celebrity Motherhood

Shelley Cobb

"Moms Gone Wild": The Limits of Celebrity and Motherhood

In the August 19, 2007 edition of *The Observer Magazine,* Alice Fisher writes, "The mother/daughter relationship isn't easy, and stardom does little for this delicate bond. Especially when mothers become celebrities off the back of their daughters." In the article, Fisher mentions a series of American and British female celebrities' troubled relationships with their mothers; however, the article focuses on the mothers of a set of intensely famous American young-adult female celebrities who experienced a series of public image meltdowns—arrest, time in jail, alcohol/drug abuse, mental health problems, time in rehab—in 2007: Paris Hilton, Lindsay Lohan, and Britney Spears (I use first names in this chapter as a way of avoiding confusion since I will inevitably refer to various members of the same families). Alongside the ambivalent censure and promotion of these three young women as celebrities in the tabloids and celebrity gossip media outlets (such as magazines *People, Us Weekly, OK,* and *Hello,* as well as online sites such as *TMZ* and *Perez Hilton*) their mothers, Kathy Hilton, Dina Lohan, and Lynne Spears have been strongly criticized in the media for not raising their daughters "well" and for not taking immediate corrective measures when their troubles began. The critiques of the mothers' past and present parenting skills are invariably founded on the public perception of their most egregious crime—pushing their daughters toward celebrity in order to gain celebrity status (and money) for themselves. All three of these mothers have been accused of "cashing in" on their daughters'

From Cobb, S. (2008). Mother of the year: Kathy Hilton, Lynne Spears, Dina Lohan, and bad celebrity motherhood. *Genders, 48.* http://www.genders.org/g48/g48_cobb.html

fame, by starring in their own reality TV shows (Lohan and Hilton) or authoring a book (Spears) thereby capitalizing on their roles as mothers of female celebrities. In these accounts, their apparent selfishness is the manifest sign of their bad motherhood and transgressive femininity, both of which can engender only more of the same in their daughters. . . .

During the Summer/Fall of 2007 *The Observer* article mentioned above was not the only mainstream news media piece in the UK and US to pick up on this refrain within the celebrity news sphere. In June 2007, the actor Jamie Lee Curtis wrote a blog on *The Huffington Post* entitled, "Mom. It's Not Right." She writes, "The sad paths of the three most popular young women— privileged but from varying backgrounds, talented, beautiful and spectacular—have ended in prison, rehab and mental illness. I hope their mothers are worried sick and wondering, 'What could I have done differently?' And our culture should be asking the same question too" (Curtis). In July of 2007 *The New York Times* reported on the mom-bashing of these women in an article titled "Sometimes Mothers Can Do No Right," taking a more balanced approach to mother-blame than Curtis's blog: "No one is saying that parents are blameless when it comes to their children's risky behavior. . . . But the amount of derision directed at mothers seems out of proportion" (Jesella). However, in November of 2007, *Vanity Fair* published an article titled "Moms Gone Wild," which appears to be, though it never states as much, a rebuttal to *The New York Times* piece. The *Vanity Fair* tagline declares, "Sure mothers always get blamed for everything. But—as a look at the women behind Paris, Lindsay, and Britney reveals—if your child is your meal ticket and career booster, it's hard to be the parent she needs" (Newman, 176).

The final phrase of the preceding line points to two cultural issues raised by the widespread critique of the mothers of young female celebrities: first, that a woman's identity as a mother and as a working person are perceived to be mutually exclusive, as opposed to the masculine ideal in which having a job means being a good father; and second, that the mother continues to be seen as the proper primary caregiver and parent to children. The "problem" with Kathy, Dina, and Lynne is that they have made motherhood and career the same thing. Consequently, according to the narrative of bad celebrity motherhood, that means they are not filling the idealized role of the "parent [their daughters] need." The young women's other parent, their fathers, play their part in the narrative by filling three different roles: Rick Hilton rarely materializes in the media, and when he does he appears to be a largely ineffectual former playboy; Michael Lohan has been generally dismissed as a "lost cause" and, more recently, as a religious freak; and Jamie Spears was hardly seen as an element in his daughter Britney's life until January of 2008 when he became conservator of his mentally ill daughter's life and estate, performing the role of father-savior in the narrative of her downfall. All three types of celebrity dads reinforce the narrative of celebrity bad motherhood. However, the cultural desire for the return of the father to save his daughter articulates western culture's ongoing need to control disruptive femininity (in this case signified through both the daughter and mother) through an image of an authoritative but kinder and gentler patriarchy, filling the role of the "parent she needs.". . .

"Spare a Thought": Moralizing Celebrity Motherhood

The public scandals and private problems of Paris, Lindsay, and Britney have been widely reported and thoroughly documented in various popular and celebrity news outlets. In the summer of 2007, their scandals seemed to reach a peak as Paris served a jail term for violating probation for her driving offences, Britney was in the midst of divorce proceedings and gave her mother a letter demanding that Lynne stay away from her young sons, and Lindsay was arrested for drunk driving and possession of narcotics for the third time. Through these episodes, Kathy, Lynne and Dina came under much public, and often vehement, censure for not being good mothers to their daughters. The criticism did not wane throughout the year and went on in to early 2008 for Dina and Lynne.

Dina's reality show, *Living Lohan,* which showcases her younger daughter Ali's initial attempts to secure fame, aired through the Spring of 2008, generally receiving bad reviews. Dina has been criticized for "pimping" Ali to celebrity culture for her own gain. Britney's younger sister Jamie Lynne, who gained her own fame as the eponymous protagonist of Nickelodeon's pre-teen girl power show *Zoey 101*, maintained a good-girl image throughout the early stages of Britney's scandals. In December of 2007, she, and her mother, announced her shock, unwed pregnancy at the age of sixteen—a turn of events that strongly clashed with her star image.

The scrutiny of Lynne increased in January of 2008 when Britney refused to hand over her children after a custody visit, and then locked herself in a bathroom, resulting in her being taken away in an ambulance and put under a psychological hold in hospital. Of all the celebrity magazines *Us Weekly* was most blunt in its blame for the troubles of the Spears daughters. Its December 26, 2007 headline declared, "Destroyed by Mama, Shame on Lynne Spears, Sold Pregnancy for $1 million. Let Jamie Lynn live with Boyfriend. 'She treats her girls like a piggybank'" (*US Weekly*). . . .

Johansson argues that celebrity culture stimulates "debate" about moral and social issues. Within the discourse of celebrity motherhood, there is some debate over the moral and social issues of mothering as a complex individual and communal experience. Most often, the discourse participates in the moralization of motherhood, removing it from any wider social or political debates and placing the responsibility for society's moral character on mothers, keeping within a long western cultural tradition of making women the guardians of society's honor.

I return now to Curtis's *Huffington Post* article as it exemplifies the moralizing of motherhood through female celebrity scandals within the media. That Curtis is a (second generation) celebrity herself as well as a mother, and that she writes in the most visited political blog on the web, only adds weight to her criticism and concern: she is someone who knows about fame, and she is dissecting it in a "serious" news context rather than within an entertainment news context. Curtis writes, "I am in no glass house. I understand only too well the pitfalls of maternal amnesia and denial" (Curtis). However, the piece never evokes her own experience of fame as an actor or what it was like to grow up as a celebrity daughter; instead she invokes only her own motherhood. . . . Moralizing the scandals of Paris, Lindsay, and Britney, she suggests that their stints in jail and rehab are just the celebrity version of what she calls a "national epidemic." For Curtis the troubles of these three young women exemplify a national disease of "omnipotent children running amok or sitting amok as they watch TV and play electronic games and shop on eBay." For her, the problem is over-indulgent "PARENTING."

Significantly though, Curtis speaks directly to and *only* to mothers: "Can we take the wrenching sight of Paris asking her mother, 'Why?' and ask it of ourselves? . . . Wake up, Mothers, and smell the denial

[sic]. . . . Instead of pointing to the cultural and political complexities of contemporary female subjectivity, Curtis speaks down to her audience (mothers) and assumes a stance of moral authority, established through her own success in surviving life in a celebrity "glass house." . . .

On Mothers Day of 2006, the *ivillage* gossip blog posted an entry title[d] "Celebrity Moms from Hell" that began, "While you reflect on the warmth of your mom this Mother's Day, I think you should spare a thought for stars like Jennifer Aniston, Drew Barrymore and Lindsay Lohan, whose mothers ain't exactly June Cleaver" ("Mothers Day"). The post features female stars' mothers who "cash-in" on their daughters' careers for money and/or fame, and asks the users, "Tired of seeing Britney's mom, Lynne, on the red carpet?" Several of the posters respond vehemently like these below:

These are obviously mothers who didn't have their chance at fame so they are doing it through their daughters now ("Mothers Day," post by jacks, May 9, 2006 2:52 PM) [sic].

None of the moms would win any prizes. They are self centered, hangers on. It's sad how many of these parents sell their kids for a buck or two. I would much rather be poor as a church mouse and have my kids love and respect ("Mothers Day," post by PepperAnn60, May 10, 2006 7:51 AM) [sic].

These mothers all have one thing in common, no shame/no pride—it's a pitiful sight for any nice young teenager to want to look up to one of these celeb types. It's really scary the image these mothers and daughters portray. It's not just a shame, it's a disgrace . . . everyone of them ("Mothers Day," post by Scared, May 10, 2006 11:22 PM) [sic].

It is important to note the 2006 date of these entries, as they appeared long before any of Paris's, Britney's, or Lindsay's most serious public scandals. At this time, the narrative of bad celebrity motherhood constructs these women as deficient mothers because they are "hangers on"—in other words, they appear to use their daughters' success to indulge their own desires for fame, money, and access to celebrity spaces (i.e. the media). Writing in 1994, Gamson called these kinds of celebrities "peripherals" and suggested that concern with them by celebrity watchers was atypical. My research on the *ivillage* gossip blog and other celebrity gossip website[s] suggests that this is no longer the case, that at least in the case of mothers who become famous because of their famous daughters, the "disdain toward the 'peripherals'" has become a regular feature in the consumption of celebrity news (Gamson, 165). In Negra's terms, these mothers are attempting to claim their value as subjects in a highly mediated postfeminist culture, in which youth, glamour, and fame have come to dominate the public image of female subjectivity.

The second comment cited above assumes that the mothers do not have their daughters' "love and respect;" which could be guessed at only in the few cases when the female celebrities make public statements about their mothers. The significance in the statement, however, is in its iteration of the ideology of "new momism," which Douglas and Michaels compare to Betty Friedan's well-known articulation of the "feminine mystique," the difference being that "the new momism is not about subservience to men . . . it is about *subservience to children.*" (Douglas and Michaels, 209, emphasis in original). The mothers to whom the post is directed are seen as self-indulgent mothers rather than self-sacrificing mothers—according to the comments. The association of motherhood with self-sacrifice has a long history, but it has become particularly virulent in postfeminist new momism as the discourse elevates and makes examples of those mothers who are perceived not to be prioritizing their children and thus challenging the conviction that motherhood is inherently self-fulfilling and an essentialized form of subjectivity. . . .

"Momagers": Celebrity Mothers/Celebrity Pimps

Three months after Jamie Lynn Spears announced her pregnancy (famously the story was sold to Britain's *OK Magazine*, reportedly by Lynne), *Us Weekly* ran the front page story mentioned above in which Lynne Spears is accused of engineering her daughters' success for her own gain. It suggests that Jamie Lynn's teenage pregnancy was Lynne's fault for "put[ting] her in situations she didn't want to be in [and] letting her live with her boyfriend" while Jamie Lynn was forced into a public life: "[Jamie Lynn] never cared about celebrity . . . she preferred Kentwood [Louisiana]" (*Us Weekly*). Additionally, the article suggests that Lynne forced her youngest daughter to sell her story of teenage pregnancy to *OK* so that her mother could have the money and that, meanwhile, her sister Britney was not told about the pregnancy before the magazine came out because Lynne did not want to lose the exclusive fee. On the *ivillage* gossip blog, one user's response to this news was simply, "Lynn Spears is a Hollywood child pimp" (FireZoey).

Multiple users refer to Kathy, Lynne, and Dina as Hollywood pimps of their own children; others use the familiar term "stage mother." By figuring these women as stage mothers, the users draw on the classed view of childhood beauty pageants as tastelessly sexualizing young girls. Their rebukes

construct the mothers and daughters as inhabiting a transgressive femininity (which evokes inappropriate class behavior) that uses sex to get ahead, situated in opposition to the middle-class femininity that hides and protects its young girls' sexuality (see Karlyn, 77 and Walkerdine).

The classed sexuality of the celebrity stage mothers and their daughters also evokes the insult "white trash" from many of the celebrity blog consumers. On the *ivillage* gossip blog, one user responded to Dina's comment, "Scarlett Johannson goes to clubs and no one cares about it, but if Lindsay goes to a club it's world news!" with the following post: "Both are sad white trash—Dina is a typical example of what's wrong with parenting aka hollywood style–both are well past there use by dates! (sic)" (natalie). The regions of the United States from which the mothers come also corroborate the view of them as white-trash in this discourse. On the celebrity gossip blog *prettyboring.com*, the blogger specifically calls Dina, "Long Island white trash" (prettyboring). Dina and her two youngest children live in North Merrick, Long Island, while the Spears are from a small town in Louisiana. Calling the Spears white-trash draws on the most common stereotype of the term: rural, poor whites of the South.

The term "poor white trash" first appears in the 1830s, and in both the pre– and post– Civil War South referred to whites who were considered lazy, dirty, sexually promiscuous, genetically defective, and inferior to Blacks and Indians. The contemporary stereotype is of the Southern "redneck." Long Island as a signifier of white trash depends on the distinction between "old money" and "new money." North Merrick is on Long Island's south shore, an area defined by working class and "new money" communities; the north shore is known for the old money of the long established New England elite. Long Island white trash conjures an image of the newly rich who join together a lack of cultural capital with the new found status of wealth. The stereotypical image includes those who vulgarly flaunt expensive, gaudy purchases, such as big gold jewelry, clothes, and ostentatious house decorations that lack a "refined" taste. In both cases, white-trash is often most easily summed up in the image of a woman with "uncontrolled" consumption practices, exhibited through sexual promiscuity or "excessive" material goods.

Calling Kathy, Dina, and Lynne—women who currently have substantial access to money—"white trash" succinctly condemns them for perceived inappropriate behavior within the socio-cultural expectations of those who are wealthy and white. For example, the *Vanity Fair* article suggests that "Hilton observers all have their favourite story about Kathy's curious lack of appropriateness," including Kathy's finding humor in Paris's *Saturday Night Live* skit—which made fun of her sex-tape scandal—while attending the taping of the show with Paris's teenage brothers. Clearly, this incident is meant to be understood as an obvious transgression of white, middle-class morality and behavior (Newman, 177). And while Lynne's white-trash credentials seemed to solidify with the announcement of her teenage daughter's pregnancy—a significant failure for a woman who claims to be a Christian at a time in America when conservative Christian values further circumscribe middle-class morality—Dina's white-trash behavioral problems, for many celebrity watchers, are found in her apparent attempts to appropriate the limelight from her children. . . .

Ultimately, the moralizing of race and class implied in the white-trash slur hinges on a need to police inappropriate female behavior. In her article "'Too Close for Comfort': *American Beauty* and the Incest Motif," Kathleen Rowe Karlyn states, "for working-class girls, glamour and sexuality are realistic vehicles toward greater social power, through work or attachment to more powerful men" (Karlyn, 77). The implication is that they "sell" their sexuality in some way whether that is through "marrying up" or through performance as a sexual object. The *Vanity Fair* article "Moms Gone Wild" notes that Kathy Hilton was told to marry for money by her mother, "Big Kathy," who herself married four times. The early-heights of Britney's pop music success caused some cultural consternation as her performance in videos for songs like "Baby One More Time" featured her sexualized school-girl uniform. At the age of seventeen she was playing what Karlyn refers to as the "nymphet," the sexually interested and active young girl who intends to seduce the middle-aged, middle-class male (Karlyn, 72). I would argue that the only thing more threatening to middle-class femininity and "family values" than the nymphet is the nymphet's stage mother. . . .

Class snobbery toward the stage mother remains because of the conflation of middle-class family values with perceptions of appropriate femininity. The soccer moms of the 1990s have [become] the security moms of post-9/11 America, and protecting their children, especially their daughters (whether that be from pedophiles or terrorists), has become the current signifying feature of middle-class motherhood (for more on this topic see Douglas and Michaels, as well as Faludi). A version of this female figure has made headlines again with Republican vice presidential candidate Sarah Palin proudly calling herself a "hockey mom," a figure which, in a convention speech joke, she likened to a bulldog with lipstick. Any suggestion that a mother might not be properly protecting her daughter or, worse, putting her daughter in harm's way, borders on the criminal. The young beauty pageant winner or aspiring child actress has an appearance of availability that implies vulnerability and the idea of a mother acquiring financial or other gains from her child's success appears to parallel the pimp who makes money off of prostitutes. The stage mother is seen to be "pimping" her daughter, as the *ivillage* poster would have it.

It is widely known that both Lynne and Dina have been stage mothers and official managers of their children's show business careers. All of Dina's children are Ford models (Lindsay signed with the agency at the age of three). Britney auditioned for *The All New Mickey Mouse Club* at the age of eight. Kathy Hilton participated in mother-daughter fashion shows with her two young girls in the late 1980s and, according to the author of *House of Hilton* (Oppenheimer), she nicknamed Paris "Star" from infancy and told her that "she would be bigger than Marilyn Monroe, bigger than Princess Di" (Newman, 177). As the *Us Weekly* cover story suggests, the perception is that these mothers have pushed, if not forced, their daughters into show business careers in order to make money off of them, and the gossip blog users suggest that they do so to relive the youths that they gave up to be mothers, making an inappropriate spectacle of themselves and their daughters.

"Bad Karma": Patriarchal Anxiety and Bad Celebrity Motherhood

As 2008 has progressed, the media narratives of Britney, Lindsay, and Paris have transformed from "girls gone wild" to stories of them as young women transformed. What is at stake in the narratives of their "wildness" and subsequent transformations is the transgression and restoration of white, middle-class femininity, as rescued from a vampiric, aging, white-trash matriarchal femininity. Kathy, Lynne, and Dina rarely benefit from their daughters' transformation narratives; Britney, Paris, and Lindsay, have,

respectively, a father, a boyfriend, and a best girl friend who have been given some credit for their "good" behavior (there is not space here to comment on the rumored lesbianism of Lindsay). Still, their mothers maintain a media presence.

In the summer of 2008, two media events involving Kathy Hilton, Dina Lohan and their daughters featured briefly in the mainstream news. The first was John McCain's presidential campaign ad comparing Barack Obama's celebrity status to Paris's and Britney's, thus associating Obama with the public image of the young female celebrities as vacuous and immature. The second was the CNN reporter Anderson Cooper's comment regarding *Living Lohan* while filling in on the *Live with Regis and Kelly* morning talk show. Chagrined at his inability to stop watching the series, Cooper said, "I can't believe I'm wasting my life watching these horrific people." He went on to say, "Then there's this seemingly nice 14-year-old girl, who looks to be about 60. She allegedly wants to be a singer, and/or actress slash performer of some sort, strip tease person, I don't know. I say that with love and concern (sic)" ("Cooper/Lohan"). Paris made her own comic video retort to the McCain ad that has been largely applauded, but which I will not spend time on here.

What I want to note is that both Kathy and Dina responded succinctly and publicly to McCain and Cooper. Kathy responded with a post on *The Huffington Blog*, calling the ad a "frivolous waste of money" (Hilton). Dina responded to Cooper saying, "People are just cruel! . . . This is bad karma for him" (Lohan).

I would argue that the McCain ad and Cooper's comments are expressions (by two representatives of white, middle-class patriarchy), of the cultural anxiety over the availability of individual success within capitalism to "inappropriate" members of American society. McCain's ad is the most pernicious with its further racist implications that Obama's image of black success is also inappropriate. Cooper's comments and his apparent "obsession" with *Living Lohan* exhibit the contradictory impulses in the anxiety over who rightfully has access to privilege in America (contradictions which are not insignificantly exemplified by Cooper's own celebrity heritage as the son of Gloria Vanderbilt).

Unsurprisingly, several blog user comments on Kathy's and Dina's responses suggested that their daughters were only getting what they deserve from more "respectable" members of the public. These comments show that mothers like Kathy, Dina, and Lynne will be closely scrutinized for using their daughters to promote themselves, but that when white men with political and cultural authority use these young women for their own self-promotion, a strong critique of their actions is not forthcoming within the media, except by the mothers of the female celebrities. For contemporary white, middle-class patriarchal society, the value of the discourse of bad celebrity motherhood is the ways in which it works as a distraction from the class prejudice, racism, and sexism that circumscribe the American promotion of capitalist individualism.

References

"Cooper/Lohan." http://www.hollywoodgrind .com/anderson-cooper-hates-living-lohan/ (accessed 5 August 2008).

Curtis, Jamie Lee. "Mom, It's Not Right," *The Huffington Post,* 10 June 2007, http://www .huffingtonpost.com/jamie-lee-curtis/mom-its-not-right_b_51507.html (accessed 18 June 2008).

Douglas, Susan J. and Meredith W. Michaels. *The Mommy Myth: The Idealization of Motherhood and How It Has Undermined All Women.* London: Free Press, 2004.

Faludi, Susan. *The Terror Dream: Fear and Fantasy in Post 9/11 America.* London: Atlantic Books, 2008.

FireZoey. December 26, 2007, 6:34pm; http://dailyblabber.ivillage.com/entrtainment/archives/2007/12/spears-family-friend-says-lynn.html (accessed 1 March 2008).

Gamson, Joshua. *Claims to Fame: Celebrity in Contemporary America.* Berkeley: University of California Press, 1994.

Hilton, Kathy. http://www.huffingtonpost.com/kathy-hilton/mccains-celebrity-adfriv_b_116593.html (accessed 5 August 2008).

Johansson, Sofia. "'Sometimes You Wanna Hate Celebrities': Tabloid Readers and Celebrity Coverage," in *Framing Celebrity: New Directions in Celebrity Culture,* eds. Su Holmes and Sean Redmond, London: Routledge, 2006, 342–358.

Karlyn, Kathleen Rowe. "'Too Close for Comfort': American Beauty and the Incest Motif," *Cinema Journal,* 44, no.1 (Fall 2004), 69–93.

"Letters." http://www.usmagazine.com/britney_spears_legal_love_letter_to_mom (accessed 20 June 2008).

Lohan, Dina. http://dailyblabber.ivillage.com/entertainment/archives/2008/08/dina-lohan-attacks-the-news.html (accessed 5 August 2008).

Moss, Kirby. *The Color of Class: Poor Whites and the Paradox of Privilege.* Philadelphia: University of Pennsylvania, 2003.

"Mothers Day." http://dailyblabber.ivillage.com/entertainment/archives/2006/05/celebrity-moms-from-hell.html (accessed 1 March 2008).

Negra, Diane. *What a Girl Wants? Fantasizing the Reclamation of Self in Postfeminism.* London: Routledge, 2008.

Newman, Judith. "Moms Gone Wild," *Vanity Fair,* November 2007, 176–181.

Oppenheimer, Jerry. *House of Hilton: From Conrad to Paris: A Drama of Wealth, Power, and Privilege.* London: Three Rivers Press, 2007.

Tasker, Yvonne and Diane Negra, eds., *Interrogating Postfeminism: Gender and the Politics of Popular Culture,* Durham, Duke University Press, 2007.

US Weekly online, http://www.usmagazine.com/ lynne_spears_sees_her_girls_as_a_piggy_bank (accessed 1 March 2008).

Walkerdine, Valerie. *Daddy's Girl: Young Girls and Popular Culture,* Cambridge: Harvard University Press, 1997.

More Than Baby Mamas

Black Mothers and Hip-Hop Feminism

Marlo David Azikwe

For nearly two decades scholars, activists and artists have broken new ground in regard to the ways we think about women and hip-hop. Through a number of necessary interventions, these artists and intellectuals have moved from critiquing the popular phallocentric swagger of hip-hop to critiquing this very critique. It is no longer appropriate to simply identify hip-hop as patriarchal and complain that its favorite son, rap music, is misogynist. Instead, our post-soul, post-modern, post-black sensibilities have allowed us to complicate how we situate women within this self-reflexive organism called hip-hop. We understand more about the ways in which black women contribute to the contours and substance of hip-hop culture. The 1980s and early 1990s produced Roxanne Shante's groundbreaking raps and Queen Latifah's Kente-adorned embodiment of the Strong Black Woman, while the late nineties and new century have given way to what Imani Perry calls [the] rise of the "sexy MC," such as Lil' Kim and Eve.[1] Despite the individual critiques that each of these artists have garnered, they together represent two generations of women in hip hop who have carved a space for black women to vocalize their independence, sexual agency and lyrical mastery.

In response, early hip-hop critics from Tricia Rose, Nancy Guevara and Cheryl L. Keyes, as well as relative new-jacks such as Joan Morgan, Imani Perry and Gwendolyn Pough have explored the ways in which black women create a progressive, feminist space within hip-hop's hyper-masculine universe.* They intervene on behalf of complexity in order to analyze black women's embrace of hip-hop identity. They sharply critique the misogyny, violence and materialism of hip-hop. Meanwhile, they also show how black women navigate the conflicting, inconsistent gray areas of hip-hop to stand up and be heard. Each of these voices, often in harmony and discord with traditional black feminist theory,

From Azikwe, M. D. (2007). More than baby mamas: Black mothers and hip-hop feminism. In G. D. Plough, E. Richardson, A. Durham, & R. Raimist (Eds.), *Home girls make some noise: Hip hop feminism anthology* (pp. 345–367). Mira Loma, CA: Parker.

*See references for selected critical readings [Ed.].

contribute to what we can now confidently call hip-hop feminism. This is a feminism that can read sexual objectification *and* agency within the same artist or textual production. It articulates the racial and sexual tensions experienced by round-the-way sistas, ghetto princesses, college students and club hoppers through the vernacular ideology of hip-hop. While our black feminist foremothers such as Barbara Smith, Barbara Christian and Michelle Wallace fought to put race and gender on the table together in order to liberate black women from a myriad of oppressions, hip-hop feminists have argued that there are realities that traditional black feminists overlook. Hip-hop feminists offer a response to a contemporary backlash against feminism among young, intelligent, progressive black women. Joan Morgan, therefore, describes a new-school desire for a functional feminism

> that possesses the same fundamental understanding held by any true student of hip-hop. Truth can't be found in the voice of any one rapper but in the juxtaposition of many. The keys that unlock the riches of contemporary black female identity . . . lie at the magical intersection where those contrary voices meet.[2]

At the intersection of those contrary voices, female hip-hop artists have addressed major feminist issues: sexual agency, domestic violence and sexual assault, female economic survival, empowerment and the strength and beauty of black women. However, the hip-hop community has neglected one key aspect of black feminist theory—discourses on motherhood. Since the Moynihan Report was issued in 1965, pathologizing black matriarchy, black feminists have sought to redefine racist and sexist notions that construct black motherhood for the dominant society. These women were compelled to action not only because Moynihan misread the lives of black American women, but also because

the implications of his "research" cleared the way for decades of violent and demoralizing public policy toward black people. In order to bring these issues to the forefront, black feminists had to distinguish themselves from their white counterparts, whose feminism sought gender equality without concern for the entanglements of other oppressions. Womanists, such as Alice Walker and Sherley Anne Williams, began to articulate a desire to synchronize group survival and women's issues into a personal politics that women could use.[3] Among their concerns were the real and imagined intricacies of black motherhood. With that brief feminist history in mind, I am interested in where issues of motherhood and procreative power stand among young women today. As far as hip-hop culture is concerned, there seem to be few popular female rappers who speak openly about their procreative lives and choices. Few portray mothers in music videos or even rhyme about procreative issues affecting the black women they represent. Furthermore, scholars and journalists who write about hip-hop and gender politics do not often address how black women navigate this highly charged political space.

This is not to say that mothering—and its attendant procreative issues such as abortion, fertility, birth control, pregnancy and child rearing—does not receive attention in hip-hop. There are a number of "mama" narratives popular in the music. Think of the strong black mother trope best remembered in Tupac's "Dear Mama" or the cautionary teen mom genre exemplified in Slick Rick's "All Alone" or another Tupac classic, "Brenda's Got a Baby." While these narratives are significant, they often work to objectify the subject position of mother. Mothers are alternatively honored or pitied. Rarely does rap music offer the chance to examine how women perceive themselves as mothers or as potential mothers, nor is there much attention paid to the intense political implications of that subjectivity.

Political rhetoric as well as legislative and legal activity surrounding social welfare, education, criminal justice and health care in the United States remains highly enmeshed with the fact of black motherhood. Moreover, medical and political technologies conjoin to manipulate not only the physical bodies of black women but also the cultural intelligibility of motherhood at all. Patricia Hill Collins notes in *Black Feminist Thought:* "African-American women's experiences as mothers have been shaped by the dominant group's efforts to harness Black women's sexuality and fertility to a system of capitalist exploitation."[4] Certainly, this has been the case in terms of the use and abuse of black women for the purpose of reproducing a slave labor force in early American history. Yet Collins' insight begs for further application within contemporary U.S. society. Black women are no longer baby machines for a plantation economy, but what about a prison economy or a low-wage welfare economy? Post-slavery regulation of black women's fertility has been, in effect, one of the major tools with which capitalist class relations have been maintained.[5] How does the dominant society manipulate the sign of the black mother in order to subdue, fix and rank groups and bodies . . . ? How can black women reclaim control of the images that are used to perpetuate a neo-slave existence? It is with these "real-world" applications that this inquiry attempts to engage. Therefore, the consideration of black women's procreative power has implications beyond my personal attraction to the issue as a black feminist scholar and mother. These issues, in fact, should be central for any individuals who align themselves with progressive struggle and social justice in the academy and beyond. What I am interested in developing are ways of reading the procreative performativity of black women and their bodies, as they are presented to us through hip-hop. . . .

I am concerned that while many black women hip-hop artists strive to assert sexual freedom, they do not attend with as much vigor to the related issue of the mothering body and how that subject position is exploited to continue to oppress all black people. Women asserting sexual freedom and agency through the language of hip-hop often trade upon patriarchal notions of the female body as weak, vulnerable and ripe for exploitation, rather than strong, confident and in control. Lauryn Hill, I will argue, flips this script and refuses to trade in the masculine narratives and metaphors to make her claims to power. Instead, much of her early work draws upon feminist language to assert mastery of her life and procreative body. Hip-hop feminists must recognize how black mothering continues to be manipulated and provide new narratives of empowerment for women; otherwise our hopes for reproductive freedom and social justice will continue to fall short of the transformative potential held within hip-hop music and culture. . . .

Reading hip-hop culture is a messy business. While we must resist simplistic readings that force us to assess what is good or bad, positive or negative for the black community, it is also possible and desirable to understand how hip-hop disrupts racist, sexist, classist and homophobic discourses that are par for the course in American culture. This is not to remove all ethical judgment from hip-hop criticism. There are aspects of hip-hop that are sexist, misogynist, homophobic, racist and exploitative. . . . Hip-hop feminist critique makes space for the gray areas, the ironies, and contradictions that are part of hip-hop and life, but it should also provide a way out of the mire of postmodern detachment to invite women and men to get down to the business of "bringing wreck" against the social forces that control their lives. . . .

Lauryn Hill: Killing Them, Softly

Lauryn Hill, as a member of The Fugees and as a solo artist, has always stood her ground among the legions of male MCs. She consistently ranks among the upper echelon of the tightest rappers to ever hold a mic, and she has maintained that control through a carefully mixed blend of conscious lyrics, undeniable flow, reggae/dub influence and R&B foundations. Unlike her female contemporaries who often defer to the power of masculinity to carve out space of empowerment for female hip-hop audiences, Hill has maintained a strident feminist stance against the hyper-masculine aesthetics that dominate the industry. . . .

Lauryn Hill has offered her subjectivity as a mother to articulate a sense of possibility and empowerment for women. Her song "To Zion," a melismatic, stirring ode to her newborn son Zion, stands as her most direct testament to motherhood. I will discuss this song in the context of Hill's own comments about the song and how it describes her struggles with having a son. Beyond that, however, I will highlight a few other textual moments made before and shortly after Hill became a mother that suggest that she seeks to empower the female body, not as a sexy gangsta, but for its "female" attributes. For Lauryn Hill, being a woman is not a curse, it is a blessing. . . .

"To Zion" is Hill's meditation on her procreative choice to have a child at the pinnacle of her artistic career. Through the confessional narrative style that has been a signature of her writing, Hill explains to her audience how she felt when she found out that she was pregnant. For Hill, her bodily experience of pregnancy initially "overwhelmed" her. Like many women who discover that they are pregnant, Hill expresses the deep sense of apprehension she feels towards the function her body had "been chosen to perform." However, she comes to see the experience as a blessing, an opportunity to bring forth "an angel" and "a man-child." Through these lines, Hill participates in a reversal of the descriptions of female embodiment expressed by her

contemporaries Eve and Missy Elliott. Hill's body, her "belly," is a space of hope and generosity. She does not see her body as necessarily vulnerable nor does she express a desire to use her body in order to entice or entrap the man in her life. She dwells on her personal connection with her body and the possibilities that it holds within. She remains future oriented and positive. She furthers her hip-hop feminist narrative as she explains the choice she makes to become a mother at such a young age. As she describes her "crazy circumstance," Hill chronicles the daunting decision of whether to continue her pregnancy or to terminate it. Hill had just come off of the success of The Fugees' CD *The Score* and was in the process of embarking on her solo career. She was young and still in college. With all of these demands, it may have seemed to her, as it does to many women, that she could not handle the added physical and emotional responsibility of a baby. Hill clearly understands that she has access to procreative choice, what she describes as a choice between her "head" or her "heart." Regardless of how she characterizes this choice, she embraces the fact that there is a choice to be made. Then, despite legitimate concerns for her career, she chooses motherhood, not as a replacement for her career, but as another aspect of her life. She seems to recognize the inherent difficulty for women facing this choice, but she seems to argue for working through the struggle.[6]

Finally, Lauryn Hill intervenes within hip-hop discourse on motherhood by simply articulating the power of the maternal figure for group survival. Taking on a womanist perspective, Hill reminds her listeners that her reasons for rapping and singing have as much to do with personal fulfillment as they do with providing narratives of black empowerment through her work. She rhymes in the song "Everything is Everything": "Let's love ourselves and we can't fail." The lyrics of this song indicate a desire to promote love and progress to her audiences. Hill wants to be a catalyst for a "better situation," which can be read as better schools, better health-care, better jobs and better opportunities for black people. Hill argues for self-love as the fail-safe method toward empowerment. She then expresses her future orientation, which relies on the power of "our seeds." Seeds, within [the] hip-hop lexicon, refers to children. Therefore, Hill's claim that "our seeds will grow" does not refer only to a metaphorical seed, but rather literally to children. In other words, Hill sees black children as the potential for progressive change within black communities. Her final admonition—"all we need is dedication"— suggests that dedication to black children represents collective struggle.[7]

Lauryn Hill does not describe this devotion toward children as a space of weakness or vulnerability. She also does not sentimentalize this notion. While her vocals in "To Zion" certainly exhibit a tender side to Hill's perceptions of mothering, her lyrics in "Everything is Everything" shows that she does not sentimentalize the political implications of mothering. She also critiques systems that work to oppress black children and adopts the lyrical hyperbole of gunplay to designate her commitment to her cause. For example, in "Lost Ones," she rhymes that she "Can't take a threat to my new-born son." Hill, who refers to herself as L-Boogie in this song, adopts the rhetoric of the civil rights struggle to illustrate her commitment to her son, the seed for the new future, within the first two lines of this verse. Hill explains that she is both down for non-violent and armed struggle depending on the situation. Threats to her "new-born son" are of the highest order, calling for the more violent response.[8]

Taken as a whole, lyrics from a number of songs by Lauryn Hill reflect an intense attention to motherhood as a legitimate contribution to the intersecting struggle for racial and gender equality. Her attention is reflected in at least three ways. First, she defends the power of the female body in and of itself against male and female rappers who render that body vulnerable and exploitable. Importantly, Hill also addresses the power of procreative choice in her song "To Zion." In this R&B song, Hill sings about the difficulty she faced in making this decision and how she ultimately finds another avenue to empowerment via the subject position of mother. Finally, Hill places mothering and children within the framework of the collective struggle for justice. She takes the stance of the revolutionary—armed if necessary who will fight against the dominant social structures designed to take advantage of black children.

Conclusion

. . . What I hope is clear is that there is room at the table for black feminists, womanists and hip-hop feminists to address the representations of black motherhood and their importance to our communities. I would love to see more women artists, especially those blessed with mainstream and popular audiences, to bring these issues to light. When Lauryn Hill sings "if I ruled the world, I'd free all my sons," she attends to the emotional desire for a mother to see her own children free and speaks the reality that so many of our "sons"—and daughters—are locked up. The life and music of the multitextual entity of Lauryn Hill offers new narratives for young black women to relate to and explore feminism.

My desire to embark on this project emerges not out of an effort to reclaim black domesticity and respectability or to add to the debates between conscious and gangsta lyricists, but out of a personal interest in what it means to be a black woman steeped in hip-hop and a mother in the twenty-first century. It means that the bedtime story I tell my sons is as likely to be Slick Rick's morality tale from 1988

("Children's Story") as anything by Hans Christian Anderson or the Brothers Grimm. It means that while I still love the music and the metaphors of hip-hop, I struggle to train my boys into men, not knuckleheads, ruffnecks or gangstas. And ultimately, it mean[s] walking the precarious line between raising the hope for generations to come—those black diamonds and pearls that Lauryn Hill sings about—or contributing to the cadre of workers/neo-slaves for a burgeoning U.S. prison and low-wage welfare economy that seeks to entrap our children within its snares. Therefore, I am arguing for a more nuanced and conscious use of hip-hop feminism, because in many cases our lives depend on it. By situating black procreative power and mothering as a theoretical space worth exploring—by contextualizing it historically as well as within its contemporary manifestations—those of us within hip-hop feminist discourse can continue to probe the possibilities and limits of the culture as a revolutionary genre.

Notes

1. Imani Perry, *Prophets of the Hood: Politics and Poetics in Hip Hop* (Durham: Duke University Press, 2004), 155.

2. Joan Morgan, *When Chickenheads Come Home to Roost: A Hip Hop Feminist Breaks It Down* (New York: Simon & Schuster, 1999), 62.

3. Sherley Anne Williams, "Some Implications of Womanist Theory," *African American Literary Theory: A Reader.* Ed. Winston Napier. (New York: New York University Press, 2000), 219.

4. Patricia Hill Collins, *Black Feminist Thought: Knowledge, Consciousness, and the Politics of Empowerment* (New York: Routledge, 2000), 50.

5. Ibid., 51.

6. The Original Hip-hop Lyrics Archive. http://www.ohhla.com/all.html. (6 January 2006)

7. Ibid.

8. Ibid.

References

Bost, Suzanne. "'Be deceived if ya wanna be foolish'; (Re)Constructing Body: Genre and Gender in Feminist Rap." *Postmodern Culture.* 12.1, 1–31.

Collins, Patricia Hill. *Black Feminist Thought: Knowledge, Consciousness and the Politics of Empowerment.* New York: Routledge, 2000.

Doyle, Laura. *Bordering on the Body: The Racial Matrix of Modern Fiction and Culture.* New York: Oxford University Press, 1994.

Keyes, Cheryl L. "'We're More than a Novelty, Boys': Strategies of Female Rappers in the Rap Music Tradition." *Feminist Messages: Coding in Women's Folk Culture.* Ed. Joan Newlon Radner. Urbana: University of Illinois Press, 1993. 203–19.

Missy Elliot. Internet, http://www.missy-elliott.com/

Morgan, Joan. *When Chickenheads Come Home to Roost: A Hip-Hop Feminist Breaks It Down.* New York: Simon & Schuster, 1999.

Moynihan, D. *The Negro Family: A Case for National Action.* Washington, D.C.: Government Printing Office, 1965.

Perry, Imani. *Prophets of the Hood: Polities and Poetics in Hip-Hop.* Durham: Duke University Press, 2004.

Potter, Russell A. *Spectacular Vernaculars: Hip-Hop and the Politics of Postmodernism.* Albany: State University of New York Press, 1995.

Pough, Gwendolyn D. *Check It While I Wreck It: Black Womanhood, Hip-Hop Culture, and the Public Sphere.* Boston: Northeastern University Press, 2004.

Rose, Tricia. *Black Noise: Rap Music and Black Culture in Contemporary America.* Hanover: Wesleyan University Press, 1994.

The Original Hip-Hop Lyrics Archive. Internet. http://www.ohhla.com/all.html.

Wallace, Michele. "When Black Feminism Faces the Music, and the Music is Rap." *The New York Times* 29 July 1990, sec. 2:20.

Williams, Sherley Anne. "Some Implications of Womanist Theory." *African American Literary Theory: A Reader.* Ed. Winston Napier. New York: New York University Press, 2000.

Discography

Elliott, Missy. "Momniy." *The Cookbook.* Atlantic Records, 2005.

———. "Work It." *Under Construction.* Electra, 2002.

Eve. "Heaven Only Knows." *Let There Be Eve . . . Ruff Ryders' First Lady.* Interscope Records, 1999.

———. "Love is Blind." *Let There Be Eve . . . Ruff Ryders' First Lady.* Interscope Records, 1999.

———. "Who's That Girl?" *Scorpion.* Interscope Records, 2001.

Hill, Lauryn. "Everything is Everything." *The Miseducation of Lauryn Hill.* Ruffhouse Records, 1998.

———. "Lost Ones." *Miseducation of Lauryn Hill.* Ruffhouse Records, 1998.

———. "To Zion." *The Miseducation of Lauryn Hill.* Ruffhouse Records, 1998.

Ol' Dirty Bastard, Raekwon and Method Man. "Raw Hide." *Return to the 36 Chambers.* Electra, 1995.

Poor Righteous Teachers. "Shakiyla." *Holy Intellect.* Profile, 1990.

Queen Latifah and Monie Love. "Ladies First." *All Hail the Queen.* Tommy Boy, 1989.

Nas and Lauryn Hill. "If I Ruled the World." *It Was Written.* Sony, 1996.

Slick Rick. "All Alone (No One to Be With)." *Behind Bars.* Def Jam, 1994.

———. "Children's Story." *Great Adventures of Slick Rick.* Def Jam, 1988.

The Fugees. "Ready or Not." *The Score.* Sony, 1996.

Tupac. "Brenda's Got a Baby." *2Pacalypse Now.* Jive, 1992.

———. "Dear Mania." *Me Against the World.* Jive, 1995.

Political Culture Jamming

The Dissident Humor of *The Daily Show With Jon Stewart*

Jamie Warner

Armed with branding techniques honed and perfected in the commercial marketplace, politicians and political parties have attempted to drown out dissident messages to better "sell" their own political policies, a dagger in the heart of deliberative democrats who argue that democracy cannot survive without open, ongoing, and rational political conversation. In fact, much of contemporary democratic theory rests on two propositions: (a) the public sphere is populated with multiple and disparate voices who can and will engage each other, and (b) these conversations will be rational. Jürgen Habermas's (1962/1989) *The Structural Transformation of the Public Sphere* is perhaps the most important of the recent statements of this position (Habermas, 1973/1975, 1998; see also Bennett & Entman, 2001; Carey, 1989; White, 1995). Indeed, many scholars posit some version of accessible, public, substantive, rational conversations among numerous and diverse participants as *the* prerequisite for a healthy democracy. . . .

Political elites and their consultants have no such concerns. Rather than fretting over possible barriers confronting marginal voices, politicians instead want their voices, agenda, and framing of issues to crowd out divergent voices because such dominant status helps contribute to the success of their specific political agendas (Lakoff, 2002, 2004). In the past two decades, politicians have increasingly utilized what are known as "branding" techniques of commercial marketers to just such an end, in the hopes of persuading the citizen/consumer to trust their "product"—their platform and policy positions—to the exclusion of all others. These branding techniques, relying on emotional rather than rational appeals, are used in the attempt to achieve automatic, unreflective trust in the branded product, whether that product is a Popsicle, a Palm Pilot, or a political party. Although such brand hegemony is obviously profitable in terms of money and/or power

From Warner, J. (2007). Political culture jamming: The dissident humor of *The Daily Show With Jon Stewart*. *Popular Communications, 5*(1), 17–36. Reprinted by permission of Taylor & Francis Ltd.

for the hegemon, it works to the detriment of the tenets of democratic theory, both by talking over viable voices and conversations in the public sphere, and by operating through calculated emotional appeals. How, in the name of the healthy democracy described previously, can one *disrupt* the transmission of the dominant political brand messages so that competing conversations can occur?

One intriguing model comes from the same realm as the original branding techniques, the media saturated world of consumer capitalism, where an insurgent movement known as "culture jamming" is at the forefront of this type of disruption. Culture jammers are a loose collection of media activists who are rebelling against the hegemony of the messages promoting global capitalism. Spearheaded by media activist Kalle Lasn of the Media Foundation and his *Adbusters* magazine, culture jammers utilize a wide variety of tactics to destabilize and challenge the dominant messages of multinational corporations and consumer capitalism. Rather than simply using factual information, rational argumentation, legal language, and traditional political tactics to oppose capitalist institutions directly, culture jamming turns the commercial techniques of image and emotion back on themselves through acts of what Christine Harold (2004) calls "rhetorical sabotage" (p. 190).

As politicians and political parties increasingly utilize the branding techniques of commercial marketers to "sell" their political agendas, it follows that similar jamming techniques could be employed to call those branding techniques into question. In this chapter, I argue that the comedian Jon Stewart and his fake news program, *The Daily Show with Jon Stewart,* act as *political* culture jammers. Through their own humorous version of news parody, *The Daily Show* writers and comedians disseminate dissident interpretations of current political events, potentially jamming the transmission of the dominant political brand message. Like other culture jammers, *The Daily Show* subversively employs emotional and aesthetic modalities similar to those employed by political branding itself, thus interrupting it from within. Unlike many culture jammers, however, *The Daily Show*'s reliance on a humorous version of parody means that they can add their voices to the conversation in a seemingly innocuous way. (After all, it is *just* a joke.) . . .

The Fetish of Political Branding

See, in my line of work you got to keep repeating things over and over and over again for the truth to sink in, to kind of catapult the propaganda. (George W. Bush, quoted in Froomkin, 2005)

. . . The basic assumption behind branding is simple: Consumers are not "rational" shoppers. Instead, they are busy people, possessing neither the time nor the inclination to do detailed comparisons of sneakers, sunglasses, or fabric softeners. This time crunch creates an opening for marketers. Knowing that many consumers cannot or will not do research based on quality and/or price, marketers instead strive to cultivate a *relationship* with consumers that inspires loyalty for that particular brand. Trust in a particular brand allows the consumer to take a time-saving shortcut at the supermarket or mall, as well as get the supposed value, and, hopefully, the status that marketers strive to attach to the brand. Thus, the key to establishing this lucrative connection with consumers is through the play of emotion, rather than the dissemination of information: "Marketing is no longer about selling. It's about creating relationships with customers that cultivate an emotional preference for your brand" (Travis, 2000, cited in Hiebert, 2001; see also Gobe, 2001, 2002). The particular relationship to be cultivated with consumers depends on the type of image that marketers believe will best sell their product to its target demographic: dependable, practical, good value for the price, safe, or the much coveted yet ever elusive "cool."

Politicians and their political consultants have fully embraced the logic and tactics of branding in the political arena. Although the normative value of the migration of these marketing tactics into the political sphere, via the media, has been widely disputed, its efficacy has not, at least from the point of view of the politicians themselves (Newman, 1999). It is obvious why parties and politicians would see brand loyalty as a desirable outcome. Citizens, like consumers, are busy people, and cultivating trust in the "Republican" or "Democratic" brand works to save the citizen/consumer time, in the form of information costs, while providing the politician or party a solid base of support. Many of the same branding techniques used to sell soap and MP3 players are exploited for political gain, including market research techniques, the proliferation of emotional messages across various media through the use of sound bites and talking points, and repetition/saturation strategies within each medium. In addition to creating a sense of familiarity, an important part of building trust, repetition of carefully researched emotional messages (e.g., talking points) helps locate a party or politician as one of the "top of mind" or "dominant" brands—the first or, hopefully, the only brand that comes to mind in response to a particular stimulus (Carter, 1999, cited in Karlberg, 2002, p. 7). The ultimate goal in political branding is the same as in commercial branding: the creation of such unquestioning trust in the brand that the citizen/consumer allows the brand [to] do the "thinking" for him or her.

Culture Jamming

How does one call these very effective branding techniques into question, so that alternative voices can get into the conversation? The success of global consumer capitalism and the marketing techniques that go with it, specifically the branding techniques mentioned previously, have spurred many internal and external critiques and rebellions, often lumped together under the term culture jamming (e.g., Klein, 2000, 2002; Roddick, 1994; Talen, 2003). Current culture jammers, such as media activist Kalle Lasn, place themselves on a "revolutionary continuum" with anarchists, Dadaists, surrealists, the Situationists, the Sixties hippie movement, and early punk rockers, among others (Lasn, 1999, p. 99; see also Dery, 1993). According to Lasn, the primary goal of culture jammers is *détournement,* a French term borrowed from the Situationists of the 1950s and 1960s. Translated literally as a "turning around," Lasn (1999) defines the concept of *détournement* as "a perspective-jarring turnabout in your everyday life" (p. xvii), which is instigated by "rerouting spectacular images, environments, ambiences and events to reverse or subvert their meaning, thus reclaiming them" (p. 103).

Specifically, Lasn and his fellow culture jammers want to reverse, subvert, and reclaim our identity as brand-trusting pawns of consumer capitalism. For example, Lasn's Web site (www.adbusters.org) constantly runs multiple ongoing antibrand campaigns, and these do utilize traditional, rational techniques such as boycotts and petition drives against heavily branded corporations such as Nike and Tommy Hilfiger. However, *Adbusters* is perhaps best known for its attempts to jam the dominant brand images with alternative images, what Lasn calls subvertisements. These images use the same branding technologies and design layouts that advertisers do, with a problematizing twist: "A well produced print 'subvertisement' mimics the look and feel of the target ad, prompting the classic double-take as viewers realize what they're seeing is the very opposite of what they expected" (Lasn, 1999, p. 131). Successful *Adbuster* subvertisments include those parodying alcohol, cigarettes, and the fast food industry, as well as the fashion establishment.

One of *Adbusters'* best-known subvertisements revolved around the Calvin Klein *Obsession* ads of the 1990s. The original and very successful print ads for the perfume featured close-ups of young, beautiful, tan, taut bodies with the words "Obsession for Men" or "Obsession for Women" across the top of the ad. Exploiting what Lasn calls "leverage points" or logical contradictions in the underlying logic of consumer capitalism, *Adbusters* attacks Calvin Klein, not with facts and figures demonstrating how the empty quest to buy beauty and status is dangerous, but instead with perverted mirror images (1999, p. 130). . . .

In what follows, I argue that *The Daily Show with Jon Stewart* functions as what I call "political culture jamming" by working in much the same way: disseminating dissident images with messages designed to provoke the same type of *détournement* or subversion of the dominant meaning that Lasn and his fellow culture jammers seek. . . .

Political Culture Jamming: *The Daily Show with Jon Stewart*

In January 2004, the Pew Research Center for the People and the Press released the results of a survey designed to discover where Americans get their political news. One of the most interesting findings involved a relatively new phenomenon: 21% of those 18–29 regularly learned about the presidential campaign and its candidates on comedy programs (compared with 23% who said they regularly learned this information from network news). Overall, 50% of the 18–29 demographic said that they at least "sometimes" learn about the campaign from these shows, compared with 27% of the 30–49 demographic and 12% of people 50 and older. . . .

One of the most popular of these comedy shows—with an estimated 1.3 million viewers per night—is *The Daily Show with Jon Stewart,* a 30-min "newscast" that airs Monday through Thursday at 11:00 p.m. EST on the cable network *Comedy Central* (Hall, 2005). . . .

The Daily Show is a funny and often sharply critical parody of a television news broadcast; the entire cast is made of up of comedians. In fact, in his videotaped acceptance of the Television Critics Association Award, Stewart recommended that one of the other, legitimate nominees, *60 Minutes* perhaps, should investigate how a *fake* news program won the award for "Outstanding Achievement in News and Information" (Kurtz, 2003). It is this seeming lack of seriousness within the serious format of a cable/network news broadcast, however, that makes *The Daily Show* both a popular and a cogent critic. Like the *Adbuster* subvertisements, *The Daily Show* inserts its voice into the political conversation by plagiarizing the aesthetics of the media, in this particular case, the news media. It is a copy, but a copy that has been strategically altered to highlight political "leverage points": factual errors, logical contradictions, and incongruities in the dominant political brand messages and the media that disseminates them.

MATTER OUT OF PLACE: PARODIC FORMAT

The first political culture jamming technique employed by *The Daily Show* is a metatechnique, one that most explicitly resembles the aesthetics of the *Adbusters'* subvertisements discussed previously: news parody format. This twisted mimicking of the newscast format is the first and most important jamming technique and the entire show makes sense only within this format. Just as the subversive parody of the *Obsession* ad must closely approximate the actual ad to be effective, the news parody must closely resemble an actual news television broadcast, and *The Daily Show* does. The anchor, Jon Stewart, presents the top stories of the day, complete with the video over his right shoulder, and conducts interviews. Correspondents, many of whom are now becoming celebrities in their own right, do segments and interviews on current events. Watching the show with the volume turned down might not alert you to the fact that this is anything other than one of the myriad news options now available. Turning the volume up should let you in on the secret. Here Stewart is interviewing "senior media analyst" Stephen Colbert about the media coverage of the U.S. invasion of Iraq in March 2003:[1]

Stewart: What should the media's role be in covering the war?

Colbert: Very simply, the media's role should be the accurate and objective description of the hellacious ass-whomping we're handing the Iraqis.

Stewart: Hellacious ass-whomping? Now to me, that sounds pretty subjective.

Colbert: Are you saying it's not an ass-whomping, Jon? I suppose you could call it an "ass-kicking" or an "ass-handing-to." Unless, of course, you love Hitler.

Stewart: [stammering] I don't love Hitler.

Colbert: Spoken like a true Hitler-lover.

Stewart: I'm perplexed. Is your position that there's no place for negative words or even thoughts in the media?

Colbert: Not at all, Jon. Doubts can happen to everyone, including me. But as a responsible journalist, I've taken my doubts, fears, moral compass, conscience, and all-pervading skepticism about the very nature of this war and simply placed them in this empty Altoids box. [Produces box] That's where they'll stay, safe and sound, until Iraq is liberated. (Miller, 2003)

This is obviously not a typical network or cable news interview. . . .

What are the consequences of choosing to intentionally misuse the newscast format? Parodying the sober and seemingly impartial language and layout of a newscast gives the content an air of legitimacy and respectability. This seemingly weighty format then allows an automatic contrast with the humorous content—out of which incongruity, a prerequisite for most humor, can flow.[2] . . .

MATTER OUT OF TIME: STRATEGIC USE OF VIDEO

The mimicking of the news format at a metalevel, however, is a necessary but not sufficient condition for the specific political culture jamming of *The Daily Show*. There is nothing inherently subversive about parody, which can just as easily be employed in the service of the dominant political message as in the critique of that message. Within the larger parodic format of the show, however, *The Daily Show* also presents the political content in a way that calls into question the *substantive* claims of the dominant brand message, as well as the media that unproblematically disseminates it.

The second technique employed by *The Daily Show*—the strategic use of video clips—thus works inside the meta-technique of the news parody. Similar to the parodic format of the show, the use of video is designed to disrupt the dominant political message by presenting various types of "matter out of time" using video clips. As previously stated, there is usually one video screen above Stewart's right shoulder just as there is on network and cable news shows. Often Stewart will turn his head and talk to the video clips, stopping the video to pose questions and make comments. . . . Stewart's own comments provide the matter that is out of time; news anchors do not usually interject such comments during "serious" news programs. . . . However, the most effective way *The Daily Show* uses video is to strategically juxtapose video clips to highlight leverage points. . . . The branding techniques are exposed as orchestrated techniques and so can be examined explicitly and critically, rather than operating in the background where they are most successful. . . .

Technically, the audience is left to draw their own conclusions, although those conclusions are channeled in a certain direction by the specific sequence of video, as the following 2003 segment demonstrates:

Stewart:	. . . When you combine the new mandate that criticizing the Commander in Chief is off limits in wartime with last year's official disbanding of the Democratic Party, we're left at the all time low in the good old fashion debate category. Now I know you're thinking: But Jon, every time I want to have a calm, honest discussion about these kinds of issues, I'm shouted down and harassed by the Dixie Chicks and their ilk. Well, tonight it all changes. . . . So first, joining us tonight is George W. Bush, the

43rd President of the United States. . . . Taking the other side, from the year 2000, Texas Governor and presidential candidate, George W. Bush.

(Split screen of Governor Bush on the left and President Bush on the right. "Bush vs. Bush" logo between them.)

Stewart:	Mr. President, you won the coin toss. The first question will go to you. Why is the United States of America using its power to change governments in foreign countries?
President Bush:	We must stand up for our security and for the permanent rights and the hopes of mankind.
Stewart:	Well, certainly that represents a bold new doctrine in foreign policy, Mr. President. Governor Bush, do you agree with that?
Governor Bush:	Yeah, I'm not so sure that the role of the United States is to go around the world and say, "This is the way it's gotta be."
Stewart:	Well, that's interesting. That's a difference of opinion, and certainly that's what this country is about, differences of opinion. Mr. President, let me just get specific: Why are we in Iraq?
President Bush:	We will be changing the regime of Iraq for the good of the Iraqi people.

Stewart: Governor, then I'd like to hear your response on that.

Governor Bush: If we're an arrogant nation, they'll resent us. I think one way for us to end up being viewed as the ugly American is to go around the world saying, "We do it this way, so should you." . . . ("Bush vs. Bush," n.d.)

Again, Stewart makes no direct comment, simply presenting the matter out of time and allowing the audience to decide how to interpret this information. Is this an example of the notorious flip-flopping [of George W. Bush]? Or does this simply represent a wise policy change due to 9/11? Stewart does not say. He simply presides over the clips. Although Stewart will often alternate looking pained or amused, as the videos are playing, rarely does he directly offer his own opinion on the video clips. By customarily adhering to this tactic, *The Daily Show* manages to stay suggestive rather than didactic, provocative rather than sermonizing or moralizing.

DIALECTICS THAT MATTER: STEWART'S SOCRATIC INTERVIEW STYLE

. . . Although the interview is a common technique used on television news broadcasts, Stewart often employs what is called "Socratic irony" as a rhetorical tactic to point out incongruities, inconsistencies, and internal contradictions in the interviewee's argument, without directly offering his own opinion, as well as without appearing confrontational. In the Platonic dialogues, Socrates routinely adopted an ignorant or tentative tone, asking simple and direct questions to his often dense interlocutors, with the seemingly innocent goal of getting to the "truth." However, his questions were

neither simple nor innocent, and Socrates would use his interlocutors' answers to suggest that they should not be quite so confident in their assertions, as well as to make his own substantive points (Colebrook, 2002, p. 87; see also Seery, 1990; Vlastos, 1991). In addition, Socrates' self-effacing demeanor and rather halting comments add to the perception of his sincerity, a mode of personal presentation that Stewart also utilizes.

Discussing the public's perception of the war in Iraq in the summer of 2005 with "senior military analyst" Stephen Colbert, Stewart, like Socrates, plays the straight man, strategically setting up the interviewee to make the substantive point for him:

Stewart: . . . When the Vice President says that the insurgency is in its last throes and Donald Rumsfeld says that that could mean 12 years, isn't that contradictory?

Colbert: Well, Jon, as a member of the cynical, knee-jerk reaction media, liberal, Ivy League, Taxachusetts elite, I can see how you would find a discrepancy between the words "last throes" and "12-year insurgency." But your mistake is looking at what's happening in Iraq on a human scale. The Administration is looking at it from a *geological* perspective. After all, it took a billion years for the earth to cool . . . ("Administrative Discrepancies," n.d.)

Here Stewart plays the calm, polite voice of reason to Colbert's vastly overstated and thus comical position. Like Socrates in the Platonic dialogues, he is *just* asking questions. . . .

By feigning ignorance and constantly insisting that *The Daily Show* is only for laughs, Stewart can operate stealthily.

Unlike his culture jamming counterparts who are openly hostile to consumer capitalism and use the violent language of revolution in their fight to be heard, Stewart's self-effacing humor fosters both a sense of trust with those interviewed on the show and a sense of camaraderie with the audience. Further, any attempts by those who were the butt of the joke to attack *The Daily Show*'s credibility could easily falter, as Stewart would be the first one to agree that he is stupid and that the show means nothing. After all, it is *just* a joke.[3] Criticizing *The Daily Show* could come close to admitting that one had no sense of humor, something nobody, especially a politician, would be eager to admit. Employing this Socratic stance—one of Socrates' most famous quotations is "All I know is that I know nothing"—Stewart can create a dissident message that raises questions about both the dominant political and media brands (Colebrook, 2002, p. 87).

Notes

1. Colbert [who now has his own spinoff show: Ed.] is also senior war correspondent, senior religious correspondent, senior UN analyst, senior White House correspondent, senior psychology correspondent, senior "death" correspondent (for stories that report on the death penalty), and senior child molestation expert (for stories on the Catholic Church).

2. George Test (1991) calls this technique the "irony of misused form" (p. 169). For a detailed discussion of the role of incongruity in humor, see Morreall (1987).

3. In his book chronicling the "new political television" of comedians Bill Maher, Dennis Miller, and Jon Stewart, Jeffrey Jones (2005) argues that Stewart's persona is like that of the court jester or fool, speaking truth to power without fear of retaliation because he has the ability to make everyone laugh.

References

Administrative discrepancies. (n.d.). *The Daily Show with Jon Stewart*. Retrieved October 2, 2005, from http://www.comedycentral.com/shows/the_daily_show/videos/stephen_colbert_index.jhtml

Bauder, D. (2004, February 29). Stewart delivers news to younger viewers. *The Associated Press*. Retrieved October 19, 2005, from http://www.washingtonpost.com/wp-dyn/articles/AI6704–2004Feb29.html

Baym, G. (2005). *The Daily Show*: Discursive integration and the reinvention of political journalism. *Political Communication, 22,* 259–276.

Bennett, W. L., & Entman, R. (Eds.). (2001). *Mediated politics: Communication in the future of democracy*. New York: Cambridge University Press.

Bush vs. Bush. (n.d.). *The Daily Show with Jon Stewart*. Retrieved August 8, 2004, from http://www.comedycentral.com/tv_shows/thedailyshowwithjonstewart/videos_corr.jhtml?startIndex=25 &p=stewart

Carey, J. (1989). *Communication as culture: Essays on media and society*. Boston: Unwin Hyman.

Colebrook, C. (2002). *Irony in the works of philosophy*. Lincoln: University of Nebraska Press.

Dery, M. (1993). *Culture jamming: Hacking, slashing and sniping in the empire of the signs*. Westfield, NJ: Open Pamphlet Series.

Froomkin, D. (2005, May 25). The ostrich approach. *Washington Post*. Retrieved August 10, 2005, from http://www.washingtonpost.com/wp-dyn/content/blog/2005/05/25/BL2005052501250.html

Gobe, M. (2001). *Emotional branding: The new paradigm for connecting brands to people*. New York: Allworth.

Gobe, M. (2002). *Citizen brand: 10 commandments for transforming brands in a consumer democracy*. New York: Allworth.

Habermas, J. (1975). *Legitimation crisis* (T. McCarthy, Trans.). Boston: Beacon. (Original work published 1973)

Habermas, J. (1989). *The structural transformation of the public sphere: An inquiry into a category of bourgeois society* (T. Burger, Trans.). Cambridge, MA: MIT University Press. (Original work published 1962)

Habermas, J. (1998). *Between facts and norms: Contributions to a discourse theory of law and democracy* (W. Rehg, Trans.). Cambridge, MA: MIT Press.

Hall, S. (2005). Colbert's "Daily Show" Spinoff. *Eonline.* Retrieved April 15, 2006, from http://www.eonline.com/News/Items/0,1,16481,00.html

Harold, C. (2004). Pranking rhetoric: "Culture jamming" as media activism. *Critical Studies in Media Communication, 21,* 189–211.

Hiebert, R. (2001). Review of *Emotional branding: How successful brands gain the irrational edge* and *Adbusters: Journal of the mental environment. Public Relations Review, 27,* 244–245.

Jones, J. (2005). *Entertaining politics: New political television and civic culture.* New York: Rowman & Littlefield.

Karlberg, M. (2002). Partisan branding and media spectacle: Implications for democratic communication. *Democratic Communique, 18,* 1–21.

Klein, N. (2000). *No logo.* New York: Picador.

Klein, N. (2002). *Fences and windows: Dispatches from the front lines of the globalization debate.* New York: Picador.

Kurtz, H. (2003, July 27). No holds barred: Alternative news outlets smack down convention coverage. *The Washington Post,* p. C1. Retrieved October 15, 2005, from LexisNexis database.

Lakoff, G. (2002). *Moral politics: How liberals and conservatives think* (2nd ed.). Chicago: University of Chicago Press.

Lakoff, G. (2004). *Don't think of an elephant!* White River Junction, VT: Chelsea Green.

Lasn, K. (1999). *Culture jam: How to reverse America's suicidal consumer binge—and why we must.* New York: Quill.

Miller, L. (2003, April 8). TV's boldest new show. Retrieved August 8, 2004, from http://archive.salon.com/ent/tv/feature/2003/04/08stewart/index_np.html

Morreall, J. (1987). *The philosophy of laughter and humor.* Albany: State University of New York.

Newman, B. (1999). *Handbook of political marketing.* Thousand Oaks, CA: Sage.

Roddick, A. (1994). *Body and soul: Profits with principles—The amazing success story of Anita Roddick & The Body Shop.* Pittsburgh, PA: Three Rivers Press.

Seery, J. (1990). *Political returns: Irony in politics and theory, from Plato to the antinuclear movement.* Boulder, CO: Westview.

Talen, B. (2003). *What should I do if Reverend Billy is in my store?* New York: New Press.

Test, G. (1991). *Satire: Spirit and art.* Tampa: University of South Florida Press.

Vlastos, G. (1991). *Socrates: Ironist and moral philosopher.* Cambridge, UK: Cambridge University Press.

White, S. (Ed.). (1995). *The Cambridge companion to Habermas.* Cambridge, UK: Cambridge University Press.

Educating *The Simpsons*

Teaching Queer Representations in Contemporary Visual Media

Gilad Padva

The visual media, mainly popular films and TV programs, offer an excellent tool for high school and university educators to encourage sexual tolerance, and in particular to promote a supportive attitude towards queer students. . . . I have selected "Homer's Phobia" as a case study here because of the significant popularity of this Emmy Award–winning 15th episode of the *Simpsons'* 8th season, aired on February 16, 1997. . . . I offer a scholarly counter-cultural analysis of this episode in regard to its politics of sexuality and gay-straight alliance, and to its visualized socio-linguistic strategies of subverting homophobia and sissy-phobia. . . .

Queering the Simpsons

. . . The popular subgenre of *animated* TV sitcoms in the late 1990s and 2000s . . . integrates semi-anarchistic humor and spectacular imagery that often challenge conventional ethnic, social, gender *and* sexual patterns of representation. This subgenre includes, for example, *Beavis & Butthead, King of the Hill, Daria, Family Guy, The Kid,* and *The Simpsons. The Simpsons,* in particular, is one of the world's most successful American television exports, syndicated in over 60 countries since 1991 (Chocano, 2001). In its imaginative, disruptive, and even surrealistic way, this subgenre often criticizes conservatism, bigotry, and prejudice with humor. . . .

Jonathan Gray (2003) suggests that *The Simpsons* has turned on its family sitcom brethren, situating its action within an anti-suburb that is depicted as xenophobic, provincial, and

From Padva, G. (2008). Educating *The Simpsons:* Teaching queer representations in contemporary visual media. *Journal of LGBT Youth, 5*(3), 57–73.

narrow-minded. Brilliantly parodying the traditional family sitcom neighborhood, *The Simpsons'* town of Springfield satirizes and challenges rather than extols the American Dream. This series criticizes the hypocrisy within the American educational system, religious, political, and even economic systems (Tingleff, 1998). Notably, through Bart, Homer, and Grandpa, *The Simpsons* even challenges categories of male sexuality. Sam Tingleff notes that the relationship between the vicious, albeit decrepit Mr. Burns, who owns the local nuclear plant, and his younger assistant Smithers, is a consistent attack on male sexual norms. Smithers' loyalty comes not from monetary desires, but his quasi-sexual attraction towards Mr. Burns.

Furthermore, the males of *The Simpsons* challenge categories of male sexuality and demonstrate its flexibility. For instance, Homer shaves his "bikini zone" for a presumed swimsuit competition; he kisses his secretary Carl (voice of the gay icon Harvey Fierstein) on the lips, and later mistakenly calls his wife "Carl" in bed; his favorite song is "It's Raining Men"; and he says Oliver North was "just poured into that uniform." And in one episode, when Grandpa Simpson can't take his pills, the elder turns into a woman, later accepting flowers and a date from a male suitor (Tingleff, 1998). Moreover, when Lenny, Homer's co-worker, is dying, he sees a heaven full of Carls. On the other hand, Homer suggests that Lisa could win a class election over Nelson by starting a rumor that he's gay. And when a Gay Pride parade passes the Simpson's house, Homer disapproves of his dog's attempt to hook up with an effeminate, leather-clad dog.

In the gay classic episode "Homer Phobia" (written by Ron Hauge and directed by Mike B. Anderson, 1997), the Simpsons befriend "John," a mustachioed kitsch trader (resembling and voiced by the cult filmmaker and gay icon John Waters). The fact that he is gay makes Homer fear his potential effect on Bart. After a series of ridiculous attempts to turn Bart into a "real man" (and consequent arguments with his wife Marge), Homer assures his son that his love for him is unconditional, whether he is straight or gay.

The anti-homophobic contribution of this episode to the empowerment of GLBT young viewers is based on its three political premises: celebrating queer counter-culture, embracing straight-gay alliance, and promoting diversity and multiculturalism.

Celebrating Queer Counter-Culture

The Simpsons' friendship with John starts during their visit to the latter's "Cockamamie's" antique store. Marge tries to sell Grandma's Civil War doll to John in order to pay an exorbitant Springfield Gas Company bill. John tells her that the doll is nothing but a Johnny Reb bottle from the early 1970s. Homer counters that it's still better than the junk that John is selling, and he wonders how a grown man can love a nostalgic box or a toy. John replies: "It's camp! The tragically ludicrous? The ludicrously tragic?" Eventually, Homer invites John over to see their home, which is "full of valuable worthless crap." John is delighted.

Camp is defined in the *Oxford Dictionary* (1996) as "Affected, theatrically exaggerated; effeminate; homosexual." Susan Sontag (1999 [1964]) categorically defined camp as a vision of the world in terms of a particular kind of style.

> It is the love of the exaggerated, the "off," of things-being-what-they-are-not . . . The androgyne is certainly one of the great images of Camp sensibility . . . What is most beautiful in virile men is something feminine; what is most beautiful in feminine women is something masculine. (p. 56)

Jack Babuscio identified camp with queer subculture based on *gay* sensibility "as a creative energy reflecting a consciousness that is different from the mainstream; a heightened awareness of certain human complications of feeling that spring from the fact of social oppression" (1999 [1978], pp. 117–18). . . .

The *Simpsons* episode's visual vocabulary is dominated by camp. For instance, John wears flamboyant, striped shirts from the 1970s and his store contains many telling artifacts: Godzilla toy, piggy bank, pink flamingo (echoing John Water[s]'s eponymous cult film), a statue of an Easter Island native head, cola bottle, floral wall decoration, etc. All these items are highly camp, as they are related to kitsch, extravagance, "good" bad taste, artificiality, style, and retrostyle, and also to feminine or "girly" behavior, demonstrated in John's clothing choices and his coy intonation and gestures.

Ironically, John finds the Simpsons extremely camp. He is thrilled by the corn-printed curtain in their kitchen, the color scheme, the rabbit ears antenna, the Hi-C soft drink and Lisa's necklace ("Pearls on a little girl! It's a fairy tale!"). Homer asks him if his records have camp value, and John flatters him: "You yourself are worth a bundle, Homer! Why I could wrap a bow around you and slap on a price tag." Homer laughs and starts dancing with John to an Alicia Bridges disco record ("I Love the Nightlife"). Marge comments that Homer has "certainly taken a shine to him."

The next morning, Homer decides to invite John and his wife over for drinks. But Marge does not think John is married. In fact, she tells Homer that "John is a ho-mo-sexual" (adopting the apparently scientific/medical definition). In response, Homer shouts hysterically.

Soon afterwards, Homer sees Bart wearing a Hawaiian shirt, choosing a pink cake over a brown one and dancing to Cher's "Shoop Shoop Song (It's In His Kiss)," wearing a large black wig with a pink bow. Bart's drag show is traumatic for his father. No confusion is allowed over his child's sexual identity and orientation (two concepts Homer repeatedly mixes up). Homer

suspects that his son is gay, not because Bart is attracted to boys, but because he does not behave manly enough. Homer sees Bart's dance, not as innocent child's play, but as a *camp* performance, identified (even in Homer's presumably straight mind) with "transvestite" gay identity, and therefore, as extremely, "problematic." He consequently resolves to "normalize" his son. . . .

While Homer is threatened by John's (homo)sexuality and its "effeminizing" influence on Bart, the female protagonists—wife Marge, their individualistic pre-adolescent daughter Lisa, and baby Maggie—sympathize with their new friend. Marge, in particular, likes gossiping with John, who demonstrates his impressive knowledge of celebrities' secret lives, and she adores him for his sense of humor, creativity, friendship, stylishness and delicacy. These qualities are contrasted to her husband's stupidity, egocentricity, misbehavior, clumsiness and machismo. It is no wonder that Marge immediately becomes John's best (female) friend, his devoted "fag hag."

Embracing Straight-Gay Alliance

The term "fag hag" dates back to the United States in the late 1960s, dismissively directed at women who were considered not attractive enough to socialize with "real men." But like so many derogatory terms, it was reclaimed in the 1990s as a stereotypic term to be worn with pride. In the ideal, gay men introduced their female friends into a world free from sexual harassment, where the emphasis was on fun and where, more often than not, they would find themselves the center of flattering and unthreatening attention. Hence, "[F]ag haggery was in fashion" (Button, 2000, p. 46). . . .

Marge's "sistership" with John is a bonding between a straight woman and a gay man who enjoys his own stylishness, neatness and effeminacy. In contrast to many straight men *and* some sissy-phobic gay men,

John celebrates rather than mocks male femininity, sissiness and stylishness. He and Marge share "feminine" insights and feelings in a friendship that signifies an alternative, equal and respectful relationship between a man and a woman in conservative small Springfield.

After Bart points a giant, phallic and colorful plastic pistol at him, Homer's worry becomes stronger. He suspects that his wife is ignoring John's malicious homosexualization of Bart, and he makes foolish attempts to save his son from gayness. For instance, he forces his Bart to look at a huge sexist advertising billboard, showing two female models in bathing suits smoking cigarettes; after a long look at the models, Bart only (homo)erotically wishes for "anything slim."

Homer decides that if he is to turn the boy into a man, Bart will need manhood and virility in his environment. During their visit to the local steel mill, Roscoe, the muscular and mustachioed manager, asks the ultravirile, muscular workers to say hello to the Simpsons. In response, they wave effeminately, "Hello-o." Homer wonders if the whole world has gone insane, watching a slender worker running-in-place while his mate theatrically slaps his back: "Stand still, there's a spark in your hair!" and the worker replies: "Get it! Get it!" Then a tanned bodybuilder in hot pants walks past Homer holding a vat of hot steel and announcing "Hot stuff, comin' through!,"—a phrase that echoes gay pornography. Roscoe states, "We work hard. We play hard" and pulls a chain. Surprisingly, a high-tech disco ball descends and the entire mill turns into a nightclub called "The Anvil," with flickering spotlights, smoke effects, dance floors, mustachioed body builders, and muscular young men at work, proudly exposing their torsos. All the workers dance to "Everybody Dance Now," except Homer, who is in shock and leaves this male-only enclave, shading Bart's eyes.

Edmund White (2000 [1980]), in his discussion of the political vocabulary of homosexuality, notes that in the past, feminization, at least to a small and symbolic degree, seemed a necessary initiation into gay life. Today, almost the opposite seems to be true. Many gay men sport beards, army fatigues, work boots, etc. They build up their bodies or are "busy arraying themselves in these castoffs and becoming cowboys, truckers, telephone line-men, football players (in appearance and sometimes also in reality)" (p. 192). In this way, the ultra-virile spectacle at the gay steel mill can be perceived as a high-camp drag show. . . .

Earl Jackson (1995) suggests that a truly subversive gay representational practice must contest not only the gay subject's experience of heterosexist persecution, but also his experience of patriarchal privilege. He notes that certain gay male cultural practices that transvalue deviance as a positive mode of self-identification contain at least an implicit critique of the normative male ideal (and the dominant heterosexual sex/gender system) from which the gay male deviates. Sam Fussell (1999 [1994]) contends that even apparently straight male bodybuilding signs a *reversal* of sex roles, with the bodybuilder taking a traditionally female role: body as object. Further, Fussell observes, "whether it be beefcake or cheesecake, it's still cake . . ." (p. 46).

David Halperin (1995) contends that gay muscles, in particular, deliberately flaunt the visual norms of straight masculinity, which impose discretion on masculine self-display and require that straight male beauty exhibit itself only casually or inadvertently. Brian Pronger (2000) also contends that gay muscles, commercialized as they are, have at least one significant character of drag performances: they are ironic. "Musculature," he notes, "within a gay ironic sensibility signifies the *subversion* of patriarchal power by acting as homoerotic *enticements* to other men" (pp. 689–690).

Homer is not only surprised by the muscular men's queerness. He is also astonished by their proud cultural identity: their dress (and undress), language ("Hot stuff, comin' through!"), behavior (dancing and having fun), and mood (happy), which contradict his image of gays as low-life, dubious and miserable people. This lively discotheque is a demonstration of power, as it presents an alternative culture, part of an alternative camp lifestyle. Homer feels threatened by the spectacular: "This is a nightmare! You're all sick!" He pathologizes gayness as deviation from the "natural" order. Camp, as a queer counter-cultural political praxis, uses its innovative and inspirational deviancy to contest the oppressive social order. This deviation is also political because camp reflects an aesthetic and ethical refusal to be visually hetero-normalized or silenced by dominance (Meyer, 1994; Padva, 2000).

Promoting Diversity and Multiculturalism

Homer's phobia primarily derived from ignorance. His negative reaction towards the gay workers/clubbers is caused by guilt for what he considers his son's deviancy. Pointedly, Homer is not demonized. From this perspective, not only gays but also straight Homer are victims of the same oppressive "natural" sexual order that stigmatizes and discriminates against sexual minorities and imposes restricting hetero-masculine codes of visibility, behavior and sexual expression on men. Although he does not recognize it, Homer too transgresses the (hetero)sexual representational regime, by wearing Hawaiian shirts, dancing with another man, etc.

Homer wonders how it could be possible that a gay son has developed in a straight family. As Eve Kosofsky Sedgwick pointed out (1990), the double-edged potential for injury in the scene of gay coming out results partly from the fact that the erotic identity of the person who receives the disclosure is also apt to be implicated in, and hence perturbed by, it.

In an earlier scene, Homer blames Marge for being "too feminine around the boy" and she replies that if there is actually a problem with Bart worth worrying over, it must be that he's not spending time with his dad. But Homer's own transgressive masculinity might be implicated in his son's suspected homosexuality.

Michael Kimmel (2001) contends that homophobia is a central organizing principle of our cultural definition of manhood. He suggests that homophobia is more than the irrational fear of gay men, more than the fear that straights might be perceived as gay men. David Leverentz (1986) points out that the word "faggot" has nothing to do with homosexual experience or even with fear of homosexuals. Rather, it arises from the depths of manhood: a label of ultimate contempt for anyone who seems sissy, untough, uncool.

Homer, horrified by the gay steel mill/dance club, decides to socialize his son into the hetero-masculine world through a male brotherhood that putatively includes himself, the paranoid local bar-owner Moe, and the town's notorious drunk Bernie—three unappealing male role models. When Bart hears about his dad's plan to go hunting with him and his friends, he whispers: "Something about a bunch of guys alone together in the woods . . . seems kinda gay." The three (straight and narrow) losers get drunk and fall asleep near the bonfire. Homer is shown gently and compassionately holding his sleeping son. Desperate to provide Bart with an animal to kill, the hunting group breaks into a reindeer pen. Homer orders him to shoot a reindeer after Bernie has assured him (ironically) that shooting a reindeer is like killing a beautiful man. Suddenly, the deer attack the unwelcome guests, who are rescued at the last moment by John's Japanese Santa Claus robot.

John has earned Homer's gratitude: "Hey, we owe this guy, and I don't want you calling him a sissy. This guy's a fruit, and a . . . no, wait, wait, wait: queer, queer, queer! That's what you like to be called, right?" and John wittily replies, "Well, that or John." Lisa remarks that this is about as tolerant as her dad gets, so John should be flattered. Here, language demonstrates the change that has occurred in Homer's thinking, when he agrees to use the other's terminology as a sign of respect.

The word "queer," as Cherry Smith (1996) points out, defines a strategy, an attitude, a reference to other identities, and a new self-understanding. "Both in culture and politics," Smith notes, "queer articulates a radical questioning of social and cultural norms, notions of gender, reproductive sexuality and the family" (p. 280).

Embracing the idea of unconditional love, Homer tells Bart in the final scene that he loves him because he is his son, gay or not. Bart looks quite surprised to be identified by his parent as gay, before he has recognized *himself* to be gay. This presents the whole identification process as questionable and contradicts Homer's (and some of the viewers') fixation over gender roles and sexual identities.

The hit song "Everybody Dance Now" (associated with the disco in the steel mill) forms the sound track for the final scene, as John's car drives off and Bart's face is shown in increasing close-ups, matching the rhythm and lyrics, "I've got the power." The makers of the "Homer Phobia" episode dedicated it to the steelworkers of America and, winking, exhorted them to "Keep reaching for that rainbow," metaphorically liberating their hyper-masculine territory from its monologic perception.

This episode's multicultural perspective, embracing diversity and open-mindedness, is based on universal ideas of freedom, liberty, equality, justice, tolerance, solidarity and compassion. The outwardly naive medium of animation here mediates sexual pluralism through (unexpected) comic situations that parody homophobia rather than homosexuals. The creators have knowingly encoded many gay expressions (e.g., "Dad, you are the living end!"), erotic innuendos (e.g., the gay steel workers' dance club is called "The Anvil"), intertextual hints (e.g., Homer recalls the hit song "It's Raining Men"; and John's car beeper plays Judy Garland's "Somewhere Over the Rainbow"). Although straight audiences too enjoy this episode, its hyperbolic scenes particularly empower gay viewers, who likely identify the linguistic maneuvers and decode the queer meanings. In "Homer's Phobia"'s Utopian vision, homophobia is just a phase; the hysterical drama queens are primarily Homer and his bigoted straight friends; and an amplified machismo is as theatrical as a flamboyant drag show.

References

Babuscio, J. (1978). The cinema of camp (aka Camp and the gay sensibility). *Gay Sunshine Journal*, 35; reprinted in Cleto, F. (Ed.). (1999). *Camp: Queer aesthetics and the performing subject* (pp. 117–135). Edinburgh: Edinburgh University Press.

Button, S. (2000). Best friends. *Attitude* 75 (July 2000), 46–48.

Chocano, C. (2001). Matt Groening. *Salon*. Retrieved April 2, 2005, from hitp://www.salon.com/people/bc/2001/01/30/groening/print.html

Fussell, S. (1994). Bodybuilder americanus. In Goldstein, L. (Ed.), (1999). *The male body: Features, destinies, exposures* (pp. 43–60). Ann Arbor: The University of Michigan Press.

Gray, J. (2003). *Imagining America: The Simpsons and the anti-suburb go global*. Paper presented at Communication in Borderlands: The 53rd Annual Conference of the International Communication Association, San Diego, California, USA. May 23–27.

Halperin, D. (1995). *Saint Foucault: Towards a gay hagiography*. New York: Oxford University Press.

Jackson, E., Jr. (1995). *Strategies of deviance: Studies in gay male representation*. Bloomington: Indiana University Press.

Kimmel, M. (2001). Masculinity as homophobia: Fear, shame, and silence in the construction of gender identity. In Whitehead, S. M. &

Barrett, F. J. (Eds.), *The masculinities reader* (pp. 266–287). Cambridge: Oxford and Malden, MA: Polity.

Leverentz, D. (1986). Manhood, humiliation and public life: Some stories. *Southwest Review,* 71.

Meyer, M. (1994). Introduction: Reclaiming the discourse of camp. In *The politics and poetics of camp* (pp. 1–23). London and New York: Routledge.

The Oxford Dictionary. (1996). Oxford and New York: Oxford University Press.

Padva, G. (2000). *Priscilla* fights back: The politicization of camp subculture. *Journal of Communication Inquiry,* 24(2), 216–243.

Pronger, B. (2000). Physical culture. In Haggerty, G. (Ed.), *Gay histories and cultures: An encyclopedia* (pp. 688–690). New York: Garland Publishing.

Sedgwick, E. K. (1990). *Epistemology of the closet.* Berkeley and Los Angeles: University of California Press.

The Simpsons (1997). Homer Phobia. Created by M. Groening; episode written by R. Hauge; directed by M. Anderson. Distributed by Gracie Films in association with 20th Century Fox Television: retrieved on June 22, 2008, from http://www.snpp.com/epidoses/4F11 .html

Smith, C. (1996). What is this thing called queer? In Morton, D. (Ed.), *The material queer: A lesbigay cultural studies reader* (pp. 227–285). Boulder, Colorado and Oxford: Westview Press.

Sontag, S. (1964). Notes on camp. *Partisan Review,* 31(4), 515–530; reprinted in Cleto, F. (Ed.), *Camp: Queer aesthetics and the performing subject* (pp. 53–65). Edinburgh: Edinburgh University Press.

Szalacha, L. (2004). Educating teachers on LGBTQ issues: A review of research and program evaluations. *Journal of Gay & Lesbian Issues in Education* 1(4), 67–79.

Tingleff, S. (1998). "I will not expose the ignorance of the faculty": *The Simpsons* as a critique of consumer culture. *The Simpsons Archive.* Retrieved on April 2, 2005, from http://www.snpp.com/olher/papers/st.paper .html

White, E. (1980). The political vocabulary of homosexuality. In Michaels, L. & Ricks, C. (Eds.), *The state of the language* (pp. 235–246). Berkeley and Los Angeles: University of California Press; reprinted in Burke, L., Crowley, T. & Girvin, A. (Eds.), *The Routledge language and cultural theory reader* (pp. 189–196). London and New York: Routledge.

"Sexy Like a Girl and Horny Like a Boy"

Contemporary Gay "Western" Narratives About Gay Asian Men

Chong-suk Han

. . . . In this chapter, I analyze the *Advocate* and *OUT* magazines from 2005, employing methods of critical discourse analysis (CDA), 'a neo-Marxist turn to the study of discourse which examines language and its usage to understand their social and political import' (Park, 2005: 11), in order to examine how images of gay Asian men are constructed and maintained within larger Western gay narratives. I argue that the response of mainstream 'gay' publications has been to marginalize gay Asian men by simply ignoring their existence or employing existing stereotypes about Asian men in general, thereby maintaining 'gay' as largely a 'white' category and relegating gay Asian men to the margins of the gay 'community.' By looking at mainstream gay publications and the way these publications marginalize gay Asian men, I hope to add another dimension to Bérubé's (2001) argument of how 'gay stays white.' More generally, I hope to contribute to the literature on the intersection of race and sexuality and how these intersections contribute to the development of various identities among multiply marginalized groups. . . .

Given the inherent power dynamics in the creation and dissemination of media images, it is not surprising to find that representations of the 'East' have a long and lurid history in the Western imagination. Through various historical periods, Asian men have routinely been portrayed as meek houseboys, asexual deviants, or domestic servants who fill 'female' roles when women are scarce (Hamamoto, 1994). It is clear that taken as a whole, these stereotypical images have worked to construct Asian men (and women) as fundamentally foreign, threatening, and perhaps most importantly, as inferior to white men (and women).

From Han, C.-S. (2008). 'Sexy like a girl and horny like a boy': Contemporary gay 'Western' narratives about gay Asian men. *Critical Sociology, 34*(6), 829–850.

For Asian men, both in the USA and abroad, stereotypes have often taken on an explicit sexual tone (Eng, 2001) as the need to ease the twin fears of the growing 'yellow peril' and miscegenation came crashing into the need to justify Western imperial thrusts into Asian territories (Lee, R., 1999). In addition, as Lowe (1996: 11) points out, 'racialization along the legal axis of definitions of citizenship has also ascribed "gender" to the Asian American subject.' Denied the ability to become citizens, the scarcity of Asian women, rigid laws barring miscegenation, and labor laws barring Asian men from the more 'masculine' trades reserved for white men, Asian men took on a decidedly feminine aura in the Western imagination.

While it is true that there have been competing images of Asian men, as Fung (1996) points out, even the 'masculine' images of Asian men have been desexualized in American media. As Nguyen Hoang points out:

Despite the recent critical attention and popularity of Asian male actors in Asian cinema and its successful crossover into Hollywood (represented by such actors as Jackie Chan, Jet Li, and Chow Yun Fat, and directors such as Ang Lee and John Woo), the representation of Asian men as sexually appealing scarcely figures into mainstream American popular culture. (Hoang, 2004: 225)

As such, even Asian 'action' heroes who are highly sexual in Asian films are desexed for the American market. A stark example is in the movie 'Romeo Must Die,' where Jet Li spends the entirety of the movie 'negotiating' a romantic affair with Aalyiah. However, the two are never shown engaging in any real act of romance. The omission of any 'real' romantic interlude between Li and Aalyiah is in stark contradiction to the normal action hero narrative when the hero virtually always ends up with the leading female character.

Clearly, all forms of media produce and reproduce inequality to varying degrees and by extension are sites of contested identity formation. Yet while narratives from novels and images on screens are often perceived to be 'fictional,' there continues to be a strong belief that narratives found in newspapers and magazines are 'factual,' and reflective of an objective 'reality.' While the 'official' goal of journalism is to provide an objective truth, in reality, journalism is a site of storytelling whereby a subjective version of reality is actually presented (Dahlgren, 1992; Storey, 1996). In fact:

[Journalistic] texts foster specific ways of seeing the world, hinder other ways, and even structure specific ways of relating to the text itself. The net outcome could in many cases be judged as ideological; that is, the ways of seeing [serve] certain social interests at the expense of others, while at the same time appearing to be neutral and natural. (Dahlgren, 1992: 13)

The subjective storytelling found in 'journalistic' pieces reinforces social inequalities by '[fostering] such feelings of collective belonging—based on class, gender, sexual preference, subcultural lifestyle or whatever' (Dahlgren, 1992: 17). On the flip side, they also foster feelings of marginalization and non-belonging along the same basis as they foster collectivism. In this way, journalistic text defines who belongs in certain categories and what that membership entails. It also works to highlight what/who is valued, and how we should think about those who are not included or valued. Given 'journalism's centrality in politics and culture, as well as its vested economic and occupational interests, [these] make questions regarding its boundaries, uses and contingencies of more than idle concern' (Dahlgren, 1992). Rather, it becomes critical to examine the role that journalism plays in maintaining and promoting social inequality by exposing journalistic practices that add to further marginalization of sub-altern groups. . . .

Where Are All the Gay Asian Men?

Looking at gay media, it is evidently clear that the strategy deployed by gay publications to maintain white male privilege is one of exclusion. Asian men, and other men of color, rarely appear as subjects of a story and are rarely represented as contributors to the debates. As such, gay print media often speaks only to white men. Advertising that 'targets' the gay community is often no better. Ads that feature white men seem to be marketing to them, while ads that feature Asian men seem to be marketing them as commodities. The invisibility of Asian men in gay media is most evident between the pages of *The Advocate,* the largest gay and lesbian news magazine in the USA.

As Bérubé (2001) would expect, gay Asian men (and other gay men of color) are virtually non-existent within the pages of *The Advocate.* During the entire year [2005], gay Asian men were the subjects of one feature story, ironically enough, about the invisibility of gay Asian men in the larger gay community. The images and narratives about gay Asian men that do make it between the covers are a reflection of their 'place' within the larger gay community, marginal members at best, commodified objects at worst. . . .

Issue 943 (July 19) of *The Advocate* featured a gay Asian man on the cover of the magazine, making him the only Asian person, man or woman, to appear on the cover of *The Advocate* in 2005. Voice-over actor James Sie, featured with his partner, musician Douglas Wood, was featured as a part of the magazine's coverage of gay parenting and adoption. In both the photos, one on the cover and the other with the story, Wood is shown holding their adopted son, while Sie is in the background. Given the 'theme' of the piece on parenting, presenting Wood as the active parent and Sie as the passive parent blatantly gives Wood primacy in the article, while relegating Sie to the background. In addition, Sie's work as a voice-over actor is only given a brief mention, while a story box promotes Wood's recently released music CD. [Thus] Wood's occupation, and by extension his role as family provider, is given primacy, while Sie's work is merely a footnote. The narrative is also symptomatic of the way the larger society, both gay and straight, views Asian Americans and other racial minorities.

In the second paragraph, the author quotes Sie as stating: 'We wanted to adopt an Asian child, and that's hard to do domestically . . . There are very few Asian women here who give their children up for adoption. It seemed like an international adoption was our best bet' (Lehoczky, 2005: 47). Later, Lehoczky explains: 'The couple were also introduced to a homophobic government from which they needed to hide their relationship . . . The adoption could be blocked if local officials found out that Sie was not in fact single' (Lehoczky, 2005: 47). While other countries are mentioned as being unfriendly towards potential gay parents, Lehoczky specifically points out China, by quoting Adam Pertman, executive director of the Evan B. Donaldson Adoption Institute, as stating: 'When Chinese officials see a single person, they grimace and start asking questions . . . They changed their rules to accommodate more married couples, which was largely a way of cutting instances of gay and lesbian adoptions' (Lehoczky, 2005: 48).

While presenting Chinese officials as being overly homophobic, and Asian women as unwilling to 'give up' their children, the article makes no mention of laws in the USA that forbid gay men and women from adopting any children, or the scarcity of white babies available for adoption. In fact, the trials endured by Wood and Sie in having to seek a child outside of the USA are blamed on Asian American women's unwillingness to 'give up' their children and the Chinese government's homophobic attitudes. Contrasted to this homophobia in 'Asian' cultures, whites, whether in the USA or elsewhere, are given a pass from blame. . . .

Adding Insult to Injury

While the treatment of gay Asian men by *The Advocate* may be lacking, at least it is not outright degrading. In fact, given the relatively small number of gay Asian men in the USA compared to gay white men, a few articles that represent the needs of a small portion of their potential readers might be expected. However, articles in *OUT* magazine seem to actively degrade gay Asian men for entertainment value, while relegating them to the margins of the gay community or placing them outside of the 'gay' community altogether. For example, the February 2005 issue of *OUT* magazine ran a column titled, 'How to Gab in Gaysian.' A pitiful and unfortunate attempt at comic relief, *OUT* magazine introduced the column in this way: 'Sometimes members of a group pepper their conversations with sexual euphemisms, saucy slang terms, and just flat-out un-PC parlance. Since there isn't an official English-Gaysian dictionary, *OUT* offers you a small menu of words you might want to know in order to verbal-vogue it like a queer Asian' (Lee, 2005, 28). Included in the list of words to be 'translated' into 'English' were *FOBulous,* an adjective meaning 'fresh off the boat and fabulous' and *dogeater,* a noun to describe a 'gaysian who unapologetically uses men for all their emotional, sexual, and financial worth, because they feel men are dogs by nature.'

First, the column works to highlight the 'foreignness' of gay Asian men compared to gay white men. From its outset, it marks gay Asians as being members of a 'group' that is outside of the gay mainstream. In implying that readers of *OUT* magazine would need an 'English-Gaysian dictionary,' the column presupposes that such readers are white. It is the implied gay white reader who is provided with a lesson on how to decipher the 'foreign' language of gay Asian men and it is the implied gay white reader who is to receive a 'lesson' about a 'foreign' group.

In addition, the column plays upon old stereotypes of Asian Americans. One, Asian men are perpetually foreign, and as such are outside of the gay mainstream. While an adjective to describe a recent immigrant is provided, there is no attempt to define slang terms that describe American born Asians. Not surprising is the inclusion of 'dogeater,' meant to conjure up stereotypical images of Asians and perceived dietary patterns. It goes without saying that such caricatures are not new. . . .

Commodifying Asian Bodies

. . . While virtually invisible in feature stories and profiles, gay Asian men are amply present in advertisements placed in gay periodicals. Full page advertisements for pornographic films with all-Asian casts are scattered generously within the pages of gay publications, all the while Asian men are excluded from the features. While advertisements in gay periodicals seem to advertise to gay white men, they advertise gay Asian men as a commodity for consumption. Perhaps nowhere is this more evident than between the pages of *Oriental Guys Magazine.* Originally published in Sydney, the recently defunct *Oriental Guys Magazine* was a nine-year advertisement of gay Asian men for white men. As Hagland (1998) notes, the Asian men who grace the pages of *Oriental Guys Magazine* and other such 'rice queen magazines'—named in reference to 'rice queens,' gay white men who prefer Asian sex partners—are meant for white male consumption, and sexual narratives regarding the men who are pictured are almost always written by white men. . . .

This commodification of gay Asian men can also be observed at gay community events. For example, the 'Mr' and 'Miss' pageants put on by the Long Yang Club (LYC)—an organization with a global network of nearly four dozen chapters that purport to cater to 'gay Asians and interested non-Asians . . .'—involve exclusively Asian contestants who are on display for white male enjoyment (Long Yang Club, 2005). Asian contestants compete with each other largely by putting their bodies on display for the approval of white judges who 'score' them and 'select' a winner. Given the true purpose of LYC, to promote inter-racial dating among gay Asian men and their 'admirers,' one wonders why only Asian men are on display. Within this structure, it becomes clear that within the inter-racial dating relationship between white men and Asian men, as facilitated by the LYC, white men have the power to objectify and select, while Asian men are objectified and selected.

Discussion

It is not surprising that the feminine image of all Asian men has been easily superimposed onto gay media. Contrasting the 'feminine' gay Asian man to the 'masculine' gay white man places gay white men in the dominant position in a society and culture that values masculinity over femininity, active over passive, and virile over submissive. In doing so, gay publications create a hierarchy of those who 'belong' in the gay 'community' and those who are simply marginal members.

Many would argue that gay publications generally tend to present only one type of image, that of young, attractive, muscular, and successful men. Certainly, in this way, gay publications are little different from 'mainstream' publications hoping to attract advertising dollars. Also, it is likely that the

focus on lean, muscular bodies has negative consequences for gay white men as well (Lorenzen et al., 2004). At the same time, these images of young, attractive white men—while problematic for other reasons—do not relegate other white men to the margins of the gay community nor actively construct them as being outside of the gay community. Rather, it works to highlight their privileged racial status allowing non-young, non-muscular, and non-successful gay white men to racially identify with the privileged position within the gay community, thereby allowing them to practice a complicit model of masculinity (Connell, 1995). As such, the results of the 'typical' images found in gay publications are different for white men who do not 'fit' the norms, and men of color.

In recent years, gay Asian American men have been active in creating their own images that go beyond the stereotypes that seem to be regurgitated in the popular 'gay' press. Sadly, *Noodle Magazine,* the only such publication produced entirely by gay Asian American men, closed after publishing just six issues between summer of 2002 and fall of 2003. In its inaugural issue, *Noodle Magazine* declared:

> What you have in your hands is something that we thought was missing in all of our lives. Sure, we've seen Asian and Pacific Islander men in a magazine or two in the past, but we kind of feel that they weren't really about us, and they talked more about us than toward us. Hey, we like the attention as much as anyone, but we don't think we've ever actually seen who we really are in print before. Not in a token article in a gay magazine, not as a sidebar in an Asian American magazine, and not as a human interest story in the newspaper. We thought it was about time we tell the stories that we want to tell. (*Noodle Magazine,* 2002: 5)

While it is clear that the producers of *Noodle Magazine* were aware of the negative stereotypes about gay Asian men within the gay community, they relied on a strategy of compensation whereby they attempted to undermine the stereotypes by 'conforming par excellence to the hegemonic ideal' (Chen, 1999: 592). By using images of muscular, and masculine, gay Asian men that mimicked the images found in magazines such as *OUT*, the producers of the magazine attempted to present gay Asian men as being similar to the hegemonic norm found within the gay press. While doing so clearly provides an alternative to the images of gay Asian men found in mainstream gay publications, and provides gay Asian men with alternative images of themselves, the same action may have unfortunate consequences. As Chan (2001: 13) notes, the desire to 'disinherit emasculating representations' simply 'reflects a willingness to adhere to a predominantly white model of masculinity.' Thus, by promoting the images of masculinity and desirability found in mainstream gay publications, these images give credit to the dominant view of 'gay' masculinity that allowed for the existence of the negative stereotypes about gay Asian men in the first place. After all, as Michael Kimmel (1994) points out, masculinity is constructed on racism, homophobia, and sexism. I would argue here that 'gay' masculinity is largely founded on transposing 'white' masculinity over that of men of color. While 'gay' masculinity can never be hegemonic, it can, nonetheless, position itself closer to the hegemonic ideal by pitting the more feminized masculinity of Asian men as a counter balance. As such, I would argue that that very masculinization of gay identity as discussed by Levine (1998) relies, to some extent, on the feminized gay Asian representations. At the same time, the entire notion of 'masculinity' is socially constructed, with the very definition of what is and is not masculine constantly negotiated and altered. Even the 'gay macho' discussed by Levine can be

seen as in flux as new models of masculinity come to dominate the gay press.

The real goal needs to be an attempt at changing the dominant view of 'masculinity' within the gay community rather than buying into the existing model provided by the gay mainstream. Doing so, however, is hardly an easy task. Rather than focusing on reproducing the dominant gay images of masculinity with Asian faces, I believe, as Chan (2000: 385) suggests, that 'an ambivalent or ambiguous model of masculinity is a more effective way to counter a hegemonic model of masculinity.' Yet as Chan (2000) finds, doing so is a daunting task. But at the same time, what other options are there if the ultimate goal is to dismantle the very system of gendered expectations that continually places gay men of color in the subordinate position to gay white men?

References

Bérubé, A. (2001) How Gay Stays White and What Kind of White It Stays. B.B. Rasmussen et al. (eds) *The Making and Unmaking of Whiteness*, pp. 234–65. Duke University Press: Durham.

Caldwell, J. (2005) Invisible No More. *The Advocate*. 15 March 2005: 28–30.

Chan, J. (2000) Bruce Lee's Fictional Model of Masculinity. *Men and Masculinities* 2(4): 371–87.

Chan, J. (2001) *Chinese American Masculinities: From Fu Manchu to Bruce Lee*. Routledge: New York.

Chen, A. (1999) Lives at the Center of the Periphery, Lives at the Periphery of the Center: Chinese American Masculinities and Bargaining with Hegemony. *Gender and Society* 13(5): 584–607.

Connell, R. (1995) *Masculinities*. University of California Press: Berkeley.

Dahlgren, P. (1992) Introduction. P. Dahlgren and C. Sparks (eds) *Journalism and Popular Culture*, pp. 1–23. Sage: London.

Eng, D. (2001) *Racial Castration: Managing Masculinity in Asian America*. Duke University Press: Durham.

Fung, R. (1996) Looking for My Penis. R. Leong (ed.) *Asian American Sexualities*, pp. 181–98. Routledge: New York.

Hagland, P. (1998) Undressing the Oriental Boy: The Gay Asian in the Social Imagination of the Gay White Male. D. Atkins (ed.) *Looking Queer: Body Image and Identity in Lesbian, Bisexual, Gay and Transgender Communities*, pp. 277–93. Harrington Park Press: New York.

Hamamoto, D. (1994) *Monitored Peril: Asian Americans and the Politics of TV Representation*. University of Minnesota Press: Minneapolis.

Hoang, N.T. (2004) The Resurrection of Brandon Lee: The Making of a Gay Asian American Porn Star. L. Williams (ed.) *Porn Studies*, pp. 223–70. Duke University Press: Durham.

Kimmel, M. (1994) Masculinity as Homophobia: Fear, Shame, and Silence in the Construction of Gender Identity. H. Brod and M. Kaufman (eds) *Theorizing Masculinities*, pp. 119–141. Sage: Thousand Oaks.

Kumashiro, K. (ed) (2004) *Restoried Selves: Autobiographies of Queer Asian/Pacific American Activists*. Harrington Park Press: New York.

Lee, D. (2005) How to Gab in Gaysian. *OUT* (February): 28.

Lee, R. (1999) *Orientals: Asian Americans in Popular Culture*. Temple University Press: Philadelphia.

Lehoczky, E. (2005) Rough Going Overseas. *The Advocate*. 19 July 2005: 47–8.

Levine, M. (1998) *Gay Macho: The Life and Death of the Homosexual Clone*. New York University Press: New York.

Long Yang Club (2005) www.longyangclub.org

Lorenzen, L., Grieve, F. and Thomas, A. (2004) Exposure to Muscular Male Models Decreases Men's Body Satisfaction. *Sex Roles* 51(11/12): 743–8.

Lowe, L. (1996) *Immigrant Acts*. Duke University Press: Durham.

Noodle Magazine (2002) Hello, My Name is Noodle. *Noodle* (Summer): 5.

Park, Y. (2005) Culture as a Deficit: A Critical Discourse Analysis of the Concept of Culture in Contemporary Social Work Discourse. *Journal of Sociology and Social Welfare* 32(3): 11–33.

Storey, J. (1996) *Cultural Studies and the Study of Popular Culture*. University of Georgia Press: Atlanta.

When in Rome

Heterosexism, Homophobia, and Sports Talk Radio

David Nylund

... *The Jim Rome Show* reflects a growing cultural trend in the United States—sports talk radio. According to sportswriter Ashley Jude Collie (2001), Jim Rome is the "hippest, most controversial, and brutally honest voice" (p. 53) in mediated sports. In addition to his nationally syndicated radio program that airs on more than 200 stations, the 40-year-old hosts ESPN's *Rome Is Burning,* a weekly 1-hr television sports talk show (and his second show on ESPN). Rome began his radio career broadcasting University of California, Santa Barbara (UCSB), basketball games. After graduating from UCSB in 1986 and serving seven non-playing radio internships, Rome earned a local weekend job at XTRA in San Diego, a powerful 77,000-watt station. The "clever fashioning of a streetwise persona" (Mariscal, 1999), his raspy voice, staccato delivery, and fiercely independent opinions separated him from the talk radio crowd, and he soon moved into hosting a primetime radio show. Eventually, his popularity earned him a television spot on ESPN2, *Talk2,* a cable show that Rome hosted in the early 90s. The Noble Sports Network syndicated Rome's radio show in 1995, and Premiere Radio Networks acquired the rights to the show 1 year later. Rome also hosted Fox Sports Net's *The Last Word,* a sports talk television program that ran from 1997 to 2002.

However, despite the variety of venues in which he plays, it is the radio show's format that contributes to Rome's controversiality and popularity. Loyal callers, whom he calls "clones," phone in with their opinion (referred to as a "take") on what's happening in the world of sports. Rome listens intently and either "runs" the caller with a buzzer (meaning he disconnects the call) or he allows them to finish their take and says, "rack 'em" (meaning he saves the call as an entry into the huge call-of-the-day contest). As opposed to other talk radio programs where there is some dialogical interaction between the caller and hosts, Rome and his callers do not engage in a back-and-forth interchange. The caller's comments

From Nylund, D. (2004). When in Rome: Heterosexism, homophobia, and sports talk radio. *Journal of Sport and Social Issues,* 28(2), 136–168. Published by Sage Publications, Inc.

are highly performative, full of insider language, and monological. Rome silently listens to the call and only comments when the caller is finished with his or her monologue or Rome disconnects the call. Rarely, if ever, does a caller disagree with Rome.[1] "Huge" calls are those that Rome considers good "smack" speech—his term for sports talk that is gloatful, uninhibited, and unbridled. According to Rome, only the strong survive in this 3-hr dose of smack and irreverence. Rome's in-group language and his unique interaction (or lack thereof) make his radio show distinctive. His "survival of the fittest" format is responsible for the show's reputation as sports version of hate-speech radio (Hodgson, 1999).

The Jim Rome Show epitomizes the growing trend of talk radio. Presented as a medium in which citizens/callers can freely "air their point of view," talk radio has become a very popular forum for large numbers of people to engage in debate about politics, religion, and sports. The media culture, with talk radio as a prominent discourse, plays a very powerful role in the constitution of everyday life, shaping our political values, gender ideologies, and supplying the material out of which people fashion their identities (Kellner, 1995). Hence, it is crucial for scholars to furnish critical commentary on talk radio; specifically, we should critique those radio texts that work to reinforce inequality.

Talk radio formats, particularly political talk radio, exploded in the 1980s as a result of deregulation, corporatization of radio, and niche marketing (Cook, 2001).[2] Deregulation, which loosened mass-media ownership and content restrictions, renewed interest in radio as a capitalist investment and galvanized the eventual emergence of its two 1990s prominent showcase formats: hate radio talk shows and all-sports programming (Cook, 2001). By the late 1990s, there were more than 4,000 talk shows on 1,200 stations (Goldberg, 1998).[3] Sports talk radio formats have, according to cultural studies scholar Jorge Mariscal (1999),

"spread like an unchecked virus" (p. 111). Currently, there are more than 250 all-sports stations in the United States (Ghosh, 1999).

As a result of deregulation and global capitalism, new media conglomerates emerged as the only qualified buyers of radio programming.[4] Infinity Broadcasting, the largest U.S. company devoted exclusively to owning and operating radio stations, owns WFAN[5] and Sacramento's local all-sports station, 1140 AM. Its competing company, Premiere Radio Network, owns the popular nationally syndicated programs hosted by Howard Stern, Rush Limbaugh, Dr. Laura, and Jim Rome. . . . Talk radio is aimed at a very desirable demographic: White middle-class men between the ages of 24 and 55 years. Research shows that talk-radio listeners are overwhelmingly men who tend to vote Republican (Armstrong & Rubin, 1989; Hutchby, 1996; Page & Tannenbaum, 1996). The most popular program, the *Rush Limbaugh Show,* has 20 million daily listeners who laugh along with the host as he rants and vents, opening a channel for the performance of the angry White male. . . . Douglas (2002) argued that although most of the research on talk radio is on the threat it poses to democracy, what is obvious, but far less discussed, is talk radio's central role in restoring masculine hegemony:

> Talk radio is as much—maybe even more—about gender politics at the end of the century than it is about party politics. There were different masculinities enacted on the radio, from Howard Stern to Rush Limbaugh, but they were all about challenging and overthrowing, if possible, the most revolutionary of social movements, feminism. The men's movement of the 1980s found its outlet— and that was talk radio. (Douglas, 2002, p. 485)

Similarly, sports talk radio, according to Goldberg (1998), enacts its White hegemony via hypermasculine posing, forceful opinions, and loudmouth shouting. Sports talk radio "pontificates, moralizes, politicizes, commercializes, and commodifies—as it entertains" (p. 213). Although Rome's masculine style is different from Limbaugh's and Stern's, all three controversial hosts have built reputations through their rambunctious, masculinist, and combative styles (Farred, 2000). With White male masculinity being challenged and decentered by feminism, affirmative action, gay and lesbian movements, and other groups' quest for social equality, sports talk shows, similar to talk radio in general, have become an attractive venue for embattled White men seeking recreational repose and a nostalgic return to a prefeminist ideal (Farred, 2000).

This chapter offers a critical analysis of the most prominent sports talk-radio program, *The Jim Rome Show*. My study does not critique and dissect *The Jim Rome Show* in isolation from other media texts or discourses about sports; rather, I aim to provide a historicized and contextualized study based in cultural studies methodology. I show how *The Jim Rome Show* is situated within a broader set of social, gender, racial, political, economic, and cultural forces. In particular, I examine the ways in which the show reinforces and (less obviously) calls into question heterosexism as well as what gender scholars call hegemonic masculinity. . . .

As a casual listener to *The Jim Rome Show* over the past 3 years, I have noticed themes of misogyny, violence, and heterosexual dominance appear to recur with considerable frequency. Rome's persona embodies an aggressive masculinity with unassailable expertise and authority. This aggressive persona climaxed in 1994 on the set of Rome's ESPN show *Talk 2* while interviewing NFL quarterback Jim Everett. During the interview, Everett knocked Rome off his chair after Rome taunted Everett by calling him "Chris" (i.e., female tennis star, Chris Evert), a veiled reference to the quarterback's reputed lack of toughness.

Rome's reference to Everett as "Chris" on the show was not the first time he had done so. In fact, Rome has used this term on Everett throughout the 1993 NFL season on his local radio show on XTRA 690 AM. This hypermasculine event increased Rome's fame and reputation among some of his audience as a host who "tells it like it is" even if it means insulting someone. However, many in the media criticized Rome's lack of professionalism and predicted the end of his career (Sports Illustrated Editors, 1994). Although Rome left ESPN2 soon after the Everett incident, his radio career slowly continued to grow to the prominence it now holds. Rome's reputation as intolerant and abusive continues to this day because his rapid-fire, masculinist-laden opinion on sports provoked OutSports.com—a Web site that caters to gay and lesbian sports fans—to refer to him as "the commentator who makes a name for himself by saying stupid things with an obnoxious style, that for some reason, attracts many straight sports fans" (Buzinski, 2000, p. 5).[6]

As a cultural studies scholar and committed sports fan, I am compelled to study *The Jim Rome Show* to examine the sexism and homophobia present in the show. When in Rome, do the clones do as the Romans do? This question led me to conduct a textual analysis that identifies those features that appear to reinforce or promote homophobia and sexism. I also researched audiences in various sports bars in the United States to achieve a better understanding of what *The Jim Rome Show* means to listeners. I was particularly curious whether certain audience members resist the dominant, hegemonic, textual themes. . . .

Hegemonic Themes

My analysis of the text confirms that much of the discourse on the show contains themes of misogyny, violence, and heterosexual dominance including themes that reinforced sexism and lesbian baiting. The following examples highlight these instances.

The first is from an infamous program dated July 23. On this date, Rome was commenting on the breaking story that several professional male athletes (Patrick Ewing, Terrell Davis, and Dekembe Motumbo) had testified in an Atlanta court that they regularly attended a strip club (The Gold Club) and engaged in sex acts with some of the club's dancers.[7] This tabloidlike story was a great opportunity for Rome to engage in his sardonic "smack" talk. Here are Rome's acerbic comments on Patrick Ewing's admission that he received free oral sex at the Gold Club:

> Want some free oral sex Patrick [Ewing]? Nah, I'm good. Maybe next time! Come on! He said he'd been there 10 times. He said he had free oral sex 2 times. And by the way, who's going to say "no" to free oral sex? I mean, clones, would you like some free oral sex? Who's going to say no to that [laughing]? Most athletes go to a club or restaurant and get comped some free drinks, chicken wings. . . . not Patrick, he gets comped free oral sex.
>
> [later in his monologue] Meanwhile, a former stripper testified. And it's a good thing. We finally have some good testimony. She testified that she performed sex acts or witnessed other dancers perform sex acts on celebrities including Terrell Davis and Dekembe Motumbo. So in response to the proverbial question, "who wants to sex Motumbo?" The answer obviously is whichever skank's turn it is at the Gold Club.

In this section of the transcript, Rome employs a very common, taken-for-granted discourse—"the heterosexual male sexual drive discourse" (Hare-Mustin, 1994). This dominant ideology is predicated on the notion that women are objects (Rome misogynistically refers to the dancers as "skanks") who arouse men's heterosexual urges, which are assumed to be "natural and compelling" (Hare-Mustin, 1994, p. 24). Accordingly, men cannot control their primitive sexual yearnings, and women are blamed for inflaming them. This assumption, reproduced by Rome's rhetorical question, "who is going to turn down 'free' oral sex," reinforces women's subjugation as they become defined as existing solely for men's pleasure.

Rome's language takes on homophobic tones later in the same program. In this excerpt, Rome ridicules a former dancer's testimony:

> Finally we are getting somewhere. I thought Ewing's testifying of getting "hummers" was going to be the best that the trial had to offer. Thankfully, it's not in fact, not even close! After Patrick was done humiliating himself, one of the hookers got on the stand. That's when it really got good. A former dancer at the club starting naming names! This is just the beginning. This "tramp" also testified that she went back to the hotel room of a former wrestling executive, to perform sex acts, not on him, but on his wife! Now, we are getting somewhere. Sex with athletes; lesbian sex acts with the wives of executives. That's what I was hoping for from the beginning! And this tramp also added that she and another dancer performed a lesbian sex show for Ewing and some friends before he was given free oral sex by other dancers. And perhaps the most amazing thing, this tramp that ratted everybody out, is now working at a day care center in Georgia. Wonderful. Who wouldn't want to leave their kids with a woman who used to be a hooker? There's no one I would trust my kids with more than a woman who used to perform lesbian sex shows for NBA centers and had sex with wrestling executives' wives. What a perfect person to have around children! Man, I can't wait to see what happens

today in the trial. I wonder who else's life will be ruined today?

Many of the callers on the September 9 program also reproduced male hegemony during their takes. Here is the call of the day:

Dan: [Contemptuously] I feel sorry for those skanks. I mean Ewing, Motumbo![8] Hopefully, the dancers got time and a half! I guess America has finally found a job worse than Assistant Crack Whore. About the only thing good to come out of this sordid mess is that Motumbo finally found a bar where his pickup line works.

Rome: [Laughing] Good job Dan!

Rome and his production staff chose this take as the call of the day, and in doing so, they support offensive, masculinist humor.[9] Dan's behavior reflects a common social practice for many men—the desire to earn the homosocial approval of other, more powerful men such as Jim Rome. Rome has power over the discourse and decides that Dan's wit gives him the right to enter the homosocial space of male privilege. Yes, Dan attempts to hold the players accountable for their behavior. However, the underlying tone of Dan's comments— "crack whore" and "skanks"—are racialized and sexist.

Rome's comments on athletes receiving oral sex at a strip club references the Clinton/Lewinsky affair and the increasing media focus on sex scandals in the lives of public figures. Although the "tabloidization" of the media has many negative consequences, Lumby (2001) posited that it is not completely destructive. In fact, the increased media attention on private sexuality is because of, in part, the "feminist project of politicizing the

private sphere and its attendant issues, such as sexual harassment, domestic violence, and child care" (p. 234). "Bad" tabloid style press may actually stem from some "good" political motives that have focused on issues that were once seen as merely personal. Yet the media focus on Clinton and Rome's focus on athletes at the Gold Club elides a feminist analysis of structures of power (Clinton with an intern or famous athletes with female sex workers). Hence, the entertainment value of sex scandals undermines the feminist goal of politicizing the private and reinforces "patriarchal sexuality morality: a proscription of sexual behavior outside the bounds of heterosexual monogamous marriage and the violation of that proscription by powerful and privileged males" (Jakobsen, 2001, p. 307).

Entertainment and Male Hegemony

How do fans themselves make sense of and respond to Rome's problematic masculinist commentary? Not surprisingly, many of the fans I spoke to found it humorous; "It's entertaining" was the most common response. In fact, 2 days after Rome's acerbic comments about the incidents at the Gold Club, the topic came up with George (all the names of my research participants have been changed to preserve anonymity), a 27-year-old White male, in a sports bar in Sacramento. While inquiring about what he finds appealing about Rome, he replied,

> I listen every day. He tells like it is. He lets it rip. He doesn't hold back. I like that! And he's entertaining! He pokes fun at people like the other day when Rome went off about the Ewing (Gold Club incident). It's funny! It reminds me of locker room humor. Yes, I get a kick out of his smack talk. It's pure entertainment.

Like when he trashes NASCAR and the WNBA.

His friend, John (a 26-year-old White male), echoed similar sentiments:

Yeah, Rome is hilarious. I thought it was hilarious when he called Jim Everett, "Chris." That's what sticks in my head when someone says something about Rome. He's kind of like the Rush Limbaugh or Howard Stern of sports talk radio. Like he thinks he's God. But I don't mind it because he's entertaining. And it's a way for him to get the ratings and the market share. I admire that because I am a stockbroker. You need to market yourself to stand out. You need to be aggressive and controversial to be successful in today's society. The show makes men cocky—like the clones. I listen to it for the entertainment. And he does know his sports.

Such comments are fairly representative of the participants that I interviewed. Many men valorize Rome's "transnational business masculinity," a term coined by Council (2000) to describe egocentrism, conditional loyalties, and a commitment to capital accumulation. In addition, as stated above, many participants found the program pleasurable because Rome is knowledgeable, authoritative, and comedic. Implied here is the notion that listening to Rome is a natural as well as an innocent pleasure. One person, when asked about the so-called harmlessness of the program, said, "If you don't like it, turn the radio dial. No one is forcing you to listen. It's just entertainment!" This is a common response to critiques of the negative effects of media culture and audience pleasure. Yet amusement is neither innate nor harmless. Pleasure is learned and closely connected to power and knowledge (Foucault, 1980). As media scholar Douglas Kellner (1995) observed,

We learn what to enjoy and what we should avoid. We learn when to laugh and when to cheer. A system of power and privilege thus conditions our pleasures so that we seek certain socially sanctioned pleasures and avoid others. Some people learn to laugh at racist jokes and others learn to feel pleasure at the brutal use of violence. (p. 39)

The media industry, therefore, often mobilizes pleasure around conservative ideologies that have oppressive effects on women, homosexuals, and people of color. The ideologies of hegemonic masculinity, assembled in the form of pleasure and humor, are what many of my participants found most enjoyable about *The Jim Rome Show*, including Rome's aggressive, masculinist, "expert" speech that ridicules others. Thus, many of the pleasurable aspects of the program may encourage certain male listeners to identify with the features of traditional masculinity.

Calling *The Rome Show:* Homosociality and Approval

I was also interested in what listeners of the program thought of callers' comments and if they had ever called the program themselves. Many enjoyed listening to callers such as Dan and found their commentary to constitute comical moments of the show. I was particularly interested in what calling in to the show might mean for men who subscribe to traditional masculinity. One of the main aspects of traditional masculine homosociality involves men's striving and competing for prestige and approval within their peer groups (Wenner, 1998). This striving provides the basis for an affiliation. Many people I interviewed stated that the ultimate compliment would be for Jim Rome to approve of their take if they called. To have your call "racked" by the leading sports media personality would be a revered honor. What's more, from within the terms of hegemonic masculinity, having one's call rejected may signify a "failure" of masculinity. The following dialogue occurred between me and Fred (a 44-year-old Black male):

David: Have you called the program before?

Fred: No, I never have called. I thought about calling but I would hate to get run [Rome disconnecting the call]. Man that would hurt! I sometimes think, "Man, I could give a good take . . . but if I call and "suck" . . . you know . . . get run, start stuttering . . . man that would be embarrassing.

David: What would be embarrassing about getting run?

Fred: It's embarrassing 'cause it's Jim Rome. He's the man [laughing]! He's the pimp in the box![10] Man, if you get racked and are the caller of the day, you're the man!

. . . When asked why *The Jim Rome Show* and other sports talk radio programs are so popular among heterosexual men, about one half of the men told me that they feel anxious and uncertain because of the changes in men's work and women's increasing presence in the public sphere. Moreover, several participants believed that sports talk provides a safe haven for men to bond and reaffirm their essential masculinity. Here's what a 27-year-old White male said in a bar in Tampa:

> It's [*The Jim Rome Show*] a male bonding thing, a locker room for guys in the radio. You can't do it at work, everything's PC (politically correct) now! So the Rome Show is a last refuge for men to bond and be men. It's just in your car, Rome, and it's the audience that you can't see. I listen in the car and can let that maleness come out. I know its offensive sometimes to gays and women . . . you know . . . when men bond . . . but men need that!

Romey's show gives me the opportunity to talk to other guy friends about something we share in common. And my dad listens to Romey also. So my dad and I bond also.

This comment is telling about the mixed effects of sports talk. On one hand, sports talk radio allows men to express a "covert intimacy"[11] (Messner, 1992) and shared meaning about a common subject matter. This bonding can bring forth genuine moments of closeness and should not necessarily be pathologized or seen as completely negative. However, much of the bonding is, as the interviewee stated, "offensive sometimes to gays and women." Many of the men I interviewed were speaking in a group context in the presence of other male peers. The gender displays (sexist and homophobic jokes, for example) by the men I interviewed in the homosocial space of a sports bar were interesting to observe as they confirmed Messner's (2002) point that men in groups define and solidify their boundaries through aggressive misogynistic and homophobic speech and actions. Underneath this bonding experience are homoerotic feelings that must be warded off and neutralized through joking, yelling, cursing, and demonizing anybody who does not conform to normative masculinity. Pronger (1990) argued the arena of sports is paradoxical: on one hand, sports is a primary site for the expression of heterosexual masculinity, and on the other hand, there is a powerful homoerotic undercurrent subliminally present in sports. Sports radio operates similarly as an extension of this paradoxically homosocial and homoerotic space. Shields (1999), in his analysis of sports radio, stated, "It would be impossible to overstate the degree to which sports talk radio is shadowed by the homosexual panic implicit in the fact that it consists almost entirely of a bunch of out-of-shape White men sitting around talking about Black men's buff bodies" (p. 50). . . .

Counterhegemonic Themes

As the above analysis illuminates, *The Jim Rome Show* reinforces male hegemony. However, a close reading of the show reveals some contradiction and fissures to hegemony. The following transcripts of the program exemplify times when the text and its voices (Jim Rome, audience members) partially subvert hegemonic masculinity and homophobia. The first example is from the show dated April 30 when the topic of bigotry was raised by Rome. Here, Rome, in his belligerent vocal style, is taking issue with the homophobic comments made by Chicago Cubs pitcher, Julian Tavarez, about San Francisco Giants fans:

> Julian Tavarez, a pitcher for the Cubs said this about San Francisco Giants fans—his words not mine—"they are a bunch of a-holes and faggots" . . . You know, it would be nice to go a week without some racist or bigot comment . . . but no, Julian. Nice job Julian. . . . And here's a thought, Julian Rocker [reference to John Rocker, a pitcher who became famous for making racist and homophobic comments during an interview in *Sports Illustrated*], just because San Francisco has a significant gay population, I would be willing to bet that not everybody at a Giants game is a homosexual. Maybe. Can't document that. Just a thought . . . I feel pretty secure in saying that? How do you come up with this garbage? I mean how do you get to the point where the proper response to heckling fans is to drop racist, anti-Semitic, or homophobic bombs on people? And even if you had those bigoted views, you would have the sense to keep it [to] yourselves. They might realize that not everybody hates everybody else. I think there is only one solution to this problem of overcrowding in the racist frat house. We are going to have to have honorary members.

In this instance, the host clearly positions himself as antiracist and antihomophobic. This stance is noteworthy and a possible contradiction to dominant sports talk discourse. Rome uses his masculine authority to stand against the intolerance often engendered by homophobia.

Rome's comments on the subject appear to be progressive and reasonable.[12] On closer examination, however, Rome's location of the problem of homophobia in a few bigoted, intolerant individuals leaves unchallenged the larger societal structures that perpetuate heterosexism. The stance taken up by the host is rooted within liberal discourse, which reduces analysis to an individual, private endeavor (Kane & Lenskyj, 2000; Kitzinger, 1987) and forecloses any serious discussion of homophobia as structural and political issues related to power, gender, and sexuality. When Rome denounces a few athletes as "bigots," it prevents a wider analysis of the link between the institution of organized sports and its heterosexual, masculinist, and homophobic agenda. Addressing the thorny questions of sexuality, politics, power, and privilege would be a risky and bold move for *The Jim Rome Show,* as it would offer a more radical challenge to the institution of heterosexual privilege and sports.

The next seemingly subversive segment relates to an editorial letter in the May 2001 issue of *Out* magazine. In that issue, the editor in chief, Brendan Lemon, stated that his boyfriend was a Major League baseball player. Lemon did not give names, but hinted that the player was from an East Coast franchise. Rome and other mainstream media programs reacted quickly to the editorial. A media firestorm resulted in a rumor mill: Players, fans, owners, and sports talk radio hosts swapped guesses and anxieties over the athlete's identity.

On May 18, Rome's monologue pondered the questions. What would happen if that person's identity became public? What would it mean for baseball, gays, and lesbians in sports in general, and for the man himself? Given that Lemon's boyfriend would be the first athlete in one of the "big four" major league team sports (baseball, football, basketball, and hockey) to come out "during" his career, what effect would this have on the institution of sport? Rome decided to pose this question to one of his interview participants that day, well-respected baseball veteran Eric Davis.

Rome: What would happen if a teammate of yours, or any baseball player, would come out of the closet and say, "I am gay"? What would the reaction be like? How badly would that go?

Eric: I think it would go real bad. I think people would jump to form an opinion because everybody has an opinion about gays already. But I think it would be a very difficult situation because with us showering with each other . . . being around each other as men. Now, you're in the shower with a guy who's gay . . . looking at you . . . maybe making a pass. That's an uncomfortable situation. In society, they have never really accepted it. They want to come out. And if that's the case, fine, but in sports, it would definitely raise some eyebrows. . . . I don't think it should be thrown at 25 guys saying, "yeah I am gay."

[Rome changes the subject . . . no follow-up]

Rome asks a pointed question to Davis whose predictable homophobic response warrants more follow-up questions. Yet Rome shifts the subject to something less problematic, letting Davis off the hook. After Rome ends the interview, he addresses Davis's comments in another monologue:

That's [Eric Davis] a 17-year respected major league ballplayer. And I think that's a representative comment of a lot of these guys. . . . He is [a] very highly regarded guy. This is why I asked him the question. And he answered it very honestly. He would be concerned about having gay teammate. . . . For instance, when he's showering. Personally, I don't agree with the take. It's my personal opinion. However, I posed the question to see what the reaction would be. And this is what I have been saying since this story broke. This is why it would not be a good thing. This is why the editor of that magazine clearly was wrong and has never been in a locker-room or clubhouse. That's why it hasn't happened. Eric Davis' reaction is what you would expect. Not everybody would feel that way, but a large majority would. It would make it nearly impossible for a gay player to come out.

Here, Rome is aware of the difficulties that would occur for an openly gay ballplayer. However, he shares his opinion in the safety of his "expert" monologue, not in the presence of Eric Davis. He does not risk compromising his masculinity or his relationship with Davis by endorsing this unusually progressive stance in the presence of a famous ballplayer such as Davis. However, when a listener calls immediately after the Davis interview, Rome responds differently:

Joe: I never imagined my first take would be on gays but I had to call. Being gay, it matters to no one but gays themselves. Why don't you guys, girls or gays . . . whatever you guys are. Just do us a favor, do yourselves a favor and keep it to yourselves. I mean . . . [Rome runs the caller with the buzzer and disconnects the call]

Rome: I think that's a very convenient response—"It's an issue only because you make it an issue." I don't agree with that, frankly. It's an issue because they are often persecuted against, harassed, assaulted, or killed in some cases. That's why it is an issue. They are fired from jobs, ostracized. It's not only an issue because they are making it an issue. What you are saying is keep your mouth shut, keep it in the closet; you are not accepting them for who they are and what they are. It's not an issue because they are making it an issue. It's an issue because of people saying things like, "keep your mouth shut. . . . We don't want you around. . . . We don't want to know you people exist." That's why it's an issue because of that treatment.

Again, Rome takes a strong stance against homophobia and demonstrates a fairly nuanced appreciation of the injustices of homophobia and heterosexism. This position is worth mentioning, particularly in the context of a program referred to as "The Jungle," with an audience of mostly men steeped in traditional masculinity and for whom heterosexuality is the unquestioned norm. Rome's antihomophobic stance represents a fissure in hegemonic masculinity. It can potentially foster a new awareness in Rome's listeners and invite new voices into this important conversation about masculinity and sexuality, potentially spurring a rethinking of masculinity and sports. Cutting off the first-time caller because of his homophobic comment could be viewed as a productive accountable maneuver, which is notable because straight men do not have a rich history of holding other straight men responsible for homophobic slurs.[13]

The historic May 18 radio show generated further substantive discussion on the issue of sports and heterosexual dominance in various media sites. This included a two-part show on Jim Rome's Fox TV show,

The Last Word, titled "The Gay Athlete." The show's guests included two out athletes: Diana Nyad and Billy Bean. The show's discussion was very rich, with the host asking fairly nuanced and enlightened questions. Since this show, Rome has interviewed other athletes who have come out since they left professional sports, including football players, Esera Tuaolo and David Kopay. In these interviews, Rome asked perceptive questions about the prevalence of homophobia in male sports and applauded their courage in coming out. ESPN also addressed the same topic and conducted a poll that showed that a substantial number of sports fans would have no problem with a gay athlete (*Outside the Lines,* 2001). What's more, the *Advocate* magazine published an article by cultural critic Toby Miller (2001) where he argued that the media firestorm generated by Brendan Lemon's article could potentially create a moment "for unions and owners of the big four to issue a joint statement in support, to show that queers are a legitimate part of the big leagues" (p. 3). . . .

It is important to note that Rome's interviewing of out athletes such as Billy Bean and David Kopay is a unique outcome in the world of heteronormative sports. To allow visibility of the gay athletes cannot be taken lightly in terms of its potential ramifications. Yet it is equally important to ask which athletes are allowed to become visible? What is their social location? How is their sexuality represented? Virtually all the gay athletes who have been on *The Jim Rome Show* are White males (an exception is Esera Tuaolo who is Samoan) who define homosexuality as an essentialist identity. Foucault (1980) contended that although visibility opens up some new political possibilities, it is also "a trap" because it creates new forms of surveillance, discipline, and limits. Sure, Bean and Kopay are given space to discuss their experience as a gay athlete, however it must be contained within a very limited, private discourse. Scholar Lisa Duggan (2001) claimed that much of the recent visibility of gays and lesbians is framed within a post-Stonewall, identitarian, private discourse. She referred to this discourse as homonormativity—"a politics that does not contest dominant heteronormative assumptions and institutions, but upholds and sustains them, while promising the possibility of a demobilized gay constituency and a privatized, depoliticized gay culture anchored in domesticity and consumption" (p. 179). According to Duggan, homonormativity is privatizing, much as heteronormativity is, and each lends support to the other. As much as Rome's recognition of gays in the sporting world is noteworthy, it is very much contained with a homonormative frame that reproduces the sex and gender binary. Hence, Rome's show, although it may be influenced by traditional gay and lesbian identity polities, is not a queer space. Athletes, including women who perform a more transgressive, non-normative sexuality, are invisible in sports radio. . . .

Notes

1. Rome's relationship with his caller, similar to most talk-show power relations between caller and host, is quite asymmetrical. Hutchby (1996) in his study of the discourse in talk radio stated that although the host has an array of discursive and institutional strategies available to him or her to keep the upper hand, occasionally callers have some resources available to resist the host's powerful strategies. Hence, Hutchby argued that power is not a monolithic feature of talk radio. Hutchby's argument does not appear to work with *The Jim Rome Show* as callers hardly ever confront Rome's authority. Rather, Rome's callers want his approval.

2. Deregulation was championed by then FCC chairman Mark Fowler who sold it as a form of media populism and civic participation. However, this public marketing campaign masked increased economic consolidation and increased barriers to entry into this market for all but very powerful media conglomerates such

as Infinity Broadcasting and Premiere Radio. Commenting about the success of conservative White male talk radio due to deregulation of the 1980s, Douglas (2002) claimed that Reaganism was successful by "selling the increased concentration of wealth as move back toward democracy" (p. 491).

3. In 1960, there were just two radio stations in the United States that were dedicated to talk radio formats (Goldberg, 1998).

4. The other significant deregulatory move in the 1980s was the abandonment of the Fairness Doctrine, which the FCC announced it would no longer enforce. The doctrine required stations to offer access to air alternative opinions when controversial issues were discussed. The goal of the doctrine was to promote a balance of views. Opponents of the doctrine, including Fowler and Reagan, felt it inhibited freedom of speech. Stations, they argued, avoided giving airtime to opinionated individuals because of the requirement to broadcast competing points of view. Unrestricted by the Fairness Doctrine's mandate for balance, Limbaugh and a legion of ultraconservative imitators took off the gloves and revived the financial state of AM radio.

5. The largest sports station in the United States, based in New York, WFAN is also the largest ad-billing radio station in the United States.

6. In a recent interview in *Sports Illustrated*, Rome stated he regrets the Everett interview and has matured into a well-reasoned interviewer. In the article, Rome stated that he was "wiser" because of being married and having a child (Deitsch, 2003).

7. The court in Atlanta was prosecuting the owner of the Gold Club for mob connections and other illegalities. This event received a great deal of media attention.

8. Ewing and Motumbo are Black men. The caller of the day, Dan, is implying that they are unattractive men. Dan's disdainful "smack talk" could be understood to reproduce racist representations of Black athletes.

9. As a sidebar, Cook (2001) challenged the common notion that radio talk shows are a natural two-way dialogue between the caller and host that allow the caller to "freely air their point of view" (p. 62). The production process

reveals that it is a complex, mediated process that constrains the dialogue through a range of in-studio control techniques. These hidden maneuvers include off-air talk decisions on what gets included on the program, what gets omitted, and time control cues. Cook argued that examining the complex relational politics in radio talk is important to examine to contest its negative power and influence.

10. The term *pimp in the box* refers to Rome's "pimping" of NHL hockey in Los Angeles during 1992–1993 when the Los Angeles Kings made it to the Stanley Cup Finals. Rome's show was the first in Los Angeles to actively talk about hockey on sports talk stations and book hockey players as guests. This made national news as Wayne Gretzky was to appear on the show following every playoff game the Kings played that season to the point where Gretzky thanked Rome during a televised interview after the Kings won Game 7 of the Western Conference Finals to advance to the finals. After thanking Kings management and players he said, "To my friend Jim Rome, we've got the karma going."

11. Messner (1992) defined "covert intimacy" as doing things together rather than mutual talk about inner lives.

12. When I refer to Rome in this section, I am referring not to Rome, the individual person. Rather, I am referring to Rome's discourse.

13. However, it is important to note that Rome asserts his authority over a person with less power—a first-time caller. Rome doesn't take this strong a stance with Eric Davis, a high-status person who likely has more influence within the sports world. This textual example reveals the power relations of talk radio; hosts and famous athletes have more authority than callers.

References

Armstrong, C. B., & Rubin, A. M. (1989). Talk radio as interpersonal communication. *Journal of Communication, 39*(2), 84–93.

Buzinski, J. (2000, July 13). *Week in review.* Available at www.outsports.com

Buzinski, J. (2001, May 20). *Give the media good marks: Coverage of closeted gay baseball player was positive and non-judgmental.* Available at www.outsports.com

Collie, A. J. (2001, August 8). Rome rants. *American Way,* pp. 50–54, 56–57.

Connell, R. W. (2000). *The men and the boys.* Berkeley: University of California Press.

Cook, J. (2001). Dangerously radioactive: The plural vocalities of radio talk. In C. Lee & C. Poynton (Eds.), *Culture and text: Discourse and methodology in social research and cultural studies* (pp. 59–80). New York: Rowman & Littlefield.

Deitsch, R. (2003, May 12). Under review: Rome returning. *Sports Illustrated, 98,* 28.

Douglas, S. J. (2002). Letting the boys be boys: Talk radio, male hysteria, and political discourse in the 1980s. In M. Hilmes & J. Loviglio (Eds.), *Radio reader: Essays in the cultural history of radio* (pp. 485–504). New York: Routedge.

Duggan, L. (2001). The new homonormativity: The sexual politics of neoliberalism. In R. Castronovo & D. D. Nelson (Eds.), *Materalizing democracy: Toward a revitalized cultural politics* (pp. 175–194). Durham, NC: Duke University Press.

Farred, G. (2000). Cool as the other side of the pillow: How ESPN's Sportscenter has changed television sports talk. *Journal of Sport & Social Issues, 24*(2), 96–117.

Foucault, M. (1980). *Power/knowledge: Selected interviews and other writings, 1972–1977* (Colin Gordon, Ed. & Trans.). New York: Pantheon.

Ghosh, C. (1999, February 22). A guy thing: Radio sports talk shows. *Forbes,* p. 55.

Goldberg, D. T. (1998). Call and response: Sports, talk radio, and the death of democracy. *Journal of Sport & Social Issues, 22*(2), 212–223.

Hare-Mustin, R. T. (1994). Discourses in the mirrored room: A postmodern analysis of therapy. *Family Process, 33,* 19–35.

Hodgson, E. (1999, August 18). King of smack. *Fastbreak—The Magazine of the Phoenix Suns,* pp. 1–5.

Hutchby, I. (1996). *Confrontation talk: Arguments, asymmetries, and power on talk radio.* Mahwah, NJ: Lawrence Erlbaum.

Jakobsen, J. K. (2001). He has wronged America and women: Clinton's sexual conservatism. In L. Berlant & L. Duggan (Eds.), *Our Monica, ourselves: The Clinton affair and the national interest* (pp. 291–314). New York: New York University Press.

Kane, M. J., & Lenskyj, H. J. (2000). Media treatment of female athletes: Issues of gender and sexualities. In L. W. Wenner (Ed.), *Mediasport* (pp. 186–201). New York: Routledge.

Kellner, D. (1995). *Media culture: Cultural studies, identity, and politics between the modern and postmodern.* New York: Routledge.

Kimmel, M. (1994). Masculinity as homophobia. In H. Brod & M. Kaufman (Eds.), *Theorizing masculinities* (pp. 119–141). Thousand Oaks, CA: Sage.

Kitzinger, C. (1987). *The social construction of lesbianism.* Newbury Park, CA: Sage.

Lumby, C. (2001). The President's penis: Entertaining sex and power. In L. Berlant & L. Duggan (Eds.), *Our Monica, ourselves: The Clinton affair and the national interest* (pp. 225–236). New York: New York University Press.

Mariscal, J. (1999). Chicanos and Latinos in the jungle of sports talk radio. *Journal of Sport & Social Issues, 23*(1), 111–117.

Messner, M. A. (1992). *Power at play: Sports and the problem of masculinity.* Boston: Beacon.

Messner, M. A. (2002). *Taking the field: Women, men, and sports.* Minneapolis: University of Minnesota Press.

Miller, T. (2001, June). Out at the ballgame. *Advocate,* pp. 1–3.

Outside the lines: Homophobia and sports. (2001, May 31). ESPN.com. Available at http://espn.go.com/otl

Page, B. I., & Tannenbaum, J. (1996). Populistic deliberation and talk radio. *Journal of Communication, 46*(2), 33–53.

Pronger, B. (1990). *The arena of masculinity: Sports, homosexuality, and the meaning of sex.* New York: St. Martin's.

Shields, D. (1999). *Black planet: Facing race during an NBA season.* New York: Crown.

Sports Illustrated Editors. (1994, April). The fall of Rome. *Sports Illustrated, 80,* 14.

Wenner, L. W. (1998). The sports bar: Masculinity, alcohol, sports, and the mediation of public space. In G. Rail & J. Harvey (Eds.), *Sports and postmodern times: Gender, sexuality, the body, and sport* (pp. 301–322). Albany: State University of New York Press.

Disability, Gender, and Difference on *The Sopranos*

Kathleen LeBesco

Gender and Disability on *The Sopranos*

Many characters on *The Sopranos* have disabilities, both traditional and metaphorical. But what is more interesting is how the audience is encouraged to adopt certain attitudes toward particular characters (disabled or not) based on the attitudes those characters exhibit toward disability, and how this happens in a gendered fashion. The dramatic conceit behind the show's first season was the conflict that would be generated when a mafia tough-guy, Tony, needed to seek therapy for his panic attacks. If panic attacks and dependence on psychological help are perceived to weaken a man, then Tony is understood as disabled by his peers.

In other scenes, we learn that Tony has learned with age to be respectful of others who are disabled. He tries to comfort his nephew Christopher, who thinks he has cancer, when Tony says, "You're just depressed." Christopher rebuffs this possibility, stating "Me? I'm no mental midget." Thus, Tony is again reminded how socially disabling any perception of difference can be. In therapy, Tony tells a story from his childhood about making fun of a neighborhood kid who had a cleft palate—Jimmy Smash, they called him—but says he finally knows what it is like to be used for someone else's amusement. Though Tony continues to make fun of Jimmy, imitating his distinctive speech pattern, he appears quite empathic nonetheless. . . .

What I propose to do in the remainder of this chapter is examine two forms of disability—one, amputeeism, considered to be of the "authentic" variety, and the other, fatness, considered to be controllable and thus "inauthentic." Many of the characterizations of women on *The Sopranos* are filtered through the experiences and attitudes of male characters, particularly Tony. I believe that a close investigation of the framing of a fat character and an amputee against this backdrop will provide a nuanced analysis of the

From LeBesco, K. (2006). Disability, gender, and difference on *The Sopranos*. *Women's Studies in Communication, 29*(1), 39–58.

preferred ideological reading of disability issues for audience members.

Case Study: Fatness and Amputeeism

Svetlana Kirilenko was introduced in the second season of *The Sopranos* as the somewhat severe Russian home health care aide for Tony Soprano's ailing mother. Through digital special effects, the nondisabled Russian actress and daughter of deaf parents Alia Kliouka appears to have lost part of one of her legs—though mostly she wears a prosthetic. Irving Zola notes the conservative tendency of television where visual depictions of certain disabilities are concerned: "There is simply a taboo against showing any missing parts, be it the result of a radical mastectomy or an amputation" (Zola, "Depictions of Disability" 11). Despite their slogan, "It's not TV, it's HBO," HBO follows suit in the depiction of Svetlana, who is rarely shown without her prosthesis. When she is shown without it, she often wears a long dress or skirt so that her stump is not visible. While early on she was a minor character relegated to the periphery of the action, Svetlana came to the forefront after Livia's death.

In season four of *The Sopranos,* Tony's Uncle Junior was ill, so Svetlana was back in the picture as she and her staff of aides cared for him. During one fateful visit to his uncle, Tony admired Svetlana's determination as she explained how she was teaching herself to build a website for her business. "You've got every reason to be in the bottle, but you're not," Tony mused. For him, Svetlana's disability signaled a free pass to alcoholism and depression, and he couldn't help but be a little awed by her pluck. This pluck, along with Svetlana's for once relaxed beauty, proved seductive; Tony and Svetlana ended up having sex on the sofa. Afterwards, in his customary brush-off, Tony told her "I'll call you in a few days." Svetlana replied, "Tony, come on. You're a nice guy, but I got my own problems. I don't want all the time to prop you up." Tony was a bit stunned by the idea that a woman who uses a prosthetic would be so nervy as to talk about propping *him* up, but he knew what she meant. What a change this is from the love affair in which the nondisabled partner manages to love the disabled one in spite of his/her disability, and in which the disabled partner feels completely unworthy.

Here we see a passionate disabled woman capable of enjoying a quick affair, but recognizing the nondisabled partner (Tony) as an emotional drain she's unwilling to take on. Svetlana is independent and sassy. In a later conversation, reacting to Tony's solipsism and self-absorption, Svetlana remarked, "Americans expect nothing bad to ever happen; the rest of the world expects only bad, and they are not disappointed." She's describing American arrogance and entitlement from a Russian perspective, but her statement is also compelling from a disability perspective.

Svetlana manages to avoid the stereotypical portrayal of people with disabilities as "sexually deviant and even dangerous, asexual, or sexually incapacitated, either physically or emotionally" (Longmore 72; see also Zola, "Depictions of Disability" II). Longmore writes that "disabled characters may be quite capable of physical love making, but spurn opportunities for romance because of a lack of self-acceptance" (73). While at first this might seem to be the case with Svetlana, in fact she doesn't pursue romance with Tony because of *his* emotional weakness. Svetlana's sex scene flies in the face of the tradition of disabled women rarely being portrayed as sexual beings (Finger 10; Lonsdale 7; Meekosha and Dowse in Barnes, Mercer, and Shakespeare 196; Zola, *Missing Pieces* 214; Garland-Thomson, "Feminist Theory" 285), and at the same time contains no cues to suggest devoteeism, either. Tom Shakespeare contends that "in modern western societies, sexual agency is considered the essential element of full adult person hood, replacing the role formerly taken by paid work: because disabled people are infantilized, and denied the status of active subjects, consequently their sexuality is undermined" (192). As both a paid worker and a sexual subject, Svetlana is accorded full personhood, even as a minor character.

Despite noteworthy commonalities, fatness differs from other more customarily recognized forms of disability in consequential ways. According to Rosemarie Garland-Thomson, "disability . . . is the attribution of corporeal deviance—not so much a property of bodies as a product of cultural rules about what bodies should be or do" (*Extraordinary Bodies* 6). Fat people, in their excessive refusal to be disciplined into culturally "acceptable" body shapes and sizes, are then as corporeally deviant as those others considered, without a second thought, to be disabled. However, for some, the key difference lies in the perceived ability to control the conditions of one's disability—in the disabled person's culpability in his or her own situation. While many commonly recognized forms of disability, like amputeeism, invite relatively little discourse about what the disabled person has done to deserve his or her loss of limb, the condition of fatness, not widely understood as a disability, tempts considerable public disdain for the fat person's weakness and lack of self-control.[1] Such presumptions manifest themselves in collective attitudes about and cultural representations of those to whom corporeal deviance is attributed.[2]

In contrast to Svetlana, Ginny Sacrimoni is desexualized—"wifed"—as the spouse of New York mob underboss and friend of Tony, "Johnny Suck." Played by Denise Borino, a fat New Jersey-ite with no prior acting experience who answered an open casting call, the minor character of Ginny is always perfectly coiffed, elegantly dressed, and what the medical establishment would call "morbidly obese." Her body size became central to the plot of *The Sopranos* in season four, when Ralph Cifaretto, a notoriously sleazy and widely

disliked member of Tony's crew, tells a joke among fellow crew members about Ginny having to have a 90-pound mole removed from her ass. Though immediately greeted with howling laughter, the joke makes its way through the grapevine back to Ginny's husband, John, who finds it no laughing matter. John explodes in anger, beating and urinating on one of Ralph's men who had laughed at the joke at the initial gathering. When Tony finds out, he confronts John, trying to understand what has made his friend so out of control: when he learns that it is the mole joke come home to roost, Tony sheepishly feigns ignorance and condemns it as deplorable.

Tony: Well if he did say it I didn't hear it, 'cause he knows better than to make a remark like that when I'm around.

John: She's fighting a weight problem since the kids were born. Weight Watchers, Richard Simmons, fasting. She works very fucking hard.

Tony: You're tellin' *me* how hard it is?

John: It's different for women: body image, self esteem. I'll tell you though, I never had a problem with her weight. To me she's beautiful—Rubenesque. That woman is my life. To think she's being mocked . . .

Tony: All right, look, I'm not gonna sit here and deny that Ralph can be a fucking asshole. And that was a horrible thing to say, but even if it was said, you can't be serious about him winding up . . . uh . . . you know. . . .

John: She's the mother of my children.

Tony: I know she is, John, I know she is. At least hear Ralph out; how long we go back, all of us?

(*The Sopranos*, episode 43: "The Weight")

John, increasingly incensed by Ralph's insensitivity, appeals to his boss Carmine to sanction a hit on Ralph in the name of Ginny's honor. Carmine agrees that the comment was inappropriate, but suggests that Ralph should be taxed, not whacked. John is unhappy with this solution. Throughout the next several scenes, John makes it known that "the ship on apologies has sailed," and that nothing short of revenge will satisfy him. His irrational behavior troubles Carmine, who orders John killed because his hotheadedness stands to undermine a profitable connection with Tony's crew. In turn, John orders a hit on Ralph to avenge Ginny's honor.

Whenever Ginny herself appears in this episode, she performs diet behavior. In one scene she weighs herself, in another she weighs her food portions, and in another she's making a fruit salad with low-fat topping. This all changes in a pivotal scene when John discovers just how much of a performance the dieting really is. Realizing he forgot something that he had planned to take on his road trip, John returns to the house to find Ginny crouched in the basement over a large box full of candy. Furious, he yells, "What the hell is this? I thought you were on the Atkins!" Ginny, petulant, guards the candy and cries, "I was. I *am*. It's hard, John; I'm trying." The exchange heats up, and viewers (but not Ginny) realize that John, who loves his wife even with her fat body, is highly agitated because he realizes he's put a hit on a man who insulted the honor of his wife—an honor not quite worth defending if she won't submit to the socially acceptable rigors of dieting. In other words, Ginny-as-fat is defensible only if Ginny is trying her damnedest not to be fat.[3]

Ginny is revealed as a woman who will not, or cannot, control her fatness through dieting. "In a culture which loves the idea that the body can be controlled, those who cannot control their bodies are seen (and may see themselves) as failures"

(Wendell, "Toward a Feminist Theory" 269). With the best of intentions, John's "don't blame the victim" mindset perniciously undermines fat subjectivity. Furthermore, it continues a dubious tradition of women with disabilities being represented as victims (Zola, "Depictions of Disability" 5; Dahl 76). "The dominant images [of disabled people] mirror the roles that are expected of men and women. These are that women must be passive and invisible and expressive, while men must be active and aggressive and instrumental" (Lonsdale 59).[4]

. . . Although I have chosen to discuss storylines highlighting two female characters, this should not be read to mean that *The Sopranos* problematizes only female bodies. The show has portrayed men living with cancer and drug addiction among other forms of affliction. Despite the presence of several fat men and at least two fat women in the cast, including the lead (James Gandolfini), fatness as a problem is never given more than a passing remark except in the case of Ginny; in fact, *The Sopranos* "repeatedly renounces the fit body and the typical means of attaining it" (Santo 73), and "has repeatedly inverted the medical establishment's denouncement of fat bodies. Contrarily, illness on the series is often equated with weight loss" (Santo 87). More than once, Tony is shown scolding his formerly chubby teenage son for his reluctance to eat—a sure sign of the value placed on bodily bulk in Tony's macho world.

Avi Santo highlights "the show's habitual use of overweight and obese bodies, particularly among its male characters" (72). Tony Soprano, Pussy Bonpensiero, Bobby Bacala, Skip Lipari, Jimmy Altieri, and Vito Spatofore surely comprise the fattest ensemble ever featured on prime time television. "With few exceptions, the male body on *The Sopranos* is regularly shown to be soft and unfit. Male fatness on *The Sopranos* is very rarely an overt signifier of failure" (72). Instead, fatness is the norm, and the male characters with whom viewers are asked to identify are rarely slim. . . .

Ideologies of Disability

. . . In the introduction to her thorough catalog of dramatic TV disability representations, Klobas discusses the problem common to most of them: "Stories are bound to a confining formula treatment where disability is a personal problem one must overcome. Viewers seldom see disabled characters as multifaceted human beings for whom physical limitations are a fact of nature. Disability is not depicted as being integrated into a busy and full life" (xiii). Though only a minor character, Svetlana avoids this diminished status. Though Tony tries to frame her as a supercrip for not being "in the bottle" and for making a website, Svetlana stands for none of that. She goes about her business, working hard (but not exactly leaping tall buildings in a single bound), loving passionately, and being a whole person, not some disabled dynamo. Her character's attitude is important because seeing someone who doesn't mourn their state of difference from a norm makes us question why we value the norm as much as we do (Hillyer 17).

Ginny, in contrast, is framed even by her loving husband as struggling intensely to overcome her fatness. In reproaching her own fatness, Ginny embodies the stereotypical disabled character who carries a "flaw" on her body, "but who hides society's and history's contempt for the disabled person by vocalizing a self-loathing or a self destructive pattern" (Hevey 424). Every shot of her in the episode "The Weight" depicts her focused on weight-changing behavior. She seems to have no other interests. Ginny comes off as what Jack Nelson describes as a "pitiable victim doomed to an unsatisfying life" (1). Even John decides Ginny's honor is no longer worth defending when he realizes that she's not dieting and fighting her weight like he thought she was. Klobas further argues that disabled characters "require help and aid to regain full personhood status" (xiv). Svetlana needs no more help in this department than the rest of us. But Ginny needs her husband's reminder that he thinks she's beautiful in order to be a whole person again after her candy binge.

In terms of social class status, it is also a lot easier for most viewers to identify with Svetlana than with Ginny. Ginny is a well-off homemaker with ample resources of time and money, whereas Svetlana lives a lower middle class life of financial concerns and wage labor. By showing us John's ultimate decision to not pursue his defense of Ginny's honor in this context, the writers are signaling that Ginny has the choice to reform herself, but can't or won't—and thus doesn't deserve the respect accorded to the likes of Svetlana.

Cumberbatch and Negrine question whether television should statistically represent society (98), and further, what constitutes "positive" imagery (102; see also Hevey 424). Ultimately, what becomes important is not the mere number of representations but the expression of a view from *within* disability culture through television—a view that counters "a history of [disability] representation that was not done by us but done to us" (Hevey 423). Jack Nelson argues that "disability activists would like to see an approach that neither denies nor emphasizes the disability portrayed" (15). Ginny's fatness is indeed overemphasized, so no points there. Furthermore, her subjectivity—whether her honor is worth fighting for—is made to hinge on how well she endeavors, through dieting, to undermine the very conditions of her own existence. But Svetlana manages to emerge victorious here; her one-leggedness is merely a fact of her existence, neither hidden nor made a big deal of. She emerges as neither supercrip nor pitiable victim, and thus stands as a politically potent example of disability represented on television.

Given that the oppression of disabled people has been described as "deriving from the economic relations of production, the . . . position of 'the flawed body' in western culture and from the anxieties of the able-bodied about their own position," examples of this type of representation constitute "a crucial tactic in diminishing the oppression of disabled people" (Hevey in Fulcher 177).

Another point of contrast in the representations of Ginny and Svetlana comes in their use of space. Zola contends that "it is increasingly less acceptable to exile problem-bearers in faraway colonies, asylums, and sanitaria. A recent compromise has been to locate them in places which, if not geographically distant, are socially distant" (*Missing Pieces* 198). On *The Sopranos*, nearly every scene featuring either Ginny or Svetlana is set in domestic space (whether the Sacrimoni manse or Uncle Junior's house)—the private sphere. These problematic women, while not institutionalized, dwell in spaces with little public influence. However, a key difference lies in the fact that Ginny is depicted in her own home, while Svetlana, as a health aide, works in the homes of others, and thus is presumed to have a greater degree of influence in the public sphere. In the most important scenes for each of these characters, their location in space is telling. Svetlana manages to emerge out of the domestic space as she stands on the porch to tell Tony to buzz off, in an act of agency. Ginny stays huddled in the basement of her home, the very bowels of the private sphere, subjected to her husband's remonstrations of her sugar lust. Ginny is trapped in the private sphere, consigned to isolation, anonymity, and shame. But in Svetlana's capacity to transcend the limitations of the private sphere to which disabled people have been relegated for too long, *The Sopranos* gives us a disabled character worthy of emulation.

Lest we become overenthusiastic about such representations, Zola cautions us about disability success stories, tales of people who have managed to overcome

their disability to accomplish great things, saying that if they "could *overcome* their handicaps so could and should all the disabled. And if we fail, it is our problem, our personality defect, our weakness" (*Missing Pieces* 205). Furthermore, "to emphasize individual personal qualities as the reason for success in overcoming difficulties (and the reason for failure if the barriers prove insurmountable) is self-serving for the individual and society" (*Missing Pieces* 235; see also Wendell, *The Rejected Body* 52). The depiction of Svetlana, who refuses to be made into a hero by Tony, refuses this logic of individualism, offering instead a more complicated ideology about disability and agency. . . .

The only evident way in which Ginny's portrayal is more forward-thinking than Svetlana's is in their casting. In contrast to the present context in which increasing numbers of reedy thespians are donning fat suits for dramatic or comedic effect, *The Sopranos* makes headway in casting an actual fat woman (as if so few exist!) as Ginny.[5] That she is not a trained actor seems beside the point, unless one considers that a fat suit would be no good for the show's realism, and serious weight gain for typically slim actresses is out of the question. Svetlana, as mentioned earlier, is played by an acclaimed non-disabled Russian actress with the help of digital wizardry. Though Alia Kliouka very capably enacts Svetlana, for some, the political significance of casting non-disabled people to play disabled ones parallels the retrograde thinking behind the minstrel shows of an earlier era.

Though obesity is not widely considered to be a disability in the popular imagination (despite its inclusion as a protected condition in the Americans With Disabilities Act), studies suggest that it has more negative connotations than other easily recognized forms of disability.[6] A study by psychologists at Rutgers and the University of Pennsylvania found that "when 10–11 year old children are asked to rate drawings of children who are either healthy, obese, or physically handicapped in order of how well they like the children depicted in the drawings, the children rate the obese youngsters lowest of all" ("Tween Girls" 12).[7] In attempting to explain an increase among girls in bias against the obese since 1961, the researchers argue that "girls' tendency to indicate stronger bias against obesity is likely a result of stronger conditioning from an early age equaling beauty with thinness. Indeed, girls as young as six are concerned about their weight and striving to be thinner" ("Tween Girls" 12; see also "Body Beautiful/Body Perfect"). . . .

Wendell protests that "now it is possible for the images of a few people to drive out the reality of most people we actually encounter . . . This tends to conflate body ideals with our concept of what is physically 'normal,' increasing the number of people whose bodies are regarded by themselves and others as abnormal and socially unacceptable" (*The Rejected Body* 86). What is sorely needed is a representational universe that begins to approach the complexity and wealth of real corporeal difference.

As I logged *Sopranos* episodes for this project, I notice[d] that a transformation began to take place in my own perceptions. Except for Ginny, whose portrayal I hope to have sufficiently problematized, fatness is neither obsessed over nor disciplined on the show. Characters exist with cancer, stroke, Borderline Personality Disorder, food poisoning, developmental disabilities, depression, panic attacks, Epstein-Barr disease, Carpal Tunnel Syndrome, sore backs, gunshot wounds to the spleen, Attention Deficit Disorder, low vision, heroin addiction, learning disabilities, obesity, amputated legs, and other conditions that are feared or reviled to different degrees in everyday life. On the show, they're mostly just another fact of life—except, of course, when they are faked. With its sharp writing and masterful acting, *The Sopranos* makes physical limitation, loss of ability, distance from body ideals, and pain comprehensible to

its audience. This accomplishment brings us one step closer to having

> less fear of the negative body, less fear of our own weaknesses and "imperfections," of our inevitable deterioration and death. Perhaps we could give up some of our idealizations and relax our desire for control of the body; until we do, we maintain them at the expense of people whose bodies do not fit the ideals, and at the expense of much of everyone's ability to live comfortably with our own real bodies. (Wendell, *The Rejected Body* 109–110)

The bodies that jar me from my daydream of reality (with its vast repertoire of human variation) transplanted to television are inhabited by the Bada Bing dancers, all strangely similar to one another with their collagen-enhanced lips, liposuctioned hips, and silicone breasts. That kind of physique has been normalized on other shows, and when it emerges as freakish in contrast to the diversity of human corporeality, it suggests that *The Sopranos* is doing interesting representational work about bodies.

Notes

1. To complicate this discussion, I invoke a 1986 study by Manna and Rogovsky (cited in Asch and Fine 243) that suggests that disabled women are viewed more negatively than disabled men, owing to the differing perceptions of the *cause* of that disability. Male disability was attributed to "external situations such as war, work injury, or accident." They attributed female disability to internal causes, such as disease. The authors suggest that attributing disability to disease may foster more negative attitudes, because disease stimulates primitive fears of contagion or of the person's inherent moral badness. Thus, the disabled woman may be viewed as "more dangerous than a similarly disabled male, more morally suspect, or more deserving of her fate" (243). The fat woman,

already viewed negatively because of her refusal to adapt to cultural body norms, is doubly cursed by virtue of her femaleness.

2. I take my cue in examining fat as disability—with its connotation of the social, cultural, and political—from April Herndon. Herndon acknowledges that there are indeed fat people who suffer impairments due to size, but chooses to focus on disability instead. "While physical impairments surely cause personal struggles, the treatment of fat/disabled people as social pariahs must be addressed first and foremost. The reliance upon biological truths about bodies . . . serves only to further pathologize individuals" (4–5).

3. Avi Santo makes a similar argument for the salvageability of Tony, claiming that his "soft, plump exterior inevitably contributes to a reading of his character as childlike and, bizarrely, well-intentioned despite his horrific behavior. Tony's base criminality is rendered more acceptable by his own desire to gain control over his body" (77; 78).

4. Adrienne Asch and Michelle Fine present a different perspective on gender roles for disabled women: "Exempted from the 'male' productive role and the female 'nurturing' one, having the glory of neither, disabled women are arguably doubly oppressed—or, perhaps, 'freer' to be nontraditional" (241). Garland-Thomson reinforces this idea of disabled women as doubly disenfranchised, claiming that "both the female and the disabled body are cast within cultural discourse as deviant and inferior, both are excluded from full participation in public as well as economic life; both are defined in opposition to a valued norm which is assumed to possess natural corporeal superiority" ("Feminist Theory" 279).

5. About Julia Roberts and Gwyneth Paltrow, Shane Watson humorously comments that "the fat suit has everything these girls could hope for in one latex, foam and spandex package. It offers them the fast track to a place as far removed from their personal experience as it is possible to go, and without having to so much as lick an M&M to get there" (5).

6. Any attempt to construct a hierarchy of disability is ultimately doomed, because the number of identity vectors that would need to be considered is great. However, I am interested in how fatness and other forms of disability converge, and at the same time, differ. I find compelling Susan Wendell's argument that "many people regard large people as unfortunate or (if they are fat) weak individuals whose abnormality creates their problems, which in itself illustrates the strength of the cultural demand that everyone meet body ideals. Nevertheless, although they are subjected to stigma, stereotypes, and cultural judgments, they are not surrounded by the same aura of hopelessness and pathology that many cultures project onto people with illnesses and injuries, nor does it seem as plausible that they should be kept out of public life" (*The Rejected Body* 46–47). Nonetheless, the expectation that fat people *can* "cure" their problem but *don't* or *won't* invites scorn of great magnitude.

7. "Recognizable" physical handicaps in this study included people using wheelchairs or crutches, as well as those with facial "deformities" or missing limbs.

References

Asch, Adrienne, and Michelle Fine. "Nurturance, Sexuality and Women With Disabilities: The Example of Women and Literature." *The Disability Studies Reader.* Ed. Leonard J. Davis. New York: Routledge, 1997. 241–59.

Barnes, Colin, Geof Mercer, and Tom Shakespeare. *Exploring Disability: A Sociological Introduction.* Malden, MA: Blackwell, 1999.

"Body Beautiful/Body Perfect: Challenging the Status Quo. Where Do Women With Disabilities Fit In?" *Disability Cool: Sexuality 'R Us* website. 17 Feb. 2002. (http://www.geocities.com/HotSprings/7319/sex.htm)

Cumberbatch, Guy, and Ralph Negrine. *Images of Disability on Television.* London: Routledge, 1992.

Dahl, Marilyn. "The Role of the Media in Promoting Images of Disability: Disability as Metaphor, the Evil Crip." *Canadian Journal of Communication.* 18.1 (Winter 1993): 75–80.

Finger, Anne. "Forbidden Fruit." *New Internationalist.* 233 (1992): 8–10.

Fulcher, Gillian. "Beyond Normalisation but Not Utopia." *Disability and Society: Emerging Issues and Insights,* Ed. Len Barton. London: Longman, 1996. 167–90.

Garland-Thomson, Rosemarie. "Re-shaping, Re-thinking, Redefining: Feminist Disability." *Feminist Disability Studies.* 20.13 (2001): 1–27.

———. *Extraordinary Bodies: Figuring Physical Disability in American Culture and Literature.* New York: Columbia UP, 1997.

———. "Feminist Theory, the Body, and the Disabled Figure." *The Disability Studies Reader,* Ed. Lennard J. Davis. New York: Routledge, 1997. 279–92.

Herndon, April. "Disparate But Disabled: Fat Embodiment and Disability Studies." *National Women's Studies Association Journal.* 14.3 (Fall 2002): 120–137.

Hevey, David. "From Self-love to the Picket Line: Strategies for Change in Disability Representation." *Disability, Handicap and Society.* 8.4 (1993): 423–429.

Hillyer, Barbara. *Feminism and Disability.* Norman, OK: U of Oklahoma P. 1993.

Klobas, Lauri E. *Disability Drama in Television and Film.* Jefferson, NC: McFarland, 1988.

Longmore, Paul K. "Screening Stereotypes: Images of Disabled People in Television and Motion Pictures." *Images of the Disabled, Disabling Images.* Ed. Alan Gartner and Tom Joe. New York: Praeger, 1987. 65–78.

Lonsdale, Susan. *Women and Disability: The Physical Experience of Physical Disability Among Women.* New York: St Martin's, 1990.

Nelson, Jack A. (1994). "Broken Images: Portrayals of Those With Disabilities in American Media." *The Disabled, the Media and the Information Age.* Ed. Jack A. Nelson. Westport, CT: Greenwood, 1994. 1–24.

Santo, Avi. "'Fat Fuck! Why Don't You Take a Look in the Mirror?': Weight, Body Image, and Masculinity in *The Sopranos.*" *This Thing of Ours: Investigating "The Sopranos."* Ed. David Lavery. New York: Columbia UP, 2002. 72–94.

Sopranos, The. Episode 43: The Weight, Dir. 6 October 2002.

"Tween Girls Stigmatize Obese Peers." *Marketing to Women.* 15.1 (January 2002): 12.

Watson, Shane. "If the Suit Doesn't Fit . . . Why Are Some of Hollywood's Skinniest Women Queuing Up to Play Fatsos?" *The Guardian* (Manchester, UK), Aug 17 2001, 2.5.

Wendell, Susan. "Toward a Feminist Theory of Disability." *The Disability Studies Reader.* Ed. Lennard J. Davis. New York: Routledge, 1997. 260–78.

———. *The Rejected Body: Feminist Philosophical Reflections on Disability.* New York: Routledge, 1996.

Zola, Irving Kenneth. "Depictions of Disability—Metaphor, Message, and Medium in the Media: A Research and Political Agenda." *Social Science Journal.* 22.4 (October 1985): 5–17.

———. *Missing Pieces: A Chronicle of Living With a Disability.* Philadelphia: Temple UP, 1982.

PART IV

ADVERTISING AND CONSUMER CULTURE

Acentral theme of the chapters in this section is the role of the media industries in the production and maintenance of an overwhelmingly consumption-oriented cultural environment in postindustrial economies like our own. Critics of such a culture point to a long list of social and political costs related to unchecked consumption of world resources, including environmental degradation, the dangerously increasing gap between rich and poor nations, erosion of political democracy, and even global warming—but the multinational corporate drive to increase levels of product consumption seems largely unaffected by these warnings.

In the consumer culture, we live in a world saturated with advertising imagery urging us to buy and consume products as a path to future happiness and self-transformation. As Sut Jhally says in "Image-Based Culture" (IV.22), which introduces this section, "In the contemporary world, messages about goods are all pervasive—advertising has increasingly filled up the spaces of our daily existence . . . it is the air that we breathe as we live our daily lives" (p. 200). Any discussion of the role of media within a capitalist economy has to foreground the role of advertising, both as an industry in its own right and, in Jhally's words, as a "discourse through and about objects" (p. 200). Because advertising legitimizes and even sacralizes consumption as a way of life, it is critical to our ability to think for ourselves that we learn to analyze not just the meanings of advertising texts but also the place of the advertising industry in our society.

As Jhally points out, "Fundamentally, advertising talks to us as individuals and addresses us about how we can become happy" (p. 200). In the past, advertisements told us that the key to happiness was our ability to keep up with the consumption patterns of our neighbors. But economist Juliet Schor, in "The New Politics of Consumption" (IV.23), points to the "upscaling of lifestyle norms" that characterizes "the new consumerism." Schor argues that a by-product of the recent economic boom times in the United States is that "luxury, rather than mere comfort, is a widespread aspiration." She shows the role of television, in particular, in contributing to this "upscaling of lifestyle norms."

> Because television shows are so heavily skewed to the "lifestyles of the rich and upper middle-class," they inflate the viewer's perceptions of what others have, and by extension what is worth acquiring—what one must have in order to avoid being "out of it." (p. 207)

After years of neglect and/or demeaning stereotyping of Blacks, Latinos, Native Americans, and Asian Americans in advertising aimed at White audiences, social protest (including boycotts) and target marketing brought significant changes to these historic practices. Especially in the case of Blacks and Latinos, significant gains in visibility and in respectful representations in mass audience advertising occurred in the 1970s. In part this was because of political pressure to change the racist representations of the past, but it also represents the recognition on the part of many companies that it would be in their economic self-interest to appeal to new target markets.

Barbara Mueller (IV.24) reviews some of the research contemporary advertisers have available to them on consumer buying patterns among African Americans, and she

provides a good example of the marketer's perspective. Mueller criticizes past advertisements featuring Black Americans for their reliance on stereotypes and points out that today "African Americans feel a strong need to be portrayed in a positive way and will appreciate marketers who do so" (p. 216). She presents detailed demographic research that breaks the African American market in general, and women in particular, into consumer profiles containing what she calls "psychographic insights" that advertisers must keep in mind when creating persuasive ads. Mueller points out in passing that credit card debt and difficulty in accumulating savings for retirement are financial issues "of concern" in many African American households. We would add that no matter how sensitive to the dignity and humanity of any target audience the advertisers may learn to be, it is still true that it is their goal to promote high levels of consumption, not to concern themselves with solving the larger social problems, including unsustainable consumer debt, to which overconsumption inevitably leads.

Moving from a focus on race to gender in relation to advertising, this part includes several chapters tracing historically several important changes in the construction of femininities in media culture over the past half century, using women's magazines and advertising directed at women as windows into this topic. We begin with an essay by Laurie Ouellette (IV.25) on Helen Gurley Brown, author of the best-selling book *Sex and the Single Girl* (1962) and later the editor who made *Cosmopolitan* magazine such a major success in the 1960s and 1970s. Ouellette shows how Brown, in her book and in the advice columns of her magazine, took on the cultural mission of showing working-class White women the path to upward mobility. According to Ouellette,

> Brown's advice offered a gendered success myth to women who found themselves taking on new roles as breadwinners, but who lacked the wages, education, professional skills, and social opportunities

to recognize themselves in more conventional, male-oriented upward-mobility narratives. (p. 230)

For these White working-class women in the prefeminist 1960s, learning to fake a middle-class version of femininity was the key to real class mobility, through ensnaring a well-off man.

At the same time Brown was urging this traditional path to success on her magazine's readers, the early women's movement was beginning to critique the very institution of marriage as an agency of women's subordination in a male-dominated social order. Advertising **images** that either confined women to roles as wives and mothers or treated women's bodies as sex objects were an early and continuing target of feminist organizing and calls for change. Recounting her experience seeking advertisers to support the pioneering feminist *Ms* magazine in its early days, Gloria Steinem reminds us, in "Sex, Lies, and Advertising" (IV.26), how advertisers targeting women as consumers subscribed to very limited notions of what constitutes femininity (i.e., dependency, concern with beauty, fixation on family and nurturance, fear of technology) and consequently "feminine" buying patterns. Feminist efforts to redefine gender ideals for advertisers in the 1970s and 1980s met with disbelief, resistance, and downright hostility. Steinem's essay reveals the extent to which advertisers also assumed the right to control editorial content of the media—citing, among other practices, efforts to censor feature stories that might conflict with the interests of advertisers.

Thanks in large part to the feminist activist work to raise awareness about **sexism** in advertising representations, as well as to social and occupational changes since the 1970s, it is no longer acceptable for advertisers to depict women in such a narrow range of occupations, nor primarily as wives and mothers. However, there is a proliferation today of marketing venues for promoting an idealized image of femininity in the form of the "beautiful bride." From websites to magazines to TV reality shows, there is a resurgence of what could be classified as the prefeminist idea that the wedding day is the triumphant moment of fulfillment for the woman. As Erika Engstrom (IV.27) writes,

> The wedding provides a venue in which women can still and are still expected to show and display others their femininity. The one day in which a woman, any woman, can be a star is her wedding day, and the reward for adhering to a hegemony of femininity is a temporary status of being a celebrity. (pp. 245–246)

Engstrom points to the new genre of wedding reality TV shows, on which the "bridal dress" and the elaborate ritual of applying cosmetics are presented as the centers of attention, as well as the agents through which "brides become 'transformed' from mere woman to bride" (p. 246).

Another current version of the femininity constructed through commercial media culture is the hypersexualized representation of the female body found in much of today's fashion advertising. Feminist scholars are not in agreement over what such hypersexualization means for women's lives. Some would argue that such representations are merely updated versions of traditional exploitation for profit ("sex sells"); others maintain that such representations depict sexual empowerment. Rosalind Gill takes on this debate in "Supersexualize Me!" (IV.28). She questions the degree to which representations of young women aggressively flaunting their sexuality are truly about female *agency* and at the same time points to the categories of women still denied any visibility in the world conjured up by advertising imagery: "older women, disabled women, fat women and any woman who is unable to live up to the increasingly narrow standards of female beauty and sex appeal that are normatively required."

Women are not the only group to be targeted with a set of images that depict a narrow standard of gender performance, since white men are increasingly targeted by an advertising industry selling idealized representations of masculinity. In his analysis of these ads, Jackson Katz (IV.29) points out the way that many of them link violence with masculinity as a way to construct a masculinity that is perceived as powerful and in control. This, he argues, is especially the case for working-class men who have less economic power and hence use their body to assert a kind of power that is based on violence. In his **content analysis** of ads from a range of genres, Katz found that

> men's magazines and mainstream newsweeklies are rife with ads featuring violent male icons, such as football players, big-fisted boxers, military figures, and leather-clad bikers. Sports magazines aimed at men, and televised sporting events, carry tens of millions of dollars worth of military ads. In the past 20 years, there have been thousands of ads for products designed to help men develop muscular physiques, such as weight training machines and nutritional supplements. (p. 262)

These images are so ubiquitous that we often fail to consider what the real-world effects could be. Katz, an antiviolence activist, is especially interested in drawing our attention to the way that violent images of masculinity could potentially legitimize actual violence against women since, he argues, images shape the way we think and provide key cultural cues as to what constitutes normative gender practices.

Gay White men constitute a particular group of men who have in the past been ignored or ridiculed by advertisers because they supposedly failed to fit the image of muscular masculinity. Ever since the discovery of the upscale gay male market niche by national advertisers in the 1970s, however, national and local magazines and newspapers have been able to court advertising dollars by selling this desirable demographic. However, again, there are many trade-offs when commercial cultural visibility (through advertising images) is embraced as a route to social equality. For one thing, only that part of the gay and lesbian community that fits the attractive demographic profile gains greater visibility—those without high incomes continue to be marginalized, even in the gay community's own media institutions, which once contained a greater diversity of images (Sender, 2007).

Thus, while on one level we can applaud the increasing visibility of some historically marginalized groups in today's ads, we must still remember the wider context of the economic and environmental costs of mass consumption. The more different groups are targeted, on both a national and an international level, the more products people will buy and the greater the level of environmental destruction. Moreover, critical media scholars point out that corporations that buy advertising space have some power to determine what types of stories and viewpoints will be represented in media. This limits free speech and lessens the possibility that alternative ways of seeing and thinking about the world will be represented across a range of texts. Ultimately, for media activists, the goal is to democratize media ownership and to diminish the power of ads, and as an important step in this direction, we need to develop the strong media literacy programs that can provide some immunization to what Neil Postman (1990) called "the eloquence of the image."

References

Postman, N. (1990). Consuming images. In *The public mind* [Video]. Washington, DC: Public Broadcasting Service.

Sender, K. (2007). *Business, not politics: The making of the gay market.* New York: Columbia University Press.

Image-Based Culture

Advertising and Popular Culture

Sut Jhally

Because we live inside the consumer culture, and most of us have done so for most of our lives, it is sometimes difficult to locate the origins of our most cherished values and assumptions. They simply appear to be part of our natural world. It is a useful exercise, therefore, to examine how our culture has come to be defined and shaped in specific ways—to excavate the origins of our most celebrated rituals. For example, everyone in this culture knows a "diamond is forever." It is a meaning that is almost as "natural" as the link between roses and romantic love. However, diamonds (just like roses) did not always have this meaning. Before 1938 their value derived primarily from their worth as scarce stones (with the DeBeers cartel carefully controlling the market supply). In 1938 the New York advertising agency of N.W. Ayers was hired to change public attitudes toward diamonds—to transform them from a financial investment into a *symbol* of committed and everlasting love. In 1947 an Ayers advertising copywriter came up with the slogan "a diamond is forever" and the rest, as they say, is history. As an N.W. Ayers memorandum put it in 1959: "Since 1939 an entirely new generation of young people has grown to marriageable age. To the new generation, a diamond ring is considered a necessity for engagement to virtually everyone."[1]

This is a fairly dramatic example of how the institutional structure of the consumer society orients the culture (and its attitudes, values, and rituals) more and more toward the world of commodities. The marketplace (and its major ideological tool, advertising) is the major structuring institution of contemporary consumer society.

This of course was not always the case. In the agrarian-based society preceding industrial society, other institutions such as family, community, ethnicity, and religion were the dominant institutional mediators and creators of the cultural forms. Their influence waned in the transition to industrial society and then consumer society. The emerging institution of the marketplace occupied the cultural terrain left void by the evacuation of these older forms.

From Jhally, S. (1990, July). Image-based culture: Advertising and popular culture. *The World and I*, pp. 506–519.

Information about products seeped into public discourse. More specifically, public discourse soon became dominated by the "discourse through and about objects."[2]

At first, this discourse relied upon transmitting information about products alone, using the available means of textual communication offered by newspapers. As the possibility of more effective color illustration emerged and as magazines developed as competitors for advertising dollars, this "discourse" moved from being purely text-based. The further integration of first radio and then television into the advertising/media complex ensured that commercial communication would be characterized by the domination of *imagistic* modes of representation.

Again, because our world is so familiar, it is difficult to imagine the process through which the present conditions emerged. In this context, it is instructive to focus upon that period in our history that marks the transition point in the development of an image-saturated society—the 1920s. In that decade the advertising industry was faced with a curious problem—the need to sell increasing quantities of "nonessential" goods in a competitive marketplace using the potentialities offered by printing and color photography. Whereas the initial period of national advertising (from approximately the 1880s to the 1920s) had focused largely in a celebratory manner on the products themselves and had used text for "reason why" advertising (even if making the most outrageous claims), the 1920s saw the progressive integration of people (via visual representation) into the messages. Interestingly, in this stage we do not see representations of "real" people in advertisements, but rather we see representations of people who "stand for" reigning social values such as family structure, status differentiation, and hierarchical authority.

While this period is instructive from the viewpoint of content, it is equally fascinating from the viewpoint of *form*; for while the possibilities of using visual imagery existed with the development of new technologies, there was no guarantee that the audience was sufficiently literate in visual imagery to properly decode the ever-more complex messages. Thus, the advertising industry had to educate as well as sell, and many of the ads of this period were a fascinating combination where the written (textual) material explained the visual material. The consumer society was literally being taught how to read the commercial messages. By the postwar period the education was complete and the function of written text moved away from explaining the visual and toward a more cryptic form where it appears as a "key" to the visual "puzzle."

In the contemporary world, messages about goods are all pervasive—advertising has increasingly filled up the spaces of our daily existence. Our media are dominated by advertising images, public space has been taken over by "information" about products, and most of our sporting and cultural events are accompanied by the name of a corporate sponsor. There is even an attempt to get television commercials into the nation's high schools under the pretense of "free" news programming. Advertising is ubiquitous—it is the air that we breathe as we live our daily lives.

Advertising and the Good Life: Image and "Reality"

I have referred to advertising as being part of "a discourse through and about objects" because it does not merely tell us about things but of how things are connected to important domains of our lives. Fundamentally, advertising talks to us as individuals and addresses us about how we can become happy. The answers it provides are all oriented to the marketplace, through the purchase of goods or services. To understand the system of images that constitutes advertising we need to inquire into the definition of happiness and satisfaction in contemporary social life.

Quality of life surveys that ask people what they are seeking in life—what it is that makes them happy—report quite consistent results. The conditions that people are searching for—what they perceive will make them happy—are things such as having personal autonomy and control of one's life, self-esteem, a happy family life, loving relations, a relaxed, tension-free leisure time, and good friendships. The unifying theme of this list is that these things are not fundamentally connected to goods. It is primarily "social" life and not "material" life that seems to be the locus of perceived happiness. Commodities are only weakly related to these sources of satisfaction.[3]

A market society, however, is guided by the principle that satisfaction should be achieved via the marketplace, and through its institutions and structures it orients behavior in that direction. The data from the quality of life studies are not lost on advertisers. If goods themselves are not the locus of perceived happiness, then they need to be connected in some way with those things that are. Thus advertising promotes images of what the audience conceives of as "the good life": Beer can be connected with anything from eroticism to male fraternity to the purity of the old West; food can be tied up with family relations or health; investment advice offers early retirements in tropical settings. The marketplace cannot directly offer the real thing, but it can offer visions of it connected with the purchase of products.

Advertising thus does not work by creating values and attitudes out of nothing but by drawing upon and rechanneling concerns that the target audience (and the culture) already shares. As one advertising executive put it: "Advertising doesn't always mirror how people are acting but how they're *dreaming*. In a sense what we're doing is wrapping up your emotions and selling them back to you." Advertising absorbs and fuses a variety of symbolic practices and discourses, it appropriates and distills from an unbounded range of cultural references. In

so doing, goods are knitted into the fabric of social life and cultural significance. As such, advertising is not simple manipulation, but what ad-maker Tony Schwartz calls "partipulation," with the audience participating in its own manipulation.

What are the consequences of such a system of images and goods? Given that the "real" sources of satisfaction cannot be provided by the purchase of commodities (merely the "image" of that source), it should not be surprising that happiness and contentment appear illusory in contemporary society. Recent social thinkers describe the contemporary scene as a "joyless economy,"[4] or as reflecting the "paradox of affluence."[5] It is not simply a matter of being "tricked" by the false blandishments of advertising. The problem is with the institutional structure of a market society that propels definition of satisfaction through the commodity/image system. The modern context, then, provides a curious satisfaction experience—one that William Leiss describes as "an ensemble of satisfactions and dissatisfactions" in which the consumption of commodities mediated by the image-system of advertising leads to consumer uncertainty and confusion.[6] The image-system of the marketplace reflects our desires and dreams, yet we have only the pleasure of the images to sustain us in our actual experience with goods.

The commodity image-system thus provides a particular vision of the world—a particular mode of self-validation that is integrally connected with what one *has* rather than what one *is*—a distinction often referred to as one between "having" and "being," with the latter now being defined through the former. As such, it constitutes a way of life that is defined and structured in quite specific political ways. Some commentators have even described advertising as part of a new *religious* system in which people construct their identities through the commodity form, and in which commodities are part of a supernatural magical world where anything is possible with the purchase of a product. The commodity as displayed in advertising plays a mixture of psychological, social, and physical roles in its relations with people. The object world interacts with the human world at the most basic and fundamental of levels, performing seemingly magical feats of enchantment and transformation, bringing instant happiness and gratification, capturing the forces of nature, and acting as a passport to hitherto untraveled domains and group relationships.[7]

In short, the advertising image-system constantly propels us toward things as means to satisfaction. In the sense that every ad says it is better to buy than not to buy, we can best regard advertising as a *propaganda* system for commodities. In the image-system as a whole, happiness lies at the end of a purchase. Moreover, this is not a minor propaganda system—it is all pervasive. It should not surprise us then to discover that the problem that it poses—how to get more things for everyone (as that is the root to happiness)—guides our political debates. The goal of *economic growth* (on which the commodity vision is based) is an unquestioned and sacred proposition of the political culture. As the environmental costs of the strategy of unbridled economic growth become more obvious, it is clear we must, as a society, engage in debate concerning the nature of future economic growth. However, as long as the commodity image-system maintains its ubiquitous presence and influence, the possibilities of opening such a debate are remote. At the very moment we most desperately need to pose new questions within the political culture, the commodity image-system propels us with even greater certainty and persuasion along a path that, unless checked, is destined to end in disaster. . . .

The visual image-system has colonized areas of life that were previously largely defined (although not solely) by auditory perception and experience. The 1980s [saw] a change in the way that popular music commodities (records, tapes, compact discs)

were marketed, with music videos becoming an indispensable component of an overall strategy. These videos were produced as commercials for musical commodities by the advertising industry, using techniques learned from the marketing of products. Viewing these videos, there often seems to be little link between the song and the visuals. In the sense that they are commercials for records, there of course does not have to be. Video makers are in the same position as ad makers in terms of trying to get attention for their message and making it visually pleasurable. It is little wonder then that representations involving sexuality figure so prominently (as in the case of regular product advertising). The visuals are chosen for their ability to sell.

Many people report that listening to a song after watching the video strongly affects the interpretation they give to it—the visual images are replayed in the imagination. In that sense, the surrounding commodity image-system works to fix—or at least to limit—the scope of imaginative interpretation. The realm of listening becomes subordinated to the realm of seeing, to the influence of commercial images. There is also evidence suggesting that the composition of popular music is affected by the new video context. People write songs or lines with the vital marketing tool in mind.

Speed and Fragmentation

In addition to issues connected with the colonization of the commodity image-system of other areas of social life (gender socialization, politics, children's play, popular cultural forms), there are also important broader issues connected with its relation to modes of perception and forms of consciousness within contemporary society. For instance, the commodity information-system has two basic characteristics: reliance on visual modes of representation and the increasing speed and rapidity of the images that constitute it. It is this second point that I wish to focus on here. . . .

The visual images that dominate public space and public discourse are, in the video age, not static. They do not stand still for us to examine and linger over. They are here for a couple of seconds and then they are gone. Television advertising is the epitome of this speed-up. There is nothing mysterious in terms of how it arose. As commercial time slots declined from sixty seconds to thirty seconds (and recently to fifteen seconds and even shorter), advertisers responded by creating a new type of advertising—what is called the "vignette approach"—in which narrative and "reason-why" advertising are subsumed under a rapid succession of lifestyle images, meticulously timed with music, that directly sell feeling and emotion rather than products. As a commercial editor puts it of this new approach: "They're a wonderful way to pack in information: all those scenes and emotions—cut, cut, cut. Also they permit you a very freestyle approach—meaning that as long as you stay true to your basic vignette theme you can usually just drop one and shove in another. They're a dream to work with because the parts are sort of interchangeable."[8]

The speed-up is also a response by advertisers to two other factors: the increasing "clutter" of the commercial environment and the coming of age, in terms of disposable income, of a generation that grew up on television and commercials. The need for a commercial to stand out to a visually sophisticated audience drove the image-system to a greater frenzy of concentrated shorts. Again, sexuality became a key feature of the image-system within this.

The speed-up has two consequences. First, it has the effect of drawing the viewer into the message. One cannot watch these messages casually; they require undivided attention. Intensely pleasurable images, often sexual, are integrated into a flow of images. Watching has to be even more attentive to catch the brief shots of visual pleasure. The space "in between" the good parts can then be filled with other information, so that the commodity being advertised becomes a rich and complex sign.

Second, the speed-up has replaced narrative and rational response with images and emotional response. Speed and fragmentation are not particularly conducive to *thinking*. They induce *feeling*. The speed and fragmentation that characterize the commodity image-system may have a similar effect on the construction of consciousness. In one series of ads for MTV, a teenage boy or girl engages in a continuous monologue of events, characters, feelings, and emotions without any apparent connecting theme. As the video images mirror the fragmentation of thoughts, the ad ends with the plug: "Finally, a channel for the way you think." . . .

Notes

1. See Edward Epstein, *The Rise and Fall of Diamonds* (New York: Simon & Schuster, 1982).

2. This is discussed more fully in William Leiss, Stephen Kline, and Sut Jhally, *Social Communication in Advertising* (Toronto: Nelson, 1986).

3. See Fred Hirsch, *Social Limits to Growth* (Cambridge: Harvard University Press, 1976).

4. Tibor Scitovsky, *The Joyless Economy* (New York: Oxford University Press, 1976).

5. Hirsch, *Social Limits*.

6. William Leiss, *The Limits to Satisfaction* (Toronto: Toronto University Press, 1976).

7. See Sut Jhally, *The Codes of Advertising* (New York: St. Martin's Press, 1987) and John Kavanaugh, *Following Christ in a Consumer Society* (New York: Orbis, 1981).

8. Quoted in Michael Arlen, *Thirty Seconds* (New York: Penguin, 1981), 182.

The New Politics of Consumption

Why Americans Want So Much More Than They Need

Juliet Schor

In contemporary American culture, consuming is as authentic as it gets. Advertisements, getting a bargain, garage sales, and credit cards are firmly entrenched pillars of our way of life. We shop on our lunch hours, patronize outlet malls on vacation, and satisfy our latest desires with a late-night click of the mouse.[1]

Yet for all its popularity, the shopping mania provokes considerable dis-ease: many Americans worry about our preoccupation with getting and spending. They fear we are losing touch with more worthwhile values and ways of living. But the discomfort rarely goes much further than that; it never coheres into a persuasive, well-articulated critique of consumerism. By contrast, in the 1960s and early 1970s, a far-reaching critique of consumer culture was a part of our political discourse. Elements of the New Left, influenced by the Frankfurt school, as well as by John Kenneth Galbraith and others, put forward a scathing indictment. They argued that Americans had been manipulated into participating in a dumbed-down, artificial consumer culture, which yielded few true human satisfactions.

For reasons that are not hard to imagine, this particular approach was short-lived, even among critics of American society and culture. It seemed too patronizing to talk about manipulation or the "true needs" of average Americans. In its stead, critics adopted a more liberal point of view and deferred to individuals on consumer issues. Social critics again emphasized the distribution of resources, with the more economistic goal of maximizing the incomes of working people. The good life, they suggested, could be achieved by attaining a comfortable, middle-class standard of living. This outlook was particularly prevalent in economics, where even radical economists have long believed that income is the key to well-being. While radical political economy, as it came to be called, retained a powerful critique of alienation in production and the distribution of property, it abandoned the nascent intellectual project of analyzing the consumer sphere. Few economists now think about how we

---

Reprinted by permission of Juliet Schor.

consume, and whether it reproduces class inequality, alienation, or power. "Stuff" is the part of the equation that the system is thought to have gotten nearly right.

Of course, many Americans retained a critical stance toward our consumer culture. They embody that stance in their daily lives—in the ways they live and raise their kids. But the rejection of consumerism, if you will, has taken place principally at an individual level. It is not associated with a widely accepted intellectual analysis, and an associated *critical politics of consumption.*

But such a politics has become an urgent need. The average American now finds it harder to achieve a satisfying standard of living than 25 years ago. Work requires longer hours, jobs are less secure, and pressures to spend more intense. Consumption-induced environmental damage remains pervasive, and we are in the midst of widespread failures of public provision. . . . Many Americans have long-term worries about their ability to meet basic needs, ensure a decent standard of living for their children, and keep up with an ever-escalating consumption norm.

In response to these developments, social critics continue to focus on income. In his impressive analysis of the problems of contemporary American capitalism, *Fat and Mean*, economist David Gordon emphasized income *adequacy.* The "vast majority of U.S. households," he argues, "can barely make ends meet. . . . Meager livelihoods are a *typical* condition, an *average* circumstance." Meanwhile, the Economic Policy Institute focuses on the distribution of income and wealth, arguing that the gains of the top 20 percent have jeopardized the well-being of the bottom 80 percent. Incomes have stagnated and the robust 3 percent growth rates of the 1950s and 1960s are long gone. If we have a consumption problem, this view implicitly states, we can solve it by getting more income into more people's hands. The goals are redistribution and growth.

It is difficult to take exception to this view. It combines a deep respect for individual choice (the liberal part) with a commitment to justice and equality (the egalitarian part). I held it myself for many years. But I now believe that by failing to look deeper—to examine the very nature of consumption—it has become too limiting. In short, I do not think that the "income solution" addresses some of the most profound failures of the current consumption regime.

Why not? First, consuming is part of the problem. Income (the solution) leads to consumption practices that exacerbate and reproduce class and social inequalities, resulting in—and perhaps even worsening—an unequal distribution of income. Second, the system is structured such that an *adequate* income is an elusive goal. That is because adequacy is relative and defined by reference to the incomes of others. Without an analysis of consumer desire and need, and a different framework for understanding what is adequate, we are likely to find ourselves, twenty years from now, arguing that a median income of $100,000—rather than half that—is adequate. These arguments underscore the social context of consumption: the ways in which our sense of social standing and belonging comes from what we consume. If true, they suggest that attempts to achieve equality, or adequacy of individual incomes, without changing consumption patterns will be self-defeating.

Finally, it is difficult to make an ethical argument that people in the world's richest country need more, when the global income gap is so wide, the disparity in world resource use so enormous, and the possibility that we are already consuming beyond the Earth's ecological carrying capacity so likely. This third critique will get less attention in this essay—because it is more familiar, not because it is less important—but I will return to it in the conclusion.

I agree that justice requires a vastly more equal society, in terms of income and wealth. The question is whether we should also aim for a society in which our relationship to consuming changes, a society in which we consume *differently.* I argue here for such a perspective: for a critique of consumer culture and practices. Somebody needs to be for quality of life, not just quantity of stuff. And to do so requires an approach that does not trivialize consumption, but accords it the respect and centrality it deserves.

The New Consumerism

A new politics of consumption should begin with daily life, and recent developments in the sphere of consumption. I describe these developments as "the new consumerism," by which I mean an upscaling of lifestyle norms; the pervasiveness of conspicuous, status goods and of competition for acquiring them; and the growing disconnect between consumer desires and incomes.

Social comparison and its dynamic manifestation—the need to "keep up"—have long been part of American culture. My term is "competitive consumption," the idea that spending is in large part driven by a comparative or competitive process in which individuals try to keep up with the norms of the social group with which they identify—a "reference group." Although the term is new, the idea is not.

Thorstein Veblen, James Duesenberry, Fred Hirsch, and Robert Frank have all written about the importance of relative position as a dominant spending motive. What's new is the redefinition of reference groups: today's comparisons are less likely to take place between or among households of similar means. Instead, the lifestyles of the upper middle class and the rich have become a more salient point of reference for people throughout the income distribution. Luxury, rather than mere comfort, is a widespread aspiration.

One reason for this shift to "upscale emulation" is the decline of the neighborhood as a focus of comparison. Economically speaking, neighborhoods are relatively homogeneous groupings. In the 1950s and 1960s, when Americans were keeping up with the Joneses down the street, they typically compared themselves to other households of similar incomes. Because of this focus on neighbors, the gap between aspirations and means tended to be moderate.

But as married women entered the workforce in larger numbers—particularly in white-collar jobs—they were exposed to a more economically diverse group of people, and became more likely to gaze upward. Neighborhood contacts correspondingly declined, and the workplace became a more prominent point of reference. Moreover, as people spent less time with neighbors and friends, and more time on the family-room couch, television became more important as a source of consumer cues and information. Because television shows are so heavily skewed to the "lifestyles of the rich and upper middle class," they inflate the viewer's perceptions of what others have, and by extension what is worth acquiring—what one must have in order to avoid being "out of it."

Trends in inequality also helped to create the new consumerism. Since the 1970s, the distribution of income and wealth has shifted decisively in the direction of the top 20 percent. The share of after-tax family income going to the top 20 percent rose from 41.4 percent in 1979 to 46.8 percent in 1996. The share of wealth controlled by the top 20 percent rose from 81.3 percent in 1983 to 84.3 percent in 1997. This windfall resulted in a surge in conspicuous spending at the top. Remember the 1980s—the decade of greed and excess? Beginning with the super-rich, whose gains have been disproportionately higher, and trickling down to the merely affluent, visible status spending was the order of the day. Slowed down temporarily by the recession during the early 1990s, conspicuous luxury consumption intensified during the recent boom. Trophy homes, diamonds of a carat or more, granite countertops, and sport utility vehicles became the primary consumer symbols of the late 1990s. Television, as well as films, magazines, and newspapers, ensure that the remaining 80 percent of the nation is aware of the status purchasing that has swept the upper echelons.

In the meantime, upscale emulation had become well established. Researchers Susan Fournier and Michael Guiry found that 35 percent of their sample aspired to reach the top 6 percent of the income distribution, and another 49 percent aspired to the next 12 percent. Only 15 percent reported that they would be satisfied with "living a comfortable life"—that is, being middle class. But 85 percent of the population cannot earn the six-figure incomes necessary to support upper-middle-class lifestyles. The result is a growing aspirational gap, and with desires persistently outrunning incomes, many consumers find themselves frustrated. One survey of U.S. households found that the level of income needed to fulfill one's dreams doubled between 1986 and 1994, and by 1999 it was more than twice the median household income.

. . . The new consumerism, with its growing aspirational gap, has begun to jeopardize the quality of American life. Within the middle class—and even the upper middle class—many families experience an almost threatening pressure to keep up, both for themselves and their children. They are deeply concerned about the rigors of the global economy, and the need to have their children attend "good" schools. This means living in a community with relatively high housing costs. For some households this also means providing their children with advantages purchased on the private market (computers, lessons, extra-curriculars, private schooling). Keeping two adults in the labor market—as so many families do, to earn the incomes to stay middle class—is expensive, not only because of the second car, child-care costs, and career wardrobe. It also creates the need for time-saving—but costly—commodities and services, such as take-out food and dry cleaning, as well as stress-relieving experiences. Finally, the financial tightrope that so many households walk—high expenses, low savings—is a constant source of stress and worry. While precise estimates are difficult to come by, one can argue that somewhere between a quarter and half of all households live paycheck-to-paycheck.

These problems are magnified for low-income households. Their sources of income have become increasingly erratic and inadequate, on account of employment instability, the proliferation of part-time jobs, and restrictions on welfare payments. Yet most low-income households remain firmly integrated within consumerism. They are targets for credit card companies, who find them an easy mark. They watch more television, and are more exposed to its desire-creating properties. Low-income children are more likely to be exposed to commercials at school, as well as at home. The growing prominence of the values of the market, materialism, and economic success make financial failure more consequential and painful.

These are the effects at the household level. The new consumerism has also set in motion another dynamic: it siphons off resources that could be used for alternatives to private consumption. We use our income in four basic ways: private consumption, public consumption, private savings, and leisure. When consumption standards can be met easily out of current income, there is greater willingness to support public goods, save privately, and cut back on time spent at work (in other words, to "buy leisure"). Conversely, when lifestyle norms are upscaled more rapidly than income, private consumption "crowds out" alternative uses of income. That is arguably what happened in the 1980s and 1990s: resources shifting into private consumption, and away from free time, the public sector, and saving. Hours of work have risen dramatically; saving rates have plummeted; and public funds for education, recreation, and the arts have fallen in the wake of a grassroots tax revolt. The timing suggests a strong coincidence between these developments and the intensification of competitive consumption. . . . Indeed, this scenario makes good sense of an otherwise surprising finding: that indicators of "social health" or "genuine progress" (i.e., basic quality-of-life measures) began to diverge from Gross Domestic Product in the mid-1970s, after moving in tandem for decades.

Can it be that consuming and prospering are no longer compatible states? . . .

Americans did not suddenly become greedy. The aspirational gap has been created by structural changes—such as the decline of community and social connection, the intensification of inequality, the growing role of mass media, and heightened penalties for failing in the labor market. Upscaling is mainly defensive, and has both psychological and practical dimensions.

Similarly, the profoundly social nature of consumption ensures that these issues cannot be resolved by pure acts of will. Our notions of what is adequate, necessary, or luxurious are shaped by the larger social context. Most of us are deeply tied in to our particular class and other group identities, and our spending patterns help reproduce them.

Thus, a collective, not just an individual, response is necessary. Someone needs to address the larger question of the consumer culture itself. But doing so risks complaints about being intrusive, patronizing, or elitist. . . .

Consumer Knows Best

The recent consumer boom rested on growth in incomes, wealth, and credit. But it also rested on something more intangible: social attitudes toward consumer decision making and choices. Ours is an ideology of noninterference—the view that one should be able to buy what one likes, where one likes, and as much as one likes, with nary a glance from the government, neighbors, ministers, or political parties. Consumption is perhaps the clearest example of an individual behavior that our society takes to be almost wholly personal, completely outside the purview of social concern and policy. The consumer is king. And queen.

This view has much to recommend it. After all, who would relish the idea of sumptuary legislation, rationing, or government controls on what can be produced or purchased? The liberal approach to consumption combines a deep respect for the consumer's ability to act in her own best interest and an emphasis on the efficiency gains of unregulated consumer markets: a commitment to liberty and the general welfare.

Cogent as it is, however, this view is vulnerable on a number of grounds. Structural biases and market failures in the operation of consumer markets undermine its general validity; consumer markets are neither so free nor so efficient as the conventional story suggests. The basis of a new consumer policy should be an understanding of the presence of structural distortions in consumers' choices, the importance of social inequalities and power in consumption practices, a more sophisticated understanding of consumer motivations, and serious analysis of the processes that form our preferences. . . .

A Politics of Consumption

. . . But what should a politics of consumption look like? To start the discussion—not to provide final answers—I suggest seven basic elements:

1. *A right to a decent standard of living.* This familiar idea is especially important now because it points us to a fundamental distinction between what people need and what they want. In the not very distant past, this dichotomy was not only well understood, but the basis of data collection and social policy. Need was a social concept with real force. All that's left now is an economy of desire. This is reflected in polling data. Just over 40 percent of adults earning $50,000 to $100,000 a year, and 27 percent of those earning more than $100,000, agree that "I cannot afford to buy everything I really need." One third and 19 percent, respectively, agree that "I spend nearly all of my money on the basic necessities of life." I believe that our politics

would profit from reviving a discourse of need, in which we talk about the material requirements for every person and household to participate fully in society. Of course, there are many ways in which such a right might be enforced: government income transfers or vouchers, direct provision of basic needs, employment guarantees, and the like. For reasons of space, I leave that discussion aside; the main point is to revive the distinction between needs and desires.

2. *Quality of life rather than quantity of stuff.* Twenty-five years ago quality-of-life indicators began moving in an opposite direction from our measures of income, or gross domestic product, a striking divergence from historic trends. Moreover, the accumulating evidence on well-being, at least its subjective measures (and to some extent objective measures, such as health), suggests that above the poverty line, income is relatively unimportant in affecting well-being. This may be because what people care about is relative, not absolute income. Or it may be because increases in output undermine precisely those factors that do yield welfare. Here I have in mind the growing worktime requirements of the market economy, and the concomitant decline in family, leisure, and community time; the adverse impacts of growth on the natural environment; and the potential link between growth and social capital.

This argument that consumption is not the same as well-being has great potential to resonate with millions of Americans. Large majorities hold ambivalent views about consumerism. They struggle with ongoing conflicts between materialism and an alternative set of values stressing family, religion, community, social commitment, equity, and personal meaning. We should be articulating an alternative vision of a quality of life, rather than a quantity of stuff. That is a basis on which to argue for a restructuring of the labor market to allow people to choose for time, or to penalize companies that require excessive hours for

employees. It is also a basis for creating alternative indicators to the GNP, positive policies to encourage civic engagement, support for parents, and so forth.

3. *Ecologically sustainable consumption.* Current consumption patterns are wreaking havoc on the planetary ecology. Global warming is perhaps the best known, but many other consumption habits have major environmental impacts. Sport utility vehicles, air conditioning, and foreign travel are all energy-intensive and contribute to global warming. Larger homes use more energy and building resources, destroy open space, and increase the use of toxic chemicals. All those granite countertops being installed in American kitchens were carved out of mountains around the world, leaving in their wake a blighted landscape. Our daily newspaper and coffee are contributing to deforestation and loss of species diversity. Something as simple as a T-shirt plays its part, since cotton cultivation accounts for a significant fraction of world pesticide use. Consumers know far less about the environmental impacts of their daily consumption habits than they should. And while the solution lies in greater part with corporate and governmental practices, people who are concerned about equality should be joining forces with environmentalists who are trying to educate, mobilize, and change practices at the neighborhood and household levels.

4. *Democratize consumption practices.* One of the central arguments I have made is that consumption practices reflect and perpetuate structures of inequality and power. This is particularly true in the "new consumerism," with its emphasis on luxury, expensiveness, exclusivity, rarity, uniqueness, and distinction. These are the values that consumer markets are plying, to the middle and lower middle class. (That is what Martha Stewart did at Kmart.)

But who needs to accept these values? Why not stand for consumption that is democratic, egalitarian, and available to all? How about making "access," rather than exclusivity, cool, by exposing the industries such as fashion, home decor, or tourism, which are pushing the upscaling of desire? This point speaks to the need for both cultural change and policies that might facilitate it. Why not tax high-end "status" versions of products while allowing the low-end models to be sold tax-free?

5. *A politics of retailing and the "cultural environment."* The new consumerism has been associated with the homogenization of retail environments and a pervasive shift toward the commercialization of culture. The same mega-stores can be found everywhere, creating a blandness in the cultural environment. Advertising and marketing are also pervading hitherto relatively protected spaces, such as schools, doctors' offices, media programming (rather than commercial time), and so on. In my local mall, the main restaurant offers a book-like menu comprising advertisements for unrelated products. The daily paper looks more like a consumer's guide to food, wine, computer electronics, and tourism and less like a purveyor of news. We should be talking about these issues, and the ways in which corporations are remaking our public institutions and space. Do we value diversity in retailing? Do we want to preserve small retail outlets? How about ad-free zones? Commercial-free public education? Here too public policy can play a role by outlawing certain advertising in certain places and institutions, by financing publicly controlled media, and enacting zoning regulations that take diversity as a positive value.

6. *Expose commodity "fetishism."* Everything we consume has been produced. So a new politics of consumption must take into account the labor, environmental, and other conditions under which products are made, and argue for high standards. This argument has been of great political importance in recent years, with public exposure of the so-called global sweatshop in the apparel, footwear, and fashion industries. Companies fear their public images, and consumers appear willing to pay a little more for products when they know they have been produced responsibly. There are fruitful and essential linkages between production, consumption, and the environment that we should be making.

7. *A consumer movement and governmental policy.* Much of what I have been arguing for could occur as a result of a consumer's movement. Indeed, the revitalization of the labor movement calls out for an analogous revitalization of long dormant consumers. We need independent organizations of consumers to pressure companies, influence the political agenda, provide objective product information, and articulate a vision of an appealing and humane consumer sphere. We also need a consumer movement to pressure the state to enact the kinds of policies that the foregoing analysis suggests are needed. These include taxes on luxury and status consumption, green taxes and subsidies, new policies toward advertising, more sophisticated regulations on consumer credit, international labor and environmental standards, revamping of zoning regulations to favor retail diversity, and the preservation of open space. There is a vast consumer policy agenda that has been mainly off the table. It's time to put it back on.

Note

1. Sources for much of the data cited in this [chapter] can be found in the notes to *The Overspent American: Why We Want What We Don't Need* (Harper Perennial, 1999) or by contacting the author.

Reaching African American Consumers

African American Shopping Behavior

Barbara Mueller

Much like their White counterparts, African American consumers spend roughly two-thirds of their incomes on housing, transportation, and food. However, beyond that, there are difference between Blacks and Whites in terms of consumption priorities and marketplace behaviors that deserve marketers' attention.

Advertisers marketing to African Americans should note some of the products and services this powerful niche is likely to purchase. [According to data from a recent market research report ("Top 50 Market Report")], Blacks index extremely high on video game systems, home security systems, luxury vehicles, and SUVs, as well as full-sized automobiles. African Americans are significantly more likely to plan on buying a luxury vehicle over the next year, and more than 439,000 (an amount that's risen more than 20% in the last five years) intend to pay at least $35,000 for that vehicle ("Force of Habit," 2006). The Lincoln division of Ford Motor Company was so impressed with the billions Blacks spent on cars that the automaker commissioned Sean "P. Diddy" Combs, the entertainment and fashion mogul, to design a limited edition Navigator replete with six plasma screens, three DVD players, and Sony Playstation 2 (Young, 2004). Miller and Kemp note that

> particular upscale, top-end brands are visible symbols of success for communicating social and economic achievements. Premium brands are a reflection of aspirations in that they provide conspicuous "badges" of social status—a means for eliminating stereotypes, fulfilling emotional needs, and staying on top of the latest trends. Because of the effects of The Filter, the use or display of upscale brands confers upscale status to African American consumers. (2005, p. 25)

From Mueller, B. (2007). Reaching African American consumers: African American shopping behavior. In *Communicating with the multicultural consumer: Theoretical and practical perspectives*. New York: Peter Lang.

According to Target Market, a company that tracks Black consumer spending, Blacks spend a significant amount of their income on depreciable products. For example, Target Market's 2005 report noted that African American households significantly increased their expenditures on consumer electronics for the home. . . .

Regarding the consumption behavior of female African Americans, research reveals the following:

- African American women are more likely to try new trends, compared with general market women (with data demonstrating an index of 134 for African American women versus an index of 90 for general market women).
- African American women would pay extra for products consistent with their image, compared to general market women (an index of 129 versus 94).
- African American women are more likely to believe that a brand name equals quality, compared to general market women (an index of 115 versus 95).
- More than their general market counterparts, African American women are more likely to purchase a two-family home.
- African American women are more likely to buy their first home in the coming year, compared to their general market counterparts. African American women are more likely to purchase homeowner/personal property insurance in the next year, compared to their general market counterparts.
- In 2005, African American women controlled $403 billion in buying power—more than Hispanic women, who controlled $346 billion in buying power.
- Over half of young African American women (eighteen to twenty-nine years of age) surveyed stated their goals were to own their own business (54%) and to own their own home (49%) (*Essence,* n.d.).

Of concern is the fact that African American households, in particular, are shown to spend larger percentages of their incomes paying credit card and other high-interest rate debt—and much of the debt they have accumulated is for those items that depreciate in value. Credit card debt has caused African American families to use critical financial resources to pay mounting monthly interest payments, instead of acquiring assets, such as real estate, or saving (Sidime, 2004). According to published reports, the Ariel Mutual Funds/Charles Schwab 2003 Black Investor Survey found that, when comparing households where Blacks and Whites had roughly the same household incomes, Whites saved nearly 20% more each month for retirement, and 30% of African Americans earning $100,000 a year had less than $5,000 in retirement savings. While 79% of Whites invest in the stock market, only 61% of African Americans do so (Young, 2004).

Beyond what African American consumers buy, where they shop is very important to them. And respect is a critical part of the retail shopping experience for Black consumers. According to a recent survey, 68% of African Americans (compared to 46% of non-Hispanic White consumers) say that how a store treats customers based on race is extremely important in deciding where to shop.

Unfortunately, over 88% of African Americans say that discrimination is still part of most African Americans' day-to-day lives (Ragland, 2005). And over half (56%) of African Americans (compared to just 17% of non-Hispanic White consumers) agreed that, "In the past I have felt a security guard/store clerk was watching me more closely than other shoppers" (Wicks, 2005). Clearly, many African Americans feel that they are being profiled while shopping. And African American shoppers' perceptions regarding racial profiling are borne out by research conducted by Harris, Henderson, and Williams (2005).

The researchers examined eighty-one federal court decisions made between 1990 and 2002 involving customers' allegations of race and/or ethnic discrimination. The authors note that consumer racial profiling can take a number of forms, including (a) *subtle degradation,* (b) *overt degradation,* (c) *subtle denial,* and (d) *overt denial,* as well as (e) *criminal suspicion. Subtle degradation* of goods and services involves cases in which customers complain they did not receive what they expected in a particular consumption setting but do not have direct evidence that this treatment was based on their race or ethnicity. In contrast, *overt degradation* occurs when it is clear that nonwhite patrons received less by way of goods and services than White customers. *Subtle denial* refers to situations in which customers allege that they were outrightly denied access to goods and services; however, they are unable to identify White patrons who received better treatment. Conversely, overt denial occurs when there is clear evidence of preferential treatment of White patrons compared with nonwhite counterparts. *Criminal suspicion* cases involve allegations that customers of color were treated with suspicion or as if they were criminals. Of course, consumer racial profiling is directed not only at African American consumers but also at Hispanic and Asian consumers, as well as those from other ethnic and/or racial groups. . . .

Real consumer discrimination remains a real problem in the U.S. marketplace. Firms that develop retail environments where ethnic consumers do not feel victimized, but rather respected, are likely to see increased revenues. And those who do not create discrimination-free environments will likely face the consequences. Ethnic consumers may opt to boycott the offending business. Indeed, one store's sales fell by more than 50% following a racial profiling incident (Bean, 2000). In other instances, individuals may choose to file a lawsuit, which is potentially costly to the marketer both in terms of dollars as well as negative publicity. A recent race discrimination lawsuit brought by eighteen current and former African American employees of a Niketown store in Chicago

has been granted class-action status, creating a potentially damaging public relations problem for the shoe manufacturer. The suit makes embarrassing allegations that African American customers, including professional athletes, such as former Chicago Bulls basketball player Tyson Chandler and three Green Bay Packer football players, were subject to greater scrutiny and monitoring at the retail outlet. The longer the case continues and the more publicity it receives, the greater the damage to the brand, which has a huge following among African American youth. It also relies on high-profile Black athletes, such as Michael Jordan and Kobe Bryant, in its marketing campaigns (Sachdev, 2006). . . .

How to Create Ads That Persuade

Marketers will be pleased to know that African Americans appear to have an affinity for advertising. According to a survey by Simmons Market Research, just 15% of African American adults don't like advertising in general, versus 37% of all adults aged eighteen and older. And 36% of Black respondents said they remembered advertised products when shopping (Price, 2005). In terms of creating messages for African American consumers, the illusion that both Blacks and Whites can be reached via identical advertisements through the same media is simply a myth, and marketers who ignore this crucial reality do so at their own risk. Many Black consumers don't feel that much, if any, of the advertising they see has any relevance to them. According to the 2005 Yankelovich Partners and Burrell Communications Group report, 60% of Black consumers feel that most television and print ads are designed only for White people. And nearly 70% of African Americans (as compared to 53% of Hispanics) say they are "extremely concerned about the practices and motives of marketers and advertisers" (Beasty, 2005). Clearly, such statistics should be a red flag to marketers and advertisers.

Most Blacks agree that there is greater need for African American representation in advertising, regardless of medium. And their representation in the media has a direct impact on their consumption behavior. Over three-quarters indicate that they are more likely to buy from companies that feature African Americans using their products and services ("How We Buy," 1998). Much progress has been made in this area. Indeed, according to several academic studies, over the last fifteen years, the number of Blacks appearing in commercials has been roughly proportional to their share of the American population. However, many general market advertising agencies rely on ethnic casting for their multicultural efforts—a matter of simply slipping an African American or other ethnic face into an otherwise traditional campaign. This approach typically rings false with many African Americans, as casting without tailoring the message to the distinctive aspects of the Black market does not make for compelling advertising. Effectively communicating with Black consumers means creating messages relevant to their lifestyle. Savvy marketers are sensitive to cultural nuances and motivators and ensure that Blacks are portrayed in a positive light in their commercial messages.

Stereotypical portrayals of African Americans in advertising have drawn criticism from civil rights groups for decades. Some of the earliest and most iconic examples of Blacks in commercial messages—Rastus the Cream of Wheat chef, Aunt Jemima, and Uncle Ben—showed Blacks in subservient roles that recalled the days of slavery. These images have been toned down over the years (Aunt Jemima's red bandanna, for example, was replaced with pearl earrings and a lace collar in 1989) and are no longer as overtly stereotypical as they once were (Peters, 2006). For the most part, African Americans in advertising today are presented in middle-class settings and as engaging in mainstream activities. But every now and then, another stereotypic portrayal manages to pop up. The most recent appears to be the image of the heavy, Black, boisterous, and, sometimes, aggressive female, who typically finds herself in either an embarrassing or confrontational situation. Large Black actresses have had recurring roles in commercials over the years and often are cast in roles where their aggressiveness is their defining trait. The heavy Black spokesperson for Pine Sol was one of the first to embrace this role. Some find the recurring use of this caricature a return to a disturbing past. "It is perpetuating a stereotype that Black females are aggressive, controlling people," notes Tommy E. Whittler, a marketing professor at DePaul University. "I don't think you want to do that" (Peter, 2006). . . .

African Americans care not only that they are represented in advertising but also about how they are portrayed. African Americans feel a strong need to be portrayed in a positive way and will appreciate marketers who do so. Miller and Kemp offer this list of culturally sensitive and positive images that celebrate Black culture rather than reinforce stereotypes:

Upscale African American individuals and their families

African American family united (including the Black father as an emotionally engaged and responsible caretaker)

African Americans working with and helping other African Americans

African American women in integrated leadership roles

African American men in integrated leadership roles

African Americans involved in technology and healthcare (2005, p. 27)

One way marketers can convey respect for African Americans' cultural heritage is via promotional activities supporting Black History Month. Originally organized as Negro History Week in 1926 by Harvard Professor Carter G. Woodson, the intent was to bring national attention to the contributions of Blacks. The week evolved into a month in 1976. Companies large and small have acknowledged Black History Month through special programming, promotions, or increased advertising in an attempt to strengthen their corporate image with Blacks. Some firms do it well. For example, Procter & Gamble sponsored the PBS documentary *African American Lives* in 2006. The same year, Target created links on its Web site to Black history facts and donated portions of the sales of a rhythm and blues (R&B) and gospel CD to the United Negro College Fund. Wal-Mart sponsored a *Voices of Color* film documentary series and curriculum kit, free for students in seventh through twelfth grades nationwide. According to Walter Guarino, president of Insight/SGW marketing firm, based in New Jersey,

> It's good business. Black History Month recognizes and celebrates blacks' contributions and reminds us of the hardships and injustices ethnic minorities have suffered over the years. Without some of these corporate sponsorships and special media programming, recognition of Black History Month would surely suffer. (Turner, 2006)

While some Blacks say they appreciate the focus on their history and culture, others view it as pandering and question a commitment that's visible only one month a year. Marketers who only nod to Blacks during the month of February are seen as exploiting Black history to sell products. Also, Miller and Kemp (2005) note that product-intensive messages may be perceived as disrespectful, or even insulting, to the very segment that the message was intended to reach. Consider the flyer from the Kmart in Maryland that proclaimed "Celebrate Black History" and then advertised "3 for $1 Jiffy Corn Muffin Mix," or the makers of Metamucil and Pepto-Bismol who ran a full-page ad in *Ebony* magazine declaring, "Black History Month is a legacy of pride and achievement leading to a

healthier tomorrow." The ad continued, "It's the same ideals you turn to when it comes to your GI (gastro-intestinal) health—a history of digestive solutions" (Thomas-Lester, 2006). Marketers must clearly exercise sensitivity when paying homage to Black history.

To successfully attract African American shoppers—or any ethnic group, for that matter—advertisers need to get inside consumers' heads. Unfortunately, to date, there has been a dearth of behavioral research on ethnic consumers. Demographic information is readily available on African Americans, Hispanics, and Asian Americans, but the body of psychographic research for these particular ethnic groups is shockingly thin, especially compared to the voluminous amounts of data available on nonethnic consumers (Popovec, 2006).

Fortunately, this is beginning to change, and the insights provided by psychographic research are invaluable. For example, recent research reveals that there is at least as much in-group variation among Blacks as there is between African Americans and other consumer groups. According to McGhee Williams Osse, co-chief executive officer (co-CEO) of Burrell Communications, one of the top-ranked advertising agencies appealing to the Black market, "The bottom line is that African Americans are no more homogeneous than other consumers. Understanding these differences will equip marketers with more practical and tactical methods of communicating to African Americans" (Wicks, 2005). The 2005 Yankelovich *Monitor* Multicultural Marketing Study revealed that the African American market can be broken into six sociobehavioral segments:

1. *Emulators* (11% of African Americans) are generally students, with a median age of seventeen, who identify with the young urban trendsetters within the African American culture but see themselves as unique and independent. They are trendsetters whose purchases reflect a need to be unconventional. But they also have a need for the social and emotional reassurance

of brands that most reflect status or achievement.

2. *Seekers* (19% of African Americans) share some characteristics with emulators but are older and more disillusioned about life. They work part-time or are temporarily unemployed. They seek image and status brands that are popular within the culture. They are a median age of forty and have a median income of $18,000.

3. *Reachers* (24% of African Americans) are strivers who are working toward the American dream but are not on the fast track. Often single parents who care for children and/or an elderly parent, they are stressed out, and they want products and services that give them the biggest bang for their buck. They are a median age of forty and have a median income of $28,000.

4. *Attainers* (27% of African Americans) are typically married with children and have a college degree. They have a more defined sense of self and a solid plan for the future. They seek and appreciate appropriate marketing and advertising that gives them useful ideas and information about how to make their lives easier and better. They have a median income of $55,000 and are a median age of forty years old.

5. *Elites* (5% of African Americans) are upwardly mobile African Americans who live and work in a more mainstream environment but retain their cultural identity and allegiances. Marketers must appeal to them through a broader range of campaigns and executions that are generally reserved for non-Hispanic Whites but can be personalized for them. They are a median age of forty-six and have a median income of $113,000.

6. *Conservers* (14% of African Americans) are an older segment with a median age of sixty-seven and an income of $38,000. This group is set in its ways and is slow to adapt to the dynamism of the African American culture. Mostly retired, their beliefs and values are deeply grounded in the experience and wisdom that helped shape their lives. Marketers must approach them in a straightforward manner (Wicks, 2005).

A second study, commissioned by *Essence* magazine publisher Essence Communications, called "Window on Our Women: How African American Women Define Success," offers insights into what ties Black women together, as well as what makes them different ("Many Shades," 2006). When African American women were asked to define success, six highly segmented consumer profiles emerged:

1. *Proud Marys* represent 21% of the female Black population and are connected to their cultural heritage, are involved in social and community activism, and value spiritual growth.

2. *Kays* represent 20% of the female Black population. They define success in financial terms, seek the stability and security that monetary success brings, and want to retire comfortably.

3. *Amazing Graces* represent 18% of Black women. They want to have it all: a career, financial success, and a happy family.

4. *Personal Beths* define interpersonal relationships as their motivation to succeed and derive satisfaction from ensuring the happiness of others. Sixteen percent of Black women fall into this category.

5. *Mother Earthas* represent 13% of Black women. They count raising children as the ultimate success and desire strong relationships with nuclear family and friends.

6. *Ultra Violets* represent 12% of Black women. For them, financial achievement is everything. These women are focused on accomplishing financial goals and spending time with close friends.

Michelle James, director of research at *Essence* explains, "It's important to note that Amazing Graces have different consumer behavior than Mother Earthas. And Proud Marys, for example, will be very connected to the social community. . . . Partnering with community organizations is the best way to reach her" ("Many Shades," 2006). The psychographic insights provided by these and future investigations will allow marketers to better tailor their commercial messages to Black consumers. . . .

References

Bean, L. (2000, December 22). Retail racial profiling charges settled by Children's Place chain. *DiversityInc*. Retrieved from http://diversityinc.com

Beasty, C. (2005, July 7). Ethnic consumers require sensitive marketing. *Destination CRM*. Retrieved from http://www.destinationcrm.com/articles/default.asp?ArticleID=5249

Essence. (n.d.). Did you know? Retrieved from http://www.essence.com/mktfacts/buying-power

Force of habit. (2006, September/October). *Marketing Management, 15*(5), 7.

Harris, A.-M., Henderson, G., & Williams, J. (2005, Spring). Courting customers: Assessing consumer racial profiling and other marketplace discrimination. *Journal of Public Policy and Marketing, 24*(1), 163.

How we buy—research says corporate reputations and trust # 1 to Black America. (1998, August 26). *The Jacksonville Free Press*, p. 1.

The many shades of the black shopping pattern. (2006, Fall). *Drug Store News*, 11.

Miller, P., & Kemp, H. (2005). *What's black about it?* Ithaca, NY: Paramount Market Publishing, Inc.

Peters, J. (2006, August 1). What's so funny? [Late edition, East Coast]. *New York Times*, p. C-1.

Popovec, J. (2006, May). Role of psychographics. *National Real Estate Investor, 48*(5), 32.

Price, M. (2005, January 17). Some analysts expect surge in corporate spending on black-targeted advertising. *Knight Ridder/Tribune Business News*, p. 1.

Ragland, J. (2005, August 15). Black shoppers feel they're unwelcome. *Knight Ridder/Tribune News Service*, p. 1.

Sachdev, A. (2006, March 24). Lawsuit against Niketown expands: Chicago employees allege discrimination. *Knight Ridder/Tribune Business News*, p. 1.

Sidime, A. (2004, November). Credit use strangles wealth. *Black Enterprise, 35*(4), 38.

Thomas-Lester, A. (2006, March 2). Black History tie-in advertising criticized. *Miami Times*, p. 1-D.

"Top 50 Market Report" (Release 5), Scarborough Research, 2005. http://www.naa.org/thesource/11.asp

Turner, T. (2006, February 1). Black History Month, brought to you by. . . . *Knight Ridder/Tribune Business News*, p. 1.

TV One and Warner Bros. Domestic Cable Distribution ink comprehensive, multi-year programming agreement for movies, series. (2006, April 10). *PR Newswire*.

Wicks, S. (2005, July 9). New report sheds light on African American shoppers. *Black Business List*. Retrieved from http://blackbusinesslist.com

Young, Y. (2004, April 2). Tough choices for tough times. *USA Today*, p. A-09.

Inventing the Cosmo Girl

Class Identity and Girl-Style American Dreams

Laurie Ouellette

I am a materialist, and it is a materialistic world.

—Helen Gurley Brown[1]

In February 1997, a former secretary named Helen Gurley Brown stepped down from her position as the editor-in-chief of *Cosmopolitan*, the hugely successful consumer magazine she developed for the "single girl" market in the mid-1960s. Still an American cultural icon, Brown was suddenly back in the media spotlight, espousing her credo on topics ranging from sex and the workplace to the Cosmo Girl, the fictionalized woman she invented to characterize the magazine's imagined 18- to 34-year-old female reader. Just as feminist historians have recognized Brown's role in partly subverting patriarchal sexual ideologies (Douglas, 1994; Ehrenreich et al., 1986), media commentators framed the departure by casting Brown as the feminine piper of the sexual revolution.[2] What cannot be explained by a singular focus on sexual politics, however, are the class-specific dimensions of Brown's message and popular appeal.

This chapter analyzes Helen Gurley Brown's early advice to women as a cultural discourse that managed some of the social and economic tensions of the 1960s and early 1970s, while also offering certain women the symbolic material to enable them to think about themselves as historical subjects in new ways. John Fiske's understanding of discourse is especially helpful for making sense of Brown's position as a capitalist media maven and an immensely popular spokeswoman for everygirl. As Fiske argues, discourse is a "system of representation that has developed socially in order to make and circulate a coherent set of meanings about an important topic area" (1987: 14). Discourses are ideological insofar as their "meanings serve the interests of that section of society within which the discourse originates and which works ideologically to naturalize those meanings into common sense," but they are not conspiratorial or "pro-duced" by individual authors or speakers (1987: 14). Rather, discourses are socially produced and often institutionalized ways of making sense of a certain topic that "pre-exist their use in any one discursive prac-tice," and that construct "a sense, or social identity, of us" as we speak them (Fiske, 1987: 14–15).

. . . I wish to show how Brown's advice spoke to major changes in women's eco-nomic and sexual roles, while also con-structing a suggested social identity for her "working girl" readers. . . . The cultural dis-course Brown articulated legitimated sexism and the capitalist exploitation of women's labor, while simultaneously expressing hard-ships and desires in a voice that spoke with credibility to an expanding class of pink-collar women.

Based on my examination of *Cosmopolitan* magazine (1965–75) as well as Brown's books, recordings and interviews during this period, I am suggesting that she articulated a girl-style American Dream that promised transcendence from class roles as well as sexual ones. Brown was one of the first mainstream figures to free women from the guilt of premarital sex by advising them to disregard the patriarchal double standard. But she was also concerned with shaping and transforming the class position of the Cosmo Girl through a combination of self-management strategies, performative tac-tics, sexuality, and upwardly mobile romance.[3] At a time when the term often seems in danger of slipping from the critical vocabulary, Brown's advice to women offers a case study in the cultural construction of class—not as an economic category or even a relationship in the Marxist sense, but as a fragmented and sexualized identity. As Brown explained,

> There are girls who . . . don't want to be that driven, to have that many affairs; they don't want more than one man or one dress at a time. They don't care about jewelry and they don't want a sable coat or Paris for the weekend. . . . But "my

girl" wants it. She is on the make. Her nose is pressed to the glass and she does get my message. These girls are like my children all over the country. Oh, I have so much advice for them. . . . (Quoted in *Guardian Weekly,* 1968)

Inventing the Cosmo Girl

In 1962, at the age of 42, Brown wrote the bestseller *Sex and the Single Girl* (1962) and became an overnight celebrity. According to Brown, the book was an unabashed self-help credo for "the girl who doesn't have any-thing going for her . . . who's not pretty, who maybe didn't go to college and who may not even have a decent family background" (quoted in Didion, 1965: 35). Drawing partly from Brown's experience as a woman who held 18 secretarial jobs before she was promoted to an advertising copywriter and then married at the age of 37, the book offered step-by-step advice on personal appearance, budget apartment dwelling, working, and, above all, flirting. Brown guided women through encounters with men who were not their husbands, instructing them how to attract the best ones, date them, cajole dinners and presents out of them, have affairs, and eventually marry the most eligi-ble man available. In a year when "married people on television slept in twin beds" (Douglas, 1994: 68) and the sexual revolu-tion remained the prerogative of men and student counterculture types, *Sex and the Single Girl* suggested that ordinary women could lead fully sexual lives outside marriage (Brown, 1962: 11). Brown critiqued manda-tory motherhood, advised birth control, con-doned divorce, encouraged women to work outside the home, and recommended sexual and financial independence within bound-aries. However, the book was by no means anti-marriage: As Brown explained, it was a response to the "man shortage," a guide to attracting desirable men while remaining "single in superlative style" ("A Proposal for *Cosmopolitan,*" n.d.).

Sex and the Single Girl was mocked by intellectuals, reviewed, as one journalist observed, "only to provide a fixed target for reviewers eager to point up (amid considerable merriment) the superiority of their own perceptions over those of Mrs. Brown" (Didion, 1965: 36). But the book appealed to hundreds of thousands of women who were living out a growing gap between "girlhood and marriage" made possible by shifting urban migration patterns and the expanding pink-collar labor force (Ehrenreich et al., 1986: 54). *Single Girl* sold more than two million copies in three weeks, due to extensive publicity and Brown's rigorous efforts to get in touch with the kind of women critics derided as "subliterate and culturally deprived" (Didion, 1965: 36). Following the book's initial success, Brown was interviewed extensively in the press, appeared as a frequent guest on radio and television talk shows, and sold the motion-picture rights to *Single Girl* to Hollywood. She wrote a series of follow-up books, including *Sex and the Office* (1964) and *Sex and the New Single Girl* (1970a), recorded best-selling lectures with names like *Lessons in Love* (1963), and wrote a syndicated newspaper column called "Woman Alone." While early feminist leaders like Betty Friedan found Brown's message "obscene and horrible," few could deny that she had developed an "astonishing rapport with America's single-girldom" (quoted in Welles, 1965: 65).

In 1965, Brown took her credo and her phenomenal sales figures to Hearst Publications, owners of *Cosmopolitan* magazine, and became the magazine's new editor-in-chief. With close monitoring by Hearst, she transformed *Cosmopolitan* from a fledgling intellectual publication into a "compendium of everything I know about how to get through the emotional, social and business shoals that confront a girl, and have a better life" (Brown, 1970a: 7). Brown maintained such strict control over the magazine that critics began to ridicule the singular, gushy voice that permeated article after article, but the editorial formula she devised drew new readers (Brown, 1965). Circulation rose by more than 100,000 the first year alone, advertising sales grew 43 percent (*Newsweek*, 1966: 60), and a series of self-help books distributed through the *Cosmopolitan* Book-of-the-Month Club were equally successful. By the mid-1970s, *Cosmopolitan* was reaching more than two million readers, advertising sales were still soaring, 12 foreign-language editions had been launched, and Brown was a celebrity who claimed to embody much of the advice she distributed through her media enterprise.[4] Due to Brown's characterizations and the "I'm that Cosmopolitan Girl" advertising campaign, which she helped write, the fictionalized Cosmo Girl had entered the cultural lexicon as a sexualized symbol of pink-collar femininity. Before elaborating on her construction, it is useful to sketch out the historical context during which she arose.

As the economist Julie Matthaei has shown, the growth of the service sector has been "central in the absorption of female labor" (1982: 282). In the 1960s, as the U.S.A. moved rapidly toward a post-Fordist economy, women entered the paid workforce in greater numbers, and began to stay there for longer periods of time, earning approximately 59 cents on the male dollar (Howe, 1977: 3). According to the U.S. Department of Labor, between 1962 and 1974, the number of employed women rose by 10 million, or 45 percent. Some women entered the male-dominated professions, but the majority entered "feminine" pink-collar jobs, and the largest gain occurred in secretarial and clerical occupations that often required no college education (Howe, 1977: 10–11). Women were already the mainstay of these occupational fields, but the capitalist expansion of the service sector was a new development, as was the growing number of women working for prolonged periods of time to support themselves (and families) in these positions.[5] *Sex and the Single Girl* spoke directly to unmarried working women, and *Cosmopolitan* was the first consumer magazine to target single "girls with jobs" with feature articles, advice columns, budget fashions and advertisements for mainly "feminine" consumer items, such as cosmetics, personal care products, lingerie, and clothing.[6] The magazine also featured advertisements for temporary employment agencies, training centers and correspondence schools where women could learn stenography, typing, and dictation and similar clerical skills. Hearst's interest in hiring Brown to address self-sufficient working women was thus linked to their emergence as a consumer market capable of purchasing certain goods and services with their own wages.[7]

Cosmopolitan's pink-collar orientation and economic base is especially clear when compared to that of its nearest competitor, *Ms.* magazine. Critics have observed that when *Ms.* debuted in 1972 as a voice of the women's movement, it tended to emphasize the goals and aspirations of liberal feminism and college-educated women. Editorial material aimed at pink-collar women was less typical, and the female consumer hailed by "dress-for-success" fashions and durable consumer goods differed from the one hailed by *Cosmopolitan* (McCracken, 1993: 278–80; Valverde, 1986: 81). Both magazines claimed to serve independent working women, but market research found *Ms.* readers had higher incomes and were more than twice as likely to have attended college. More than a third of *Ms.* readers (as opposed to virtually no *Cosmopolitan* readers) also held advanced degrees (Harrington, 1974). Critics, however, downplayed the social and economic basis of the skew and blamed Brown for the "Two Faces of the Same Eve," explaining that intelligent women with graduate degrees were not apt to be called "little Cosmo Girl" or buy a magazine whose editor insists that ideas be made "baby simple" (Harrington, 1974: 12). With considerable scorn, Brown was characterized as the "working girl's Simone de Beauvoir" of her era (*Newsweek*, 1966: 60).

In the U.S.A., women's mass entry into the workforce is often attributed to the second wave of the women's movement. However, when we consider the stratification within the female labor force, Barbara Ehrenreich's thesis that "male revolt" from the traditional breadwinning role was an earlier and more significant catalyst seems highly plausible. Breadwinning, according to Ehrenreich, was an informal economic contract rooted in the family wage system, and as such it was dependent upon the voluntary cooperation of men:

Men are favored in the labor market, both by the kinds of occupations open to them and by informal discrimination within occupations, so that they earn, on the average, 40 percent more than women do. Yet nothing compels them to spread the wealth to those—women and children—who are excluded from work or less generously rewarded for it. Men cannot be forced to marry; once married, they cannot be forced to bring home their paychecks, to be reliable job holders, or, of course, to remain married. In fact, considering the absence of legal coercion, the surprising thing is that men have for so long, and, on the whole, so reliably, adhered to what might be called the "breadwinner" ethic. (1983: 11)

Once held together by popular culture, expert opinion and religious expectations, the breadwinning ethic began to unravel around the time the Beats, with their flagrant celebration of male freedom, appeared on the scene, says Ehrenreich (1983: 12; 52). When *Playboy* magazine debuted in 1953, she argues, "male revolt" was expressed in a broader context. While *Playboy* is often associated with the mainstreaming of soft-core pornography, it also promoted a "Dale Carnegie–style credo of male success" rooted in free enterprise, a strong work ethic and materialistic consumption. The only difference between conventional success mythology and Hugh Hefner's message was that men were not encouraged to share their money, says Ehrenreich. Wives and single women were depicted as shrews and "gold-diggers," while bachelors were advised to pursue sex on a casual basis to avoid getting snared in a "long term contract" (1983: 46). By the 1970s, alimony reductions and no-fault divorce laws—however progressive in the feminist sense—had legitimated male revolt at the official level of the state. For the first time in U.S. history, observed sociologist Jane Mansbridge, "society was beginning to condone a man leaving his family on the sole grounds that living with them and providing for them made him unhappy" (1986: 108).

Brown's advice spoke to the social and economic flux generated by these shifts by offering a modified sexual contract, and by presenting certain women, who may no longer have recognized their place in male-oriented American Dream mythology, with the discursive material to envision themselves as upwardly mobile sexual agents. Brown was clear in her wish for women to see themselves in the fictionalized persona of the Cosmo Girl. "A guy reading *Playboy* can say, 'Hey, That's me.' I want my girl to be able to say the same thing," she explained (quoted in *Providence Journal*, 1965). While her advice was often antagonistic, the social structure that was the cause of the dilemma was never challenged. . . .

The Beautiful Phony

. . . Brown's credo required an understanding of identity as something that could always be reworked, improved upon, and even dramatically changed. *Sex and the Single Girl* promised every girl the chance to acquire a stylish and attractive aura by copying fashion models and wealthy women (Brown, 1962: 189–94). Expenditures on clothing, cosmetics, and accessories were presented as necessary investments in the construction of a desirable (and thus saleable) self. *Cosmopolitan* columns with names like "So You're Bored to Death with the Same Old You" (1972) extended these possibilities by offering women the ability to construct a "whole new identity," defined in terms of fashion and style. According to the

column, "A new lipstick will really not work a sudden transformation, but have you considered going further? Perhaps even to the point of changing everything (hair, makeup, clothes, manner), in short, changing your type?" (*Cosmopolitan*, 1972: 172). Other articles with names like "Yes, You Can Change Your Image" (De Santis, 1969) stressed the fluidity of female subjectivity, encouraging readers to make themselves over and even construct multiple selves, often to meet the demands and opportunities of prolonged courtship.

To "get into the position to sink a man" it was not necessary that a woman be beautiful, but she had to know how to create "an illusion of beauty" (Brown, 1962: 204). Phoniness was often celebrated as a form of trickery—a way to create a prettier, sexier, and more desirable self beyond one's allotted means. Even the *Cosmopolitan* cover girl was exposed as a "fake," her breasts made to appear more alluring with masking tape and Vaseline (Kent, 1972; Reisig, 1973). According to another column called the "The Beautiful Phony" (*Cosmopolitan*, 1966a), "naturalness" was an imposed value that destroyed the possibility of such illusions. Taking sides with the imagined reader, it opened with the advice:

> They're always telling you to be the most natural girl in the world and you want to cooperate but, well, they just ought to see you in your natural state. Pale, lashless, lusterless, bustless and occasionally, after a grinding day at the typewriter, almost fingernail-less! Darling, not another apology! (1966a: 104)

Instead, "new looks" created with wigs, and false eyelashes, tinted contact lenses, fake beauty spots, false toenails, false fingernails, nose surgery, padded bras, false derrieres, and fake jewelry were recommended. Another article explaining "Why I Wear My False Eyelashes to Bed" (Cunningham, 1968) presented the problem of a shower with a lover, a situation where the investments of a highly produced femininity (and hence its material rewards) might be erased. Recommending hurling soap suds in his eyes so "he won't be able to see how you look" (Cunningham, 1968: 18), it got to the core of Brown's advice by linking femininity to the modified sexual contract she espoused.

The aspirations of the Cosmo Girl were white, heterosexual, and upper-middle class. "Other" women were sometimes acknowledged in *Cosmopolitan* articles like "What It Means to Be a Negro Girl" (Guy, 1966), but they were not presented as models for emulation, primarily because Brown's mobility credo forbade it. White working-class culture appeared more often, but as a reference point for makeover and improvement. Similar to femininity, class was presented as a malleable identity that could be easily changed through performative tactics, covert strategies, and cultural consumption.

Unlike her feminist contemporaries who believed in the possibilities of a female sex class (Firestone, 1970; Millett, 1970), Brown was especially concerned with improving the lot of women stuck lower on the economic ladder. While her most radical suggestion may have been to carry Karl Marx's *Das Kapital* as a way to meet potential eligibles (1962: 63), the Cosmo Girl was often addressed as a have-not, and was offered instructions to remedy the situation. Instead of critiquing the capitalist distribution of resources or the politics of wage labor, reworking one's identity was presented as an individual route to mobility. The extent to which these narratives constructed a feminine version of American Dream mythology is revealed by Brown's own version of the Horatio Alger story:

> We have two Mercedes-Benzes, one hundred acres of virgin forest near San Francisco, a Mediterranean house overlooking the Pacific, a full-time maid and a good life. I am not beautiful, or even pretty . . . I didn't go to college. My family was, and is, desperately poor and I have always helped support them. . . . But I don't think it's a miracle that I married my husband. I think I deserved him!

> For seventeen years I worked hard to become the kind of woman who might interest him. (Brown, 1962: 4–5)

Drawing from John Berger (1972), Ellen McCracken has shown how commercial women's magazines trade on female insecurities by offering a temporary "window to a future self" rooted in male visions of idealized femininity and consumer solutions (1993: 13). Jackie Stacey discusses something similar in her analysis of women and film stars, but proposes that the perpetual gap between "self and ideal" is the subjective space where female identities are negotiated (1993: 206). In *Sex and the Single Girl*, Brown extended these processes by constructing an idealized, but never fully realized, class subjectivity for her readers, which then manifested in the fragmented identity of the fictionalized Cosmo Girl. Although rooted in upper-class reverence and materialistic desires, her advice is difficult to dismiss as entirely co-optive or advertising-driven, because it was presented as a guide to overcoming the gendered class barriers Brown encountered. Her path to success stressed the conventional motto of hard work and conspicuous consumption, but it also required covert strategies and performative behaviors on the part of the Cosmo Girl. As I see it, the tenuous sense of agency Brown's advice offered is central to the tension between class fluidity and class consciousness in the politicized sense.

Women were essentially advised to "pass" as members of the bourgeoisie, by studying and copying its presumably superior tastes, knowledges, and cultural competencies. This performative strategy was rooted in the unauthorized acquisition of what Pierre Bourdieu (1984) calls "cultural capital," or the symbolic resources that signify and legitimate class dominance in capitalist democracies. In the U.S.A., the myth of equality of opportunity proposes that anyone can gain access to economic capital (what wealth buys) through individual effort and talent, while the cultural capital that breeds success is inherited via "proper" family socialization or acquired through extended years of schooling (Jhally and Lewis, 1992: 69). Brown subverted these intersecting mythologies in a roundabout way by revealing pink-collar barriers to the American Dream, and by partly subverting the uneven distribution of cultural capital. According to Brown's girl-style American Dream, anyone—even the Cosmo Girl—could appropriate the surface markers of cultural capital. Once acquired, these surface markers of class position could be traded for economic capital (or access to it) on the dating and marriage market.

The credibility of this advice was rooted in the fact that women who may have married directly into the lower classes were spending longer periods of time working as office workers. Under the ambiguous label "pink collar," they encountered men with more education, money, and resources. Brown's advice encouraged women to exploit these opportunities, and prepared them to do so by offering a basic introduction to upper-class customs and cultural traditions. "Some girls have it . . . some don't. But that elusive little quality separating the haves from the [have-]nots is within everyone's grasp," claimed one *Cosmopolitan* article (Geng, 1970: 92).

Since the advice was always tempered to the experience of the Cosmo Girl, the reader was allowed to participate in two class cultures simultaneously, which encouraged a fragmented class subjectivity. However, the point of the lessons was to conceal one's working-class lineage. Thus, *The Cosmo Girl's Guide to the New Etiquette* warned women about common phrases that were "instant lower-class betrayals" (Brown, 1970b: 55). Similarly, *Cosmopolitan* articles with names like "Poor Girl Paintings" (*Cosmopolitan,* 1966c), "If You Don't Know Your Crepes From Your Coquilles" (Matlin, 1969), "Go Ahead, Pretend You're Rich" (Barnes and Downey, 1968), "Good Taste" (Johnson, 1974), and "Live Beyond Your Means" (de Dubovay, 1975) presented lessons on the ways of the educated, wealthy, and culturally sophisticated.

This advice often involved appropriating cultural signifiers of class, particularly European cuisine, art, foreign languages, and good books. One especially vivid example here was "A Handbook of Elegant Starvation," a *Cosmopolitan* guide to maintaining a "desirable image" while pursuing the arts and getting by on unemployment insurance (Dowling, 1966). According to the article, which offered detailed instructions for serving "Bogus Beef Bourguignon" to a male dinner guest, "The clue to faking it on $12.50 a week is a front. You've got to keep up a front—an aura of prosperity—at all times" (1966: 30). Another article proposed that an ordinary secretary, who "would probably expire from malnutrition if she didn't have a dinner date at least two nights a week," could easily pass as a member of the New York "jet set" or a corporation president's daughter (Tornabene, 1966: 43). By extending the aura of cultural capital to the female masses, this discourse subverted the myth that class is inevitable or natural. However, it also upheld the class pyramid and reproduced social and cultural hierarchies. . . .

Pink-Collar Sexuality

Feminist historians have suggested that what was potentially transforming about *Cosmopolitan* magazine was the emphasis placed on female sexuality (Douglas, 1994; Ehrenreich et al., 1986).[8] Features on female orgasm, birth control, masturbation, casual sex, and sexual experimentation appeared under Brown's editorship, while quizzes with names like "How Sexy Are You?" (*Cosmopolitan,* 1969) invited ordinary women into the sexual revolution, and *Cosmopolitan's Love Book* (Brown, 1972) offered them instructions on the new sexual protocol. At the close of the 1970s, Brown hired a sociologist to survey the sexual practices of *Cosmopolitan* readers, and they were found to be the most experienced group in western history (Wolfe, 1981).

However, what a focus on sexual politics cannot fully explain are the class dimensions of Brown's discourse on female sexuality, as epitomized by her credo "Poor girls are not sexy!" (1962: 108).

. . . Sexual fantasies presented in *Cosmopolitan* fiction excerpts and in *Cosmopolitan's Love Book* encouraged women to identify with female heroines whose male sexual partners (or desired partners) were above them socially and economically. . . . Female desire was linked to what the male object represented socially and economically. As Brown explained in *Sex and the Single Girl,* a woman is "more favorably disposed toward a man who is solvent and successful than someone without status. She prefers a tycoon to a truck driver no matter how sexy the latter looks peering down at her from the cab of his chrome chariot" (1962: 227).

Cosmopolitan's "Bachelor of the Month" column was similarly constructed. This sought-after eligible was always solvent and socially established, as were the men presented as desirable in articles like "It's Just as Easy to Love a Rich Man" (Lilly, 1965), "How Much Will He Earn?" (Sloane, 1966), "The Big Catch" (Blyth, 1972), and "Used Men: A Definitive Guide for the Selective Shopper" (Price, 1972). When acknowledged, working-class men were almost always presented as undesirable, as epitomized by the juxtaposition in February 1966 of two *Cosmopolitan* profiles, one featuring "Six Current (But Perennial) Fascinators" (1966d), the other featuring "10 Most Wanted Men (by the FBI)" (Reed, 1966). While the first roster was comprised of men characterized as rich, famous, successful, charming, and attractive, the second opened with the warning "You've seen the most fascinating men, now read about the most feared" (Reed, 1966: 72). Police mug shots were accompanied by one-liners detailing the physical characteristics of the men as well as their occupations, which included clerk, dishwasher, hospital orderly, tractor driver, and mason's helper.

While female sexual desire was linked to upward mobility through men, the construction of female sexual desirability in *Cosmopolitan* was linked to the cultural codes of the working-class prostitute. Indeed, sexually explicit representations of women were the only places readers were encouraged to forge positive identifications with working-class traditions. Bourgeois tastes were transgressed by these images, especially on the cover, where the desirability of the model was constructed through class-coded signifiers such as exposed cleavage, teased hair, heavy make-up, and flamboyant and suggestive costumes.[9] The sexualized Cosmo Girl was not the wholesome middle-class sex object of the era, and she appeared to contradict Brown's discreet schemes for mobility. However, the sexualized imagery also offered an entry point into the modified sexual contract Brown espoused.

In the 1960s, when college-educated women were beginning to demand and sometimes secure equality in the professional workplace, most pink-collar office workers were not so fortunate. Brown articulated an alternative way to get men to part with their disproportionate share of power and resources. She subverted the moral shame surrounding sex and reframed the sexual code as an individual ethic and a commodity exchange. In this sense, her advice was rooted in the history of working-class women's sexual practices.

Kathy Peiss, for example, has shown how a turn-of-the-century system of "treating" allowed young, unmarried workers to trade "sexual favors" ranging from flirting and kissing to sexual intercourse for small presents, meals, and admissions to amusement parks, which they could not otherwise afford (1983: 78). Some "charity girls" appropriated the look of a prostitute, using "high-heeled shoes, fancy dresses, costume jewelry, elaborate pompadours and cosmetics" to attract male attention (1983: 78). The system of treating was also present in the workplace, says Peiss, where sexual harassment was rampant (1983: 78–9). Brown's advice articulated an updated sexual barter system, by encouraging the Cosmo Girl to never go dutch, but to instead coax gifts, dinners, vacations, groceries, and cash presents from male dates, bosses, colleagues, and partners. Her revised sexual contract promoted women's sexual freedom and financial independence, while also encouraging the exchange of sexual "favors" for material comforts and luxuries. Perhaps the most significant difference between the system Peiss describes and what Brown articulated is that the Cosmo Girl was encouraged to pursue men who may have been off limits in earlier eras. . . .

While the mainstream women's movement strove for equality in the workplace, Brown often framed sexual activity in terms of work and achievement. "Sex is a powerful weapon for a single woman in getting what she wants from life," she explained to an interviewer (quoted in *San Francisco*, 1962). A similar message was conveyed in her memoir, where Brown described the ability to bring a man to orgasm as a "specialty" every upwardly mobile girl should acquire (1982: 212). Occasionally, *Cosmopolitan* explained the advantages of being "kept" and "slightly kept" girls (Baumgold, 1970; Condos, 1974), and articles glamorizing upscale prostitution were not uncommon. However, these explicit cases of sexual trading were not nearly as prevalent as the sexualization of the office, especially the relationship between male superiors and female secretaries. Again, this pattern drew from and reworked historical assumptions about the role of women in offices. . . .

By the 1960s, office work was a rapidly growing occupational field, and women were an expanding part of the labor force. By the time *Sex and the Single Girl* appeared, almost one of every three employed women worked in clerical and secretarial jobs (Matthaei, 1982: 282), and by 1974 women held four out of five jobs in this category (Howe, 1977: 10). The capitalist expansion of the service sector opened the field to women outside the middle class, while

women with college degrees were struggling to move into male-dominated professions. What remained was the middle-class respectability of office work compared to factory work and other working-class wage labor (Matthaei, 1982: 282). Despite the low pay and dead-end nature of most pink-collar jobs, this made it easier for women to see themselves as upwardly mobile. . . .

Cosmopolitan elevated the sexual worth of the secretary by suggesting that "a secretary is not necessarily rich, beautiful or brilliant, but she is the most sought-after female since King Kong chased Fay Wray" (Lewis, 1969: 133). Likewise, the rewards for working for women were defined through the types of men one encountered. In *Sex and the Single Girl*, Brown promoted secretarial jobs because they were "all-time great spots" for meeting men (1962: 37). *Cosmopolitan* articles with titles like "Secretaries Who've Made Very, Very Good" (James, 1969), "Be a 9-to-5 Show Off" (Fisher, 1970), and "Hollywood Secretaries" (*Cosmopolitan*, 1975a) also glamorized secretarial jobs as excellent places to meet well-connected bosses, dreamy executives, and traveling salesmen with expense accounts. One article even recommended "A Different Job Every Day" (Fahey, 1966), contracted through temporary employment agencies, as a chance to meet dozens of eligible men in a single week. The low pay, insecurity, and lack of benefits offered by the growing temporary workforce were obscured. . . .

Brown clearly understood women's subordination in the office, but she did not directly challenge it because "in an ideal world, we might move onward and upward by using only our brains and talent, but since this is an imperfect world, a certain amount of listening, giggling, wriggling, smiling, winking, flirting and fainting is required in our rise from the mailroom" (1964: 3). . . .

There were exceptions to these patterns, especially after 1970, when Brown proclaimed herself a friend of women's lib and *Cosmopolitan* began to negotiate feminist discourse, however haltingly. Several feminist articles were published, including an excerpt in November 1970 from Kate Millett's book *Sexual Politics* (1970) critiquing the gendered aspects of economic inequality and the ideology of heterosexual romance. As was typical, however, it was shockingly out of place, juxtaposed with a fashion spread proclaiming "Be His Fortune Cookie in Our Gala Gypsy Dress" (*Cosmopolitan,* 1970). Liberal feminist demands for professional equality had a more lasting impact on Brown's thinking, and on the partial incorporation of conventional success mythology in *Cosmopolitan.* While she continued to value street smarts over a college degree and to promote the sensational opportunities offered by secretarial work, Brown modified her credo to suggest that the Cosmo Girl might be both a sex object and a "high powered" executive (Brown, 1982: 19–20).

Girl-Style American Dreams

Many pink-collar women may have found the Cosmo Girl's fragmented identity as an upwardly mobile sexual agent more attractive and even more feasible than what the mainstream women's movement offered. Brown's advice offered a gendered success myth to women who found themselves taking on new roles as breadwinners, but who lacked the wages, education, professional skills, and social opportunities to recognize themselves in more conventional, male-oriented upward-mobility narratives. She articulated, in feminine terms, the materialistic desires that so often underpin popular structures of feeling in a consumer-oriented nation where the class structure is officially denied. Brown's reworking of American Dream mythology involved the construction and reconstruction of a desirable self, the presentation of identity as self-made, the valorization of femininity as a creative production, the partial subversion of natural class distinctions, the refusal of

Victorian sexual norms, and the expression of multiple hardships and frustrations—all within a framework that legitimated capitalism, consumerism, and patriarchal privilege. However, to dismiss the fragmented, sexualized class identity she promoted as wholly co-optive or less than "real" would be to lose touch with the way social beings construct a sense of self.

As Stuart Hall suggests with his theory of articulation, there is no necessary link between economics and class. Class awareness is a social construct, produced in a political sense only when individual experiences are articulated as a "political force," enabling subjects to enter the stage as historical agents (Hall, 1986: 55). Brown's advice encouraged women to rework their identities on the basis of upper-class ideals, and to assess their current situations and future possibilities on the basis of those constructions. One of the consequences of the discourse may have been the way it positioned women as individual competitors in the quest for mobility, rather than part of a growing female labor force with many differences, to be sure, but with collective interests and bargaining power. Characterizing her own self-transformation, for example, Brown explained that "early on you have to separate yourself in the head from those people (friends, family, colleagues) you don't want to be like . . . be one of the girls, but also don't be one of the girls" (1982: 38).

Helen Gurley Brown's historical resonance as the "working girl's Simone de Beavoir" suggests the need to take the cultural construction of class seriously. . . .

Notes

1. Quoted in *Time* (1965: 60).
2. See, for example, Brown's appearance, 25 January 1997, on CNN's *Larry King Live.*
3. Mariana Valverde (1986) also observed the promotion of mobility in *Cosmopolitan,*

arguing that what both the Cosmo Girl and the Ms. woman of the 1980s wanted, despite their different paths to achievement (e.g., getting a man vs. merit), was to be white, upper-middle class, and heterosexual. While she sees both magazines imposing unified capitalist and patriarchal ideologies on women (a view similar to early feminist Marxist criticism), I see Brown's advice in poststructuralist terms, as a contradictory, historically specific and productive discourse that constructed a social identity for pink-collar women.

4. Harrington, 1974. In 1997, *Cosmopolitan* had a U.S. circulation of 2.5 million, resulting in $156 million in estimated annual advertising revenue (Pogrebin, 1997).

5. In 1940, about one-third of employed Americans were in white-collar occupations, while in 1959 nearly half were due to the expanding service economy and the growing number of women who joined the "white-collar ranks." However, many of these jobs were "essentially manual" in that they were routine, repetitive, and sometimes minimally skilled. They paid less than the professions and often less than skilled blue-collar work, but were "rated" above traditional working-class wage labor because they were perceived as "cleaner" and more "dignified" (Packard, 1959: 25–6). Advertisers played on the social ambiguity, promising status through consumer goods. In this [chapter] I refer to non-professional white-collar jobs taken up predominantly by women as pink-collar. For more on the post-Fordist economy see Harvey (1990: 121–97).

6. Brown envisioned the "untapped" market for *Cosmopolitan* as single women, divorcees, and widows, separated, and "otherwise neglected wives" who worked outside the home. Working married women who were (because of their independent attitude) "women on their own" were considered a secondary market ("A Proposal for *Cosmopolitan*," n.d.; "Statement for Advertisers," n.d.). Early marketing discourse inflated the spending power of the magazine's readers, describing them as well educated, high income, and "working in top occupations," despite statistic[s] that contradicted these generalizations. Thus, there was overlap between the

class performativity Brown encouraged and the strategies used to court advertisers. While the Cosmo Girl was constructed as single and sexually free, a high percentage of readers were married. This would suggest that they too were drawn to the magazine's guide to changing sexual and economic roles.

7. Products and services said to be bought by *Cosmopolitan* readers included cosmetics, perfumes, fashion and personal products, wines and liquors, travel, miscellaneous, and mail order (*Cosmopolitan* Advertising Kit, 1965). The first three categories comprised most of the advertising according to my research.

8. Ehrenreich et al. note that Brown championed independence and guiltless sex at a time when few women "could imagine options other than marriage and full-time motherhood" (1986: 56). Susan Douglas (1994) also cites Brown as a key figure in the transformation of female sexuality.

9. As McCracken argues, "If the *Cosmopolitan* cover photo presents women with an ideal image of their future selves, it is an image at the other end of the social spectrum from that of the affluent *Vogue* or *Bazaar* cover" (1993: 158). While she sees this image as an invitation to male fantasy and sexual voyeurism, I see it rooted in the class dimensions of Brown's revised sexual code.

References

Barnes, J. and M. Downey (1968) "Go Ahead— Pretend You're Rich," *Cosmopolitan* (July): 54–5.

Baumgold, J. (1970) "The Slightly Kept Girl," *Cosmopolitan* (Sept.): 154.

Berger, J. (1972) *Ways of Seeing*. London: Penguin Books.

Blyth, M. (1972) "The Big Catch," *Cosmopolitan* (Jan.): 128–36.

Bourdieu, P. (1984) *Distinction: A Social Critique of the Judgment of Taste*. Cambridge, MA: Harvard University Press.

Brown, H. G. (1962) *Sex and the Single Girl*. New York: Bernard Geis Associates.

Brown, H. G. (1963) *Lessons in Love.* New York: Crescendo Records.

Brown, H. G. (1964) *Sex and the Office.* New York: Bernard Geis Associates.

Brown, H. G. (1965) "New Directions for *Cosmopolitan," The Writer* (July): 20.

Brown, H. G. (1970a) *Sex and the New Single Girl.* New York: Bernard Geis Associates.

Brown, H. G. (ed.). (1970b) *The Cosmo Girl's Guide to the New Etiquette.* New York: Cosmopolitan Books.

Brown, H. G. (ed.). (1972) *Cosmopolitan's Love Book: A Guide to Ecstasy in Bed.* New York: Cosmopolitan Books.

CNN Television. (1997) Interview with Helen Gurley Brown, *Larry King Live* (25 Jan.).

Condos, B. (1974) "I Was Kept," *Cosmopolitan* (May): 60, 66–74.

Cosmopolitan Advertising Kit, July 1965, HGB papers, Box 8, Folder 12.

Cosmopolitan (1966a) "The Beautiful Phony" (March): 104–7.

Cosmopolitan (1966b) "*Cosmopolitan* Interviews Hugh M. Hefner" (May): 76–81.

Cosmopolitan (1966c) "Poor Girl Paintings" (Aug.): 88.

Cosmopolitan (1966d) "Six Current (But Perennial) Fascinators" (Feb.): 66–71.

Cosmopolitan (1969) "How Sexy Are You?" (April): 54–6.

Cosmopolitan (1970) "Be His Fortune Cookie in Our Gala Gypsy Dress" (Nov.): 104.

Cosmopolitan (1975a) "Hollywood Secretaries" (Aug.): 36.

Cosmopolitan (1975b) "How to Sink into a Man" (Nov.): 48–9.

Cunningham, L. (1968) "Why I Wear My False Eyelashes to Bed," *Cosmopolitan* (Oct.): 46–51.

de Dubovay, D. (1975) "Live Beyond Your Means," *Cosmopolitan* (Aug.): 132–4.

De Santis, M. (1969) "Yes, You Can Change Your Image," *Cosmopolitan* (April): 91–3.

Didion, J. (1965) "Bosses Make Lousy Lovers," *Saturday Evening Post* (30 Jan.): 34–8.

Douglas, S. (1994) *Where the Girls Are: Growing Up Female with the Mass Media.* New York: Time Books.

Dowling, C. (1966) "A Handbook of Elegant Starvation," *Cosmopolitan* (Oct.): 30–2.

Ehrenreich, B. (1983) *The Hearts of Men.* New York: Anchor Books.

Ehrenreich, B. et al. (1986) *Re-Making Love: The Feminization of Sex.* New York: Anchor Books.

Fahey, P. (1966) "A Different Job Every Day," *Cosmopolitan* (Oct.): 128–31.

Ferguson, M. (1983) *Forever Feminine: Women's Magazines and the Cult of Femininity.* London: Heinemann.

Firestone, S. (1970) *The Dialectic of Sex.* New York: Quill Press (repr. 1993).

Fisher, K. (1970) "Be a 9-to-5 Showoff," *Cosmopolitan* (Nov.): 150–1.

Fiske, J. (1987) *Television Culture.* New York: Routledge.

Geng, V. (1970) "A Little Bit of Class," *Cosmopolitan* (Oct.): 92–7.

Greller, J. (1966) "Night School Isn't All Education," *Cosmopolitan* (July): 87–8.

Guardian Weekly (1968) newspaper clipping (12 Nov.) HGB papers, Box 7, Folder 3.

Guy, R. (1966) "What It Means to Be a Negro Girl," *Cosmopolitan* (July): 76–81.

Hall, S. (1986) "On Postmodernism and Articulation: An Interview," *Journal of Communication Inquiry* 10(2): 45–60.

Harrington, S. (1974) "Two Faces of the Same Eve: *Ms.* Versus *Cosmo," New York Times Magazine* (11 Aug.): 10–11, 36, 74–6.

Harvey, D. (1990) *The Condition of Post-modernity.* London: Blackwell.

Hennessy, R. (1993) *Materialist Feminism and the Politics of Discourse.* New York: Routledge.

Howe, L. (1977) *Pink Collar Workers.* New York: G. P. Putnam's Sons.

James, T. (1969) "4 Secretaries Who've Made Very, Very Good," *Cosmopolitan* (June): 134–5.

Jhally, S. and J. Lewis (1992) *Enlightened Racism: The Cosby Show, Audiences and the Myth of the American Dream.* Boulder, CO: Westview.

Johnson, N. (1974) "Good Taste!" *Cosmopolitan* (Feb.): 122–31.

Joyce, P. (ed.) (1995) *Class.* New York: Oxford University Press.

Kent, R. (1972) "Cover Girl: Behind the Scenes," *Cosmopolitan* (Aug.): 94–117.

Lewis, B. (1969) "Today's Secretary—Wow!" *Cosmopolitan* (June): 133.

Lilly, D. (1965) "It's Just as Easy to Love a Rich Man," *Cosmopolitan* (July): 66–9.

Mansbridge, J. (1986) *Why We Lost the ERA.* Chicago: University of Chicago Press.

Matlin, P. (1969) "If You Don't Know Your Crepes From Your Coquilles, Or How to Order From a French Restaurant," *Cosmopolitan* (April): 96–9.

Matthaei, J. (1982) *An Economic History of Women in America.* New York: Schocken.

McCracken, E. (1993) *Decoding Women's Magazines.* New York: St Martin's.

Millett, K. (1970) *Sexual Politics.* Garden City, NY: Doubleday.

Newsweek (1966) "Down with "Pippypoo" (18 July): 60.

Packard, V. (1959) *The Status Seekers: An Exploration of Class Behavior in America.* New York: David McKay.

Peiss, K. (1983) "'Charity Girls' and City Pleasures: Historical Notes on Working-Class Sexuality, 1880–1920," pp. 74–87 in Ann Snitow et al. *Powers of Desire.* New York: Monthly Review Press.

Pogrebin, R. (1997) "Changing of Guard at Cosmo," *New York Times* (13 Jan.): D1.

Price, R. (1972) "Used Men: A Definitive Guide for the Selective Shopper," *Cosmopolitan* (Aug.): 68–73.

"A Proposal for Cosmopolitan from Helen Gurley Brown" (n.d.) Helen Gurley Brown papers, Sophia Smith Collection, Smith College, Northampton, MA (hereafter HGB papers), Box 14, Folder 4.

Providence Journal (1965) newspaper clipping (1 July) HGB papers, Box 8, Folder 1.

Reed, R. (1966) "10 Most Wanted Men (by the FBI)," *Cosmopolitan* (Feb.): 72–81.

Reisig, R. (1973) "The Feminine Plastique," *Ramparts* (March): 25–9, 53–5.

San Francisco News Call Bulletin (1962) "Single Gal's Quandary" (6 July) HGB papers, Box 8, Folder 3.

Sloane, L. (1966) "How Much Will He Earn?" *Cosmopolitan* (Feb.): 30–7.

Stacey, J. (1993) *Star Gazing: Hollywood Cinema and Female Spectatorship.* London: Routledge.

"Statement from Helen Gurley Brown for Advertisers" (n.d.) HGB papers, Box 14, Folder 3.

Time (1965) "Big Sister" (9 Feb.): 60.

Tornabene, L. (1966) "How to Live Beautifully on $100 a Week," *Cosmopolitan* (Aug.): 42–7.

Valverde, M. (1986) "The Class Struggles of the Cosmo Girl and the Ms. Woman," *Heresies* 18: 78–82.

Welles, C. (1965) "Soaring Success of the Iron Butterfly," *Life* (19 Nov.): 65–6.

Wolfe, L. (1981) *The Cosmo Report.* New York: Arbor House.

Sex, Lies, and Advertising

Gloria Steinem

. . . When *Ms.* began, we didn't consider *not* taking ads. The most important reason was keeping the price of a feminist magazine low enough for most women to afford. But the second and almost equal reason was providing a forum where women and advertisers could talk to each other and improve advertising itself. After all, it was (and still is) as potent a source of information in this country as news or TV and movie dramas.

We decided to proceed in two stages. First, we would convince makers of "people products" used by both men and women but advertised mostly to men—cars, credit cards, insurance, sound equipment, financial services, and the like—that their ads should be placed in a women's magazine. Since they were accustomed to the division between editorial and advertising in news and general interest magazines, this would allow our editorial content to be free and diverse. Second, we would add the best ads for whatever traditional "women's products" (clothes, shampoo, fragrance, food, and so on) that surveys showed *Ms.* readers used. But we would ask them to come in *without* the usual quid pro quo of "complementary copy."

We knew the second step might be harder. Food advertisers have always demanded that women's magazines publish recipes and articles on entertaining (preferably ones that name their products) in return for their ads: clothing advertisers expect to be surrounded by fashion spreads (especially ones that credit their designers); and shampoo, fragrance, and beauty products in general usually insist on positive editorial coverage of beauty subjects, plus photo credits besides. That's why women's magazines look the way they do. But if we could break this link between ads and editorial content, then we wanted good ads for "women's products," too. . . .

I thought then that our main problem would be the imagery in ads themselves. Carmakers were still draping blondes in evening gowns over the hoods like ornaments. Authority figures were almost always male, even in ads for products that only women used. Sadistic, he-man campaigns even won industry praise. (For instance, *Advertising Age* had hailed the infamous Silva Thin cigarette theme. "How to Get a Woman's Attention: Ignore Her," as "brilliant.") Even in medical journals, tranquilizer ads showed depressed housewives standing beside piles of dirty dishes and promised to get them back to work.

Excerpts reprinted from *Ms. Magazine*, July/August 1990, by permission of Gloria Steinem.

Obviously, *Ms.* would have to avoid such ads and seek out the best ones—but this didn't seem impossible. *The New Yorker* had been selecting ads for aesthetic reasons for years, a practice that only seemed to make advertisers more eager to be in its pages. *Ebony* and *Essence* were asking for ads with positive black images, and though their struggle was hard, they weren't being called unreasonable. . . .

The fact that *Ms.* was asking companies to do business in a different way meant our saleswomen had to make many times the usual number of calls—first to convince agencies and then client companies besides— and to present endless amounts of research. I was often asked to do a final ad presentation, or see some higher decision maker, or speak to women employees so executives could see the interest of women they worked with. That's why I spent more time persuading advertisers than editing or writing for *Ms.*, and why I ended up with an unsentimental education in the seamy underside of publishing that few writers see (and even fewer magazines can publish).

Let me take you with us through some experiences, just as they happened:

1. Cheered on by early support from Volkswagen and one or two other car companies, we scrape together time and money to put on a major reception in Detroit. We know U.S. carmakers firmly believe that women choose the upholstery, not the car, but we are armed with statistics and reader mail to prove the contrary: a car is an important purchase for women, one that symbolizes mobility and freedom.

But almost nobody comes. We are left with many pounds of shrimp on the table, and quite a lot of egg on our face. We blame ourselves for not guessing that there would be a baseball pennant play-off on the same day, but executives go out of their way to explain they wouldn't have come anyway. Thus begins ten years of knocking on hostile doors, presenting endless documentation, and hiring a full-time

saleswoman in Detroit: all necessary before *Ms.* gets any real results.

This long saga has a semi-happy ending: foreign and, later, domestic carmakers eventually provided *Ms.* with enough advertising to make cars one of our top sources of ad revenue. Slowly, Detroit began to take the women's market seriously enough to put car ads in other women's magazines, too, thus freeing a few pages from the hothouse of fashion-beauty-food ads.

But long after figures showed a third, even a half, of many car models being bought by women, U.S. makers continued to be uncomfortable addressing women. Unlike foreign carmakers, Detroit never quite learned the secret of creating intelligent ads that exclude no one, and then placing them in women's magazines to overcome past exclusion. (*Ms.* readers were so grateful for a routine Honda ad featuring rack and pinion steering, for instance, that they sent fan mail.) Even now, Detroit continues to ask, "Should we make special ads for women?" Perhaps that's why some foreign cars still have a disproportionate share of the U.S. women's market.

2. In the *Ms.* Gazette, we do a brief report on a congressional hearing into chemicals used in hair dyes that are absorbed through the skin and may be carcinogenic. Newspapers report this too, but Clairol, a Bristol-Myers subsidiary that makes dozens of products— a few of which have just begun to advertise in *Ms.*—is outraged. Not at newspapers or newsmagazines, just at us. It's bad enough that *Ms.* is the only women's magazine refusing to provide the usual "complementary" articles and beauty photos, but to criticize one of their categories—*that* is going too far.

We offer to publish a letter from Clairol telling its side of the story. In an excess of solicitousness, we even put this letter in the Gazette, not in Letters to the Editors where it belongs. Nonetheless—and in spite of surveys that show *Ms.* readers are active women who use more of almost everything Clairol makes than do the readers of any other women's magazine—*Ms.* gets almost none of these ads for the rest of its natural life.

Meanwhile, Clairol changes its hair coloring formula, apparently in response to the hearings we reported.

3. Our saleswomen set out early to attract ads for consumer electronics: sound equipment, calculators, computers, VCRs, and the like. We know that our readers are determined to be included in the technological revolution. We know from reader surveys that *Ms.* readers are buying this stuff in numbers as high as those of magazines like *Playboy*, or "men 18 to 34," the prime targets of the consumer electronics industry. Moreover, unlike traditional women's products that our readers buy but don't need to read articles about, these are subjects they want covered in our pages. There actually *is* a supportive editorial atmosphere.

"But women don't understand technology," say executives at the end of ad presentations. "Maybe not," we respond, "but neither do men—and we all buy it."

"If women *do* buy it," say the decision makers, "they're asking their husbands and boyfriends what to buy first." We produce letters from *Ms.* readers saying how turned off they are when salesmen say things like "Let me know when your husband can come in."

After several years of this, we get a few ads for compact sound systems. Some of them come from JVC, whose vice president, Harry Elias, is trying to convince his Japanese bosses that there is something called a women's market. At his invitation, I find myself speaking at huge trade shows in Chicago and Las Vegas, trying to persuade JVC dealers that showrooms don't have to be locker rooms where women are made to feel unwelcome. But as it turns out, the shows themselves are part of the problem. In Las Vegas, the only women around the technology displays are seminude models serving champagne. In Chicago, the big attraction is Marilyn Chambers, who followed Linda Lovelace of *Deep Throat* fame as Chuck Traynor's captive and/or employee. VCRs are being demonstrated with her porn videos.

In the end, we get ads for a car stereo now and then, but no VCRs; some IBM personal computers, but no Apple or Japanese ones. We notice that office magazines like *Working Woman* and *Savvy* don't benefit as much as they should from office equipment ads either. In the electronics world, women and technology seem mutually exclusive. It remains a decade behind even Detroit.

4. Because we get letters from little girls who love toy trains, and who ask our help in changing ads and box-top photos that feature little boys only, we try to get toy-train ads from Lionel. It turns out that Lionel executives *have* been concerned about little girls. They made a pink train, and were surprised when it didn't sell.

Lionel bows to consumer pressure with a photograph of a boy *and* a girl—but only on some of their boxes. They fear that, if trains are associated with girls, they will be devalued in the minds of boys. Needless to say, *Ms.* gets no train ads, and little girls remain a mostly unexplored market. By 1986, Lionel is put up for sale.

But for different reasons, we haven't had much luck with other kinds of toys either. In spite of many articles on child-rearing—an annual listing of nonsexist, multiracial toys by Letty Cottin Pogrebin; Stories for Free Children, a regular feature also edited by Letty; and other prizewinning features for or about children—we get virtually no toy ads. Generations of *Ms.* saleswomen explain to toy manufacturers that a larger proportion of *Ms.* readers have preschool children than do the readers of other women's magazines, but this industry can't believe feminists have or care about children.

5. When *Ms.* begins, the staff decides not to accept ads for feminine hygiene sprays or cigarettes: they are damaging and carry no appropriate health warnings. Though

we don't think we should tell our readers what to do, we do think we should provide facts so they can decide for themselves. Since the antismoking lobby has been pressing for health warnings on cigarette ads, we decide to take them only as they comply.

Philip Morris is among the first to do so. One of its brands, Virginia Slims, is also sponsoring women's tennis and the first national polls of women's opinions. On the other hand, the Virginia Slims theme, "You've come a long way, baby," has more than a "baby" problem. It makes smoking a symbol of progress for women.

We explain to Philip Morris that this slogan won't do well in our pages, but they are convinced its success with some women means it will work with *all* women. Finally, we agree to publish an ad for a Virginia Slims calendar as a test. The letters from readers are critical—and smart. For instance: Would you show a black man picking cotton, the same man in a Cardin suit, and symbolize the antislavery and civil rights movements by smoking? Of course not. But instead of honoring the test results, the Philip Morris people seem angry to be proven wrong. They take away ads for *all* their many brands.

This costs *Ms.* about $250,000 the first year. After five years, we can no longer keep track. Occasionally, a new set of executives listens to *Ms.* saleswomen, but because we won't take Virginia Slims, not one Philip Morris product returns to our pages for the next 16 years.

Gradually, we also realize our naiveté, in thinking we *could* decide against taking cigarette ads. They became a disproportionate support of magazines the moment they were banned on television, and few magazines could compete and survive without them: certainly not *Ms.*, which lacks so many other categories. By the time statistics in the 1980s showed that women's rate of lung cancer was approaching men's, the necessity of taking cigarette ads had become a kind of prison.

6. General Mills, Pillsbury, Carnation, Del Monte, Dole, Kraft, Stouffer, Hormel, Nabisco: you name the food giant, we try it. But no matter how desirable the *Ms.* readership, our lack of recipes is lethal.

We explain to them that placing food ads *only* next to recipes associates food with work. For many women, it is a negative that works *against* the ads. Why not place food ads in diverse media without recipes (thus reaching more men, who are now a third of the shoppers in super-markets anyway), and leave the recipes to specialty magazines like *Gourmet* (a third of whose readers are also men)?

These arguments elicit interest, but except for an occasional ad for a convenience food, instant coffee, diet drinks, yogurt, or such extras as avocados and almonds, this mainstay of the publishing industry stays closed to us. Period.

7. Traditionally, wines and liquors didn't advertise to women: men were thought to make the brand decisions, even if women did the buying. But after endless presentations, we begin to make a dent in this category. Thanks to the unconventional Michel Roux of Carillon Importers (distributors of Grand Marnier, Absolut Vodka, and others), who assumes that food and drink have no gender, some ads are leaving their men's club.

Beermakers are still selling masculinity. It takes *Ms.* fully eight years to get its first beer ad (Michelob). In general, however, liquor ads are less stereotyped in their imagery—and far less controlling of the editorial content around them—than are women's products. But given the underrepresentation of other categories, these very facts tend to create a disproportionate number of alcohol ads in the pages of *Ms.* This in turn dismays readers worried about women and alcoholism.

8. We hear in 1980 that women in the Soviet Union have been producing feminist *samizdat* (underground, self-published books) and circulating them throughout the

country. As punishment, four of the leaders have been exiled. Though we are operating on our usual shoestring, we solicit individual contributions to send Robin Morgan to interview these women in Vienna.

The result is an exclusive cover story that includes the first news of a populist peace movement against the Afghanistan occupation, a prediction of *glasnost* to come, and a grass-roots, intimate view of Soviet women's lives. From the popular press to women's studies courses, the response is great. The story wins a Front Page award.

Nonetheless, this journalistic coup undoes years of efforts to get an ad schedule from Revlon. Why? Because the Soviet women on our cover *are not wearing makeup*.

9. Four years of research and presentations go into convincing airlines that women now make travel choices and business trips. United, the first airline to advertise in *Ms.*, is so impressed with the response from our readers that one of its executives appears in a film for our ad presentations. As usual, good ads get great results.

But we have problems unrelated to such results. For instance: because American Airlines flight attendants include among their labor demands the stipulation that they could choose to have their last names preceded by "Ms." on their name tags—in a long-delayed revolt against the standard, "I am your pilot, Captain Rothgart, and this is your flight attendant, Cindy Sue"— American officials seem to hold the magazine responsible. We get no ads.

There is still a different problem at Eastern. A vice president cancels subscriptions for thousands of copies on Eastern flights. Why? Because he is offended by ads for lesbian poetry journals in the *Ms.* Classified. A "family airline," as he explains to me coldly on the phone, has to "draw the line somewhere."

It's obvious that *Ms.* can't exclude lesbians and serve women. We've been trying to make that point ever since our first issue included an article by and about

lesbians, and both Suzanne Levine, our managing editor, and I were lectured by such heavy hitters as Ed Kosner, then editor of *Newsweek* (and later of *New York Magazine*), who insisted that *Ms.* should "position" itself *against* lesbians. But our advertisers have paid to reach a guaranteed number of readers, and soliciting new subscriptions to compensate for Eastern would cost $150,000, plus rebating money in the meantime.

Like almost everything ad-related, this presents an elaborate organizing problem. After days of searching for sympathetic members of the Eastern board, Frank Thomas, president of the Ford Foundation, kindly offers to call Roswell Gilpatrick, a director of Eastern. I talk with Mr. Gilpatrick, who calls Frank Borman, then the president of Eastern. Frank Borman calls me to say that his airline is not in the business of censoring magazines: *Ms.* will be returned to Eastern flights.

10. Women of color read *Ms.* in disproportionate numbers. This is a source of pride to *Ms.* staffers, who are also more racially representative than the editors of other women's magazines. But this reality is obscured by ads filled with enough white women to make a reader snowblind.

Pat Carbine remembers mostly "astonishment" when she requested African American, Hispanic, Asian, and other diverse images. Marcia Ann Gillespie, a *Ms.* editor who was previously the editor in chief of *Essence*, witnesses ad bias a second time: having tried for *Essence* to get white advertisers to use black images (Revlon did so eventually, but L'Oréal, Lauder, Chanel, and other companies never did), she sees similar problems getting integrated ads for an integrated magazine. Indeed, the ad world often creates black and Hispanic ads only for black and Hispanic media. In an exact parallel of the fear that marketing a product to women will endanger its appeal to men, the response is usually, "But your [white] readers won't identify."

In fact, those we are able to get—for instance, a Max Factor ad made for *Essence* that Linda Wachner gives us after she becomes president—is praised by white readers, too. But there are pathetically few such images.

11. By the end of 1986, production and mailing costs have risen astronomically, ad income is flat, and competition for ads is stiffer than ever. The 60/40 preponderance of edit over ads that we promised to readers becomes 50/50; children's stories, most poetry, and some fiction are casualties of less space: in order to get variety into limited pages, the length (and sometimes the depth) of articles suffers; and, though we do refuse most of the ads that would look like a parody in our pages, we get so worn down that some slip through. . . . Still, readers perform miracles. Though we haven't been able to afford a subscription mailing in two years, they maintain our guaranteed circulation of 450,000.

Nonetheless, media reports on *Ms.* often insist that our unprofitability must be due to reader disinterest. The myth that advertisers simply follow readers is very strong. Not one reporter notes that other comparable magazines our size (say, *Vanity Fair* or *The Atlantic*) have been losing more money in one year than *Ms.* has lost in 16 years. No matter how much never-to-be-recovered cash is poured into starting a magazine or keeping one going, appearances seem to be all that matter. (Which is why we haven't been able to explain our fragile state in public. Nothing causes ad-flight like the smell of nonsuccess.)

My healthy response is anger. My not-so-healthy response is constant worry. Also an obsession with finding one more rescue. There is hardly a night when I don't wake up with sweaty palms and pounding heart, scared that we won't be able to pay the printer or the post office; scared most of all that closing our doors will hurt the women's movement.

Out of chutzpah and desperation, I arrange a lunch with Leonard Lauder,

president of Estée Lauder. With the exception of Clinique (the brainchild of Carol Phillips), none of Lauder's hundreds of products has been advertised in *Ms.* A year's schedule of ads for just three or four of them could save us. Indeed, as the scion of a family-owned company whose ad practices are followed by the beauty industry, he is one of the few men who could liberate many pages in all women's magazines just by changing his mind about "complementary copy."

Over a lunch that costs more than we can pay for some articles, I explain the need for his leadership. I also lay out the record of *Ms.*: more literary and journalistic prizes won, more new issues introduced into the mainstream, new writers discovered, and impact on society than any other magazine: more articles that became books, stories that became movies, ideas that became television series, and newly advertised products that became profitable: and, most important for him, a place for his ads to reach women who aren't reachable through any other women's magazine. Indeed, if there is one constant characteristic of the ever-changing *Ms.* readership, it is their impact as leaders. Whether it's waiting until later to have first babies, or pioneering PABA as sun protection in cosmetics, *whatever* they are doing today, a third to a half of American women will be doing three to five years from now. It's never failed.

But, he says, *Ms.* readers are not *our* women. They're not interested in things like fragrance and blush-on. If they were, *Ms.* would write articles about them.

On the contrary, I explain, surveys show they are more likely to buy such things than the readers of, say, *Cosmopolitan* or *Vogue*. They're good customers because they're out in the world enough to need several sets of everything: home, work, purse, travel, gym, and so on. They just don't need to read articles about these things. Would he ask a men's magazine to publish monthly columns on how to shave before he advertised Aramis products (his line for men)?

He concedes that beauty features are often concocted more for advertisers than readers. But *Ms.* isn't appropriate for his ads anyway, he explains. Why? Because Estée Lauder is selling "a kept-woman mentality."

I can't quite believe this. Sixty percent of the users of his products are salaried, and generally resemble *Ms.* readers. Besides, his company has the appeal of having been started by a creative and hardworking woman, his mother, Estée Lauder.

That doesn't matter, he says. He knows his customers, and they would *like* to be kept women. That's why he will never advertise in *Ms.*

In November 1987, by vote of the Ms. Foundation for Education and Communication (*Ms.*'s owner and publisher, the media subsidiary of the Ms. Foundation for Women), *Ms.* was sold to a company whose officers, Australian feminists Sandra Yates and Anne Summers, raised the investment money in their country that *Ms.* couldn't find in its own. They also started *Sassy* for teenage women.

In their two-year tenure, circulation was raised to 550,000 by investment in circulation mailings, and, to the dismay of some readers, editorial features on clothes and new products made a more traditional bid for ads. Nonetheless, ad pages fell below previous levels. In addition, *Sassy,* whose fresh voice and sexual frankness were an unprecedented success with young readers, was targeted by two mothers from Indiana who began, as one of them put it, "calling every Christian organization I could think of." In response to this controversy, several crucial advertisers pulled out.

Such links between ads and editorial content was a problem in Australia, too, but to a lesser degree. "Our readers pay two times more for their magazines," Anne explained, "so advertisers have less power to threaten a magazine's viability."

"I was shocked," said Sandra Yates with characteristic directness. "In Australia, we think you have freedom of the press—but you don't."

Since Anne and Sandra had not met their budget's projections for ad revenue, their investors forced a sale. In October 1989, *Ms.* and *Sassy* were bought by Dale Lang, owner of *Working Mother, Working Woman,* and one of the few independent publishing companies left among the conglomerates. In response to a request from the original *Ms.* staff—as well as to reader letters urging that *Ms.* continue, plus his own belief that *Ms.* would benefit his other magazines by blazing a trail—he agreed to try the ad-free, reader-supported *Ms.* you hold now, and to give us complete editorial control.

Unraveling the Knot

Political Economy and Cultural Hegemony in Wedding Media

Erika Engstrom

The U.S. bridal industry is estimated at between $50 and $70 billion annually; the potential for this market is huge: Nearly 2.4 million marriages are performed each year (Gibbons, 2003). The investment of money and time that goes into the traditional wedding, with the average "big" wedding costing some $20,000, makes it not only a major event, but also a major expense for those starting married life; more than half of couples who choose to hold a wedding pay for it all themselves (Ellerbee & Tessem, 2001), which can lead to their starting their married life in debt (Currie, 1993). . . .

Bridal media in general "rev up" expectations for big weddings by exalting the complexity and cost of the event, contended Gibbons (2003). Today, one easily finds myriad bridal and wedding gown magazines at any supermarket or newsstand, with titles such as *Bride's, Modern Bride, Elegant Bride, Bridal Guide, Bliss for Brides, BrideNoir* (for women of color), *Martha Stewart's Weddings, Wedding Dresses Magazine,* and newer, specialized titles such as *The Wedding Channel.com's Wedding Bells, InStyle Weddings,* and *Allure Bride* (from the publishers of *Allure* magazine). These publications concentrate on bridal accoutrements, such as gowns, accessories, party favors, jewelry, and cosmetics, rather than on the meaning and subsequent relationship created by the wedding ceremony (Filak, 2002).

In addition to gala weddings as portrayed in Hollywood films, various reality television programs have been added to the bridal media milieu. Focused on the experience of ordinary people in actual, unscripted environments (Deery, 2004), documentary-style wedding programs record couples' efforts to escape their current habitus by creating the perfect wedding (Herr, 2005). For example, The Learning Channel's *A Wedding Story,* one of the first programs in the wedding reality genre, offers viewers a familiar version of the wedding, which requires the white wedding gown for the bride, a church ceremony, and outward indication of expense at the reception (Engstrom, 2003; Engstrom

From Engstrom, E. (2008). Unraveling the knot: Political economy and cultural hegemony in wedding media. *Journal of Communication Inquiry, 32,* 60–82. Published by Sage Publications, Inc.

& Semic, 2003). Lifetime's ("Television for Women") *Weddings of a Lifetime* specials gave viewers fairy tale weddings that served as thinly disguised advertisements for particular venues and services, specifically, Walt Disney World's Fairy Tale Wedding Pavilion (Levine, 2005).

Taken together, bridal magazines and the portrayal of the lavish wedding across media forward the message that weddings serve as the endpoint of romantic relationships and, relevant to this study, *the* life goal for women. . . .

The current study examines the hegemonic messages about today's wedding in American society, and, by extension, its accompanying dictates of consumption and the role of women, disseminated by The Knot, a bridal media company. The Knot, self-proclaimed as the "#1 wedding website," with 2.1 million unique visitors a month, consists of brand extensions in print, with the publication *The Knot Magazine* and a series of books. Most recently, it has ventured into the world of television, with its reality television program *Real Weddings from The Knot,* produced in partnership with the cable outlet Oxygen.

With its various crossover alliances and relationships with major retailers and other media, such as Oxygen, The Knot serves as a prime example of the political economy of the media.[1] Not only does The Knot's structure reflect media economy, its product can be viewed as cultural "work," the product of media messages central to "the production and reproduction of the social relationships within capitalism" (Carragee, 1993, p. 330). Indeed, one can argue that weddings and their requisite expense, through capitalism, create and legitimize social relationships, namely, marriage. . . .

Unraveling The Knot's Media Ties

TheKnot.com launched on America Online in September 1996. Founded by "four good friends, two of whom had barely survived

their own wedding, due to the lack of updated information and real-world resources available" (*Company Milestones,* 2007), The Knot now serves as "wedding central" online, with links to various wedding item retailers, and claims to be the largest online retailer of wedding favors and supplies. Brides- (and grooms-) to-be can click on links such as "Wedding Planning," "Wedding Budgeter," "Wedding Fashion," "Bridal Beauty," and "Grooms" (who only have one link dedicated to them). The site even offers a link to apply for a "The Knot" American Express credit card. TheKnot.com promotes itself as the only wedding brand on AOL, MSN, and Yahoo Internet portals, and also has established marketing alliances with May Department Stores Company, the umbrella company of Robinsons-May, Filene's, and Famous-Barr, under which The Knot promotes these stores' wedding registry services (*The May Department Stores,* 2002). . . .

In March 2005, The Knot announced the debut of its online TV channel, The Knot TV, linked to its main Web site's "Talk" section (Tedeschi, 2005). The program schedule relies on *Real Weddings from The Knot* and short videos of bridal makeovers and "fashion reports," featuring streaming video of runway shows of designer wedding gowns. Visitors can view fashion reports on demand, but must wait for a short commercial first (such as for Crest's Whitening Strips tooth bleach). Thus, even "on demand" video on The Knot is accompanied by some form of external sponsorship.

The Knot's media holdings continue to expand, with the acquisition of Great Boyfriends.com, a site where women recommend men to other women, and TheNest .com, a site devoted to all the domestic necessities of newlyweds just setting up house. TheNest.com, aimed at the "freshly married," offers blogs, advice columns, and recipes, in addition to guiding its visitors to retail merchants of housewares, appliances and automobiles, and lending companies for home mortgages (Oser, 2005).

The Knot Magazine includes full-page promotions for these Web sites, with directions for readers to consult TheKnot.com Web site throughout its editorial content.

Though it appears to Web site visitors as a one-stop shop for everything bridal, advertising comprises the bulk of The Knot's income. According to its annual report of earnings, in 2004 The Knot's net revenues totaled $41.4 million. Most of it ($17.6 million) came from sponsors and advertising, including local vendor and national advertising sales, with merchandising accounting for $13.1 million, and its publishing ventures bringing in $10.7 million (*Annual Report*, 2005). In 2005, net revenues increased to $51.4 million, with revenues from online advertising and sponsorships increasing to $25.8 million, while merchandise revenue declined by $0.5 million (*Form 10-K for The Knot, Inc.*, 2006). The Knot's publishing revenues increased to $13 million in 2005. These figures point not only to the company's success in securing advertising and sponsors, but also to the demand for bridal media and the need for wedding products and services. . . .

Cultural Hegemony in *Real Weddings from The Knot*

"Weddings, marriage, romance, and heterosexuality become naturalized to the point where we consent to the belief that marriage is necessary to achieve a sense of well-being, belonging, passion, morality, and love," wrote Ingraham (1999, p. 120). This hegemony encompasses our commonsense and unquestioned notions about marriage, such as the expectation that women buy into, literally, the wedding ideal. Several studies have used hegemony theory specifically to analyze wedding-related media. Lewis (1997) used hegemony to examine the gendered messages contained in wedding photography and concluded that wedding photography illustrates notions of perfection, "ideal" body language, and glorification of the bride in all her finery,

and legitimizes consumerism through the acceptance of its high cost and necessity.

Reality TV wedding shows, Herr (2005) observed, "could be considered the next logical step in the professionalization and commercialization of the American wedding" (p. 24). . . .

Real Weddings from The Knot debuted in 2003 as a joint venture between The Knot and the Oxygen cable network. Oxygen, cofounded by Oprah Winfrey, is independently owned and operated and available to 52 million cable households (*About Oxygen*, 2007). Its mission, according to its Web site, is "to bring women (and the men who love them) the edgiest, most innovative entertainment on television" (*About Oxygen*, 2007). Presented on Oxygen during cross-promoted "Wedding Weeks" about twice a year, the program features couples from "all walks of life with all kinds of weddings" (*Oxygen Proposes to The Knot*, 2004). . . .

Each 30-minute episode follows the wedding couple as they prepare for their wedding, often weeks in advance. Voiceover narration from the bride introduces and concludes each episode; other audio comes from natural sound and participants (e.g., the groom, parents, family members, wedding coordinators) who speak directly into the camera. Viewers watch as couples write their own vows, choose flowers, put together party favors, and perform other wedding-related activities. For each season of *Real Weddings from The Knot*, episodes are presented in weekend marathons, ending with a special "wedding gown" fashion show. . . .

Major Content Themes

BRIDE AS PHYSICAL OBJECT

The wedding provides a venue in which women are still expected to show, and display to others, their femininity. The one day in which a woman, any woman, can be a star is her wedding day, and the reward for adhering to a hegemony of femininity is a temporary status of being a celebrity, as noted by Boden (2003): "Overwhelmingly, femininity is conceptualized as 'picture-perfect,' triggering visual pleasure for the bride as well as her audience for conforming to the cultural requirements for a successful bridal appearance" (p. 62).

Of all the required accoutrements of the wedding, the bridal gown holds utmost importance in *Real Weddings from The Knot*. In all episodes, brides wear some type of formal, white (or cream-colored) dress. Brides are often shown being fitted for their dresses, many times with female onlookers, such as mothers, tearfully expressing how beautiful they look. The term *princess* is used repeatedly as brides become the object of their own gaze, as illustrated by the following: "I feel really pretty. I feel like a princess," comments 23-year-old Jen, a former recording artist who has given up her career in favor of marriage; "It's starting to hit home, the whole reason why we're here is this dress. . . . Oh, my god, I feel like a princess," says Orisha, whose marriage to John comes after they have already been living together and have a daughter.

For Cara, who claims in her voiceover introduction, "Every bride dreams of being a princess on her wedding day," her dress serves as a source of unhappiness, as she tries on her ill-fitting, custom-made gown: "I don't love it. It's not what I imagined." Her comments point to the significance a piece of apparel holds—her happiness hinges on how this dress looks and feels. The "magic" surrounding the perfect dress holds significance for many of these brides; several seek that perfection by hiring designers to make a one-of-a-kind gown, such as Amy, who started looking for dresses a year before the wedding, and after trying on "100" dresses and not finding the "right one," had a couturier make one for her. Tiffany, who has overseen every detail of her New York Harlem Renaissance wedding, is shown being fitted in a Vera Wang gown, and is given walking lessons by prominent *Vogue* editor Andre Leon Talley.

More so than the bride herself, it is her *dress*—her "packaging" (Goldstein-Gidoni, 1997)—rather than her person as a human being—that serves as the center of attention. Brides are seen getting dressed on the wedding day, often assisted by others, due to the elaborateness and complexity of the "costuming." Recurrent images also include the bride being formally photographed, with the white dress serving as the focus of the viewer's gaze. In sum, women about to be married are *transformed* into "real" brides once they wear the wedding gown, which this program promulgates as the true mark of the princess bride.

The other requirement women must meet to become a bride is that they be made up with cosmetics and their hair be done in a special coiffure. Makeup's transformative power becomes magnified on a woman's wedding day. While making up has become a tangible way for women to confirm their feminine identities (Peiss, 1996), similarly, through special application of cosmetics, and hairstyling, brides become "transformed" from mere woman to bride. In nearly all episodes, brides, and their female attendants, are shown at beauty salons on the wedding day and/or having their cosmetics applied by either a makeup artist or themselves. For example, Katie, a model and dental hygienist, insists on doing her sisters' makeup and hair herself because she wants them to "look perfect."

While these brides all undergo beauty regimens of some sort, the notion that beauty requires pain is especially noteworthy. For example, 20-something Kaijsa has her hair done in an "up do" at a beauty salon and says, "I don't like pain, but if it makes me look good, I don't care," while wincing as her tiara and veil are positioned into her coiffure. Especially telling is how this idea of pain equaling beauty extends to younger female bridal party members. One of Lori's two young stepdaughters-to-be (she is marrying Mark, a divorced father) cries in pain because her hair pins hurt, as the other comments, "Beauty is pain." Thus, this example illustrates that not only do brides expect to experience some kind of pain or discomfort, but young girls already understand that beauty involves some amount of sacrifice, sometimes to the point of crying.

The emphasis on female beauty becomes even more heightened with the juxtaposition of images of grooms getting dressed and ready for the wedding day. The most common image among these episodes features the groom visiting a tuxedo shop a day or two prior to the wedding for a final fitting, or getting dressed on the wedding day. Even this aspect is implied to be controlled by the bride, as the men on the program are not shown actually *selecting* their attire. For example, in Orisha and John's episode, John and his attendants make their requisite visit to the tuxedo shop to have a last-minute fitting, with Orisha and other female family members supervising. Speaking into the camera, Orisha reminds viewers, "*I picked the color for the tux. It's my theme here.*" Typically, however, attention to men's apparel is confined to brief visits to the tuxedo shop or making last-minute adjustments to neckties on the day of the wedding. While brides are shown at length trying on and admiring their gowns and being assisted by other women on the wedding day, men's apparel receives little attention, if at all.

The importance of brides' physical beauty becomes further underscored as women are consistently shown having their makeup applied by someone else, appearing on camera with a facial mask (Orisha has a mud mask and Kaijsa is shown taking a bath with cold cream and cucumber slices over her eyes), or having their hair coiffed in a salon. In contrast, while John has his braids done by a female family member at home and Todd has his hairdresser brother coif his hair, men are never seen shaving or applying beauty products. The absence as a rule of such images of men attending to their visage makes the occasional exception even

more jarring, as in the case of Catina and Todd's episode. In addition to doing his hair, his hairdresser brother applies facial makeup to Todd, explaining that doing so will prevent Todd's face from being too shiny for the wedding photographs. Todd's other brothers laugh as they look on, which further emphasizes that such treatment is inappropriate for men.

In sum, physical appearance is clearly a much more important aspect of "looking the part" for women than for men on the wedding day (and, indeed, every day). . . . One can consider the process of the wedding, that is, the "making" of the bride, as a disciplinary practice that creates ideal feminine beauty. The special attention given to the application of makeup on the female face further emphasizes the unpainted female face as "defective" (Bartky, 1988), and in need of correction, in contrast to the male face. When the male face *is* subjected to similar treatment, as in the case of Todd, and with justification (to ensure aesthetically pleasing wedding photographs), the male is apt to be ridiculed. The application of makeup for women, however, is "natural," in that, as Hall and Hebert (2004) noted, makeup creates feminine identity; women are not truly women without it, or without the accompanying discomfort (including starving oneself) required to look beautiful.

SUPERBRIDE/MANAGER

In *Real Weddings from The Knot,* the bride's major responsibilities are to look beautiful and to oversee the planning of her wedding. Boden's (2003) "superbride" serves as the role model for the brides in these episodes, with a common theme pointing to the traditional view that wedding planning, centered on shopping and attainment of material goods, falls into the feminine realm (Lowrey & Otnes, 1994). As they decide every detail of what is supposed to be their "special day," these superbrides frantically make arrangements, run errands, and ensure everything from wedding rings to bouquets are accounted for, all the while commenting to the viewer that they don't mind being frazzled, because it is "worth it."

Brides in this program consistently direct ceremony rehearsals, tell people what to do and how to act, and oversee catering, decorating, and their own and others' apparel, even when they hire wedding coordinators. For example, Catina, who will marry Todd in a big church, choreographs the dance numbers for her elaborate wedding, and Katie orders her bridesmaid sisters to "stand up straight," just as they are to walk into the ceremony. While their grooms do participate at times, such as by making party favors or going to food tastings to choose their reception menus, final decisions are made by the brides.

The episode featuring Amy, who has been with Mark for 5 years, serves as a notable example of an extreme "superbride."[2] This episode is marked by Amy's constant bossiness, penchant for tirades, and verbal abuse of her parents (which includes constant profanity and directives for them to "shut up")—which they seem to take in stride. Amy oversees every minute aspect of her wedding at a mansion in the New York countryside, including the coordination and assemblage of gift baskets for guests, and even gluing artificial flowers to guests' flip flops. Her mother comments, "She's a girl with a mind of her own, she knows what she wants." Her future husband, Mark, even acknowledges her controlling nature when he explains to the viewer that "Amy wears the pants. She's the boss of the family." Indeed, Mark is rarely seen in this episode; he goes off-roading on motor bikes just hours before the wedding and mainly stays out of Amy's way.

On the wedding day, she becomes upset to find her bouquet is the wrong color, and her parents nag her about being late to the ceremony, as she calmly smokes a cigarette. Ironically, this "superbride" is 45 minutes late to her own wedding. However, Amy's controlling nature apparently doesn't bother

Mark, as he tells her, in front of the wedding audience, "You are my sunshine, my angel." Amy's seemingly stressful wedding preparations all work out in the end, and as she says in the voiceover conclusion, "In the future, I'll forget all the worry and stress that went into planning this wedding."

Even as Amy serves as the extreme superbride, all the brides in these episodes illustrate superbride behavior in one form or another. In contrast, the grooms generally serve either as companions or assistants to their future wives (Bill accompanies Amy to a meeting with their cake designer, John and Danielle visit their florist, Kaijsa and Ryan go food tasting together), or stay out of the planning altogether. For example, Lori does the planning for her and Mark's destination wedding. "It doesn't bother me that I'm doing most of the planning by myself, because Mark does all the work when we're at home all week long," Lori comments.

Grooms who do participate usually do so in a secondary capacity: Ryan helps Kaijsa with seating assignments for the reception; Jeff builds special platforms for the wedding lanterns for his and Jessa's budget wedding and goes shopping with her at Wal-Mart; Gus runs errands based on Katie's "to-do" list to "help relieve some of Katie's stress." However, even as some grooms try to be helpful, brides often become frustrated when their men fall short on even the seemingly simplest tasks. For example, Sarah-Jane does all the planning for her wedding with Nate, constantly making to-do lists every day and stressing out over the "68 things" she must do. Nate's major task is to learn how to dance for their reception. Sarah-Jane becomes upset when Nate still can't remember the dance, after 8 months of lessons. At Kaijsa and Ryan's wedding rehearsal, Kaijsa asks Ryan to help her direct the intricate Jewish ceremony. After it becomes clear that nobody listens to her instructions, she finally throws her hands up in frustration.

Overall, brides assume responsibility for most of the wedding planning, details, and errand running. In the case of millionaire John and his bride Danielle, viewers see them visit their florist together, and discussing wedding and reception details on camera. John appears intricately involved with every aspect of their glamorous Newport, Rhode Island, wedding, which involves two reception sites, one for cocktails at the Tennis Hall of Fame and another for the "real" reception at a mansion that John had chosen as a wedding site when he was a boy. However, he makes a point to explain to their guests at their rehearsal dinner and again at their reception that Danielle has made most of the decisions. "We've put—*she's* put—a lot of planning into this for the last two years," he says while making a toast at their reception, making clear that she has been the one in charge. Overall, then, while grooms may participate in various ways in the wedding planning, the main responsibility falls to the brides. . . .

WEDDING DETAILS AND CONSUMERISM

As viewers watch the wedding plans unfold, noticeable attention is given to items specifically chosen for the ceremony, such as the aforementioned all-important wedding gown, shoes, bridesmaids' dresses, flowers, wedding cake, entertainment in the form of live bands and recorded music, and locale. Larger scale weddings take place at some sort of unique venue, such as an historic mansion or hotel, country estate, or exclusive club. For example, writer Susan Orlean (*The Orchid Thief*) and husband John hold their upscale Manhattan wedding at The Explorer's Club, and hire a gospel choir to provide music; millionaire John and model Danielle marry at a Newport, Rhode Island, mansion; and Alison, an antiques store owner, and Tommy, a stockbroker, hold their wedding at Alison's parents' horse farm, complete with 7,000 flowers and a 9,000 square-foot tent to hold their 800 guests.

Attention to details such as party favors for guests emphasizes the importance of items and gifts as ways for couples to imbue their weddings with a personal touch. For example, John and Danielle give boxes of Krispy Kreme donuts to guests, specially delivered in a vintage-style Krispy Kreme truck. Specifics on wedding cakes also get attention, as the viewer goes along with Amy and Bill as they consult with their wedding cake baker on their novelty, shopping-themed cake, or watches Jessa, a research scientist and bride "on a budget," bake and decorate her own wedding cake.

The wedding budget serves as the central theme of Jessa's wedding with Jeff, a medical student. In their episode, viewers are told simply that they are on a budget, and watch them shop for wedding supplies at Wal-Mart. While the television version of their story emphasizes their tight budget and the amount of work they put into creating their version of the dream wedding, the online synopsis of their episode terms their wedding as being on "a graduate student budget of only $6,000." The emphasis on the "homemade" quality of their wedding—with even the couple commenting that others might call them "cheap" but they prefer "thrifty"—conveys the message that Jessa and Jeff cannot do much with "only" $6,000, and suggests that couples with similarly "small" budgets should expect to bake their own cakes as well. Juxtaposed with the more usual sumptuous weddings, Jessa and Jeff's homemade country wedding, as well as Whitney and Jeff's country-style barbeque reception, look shabby; the resulting message to viewers reinforces the "big, white wedding" ideal, in which guests are treated to lavish parties and gifts. . . .

Discussion

As a producer of cultural work, The Knot serves as an ideal example of the modern media conglomerate, but even more so of media synergy, as a single corporation's several outlets "can use each other to move content and promote themselves" (McAllister, 2000, p. 109). Media synergy allows The Knot to promote itself through its Web site, magazine, specialty publications, and reality television series. Similar to the "synergistic melding" of the Lifetime cable channel, its owner, ABC, and ABC's owner, the Walt Disney Company, that resulted in *Weddings of a Lifetime* (Levine, 2005), The Knot's foray into the world of reality television provides another means by which it can self-promote and further its reach among its target audience—immediate and potential brides.

If American society in general consists mostly of a middle class, then weddings, according to Herr (2005), allow for the creation of a "spectacle," with the goal of "moving up," so to speak, to a higher class for one special day. *Real Weddings from The Knot* and its online and print counterparts create and provide for women an escape, albeit temporary, from the monotony of a middle-class habitus. While *Real Weddings* offers viewers a range of weddings, from down-home to glamorous, the program's underlying message instills the notion that no matter what one's socioeconomic status, the wedding requires some degree of special effort that always involves additional work and money. All these weddings involved the wearing of special clothing (wedding gown and tuxedos), reception with elaborate decorations, music, and specialty items (e.g., a wedding cake), which create a clear departure from the everyday. Even the sumptuous receptions of John and Danielle, the millionaire and the model, serve as departures from their already upscale daily life. . . .

The feminine ideal forwarded by *Real Weddings from The Knot,* and bridal media in general, provides a contrast to a wider picture of the status of women in American society today. While the program portrays strong women who "know what they want" and have established successful careers for themselves, the wedding demands them to play roles that remain decidedly feminine. This was illustrated by Cara, a Wall Street broker who has earned a seat on the New York Stock Exchange, who plans and gets her "fairy tale" wedding. However, even as women like Cara make progress in the male-dominated business world, and seemingly promote feminism, in terms of creating equality in that sphere of social life, they still symbolize the feminine values embodied in the self-image of beautiful, finely dressed "princess" (a term denoting a secondary royal status, an ideal embraced by the program).

In sum, while the take-control, almost-masculine attitudes of "superbrides" such as Cara and Amy demonstrate on the surface their independent attitude, they still adhere to feminine ideals of physical beauty and play the role of demure bride on their wedding day. Thus, ironically, even as they control their "special day," they succumb to and happily accept the stress, worry, and even pain required to look the part of the blushing bride. The acceptance of the disciplinary practices surrounding the bridal role illustrates what Bartky (1988) called "the economy of enforcement," in which women both dictate and subject themselves to such rules, and "men get off scot-free" (p. 81). The imbalance between the genders in this regard, with women dedicating their time toward making themselves beautiful and creating the perfect dream wedding, and men for the most part left out of wedding planning, further demarcates the line between the feminine and masculine. In this sense, weddings remain "women's work," rather than an endeavor whose labor is shared by both partners.

Conclusion

Regarding this particular media corporation, the name *The Knot* seems more than apropos. Through its reality television show, The Knot ties entertainment, information, and ultimately, merchandising together to create what Mosco (1996) termed an "institutional circuit of communication products" that links the bridal industry, the primary producers of bridal products, to consumers, by presenting the weddings of ordinary people. As a "one-stop" shop for all things bridal, it provides its readers and viewing audience, through a variety of media, formalized instruction in the art of party planning, a social endeavor one does not normally learn in school. It also has established relationships with its advertisers by providing its Web visitors direct access to an array of retailers, including its own online store. Wedding accessories thus can be purchased simply by clicking an icon of one's choice. In this sense, its media side supports its business side quite efficiently. In terms of political economy of the media, then, The Knot creates not only media products supported by advertising revenue but also directly encourages retail sales for its advertisers' financial success.

In turn, because The Knot's survival depends on its advertisers' sales, the messages it sends through its own media product, in the guise of the editorial sections of its magazines, Web site, and its reality television program, promote the need for the items its advertisers sell. These messages relay to its female audience a repeated and uniform version of the wedding, disallowing alternatives that would negate the importance of seemingly vital elements, namely, those that The Knot's advertising and editorial content feature. Because hegemony exists only when the possibility for counter-hegemony exists, The Knot must constantly remind its audience that other wedding styles either are undesirable (cheap) or—as is implied by ignoring them—do not exist. In this way, The Knot also advances a cultural hegemony regarding how one can and is supposed to enact the wedding, a personal commitment made publicly.

The public nature of the wedding creates another dimension that The Knot addresses, that of instructing women to perform the role of bride in the correct manner. In that hegemony exists not by state-imposed force but by consent, women who wish to marry correctly, then, adhere to the rules suggested by The Knot and other bridal media. Fear of deviating from the correct wedding script thus leads to what Landy (1994) termed a "convenience of conformity," wherein brides follow the rules set by the experts. In the process, The Knot reestablishes the big, intricately planned wedding as *the* ideal, and the image of the beautiful and beautifully dressed bride as the pinnacle of femininity.

While The Knot concentrates on weddings (and with its new Web site TheNest, the proper way of setting up one's new marital home), its media product/cultural work provides additional instruction in the proper way women should fulfill non-bridal roles. As discussed above, many of the women featured in *Real Weddings from The Knot* also have careers, and successful ones at that. In this sense, the very inclusion of such facts can allow one to view it as feminist. However, the program gives even more time to depictions of these same women undergoing beauty regimens, being fitted for bridal gowns, and devoting large amounts of time to a clearly feminine project.

"Sometimes consumerism has been seen as the principal source of women's oppression in the twentieth century, as a force, which by promoting a falsely feminine identity, distracts them from what would otherwise be their true identities, as humans and/or women," observed Bowlby (1996, p. 381). The subtle, and not so subtle, messages that associate happiness with consumption and perfection with femininity, conveyed by *Real Weddings from The Knot* and similar programs in the reality genre, provide additional evidence for such a claim. The resulting cultural work points to an image of the successful woman as fulfilling the role of beautiful consumer.

Regarding The Knot's emphasis on femininity and its relation to feminism, the amount of time and effort required to organize the kinds of weddings presented on this program and others like it thus serves to distract women from otherwise devoting that time to other facets of their lives, including activities that would put them in competition with men in the working world. Moreover, the additional self-enforcement of the disciplined bridal body provides evidence for Bartky's (1988) assertion that "normative femininity" has become more and more centered on women's appearance, even as older forms of patriarchal domination erode (p. 81). Thus, while American women continue their progress toward equality in larger society, one can view the cultural hegemony forwarded by bridal media as an acceptable means by which patriarchal values and traditions endure.

Notes

1. Political economy of the media here refers to the study of power relations involved in the production, distribution, and consumption of resources and products of communication, with media products and audiences serving as both (Mosco, 1996). Regarding communication studies, political economists examine the structure of media industries and their relationships with other economic sectors within a capitalistic system (Steeves & Wasko, 2002) and how media and communication systems and content "reinforce, challenge, or influence existing class and social relations" (McChesney, 2000).

2. Amy's behaviors are illustrative of demanding behaviors of brides as described in the popular book *Bridezilla: True Tales From Etiquette Hell* (Spaemme & Hamilton, 2002). Though the book uses a humorous approach in discussing bad manners exhibited by brides who seek to create the perfect wedding, it offers insight into how obsessive wedding planning can go awry and the problems created by some brides' overly materialistic concerns.

References

About Oxygen. (2007). Retrieved May 4, 2007, from http://www.oxygen.com/basics/about .aspx

Annual report. (2005, March 21). Retrieved March 28, 2005, from http://biz-yahoo.com/ e/050321/ knot.ob10-k.html

Bartky, S. L. (1988). Foucault, femininity, and the modernization of patriarchal power. In I. Diamond & L. Quinby (Eds.), *Feminism and Foucault: Reflections on resistance* (pp. 61–86). Boston: Northeastern University Press.

Boden, S. (2003). *Consumerism, romance, and the wedding experience.* New York: Palgrave Macmillan.

Bowlby, R. (1996). Soft sell: Marketing rhetoric in feminist criticism. In V. deGrazia, with E. Furlough (Eds.), *The sex of things: Gender and consumption in historical perspective* (pp. 381–387). Los Angeles: University of California Press.

Carragee, K. M. (1993). A critical evaluation of debates examining the media hegemony thesis. *Western Journal of Communication, 57,* 330–348.

Company milestones. (2007). Retrieved May 4, 2007, from http://www.theknot.com/au_ milestones.shtml

Currie, D. H. (1993). Here comes the bride: The making of a "modern traditional" wedding in Western culture. *Journal of Comparative Family Studies, 24,* 403–421.

Deery, J. (2004). Reality TV as advertisement. *Popular Communication, 2,* 1–20.

Ellerbee, L., & Tessem, R. (Executive Producers). (2001, February 25). *The American wedding* [Television cablecast]. New York: Lucky Duck Productions. (Available from A&E Television Networks, http://www.aande.com)

Engstrom, E. (2003). Hegemony in reality-based TV programming: The world according to *A Wedding Story. Media Report to Women, 31,* 10–14.

Engstrom, E., & Semic, B. (2003). Portrayal of religion in reality TV programming: Hegemony and the contemporary American wedding. *Journal of Media and Religion, 2,* 145–163.

Filak, V. (2002, August). *Marriage, magazines and makeup tips: A comparative content analysis of* Bride's *magazine and* Glamour *magazine.* Paper presented at the annual meeting of the Association for Education in Journalism and Mass Communication, Miami, FL.

Form 10-K for The Knot, Inc. (2006, March 17). Retrieved May 16, 2006, from http://biz .yahoo.com/ e/060317/knot10-k.hmtl

Gibbons, S. (2003, June 4). Bridal media promote merchandise, not marriage. *Women's eNews.* Retrieved June 23, 2003, from http://www .wenews.org/article.cfm/dyn/aid/1353/

Goldstein-Gidoni, O. (1997). *Packaged Japaneseness: Weddings, business and brides.* Honolulu: University of Hawai'i Press.

Hall, A., & Hebert, L. (2004, August). *The evolution of the makeover from print to television: An analysis of the social construction of the female body image.* Paper presented at the annual meeting of the Association for Education in Journalism and Mass Communication, Toronto, Canada.

Herr, R. A. (2005, May). *The dream and the reality of the American wedding: Taste, style, and reality television.* Paper presented at the annual meeting of the International Communication Association, New York.

Ingraham, C. (1999). *White weddings: Romancing heterosexuality in popular culture.* New York: Routledge.

Landy, M. (1994). *Film, politics, and Gramsci.* Minneapolis, MN: University of Minnesota Press.

Levine, E. (2005). Fractured fairy tales and fragmented markets: Disney's *Weddings of a Lifetime* and the cultural politics of media conglomeration. *Television & New Media, 6,* 71–88.

Lewis, C. (1997). Hegemony in the ideal: Wedding photography, consumption, and patriarchy. *Women's Studies in Communication, 20,* 167–187.

Lowrey, T. M., & Otnes, C. (1994). Construction of a meaningful wedding: Differences in the priorities of brides and grooms. In J. A. Costa (Ed.), *Gender issues and consumer behavior* (pp. 164–183). Thousand Oaks, CA: Sage.

The May Department Stores Company and The Knot announce marketing alliance [Press release] (2002, February 25). Retrieved March 4, 2005, from http://www.theknot .com/02.25.02.shtml

McAllister, M. P. (2000). From flick to flack: The increased emphasis on marketing by media entertainment corporations. In R. Andersen & L. Strate (Eds.), *Critical studies in media commercialism* (pp. 101–122). New York: Oxford University Press.

McChesney, R. W. (2000). The political economy of communication and the future of the field. *Media, Culture and Society, 22,* 109–116.

Mosco, V. (1996). *The political economy of communication: Rethinking and renewal.* Thousand Oaks, CA: Sage.

Oser, K. (2005, May 23). TheKnot.com seeks to extend its engagements. *Advertising Age,* 76(21), 144.

Oxygen proposes to The Knot: 10 more episodes of Real weddings from the knot [Press release] (2004, March 1). Retrieved October 4, 2004, from http://www.theknot .com

Peiss, K. (1996). Making up, making over: Cosmetics, consumer culture, and women's identity. In V. deGrazia, with E. Furlough (Eds.), *The sex of things: Gender and consumption in historical perspective* (pp. 311–336). Los Angeles: University of California Press.

Spaemme, N., & Hamilton, J. (2002). *Bridezilla: True tales from etiquette hell.* Plano, TX: Salado Press.

Steeves, H. L., & Wasko, J. (2002). Feminist theory and political economy: Toward a friendly alliance. In E. R. Meehan & E. Riordan (Eds.), *Sex and money: Feminism and political economy in the media* (pp. 16–29). Minneapolis, MN: University of Minnesota Press.

Tedeschi, B. (2005, March 14). Websites try offering TV shows. *New York Times E-Commerce Report.* Retrieved March 28, 2005, from http://www.nytimes.com/2005/ 03/14/technology/14ecom.html?ei=5088& en=2adcb055d1d

Supersexualize Me![1]

Advertising and the "Midriffs"

Rosalind Gill

. . . For the last four decades the notion of objectification has been a key term in the feminist critique of advertising. Its centrality to the feminist critical lexicon lay in its ability to speak to the ways in which media representations help to justify and sustain relations of domination and inequality between men and women. In particular, processes of objectification were held to be the key to understanding male violence against women:

> Adverts don't directly cause violence . . . but the violent images contribute to the state of terror. Turning a human being into a thing, an object, is almost always the first step towards justifying violence against that person . . . This step is already taken with women. The violence, the abuse, is partly the chilling but logical result of the objectification. (Kilbourne, 1999: 278)

It is difficult to over-estimate the importance of this argument for feminism (and also for understandings of racism and other relations of brutality); it has been central to feminist activism around advertising and media representations more generally. However, I want to suggest that a number of significant changes have taken place in the regime of representation that mean that the notion of objectification no longer has the analytic purchase to understand many contemporary constructions of femininity. Increasingly, young women are presented not as passive sex objects, but as active, desiring sexual subjects, who seem to participate enthusiastically in practices and forms of self-presentation that earlier generations of feminists regarded as connected to subordination. . . .

This shift was emblematic of a wider transformation happening in advertising in the early 1990s. Robert Goldman (1992) has argued that advertisers were forced to respond to three challenges at this time. First, there was the growing experience of 'sign fatigue' on the part of many media audiences fed up with the endless parade of brands, logos and consumer images.

From Gill, R. (2009). Supersexualize Me! Advertising and the 'Midriffs.' In F. Attwood (Ed.), *Mainstreaming sex: The sexualization of Western culture* (pp. 93–99). New York: I. B. Taurus.

Like its millennial sibling, compassion fatigue, sign fatigue showed itself in what we might call a weariness of affect, an ennui and a disinclination to respond. Secondly, advertisers had to address increasing 'viewer scepticism,' particularly from younger, media-savvy consumers who had grown up with fast-paced music television and were the first generation to adopt personal computers and mobile phones as integral features of everyday life. To get through to this generation, who regarded themselves as sceptical and knowing in relation to commercial messages, advertisers had to adapt. They increasingly came to produce commercials that mocked the grammar and vocabulary of advertising and effaced their own status as advertisements. Thirdly, advertisers needed to address feminist critiques of advertising and to fashion new commercial messages that took on board women's anger at constantly being addressed through representations of idealized beauty.

Goldman argued that advertisers' response to this third challenge was to develop what he called 'commodity feminism'[2]—an attempt to incorporate the cultural power and energy of feminism whilst simultaneously domesticating its critique of advertising and the media. Commodity feminism takes many different forms. It consists of adverts that aim to appease women's anger and to suggest that advertisers share their disgruntlement with images of thin women, airbrushed to perfection. It is found in adverts that attempt to articulate a rapprochement between traditional femininity and characteristics which are coded as feminist goals; independence, career success, financial autonomy. It may be identified in gender-reversal adverts or in revenge adverts that mock or turn the tables on men. Elsewhere I have considered a number of shifts in the representation of gender in advertising in some detail (Gill, 2007a).[3] In the remainder of this chapter, however, I will turn my attention to perhaps the major contemporary shift in the sexual representation of women: the construction of a young, heterosexual woman who knowingly and deliberately plays with her sexual power and is forever 'up for it': the midriff.

Sexualization and the Midriffs

The midriff is a part of the body between the top of the pubis bone and the bottom of the rib cage. This part of the female body has been the site of erotic interest in many non-Western cultures for a long time. In the West, the recent upsurge of interest in the midriff can be traced back to the visual presentation of Madonna in the late 1980s in which her pierced belly button and toned abdomen became features for erotic display in dance routines. For almost a decade, between the mid-1990s and the mid-2000s, revealing the midriff was central to young women's fashion in the West, with low-hung hipster jeans and cropped or belly top, exposing a pierced navel at the front and the familiar 'whale back' (visible g-string) from behind. Increasingly, the lower back has also become a site for elaborate tattoos.

This style was so widespread for such a long time that the term 'midriffs' has become a shorthand employed by advertisers and marketing consultants (Quart, 2003). In one sense it signals a generation—primarily women in their 20s and 30s, but sometimes also girls in their teens and women in their early 40s—defined by their fashion tastes. More tellingly, the midriffs can be understood in relation to a particular sensibility: a sensibility characterized by a specific constellation of attitudes towards the body, sexual expression and gender relations.

Advertising aimed at the midriffs is notable for its apparently 'sexualized' style but this is quite different from the sexual objectification to which second-wave feminist activists objected. In today's midriff advertising, women are much less likely to be shown as passive sexual objects than as empowered, heterosexually desiring sexual subjects, operating playfully in a sexual marketplace that is presented as egalitarian or actually favourable to women.

Midriff advertising has four central themes: an emphasis on the body, a shift from objectification to sexual subjectification, a pronounced discourse of choice and autonomy, and an emphasis upon empowerment.

Perhaps the most striking feature of midriff advertising is the centrality of the body. If in the 1950s the home was the ideal focus for women's labour and attention, and the sign used to judge their 'worth,' in the new millennium it is the body. Today, a sleek, controlled figure is essential for portraying success, and each part of the body must be suitably toned, conditioned, waxed, moisturized, scented and attired. In advertising, more and more parts of the body come under intense scrutiny: Dove's summer 2006 campaign alerts us that the newest must-have accessory is beautiful armpits, lest we forget to use all the products necessary to render this part of the body acceptable.

Today, the body is portrayed in advertising and elsewhere as the primary source of women's capital. This may seem obvious and taken-for-granted, but it is, in fact, relatively new. Surveillance of women's bodies constitutes perhaps the largest type of media content across all genres and media forms. Women's bodies are evaluated, scrutinized and dissected by women as well as men and are always at risk of 'failing.' This is most clear in the cultural obsession with celebrity which plays out almost exclusively over women's bodies. . . . In the very recent past, women's cooking, domestic cleanliness or interior design skills were the focus of advertisers' attention to a much greater extent than the surface of the body. But there has been a profound shift in the very definition of femininity so that it is now defined as a bodily property rather than a social or psychological one. Instead of caring or nurturing or motherhood, it is now possession of a 'sexy body' that is presented as women's key source of identity. . . .

There has also been a shift in the way that women's bodies are presented erotically. Where once sexualized representations of women in the media presented them as the passive, mute objects of an assumed male gaze, today women are presented as active, desiring sexual subjects who choose to present themselves in a seemingly objectified manner because it suits their liberated interests to do so. . . . The notion of objectification does not seem to capture this; a better understanding would come from the Foucaultian idea of (sexual) subjectification, which speaks to the way that power operates through the construction of particular subjectivities.

A crucial aspect of both the obsessional preoccupation with the body and the shift from objectification to sexual subjectification is that this is framed in advertising through a discourse of playfulness, freedom, and, above all, *choice*. Women are presented not as seeking men's approval but as *pleasing themselves*; in doing so, they just happen to win men's admiration. . . .

Dee Amy-Chinn (2006) eloquently captures this double-edged postfeminist emphasis on women pleasing themselves, in the title of her article about lingerie advertising: 'This is just for me(n).' Such advertising hails active, heterosexual young women, but does so using a photographic grammar directly lifted from heterosexual pornography aimed at men. The success—and this is what is novel about this—is in connecting 'me' and 'men,' suggesting there is no contradiction—indeed no difference—between what 'I' want and what men might want of 'me.' This is clearly complicated. There is no necessary contradiction or difference between what women and men want, but equally it cannot be assumed that their desires are identical. What is most interesting is the sophisticated 'higher' development of ideology and power relations, such that the ideological is literally made real. This takes the form of constructions of femininity that come straight out of the most predictable templates of male sexual fantasy, yet which must also be understood as authentically owned by the women who produce them. Part of their force lies precisely in the fact that they are not understood as ideological, or indeed are understood as *not* ideological. . . .

Almost as central to midriff advertising as the notions of choice and 'pleasing one's self,' is a discourse of feminine *empowerment*. Contemporary advertising targeted at the midriffs suggest, above all, that buying the product will empower you. . . . What is on offer in all these adverts is a specific kind of power—the sexual power to bring men to their knees. Empowerment is tied to possession of a slim and alluring young body, whose power is the ability to attract male attention and sometimes female envy. . . . A US advert for lingerie dares to make explicit that which is usually just implied. Showing a curvaceous woman's body from the neck down, clad in a black basque and stockings, the advert's text reads, 'while you don't necessarily dress for men, it doesn't hurt, on occasion, to see one drool like the pathetic dog he is.'[4] This is 'power femininity': a 'subject-effect' of 'a global discourse of popular post-feminism which incorporates feminist signifiers of emancipation and empowerment, as well as circulating popular postfeminist assumptions that feminist struggles have ended, that full equality for all women has been achieved, and that women of today can "have it all"' (Lazar, 2006).

Supersexualize Me: Midriff Advertising and Postfeminism

What, then, are we to make of the shift in the way that women are presented sexually? In offering up representations of women who are active, desiring sexual subjects, who are presented as powerful and playful, rather than passive or victimized, has advertising pointed to more hopeful, open or egalitarian possibilities for gender relations? I do not think so. On the contrary, I want to argue that midriff advertising re-sexualizes women's bodies, with the excuse of a feisty, empowered postfeminist discourse that makes it very difficult to critique.

Let us examine first some of the exclusions of midriff advertising. Most obviously this includes anyone living outside the heterosexual norm. Contemporary midriff advertising operates within a resolutely hetero-normative economy, in which power, pleasure and subjectivity are all presented in relation to heterosexual relationships. Indeed, the parallel growth of a kind of 'queer chic' (Gill, 2008) seems to locate homosexuality in terms of style and aesthetics rather than sexuality. A cynic might suggest that the greater visibility of hyper-feminine/hyper-sexualized lesbians in advertising may be a way for advertisers to evade charges of sexism, whilst continuing to present women in a highly objectified manner.

Others excluded from the empowering, pleasurable address of midriff advertising are older women, disabled women, fat women and any woman who is unable to live up to the increasingly narrow standards of female beauty and sex appeal that are normatively required. These women are never accorded sexual subjecthood. The figure of the 'unattractive' woman who seeks a sexual partner remains one of the most vilified in popular culture. . . .

Sexual subjectification, then, is a highly specific and exclusionary practice, and sexual pleasure is actually irrelevant here; it is the power of sexual attractiveness that is important. Indeed, the two are frequently and deliberately confused in midriff advertising.

The practice is also problematic for what it renders invisible, what Robert Goldman has called the 'diverse forms of terror experienced by women who objectify themselves.' He explains:

> There is the mundane psychic terror associated with not receiving 'looks' of admiration—i.e., not having others validate one's appearance. A similar sense of terror involves the fear of 'losing one's looks'—the quite reasonable fear that ageing will deplete one's value and social power. A related source of anxiety involves fear about 'losing control' over body weight and appearance . . . and there is a very real physical terror which may accompany presentation of self as

an object of desire—the fear of rape and violence by misogynist males. (1992: 123)

Midriff advertising is notable not only for its success in selling brands but also—much more significantly—for its effective rebranding or reconstruction of the anxieties and the labour involved in making the body beautiful, through a discourse of fun, pleasure and power. The work associated with disciplining the feminine body to approximate the required standards is made knowable in new ways that systematically erase pain, anxiety, expense and low self-esteem. See, for example, the way that the application of boiling wax to the genital region and then its use to pull out hairs by their roots can be discursively (re)constructed as 'pampering' (Sisters, I don't think so!).

Goldman is correct, too, to point to the erasure of violence in such advertising. It seems literally to have been conjured away. In one advert, an attractive young woman is depicted wearing just a bra, her arm stretched high in the internationally recognized gesture for hailing a taxi. 'I bet I can get a cab on New Year's Eve 1999,' she declares, laughing. Here, again, exposed breasts are a source of male attention-grabbing power, a way to defeat the notorious concerns about taxi queues on the millennium eve. But the representation is entirely shorn of any suggestion of the violence that might threaten a woman so scantily attired, late at night, in the midst of large numbers of men who are drinking heavily. More generally, the depiction of heterosexual relations as playful, and women as having as much—if not more—power as men in negotiating them, is at odds with statistics, which give an extraordinarily sobering picture of the levels of violence by men against women.[5] . . .

Midriff advertising articulates a thoroughgoing individualism in which women are presented as entirely autonomous agents, no longer constrained by any inequalities or power imbalances. The pendulum swing—from a view of power as something obvious and overbearing which acts upon entirely

docile subjects, towards a notion of women as completely free agents who just 'please themselves'—does not serve feminist or cultural understandings well. It cannot explain why the look that young women seek to achieve is so similar. If it were the outcome of everyone's individual, idiosyncratic preferences, surely there would be greater diversity, rather than a growing homogeneity organized around a slim, toned, hairless body. Moreover, the emphasis upon choice sidesteps and avoids all the important and difficult questions about how socially constructed ideals of beauty are internalized and made our own.

The notion of choice has become a postfeminist mantra. The idea that women are 'pleasing themselves' is heard everywhere: 'women choose to model for men's magazines,' 'women choose to have cosmetic surgery to enhance the size of their breasts,' 'women choose to leave their children in Eastern Europe or in the Global South and come and make a better life in the rich countries.' Of course, at one level, such claims have some truth: some women do make 'choices' like this. However, they do not do so in conditions of their own making, and to account for such decisions using only a discourse of free choice is to oversimplify, both in terms of analysis and political response. We need urgently to complicate our understandings of choice and agency in this context (Gill, 2007b).

Finally, I would argue that midriff advertising involves a shift in the way that power operates: it entails a move from an external, male-judging gaze, to a self-policing, narcissistic gaze. In this sense it represents a more 'advanced' or pernicious form of exploitation than the earlier generation of objectifying images to which second-wave feminists objected—because the objectifying male gaze is internalized to form a new disciplinary regime. Using the rather crude and clunky language of oppression, we might suggest that midriff advertising adds a further layer of oppression. Not only are women objectified, as they were before, but *through sexual subjectification they must also now under-stand their own objectification as pleasur-able and self-chosen.* If, in earlier regimes of advertising, women were presented as sexual objects, then this was understood as something being done to women. In contemporary midriff advertising, how-ever, some women are endowed with the status of active subjecthood so that they can 'choose' to become sex objects, because this suits their liberated interests. One of the implications of this shift is that it renders critique much more difficult.

. . . Goldman's analysis of commodity feminism discussed earlier in this chap-ter . . . stresses the ongoing struggle between advertising and feminism, . . . that, so far, . . . has largely been resolved in favour of the advertising industry, with feminist ideas ransacked, cannibalized, incorporated, and "domesticated." To contest this, there are three fronts on which feminists must engage: first, to articulate a language and cultural politics of resistance to midriff advertising, preferably one that is funny, feisty, sex-positive and inclusive; second, to rethink agency and choice in more sophisticated terms that reject the existing dualisms; and finally, to push for—or create—more diverse representa-tions of gender and sexuality.

Notes

1. This title owes a debt to Morgan Spurlock's powerful critique of the fast-food industry, *Super Size Me* (2004).

2. Commodity feminism is, of course, an homage to Marx and Engels's notion of com-modity fetishism.

3. See also Gill (2008) for a discussion of sexualization that looks at the rise of 'queer chic' in advertising, the erotic depiction of men's bod-ies, and the increasing use of the grammars of heterosexual pornography in advertising.

4. Elsewhere (2007a) I have considered the offensive depiction of male sexuality in such adverts.

5. It is estimated that there were 190,000 incidents of serious sexual assault and 47,000 female victims of rape in 2001 in England and Wales. Research by Amnesty International in the UK published in November 2005 found that a blame culture exists against women who have been raped, with up to one-third of people who were questioned seeing a woman as responsible if she was wearing revealing clothing, had been drinking or had had a number of sexual partners.

References

Amy-Chinn, D. (2006). "This is just for me(n): Lingerie advertising for the post-feminist woman." *Journal of Consumer Culture* 6(2).

Gill, R. (2007a). "Critical respect: Dilemmas of choice and agency in feminism (A response to Duits and Van Zoonen)." *European Journal of Women's Studies* 14(1).

Gill, R. (2007b). "Postfeminist media culture: Elements of a sensibility." *European Journal of Cultural Studies*.

Gill, R. (2008). "Beyond 'sexualization': Sexual representations in advertising." *Sexualities*.

Goldman, R. (1992). *Reading ads socially*. London; New York, Routledge.

Kilbourne, J. (1999). *Can't buy my love: How advertising changes the way we think and feel*. New York, London, Touchstone.

Lazar, M. (2006). "'Discover the power of fem-ininity!' Analysing global 'power femininity' in local advertising." *Feminist Media Studies* 6(4).

Quart, A. (2003). *Branded: The buying and sell-ing of teenagers*. London, Arrow Books.

Rushkoff, Douglas. (2001). *The Merchants of Cool*. Documentary film aired on Frontline, PBS.

Spurlock, Morgan. (2004). *Super Size Me*. Documentary film.

Walby, Sylvia and Jonathan Allen. (2004). *Domestic Violence, Sexual Assault and Staulking: Findings from the British Crime Survey*. Home Office Study 276. Home Office Research, Development and Statistics Directorate.

Advertising and the Construction of Violent White Masculinity

From BMWs to Bud Light

Jackson Katz

Since the late 1990s, there has been growing attention paid in media and cultural studies to the power of cultural images of masculinity. Nonetheless, there has been little attention paid, in scholarship or antiviolence activism, to the relationship between the construction of violent masculinities[1] in what Sut Jhally (1990) refers to as the "commodity image-system" of advertising and the pandemic of violence committed by men, young men, and boys in the homes and streets of the United States.

This chapter is an attempt to sketch out some of the ways in which hegemonic constructions of masculinity in mainstream advertising normalize (White) male violence and to point to some new developments and continuities in the way this is achieved. Theorists and researchers in profeminist sociology and men's studies have developed the concept of *masculinities,* as opposed to *masculinity,* to more adequately describe the complexities of male social position, identity, and experience. At any given time, the class structure and gender order produce numerous masculinities stratified by socioeconomic class, racial and ethnic difference, and sexual orientation. The central delineation is between the hegemonic, or dominant, masculinity (generally, White, heterosexual, and middle class) and the subordinated masculinities (e.g., men of color, gays, poor, and working class).[2]

But although there are significant differences between the various masculinities, in patriarchal culture, violent behavior is typically gendered masculine. This doesn't mean that all men are violent but that violent behavior is considered masculine (as opposed to feminine) behavior. One need not look very closely to see how pervasive is the cultural imagery linking various masculinities to the potential for violence. One key source of constructions of dominant masculinity is the Hollywood movie industry, which has introduced into the culture a seemingly endless stream of violent male icons. For several decades, tens of millions of people, disproportionately male and young, have flocked to theaters and rented videocassettes and DVDs of the "action-adventure" (a Hollywood euphemism for *violent*) films of White male icons such as Arnold Schwarzenegger, Sylvester Stallone, Jean-Claude Van

Damme, Bruce Willis, Christian Bale, Matt Damon, and so on.

The first wave of these cultural heroes rose to prominence in an era, the mid-to-late 1970s into the 1980s, in which working-class White males had to contend with increasing economic instability and dislocation, the perception of gains by people of color at the expense of the White working class, and a women's movement that overtly challenged male hegemony. In the face of these pressures, then, it is not surprising that White men (especially but not exclusively working class) would latch onto big, muscular, violent men as cinematic heroes. For many males who were experiencing unsettling changes, one area of masculine power remained attainable: physical size and strength and the ability to use violence successfully.

Harry Brod (1987) and other theorists have argued that macro changes in postindustrial capitalism have created deep tensions in the various masculinities. For example, according to Brod,

Persisting images of masculinity hold that "real men" are physically strong, aggressive, and in control of their work. Yet the structural dichotomy between manual and mental labor under capitalism means that no one's work fulfills all these conditions. Manual laborers work for others at the low end of the class spectrum, while management sits at a desk. Consequently, while the insecurities generated by these contradictions are personally dissatisfying to men, these insecurities also impel them to cling all the more tightly to sources of masculine identity validation offered by the system. (p. 14)

One way that the system allows working-class men (of various races) the opportunity for what Brod (1987) refers to as "masculine identity validation" is through the use of their body as an instrument of power, dominance, and control. For working-class

males, who have less access to more abstract forms of masculinity-validating power (economic power, workplace authority), the physical body and its potential for violence provide a concrete means of achieving and asserting "manhood."

At any given time, individual as well as groups of men are engaged in an ongoing process of creating and maintaining their own masculine identities. Advertising, in a commodity-driven consumer culture, is an omnipresent and rich source of gender ideology. Historically, use of gender in advertising has stressed difference, implicitly and even explicitly reaffirming the "natural" dissimilarity of males and females. In early 21st-century U.S. culture, advertising that targets young White males (with the exception of fashion advertising, which often features more of an androgynous male look) has the difficult task of stressing gender difference in an era characterized by a loosening of rigid gender distinctions. This requires constantly reasserting what is masculine and what is feminine. One of the ways this is accomplished, in the image system, is to equate masculinity with violence, power, and control (and femininity with passivity).

Ads that link masculinity to violence are ubiquitous. Contemporary ads contain numerous images of men who are positioned as sexy because they possess a certain aggressive "attitude." Men's magazines and mainstream newsweeklies are rife with ads featuring violent male icons, such as football players, big-fisted boxers, military figures, and leather-clad bikers. Sports magazines aimed at men and televised sporting events carry tens of millions of dollars worth of military ads. In the past 20 years, there have been thousands of ads for products designed to help men develop muscular physiques, such as weight training machines and nutritional supplements.

By helping to differentiate masculinity from femininity, images of masculine aggression and violence—including violence against women—afford young males across class a degree of self-respect and security (however illusory) within the more socially valued masculine role. In addition, as automation, globalization, and the demise of the domestic manufacturing industry and other macroeconomic shifts have contributed to a decline both in employment and real wages for working-class White men, images of violent masculinity in the symbolic realm of media and advertising function, in part, to bolster masculine identities that have increasingly less foundation in the material world.

Violent White Masculinity in Advertising

The appeal of violent behavior for men, including its rewards, is coded into mainstream advertising in numerous ways: from violent male icons (such as particularly aggressive athletes or superheroes) overtly threatening consumers to buy products to ads that exploit men's feelings of not being big, strong, or violent enough by promising to provide them with products that will enhance those qualities. These codes are present in all forms of advertising, but this chapter focuses primarily on mainstream American magazine ads (*ESPN* magazine, *Esquire*, *Men's Journal*, *Sports Illustrated*, *GQ*, *Maxim*, *Rolling Stone*, etc.), ads from special-interest men's magazines (e.g., *PC Gamer* and *UFC* magazine), and TV and web-based ads from the early 2000s through 2010.

Several recurring themes in advertising targeting men help support the equation of White masculinity and violence: the angry, aggressive, White working-class male as anti-authority rebel (21st-century version); violence as genetically programmed male behavior; the use of military and sports symbolism to enhance the masculine appeal and identification of products; and the association of muscularity with ideal masculinity.

THE ANGRY, AGGRESSIVE, WHITE WORKING-CLASS MALE AS ANTI-AUTHORITY REBEL (21ST-CENTURY VERSION)

The rock, heavy metal, and rap-metal cultures of recent decades have produced numerous male artists who perform a White, working-class "rebel" masculinity that embodies all sorts of violent angers and resentments and seeks validation in the defiance of middle-class manners and social conventions. Not surprisingly, advertisers have sought to use this young-White-man-with-an-attitude in their marketing of products to young males. In one characteristic example, a 2001 ad for JVC audio equipment features Nikki Sixx of the 1980s metal band Motley Crue with an angry expression on his face. Prominently placed in the foreground (visually "in your face") is a large speaker system and CD/cassette unit. The copy reads "Big, Mean, Loud." More recently, in a 2009 ad for WWE Shop, a clothing line owned by World Wrestling Entertainment (WWE), the professional wrestler John Cena—whose character and clothing are meant to represent those of a thuggish White working-class rapper—is pictured in his trademark baseball cap, jean shorts, wrist bands, and T-shirt emblazoned with a cartoon drawing of a wrestler about to violently toss another man off his shoulders and to the ground, with the words "Attitude Adjustment."

The superstar White rap artist Eminem (nee Marshall Mathers) is arguably the most well known of the contemporary "angry White males" with attitude who, for the past decade, have been skillfully marketed to young people—especially White boys—as anti-authority "rebels." The rage-rock group Limp Bizkit and the metal band Slipknot are other notables in this genre. Compared to the aggressive rockers of the classic rock era of the 1960s and 1970s, these 21st-century artists affect a much more overtly violent, aggressive, and nihilistic demeanor.

Eminem, for example, in ads for his music CDs and other projects, is almost always portrayed with scowls on his face or with looks of grim seriousness. For the past decade, in magazine layouts that function as de facto unpaid ads, Eminem has been portrayed in cartoonishly violent guises. In one 2000 layout in the hip-hop magazine *The Source,* he appeared in an old hockey goalie's mask (a homage to the serial murderer Jason from the film *Friday the 13th*), holding a chainsaw. The article was entitled "American Psycho," the page smeared with a bloodied handprint. In a video ad for his 2009 album *Relapse,* a psychopathic-appearing Eminem is pictured naked in a pool of blood. Judging by the number of violent poses struck by Eminem in similar magazine articles, online videos, and other promotional materials, it is safe to say that violent posturing—especially toward women and gays—is central to Eminem's constructed identity as a rebellious White rapper who's "keepin' it real." But it is never exactly clear what a White rapper like Eminem is rebelling *against.* Powerful women who oppress weak and vulnerable men? Omnipotent gays and lesbians who make life a living hell for straight people? Eminem's misogyny and homophobia, far from being "rebellious," are actually extremely traditional and conservative. But the homicidal and rape fantasies in his lyrics continue to upset a lot of parents, so kids can "rebel" against their parents' wishes and middle-class norms by listening to him, buying his CDs, and so on. The irony is that buying into Eminem's "bad boy" act turns them into obedient consumers. ("If you want to express your rebellious side, we have just the right product for you! The Marshall Mathers LP! Come get your Slim Shady!) It's rebellion as a purchasable commodity.

Advertisers for the music and movie industries are constantly developing marketing strategies to appeal to the lucrative markets of young consumers of all socioeconomic classes. In recent years, one of the most successful of these strategies involves praising young consumers for their media smarts, especially in contrast with their parents and other older people. Then, as the young consumers absorb props for their sophistication, they are sold CDs, movies, and myriad other products whose purchase purportedly proves how hip these consumers are. This process would be laughable were it not for the fact that some of the products (e.g., Eminem) often simply reinforce or legitimate violent masculinity—and other cultural pathologies—as rebellious, humorous, or "cool."

Over the past decade, the skateboarding, snowboarding, motocross racing, and extreme sports cultures have contributed to the creation of another type of White working-class rebel masculinity that is then packaged and sold to consumers. In the advertising universe, this masculinity is characterized by the willingness to take dangerous risks; the potential for violent injury and even death is omnipresent. A Children Now study found that 27% of the commercials during televised extreme sports events placed actors in dangerous situations (Brown, Lamb, & Tappan, 2009). One ad for Boost Mobile phone company depicts a close-up of Rick Thorne, a heavily tattooed professional BMX rider. The text reads "Broke my arm, my leg and teeth. But not my bank." Monster Energy drinks employs several high-profile skaters and bikers as product pitchmen, and their ads are particularly aggressive. One ad reads, "The MONSTER packs a vicious punch but has a smooth kick ass flavor you can really pound down. So when it's time to unleash the beast within, grab a MONSTER and GO BIG!"

VIOLENCE AS GENETICALLY PROGRAMMED MALE BEHAVIOR

One way that advertisers demonstrate the "masculinity" of a product or service is through the use of violent male icons or types from popular history. This helps to associate the product with manly needs and pursuits that we are led to believe have existed from time immemorial. It also furthers the ideological premise, disguised as common sense, that men have always been aggressive and brutal and that their dominance over women is biologically based. "Historical" proof for this is shown in a multitude of ways.

A 2010 ad for a protein supplement by Nutrabolics depicts the mixed martial arts champion Frank Mir shirtless, with his arms folded, and a scowl on his face. Behind him is a drawing of the Roman Coliseum. The text reads "Fuel Your Next Conquest." It further states that "A true warrior does not relinquish to fatigue, rather he supplies his body with the arsenal needed to win a multitude of battles." An ad for the Toyota 4Runner depicts a photograph of two men eating an outdoor meal while camping, with a cartoon skunk looking over them. The text promises "reclining fold-flat second-row seat and improved driver comfort." But lest potential customers think that desiring such comforts is not masculine, it continues with a tongue-in-cheek reference to a celebrated frontiersman from the 19th century: "Not that you need to be pampered, you element-hardened, modern-day Davy Crockett."

An ad for Trojan condoms features a giant-sized Roman centurion, in full uniform, muscles rippling, holding a package of condoms as he towers over the buildings of a modern city. Condom manufacturers know that the purchase and use of condoms by men can be stressful, partially because penis size, in popular Western folklore, is supposedly linked to virility. One way to assuage the anxieties of male consumers is to link the product with a recognizably violent (read: masculine) male archetype. It is no coincidence that the leading brand of condoms in the United States is named for an ancient warrior (Trojan). Ancient warriors have also proven to be big box-office draws in the 21st century, and action-packed trailers for movies such as *300* (2007), about the Battle of Thermopylae, and print ads for

the Starz television series *Spartacus: Blood and Sand* (2010)—replete with a sword-wielding warrior—appear all over mainstream television and magazines.

An even more sinister use of historical representations involves portraying violence that would not be acceptable if shown in contemporary settings. Norwegian Cruise Line, for example, in an ad that ran in the 1990s in major newsweekly magazines, depicted a colorful painting of a scene on a ship's deck, set sometime in the pirate era, where men, swords drawn, appear simultaneously to be fighting each other while a couple of them are carrying off women. The headline informs us that Norwegian is the "first cruise line whose entertainment doesn't revolve around the bar."

It is highly doubtful that the cruise line could have set what is clearly a rape or gang rape scenario on a modern ship. Controversy is avoided by depicting the scene as historical. A more recent—and much subtler—variation on this theme can be seen in the popular Captain Morgan spiced rum ads, which feature a cartoon pirate, "the Captain," inserted into contemporary party scenes, often with attractive young women and overt sexual suggestion. In one ad, the Captain is depicted aboard a sailboat with three young White women, one in a skimpy bikini. The text reads "Catch of the Day." The tagline in many *Captain Morgan* ads, "Got a little captain in you?" poses an implicit challenge to young men as it reinforces the idea that "real men" (pirates, swashbucklers) have always treated women as objects, or as less-than-fully human, a dehumanizing process that can lead to violence.

THE USE OF MILITARY AND SPORTS SYMBOLISM TO ENHANCE THE MASCULINE IDENTIFICATION AND APPEAL OF PRODUCTS

Well before the September 11, 2001, attacks prompted an upsurge in advertisers' use of martial displays of patriotic sentiment, advertisers who wanted to demonstrate the unquestioned manliness of their products could do so by using one of the two key subsets in the symbolic image system of violent masculinity: the military and sports. Uniformed soldiers and players, as well as their weapons and gear, appear frequently in ads of all sorts. Advertisers can use these signifiers in numerous creative ways to make their products appear manly.

A 2010 ad for MTM watches depicts a man wearing a dark, military or police-style jacket. He is wearing the watch over the long sleeve of the jacket; the text reads: "Special Ops." One ad in the early 2000s for *The Economist* magazine manages to link the magazine with White heterosexual sexism, military masculinity, and imperialist aggression, presented in a spirit of ironic hyperbole, all in one page. In the top left corner is a photo of a classic (White) "pinup girl" from the 1940s at the beach in a bathing suit. The text reads "Sex Symbol." In the top right corner is a picture of a U.S. fighter jet in flight. The text reads "Power Symbol." Front and center is a picture of the magazine's cover, with a distorted map of North America portrayed as towering over Central and South America; Africa and Asia are small and off to the side. The map is headlined "America's world" and features one-word designations of various geographical areas: "Surfin'" in the Pacific; "Huntin'" in northwest Canada; "Exploitin'" in Central America; "Fishin'" in the Caribbean; "Fightin'" in Africa and Asia. The bold text underneath says simply: "Status Symbol." It might as well say "This magazine is for 'real' men, and ('wink, wink, nudge, nudge') real men are sexist and violent."

Ads for the military itself also show the linkage between masculinity and force. The U.S. military spends over $600 million annually on advertising (RAND Corporation, 2009). Not surprisingly, armed services advertisements appear disproportionately on televised sporting events and in sports and so-called men's magazines. Military ads are characterized by exciting outdoor action scenes with accompanying text replete with references to "leadership," "respect," and "pride." Although these ads sometimes promote the educational and financial benefits of military service, what they're really selling to young working-class White males is a vision of masculinity—adventurous, aggressive, and violent—that provides men of all classes with a standard of "real manhood" against which to judge themselves.

Boxers and football players appear in ads regularly, promoting products from underwear to deodorants. The text for a 2010 ad depicting the BMW M3 reads "Heavyweight power. Welterweight package." An ad for the energy drink 5-Hour Energy depicts an urban scene with three men in business suits on stone steps in what looks like a big city business district, with glass and steel office towers in the background. One of the men appears to have just kicked the other two into the air. The text reads: "Because life gets pretty hairy outside the ring, too."

In the early 2000s, a black and white photo of a young White man in uncovered football shoulder pads adorned Abercrombie and Fitch advertising layouts. In Abercrombie and Fitch mall stores, a dramatically enlarged version of this photo greeted customers as they entered the store. Abercrombie and Fitch does not sell football equipment, of course. Rather, the clothing company— which has built brand recognition for the past two decades with its "racy" and sexually suggestive layouts of scantily clad teenagers—was presumably seeking to accentuate its appeal to adolescent males by creating brand identification with the archetypally masculine young man: the football player.

Football themes abound in advertising, including in ads for products with little or no discernible relationship to football. An ad for Nissan Altima shows the car driving on a rough stone surface, with water spraying all around. The caption reads "Necessary roughness." (Unnecessary roughness is a major penalty in football.) A newspaper ad for a Southern California John Elway Toyota dealership shows—amid the banner headlines of cost-saving special deals—an action shot of the long-retired star quarterback Elway in full football uniform. The photo has no relation to the product or the ad except, perhaps, to appeal to men's (and women's?) yearning for a kind of reflected glory by reminding potential buyers of the masculine prowess of the dealership's namesake. Sometimes football players are positioned simply to sanction the masculinity of a suspect product line. For example, a 1999 ad for a cologne by Clinique depicts a clean-cut young White man in a football uniform, holding a football and running toward the camera. Standing beside him is a young White woman, in a white dress, holding a white frosted birthday cake with candles. The only copy says, in bold letters, "Clinique Happy. Now for Men." It seems reasonable to infer that the goal of this ad was to shore up the masculine image of a product whose name (Clinique) has feminine connotations. The uniformed football player, a signifier of violent masculinity, achieves this task by visually transmitting the message: Real men can wear Clinique. The birthday cake in the woman's arms, of course, sends a signal to women that this product is an acceptable present for their (masculine) boyfriends.

Advertisers know that using high-profile violent male athletes can help to sell products, such as yogurt and light beer, that have historically been gendered feminine. Because violence establishes masculinity, if these guys (athletes) use traditionally "female" products, they don't lose their masculinity. Rather, the masculinity of the product—and hence the size of the potential market—increases. Miller Brewing Company proved the efficacy of this approach in their long-running television ad campaign for Lite beer. The Miller Lite campaign, which first appeared in the early 1970s, helped bring Miller to the top of the burgeoning light beer market and is often referred to as one of the most successful TV ad campaigns in history. A recent example of this strategy is a Bud Light ad (2010) that depicts an Ultimate Fighting Championship bout, with the fighters hitting each other's bodies. The

text reads: "From the first round to last call. America's favorite beer is proud to sponsor America's hardest-hitting sport."

THE ASSOCIATION OF MUSCULARITY WITH IDEAL MASCULINITY

Men across socioeconomic class, race, and ethnicity might feel insecure, relatively powerless, or vulnerable in the economic sphere and uncertain about how to respond to the challenges of women in many areas of social relations. But, in general, males continue to have an advantage over females in the area of physical size and strength. Because one function of the image system is to legitimate and reinforce existing power relations, representations that equate masculinity with the qualities of size, strength, and violence thus become more prevalent.

The anthropologist Alan Klein (1993a)[3] has looked at how the rise in popularity of bodybuilding is linked to male insecurity. "Muscles," he argues, "are about more than just the functional ability of men to defend home and hearth or perform heavy labor. Muscles are markers that separate men from each other and, most important perhaps, from women. And while he may not realize it, every man—every accountant, science nerd, clergyman, or cop—is engaged in a dialogue with muscles" (p. 16).

Advertising is one area of the popular culture that helps feed this "dialogue." Sports and other magazines with a large male readership are filled with ads offering men products, supplements, and services to enhance their muscles—or their penis size. Often these ads explicitly equate muscles with violent power, as in an ad for a Marcy weight machine that tells men to "Arm Yourself" under a black and white photograph of a toned, muscular White man, biceps and forearms straining, in the middle of a weight-lifting workout. The military, too, offers to help men enhance their bodily prowess. An ad for the Army National Guard shows three slender young men, Black and White, working out, over copy that reads "Get a Part-Time Job in Our Body Shop."

The discourse around muscles as signifiers of masculine power involves not only working-class men but also middle- and upper-class men. This is apparent in the male sports subculture, where size and strength are valued by men across class and racial boundaries. But muscularity as masculinity is also a theme in advertisements aimed at upper-income males. Many advertisers use images of physically rugged or muscular male bodies to masculinize products and services geared to elite male consumers. An ad for the business insurance firm Brewer and Lord uses a powerful male body as a metaphor for the more abstract form of (financial) power. The ad shows the torso of a muscular man curling a barbell, accompanied by a headline that reads "the benefits of muscle defined." The text states that "the slow building of strength and definition is no small feat. In fact, that training has shaped the authority that others see in you, as well."

Saab, targeting an upscale, educated market in the early 1990s, billed itself as "the most intelligent car ever built." But in one ad, it called its APC Turbo "the muscle car with a social conscience"—which signaled to wealthy men that by driving a Saab they could appropriate the working-class tough guy image associated with the concept of a "muscle car" while making clear their more privileged class position. In a 2001 version of the same phenomenon, Chevy, in an ad for the expensive Avalanche SUV, showed a close-up photo of the big vehicle turning sharply on a dusty road. The text reads "Rarely do you get to see the words 'ingenious' and 'muscle-bound' in the same sentence."

Throughout the 2000s, Ford Motor Company employed classic blue-collar masculine iconography in its truck ads (Ford trucks, such as the F-150, hauling heavy loads, driving off-road on rugged terrain) to sell its trucks as symbols of masculine power, prowess, and control. If the television

ads' storylines didn't adequately convey the message, the signature ending did: Built Ford Tough. One print ad for the Ford Escape (2006) used middle-class White men's fear of working-class White men to sell them on speed and engineering as important features of self-protection in a dangerous world. The ad depicts two White men in European-style bike gear getting into their Escape at a desert truck stop. Along with their clothing, their bicycles, strapped to the roof of their vehicle, signify their middle-class masculinity, which is, stereotypically, less than physically tough. Right next to them, looking menacing and confrontational, are three White men in black leather and tattoos; one has a black T-shirt with the inscription "Hellbound." They are positioned next to their motorcycles, possibly Harley Davidsons, signifying their working-class masculinity and establishing them, stereotypically, as physically tough and intimidating. The visuals of the ad play to the anxieties and fear of the middle-class men, but for good measure, the text clarifies the point: "V6 power for long, leisurely drives, or quick, exciting ones."

Conclusion

Media play an important role in constructing and normalizing violence, both at the interpersonal and the state levels. In light of the ongoing, worldwide crisis of men's violence against women, children, and other men, antiviolence educators and activists should advocate for a dramatic expansion of critical media literacy education at age-appropriate levels from Grades K–12, and in all manner of college and graduate programs, that helps to lay bare the gender norms that underpin and legitimate much of this violence. The kinds of critical media literacy analyses contained in this chapter need also to be incorporated into community-based violence prevention initiatives, as well as into prevention education work funded by local, state, and federal government. To some extent, this is already happening. For example, many domestic and sexual violence organizations, batterer intervention programs, and gang violence prevention initiatives use my video, *Tough Guise* (Katz & Earp, 2000), or Byron Hurt's video *Hip Hop: Beyond Beats and Rhymes* (2007), to engage young men and women in lively debates about masculinities and media.

This chapter focuses attention on constructions of violent White masculinity in mainstream advertising. We need also to study more comprehensively a number of other cultural sites where violent masculinities are produced and legitimated: video games, comic books, toys, the sports culture, professional wrestling, comedy, popular music, and pornography. This will help us to understand more fully the links between the construction of gender, other macrosocial processes, and the prevalence of violence, which might then contribute to more sophisticated and effective antiviolence interventions.

Notes

1. *Violence* refers to immediate or chronic situations that result in injury to the psychological, social, or physical well-being of individuals or groups. For the purpose of this chapter, I will use the American Psychological Association's (APA's) more specific definition of interpersonal violence. Although acknowledging the multidimensional nature of violence, the APA Commission on Violence and Youth defines interpersonal violence as "behavior by persons against persons that threatens, attempts, or completes intentional infliction of physical or psychological harm" (APA, 1993, p. 1).

2. Although hegemonic constructions of masculinity affect men of all races, there are

important variables due to racial/ethnic differences. I have chosen to focus on the constructions of various White masculinities, at least in part because while masculinity is often hidden in the national conversation about violence, so is whiteness.

3. The article cited here was excerpted from Klein's (1993b) book *Little Big Men: Bodybuilding Subculture and Gender Construction.*

References

American Psychological Association (APA). (1993). *Violence and youth: Psychology's response.* Washington, DC: Author.

Brod, H. (Ed.). (1987). *The making of masculinities: The new men's studies.* Boston: Allen & Unwin.

Brown, L., Lamb, S., & Tappan, M. (2009). *Packaging boyhood: Saving our sons from superheroes, slackers and other media stereotypes.* New York: St. Martin's.

Hurt, B. (2007). *Hip hop: Beyond beats and rhymes* [Documentary video]. Plainfield, NJ: God Bless the Child Productions.

Jhally, S. (1990, July). Image-based culture: Advertising and popular culture. *The World and I,* pp. 508–519. [See Chapter 22 in this volume.]

Katz, J., & Earp, J. (2000). *Tough guise: Violence, media and the crisis in masculinity* [Educational video]. Northampton, MA: Media Education Foundation.

Klein, A. (1993a, January). Little big men. *Northeastern University Magazine,* pp. 14–19.

Klein, A. (1993b). *Little big men: Bodybuilding subculture and gender construction.* Albany: State University of New York Press.

RAND Corporation. (2009). National Defense Research Institute. Retrieved on March 21, 2010, from http://www.rand.org/pubs/documented_briefings/2009/RAND_DB565 .pdf

PART V

REPRESENTING SEXUALITIES

No contemporary book on popular culture can ignore what some scholars are calling the "pornification" of the culture. As Karen Boyle (V.32) defines this concept, it encompasses both the increased availability of hardcore and the use of its codes and conventions in a range of representations and activities which are not themselves pornography. In this part, we have included chapters that illustrate the way in which soft-core pornographic conventions have moved inexorably into mainstream commercial media culture. These chapters are intended to help students think and debate about this important feature of our contemporary world. We also include chapters that speak to the possibilities of representing sexualities in media culture in a less exploitive way.

We start with what the pornography industry calls "gonzo" (or hardcore) pornography, because in the Internet age, this has indeed become the mainstream form. The slang term *gonzo* originally derived from a type of visual journalism pioneered by Hunter S. Thompson. Currently, it refers to filmed pornography that "puts the camera right into the action—often with one or more of the participants both filming and performing sexual acts—without the usual separation characteristic of conventional porn and cinema" (www.en.wikipedia.org/wiki/Gonzo_pornography). As soft-core pornography continues to migrate into popular culture, it becomes important for the pornography industry to offer ever more explicit and body punishing images to distinguish itself from mainstream media imagery.

This continual process of "hardening" of hardcore has implications for the future of sexual representation in pop culture.

Pornography has been held up to feminist scrutiny and debate for many years, and it is not our intent in this part to provide a thorough introduction to the strongly conflicting perspectives seen in these debates. However, frequently ignored in these divisive discussions is the way race works to intensify and sexualize the gender domination that is threaded through hardcore pornography codes and conventions. As Gail Dines writes in her chapter (V.30), "Analyzing the role of racial representations in pornography is . . . key to understanding how pornography works as a discourse."

If, as radical feminists argue, pornography is pleasurable because it sexualizes inequality between women and men, then the more degraded and abused the woman, the greater the sexual tension and thrill for the male viewer. It is hard to conceive of a better way to degrade white women, in a culture with a long and ugly history of racism, than having them penetrated again and again by a body that has been constructed, coded, and demonized as a carrier for all that is sexually debased, namely the black male. (p. 275)

Although gonzo or hardcore is the dominant form of mainstream pornography, the Internet and other technologies have also enabled the proliferation of homemade amateur materials, including what media scholar Feona Attwood (V.31) calls "smart smut" or (alternative) "altporn," consisting of "softcore images, that is, photographs of women shot in tasteful pin-up or art styles rather than images of explicit display or sexual activity" (p. 285). Attwood looks at two prominent altporn websites, *Nerve* and *SuicideGirls*, arguing that their codes and conventions differ from those found in mainstream Internet porn. The chapter speaks to the blurring of hard and fast lines between producers and consumers or media culture— a theme found elsewhere in this book, particularly in the chapters in Part VIII. One of

Attwood's key points is that on these sites, "sexual display becomes an important part of individual and collective self-definition. It is used to signify a response and an alternative to the way sex is presented elsewhere— particularly in mainstream commercial porn" (p. 285).

Articles in *Adult Video News*, the trade paper of the pornography industry, suggest that mainstream porn continues to attract a largely male audience (not surprisingly, given how it overwhelmingly adopts the "male gaze" through its filming conventions). While women are not major consumers of mainstream gonzo porn, Karen Boyle (V.32) argues that the **pornography** industry is depicted within TV media culture in a way calculated to attract a mainly female audience. In focusing on a hit reality show on E! Television, Boyle shows how *Playboy* magazine's "entertainment for men" is "transformed into a hit TV show for women and girls."

In *The Girls Next Door*, three working-class young women from small towns who live in Hugh Hefner's Playboy mansion are followed as they morph into celebrities who live in lavish surroundings and can afford to shop for high-end products (though Hefner's financial control over these shopping expeditions is concealed from the viewer). By focusing on the glamour of the models' working lives and the desirability of their consumption practices, Boyle argues, the women's involvement in the pornography industry is represented as a form of female empowerment. At the same time, in her interpretation,

The show promotes a particular version of the Playboy brand to women and . . . in doing so, it largely ignores the sex (commercial and otherwise) that lies at the heart of the enterprise. (p. 299)

The once-clear line between the pornography industry and mainstream popular culture was obviously already blurred by the time *The Girls Next Door* debuted in 2005. Just one year earlier, Paris Hilton, the hotel heiress who was already somewhat of a celebrity, was catapulted into mega-celebrity status by the circulation of an amateur sex video featuring herself and her then boyfriend, Rick Solomon. Picked up by the porn industry, this video depicts Hilton submitting to the control of Rick Solomon, a submissiveness that "can be read in terms of humiliation—a pleasure presumably comes from seeing an heiress on her knees, so to speak." While Hilton's wealth allows her to maintain her celebrity status despite (or some would because of) the wide circulation of this video, this celebrity status is also a double-edged sword. According to Thomas Fahey (V.33), who analyzes Hilton's representations across several media culture formats, people are free to express their resentment of Hilton because she is a celebrity, and class antagonism clearly underlies this resentment.

Jane Caputi (V.34) further develops the theme of sexual degradation in pornography-inspired pop culture imagery in her chapter, "The Pornography of Everyday Life." Closely analyzing mostly advertising images in fashion magazines targeted to women consumers, Caputi argues that when the codes from "degradation porn" filter into mainstream culture, "these are not generally perceived as humiliation and torture; rather they are perceived as sex." Even when "everyday" porn is not representing sexuality as entwined with female degradation, according to Caputi, it is still "founded in very conventional notions of gender: Women and men are said to be opposites and unequal, with specific gendered attributes such as masculine aggression and female-identified passivity" (p. 312).

Some would argue that hip-hop representations of women as "bitches and hoes" clearly contribute to the degradation of Black women, within a society that already has a long and ugly history of sexualized racism. In a section from *The Hip Hop Wars,* Tricia Rose (V.35) engages with the longstanding and contentious debates within the Black community over representations of African American women and sexuality within hip-hop narratives, language, and visual imagery. For Rose, "although hip hop isn't primarily responsible for America's sexism, it is the most visible and extreme engine

for it in black popular culture, which means that it has a special impact on black women and men who, because of the racist and sexist world in which they live, rely on black culture as a source of reflection, support, and affirmation" (p. 325). Complicating this discussion, Rose looks at how some hip-hop celebrities attempt to deflect accusations of sexism by asserting that many young Black women freely comply with their own sexist treatment, as both participants in music videos and as fans of hip-hop's street culture. But as Rose points out,

> For many young black women, the language of commercial hip hop about black sexuality has influenced their understanding of black women, not just reflected it. (p. 322)

To criticize representations of women as "bitches and hoes" within hip-hop culture is not to be "anti-sex," from Rose's perspective, but simply to offer a thoughtful analysis of the way sex is packaged and consumed within commercial pop culture. She argues for what she calls "a genuine sexual freedom of expression," but one that is not "tied to sexist male fantasies or to male-dominated sex trades in which women are demeaned and degraded in order to appear to be sexually free" (p. 324).

Of course, African American women are not the only women of color to be subjected in distinctively racialized ways to hypersexualization in pop culture, as Debra Merskin (V.36) shows in her chapter on the Latina character played on *Desperate Housewives.* Pointing to several preexisting stereotypes of Latinas circulating in largely White-produced and White-consumed media culture, Merskin shows how the hero and role model potential of the television series character is "undermined" by such stereotypes. She argues that

> Longoria's prime time pinup status and promotional positioning in magazines reinforce the already prominent, over-sexed, under-dressed decisive and divisive character she embodies on *DH.* (p. 327)

Questionable sexual representations in media culture are also of strong concern within the GLBT (gay, lesbian, bisexual, transgender) community. Despite some important advances in gay and lesbian visibility in media culture in recent years, representations of sexuality in mainstream pop culture continue to be, for the most part, rampantly heterosexual. Part of the reason for this is the continuing homophobia that producers assume continues to characterize the majority of media consumers in most targeted audiences. Although progress has been made by activists in raising awareness of new audiences for complex representations of nonnormative sexuality and gender, producers of mainstream media culture still shy away from representing sexual and gender minorities in richly textured ways. For example, gay men are still frequently stereotyped in television culture as feminine, as was the character of Jack on the popular show *Will & Grace* of a few years ago.

Jay Clarkson (V.37) studies "the politics of gay representation" through an examination of "the discourse of the discussion board of StraightActing.com, an Internet discussion board for self-identified straight-acting gay men." He argues that in their discussions about "the nature of their and other gay men's visibility . . . they demonize an effeminate gay stereotype, which they perceive as dominating media representations of gay men" (p. 336). Viewing "the flamer" and other gender transgressives as limiting the progress of full gay and lesbian integration into the society's mainstream, they "argue that increased visibility of straight-acting gay men has the potential to undo what they see as the negative consequences of the prevalence of effeminate gay stereotypes" (p. 340). But for Clarkson, such a conservative and defensive visibility strategy is wrongheaded and would only contribute to the narrowing of public understanding of the complexities of gender and sexuality. In his view, "It does not challenge the fear or hatred of gayness."

While their argument seems to be that their increased visibility will lead to greater acceptance of homosexuals, they fail to acknowledge that the root of homophobia remains homosexuality. (p. 340)

In the case of lesbians, most media scholars and activists would acknowledge that *The L Word*, a drama series introduced in 2004 about a largely lesbian community in Los Angeles, has been groundbreaking. Marnie Pratt (V.38) argues that by making the majority of its main characters lesbians and by depicting their lives, relationships, and social and political issues as the focus of the show, *The L Word* sets itself apart from other shows that have lesbian characters. Moreover, according to Pratt, the show

deserves to be commended for a wealth of great features. For example, the characters are believable and complex and the series has dealt with a variety of tough topics in smart ways, such as coming out, childbearing, abuse/exploitation of women, substance addiction, and gay marriage. The show has also been cutting edge in many of its depictions of sexual encounters. Sexual practices are discussed frankly and realistically through the depictions of both long-term committed and "one night stand" relationships. (p. 340)

But for all this, it has also been criticized by its fans for its lack of racial and ethnic diversity, for its use of actresses who conform completely to beauty standards from Hollywood, and for its overemphasis on "femmes" ("feminine"-appearing and -acting lesbians). Taking these criticisms seriously and acting accountable to the community of fans who offer them, the show's producer, Ilene Chaiken, moved after the first season to introduce new characters, new plots, and more gender diversity. While Pratt does not argue that all the representation issues in the show have been resolved through such changes, she sees *The L Word* as a hopeful example of collaboration between producers and loyal fans in generating a more responsible presentation of a community's sexual and gender diversity—something that could inspire future producers and fans concerned with other kinds of diversity as well.

The White Man's Burden

Gonzo Pornography and the Construction of Black Masculinity

Gail Dines

ecent articles in *Adult Video News* (*AVN*)[1] have called attention to the fact that the fastest growing and most bootlegged internet pornography is "interracial pornography" (IP). While web sites advertise a multicultural mix of males and females, by far the dominant performers are black men and white women. With titles such as *Black Poles in White Holes, Huge Black Cock on White Pussy,* and *Monster Black Penises* and *Tight White Holes,* the male viewer knows what to expect when he punches in his credit card numbers. Although there are sites that advertise Asian and Latina women, there are very few sites with Latino and Asian men and white women. Indeed, if the heterosexual male wants to gaze at Asian or Latino men, then he has to move into a truly forbidden world for straight pornography, namely gay pornography.

Analyzing the role of racial representations in pornography is, I argue, key to understanding how pornography works as a discourse, as it explicates taken-for-granted assumptions about what makes pornography pornographic. If, as radical feminists argue, pornography is pleasurable because it sexualizes inequality between women and men, then the more degraded and abused the woman, the greater the sexual tension and thrill for the male viewer. It is hard to conceive of a better way to degrade white women, in a culture with a long and ugly history of racism, than having them penetrated again and again by a body that has been constructed, coded, and demonized as a carrier for all that is sexually debased, namely the black male.

Pornography and Masculinity

In order to explore the way that race functions in pornography, it is important to first examine the contemporary world of internet pornography, since the explosion of electronic

Reprinted with permission of the *Yale Journal of Law and Feminism* from the *Yale Journal of Law and Feminism,* Vol. 18, No. 1, pp. 283–297.

pornography has had enormous implications for content as well as form. Mainstream pornography today looks nothing like the scrubbed, sanitized world of *Playboy*. In place of the "girl next door," smiling suggestively at the camera with her legs partially spread, is the girl that pornography consumers wish lived next door. Mainstream movies today are populated with what the male performers call "cum buckets," "sluts," and "cunts," who love pounding anal, oral, and vaginal sex, who enjoy being smeared with semen, and who see their lives' goals as breaking the record for the greatest number of "gang bangs" within a twenty four-hour period. Threaded throughout all these movies is an overt hatred for women that is evidenced in the dialogue and the fascination with body-punishing sex, such as frequent references to how much the woman can take before she breaks. Paul Little, AKA Max Hardcore, became famous (and rich) for his particular style of pornography that specializes in extremely violent and degrading sex. . . .

This type of violent pornography popularized by Max Hardcore helped to define the contours of present-day gonzo pornography.[2] By far the biggest moneymaker for the industry, this type of pornography makes no attempt at a storyline, but is just scene after scene of violent penetration in which the woman's body is literally stretched to its limit. . . . To argue that the pleasure of heterosexual pornography for men is not somehow wrapped up in the degradation of women is to ignore the multiple verbal and image-based cues that form the codes and conventions of mainstream pornography.[3] Moreover, failure to see pornography as a text about the elevation of men and the degradation of women also misses the role that pornography plays in the production of masculinity as both a category of material existence, and an identity that is contested, negotiated, and in need of constant reproduction.[4]

It is now a given in much of academic feminism that masculinity and femininity are social constructs that work together to produce a gender system that is fused with inequality, hierarchy and violence.[5] Until recently, much of the analysis of masculinity sought to explain how hegemonic masculinity is defined in opposition to femininity, where hegemonic masculinity is unproblematically coded as white. However, as many black scholars have argued,[6] white hegemonic masculinity is always in negotiation with black masculinity, as the two exist in what James Snead calls "a larger scheme of semiotic valuation,"[7] in that the elevation and mythification of white masculinity relies on the debasement of black men as sexual savages, Uncle Toms, and half-wits such as Stepin Fetchit. Patricia Hill Collins goes further by arguing that black masculinity is so debased by white culture that it becomes a fluid category whereby any man of color can become marked as black should he in any way fail to conform to the strict disciplinary practices of white masculinity.[8]

However, what constitutes hegemonic white masculinity is itself a moving target that depends on the socioeconomic dynamics of a given time and place. In the United States, and indeed most of the Western world, there is a general consensus that a real man (read: white) works hard, puts food on the table and an SUV in the driveway, shows some interest in his children's welfare, and exhibits a somewhat restrained set of sexual practices within state-sanctioned heterosexual marriage. On virtually every level, black men are defined by white culture as failing to meet the standards of white hegemonic masculinity. They are portrayed as shiftless, they need welfare to get food for their families, they drive pimp cars (when they can afford cars), and they engage in what Cornel West mockingly refers to as "dirty, disgusting, and funky sex."[9] And this is the problem for white men. While they would not swap their material privileges with black men, many white men would indeed like "black" sex as it is seen in the white racist imagination, as "more intriguing and interesting."[10] It is argued in this chapter that this white racist construction of black male sexuality is what drives IP and serves to heighten the sexual tension in the pornography, while simultaneously making this country an increasingly hostile and dangerous place for people (especially blacks) who fall outside the markers of whiteness. . . .

According to *AVN*, IP is emerging as the biggest single growing category, with nearly one in four new films fitting into this subgenre.[11] A recent article quotes a producer, who says, "[r]ight now interracial gonzo is probably the strongest genre. . . . The demand for interracial far outweighs all the other formats of gonzo."[12] While there are both black and white pornography producers and directors, the audience for IP is overwhelmingly white, according to the ongoing studies conducted by Dr. Robert Jensen.[13] The obvious question here is: why do white men want to gaze at, and masturbate to, black penises penetrating white women's vaginas, mouths, and anuses, given the historical coding of the black penis as defiler of white womanhood and emasculator of white masculinity?

Interracial Pornography: Looking for the Primitive (Black) Male

The most startling fact that jumps out at anyone who surfs these sites is the absence of men of color who are not black. A more precise term for interracial would be black men and white women, but in a society where the color line is defined by the binary black/white categorization, such precision would be redundant. This binary system has engaged many theorists who seek to interrogate how race has been constructed in American history against the backdrop of slavery. One insightful analysis is offered by James Snead, who writes, following W.E.B. Du Bois, that the "Negro" is "the metaphor . . . the major figure in which these power relationships of master/slave, civilized/primitive, enlightened/backward, good/evil, have been embodied in the American subconscious."[14] This does not mean that other races don't exist in America, but that blacks are the "idealized" other, and different racial groups float between the two poles of the color line, depending on their economic, social, and cultural status.[15] And since pornography is not a genre known for its subtlety, when it deals with race, it deals with the clear, uncomplicated racial categories that define American society, ideologically if not materially.

Since the race of the performers is the key to marketing IP, it is not surprising that the black male tends to be very dark-skinned and the white woman very blonde. While skin color can vary among blacks, blonde hair is a clear signifier of white womanhood. . . .

One of the most popular series of IP movies is called Blacks on Blondes, which features blonde women with multiple black men. As in most IP, the blonde performer is "applauded" for being able to take a black penis in her white mouth, vagina, and anus. In one particular movie with "Liv Wylder," we see an example of a theme running through IP, namely the emasculation of the white man by the big black penis. The text on the site reads:

> Bring out the cuckold mask again! Time for another white couple to live out their naughtiest fantasy, and thanks to Blacks on Blondes for making it happen! Liv and Hubby have been married for a few years, and she wears her ring proudly. But lately the spark has left the bedroom, if you know what I mean. A few e-mails later, and we've got Hubby in a cage while Boz and Mandingo work Liv over. And when I say they work her over, we mean it. She takes so much black dick it amazed even us. The best part of this whole deal was the end: after Liv has about a gallon of cum all over her face and clothes, and grabs a plastic bowl—for Hubby to beat off in. He does, and his wad was weak, and Liv lets him know that.[16]

The white man's body is literally and metaphorically contained in this movie by both his whiteness and the physical cage in which he is locked during the sex scenes. References to his poor performance in bed ("the spark has left the bedroom") and his ineffectual semen ("his wad was weak") stand in sharp contrast to the size of the black men's penises, the skill of their sexual performance ("they work her over, we mean it") and the amount of semen they produce ("a gallon of cum"). And to illustrate where the white woman's allegiance lies, the last line lets us know that Liv is only too happy to ridicule the husband in front of the black men. Indeed, in many such movies, regular reference is made to the white woman's distaste for white penises after she has sampled a "real man's" penis. It is thus apparent why one popular series of IP films is called *Once You Go Black . . . You Never Go Back.*[17]

In heterosexual non-interracial pornography, it is the woman's body that is scrutinized, talked about, focused on, and visually interrogated. In IP it is the black penis that becomes the star of the show. Indeed, on one site where users post their reviews of movies, there is a debate going on about the apparent authenticity of the black penis in the movie, *White Meat on Black Street.*[18] Some of the viewers are clearly disturbed by what they see as the fake quality of the penis, while others express a desire to have such a penis. While the race of the user is not clear from the name (most use "anonymous"), the tone of the posts suggests white male readers. One particularly observant viewer, "ramjet" wrote on February 9, 2006:

> If you want the best available proof of the fake penis being used, check out the 5th MPEG video in respect of Ruby at the 1:30 mark. The dick is a different color to its "owner" and, more importantly, YOU CAN SEE WHERE IT ENDS AND HIS REAL COCK FITS IN TO IT. The fake has fully come away from his body and his real balls have fallen out underneath. Case closed.[19]

This "heterosexual" viewer seems more entranced by the black penis than by the white woman's body: his sense of betrayal at having paid to see a real black penis, and instead getting what he sees as a fake one, is palpable. . . .

In addition to the text that foregrounds the black penis, there are secondary themes that suggest that it is not just any black man who can perform. The black men are often described as thugs, pimps, hustlers, Hip-Hoppers, mofos, and bros who live in the "hood" and drive "pimp-mobiles." The class markers here make apparent that it is working class black men who are sexual savages, and the most esteemed is the "black pimp," who keeps his girls in line and has taught them all they need to know about being a "ho." Pimp-themed movies abound in IP, where the black pimp is defined as the "king of the hood," who uses the particular skill that black men "innately" have, of combining sex and violence, to turn black "bitches" into "hos." . . .

The pimp, thug/hustler black man of the "hood" with the out-of-control body is not only a favorite of white straight men, but also seems to be a popular object of desire for gay white men. Titles such as *Blacks on White Boys, Ebony Dicks in White Ass Holes,* and *Black Bros and White Twinks* make clear who does what to whom in interracial gay porn. The "hood" once again figures largely on the websites where users are encouraged to become site members by clicking the mouse, which will let them "Join Our MemberHood."[20] It seems that white gay men can buy their way into the hood for a short, and contained, time.

In his analysis of the visual and verbal clues that inform the fetishized and commodified black males in IP gay porn, Dwight A. McBride suggests that such images "presume a viewer who is other to the experience of the man represented in the films."[21] Moreover, the racial ideologies that make these images intelligible and pleasurable are the very ideologies that underscore mainstream white racism. As McBride argues:

> [H]ere in the form of typical images of black men in the mediated context of black gay porn, the viewer can enjoy fantasies about his sexual relationship to blackness, without having to account for the possibly troublesome dimensions of the brand of thinking about race that he must necessarily bring to these images for them to work their magic, so to speak.[22]

These "troublesome dimensions" are what need to be explained, not only for gay IP but also straight IP, and indeed for many of the images that have circulated and continue to circulate in white-owned and white-consumed media. IP does not exist in a world of its own, but rather draws from, and contributes to, the hegemonic ideologies of race in America that have justified, legitimized, and condoned deeply-rooted systems of racial oppression. However, the way that IP articulates and rearticulates these ideologies is linked to the particular form of pleasure that it offers its readers, namely (white) masculinized sexual pleasure.

Interracial Pornography as the New Minstrel Show

The pleasure that white audiences receive from consuming images of blacks is complex and rooted in the politics of whiteness as an identity that affords status, privileges, and a sense of belonging to some mythical (glorified) racial group.[23] The above mentioned argument articulated by James Snead, that the debasement of blacks is linked to the elevation of whites, is not hard to grasp, given the vicious stereotypes of blacks as savages, Coons, half-wits, Mammies, and Jezebels. Whiteness, as an identity, is a meaningless concept outside of the constructed notions of blackness that whites have produced and circulated in popular culture. Thus, in this wholly mythical world, to be white is to be the opposite of black: hardworking, law abiding, intellectual, rational, and sexually restrained and controlled. These are all traits that in the everyday world have very real currency, providing status to those who operate with a clear allegiance to the culture of whiteness.

However, the world of pornography is actually a parallel universe where, for at least the time it takes to get aroused and ejaculate, the currency is one that is in direct contradiction to whiteness. In this world, the traits of whiteness are indeed a burden for the white man, since restraint of any type threatens to undermine the full sexual pleasure that can be achieved with a bevy of "sluts," "whores," and "cum buckets," willing to do anything you want. In this world, the mythical black man, who is uncontrolled, unrestrained, animalistic, and savage, will always trump the uptight, contained, and penis-challenged white guy. Why, then, do white men who do not, in the real world, take kindly to seeing themselves as demasculinized by black men, buy IP?

To look for possible answers to this conundrum, I suggest we go back in time and examine another genre that poses similar questions for historians of race, namely, the blackface minstrel shows that swept through America in the 1830s and 1840s. Much has been written about the politics of these shows, the ways in which they encoded blackness, and the pleasures they afforded the white, mostly male, audiences through displays of white actors in blackface performing "blackness" by singing and dancing.[24] Gerald R. Butters suggests that once given the mask of blackness, white men could "sing, dance, speak, move, and act in ways that were considered inappropriate for white men."[25] While there is general agreement that these shows were unapologetically racist, historians suggest that multiple and contradictory pleasures were afforded to the audiences, in that they identified both with and against the white performers in black face.

Part of the identification process was facilitated by the fact that these shows did not employ unrecognizable songs or melodies; instead, the musical style and structure borrowed heavily from European patterns. What was different, however, according to Deane Root, was the style of the performance of the songs, which was "much cruder. It was . . . foreign. Out of the culture. . . . They were trying to exaggerate and make [something] (sic) exotic."[26] In IP, the "songs or melodies"[27] are indeed similar to white-on-white porn, since the sex acts between black men and white women are the recognizable anal, vaginal, and oral penetrations. However, the style is, in a sense, exaggerated and cruder, in its focus on "big black dicks" pounding away at "small white orifices" that are stretched. . . to foreign proportions.[28] The aim here, however, is not so much to make the performance exotic as it is to make it erotic, since the sexual pleasure of IP is intensified by the increased sexual abuse of the woman, and the (partial) identification of the viewer with the hypersexual black male.

The fact that black men perform black pornography, rather than white men in blackface, speaks to the ways in which white ownership of media and pornography has defined, and continues to define, the contours of blacks playing blacks *as whites see them*. When black men were eventually allowed on to the stage in minstrel shows, they also had to cork their faces and behave as the whites did in black face.[29] The reason for this, argues Mel Watkins, is that whites assumed that the minstrel shows depicted something real and essential about blacks, because the shows "[w]ere advertised as the real thing. In fact, one group was called 'The Real

Nigs' . . . they were advertised as 'Come to the theatre and get a real look into what plantation life was like' . . . It was advertised as a peephole view of what black people were really like."[30]

Rather than a peephole, IP porn is a peepshow for whites into what they see as the authentic black life, not on the plantation, but in the "hood," where all the conventions of white civilized society cease to exist. The "hood" in the white racist imagination is a place of pimps, ho's and generally uncontrolled black bodies, and the white viewer is invited, for a fee, to slum in this world of debauchery. In the "hood," the white man can dispense with his whiteness by identifying with the black man, and thus can become as sexually skilled and as sexually out-of-control as the black man. Here he does not have to worry about being big enough to satisfy the white woman (or man), nor does he have to concern himself with fears about poor performance or "weak wads," or cages, like poor hubby in Blacks on Blondes. Indeed, the "hood" represents liberation from the cage, and the payoff is a satiated white woman (or man) who has been completely and utterly feminized by being well and truly turned into a "fuckee."

But before we celebrate the IP text as subversive and liberatory, we need to put the text in the context of the material world of racist America. The body that is celebrated as uncontrolled in IP is the very same body that needs to be controlled and disciplined in the real world. Just as white suburban teenagers love to listen to hip-hop and white adult males gaze longingly at the athletic prowess of black men, the white pornography consumer enjoys his identification with (and against) black males through a safe peephole, in his own home, and in mediated form. The real, breathing, living black man, however, is to be kept as far away as possible from these living rooms, and every major institution in society marshals its forces in the defense of white society. The ideologies that white men take to the pornography text to enhance their sexual pleasure are the very ideologies that they use to legitimize the control of black men: while it may heighten arousal for the white porn user, it makes life intolerable for the real body that is (mis)represented in all forms of white controlled media.

Notes

1. See, e.g., DRM Versus P2P: Point, Counterpoint (Tripp Darnels ed.), Adult Video News Mag., May 2003, http://www.avnon1ine.com/index.php?Primary_Navigation=Editorial&Action=Print_Artic1e&Contcnt_ID=105809 (last visited Apr. 10, 2006).

2. For a discussion of Max Hardcore's role in making pornography sexually violent, see Max Hardcore Porn Star, http://max-hardcore.excaliburfilms.com/AVN/Max-Hardcore-Biography.htm (last visited Apr. 16, 2006).

3. For a fuller discussion on the ways that the pornographic text constructs women as the degraded "other," see Robert Jensen, Cruel to be Hard: Men and Pornography, Sexual Assault Report 33 (2004), available at http://uts.cc.utexas.edu%7Erjensen/freelance/pornography&cruelty.htm.

4. For an analysis of how pornography is implicated in the construction of hegemonic masculinity, see John Stoltenberg, Refusing to Be a Man (1989).

5. See, e.g., R. W. Connell, Masculinities (1995); Hazel Carby, Race Men (1998).

6. See, e.g., Dwight A. McBride, Why I Hate Abercrombie and Fitch: Essays on Race and Sexuality in America (2005); Mark Anthony Neal, New Black Man (2005).

7. James Snead, White Screens/Black Images: Hollywood from the Dark Side 4 (1994).

8. Patricia Hill Collins, Black Sexual Politics 186–87 (2004).

9. Cornel West, Race Matters 83 (1993).

10. Ibid.

11. Ethnic Diversity in Adult: Can't We All Just Fuck Along?, Adult Video News Mag., May 2003, http://www.adultvideonews.com/cover/cover0905_01.htmt (last visited Apr. 18, 2006).

12. Ibid.

13. Telephone Interview with Dr. Robert Jensen, Professor of Journalism, University of Texas at Austin (Apr. 3, 2006).

14. Snead, supra note 7, at 2.

15. The study of how different racial and ethnic groups became "white" illustrates the fluid nature of "race" and identity in this country. For a particularly insightful analysis, see Noel Ignatiev, How the Irish Became White (1995).

16. BlacksonBlondes.com, http//blackson blondes.com/main.php?pg-6 (last visited Mar. 20, 2006).

17. For a description of the content of these movies, see searchextreme.com, Once You Go Black . . . You Never Go Back, http://www.search extreme.com/series/Once_You_ Go_Black . . . _ You_Never_Go_Back/97899206841 (last visited Mar. 20, 2006).

18. See Sir Rodney's Guide to Online Erotica, http://www.sirrodney.com/singlereview/White+Meat+On+Black+Street#readerreviews (last visited Apr. 3, 2006).

19. Sir Rodney's Guide to Online Erotica, http://www.sirrodney.com/singlereview/White+Meat+On+Black+Street+#readerreviews (last visited Apr. 3, 2006).

20. Twinks from the Hood, http://www.twinksfromthehood.com/?revid=14522&pid=51&track (last visited Apr. 2, 2006).

21. McBride, supra note 6, at 103.

22. Ibid.

23. For a fuller discussion on how whiteness is socially constructed, see George Lipsitz, The Possessive Investment in Whiteness: How White People Profit from Identity Politics (1998); Ignatiev, supra note 15; and David R. Roediger, The Wages of Whiteness (1991).

24. For a fuller discussion of the politics of black face, see Gerald R. Butters, Jr., Black Manhood on the Silent Screen (2002); Eric Lott, Love and Theft: Black Face Minstrelsy and the American Working Class (1995); and Michael Rogin, Blackface, White Noise: Jewish Immigrants in the Hollywood Melting Pot (1998).

25. Butters, supra note 24, at 10.

26. Excerpts from the PBS program, American Experience, Stephen Foster, http://www .pbs.org/wgbh/amex/foster/sfeature/sf_minstrelsy_ 3.html (last visited Mar. 20, 2006).

27. For an analysis of how pornographic films can be likened to musicals, see Linda Williams, Hard Core: Power, Pleasure and the 'Frenzy of the Visible' 130–52 (1989).

28. See infra p. 284 and note 8.

29. This is not to argue that blacks simply mimicked the whites in black face as there were some real attempts by black actors to provide a more humanized, authentic version of black life. However, there were very real limits to this. Butters, supra note 24, at 11–12.

30. Excerpts from the PBS program, American Experience, Stephen Foster, http://www.pbs.org/ wgbh/arnex/foster/sfeature/sf_minstrelsy_5.html (last visited Mar. 20, 2006).

No Money Shot?

Commerce, Pornography, and New Sex Taste Cultures

Feona Attwood

This chapter is concerned with new internet websites where sex is the focus of participatory cultures and where commerce and community are combined. . . . The chapter focuses on two sites—Nerve, a magazine launched in the late 1990s and dedicated to what it calls 'smart smut,' and SuicideGirls, an altporn[1] site created by duo 'Spooky' (Sean Suhl) and 'Missy Suicide' (Selena Mooney), in 2001. It investigates how these sites combine commerce and community, how they classify their modes of production and consumption as sexy and sophisticated, and how they may be understood in the broader context where the boundaries between sexual representation and self-presentation are increasingly blurred, and where commerce is increasingly part of the way identity and community are produced.

Participation and Consumption: New Sex Cultures Online

The notion of participatory culture is crucial in understanding the emergence of new kinds of cultural production and consumption at the beginning of the 21st century. Writers such as Henry Jenkins (2006) have documented a move towards an era of cultural convergence, in which commercial and amateur media production increasingly sit side by side, and in which people take hold of media technologies to construct communities in ways that have not been possible in the past. As Jenkins writes, 'Rather than talking about media producers and consumers as occupying separate roles, we might now see them as participants who interact with each other according to a new set of rules that none of us fully understands' (2006: 3). This is

From Attwood, F. (2007). No money shot? Commerce, pornography, and new sex taste cultures. *Sexualities, 19*(4), 441–456.

particularly evident online where technology has expanded the possibilities of participation enormously, and where many new applications depend on networks, as in popular sites such as MySpace, YouTube[2] and Second Life. While online networks initially worked as meeting places for subcultures and fan cultures—and continue to function in this way—they also increasingly pull in the 'ordinary' consumer. Convergence, networks and participation are thus reconfiguring media production and consumption on an increasingly broad scale. This complicates established ways of viewing cultural production and consumption as a linear process, where ordinary people 'receive' media and other products from media professionals.

These changes are also evident in the development of sexually explicit representations online. Until recently, most discussions about online pornography saw it simply in terms of increasing and extending the distribution of existing commercial porn, but new opportunities for sexual production and consumption are becoming clearer. It is now possible to create, distribute and access a much more diverse set of sexual representations than before. Pornographers may operate independently of the established industry in new and alternative ways, while small groups of independent and 'savvy media practitioners' are producing and distributing alternative porn in online arenas for peer-to-peer sharing, sex activist and art networks. This is 'a collaborative producing of porn,' the beginnings, in Katrien Jacobs' view (2004b), of a democratization of porn which challenges existing frameworks for representing sex.

The migration of porn to the internet not only complicates existing models of cultural production and consumption, but makes it much harder to classify as a form of commercial sex. Although paysites continue to flourish, an enormous amount of pornographic material is now free to view. Dougal Phillips (n.d.) notes how the file-sharing of online porn dramatically alters the economy of pornographic distribution, producing 'a community of exchange' in which participants are simultaneously vendor and consumer. Porn file-sharing challenges the existing commercial structures within which porn operates, and it has the potential to alter existing concepts of pornographic production and consumption.

While some new pornographers rely on 'gift-giving' rather than financial transactions, communities are created and participation is possible, even where some commodities must be paid for in a 'community friendly commodity environment' (Jacobs, 2004a: 77). The sites that I discuss here fall into this category. They have adopted a subscription model, allowing different levels of access. At Nerve, readers can look at any materials posted in the previous 30 days and some of the photography galleries for free. Membership costs $7 per month and allows access to all of Nerve's archives which contain essays, poetry, fiction, advice, blogs, photography and personals, and also to premium photography galleries. SuicideGirls' membership is $12 per month and offers extra content to subscribers, plus the opportunity to interact with other members of the SuicideGirls community through groups, chat rooms and webcams. Both sites offer special deals which give a lower membership rate for longer subscriptions. The 'Suicide Girls,' whose picture sets, videos, journals and blogs make up the bulk of the site, are paid a fee for their work, but the distinction between model and reader, evident in most forms of pornography, is very blurred here. Suicide Girls are members of the SuicideGirls community, distinguished only from other members by their modelling, the fees they attract for this, and by the lifetime memberships their status as Suicide Girls also earns them.

On such sites, access is related simultaneously to commerce and community: the more you pay, the more you belong. Both sites also engage in more traditional commercial activities; SuicideGirls has moved into merchandising (selling clothes and jewellery), publishing (a SuicideGirls book appeared in 2004), and performance (there are neo-burlesque tours which are also available to view on DVD). Nerve has concentrated its efforts in publishing, with books on sex advice and etiquette, literature and photography.

Nerve and SuicideGirls are good examples of new forms of alternative pornography and of participatory cultures which serve corporate and community needs, enabling a 'collaborative eroticism' (Van der Graf, 2004). In both, sexual display becomes an important part of individual and collective self-definition. It is used to signify a response and an alternative to the way sex is presented elsewhere—particularly in mainstream commercial porn, which the sites characterize as standardized, bland and anodyne. In this respect, issues of taste and aesthetics become a significant component in the way the communities construct themselves. Nerve 'consciously seeks to blur the boundaries between pornography and avant-garde art' (Jenkins, 2004: 6), while SuicideGirls describes itself as an 'art-sleaze phenomenon.'[3] *Wired* magazine contrasts 'stylish subculture sites' like SuicideGirls, with their 'artful nude photos of women who are more likely to be purple-haired, pale and pierced,' with mainstream porn sites which feature 'ugly Web design, annoying pop-up ads, and badly lit pictures of big-haired breast-implanted blondes' (Barron, 2002). Here, *stylishness*—of genre, body display and web design—is crucial in the sites' definitions of themselves.

Nerve and SuicideGirls differ in style and content from commercial hardcore porn, which is still organized around a set of sexual 'numbers' derived from 1970s hardcore video. These are the oral, vaginal and anal penetration of women by men, girl-on-girl scenes, and threesomes. Porn of this kind tends to focus on the explicit display of women's bodies, with male display limited to ejaculation, usually onto the body or into the mouth of a woman—the so-called 'money shot.' This focus on flesh and ejaculation—or 'meat' and 'money'

(Williams, 1989)—is rarely found in smart smut and altporn sites, which favour softcore images, that is, photographs of women, shot in tasteful pin-up or art styles—rather than images of explicit display or sexual activity.[4] In addition, on smart smut and altporn sites, sexual content is combined with coverage of music, news, art, culture and counterculture, so that sex is placed in a much broader cultural context than in more mainstream porn sites. Nerve calls itself a magazine about 'sex and culture,' for an audience that appreciates 'original, award-winning writing and photography, as well as discerning coverage of the best films, television, books and music,' while SuicideGirls emphasizes its combination of 'the best music and alternative culture sites with an unapologetic, grassroots approach to sexuality.' Porn is therefore able to take its place alongside other forms of culture and subculture, becoming a focus for engaging in community and culture building.

The combination of amateur and professional production and the incorporation of forms of interaction such as blogs, discussion groups and message boards associated with non-sexual online communities also works to construct the sites as forms of community. Nerve places amateur writing in the dating profiles of 'young, urban trendsetters' alongside professional work, thereby presenting the site as a community, online media as a tool for public self-expression, and sex as a form of self-presentation and relation. Altporn sites tend to address their target communities more narrowly, drawing on the iconography of subcultures, such as goth or hippie, and they are often characterized by the 'do-it-yourself' amateur aesthetic associated with the subcultural production of art, fashion and music. SuicideGirls belongs to this category, presenting itself as a showcase for 'postmodern pin-up girls for the alternative nation.' Young women, often heavily tattooed and/or pierced, appear in a range of forms, including pin-up imagery, profiles, journals, blogs and cams. The site is a commercial environment and a community at several levels; it belongs to its founders and owners, who run it as a business; it belongs to the Suicide Girls themselves, who are paid to appear on the site, and who 'embody' the community; and it belongs to the members, who are paying subscribers and who participate in the community: on SuicideGirls, both Suicide Girls and subscribers can create a profile and journal; they can chat, use cams, share photos and join groups. What unites them all is their membership of a taste culture which functions to bind them together in relations of economic and cultural production and consumption, which are also relations of community.

ClassySex.com

Sites like Nerve and SuicideGirls are concerned with formulating a sexual sensibility for audiences that have traditionally been neglected by porn—young people and women. For example, Nerve.com promotes itself as a 'smart sex' magazine for 'young, urban, over-educated hipsters.' This involves a recasting of sexual interest as literate and cool, consonant with the late modern association of hedonistic sexuality with a new petitebourgeoisie, of 'classy' sex with women (Juffer, 1998), and with the emergence of porn chic (McNair, 2002). Through the development of particular kinds of tasteful sexual representations for specific taste cultures, new porn audiences are defined as sophisticated and liberated consumers (Jancovich, 2001). This marks a departure in the presentation and marketing of porn which has generally been understood as a low, crude and 'dirty' form of cultural production. The aestheticization of sex can also be traced in other media such as subscription cable television, where it is possible to narrowcast relatively sexually explicit material to a commercially attractive audience of middle-class 'bourgeois

bohemians'—most notably and successfully in the postfeminist drama, *Sex and the City* (Arthurs, 2003). . . .

Altporn Aesthetics and the New 'Porn Star'

The hybridity of these images and the complex readings made of them are related to an aestheticization of sex, which is evident in other areas of popular culture and commerce, for example in lingerie adverts, erotic literature, and the marketing of sex toys (Attwood, 2005; Juffer, 1998). Jane Juffer has characterized this as a domestication of porn, which recasts the consumption of some sexually explicit representations as a marker of distinction, sophistication and taste. In the production and consumption of these, a set of concerns with sexual aesthetics, authenticity and self-expression is foregrounded. This set of concerns can also be found in the amateur pornography that Sergio Messina has dubbed 'realcore,' and defined as representations of 'real people with real desires, having real sex in real places' (n.d.). According to Messina, realcore originated in the BDSM [Bondage, Discipline, Sadism, and Masochism] community, appearing online in the late 1990s. By definition, it has worked to expand the vocabulary of sexual expression, making visible many more types of sexual practice than are generally represented in porn. In both style and content, it has pushed the boundaries of what is understood as porn and as 'real sex.' This kind of representation can be understood as part of 'a broad postmodern taste for "authentica,"' which includes webcam culture, celebrity nudity, amateur porn and reality TV, and which focuses on new public displays of 'the ordinary,' which often make use of images of naked bodies (Barcan, 2000: 145–6).

Although sites like Nerve and SuicideGirls are clearly related to the rise of realcore, they are very different in aesthetic terms. Realcore is characterized by wide-angle shots, low-fi presentation, a lack of technical gloss, and a form of performance by its 'models' which acknowledges the presence of the camera and speaks its 'reality' (Messina, n.d.). The aesthetic of Nerve and SuicideGirls is instead derived from glamour and pin-up photography, which in turn draw on the codes of fashion and portraiture. It is also related to the practice of boudoir photography described by Ruth Barcan, whereby ordinary people employ professional photographers to create glamorous pictures of them, thereby imitating 'the images of perfection associated with stars' (2004: 249).

The SuicideGirls aesthetic also involves the recycling of the codes and conventions of retro and contemporary subculture imagery. Missy Suicide describes how the site was inspired by the post-punk style of Portland, Oregon, 'where everyone was an artist and everyone created something,' and by pin-up photography of 1950s' models like Bettie Page, who she saw as 'self-confident, elegant and upbeat' (Barcan, 2004: 7). SuicideGirls is dedicated to the 'post-punk girls who haunted Pioneer Street, listening to Ice Cube on their iPods, decked out in Minor Threat hoodies and miniskirts, with a skateboard in one hand, a cup of coffee in the other, and a backpack of Kerouac and Hemingway slung over one absent-mindedly exposed shoulder' (2004: 8). Despite this delineation of a 'type' of girl who can be defined so precisely by her forms of cultural consumption—young, literate and cosmopolitan with tastes derived from punk and riot grrrl—Missy's vision was to create 'new Pin-Up girls, each with their own ferociously unique style and outlook' (2004: 8).

The characterization of a cool, contemporary, sexy, clever, stylish and urbane femininity—'the girls next door, but more colorful and with better record collections' as the SuicideGirls site puts it—can be contrasted with most mainstream porn representations, where women are defined only in terms of their availability for sex or their sexual prowess. The bodies of Suicide Girls may be 'sexy,' but their tattoos and piercings also insistently reference individual style and membership of subculture communities. They are hot and cool, sexy and beautiful, and although they may require as much work as the bodies of porn stars, they also signify an authenticity derived from a high glamour tradition, in which 'personality' is indicated through 'image' (Tolson, 1996: 117–18). This recycling of representational codes associated with celebrities works to glamorize and exalt the models, simultaneously refusing the connotations of porn imagery, which 'objectifies' and depersonalizes its subjects. The use of journals and other forms of self-expression on the site also works to construct Suicide Girls as really real, 'emotionally fleshed out' (Tomlin, 2002), as 'whole people' rather than 'just bodies' (in N. Phillips, 2005).

New sex taste cultures such as SuicideGirls complicate traditional ways of representing the self; combining forms associated with objectification and commodification and those associated with the expression of the unique self. This is further emphasized by the way they draw on the visual conventions of glamorous pin-up girls such as Bettie Page, who straddles the border between porn star, glamour model, celebrity and film star. In the process, the women who appear on SuicideGirls may themselves become 'micro-celebrities.'[5] An insistence on the authenticity of the girls is set against the artificiality of professional porn stars—they are average but unique, where porn stars are spectacular but inhuman. In this sense, an aesthetic of glamour is made to connote authenticity and the everyday, rather than the artificial and fantastic world of mainstream commercial porn.

Empowered Eroticism

The aesthetic of sites such as Nerve and SuicideGirls is part of the way new sex taste cultures attempt to define themselves, through a variety of oppositions to mainstream culture—and especially mainstream porn—as creative, vibrant, classy, intelligent, glamorous, erotic, radical, varied, original, unique, exceptional and sincere, compared to the unimaginative, dull, tasteless, stupid, sleazy, ugly, hackneyed, standardized, commonplace, trite, mediocre, superficial and artificial. In the process, a system of aesthetics is evoked as a form of ethics. Indeed, a number of alternative online producers have explicitly linked porn and political activism. The Sensual Liberation Army, which provides links to porn images, asks its readers to visit sites such as The American Red Cross and Democracy Now. The producers of FuckforForest (n.d.) exchange porn for money, which they donate to environmental causes. Furry Girl's VegPorn site donates money from sales at its online sex shop to Scarleteen, the sex education resource for teenagers (FurryGirl, n.d.).

Some altporn practitioners are also concerned with developing an ethical framework for new forms of sexual representation. FurryGirl argues that altporn should revalue models, by inviting them 'to express themselves and have a say in how they are presented,' and by portraying them 'as multidimensional beings, with interests other than sex.' It should defy conventions of beauty, body type and style and challenge 'stereotypes and negative attitudes about race, size, gender, and sexual orientation.' It should be sex positive and uphold 'the idea of safe, sane, and consensual sex play.' It should also work towards building a participatory culture. This should involve 'people who are a part of each other's lives outside of porn,' so that porn becomes 'an expression of the people who make it.' Altporn producers should work 'to foster community on the site,' through forums, journals, chat rooms, and on the web, through networking, making connections and helping each other out (in Watson, n.d.). Similarly, TastyTrixie's Webwhore Manifesto (n.d.) calls for a recognition of the wide range of skills necessary for good webwhoring, which she defines as 'providing sex fantasy entertainment on the internet,'

and the contribution that sex work makes to society, and for 'solidarity in smut'—the promotion of links with other sex workers and the development of a professional code of ethics.

The ethical framework invoked here is one developed by writers such as Annie Sprinkle and Pat Califia, and espoused more recently in collections such as Marcelle Karp and Debbie Stoller's *The Bust Guide to the New Girl Order* (1999), Lee Damsky's *Sex and Single Girls* (2000), and Merri Lisa Johnson's *Jane Sexes It Up: True Confessions of Feminist Desire* (2002). Although these retain a critical focus, they tend towards the embracing and shaping of cultural and commercial sexual practices, rather than focusing on their regulation and censorship. The attempt to develop a sexual ethics beyond existing moral frameworks, also exemplified in books like *The Ethical Slut* (1998), by Dossie Easton and Catherine Listz, which is referenced by altporn practitioners such as FurryGirl, provides an important context for the development and analysis of new sex taste cultures, because of its refusal of traditional assumptions that commercial sex is wrong or necessarily harmful.

The most sustained counter-claim to the empowered eroticism of SuicideGirls came in 2005, when nearly 40 models left the site amid claims that the site's male president, Spooky, was abusive to models and used Missy as 'a pro-woman front' (Fulton, 2005). SuicideGirls was criticized for the poor pay and restrictive contracts it offers its models,[6] and for its heavy-handed responses to the criticisms made by disenchanted SuicideGirls, removing dissenters and their critical posts from the community (Koht, 2006), and filing legal actions against rival sites when models, allegedly still under contract to SuicideGirls, began working for them (Demsky, 2006). While it is difficult to establish the truth of these allegations, paying attention to the *details* of how new sex taste cultures do and do not work, rather than making assumptions about sexual representation and commercial sex, will provide a good starting point if we are to begin to make sense of them in ethical terms.

As long ago as 1987, Kathy Myers suggested that we might move beyond the tired and abstract debates about an imaginary monolithic pornography if we started to ask specific questions about how models are selected, how images are produced, what power relationships exist between photographers and models, how images are framed and distributed, and what kinds of contexts they are consumed in. For some writers, these kinds of questions make little difference to 'the fundamentally problematic relationship between viewer and viewed that lies at the heart of all pornography' (N. Phillips, 2005), but in the contemporary climate, when we are witnessing radical shifts in the ways we create and access sexual images, it is crucial that we abandon assumptions about what is 'fundamentally' problematic about new sex taste cultures, such as SuicideGirls, and move on.

Pornography as Self-Presentation

Danielle DeVoss (2002) has argued that women's self-published porn sites can be seen as '*identity projects*' (2002: 76), and Ruth Barcan maintains that more generally, images—particularly those of nudity—now play an important part in the way we form our identities, constituting, to use Foucault's term, a major 'technology of the self' (2004: 212). In this context it is important to develop an understanding of the key forms of nudity that contemporary culture privileges—celebrity nudity, glamour nudity and homemade nudity (2004: 212). Since the early 1990s female celebrity nudity has increasingly been presented as 'a sign of liberation,' in which 'economic freedom . . . sexual liberation and freedom of choice' happily coincide (2004: 242), and in which porn is able to become 'chic' (McNair, 2002). Glamour photography works to allow ordinary people to participate in the kind of 'image-work' previously

associated only with celebrities, and is often undertaken at times when 'identity and/or body image have become self-conscious or precarious in some way' (Barcan, 2004: 249). Homemade nudity is most evident in the explosion of interest in sexually explicit material featuring real people—in realcore, reality TV shows and chat rooms. The accessibility of all these new forms has made sexually explicit imagery more culturally visible, whether it is accessed by individuals or not (Barcan, 2004: 254).

Digital technologies are changing the kinds of 'identity work' performed in western cultures, and self-presentation is increasingly mediated. Barcan argues that we can make sense of new forms of image and identity work as part of a shift towards understanding identity in terms of a 'staged authenticity,' which combines 'desire for the real, fetishization of the real, resignation to the fact that the real is always elusive, fun in fakery, and celebration of the delights of role-play and performance' (2004: 255). In this context, commercial sex inevitably takes on new significance, by providing resources for the development of sexual identities, and by providing arenas for presenting those identities.

The success of SuicideGirls has dramatically increased interest in alternative pornography and the number of altporn sites is growing fast. The aesthetic of these kinds of sex taste cultures, and the way they address young hip consumers, has also sparked some interest from the mainstream porn industry. An article in *Adult Video News* about porn for the youth market recommends that porn producers, 'Hook in the currently secondary non-mainstream buyers now, and hold on to them as they mature and their favored product gains acceptance' (Stokes, 2005). It argues that if it is to appeal to young, sophisticated consumers, porn must be presented in a form they can relate to aesthetically, and it must fit into their existing practices of media consumption.

There are already signs that the aesthetic and address developed by sites like

SuicideGirls is being appropriated by large porn production companies. Filmmaker Eon McKai, whose work fits the SuicideGirls aesthetic and demographic, has been hired by VCA Pictures, which is owned by *Hustler,* to make porn for the youth market. Dismissing contemporary mainstream porn as 'tired out and out of touch,' and noting how ground-breaking SuicideGirls has been, McKai argues that 'There's a ton of kids like me who listen to emo, punk-rock, goth, electro, or drum and bass . . . and there's no smut for us.' McKai's film, *Art School Sluts* (2004), is made 'from the scene for the scene,' and features Suicide Girls as extras, girls 'you could catch dancing . . . around town on any night of the week' (McKai, n.d.).

Sex taste cultures like SuicideGirls and Nerve are the nearest thing we currently have to the kind of porn recommended by *Adult Video News,* and they provide a model of the ways that commercial sex representations may develop in the future, both within community sites and within the existing porn industry. They are part of a 'reconfiguration of erotic life' in which sex and commerce are combined (Bernstein, 2001: 397). The rapid growth of new forms of online pornography and the taste cultures that grow up around them are blurring the boundaries between porn and other aesthetics, between commercial and non-commercial forms of sex, between consumption and community, and between sex as representation and self-presentation, recreation and relation. It poses new questions about what we mean by commercial sex and how we might develop its study.

Notes

1. Altporn is sometimes also called punk porn or indie porn, and, as these names suggest, has a particular subculture focus.

2. A porn clone of this site now exists at http://www.pornotube.com/ (accessed 10 January 2007).

3. The *Los Angeles Times,* quoted on the SuicideGirls site, http://suicidegirls.com/tour/ (accessed 9 September 2006).

4. Some altporn sites portray a much wider range of sexual practices than is generally depicted in porn—the BellaVendetta site organizes its galleries according to 'fetish' and 'kink' categories, including asphyxiation, bathrooms, blood sex, clown porn, crafts and hobbies, food, glasses, horror, menstrual art, love letters, smoking, tickling, weapons, and wheels. See BellaVendetta (n.d.). See Burning Angel for examples of altporn video, http://www.burningangel.com/ (accessed 15 January 2007).

5. The term is used by Terri Senft (2005) in her discussion of the fame achieved by women producers of webcam sites, or 'camgirls.'

6. According to a report by Deidre Fulton (2005) Suicide Girls 'get $300 per photo set, plus additional money if they go on tour, shoot videos, or pose in photos with another girl.'

References

Arthurs, Jane (2003) '*Sex and the City* and Consumer Culture: Remediating Postfeminist Drama,' *Feminist Media Studies* 3(1): 83–98.

Attwood, Feona (2005) 'Fashion and Passion: Marketing Sex to Women,' Special Pleasure and Danger Revisited Anniversary Issue, *Sexualities* 8(4): 395–409.

Barcan, Ruth (2000) 'Home on the Rage: Nudity, Celebrity, and Ordinariness in the Home Girls/Blokes Pages,' *Continuum: Journal of Media and Cultural Studies* 14(2): 145–58.

Barcan, Ruth (2004) *Nudity: A Cultural Anatomy.* Oxford and New York: Berg.

Barron, Jess (2002) 'When Sub-Pop Meets Porn,' URL (accessed 23 October 2006): http://www.wired.com/news/culture/0,1284,53034,00.html

BellaVendetta (n.d.) URL (accessed 2 November 2006): www.bellavendetta.com/

Bernstein, Elizabeth (2001) 'The Meaning of the Purchase: Desire, Demand and the Commerce of Sex,' *Ethnography* 2(3): 389–420.

Califia, Pat (n.d.) URL (accessed January 2007): http://www.patcalifia.com/

Damsky, Lee (ed.) (2000) *Sex and Single Girls: Straight and Queer Women on Sexuality.* Seattle: Seal Press.

Demsky, Ian (2006) 'How a Punk-Porn Empire is Trying to Protect its Piece of the Pie,' URL (accessed 27 October 2006): http://www.wweek.com/editorial/3210/7126/ Suicide Defense

DeVoss, Danielle (2002) 'Women's Porn Sites—Spaces of Fissure and Eruption or "I'm a Little Bit of Everything"', *Sexuality and Culture* 6(3): 75–94.

Easton, Dossie and Liszt, Catherine A. (1998) *The Ethical Slut: A Guide to Infinite Sexual Possibilities.* San Francisco, CA: Greenery Press.

FuckForForest (n.d.) URL (accessed January 2007): http://www.fuckforforest.com/

Fulton, Deidre (2005) 'SuicideGirls Revolt,' URL (accessed 23 October 2006): http://www.portlandphoenix.com/features/other _stories/documents/05018238.asp

FurryGirl (n.d.) URL (accessed January 2007): http://www.furrygirl.com/

Jacobs, Katrien (2004a) 'Pornography in Small Places and Other Spaces,' *Cultural Studies* 18(1): 67–83.

Jacobs, Katrien (2004b) 'The New Media Schooling of the Amateur Pornographer: Negotiating Contracts and Singing Orgasm,' URL (accessed 2 June 2006): http://www.libidot.org/katrien/tester/articles/negotiating-print.html

Jancovich, Mark (2001) 'Naked Ambitions: Pornography, Taste and the Problem of the Middlebrow,' *Scope,* URL (accessed 22 May 2001): http://www.nottingham.ac.uk/film/journal/articles/naked-ambition.html

Jenkins, Henry (2004) 'So You Want to Teach Pornography,' in Pamela Church Gibson (ed.) *More Dirty Looks: Gender, Pornography and Power.* London: BFI.

Jenkins, Henry (2006) *Convergence Culture: Where Old and New Media Collide.* New York: New York University Press.

Johnson, Merri Lisa (ed.) (2002) *Jane Sexes it Up: True Confessions of Feminist Desire.* New York: Thunder's Mouth Press.

Juffer, Jane (1998) *At Home with Pornography: Women, Sex and Everyday Life.* New York and London: New York University Press.

Karp, Marcelle and Stoller, Debbie (eds) (1999) *The BUST Guide to the New Girl Order.* New York: Penguin.

Koht, Peter (2006) 'Obscene but Not Heard,' URL (accessed 30 October 2006): http://www.metroactive.com/papers/metro/01.04.06/suicidegirls

McKai, Eon (n.d.) 'WHO THE FUCK IS EON McKAI ANYWAY?' URL (accessed 2 November 2006): http://www.eonmckai.com/

McNair, Brian (2002) *Striptease Culture: Sex, Media and the Democratization of Desire.* London and New York: Routledge.

Messina, Sergio (n.d.) 'Realcore: The Digital Porno Revolution,' URL (accessed 11 October 2006): http://realcore.radiogladio.it/

Missy Suicide (2004) *SuicideGirls.* Los Angeles, CA: Feral House.

Myers, Kathy (1987) 'Towards a Feminist Erotica,' in Rosemary Betterton (ed.) *Looking On: Images of Femininity in the Visual Arts and Media,* pp. 189–202. London and New York: Pandora.

Nerve.com (2005) 'About Us,' URL (accessed 22 April 2005): http://www.nerve.com/aboutus/advertising/

Phillips, Dougal (n.d.) 'Can Desire Go On Without a Body? Pornographic Exchange and The Death of the Sun,' *Culture Machine,* URL (accessed 5 May 2006): http://culturemachine.tees.ac.uk/InterZone/dphillips.html

Phillips, Nick (2005) 'Cynical, Bitter, Jaded As Hell. Also Naked,' URL (accessed 13 May 2005): http://www.citypages.com/databank/23/1147/ article10895.asp

Scarleteen (n.d.)URL (accessed January 2007): http://www.scarleteen.com/

Senft, Terri (2005) 'Camgirls: Gender, Micro-Celebrity and Ethics on the World Wide Web,' URL (accessed 6 May 2005): http://www.echonyc.com/~janedoe/diss/intr01.html

Sensual Liberation Army (n.d.) URL (accessed January 2007): http://sensuallib.com/

Sprinkle, Annie (n.d.) URL (accessed January 2007): http://www. anniesprinkle.org/

Stokes, Peter (2005) 'We Want Our Porn and We Want It Now! The Youth Market: Who Is It, Why Is It, and What Does It Mean for Retailers?' URL (accessed 24 October 2006): http://www.adultvideonews.com/cover/ cover1105_01.html

SuicideGirls (n.d.) URL (accessed January 2007): http://suicidegirls.com/

TastyTrixie (n.d.) 'WebWhore Manifesto,' URL (accessed 2 November 2006): http://tastytrixie.com/manifesto.html

Tolson, Andrew (1996) *Mediations: Text and Discourse in Media Studies.* London: Arnold.

Tomlin, Annie (2002) 'Sex, Dreads, and Rock 'n' Roll: SuicideGirls' live nude punks want to be your porn alternative,' URL (accessed 24 November 2006): http://www.bitchmagazine.com/archives/12_02sg/sg.shtml

Van der Graf, Shenja (2004) 'Blogging Business: SuicideGirls.com,' *M/C Journal* 7(4) URL (accessed 2 April 2005): http://journal.media-culture.org.au/0410/07_suicide.php

VegPorn (n.d.) URL (accessed January 2007): http://www.vegporn.com/

Watson, Paul (n.d.) 'alternaporn: we sing the body politic,' URL (accessed 23 November 2006): http://www.lazaruscorporation.co.uk/v4/articles/alternaporn.php

Williams, Linda (1989) *Hard Core: Power, Pleasure and the 'Frenzy of the Visible.'* London: Pandora.

"That's So Fun"[1]

Selling Pornography for Men to Women in *The Girls Next Door*

Karen Boyle

Pornification

This chapter focuses on the hit U.S. TV show, *The Girls Next Door* (*GND*),[2] a "reality" series following the lives of three women—Holly Madison, Bridget Marquardt, and Kendra Wilkinson—who, until 2008, lived at the Playboy mansion as Hugh Hefner's "girlfriends."[3] *GND* has been phenomenally successful for *E!*: In 2007, it was the cable channel's most watched show, with women making up 70% of the audience (Kaplan, 2007). According to Lisa Berger, *E!*'s executive vice president of programming and development, women's embrace of the show was something of a surprise: "I thought that [female viewers] were going to hate these women" (Kaplan, 2007). Counter to Berger, I want to argue that *GND* very deliberately courts a female audience—and, specifically, a *young* female audience—but that to do so involves a marginalization of Playboy's raison d'être, euphemistically encapsulated in *Playboy* magazine's strap line: "entertainment *for men*." How "entertainment for men" is transformed into a hit TV show for women and girls is the main concern of this chapter.

However, I want to begin by placing this analysis in a broader context. To note that the boundaries between the pornographic and the mainstream have become increasingly blurred in recent years is hardly news: This has been a theme in academic and popular commentary for some time now. And this process has been given a variety of labels: porno-chic, pornification, pornographication. What is of most significance for this chapter, however, is the way that these labels can be used to bring together a series of quite disparate processes. Specifically, such labels are often taken to encompass *both* the increasing availability of porn—hard and soft core—*and* shifting mainstream conventions around the representation, pervasiveness, and public visibility of sexual practices and products. If what you are interested in is the sexualization of the public sphere, there is a certain logic in bringing these processes together. But it is important not to collapse one into the other (as many pro-porn writers do), as they typically involve very different patterns of production and consumption.

To give just one example, it is not uncommon to see the increased availability of hardcore porn discussed alongside the wider merchandising of sex toys or the popularity of pole dance exercise classes.[4] Vibrators and audiovisual pornography may both be products sold with the promise of sexual arousal, but that is where the similarity ends: One activity depends on the use of the bodies of *other* human beings for your sexual arousal; the other does not. Similarly, while fitness DVDs and classes focusing on striptease and pole dancing are clearly influenced by the commercial sex industry—indeed, there is a *GND* workout DVD—these activities align their female consumers with the "objects" to be bought (the porn performer, stripper, lapdancer) and not with the buyer of commercial sex. The casual equation of these activities makes commercial sex appear less misogynistic by suggesting that women are also consumers of sex. This conveniently sidesteps that what is being sold to women is often a way of working on *their own* bodies, rather than sexual access to the bodies of others.

This failure to recognize the important difference in what is being sold to women and men in this process of pornification means that female sexual desire is too often reduced to a willingness to sexually objectify oneself (Levy, 2005). Some women clearly do make choices about their involvement in pornography and other forms of commercial sex, and these choices are not immaterial (Whisnant, 2004). However, an individual's choice does not disrupt the realities of the sex industry (of which *Playboy,* my focus in this chapter, is a part). It remains an industry built on providing straight men with sexual access to a wide array of women for profit, independent of the women's own sexual pleasure. That some women—including those portrayed in *GND*—may have something to gain in this scenario (in terms, for instance, of wealth, opportunities, and recognition) does not negate this fundamental inequality.

Yet, the porn consumer is often invisible in contemporary accounts. Too often, women

(performers) are pitted against women (feminist critics), meaning that a political analysis of the industry is reduced to little more than a catfight in which one group is "mean" to the other. As we will see, this is a device used in *GND,* but it is by no means unique to this show: Being "judged" (by other women and also by some men) is portrayed as the most damaging aspect of women's involvement in prostitution and pornography in a range of contemporary film and television texts. This is consistent with the framing of commercial sex as a narrative about women that cuts across mainstream representations of the subject in many genres and, indeed, has become so commonsensical that it is virtually unquestioned (Boyle, 2008, in press-a, in press-b; McLaughlin, 1993). Prostitution = prostitute; pornography = porn star; sex work = sex worker: Whatever political position commentators take on the issue, the equation of commercial sex with the women bought and sold within it naturalizes male demand, suggesting it is inevitable, lacking in complexity, and not worthy of investigation.

This is, then, the context in which *GND* emerged, a context in which pornography was more available than ever before and widely referenced in the codes and conventions of popular culture. At the same time, the discourse around pornography and pornification had diverted attention away from the specificities of pornographic production and consumption practices to make pornography seem more women-friendly. In the remainder of this chapter, I will try to unpack *how GND* has been so successful in making porn for men palatable to a female audience, securing their buy-in to the Playboy brand and its worldview.

Playing at Porn With *The Girls Next Door*

Despite Berger's apparent surprise about *The Girls Next Door*'s female appeal,

Playboy merchandising has long targeted women and girls. The brand has also achieved a degree of mainstream visibility in fictions aimed at women, including *Sex and the City* ("Sex and Another City," 3.14) and, more recently, *The House Bunny*, a teen comedy in which a former resident of the Playboy mansion transforms the lives and bodies of a sorority house on the brink of closure by performing a series of makeovers and throwing some great parties.[5] What these representations share is an emphasis on fashion, appearance, and relationships between women, and this is also central to *GND*.

GND centers on the three "girls"— Holly, Bridget, and Kendra—with Hefner a key, but peripheral, figure. While it is assumed that the "girls" will be unknown to viewers—at least at the beginning (the first episode is entitled "Meet the Girls")— Hefner needs no introduction. The show's original opening credits illustrate this nicely and point to many of the other arguments I want to develop in this chapter.

Each woman is introduced in turn, using short cartoonish segments in which they appear as bobble-headed figures, their enlarged heads making them both comic and childlike in appearance (reminiscent of figures like Hello Kitty).[6] The introductions to each of the women caricature their personalities and interests while also providing a mini-narrative of transformation: a before (-Hefner) and after (-Hefner). Before, Holly was a small-town cheerleader in an unremarkable, generic locale; after she is the lady of the house, dressed in a sequined gown and positioned in a room with a chandelier, roll-top bath, and decadent furnishings. Before, Bridget was a bookish, albeit cheeky, student; after she is the girlish girlfriend, her books incorporated into a pink, glittery room that would be many a young girl's fantasy space. Before, Kendra was a tomboy; after, she retains her sports interests but is now surrounded by expensive gadgetry in a room of her own that is both spacious and chaotic.

Hefner, in contrast, is assumed to be familiar to the audience, and in the credit sequence, his role is both to bring the women together (up until he appears they are only shown separately) *and* to establish a wider context of luxury: while the women are associated with personalized spaces, the whole mansion with its servants, gardens, birds, and exotic animals is his domain. Moreover, in contrast to the women—who all have name tags appearing on screen during the credits—Hefner is not introduced by name: He just *is*. In this brief sequence, then, it is established that it is the women who are the objects of scrutiny but that they are, to use Gail Dines's (2009) phrase, "childified" women, dependent on a wealthy, benevolent patriarch. It is also notable that there is nothing obviously "pornographic" about the credit sequence: It could be the opening for any family-orientated reality series.

In the first season in particular, there is an awareness that Hefner's living arrangements may incite critique, but it is the *women* who have to answer the criticisms. In a short interview included in the Season 1 DVD, Holly notes, with exasperation,

> People want to ask you the same questions. "Do you really sleep with him? How many girls live there? How much do you get paid? Or how did you get this job?" And I'm like, "It's not a job, fuck off." . . . I don't want to be asked a million stupid questions. . . . People think I'm just some gold-digger who's here because I wanna be a Playmate or something and they always want to know, "Oh what are you going to do after, when are you leaving, how much do you get paid." And I'm just like, "God, my whole life revolves around Hef and this" and it's so irritating to be asked a question like that because, you know, these people don't know me.[7]

At various points, all three women make frustrated reference to these questions (or others like them) and perceptions that they are sluts or gold-diggers. But as Hefner himself is *never* interviewed, it is the *women's* behavior that is under scrutiny here too (why do they do it? how could they?) in more or less explicit ways.

Other accounts of life at the Playboy mansion offer some opportunity to consider Hefner's behavior: St. James (2009), for instance, describes how Hefner determines where, when, and how sex takes place, as well as setting a series of rules that his "girlfriends" must live by (which include a ban on dating other men and a 9 p.m. curfew). She also describes Hefner's financial control over his "girlfriends," encapsulated in the weekly "allowance" they receive. Most of this goes unremarked in *GND*. The show is purposefully opaque about the women's sexual relationships with Hefner. He may be an icon, a role model for male viewers, but he is never portrayed through the women's eyes as *sexually* desirable. This allows the show to sidestep Hefner's controlling behavior because not only do the women consent to it, but their apparent lack of sexual desire makes this a nonissue. When the women are asked questions on this topic, they insist on their right to privacy, and those asking the questions are made to seem rude, invasive, and driven by prurient interest.

This is perhaps most obvious in the episode "I'll Take Manhattan" (1.12), in which the women go to New York with Hefner to do publicity for their forthcoming *Playboy* pictorial, including a television interview with veteran journalist Barbara Walters. Walters's interview is not shown but is described by the women, who emphasize how inappropriate and rude the questioning was, describing Walters herself as "mean." The women talk about feeling set up by Walters's interview and not being allowed to speak on screen, side-stepping—in the process—the actual questions asked by Walters and the answers to them. By so resolutely focusing on Holly, Bridget, and Kendra and having them embody the Playboy brand, the show ensures that any criticism of the show, or of Playboy,

becomes a criticism of the three women. Given their infantilization, this comes across as a form of bullying.

So how is it that these three women embody Playboy within the show? Most obviously, the women's wardrobes are dominated by Playboy brand gear (jewelry, vests, T-shirts, sweatshirts, bags), and the women are often shot against a backdrop of Playboy merchandise: From chairs to a pinball machine, cushions to bottled water, the bunny is everywhere. The use of the women's bedrooms as a backdrop for many interview segments enhances the sense that we are being given a privileged insight into their thoughts and feelings. That the Playboy bunny is so seamlessly integrated into these personal spaces is a comment on its unremarkable ubiquity in the wider culture as well as in the show. But this also resonates with arguments that a domestication of pornography accompanies its address to women, and the domestic dramas of the show reinforce this sense that we are "at home" with Playboy (Juffer, 1998).

More insidiously, in *GND*, Playboy is embedded in a childlike culture. This can be seen in the opening credits where the women's childified alter egos are imagined as cheerleader, student, and tomboy, before being relocated to the mansion where they are placed within a bedroom culture. Like the young female audience watching the show, the "girls" live in their bedrooms, where they gossip with each other, plan parties, and confess to the camera. Bridget, the oldest of the three, is particularly "childified": In her room, Playboy bunnies sit next to Hello Kitty, Mr. Potato Head, and numerous teddies, and in interviews, she speaks in a slightly breathless, girlish voice with infectious excitement, lots of giggling, and occasional tears. Indeed, "That was so *fun*" is Bridget's most frequent assessment of the photo shoots, shopping trips, parties, events, and excursions that make up their lives.

Pornography is just one more thing "girls" like to play at. And it's something all girls in *GND* want a shot at. Virtually all the women in the show are potential, current, or past Playmates or Hefner girlfriends, and it's a real family affair with second-generation Playmates, mother/daughter fans, and the women's own female family members making regular appearances. Most disturbing of all, however, in the fifth season episode, "Third Time's The Charming," the 2-year old daughter of a former Playmate is introduced with the on-screen caption "Future Playmate." It's not just that the women are childified playmates, then, but that girl children are porn stars in waiting.

For the adult women, much of their lives center on dressing up, having hair and makeup done, and finding the right costume for an activity or themed party. There is an obvious childishness to this, but the emphasis on appearance and transformation clearly resonates with women's culture more generally: The women are shown shopping for themselves and others, getting ready at salons and in their bedrooms, and endlessly looking in mirrors.

In the first season, Bridget's younger sister, Anastasia, is given a makeover for the midsummer party at the mansion. To anyone familiar with makeover shows, the framing of Anastasia's makeover will be instantly recognizable. Having looked on enviously from the sidelines as the women shot their *Playboy* pictorial in the previous episode ("Just Shoot Me," 1.07), the makeover allows Anastasia to briefly become the narrative and visual center. It is discursively framed as a process of self-realization and empowerment ("I feel so much better about myself," she says). During the emotional final "reveal," as Anastasia descends the mansion staircase in soft-focus slow motion to rapturous applause, it is the reactions of the "girls" and Anastasia's mother that are privileged both in real time and in retrospective interview segments. Dressing up (or down) in *GND* is primarily undertaken for an audience of *other women*.

This emphasis on appearance is apparent even in episodes where it is not the narrative focus. In a typical episode, the three central characters wear between 8 and 14 different outfits each. This is particularly striking when you consider that many episodes are supposedly confined to one day. Holly, Bridget, and Kendra routinely comment on their own and other women's appearances both on screen and in their DVD commentaries. The vast majority of this commentary is complimentary, and the community of women in *GND* is imagined as a largely supportive, friendly one. As the example of Anastasia's makeover suggests, there is an inclusive tone to this: With a bit of work, some shopping, and the right girlfriends, any young girl can be this kind of beautiful. No special skills are required: Indeed, the women's *lack* of knowledge and experience are (along with dyed blonde hair and large breasts) their defining characteristics. Paradoxically, this both speaks to their current wealth (they don't need to be able to cook, tidy up, or drive, as there are always other people to do it for them)[8] *and* their more "lowly" backgrounds (Hefner expands their horizons, and they experience many things for the first time with him).

However, despite Hefner's wealth and the opulence of the women's lifestyle, their own consumption practices—particularly in the early seasons—are decidedly accessible and replicable. Yes, within the show, the Playboy goods are embedded within a world that is out of the reach of the average viewer, but the goods themselves are affordable, everyday. The women's entry into the exclusive world is, initially at least, dependent on Hefner: When they travel with Hefner, they travel in a private jet, stay in opulent hotel suites, and visit expensive and exclusive restaurants and clubs. When left to their own devices, they buy tacky gifts in souvenir shops and roadside diners and give "novelty" gifts to each other and the Playmates. When he holds parties, Hollywood actors, sportsmen, and TV stars show up; when the girls hold parties, they involve store-bought decorations, homemade costumes, and a guest list of Playmates. The women domesticate and feminize the Playboy brand, but they also glamorize its mass marketing, placing Playboy-branded goods in a luxury context where they are celebrated and enjoyed by women. The women's back stories (revisited at various points) emphasize their small-town roots, and in the interview segments, they reiterate their gratitude to Hefner for the opportunities he has given them. Their lifestyle is Hefner's gift, and he is shown to be a very generous man: Part of the appeal of the series might well be that the women's lifestyle is made to seem accessible.

This is also where the show's allusions to other reality formats are important. I have already referred to makeover shows, but there are also connections with "talent" or other "search" formats. Playboy is always on the lookout for new "girls." The fifth season search for the 55th Anniversary Playmate (which takes up four episodes) clearly references shows like *American Idol* (2002–) as the celebrity judge (Holly) takes her show on the road, with open auditions in four cities where hopefuls try out for the magazine. The first two episodes ("Girl Crazy" Parts 1 & 2) recall early season episodes in other talent shows: They are inundated with applicants, many of whom are made to appear comically deluded about their potential. As on other "talent" shows, we are invited to look at and judge the contestants along with the celebrity judge and, perhaps, to imagine whether we could do better (the auditions are, after all, open to any woman). Although it is a man who takes the photographs and shoots the video at the auditions, we are never shown his reactions: Instead, cutaways to Holly and Bridget cue our responses to the auditioning women, while underlining the distance between actual and aspiring playmates. The second two episodes ("Pleading the 55th" Parts 1 & 2) involve the chosen few performing for the camera as the hopefuls are narrowed from thousands, to six, then three, and, finally, the announcement of the winner is met with obligatory tears, hugs, and gushing proclamations of dreams coming true. This is Playboy's version of the American Dream, and while fulfilling that dream is Hefner's gift, the search—the process of *looking at* and *judging* nude women—is Holly's.

The 55th anniversary episodes are not, however, unusual in making the gaze at *Playboy*'s pages and models a female one. Throughout the show's five seasons, the women repeatedly look at and comment upon their own and other women's nude spreads for the magazine. In the second episode ("New Girls in Town"), the women attend a party for Playmate-of-the-year and talk to the camera about their own dreams of Playboy stardom. For Holly, this dream is presented as a validation of her relationship with Hefner; for Bridget, as a long-term dream that she dates to seeing beautiful women in her father's *Playboy* at the age of 4; and for Kendra, it is a motivation to "stay healthy." Pornography is thus framed as fulfilling *women's* and *girls'* aspirations related to love, family, beauty, and health. My concern here is not whether this is true or even whether this is a desirable aspiration but rather that this renders the demand side of the equation, as well as its gendered dynamic, invisible. In *GND*, pornography exists because women want to be in it and, to a lesser extent, because they want to look at it.

Indeed, it is *women* who repeatedly look at and comment on the pictorials within the show: Holly, Bridget, and Kendra are often present at photo shoots, offering encouragement to their Playmate friends; models look at their own pictorials with nervous excitement; and Playboy centerfolds are the everyday art adorning the walls of the mansion, including in the girls' more private spaces. When Holly, Bridget, and Kendra are themselves in front of the camera for the first time, Anastasia is on the sidelines, and it is her admiring and envious gaze that directs the viewer's. From Season 3 onwards, the female gaze is formalized as Holly takes on a role as a photo editor. While Hefner retains ultimate control—and the "drama" hinges on Holly's anxiety as to whether he will approve of her choices (e.g., "My Bare Lady," 3.04)—his distance from the set means that his gaze is not determining. As he is rarely present at the photo shoots,[9] he is distanced from the construction of the image, reinforcing the sense that these are expressions of female subjectivity. Unsurprisingly, the women comment on beauty and never on the masturbatory potential of the image. In short, there is no sense that the *Playboy* images included in *GND* are produced for men, or that they speak to a male fantasy of female sexual availability. The show feminizes and naturalizes the pornographic gaze: This isn't male fantasy; it's a celebration of women at their most beautiful.

Conclusion

As this discussion of *The Girls Next Door* suggests, contemporary popular culture privileges certain frameworks for understanding pornography at the expense of others. Disappointingly, much recent academic work, while offering useful insights into aspects of pornography, has nevertheless adopted some of these frameworks fairly uncritically: for instance, by assuming that we can analyze pornography by analyzing the women within it or by conflating commercial sex with sex. *GND* exploits this context by focusing on the three women who live with Hugh Hefner and positioning the pornography that his empire is built upon relative to their lives and as the object of their gaze. In seeking to appeal to a core female audience, the show disguises the fundamental nature of Playboy (the magazine and the brand) as a form of *sexual* "entertainment *for men*" and, rather, fosters the illusion that pornography exists because women want to be in it.

One of the benefits of analyzing pornography through its televisual representation in this way (see also Boyle, 2008, in press-a, in press-b) is that it allows us to move away from debates about individual women and their choices to consider, instead, the

generic qualities of these stories and how they, collectively, function to legitimate the industry. In short, I am not concerned here with whether Holly, Bridget, and Kendra are telling the truth—or even a truth—about their lives at the Playboy mansion in this show (although their glossy account is significantly different from Izabella St. James [2009], as I have indicated). Rather, my concern is with how the show promotes a particular version of the Playboy brand to women and how, in doing so, it largely ignores the sex (commercial and otherwise) that lies at the heart of the enterprise. Although clearly approved as a celebratory account of Playboy life, this unwittingly gets at one central element of the feminist critique of commercial pornography: It has nothing to say about women's sexual desires but everything to say about men's fantasies of power and control. The women are there because of Hefner, for Hefner, and subordinate their own desires to his. That *E!* has been so successful in selling this vision to women is a damning indictment of our contemporary culture and the way women are encouraged to see and value themselves within it.

Notes

1. "That's so fun" is one of Bridget's favorite phrases both in the show and on the DVD commentaries.
2. European title: *The Girls of the Playboy Mansion*.
3. Holly, Bridget, and Kendra all split with Hefner after the fifth season. The sixth season introduced Hefner's new girlfriends: Crystal Harris (age 23) and twins Karissa and Kristina Shannon (age 19). This chapter focuses on the show's first five seasons.
4. See, for example, McNair (2002), Williams (2004, p. 12), and Smith (2007, p. 167).
5. The consumer guidance provided on the UK DVD for *The House Bunny* is revealing: It was given a 12-certificate due to "one use of strong language and moderate sex references."

[In the British rating system for home media products, this indicates material not suitable for children under age 12. Ed.] That a comedy about Playboy should contain only *moderate* sex references speaks volumes about the ways in which young women are being invited to buy into a sanitized brand that has nothing to say about their own sexualities and desires but rather emphasizes their need to be *seen* as desirable (the film's tagline is "The student body is about to get a makeover.").

6. Unsurprisingly, bobble-headed figurines of the women are among the show's merchandising tie-ins.

7. "All About the Girls": Season 1 DVD Special Features (Region 2).

8. This is, of course, the premise of another successful reality series: Paris Hilton and Nicole Richie's *The Simple Life* (2003–2007). Hilton herself makes a number of appearances in *GND* and, indeed, her own media stardom is largely indebted to a sex tape: a trajectory followed by another *E!* reality star and *Playboy* Playmate, Kim Kardashian.

9. In the episode "Go West, Young Girl" (4.08), Hefner makes his first visit to Playboy Studio West in 15 years.

References

Boyle, K. (2008). Courting consumers and legitimating exploitation: The representation of commercial sex in television documentaries. *Feminist Media Studies, 8*(1), 35–50.

Boyle, K. (In press-a). The dark side of hard core: Critical documentaries on the sex industry. In C. Hines & D. Kerr (Eds.), *Hard to swallow: Hard-core pornography on screen*. London: Wallflower.

Boyle, K. (In press-b). Selling the selling of sex: Secret diary of a call girl on screen. *Feminist Media Studies, 10*(1).

Dines, G. (2009). Childified women: How the mainstream porn industry sells child pornography to men. In S. Olfman (Ed.), *The sexualization of childhood*. Westport, CT: Praeger.

Juffer, J. (1998). *At home with pornography: Women, sex & everyday life*. New York: New York University Press.

Kaplan, D. (2007, August 6). Why women love *Girls Next Door. New York Post*.

Levy, A. (2005). *Female chauvinist pigs: Women and the rise of raunch culture*. London: Simon & Schuster.

McLaughlin, L. (1993). Chastity criminals in the age of electronic reproduction: Re-viewing talk television and the public sphere. *Journal of Communication Inquiry, 17*(1), 41–55.

McNair, B. (2002). *Striptease culture: Sex, media and the democratisation of desire*. London: Routledge.

Smith, C. (2007). Designed for pleasure: Style, indulgence and accessorized sex. *European Journal of Cultural Studies, 10*(2), 167–184.

St. James, I. (2009). *Bunny tales: Behind closed doors at the playboy mansion*. Philadelphia: Running Press.

Williams, L. (2004). Porn studies: Proliferating pornographies on/scene: An introduction. In L. Williams (Ed.), *Porn studies* (pp. 1–23). Durham, NC: Duke University Press.

Whisnant, R. (2004). Confronting pornography: Some conceptual basics. In C. Stark & R. Whisnant (Eds.), *Not for sale: Feminists resisting prostitution and pornography*. Melbourne, Australia: Spinifex.

One Night in Paris (Hilton)

Wealth, Celebrity, and the Politics of Humiliation

Thomas Fahy

For many Americans, Paris Whitney Hilton washed up on the shores of celebrity in the September 2000 issue of *Vanity Fair*. The article, "Hip-Hop Debs," presents Paris and her sister, Nicky, as the new generation of media-hungry Hiltons. Modeling themselves after their great-grandfather, Conrad Hilton, who built the hotel empire and forged a public persona based on his association with celebrities (from L. A. showgirls to his second wife, Zsa Zsa Gabor) and their grandfather, with his short-lived yet highly publicized marriage to Elizabeth Taylor, the Hilton sisters seem to be extending this family tradition with élan. Of course, they have been making appearances at high-society events and parties since the late 1990s, but their debut in *Vanity Fair* marked a new beginning of sorts—an attempt on the part of their family to catapult them into the upper stratosphere of celebrity and to shape the ways in which the media would interpret them.

In many respects, "Hip-Hop Debs" accomplished these goals, albeit ironically. It moved the sisters, particularly Paris, from "Page Six" to cover story material. Yet much to the Hilton family's dismay, Nancy Jo Sales's sardonic text and David LaChapelle's controversial images helped establish the terms that would continue to characterize Paris Hilton as a vapid, narcissistic, spoiled, and highly sexualized figure who desires one thing above all else—fame. Sales reports one anonymous friend as saying that "all [Paris] wants to do is become famous . . . to wipe out the past, to become somebody else."[1] Certainly the accompanying photographs of the nineteen-year-old heiress reinforce this notion. But just like the glaring contradictions between Paris Hilton's ostentatious public image and the ways in which she tries to characterize herself as "a normal kid,"[2] a tension underlies her celebrity status and her privileged place in America's hereditary aristocracy.

Celebrities must continually negotiate the public's desire to both elevate and denigrate the famous. As Leo Braudy explains in *The Frenzy of Renown: Fame and Its History*, "modern

---

fame is always compounded of the audience's aspirations and its despair, its need to admire and to find a scapegoat for that need."[3] Paris Hilton, a celebrity who is both desired and despised, would seem to fulfill these needs. Unlike public figures who achieve recognition from acting, performing, writing, athletics, and/or politics, however, Hilton's fame hasn't come from any discernible talent or skill. It is inherited, like her wealth, and this complicates how we read and understand her image. Not only is there less to admire about Paris Hilton, but she also fails to embody the typical promise of modern-day celebrity—that anyone can achieve the same. . . .

Despite her claims that any woman can tap into her "inner heiress," Paris Hilton repeatedly acknowledges that "heiresses are born with privileges."[4] She has even claimed to be "American royalty."[5] But who among us will inherit tens of millions? Who has the opportunity to live in the Waldorf-Astoria on Park Avenue and to get unrestricted access to red-carpet events with famous actors and rock stars? If, as Leo Braudy reminds us, fame "requires that uniqueness be exemplary and reproducible,"[6] what exactly is the source of Paris Hilton's appeal? Why does she receive so much public attention?

Two photographs from the *Vanity Fair* article offer a clue about her celebrity. The picture entitled "Sweetie Pie," for example, shows Paris in an act of youthful rebellion as she stands near the entryway of her grandmother's lavish Beverly Hills living room. The elegant, wealthy furniture in the background clearly belongs to another, much older, generation, and a robe lies on the floor as if it has just fallen off her shoulders, revealing Paris's scantily clothed body. Her legs are wide apart. A short, tight skirt barely covers her crotch, and a fishnet tank top reveals her breasts and nipples. The straps of her high-heeled shoes almost blend into a nearby phone cord (the most contemporary and anachronistic object in the room). Reflective sunglasses hide her eyes, and she extends her middle finger to the viewer. On one level, her brazen pose seems directed at members of the

media and the general public who both desire her image and criticize her at the same time. On another, perhaps more obvious level (the one probably uppermost in Hilton's mind at the time), the photograph suggests Paris's rejection of her upper-class heritage— leaving behind the values of old money (as embodied in the furniture) and saying "fuck off" to the social propriety expected of someone of her economic class. Even the robe on the floor and her cut-off gloves imply a casting off of sorts. A robe and gloves would hide her body; they suggest an investment in privacy and, arguably, propriety. But Paris Hilton has largely defined herself as the antithesis of these things.[7] Here, she wears an outfit that has more in common with a prostitute than an heiress. It is an outfit that suggests public (as well as sexual) access, not private reservation. And in the context of this Beverly Hills estate, her clothing and exposed body elide class divisions between her and her audience; they promise intimate access to— and even the possible violation of—this world of privilege.

The most striking photograph, "California Girl," also works to mitigate Paris Hilton's elite status through sexual objectification and erotic desire. In this image, Paris's body has washed up onto Zuma Beach. Her eyes are closed, and her mouth is open in an ecstatic smile—perhaps in the hopes of mouth-to-mouth resuscitation from either the nearby men or an anonymous public. The top of her swimsuit has been lowered to reveal her right breast, and her legs, once again, are spread apart. Twenty-dollar bills and a few makeup bottles (trappings of her class or of prostitution) surround her body in the wet sand, while several surfers stand nearby, holding their long, phallic surfboards. These details invite the viewer to watch two things: Paris Hilton's inert, seemingly lifeless body and the surfers who gaze at her. The money reinforces the idea that part of her allure stems from her association with the Hilton family fortune. But her nudity and vulnerability, suggested by the position of her body and the men who surround her with their large surfboards, casts her as an object of desire and potential violation. One might not have riches to inherit, but one can engage in the fantasy of sexual congress with such money through a figure like Paris Hilton.[8] It is both her wealth and sexually exposed/available body, therefore, that titillate the public. Together these things are presented as—and continue to be—defining terms of her celebrity.

Just as these photographs can be read as a critique of the public attention given to such a superficial individual, they also function ironically in relation to the article. Most obviously, they undermine the ways in which Mrs. Hilton insists, for example, that Paris is a "sweet kid" and "the most modest girl."[9] But in many respects, these photographs and the dynamic created by their juxtaposition with the text also set the stage for the ways in which Paris Hilton—and by Paris Hilton I mean all of the people who construct her image (her family, managers, agents, publicists, the media, a complicit public, etc.)—would make immodesty and, more importantly, humiliation significant components of her success. From her autobiography, *Confessions of an Heiress,* and reality television show, *The Simple Life,* to her controversial commercial for Carl's Jr. and her pornographic videos, particularly *One Night in Paris,* Paris Hilton's highly eroticized image promises an erosion of the economic boundaries that typically separate the upper class from the rest of society. As P. David Marshall reminds us, "celebrities reinforce the conception that there are no barriers in contemporary culture that the individual cannot overcome."[10] And Paris Hilton has made this message an essential part of her appeal.

"How to Be an Heiress": Deception, Boredom, and the Not So Simple Life

In January 2006, the Economic Policy Institute published a report on the growing disparity between the rich and poor in the United States. Authors Jared Bernstein, Elizabeth McNichol, and Karen Lyons attribute this problem to a number of factors, including wage inequality (which has been exacerbated by globalization, increased immigration and trade, long periods of unemployment, deregulation, and the weakening of unions), investment income that typically benefits the wealthy, corporate profits, and government policies ("both what governments have done and what governments have not done"[11]). The report argues that the economic inequalities of the last twenty-five year have led to a decline in most people's living standards, a decline that has social and political implications:

> The United States was built on the ideal that hard work should pay off, that individuals who contribute to the nation's economic growth should reap the benefits of that growth. Over the past two decades, however, the benefits of economic growth have been skewed in favor of the wealthiest members of society. . . . A widening gulf between the rich on the one hand and the poor and middle class on the other hand can reduce social cohesion, trust in government and other institutions, and participation in the democratic process.[12]

In part, the EPI's report, entitled "Pulling Apart: A State-by-State Analysis of Income Trends," views this widening economic gulf as a corrosive agent of the ideals of American democracy and society—a metaphoric and potentially literal "pulling apart" of the United States. It also implies that this gap can have dangerous consequences, including the weakening of social cohesion and the public trust.

The media quickly characterized this report—along with the conference hosted by the Economic Policy Institute in the same month—as a signal of impending "class warfare."[13] And this interpretation resonates with the analyses of political and economic historian Kevin Phillips. In his book *Wealth and Democracy,* Phillips argues that the

United States has long since abandoned the egalitarianism of the Founding Fathers and has, in fact become a plutocracy. One dimension of his critique involves the "hereditary aristocracy." He explains that early-twenty-first-century America is both the "world's richest major nation" and "the West's citadel of inherited wealth. Aristocracy [is] a cultural and economic fact, if not a statutory one."[14] And Phillips considers the ability of the rich to pass on their estates to be a significant factor in this growing economic inequality: "The United States in turn entered the new century with the Republican Party having begun the elimination of federal estate and gift taxes in order to let the great wealth accumulations of the late twentieth century pass minimally hindered to the next generation."[15] Philips concludes that this type of disparity often leads to a "politics of resentment"—resentment that is typically manifested in radicalism and sweeping political reform.

Paris Hilton is a clearly a beneficiary of policies that help safeguard inherited wealth, and as a celebrity who represents this aristocratic culture, a great deal of public resentment about class inequality has been directed at (and mitigated by) her image. Oftentimes, upper-class society, just like celebrity culture, is linked to a democratizing impulse associated with the American Dream. Both imply that anyone can potentially achieve fame and wealth. At a time when the gap between rich and poor is greater than at any point in U.S. history and when political resentment seems to be growing over policies that favor the rich, however, Hilton's association with hereditary wealth (which by its very nature is exclusive) could have been a liability for her public image. Yet it hasn't been. In fact, it has been a crucial part of her popularity and success. Paris Hilton—at her most glamorous, most erotic, and most embarrassed—provides her audience, particularly those who feel disenfranchised by economic inequality, with an outlet for their fantasies and frustrations. Her eroticized body promises intimate access to the world of celebrity and upper-class privilege, while images of her that are

intended to humiliate (as evident in the ironic subtext of the *Vanity Fair* article, *The Simple Life,* and *One Night in Paris*) enact a kind of politics that closes the socio-economic gap between herself and the majority of those who consume her image. In this way, Paris Hilton's image is not only an effective tool for examining contemporary tensions about wealth, but it also offers greater insight into the ways in which popular culture can mitigate—and even defer—the kind of resentment that would lead to social and political change. . . .

Hamburgers, Wine, and Home Videos: The Pornification of Paris

Early in the 1967 film *Cool Hand Luke,* a chain gang is clearing the debris alongside a country road when a young woman with long, blonde hair steps outside her farmhouse and begins washing a dirty car. As the shirtless, sweaty prisoners watch her with increased desire and agitation, a simulated sex scene begins. The camera focuses first on her hands unscrewing the nozzle of the hose as she sprays the car and then lathers it with soap. Though she mostly avoids looking at the men directly, she watches them in the reflection of the hubcap, watching her. At one point, she lies across on the hood at an angle that is preposterous for the cleaning job at hand but ideal for allowing the men to ogle her buttocks and exposed legs. She continues washing with increasing vigor, licking her lips and smiling as the music, which plays from a transistor radio that she has placed nearby, gets louder and faster. She then squeezes the soapy sponge in front of her body, the suds spilling onto her stomach like a "money shot" in pornography films. She wipes it off while her cotton frock clings with increasing tightness to her damp body. Finally, she washes the roof, pushing her sudsy breasts against the driver-side window.

This scene is not just about the erotic pleasure and the power that the woman enjoys by knowing that she is being watched and desired, suggested by her sly smile and performative behavior. This scene is also about perception. The shot/reaction shot sequence enables the audience to observe how these men respond to the woman, how they fantasize and interpret her body in different, self-serving ways. Dragline (George Kennedy) sees her as a Madonna/whore figure, naming her Lucille because "anything so innocent and built like that just got to be named Lucille." Another man defends her purity and innocence, arguing that "she doesn't know what she is doing." But Luke Jackson (Paul Newman), who embodies the nonconformist spirit of the film, recognizes that her behavior is about the power of sexuality: "Oh boy, she knows exactly what she is doing—driving us crazy and loving every minute of it."[16]

It is this scene that commercial director Chris Applebaum used as inspiration for Paris Hilton's controversial Carl's Jr. spot. He told Krista Smith of *Vanity Fair* that "I was one of those people who always felt that glorifying the acquisition of fame and wealth is an ugly thing about our society, and that [Paris] sort of symbolizes that. When I finally got to [the commercial], I found a girl who is so in on the joke and so ready to laugh at herself."[17] What he means by "in on the joke" is a bit unclear here. Is it the recognition that she is playing into the public's desire—not so unlike the chain gang in *Cool Hand* Luke—to see women purely in terms of sexuality? Is it the joke that Paris recognizes her true investment in selling herself as a sexual object for fame and public recognition? Or both? In any case, the Carl's Jr. advertisement recasts this scene in Hilton-esque terms. Instead of walking out of a farmhouse, Hilton walks into a hangar/studio to wash a Bentley (the kind of car that she would presumably be driven around in). Wearing both the trappings of her class (a diamond necklace, jeweled bracelets, rings, and a fur that she drops to the ground in a striptease) and a one-piece leather garment that suggests an association with call girls and strippers, she crawls across the car and

the floor in a sudsy fervor. Unlike the woman from *Cool Hand Luke,* Paris looks directly at the audience throughout the scene; in and outside of this advertisement, there is nothing shy about the power and pleasure that Hilton gets from being an object of both sexual and economic desire. The commercial ends after she bites into an enormous, 1000-calorie hamburger and then squirts a nearby hose at the camera with ejaculatory pleasure. The music throughout is fitting for both a strip club and a pornographic film, and much like the videotaped sequences of Paris Hilton in the remake of *House of Wax* (2005), it clearly alludes to her infamous pornographic videos, particularly *One Night in Paris* [filmed with her boyfriend of several years, Rick Salomon].[18]

Arguably, it is Paris Hilton's inextricable association with amateur porn that made this commercial controversial. Certainly, one can see half-naked women draped over cars in any number of NASCAR-type calendars, but the Parent's Television Council launched a highly visible and successful campaign to remove this advertisement from primetime television. In September 2005, PTC president Brent Bozell maintained that the Hilton commercial hurt the fast-food chain, citing an Associated Press report that the company recently saw a 30% drop in stock for the year. "Once again," Bozell concludes, "we see the evidence that Carl's Jr. and Hardee's racy Paris Hilton ad failed to increase sales. . . . The soft porn Paris Hilton ad has alienated millions of families and exposed millions of children to raunchy content that has no place on television during primetime hours."[19] Bozell's comments make Hilton's association with pornography and "raunch culture"[20] grounds for censorship here. Paris is bad for families, for children, so she should be banned from primetime. Even in an era when nudity, profanity, and simulated sex scenes are increasingly part of primetime television, Bozell's hysterical response is not entirely surprising, however. As Walter Kendrick argues in The *Secret Museum: Pornography in Modern Culture,* the history of pornography is also a history of censorship.

"Once 'pornography' was labeled and its threat identified, the methods employed to control it were borrowed unchanged from the long tradition of political and religious persecution that preceded 'pornography' and outlives it."[21] Yet censoring Hilton's advertisement from television didn't prevent people from reading about it in newspapers and, more significantly, watching it on the internet. The controversy actually seems to have drawn more attention to the commercial as a result. One newspaper report sarcastically points out that a link to the advertisement on the PTCs website ("You can't be outraged if you can't watch it a few times to be sure"[22]) helped contribute to the immense internet traffic promoting it.

Nevertheless, Kendrick reminds us that these acts of censorship expose the ways in which pornography is a highly politicized genre: "The history of 'pornography' is a political one."[23] So what exactly are the social and political implications of Paris Hilton's association with pornography? What explains the extraordinary interest in her video *One Night in Paris*? A four-minute version first became available on the internet in November 2003, one month before the premiere of *The Simple Life*; a thirty-eight-minute version then appeared on Rick Salomon's own website in February 2004 (for $50); and the current tape, which is approximately forty-five minutes long and includes generic footage of the couple from May 2001, is one of the best-selling pornography "films" in the industry. (According to *The New York Times*, for example, Red Light District, which obtained distribution rights and began selling the Hilton tape in June 2004, had sold over 600,000 copies as of March 2006.).[24] . . .

As my discussion of Hilton has suggested, pornography seems to be a logical extension of her career; placing her exposed, serialized body and money on display for public consumption and voyeuristic pleasure. *One Night in Paris* plays into these aspects of her celebrity and has significantly raised her public profile, helping to promote various projects such as *The Simple Life, Confessions of an Heiress*, jewelry lines, perfumes, clubs, video games, and even a music CD whose title song is "Screwed." Specifically, *One Night in Paris* offers both the illusory promise of discovering something beyond Hilton's public image and the desire to see someone of her economic standing humiliated through sexual objectification and exposure.

One of the most striking aspects of *One Night in Paris* is the surprising lack of intimacy on the tape. Rick and Paris do not share deeply personal sentiments (even when they use the word "love," which I will discuss later), nor do they seem invested in mutual pleasure. In fact, they mostly come across as two people with very different desires: Rick for voyeuristic sex and personal pleasure, Paris for posing before the camera and satisfying Rick by complying with his commands. Rick prods—and practically forces—her to perform for the camera and for himself, telling her to strip, to sit on his cock, to lie down, to open her legs, to show her "gorgeous pussy," and to perform fellatio ("suck it"); whereas Paris Hilton looks noticeably bored during intercourse—and heiresses should never be bored, right? This boredom clearly contrasts with the pleasure that she takes in being in front of the camera. Hilton continually seems to pose for and to be fully conscious of how her body is appearing on film. In the opening sequence of Salomon's thirty-eight-minute web version, for example, the camera shows a close-up of breasts and then gradually rises to reveal Paris Hilton's face. She then points the camera back onto her breasts, as if she is taking pleasure in recording herself for later viewing/consumption. This moment of posing, studying, and presenting her own body is when she seems most familiar and, sadly, most comfortable. It is a moment that encapsulates her public and, as suggested here, private life.[25]

After the opening shot of Paris's topless body, the tape cuts to approximately twenty minutes of explicit sex in the greenish hue of night-vision. Their glowing white eyes, which reflect the bright, unnatural light of the camera, and the grainy green-black color make them appear unreal and even ghoulish. These shots (many of which feature close-ups of penetration) could be of anyone; they are so close and/or distorted by the night-vision that they are difficult to "figure out" initially. Once again, this helps to keep Paris Hilton's body in the realm of the ambiguous, interpretable image. She is not individualized here; she is just a set of body parts on display: neck, breasts, back, vagina, legs, buttocks, etc. In fact, without the opening bathroom sequence, we couldn't be sure who is having intercourse. A few moments later, Rick orchestrates rear-penetration sex, setting up the camera on a nearby surface and ordering Paris into various positions. Her head is off-screen for most of this, except when Rick periodically stops to adjust the camera. During these breaks, Paris crawls into view to smile for the camera—a somewhat eerie image that seems more reminiscent of a photographic negative than a real person, as if her private, sexual life occurs in a kind of darkroom, a place where more poses and images are waiting to be produced for public consumption.

Only when Paris first climbs on top of Rick and faces the camera during intercourse do we get a sustained opportunity to watch Hilton's face. Here she seems utterly bored and far more interested in looking at the camera than in what Rick is doing beneath her. This boredom not only raises issues about the role of women's pleasure in pornography, but it also returns us to the importance of appearances for Hilton's persona. As Ariel Levy sarcastically points out in *Female Chauvinist Pigs: Women and the Rise of Raunch Culture*, "any fourteen-year-old who has downloaded her sex tapes can tell you that Hilton looks excited when she is posing for the camera, bored when she is engaged in actual sex. . . . She is the perfect sexual celebrity for this moment, because our interest is in the appearance of sexiness, not the existence of sexual pleasure."[26] This reading resonates with the portrayal of Hilton's celebrity in her photo-centric autobiography, which is about appearing to be a

glamorous, sexually accessible jet-setter and party girl; the pornographic overtones of the Carl's Jr. commercial (where the principal pleasure comes from being watched); her self-involved dancing in *The Simple Life*, and her highly staged romance with "Chops" on the same show. For Levy, Hilton's current cultural function is emblematic of a larger problem among young women today who embrace an overt and public sexualization of the body as a means for empowerment. This critique also resonates with Linda Williams's concerns about pornographic representations of female pleasure in her study *Hard Core: Power, Pleasure, and the "Frenzy of the Visible"*: "[Pornography has] long been a myth of sexual pleasure told from the point of view of men with the power to exploit and objectify the sexuality of women."[27] Both of these analyses point to problematic notions of power in relation to women's sexuality and the consumer marketplace. Exposing one's breasts on the pages of *Playboy*, for *Girls Gone Wild*, or in the context of a pornographic film, for example, does not empower women, yet many women embrace this kind of "raunch culture," as Levy calls it, to assert a certain degree of sexual and personal liberation. Certainly, Hilton has used this type of sexualized exposure to claim her independence from an aristocratic privilege and, by extension, her individuality.

Without a doubt, raunch culture has significantly contributed to Paris Hilton's fame, yet the power and pleasure in *One Night in Paris* center around Rick Salomon. His forceful, often degrading, treatment of Hilton completely plays into the socio-economic politics of the video and her public persona more broadly. The Paris Hilton of this video is submissive, easily embarrassed, and in many ways humiliated—a far cry from her aggressive pose in the 2000 *Vanity Fair* photograph "Sweetie Pie." Given her highly publicized place in America's hereditary aristocracy and her association with corporate culture, this is certainly part of the video's appeal. A quick search of recent pornography titles reveals numerous films that feature settings and/or characters associated with upper-class society and wealth: *Upper Class* (2002), *Rich and Horny* (2004), *Rich Girls Love Anal* (2004), *Filthy Rich* (2005), and not surprisingly, *The Not So Simple Porn Life*, Volume 1 (2005). In many ways, *One Night in Paris* can be read as contributing to this genre in that it casts such wealth in the context of pornographic fantasy. As one of the customer reviews of *One Night in Paris* on Adult DVD Empire suggests, the portrayal of the upper class in pornography is often linked to the pleasure of seeing degrading images of the rich: "No matter what, it's nice to know this little trust fund girl can take cock like a champ. It's too bad she takes a shot to the chest in the end, as a facial would have made this home porno even hotter. Buy this video . . . you will not regret it!"[28] Locker-room rhetoric aside, this endorsement suggests that the video's value comes, in part, from the revelation that "this little trust fund girl can take cock like a champ"; to see Hilton performing sexually, erodes some of the distance between her privileged, trust-fund life and her low-brow associations with pornography.

Likewise, Hilton's submissiveness to Rick Salomon contributes to the ways in which the video can be read in terms of humiliation—a pleasure presumably comes from seeing an heiress on her knees, so to speak. I'm not suggesting that pornography is synonymous with humiliation and the misogynistic objectification of women, though much of it does this. But the context surrounding the release of *One Night in Paris* and the ways in which we read Paris Hilton's celebrity and shameless self-promotion contribute to this reading. When Paris Hilton first learned of the tape, for example, she claims to have been heartbroken and humiliated:

> Someone sent it to me and I was, like, crying, I was so embarrassed. . . . It was humiliating . . . . I used to think it was so bad, but it's like, everyone has sex. I'm sure everyone has filmed a tape. It's not like it was some random person. I was in love with that man. I was with him for three and a half years. We were together.

I don't even really remember filming it, I was so out of it on that tape . . . He is making so much money. It makes me so mad. We were suing in the beginning, but everyone has already seen it. . . . . I don't want to go to court. He will fight me. I just want to get on with my life.[29]

Hilton highlights two issues here: her emotional and financial violations. On the one hand, she feels that the tape violates the private context in which it was filmed and the love she shared with Rick, who was married to someone else during part of this three-and-a-half year courtship.[30] On the other hand, Hilton expresses resentment about Rick's ability to profit from her image, which she feels more entitled to: "He is making so much money. It makes me so mad." Though she has repeatedly claimed that she doesn't earn anything from the sale of the tape, her lawyer, Peter Lopez, has stated otherwise, explaining in a 2005 interview that Paris does, in fact, receive profits from the tape.[31] Regardless, the link between the emotional heartbreak of this exposure for Hilton and the financial exploitation that resulted makes any viewer a participant in this dual violation. We are, in effect, investing money in witnessing and perpetuating this humiliation of Paris Hilton.[32]

The absence of Hilton's own sexual (and arguably emotional) pleasure in *One Night in Paris* can largely be attributed to Rick Salomon's degrading and humiliating treatment of her. Throughout the video, he refers to Hilton as a "bitch," "a fucking scumbag," "a beautiful beast," and "an animal"; even though some of these labels are presented playfully (he doesn't seem capable of speaking without giggling), the terms are degrading nonetheless. At one point, Hilton even protests: "Don't talk to me like I'm an animal." Yet this protest doesn't change Rick's behavior, which is increasingly domineering and objectifying, or hers, which is increasingly compliant. This animalistic and abusive language also undermines the rhetoric of love in the video. At one point, Paris asks Rick to say "I love you," and he only does so because he wants her to show him her "pussy" ("You'd better show me that fucking pussy right now"). He then offers a disingenuous "I love you," mimicking her voice and immediately asking, "Can I please take off your pants?" In fact, Rick Salomon's use of "love" only occurs in tandem with either an objectifying comment about her body, a self-congratulatory remark about his penis, or in the midst of his own pleasure (specifically when she performs fellatio on him at the end of the video). These proclamations of love are ultimately undercut by this behavior, and one never gets the sense that Rick actually loves Paris. Though a certain degree of truthfulness can be heard in Hilton's voice when she proclaims her love for him, these words cannot be understood apart from the sexual gambit that is going on here. Rick is only willing to give her what she wants (a verbal statement of love) for sex. This fairly conventional, almost clichéd division—a woman desiring emotional fulfillment and a man desiring physical gratification—fits into the misogynistic undercurrent the runs throughout *One Night in Paris* and adds another layer to the humiliation that can be read into it.

Prior to the final scenes of missionary sex and fellatio, Paris removes her panties for him (and the camera) while sipping from a bottle of wine and holding it between her legs. At one point, Rick asks, "Are you going to sit on that bottle?" A few moments later his penis will substitute for the bottle that has been between her legs and in her mouth. In the meantime, we watch Paris Hilton on the divans and plush chairs of the elegant hotel room, wearing a black bra and holding that bottle. The white wine and the rest of the furniture function, to some extent, as props for her wealth and class. This isn't Motel 6, and they aren't drinking beer. Normally, this setting would require money to get access to, but through this video, the viewer gets intimate access both to this affluence and Hilton's body. As Rick proceeds to put his penis inside her, first pressing her legs against his chest as she lies on the bed beneath him and then rolling her over, she moans more in pain than pleasure, and says

repeatedly that it hurts. Unlike the closing minutes of the video, which provide a close-up of her fellatio, this sex is about not Rick's pleasure but his control. It is a control that comes from Rick's persistent objectification and his forcefulness—he slaps her buttocks during this sequence as well, insists that she loves his "big cock," and later presses her head onto his penis even after she protests that he is choking her ("Sorry," he says with a trademark giggle. "I was sort of trying to [choke you]."). It is this kind of dominance that *One Night in Paris* invites and enables us to participate in. It is this kind of dominance that mitigates what is alien, elite, and inaccessible about Hilton's vast fortune and her place of privilege in American society.

Notes

1. Nancy Jo Sales, "Hip-Hop Debs." *Vanity Fair* (September 2000): 378.

2. Sales, "Hip-Hop Deb," 381.

3. Leo Braudy, *The Frenzy of Renown: Fame and Its History* (New York: Oxford University Press, 1986), 9.

4. Paris Hilton and Merle Ginsberg, *Confession of an Heiress: A Tongue-in-Chic Peek Behind the Pose* (New York: Fireside Books, 2004), 6.

5. Reported in Sales, "Hip-Hop Debs," 352.

6. Braudy, *The Frenzy of Renown*, 5.

7. In many ways, Paris Hilton comes across as incapable of privacy—to such an extent that she has reportedly claimed to be so accustomed to being photographed that "she hears clicking noises even when there are no cameras." This quote comes from paparazzo photographer Ron Galella. See Krista Smith, "The Inescapable Paris," *Vanity Fair* (October 2005): 284.

8. It is also worth mentioning that almost all of the bodies in the photograph are fragmented in some way or another, the image is cropped to remove the heads of three of the men, to show only the leg and hip of another man at the far right, and to cut off the bottom part of Paris's right leg. Each of the surfers also shares the same basic shape and build, and the two

male faces that are visible have strikingly similar features (dark eyes as well as dark, shoulder-length hair). These details—particularly the group of indistinguishable men whose partial bodies suggest that there are more of them staring at her off camera—imply a desire for Paris Hilton that is infinitely reproducible.

9. Sales, "Hip-Hop Debs," 378.

10. Marshall, *Celebrity and Power,* 24b.

11. Jared Bernstein, Elizabeth McNichol, and Karen Lyons, "Pulling Apart: A State-by-State Analysis of Income," *Economic Policy Institute* (January 2006): 4, http://www.epinet.org/content.cfm?id=2246.

12. Bernstein, McNichol, and Lyons, "Pulling Apart," 11.

13. Founder and former president of the Economic Policy Institute, Jeff Faux spoke at this conference and warned of impending "political unrest." For more on this, see Andrew Leonard, "Class Warfare, Anyone?" Salon.com. http://www.salon. corn/tech/htww/2006/01/24/faux/index.html/. Steven Pearlstein of *The Washington Post* sees the need for "fundamental tax reform" (including "a reasonable inheritance tax") as a far cry from "class warfare." See Steven Pearlstein. "Solving Inequality Problem Won't Take Class Warfare," *The Washington Post,* March 15 2006, DO1. And for a critical response to the Economic Policy Institute's report, see Tim Kane, "Income Relativism," *National Review Online,* January 30, 2006, http://article.nationalreview.com/?q=ZmVjZD120TYZTdiYTEwOWViNDViyzdiYzY0OTC=.

14. Kevin Phillips, *Wealth and Democracy* (New York: Broadway Book, 2002), 124.

15. Ibid., 392.

16. *Cool Hand Luke,* DVD, directed by Stuart Rosenberg (1907; Los Angeles, CA: Warner Home Video, 1997).

17. Smith, "The Inescapable Paris," 288.

18. In September 2004, another sex tape featuring Hilton started circulating on the internet. This video featured Hilton "with Nick Carter, a former member of the band Backstreet Boys, and Jason Shaw, a Tommy Hilfiger model." See Ariel Levy, *Female Chauvinist Pigs: Women and the Rise of Raunch Culture* (New York: Free Press, 2005), 28.

19. To see these comments, visit the PTC website at: http//www.parentstv.org/ptc/advertisersasp.

20. I am borrowing this phrase from Ariel Levy's *Female Chauvinist Pigs: Women and the Rise of Raunch Culture,* which I discuss later in the essay.

21. Walter Kendrick, *The Secret Museum: Pornography in Modern Culture* (New York: Viking Press, 1987), 95.

22. Rick Kushman, "Paris Hilton and the Future of Advertising," *Sacramento Bee.* June 7, 2005, Entertainment.

23. Kendrick, *The Secret Museum,* 281.

24. This number does *not* include the version sold via the internet by Rick Salomon, the co-star, prior to his deal with Red Light. According to *The New York Times,* this video also received an award from "a porn industry trade group for Top Selling Title of the Year in 2005." See Lola Ogunnaike, "Sex, Lawsuits, and Celebrities Caught on Tape," *The New York Times,* March 19, 2006, sec 9: 1.

25. Not surprisingly, this moment will be repeated at the end of the night-vision sequence, operating both as a frame device for the first part of the tape and as marker that divides the night-vision segment from the footage filmed in color. It is frame that blurs the line between Paris Hilton's private and public life, suggesting that in both spheres she is preoccupied with presenting herself for public consumption.

26. Levy, *Female Chauvinist Pigs,* 30.

27. Williams, *Hard Core,* 22.

28. This customer review, "Cum for Paris, Stay for Porn," was posted on June 14 2004 by Master Lang.

29. Quoted in Smith, "The Inescapable Paris," 288.

30. Salomon was married to Shannen Doherty briefly between 2002–2003.

31. See Ogunnaike, "Sex, Lawsuits and Celebrities Caught on Tape," *The New York Times,* March 19, 2006, sec 9.

32. In January 2005, Paris Hilton was so upset about the video that she reportedly stole a copy from a street vendor in Hollywood. See "Paris Hilton Cleans Up Smut Shop," UPI, February 2, 2005.

The Pornography of Everyday Life[1]

Jane Caputi

The subject of sexualized degradation flooded world consciousness after May 2004, when trophy photos that American soldiers took of their abuse of Iraqi prisoners at Abu Ghraib prison were released to the public. They showed Iraqi men stripped, bound, and forced into situations both sides believed to be denigrating—simulating homosexual sex, acting like animals, posing for sexual display, and wearing women's underwear on their heads. In one photo, naked men are made to pile on top of one another, with their buttocks in the air. Standing nearby, smiling and giving a "thumbs-up" gesture, are a male and a female soldier. Shocked and appalled, many recognized the behavior in these photos as sexual torture.

What was not widely acknowledged, however, was how often we see women being posed and treated in precisely these ways, not only in pornography but also in fashion magazines, music videos, and advertising. And these are not generally perceived as humiliation and torture; rather, they are perceived as "sex." For example, a photo in an issue of *Vibe* magazine (which appeared before the release of the Abu Ghraib photos) is structured around a scene that is eerily similar to one I just described. Two Black men are seated at a bar. To their left, a Black woman in a very short skirt and stiletto heels bends over the bar, exposing her "panties" and baring part of her buttocks. One grins widely and the other gives a "thumbs-up" gesture. Just recently, an ad for a new TV action series shows a White man posing on a ladder leading up into a helicopter. He stares out with an expression as firm as his chin; his outstretched hand brandishes a big gun. Higher up on the ladder, we see a White woman getting into the helicopter. Well, we don't really see her—just her bare legs, red stiletto heels, and the red dress clinging to her bent-over buttocks. In both of these displays, it's not hard to figure out who is in charge and who is the "butt" of the misogynist joke.

As these examples indicate, this article is not about X-rated porn. Rather, it is about a "habit of thinking" (Williams, 1995, p. 123), an everyday pornographic discourse (including words and pictures) that sexualizes denigration and domination as it also genders it, with "the man" being the one on top, and the objectified, exposed, and denigrated one on the bottom being "the woman" (even when sometimes a woman plays the masculine role and vice versa).

Catharine MacKinnon and Andrea Dworkin (Dworkin, 1989, pp. 253–275) originally shifted the debate around pornography from the issue of "morality" to one of power relations. In so doing, they define pornography not as all sexually explicit materials but only those that enact "the graphic, sexually explicit subordination of women" or men, children or transsexuals "used in the place of women." Their extended discussion delineates specific elements, including women being put into "postures or positions of sexual submission, servility or display," "scenarios of degradation, injury, abasement, torture," and "dehumanizing objectification." Pornography, in this view, is not about the "joy of sex" but about the domination and "denigration of women and a fear and hatred of the female body" (Kaplan, 1991, p. 322).

My plan in this chapter is to criticize select popular representations that transmit and normalize this pornographic paradigm. Some readers might see them the same way I do; others might not. Popular culture is not monolithic, and representations are open to interpretation. My intent is to suggest that the pornographic "habit of thinking" underlies and supports oppressions, including not only sexism but also homophobia, racism, colonization,[2] and violence against the Earth, elements, and creatures. Pornography is everyday, not just in the sense that coded versions of it populate mainstream images but also because its precepts underlie mainstream ideas and practices.

Gender Pornography

Mainstream heterosexual pornography is founded in very conventional notions of gender: Women and men are said to be opposites and unequal, with specific gendered attributes such as masculine aggression and female-identified passivity. However different and unequal, the story goes, men and women still are (and should be!) attracted to each other—and *only* to each other. These gender norms thereby sexualize inequality, domination, and even violence and are reflected in conventional representations of "ideal" *straight* (in the senses both of heterosexual and noncomic) couples. In these, the man is upright, taller, stronger, richer, older, bolder, and colder—in short, more powerful. The woman is reclining or constrained. She is "put down" (often literally on the floor) or constrained (often, literally up against a wall) and is shorter, weaker, vulnerable, younger, and warmer—in short, socially powerless.

Calvin Klein ads, for example, are especially known for their erotic charge. Consider a 2007 ad for CKIN2U fragrance. It shows a young White couple in an amorous situation. They are posed up against a gray concrete wall. He is taller and leaning over her, while her back is against the wall. His left hand presses into the wall, while his right tugs on her long hair. His look is determined, while hers is dazed. Both wear jeans, but hers are low cut and a good deal of skin is showing. His belt is undone and her hand is wrapped limply around its end. The situation is clearly sexual, but with an obvious power differential. He seems determined to get "into her," but she is largely passive. Moreover, she is backed up against that unyielding barrier. The phrase "up against the wall" means literally to be trapped, cornered, and put into a situation with no escape and no options. Pressure and coercion, not consent, is the sexually charged dynamic here.

This same version of power-over sex is obvious in another fragrance ad from the same year. This one is for "Sean Jean Unforgivable Woman," a product line created by hip-hop star P. Diddy Coombs. An African American couple is featured in what appears to be a sexual situation, once again with a wall as backdrop. This time, the man (Coombs) crushes the woman, whose back is to him, up against that wall. Both of his arms are around her, holding her there. In profile, her eyes are closed, her right arm flails back as if in futile resistance. The perfume's name, "Unforgivable Woman," implies that she has done something to deserve this sexualized punishment. When taking in such images, we should know that two to four million women are victims of domestic violence every year in the United States, that rape is a core element in that abuse, and that Black women experience domestic violence at a rate 35% higher than that of White women and about 2.5 times the rate of women of other races (Rennison & Welchans, 2000).

The normalcy of male sexual domination of women is assumed, even when there seems to be a challenge. A photo illustrating a 2007 *Cosmopolitan* article (Benjamin, 2007) shows a woman lying on top and clearly over a man in bed. The theme of the piece is that some men entertain a fantasy of a girlfriend playing the role of "boss lady" in bed. But nothing is really that different here. The sexuality is still focused on domination and submission, and his "boss lady" fantasy is something "secret," to be enacted only "every once in a while" and only in the bedroom. Proper gender roles remain in place: The onus is placed on the woman to fulfill the man's fantasies.

Violence Porn

Slang words for sexual intercourse equate it with violence: *fucking, nailing, screwing, banging,* and so on. Implicit in this is the idea that it is the man (or masculine-identified partner) who is doing the "fucking" and the feminine-identified partner who is getting "fucked." Hegemonic masculinity demands that "real men" must have no trace of what is defined as "feminine," and this is one of the principal bases of homophobia as well as sexism. When boys and men sexually harass other boys and men with words, they call them *woman, whore, pussy, bitch,* as well as *sissy, faggot,* and *punk,* putting them in the place of the woman. To reclaim heterosexuality and manhood, men have to assert domination, most efficiently and most effectively by being violent (Gilligan, 1997).

A 2009 ad for Dockers enacts this scenario by showing a male figure from the top of his head to his knees. From the waist down, he is wearing the Dockers. Above, an outline of his body is filled in by a stream of words scolding men and proclaiming that a "genderless" society has stripped them of their manhood and left them "stranded on the road between boyhood and androgyny" (Wear the Pants Dockers, 2009). Dockers demands that men "answer the call of manhood," t[ake] charge, and "WEAR THE PANTS." This is a resounding call for gender conformity and sexist dominance. In mainstream culture, men who cross-dress can be acceptable if they present themselves as obvious comic characters, whose maleness, as well as heterosexuality, is still apparent; otherwise, they are subjected to mockery. Cross-dressing women, as long as they are clearly feminine, seductive, often partly undressed, and heterosexually coded, can be presented as titillating. If not, they too are punished (more on this later).

Dockers' mandate to "wear the pants" also intends to make us think of what is inside the pants and fall prey to the pornographic notion that the penis inherently is an instrument of violence. Male heroes in popular culture invariably are pictured not only wearing pants but also wielding weapons, the bigger the better. In Freudian psychoanalysis, as well as popular understandings, these weapons are phallic symbols. One of the more unnerving instances of this theme can be found in an illustration for an article on male infertility that appeared in a 2007 edition of *Details* magazine. It shows a large and fully loaded handgun aiming directly at the viewer. The headline reads, "Why Isn't Your Wife Pregnant Yet? Alarming new infertility research says you may be shooting blanks." Another penis-gun parallel appeared in a photo illustrating an article on male athletes and guns in *Vibe*. It showed the naked torso of a well-muscled Black man. Protruding from the top of his red sweatpants is the head of a pistol (the barrel, obviously, occupies the same space as his penis).

Rape Porn

In pornography, sexualized domination is enacted via explicit scenes of rape, bondage, abuse, and torture. In everyday porn, these same behaviors are suggested with varying degrees of subtlety. Sharon Marcus (1992) argues that a "rape script" is coded into the ways that our culture habitually represents men's bodies as penetrating, powerful forces (weapons) and women's bodies as inner spaces that can be invaded and owned, without will or capacity for violence, including defensive violence.

These themes inform a 2007 ad for business loans offered by J. P. Morgan Chase set in a dress store. A young, demure Asian woman stands, holding a sign at womb level reading "OPEN," her eyes and head downcast. Flanking her are frocks, draped on headless mannequins. The woman, too, is for sale; she is completely available, has no sovereign will (indicated by her lowered, submissive gaze) and no voice to protest (the headless mannequins). A 2005 ad for St. Pauli Girl beer draws on that same rape script and indicates that alcohol facilitates the process: "It's hard to get some girls to open up. Others just need a bottle opener."

One of the most extreme, and notorious, rape-friendly ads is one for Dolce & Gabbana (D&G) that appeared in 2007. It shows a blank-looking White woman in a bathing suit pinned to the ground by one White man, while four others look on. International protests ensued for its too obvious suggestion of gang rape, and D&G pulled the ad. Within a year, the same company again took up this theme, again with an all-White group, though this time with a young man as victim. There was no widespread protest. Due to homophobia and gender norms, the subject of male-on-male rape is still so locked up in taboo that any outcry was foreclosed.

Everyday Child Porn

When women demand and express their intellectual, sexual, and emotional freedom, society responds with both overtly woman-hating representations as well as the increased sexualization of children. In pornography, women are marked with clothing and hairstyles to suggest that they are children or teenagers (Jensen & Dines, 1998, p. 87). Everyday porn also shows women in poses and clothing that suggest they are little girls. An ad for Akademiks jeans arranged a Black woman, on her knees on the floor. Her thumb is posed in front of her mouth, as if she were about to begin sucking on it, and she looks around to seductively gaze at viewers. Her hair is in pigtails; she wears only high heels, a pink sweater, and a pair of underpants, with *akademiks* emblazoned across the rear. A 2009 ad for Juicy Couture arranges two adult White women on the floor, dressed in childish hats and dresses and staring out with a blank gaze suggesting passivity, trauma, or mental incompetence.

THE PURE AND THE DIRTY

Porn enthusiasts unhesitatingly recommend that porn stay "dirty" and stress that it must continually break new taboos to remain exciting. Although many think that pornography and religious moralism or "family values" are opposites, this is not the case. Rather, mainstream porn shares with patriarchal religion not only the idea of sex as "dirty" but other fundamental beliefs, including that women are inferior to and in service to men, and a mind-body split, which deems sexuality to be spiritless and mindless (all body) and thought to be ideally emotionless or objective (no body).

A sexual double standard is derived from these ideas, one that allows men greater sexual latitude, defines women in relation to men, and splits women into pure or dirty, "virgins" or "whores," "keepers" or "trash," good "goods," or "damaged goods," often along race and class lines. An ad for liquor shows two women, one Asian wearing black, the other White, blonde, and wearing a white dress. They are in front of a mirror, and the Asian woman, applying lipstick, appears to be gazing directly at the viewer. She is labeled a "man eater," while the White woman, staring off blankly, is a "vegetarian." "Bad girls" are defined as "others"—treacherous, dirty, hypersexual, not properly feminine, fit only for prostitution and pornography.

These notions of purity and dirtiness underlie not only sexism but also racism and homophobia. Those who claim to be the most "pure" tend to project all that they deny and fear in themselves onto people whom they then classify as "dirty," "savage," and so on. One ad for soap (1995) shows an upright, young blonde White woman in a white blouse, alongside the word *PURE*. It looks, on one hand, like an endorsement of female chastity. On the other, it might remind us of a neo-Nazi poster evoking racist notions of "purity" of blood. Of course, patriarchal and racist cultures severely police women's chastity to ensure children's "legitimacy" and "purity," paternally and racially.

Distorted notions of purity and dirtiness also are used to foment and justify homophobia and transphobia. In March 2005, an extraordinary interfaith alliance of male religious leaders in Jerusalem formed to try to stop an international gay pride festival in Jerusalem. One Islamic leader stated the group's aim: "We can't permit anybody to come and make the Holy City dirty" (Goodstein & Myre, 2005). A 2004 ad for gum makes a similar point. It shows a young White woman, with short brown hair, minimal makeup, and wearing a button-down shirt and tie. A sewer cover is shoved into her mouth. The copy reads: "Dirty Mouth, Clean it up with Orbit." The implication here is that it is the cross-dressing/lesbian woman who is dirty and should be abused, silenced, and "cleaned up."

OBJECTIFICATION

Patriarchal definitions of women as property and commodities are behind the sexual objectification of women, along with an ensuing alienation from the human body, with its individual and changeable nature. A 2008 ad for a center for cosmetic surgery shows an Asian woman naked except for fetish-wear underpants. Lines are drawn from key zones of her body, indicating where she has been worked on, for example, "breast augmentation." The headline,

addressing male viewers, claims, "WE CAN REBUILD HER." The unmodified female body is a turn-off to a pornographic culture steeped in misogyny, body loathing, and the technological "fix."

To objectify someone is to deny them autonomy and to use them as a tool for your own purposes, to act as if they are a thing that you own, to make them into a kind of replaceable commodity (Nussbaum, 1999). Numerous images do this overtly by blending women into literal things— furniture or vehicles, as in a 2006 ad for the Ford Fusion that showed a Black woman's heavily made-up face merging with the car, her eye becoming one of the headlights.

The classic symbol of objectification is the doll, mannequin, or "fembot," which appears in advertisements for everything from antidepressants to window treatments, sports gear, and liquor. A 2007 Heinecken television commercial, which retains a following on YouTube, features a platinum blonde, White-skinned robot who dances, sprouts an additional set of mechanical arms, and produces from her torso a keg of Heinecken, from which she pours a glass of beer and offers it to viewers. She then splits into three identical models. Here is the ultimate sex object—fungible, decorative, entertaining, and with no possibility of a will of her own, existing only to serve. Numerous YouTube commentators affirm their sexual attraction to this robot, one (Dominatorxxx) deeming her the "perfect woman."[3]

"Perfection" actually characterizes pornographic objectification's exact fit with a capitalist consumer society. Sexuality conflated with objectification leads to an inability to relate or connect. It then can be manipulated and channeled into a desire to acquire things, and when these don't (as they can't) really satisfy, the consumer can throw them away and get new things.

SLAVERY PORN

The institutionalization of sexualized domination historically began with the establishment of slavery at the inception of patriarchal organization (some five to seven thousand years ago) when elite men enslaved women from conquered groups (Lerner, 1986). Later, they also enslaved subordinated men. Enslaved men could be and sometimes were raped by masters and mistresses, but for women, "sexual exploitation marked the very definition of enslavement" (Lerner, 1986, p. 89).

Patricia Hill Collins (1990) argues that the history of racist enslavement and attendant sexual exploitation of African American women forms a "key pillar on which contemporary pornography rests" (p. 168). In the United States, White slaveholders and masters put naked Black people on display on the auction block and treated them as commodities for purchase, justifying this by saying Africans were more animal than human (all within a belief system that says that animals are inferior to humans). They bound, gagged, and whipped those they enslaved, routinely raping the women and some of the men. These themes are reproduced in pornography and everyday pornography. One 1995 ad for Moschino clothing shows a dark-skinned woman in animal prints against a pink fabric background. Her arms and legs are outspread, and she wears a dazed expression. Looking closely, you can see that she actually is stapled to the fabric, like a doll, or a slave awaiting purchase.

Bondage literally means a state of enslavement. A fashion jewelry spread in *Jamaque* magazine (2009) showed a light-skinned woman, naked and seated on the floor with her back to the viewer. A necklace is draped over her shoulder blades, while two jeweled bracelets hold her hands behind her buttocks as if she were handcuffed. A 2007 ad for Intel informed by an outrageous fantasy of sexual/racial dominance is set in a workplace. An ordinary, clothed White man stands upright in the middle of the room; on both sides, heavily muscled and dark-skinned Black men in skimpy spandex athletic-type suits bow down to him.

Some of these sexually racist themes show up not only in White but also in Black popular culture (Cole & Guy-Sheftall, 2003; Collins, 2004). Janell Hobson (2005, p. 102) argues that many music videos and concerts pornographically "overexpose black female rear ends," much in the ways that 19th-century European culture fetishized the buttocks of Sara Baartman, who was dubbed the "Hottentot Venus" and stripped and displayed for profit. One video, "P-Poppin" by Ludicris, is built around a strip club. Marcus Flowers, a community educator at an Atlanta organization, Men Stopping Violence, critiques it: "The way that the women are paraded in front of fully clothed customers, their bodies for sale, reminds me of how half-naked slaves were exhibited to white buyers at auctions, as if they were animals" (Mendez Berry, 2005, p. 166). Of course, animals shouldn't be treated that way either. Many ecofeminist thinkers (e.g., Adams, 2003; Collard, 1988) argue that the ways that an oppressive culture treats women and other oppressed groups are directly related to the ways that it treats nonhuman nature, including animals.

SNUFF

In the February 2009 issue of *Details,* a photograph illustrating a story about dating during the economic recession showed a White woman turned upside down and dumped in a garbage can. All we can see is her high-heeled feet and legs, jutting up in the air. Similarly abusive images are just as common in women's popular publications. In *Cosmopolitan's* November 2009 issue, the illustration for an article on "26 Ways to Make a Fresh Start" showed a White woman's black-stocking-clad legs and high-heeled feet jutting up into the air from the seat of a couch. The rest of her body had been buried into the space between the cushions and the back of the couch. This theme of women's severed legs waving in the air is a common one. When Juergen Teller photographed Victoria Beckham in an ad for Marc Jacob's designs, he didn't present her as a glamorous celebrity but as something less than human, a kind of dismembered "living doll" (Horyn, 2008). In one photo, we see only her bare, high-heeled legs flopping spread-eagled over the side of a shopping bag.

Symbolic dismemberments have long been the norm in fashion photography (Caputi, 1987) and usually are not recognized as such, so habituated are we to them. We might notice them if they were being done to male bodies, but they are not in any comparable way.

An extreme form of violent pornography is the snuff film or photograph, which documents someone actually being murdered. A "virtual snuff" sensibility informs countless fashionable images that have appeared in advertising and fashion tableaux since the 1970s. Models are showcased in positions suggesting that they are dead: suffocated under plastic bags; heads without bodies, bodies without heads; laid out in gift boxes; sprawled brokenly on stairs, streets, and boutique floors. A 2004 ad for Giuseppe Zanotti shows the body of a thin White woman, on her back and clothed in fetish lingerie, dumped into a car trunk. Her head disappears; her torso and what might be prosthetic legs are stretched out for display.

So normalized has the image of a murdered woman become that "America's Next Top Model," in a 2008 show, asked contestants to pose as victims of violent death.[4] Monica Sjöö and Barbara Mor (1991) suggest that such tortured and mutilated "images. . . . of female flesh . . . are really our species' maps of the mutilated earth" (p. 411). A 2009 ad for Global Fruits juice shows the Earth being compressed and squeezed dry by a pair of male hands. Paralleling the abused images of women in our popular culture are countless such images of the Earth carved up, strangled, objectified, targeted, and otherwise violated (Caputi, 2004).

ALTERNATIVE VISIONS

A 2007 ad for Chanel lipstick shows a partial image of the bottom of a White woman's face. Stretching across her mouth is a gold chain with a large pearl in the middle, held just between her teeth. This jewelry item looks like, and is being used as, the kind of a gag that uses a ball to force the mouth open and to silence the one who is gagged (such a gag appears in the "torture-porn" film *Hostel*). This image sums up pornographic intention to keep women (and those used in the place of women) *open* for violation and at the same time to *shut* them up—silencing not only speech but also a resistant imagination.

So imbued is the pornographic worldview, it is extremely difficult to imagine a sexuality outside of it. This inability to imagine an alternative is itself an effect of abuse. Violence, including violence in intimate relationships, does not always take the form of physical blows. Abuse takes an emotional/psychological form as well, one that is meant to destroy the self-esteem of the victim while enhancing that of the abuser. It appears as verbal assaults, belittlement, cultivation of anxiety and despair, humiliation, blaming, accusation, denigration, disrespect, and reality control, which includes denying the harm of the abuse, creating an atmosphere of threat, and blocking awareness of alternative ways of living and being.

Repeated, negative mass representation of a group is a public form of psychological abuse. It too serves as a form of destruction meant to squelch resistance and destroy self-esteem. It, too, feeds the sense of omnipotence of the dominators. And it, too, serves as a form of reality control. It tells us that this is the only world possible, blocks awareness of alternative ways of living and being, and stifles the development of an imagination other than the pornographic one.

Numerous theorist/activists counter with alternatives. Sharon Marcus (1992) celebrates a discourse of the female body/mind as no longer "object, property, and . . . inner space" but as powerful, capable of will and even violence. bell hooks (1993) asks heterosexual women to cease sexualizing the dominating "hard man" and to eroticize, instead, equal and respectful relationships. Patricia Hill Collins (2004) puts forth an ethic of "honest bodies that are characterized by sexual autonomy and soul, expressiveness, spirituality, sensuality, sexuality, and an expanded notion of the erotic as a life force" (p. 287).

Collins draws on poet Audre Lorde (1984), who extols what she calls the "erotic," a cosmic force of connectivity and creativity that courses through unfettered sexuality as well as creative work and play. The erotic rejoins body and mind, sex and spirit and is, Lorde claims, our birthright, our bodily access to forces of creativity, ecstasy, and connection, and also the energy source that enables us to resist oppression and transform ourselves and our world.

In ancient understandings, the erotic as a cosmic creative force was represented by the figure of a (Sex) Goddess, sometimes a bisexual divinity. She is pictured variously as naked, surrounded by animals or herself part animal, and with spread legs to signify the vulva as sacred and powerful. Patriarchal religions came to power, in part, by defaming and profaning that Goddess and ultimately turning her into pornography (Caputi, 2004). Susan L. Taylor (2006), former editorial director of *Essence* magazine, proclaims that now is the time for "Goddess to awaken from patriarchy's trance." She claims that this happens every time "women step into our power." Some will resonate with this symbol; others will generate new ones. This is as it should be, for diversity—as well as fun, pleasure, joy, care, freedom, and respect for others—is fundamental to the erotic principle.

Notes

1. My film, *The Pornography of Everyday Life,* distributed by Berkeley Media (www

.berkeleymedia.com), incorporates much of this material. This article is an updating and revision of my article "Everyday Pornography," which appeared in the earlier edition of this anthology. I also draw on several other pieces, including one in Caputi (2004). I thank Lauren Walleser, Ann Scales, Mary Caputi, Peter Cava, Andria Chediak, Rebecca Whisnant, Nicole Calvert, and many students who gave me some of these materials and/or discussed them with me.

2. Andrea Smith (2005) provides insightful analysis on issues of sexualized invasion and the ways that notions of purity and filth are manipulated to further colonization and genocide.

3. Ad and comments at http://www.you tube.com/watch?v=1 -NfrBgYIEQ (last visited January 24, 2010).

4. You can view pictures from the show and read a transcript at www.zap2it.com/news/custom/ photogallery/zap-photogallery-antm8-crime scenevictims,0,698280.photogallery (last visited January 24, 2010).

References

Adams, C. (2003). *The pornography of meat.* New York: Continuum.

Benjamin, J. (2007, September). The sex he secretly craves. *Cosmopolitan.*

Caputi, J. (1987). *The age of sex crime.* Bowling Green, OH: Bowling Green State University Press.

Caputi, J. (2004). *Goddesses and monsters: Women, myth, power and popular culture.* Madison: University of Wisconsin Popular Press.

Cole, J. B., & Guy-Sheftall, B. (2003). *Gender talk: The struggle for women's equality in African American communities.* New York: Ballantine.

Collard, A. (with Contrucci, J.). (1988). *Rape of the wild: Man's violence against animals and the Earth.* Bloomington: Indiana University Press.

Collins, P. H. (1990). *Black feminist thought: Knowledge, consciousness, and the politics of empowerment.* New York: Routledge.

Collins, P. H. (2004). *Black sexual politics: African Americans, gender, and the new racism.* New York: Routledge.

Dworkin, A. (1989). *Letters from a war zone.* New York: Putnam.

Gilligan, J. (1997). *Violence: Reflections on a national epidemic.* New York: Random House.

Goodstein, L., & Myre, G. (2005, March 31). Clerics fighting a gay festival for Jerusalem. *New York Times.*

Hobson, J. (2005). *Venus in the dark: Blackness and beauty in popular culture.* New York: Routledge.

hooks, b. (1993). Seduced by violence no more. In E. Buchward, P. Fletcher, & M. Roth (Eds.), *Transforming a rape culture.* Minneapolis: Milkweed.

Horyn, C. (2008, April 10). When is a fashion ad not a fashion ad? *New York Times.*

Jensen, R., & Dines, G. (1998). The content of mass-marketed pornography. In G. Dines, R. Jensen, & A. Russo (Eds.), *Pornography: The production and consumption of inequality* (pp. 65–100). New York: Routledge.

Kaplan, L. J. (1991). *Female perversions: The temptations of Emma Bovary.* New York: Doubleday.

Lerner, G. (1986). *The creation of patriarchy.* New York: Oxford University Press.

Lorde, A. (1984). *Sister outsider.* Trumansburg, NY: The Crossing Press.

Marcus, S. (1992). Fighting bodies, fighting words: A theory and politics of rape prevention. In J. Butler & J. W. Scott (Eds.), *Feminists theorize the political.* New York: Routledge.

Mendez Berry, E. (2005, March). Love hurts: Rap's 'Black Eye.' *Vibe,* pp. 163–168.

Nussbaum, M. C. (1999). *Sex and social justice.* New York: Oxford University Press.

Rennison, M., & Welchans, W. (2000). *Intimate partner violence* (NCJ 178247). Washington, DC: U.S. Department of Justice, Office of Justice Programs, Bureau of Justice Statistics.

Sjöö, M., & Mor, B. (1991). *The great cosmic mother: Rediscovering the religion of the Earth* (2nd ed.). San Francisco: Harper SanFrancisco.

Smith, A. (2005). *Conquest: Sexual violence and American Indian genocide.* Boston: South End Press.

Taylor, S. L. (2006, October). The goddess within. *Essence.*

Wear the Pants Docker. (2009, December 6). *New York Times.*

Williams, P. J. (1995). *The rooster's egg: On the persistence of prejudice.* Cambridge, MA: Harvard University Press.

List of Advertising Images Discussed Above

1. Royal Elastics, 2005, source unknown.

2. http://www.antiwar.com/news/?article id=8560, last visited January 24, 2010.

3. Love's "Baby Soft," Love Cosmetics, 1975, source unknown.

4. "Bottoms UP," Photograph by Natasha Papadopoulou, *Vibe,* ca. 2002.

5. Ad for Human Target, *New York Times,* January 3, 2010.

6. CKIN2U, appearing in *Cosmopolitan,* 2007.

7. Sean Jean Unforgivable Woman, 2007. You can see the ad and read feminist commentary at http://shake spearessister.blogspot.com/2007/09/ assvertising_21.html, last visited January 24, 2010.

8. Wear the Pants Dockers, © 2009 Levi Strauss & Co., *New York Times,* December 6, 2009.

9. Photograph by Greg Broom, *Details,* February 2007, http://www.details .com/sex-relationships/marriage-and-kids/200702/male-infertility-paranoia, last visited January 24, 2010.

10. Photographer unknown, *Vibe,* April 2009.

11. JPMorganChase, 2007.

12. St. Pauli Girl Beer, 2005, © Imported By Barton Beers, Ltd., Chicago, Illinois.

13. Dolce Gabbana, 2007. You can view the ad at www.adrants.com/2007/02/dolce-gabbana-ad-cartoonish-edginess-or-g.php, last visited January 24, 2010.

14. Dolce Gabbana, 2008. Can be viewed at www.bilerico.com/2008/06/dolce_gabbana_sells_gang_rape.php, last visited January 24, 2010.

15. Steve Madden, ca. 2005.

16. akademiks, appearing in *Vibe,* ca. 2005.

17. Juicy Couture, *New York Times Style Magazine,* Holiday, 2009.

18. Love's Baby Soft, Love Cosmetics, 1975.

19. Hennessy [Vegetarian/Maneater], © 2001 Schiefflin & Somerset Co., New York.

20. "Pure," © 1994 Neutrogena Corp.

21. Diesel, source unknown, ca. 1994.

22. "Dirty Mouth," © 2004 Wm. Wrigley Jr. Co.

23. Hustler, 2005.

24. Cesare Paciotti, 2009.

25. New Beauty Center, *Ocean Drive,* September 2008.

26. Ford Fusion, advertisement, *Vibe,* March 2006.

27. Heinecken ad, 2007, http://www.youtube.com/watch?v=1-NfrBgYIEQ, last visited January 24, 2010.

28. Moschino, *Elle* magazine, © 1999.

29. *Jamaque International Magazine,* vol. 2, #1, 2009. http://www.jamaquemagazine.com/v1/, last visited January 24, 2010.

30. Intel ad, 2007. You can view at (http://gizmodo.com/284037/intel-ad-might-be-racist-but-boy-does-it-make-me-want-a-core-2-duo), last visited January 24, 2010.

31. Photograph by Matthew Donaldson, *Details,* February 2009.

32. Photographer unknown, *Cosmopolitan,* November 2009.

33. Photo in *New York Times,* April 10, 2008, accompanying the article by Horyn.

34. Giuseppe Zanotti Designs, advertisement, *In Style,* March 2004.

35. Global Fruits, *Backpacker Magazine,* 2009.

36. Chanel, Inc.

"There Are Bitches and Hoes"

Tricia Rose

One of the signature icons that drives commercial hip hop is the pimp. An important facet of urban street cultures and illicit economies, and once relegated to folklore, underground vernacular culture, and the margins of mainstream society, pimps have become popularized and mainstreamed. Building on the glamorization of black pimp culture in blaxsploitation films of the 1970s and on the influence of raw sexual hierarchies exported from prison culture, many rappers began drawing from pimp culture, style, slang, and attitude as part of their identities. Rappers such as Too Short, Snoop Dogg, Ice T, now deceased Pimp C, Dr. Dre, David Banner, 50 Cent, Nelly, and Lil' Pimp brag about controlling women like pimps, being stylish like pimps, and about being pimps themselves; promote pimp-based products (e.g.. Nelly's energy drink, Pimp Juice); and elevate former pimps like the Archbishop Don "Magic" Juan to cult-like status. Pimp culture has saturated commercial hip hop. As T. Denean Sharplev-Whiting has put it: "The 'g's up, ho's down mentality of late 1980s hip hop laid the groundwork for the pimp-playa-bitch-ho' nexus that has come to dominate hip hop." Strippers and groupies, already praised and demeaned for their sexual actions, are now also being promoted and contained within this pimp-ho framework. Pimping style and attitude have migrated into other facets of mainstream popular culture, such as the car-customizing show *Pimp My Ride,* "Pimp and Ho" Halloween and theme parties, the film *Hustle and Flow,* and cable network programming exposing pimp culture. Pimping is everywhere these days.[1]

Despite the cuddly, fuzzy-hat image of pimps in some mainstream outlets and celebrated films like *Hustle and Flow* that attempt to generate sympathy for pimps, pimp ideology and its expression in popular culture are fundamentally exploitative to women. Dominating prostitutes and living off of their sex work, street pimps use physical violence (including rape) as well as emotional and psychological manipulation to control prostitutes. Phrases like Snoop Dogg's famous rap lyric "Bitches ain't shit but hoes and tricks" capture pimps' fundamental attitude: Women are bitches, and bitches are whores and prostitutes.

From Rose, T. (2008). "There are bitches and hoes." In *The hip-hop wars* (pp. 167–185). New York: Perseus.

Taking a brash attitude in defense of these exploitative terms, most defenders of this trend in hip hop rely on the idea that they are talking about a reality of life and dare people to deny it. . . .

Some hip hop artists defend their endless self-aggrandizing talk about dominating "bitches and hoes" by saying that they are not talking about all women. But "bitches and hoes" are all the women they talk about. The valorization of the gangsta and pimp also highlights and celebrates the very women they degrade, encouraging young women fans to emulate the behaviors of "bitches and hoes" to get attention, to be desired, and to be considered sexy. Bitches and hoes get all the attention in hip hop. Of course, many women participate in the videos and other aspects of the culture that demeans them—and female fans emulate these behaviors, too. Some point to women's cooperation with sexism in hip hop to say that it cannot, therefore, be that bad and that women must not really mind. While being a black gangsta is the primary means of gaining recognition, money, and fame for males in hip hop, behaving in hyper-sexual ways is, for some women, the only means of making any gains at all. Men have gangs, drug dealing, and pimping; sex is the street economy open to women. Pointing to women's participation in a system that exploits them to prove it isn't sexist falsely assumes that sexism is sexism only when all women label it so. It also denies the power of socialization in creating our collusion with social relationships that hurt us. Again, since sexism socializes all men and women, we have to work against it; being anti-sexist doesn't come naturally in a system that rewards us for participating.

Because street culture and the exploitative culture on which it is based have become such key sources of black identity in the hip hop generation, many young black women parrot the sexist ideas that are so widely circulated in hip hop; it's a key to belonging. For many young black women,

the language of commercial hip hop about black sexuality has influenced their understanding of black women, not just reflected it. Sexism works best when women are isolated from and pitted against one another (as detailed in the song "Bitches and Sisters"). Isolation and conflict ensure that they will sustain and internalize the terms of insult and control used to keep things as they are. Women are rewarded by men for participating in this system.

Young women are also coerced into participating by the dictates of record-industry marketing. As noted by Glen Ford, a veteran radio and rap video programmer and current executive editor of the *Black Agenda Report,* the consolidation of these limited identities is directly related to corporate pressure:

> The term "street" became a euphemism for a monsoon or profanity, gratuitous violence, female and male hyper-promiscuity, the most vulgar materialism, and the total suppression of social consciousness. A slew of child acts was recruited to appeal more directly to the core demographic. Women rappers were coerced to conform to the new order. A young female artist broke down at my kitchen table one afternoon, after we had finished a promotional interview. "They're trying to make me into a whore," she said, sobbing, "They say I'm not 'street' enough." Her skills on the mic were fine. "They" were the A&R [Artists and Repertoire] people from her corporate label.[2]

Some young women who are angered by this hyper-sexism speak out, but many do not. To be publicly and strongly against sexism in the music industry is to guarantee one's marginality. And to challenge sexism in the black community (as in larger society) is to discourage public support; in fact, doing so is often perceived as an anti-black community action and can make one a target. For black women—who are already marginal in larger society—taking a stand in a way that might alienate them from their local community is painful and difficult and often not worth it. So, instead, there is a great deal of silence or skirting of the issue, as black women try to find ways to manage what is a hurtful, insulting, and discriminatory language of belonging. One such way is to agree that "there are bitches and hoes." . . .

The constant public labeling of black women in hip hop as "bitches and hoes" has forced young women to stake out a position. Some embrace "bitch" as a term of empowerment and also try to reverse the sexual-power exchange, calling men "hoes." Women who use "bitch" in this subversive way are trying to challenge the language of sexism; men who use "bitch" are ultimately supporting such language. Many women and girls say that since they are not "bitches and hoes," these rappers are "not talking about me" because I don't "behave that way." So, "it doesn't impact me." In some cases, this kind of distorted self-defense is a valiant but tragic effort to pretend that such labeling is not hurtful to all women no matter how one acts. It's often a matter of survival to craft this defense, as the distinction is mostly a fiction. In the film *Hip Hop: Beyond Beats and Rhymes,* Byron Hurt makes the following point to a young woman who tries to use this defense: "It's funny when I hear women say, 'when these rappers are calling women bitches and ho's, they're not talking about me." It's like, yo, they *are* talking about you. If George Bush was to get on national TV and make a speech, and he started calling black people niggers, would you be like, 'I don't know who George Bush is talking about, but he ain't talking about me?" . . .

Although the roots of the common portrayal of black women as ugly, aggressive, and hypersexual were formed long ago, there is a more recent term that bears importance here. The term "welfare queen," coined by Ronald Reagan in the 1980s, typecast poor black women on welfare as sexually irresponsible, money-hungry and lazy. To drum up support for drastic reductions in public welfare assistance, those who used this term accused economically limited black women of manipulating and cheating the welfare system by having babies to increase their welfare assistance payments. The label "welfare queen" relied on the already sedimented idea that black women are sexually deviant and untrustworthy. Now, as the term implied, they were whoring themselves for state assistance.

This kind of racist and sexist name-calling is pretty similar to what Snoop claims about the "bitches and hoes" in his 'hood: "that ain't doin' shit, that's trying to get a nigga for his money." It's just that he says he has a right to do it because he knows them from personal experience. Snoop's attitude about poor black women isn't any better than that of many of the conservatives who attack him.

Snoop's "I know them from personal experience" defense also uses a racial authenticity argument to justify his sexism. Snoop and many other multi-platinum rappers from tough, poor black and brown neighborhoods continue to *choose to represent a sexist perspective about reality they no longer have.* There are many men and women in the 'hood who don't hold his sexist views, and he can't legitimately rely on his so-called reality to justify his own perpetuation of this image of black women. After several years of hits and celebrity living and socializing out of the 'hood, traveling the world, and having access to nearly any and all manner of ideas, knowledge, and new forms of socialization, to act as if they have no meaningful relationship to women beyond the ones they call "bitches and hoes" is ridiculous. Like they still live in a rented apartment in the 'hood and a brigade of money hungry black women are figuring out ways to take their riches?

Rappers are not under assault by black women whose behavior they don't like. The gangsta rapper image *needs* "bitches and hoes," and so they continually invent them. Women, so labeled, add lots of status and value to gangsta and pimp images. If you can't have lots of women serving and servicing you, then how can you be a real player, a real pimp? So, the process of locating, labeling, partying with, and then discarding black women is part of the performance that enhances gangsta- and pimp-style rappers' status and, thus, their income. If, as Jay-Z raps in "99 Problems," "I got 99 problems but a bitch ain't one," then why bother telling us about her inability to give him problems—unless controlling bitches is part of his power? Similarly, Snoop and other rappers at his level don't have any reason to fraternize with women whom they feel are out to "take their money." So, if they're "just keeping it real," then they need to stop pretending that they are victims of black women out to take their money. That's nonsense. If they're so good at identifying women they insist should be called bitches and hoes, then it shouldn't be too hard to stay away from them. And, if they're able and want to stay away from them, then there's no reason to rap about them constantly.

I'm not saying that all women are above criticism. But if people want to challenge someone's behavior because they don't like it, they should talk about the behavior and say why it's problematic rather than using generalized, sexist, or racist language and labeling. The culture of women's sexual behavior promoted by hip hop videos shapes the actions of young black women in ways that will bring them attention and status. So, in a sense, hip hop is becoming a "bitches and hoes" factory, encouraging girls and young women to play the limited roles assigned to them.

Conservative responses to hyper-sexual popular culture usually involve an anti-sex agenda, one that functions to contain women's sexuality while failing to fight sexism or to work toward women's overall freedom. Rappers and corporate industry representatives highlight the sexually repressive tone and agenda of conservative attacks on hip hop in order to encourage women's complicity with their own exploitation. Indeed, the two positions—sexual exploitation and sexual repression—are birds of a feather. I am not interested in a less sexually open society or in sexual censorship, and I am not against sex workers or a gender-equal sex industry that protects women's rights and work conditions. Rather, I am concerned about black women's overall freedom and equality. This involves genuine sexual freedom of expression—not freedom of expression tied to sexist male fantasies or to male-dominated sex trades in which women are demeaned and degraded in order to appear to be sexually free. Nor does it involve women's sexual repression—a returning to sexual determination of women through sexual repression in the interests of patriarchal male control. Sexual explicitness does not have to be sexually exploitative. If we don't make this distinction when we fight against the constant barrage of "there are bitches and hoes," then we wind up with a sexually repressive call for less sexuality.

The problem in commercial hip hop as it has evolved over the past fifteen years is that terms of sexual exchange are now so exploitative and overarching that nearly everyone is cast as either a player (the one in control) or the one getting played (the one being dominated). Women are nearly always on the latter end of this exchange and their only way out is to either confine their sexuality or try to become players. Those who reverse the terms and do try to become players are often relabeled "bitches and hoes" who are "trying to take a nigga's money." So, either way, they lose. This blending of sexual explicitness with sexual exploitation is hurtful and destructive for black women and for black male/female relationships and the black community generally.

So, although hip hop isn't primarily responsible tor America's sexism, it is the most visible and extreme engine for it in black popular culture, which means that it has a special impact on black women and men who, because of the racist and sexist world in which they live, rely on black culture as a source of reflection, support, and affirmation. This is one key reason why it's important to make sure that black popular culture is not overrun by the worst forms of domination and inequality. Making sexism sexy only makes life harder for everyone, especially black women and others in the black community who already have too many unfair hurdles to overcome.

Instead, let's demand that empowered women be in charge of their own sexual imagery and give them the freedom to express themselves as they see fit. There is no evidence that most young women want to replace the more sexually explicit brand of sexism they currently manage with a repressed version of sexism. This less-repressed one gives them more day-to-day freedom, even though it is often highly exploitative. The anti-sex agenda of many conservatives is unappealing, disempowering, and uninterested in promoting women's rights or fighting sexism.

We have to work hard against what destroys who we are, what prevents us from reaching our best selves and stalls our efforts to create a truly just society. Many of the artists and executives who deflect legitimate criticism with the kinds of excuses presented here defend their constant use of highly insulting racist and sexist ideas about black women while profiting from it. We need to understand the roots of sexist images and work to reduce their impact, visibility, and perpetuation everywhere, not only in hip hop. We also have to confront the reason why these images are so successful as products sold to millions of people from all racial backgrounds. . . .

When asked about their lyrics, many rappers respond to the terms set out by conservatives who attack them, not to the many black women who have generally supported hip hop but find this escalation of highly destructive imagery a problematic betrayal. The fact that conservatives attack male rappers doesn't mean that these rappers' lyrics and their too-easy defense of their portrayals of black women are worthy of progressive defense. Save the defense for the young men and women who are willing to stand up for what is right, not for those who pander to what is clearly wrong and unjust because "it's the way it is," "other people do it," "I get unfairly attacked for it," and "conservatives don't understand or like it." We can attack the conservatives about plenty of issues, but we shouldn't marshal black people's solidarity in the service of defending sexist attacks on black women. Not in hip hop, and not anywhere else.

Notes

1. T. Denean Sharpley-Whiting, *Pimps Up, Ho's Down: Hip Hop's Hold on Young Black Women* (New York University Press, 2007), p. xvii.

2. Glen Ford, "Hip Hop Profanity, Misogyny and Violence: Blame the Manufacturer," available online at www.peaceandjustice.org/article.php/20070507114621137/print.

Three Faces of Eva

Perpetuation of the Hot-Latina Stereotype in *Desperate Housewives*

Debra Merskin

One of most popular network television programs to come along in years, *Desperate Housewives* (*DH*), enjoys a viewership of more than 21 million women and men (Arthur, 2006, p. E5). In its 9:00 p.m. Sunday nighttime slot, *DH* presents the intimate lives of five attractive women living in a middle-to-upper-middle-class neighborhood somewhere in America. One of these women, Gabrielle Solis (played by Eva Longoria) is Latina. At first blush, hers appears to be a breakthrough role in terms of media representations of Latinas. Visibility as a lead character in a highly successful television program is a rarity for Latino women and for men. Unfortunately, however, a critical reading of the program shows that the opportunity to advance the image of Latinos is lost, as dialogue, the presentation of Gabrielle, and the off-screen life of Longoria fulfill Keller's (1994) tripartite typology of Latina stereotypes (Cantina Girl, Suffering Señorita, and Vamp). . . .

In a "cultural climate where Latinas are hot and hot Latinas are on fire," *DH*'s Eva Longoria sizzles (Papps, 2005, p. 21). As Wisteria Lane's hoop-earringed hottie, Gabrielle Soles, Longoria's role as well as her public personae consistently present the entire spectrum of the hot Latina stereotype.[1] Longoria's prime time pinup status and promotional positioning in magazines reinforce the already prominent, oversexed, under-dressed decisive and divisive character she embodies on *DH*. . . . The steamy similarity in character and promotion of Longoria/Solis is seamless. . . .

From Merskin, D. (2007). Three faces of Eva: Perpetuation of the hot-Latina stereotype in *Desperate Housewives. Howard Journal of Communications, 18*, 133–151. Reprinted by permission of Taylor & Francis Ltd.

Latina Stereotypes in U.S. Popular Culture

During the 1920s through 1940s, Latina stars such as Carmen Miranda broke through racial/ethnic barriers to celebrity and success in U.S. popular entertainment. Yet, the physical and performative requirements for success simultaneously established not only the Latina "look" in film, but also the look as a symbol of lower social class. Carmen Miranda ("the lady in the tutti-frutti hat"), Dolores del Rio, and Lupe Velez (the "Mexican Spitfire"), projected not only exotic, inviting, and flamboyant sexuality, but also a particular social class look derived from a perceived ethnicity. In 1945, Carmen Miranda, for example, was America's highest paid woman (O'Neil, 2005). Her fame, however, carried a high price, as fruit-feted hats, an accent thick as picante, and ever-zanier roles undermined whatever strides she had taken for Latinas in Hollywood (O'Neil, 2005). . . .

Stereotypical behavioral characteristics assigned to Latinas include "addictively romantic, sensual, sexual, and even exotically dangerous" (Mastro & Behm-Morawitz, 2005, p. 125), self-sacrificing, dependent, powerless, sexually naive, childlike, pampered, and irresponsible (Arredondo, 1991; Gil, 1996; King, 1974; Lott & Saxon, 2002). Stereotypical Latinas "all make good domestics," mispronounce words, speak Spanish, are Catholic, are impulsive dancers, and are known for "cooking up a spicy storm" (Cofer, 2005, p. 247)—not only in a culinary sense. Comprised of "bright colors, rhythmic music, and olive or brown skin," Latina tropicalism erases differences between specific Latino groups and conflates characteristics of people from African, Caribbean, and Latin American cultures into a single, pan-Latino/a identity (Guzmán & Valdivia, 2004, p. 211). . . .

Keller (1994, p. 40) organized these stereotypes under three categories which "epitomize the range of representations of women in Hispanic" and Anglo television and film.

1. *Cantina Girl.* "Great sexual allure," teasing, dancing, and "behaving in an alluring fashion" are hallmark characteristics of this stereotype. She is most often represented as a sexual object, a "naughty lady of easy virtue" (p. 40).

2. *Faithful, Self-Sacrificing Señorita.* This woman usually starts out good, but goes bad by the middle of the film or television program. This character realizes she has gone wrong, and is willing to protect her Anglo love interest by placing her body between the bullet/sword/posse/violence intended for him.

3. *Vamp.* Whereas Cantina Girl is most often presented physically as an available sexual object, the Vamp uses her intellectual and devious sexual wiles to get what she wants. She often brings men to violence and enjoys doing so. She is a psychological menace to males who are ill equipped to handle her.

Keller (1994) noted that the three major stereotypes function mainly in relationship to an Anglo love interest. Sex, passion, manipulation, and physical beauty are common to each of the characters, who are coded with particular types of clothing, postures, motivations, speech, and behavior. This portrait epitomizes stock Latina attributes that set the stage for the character of Gabrielle to appear (to Anglo audiences) as natural.

Although all of the women on *DH* are, in some way, sexual, Gabrielle's libido is on fast-forward in a way different from the highly sexual Edie, for example. Susan (Teri Hatcher) is meek; Lynette (Felicity Huffman), mother of four, avoids sex so as not to get pregnant again; and Bree (Marcia Cross), described as "Martha Stewart on steroids" is repressed. Edie (Nicollette Sheridan) is single and uses sex to get what she wants in a somewhat mindless and obvious manner, whereas Gabrielle is tactical, risky, and sensual (shown in her bra and panties or tiny teddies) and iconicized in the larger-than-life portrait that hangs above the Solis's fireplace.

The character Gabrielle and the actor Eva Longoria present a mediated, pan-ethnic identity in the process of "tropicalization" (Aparicio & Chavez-Silverman, 1997). Both the role and the public appearances are consistent with one another. Through these representations, both as character and celebrity, Gabrielle/Eva becomes a key tropicalizer, embodying panethnic traits of Latinidad that draw from and affirm dominant stereotypes of Latina-ness. . . .

Spicy Paella

Most of the characters on *DH* enter *tabla rasa*. In nearly every episode, drop by delicious drop, the characters' personalities blossom, their pasts are slowly revealed, and, however tarnished, their true natures shine through.

In the show's pilot (Cherry & McDougall, 2000) episode, Whiteness is established as the central signifier of culture on Wisteria Lane. In this episode the viewer first meets Gabrielle Solis, as the camera pans to her from a handsome Hispanic man we later come to know as her husband, Carlos. In a skin-tight, slinky black dress, stunning jewelry, and spiky high-heeled shoes, Gabrielle carefully navigates the front steps, all while carrying a steaming dish. Gabrielle and Carlos are on their way to a wake for a friend (Mary Alice) who committed suicide (she becomes the disembodied, omniscient narrator/voice over for the show). The omniscient narrator (Mary Alice) introduces Gabrielle to the audience this way: "Gabrielle Solis, who lives down the block, brought a spicy paella."

In this introductory scene, we learn a lot about Gabrielle. She is immediately constructed as Latina in her dress, mannerisms, and by the food she contributes to the wake. We learn she married Carlos not out of deep love, but for economic reasons. That fact is no secret to Carlos who is well aware of, and takes seriously, this arrangement and his power to control it. Mary Alice tells the viewer, "Since her modeling days in New York, Gabrielle had developed a taste for rich food and rich men." We quickly learn that Gabrielle quit her high fashion modeling career (a form of bodily selling), with the understanding that Carlos would keep her bejeweled, pampered, and wanting for nothing. In return, she sleeps with him, makes herself available, and, because of her good looks, is an asset in his business dealings in the (implied) Anglo world. The audience is told, "Gabrielle liked her paella piping hot. However, her relationship with her husband was considerably cooler."

Gabrielle is Carlos's property. More than a trophy wife, more than arm candy, Gabrielle makes herself available for his use (at least initially). This arrangement is evidenced by his willingness to "pimp" her for his own gain, and her willingness to go along with it. As a Cantina Girl, she knows what she's got, and as a Vamp, she works it to her advantage. For example, before a party with one of his important clients, Gabrielle shouts that Carlos cannot order her around or force her to go:

Carlos: "It's business. Tanaka expects everyone to bring their wives."

Gabrielle: "Every time I'm around that man, he tries to grab my ass."

Carlos: "I made over $200,000 with him last week. If he wants to grab your ass, you let him."

Gabrielle has mixed feelings about their agreement and how things are turning out in her life. Later in the same episode, Gabrielle tells Carlos she hates the way he talks to her, to which he replies, "and I really hate that I spent $50,000 on a diamond necklace that you couldn't live without. But I've learned to deal with it." When Carlos apologetically gives Gabrielle a convertible with a big red ribbon on it, she says, "Carlos, what have you done?" He replies, "I saw it when I drove by the dealership. I thought, 'Gabrielle would look so beautiful in this.'" "Carlos!" she exclaims, playfully shoving him. Mary Alice's narration tells us "Gabrielle could see what this gesture had cost Carlos so *she responded the only way she knew how*" [italics added]. The scene ends with Gabrielle, in Cantina fashion, kissing Carlos, jumping up, and wrapping her legs around him. . . .

"To-be-looked-at-ness" is an important aspect of the construction of Gabrielle (Mulvey, 2001, p. 397). Her body is a central marker of Latinidad conflated with sexuality; therefore, her clothing is always bright and tight fitting, for example, to show off her toned and lithe body in a way that has "strong visual and erotic impact," connotes availability, and exudes willingness (p. 397). In Episode 17 ('Children Will Listen'), Gabrielle's priorities are reasserted: "There were many things Gabrielle Solis knew for certain. She knew red was her color. She knew diamonds went with everything, and she knew men were all the same."

The Cantina Girl in Gabrielle thrives on, and feels validated by, attention to her appearance. In nearly every episode she is shown working out, or on her way to, or back from, doing so. While Gabrielle wants her affair with John, her 17-year-old "gardening toy boy lover" (Papps, 2005, p. 21), to be a secret, she does not mind attention and admiration from others. For example, in Episode 4, she asks John, "Why are your friends staring at me? Did you tell them about us?" John exclaims, "No! They're staring because they think you're hot." Gabrielle replies, smiling, "Oh! Okay!" (Cherry, Spezialy, & Melman, 2004). In Episode 5 (Cunningham, 2004), Gabrielle's vanity is apparent when she assures her friend, Susan, that she knows when people aren't looking at her;

"Honey, trust me. When they're not staring at me, I notice." . . .

Promiscuity, passion, sex, and risk taking are characteristics of Gabrielle as her psychic (Vamp) personality emerges (Keller, 1994). For example, Gabrielle finds her encounters with John exciting, not only for the sex, but also because she is fooling Carlos, and is stimulated by fear of his wrath. She spites Carlos and his money when she lures John into the kitchen (while Carlos is outside examining the lawn; Papps, 2005, p. 21). John watches Gabrielle take off her blouse and lean back seductively on the kitchen table. She tells him the table is hand-carved, imported from Italy, and cost Carlos $23,000. John laughs and asks her, "So you wanna do it on the table this time?" Gabrielle replies, "Absolutely."

In order to keep her affair with John going, yet secret, Gabrielle vacillates, and sometimes sacrifices for Anglo love interest John (as Carlos suspects it is not the garden John is tending). In the middle of the Tanaka party, for example, Gabrielle-the-Vamp makes sure her husband is well supplied with alcohol, and rushes home to mow the lawn herself. Wearing an elegant evening gown and spiky high heels, the Suffering Señorita pulls the lawnmower out of the garage and, under cover of darkness, frantically mows, rushes back to the party, no worse for wear (except for the telltale leaf she removes from her hair, moments before returning, flirtatiously, to her husband's side). . . .

During the first season of *DH*, the Gabrielle Solis character transmogrifies from Cantina Girl, to Suffering Señorita, to Vamp. In the process, she does not lose any of the characteristics of the individual types: rather, as her character develops, the trio comes together, as she becomes a fully realized hot Latina stereotype.

In her public life, the actor Eva Longoria picks up where Gabrielle leaves off. In her off screen appearances, Longoria, the "Latina temptress" (Papps, 2005, p. 21), does little to dispel a view of her behaviors, attitudes, and beliefs as identical to Gabrielle's.

For example, in a magazine interview (in which she was later proclaimed the number 1 out of 100 sexiest women), Longoria said, "There's something very sexy about being submissive. Because your guard is down, you have to totally surrender to something like that" (Maximonline.com, 2003, ¶3). She plays the fantasy card when she admits she dresses a lot like her on-screen role: "I wear G-strings every day, all the time. I actually don't even own a full-bottom pair of under-wear. I also love lingerie, and I love high heels, but I prefer total nakedness overall. That, to me, is so much sexier" (Maximonline .com, 2003, ¶3).

Because I'm Worth It

In late 1990s publicity, celebrity A-lister Jennifer Lopez stated she is an "actress who is Latin—not a Latin actress, as in one who just does Latina roles" (Beltrán, 2002, p. 77). While this might have been part of a public relations strategy to position Lopez as an actor, moving away from pre-vious publicity about her buttocks,[2] Longoria, in contrast, presents a public and media persona consistent with her hot Latina *DH* role. In an interview, Longoria responded to the question "What's the best thing about being a woman?" in a way consistent with Keller's (1994) stereotypi-cal "triplets" in her *DH* role:

> Everything, everything. The sexiness that we get to exude. The femininity of hav-ing soft skin. The desire of always want-ing to be pretty and put on make-up and wear heels. I love being a woman. I love shopping. I love wearing dresses and heels and jewelry. I love being sexy and feeling sexy. But the best thing about being a woman is the power we have over men. (oyemag.com, 2005)

In a *Rolling Stone* interview, Longoria was described as "the hottest, juiciest of the Wisteria Lane housewives," who, "when she isn't shopping or mowing the front lawn in a pink party gown, she's doing the nasty with her seventeen-year-old hunk of a gardener." In response to the question, "What was the best sex you had all year?" she replies, in Gabrielle-esque vamp form,

> Probably with my vibrator. I own two. I have the rabbit one, and I give that as a gift all the time to other girls for a birthday or the like. It's the best gift to give: an orgasm. And if I can't do it for ya, I'll give you the tools to succeed! I have one rabbit and a Pocket Rocket. (Hedegaard, 2005)

Longoria's sexy girl-ness transcends her role in *DH* in the advertising arena. Wearing a black skin-tight, criss-cross backed evening gown she longingly and liq-uidly lounges on a white bedspread, slither-ing forward and rolling from stomach to back, extolling the virtues of L'Oreal's VIVE shampoo. This commercial is the first among many she will do as the first and only Latina spokes model for the world's largest cosmetic company (Foster, 2005, p. 30), as she lends her name and body to the beauty product monolith's array of goods (L'Oreal, 2005). Longoria went with the company because, "L'Oreal is one of the few companies that really reflect my values. Their company philosophy and their leg-endary phrase 'Because I'm Worth It,' go hand-in-hand with who I am as a person. This is it, the best, the culmination of an amazing year" (Femalefirst.com, 2005).

Thirty-year-old Longoria "joins a bevy of beauties" who have contracted with L'Oreal, including Andi MacDowell, Beyonce Knowles, and Jennifer Aniston (Fashionspot.com, 2005). Although Longoria may have fol-lowed Aniston's footsteps to the door of the house of L'Oreal, it was for Aniston's bed-room she volunteered her services. Intended as humor, in light of publicity surrounding the Jennifer Aniston/Brad Pitt split (allegedly over Aniston's unwillingness, and Pitt's desire, to have children), Longoria joined other American women in donning a pink "I'll have Brad's babies" t-shirt. Friends and fans were shocked by Longoria's lapse in judgment. She later apologized for the display of poor taste and the insult to Aniston. What is interesting, however, is that Longoria was keeping in character by playing the happy-when-pregnant, hot Latina, Cantina Girl stereotype.

Longoria's public appearances do much to bolster her onscreen role. Voted by *Variety* as one of the "Ten New Faces of Fall" (quoted in torontofashion.com, 2004), she extends her seductive reach to daytime and evening (mostly female) viewing audiences, with an appeal (and giggle) that will inevitably include men. Good marketing? Sure. However, as predicted by Accumulation Theory (DeFleur & Dennis, 1998), the combination of on-screen, off-screen, and in-print activities work to reinforce the hot Latina stereotype. In an interview, in defense of her role and as a response to criticism of perpetuating Latina stereotypes, Longoria stated:

> I don't think they're detrimental. It's great to be represented in any way. Ricardo Montalban said something about that in the documentary, *The Brown Screen*. He said, "What's wrong with being a Latin Lover? Why is that a bad stereotype? I consider that a compliment." Same thing with Latinas always being cast as the sexy girl. It's a good thing! (oyemag.com/eva.html, 2005)

Discussion

... Based on this analysis, the role of Gabrielle Solis (Eva Longoria) contributes to and perpetuates long-standing stereotypes of Latinas in American movies and television programs as identified by Keller (1994). Longoria's off-screen activities and antics further reinforce and conflate the character with the person. It is often difficult to determine whether the media are referring to Longoria's character or to her as celebrity when they describe her as a "firecracker" (Fernandez, 2004, ¶32), a "hot tempered siren" (Wittstock, 2005, ¶12), and one of the "titular horny homemakers" (FHM.com, 2004, ¶1). Referring to Longoria's "coverage" in its October 2004 issue, *FHM* magazine states, "Given the theme of Eva's new show, it seemed only appropriate that the 29-year-old's *FHM* photo shoot involved doing domestic work in her delicates. 'It wasn't a new experience—that's standard operating procedure in my household,' she says. 'Who doesn't do housework in their underwear?'" (FHM.com, 2004). ...

The representational politics of Gabrielle/Eva position the Latina character in a way that functions to provide justification for a narrow perception, resulting in a continuation of the hot Latina stereotype. This "mainstreaming" of stereotypical images exists in a climate that supports hegemonic ideals of Anglo (White) heterosexual, male privilege (Gerbner, Gross, Morgan, & Signorielli, 1994). As it largely remains unchallenged by alternative portrayals, the Hot Latina stereotype takes on the appearance of naturalness. ... The character Gabrielle Solis and the actor Eva Longoria conflate in the public eye, as both on-screen and off-screen women are consistent with one another. If Anglos, by way of media-supplied information, come not to expect much of Latinas and, because of the function of internalized oppression, Latinas do not expect much for themselves, the cycle of oppression continues uninterrupted. ...

Notes

1. In this chapter, the terms *Hispanic, Latino,* and *Latina* are used interchangeably as is consistent with marketing, media, and government terminology (Davila, 2002).

2. She made this announcement before *Maid in Manhattan* (2002) was released.

References

Aparicio, F. R., & Chavez-Silverman, S. (1997). *Tropicalizations: Transcultural representations of Latinidad.* Hanover, NH: University Press of New England.

Arredondo, P. (1991). Counseling Latinas. In C. C. Lee & B. L. Richardson (Eds.), *Multicultural issues in counseling: New approaches to diversity* (pp. 143–156). Alexandria, VA: American Association for Counseling and Development.

Arthur, K. (2006, March 28). *Housewives* carries ABC. *New York Times,* p. E5.

Beltrán, M. C. (2002). The Hollywood Latina body as site of social struggle: Media constructions of stardom and Jennifer Lopez's 'Crossover butt.' *Quarterly Review of Film and Video, 19,* 71–86.

Cherry, M. (Writer) & McDougall, C. (Director). (2004). Pilot [Television series episode]. In M. Cherry (Executive Producer), *Desperate Housewives.* American Broadcasting Company.

Cofer, J. O. (2005). The myth of the Latin woman: I just met a girl named Maria. In R. Riske-Rusciano & V. Cyrus (Eds.), *Experiencing race, class, and gender in the United States* (4th ed.) (246–248). Boston, MA: McGraw Hill.

Cunningham, A. (Writer). Come in, Stranger. [Television series episode] In M. Cherry (Executive Producer), *Desperate Housewives.* American Broadcasting Company.

Davila, A. (2002). *Latinos Inc.: The marketing and making of a people.* Berkeley: University of California Press.

DeFleur, M. L. & Dennis, E. E. (1998) *Understanding mass communication* (6th ed.). Boston: Houghton Mifflin.

Fashionspot.com. (2005). *Eva Longoria signs with L'Oreal* (online). Retrieved July 30, 2005, from, http://www.thefashionspot.com/forums/archive/index.php/t-24613.html

Femaletirst.com. (2005). Desperate Housewives *Eva Longoria face of L'Oreal.* Retrieved July 29, 2005, from http://www.femalefirst.co.uk/fashion/5582004.htm

Fernandez, M. L. (2004, September 5). Desperation row [Electronic version]. *L.A. Times.* Retrieved April 20, 2005, from http://www.geocities.com/Hollywood/4616/lat0905b.html

FHM.com (2004). *Eva Longoria* [Electronic version]. Retrieved April 20, 2005, from http://www.fhmus.com/girls/covergirls/290/

Foster, L. (2005, April 13). Former Gucci team links with Lauder. *Financial Times,* p. 30.

Gerbner, G., Gross, L., Morgan, M., & Signorielli, N. (1994). Growing up with television: The cultivation perspective. In J. Bryant & D. Zillmann (Eds.), *Media effects: Advances in theory and research* (pp. 43–67). Hillsdale, NJ: Lawrence Erlbaum.

Gil, R. M. (1996). Hispanic women and mental health [Electronic version]. In J. A. Sechzer, S. M. Pfafflin, F. L. Denmark, A. Griffin, & S. J. Blumenthal (Eds.), *Women and mental health* (pp. 147–159). *Annals of the New York Academy of Sciences, 789.*

Guzmán, I. M., & Valdivia, A. N. (2004). Brain, brow, and booty: Latina iconicity in U.S. popular culture. *The Communication Review, 7,* 205–221.

Hedeggard, E. (2005, December 15). Eva Longoria: A year of 'sex' for the *Desperate Housewives* star [Electronic version]. *Rolling Stone.* Retrieved June 5, 2005, from http://www.rollingstone.com/poylongoria/?rnd=1126115925047&has-player=true

Keller, G. D. (1994). *Hispanics and United States film: An overview and handbook.* Tempe, AZ: Bilingual Review/Press.

King, L. M. (1974). Puertorriquenas in the United States: The impact of double discrimination. *Civil Rights Digest, 6*(2), 20–28.

L'Oreal. (2005). Retrieved August 20, 2005, from lorealusa.com

Lott, B., & Saxon, S. (2002). The influence of ethnicity, social class, and context on judgments about U.S. women. *The Journal of Social Psychology, 142,* 481–499.

Mastro, D. E., & Behm-Morawitz, E. (2005). Latino representations on primetime television. *Journalism and Mass Communication Quarterly, 82*(1), 110–127.

Maximonline. (2003). Girls of *Maxim*. Retrieved from http://www.maximonline.com/girls_of_maxira/html/girl_1021.html

Mulvey, L. (2001). Visual pleasure and narrative cinema. In *Media and cultural studies: Key works* (pp. 393–404). Malden, MA: Blackwell.

O'Neil, B. (2005). Carmen Miranda: The high price of face and bananas. In V. L. Ruiz & V. S. Korrol (Eds.), *Latina legacies: Identity, biography, and community* (pp. 193–208).

Oxford, England: Oxford University Press.

oyemag.com. (2005). Eva fever. *Open Your Eyes*. Retrieved July 10, 2005, from http://www.oyemag.com/eva.html

Papps, N. (2005, April 10). The Latina temptress, *The Sunday Telegraph*, p. 21.

Torontofashion.com (2004). Ten new faces of fall. Retrieved March 8, 2005, from toronto.fashion-monitor.com/news.php/news/2005041001eva_longoria

Wittstock, M. (2005). Mothers of suburbia [Electronic Version]. *Observer/Guardian*. Retrieved March 8, 2005, from http://observer.guardian.co

The Limitations of the Discourse of Norms

Gay Visibility and Degrees of Transgression

Jay Clarkson

Painful.

Both my partner and I are totally straight-acting, very masculine, and when we're in mixed company with someone who's . . . um . . . well, let's just say they open their mouth & their purse falls out, well, we get rather uncomfortable.

Case in point: a big get-together of a bunch of friends last year at the local Macaroni Grille (chain Italian restaurant). Thing is, this is suburban Detroit, not the Castro, and a table full of fourteen guys in a busy restaurant full of middle-class families might get noticed of its own accord!

Add in one of our friends, let's call him "Bill." Not his real name. Bill's 23, lives at home, has no responsibilities, and is finishing up interior design school. He's emaciated thin; we think he lives on ice chips, Dolce & Gabbana anything, and Swarovski crystal trinkets. Both he and another member of our crew decided that this would be the perfect place to turn up their flames from "dull glow" to "viewable-from-space." It was all I could do not to either 1. smack him or 2. flee the building.

Because my one pet peeve, more than anything else with regards to gay men (besides the idiots who believe that HIV is a curable disease and therefore don't use protection) are fags who don't recognize the conditions of their environment. There's a time to flame out (greeting friends in the gay bar) and a time to tone it down (the sideline at an NFL game). Boys who don't change their temperament in accordance with their conditions endanger themselves and those they're with, in my opinion. (roadster_guy)

At the heart of the politics of gay representation are two intersecting considerations: the meanings and functions of visibility, and the role of gender performance in our understanding of sexuality. This chapter continues the discussion of gay visibility and gender transgression that

From Clarkson, J. (2008). The limitations of the discourse of norms: Gay visibility and degrees of transgression. *Journal of Communication Inquiry, 32*(4), 368–382. Published by Sage Publications, Inc.

has emerged as a key concept in recent scholarship of GLBTQ (gay, lesbian, bisexual, transgender, and queer) representation in the media. I explore the discourse of the discussion board of StraightActing.com, an Internet discussion board for self-identified straight-acting gay men, to demonstrate how current popular understandings of representational power create divisiveness among groups of gay men who seek to normalize a particular set of gender performances as acceptably gay, at the expense of other performances perceived as more transgressive. . . .

The discourse of visibility on Straight Acting.com is useful because the online space functions for self-proclaimed straight-acting gay men to make themselves visible to other gay men. Their discussions include significant debate about the nature of their and other gay men's visibility, of which I have chosen a representative sample. Their discourse mirrors critical understandings of the power of visibility and gender transgression. They demonize an effeminate gay stereotype, which they perceive as dominating media representations of gay men, because they fear that it functions to construct a normative gay identity that is promoted by other gay men and can only be undone with increased visibility of straight-acting gay men. . . . Their argument assumes that transgressive gender performance, not just same-sex desire, is the root of antigay attitudes. Homophobia in this formulation is reduced to a fear of particular gender performances, and not a deeper cultural fear of same-sex attraction. The visibility of straight-acting gay men, or men who cannot be read as gay, may challenge the notion of a hegemonic and monolithic gay identity, but they reflect the historic need for the marginalized to remain obedient, silent, and invisible in order to be recuperated into dominant ideologies (Owen, Vande Berg, & Stein, 2007). I argue that for gay visibility to challenge the hegemonic gender regime, the acceptance of outspoken, disobedient, visible gay men and lesbians is necessary to raise acceptance of all gay people, including those who identify as straight acting, and to recognize the diversity of gay identities.

Conceptualizing Visibility

It is important to remember that visibility is not in itself an unproblematic concept. Peggy Phelan criticizes identity politics for its reliance on the assumption that a lack of media visibility of a minority group reflects and reproduces inequality, and accordingly, these groups should seek great power through increased visibility. Phelan has quipped, "If representational visibility equals power, then almost-naked young white women should be running Western Culture" (Phelan, 1993, p. 10). She recognizes that equating visibility with power is problematic, for in its supposed promise of liberation it invites increased surveillance. . . . The notion that the power visibility promises may be reduced to quantity is nonsensical, since visibility is often used to signify deviance and not to promote tolerance (see, e.g., Sloop, 2004). . . .

Gay and lesbian media critics have long recognized that media visibility of gay men and lesbians often functions only to make a certain type of homosexual natural and normal (Battles & Hilton-Murrow, 2002; Dyer, 1977; Shugart, 2003). It is important therefore for critics to analyze gay and lesbian visibility to see how it is being used by heterosexual society to define homosexuality. . . . Despite the widely accepted notion that GLBTQ people turn to the media to understand homosexuality, there remains a relative void in research detailing the ways that actual gay people conceptualize visibility in the media or in actual social practice. It is important to look beyond merely examining media texts to determine how transgressive performances may be constructed, and to actually observe how these transgressive performances are read by those who oppose them. . . .

DEGREES OF TRANSGRESSION AND THE LIMITS OF NORMALIZATION

The passage from roadster_guy that begins this chapter reveals the tension over gay visibility that exists even within gay communities.[1] In answering the question "How have your experiences with nelly men been," roadster_guy blames those who are read as gay for their own oppression and advocates invisibility for gay men. He demonstrates a homophobic, but widely accepted and repeated, view: those who do not alter their behaviors to avoid the risk of offending potentially homophobic bystanders are responsible for any disciplinary action that those homophobes may choose to inflict. Furthermore, the fact that he would consider smacking his friend for displaying any sort of gender transgression reveals his reliance on blending into a presumably heterosexual environment at any cost, and his assumption that gender performance is an overtly agentic set of choices to be made.

Given roadster_guy's obvious discomfort with Bill, even before he broadcast his flaming performance to space, it is unclear why Bill is his friend at all. His reaction does reveal how gender transgressors are disciplined differently than those who conform. Most importantly, it reveals that selective homophobia is alive and well within gay communities. It suggests that some gay men fear the gender performances they see as flaming, not only because they do not like them, but also because they fear what those performances may mean to straight people. However, it is these flaming gender performances which represent a heightened degree of transgression that, as the visibility of gay men grows, remains a barometer for gay rights and highlights how the gender and sex regime continues to operate even within gay communities. Potentially, as Halberstam (1998) argues, these transgressors are not simply saying no to the dominant gender regime, but are in fact saying "I don't care" to the system of power, and thus it is more difficult for disciplinary forces to cope with this transgression.

I submit "degrees of transgression" as a metaphor for discussing the political potential of rethinking "normalization" of gay visibility as "conventionalization." This phrasing should remind critics that "flaming gays" remain among the most marginalized members of society, even in some gay communities. Even when these flamers are represented in the media, audiences, including gay men, often are positioned to laugh at gender transgression, not to identify with those who perform it. Furthermore, many assume that the presence of a flamer positions the reader to laugh at the transgression, even if the audience is positioned to identify with the transgressor. The flamer needs to be validated in media texts, and by media audiences, as a critical first step toward the acceptance of these gender performances as legitimate conventions of the larger and more diverse gay community. . . .

Negating Transgression in Representations of Gay Pride

The limits of normalization and the fear of heightened degrees of transgression can be observed in the discourse of Straight Acting.com. Several of its members suggest that gay visibility would improve in quality if gay pride parades were abolished and gay men implemented a strategy of being "quietly gay":

I'm not sure gay pride is working. A gay author, Dan Savage, I think, suggested that once the disease is cured, the cure becomes toxic. Once the cancer is gone, the chemo will kill you. I think the Stonewall/Gay Pride movement was a necessary cure, and brought the gay world to people's attention. But I think that what was once the cure is now toxic. I see more and more of our rights taken away, and more hate crimes, because the flamboyant elements of the gay movement have remained in power after they have ceased to be effective, IMHO.[2]

I suggest a movement called "quietly gay." I think it's important for me to be out to the people closest to me, but as for the rest of the world, they can "do the math." I don't need to be vocal or up front with the world at large. And I think the world would be more accepting if we just lived our lives in our own little world. I think that we are losing because people continue to shove their orientation in people's faces. I think a new vanguard of "normal" men living normal lives would help the movement more at this moment in time. Thought I'd toss that out for discussion. (James)

James is interpreting Dan Savage, a controversial gay columnist, correctly. Savage does argue that pride has outlived its usefulness and may be more of a hindrance than a help. The article that James is citing argues that gay pride functions to suggest that there is a unified gay community, and warns of the danger of assuming that all gay people look out for each other.

Of course, Savage is correct in asserting that not all gay people are allies, as the discourse of this Web site reveals; however, he is wrong to assume that we are at the point where a cure for societal homophobia is no longer needed. I am not arguing that pride is the solution to homophobia, but Savage's perspective that gay rights have been won is tragically optimistic and ignores the growing amount of antigay physical and political violence, as well as the overwhelming body of legislation that has passed to prevent GLBTQ people from enjoying equal access to citizenship.[3]

James, in his post above, reveals that antigay sentiment is still quite strong among large sections of the American population. However, James attributes this sentiment, and an increase in hate crimes, to the visibility of "flamboyant" gay people, and argues that we should move toward a gay identity that conforms to normative standards of gender identity while retaining nonnormative sexual identities. His comments suggest that invisibility is his preferred strategy and that normalization of his particular gender identity is more important than the acceptance of other conventions of gay identity. James's insistence on reduced visibility for particular types of gay people does recognize that diversity exists, but his strategy of reduced visibility attempts to rhetorically douse those who perform higher degrees of transgression. . . .

James's perspective represents only one side of the debate about visibility on StraightActing.com. Xaphan is the first to challenge James's understanding of the power of gay visibility:

Ahh, but the chemo doesn't get all the cancer during the first treatment. You need to have repeated treatments and follow up to make sure it's gone. Pride is that treatment. And each year, society as a whole gets a little dose of Queer Chemo.

Pride in Boston started 35 years ago. Since that time we've become more visible, less discriminated against, have more rights, less fears, and now we can marry. We're getting to be cured of the homophobic cancer. Will it all go away? Nope. There are still people that think blacks should go back to Africa and women shouldn't be independent. But, can we improve conditions for a more equal world, yes.

So while Pride is seen by people with clouded vision (nice way of saying ignorant fools) as a show of flamboyance, it is in fact exposure, a dose of the variation of life. If Pride is a foolish display of homosexuality, then what of Mardi Gras, Carnival, and Spring Break. What do these things say of heterosexual people? What do they say of young people? And these are groups who don't require any visibility or more acceptance.

So Pride is the continuation of the homophobia chemotherapy. (Xaphan)

Xaphan recognizes that gay rights have increased since the inception of gay pride events, although whether this is as a consequence is impossible to determine. His comment reveals the assumptions of identity politics: that increased visibility results in increased power, which here is framed as acceptance and civil rights. More importantly, he reveals the power of exposing the invisible in order to challenge interpretations of the visible. His comparison of the heterosexual displays of Spring Break and Mardi Gras to the homosexual "flamboyance" of gay pride reveals the ways in which homosexuality is seen and heterosexuality remains unmarked, because these expressions of heterosexuality are contextualized, and thus seen as only one convention of heterosexuality. Few complain about the display of heterosexuality during Spring Break, although some complain about its graphic nature. Furthermore, this distinction recognizes the diversity in heterosexual sexuality—not just their straightness, but the ways that they may employ their sexuality in public or in private. However, the assumption that Xaphan is revealing is that gay sexuality is defined for the public by the gay pride events: that the norm is public displays of sex and sexuality, not that these are indicative of a particular group within the gay community.

What the discourse about gay pride reveals is not that some of these men believe that visibility does not lead to social change, but instead that they see only specific types of representation leading to social change. The flaming performances that are traditionally associated with gay pride are rejected when James advocates that gay people should quietly emulate heterosexual relationships. In the following comment James elaborates on what "quietly gay" means to him. In doing so he assumes that one can be publicly gay without revealing the private desires that homosexuality entails:

> For me, the couples standing in line to get licenses in San Francisco was a powerful, quiet witness. It said something strong and true about the gay experience, and didn't require any costumes. I'm not asking anyone to sit down and shut up—I'm thinking of becoming visible in a different set of roles. I don't think the public at large benefits from knowing about my private desires, but they can see me working for a candidate, cleaning up a park, being a churchgoer, etc., and do the math from the way I live my life. I think the last election has shown that rather than gaining us rights, the gay pride movement is galvanizing people against us. Showing that we are the same as everybody else, and living our lives with our orientation blended in with the rest of the flavors of our lives, would do more to help the cause now, IMHO. (James) . . .

Conclusion

The important difference between norm and convention lies in the insistence on a plurality. However, the intragroup struggle over a dominant convention, revealed in the discourse of StraightActing.com, reveals the danger of the current conceptualization of visibility among gay men. The reliance on this discourse of normalization suggests that what media representations contribute to is a single norm for gay men, and all else are abnormal or less than acceptable. Formulating representational power as normalizing, and not conventionalizing, promotes divisiveness among members of the gay community, struggling over which of their identities may become normalized. Just as heterosexuality is not reduced to a single norm, with its recurring representation in MTV's variety of Spring Break specials and coverage of overt sexual display at Mardi Gras celebrations, homosexuality at gay pride parades may be thought of as contextualized within that moment. The displays of homosexuality are conventions that occur within a particular moment and do not represent homosexuality as a whole, and may not even represent the lives of those who engage in these displays at pride events. A discursive shift to conventionalization may reduce the intergroup struggle over who is represented, by assuming a wider range of degrees of transgression.

The discourse of media stereotypes of gay men reveals both pro- and anti-visibility perspectives. In their calls for inclusion, these men focus on inclusion for those men who adhere to the traditional and perhaps conventional expectations of male behavior. In this discussion group, these particular men want to see a change in the ways gay men are represented. They are angered by the seeming focus on feminine gay representations and want to shift the focus to gay men who act just like "normal" heterosexual men, thus returning feminine gay men to a closet of symbolic annihilation. Indeed, they want to return to the privileged position of seeming to be just like heterosexual men, so that they can assume some of the power that this position entails. . . .

Some of these men, as well as some media critics, argue that increased visibility of straight-acting gay men has the potential to undo what they see as the negative consequence of the prevalence of effeminate gay stereotypes and those who uphold them. They fail to recognize the liberatory potential of representing higher degrees of transgression. While their argument seems to be that their increased visibility will lead to greater acceptance of homosexuals, they fail to acknowledge that the root of homophobia remains homosexuality. They seek to normalize gay men as "real men," but their strategy for confronting homophobia is limited to challenging the conflation of gender and sexuality, and does not seek acceptance for those whose degrees of transgression are higher. It does not challenge the fear or hatred of gayness. . . .

Notes

1. StraightActing.com is a privately funded Web site for self-proclaimed straight-acting gay men that can be read by all, but users must register (at no cost) to post. The site is based around the discussion area called the Butch Boards, but also includes a series of straight-acting quizzes and, before a massive server crash in the summer of 2004, personal ads, home pages, and other services. The Butch Boards and the quiz have been restored, but unfortunately the previous content has been irreparably lost, and the discussion boards started anew early in October 2004. In June 2005, the Butch Board included 18 forums ranging from 41 to 310 topics in each. Overall, there were slightly less than 55,000 total posts, ranging widely in length and content. While the forum descriptions suggest that the discussion topics are well organized, there is considerable overlap in topic area from forum to forum. As part of a larger study, I engaged all areas of the discussion board in order to avoid overlooking certain perspectives or favoring one forum's most active posters. This chapter focuses exclusively on the discourse of visibility in these forums.

2. IMHO is a common acronym for "In my humble opinion."

3. Five more states voted to ban same-sex marriage in the 2006 election, bringing the total number to 24.

References

Battles, K., & Hilton-Morrow, W. (2002). Gay characters in conventional spaces: *Will & Grace* and the situation comedy genre. *Critical Studies in Media Communication, 19*(1), 87–106.

Dyer, R. (1977). *Gays and film*. London: British Film Institute.

Halberstam, J. (1998). *Female masculinity*. Durham, NC: Duke University Press.

Hequembourg, A., & Arditi, J. (1999). Fractured resistances: The debate over assimilationism among gays and lesbians in the United States. *Sociological Quarterly, 40*, 663–680.

Owen, A. S., Vande Berg, L. R., & Stein, S. R. (2007). *Bad girls: Cultural politics and media representations of transgressive women*. New York: P. Lang.

Phelan, P. (1993). *Unmarked: The politics of performance*. London: Routledge.

Shugart, H. A. (2003). Reinventing privilege: The new (gay) man in contemporary popular media. *Critical Studies in Media Communication, 20*(1), 67–92.

Sloop, J. M. (2004). *Disciplining gender: Rhetorics of sex identity in contemporary U.S. culture*. Amherst: University of Massachusetts Press.

Squires, C. R., & Brouwer, D. C. (2002). In/discernible bodies: The politics of passing in dominant and marginal media. *Critical Studies in Media Communication, 19*(3), 283–311.

"This Is the Way We Live . . . and Love!"

Feeding on and Still Hungering for Lesbian Representation in *The L Word*

Marnie Pratt

Lesbians Find Their Way to the Small Screen

The L Word is, of course, not the first television program to have lesbian characters. There have been lesbian characters on several cable and regular network series throughout recent years, such as on *ER, Friends, Queer as Folk, Buffy the Vampire Slayer,* and, of course, *Ellen.* The majority of the lesbian characters on these programs were either peripheral or secondary characters. *Ellen's* main character, Ellen Morgan (Ellen DeGeneres), was a groundbreaking exception; however, the character was unfortunately short-lived after actually coming out. What sets *The L Word* apart is not only the fact that the majority of its main characters are lesbians, but also that these characters' lives, relationships, and political or social issues are the focus of the series. Creator Ilene Chaiken pitched the project (then called *Earthlings*), loosely based on her own life experiences, to an uninterested Showtime in the late 1990s (Rosenduft 20). Shortly thereafter, however, Showtime scored a big hit with *Queer as Folk* and HBO had high ratings with *Sex and the City.* These shows proved that there were significant audiences for both all queer and all female character lineups. In 2001, Showtime went back to Chaiken to see whether she was still interested in combining the two (Rosenduft 23).

The L Word became an overnight sensation for Chaiken and Showtime. It debuted in January 2004 to mostly positive media reviews, has since reached more than 500,000 viewers per season (Cole, 'Season 3" para. 2), and became the most quickly renewed series in Showtime's history (Rosenduft 23). It was renewed for a second season after only two

From Pratt, M. (2008). "This is the way we live . . . and love!" Feeding on and still hungering for lesbian representation in *The L Word.* In R. Beirne (Ed.), *Televising queer women: A reader* (pp. 135–147). New York: Palgrave Macmillan.

episodes and for a third season before the premier episode of season two (McDermott 26). *The L Word*'s success has also been felt in the second market of DVD sales, which according to Chaiken "are through the roof" (quoted in Stockwell 48). This success also reflects *The L Word*'s highly devoted fan base. "Enthusiastic fans trade show secrets and leak spoilers or plot lines through weblogs, unofficial websites, and gossip circles" (Rosenduft 19). In fact, online fan communities began appearing before the pilot episode even aired. Most notable of these are www.l-word.com and www.thelwordonline.com. The former has over 30,000 members and around 150,000 visitors per month (Jacky) and the latter averages around 11,000 visitors a day ("The L Word Online—Site Summary"). Anne Ramsay (Robin), a guest actor on *The L Word*, attempted the following explanation for the overwhelming fan response: "I think [the lesbian community] is starving, and has been for years" (quoted in McDermott 27). However, a downside to the program's pioneer status and resultant hungry fans is that this audience is also expectant and demanding. The show's most loyal fans have become its most challenging critics. Actor Leisha Hailey (Alice) explains, "There's so much pressure on this one show, the first of its kind, to represent every dyke or lesbian in the world" (quoted in Champagne para. 14). However, Chaiken remains positive about the criticism, "I love that we have a passionate audience who seem to love the show but also take[s] issue with lots of things we do. I welcome that exchange" (quoted in Wilkinson 24). It is within this exchange that viewers have the opportunity to rethink the definition of representation.

The L Word as "Image of" Representation

It cannot be denied that *The L Word* is groundbreaking television and that it deserves to be commended for a wealth of great features. For example, the characters are believable and complex and the series has dealt with a variety of tough topics in smart ways, such as coming out, childbearing, abuse/exploitation of women, substance addiction, and gay marriage. The show has also been cutting edge in many of its depictions of sexual encounters. Sexual practices are discussed frankly and realistically through the depictions of both long-term committed and "one night stand" relationships. A pregnant character was maintained as a sexually viable individual throughout season two. When the often-stereotyped topic of strap-on dildos surfaced, not only was it depicted on screen, but the accompanying discussion also broke down common cultural assumptions by stressing that their use was not because lesbians need penises for sex (2.9). And, finally, the show strays from many other queer depictions in that it has shown relatively little homophobia or violence against its characters. The show depicts a somewhat utopian environment. According to Joy Press of *The Village Voice*, "Everywhere they go resembles a hermetically sealed world of lesbian loveliness" (para. 7). While this has sometimes become a point of critique for the show, it also serves as a very necessary counterpoint to a wealth of other films and television programs dealing with serious, and often depressing, topics related to lesbian life. In other words, for viewers who deal with discrimination on a daily basis, sometimes it can be important to escape, and *The L Word* fulfills this need. For example, one fan explains in a letter reprinted from L-word.com in the "bonus features" section of the season two DVD set, "The show was my only source of comfort, an escape from my own reality" (Colenickel). Another fan clarifies, "We [are] able to find women in a homonormative environment . . . if I wanted to see real life I would look in the mirror" (Angelak).

Similar to this concept of escapism is the necessity of community. Performance artist Tim Miller and theater scholar David Roman discuss how queer performance is often written off by mainstream culture as "preaching to the converted" (172). In a predominantly homophobic culture that consistently discriminates against and further limits the rights and voices of its homosexual members, however, these performances can be important, if not critical, for the communities they represent (Miller and Roman 172). Miller and Roman describe the importance of queer performance spaces:

> lesbians and gay men interested in theatre that spoke explicitly about lesbian and gay issues now [post-Stonewall, as queer, community-based theaters developed] had a theatre within the public sphere where subcultural codes, vernaculars, and customs could be articulated and shared, negotiated and contested . . . Together these people forged energies to simulate and enact a sense of queer history and queer community . . . The idea of forging community, however tentative or utopian, rested on the assumptions that community is a political necessity and a viable possibility. (173–174)

In other words, queer performance spaces become a safe venue for individuals to create a community, find support, make their voice be heard, and "be absorbed into a critical mass of subcultural resistance to the heteronormative muscle [they] must encounter continually in [their] daily lives" (Miller and Roman 176). The community of viewers that has developed around *The L Word* is definitely reminiscent of Miller and Roman's queer performance space. Fans on websites created around the show have developed friendships, shared coming out stories, traded fan fiction,[1] and communicated advice and support for each other.

All of these aspects of *The L Word* and what it offers its audience should be commended, with the hope that they will break down stereotypes as part of what Chaiken describes as the "evolution of cultural attitudes" (quoted in "Lesbian life, love on *The L Word*" para. 25). However, while the

series may at times be the aforementioned "lesbian loveliness" (Press para. 7), the representations are not always "the way we live and love," as the show's theme song suggests (Betty).

Without a doubt, the most highly critiqued aspect of the show (by fans and critics alike) is the appearance of the main characters. Writer and actor Guinevere Turner explains:

> One of the biggest complaints I hear from lesbians about the television show . . . is that the women on the show are all so girly and un-gay-looking. "Where's the big old truck-driving tattooed dyke?" one woman stood up and asked at a panel discussion with the creative team of the show. "I don't know any women who look like those women!" (para. 2)

In early reviews of the show, journalists discussed the look of the women on the show as "cute and shiny" (Theobald 5), "beautiful" (Hensley 48), and "smart, successful, impossibly thin women with perfect, choppy haircuts" (Press para. 3). The women are all very thin, conventionally attractive, well groomed, heavily made up, and highly fashionable. In fact, more than one of the actors has spent some time in modeling; in the 1980s, Jennifer Beals (Bette) was rated the top "pin up" girl after her success in *Flashdance,* and Sarah Shahi (Carmen) is a former Dallas Cowboys cheerleader. In the lesbian community, these women would all be considered "femmes."

A similar critique often leveled at the show regarding its representation of the lesbian community deals with its lack of racially and ethnically diverse characters. Almost all of the characters are white, with the exception of Bette, who is biracial, and Carmen, who is Latina. However, Carmen did not join the cast until the second season, after the show had received some of this criticism. Even more interesting, there is one core African American character on the show, Kit (Pam Grier); however, Kit is not a lesbian. She is one of the two main cast members who are straight (the other is male). Kit is also the only larger-bodied woman on the show. All of these things taken together create the impression that the show is equating very specific conceptions of beauty, race, and ethnicity with queerness.

During the first season and shortly afterward, the most common response to these early criticisms from those involved with the show is that the cast is realistic for L.A. "It's just the way L.A. is" (Turner para. 3). Another popular response is that since the show is loosely based on Chaiken's life, these people represent her personal experiences. One of *The L Word's* directors, Rose Troche, explains, "These characters are not every woman. They are not every lesbian. They're a very real depiction of a group of L.A. lesbians based on Ilene's own experiences" (quoted in Hensley 48). While both of these responses may be reasonable,[2] what makes them particularly problematic for the represented community is that *The L Word* is the first show of its kind. As a result, it is painting one of the initial pictures of lesbian life for the rest of the world. In addition, it is feeding the needs of a represented community that has had very few previous television images of themselves.

Another aspect of the show that is problematic regarding representation is how it has dealt with transgender issues. Near the end of season one, the character Ivan (Kelly Lynch) was introduced as a love interest for Kit. It was suggested that Ivan identified as a man and he appeared to be placed in the show to represent and discuss issues of the transgender community's intersection with the lesbian community. The show began to intelligently explore these issues through discussions between Bette and Kit, where Kit defends Ivan as being able to be who he wishes to be. Bette insists that he is a woman and that the heterosexual Kit should not get involved with him (2.1). However, shortly into the second season, Ivan is quickly removed from the plot. . . .

Mediating Representation With *The L Word*

Chaiken has often proclaimed that Showtime has little control over her creative process with the show. In fact, according to one interview, the network has made only one demand of her. Showtime required her to include a straight male character in season two (Fonseca 41). This character was intended to cater to the straight male audience of the show. As Showtime's President of Entertainment Robert Greenblatt explains, "We thought it would be good for the male audience to have a guy they could relate to" (quoted in Fonseca 41). However, it also seems possible that Showtime's executives may have a bit more influence than simply this one character request. In another interview, Greenblatt has stated, "[I]t must be liberating for Ilene to do a series about her own experiences, but ultimately, we want people everywhere to buy it. So yes, the women are all attractive and we make no apologies about that. It's television. Who wants to watch unattractive people, gay, straight or whatever?" (quoted in Glock 38). Not only does this comment indicate an unaddressed level of control on the part of Showtime, but it also indicates that they appear to be designating what is to be considered "attractive" for the rest of the world. Regardless of the fact that Greenblatt himself is a gay man, *The L Word* clearly appears to be under the same heteronormative conceptions of gender and beauty as most other aspects of popular culture.

These types of control are what Richard Dyer labels as power relations. He explains that they plague popular media representations because they "put the weight of control over representation on the side of the rich, the white, the male, [and] the heterosexual" (Dyer 2). Since media representations are so pervasive and have such a powerful cultural influence, the possibility of shifting the control of this media could be of great cultural importance. Or, as scholar

Jennifer Pozner asserts in an article on feminist media, "Control of the media is the single most important issue of our time" (37). What makes *The L Word* most interesting (and most applicable to this study) is that it does appear to have made an effort to respond to, or "converse with" its critics (fan and otherwise). In doing so, the creators have allowed the audience to think of the series' representations as both "image[s] or like-ness[es]" and "official delegate[s], agent [s], or spokes[people]" (*American Heritage Dictionary* 1180). This has altered the dynamic of power relations and control described by Dyer.

Before discussing how the conversation between the audience and creators of *The L Word* has played out and impacted the show, it is critical to establish its actual existence. The easily ascertained side to the conversation is the audience. They are clearly communicating about the show with each other and with the intention of reaching the creators. As has already been mentioned, websites are filled with discussion boards, editorials, reviews, petitions, and blogs. One way in which it has been made evident that Showtime and Chaiken are interested in the input of this audience is that the show's official website (www.sho.com) encourages these discussions by including the same types of material as the fan-based sites. Showtime's website includes message boards, editorials, blogs, and fan fiction links specifically related to *The L Word*. Showtime and the creators even held a web-based contest in 2006 for fan fiction writers to create their own episode of the series, which they called "the fanisode." Furthermore, Chaiken and the cast have made it abundantly clear through interviews that they are willing to hear from the audience on fan websites, as well.

In numerous interviews (some even with the developers of these types of sites), cast and crew members have mentioned reading, frequenting, and even being members of fan websites, such as www.l-word.com and www.thelwordonline.com. For example, at

an autograph signing with Chaiken and actor Pam Grier in Atlanta, GA, the two interviewed with the fan website www.l-word.com, and both admitted in the interview that they frequent and enjoy the site. In fact, Grier stated, "Hey, I go to the site, too. I belong to the site" (Cole para. 2). At a fan convention interview in the United Kingdom, cast member Laurel Holloman (Tina) mentions both reading fan mail and visiting the fan websites. "I've been there [www.l-word.com]. It's the biggest website we have . . . And I think the other girls visit it too. I know Leisha does and Kate [Moennig, who plays Shane] does" (Watson para. 62). Even actors who play more peripheral characters admit to reading the fan sites. In an interview with Meredith McGeachie (Tonya) by www.l-word.com, she confirms, "I think the website is fantastic. Erin [Daniels, who plays Dana] told me at one point that there was a Tonya thing so just to go and look and I did and I was like, 'wow'" (Watson para. 11).

However, frequenting websites and reading fan mail do not necessarily confirm that the creators are willing to let what they read influence their actual creative process. For that, we will turn once more to Chaiken:

> I try to strike a balance when I read the message boards, which I do occasionally, and when I hear from fans and viewers. I'm interested and enlightened and probably subconsciously influenced. I care a lot about what the show's fans think. The writers and I ultimately will tell the stories that we believe are the right stories, that are the truest stories, but it's significant to us what the people who have been watching the show think about the characters and their lives. (Chaiken para. 6)

It seems clear that not only is there an audience and creator interaction, but there is also openness for that interaction to impact the series and its representations.

As the series progressed into seasons two and three, it began to appear as if it was responding directly to some of the critiques leveled at its content. A wider variety of queer individuals began to appear in these seasons. Not only was Latina lesbian Carmen added to the main cast in season two, but there are also more women of color and gender-variant peripheral or supporting characters. . . .

In addition, season three addressed the tensions created among audience members over the poor representation and eventual loss of the character Ivan with the introduction of Moira (Daniela Sea). Moira became the first self-identifying and visibly "butch" character for the main cast of the show. Moira is a friend and love interest for Jenny (Mia Kirshner), who moves with Jenny from Illinois to L.A. Shortly after arriving, it is revealed that Moira actually wishes to become Max and he then begins to transition throughout the season. Max's transition became one of the main plotlines of the season, and is, therefore, given a significant amount of screen time and discussion. While some of the dialogue over Max's story arc appeared forced and rudimentary, the show also appeared to have done at least some of its homework by addressing issues such as the financial difficulties of transitioning, social repercussions, violence, and the emotional strain sometimes felt by transitioning individuals. Intersections between transgender and lesbian communities are also addressed in conversations that deal with difficult arguments about "giving up being a woman" or "losing all the strong butch warriors" (3–9). And tensions are depicted between a character who undergoes a mastectomy due to breast cancer and Max, who is anxious to undergo top surgery (3.8). . . .

The communicative approach taken by *The L Word*'s audience members appears to have created a sense of responsibility on the part of its creators and enabled the series' representations (images of) to simultaneously be representatives (delegates or spokespeople) for the lesbian and queer community. And while creator Chaiken often tries to maintain that her main responsibility is to storytelling instead of that community, she also appears well aware of whose stories she is actually telling. "Representation is so important to people," she explains. "Lesbians have never had a show of our own before, so I understand all of the fan ranting and raving out there about it. Even more so than with other shows, the fans own this show. It's not my show; it's theirs" (quoted in Littleton 13).

Looking Forward

At a lecture given by Ilene Chaiken during a seminar on queer television, an unidentified audience member stood up with tears in her eyes to proclaim her gratitude to Chaiken. "I grew up in the 60s. When I was a teenager it was rough. You are doing something besides making entertainment. You are performing a public service. You're not just creating television. You are saving lives" (quoted in Glock 26). I am alternately touched and concerned by this quote. On one hand, the heartfelt and painful honesty that this reveals regarding the importance of media representations for lesbian communities is moving. However, I am also profoundly troubled by the level of investment it indicates some viewers are experiencing for this television program. What is it about popular media representations that would lead an individual to this type of statement regarding a commodity of popular culture? I believe that this audience member's investment is tied to queer culture's long struggle with "the closet" and visibility.

In her landmark work *Epistemology of the Closet*, Eve Sedgwick states, "Vibrantly resonant as the image of the closet is for many modern oppressions, it is indicative for homophobia in a way it cannot be for other oppressions. Racism, for instance, is based on a stigma that is visible in all but exceptional cases . . . so are the oppressions based on gender, age, size, physical handicap" (75). While some may argue that Sedgwick's statement is a bit generalizing, I still wonder if this does not indicate something specific for queer communities and their relationship with representational visibility. For a group of individuals so indoctrinated by the concept of the closet, of hiding something significant to their beings, is it not possible that visibility is somehow more crucial? It is the "fundamental feature of social life" that the closet creates that I believe makes popular culture representations so critical to queer culture and the queer movement (Sedgwick 68). These images are long overdue representatives as well as representations.

The L Word has provided its audience the very critical validation through visibility it desires and even though the series is still struggling to achieve positive representations, it is crucial that the show exists and succeeds. After all, without *The L Word's* success, television executives, creators, and writers will not be interested in creating more shows like it. However, it is also critical that its audience continue to mediate how the term *representation* is thought of in popular culture. This mediated definition and conversational approach allows for the struggle over media representations to be both about the existence of images and the accuracy of those images when they do exist.

Notes

1. In an essay from *The Gay and Lesbian Review Worldwide,* author Marianne MacDonald described fan fiction (or "fanfic") as "fiction written by the fans of any popular narrative, be it a novel, a TV series, or a film" (28). These stories are published both online and within fan-based magazines. For further information on fan fiction see Henry Jenkins's 1992 book *Textual Poachers: Television Fans and Participatory Culture.*

2. In the director commentary section for the lesbian film *Mango Kiss*, director Sascha Rice discusses a similar situation when she states that she could "not find a butch [actor] in L.A." This film is set in San Francisco, but was cast in L.A.

References

Angelak. "Fan Mail [DVD Extras]." The L Word Complete Second Season. DVD edition. Showtime, 2005.

Betty. "The L Word Theme (The Way That We Live)." The L Word: The Second Season Sessions—Original Score. Silver Label. 2004.

Chaiken, Ilene. "Chat Transcript." L-Word.com: In the News. April 11, 2004. September 5, 2006. http://www.l-word.com/news/chaiken.php.

Champagne, Christine. "Gaywatch: The L Word." Planet Out. January 9, 2004. September 7, 2006. http://www.planetout.com/pno/entertainment/news/splash. html?sernum=625.

Cole, Pam. "Chaiken and Grier Interview." L-Word.com: In the News. January 4, 2006. September 5, 2006. http://www.l-word.com/news/autograph_interview_l.php.

Colenickel. "Fan Mail [DVD Extras]." The L Word Complete Second Season. DVD edition. Showtime, 2005.

Dyer, Richard. The Matter of Images: Essays on Representation. New York: Routledge, 1993.

Fonseca, Nicholas. "Return of the Pink Ladies." Entertainment Weekly February 18, 2005: 39–41.

Glock, Alison. "She Likes to Watch." New York Times Febuary 6, 2005, late ed. sec. 2:26+.

Hensley, Dennis. "L is for Leisha." The Advocate. February 17, 2004: 41–53.

Jenkins, Henry. Textual Poachers: Television Fans and Participatory Culture. New York, Routledge, 1992.

"The L Word Online—Site Summary." Sitemeter.com. 2006. September 1, 2006. http://www.sitemeter.com/?a=stats&s=s17word online.

"Lesbian Life, Love on 'The L Word.'" CNN January 15, 2004. September 7, 2006. http://www.cnn.com/2004/SHOWBIZ/TV/01/15/apontv.thelword.ap/.

Littleton, Cynthia. "Popularity of 'The L Word' Being Seen all Over." Chicago Sun Times March 3, 2005, final ed.:NC40.

MacDonald, Marianne. "Harry Potter and the Fan Fiction Phenom." The Gay and Lesbian Review Worldwide 13 (2006): 28–30.

McDermott, Eileen. "The L Word: They're Back!" GONYC. February 2005: 26–27.

Miller, Tim and David Roman. "Preaching to the Converted." Theater Journal. 47 (1995): 169–188.

Pozner, Jennifer L. "The 'Big Lie': False Feminist Death Syndrome, Profit, and the Media." Catching a Wave: Reclaiming Feminist for the 21st Century. Ed. Rory Dicker and Alison Piepmeier. Boston: Northeastern University Press, 2003. 31–56.

Press, Joy. "Sapphic Lights." The Village Voice. January 7–13, 2004. September 7, 2006. http://www.villagevoice.com/arts/0401,tv,50047,27.html.

Rosenduft, Raimy. "Now it's Our Party." Velvet Park, Winter 2005: 19–27.

Sedgwick, Eve Kosofsky. Epistemology of the Closet. Berkeley: University of California Press, 1990.

Stockwell, Anne. "One Family's Value." The Advocate January 30, 2001. September 25, 2002. http://www.advocate.com/html/stories/30/830_cvr_brooke.asp.

Theobald, Stephanie. "From Icon to Dykon." Guardian September 4, 2004, final ed., sec. The Guide: 4–6.

Turner, Guinevere. "Lipstick Los Angeles." OUT Traveler Magazine. December 2004, September 7, 2006. http://www.thelwordonlin.com/lipstick_LA.shtml.

———. Personal Interview with Candace Moore. March 28, 2005.

Watson, Tracey. "L-Word Exclusive Interview with Meredith McGeachie." L-Word.com: In the News. January 30, 2006. September 5, 2006. http://www.l-word.com/news/meredith_1.php.

Wilkinson, Kathleen. "We Lucky Lesbians." Lesbian News, January 2005: 24–5.

PART VI

GROWING UP WITH CONTEMPORARY MEDIA

The potential effects of mass media culture on children and young people have always generated much anxiety and controversy and even, on occasion, media activism. Educators have argued that young children are a particularly vulnerable population, given their limited experience of the world and the likelihood that their sense of the boundaries between media representations and the real world is less well established than (ideally) that of adults. According to Dafna Lemish (VI.39),

> Most pronounced are concerns over the effects of television violence on children, as well as the potential harm of exposure to sexual portrayals, the effects of advertising on consumer culture, and the more general concern over children's passivity and social disengagement. (p. 355)

In the age of **globalizing media,** concerns around children's television are now being studied on an international level. Lemish explores the current state of the research and argues that

> In summary, empirical evidence suggests that children's television around the world consists primarily of fictional animation programs not produced domestically but purchased from abroad, mainly from the United States and Canada. These programs feature mostly light

skin characters with an overwhelming presence of males. Therefore, the White male hegemony seems to be numerically dominant in children's television around the world, just as it is in other aspects of popular culture. (p. 358)

Despite this critique of the status quo, Lemish offers a somewhat hopeful account of the continuing positive potential of media and television in particular—if reformed by creative and responsible professionals who see it as a "social resource"—for opening up children's imaginations and giving "voice to their multiple perspectives and experiences."

A less sanguine view is offered by Juliet Schor (VI.40) in her analysis of the impact of the commercial nature of children's media in the United States today. Schor introduces us to the "commercialized child," analyzing the ways in which childhood is being defined and manipulated in marketing and advertising. Although targeting young children is not new for the sellers of food, kids' clothes, and toys, there has been a significant "upscaling" of kids' products in recent years, in part through the marketing strategy of emphasizing social exclusivity as "cool." In contrast to earlier times when "cheap stuff dominated kids' consumer worlds," Schor tells us,

> Now that kids have access to so much more money, status and its underlying values of inequality and exclusion have settled at the heart of the kid consumer culture. . . . Marketers convey the view that wealth and aspiration to wealth are cool. . . . Living modestly means living like a loser. (pp. 367–368)

Schor also calls our attention to the "naturalization" of both childhood and gender that dominates the thinking of the marketing professionals in relation to targeting young consumers: Almost all products, messages, and campaigns are subjected to gender analysis that asks, "Is it for boys, or is it for girls?" While there has been some updating of the formulas related

to femininity (primarily to include "girl power" themes, a concept that some argue is itself an attempt to co-opt feminism), there are still very clear conservative gender conventions for representing girls and boys in advertising, reflecting the belief that "boys are more skittish about gender identities and highly sensitive to anything that smacks of the feminine" (p. 366).

As a preeminent icon of girl consumer culture, Mattel Corporation's Barbie doll continues to reflect and construct racialized gender ideology and to attract critical analysis from media scholars and activists. The original Barbie encoded an idealized White American teenaged girl, whose ethnic neutrality was useful for a marketing strategy that stressed "Americanness." However, over the 40 years since her first release on the toy market, in part because of a changed marketing strategy, one that targets "ethnic" U.S. consumers and a global market, Mattel has sold "more than one billion dolls" in 150 countries—making Barbie what Karen Goldman calls (VI.41) "one of the world's most ubiquitous plastic objects." In her essay, Goldman traces the evolution of "official" Mattel representations of Latina femininity, such as Hispanic Barbie and various "Dolls of the World" Barbies. According to Goldman,

> Behind Mattel's portrayal of Latino/a identity lies a system of representation that sells itself as authentic but that ultimately either depicts Latino/a culture as homogeneous and exotic or repackages the doll's Latinidad in an assimilated form, whether to make her more attractive to more assimilated Latinos or to market her more effectively in places where ethnic diversity is not particularly marketable. (p. 378)

No discussion of children's commercialized pop culture would be complete without paying attention to the impact of the Disney company on our archive of media representations that are formative in childhood. As Lee Artz says in his chapter on

Disney's animated films (VI.42), "Disney leads the world in the production and distribution of popular culture" (p. 383). In an attempt to understand why Disney animation has achieved such global dominance, Artz looks at the political economy of Disney, exploring it both as industry and producer of ideology. Through textual analysis of the ideology encoded in animated feature films of the past decade, Artz argues that Disney's dreamworld of individual heroes and royalty rests on cultural privilege, social inequality, and human alienation and that Disney's symbolic production parallels the social production of global capitalism.

So far, our chapters in this part have featured primarily text analysis, but we now turn to an audience response study that focuses on how a particular group of adolescent South Asian American girls are actually making sense of the popular culture in their lives. In Meenakshi Gigi Durham's words, her study (VI.43) "explored South Asian immigrant girls' experiences of coming of age among contemporary global mediascapes, through a series of interviews that brought to the surface the dynamic intersections of body politics, culture-crossing, and myths of homeland. These issues emerged in a constant interplay with the narratives of gender and sexuality in contemporary consumer-oriented teen media" (p. 389). Durham looked closely at how these girls consume but also critically resist some of the central messages about sexuality and romance encoded in both American TV shows and Bollywood films, using these to help them negotiate identity issues as "diaspora" adolescents—neither fully at home in the United States nor fully adopting their parents' Indian culture. In their questioning of both types of "monocultural" texts, Durham views the girls as creating "the potential for new sexual identities that have emancipatory possibilities for them as girls in-between" (p. 396).

How young audiences make meaning from media texts is also the focus of Kathleen Farrell's chapter, "HIV on TV: Conversations with Young Gay Men" (VI.44).

She was specifically interested in how gay college-age men read the popular cable TV dramatic series *Queer as Folk,* "the first television drama in the USA to deal explicitly with queer culture" by representing an almost entirely GLBT (gay, lesbian, bisexual, transgender) community in which characters lead "gay-affirming lives that center on their close friendships with one another." Farrell points out that in *Queer as Folk,* in contrast to other dramatic treatments of HIV/AIDS in television programs of the past, contracting HIV is not automatically presented as a death sentence. Rather, living with HIV is just one problem that characters may face among many others, including "gay bashing, workplace discrimination, and coming out to family members."

Farrell's research observed how focus groups discussed a storyline in which a central character began to date someone who was HIV positive. Given that many of the focus group participants were not directly familiar with real people living with HIV, many were surprised and initially unsettled by "new ideas" suggested by the matter-of-fact presentation of HIV as a chronic disease. In Farrell's analysis, group discussions of the show also clearly provided focus group participants with an opportunity to increase their knowledge about HIV transmission. The show itself was seen by the focus group participants as a valuable educational tool, promoting safe-sex practices in an entertaining way, without coming across as too preachy, conservative, or critical of casual sex or gay lifestyles.

Taking a similarly optimistic view of the potential pedagogical value of media for youth, danah boyd's chapter on the social networking behavior of high school age teens (VI.45) stresses the importance of creating online communities as part of young people's process of learning how to navigate what Boyd calls a "networked public space"—that is, spaces and audiences that are bound together through technological networks. In the case of the wildly popular social network sites such as MySpace and

Facebook, where members are encouraged to develop "their own" semi-private homepage environments, including self-expressive "profile" texts, the networked public space creates potential problems for teens, their parents, and school authorities. Boyd points out that the social network profile can be seen as a form of digital body where individuals must write themselves into being, and in the case of most teens, the online identity created and presented is one that they believe their primary audience of peers will receive as "cool." When parents monitor the online identities of their children, teens frequently respond by creating what Boyd calls "mirror networks" with their friends, where forbidden materials may be displayed on a second profile that is kept well hidden from parents.

Parents are not the only ones interested in how teens are using Internet technologies to create communities with one another. As Kathryn Montgomery points out in "Born to Be Wired" (VI.46), marketers recognize that teens have been a driving force behind the Internet revolution through their enthusiastic adoption of the new digital media. One of the reasons for the "pivotal role" that interactive digital media are playing in teenagers' lives, according to Montgomery, is that there is an excellent match between the properties of these media and the developmental needs of young people.

> Online communication tools enabled instantaneous and constant contact with peers; personal Web pages offered compelling opportunities for self-expression and identity exploration; and ubiquitous portable devices facilitated mobility and independence. (p. 419)

Taking advantage of adolescent vulnerability, adventurousness, and naïveté, marketers developed new digitally savvy techniques to exploit this valuable demographic. One example is peer-to-peer "viral" marketing or "buzzing," which was particularly useful in launching Elizabeth Arden's new perfume, Britney Spears's Curious, in 2004. The campaign, using websites popular with girls, offered a 45-second recorded voicemail message from Spears in exchange for cell phone numbers and ZIP codes from teen cell phone users. The teens who volunteered forwarded Spears's message to friends and in turn received text messages from Spears. Within 4 months, 300,000 girls had been contacted, and $36 million worth of product had been sold.

When considering the experience of youth growing up in daily contact with media culture, we must include substantial attention to electronic and online games, which take up such a large proportion of the leisure time of children, young people, and even older people today. As John Sanbonmatsu (VI.47) points out, "In the US alone, an estimated 170 million people—more than half the population—play video games" (p. 427). In his provocative essay, he calls our attention to the potential dangers of the alluring, highly realistic simulations that draw so many players into these virtual worlds.

Sanbonmatsu argues that many of the most popular video games reproduce sexist and racist depictions, while also legitimizing a consumerist militaristic society that undermines the well-being of individuals, cultures, and the ecosystem. Placing video game playing within the socioeconomic context of our contemporary life, he questions why they are so popular, not only with men and boys but increasingly with women and girls. For Sanbonmatsu, the answer lies in our society's many alienating problems—the increasing financial problems that working people face, a delegitimization of the state, and the destruction of the environment—all issues that people feel are out of their control. He suggests that confronted with these problems, "We ourselves seem to hunger for escapist forms of entertainment that restore to us, albeit only in virtual form, precisely that which many of us feel we are losing in real life" (p. 428).

While it might be hard to argue for the socially or intellectually redemptive value of a commercially successful "entertainment" game like *Grand Theft Auto,* there is increasing interest among game designers and teachers in reclaiming this compelling interactive digital technology for educational purposes. As Kevin Schut (VI.48) writes, the multifaceted, complicated, yet intuitive interaction with virtual worlds that computers make possible can potentially be a whole new way for people to experience or learn about history. However, as Schut goes on to warn in his chapter, "Strategic Simulations and Our Past," we should regard even "historical simulations . . . with something of a critical eye." Looking at several examples of "historically themed game simulation series," Schut argues that "a kind of masculine slant is exceptionally clear in game presentation of history." For example, he points out, while professional historians have long since broadened the scope of history to include the lives and voices of marginalized or less powerful people, most historical digital games "ignore these trends and almost exclusively focus on politics, economics, and war" (p. 439).

A conventional masculinist gender bias is not only displayed in the texts of most interactive digital games, as seen already, but also appears in the actual playing of games by fans. Elena Bertozzi (VI.49), who teaches digital game design, looks at observed gender differences in digital play, finding that despite increased female participation in digital play, "researchers have documented the ways in which gender politics are reconstructed in digital worlds" (p. 444).

Given that digital play offers a considerable amount of gender plasticity through avatars, it might seem illogical for gender stereotypes and concerns to persist in digital gaming, but they do. (p. 444)

Bertozzi hypothesizes that such differences "are strongly influenced by the unwillingness of both genders to cross traditional, culturally gendered play lines" (p. 444). She is especially interested in female resistance to competing fiercely with men in games, because of the real-world implications of continuing to associate competitive success with masculinity. On the positive side, she reminds us, many women are now using game/play activities as a way of practicing competing "at the same level as males." As she writes, "If we recognize the significance and level of difficulty of challenging existing norms, we can better support their initiatives and create structures to help others join them" (p. 444).

The Future of Childhood in the Global Television Market

Dafna Lemish

Television and Children: A Global Issue[1]

The nature of relations between children and television is a global issue for a variety of compelling reasons. First, children of both genders as well as of all ages, races, religions, classes, and geographic regions of the world watch television on a regular basis, enjoy it tremendously, and may well learn more about the world from it than from any other socializing agent. Very few other social phenomena can be claimed with such confidence to be an experience shared by most children in today's world. Whether they view TV in their bedroom, download it on their computer or mobile phone, share the family set in the living room, or watch it in the classroom or the community center, it is part of the taken-for-granted everyday experience of most children. No other cultural phenomenon has achieved such a magnitude of penetration or global status.

The global status of television can be claimed because very similar debates over television's role in the lives of children have emerged globally. On one hand, high hopes and great expectations have been expressed worldwide that television would enrich children's lives, stimulate their imagination and creativity, broaden their education and knowledge, encourage multicultural tolerance, narrow social gaps, and stimulate development and democratization processes. On the other hand, there has been and continues to be great anxiety about the ability of television to numb the senses, develop indifference to the pain of others, encourage destructive behaviors, lead to a deterioration of moral values, suppress local cultures, and contribute to social estrangement.

These oppositional stances in regard to the medium of television—as a "messiah" on one hand and "demon" on the other—have been discussed widely in public debates in every society that has absorbed the medium. Most pronounced are concerns over the effects of television violence on children, as well as the potential harm of exposure to sexual portrayals, the effects of advertising on consumer culture, and the more general concern over children's passivity and social disengagement. Media debates, public forums, parents and community newsletters, legislative bodies' hearings, educational leaders, broadcasting policy makers—all contributed to these popular debates framed as "moral panics," exerting public pressure on governing institutions.

The relations of television and children have interested scholars worldwide, mainly in the fields of psychology, media studies, sociology, education, and health professions (see, e.g., Lemish, 2007; Pecora, Murray, & Wartella, 2007). Their varied disciplinary homes have made a great deal of difference to the kind of theoretical underpinnings brought to their research, the questions posed, the methods applied, and, accordingly, the kinds of findings reported and their interpretation. Furthermore, in this respect, the academic field concerned with the reciprocal relationships between children and television reflects in large degree the changes that have taken place in the various disciplines nourishing this scholarly field, in general, and the study of mass media, in particular.

Psychology, the most prominent of the disciplines applied to this area, has focused on the individual child and a host of related issues, such as social learning from television, the effects of television on behavior, development of comprehension of television content, or the uses children make of television and the gratifications they acquire from their viewing behaviors. As the body of literature grew, mainly from Western academic institutions, it became clear that the "strong effects" conclusion that assumes a unidirectional television effect on children is too oversimplistic. Other research demonstrated something that common sense and anecdotal data posited for a long time: Children are not passive entities, a la the proverbial "tabula rasa," upon which television messages leave their marks. On the contrary, children are active consumers of television: They react to, think, feel, and create meanings. They bring to television encounters a host of predispositions, abilities, desires, and experiences. They watch television in diverse personal, social, and cultural circumstances that, too, influence and are part of their discourse and interactions with television. Thus, it has become clear that asking "What do children do with television?" is just as important a question as "How does television influence them?"

This paradigm shift led to highlighting the need for cross-cultural research. Clearly, comparative research of this global phenomenon can illuminate many of the questions on the research agenda: Does televised violence affect children differently if they are living in a violent urban center in comparison to a tranquil isolated village? Are children more frightened by news coverage of war when they are growing up amid armed conflict in comparison to children for whom war is a fictitious concept? Do children react differently to actors and actresses of European descent who appear in their favorite soap operas and situation comedies if they are living in a dominantly Euro-American society in comparison to African, Latino, or Asian ones? And what about consumerism—would children raised in rich consumer cultures amid an abundance of products from which to choose interpret advertising differently than those with no financial resources or limited personal property? Pursuing such questions related to children and television has become a global endeavor for researchers to study, as no single body of knowledge based on contextualized studies in one culture, be it as rich and diverse as possible, can provide us with the in-depth, multifaceted picture necessary to understand this phenomenon in its full global manifestation.

The topic of children and television is of global interest for an additional crucial reason. Today, children are part of a global audience that transcends local or even regional physical and cultural boundaries in consumption of television programs. As a global phenomenon, television promotes mainly what has been termed as "late modernity" values, typified primarily by commercialism, globalization, privatization, and individualization. This is "achieved" as a result of the fact that children all over the world watch, for example, American-produced cartoons, situation comedies, soap operas, action-adventure serials, and Disney and Hollywood movies. However, they also watch programs that come from other parts of the world, such as Latin-American telenovelas, localized versions of Japanese animations, or the local coproductions of the American *Sesame Street* and the United Kingdom's *Teletubbies*. Worldwide, children complete their homework or chores to the sounds of popular music on MTV and fantasize on love and adventure over blockbuster movies broadcast at a later time on their local channels or downloaded on their computers. They cheer for their favorite sports team across continents and seas, follow the news of armed conflicts worlds apart, and admire many of the same celebrities, collect their memorabilia, hang their posters, wear their T-shirts, and follow their private lives in the magazines and websites.

Therefore, the study of media and children can no longer remain bound within national borders, as media, children, and young people's well-being are international as well as transnational phenomena involving important issues such as the political economy of media corporations; implications of the centrality of new, border-free technologies; massive migration movements; and rapidly changing understandings and theorizing of multiculturalism, cultural hybridity, and diasporic identities. The monies invested in children and child-targeted entertainment media advance a global market of enormous proportions and varying value. For huge entertainment corporations, children are not future citizens; rather, they are first and foremost consumers.

Childhood is not a distinct period in the life cycle from the commercial point of view, one that should be attended to with compassion and responsibility. Rather, on the contrary, it is a distinct market opportunity requiring strong socialization to consumer-centered lifestyle. Thus, any attempts to advance or lobby for change in the contents of television programs and movies directed at children, to legislate internet safety, or to develop less violent and more creative computer games for children can no longer be redressed in national isolation. Indeed, cross-cultural studies have demonstrated

their potential to reveal the deep ethnocentrism and cultural biases inherent in so many of these texts, understand the complex intertwining of culture and media, and at the same time highlight those aspects of children's lives, their needs, aspirations, pleasures, and anxieties, that seem to be shared universally.

Content Characteristics of Children's Television Circulating Globally

Given this broad overview, we can discuss one of the pressing questions at the center of studies of children's television: What kind of television programs are traveling around the world? A recent analysis of children's television programs in 24 countries (Götz et al., 2008) presented compelling evidence of the global flow of children's programs. The analysis of 9,000 individual programs (out of about 20,000 recorded in the sample that aired during 2,400 hours of explicit children's television) found that only 23% of the programs were produced or coproduced domestically around the world, while 77% of all fictional programs were "imported." The United States and the United Kingdom, with 83% and 67% shares of the market, respectively, were the countries with the highest percentages of local production, followed by China (53%) and Canada (45%). At the other end of the spectrum, only 1% of the programs broadcast in Hong Kong, Kenya, and New Zealand were produced domestically. The biggest export region of children's television programs was North America, where 60% of the world children's television production originated, followed by Europe with 28% and Asia with 9%.

Among the sample of programs studied, 69% were fictional shows, 17% were nonfiction, and 7% were mixed genres. Animated programs comprised the main share of the fictional programs (84%). There was a much smaller share of children's programs that featured real human beings (9%), mixed formats (5%), or puppet shows (2%).

Another central finding was that there were more than twice as many male characters (68%) than female characters (32%) in children's programs. The percentage of females was much lower in programs without human characters, where creators have the most freedom to construct images (25% as animals, 21% as monsters, 16% as robots, and 13% as other fictional beings). Differences between the various countries were not significant, highlighting that this is a universally biased characteristic. In addition, on the average, 72% of all main characters were coded as Caucasian, including in countries where the dominant skin color is black (e.g., 69% of characters in children's programming in Kenya and 81% in South Africa were white).

In summary, empirical evidence suggests that children's television around the world consists primarily of fictional animation programs not produced domestically but purchased from abroad, mainly from the United States and Canada. These programs feature mostly light skin characters with an overwhelming presence of males. Therefore, the White male hegemony seems to be numerically dominant in children's television around the world, just as it is in other aspects of popular culture.

Implications for Future Childhoods Around the Globe[2]

Analysis of the characteristics of the global children's television market can be grounded in the more general discourse of critical approaches to media globalization and its influences on local cultures, indigenous traditions, heritages, and values. Globalization, in this sense, rarely means universal but rather refers to the spread of Western mediated products and images around the globe.

The claim that we live in a world increasingly characterized by Americanization has

been put forth repeatedly in intellectual and political thought (e.g., Bloch & Lemish, 2003; Held & McGrew, 2003; Ritzer, 1993). Most notably, in the children's television domain, there are three main American corporations (following recent purchasing and realignments) controlling the market in the United States as well as the rest of the world—the Disney Channel, Nickelodeon, and Cartoon Network ("Kidscreen," n.d.). The competition between television networks for their share of the children's market drives them to differentiate themselves from one another and to create brand identity and loyalty (White & Hall Preston, 2005), characterized, among other markers, by a specific gender and age appeal. Their global success suggests that they have succeeded in maximizing their appeal worldwide. Given these structures of market forces, what, then, are the possible implications of the dominance of North American television programs in constructing childhoods around the world? Let us consider some of the most central influences that emerged in a grounded theory of mediated childhood, via analysis of 135 interviews with producers of children's television from 65 countries around the world (Lemish, 2010).

LOSS OF THE LOCAL

While this is not a new argument in the discourse of cultural imperialism (Morley, 2006), American programming for children has been strongly criticized around the world on many levels: for being stereotypical of gender and race, for being irrelevant to indigenous cultures, for being too limited in scope of content and issues for children as they mature, for unnecessarily accelerating adulthood, and for encouraging wasteful consumerism. In this study, the longing for more visibility of one's own culture has been a very strong theme. Direct blame has been directed at exported American television for children and its role in perpetuating inappropriate values, including flooding the children's television market with stereotypical representations of an imagined, idealized portrayal of the American way of life with associated hegemonic-oriented representations of gender and race roles. A partial list of the critique of values identified in the forms of American television broadcast to children around the world includes heavy consumerism, over-preoccupation with sex and romance, lack of respect for adults and local cultural traditions, individualism and estrangement from the collective, dominance of the English language and slang, dominance of popular culture, and celebrity adoration. Critiques also cite what is absent in these programs, including the lives, values, and concerns of lower-class children as well as children growing up in poor-resource societies, in conflict and crisis situations, in nontraditional family arrangements, or on the streets. The lack of buying power of such populations means that they are transparent to the industry, according to the rules by which this system operates. Accordingly, their needs, aspirations, pleasures, fantasies, and realities are not catered to or reflected on the screens to which children and youth are exposed.

Major social issues shared throughout the world that are of central concern for young people are nonexistent in the lives of the middle-class children portrayed on screens around the world—for example, schooling, life as HIV/AIDS orphans, domestic and sexual violence, safety, health, and plain survival. Rarely, too, are the historical values and tales, music, customs and mores, sights and sounds, foods, habits, languages, and ways of lives different from those of the "imaginary center" of the Western world (Appaduari, 1990). As a result, most young viewers neither see themselves nor their lives reflected or presented in authentic ways. Rather, among the results of the heavy dominance of the *imagined* Western world is exposure and informal socialization to a social world where they, and those like them, are marginal, unimportant, even nonexistent. Here,

according to the cultivation hypothesis advanced in media studies (Signorielle & Morgan, 1990), we can argue that accumulated exposure to a particular worldview fosters an internalization of that world as an accurate and normative perspective to life. Accordingly, many scholars and media educators argue that media literacy programs should enable participants to challenge images that entrench a perspective of oneself as an "other" as well as to engage children of privileged hegemonies in questioning self-perceptions and life experiences as standing for all children.

THE DOMINANCE OF THE WESTERN BEAUTY MYTH

In a related argument, children's television is a partner with other industries in perpetuating an unattainable beauty model, particularly for girls. This model exemplifies the intertwining of gender and postcolonial theories, as it relates to what Wolf (1991) referred to as the Western "beauty myth": a homogenization of the desired female "look" as mostly young, thin, attractive, heterosexual, wealthy, and predominantly White. Evidence from the global study presented above (Götz et al., 2008), as well as additional studies (e.g., Bramlett-Solomon & Roeder, 2008; Northup & Liebler, 2010), demonstrates the priority given to selected images of Whiteness on television viewed by children, all of which convey the message that Western beauty is superior to any other racial forms. Scholars claim that the implications of such images are that they are disempowering for children worldwide with impacts on self-identity, national pride, and behavior (including the purchase of products in the pursuit of the unattainable look and plastic surgery that imitates Caucasian features). Concern for young people's desire to forsake their identity and even to abandon their distinct racial physical characteristics was among the sources of producer grievance around the world (Lemish, 2010).

Thus, the beauty myth has been perceived to be a well-disciplined effort to control girls as well as a racial form of inequity and discrimination. Indeed, Hall (1997) claimed this to be an example of "internal colonization" that occurs when adoption of a dominant representation "succeeds" so that people see and experience themselves as an Other. Black, Filippina, or Latina girls, for example, learn to see themselves through the White masculine perspective that represents and speaks for them. In doing so, they internalize an oppressive point of view of themselves and participate in a "process of whitening that attempts to modernize these identities while bleaching ethnicities" (Nayak & Kehily, 2007, p. 24). Others have referred to this as a form of discrimination based on skin color that is a process of internalized "colorism" (Banks, 2000). Thus, even skin tone may determine different "shades" of racism and create status hierarchies and inequalities within the colored community itself (Celious & Oyserman, 2001).

The struggle to attain the "Western look" also imposes an economic strain on children and their families as it encourages heavy consumption of leisure goods that in turn fuels production of a variety of products, including clothing, fashion accessories, costly surgeries, and multiple exemplars of Western popular culture. A related concern is that the popular beauty ideals distributed by television for children promote deficit self body-image and glorification of thinness, as well as encourage destructive eating disorders (Harrison & Hefner, 2006). On the other hand, the unhealthy eating habits promoted by the American "fast-food" industry along with a passive physical life encouraged by heavy consumption of television have been found to be correlated with growing obesity among young people (Vandewater & Cummings, 2008) in Western societies and are raising anxiety over possible similar influences worldwide.

GENDER SEGREGATION

The dynamics of the television industry in the United States and the insatiable economic needs that drive them contribute in numerous ways to television's gender segregation worldwide. For example, they continue to promote a worldview through which boys and girls are encouraged to inhabit different electronic and cultural spaces. They do so through the contents offered, as well as by serving as a model for younger, resource-poor television industries. The Disney Channel, for example, with its big global hits (e.g., *High School Musical; Hannah Montana*) is clearly perceived as "girls oriented," while the Cartoon Network has been traditionally associated with action-adventure cartoons and a boys' audience. Originally, Nickelodeon was involved in extensive gender experimentation and was a somewhat gender-neutral channel. While its programming decisions have shifted, the channel retains a more balanced approach in its programming than any of the other major networks. Yet, it is still perceived by industry professionals to be skewed toward girls (Lemish, 2010). This general division among the networks is strongly reinforced by the truism that has become the industry's working axiom: Although girls will watch boys' shows, boys will not watch girls' shows. Scholars have found that this central belief is shared throughout the industry (Alexander & Owers, 2007; Banet-Weiser, 2004; Lemish, 2010; Seiter & Mayer, 2004).

Similar forms of audience fragmentation, particularly along race and sexuality lines (e.g., African American programs, Hispanic programs, gay programs) and their intersection with gender identities, have been found to contribute to the identity project of individuals in this era of late modernity. These trends are gradually shifting due to economic pressures and growing gender equity awareness so networks are now making an effort to address the issue of channel segregation by employing strategies such as selecting lead characters from both genders, diversifying program genres and narrative styles, and packaging and naming strategies. However, it is interesting to note that expanding the audience to include both boys and girls is clearly understood as a marketing strategy. Take, for example, Disney's efforts to attract 6- to 14-year-old boy viewers to the new Disney XD cable channel and website (Barnes, 2009). This plan does not seem to be aimed at blurring gender segregation or erasing stereotypes; rather, on the contrary, it is geared to offering a clearly defined "boys' world"—an X Disney—in addition to the existing girls' one.

Television professionals' construction of their young audiences as largely inhabiting two very different gendered cultural worlds draws heavily on developmental theories as well as market and academic research findings. Studies suggest that the tendency for children to segregate themselves by gender and to play more compatibly with same-sex partners is already evident in early childhood and progressively gains strength by mid-childhood. The causes and consequences of this segregation are a major topic of investigation in child psychology and education (Maccoby, 1998; Mehta & Strough, 2009). Suffice to say, for our purposes, that gender-segregated childhoods provide different contexts for children's social development. This does not necessarily prepare them for mutual understanding and collaboration. This segregation runs parallel to the current popularity of the "Mars and Venus" metaphor (Gray, 1991), according to which men and women are perceived to be essentially different beings with opposing communication styles and emotional needs. This perspective has recruited to its service key elements of the postfeminist sensibility, best represented by the slogan "different but equal" (Shifman & Lemish, in press). Television and toy industries seem to be capitalizing quite successfully on this popular trend, pushing it to its extremes in their pursuit of ever-expanding markets and profits worldwide.

Earlier research on the gendered nature of media consumption by children and youth found that while, overall, girls do develop an interest in traditional masculine genres, on the whole, boys continue to show no interest in female genres (Lemish, Liebes, & Seidmann, 2001). While the largely descriptive evidence gathered does provide empirical support for the popular axiom applied by children's entertainment industry and media professionals cited above, we lack critical analyses that are the product of unpacking and identifying the mechanisms creating this phenomenon. For example, according to the feminist analysis of social change, this process can be partly explained through the observation that, more generally, girls as well as women have learned to gradually incorporate typical male perspectives and values into their lives while not abandoning their traditional female responsibilities and interests. This echoes other situations where efforts at improving status and positions are advanced through the process of subordinated social groups adjusting "up" socially. Perhaps the trend of girls' interests in boys' genres represents their growing sensitivity to the advantageous position that boys hold in societies around the world and the higher value associated with their tastes and interests.

Serving the Needs of Children— Proactive Conclusions[3]

Television programs for children that travel around the world are big business. As such, profit is the main interest of the executives who manage these programs, rather than the aim of bettering children's lives. However, I submit that critical analyses of the content offerings of this major socializer raise serious questions and ethical challenges about the industry's conduct and social responsibility.

As delineated in the United Nations Convention on the Rights of the Child (1989), the rights of children include a variety of communication rights: the right to be heard and to be taken seriously, to free speech and to information, to maintain privacy, to develop cultural identity, and to be proud of one's heritage and beliefs. Yet, whether girls and boys live in deprived and resource-poor societies or in overwhelmingly commercialized and profit-driven ones, their voices are for the most part neither heard nor taken seriously. They have limited opportunities to express their needs and opinions or to access much-needed information, available to youth and adults. Many mass communication efforts do not respect children's privacy and dignity or foster their self-esteem and confidence. Even in the cases in which, seemingly, they are allowed to "voice" their concerns, it is often only "token" in nature, reflects adults' perspectives, and does not necessarily contribute to their holistic development or problem-solving skills (Kolucki & Lemish, in press).

Children around the world face similar issues of personal safety, as well as anxiety over the future of the globe and their place in it. Television has a responsibility to help all children become courageous adults and active citizens of this world. Offering girls and boys a symbolic "safe space," with images of children who are not afraid to divert from traditional gender and cultural norms as well as break away from them in seeking to make the world a better place for themselves and for others, may be just what this "safe space" can symbolically do.

Part of the effort to provide children with a "safe space" includes advancing programs that enable them to understand what it is like to live in a society of inclusion. A diverse screen provides more realistic, humane portrayals of current societies around the world and is also central to the well-being of the children growing within them. It celebrates girls and boys as children who share the same challenges, aspirations, morality, dreams, and hopes; children who need love and friendships, have adventures, and overcome difficulties; children who are curious and eager to explore their surroundings and who struggle with their multiple identities; children who try to carve their place in the world. Children's television needs to present young persons who are self-willed, are positive, and share their problems and accomplishments. Breaking stereotypes and opening up the screen to blurring gender and racial differences and offering children real choices that cut across divides can foster a safer and healthier environment for growth and development. Young viewers can be exposed to a range of possibilities relevant to their own lives that also challenge the ways in which they are brought up to think about their own identities.

While these suggestions may seem naive given the competitive nature of the now well-established global television market, it is crucial to remember that we can build upon and expand many of the efforts taking place worldwide by dedicated professionals who see television as a social resource that needs to be taken seriously and responsibly. Indeed, there are professionals working, too, within the commercial world to introduce change from within the system. Others operate in organizations driven by social goals that are not solely profit driven, as well as not-for-profit alternative and citizen media who, collectively, offer a spectrum from the conservative to radical and subversive contents (Downing, 2001). These efforts can be framed as part of media reform and democratization movements that seek not only to rebut but also to offer alternatives to the hegemonic control by media corporations (McChesney & Nichols, 2002).

Indeed, many such efforts are integrated within public broadcasting systems funded by the state, particularly in Europe. Many of these efforts in the realm of television for children are dedicated to contextualizing their productions within local cultures and children's needs (Lemish, 2010). Some of the best efforts of such work are presented in international events that bring together professionals involved in creating quality television for children around the globe, such as the *Prix Jeunesse* in Munich and the *Japan Prize* in Tokyo, among others (see Cole, 2007). Therefore, the debate over the future of public broadcasting, free journalism, and democracy (e.g., McChesney & Nichols, 2010) also has serious implications for broadcasting to children—a unique population devoid of political and economic power or opportunities to lobby, protest, or bargain for their rights.

Through incorporating concerns for children's well-being and healthy development, television can be enriching and inspiring. It can offer a diverse range of possibilities for children and complex characters that are not bound by stereotypes, and it can give voice to their multiple perspectives and experiences. It may constitute a safe environment in which to explore the full range of roles children might wish for themselves, a vision for a different reality, and aspiration for a better world.

Notes

1. This section is reprinted with some changes from my earlier work, Lemish (2007, pp. 1–4).

2. This section draws upon my earlier work published in Lemish (2010, chaps. 3 and 4).

3. This section draws upon my earlier work published in Lemish (2010, chaps. 7 and 8).

References

Alexander, A., & Owers, J. (2007). The economics of children's television. In J. A. Bryant (Ed.), *The children's television community* (pp. 57–74). Mahwah, NJ: Lawrence Erlbaum.

Appadurai, A. (1990). Disjuncture and difference in the global economy. *Theory, Culture and Society, 7,* 295–310.

Banet-Weiser, S. (2004). Girls rule! Gender, feminism, and Nickelodeon. *Critical Studies in Media Communication, 21*(2), 119–139.

Banks, T. L. (2000). Colorism: A darker shade of pale. *UCLA Law Review, 47*(6), 1705–1746.

Barnes, B. (2009, April 14). Disney expert uses science to draw boy viewers. *The New York Times.*

Bloch, L. R., & Lemish, D. (2003). The megaphone effect: International culture via the US of A. *Communication Yearbook, 27,* 159–190.

Bramlett-Solomon, S., & Roeder, Y. (2008). Looking at race in children's television: Analysis of Nickelodeon commercials. *Journal of Children and Media, 2,* 56–66.

Celious, A., & Oyserman, D. (2001). Race from the inside: An emerging heterogeneous race model. *Journal of Social Issues, 57*(1), 149–165.

Cole, C. F. (2007). A guide to international events in children's media. *Journal of Children and Media, 1*(1), 93–100.

Downing, J. (2001). *Radical media: Rebellious communication and social movements.* Thousand Oaks, CA: Sage.

Götz, M., Hoffman, O., Brosius, H. B., Carter, C., Chan, K., Dobnald, S. H., et al. (2008). Gender in children's television worldwide. *TelevIZIon, 21*(E).

Gray, J. (1991). *Men are from Mars, women are from Venus: A practical guide for improving communication and getting what you want in your relationships.* New York: HarperCollins.

Hall, S. (1997). *Representation: Cultural representations and signifying practices.* Milton Keynes, UK: Open University Press.

Harrison, K., & Hefner, V. (2006). Media exposure, current and future body ideals, and disordered eating among preadolescent girls: A longitudinal panel study. *Journal of Youth and Adolescence, 35,* 153–163.

Held, D., & McGrew, A. (Eds.). (2003). *The global transformations reader: An introduction to the globalization debate* (2nd ed.). Cambridge, UK: Polity.

Kidscreen ratings watch. (n.d.). Retrieved January 30, 2010, from http://www.kidscreen.com/articles/news/20091223/ratingswatch.html

Kolucki, B., & Lemish, D. (In press). *Communication for children and youth: Good*

practices that nurture, inspire, excite, educate, and heal. New York: UNICEF.

Lemish, D. (2007). *Children and television: A
global perspective.* Oxford, UK: Blackwell.

Lemish, D. (2010). *Screening gender in
children's TV: The views of producers
around the world.* New York: Routledge.

Lemish, D., Liebes, T., & Seidmann, V. (2001).
Gendered media meaning and use. In
S. Livingstone & M. Bovill (Eds.), *Children
and their changing media environment*
(pp. 263–282). Hillsdale, NJ: Lawrence
Erlbaum.

Maccoby, E. E. (1998). *The two sexes: Growing
up apart—coming together.* Cambridge,
MA: The Belknap Press of Harvard
University Press.

McChesney, R., & Nichols, J. (2002). *Our
media, not theirs: The democratic struggle
against corporate media.* New York: Seven
Stories Press.

McChesney, J., & Nichols, J. (2010). *The death
and life of American journalism: The media
revolution that will begin the world again.*
Philadelphia: First Nation Books.

Mehta, C. M., & Strough, J. (2009). Sex segregation in friendships and normative contexts across the life span. *Developmental
Review, 29,* 201–220.

Morley, D. (2006). Globalisation and cultural
imperialism reconsidered: Old questions in
new guises. In J. Curran & D. Morley (Eds.),
Media and cultural theory (pp. 30–43).
New York: Routledge.

Nayak, A., & Kehily, M. J. (2007). *Gender,
youth and culture: Young masculinities and
femininities.* Hampshire, UK: Palgrave.

Northrup, T., & Liebler, C. (2010). The good, the
bad, and the beautiful: Beauty ideals on the
Disney and Nickelodeon channels. *Journal
of Children and Media, 4*(3), 265–282.

Pecora, N., Murray, J. P., & Wartella, E. A.
(Eds.). (2007). *Children and television:
Fifty years of research.* Mahwah, NJ:
Lawrence Erlbaum.

Ritzer, G. (1993). *The McDonaldization of
society.* Thousand Oaks, Pine Forge Press.

Seiter, E., & Mayer, V. (2004). Diversifying representation in children's TV: Nickelodeon's
model. In H. Hendershot (Ed.), *Nickelodeon
nation: The history, politics, and economics
of America's only TV channel for kids*
(pp. 120–133). New York: New York
University Press.

Shifman, L., & Lemish, D. (In press). "Mars and
Venus" in virtual space: Post-feminist
humor and the Internet. *Critical Studies in
Media Communication.*

Signorielle, N., & Morgan, M. (Eds.). (1990).
*Cultivation analysis: New directions in
media effects research.* Newbury Park, CA:
Sage.

Vandewater, E. A., & Cummings, H. M. (2008).
Media use and childhood obesity. In
S. L. Calvert & B. J. Wilson (Eds.), *The
handbook of children, media, and development* (pp. 355–380). Oxford, UK: Blackwell.

White, C. L., & Hall Preston, E. (2005). The
spaces of children's programming. *Critical
Studies in Media Communication, 22*(3),
239–255.

Wolf, N. (1991). *The beauty myth: How images of
beauty are used against women.* New York:
Doubleday.

From Tony the Tiger to
Slime Time Live

The Content of Commercial Messages
in Children's Advertising

Juliet B. Schor

. . . The 1980s brought major changes in children's advertising. Companies began to see more potential in selling to kids. Credit for this realization is typically given to James McNeal, whose estimates of children's purchasing power were widely circulated in the industry. McNeal reports that in the 1960s, when he pitched his expertise to firms, his message fell on deaf ears: "They practically laughed me out of the place. 'Kids as a market? You gotta be kidding.'"[1] By the late 1980s, when his first book appeared, companies were taking children far more seriously. McNeal's estimates helped to expand the types of products that were marketed to kids, as well as increase the volume of dollars companies were willing to commit in categories such as food and leisure. Kraft started targeting kids for cheese, pasta, Jell-O, and puddings, in addition to longstanding child foods such as snacks and cereals. As Paul Kurnit, one of the deans of kid marketing explained to me, "There was the recognition that you could drive macaroni and other foods to kids themselves, you know, 'Mom, please get me Kraft macaroni and cheese.'"[2]

A second development was that the expansion of children's media offered new opportunities for advertisers. In the 1980s, cable television stations specifically designed for children were introduced. And although some of them, such as Nickelodeon, did not initially accept ads, those policies eventually changed. Cable became an inexpensive and effective venue for advertisers. The emergence of Fox as a fourth network also helped propel the kids' market. Fox skewed toward youth, using edgy new formats with "cool" and African American, urban themes that appealed to children who hadn't yet reached adolescence.

Finally, the 1980s witnessed the dramatic upsurge in kids' influence power. There were fewer of what marketers called the "authoritarian mom"—the woman who, in the words

Excerpt from Schor, J. (2004). *Born to buy: The commercialized child and the new consumer culture*. New York: Scribner/Simon & Schuster.

of Paul Kurnit, said, "No way, no how is there going to be a pre-sweetened cereal in our house, no matter how hard Johnnie tries to convince her." Instead, 1980s mothers were far more likely to be permissive or ambivalent moms, willing to buy the products. "Another piece of it is that today's mom grew up with all this stuff, so she tends to be much more of a culture creature herself, and if her parent wasn't authoritarian, why should she be?"

By the 1990s the stage was set for a thorough revolution in youth marketing. Kids had unprecedented spending power. They had unprecedented influence over their parents' spending power. They were watching unprecedented levels of television. And they were on their own far more than the previous generation had been. Now the trick was to get them to buy the products on offer.

The companies responded by upping their ad budgets substantially. Once that happened, the agencies needed to bring in more expertise. In the past kid marketers had mostly relied on personal intuition and the experiences they themselves had as parents. With so many more dollars at stake, that strategy was risky, so companies hired psychologists, child development specialists, anthropologists, and sociologists to help craft more compelling messages. They developed far more capacity for testing and research and they began delivering those messages in new ways. . . .

The Child Psyche According to Marketers

In contemporary marketing, the naturalization of consumer desires has been codified into a set of timeless emotional needs all children are believed to possess.[3] Standard practice consists of matching those universal needs to particular products and advertising messages, in which the role of the ad or product is to satisfy the need. Kids need

to be scared to help them overcome their fears, so make a scary movie. Kids need to belong, so suggest that if they buy brand X, they'll have friends.

These needs are defined similarly throughout the field. The first "need" is for gender differentiation. Virtually every marketing professional I encountered contends that boys and girls like different products and need segregated marketing. With the exception of food, almost all products, messages and campaigns are subjected to gender analysis that asks, Is it for boys, or is it for girls? (Some products do emerge as unisex.) Despite efforts to raise awareness about the role of toys in the reproduction of unhealthy gender stereotypes, the major toy chains still segregate by gender.[4] The so-called timeless emotional needs also skew in one direction or another, and boys get a wider range of messages. The conventional wisdom is that boys want power. Boys also want action, and they want to succeed. By contrast, girls are thought to want glamour. And although girl power (the idea that girls are powerful and active) has now entered the pantheon of innermost needs, girls are still thought of in stereotypical ways and remain tethered to traditional ideals of glamour and femininity, even when they're powerful.

In ads, these ideas play out in standard formulas. The old themes of car crashes for boys and pink-washing for girls have by no means disappeared, but they are less common, and the gender rules have become more subtle. For example, boy characters and masculine messages must dominate in ads for any products that are aimed at boys or both sexes. If four children are used to advertise a unisex or boy product, the rule is that at least three will be boys. Three girls are used only for girl products. The rationale for these conventions is that boys are more skittish about gender identities and highly sensitive to anything that smacks of the feminine.[5] As a consequence, boys are still preferred when casting ads. Other gender differences are that girls remain more likely to be portrayed in indoor domestic spaces, and boys are shown out of doors. While passivity is no longer required for girls, behavioral differences remain, such as the fact that boys are frequently shown engaging in antisocial behavior, while girls act only in socially sanctioned ways.

Despite the growth of girl heroines, gender imbalance remains in certain programming mediums. A 1997 Kaiser Family Foundation study found that 63 percent of movie characters arc male, as are 78 percent of those in music videos.[6] (The breakdown on television is now closer to parity, with 55 percent male characters.) But there are some signs that the consensus is cracking. The phenomenon of gender blending has been getting attention recently, with examples such as boys wearing nail polish or girls liking "gross."[7] However, for a field that portrays itself as on the cutting edge, the extent to which gender stereotypes still predominate is striking. . . .

The Marketing of Cool

Cool has been around for decades. Back in the fifties, there were cool cats and hipsters. In the sixties, hippies and the Beatles were cool. But in those days, cool was only one of many acceptable personal styles. Now it's revered as a universal quality—something every product tries to be and every kid needs to have.[8] Marketers have defined cool as the key to social success, as what matters for determining who belongs, who's popular, and who gets accepted by peers. While there is no doubt that the desire for social acceptance is a central theme of growing up, marketers have elevated it to the sine qua non of children's psyches. The promotion of cool is a good example of how the practices of marketing to teens, for whom social acceptance is even more important, have filtered down to the children's sphere. In a recent survey of 4,002 kids in grades 4 through 8, 66 percent reported that cool

defines them.[9] Part of why is that cool has become *the* dominant theme of children's marketing.

Part of the genius of cool is its versatility. Cool isn't only about not being a dork. Cool takes on many incarnations. It can incorporate dork and jock, if necessary. It can be driven by neon or primary colors; it's retro or futuristic, techno or natural. Today, Target is cool. Yesterday it was the Gap. Good-bye Barney. Hello Kitty. By the time you read these words, today's cool will not be. But although cool is hard to pin down, in practice it centers on some recurring themes, and these themes are relentlessly pushed by marketers in the conception and design of products, packaging, marketing, and advertising. At every step, these principles apply.

One theme is that cool is socially exclusive, that is, expensive. In an earlier era, cheap stuff dominated kids' consumer worlds, mainly because they didn't have much money. They bought penny candy, plastic toys, and cheap thrills. In those days, the functional aspects of products were paramount, such as the fact that the toy is fun to play with or the candy tastes good. Social symbolism and status weren't wholly absent, but they were far less important. Now that kids have access to so much more money, status and its underlying values of inequality and exclusion have settled at the heart of the kid consumer culture. Branding expert Martin Lindstrom reports that for tweens, the brand took over from function as the main attraction of products in the 1990s.[10] From video games, to apparel, to that ubiquitous symbol of status, the athletic shoe, kids' products have upscaled, in the process becoming both more unaffordable and more desirable. Gene Del Vecchio, former Ogilvy and Mather executive and author of *Creating Ever-cool: A Marketer's Guide to a Kid's Heart,* is more candid than most others about the exclusionary nature of cool. "Part of cool is having something that others do not, that makes a kid feel special. It is also the spark that drives kids to find the next cool item."[11] When Reebok introduced its computerized Traxtar shoe, it was banking on a message of "superiority" ("I have Traxtar and you don't"), according to the people who designed the program.[12] The shoe became the top seller in its category, a notable accomplishment given its significantly higher price. Marketers convey the view that wealth and aspiration to wealth are cool. Material excess, having lots of money, career achievement and a lifestyle to go with it are all highly valued in the marketing world's definition of what's hot and what's not. Living modestly means living like a loser.

Cool is also associated with being older than one's age. Marketers and advertisers take this common desire of kids and play into it in a variety of ways.[13] They put a few older kids in ads that are targeted to younger kids. They have young kids in ads morph into older kids or into adults. They use adult celebrity endorsers for products or brands that kids buy. They depict fantasy worlds in which a young kid sees himself or herself grown up. Cool is also associated with an anti-adult sensibility, as ads portray kids with attitude, outwitting their teachers and tricking their parents. Finally, cool is about the taboo, the dangerous, the forbidden other. Among advertisers *edgy* has been and remains the adjective of the moment—not "over the edge," because that is too dangerous, but "at the edge," "pushing the edge."

Edgy style has associations with rap and hip-hop, with "street" and African American culture. In the 1990s, ads aimed at white, middle-class Americans began to be filmed in inner-city neighborhoods with young black men as the stars. The ads made subtle connections to violence, drugs, criminality, and sexuality—the distorted and stereotypical images of young black men that have pervaded the mainstream media. As Harvard University's Douglas Holt wrote in 1999 in a paper we coauthored, "Street has proven to be a potent commodity because its aesthetic offers an authentic threatening edginess that is very attractive both to white suburban kids who perpetually recreate radical youth culture in relation to their parents' conservative views about the ghetto, and to urban cultural elites for whom it becomes a form of cosmopolitan radical chic. . . . We now have the commodification of a virulent, dangerous 'other' lifestyle . . . Gangsta."[14]

The story of how street came to be at the core of consumer marketing began more than thirty years ago. Chroniclers of the marketing of "ghetto" point to the practices of athletic shoe companies, starting with Converse in the late 1960s and, more recently, Nike and its competitors. The shoe manufacturers intentionally associated their product with African American athletes, giving free shoes to coaches in the inner cities, targeting inner-city consumers in their research, attaching their brand to street athletics and sociability. The also developed a practice dubbed "bro-ing" by industry insiders, that is, going to the streets to ask the brothers which designs deserve the moniker of cool.[15] Apparel companies, beginning with Tommy Hilfiger, became active in this world, giving rap stars and other prominent tastemakers free samples of their latest styles.[16] While the connection to inner-city life may sound like a contradiction with the idea that cool is exclusive and upscale, it is partially resolved by the fact that many of the inner-city ambassadors of products are wealthy, conspicuous consumers such as rap stars and athletes driving fancy cars and living luxurious lifestyles.

Eventually soft drink companies, candy manufacturers, culture producers, and many others that sell products to teens and kids would be on the street, trying desperately to get some of that ineluctable cool to rub off on their brand. As advertiser Paul Kurnit explains, "What's going on in white America today is [that] the inner city is very much a Gold Standard. We've got lots of white kids who are walking around emulating black lifestyle."[17] Of course, mere association with ghetto style is not a guarantee of success. Some campaigns have been flat-footed with their mimicry. Others lack basic credibility, such as preppy tennis shoe K-Swiss, which tried to position itself as a street brand. The brands that have been skilled at this approach are those with images that are more plausibly and authentically connected to it.

Although many aspects of African American culture have had a long historical association with cool, such as jazz and sartorial styles, as well as a legacy of contributions to popular culture, what's happening now is unique. Never before have inner-city styles and cultural practices been such a dominant influence on, even a primary definer of, popular culture. The process is also no longer one of mainstreaming, in which a cultural innovation from the margins is incorporated into the larger culture. Rather, in the words of Douglas Holt again, "It is now the local, authentic qualities of Street culture that sell. Instead of black cultural products denuded of their social context, it is now primarily the context itself—the neighborhood, the pain of being poor, the alienation experienced by black kids. These are the commodifiable assets." The other new development is the role of large corporations in the movement of styles and cultural forms from the ghetto to the suburb. The process no longer develops through an organic movement as it once did. Instead, cool hunters manage the process of cultural transmission. Another novel aspect is the evolution of a back-and-forth dynamic between the companies and the grass roots, with cool-hunting and street marketing creating what media critics have called a feedback loop.

The feedback loop is a sharp departure from decades past, when consumers blindly followed where advertisers led. In Holt's words, marketers once possessed a monopoly on "cultural authority," in which they set the tone and agenda, and consumers eagerly looked to them to learn what to wear, eat, drive, and value.[18] That cultural authority has virtually disappeared. Its demise can be traced to the backlash against advertising that originally emerged in the 1950s with the popularity of books such as John Kenneth Galbraith's *The Affluent Society* and Vance Packard's *The Hidden Persuaders*. By the 1960s some of the most successful marketers were those who took their cues from consumers. Since then, advertisers have increasingly attempted to figure out what people already value and let those findings direct ads.[19] With youth, the process has gone a step further, because they know the advertisers are relying on them, and consciously play to their influence. That's the feedback idea, which has been identified by observers such as Douglas Kellner, Holt, and Douglas Rushkoff. As Rushkoff explains, in a plea to the industry: "It's turned into a giant feedback loop; you watch kids to find out what trend is 'in,' but the kids are watching you watching them in order to figure out how to act. They are exhibitionists, aware of corporate America's fascination with their every move, and delighting in your obsession with their tastes."[20] Although there's a democratic veneer to the feedback loop, that perspective obscures the fact that giant businesses orchestrate, control, and profit from the process. Furthermore, kids are increasingly pulling outrageous and even dangerous stunts to get themselves noticed by the great big marketing machine.

Originally, the marketing of edgy was a teen and young adult development. Now it too has trickled down to the children's market, though with some adjustments. Kid advertisers had to become far more discriminating, screening out what had become an anything-goes ethic. By way of illustration, consider the heroin-chic fashion photography of the mid-1990s. At that time cool hunters routinely included drugs, including hard ones, on their lists of what's hot and what's not. As one now-famous accounting from a cool-hunter publication that appeared in the *New Yorker* had it: "In San Francisco it's Nike, heroin, and reggae;

in Chicago, Jungle music, Tag watches, and drugs."[21] Similarly, in kids' ads, violent images are more restricted, although this is less the case in movie ads, video games, and on the Web. The situation is similar with sexuality, exploitative racial imagery, and certain antisocial themes, all of which are prominent in cultural forms for teens and young adults. While going edgy can almost guarantee cool, it can also jeopardize a brand that depends on maintaining its wholesome image. Advertisers calibrate the degree of edginess and strive to go as far as, but not beyond, what a brand's image can tolerate. . . .

Age Compression

One of the hottest trends in youth marketing is age compression—the practice of taking products and marketing messages originally designed for older kids and targeting them to younger ones.[22] Age compression includes offering teen products and genres, pitching gratuitous violence to the twelve-and-under crowd, cultivating brand preferences for items that were previously unbranded among younger kids, and developing creative alcohol and tobacco advertising that is not officially targeted to them but is widely seen and greatly loved by children. "By eight or nine they want 'N Sync," explained one tweening expert to me, in the days before that band was eclipsed by Justin Timberlake, Pink, and others.[23]

Age compression is a sprawling trend. It can be seen in the import of television programming specifically designed for one year olds, which occurred, ironically, with Public Broadcasting's *Teletubbies*. It includes the marketing of designer clothes to kindergarteners and first graders. It's the deliberate targeting of R-rated movies to kids as young as age nine, a practice the major movie studios were called on the carpet for by the Clinton administration in 2000.[24] It's being driven by the recognition that many

children nationwide are watching MTV and other teen and adult programming.[25] One of my favorite MTV anecdotes comes from a third-grade teacher in Weston, Massachusetts, who reported that she started her social studies unit on Mexico by asking the class what they knew about the country. Six or seven raised their hands and answered, "That's the place where MTVs Spring Break takes place!"[26] For those who haven't seen it, the program glorifies heavy partying, what it calls "bootylicious girls," erotic dancing, wet T-shirt contests, and binge drinking.

A common argument within the marketing world is that age compression is being caused by social trends that make contemporary children far more sophisticated than their predecessors. These include the increased responsibilities of kids in single-parent or divorced families, higher levels to exposure adult media, children's facility with new technology, early puberty, and the fact that kids know more, earlier. In the 1980s, Hasbro sold its GI Joe action figure to boys aged eleven to fourteen. Now Joe is rejected by eight year olds as too babyish.[27] Twenty years ago, *Seventeen* magazine targeted sixteen year olds; now it aims at eleven and twelves.[28] In a telling gesture the toy industry has officially lowered its upper age target from fourteen to ten.

Marketers have even coined an acronym to describe these developments. It's KAGOY, which stands for Kids Are Getting Older Younger. The social trends become part of the license for treating kids as if they were adults. Indeed, some advertisers are even arguing that current approaches are too protective of children. In a presentation at the 2001 annual Marketing to Kids Conference, executive Abigail Hirschhorn of DDB New York argued that it's time to stop talking down to kids and start "talking up" to them and that too much advertising denies kids what they really crave—the adult world. She argued for more "glamour, fashion, style, irony, and popular music."

Nowhere is age compression more evident than among the eight- to twelve-year-old target. Originally a strategy for selling to ten to thirteen year olds, children as young as six are being targeted for tweening. And what is that exactly? Tweens are "in-between" teens and children, and tweening consists mainly of bringing teen products and entertainment to ever-younger audiences. If you're wondering why your daughter came home from kindergarten one day singing the words to a Britney Spears or Jennifer Lopez song, the answer is that she got tweened. Tween marketing has become a major focus of the industry, with its own conferences, research tools, databases, books, and specialty firms.[29] Part of why tweening is so lucrative is that it involves bringing new, more expensive products to this younger group. It's working because tweens have growing purchasing power and influence with parents. The more the tween consumer world comes to resemble the teen world, with its comprehensive branding and intense levels of consumer immersion, the more money there is to be made.

In some cases, it's the advertisers pushing the trend with their clients. But clients are also initiating the process. Mark Lapham (pseudonym), president of a company that has focused almost exclusively on the teen market, says, "We're being asked all the time about it" by makers of school supplies, apparel manufacturers, cosmetics companies. Lapham explains how his clients are thinking: "Hey, we can actually sell a cosmetic, not just bubble gum lip gloss. . . . We can sell foundation possibly . . . nail polish."

Abigail Hirschhorn's plea for industry change is well behind the times. Children are being exposed to plenty of glamour, fashion, style, irony, and popular music, that is, sex. Even the family-friendly Disney Channel is full of sexually suggestive outfits and dancing. One radio Disney employee explained to me that the company keeps a careful watch on lyrics but is hands-off with the other stuff. A stroll down the 6X–12 aisles of girls' clothing will produce plenty

of skimpy and revealing styles. People in advertising are well aware of these developments. Emma Gilding of Ogilvy and Mather recounted an experience she had during an in-home videotaping. The little girl was doing a Britney Spears imitation, with flirting and sexual grinding. Asked by Gilding what she wanted to be when she grew up, the three year old answered: "A sexy shirt girl." As researcher Mary Prescott (pseudonym) explained to me in the summer of 2001, "We're coming out of a trend now. Girl power turned into sex power. A very sexy, dirty, dark thing. Parents were starting to panic." While Prescott felt that a reversal toward "puritanism" had already begun, other observers aren't so sure. Not long after Prescott's prediction, Abercrombie and Fitch came under fire for selling thong underwear with sexually suggestive phrases to seven to fourteen year olds.[30] And child development expert Diane Levin alerted parents to the introduction of World Wrestling Entertainment action figures recommended for age four and above, which include a male character with lipstick on his crotch, another male figure holding the severed head of a woman, and a female character with enormous breasts and a minimal simulated black leather outfit and whip.[31] Four year olds are also targeted with toys tied to movies that carry PG-13 ratings.[32]

Some industry insiders have begun to caution that tweening has gone too far. At the 2002 KidPower conference, Paul Kurnit spoke out publicly about companies "selling 'tude' to pre-teens and ushering in adolescence a bit sooner than otherwise." Privately, even more critical views were expressed to me. Mark Lapham revealed that he finds this "kind of an amazing thing . . . this is where personally my guilt comes out, like gosh, it's not really appropriate sometimes." But, he continues, "that's where society's going, what do you do?" Prescott, who is more deeply immersed in the world of tweening, confessed that "I am doing the most horrible thing in the world. We are targeting kids too young with too many inappropriate things . . . . It's not worth the almighty buck."

Notes

1. For James McNeal on his expertise falling on deaf ears, see the Preface to McNeal (1999).

2. Kurnit quotes and Kraft examples from my interview with Kurnit in Chappaqua, New York, November 15, 2002.

3. On children's timeless emotional needs, see Del Vecchio (1997), p. 28. For a related list of marketers' themes, see Nader (1996).

4. On sexual stereotyping and toys, see Seiter (1993).

5. On gender conventions in ads, Paul Kurnit articulated the conventional wisdom: "Capturing the boy is more difficult than capturing the girl, and that gets to some of the sexuality issues. . . . Girls in the marketing space tend to be a lot more relaxed in their skin than boys are."

6. On Kaiser findings on gender imbalance in programming and 63 percent, 78 percent, and 55 percent figures, see Signorielli (1997), Table 2, available at www.kkf.org.

7. Gender blending and examples trend from Rachel Geller of the Gepetto Group, presentation at KidPower 2002. For a perspective that begins with gender blurring but ends up stressing gender difference, see Gross (2002a).

8. For a now classic account of cool-hunting, see Gladwell (1997), reprinted in Schor and Holt (2000).

9. A recent survey in which 66 percent of kids say cool defines them is from the KidID survey of justkid Inc. Data provided to the author and presented by Wynne Tyree at KidPower 2002.

10. On the shift from function to brand as the main attraction, sec Lindstrom (2003), p. 82.

11. Gene Del Vecchio quote "part of cool" is from Del Vecchio (1997), p. 121.

12. On Traxtar marketing and its success, see Siegel et al. (2001), pp. 179–190.

13. On kids wanting to be older than they are, this is what Paul Kurnit had to say in our interview. "Emulation and aspiration work up, but only to a certain point. So if you want to capture six to eleven year olds, your bull's-eye is probably in a commercial casting a twelve or thirteen year old boy."

14. Douglas Holt quote on street as a potent commodity is from Holt and Schor (1998).

15. On sneaker marketing in the inner city, see Vanderbilt (1998), ch.1.

16. On Hilfiger, see Smith (1997) and Spiegler (1997).

17. Paul Kurnit quote from his interview with O'Barr (2001).

18. On the cultural authority of marketers, see Holt (2002).

19. On these issues, see Kellner (1998), Holt (2002), and Frank (1997) on the backlash against advertisers and the subsequent marketing of cool.

20. The feedback loop is explored in the PBS special *Merchants of Cool*, available online at pbs.org frontline/shows/cool/. Douglas Rushkoff quote from his essay "The Pursuit of Cool: Introduction to Anti-Hyper-Consumerism," available online at http://www.rushkoff.com/essay/sportswearinternational.html.

21. On cool-hunters' lists of what's hot and what's not see Gladwell (1997), from which these items are drawn.

22. On age compression, see Neil Postman's classic discussion (1994) from the point of view of the "disappearance of childhood." See also Hymowitz (1999), ch. 4, on what she calls the "teening of childhood."

23. "By eight or nine they want 'N Sync" quote from Mary Prescott in 2001.

24. On the deliberate targeting of R-rated movies, see the prepared statement of the Federal Trade Commission,"Marketing Violent Entertainment to Children: Self-Regulation and Industry Practices in the Motion Picture, Music Recording, and Electronic Game Industries," available at www.ftc.gov/os/2001/07/violencetest.htm. For a discussion, see Grier (2001). On screening movies to nine and ten year olds, see Carvajal (2000).

25. On MTV watching, see Stanger and Gridina (1999), p. 11. My survey finds a third of ten to thirteen year olds watch MTV.

26. One of my favorite MTV anecdotes is from a seminar I gave to teachers in May 2002.

27. GI Joe age figures are from Paul Kurnit, who worked on the GI Joe account some years ago, from his KidPower 2002 presentation.

28. On *Seventeen* magazine's target audience, see Grier (2001), p. 12.

29. On the idea of the tween and its evolution from earlier categories of sub- and pre-teens, see Cook and Kaiser (2003).

30. On Abercrombie and Fitch thong underwear, an Associated Press (2002) story reports that the underwear has the words *eye candy* and *wink wink* printed on the front. These items prompted a protest e-mail campaign from two Christian groups, the American Family Association and the American Decency Association.

31. On WWE action figures, see Diane Levin (2003). See www.bicp.org for more information on WWE, as well as a campaign to oppose its marketing practices.

32. On four year olds targeted with toys tied to PG-13 movies, see Carvajal (2000).

References

Associated Press. "Abercrombie and Fitch Is Coming Under Fire—Again." May 22, 2002.

Carvajal, Doreen. "How the Studios Used Children to Test Market Violent Films." *New York Times*, September 27, 2000.

Cook, Daniel Thomas, and Susan B. Kaiser. "Betwixt and Be Tween; Age Ambiguity and the Sexualization of the Female Consuming Subject." Unpublished paper, 2003.

Del Vecchio. Gene. *Creating Ever-Cool: A Marketer's Guide to a Kid's Heart.* Gretna, LA: Pelican Publishing Company, 1997.

Federal Trade Commission Staff report, Marketing Violent Entertainment to Children. Washington, D.C.: U.S. Government Printing Office, 2000.

Frank, Thomas. *The Conquest of Cool.* Chicago: Chicago University Press, 1997.

Gladwell, Malcolm. "The Coolhunt." *New Yorker*, March 17, 1997.

Grier, Sonya A. "The Federal Trade Commission's Report on the Marketing of Violent Entertainment to Youths." *Journal of Public Policy and Marketing* 20(1): 123–141. 2001.

Gross, Holly. "Spotting the Marketing Opps in Blurring Gender Lines." *Kidscreen,* September 2002a. p. 53.

———. "Cracking the Tween Connection Code." *Kidscreen,* March 2002b, p. 36–37.

Holt, Douglas and Juliet B. Schor. "Consumerism, the Commodification of Ghetto Violence, and Underclass Status." Unpublished report, Harvard University, 1998.

Holt, Douglas B. "Why Do Brands Cause Trouble? A Dialectical Theory of Consumer Culture and Branding." *Journal of Consumer Research* 29(1):70–90, 2002.

Hymowitz, Kay S. *Ready or Not: Why Treating Children as Small Adults Endangers Their Future and Ours.* New York Free Press, 1999.

———. "The Contradictions of Parenting in a Media Age." In Diane Ravitch and Joseph P. Viteritti, eds., *Kid Stuff: Marketing Sex and Violence to America's Children.* Baltimore: Johns Hopkins University Press, 2003.

Kaiser Family Foundation. *Kids and Media @ the Millennium.* Menlo Park, CA Kaiser Family Foundation, 1999.

Kellner, Douglas. "Beavis and Butt-Head: No Future for Postmodern Youth." In Shirley Steinberg and Joe Kincheloe, eds., *Kinderculture.* Boulder, CO: Westview Press, 1998.

Levin, Diane. *Remote Control Childhood? Combating the Hazards of a Media Culture.* Washington, D.C: National Association for the Education of Young Children, 1998.

———. *Teaching Young Children in Violent Times: Building a Peaceable Classroom* (2nd ed). Cambridge, MA, and Washington, D.C: Educators for Social Responsibility and the National Association for the Education of Young Children, 2003.

Lindstrom, Maran. *Brandchild.* London: Kogan-Page, 2003.

McNeal, James. *The Kids Market: Myths and Realities.* Ithaca, NY: Paramount Publishing, 1999.

Nader, Ralph. *Children First! A Parents' Guide to Fighting Corporate Predators.* Washington, D.C: Corporate Accountability Research Group, 1996.

O'Barr, Mack. "Interview with Paul Kurnit." *Advertising and Society Review* 2:2, 2001.

Postman, Neil. *The Disappearance of Childhood.* New York: Vintage, 1994.

Schor, Juliet B., and Douglas Holt. *The Consumer Society Reader: An Anthology.* New York: New Press, 2000.

Seiter, Ellen. *Sold Separately: Parents and Children in Consumer Culture.* New Brunswick, NJ: Rutgers University Press, 1993.

Siegel, David L., Timothy J. Coffey, and Gregory Livingston. *The Great Tween Buying Machine: Marketing to Today's Tweens.* Ithaca, NY: Paramount Market Publishing, 2001.

Signorielli, Nancy. *A Content Analysis: Reflections of Girls in the Media.* Menlo Park, CA: Kaiser Family Foundation, 1997. Available at www.kkf.org.

Smith, Paul. "Tommy Hilfiger in the Age of Mass Customization." In Andrew Ross, ed. *No Sweat: Fashion, Free Trade, and the Rights of Garment Workers.* New York: Verso, 1997.

Spiegler, Marc. "Marketing Street Culture." *American Demographics* 18(11):28–32, 1997.

Stanger, Jeffrey D., and Natalia Gridina. *Media in the Home: The Fourth Annual Survey of Parents and Children.* Philadelphia: Annenberg Public Policy Center of the University of Pennsylvania, 1999.

Vanderbilt, Thomas. *The Sneaker Book.* New York: New Press, 1998.

La Princesa Plastica

Hegemonic and Oppositional Representations of *Latinidad* in Hispanic Barbie

Karen Goldman

In the forty-some years since she emerged from her original mold, Mattel's Barbie doll has become, both as cultural icon and children's plaything, one of the world's most ubiquitous plastic objects. The doll's embodiment of a diversity of feminine images reflects Mattel's efforts to market to continuously changing and increasingly diverse groups of U.S. and international consumers. But is it true, as some observers have contended, that, given the preeminence and persistence of the image of "rich, blonde Barbie" worldwide, resistance, cultural or otherwise, to hegemonic Barbie culture is futile? Barbie scholar Erica Rand (1995) points out that there is often a wide gap between the contexts and narratives that are produced for Barbie by Mattel, which are far from monolithic themselves, and the meanings that are generated by her consumers, whether children at play, collectors, or those who find in Barbie's carefully constructed persona an irresistible target for parody and subversion (26–28). . . .

The often quoted statistics on Barbie's global presence are staggering: more than one billion dolls sold in 150 countries, representing forty-five different nationalities (Barbie Collectibles, 2002). Although there is today a multitude of manifestations of Barbie culture, both hegemonic and oppositional, the point from which they all depart is the original, blue-eyed, blonde Barbie. Barbies are marked as "ethnic" or foreign only to the extent to which they differ from the original doll. In her "unauthorized biography," *Forever Barbie* (1994), M. G. Lord begins a chapter on ethnic Barbie by drawing an analogy between the development of Ruth Handler's original doll and the creation of Caucasian, all-American Hollywood star icons by largely Jewish-run movie studios. Lord asserts that original

Barbie's ethnic neutrality differs from and surpasses that of the flesh-and-blood female stars that she resembles because, unlike "real" actresses, Barbie had no biological heredity and was, in fact, better suited than a human actress to exemplify an impossible ideal: "There was no tribal taint in her plastic flesh, no baggage to betray an immigrant past. She had no navel; no parents; no heritage" (160). Barbie's plasticity afforded her creators the luxury of designing her from scratch and literally molding every aspect of her appearance.

Like Hollywood promoters, who need to "design" stars that will engage the identification of the largest number of viewers, Mattel strove to develop a Barbie that would appeal to the greatest number of the doll's target audience: white, middle-class American parents and their daughters. Thus, the company's marketing strategy involved stressing, above all else, the doll's "Americanness." She had to be, in the words of Barbie's admiring biographer, BillyBoy (1987), "the personification of the all-round American girl" (28). In the social environment of the United States of the late 1950s, this meant she had to be Caucasian, blonde, light-skinned, and free of any obvious ethnic markers.

The original Barbie's ethnic neutrality not only served to emphasize the association of middle-class Caucasian femininity with "Americanness," it also served to bolster what Erica Rand refers to as Mattel's "language of infinite possibility" (28). Citing the need to allow children to project their own imagination onto the doll, Ruth Handler went to great lengths to expunge what she perceived as distinguishing characteristics that would give Barbie a distinct look or persona. In a 1990 interview she remarked, "the face was deliberately designed to be blank, without a personality, so that the projection of the child's dream could be on Barbie's face" (quoted in Rand, 40). But, like any cultural product, and despite the claims of her inventor, Barbie has indeed "always already" been inscribed in a manufactured narrative that is strictly circumscribed and defined by her producers. Clearly, within the rigid parameters of the doll's image as projected by Mattel, the possibilities for imagining a nonhegemonic Barbie were limited.

By 1961, Mattel had made the decision to allow Barbie to acquire a specific biography beyond her first name and the qualifier "teenage fashion model." During the early sixties, Barbie was appearing in books, records, and other texts as a blonde ponytailed teenage fashion model with a personality, an address, a last name, and a boyfriend. While Barbie's and Ken's first names were taken from the real names of Ruth and Elliot Handler's two children, the other names are a veritable tribute to hyperbolic anglocentrism: Barbie's full name is Barbara Millicent Roberts. Ken's surname is Carson, and the two names together are, appropriately, an homage to Mattel's advertising firm: Carson/Roberts. Barbie's parents' names are identified as George and Margaret (only a minor variation of George and Martha, those archetypical grandparents of the nation). Barbie lives a glamorous but otherwise typical teenage life in a small American town called Willows.

Mattel has periodically adjusted Barbie's body, face, and hair in the interest of keeping up with styles and social realities of the day. But during the early years of her existence it was above all clothing and accessories that allowed her to (at least superficially) diversify her look. At first, the outfits marketed for Barbie fell into categories that emphasized her elegance ("Evening Splendor," "Silken Flame"), career aspirations ("Ballerina," "Registered Nurse"), leisure activities ("Ski Queen," "Movie Date"), or special occasions ("Easter Parade," "Bride's Dream"). None of these outfits departed in any substantial way from the standard of Barbie's (and later Ken's) middle-class Caucasian Americanness. By 1964, Barbie and Ken had already acquired many of the accoutrements of the American dream, for example, those appropriately named "dream" accessories: the "dream kitchen" (1964), the "dream house" (1964), and the sports car (1962). For members of the postwar American middle class who had already attained these assets, travel, particularly to an exotic location, became a status-bearing consumer item, akin to owning a nice house or car (Urry, 2002). In 1964, in a miniature reenactment of the U.S. middle-class's increasing tendency to dedicate capital and leisure time to long-distance travel, Mattel launched the Travel Costume series, and Barbie and Ken become tourists, visiting Japan, Switzerland, Holland, Hawaii, and Mexico. Each travel costume outfit included "charming traditional costumes" for Barbie and Ken, as well as a miniature storybook that narrated the pair's travel adventures.

Central to Barbie's Mexican travel experience is the fact that the dolls (with or without the storybook provided with the outfit) come with a ready-made Mattel-produced narrative that highlights the pair's status as Caucasian Americans enjoying leisure adventures, oblivious to the larger narrative that is the largely mestizo Mexican nation and its people. No images of other compete as meaning producer with the Mattel master narrative, for there are no traces of actual people (or doll personalities) in the narrative other than the costumed Caucasian Barbie and Ken. . . .

Mexico is a backdrop for Barbie's and Ken's travel adventure, not unlike the stories of the Little Theatre Costume sets that were sold concurrently, featuring Barbie as a princess of the Arabian Knights, Little Red Riding Hood, Guinevere, and Cinderella. Like the memorable figure of Donald Duck wearing a sombrero and traveling through Mexico on a flying serape in the 1989 Disney cartoon film, *The Three Caballeros,* Ken and Barbie perform their jovial masquerade against a background in which the totality of Mexico is represented as a storybook land. The story and the outfits depict folkloric or traditional elements of Mexican culture that, through caricature, are rendered no more unfamiliar or threatening to American cultural hegemony than the storybook characters. Thus, Ken's and Barbie's masquerading in the Mexico set functions

more as an affirmation of the doll's implacable whiteness than any attempt to represent a multicultural opening. . . .

Following a traditional pattern of imperialist penetration, Barbie's (and Mattel's) entry into an international, intercultural environment begins from the position of tourist, that of postcolonial traveler to exotic locations. However, and in spite of the Travel Collection's clear affirmation of the dolls as Anglo and American, even this limited acknowledgment of worlds beyond the United States points, however tenuously, to Barbie's (and Mattel's) imminent initial foray into global expansion. It marks the beginning of what would eventually become the breakup of the monolithic Barbie narrative, in which nonwhite others are not only invisible, but their existence is never even an issue, for it simply does not come into play.

By the late sixties, Barbie's privileging of Caucasian femininity as the standard of American beauty, anachronistically silhouetted against a background of the civil rights movement and increasing ethnic and racial diversity in the United States, was becoming an encumbrance to Ruth Handler's notion that all girls must be able to identify with Barbie. Mattel decided to alter its master narrative in a reversal that reined in Barbie's biography and reintroduced the "language of infinite possibility." In 1967, Mattel launched a rather unconvincing Black Francie doll, followed, in 1968, by Barbie's Black friend Christie. In 1980, Mattel introduced Black and Hispanic Barbie, as well as a "Dolls of the World" Collection. In 1988, Teresa, an Hispanic doll, was introduced, followed by a line of African American "friends of Barbie." In a 1990 interview for *Newsweek,* Mattel product manager Deborah Mitchell proudly announced, "now, ethnic Barbie lovers will be able to dream in their own image" (duCille, 1995, 554).

While it is clear that Mattel was intent on capturing the growing ethnic markets in the United States by developing dolls meant to allow identification by ethnic "others," there is much debate regarding how authentically the dolls actually represent diversity. The representation of Latinidad in the marketing of Hispanic Barbie dolls has followed the recent pattern of many products aimed at Latino consumers. Media scholar Clara Rodriguez (1997) argues that in the popular media in the United States today, Latinos are typically either absent or misrepresented. When they are represented, it is often as negative stereotypes or as exotic foreigners (13–30). Behind Mattel's portrayal of Latino/a identity lies a system of representation that sells itself as authentic but that ultimately either depicts Latino/a culture as homogeneous and exotic, or repackages the doll's Latinidad in an assimilated form, whether to make her more attractive to more assimilated Latinos or to market her more effectively in places where ethnic diversity is not particularly marketable. . . .

The first Hispanic Barbie doll's bilingual box introduced her as Barbie Hispanica (not the grammatically correct Hispaña). Like the earlier Mexico Travel Barbie, she is stereotypically dressed in a white peasant blouse and a full red skirt, a lace mantilla over her shoulders and a red rose tied around her neck. If the standard for Caucasian Barbie is light-skinned, blonde, and blue-eyed, the U.S. Hispanic version presents those contrasting physical attributes stereotypically associated with Latinas: dark hair, dark eyes, and darker skin. However, in few of the dolls designed to represent Hispanic (or Latina) women is skin tone ever darker than the suntanned Malibu Barbie dolls. Facial features never hint at indigenous or African heritage. What most prominently distinguishes the original Hispanic Barbie from any of the brunette Caucasian Barbies is the doll's paratextual items: clothing and accessories, or, more accurately, her costume. The original Hispanic Barbie, as well as subsequent special editions that celebrate occasions culturally specific to Latinos, such as the Quinceañera Barbie, all sport traditional folkloric clothing that is intended to mark them very clearly as Latinas, and therefore as foreign, exotic other.

In her physical characteristics, posture, and dress, the original Hispanic Barbie very closely resembles the international Hispanic (read: foreign) Dolls of the World, which are designed to reflect "typical" national attributes and dress in folkloric clothing. To Caucasian Barbie's quintessential Americanness, the Dolls of the World represent a quintessentially foreign counterpoint. But, as Wendy Varney argues in her convincing analysis of Australian Barbie, they are essentially American products and bear the Stamp of U.S. cultural imperialism, no matter what the guise. With respect to Latina identity, the Dolls of the World tend to negotiate difference by representing those Latinas as either hyperbolically folkloric (Mexico, Peru) or splashy and exotic (Brazil). Mattel's stated goal in offering the Dolls of the World Collection is to foster international understanding and appreciation of cultural differences. Significantly, the Andalusian Barbie and Mexican Barbie, both of whom are included in the Dolls of the World Collection, differ only superficially from U.S. Hispanic Barbie. They all have fair complexions and long dark hair, each with a large red rose tucked behind one ear. They wear full skirts and blouses, and all three dolls' clothes feature bright red as the predominant color, a characteristic that persists in Mattel's representations of Hispanics. Cultural differences among diverse groups and nationalities are elided, as Latinidad is reduced to one easily consumable, stereotypical identity-in-a-box.

The Peruvian doll, issued in 1999, provides a good example of how notions of Latin American class, race, and ethnicity play out in the real or implied narrative that frames the doll's paratextual positioning. For one thing, the doll is clearly meant to portray the identity of an indigenous Peruvian woman, with her long braids, round face, traditional woven shawl, and matching skirt. However, her facial features are wholly Caucasian, as is her rosy skin tone. In a clear and rather surprising break with standard Barbie design and Mattel's custom of representing racial differences only through what Ann duCille calls the "tint of the plastic," Peruvian Barbie carries a baby, who presumably is meant to be her own. One thing that has consistently defined the essence of Barbie has been her status as a single woman. While she is often depicted as a big sister or caring for children, and she has long been available as a bride, there has never been such a thing as a "Married Barbie," much less a maternal Barbie. Until the recent release of the "Happy Family" dolls, including a "Pregnant Midge" (not Barbie), that comes with a belly containing a removable baby, maternity has been wholly absent in the world of Barbie dolls. In the case of Midge, the issue of paternity is never in question, since, in a throwback to the early years of Mattel's use of heavy-handed biography, the doll wears a wedding ring, and her box provides a narrative identifying the father as Midge's husband, Alan.

The Peruvian doll comes with no such disclaimer. The baby is one more accessory, like Hispanic Barbie's lace mantilla, that identifies her as ethnically other. The representation of the Peruvian Barbie as mother is possible precisely because she is a Doll of the World, that is, she is foreign, and not subject to the rigid conventions of the "American" dolls. In addition, Peruvian Barbie's representation responds to principles of marketing and stereotypes that view Latinos as extremely family-oriented and conservative on the issue of nontraditional roles for women (Deanne et al., 2000). The presence of the baby, with or without an implied father, is a much more important signifier of Mattel's notion of Latina femininity than any national costume or textual commentary might be.

Following the introduction of the first Hispanic Barbie in 1980, which differed little from the "foreign" Dolls of the World, Mattel favored more culturally assimilated Hispanic dolls that differed little from nonethnic Barbies, beyond adjustments to physical characteristics such as hair color and skin tone. Hispanic Barbie and African American Barbies were simply marketed as differently tinted versions of Caucasian Barbies. Such not-*too*-ethnic dolls were attractive to both ethnic minorities and majority Caucasian buyers, and thus served the dual purpose of appearing to foster diversity while increasing profits. In 1988, Mattel introduced Teresa, a bona fide Latina friend of Barbie. Like Barbie, Teresa has been produced with a multitude of physical characteristics over the years, morphing from a doll with consistently darker skin and hair to one that is often indistinguishable from nonethnic Barbie.

Today, all ethnic Barbie dolls vary in skin tone and hair color, but they typically wear the same clothes and accessories as Caucasian Barbie. It is tempting to consider that Teresa's changing looks signal Mattel's acknowledgment of the tremendous diversity among Latino populations world-wide. But beyond the dye that is used to tint her plastic body, it is hard to appreciate any substantial difference between Teresa and brunette Caucasian Barbies. What renders them similar is far more compelling than what sets them apart. Since recent issues of the Teresa doll don't even include Spanish text on the box, the only remaining link to Teresa's Latina identity is her name, Teresa (whose echo of the distant Spanish mystic Santa Teresa does not go unnoticed by many). . . . Even when Teresa is sold in a way that culturally marks her as Hispanic— for example, as Quinceañera Teresa—she more closely resembles Caucasian Barbie than the Latin American or Spanish Dolls of the World. The ultimate confirmation of her degree of assimilation is her marketing success in regions of the United States that do not have high concentrations of Latinos.

While Mattel has been congratulating itself for promoting diversity in the United States by including Hispanic Barbie and Teresa along with other dolls of color among its products, in Latin American countries where licensed Barbies are produced by regional subsidiaries, the dolls are nearly always modeled on the traditional Hollywood-inspired brands of American beauty: Caucasian and blonde. And although Caucasian blonde Barbie is certainly popular among Latina girls in the United States (Budge, 2003), it is unusual for a Hispanic doll to be marketed in the United States that does not possess those physical characteristics typically attributed to Latinas: darker skin, hair, and eyes. That Hispanic Barbies in the United States are not generally sold as blondes, whereas they very often are in Latin America, points to some of the complexities of racial and ethnic identification and marketing in both countries. As is evident in the success of female celebrities from Eva Peron to XuXa, in Latin American popular culture it is, ironically, the Hollywood-inspired ideal of blonde feminine beauty that prevails. And, given Barbie's relatively hefty price tag in Latin America (about $20), it is precisely the mostly white elite to whom Barbie dolls are marketed. The highest proportion of Barbie ownership in Latin America (outside of Puerto Rico, where a whopping 72 percent of girls own Barbies, is in Argentina (44 percent) and Chile (49 percent), nations that also have the lowest proportion of indigenous peoples, blacks, and mestizos, and the highest proportion of European-descended Caucasians ("Barbie Dolls in Latin America," 2002). Not surprisingly, the most popular Argentine Barbies tend to be those with the most Caucasian features. . . .

Barbie's hegemonic identity and her very ubiquity have always made her an attractive target for parodical representations of subversive intent. These counterhegemonic efforts include guerrilla tactics, such as the Barbie Liberation Organization, which sabotaged toys on store shelves. Other examples include works of criticism and literature that revisit and reinterpret the Barbie image, such as *Mondo Barbie* and *The Barbie Chronicles,* works of visual art, a multitude of Internet sites such as visiblebarbie.com and distortedbarbie.com, as well as the notable 1987 film *Superstar* by Todd Haynes. This film narrates the life of pop music star Karen Carpenter, who died of anorexia in 1983, using Barbie dolls to stand in for the human figures. Like Haynes's

film, the majority of these counterhegemonic and often feminist-inspired criticisms target Barbie's absurd body proportions, her flawless physiognomy, her anachronistic femininity, and the culture of consumption she promotes. Few of them problematize the issues of race, ethnicity, class, and the privileging of U.S. perceptions of foreign others in their analyses. . . .

The Internet has been a prodigious global source of Barbie resistance, parody, and criticism. Pocho.com is a Web site based on *Pocho Magazine,* which has been around since the late eighties. The site, subtitled "Aztlán's número uno source for satire y chingazos," features irreverent and biting satire, a longstanding tradition in Mexican journalism. Though *pocho* literally means faded, it is a disparaging term often used by Mexicans to describe U.S.-assimilated Mexican Americans. The magazine's and Website's appropriation of the term reflects a sentiment that has grown consistently as people of Mexican heritage in the United States proudly embrace their identity as one of fluidity and hybridity. On the site, as in the lives and cultures of Chicanos and other Latinos in the United States, English and Spanish are mixed freely, and articles on Mexican president Vicente Fox are juxtaposed with ones on Ron Unz and Monica Lewinsky. The April 28, 2000, edition featured a satirical story titled "New Latina Barbies Unveiled," announcing that Mattel had launched a line of Barbies in the likeness of Latina celebrities Cameron Diaz, Christina Aguilera, and Jennifer Lopez, as well as a new "Hispanic Family."

The text says, in part, "These dolls accurately capture the cultural pride felt by all of these strong Latina women. . . . We hope little Latina girls feel validated each time they look at their realistic and culturally accurate Latina Barbie dolls" (Sanchez-McNulty, 2000). Of course, the joke, one that Mattel (and Hollywood) never gets, is that all of the dolls look the same; they are blonde, blue-eyed, and have perfectly symmetrical Caucasian features. Of course, this begs the question, posed by duCille with regard to black African American dolls: "What would it take to produce a line of dolls that more fully reflects the wide variety of sizes, shapes, colors, hair styles, occupations, abilities, and disabilities that African Americans—like all people—come in?" (duCille, "Dyes and Dolls," 1995, 559). Clearly, the answer to that question does not lie with Mattel, which proudly asserts that "Today, in her 43rd year, Barbie reflects the dreams, hopes and future realities of an entire generation of little girls who still see her as representing the same American dream and aspirations as when she was first introduced in 1959!" (Barbie.com, 2002).

Perhaps, as she straddles cultures, Hispanic Barbie must strive to (and be animated to) embody what Latina writer and critic Gloria Anzaldua (1999) describes as "a tolerance for ambiguity" that characterizes the new mestiza: "She learns to juggle cultures. . . . Not only does she sustain contradictions, she turns ambivalence into something else" (101). Or perhaps, as Wendy Varney suggests, the Barbie phenomenon is itself inextricably, irrevocably bound up in a white, middle-class American context (3). As such, it is hard to resist the temptation to glimpse, behind each Barbie, regardless of her skin and hair color, facial characteristics and dress, or even the language that she speaks, a little blonde blue-eyed Barbie named Barbie Millicent Robert from Willows.

References

Ananova. "Lesbian Barbie Film Banned in Mexico." http://www.ananova.com/news/story/sm_540282.html?menu=news.quirkies (accessed November 11, 2002).

Anzaldua, Gloria. *Borderlands/La Frontera: The New Mestiza* (2nd ed.). San Francisco: Aunt Lute Books, 1999.

Barbie Collectibles, http://www.barbiecollectibles.com/inciex-home.asp (accessed November 12, 2002).

Barbie.com. Mattel Corporation, http://www.barbie.com/ (accessed October 10, 2002).

"The Barbie Doll Story." Mattel Corporation, http://www.shareholder.com/mattel/news/20020428–79139.cf (accessed October 22, 2002).

"Barbie Dolls in Latin America." Zona Latina. http://www.zonalatina.com/Zldata37.html (accessed December 22, 2002).

BillyBoy. *Barbie, Her Life and Times.* New York: Crown Trade Paperbacks, 1987.

Budge, David. "Barbie Is No Living Doll as a Role Model." *Times Education Supplement,* January 7, 2003.

Deanne, Claudia, et al. "Leaving Tradition Behind: Latinos in the Great American Melting Pot." *Public Perspectives* 11, no. 3 (May/June 2000): 5–7.

duCille, Ann. "Barbie in Black and White." In *The Barbie Chronicles: A Living Doll Turns Forty.* New York: Touchstone, 1999.

———. "Dyes and Dolls: Multicultural Barbie and the Merchandising of Difference." In *A Cultural Studies Reader,* ed. Jessica Rajan and Gita Rajan. London: 1995.

"Life in Plastic." *Economist,* December 21, 20–23, 2002.

Lipsitz, George. *Dangerous Crossroads: Popular Music, Postmodernism and the Poetics of Place.* Verso: London, 1994.

Lord, M. G. '*Forever Barbie*' The Unauthorized Biography of a Real Doll. New York: William Morrow, 1994.

Pratt, Mary Louise. *Imperial Eyes: Travel Writing and Transculturation.* London: Routledge, 1992.

Rand, Erica. *Barbie's Queer Accessories.* Durham, NC: Duke University Press, 1995.

Rodriguez, Clara, ed. *Latin Looks: Images of Latinas and Latinos in the U.S. Media.* Boulder, CO: Westview Press, 1997.

Sanchez-McNulty, Maria. "New Latina Barbies Unveiled." *Pocho.* http://www.pocho.com/new/2001/barbies21200barbies31700.htm.

Urry, John. *The Tourist Gaze* (2nd edition). London: Sage, 2002.

Varney, Wendy. "Barbie Australis: The Commercial Reinvention of National Culture." *Social Identities* 4 (June 1998): I6I. http://search.epnet.com/direct.asp?an=873697&db=abh (accessed October 2, 2002).

Monarchs, Monsters, and Multiculturalism

Disney's Menu for Global Hierarchy

Lee Artz

Disney leads the world in the production and distribution of popular culture. Although AOL–Time Warner may be the media giant in assets, none challenges Disney as the primary purveyor of entertainment nor approach its perennial popularity and box-office success in animated feature films. Indeed, animation is central to Disney's economic vitality and cultural influence. In the last decade, Disney has sold over $3 billion in toys based on characters from its animated features. Disney theme parks, featuring popular film characters and settings, now have more visitors each year than all of the fifty-four national parks in the United States.

Although Disney produces nonanimated films through its Miramax and Touchstone movie studios, its economic and cultural strength remains in animation. Using profits from its global sales of animated films, Disney has acquired the ABC television network, mass-market radio stations, and cable channels such as ESPN and A&E. . . .

The centrality of animation to Disney's corporate success and the corresponding centrality of Disney animation to global popular culture forms and themes require some exploration. This inquiry should entail both a political-economic and a cultural studies approach, given the apparent parallels between Disney's corporate practices (from investment and workplace practices to technological production and mass distribution) and the ideological themes of Disney's animated narratives (including race and gender equality). Investigating the construction, content, and persuasive appeal of Disney animations suggests that Disney consistently and programmatically produces "commodities-as-animated-feature films" that promote an ideology preferred by Disney and global capitalism—an ideology at odds with democracy and creative, participatory social life. . . .

In a society and culture ostensibly democratic, it is unsettling to find the major distributor of global entertainment promulgating narratives that simultaneously soften and defend messages of social-class hierarchy and antisocial hyper-individualism. . . .

Naturalizing Hierarchy

Hierarchy in a social order indicates a ranking according to worth, ability, authority, or some other attribute. In Disney, these values are combined with goodness and physical appearance such that, in each animated narrative, heroes and heroines are invariably good, attractive, capable, worthy, and ultimately powerful, while in service to the narrative's social order.

From the opening "circle of life" scene in *The Lion King* we cannot mistake the social order and its validity. All species bow before the rightful king. The heavens open and a (divine?) light shines on the new lion cub. This future king is held before a multitude of reverent and bowing beasts whose happiness and very existence depend on the maintenance of the established and rightful hierarchy. The visual metaphors of good and evil are simple and transparent: a regal king and his heir; an evil uncle who covets the kingdom; and lesser passive animal-citizens overrun by social undesirables in need of leadership. The meanings are animationally inescapable—the King and his son, Simba, are brightly drawn, muscular, and smoothly curved; the villainous uncle, "Scar," is dark, angular, thin, and disfigured; the hyenas, likewise, are angular and unmistakably Black and Latino (in the voice, diction, and verbal styles of Whoopi Goldberg and Cheech Marin); the socially irresponsible meerkat and boar, more cartoonish, less naturalistically drawn, live beyond the pride lands. The dialogue and action indicate importance, as well. Mustafa

speaks in the King's English, usually from on high. Scar, the villain, lurks in shape and movement, languid, lazy, and foppish, narratively manipulating other characters through deceit. The hyenas have secondary roles with fewer lines, delivered comically, with slapstick interactions that are nonetheless understood as relationships of power that are maintained throughout. . . .

The narratives of *Pocahontas, Mulan, Tarzan* and other Disney animations are formed from the same redundant template of elite hierarchy, albeit with hegemonic variation. In *Pocahontas,* the standard Disney coming-of-age romance has been updated with a feisty, independent heroine in a narrative advocating cultural tolerance but following the trail of all Western captivity narratives with its "noble" Powhatan, "savage" warrior Kocoum, and "Indian princess" Pocahontas.[1] John Smith, blond, smoothly muscular, and athletically animated, fulfills the heroic ideal in vision and plot, while Chief Powhatan appears more sedate in bold, symmetrical strokes, with slower, more dignified screen movements and dialogue. These two elites survive the actions of the reactionary Kocoum and villainous Ratcliffe. The stoic, irrational Kocoum has few lines, and dies at the hands of a naive colonialist. The Ratcliffe character reveals in dialogue that he is indulgent, pompous, greedy, incompetent, and not respected by the British nobility. He appears as the largest figure in the film, obese, with a huge nose, big lips, and pencil-thin triangular mustache. The narrative's social relations are hierarchical: lower-class Anglos work for Ratcliffe or Smith; native soldiers and villagers follow Powhatan's directives. In the end, the "good" colonialist John Smith intervenes to save Powhatan and order the arrest of Ratcliffe; Pocahontas presumably finds her true path as a peacemaker and daughter; and the rest of the natives and English adventurers assume their prescribed subordinate positions, awaiting further orders from their superiors. In *Pocahontas,* two hierarchical orders are defended and left intact, although the extended visual metaphor of John Smith saving Powhatan and wanting to civilize Pocahontas indicates that the colonial is dominant over the indigenous. . . .

While the hero and heroine are always noble and attractive by birth, villains are privileged and titled only because of the misplaced magnanimity or whim of a legitimate superior. Villains are unattractive, semi-elite social misfits. Jafar is grand vizier, adviser to Sultan; Scar is King Mustafa's disgruntled brother, ineligible for legitimate succession; and Ratcliffe's governorship is a reluctant sop from more worthy elites. Randall remains on the monsters' payroll only through his deceit, which ultimately is discovered by the hero, Sully. In each of these narratives and many others (e.g., *Little Mermaid, Beauty and the Beast, Fox and Hound*), the dominant social class has no villainy, producing only good souls who never abuse their authority. We understand this viscerally by the soft, cuddly caricatures that Disney creates. Abuse comes solely from those elevated beyond their goodness, villains who would reach beyond their status and disrupt the social order. . . . In the fairy-tale world of the dominant, class rules apply: a frog becomes a prince only if he was a prince before. Rulers may change among the elite (from Mustafa to Simba, from Sultan to Aladdin, Flik gets royal privilege), but the rules and ruled remain. And, in Disney's world, the only just rule is class hierarchy. . . .

Evil henchmen, such as Clayton's sailors or the Huns, are consistently shabbily dressed or disheveled, dark, often bearded, usually armed, speak harshly in short sentences, and mete out their brutality only as long as the villain commands. In Disney, lower-class characters do not act on their own. Large groups are often cast as mob-like in action and graphic: jeering primates terrorize Jane; wildebeest stampede without regard for others in *The Lion King;* native warriors huddle around the fire waiting for orders to attack; the Huns shout and howl above the thunder of their horses' hooves; grasshoppers and sharks indiscriminately attack. Whether African, Arabian, North American, Chinese, or nonhuman, few from the good citizenry or evil troops are individualized; even fewer have articulate voices, appearing but as replicates from two or three stencils, graphically reflective of their necessarily subordinate position in Disney's hierarchy. In sum, Disney films all play a similar refrain: a stylized, naturalized, and Westernized elite hero combats a privileged antisocial oversized villain, while cute animal sidekicks and thuggish rebels knock about in front of a shapeless, faceless humanity. Animating hierarchy centers Disney's vision, whatever the era, geography, or species.

Ordering Coercion and Power

To underscore this essential Disney law, narrative resolution in each film defends and reinforces the status quo. Nothing is resolved until the preferred social order is in place. No one lives happily ever after until the chosen one rules. All is chaos and disorder in the pride lands until Simba returns as monarch. Even nature withholds its bounty, pending the proper social hierarchy. Nemo's mistake is curiosity about another world: when he leaves the security, safety, and proper place of the coral reef, disaster strikes. Saving China is only a youthful adventure: Mulan's "place in life" is in the family garden. Even the wisest of apes knows Tarzan is superior. . . .

We all need true rulers who are wise, benevolent, and powerful. Any other arrangement is unworkable. Villains may attain power, but as nonelite, false leaders, they are ill equipped to rule. Their reign is disastrous and temporary. Soon the hero will save the day and the hierarchy. "As evil is expelled, the world is left nice and clean," and well ordered.[2] Thus, zebras bow, faceless Chinese cheer, and, in general, the working masses rejoice (and happily resume their subservience) upon the triumphant defense of the hierarchy. The pleasant narrative outcome verifies the virtue of hierarchy and models Disney's actual institutional hierarchy, in everything from animation production to cruise ships, theme parks, and town life in Celebration, Florida.[3] In its digital production, Disney replaces piecework animation artists with piecework technicians in a hierarchical structure dedicated to marketing entertainment commodities for shareholder profit—no cooperative here, no creative exchange between artists, technicians, and citizen-parents. The story scripts in narrative and in production and distribution conform to market dictates and capitalist production norms, including corporate elite control.

Preference and justification for elite control can be observed in the attributes of each narrative's leading authority: this character is morally good and invariably benevolent. The sultan may be disoriented, but he is a gentle soul, impervious to evil. A compassionate John Smith—"the perfect masculine companion"—is willing to sacrifice his own life to avoid further bloodshed.[4] In contrast to the malevolent Huns, Mulan's emperor exudes warmth to his docile subjects. Tarzan demonstrates his human compassion and species superiority in saving his ape family (and Jane). For Disney, all elite authority figures are good, caring, and protective of their wards. In a telling statistical analysis of eleven Disney animations, Hoerner found that heroic protagonists exhibit 98 percent of all pro-social behavior in the films.[5]

... A consistent haloing of hierarchal power as preferable for all organizes the films' moral conflicts and elite responses to challenge. In all cases, elite heroes and heroines use coercion with impunity, continuing a Disney tradition that dates back to Snow White. Elite coercion varies, from the Beast's abuse of Belle, to the colonialist's murder of Kocoum. Mulan slaughters dozens of Huns; Tarzan wrestles with Clayton, who accidentally falls to his own death. Villains Randall, Waterhouse, Hopper, and various aliens are similarly dispatched by elite violence.

In addition to coercion, elites frequently employ deceit. Everywhere and always Disney's heroic elites are stronger, smarter, and victorious in the final conflict (even when performing antisocial acts). In each case, the protagonist earns riches, power, and happiness.

In contrast, villains—who almost exclusively exhibit antisocial behavior and violence—suffer calamity or death: Jafar is imprisoned for thousands of years; Scar dies; Kocoum dies; Ratcliffe is arrested; the Hun dies; Clayton dies; Randall and Hopper are ultimately dispatched. One need not consult a literary critic to understand the moral of these stories. In all fairy tales, good triumphs over evil, but for Disney good is the exclusive genetic and social right of the elite. Elites are attractive, benevolent, good, and successful; villains are misshapen, treacherous, and evil, and cannot win. The rest of the Disney world is undifferentiated, passive, dependent on elite gratuity, and largely irrelevant, except as narrative fodder.

Community and Democracy

.... In focusing exclusively on individual elites, Disney dismisses group solidarity and the public interest as unimportant to the story. Although each narrative includes dozens of nonelite characters, they appear primarily as background or as proxies to the protagonists—as exhibited by Nemo's "tank guy" buddies. In fact, "every Disney character stands on either one side or the other of the power demarcation line. All below are bound to obedience, submission, discipline, humility. Those above are free to employ constant coercion, threats, moral and physical repression and economic domination."[6]

.... Individualism and competition— buzzwords for capitalism—are reserved for Disney's fantasy elites, who have no moral or social peer. Elite ideas and actions are right, good, and ultimately successful. Villains may have ideas and take action, but they are wrong, bad, and doomed to fail. In such a fantasy world, no other ideas or actions are needed; hence Disney's animated public seldom speaks, exhibits limited thought, and undertakes little independent action—and never, ever, does a nonelite character freely broach the question of equality, democracy, or social justice.

. . . . At most, Disney's animated populations appear as "average" characters, either acting irresponsibly as inferiors, squabbling over trifles or passively waiting for mobilization orders from a superior. Most secondary castings are not particularly bright in dialogue or graphic portrayal, except for aides, who are often mischievous but harmless, comic animals. Less enlightened nonelites tend toward antisocial behavior as thieving hyenas, tormenting monkeys, or devious monsters. Having baser instincts, "bad" nonelites (unshaven, partially dressed, usually large) are also prone to violence and easily misled by nefarious Disney antagonists: Arab bandits work for Jafar; sailors join Clayton in kidnapping; hordes follow the Hun; Randall directs his monster minions; and grasshoppers pillage for Hopper.

Predictably, according to Disney, most nonelites tacitly or enthusiastically understand that hierarchy is good and support the social order no matter who rules. The citizens of Agrabah bow to the sultan, Jafar, then Aladdin on each successive command; no animals rise up against Scar; the colonists obey Ratcliffe, then Smith; and all apes obey Kerchak, then Tarzan; the Queen rules over all bugs: long live the monarchy!

According to Disney, workers, sailors, farmers, and other producers are wretched, irrational, chaotic, and passive, unable to act in their own interests—at best they may be motivated to protect the hierarchical social order. Some may be roused to mob action under the wrong leader, but all will be happier if the proper order is fulfilled—the hierarchical natural order of the animal kingdom, or the hierarchical social order of an Arab sultanate, Chinese empire, British

or ant colony, toy room, scare factory, or ocean. Group action, in other words, occurs only at the whim of the powerful.

. . . . Moreover, in Disney animations, actions by leading characters thoroughly shred any semblance of collective interest. Aladdin deserts the orphans and his neighborhood; Pocahontas betrays her nation; Tarzan betrays his family; Mulan deceives her family and compatriots; Simba returns to the pride lands only out of royal duty; Flik imperils the colony; Marlin has no concern beyond Nemo. Disney never animates democracy or social responsibility. Disney heroes in all their wit and wisdom never seek happiness or fulfillment through commitment to improving the human condition. Instead, all Disney animated stars indicate that acting against the public interest in one's search for individual gratification is natural, legitimate, and preferred. . . .

The Realities of Fantasy

Disney is a world leader in mass entertainment implicated in the globalization of capitalism and a concerted effort to deregulate and privatize world culture. A highly proficient producer and international distributor of capitalist cultural products, Disney advances an ideological content that parallels the social and political requirements of capitalist economic activity: hierarchy, elite coercion, hyper-individualism, and social atomism.[7] In particular, Disney's animated features communicate a clear message to the world: The individual elite quest for self-gratification, adventure, and acquisition is good and just. . . .

Disney themes, characters, and animation style have been thoroughly institutionalized in practice and procedure—from the scriptwriters, animators, and technical producers, who create the actual films, to the market researchers and integrated marketing directors, who conduct product research and focus groups to spot trends and advise editors on socially sensitive issues—all are geared to maximizing corporate profits. Pixar's innovations digitally improve Disney content and productively improve Disney's market dominance. Furthermore, dominance in the production of commodified animation and its spin-offs indicates that Disney's narratives resonate with appreciative mass audiences, suggesting that Disney's hierarchical themes are also culturally acceptable, at least tacitly. Individual pleasures or meanings derived from Disney commodities reinforce, but should not be confused with, the overarching, consistent themes of self-fulfillment through consumption.

Disney's ability to market popular films and the public's delight in consuming their little pleasures can best be understood as a negotiated hegemonic activity.[8] Like modern advertising, Disney worlds are fanciful, optimistic, and tidy.[9] And like advertising, Disney has become part of everyday life, commercially and culturally institutionalized by design.[10] But in Disney's case the medium is also the advertisement. Disney products are themselves advertisements for Disney and for its ideological and cultural themes. . . .

The interpretation of Disney animation presented here is intended only as an entry to discussing Disney's vision of globalization. Understanding Disney clarifies the global intent of corporate capitalism. Without deviation Disney animates and narrates myths favorable to a corporate culture, including its own. The emerging world capitalist culture revels in the ideology distributed by Disney, an ideology that aligns the morals of every animated film to class hierarchy, thereby denigrating and dismissing solidarity, democracy, and concern for community needs and interests. . . .

Notes

1. Michael T. Marsden and Jack Nachbar, *The Indians in the Movies: Handbook of North American Indians* (Washington, D.C.: Smithsonian Institution, 1988).

2. Ariel Dorfman and Armand Mattelart, *How to Read Donald Duck: Imperialist Ideology in the Disney Comic* (New York: International General, 1975), 89.

3. Celebration, Florida, is Disney's model perfect community located five miles from Disney World with state-of-the-art schools, pedestrian malls, and public spaces—all closely governed by the Disney Corporation.

4. Derek T. Buescher and Kent Ono, "Civilized Colonialism: Pocahontas as Neocolonial Rhetoric," *Women's Studies in Communication* 19 (1996): 117–153. (Quoted on p. 140.)

5. Keisha L. Hoerner, "Gender Roles in Disney Films: Analyzing Behaviors from Snow White to Simba." *Women's Studies in Communication* 19 (1996): 213–228. (Quoted on p. 222.)

6. Dorfman and Mattelart, *How to Read*, 35.

7. Goran Therborn, "Why Some Classes are More Successful Than Others," *New Left Review* 138 (1983): 37–55.

8. Antonio Gramsci, *Selected Writings, 1916–1935*, ed. David Forgacs (New York: Schocken, 1988). Lee Artz and Bren Murphy, *Cultural Hegemony in the United States* (Thousand Oaks, Calif: Sage, 1990).

9. Paul J. Croce, "A Clean and Separate Space: Walt Disney in Person and Production," *Journal of Popular Culture* 23, no. 3 (1991): 91–103. (Quoted on p. 91.)

10. Pamela C. O'Brien, "The Happiest Films on Earth: A Textual and Contextual Analysis of Walt Disney's *Cinderella* and *The Little Mermaid*," *Women's Studies in Communication* 19 (1996): 155–181. (Quoted on pp. 173–75.)

Constructing the "New Ethnicities"

Media, Sexuality, and Diaspora Identity in the Lives of South Asian Immigrant Girls

Meenakshi Gigi Durham

. . . . To gain insight into how media narratives and images figure into the negotiation of diaspora adolescent sexuality, in this study I explored South Asian immigrant girls' experiences of coming of age among contemporary global mediascapes, through a series of interviews that brought to the surface the dynamic intersections of body politics, culture-crossing, and myths of homeland. These issues emerged in a constant interplay with the narratives of gender and sexuality in contemporary consumer-oriented teen media. . . .

In recent globalization theory, the notion of hybridization has been used to address the multiple discontinuities and meldings of global and local symbolic practices and their material implications. For diaspora women and girls, sexuality marks the locus at which competing discourses of embodiment and agency intersect, where global/local power relations play out. Deterritorialized women encounter drastic differences in the ways in which female sexuality is conceptualized and governed in different cultural contexts, and these differences have real-world physical and psychic consequences. Appadurai (1996) notes that the politics of gender and violence are deeply imbricated in global shifts and their attendant mediascapes: "as fantasies of gendered violence dominate the B-grade film industries that blanket the world . . . the honor of women becomes increasingly a surrogate for the identity of embattled communities of males" (p. 45), and female sexuality becomes an arena for power struggles.

Recent research on immigrant girls reveals that these relations of power play out in the sexual dynamics of diaspora families. For example, Espiritu (2001) found that immigrant Filipino American families exercised a great deal of control over their daughters' sexual activity, restricting it severely, and that this "policing" led to tensions and hierarchies within the families, especially because of the differential treatment of girls and boys. Ward and Taylor (1991) found that immigrant teenagers from Vietnamese, Haitian, Hispanic and Portuguese families could not talk with their parents about sex, and that girls would be punished for evidence of sexual activity (while boys would not). Maira (2002) similarly found "a gendered double standard that is more lenient on males than females" (p. 155) among parents of second-generation immigrant South Asian youth in New York. This curtailment of girls' sexuality is tied, Maira argues, to national ideologies in which women's bodies are seen as repositories of tradition and weapons of defense against cultural violations. Gillespie (1995) made the same point in an early study of South Asian immigrant teenagers in London, noting that in this diaspora group "family honour, or izzat, ultimately depends on the chastity of daughters" (p. 152).

As Goodenow and Espin (1993) have noted, "while males are often encouraged to Americanize rather quickly, females are more frequently expected by their families to maintain traditional roles and virtues. Conflict is particularly likely to arise with regard to issues of appropriate sex role behavior and sexuality" (p. 174). Several studies indicate that female immigrants to the U.S. adapt, in general, more quickly to American sex and gender roles than men (Ghaffarian, 1989; Robinson, Ziss, Ganza, Katz, & Robinson, 1991; Tohidi, 1993); this differential adaptation tends to result in intra-familial conflict.

At the same time that immigrant families exercise rigid restraint over adolescent girls' sexuality, Western culture continues to hypersexualize girls and women of color (Parmar, 1993; Tajima, 1989; Yegenoglu, 1998). Western media promote certain displays of female sexuality—ones that call for body exposure and heterosexual voracity (McNair, 2002)—that may be in conflict with certain aspects of non-Western cultural conventions for women, while resonating with the desire for sexual agency that contemporary young women seek. . . .

All of the girls [who participated in this study] noted that their parents had either strict limits or actual prohibitions on dating and interactions with boys. These limits extended to restrictions over the girls' interactions with "American" (non-Indian) girl friends. The restrictions, the girls believed, had to do with parental fears of the possibility of sexual misbehaviors as well as other forms of delinquency, such as drug abuse or drinking. These fears played out in the form of a "discipline of the body" that extended to clothing and demeanor, and that was related to issues of sexuality.

Malini: They won't let us wear, like, short skirts or tank tops . . .

Kiran: I guess they think boys will look at us or something.

While tensions with parents are a common aspect of adolescence, not unique to the immigrant experience, these conflicts became more acute with regard to culturally specific issues. For example, all three 15-year-olds were involved in an ongoing debate with their parents about attending their school's junior prom the following year. The Indian parents had all forbidden their daughters to attend, because, the girls said, of their fears of an unfamiliar cultural ritual, understood only through salacious media frames. As Divya noted, "I can't go to prom because of what they think might happen," a view supported by Ria.

Ria: I know I'll go. I know I'm going to go. I know I'm going to go. With a boy. But my parents are like, I don't want you to go because of what's going to happen after the dance.

Researcher: What do they think is going to happen after the prom?

Ria: We're going to get all drunk and get a hotel room and have sex.

Malini: That is such a teenage movie stereotype!

Ria: I know! That's what's in all the movies about the prom, but it isn't what everybody does!

Further discussion emphasized parental fears of sexual transgressions that were, the girls believed, based on media stereotypes.

Divya: We are not allowed to go to dances because they're afraid of things that might happen. If a guy calls and my dad answers the phone and he asks to speak to me, I will hear a whole series of questions—"Who is that? What did he want? Why is he calling you?"—Oh my god, it's so crazy. And like dances . . . my mom, I don't think she cares, but my dad . . . they ask about them, and find out what we did and they don't trust me, or, I don't know, they trust me but they think I'll be tempted by drugs or alcohol and all that . . . They think that, "oh my god, everybody's doing it and she's going to get hooked on it too."

All of the girls claimed that they were on the whole prohibited from attending parties and other social events with peers, even those organized by their schools. As Ria explained,

My parents, they don't want me to go to dances. Because there's all these stories about robberies and guns and alcohol and stuff at like schools, and like pot and stuff. My parents always ask me questions when I come home and before I go. They ask me stuff like, "was anybody smoking? Was anybody doing drugs? Was anybody in the bathroom most of the time? Did anybody come out looking funny?" Stuff like that. And

I'm like, "No! Believe me! There was nothing like that!" and they go, "Do you hang out with anybody who does bad stuff?" And I'm like, "no. I don't hang out with people like that." I'll be like, "mom, why does it matter?" . . . and it really gets on my nerves. I feel like they don't trust me at all.

The girls chalked some of these restrictions up to cultural differences, but they also pinpointed the media as key factors in this parental dictum:

Malini: They never went to a prom, they don't know about things here, and they believe what's in the movies . . .

Divya: Everybody knows that those movies are nothing like real life! High school is never like that! But I think our parents believe it.

In fact, the girls perceived their parents to rely on media characterizations of American high school life in the absence of first-hand experience of it. As they pointed out, their parents were unfamiliar with the realities of the U.S. secondary school experience and so obtained their information from largely mediated sources, which the girls dismissed as unrealistic and exaggerated. . . .

Media scripts of adolescent sexuality as a crisis were identified by the girls as being particularly influential in guiding parental restrictions over the girls' activities.

Lekha: Another thing is teen pregnancy. I mean, yeah, there's a really high teen pregnancy birth rate and like all that stuff, and yeah it's pathetic, and I would never ever dream of doing that. But my parents like say, when they see commercials like that or TV shows about teens having sex, they're like, "Do you know anybody who does this? Do you do this?" and they like think I'm the worst person in the world when it comes to sex.

Kiran: They think that everything on TV totally applies to you. . . .

As Appadurai (1996) observes, the media offer a furious flow of images and texts in which reality and fantasy are mixed, and

> the farther away . . . audiences are from the direct experience of metropolitan life, the more likely they are to construct imagined worlds that are chimerical, aesthetic, even fantastic objects, particularly if assessed by the criteria of some other perspective . . . (p. 35)

In these scenarios, the girls' perspectives and experiences collided with their parents' media-derived understandings of the world of the American teenager. Yet the girls themselves consumed mainstream media; while they saw themselves as more media-savvy and sophisticated than their parents, their consumption patterns indicated a different kind of reliance on media scripts, particularly of gender and sexual behavior.

Crossing Pop Culture Borders

Divya and Lekha self-defined as the heaviest users of mainstream media. Both confessed to enjoying mainstream movies and television shows. Divya said she listened to pop music, especially the Backstreet Boys and 'N Sync, but none of the others shared those interests, which at the time of the interviews enjoyed enormous popularity among teenagers.

The other girls said they did not watch television or movies, except for the TV sitcom *Friends,* which all five girls watched regularly, participating in a fan culture that they shared with "American" friends at school. They enjoyed the show so much that they bought and exchanged DVDs of

different episodes, but they consistently characterized themselves as critical viewers:

Ria: Last year I really got into the show *Friends.* Which I guess is unrealistic and I know is so stupid and stereotypical but I'm not really influenced by it, if you want to talk about media influences . . . but, I don't know, I just love watching it, I love like how fun they are and how much fun they have . . .

Divya: Sometimes they're really stupid, but it isn't as bad as *Dawson's Creek.*

Malini: Like *Dawson's Creek* is so retarded. It's just about a bunch of teens, and they do this typical teen stuff, and none of it is real . . . And I guess we like watching the stupid chick flicks, but not because we think it's real or we want to do it . . .

Ria: We think it's funny and hopefully we're not influenced by it.

Malini: We are not at all.

Again, the girls believed their own oppositional decoding of the television text was diametrically opposed to their parents' dominant reading; the latter, they felt, was unfairly transferred to their own reception of the texts.

Ria: On *Friends* they're always sleeping with different guys, and hopefully I'll never, ever do that. I don't want to use that as an example of what a relationship should be.

Divya: We own DVDs of *Friends* . . . But my parents are worried about it. They think, if they see me watching *Friends,* "oh my God, she's watching this, and she'll think they're role models, and she's going to go do all these things" . . . but it's, like, no.

Kiran: Yeah, I asked my mom to watch it with me once, and it happened to be an episode all about like, sexual stuff, and I guess it kind of revolved around sex, but not so much that that was all they talked about, and my mom was like, "oh, so you like watching this because it's all about sex" . . . [Laughter]

A significant common theme that emerged in terms of media use was the girls' critique of, and dissociation from, what they declared to be "American" media, which seemed to translate as "white mainstream" popular culture. *Friends* was the only American television show they admitted to watching regularly; while they said they enjoyed the show because it was "fun," they were dubious about their own susceptibility to the ways of life it espoused, and their use of the show was partly a matter of communicatory utility: they watched it in order to be able to converse with non-Indian peers at school. As Ria explained, "At school, if you don't have anything else to talk about, it's like, 'Oh, did you see this movie, or did you watch the Grammys or last night's *Friends?*'"

On the other hand, the girls were avid consumers of Indian popular culture, which they actively imported into their lives in various ways. They rented Indian (usually Hindi-language) movies from local Indian grocery stores and restaurants, as well as acquiring them through social networks, they downloaded Indian pop music from the Internet, and they attended Indian movies at local showings. Music was an important arena of cultural consumption for all five of the girls; their musical tastes varied somewhat, as did the meanings they accorded to their listening practices. But all five girls expressed a predilection for Indian popular music, which was closely related to film watching.

Malini: All the CDs I own are Indian CDs, and that's all I ever listen to. All I ever listen to are Indian soundtracks and stuff, and that's what I like. It has to have a good downbeat and the words have to make sense.

Researcher: Where do you get it?

Malini: We download it off the Internet.

Ria: I *love* Hindi film songs. I *love* Hindi films songs. Even though, like, I don't even know what they mean—I mean I can understand some things, but sometimes I'm like, um, I don't know what they're saying, but I like the beat and I always end up dancing to them and stuff like that. I don't know, they're just cool, they're just better than American songs. I love listening to them.

Researcher: Do you watch the movies, too, that the songs are from?

Girls: Yeah.

Lekha: All of our . . . like my mom's friends with all these Indian people . . . like they'll all get Indian movies and we share them . . .

Researcher: Do you get together and watch them?

Girls: Yeah, we do.

Divya: I love Indian movies.

The girls' embrace of "Bollywood" films and pop culture typifies contemporary trends. Indian films are currently enjoying burgeoning popularity in the West, but their global distribution has been great for many years, particularly in the Middle East and Europe; the Indian motion picture industry produces some 800 films a year, outstripping Hollywood in its productivity and destabilizing traditional notions of West-to-East cultural and monetary flows (Aftab, 2002; Chute, 2002; Cieko, 2001; La Ferla, 2002; Murphy, 2001; Passage from India, 2000). Aftab (2002) notes that the biggest audience for Indian pop culture has, of late, been so-called "NRIs," or nonresident Indians, loosely defined as anyone of Indian heritage living outside of India. He points out that even people born abroad to Indian parents self-identify as NRIs, which, he says, "suggests that the term Indian denotes a mental rather than a physical state, the community joined up not so much by geography as by a web of shared cultural influences" (Aftab, 2002, p. 92). In Kaleem's analysis, Indian cinema is a key factor in this identificatory cultural web. In this study, too, Indian cinema and its music ranked high as a source of cultural identification.

But the girls were clear that they did not see Indian movies as any more realistic than American ones; cinema texts, for them, offered social constructions that marked the fantastic extremes of the two cultures:

Ria: The movies are not about Indian culture. It's Indian people's fantasies. Because in the movies all those people are rich and they're all, like, they always wear clothes like we do, in fact they wear shorter clothes and more expensive, it's always like a fashion show—they don't really wear Indian clothes.

Malini: I think soon enough Indian movies and American movies are going to be identical.

Significantly, while the girls partly saw Indian films as having the same sort of communicatory utility as *Friends,* they also regarded them as connecting them with the Indian community. Ria said:

The movies give us something to talk about with other Indian people, I guess. They can make us feel more like part of an Indian community, the way Bal Vihar[1] does too.

Their valorization of Indian popular culture was a marker of their need to connect to an India that was, for them, an imaginary world, as distant and unfamiliar as their American school experiences were to their parents. They were largely uncritical of Indian films and music, refusing to dismiss them as "stupid" or "retarded," as they had American cultural texts. In this, their orientation to a diasporic homeland was one of affirmation and longing. . . .

The girls saw a different role in their lives for the cinema of the South Asian diaspora. Familiar with such films as Mira Nair's *Mississippi Masala,* Gurinder Chadha's *Bend It Like Beckham,* and Piyush Dinker Pandya's *American Desi,* they expressed an emotional connection with these films that was distinctly different from the ways in which they related to other media.

Ria: If there's a film like that playing in town, I'll go see it before I go see anything else. It's like they're about us.

Malini: Those kinds of movies are more real than any others . . . I mean. I know they're exaggerations, too, but they are familiar situations.

Ria: They're sort of like inside jokes. We get them.

The girls all singled out the films' narratives of love and sex, referring specifically to the taboo relationships between Indian girls and men of different racial/cultural backgrounds in both *Bend It Like Beckham* and *Mississippi Masala.* They identified these storylines as salient to their interests. All five girls said they envisioned eventually falling in love with and marrying men—what Malini described as a "Western marriage"—and some of the girls were certain that such a move would precipitate conflicts with their parents, an extension of the frictions they were dealing with as teenagers. Yet in a sense, these diasporic media offered hope. The girls often watched these films with their parents, and sometimes the narratives opened up topics of discussion that eased the cultural chasms between them. "My dad hates *American Desi*," said Kiran. "He thinks we are laughing at him, when we laugh at the Indian accents and everything. But my mom likes it and we've had a lot of good discussions about what Indian girls are supposed to be like, and stuff like that." Lekha, on the other hand, found that these films further reinforced her parents' resistance to and fear of Western culture. "They think I'm about to fall in love with or sleep with every white guy who comes along. They really have no clue."

Conclusions: Media, Culture, and Difference

Overall, the girls saw themselves as outsiders to both of the spheres they inhabited; they did not self-identify as American, though all of them had been raised in the U.S. and held citizenship. They did classify themselves as Indian, but recognized that their Indianness differed from that of their parents. In fact, the issues of sexuality that marked the divisions between themselves and their parents also demarcated lines of difference between themselves and their American peers. Their grappling with these issues of culture and difference vis-à-vis the media environment demanded the exercise of an imaginative agency in carving out a space of gender/sexual identity. As two of the girls observed:

Ria: I'm figuring things out for myself. The way we have to think about this stuff is different. It's nothing like the relationships on TV,

where like the popular guy and the popular girl get together . . . never in my life would I imagine that the way things are on TV are real.

Divya: When I talk to my friends about like certain things, I've even talked to guy friends about this, I've told them I think sex before marriage is wrong, and I don't want to drink. I don't want to do drugs, and they understand that, and some of them feel the same way, they accept it. And some of my other friends—I'm surprised that they can be so stupid when it comes to these things. But we, all of us here, we have to think about these things in a different way, because of Indian values and all that . . . We can talk to each other.

A number of scholars have commented on the complicated politics of race that position Indian American identities as being something between "near white" and "near black" (Maira, 1998; Mazumdar, 1989; Okihiro, 1994). Sunaina Maira's studies of second-generation Indian American youth and the New York club scene suggest that club "remix" music, which combines traditional Indian rhythms with rap, is an attempt by these youth "to mediate between the expectations of immigrant parents and those of mainstream American culture, by trying to integrate signs of belonging to both worlds" (1998, p. 360).

By contrast, the girls in this study saw both Indian and American popular culture as marking the boundaries of those two worlds, neither of which they claimed as their milieu. Rather than attempting to find a place in both cultural spheres, they recognized the need to assert a new identity position that, in a sense, rejected the options offered by Indian as well as American media texts. As consumers, therefore, their textual readings involve a radical questioning of the sexual mores instantiated by the television shows, films, and popular music they consumed. . . .

A number of studies indicate that viewers who are socially marginalized are better able to read media oppositionally than mainstream audiences (see Bobo, 1995; Cohen, 1991; Lind, 1996; Morley, 1992). Given this, it would be a mistake to dismiss the girls' critiques of the texts as naïve or unthinking: their recognition of the identity politics at play speaks to a different interpretation of their viewing positions. . . . The girls' lives at home and at school are circumscribed and colored by the cross cultural currents that traverse them, and their experiences in these "border zones" of youth culture are not represented in the mainstream media.

In contrast, the cinema of the diaspora, with its themes of inter-ethnic love and romance within and outside of the family sphere, offered a framework that resonated with the girls. Perhaps this is because the diaspora films encapsulate and explore the themes of cultural hybridization that the girls are negotiating in their daily lives. If we think of hybridization in terms of the interlacing of the global and the local, a way of understanding the symbolic and material collisions and fusions that mark the new global landscape, then these cinematic representations offer a cultural form in which the seemingly irreconcilable differences between cultures are articulated and worked out. Monocultural forms, by contrast, as the girls observed, mark the poles and never engage in analyses of the complexities of cultural globalization. In representing sexuality, in particular, the micropolitics of cultural hybridity are invisible and therefore untenable. . . .

For the girls in this study, sexual self-identification is a political project that is articulated to gender, race, and culture. Inherent in it is a critique of the dominant discourses of assimilation, that would draw them into the culturally fetishized role of the hypersexual woman of color, and a concomitant critique of the essentialized, marginal sexual script of

the Indian immigrant with its "fantasies of sexual purity and fears of polluting seductiveness [that] are part of a larger ideology of ethnic authenticity at work" in its popular culture forms (Maira, 1998, p. 361). In deploying these critiques, these adolescent girls create the potential for new sexual identities that have emancipatory possibilities for them as girls in-between, or girls embarking on the project of forging new ethnicities in the interstitial cultural spaces that allow for new imaginings of gender and sexuality.

Note

1. Bal Vihar refers to the Hindu religious educational program that three of the girls (Ria, Kiran, and Divya) attended.

References

Aftab, K. (2002). Brown: The new black! Bollywood in Britain, *Critical Quarterly, 44,* 88–98.

Appadurai. A. (1996). *Modernity at large: Cultural dimensions of globalization.* Minneapolis: University of Minnesota Press.

Bobo, J. (1995). *Black women as cultural readers.* New York: Columbia University Press.

Chute, D. (2002). The road to Bollywood. *Film Comment, 38,* 36.

Cieko, A. (2001). Superhit hunk heroes for sale: Globalization and Bollywood's gender politics. *Asian Journal of Communication, 11,* 121–143.

Cohen, J. R. (1991). The "relevance" of cultural identity in audiences' interpretations of mass media. *Critical Studies in Mass Communication, 8,* 442–454.

Espiritu, Y. L. (2001). "We don't sleep around like white girls do": Family, culture, and gender in Filipina Americans' lives. *Signs, 26,* 415–440.

Ghaffarian, S. (1989). *The acculturation of Iranians in the United States and the implications for mental health.* Unpublished doctoral dissertation, California School of Professional Psychology, Los Angeles.

Gillespie, M. (1995). *Television, ethnicity and cultural change.* New York: Routledge.

Goodenow, C., & Espin, O. M. (1993). Identity choices in immigrant adolescent females. *Adolescence, 28*(109), 173–184.

La Ferla, R. (2002, May 5). Kitsch with a niche: Bollywood chic finds a home. *New York Times,* p. K1.

Lind, R. A. (1996). Diverse interpretations: The "relevance" of race in the construction of meaning in, and the evaluation of, a television news story. *Howard Journal of Communication, 7,* 53–74.

Maira, S. (1998). Desis reprazent: Bhangra remix and hip hop in New York City. *Postcolonial Studies, 1,* 357–370.

Maira, S. (2002). *Desis in the house: Indian American youth culture in New York City.* Philadelphia: Temple University Press.

Mazumdar, S. (1989). Racist responses to racism: The Aryan myth and South Asians in the United States. *South Asia Bulletin, 9,* 47–55.

McNair, B. (2002). *Striptease culture: Sex, media, and the democratisation of desire.* Routledge: London and New York.

Morley, D. (1992). *Television audiences and cultural studies.* New York: Routledge.

Murphy, D. E. (2001, April 27). A little bit of Hollywood starring India. *New York Times,* p. B1.

Okihiro, G. Y. (1994). Is yellow black or white? In G. Y. Okihiro (Ed.), *Margins and mainstreams: Asians in American history and culture* (pp. 31–63). Seattle: University of Washington Press.

Parmar, P. (1993). That moment of emergence. In M. Gever, J. Greyson, & P. Parmar (Eds.), *Queer looks: Perspectives on lesbian and gay film and video* (pp. 3–11). New York: Routledge.

Passage from India. (2000, October 21). *The Economist, 357*(8193), 80.

Robinson, I., Ziss, K., Ganza, B., Katz, S., & Robinson, E. (1991). Twenty years of the sexual revolution, 1965–1985: An update. *Journal of Marriage and the Family, 53,* 216–220.

Tajima, R. E. (1989). Lotus blossoms don't bleed: Images of Asian women. In Asian Women United of California (Eds.), *Making waves: An anthology of writings by and about Asian American women* (pp. 308–317). Boston: Beacon.

Tohidi, N. (1993). Iranian women and gender relations in Los Angeles. In R. Kelley, J. Friedlander, & A. Colby (Eds.), *Irangeles: Iranians in Los Angeles* (pp. 175–217). Berkeley: University of California Press.

Ward, J. V., & Taylor, J. M. (1991). Sexuality education for immigrant minority teenagers: Developing a culturally appropriate curriculum. In J. Irvine (Ed.), *Sexual cultures and the construction of adolescent identities* (pp. 51–68). Philadelphia: Temple University Press.

Yegenoglu, M. (1998). *Colonial fantasies: Toward a feminist reading of Orientalism.* Cambridge, UK: Cambridge University Press.

HIV on TV

Conversations With Young Gay Men

Kathleen P. Farrell

. . . . As the current HIV epidemic in the United States continues to affect gay communities, it is important to understand how young gay and bisexual men understand this phenomenon in relation to themselves, their friends, and their futures. While in colleges and universities across the country, oftentimes far from large, established gay communities such as in New York City and San Francisco, many young gay men have never met anyone living with, or directly affected by, HIV. Instead, these students only have access to media and popular culture representations of people with HIV and the HIV epidemic, more generally.

This study draws on a unique storyline from the popular groundbreaking series, *Queer as Folk,* to address the different ways that several groups of undergraduate gay males make sense of HIV and its representation in a fictional TV storyline. This research is important since it adds to the minimal published accounts of televised HIV content by moving past textual analysis and, instead, learning from audience members how these representations are understood by them. In addition to gaining a better understanding of how some gay audiences consume these HIV related stories and incorporate them into their own lives, these findings also illuminate the possibilities for HIV prevention through entertaining television programs that appeal to young nonheterosexual audiences, as well as the possibility of focus group research as a prevention source in and of itself. . . .

A Brief History of HIV on TV

On 7 July 1981, CNN aired a story on Kaposi's sarcoma and marked the first time the syndrome, later known as AIDS, was mentioned on TV (Kinsella, 1989: 260). Two and a half years later, *St. Elsewhere* became the first prime-time drama to include a story of a gay or bisexual man with AIDS, although the next gay-themed AIDS drama did not air until late

From Farrell, K. P. (2006). HIV on TV: Conversations with young gay men. *Sexualities*, 9(2), 193–213.

1985. During this time, networks reportedly feared that AIDS dramas would encourage backlash from both gay rights groups and right-wing activists and chose, instead, to deal with AIDS on talk shows and news programs, where audiences were often shown depictions of emaciated AIDS patients dying in hospital rooms. However, when NBC's *An Early Frost* (1985), the first TV movie to focus on AIDS, aired, it received exceptional ratings and even Emmy nominations. The timing was perfect: AIDS was headline news following Rock Hudson's confirmation of infection, and the movie provided accurate medical facts to millions of viewers who knew little of the emerging epidemic. Also around this time, ABC and CBS were working on TV movie proposals about young gay men and AIDS (Capsuto, 2000).

While NBC treated *An Early Frost* as 'a prestige piece', some gay activists criticized the film and subsequent TV AIDS dramas featured throughout the late 1980s and early 1990s for their consistent shortcomings (Capsuto, 2000; Gross, 2001; Netzhammer and Shamp, 1994; Russo, 1987; Seidman, 2002). Gross (2001) describes gay characters on television, in general, as primarily being defined by their problems and absent from any sort of larger gay culture, and these AIDS stories were no exceptions. In fact, gay and bisexual male characters with AIDS at this time were always classified by their illness, used as a 'dramatic device'.[1] In addition, a repeated feature of all TV AIDS dramas was a focus on individual people who have AIDS, and perhaps their heterosexual family, but with no recognition of gay communities or AIDS activists (Gross, 2001). Gross (2001) argues that this type of representation suggests that people with AIDS are abandoned until their birth family comes and saves them from being alone. *An Early Frost* is one such film: it focuses on how a heterosexual family deals with their son being forced out of the closet by AIDS, but little consideration is given to the fact that this is happening to their son, *not them*, and the film does not include

any attention to how this young man struggles with his illness in his own circle of friends (Russo, 1987).

Critics also note how AIDS dramas of this time period, whether 'about' gay men or not, were sanitized, often portraying 'white people with bad luck' (Gross, 2001: 144). A newspaper editorial from 1988 explains, '[o]n TV, AIDS is primarily a disease of middle-class white children, who get it from blood transfusions, and, secondarily, of middle-class white heterosexuals, who get it from prostitutes, and middle-class white homosexuals, who get it from a single lover who committed a single indiscretion.'[2] These were the dramas that depicted the innocent victims of AIDS and their families, and were primarily 'message' scripts with lessons like 'Be nice to people with AIDS' and 'Protect yourself from HIV', reminding audiences to be compassionate to these 'victims' (Capsuto, 2000). On the other hand, Gross (2001) describes an (also unfavorable) alternative to this popular family-centered model—those films that portrayed 'AIDS villains': people who carelessly or deliberately place others at risk of becoming infected. One example, from 1988, is *Midnight Caller,* a dramatic series on NBC, which featured an episode with a bisexual man who intentionally spreads HIV to numerous unsuspecting sexual partners.

Since the 1980s, the presence of HIV on TV has been a relatively rare event, especially on shows that may appeal specifically to young gay audiences. Although Hollywood films continue to address HIV on the big screen, in such films as *Philadelphia* (1993) and the more recent *The Hours* (2002), HIV has become relegated on television to daytime programming with audiences containing large numbers of heterosexual female viewers, such as afternoon soap operas, or health/scientific news stories on the evening news. While gay characters, in general, have become more commonplace on network television, including prime-time sitcoms, dramas, and reality TV programs, there continues to be an absence of HIV-positive gay men. Additionally, when one of these characters does appear, he is usually portrayed as one single gay person with HIV among his heterosexual and HIV-negative friends and family.

The Text: *Queer as Folk*

Queer as Folk is a weekly television drama [U.S. run was from 2001 to 2006], and one-time highest rated program on the premium cable network, Showtime. Although *Queer as Folk* centers on a group of middle-class white characters (a criticism offered by both activists and focus group participants), it also deserves recognition for its departure from the patterns of televised AIDS stories from the last two decades.

The show originated in Britain, and its American counterpart was the first television drama in the USA to deal explicitly with queer culture: almost all its primary characters are gay men and lesbians who are active members of a larger queer community including gay nightclubs and bars, stores, gyms and even gay-themed restaurants. In addition, the characters often come into contact with other gay people at their work and even on the street. In fact, one character is an advertising executive who frequently wins clients by creating advertisements that are meant to appeal specifically to gay audiences. The main characters of the show are not ashamed of their sexuality—they lead complex lives with good days as well as bad days; bad days that sometimes involve dealing with homophobia from the larger society without being portrayed as victims. Instead, this group of characters leads gay-affirming lives that center on their close friendships with one another. Although it received less controversy than initially expected, *Queer as Folk* was often considered problematic by both gay and straight audiences primarily in reaction to the abundance and explicitness of its sex scenes. Some audiences seemed to be uncomfortable with the frankness of these scenes,

while other audiences criticized the stereotypical representations of gay men as hanging out in dance clubs looking for sex. Supporters of the show often argue that *Queer as Folk* simply offered a representation of one aspect of gay culture, and felt that the storylines were compelling and true to life.

Unlike television's attention to HIV in the late 1980s as an issue for the movie of the week, the American *Queer as Folk* incorporates HIV storylines throughout the series. In fact, HIV does not appear as a special dramatic topic that the show's characters encounter in one or two heartfelt episodes, but rather, it is presented simply, and matter-of-factly, as one problem with which these characters must struggle in the context of other storylines about gay bashing, workplace discrimination, and coming out to family members. Specifically, *Queer as Folk* has included stories of its leading characters being tested for the virus; an episode where a good friend of a main character dies of AIDS; an episode centered on raising money for an AIDS-care organization; and several other explicit references to condom use to protect from sexually transmitted diseases, including HIV. Also, quite notably, one of the featured characters, although not a lead role, is the uncle of the primary character Michael, Vic, who has been living with AIDS for over a decade. Although the audience is sometimes reminded that Vic has AIDS, it is not the central concern in most of his scenes. Instead, he is Michael's uncle, an older gay man who happens to have AIDS.

The Current Project

This project focuses on one of the HIV-related storylines from the second season, in which the primary character, Michael, begins to date Ben, who is HIV-positive. Audience members watch as Michael struggles to negotiate his feelings for someone with HIV, while members of his support system voice their opposition to the relationship, citing their fear that Michael will also become infected. In the story, Ben's HIV status is revealed to Michael soon after they kiss on their first official date. Michael chooses not to advance the sexual contact that night, but continues to date Ben, despite fierce confrontations with his good friend, Ted, and his mother, Debbie. When Michael and Ben are about to have sex for the first time, Michael sees Ben's HIV medications and gets too scared about the possibility of becoming infected, causing him to end the relationship with Ben.[3] However, later in the season, Michael has realized the extent of his romantic feelings for Ben, and fights to resume their relationship. Their relationship continues throughout the series, as we see them become a sexually intimate couple and work to gain approval from Debbie and Ted. We also see Ben, sick with an HIV-related complication, go to the hospital. Ultimately, he recovers and, at the end of the season, his relationship with Michael is going strong, supported by both Debbie and Ted. Michael has not become infected with the virus.

As an HIV story that focuses on the relationship between two gay men surrounded by family, gay friends and a larger gay culture, the romance of Michael and Ben is exceptional and worthy of investigation. This couple continues to be sexual, in spite of HIV (an occurrence which is rare for any gay couple on TV), and their participation in the show is not limited to the HIV aspect of their relationship. Instead, there are many accounts of Michael and Ben doing everyday things, without any mention of Ben's HIV status or of Michael's reaction and negotiations of it. This HIV storyline from *Queer as Folk*, then, provides a unique opportunity to investigate the various ways that audiences make sense of HIV and its dramatic representation. Primarily, I wanted to learn how gay undergraduate males engage with and discuss the fictional television portrayal of a serodiscordant gay couple (that is, mismatched HIV status)

who are struggling with their relationship. How are these young men making sense of HIV on TV, and in their own lives?

Method

In order to gain access to the perspectives of *Queer as Folk* audience members, I organized a series of small focus groups. Each group meeting lasted 3-4 hours and took place in a seminar/conference room or an empty classroom. In these groups participants were asked to watch three separate 20-minute collections of edited clips from the second season of the U.S. *Queer as Folk*. The clips were organized so that Ben and Michael's relationship was highlighted, although some other sequences from the series were also included. After viewing each 20-minute segment, I turned the discussion over to the participants to talk about whatever interested them the most, and I recorded these interactions on audiotapes. Although I guided the conversations, and often interjected with probing follow-up questions (such as 'What did you think of that scene?' or 'Can you tell me more about why you think that?'), most of the talk took place among the focus group members and centered on their opinions of the stories and characters that they viewed. After transcribing these tapes, I carefully reviewed the conversations and coded them according to emergent themes. These focus groups proved to be a very useful way to collect rich data from my study participants. . . .

Results

TALKING ABOUT HIV (ON TV)

Like all socially constructed phenomena, the meaning of HIV in society, and in the lives of the young men I talked with, can be complex and multi-layered. In this chapter

I will address several of the primary themes relating to HIV that emerged from our focus group meetings: the way that HIV was most often described in the context of our discussions (what I refer to as the social definition of HIV); how most participants recognized that the HIV storyline from *Queer as Folk* is a sharp departure from previous televised representations of HIV and their opinions of this shift; the attitudes toward condom use and safe-sex behavior in the real lives of the focus group members; as well as the safe-sex messages they perceive this TV show to be imparting. Overall, these discussions expose the many ways that these young men are making meaning of this HIV storyline in relation to their own lives and their understanding of gay culture. . . .

Despite reporting that HIV awareness and prevention has become a routine aspect of their sexual existence, study participants did not express any level of comfort or indifference when discussing their ordinary, everyday negotiations of HIV. Instead, participants referred to asking a potential sex partner's HIV status as 'daunting', 'a very sensitive situation', and one focus group member reported that asking someone's HIV status 'somehow seems like it would be rude'. Moreover, study participants did not share an understanding of HIV as a chronic illness, rather than a fatal disease.

On *Queer as Folk*, Ben, who is HIV-positive, refers to revealing his HIV status to Michael as 'dropping a bomb'. . . . Many of the focus group participants were surprised when Michael chose to continue dating Ben, and most agreed that, while Ben appeared to be a great match for Michael before he 'dropped the bomb', once his HIV status was known, Ben's attractiveness rating dropped also:

Pete: When I first heard it I guess I was disappointed because his perfect image was destroyed. And, you know, before that, he was seen as perfect: all the men were looking at him, they all wanted him, but

after this happened, he's not as perfect anymore.

George: [referring to Ben's HIV status] That's a deal breaker.

While some focus group members did not fully subscribe to the thinking presented here, it became very clear through our discussions that the exposure many of these young men have had to HIV scared them. Regardless of whether participants supported Michael and Ben's relationship or not, they all expressed fear of contracting HIV; they all thought that life, as they know it, would change completely. Since all but five of the focus group participants reported that they have never known anyone, in their real lives, who is directly affected by, or infected with, HIV, it seems logical that HIV information, whether viewed in prevention literature, in schools or through the mass media, has contributed to an understanding of HIV as something extraordinary, negative and frightening. This social definition of HIV was shared by all members of my focus groups.

HIV ON TV IN 2003: LIFE WITH HIV

Many times throughout my research, participants noted how the depiction of Ben, as a character *living* with HIV, is groundbreaking. . . .

We never really see this side of the happy HIV person, that's kind of sad . . . I think it's actually a great thing that they have it on a television show, have someone talk about HIV and their life and not talk about just the end part of the cycle, rather than the middle part—about living their life and . . . that they are able to live a healthy life having AIDS, having a relationship . . . I think it's great and I really enjoy, I love, watching it.

. . . John, impressed with Ben's character not being celibate, said:

I think it is an interesting twist considering the person with AIDS [wants to have sex] which is different 'cause that's something, that isn't something, like a requirement that you'd expect someone with AIDS to have . . . I thought that was a pretty good portrayal of someone with AIDS because it shows them as being sexual people.

Pete elaborated on this by explaining that Ben, as a young, good-looking and physically fit HIV-positive character, challenges stereotypical television portrayals of people with HIV/AIDS:

I guess just the fact that he was seen as perfect sends the message that not all people with HIV are old, nasty, gay men that look sickly and everything. . . .

While academic and medical reports of HIV emphasize this fact, that HIV-positive people can live in excellent health and form for decades, study participants point out that many audience members may not be aware of this fact, and that their comprehension of HIV-positive people would be expanded through these characters. . . .

Repeatedly, focus group members described how *Queer as Folk* extended their knowledge of *people* with HIV, and criticized their formal schooling for not addressing these issues:

Mike: Like, you learn about it [HIV/AIDS] in school, you learn about it, whatever, and it's . . . you learned about the virus, you didn't learn about the people.

Pete: When people do learn about AIDS prevention and everything, you just are told like, 'ok, this could happen to you, and so and so and so, and you can get sick, and you'll have to take medicine, whatever,' but they don't actually tell you what happens, how you live your life and how you . . . the medical terms and everything.

. . . Generally, focus group members felt that TV shows like this help people understand that people living with HIV are living with 'one more thing to deal with,' instead of always being consumed with the possibility of death or illness. Repeatedly many of these young men reported that these were new ideas for them; they had not really considered HIV-positive people as living 'regular lives', dating HIV-negative people, promoting casual sex to their friends (as opposed to warning them of the dangers and suggesting that casual sex will inevitably lead to HIV infection), and not being particularly preachy about HIV awareness. In these ways, *Queer as Folk* has increased their understanding of the social dimensions of HIV.

Beyond what they watched on-screen, participants' knowledge about HIV was also transformed through their involvement in these focus groups. In fact, misconceptions about how HIV is transmitted, the medical implications of a positive HIV test result, and other incorrect assumptions regarding the virus and its treatment, were voiced and frequently dismantled during these focus group meetings. . . .

CONDOM USE: AN ISSUE OF TRUST

Consistently, focus group participants reported that condom use is required in order for them to have sex whenever a partner's HIV status is uncertain. Here, George describes what he was thinking, during a scene in which two of the main characters accidentally walk into a party and immediately leave, disapprovingly, when they see that many attendees were having unprotected sex:

It was just shocking, because you, for us, well, for me, anyway, you're just always going to have the image of having a condom. Like always. Like, it's like health or whatever, but you know [you need] to have a condom . . . [having sex without a condom] that's not really cool.

. . . By openly enforcing the notion that condoms are essential, focus group members are creating and recreating the sexual norms which pertain to their lives. *Queer as Folk*, as a TV show, is also contributing to these sexual scripts by including storylines containing explicit references to condom use, and by communicating, through the use of fictional characters, that unprotected sex is improper. In the context of these focus groups, both the participants and the TV show are promoting lessons about consistent condom use, by criticizing men who do not use them and praising those who do.

In reference to why some gay men do not use condoms regularly, explanations such as 'ignorance', 'stupidity', and 'because some people just don't seem to be getting it' were offered by most focus group members. However, while condom vigilance initially was reported as essential, some participants later revealed that exceptions to this rule are acceptable [when] carried out in the context of a 'serious' relationship in which the HIV status of both partners is known, or, in one participant's terminology, when he knows that his partner is 'clean'. Furthermore, focus group discussions uncovered that having sex without a condom, in a long-term romantic relationship, is the 'ultimate sign of trust' for some of these young men:

Rhyse: I think part of that has to do with trust, that, the whole HIV/AIDS issue partially is one of trust, and so, in order to say that you fully trust the person you're with, well, lose the condom. You know, I mean, if you trust them that much, and they said they don't

have anything, you believe them, and you're going to prove that at any cost . . . that's not to say that the words 'I love you' or that the words 'I trust you' are meaningless, but actions speak louder than words and that's a huge action.

Elliot: And, kind of going along with that, when you put your life into somebody's hands . . . that's the ultimate sign of trust. And sexual acts without a condom, is really, there's a ton of danger that goes along with that, and you're totally putting yourself out there, in the control of someone else.

This conversation took place after viewing a scene in which one primary character, Justin, discusses how his sexual relationship allows certain behaviors, such as sex without a condom, because both he and his regular partner are both HIV-negative. In this scene, Justin is noting how a serodiscordant couple, such as Ben and Michael, will never be able to engage in these activities, due to the risk of infection. Justin's partner, Brian, immediately and emphatically corrects Justin's naive statement, expressing that unprotected sex with anyone is always a bad idea. After all, Brian argues, Ben contracted HIV from unprotected sex with a serious boyfriend who was also believed to be HIV-negative.

While some focus group members agreed that Justin's partner was speaking words of wisdom, others, such as Rhyse and Elliot, quoted earlier, did not seem to be persuaded by this on-screen lesson. What is noteworthy here is the way that the fictional story imparts a message that is counter to the risky sexual practices in which some of these young men choose to engage. There is an opportunity here for the show to begin challenging audiences' ideas regarding what types of behavior are acceptable or 'safe' and in what contexts. While many of the focus group participants already subscribed to the idea of persistent condom use outside of 'serious' relationships, there is much room for change in behavioral norms regarding the strict use of condoms within these relationships. Is there potential for a TV show to provide sexual scripts that effectively communicate this necessity?

TV as Safe-Sex Education?

. . . . Although initially attracted to the show for entertainment, many focus group members recognized that this show also functions as an educator regarding many aspects of gay culture, including HIV awareness and prevention. While a few participants, including Schyler, felt some of these informative attempts were a bit 'heavy handed', 'contrived and really irritating', most other focus group members were not bothered by these messages and, instead, had only positive things to say regarding the way that the storylines were presented. However, even some of these focus group members cautioned that the safe-sex messages could easily become 'over the top' and feel 'preachy' if handled in a more focused or explicit way. The following statements by Charles and Mikey provide instructive warnings for TV stories attempting to offer informational messages regarding HIV-positive people and/or safe sex:

Charles: If they would have elaborated on that scene [regarding condom use] I'm not sure if the audience would have liked that, because it would have put too much emphasis on the suggestion that it needs to be dealt with, and like they're trying really hard to deal with this issue, you know, trying to teach a lesson.

Mikey: I think they don't overemphasize the issue, or they don't make it too out there . . . they refer to it

in very brief moments, but it's not the focus of it, that's where the entertainment comes into play. When you beat down the issues such as this, not using condoms, it just gets to be boring to the person watching it.

In fact, common published critiques of media-based HIV prevention campaigns, which rely heavily on the use of Public Service Announcements (PSAs) aired during televised commercial breaks, are that these messages often do not appeal to gay audiences; they often inspire feelings of guilt within gay communities; they are frequently perceived to be insensitive or too moral; and audiences are turned off due to feeling that they are receiving a lecture (Dejong et al., 2001; Salmon, 2000; Turner, 1997). Instead, as outlined by Charles and Mikey, entertainment-based media campaigns should be designed to incorporate responsible sexual heath messages, using more subtle, positive reinforcement strategies in TV programs that appeal specifically to their target audience (Dejong et al., 2001; Keller and Brown, 2002; Steele, 1999; Turner, 1997). The challenge here is to continue entertaining, as the educational messages are being consumed. For audiences who were learning sexual scripts through their consumption of popular culture, *Queer as Folk* provided them with attractive material from which they could begin to understand the necessity of condom use. These audiences, in a sense, were seeking out these safer-sex lessons by repeatedly tuning in on a weekly basis, where their education continued. . . .

Notes

1. In *The Celluloid Closet*, Vito Russo writes, '[i]n Hollywood films . . . homosexuals have not been people; they have been a dramatic device used to shock and sell' (Russo, 1987: 248).

2. *San Jose Mercury News,* 1988, cited in Capsuto (2000).

3. Michael's decision not to continue his relationship with Ben was followed by protests from AIDS activist groups (*Larry King Live,* 2002).

References

Capsuto, S. (2000) *Alternate Channels: The Uncensored Story of Gay and Lesbian Images on Radio and Television.* New York: Ballantine Books.

Dejong, W., Wolf, R. C. and Austin, S. B. (2001) 'US Federally Funded Television Public Service Announcements (PSAs) to Prevent HIV/AIDS: A Content Analysis', *Journal of Health Communication* 6 (3): 249–63.

Gross, L. (2001) *Up From Invisibility: Lesbians, Gay Men, and the Media in America.* New York: Columbia University Press.

Keller, S. N. and Brown, J. D. (2002) 'Media Interventions to Promote Responsible Sexual Behavior', *The Journal of Sex Research* 39 (1): 67–72.

Kinsella, J. (1989) *Covering the Plague: AIDS and the American Media.* New Brunswick, NJ: Rutgers University Press.

Larry King Live (2002) Interview with Cast of *Queer as Folk.* Air date: 24 April CNN.

Netzhammer, E. C. and Shamp, S. A. (1994) 'Guilt by Association: Homosexuality and AIDS on Prime-Time Television', in R. J. Ringer (ed.) *Queer Words, Queer Images: Communication and the Construction of Homosexuality,* pp. 91–106. New York and London: New York University Press.

Russo, V. (1987) *The Celluloid Closet: Homosexuality in the Movies* (revised edn). New York: Harper & Row Publishers.

Salmon, C. T. (2000) 'Summary Report: Setting a Research Agenda for Entertainment-Education', in Centers for Disease Control and Prevention, Office of Communication, URL (retrieved September 2003): http://www .cdc.gov/communication/eersrcha.htm

Seidman, S. (2002) *Beyond the Closet: The Transformation of Gay and Lesbian Life.* New York: Routledge.

Steele, J. R. (1999) 'Teenage Sexuality and Media Practice: Factoring in the Influence of Family, Friends, and School', *The Journal of Sex Research* 36(4): 331–341.

Turner, D. C. (1997) *Risky Sex: Gay Men and HTV Prevention.* New York: Columbia University Press.

Why Youth (Heart)
Social Network Sites

The Role of Networked Publics in
Teenage Social Life

danah boyd

. . . . The rapid adoption of social network sites by teenagers in the United States and in many other countries around the world raises some important questions. Why do teenagers flock to these sites? What are they expressing on them? How do these sites fit into their lives? What are they learning from their participation? Are these online activities like face-to-face friendships—or are they different, or complementary? . . .While particular systems may come and go, how youth engage through social network sites today provides long-lasting insights into identity formation, status negotiation, and peer-to-peer sociality. . . .

I argue that social network sites are a type of networked public with four properties that are not typically present in face-to-face public life: persistence, searchability, exact copyability, and invisible audiences. These properties fundamentally alter social dynamics, complicating the ways in which people interact. I conclude by reflecting on the social developments that have prompted youth to seek out networked publics, and considering the changing role that publics have in young people's lives. . . .

Networked Publics

Defining the term *public* is difficult at best.[1] As an adjective, it is commonly used in opposition to *private*. When referring to locations, *public* is used to signal places that are accessible to anyone (or at least anyone belonging to a privileged category like adults). In

From boyd, d. (2007). Why youth (heart) social network sites: The role of networked publics in teenage social life. In D. Buckingham (Ed.), *Youth, Identity, and Digital Media*, pp. 1, 7–9, 15–19, 21–22. © 2008 Massachusetts Institute of Technology, used by permission of MIT Press.

reference to actions or texts, *public* often implies that the audience is unknown and that strangers may bear witness.

As a noun, *public* refers to a collection of people who may not all know each other but share "a common understanding of the world, a shared identity, a claim to inclusiveness, a consensus regarding the collective interest."[2] In some senses, *public* is quite similar to *audience* as both refer to a group bounded by a shared text, whether that is a world view or a performance.[3] These words often collide conceptually because speaking to the public implies that the public is acting as an audience. . . .

In this chapter, I move between these many different meanings of public. Social network sites allow publics to gather. At the same time, by serving as a space where speech takes place, they are also publics themselves. The sites themselves also distinguish between public and private, where public means that a profile is visible to anyone and private means that it is friends-only.

The types of publics that gather on social network sites and the types of publics that such sites support are deeply affected by the mediated nature of interaction. . . .

Networked publics are one type of *mediated public;* the network mediates the interactions between members of the public. Media of all stripes have enabled the development of mediated publics. . . .

In unmediated environments, the boundaries and audiences of a given public are structurally defined. Access to visual and auditory information is limited by physics; walls and other obstacles further restrain visibility. Thus when I say that I embarrassed myself in public by tripping on the curb, the public that I am referencing includes all of the strangers who visually witnessed my stumble. The audience is restricted to those present in a limited geographical radius at a given moment in time. The public that I conceptualize might also include all of those who might hear of my accident through word-of-mouth; although the likelihood of others sharing the event is dependent on my status

in the public and the juiciness of the story. While I might think that the whole world must know, this is not likely to be true. More importantly, in an unmediated world, it is not possible for the whole world actually to witness this incident; in the worst-case scenario, they might all hear of my mishap through word of mouth.

Mediating technologies like television, radio, and newsprint change everything. My fall could have been recorded and televised on the nightly news. This changes the scale of the public. Rather than considering all of the people who *did* witness me visually, I must also consider all of the people who *might* witness a reproduction of my fall. The potential audience is affected by the properties of the mediating technologies, namely *persistence, replicability,* and *invisible audiences.* Networked publics add an additional feature—*searchability*—while magnifying all of the other properties. While broadcast media take advantage of persistence, it is not as if anyone could go to the television and watch my fall whenever they wish; but if my fall is uploaded to YouTube or MySpace Video, this is possible.

These four properties thus fundamentally separate unmediated publics from networked publics:

1. *Persistence:* Unlike the ephemeral quality of speech in unmediated publics, networked communications are recorded for posterity. This enables asynchronous communication but it also extends the period of existence of any speech act.

2. *Searchability:* Because expressions are recorded and identity is established through text, search and discovery tools help people find like minds. While people cannot currently acquire the geographical coordinates of any person in unmediated spaces, finding one's *digital body* online is just a matter of keystrokes.

3. *Replicability:* Hearsay can be deflected as misinterpretation, but networked public expressions can be copied from one place to

another verbatim such that there is no way to distinguish the "original" from the "copy."[4]

4. *Invisible audiences:* While we can visually detect most people who can over-hear our speech in unmediated spaces, it is virtually impossible to ascertain all those who might run across our expressions in networked publics. This is further compli-cated by the other three properties, since our expression may be heard at a different time and place from when and where we originally spoke. . . .

Identity Performance

In everyday interactions, the body serves as a critical site of identity performance. In conveying who we are to other people, we use our bodies to project information about ourselves.[5] This is done through movement, clothes, speech, and facial expressions. What we put forward is our best effort at what we want to say about who we are. Yet while we intend to convey one impression, our performance is not always interpreted as we might expect. Through learning to make sense of others' responses to our behavior, we can assess how well we have conveyed what we intended. We can then alter our performance accordingly. This process of performance, interpretation, and adjustment is what Erving Goffman calls *impression management.*[6] . . .

Learning how to manage impressions is a critical social skill that is honed through experience. Over time, we learn how to make meaning out of a situation, others' reactions, and what we are projecting of ourselves. As children, we learn that actions on our part prompt reactions by adults; as we grow older, we learn to interpret these reactions and adjust our behavior. Diverse social environments help people develop these skills because they force individuals to re-evaluate the signals they take for granted.

The process of learning to read social cues and react accordingly is core to being socialized into a society. While the process itself begins at home for young children, it is critical for young people to engage in broader social settings to develop these skills. Of course, how children are taught about situations and impression manage-ment varies greatly by culture,[7] but these processes are regularly seen as part of com-ing of age. While no one is ever a true mas-ter of impression management, the teenage years are ripe with experiences to develop these skills.

In mediated environments, bodies are not immediately visible and the skills people need to interpret situations and manage impressions are different. As Jenny Sundén argues, people must learn to *write them-selves into being.*[8] Doing so makes visible how much we take the body for granted. While text, images, audio, and video all pro-vide valuable means for developing a virtual presence, the act of articulation differs from how we convey meaningful information through our bodies. . . .

In some sense, people have more control online—they are able to carefully choose what information to put forward, thereby eliminating visceral reactions that might have seeped out in everyday communication. At the same time, these digital bodies are funda-mentally coarser, making it far easier to mis-interpret what someone is expressing. . . .

Privacy in Public: Creating *MY* Space

My mom always uses the excuse about the internet being "public" when she defends herself. It's not like I do any-thing to be ashamed of, but a girl needs her privacy. I do online journals so I can communicate with my friends. Not so my mother could catch up on the latest gossip of my life.—Bly Lauritano-Werner, 17[9]

For Lauritano-Werner, privacy is not about structural limitations to access; it is about being able to limit access through social conventions. This approach makes sense if you recognize that networked publics make it nearly impossible to have structurally enforced borders. However, this is not to say that teens do not also try to create structural barriers.

Teens often fabricate key identifying information like name, age, and location to protect themselves. While parents groups often encourage this deception to protect teens from strangers,[10] many teens actually engage in this practice to protect themselves from the watchful eye of parents.

Fabricating data does indeed make search more difficult, but the networked nature of MySpace provides alternate paths to finding people. First, few teens actually lie about what school they attend, although some choose not to list a school at all. Second, and more problematically, teens are not going to refuse connections to offline friends even though that makes them more easily locatable. Parents simply need to find one of their child's friends; from there, it is easy to locate their own kid. While teens are trying to make parental access more difficult, their choice to obfuscate key identifying information also makes them invisible to their peers. This is not ideal because teens are going online in order to see and be seen by those who might be able to provide validation.

Another common structural tactic involves the privacy settings. By choosing to make their profile *private*,[11] teens are able to select who can see their content. This prevents unwanted parents from lurking, but it also means that peers cannot engage with them without inviting them to be Friends. To handle this, teens are often promiscuous with whom they are willing to add as Friends on the site. By connecting to anyone who seems interesting, they gain control over the structure. Yet, this presents different problems because massive Friending introduces a flood of content with no tools to manage it.

Another structural approach intended to confound parents is creating *mirror networks*. When Stacy's mom found her profile, she was outraged. She called the moms of two of Stacy's friends—Anne and Kimberly. All three parents demanded that their kids clean up their profiles and told them to tell their friends the same or else more parents would be called. Steamed by the prudish response of their parents, Stacy, Anne, and Kimberly reluctantly agreed to change their profiles. Then, they each made a second account with fake names and details. Here, they linked to each other's second profile and uploaded the offending material, inviting their friends to do the same. In doing so, they created a network that completely mirrored the network that their parents had seen. Their parents continued to check their G-rated profiles and the girls continued to lead undercover lives.

While deception and lockdown are two common structural solutions, teens often argue that MySpace should be recognized as *my* space, a space for teenagers to be teenagers. Adults typically view this attitude as preposterous because, as they see it, since the technology is public and teens are participating in a public way, they should have every right to view this content. This attitude often frustrates teenagers who argue that just because anyone *can* access the site doesn't mean that everyone *should*.

When teens argue for having *my* space in a networked public, they are trying to resolve the social problems that emerge because the constructions of public and private are different online and off. In unmediated spaces, structural boundaries are assessed to determine who is in the audience and who is not. The decision to goof off during lunch is often made with the assumption that only peers bear witness. In mediated spaces, there are no structures to limit the audience; search collapses all virtual walls.

Most people believe that *security through obscurity* will serve as a functional barrier online. For the most part, this is a reasonable assumption. Unless someone is of particular note or interest, why would anyone search for them? Unfortunately for teens, there are two groups who have a great deal of interest in them: those who hold power over them—parents, teachers, local government officials, etc.—and those who wish to prey on them—marketers and predators. Before News Corporation purchased MySpace, most adults had never heard of the site; afterwards, they flocked there either to track teenagers that they knew or to market goods (or promises) to any teen who would listen. This shift ruptured both the imagined community and the actual audience they had to face on a regular basis. With a much wider audience present, teens had to face a hard question: what's appropriate?

This problem is not unique to social network sites; it has been present in all forms of mediated publics. Consider Stokely Carmichael's experience with radio and television.[12] As an activist in the 1960s, Carmichael regularly addressed segregated black and white audiences about the values and ideals of the burgeoning Black Power movement.

Depending on the color of his audience, he used very different rhetorical styles. As his popularity grew, he started attracting media attention and was invited to speak on TV and radio. This opportunity was also a curse because both black and white listeners would hear his speech. As there was no way to reconcile the two different rhetorical styles he typically used, he had to choose. By maintaining his black roots in front of white listeners, Carmichael permanently alienated white society from the messages of Black Power. Faced with two disjointed contexts simultaneously, there was no way that Carmichael could successfully convey his message to both audiences.

Teenagers face the same dilemma on MySpace. How can they be simultaneously cool to their peers and acceptable to their parents? For the most part, it is not possible. While most adults wish that kids would value what they value, this is rarely true.

It is easy to lambaste teens for accepting the cultural norms of the 'in' crowd, but social categories[13] and status negotiation[14] are core elements in teen life; this is part of how they learn to work through the cultural practices and legal rules that govern society. The behaviors that are typically rewarded with status in school are often resistant to adult values. On MySpace, teens are directly faced with peer pressure and the need to conform to what is seen to be cool. Worse, they are faced with it in the most public setting possible—one that is potentially visible to all peers and all adults. The stakes are greater on both sides, but the choice is still there: *cool or lame?*

Unfortunately, the magnified public exposure increases the stakes. Consider a call that I received from an admissions officer at a prestigious college. The admissions committee had planned to admit a young black man from a very poor urban community until they found his MySpace. They were horrified to find that his profile was full of hip-hop imagery, urban ghetto slang, and hints of gang participation. This completely contradicted the essay they had received from him about the problems with gangs in his community, and they were at a loss. Did he lie in his application? Although confidentiality prevented me from examining his case directly, I offered the admissions officer an alternative explanation. Perhaps he needed to acquiesce to the norms of the gangs while living in his neighborhood, in order to survive and make it through high school to apply to college?

Situations like this highlight how context is constructed and maintained through participation, not simply observation. When outsiders search for and locate participants, they are ill prepared to understand the context; instead, they project the context in which they relate to the individual offline onto the individual in this new online space. For teens, this has resulted in expulsions, suspensions, probations, and being grounded.[15] In Pennsylvania, a student's parody of his principal was not read as such when the principal found this profile on MySpace; the student was removed from school and lawsuits are still pending.[16] Of course, not every misreading results in the punishment of youth. Consider the story of Allen and his daughter Sabrina. Because Sabrina thinks her dad is cool, she invited him to join her on MySpace. Upon logging in, Allen was startled to see that her profile included a quiz entitled *"What kind of drug are you?"*, to which she had responded, *"cocaine."* Confused and horrified, Allen approached his daughter for an explanation. She laughed and explained, *"it's just one of those quizzes that tells you about your personality . . . but you can kinda get it to say what you want."* She explained that she didn't want to be represented by marijuana because the kids who smoked pot were lame. She also thought that acid and mushrooms were stupid because she wasn't a hippie. She figured that cocaine made sense because she heard people did work on it and *"besides Dad, your generation did a lot of coke and you came out OK."* This was not the explanation that Allen expected.

Teens are not necessarily well-prepared to navigate complex social worlds with invisible audiences, but neither are adults. While Allen was able to talk with his daughter about other possible interpretations of her choice in presentation, he recognized that her profile was not meant for such audiences. How could he teach her how to engage in identity presentation while navigating multiple audiences? While MySpace is public, it is unlike other publics that adults commonly face. This presents a generational divide that is further complicated by adults' mis-readings of youth participation in new media.

But Why There?

The power that adults hold over youth explains more than just complications in identity performance; it is the root of why

teenagers are on MySpace in the first place. In the United States, the lives of youth—and particularly high school teenagers—are highly structured. Compulsory high school requires many students to be in class from morning to mid-afternoon; and many are also required to participate in after-school activities, team sports, and work into the evening. It is difficult to measure whether today's high school teens have more or less free time than previous generations, but the increased prevalence of single working parent and dual-working parent households implies that there are either more latchkey kids or more after-school programs watching these kids.[17] Given the overwhelming culture of fear and the cultural disdain for latchkey practices, it is likely that teens are spending more time in programs than on their own. Meanwhile, at home in the evenings, many are expected to do homework or spend time with the family. While the home has been considered a *private* sphere where individuals can regulate their own behavior, this is an adult-centric narrative. For many teens, home is a highly regulated space with rules and norms that are strictly controlled by adults.

Regardless of whether teens in the United States have the time to engage in public life, there are huge structural and social barriers to them doing so. First, there is an issue of mobility. While public transit exists in some urban regions, most of the United States lacks adequate transportation options for those who are unable to drive; given the suburbanization of the United States, teens are more likely to live in a region without public transit than one with public transit There is a minimum age for drivers in every state, although it varies from 16–18. A license is only one part of the problem; having access to a car is an entirely separate barrier to mobility. This means that, for many teens, even if they want to go somewhere they are often unable to do so.

American society has a very peculiar relationship to teenagers—and children in general. They are simultaneously idealized and demonized; adults fear them but they also seek to protect them.[18] On one hand, there has been a rapid rise in curfew legislation to curb teen violence[19] and loitering laws are used to bar teens from hanging out on street corners, in parking lots, or other outdoor meeting places for fear of the trouble they might cause. On the other hand, parents are restricting their youth from hanging out in public spaces for fear of predators, drug dealers, and gangs. Likewise, while adults spend countless hours socializing over alcohol, minors are not only restricted from drinking but also from socializing in many venues where alcohol is served.

Moral entrepreneurs have learned that "invoking fears about children provides a powerful means of commanding public attention and support."[20] This ongoing *culture of fear* typically overstates the actual dangers and obfuscates real risks in the process.[21] Yet, the end result of this is that youth have very little access to public spaces. The spaces they can hang out in are heavily controlled and/or under surveillance:

> My [guardian] is really strict so if I get to go anywhere, it's a big miracle. So I talk to people on MySpace . . . I know she means well, I know she doesn't want me to mess up. But sometimes you need to mess up to figure out that you're doing it wrong. You need mistakes to know where you're going. You need to figure things out for yourself.—Traviesa, 15

Many adults believe that these restrictions are necessary to prevent problematic behaviors or to protect children from the risks of society. Whether or not that view is valid, restrictions on access to public life make it difficult for young people to be socialized into society at large. While social interaction can and does take place in private environments, the challenges of doing so in public life are part of what help youth grow. Making mistakes and testing limits are fundamental parts of this. Yet, there is a

pervading attitude that teens must be protected from their mistakes. . . .

While the jury is still out on whether or not the Internet is democratizing, online access provides a whole new social realm for youth. Earlier mediated communication devices—landline, pager, mobile—allowed friends to connect with friends even when located in adult-regulated physical spaces. What is unique about the Internet is that it allows teens to participate in unregulated publics while located in adult-regulated physical spaces such as homes and schools. Of course, this is precisely what makes it controversial. Parents are seeking to regulate teen behavior in this new space; and this, in turn, is motivating teens to hide.

> A few of my friends won't even dare to tell their parents about their MySpace cause they know they'll be grounded forever. I know two kids who got banned from it but they secretly got back on.— Ella, 15

Yet, putting aside the question of risk, what teens are doing with this networked public is akin to what they have done in every other type of public they have access to: they hang out, jockey for social status, work through how to present themselves, and take risks that will help them to assess the boundaries of the social world. They do so because they seek access to adult society. Their participation is deeply rooted in their desire to engage publicly, for many of the reasons we have discussed earlier. By prohibiting teens from engaging in networked publics, we create a *participation divide*,[22] both between adults and teens and between teens who have access and those who do not.

Conclusion

Publics play a crucial role in the development of individuals for, as Nancy Fraser explains, "they are arenas for the formation and enactment of social identities."[23] By interacting with unfamiliar others, teenagers are socialized into society. Without publics, there is no coherent society. Publics are where norms are set and reinforced, where common ground is formed. Learning society's rules requires trial and error, validation and admonishment; it is knowledge that teenagers learn through action, not theory. Society's norms and rules only provide the collectively imagined boundaries. Teenagers are also tasked with deciding how they want to fit into the structures that society provides. Their social identity is partially defined by themselves, partially defined by others. Learning through *impression management* is key to developing a social identity. Teenagers must determine where they want to be situated within the social world they see and then attempt to garner the reactions to their performances that match their vision. This is a lifelong process, but one that must be supported at every step. . . .

Teens today face a public life with unimaginably wide possible publicity. The fundamental properties of networked publics—persistence, searchability, replicability, and invisible audiences—are unfamiliar to the adults that are guiding them through social life. It is not accidental that teens live in a culture infatuated with celebrity[24]—the "reality" presented by reality TV and the highly publicized dramas (such as that between socialites Paris Hilton and Nicole Richie) portray a magnified (and idealized) version of the networked publics that teens are experiencing, complete with surveillance and misinterpretation. The experiences that teens are facing in the publics that they encounter appear more similar to the celebrity idea of public life than to the ones their parents face.

It is not as though celebrities or teenagers wish for every conversation to be publicly available to everyone across all time and space, but mediated publics take the simplest public expressions and make them hyperpublic. Few adults could imagine every conversation they have sitting in the park or drinking tea in a cafe being available for such hyperpublic consumption, yet this is what technology enables. Unfortunately, there is an ethos that if it is possible to access a public expression, one should have the right to do so. Perhaps this is flawed thinking.

While we can talk about changes that are taking place, the long-term implications of being socialized into a culture rooted in networked publics are unknown. Perhaps today's youth will be far better equipped to handle gossip as adults. Perhaps not. What we do know is that today's teens live in a society whose public life is changing rapidly. Teens need access to these publics—both mediated and unmediated—to mature, but their access is regularly restricted. Yet this technology and networked publics are not going away. As a society, we need to figure out how to educate teens to navigate social structures that are quite unfamiliar to us, because they will be faced with these publics as adults, even if we try to limit their access now. Social network sites have complicated our lives because they have made this rapid shift in public life very visible. Perhaps instead of trying to stop them or regulate usage, we should learn from what teens are experiencing? They are learning to navigate networked publics; it is in our better interest to figure out how to help them.

Notes

1. For a primer on some of the key debates concerning 'public' and 'public sphere,' see Calhoun, Craig. 1992. *Habermas and the Public Sphere* (Cambridge, MA: MIT Press).

2. Livingstone, Sonia. 2005. "Introduction" and "On the relation between audiences and publics." *Audiences and Publics: When Cultural Engagement Matters for the Public Sphere* (ed. Sonia Livingstone) Portland: intellect. 9.

3. Ibid., 9–41.

4. Negroponte, Nicholas. 1996. *Being Digital.* New York: Vintage.

5. Davis, Fred. 1992. *Fashion, Culture and Identity.* Chicago: University of Chicago Press.

6. Goffman, Erving. 1956. *The Presentation of Self in Everyday Life.* Edinburgh: University of Edinburgh.

7. Briggs, Jean. 1999. *Inuit Morality Play: The Emotional Education of a Three-Year-Old.* New Haven: Yale University Press.

8. Sundén, Jenny. 2003. *Material Virtualities.* New York: Peter Lang Publishing.

9. Lauritano-Werner, Bly. 2006 ."Reading My LiveJournal." *Youth Public Radio.* June 28. http://youthradio.org/society/npr060628_online journal.shtml

10. Farnham, Kevin and Dale Farnham. 2006. *MySpace Safety: 51 Tips for Teens and Parents.* Pomfret, CT: How-To Primers.

11. Private profiles in MySpace are visible to Friends only. When strangers visit their page, they are shown the primary photo, name, location, age, and a saying. They must become Friends with that person to see the rest of the content.

12. Meyrowitz, Joshua. 1985. *No Sense of Place.* New York: Oxford.

13. Eckert, Penelope. 1989. *Jocks & Burnouts: Social Categories and Identity in the High School.* New York: Teachers College Press.

14. Murray, Milner, Jr. 2004. *Freaks, Geeks. and Cool Kids: American Teenagers, Schools, and the Culture of Consumption.* New York: Routledge.

15. Koppelman, Alex. 2006. "MySpace or OurSpace?" *Salon.* June 8. http://www.salon.com/mwt/feature/2006/06/08/myspace/

16. Poulson, Kevin. 2006. "Scenes from the MySpace Backlash." *Wired News* February 27. http://www.wired.com/news/politics/1,70254–0.html

17. Johnson, Julia Overturf, Robert Kominski, Kristin Smith, and Paul Tillman. 2005. "Changes in the Lives of U.S. Children 1990–2000." Working Paper No 78, United States Census Bureau, November.

18. Austin, Joe and Michael Nevin Willard. 1998. "Introduction: Angels of History, Demons of Culture." *Generations of Youth: Youth Cultures and History in Twentieth-Century America* (ed. Joe Austin and Michael Nevin Willard). New York: New York University Press, 1–20.

19. Ruefle, William and Kenneth Reynolds. 1995. "Curfew and Delinquency in Major American Cities." *Crime and Delinquency* 41:347–363.

20. Buckingham, David. 2000. *After the Death of Childhood.* Oxford: Polity, p. 11.

21. Glassner, Barry. 2000. *The Culture of Fear: Why Americans Are Afraid of the Wrong Things.* Basic Books.

22. Jenkins, Henry. 2006. "Confronting the Challenges of Participatory Culture: Media Education for the 21st Century." White Paper for MacArthur Foundation.

23. Fraser, Nancy. 1992. "Rethinking the Public Sphere: A Contribution to the Critique of Actually Existing Democracy." *Habermas and the Public Sphere* (Craig Calhoun, ed.). Cambridge, MA: MIT Press. 125.

24. Halpern, Jake. 2007. *Fame Junkies: The Hidden Truths Behind America's Favorite Addiction.* Houghton Mifflin.

Born to Be Wired

Kathryn C. Montgomery

. . . . In many ways, teens were the *defining users* of digital media culture. With nearly three-quarters of twelve- to seventeen-year-olds online by the end of the twentieth century, teenagers embraced this new online world with great enthusiasm, responding eagerly to its invitation to share ideas, contribute content, and otherwise place their stamp on a media system that they themselves could create and manage. The Internet played a pivotal role in their lives, influencing their family and social relationships. Teens far exceeded adults in their use of instant messaging, visits to chat rooms, and playing or downloading games.[1] At the forefront of technological innovation, they eagerly adopted cell phones, pagers, and other new electronic gadgets that offered unprecedented levels of communications and information retrieval at their fingertips.[2] The properties of the interactive media were uniquely suited to their developmental needs. Online communication tools enabled instantaneous and constant contact with peers; personal Web pages offered compelling opportunities for self-expression and identity exploration; and ubiquitous portable devices facilitated mobility and independence. The Internet's extensive reach and its promise of anonymity created an environment that encouraged information-seeking on a wide variety of topics inaccessible or taboo for earlier generations. Anonymous chat rooms and forums allowed teens to engage in discussion and debate without fear of exposure. The digital media were challenging many of the conventions and institutions of the past, blurring or obliterating the boundaries between public and private, commercial and noncommercial, school and home, local and global.

Teens were also playing a central role in the new digital marketplace. Long before the advent of the Internet, market researchers engaged in an ongoing campaign to track the valuable—but elusive and quixotic—teen demographic, frequently enlisting teenagers in a variety of street marketing and "coolhunting" schemes to identify the latest fashion and music trends.[3] The rapid growth of interactive technologies enabled marketers to gain unprecedented direct access to teenagers. "Cyberteens" were key pathfinders in the unfolding digital landscape. "The current generation of teens is more tech savvy than any segment of the population," noted a report by Cheskin Research. "As this generation matures, their attitudes and experiences on the Internet will vastly influence its future evolution. By investigating teen behaviors and

From Montgomery, K. C. (2007). Born to be wired. In K. C. Montgomery, *Generation Digital: Politics, Commerce, and Childhood in the Age of the Internet,* pp. 107–108, 125–127, 130–131, 134–135. © 2007 Massachusetts Institute of Technology, by permission of MIT Press.

attitudes today, companies can not only address the needs of this market, but also predict future trends in technology."[4]

Unrestrained by government regulation and largely under the radar of parents and policymakers, advertisers were able to develop a full array of new digital-marketing strategies, especially tailored to the developmental needs and interests of adolescents. Enlisting the expertise of psychologists and anthropologists, marketers continued to probe the inner workings of the teen psyche, designing marketing strategies that would cater to them. The interactive media ushered in an entirely new set of relationships, breaking down traditional barriers between content and commerce, and creating unprecedented intimacies between teens and marketers. Marketers were able to shadow teens' every move through the expanding media environment, identifying new targeting opportunities along the way. Brands and corporate logos tagged along with teens in their journeys through cyberspace, inserting themselves into instant messages and chat rooms, popping into e-mail in-boxes, and beckoning from cell-phone screens.

As the features and functions of this new digital online marketplace were being tested and refined, teens served as subjects for continuous and pervasive market research, connected through electronic umbilical cords to a phalanx of companies that monitored their every online move. As a consequence, a unique symbiosis developed between the corporate creators of this digital culture and its most avid users; many teens were eager and willing partners in the design and implementation of an array of cultural products and practices that would help shape the electronic media system in the twenty-first century. . . .

Commercializing Culture

As marketers closely watch how youth are interacting with digital media, they continue to probe the psychological links between technology and adolescent development. "The Internet has evolved to become the 'hub'—or primary medium" for young people, explained the market research report, *Born to Be Wired*. "Teens and young adults are searching for independence and control, and the Internet gives it to them like no other media can." To develop the most effective strategies, Greg Livingston of the Wonder Group advised, brands need to take into account the "basic motivators" for this developmental stage—"freedom, independence, power, and belonging." But companies also must understand fully how members of the Millennial Generation are engaging with digital media. With this knowledge, marketers can "be part of the communication structure of teens."[5]

Exploring the subcultural terrain of the Digital Generation, market researchers divide teen consumers into clearly definable market segments, based on their use of new media. "Chic Geeks" are "early adopters of technology and heavy users of gadgetry . . . with cell phones as constant companions." They have "wide social networks that they actively cultivate," and they are "conspicuous consumers, . . . looking to brands to get them noticed" and desiring "new news in their messaging . . . to be the first to hear it." Therefore advertisers should "give them a sense of exclusivity with the information you provide to them," remembering that "image is important to them." The "Now Crowd" also are heavy media users with large social networks. A "young segment, largely suburban," with "a relatively high proportion of African-Americans," the Now Crowd are "wannabe" leaders. To best appeal to this group, marketers are advised to offer them "social currency—information that will raise their standing and credibility" among their peers. "The role of brands to the Now Crowd is to help 'brand' them as being the 'Now' Crowd." But companies are warned not to let members of this subgroup down because "they are influential and can spread negative word-of-mouth quickly."[6]

In their efforts to become part of the communication structure of young people, marketers have developed a set of practices specifically designed to target teenagers, tweens, and young adults. These practices, forged in the formative period of Internet ecommerce, have evolved and migrated to mesh with a growing number of pastimes and "platforms," as companies seek to ensure their brands become a pervasive presence throughout the digital media culture.

Mobilizing the Tremor Nation

Procter & Gamble (P&G) has been at the forefront of innovative teen-marketing strategies, launching its peer-to-peer network Tremor in 2002.[7] The venture is designed to identify those teen "connectors" who are socially active and can influence their peers' buying decisions.[8] This select group of young people—largely female (60 percent)— is then given inside information about new products and previews and programs and encouraged to tell their friends about them.[9] Not any tween or teen can become a "Tremorite." P&G carefully chooses its members based on "Internet usage, social networks, and willingness to advocate to peers" and then gives them coupons, new product samples, and advance copies of TV-program scripts to encourage their participation in research and promotion. Tremor claims great successes for its clients, which have included entertainment companies such as WB, AOL, and Time Warner, as well as numerous product brands. Savvy Tremorites are credited with helping Coca Cola choose "Nothing Else Like It" as a billboard slogan.[10] And when Tremor sent teens in one city an advance script for an episode of *Dawson's Creek,* the ratings for the popular show tripled in that market.[11]

Within two years of Tremor's launch, P&G boasted "a sales force of 280,000 teens . . . part of a massive focus group and word-of-mouth marketing drive to counter the eroding influence of conventional advertising." The company predicted that its Tremor Nation was only the "first of what's expected to be a mass movement as advertisers seek new ways to attract audiences and build loyalty." Through its partnership with Blue Dingo, a New York ad agency specializing in "building Web-based interactive marketing programs and online social networks," P&G created a high-powered new Web site for its Tremorites, billed as "the virtual equivalent of a gated community, a members-only Web site replete with word-of-mouth and community building features." Underscoring this exclusive insider status, the site spells out the various perks of membership:

> Tremorites can quickly view Tremor programs currently available to them, search for and hook up with other members with similar interests whom they can Instant Message, send personal messages to one another and receive notes from the Tremor Team, see what's hot and happening in their own hometown and throughout the U.S., access unreleased music and get special offers negotiated exclusively for Tremorites.[12]

Peer-to-peer marketing (sometimes called "buzz" or "viral marketing") has become a staple among youth advertisers.[13] The practice spawned its own Word-of-Mouth Marketing Association (WOMMA). Its Web site features mini-case studies of successful campaigns, offering a rare glimpse into the inner workings of online marketing. When Elizabeth Arden launched its new perfume, Britney Spears's Curious, its debut took place with almost no publicity. Yet within only four months, it had become the leading fragrance launch for 2004, generating sales of $36 million. "How did a mature, fit-for-the-elderly brand like Elizabeth Arden manage to attract teenage girls in such a discreet and succinct manner?" the Web site asked. "The answer: Unconventional/Viral marketing." In the weeks before the perfume was launched, "a discreet banner with a photo of Britney" was placed on five Web sites popular with teens, including Bolt.com and Alloy.com. The ads asked girls to provide their cell phone numbers and zip codes. Almost 30,000 girls responded in order to receive a 45-second recorded voice mail from Britney herself, in which the pop star thanked her fans and shared her excitement about the new fragrance she was working on. "This marketing campaign worked because it was done in non-marketing speak," explained the Web site. "Since these girls felt like they knew a secret from Britney about Britney, they forwarded the voice mail to their friends, even posting the text on Britney-related online forums." To keep the buzz going about the yet-to-be-released product, marketers followed up with a series of text messages from Britney, including a list of nearby stores where the girls would be able to buy Curious. "In the end, with its viral effect, the campaign reached about 300,000 girls. The strategy was a first for the fragrance industry."[14] . . .

Advergaming, Game-vertising, and Immersive Advertising

The growing popularity of video games among young people has created an opportunity that advertisers simply cannot pass up. By 2005, 81 percent of the online teens—or two-thirds of the teenage population—were playing video games, a 50 percent increase from four years earlier.[15] Video games have become the fastest-growing form of entertainment, with teens and young adults at the forefront. Gaming takes place across many digital platforms in addition to the Internet—from consoles, to hand-held devices such as Nintendo, to cell phones.[16] In industry surveys, youth consumers consistently rank the Internet and videogames higher than television in importance.[17] More than 70 percent of young men have become avid gamers, spending as much time or more playing games as they did watching television.[18] And games are not the exclusive domain of young males; one third of gamers are women. Video games in the United States have grown into a $9.4 billion business, surpassing even the movie box office in earnings. "Video games are part of the DNA of the youth market—they're in the bloodstream," Howard Handler, Virgin Mobile's chief marketing officer, told the press, "The contemporary youth lifestyle is music, action sports and video gaming all blurred together."[19]

Games also provide the perfect "immersive environment" for incorporating brand messages seamlessly into the content. The quintessential sticky content, video games can engage players for hours on end, inviting them to come back again and again to play. "Because players spend so much time with a single game—on average, between two and four hours at a time—brands want to be part of that hyper-reality," reported *Advertising Age*.[20] "Advergaming" is considered particularly effective with young audiences who tend to get annoyed with Internet banners and pop-up ads.[21]

Not surprisingly, marketers have been flocking to videogames.[22] Some of the biggest brands in the youth market have been woven into the content of popular games, including Levis, Coke, McDonalds, Kraft, Nike, AT&T Wireless, and Nokia.[23] In-game advertising is considered particularly ideal for "reaching that elusive male youth demo," explained one trade publication. Massive, a New York–based advertising network, offers opportunities for "dynamic product placement (which allows advertisers to update ads) in video games like Ubisoft's Splinter Cell: Chaos Theory and Funcom's Anarchy Online." The company signed deals with a dozen U.S. advertisers, including Paramount Pictures, Nestle, Honda, and Dunkin' Donuts.[24]

Internet games create unique opportunities to microtarget individual game players. In addition to integrating brands into the storyline of a game, advertisers can respond to a player's actions in real time, changing, adding, or updating advertising messages to tailor their appeal to that particular individual. "The silver bullet is really doing custom solutions for clients," explained one industry executive.[25] The technology also enables precise measurements of customer reactions to the online advertising.[26] Digital marketers have perfected software for tracking consumer behavior in the interactive market. Doubleclick's Motif, for example, offers a full spectrum of sophisticated tools in its Audience Interaction Metrics Package. "You'll automatically get metrics on how long each ad was displayed or how the viewer interacted with the ad . . . so you know what works best. . . . You can track audience video plays, completions, pauses, stops, restarts, mutes, average view time, and custom video interaction metrics." Among the hundreds of Web sites subscribing to Doubleclick's Motif service are some of the top destinations for children and teens, including: Alloy.com, DELiA*s.com, AIM, KidsWB.com, Nick and Nickjr.com, TeenPeople.com, and Timeforkids.com.[27]

Online games are a particularly good vehicle for advertising snacks and other impulse food products. According to Nielsen//Net Ratings, buyers of Tombstone Pizza were among the most avid players of such online games as cheatplanet.com, addictinggames.com, and Lycos Network entertainment.[28] In 2005, Sony partnered with Pizza Hut to take "dynamic product placement" a step further, building into its Everquest II videogame the ability to order pizza. "All the player has to do is type in the command 'pizza,' and voila—Pizza Hut's online order page pops up," explained the trade publication *Strategy*. "While it's just pizza now, the in-game purchasing potential is wide open."[29] One expert predicted that advertising and product placement will soon be as integral to video games as story lines and action.[30]

When Nickelodeon bought the highly popular online game site Neopets in 2005, to become part of the new TurboNick Web site, one of its goals was to "monetize" the huge amount of traffic the site enjoyed

by inserting more brands. Already, McDonalds and other familiar icons can be found among the businesses in the site's Shop section. In a game where the object is to keep your neopet alive by feeding her regularly (ensuring your repeated visits to the site), executives envision a future scenario in which game players "will be feeding their pets with food products from major brands."[31] . . .

The Social Network Sell

Social networking sites like MySpace.com, Friendster.com, and Facebook.com enable users to create personal Web sites, where they can post profiles, photos, videos, and music. But unlike standard Web-hosting services, these sites are designed to serve as powerful word-of-mouth engines, where people can find new friends, connect with old ones, and manage their social lives. Like IM, social-networking sites have transformed the informal social relationships that are part of everyday life into digitized personal networks.[32] In a very short time, these sites exploded in size and influence, becoming particularly popular with teen girls. "Teenagers say they get hooked on building and browsing the social networks, playing online games and music posted by their friends, answering lifestyle quizzes, and exchanging comments online into the wee hours," writes Andrew Trotter in *Education Week*.[33] Such "super hot sites," noted *Advertising Age*, offer "a potential eyeball windfall to advertisers."[34]

MySpace began as a way for musicians to promote themselves and their music, enabling fans to gather together and talk about their favorite celebrities.[35] Within a year, more than 20,000 established and up-and-coming artists had taken up online residence there, attracting a huge fan base, with more than 40 million members by 2005. The small upstart had become such a hot property that Rupert Murdoch's NewsCorp (owner of the Fox entertainment empire) quickly bought it up. MySpace also attracted hundreds of advertisers eager to tap its rich demographic mother lode. Procter & Gamble chose MySpace as the place to introduce teen girls to its new brand of deodorant, Secret Sparkle. By placing the product logo on the home page for singer Hillary Duff, the company encouraged teens to promote the brand to each other through their social networks. The campaign also featured an iPod sweepstakes. "We have to be where they are in this online world," a company spokesperson told the press.[36]

As companies insert themselves into these new social networks, they are intentionally seeking to blur the lines between advertising and content. Social networks are "breaking down that wall between what is marketing and what isn't," commented one youth marketing expert. "[S]ometimes the marketing is so embedded in the social network sphere that it draws users to interact with the brand as if they were e-mailing friends," explained an article in *Marketing*. For example, to promote its film *The Ringer*, Twentieth Century Fox created special Web pages on MySpace for the fictional characters, as if they were real users. The tactic proved successful. The character Steve "has more than 11,000 friends," observed the article, "in other words, more than 11,000 consumers who visited his page and requested to become a part of it. They respond to Steve's fictional blog entries and become involved in the story."[37]

The social-networking phenomenon is likely to grow into an even more successful venue for advertising and marketing. In October 2005, MySpace.com alone accounted for 10 percent of all ads viewed online.[38] Marketers are particularly eager to take advantage of the large, highly detailed user profiles and expanding lists of "friends" on these sites. "The targeting we can do is phenomenal," one industry executive told the press.[39] . . . .

Notes

1. Amanda Lenhart, Lee Rainie, and Oliver Lewis, *Teenage Life Online: The Rise of the Instant-Message Generation and the Internet's Impact on Friendship and Family Relationships* (Washington, DC: Pew Internet and American Life Project, 2001), 37, http://www.pewinternet.org/pdfs/PIP_Teens_Report.pdf. The study showed that 45 percent of all American children under the age of 18 go online. Almost three quarters (73 percent) of those between 12 and 17 go online. In contrast, 29 percent of children 11 or younger go online.

2. Some of the research for this section was published in CME's 2001 report: *TeenSites.com: A Field Guide to the New Digital Landscape* (Washington, DC: Center for Media Education, 2001). See Lee Rainie and Dan Packel, *More Online, Doing More* (Washington, DC: Pew Internet & American Life Project, Feb. 2001). Lenhart, Rainie, and Lewis, *Teenage Life Online*, 37.

3. Malcolm Gladwell "The Coolhunt," *New Yorker*, March 17, 1997, 78–89.

4. Cheskin Research, "Online Teens Give Clues to the Future of the Web," August 23, 1999, www.cheskin.com/who/press/release_net-teens.html (accessed March 24, 2001)

5. Comments by Greg Livingston, speaking at the "Born to Be Wired" conference, Yahoo! headquarters, Sunnyvale, California, July 24, 2003. I was a presenter at this conference.

6. "A New Media Landscape Comes of Age," Executive Summary, *Born to Be Wired: The Role of New Media for a Digital Generation*, commissioned by Yahoo! and Carat Interactive. Research conducted by Harris Interactive and Teenage Research Unlimited, July 23, 2003. From the author's personal files.

7. Cliff Peale, "P & G Targets Teenage Buyers," *Cincinnati Enquirer*, Sunday, October 27, 2002, http://enquirer.com/editions/2002/10/27/biz_tremor27.html.

8. Malcolm Gladwell discusses the notion of "connectors" as a key strategy in peer-to-peer marketing at length in his popular book *The*

Tipping Point. Malcolm Gladwell, *The Tipping Point: How Little Things Can Make a Big Difference* (Boston: Little, Brown, 2000). For a discussion of this and other similar strategies used to market to teens, see Alissa Quart, *Branded* (New York: Basic Books, 2003).

9. Peale, "P & G."

10. PR Newswire, "Blue Dingo Puts the Shakes in Tremor; Online Teen Social Network Goes to Work for Proctor & Gamble," March 22, 2004.

11. Peale, "P & G."

12. PR Newswire, "Blue Dingo Puts the Shakes in Tremor; Online Teen Social Network Goes to Work for Proctor & Gamble," March 22, 2004; http://www.tremor.com/login/about_us .aspx.

13. See Martin Lindstrom and individual contributors, *Brandchild* (London: Kogan Page, 2003), 137–156. See also Mark Hughes, *Buzzmarketing: Get People to Talk about Your Stuff* (New York: Portfolio, 2005); Buzz Marketing, http://www.buzzmarketing.com/index .html; Emanuel Rosen, *The Anatomy of Buzz: How to Create Word of Mouth Marketing* (New York: Doubleday, 2000).

14. Burston Marseller, "Unconventional Marketing Becomes the Convention," e-Fluentials Blog, September 26, 2005, http://blog.efluentials .com/index.php?title= unconventional_marketing_ becomes_the_con&more=1&c-1&tb=1& pb=1.

15. Amanda Lenhart, Mary Madden, and Paul Hitlin, *Teens and Technology* (Washington, DC: Pew Internet and American Life Project), July 27, 2005, http://www.pewinternet.Org/PPF/ r/162/report_display.asp.

16. In 2004, there were 100 million gaming consoles in households, 60 million hand-held games and a growing number of game-enabled cellphones. T. L. Stanley, "Video Games: The New Reality of Youth Marketing," AdAge.com, March 22, 2004.

17. Stanley, "Video Games."

18. Massive Incorporated, http://www.massive incorporated.com/site_advert/ advert_home.htm (accessed February 2, 2005).

19. Stanley, "Video Games."

20. Stanley, "Video Games."

21. Michael McCarthy, "Disney Plans to Mix Ads, Video Games to Target Kids, Teens," *USA Today,* January 18, 2005, 6B.

22. Marketers in the category spent $414.1 million in advertising in the first 11 months of 2003. Stanley, "Video Games."

23. Stanley, "Video Games"; Beth Snyder Bulik, "Advergaming Grows in Reach and Power," AdAge.com, May 24, 2004.

24. Annette Bourdeau, "The Kids Are Online," *Strategy,* May 1, 2005.

25. Bulik, "Advergaming."

26. Massive Entertainment specializes in advergaming and other immersive advertising strategies, promising its clients customized reports on consumer interaction with brand messaging that would allow for a level of accountability and evaluation of the effective- ness of the ad placements that is impossible in other traditional broadcast and print outlets. The internet link "allows Massive's software to modify the ads as players progress through a game." In 2005, the company predicted it would put its software into "40 games by the end of the year," and reported it had signed agreements with advertisers such as "Dunkin' Donuts, Intel, Paramount Pictures, Coca-Cola, Honda and Universal Music Group." Massive Incorporated, http://www.massiveincorporated.com/site.adver t/advert_home.htm (accessed February 2, 2005).

27. Dart Motif, http://www.dartmotif.com (accessed September 27, 2005).

28. Michael Saxon, Vice President, Media Products-NetRatings, Inc. "Moving Towards Marketing's Holy Grail: Connecting Online and Offline User Behavior," Nielsen/NetRatings, http://thearf.org./downloads/Councils/Online/ 2004–05–17_ ARF_NetRatings.pdf (accessed September 25, 2005).

29. Bourdeau, "The Kids Are Online."

30. Matt Richtel, "A New Reality in Video Games: Advertisements," *New York Times,* April 11, 2005, C1.

31. Mike Shields, "Surfing Lessons," *Mediaweek,* July 25, 2005; Joe Pereira, "Junk- Food Games," *Wall Street Journal,* May 3, 2004, B1–B4. The Walt Disney Company launched its own "branded entertainment" site in 2005, with the interactive multi-player game

Virtual Magic Kingdom. With a target market of tweens and young teens, the site beckoned visitors on a fun-filled virtual tour of Disney's five global resorts and eleven theme parks, where they could engage in free online games based on real rides, including the Haunted Mansion and Jungle Cruise. They could also chat, create their own avatars, and earn virtual points that could be redeemed for prizes when visiting the actual theme parks. McCarthy, "Disney," 6B.

32. Friendster, explained *Wired News*, "helps users find dates and new friends by referring people to friends, or friends of friends, or friends of friends of friends, and so on." Leander Kahney, "Making Friendsters in High Places," *Wired News*, July 17, 2003.

33. Andrew Trotter, "Social-Networking Web Sites Pose Growing Challenge for Educators," *Education Week*, February 15, 2006, 8.

34. Kris Oser, "MySpace: Big Audience, Big Risks," *Advertising Age* (Midwest region edition), February 20, 2006, 3. As columnist Nat Ives observed, "Marketers hope these sites will make it easier to start and track communication about brands among friends and contacts," Nat Ives, "A New Type of Pitch to the Online Crowd Mixes Pop Stars and Personals," *New York Times*, December 3, 2004, C6.

35. Jessi Hempel and Paula Lehman, "The MySpace Generation," *Business Week*, December 12, 2005, 86.

36. Ives, "A New Type of Pitch," C6.

37. Michelle Halpern, *Marketing* 111, no. 3 (2006): 5

38. Hempel and Lehman, "The MySpace Generation," 86.

39. The quote in Bourdeau, "The Kids Are Online," is from Rob Davy, commercial manager at Nexopia, which is based in Edmonton, Canada.

Video Games and Machine Dreams of Domination

John Sanbonmatsu

The computer video game has emerged in the space of a few short decades from the shadows of "geek" subcultural obscurity to become the most pervasive entertainment medium in the industrialized world. In the United States alone, an estimated 170 million people—more than half the population—play video games (John, 2009).[1] By comparison, about 75 million go each year to professional baseball games, and 39 million play chess ("National Chess Survey," 2003). In 1980, the video game industry barely existed. Today, it dwarfs almost every other media industry. Sales of video game software, hardware, and accessories totaled about $20 billion in 2009—twice what Hollywood brought in the box office that year.

If media theorist Marshall McLuhan was right, a generation ago, to say of the new mass media of his time, television, that "the medium *is* the message," what message is being signaled by the aggressive new medium of video games? What does the popularity of technologically mediated forms of play tell us about the social forces and myths shaping life today in advanced capitalist culture? Why have video games become as pervasive as they have? Might video games *play us* as much as we play them?

While some critics have depicted video games (as well as cyberspace and the new interactive digital media more generally) as liberatory phenomena—for example, praising them as spaces where players can subvert repressive gender norms by assuming fluid identities—others have argued that, far from being a utopian force in society, the video game is both a mirror of existing relations of power and authority in society and a powerful cultural force in its own right. Thus, feminists have observed that the content of video games mirrors the worldview of the White, heterosexual men who overwhelmingly create and play them, noting that exaggerated sex stereotyping, misogyny, and simulated violence against women are the norm. The vast majority of game protagonists and heroes are male, and the latter conform closely to the hegemonic norm of masculinity—the aggressive, dominating man authorized by the wider patriarchal culture (Alloway & Gilbert, 1988; Hill, n.d.). Few games model a range of female body types for players to inhabit as avatars: Women are White and young (or exoticized women of color) with unrealistic body proportions and depicted either semi-nude or in clinging body suits (*Lara Croft*). Games like *Dead or Alive: Extreme Volleyball* are indistinguishable from soft-core pornography; others, like *Grand Theft Auto,* invite the player to exploit women sexually. Critical race theorists similarly note the prevalence of racist representations of people of color in many games. Asians are depicted as martial arts experts or sinister villains, never as political leaders, accountants, or composers; African Americans and Latinos are depicted as drug kingpins or prostitutes, not hard-working migrant laborers or professors of literature; Arabs are blood-thirsty savages and terrorists, never citizens of particular nations and cultures, or parents with children, and so on (see Chan, 2005; Leonard, 2004).

Video games are thus potent conduits of the dominant ideologies, myths, and norms of society (i.e., those most conducive to maintaining the status quo in unequal social and property relations). Like other forms of mass media, video games do more than just represent our world; they actively *shape* that world, conforming reality to particular ideologies, social expectations, and collective fantasies. As Ian Bogost (2007) observes, "The logics that drive our games make claims about who we are, how our world functions, and what we want it to become" (p. 340). The very immersive and participatory qualities of video games make them especially persuasive mechanisms of social indoctrination and control. Anyone who has careered down the virtual streets of Chicago in *Gotham Racing* or joined a platoon of Marines patrolling the dusty streets of a Middle Eastern city in *Call of Duty 2* can attest to the visceral power of the medium—the degree to which intense player involvement heightens the psychological connection between human and machine. While the industry disavows real-world connections between kids shooting virtual humans in the head and real-life mass shootings by children in our schools, that same industry, in other market sectors, brags that

video games are without peer among media in shaping human behavior and psychology. As Penny observes, "Psychotherapists employ simulation technologies precisely because they have effect in people's lives," while the Pentagon invests heavily in game simulations because of their proven effectiveness in conditioning soldiers to kill or to learn new battlefield tactics (Penny, 2004). Computer simulations are now widely used in corporate culture—by the aviation industry to train pilots, by hospital schools to teach surgical techniques, by the finance industry to simulate trading transactions, and by companies to train sales personnel in the arts of persuasion. There is no doubt, therefore, that the simulations we ourselves enact as ordinary consumers of video games are educating our senses and structuring our perceptual world too. The question is, what are we being "educated" into?

My argument is that video game culture "hails" or conditions us into an aggressive, socially destructive form of consciousness. By training the player into an *instrumentalist* conception of human thought and action—inviting him or her to conceive of the world as little more than an arena for demonstrating his or her own mastery and control—video games facilitate the ever more fateful intrusion of capitalism, technological fetishism, and masculine fantasies of domination into the fabric of daily life. At the same time, the process of "society's ingression into the psyche," as the philosopher Herbert Marcuse termed it, could not gain traction without our own tacit collusion or consent (Marcuse, 1968, p. 254). We ourselves seem to hunger for escapist forms of entertainment that restore to us, albeit only in virtual form, precisely that which many of us feel we are losing in real life—namely, a sense of our own efficacy and power in a chaotic, terrifying, and alienating world that seems increasingly out of our control. Paradoxically, however, the more we participate in simulations of life, the less involved we become in real life, forsaking those forms of speech and action that could *matter.*

War Simulation and the Militarization of Everyday Life

To frame my discussion, I want to draw on Herbert Marcuse's analysis of how media and technology serve to integrate consciousness into the circuits of capitalism and imperialism. Marcuse argued that the repression of human libidinal or instinctual needs by Western society yields ever more destructive forms of culture. As capitalism becomes more advanced, a gap opens up between, on one hand, the creative and productive forces of society, our potential to make the world a livable one, and, on the other, pathological forms of social life and behavior that are in reality quite harmful: mobilization for perpetual war, destruction of nature, and heightened aggressiveness in all arenas of life and culture. The result is "a suicidal tendency on a truly social scale" (Marcuse, 1968, p. 268). Such a system meanwhile requires a particular form of human personality or consciousness to maintain itself. Freud believed that the repression or taming of our biological instincts was the price we paid for our entry into society. The healthy human individual channels or "sublimates" his or her instinctual needs into socially productive activities—art, work, family relations, and so on. However, Marcuse argued that in the context of a pathological social order, society might cause such strain in the individual as to produce what he termed "surplus" repression, in effect taking the individual's libidinal instincts and channeling them into socially *destructive* forms.

Technology is the characteristic mechanism of such aggression. As the distillation of an "instrumentalist" mentality, technology strengthens the life-denying system and effectively shields it from possible revolt by those whom it has stripped of power and dignity. Particularly, in the sphere of mass media, the dominant culture blurs together or integrates existential opposites—death and life, killing and culture, sadism and joy. The new "unities" then get sold back to us as commodities. As Marcuse (1968) wrote,

The brutalization of language and image, the presentation of killing, burning, and poisoning and torture inflicted upon the victims of neocolonial slaughter is made in a common-sensical, factual, sometimes humorous style which integrates these horrors with the pranks of juvenile delinquents, football contests, accidents, stock market reports, and the weatherman. (p. 259)

Marcuse's framework is helpful in revealing the hidden meaning of contemporary video game culture. For, notwithstanding the seeming diversity of video games on the market today—for example, massively multiple-player online role-playing games (MMORPGs), puzzle and educational games, driving simulations, sports and fashion games, and so on—themes of violence, aggression, and war predominate. In 2008, the three most popular new online games were *Grand Theft Auto IV; Star Wars: Force Unleashed,* a futuristic battle game; and *Fallout 3,* a futuristic first-person shooter and combat strategy game. The other top 10 online games included the violent first-person shooter war games *Gears of War 2, Call of Duty,* and *Metal Gear Solid 4: Fable II,* a fantasy adventure game in which the hero fights various dangerous enemies; *Super Smash Mario Brothers Brawl,* a Hobbesian "war of all against all," using popular animated characters; *Madden N.F.L. '09,* a complex simulation of commercial male football; and *WWE Smackdown vs. Raw '09,* an ultra-violent simulation of the misogynistic cable program, World Wrestling Entertainment, in which players inhabit the avatars of muscular male fighters and use extreme fighting techniques to kill their opponent—by setting their opponents' bodies on fire (Freierman, 2008). As this list suggests, many of the leading games are both *masculinist* and *militaristic.* To understand why, it is essential to appreciate the institutional origins of the medium in the U.S. national security state apparatus, where patriarchal dreams of "virtuous" domination and control of others materialized into functional high-tech weapons systems.

The emergence of a permanent war economy in the United States after World War II, and with it the functional integration of capitalist industry and academic institutions into cold war nuclear war planning, led to computerization and a new culture of simulation. A watershed came in 1961 when academic researchers working for the Department of Defense at M.I.T. developed a digital game called *Spacewar*. Other researchers soon grasped the military potential of combining traditional war game simulations with computerization. In the late 1970s, the Office of Naval Research established the "Theater-Level Gaming and Analysis Workshop for Force Planning," and by the early 1980s, the United States was spending many millions of dollars on computer simulations like SIMNET, which allowed dispersed participants to engage in real-time "war" over a virtual battlefield (Lenoir & Lowood, 2005). By the 1990s, finally, the Pentagon had built an elaborate network bringing together commercial video game design companies, university researchers, and U.S. military personnel to create what critics have called a "military-industrial-academic-entertainment complex."

Today, the video game is the sine qua non of modern high-tech war fighting, an indispensable tool at all stages of conflict, from recruitment (e.g., *America's Army*, a MMORPG released by the U.S. Army in 2002 and since played by millions; Nichols, 2010) through training (e.g., *Marine Doom*, the military adaptation of the FPS video game, *Doom*, which teaches soldiers to kill unreflexively) to actual battlefield use. Among today's war game centers is DAR-WARS, a program funded by the Defense Advanced Research Projects Agency (DARPA) for the U.S. Joint Chiefs of Staff and Marine Corps, which uses "webcentric, simulation-based trainers [to] take advantage of widespread PC-based technology, including multi-player games, virtual worlds, intelligent agents, and online communities."[2] Meanwhile, in Afghanistan, NATO pilots trained, perhaps, at PEO STRI (the U.S. Army's Program Executive Office for Simulation, Training, and Instrumentation, headquartered in Orlando, Florida) use computer-mediated weapons to drop real munitions on real people. And in Nevada and Arizona, U.S. Air Force pilots and CIA-sponsored mercenaries remotely operate robotic Predator and Reaper drones to launch lethal missile attacks in Syria or Pakistan, 7,500 miles away.

As Marcuse emphasizes, the form and content of technological artifacts and mass culture in a repressive or destructive order tend to serve the ideological and practical needs of that order. In this regard, commercial video games do critical ideological work in preparing the population for permanent war mobilization and military aggression, by normalizing and dehistoricizing state violence and demonizing "authorized" enemies of the U.S. state. While many Americans believe they live in a nation that uses violence as a last resort and then only in self-defense, the facts of U.S. foreign policy over the past century tell a different story, of illegal military intervention, counterrevolutionary warfare, support for pro-U.S. dictatorships around the world, and paroxysms of ruthless violence (Johnson, 2004). Yet military FPS (first-person shooter) games, including historical games depicting past wars, uncritically celebrate U.S. military and technological supremacy and depict America's enemies as dangerous savages worthy of extermination. The narrative content of many post-9/11 games in particular reiterates the values and policy assumptions of the so-called war on terror, mapping the world cognitively to prepare American soldiers and citizenry alike "for colonial exercises of spatial domination" (King & Leonard, 2010, p. 91). As Höglund (2008) observes, such games serve the interests of the U.S. state by constructing the entire Middle East "as a frontier zone where a perpetual war between U.S. interests and Islamic terrorism" can be enacted.[3] The result is a new Orientalism in which "the gamer involved in a military shooter set in the Middle East is forever performing . . . strategic containment of the Other"—the dark-skinned barbarian perpetually threatening the innocent redoubt of Western civilization.

In sum, as Kline, Dyer-Witheford, and de Peuter (2003) observe, the video "game industry, conjured into being by technologically adept and culturally militarized men, made games reflecting the interests of its creators, germinating a young male subculture of digital competence and violent preoccupations" (p. 257). What is disturbing is how widespread and "normal" such "violent preoccupations" have become, as young men and boys routinely play at war using forms of software and hardware that are functionally indistinguishable from the ones being used at DARWARS or in the Afghan "theater." Gaming culture has indeed become the central mechanism for socializing the nation's boys and young men into an unthinking, pro-U.S. military perspective. Children and adults now play at war using highly realistic virtual weapons—the AK-47, M16A4, M1 Garand, Walther PPK, sniper rifle, and so on—whose technical specs and behavior in the field mimic the real thing. (Meanwhile, to capitalize on the fact that virtually every young male growing up today attains technical prowess in destroying virtual objects and enemies using commercial game controllers, the military has begun integrating Xbox and Wii controllers into the controls of its actual weapons and robotics equipment [Derene, 2008].)

What has enabled such realism and fidelity is the seamless integration of the private video game industry with the Pentagon. Not only do designers cycle back and forth between the U.S. military and private corporations, but commercial companies scrupulously model games on the latest in U.S. military doctrine, equipment, and weaponry. Some game companies even manufacture hardware or software for actual weapon systems. SEGA, which has a lucrative contract with the Boeing corporation to produce computer boards for a real tactical fighter plane, also produces *After Burner Climax,* which invites players to select "aircraft from

the F-14D Super Tomcat by Northrop Grumman to the F-15E Strike Eagle and F/A-18E Super Hornet by Boeing."

In November 2009, Activision shattered the previous record for the opening of a video game (previously held by *Grand Theft Auto IV*) with its release of *Call of Duty 2: Modern Warfare,* a military shooter game that raked in more than $300 million on its first day alone. *Call of Duty 2* was widely praised for its attention to "realism." And indeed, to see the command protocols, infrared images, the tactical ballistics, and flight characteristics of the C-130 attack aircraft experienced by the player of *Call of Duty 2* side by side with those evident in actual video footage of U.S. pilots strafing real human beings from a C-130 during a night raid in Afghanistan is to be awed by the realism.[4] But as in other games, what counts as verisimilitude is technological fetishism, not historical or psychological truth. Elided in such war simulations are the actual human consequences of combat—loss, trauma, suffering, the deaths of children, the cries of wounded soldiers and animals.

Virtual warfare is no longer limited to the military battlefield, either: Civil society itself becomes a war zone for symbolically enacting aggression and playing out the destructive "scripts" authorized by the wider culture. Violence against women (a social class whose objectification and subordination is still widely sanctioned by the society) is an especially prominent theme in some of the leading games. Thus, the popular Japanese video game *Rape-lay* consists of raping girls and young women (e.g., on deserted subway platforms), while sexual violence is one of the draws of the *Grand Theft Auto* series (a role-playing [RPG] game set in highly realistic urban settings). On YouTube, young men from different countries post homemade videos showing their favorite ways of killing prostitutes in *GTA IV.* The players' avatars drive women in the game to remote, desolate spots in the *GTA* world, and then murder them in various ways—bludgeoning them with tire irons, knifing them, shooting them in the head or stomach, burning them alive, drowning them, or dismembering them with a hand grenade. The bodies of the women writhe and fall apart in a fair simulation of the way a real woman's body might behave in real life, showing the detail that male software engineers specializing in "frag physics" lavish on simulated violations of the human body. The question here is not whether playing *GTA IV* directly causes violence against women but whether games that invite male players to participate in such simulated atrocities do not trivialize actual male violence against women—an epidemic in our and other societies—and legitimate and reinforce existing misogynistic attitudes. The evidence suggests that playing such games in fact does dull players' empathetic responses to real-world victims of violence, including women.[5]

Militarism and symbolic violence have become so pervasive that even ostensibly benign children's games are often inflected with technological aggression and masculine dreams of domination. In *Pokémon*, the player's avatar roams the world trying to enslave "as many of several hundred elusive creatures" as possible. "Once you leash one and it becomes part of your menagerie, you then train it and make it more powerful by carrying it around and deploying it in battles against other trainers" (Schiesel, 2010, p. C3). On the Arcademic Skill Builders website, meanwhile, children learn mathematical division by blasting away at a phalanx of advancing tanks ("Demolition Division") or learn multiplication by shooting at asteroids. Few children's games are in fact entirely free of militarization, and fewer from the drive to instrumentalize nature.

Capitalism and Instrumental Reason

Even when the content of games is not explicitly violent, the medium itself conveys an educative "message" that instrumental

manipulation of the world, of self and other, is natural and socially productive. One striking feature of the computer video game is the extent to which the player's fundamental cognitive and behavioral modality is oriented toward *manipulation* of the representational world, rather than *receptivity* toward it. In this regard, the computer video game may represent the ideal distillation of what Marcuse and other critics have termed *instrumental reason*. By this I mean, first, the prejudice of the modern capitalist age that things in the world have no value outside of our ability to manipulate them and, second, a mode of thinking and action whereby qualitative experiences, processes, and modes of being are reduced to *quantitative* measures. Hannah Arendt (2003) observed these "typical attitudes" in *homo faber* or "Man the maker,"

His instrumentalization of the world, his confidence in his tools and in the productivity of the maker of artificial objects; his trust in the all-comprehensive range of the means-ends category, his conviction that every issue can be solved and every human motivation reduced to the principle of utility; his sovereignty, which regards everything given as material and thinks of the whole of nature as [a mere thing to be made into whatever we wish]. (p. 364)

The roots of this "instrumentalization of the world" are deep—they go back at least far as ancient Greek culture and myth, which celebrated the "cunning" of human reason in its capacity to master and dominate the world. With the emergence of capitalist social relations in modern Europe, Nature came to be viewed as "thing-like," as dead matter to be manipulated at will. The logic of the commodity, which is the logic of abstraction and numerary—the "mathematization of nature"—meanwhile became the dominant perceptual template through which Western culture viewed the world (Husserl, 1970). Computerization in some ways represents the ultimate triumph of this process, a victory of the quantitative over the qualitative in our encounters with the real. As critic Michael Heim (1993) notes, however, what we "gain in power" through the system of technological abstraction comes at the expense "of our direct involvement with things" (p. 18). We learn to think and perceive in fragments, to "outsource" our skills and consciousness to machinic entities, and to treat one another with brutal, offhand indifference. Reality collapses into solipsism: The world seems to organize itself around *my* needs and desires. The human and animal body—the true ground of all our experiences and ways of knowing—is diminished, as virtual reality leads to a sense of *disembodiment*.

This instrumentalist conception of the world achieves its fullest expression in first-person shooter games, where the subject's interaction with others is most likely to be represented by a disembodied weapon floating in mid-air, and in strategy games, which reduce history to instances of technological social Darwinism (groups of humans dominating and subduing one another on the basis of their artifacts; Friedman, 1999; see also Galloway, 2006). But instrumentalism stalks even ostensibly innocent games like those in the lucrative *Sims* franchise, where living processes— whether life in the suburbs or life evolving on another planet (as in *Spore*)—are reduced to a series of cost-benefit decisions. In the original *Sims,* the player lives in a middle-class White suburban neighborhood, shops, raises a family, pursues a career, forms friendships, dates, and so on, all the while keeping an eye on quantitative status bars that allow him or her to monitor the Sims' biological functions, social status, and so on. Life is reduced to a sequence of strategic moves to maximize one's individual interests, with the Sim player assuming the role of a technocratic manager over his or her life—"controlling and predicting and directing the behaviour of a very finely tuned market niche, a 'segment of one'" (Kline et al., 2003, p. 278). As J. C. Herz (2000) writes, "Everything is

an object that yields a measurable benefit when some action is performed on it" (p. G10). Other human beings are viewed in the same light, as a means for maximizing one's own self-interest. "Even having children is a means to an end," Kline et al. (2003) observe of *The Sims,* "since it is through the interaction of your Sims' kids with the neighbours that adult Sims get to know each other" (p. 276), and it is through such interactions that one builds the connections one needs to advance one's career and increase one's income.

The fact that such instrumental egoism is by no means accidental but is "formally engineered into the game-play" can be traced to the ultimate objective of commercial gaming culture, which is to integrate the player into the circuits of real-world capitalist production and consumption (Herz, 2000). Ideologically, the worldview of *The Sims* is in fact indistinguishable from neoliberal economics. As economist (and capitalist apologist) Milton Friedman once wrote, "Children are at one and the same time *consumer goods* and potentially responsible members of society" (Friedman, 2002, p. 33, emphasis added), confirming the hidden logic of capital, which is to reduce all labor, all living beings, to the status of *things.*[6] Today, the computer video game is the "ideal commodity" of post-Fordist capitalism, the paradigmatic form of a system that now requires "a ceaseless stream of new commodities with ever-shortening product cycles and life-spans" (Kline et al., 2003, p. 66). Kline et al. (2003, pp. 60–77) relate the emergence of the video game as *the* significant consumer commodity of the 21st century to the need of the world capitalist system to stave off systemic crisis. The information revolution, they suggest, made it possible for capital to circumvent the objective limits of an older "regime" of capital accumulation. Just as the post-1980s era of speculative finance capital led banking institutions and consumers to invest wildly in "virtual" or fictive financial commodities—credit default swaps and other esoteric derivatives—the need of capital to colonize new markets led to the extension of commodity fetishism into the *virtual* realm. Where once computer games had to be tethered to bulky media like cathode-ray TVs or hulking, stationary consoles at the arcade, today they leap nimbly from cell phones and laptops to PCs and from HD televisions to the DIS (Disney Information System), heedless of spatial or temporal limits. Whereas chess can be played for free and has withstood the centuries with few modifications (and those rendered through folk adaptation), today's virtual games are expensive and designed to be obsolete within days or weeks, requiring the consumer to spend money continuously. Game content itself becomes commodified: In *Second Life,* players buy virtual clothes from the Gap or other mainstream retail chains, using real dollars, and hire real sweat-shop labor in China to mine virtual gold in *World of Warcraft* (see Castronova, 2005, pp. 170–204).

While the appeal of simulation games like *The Sims* or *Spore*—or *GTA*—is that they offer the player the illusion of complete freedom and power, in reality they tap into the thwarted libidinal energies of players and spin virtual flax into the real gold of the capitalist economy. Multinational corporate behemoths like Sony, Entertainment Arts, and Activision spend billions on marketing campaigns to manipulate the consciousness and behavior of the millions of children, teenagers, and young adults in the wealthy North who together make up the lucrative youth market (in 2000, worth up to $164 billion; Kline et al., 2003, p. 221). As Kline et al. (2003) point out,

> [When] one looks at the . . . economic, technological, and cultural forces shaping *The Sims* gamer—not merely as the participant in a . . . scripted and designed play scenario but also as a member of a population among which certain levels of technological familiarity are increasingly normalized, required, and rewarded, and as the target of a high-intensity marketing regime designed to elicit certain

levels of consumption activity—much of [his] apparent autonomy and empowerment evaporates. The player reappears as object, not subject, the product of a system . . . partially programmed . . . as much played upon as player. (p. 279)

On one hand, the player himself colludes in this process, knowing full well that the real game in town is the game of consumerism and profit realization. On the other hand, he barely comprehends the degree to which his own behavior, his consciousness, his values, his desires, have been effectively commandeered and subordinated to reinforce a regime of power whose destructive features are rendering his sovereignty as a political subject, his own consciousness itself, *obsolete.*

Conclusion

The more ubiquitous the video game form becomes and the more lifelike its simulations of reality, the more its characteristic phenomenology comes to assume the form of a *paradigm,* a structuring set of knowledge practices and theories with the power to shape the way we see and experience the world. The trouble is, the more we paradoxically seek solace in the womb of the machine itself—that is, in a limitless virtual realm where the very masculinist and "instrumentalist" approach that has failed us in the real world yet retains its aura of potency—the more we flee the actual public sphere, that realm of appearances where *action and speech* might still matter. Political theorist Sheldon Wolin warns of a creeping "inverted totalitarianism" in which powerful interests rule not by whipping the masses up to a frenzied unity (as in fascism) but by turning us into quiescent spectators. Meanwhile, our own deep anger over being treated as mere things—by our employers, by our government, by the anonymous corporate bureaucracies we are forced to interact with every day—gets channeled into socially destructive forms: addictive online behaviors, simulations of atrocities, real bombs, and missiles raining on real people in foreign lands. By thus adapting life instincts to the external needs of an unjust social order, the individual in effect (to quote Marcuse again) "collaborates in his own repression, in the containment of potential individual and social freedom, [and hence] in the release of aggression" (Marcuse, 1968, p. 254). The individual comes to bear "the marks of a mutilated human being." For while the behaviors, forms of culture and play, and so on called into being and sanctioned by the system may be productive for that system itself, they are fundamentally destructive from the vantage point of actual human happiness and planetary well-being.

Notes

1. The original report was released by the NPD Group, a market research firm.

2. DARWARS website (http://www.darwars .org/about/index.html), accessed March 10, 2010. I am indebted to Nina Huntemann for her research on military uses of video game technologies.

3. As David Nieborg points out, the U.S. Army's *America's Army* MMORPG "has become a powerful vessel for disseminating U.S. Army ideology and foreign policy to a global game culture" (Höglund, 2008, p. 9).

4. Both the real C-130 footage and the simulacral footage were available on YouTube in April 2010. I want to thank Darius Kazemi for bringing this footage to my attention.

5. "In violent video games," the authors of one study of the effects of violent media on children's behavior conclude, "empathy is not adaptive, moral evaluation is often non-existent, but proviolence attitudes and behaviors are repeatedly rewarded" (Funk, Baldacci, Pasold, & Baumgardner, 2004, p. 34).

6. South Korea, a nation so obsessed with video games that some individuals have literally played themselves to death, became a tragic proving ground for this theory of human disposability

when authorities there arrested a couple for child abuse and neglect after the parents left "their 3-month-old daughter to starve to death while they raised a virtual daughter online during 12-hour bouts at a cyber cafe." The couple had become addicted to *Prius Online*, a game akin to *Second Life* where players engage in virtual work and virtual relationships, and "[earn] an extra avatar to nurture once they reach a certain level." One police officer observed, "The couple seemed to have lost their will to live a normal life because they didn't have jobs and gave birth to a premature baby. . . . They indulged themselves in the online game of raising a virtual character so as to escape from reality, which led to the death of their real baby." The virtual child, ironically named *Anima* (the Latin word for "breath" or "soul," which in ancient usage meant a *living being*) flourished; meanwhile, the real baby perished from "severe dehydration and malnutrition" (Frayer, 2010). While one must be careful not to make too much of a single case, the incident nonetheless serves as a reminder of what can happen when flesh and blood human beings become subordinated to, and indeed absorbed into, the realm of virtual commodities.

References

Alloway, N., & Gilbert, P. (1988). Video game culture: Playing with masculinity, violence, and pleasure. In S. Howard (Ed.), *Wired-up: Young people and the electronic media* (pp. 95–114). London: University of London College Press.

Arendt, H. (2003). The human condition. In R. C. Scharff & V. Dusek (Eds.), *Philosophy of technology: The technological condition*. New York: Blackwell.

Bogost, I. (2007). *Persuasive games: The expressive power of video games*. Cambridge: MIT Press.

Castronova, E. (2005). *Synthetic worlds: The business and culture of online games*. Chicago: University of Chicago Press.

Chan, D. (2005). Playing with race: The ethics of racialized representations in e-games.

International Review of Information Ethics, 4(12), 24–30.

Derene, G. (2008, May 29). Wii all you can be? Why the military needs the gaming industry. *Popular Mechanics.* http://www.popular mechanics.com/technology/military_law/42 66106.html

Frayer, L. (2010, March 10). Baby starved as couple nurtured virtual kid. AOL News. http://www.aolnews.com/crime/article/south-korean-couple-nurtured-virtual-child-as-their-baby-starved-police-say/19384636

Freierman, S. (2008, November 10). Popular demand: Video games. *New York Times,* p. B10.

Friedman, M. (2002). *Capitalism and freedom* (40th anniversary ed.). Chicago: University of Chicago Press.

Friedman, T. (1999). Civilization and its discontents: Simulation, subjectivity, and space. In G. Smith (Ed.), *Discovering discs: Transforming space and place on CD-ROM* (pp. 132–150). New York: New York University Press.

Funk, J. B., Baldacci, H. B., Pasold, T., & Baumgardner, J. (2004). Violence exposure in real-life, video games, television, movies and the Internet: Is there desensitization? *Journal of Adolescence, 27,* 23–39.

Galloway, A. (2006). *Gaming: Essays on algorithmic culture.* Minneapolis: University of Minnesota Press.

Heim, M. (1993). *The metaphysics of virtual reality.* Oxford, UK: Oxford University Press.

Herz, J. C. (2000, February 10). The Sims who die with the most toys wins. *New York Times,* p. G10.

Hill, N. (n.d.). Playing with patriarchy. *Cerise Magazine.* http://cerise.theirisnetwork.org/archives/9

Höglund, J. (2008, September). Electronic empire: Orientalism revisited in the military shooter. *Game Studies: The International Journal of Computer Game Research.* 8(1). http://gamestudies.org/0801/articles/hoeglund

Husserl, E. (1970). *The crisis of European sciences and transcendental phenomenology.* Evanston, IL: Northwestern University Press.

John, Tracey, "170 Million Americans Play Video Games, Study Finds." *Wired Magazine,* Aug. 3, 2009. (http://www.wired.com/gamelife/2009/08/npd-games/).

Johnson, C. (2004). *Blowback: The costs and consequences of American empire.* New York: Holt.

King, C. R., & Leonard, D. J. (2010). Wargames as a new frontier: Securing American empire in virtual space. In N. B. Huntemann & M. T. Payne (Eds.), *Joystick soldiers: The politics of play in military video games.* New York: Routledge.

Kline, S., Dyer-Witheford, N., & de Peuter, G. (2003). *Digital play: The interaction of technology, culture, and marketing.* Montreal, Quebec, Canada: McGill-Queen's University Press.

Lenoir, T., & Lowood, H. (2005). Theaters of war: The military-entertainment complex. In H. Schramm, L. Schwarte, & J. Lazardzig (Eds.), *Collection—Laboratory—Theater: Scenes of knowledge in the 17th century* (pp. 427–456). Berlin: Walter de Gruyter.

Leonard, D. (2004). Unsettling the military entertainment complex: Video games and a pedagogy of peace. *Studies in Media & Information Literacy Education, 4*(4).

Marcuse, H. (1968). *Negations: Essays in critical theory* (J. J. Shapiro, Trans.). Boston: Beacon.

National chess survey reveals the truth about chess: Why people play and what scares them away. (2003, December 2). *Business Wire.*

Nichols, R. (2010). Target acquired: *America's Army* and the video games industry. In N. B. Huntemann & M. T. Payne (Eds.), *Joystick soldiers: The politics of play in military video games* (pp. 39–52). New York: Routledge.

Penny, S. (2004). Representation, enaction, and the ethics of simulation. In N. Wardrip-Fruin & P. Harrigan (Eds.), *First person: New media as story, performance, and game.* Cambridge: MIT Press.

Schiesel, S. (2010, March 19). Look kids: A way to slip Pokémon past mom. *New York Times,* p. C3.

Strategic Simulations and Our Past

The Bias of Computer Games in the Presentation of History

Kevin Schut

Education and Historical Simulations

A growing number of educators are starting to champion the use of digital games as teaching tools.[1] Anyone who has played a substantial number of games probably already realizes that this new medium has several educational benefits. But aside from the obligatory copy of *Oregon Trail* (Learning Company, 1997) or other relatively simple and limited edutainment CD-ROMs hanging around the classroom computer, computer games have not been commonly used to teach in a systematic manner. Now an increasing number of voices are speaking up for just that.

In a recent guest editorial in *Wired* magazine, famed game designer Will Wright (2006), who designed *SimCity* (Maxis Software, 1989) and *The Sims* (Maxis Software, 2000), touts the ability of games to encourage scientific thinking. Likewise, writer Steven Johnson (2005), in his engaging book *Everything Bad Is Good for You*, argues that video games have been a perfect vehicle for encouraging increasingly complex thought patterns. This echoes recent publications in education theory. James Paul Gee's (2003) book *What Video Games Have to Teach Us About Learning and Literacy* is a very readable treatise on how good digital games model good learning practices. The book puts together a persuasive case for the ability of games to make meaning situated, to help create motivated, tailored, and incremental discoveries, and to encourage social sharing of knowledge, among other things. Although evidence-based research is still not available in large quantities—and much of what *is* available is methodologically questionable—Kurt Squire (2004b, 2005; Squire & Jenkins, 2003) is one prominent education researcher who has widely published about using the game *Civilization III* (described in more detail below) in actual classrooms. Although he

From Schut, K. (2007). Strategic simulations and our past: The bias of computer games in the presentation of history. *Games and Culture: A Journal of Interactive Media*, 2(3), 213–235.

sees potential drawbacks, Squire believes that digital games are potentially powerful teaching tools. Gee, Squire, and others do not argue that games are a panacea for all that ails schools today; rather, these theorists see computer and video games as valuable tools when coupled with proper guidance and other media resources.

Personally, I strongly support the idea of integrating games with teaching. As a lifelong game player, I have experienced many of the benefits of gaming that Squire, Gee, and others describe. But there is no such thing as a perfect tool. Games have significant strengths and limitations. This does not mean we should abstain from historical simulations; it simply means we should approach them with something of a critical eye. The current educational research on games certainly notes the pragmatic limitations of using them in standard school settings. . . . I think, however, that these analyses could go a little further.

I take my cue for this article partly from a question asked in a recent article by the educators at the University of Wisconsin who are leading the charge for the use of games in classrooms (Shaffer, Squire, Halverson, & Gee, 2005). The authors end the piece with a call for more research on games, and specifically wonder "how inhabiting a virtual world develops situated knowledge— how playing a game like *Civilization III*, for example, mediates players' conceptions of world history" (p. 111). It is at this level that I think educators and players need to be aware of some of the limitations and tendencies of the medium.

Media Ecology and the Ideology of Games

As games have moved from niche-culture status to mainstream, intellectuals have started to pay more attention to the ideologies that a game appears to support, in spite of the apparent freedom of play. Although a digital game may seem to give greater latitude to gamers than do other media, the procedural authors of games set limits and boundaries to activity (Frasca, 2003). As Shoshana Magnet (2006) argues, in her critique of *Tropico* (PopTop Software, 2001), capitalist or ethnocentric assumptions can be built right into a game's virtual landscape (its "gamescape," as she puts it). Barkin (2002) and Chen (2003) likewise criticize *Civilization III* (Firaxis Games, 2001) for the problematic assumptions built into the game's model of culture. In their seminal textbook *Rules of Play*, Katie Salen and Eric Zimmerman (2004) also extensively talk about the possibility of specific games encoding ideologies.

Although this kind of single-game analysis is valuable, we can draw a larger picture: a consideration of the ideological implications of the medium as a whole. As Ted Friedman (1999) puts it, "Any medium . . . can teach you how to see life in new ways" (p. 133). By being able to "reorganize perception," to use Friedman's term, the digital game medium can have profound implications for how we understand the world and how it works. Educators and players in general would be well served to consider how computer and video games provide new ways to see and understand history.[2] . . .

MASCULINE HISTORY

Both computers and computer games have a strongly masculine history that still manifests itself in numerous ways. Although it is widely believed that the first computer programmer was a woman—Ada Lovelace is reputed to have written theoretical programs for Charles Babbage's never-constructed Analytical Engine—the roots of the modern computer are in thoroughly masculine contexts, such the cold war–era U.S. military, academic engineering departments of major research universities, and the early hacker culture.[3] Although the gender balance has clearly shifted during the past two or three decades, it is clear that computers are still very male items in many ways (Cassell &

Jenkins, 1998). For example, recent statistics from the U.S. Bureau of Labor Statistics (2005) list women as occupying only 27.0% of positions in "computer and mathematical occupations," and a recent survey completed by the International Game Developers Association found that women form only 11.5% of the game industry's total workforce and only 5.0% of its programmers (Gourdin, 2005).

This latter statistic is not a new development: Computer games have also had a very male-dominated history. A few prominent female designers, such as Roberta Williams, have managed to make their mark on game culture, but, by and large, the people who made the digital game industry what it is today were men. A look at any list of credits today shows that although there are ever-greater numbers of women working in the game-making industry, the vast majority are still male. In short, one of the most salient features of the digital game medium—both in terms of computer technology and the game industry itself—is that it is very masculine in nature. It should be clear that there is nothing essentially masculine about either games or computers; nevertheless, a masculine bias has been a major feature of the social construction of the digital game medium throughout its history.[4]

For decades now, critical historians have struggled to counteract the manner in which the standard Western histories of Great White (dead) Men have written marginal social groups out of our cultural historical consciousness. Although the discipline of history has been busy correcting this significant problem, digital games tend to reinscribe it. A kind of masculine slant is exceptionally clear in game presentation of history. For one thing, practically all history in digital games is focused on some combination of politics, economics, and war. For another, all of the historical games examined for this article demonstrate the centrality of aggressive power and/or acquisition. The centrality of these features displays the importance of stereotypical manhood to historical simulations.

The first evidences of this masculine bias are the types of historical focuses of the game simulations. Partly as an attempt to correct the hegemonic bias of traditional historical research, the discipline of history has broadened its scope to include a great diversity of subjects. Social, cultural, and critical histories are particularly valuable for emphasizing the significance of people ignored in the traditional accounts of monarchs, merchants, and military campaigns. Most historical digital games, however, ignore these trends and almost exclusively focus on politics, economics, and war. Strategy games that are historical simulators almost always have an economic component and frequently have a political dimension as well. A major part of *Civilization* and the *Total War* games—and, to a lesser extent, *Pirates*—consists of balancing income and expenses, developing commercial trade, exploiting resources, investing in economic infrastructure, and so on. Another part of these same games is dedicated to developing and maintaining advantageous relationships with other factions or powers in the games (whether they are played by humans or the computer): making and breaking alliances, trading deals, and other diplomatic agreements. Both *Civilization* and the *Total War* games have an internal political element as well, requiring the player to keep his or her own population content enough to avoid rebellion.

More blatant than the two themes of economics and politics, however, is the centrality of war. Practically all commercial historical digital games feature some kind of military- or combat-oriented activity, even if it is not the only option available to players. *Pirates* allows the player to be a peaceful merchant instead of a bloodthirsty privateer, and the *Civilization* player may win the game without conquering anyone or anything. In both cases, however, it would be extremely challenging to make it all the way through the game without a single battle. In addition, the mechanics of these games, their manuals, and even their promotional literature clearly indicate that game makers wish violence and combat to prominently feature in gameplay. In many other historical simulations, war is the raison d'être, as clearly evidenced by the titles of the *Total War* and *Battlefield* games. Playing these games in a nonconfrontational or nonviolent way would be to deliberately subvert the games' purposes (which, of course, is possible).

Other kinds of historical focuses certainly do appear in historical representations of the past. All of the games except for the *Battlefield* series feature broader cultural issues. *Civilization* has numerous cultural and social technologies, such as mysticism or nationalism, and buildings, such as coliseums or cathedrals. In addition, its encyclopedic descriptions of the various game units, improvements, and concepts give a great deal of historical depth that often moves beyond political, economic, and military considerations. In *Pirates*, one of the major mini-games is the decidedly artistic activity of ballroom dancing. But, as a whole, these social and cultural pictures of history are subservient to the political, economic, and military focuses of the game mechanics: Their game function is to help the player become more politically, economically, and militarily successful. Successful dancing in *Pirates*, for example, leads the charmed governor's daughter to give gifts or tips about financially rewarding quests.

When culture is apparently autonomous, it ends up functioning in much the same manner as an economic system. In the last two versions of *Civilization*, a player may win the game by achieving cultural dominance. Buildings such as libraries or theaters produce "culture points." These accumulate throughout the game, extending the territory of the player and even leading to enemy cities defecting to a dominant neighboring civilization. If a player's culture is powerful enough, he or she wins the game. Although the game uses the word *culture*, this is obviously misleading: Culture in reality is a complex, particular, multifaceted phenomenon (Barkin, 2002; Chen, 2003). What we are seeing here is currency, dressed up as culture points. Even when the game tries to get away from

politics, economics, and war, it cannot escape the well-worn pattern.

In fact, *Civilization*'s culture system is also a good illustration of another masculine theme: Games typically present history as a matter of aggressive power. In the *Battlefield* games, this is particularly clear: The player must kill or be killed—the player's team must physically destroy the opposition with firearms or military vehicles. In the strategy games, the focus can be on this kind of conquest-oriented militaristic power drive, but just as often, the key motive of the game is aggressive acquisition. In *Total War*, the player tries to get as much territory and as large an army as possible. In *Civilization*, the player has several options, but whether he or she chooses a military, cultural, or technological route to success, the game consists of trying to get as much stuff as possible, often forcefully. In *Pirates*, we see the modern suburban dream of acquiring a career, wife, and house with a yard, written onto a 17th century Caribbean setting; the player's score is dependent, among a few other things, on the amount of treasure acquired, the amount of land rewarded by grateful governors, and the attractiveness of the wife.[5] Again, the player achieves this primarily via sword fights, ship-to-ship combat, and ground-based invasions.

It is of course important to note that politics, economics, and even war are not inherently male spheres of life, nor do only men desire power or focus on acquisition (or that not all men wish for these things). However, all of these themes are stereotypically male; they fit widely publicized, rough masculine ideals of aggressiveness and domination (e.g., Douglas, 1999; Faludi, 1999; Jeffords, 1994). More importantly, these themes crowd out or subvert things that are not stereotypically masculine, especially in the presentation of historical games. Many, including myself, have reasonable hope that this might change. There are a growing number of popular digital games that break the hyper-masculine mold—notably best-sellers *SimCity* and *The Sims*—although virtually none take place in historical settings. M.I.T.'s "Games-to-Teach" project developed a historical multiplayer role-playing game that also suggests that the representation of history in games is not locked into the stereotypically masculine interests (Squire & Jenkins, 2003). For the moment, however, the bias of the medium is pretty thoroughly in favor of one gender, and it will take work to change that. . . .

Notes

1. Discussion about the educational value of games has actually gone on for a long time (Egenfeldt-Nielsen, 2004; Squire, 2004a). According to Squire (2004a), teaching with games was somewhat in vogue during the 1970s, but these games rarely used computers, and they fell out of favor in the 1980s. What we are seeing now is a renaissance of interest from a distinctively constructivist educational theory viewpoint.

2. Squire's (2006) recent writing, "Videogames as Designed Experience," is an excellent example of a broad ideological critique of the digital game medium. He touches some of the same issues as this article does, but his main focus is on educational ideology—the way game playing and game design encode the character of learners. Another contrast with this piece is that Squire's article spends much more time talking about the performance of gameplay.

3. Although none of these observations are particularly controversial, a good game-oriented discussion of some of these issues is in *Digital Play* (Kline, Dyer-Witheford, & De Peuter, 2003).

4. Again, for a good discussion of the "militarized masculinity" in games, see *Digital Play* (Kline et al., 2003). Also see Cassell and Jenkins (1998) and Herz (1997).

5. This is actually ranked in the game; the three varieties are "plain," "attractive," and "beautiful."

References

Barkin, G. (2002, January 15). The culture of Civilization III. Message posted to http://web.archive.org/web/20020201200724/www.joystick101.org/?op=displaystory&sid=2002/1/12/222013/422

Cassell, J., & Jenkins, H. (1998). Chess for girls? feminism and computer games. In J. Cassell & H. Jenkins (Eds.), *From Barbie to Mortal Kombat: Gender and computer games* (pp. 2–45). Cambridge, MA: MIT Press.

Chen, K. (2003). Civilization and its disk contents: Two essays on civilization and Civilization. *Radical Society, 30*(2), 95–107.

Douglas, S. (1999). *Listening in: Radio and the imagination, from Amos 'n Andy and Edward R. Murrow to Wolfman Jack and Howard Stern.* New York: Times Books.

Egenfeldt-Nielsen, S. (2004). Practical barriers in using educational computer games. *On the Horizon, 12*(1), 18–21.

Faludi, S. (1999). *Stiffed: The betrayal of the American man.* New York: William Morrow.

Ferguson, N. (Ed.). (1997). *Virtual history: Alternatives and counterfactuals.* London: Picador.

Firaxis Games. (2001). Sid Meier's civilization III [Computer game]. Lyon, France: Infogrames.

Firaxis Games. (2004). Sid Meier's pirates! [Computer game]. New York: Atari.

Firaxis Games. (2005). Sid Meier's civilization IV [Computer game]. New York: 2K Games.

Fiske, J. (1987). *Television culture.* New York: Routledge.

Frasca, G. (2003). Simulation versus narrative: Introduction to ludology. In M. J. P. Wolf & B. Perron (Eds.), *The video game theory reader* (pp. 221–235). New York: Routledge.

Friedman, T. (1999). Civilization and its discontents: Simulation, subjectivity and space. In G. M. Smith (Ed.), *On a silver platter: CD-ROMs and the promises of a new technology* (pp. 132–150). New York: New York University Press.

Gee, J. P. (2003). *What video games have to teach us about learning and literacy.* New York: Palgrave Macmillan.

Gourdin, A. (2005). *Game developer demographics: An exploration of workforce diversity.* San Francisco: International Game Developers Association.

Herz, J. C. (1997). *Joystick nation: How videogames ate our quarters, won our hearts, and rewired our minds.* Boston: Little, Brown.

Huizinga, J. (1949). *Homo ludens: A study of the play-element in culture* (R. F. C. Hull, Trans.). London: Routledge and Kegan Paul. (Original work published 1938)

Jeffords, S. (1994). *Hard bodies: Hollywood masculinity in the Reagan era.* New Brunswick, NJ: Rutgers University Press.

Jenkins, H. (1992). *Textual poachers: Television fans and participatory culture.* New York: Routledge.

Jenkins, H. (2002). Game design as narrative architecture. In N. Wardrip-Fruin & P. Harrigan (Eds.), *First person: New media as story, performance, and game* (pp. 118–130). Cambridge, MA: MIT Press.

Johnson, S. (2005). *Everything bad is good for you: How today's popular culture is actually making us smarter.* New York: Riverhead Books.

King, B., & Borland, J. (2003). *Dungeons and dreamers: The rise of computer game culture from geek to chic.* New York: McGraw-Hill/Osborne.

Kline, S., Dyer-Witheford, N., & De Peuter, G. (2003). *Digital play: The interaction of technology, culture, and marketing.* Montreal, Quebec, Canada: McGill-Queen's University Press.

Latour, B. (1996). *Aramis, or the love of technology.* Cambridge, MA: Harvard University Press.

Learning Company. (1997). The Oregon trail (3rd ed.) [Computer game]. San Francisco: Author.

Magnet, S. (2006). Playing at colonization: Interpreting imaginary landscapes in the video game Tropico. *Journal of Communication Inquiry, 30*(2), 142–162.

Manovich, L. (2001). *The language of new media.* Cambridge, MA: MIT Press.

Maxis Software. (1989). SimCity [Computer game]. Eugene, OR: Broderbund.

Maxis Software. (2000). The Sims [Computer game]. Redwood City, CA: Electronic Arts.

McMahan, A. (2003). Immersion, engagement, and presence: A method for analyzing 3-D video games. In M. J. P. Wolf & B. Perron (Eds.), *The video game theory reader* (pp. 67–86). New York: Routledge.

Murray, J. H. (1997). *Hamlet on the holodeck: The future of narrative in cyberspace.* Cambridge, MA: MIT Press.

PopTop Software. (2001). Tropico [Computer game]. New York: Gathering of Developers.

Salen, K., & Zimmerman, E. (2004). *Rules of play: Game design fundamentals.* Cambridge, MA: MIT Press.

Shaffer, D. W., Squire, K. R., Halverson, R., & Gee, J. P. (2005). Video games and the future of learning. *Phi Delta Kappan, 87*(2), 105–111.

Squire, K. (2004a). *Replaying history: Learning world history through playing Civilization III.* Unpublished doctoral dissertation, Indiana University, Bloomington.

Squire, K. (2004b). Review: Sid Meier's civilization III. *Simulation and Gaming, 35*(1), 135–140.

Squire, K. (2005). Changing the game: What happens when video games enter the classroom? *Innovate Journal of Online Education, 1*(6). Retrieved June 8, 2006.

Squire, K. (2006). From content to context: Videogames as designed experience. *Educational Researcher, 35*(8), 19–29.

Squire, K., & Jenkins, H. (2003). Harnessing the power of games in education. *Insight, 3,* 5–33.

Starr, P. (1994). Seductions of Sim. *American Prospect, 5*(17). Retrieved July 18, 2006, from http://www.prospect.org/print/V5/17/starr-p.html

Suits, B. (1978). *The grasshopper: Games, life and utopia.* Toronto, Ontario, Canada: University of Toronto Press.

U.S. Bureau of Labor Statistics. (2005). *Women in the labor force: A databook* (Publication No. 985). Retrieved June 12, 2006, from http://www.bls.gov/cps/wlf-databook-2005.pdf

Wright, W. (2006, April). Dream machines: Will Wright explains how games are unleashing the human imagination. *Wired, 14*(4), 110–112.

"You Play Like a Girl!"

Cross-Gender Competition and the Uneven Playing Field

Elena Bertozzi

Much has been written about why females do not play the same games or as many digital games as males do. It is now estimated that females play digital games at least as often as males do, but the levels of complexity of games varies widely (Dillon, 2006). Lucas and Sherry (2004) define casual/traditional games (those preferred by females) as 'non-mental rotation games' and console or complex PC games (preferred by males) as 'mental rotation games.' These terms suggest that playing 'mental rotation' games requires an additional level of training and immersion not required by traditional games. The lack of female engagement in this sphere matters because participating in complex digital play[1] is a predictor of confidence in and competence with digital technology (AAUW, 2000; Bertozzi and Lee, 2007; Oxford, 2005). Some have suggested that the representation of women as passive sex objects prevents women from fully engaging in the medium, while others have posited that the emphasis on violent/shooting-based conflict keeps females from being interested in this type of play (Cassell and Jenkins, 1998; Heintz-Knowles, 2001; Oxford, 2005; Schleiner, 1998). For years, it has been argued that females value social behavior and positive values, and that as soon as games of this type emerge, females will play them. Over the last couple of years, several games have been published that meet these criteria (*Final Fantasy, Animal Crossing, World of Warcraft* [*WOW*], *SIMS*) and there have been significant increases in female players of these games.[2] If anything though, the popularity of these games among males demonstrates that males do not require stereotypical representations of females or violence to enjoy digital gameplay, and that they value social interaction as much as females do.

The lack of female engagement in digital play is related to deeply rooted understandings of gender differences in the culture at large. Playgrounds such as poker tables, Monopoly

From Bertozzi, E. (2008). 'You play like a girl!' Cross-gender competition and the uneven playing field. *Convergence, 14*, 473–487.

boards or levels of Halo are affected by gender politics in the larger culture. Players can certainly make a conscious decision to avoid or ignore them, but they exist and affect the play process in both conscious and unconscious ways. It is possible that males seek to play with males and females with females in part because single gender playgrounds are arenas in which players feel somewhat freed from having to deal with the complexities of cross-gender interactions which affect every other area of their lives.

Researchers have documented the ways in which gender politics are reconstructed in digital worlds (Schleiner, 1998; Taylor, 2006; Yee, 2004, 2006). In *Everquest,* for example, players can choose to play as either male or female avatars. The gender of the avatar makes absolutely no difference to the actual abilities or capacities of the avatar. The world is constructed to be gender neutral. Players, however, are affected by the sex of the avatar, in that they treat avatars differently based on their appearance. A delicate-looking female avatar will receive more offers of help and collaboration than a male ogre avatar will. Players are very sensitive to gender politics and are often very savvy about playing as a certain type of avatar when they wish to solicit different types of reactions from other players. Many players will play as both male and female avatars under different circumstances, either for strategic advantage, or because it allows them to replay a game and experience a different set of circumstances.

Given that digital play offers a considerable amount of gender plasticity through avatars, it might seem illogical for gender stereotypes and concerns to persist in digital gaming, but they do.[3] Players of digital games are sexed and the sex of the player matters. The preponderance of male players in complex digital games makes it virtually certain that females who play these digital games will be playing against males.

This chapter considers the possibility that gender differences in digital play are strongly influenced by the unwillingness of both genders to cross traditional, culturally gendered play lines. The fact that females are routinely punished for challenging males on what is perceived to be their turf may be an important factor in deterring women from digital play. When males play against players whom they believe to be female, they are affected by a range of cultural norms including: standards of civility, their own self definition as male, and culturally sanctioned expressions of sexual desire. When females play against players whom they believe to be male, they are affected by similar issues, but from a different perspective. Analysis of gender differences in digital play behavior should consider these factors. In a huge range of game/play activities, including digital gameplay, some females are competing or attempting to compete at the same level as males. They are forging new paths in difficult territory. If we recognize the significance and level of difficulty of challenging existing norms, we can better support their initiatives and create structures to help others join them.

Civility and Chivalry

When males and females play against one another, problems arise. Although there has recently been much lamenting about the death of civility, and concern that young people are growing up without manners, we still have very strongly felt beliefs about how males and females should interact with one another. One of the most relevant, in terms of play, is that it is wrong for males to be aggressive towards females. Our cultural history includes the understanding that males should be protective of women and seek to help them. This understanding was, of course, based on the idea that females are the 'weaker sex,' and required protection and dominance from a strong male. Although we are moving past this perception to some degree, there is no question that public demonstration of violence or aggression from a male towards a female remains culturally unacceptable. Such behavior brings to mind issues of wife beating, rape and other serious crimes. Many males are thus understandably reluctant to engage in any behavior that might even suggest aggression towards a female, for fear that this might be misinterpreted (Hargreaves, 1990).

> A boy on a co-ed football squad—or playing against a co-ed squad—faces an irreconcilable conflict between his duty as a man and his duty as a player. As a man, he must never strike a woman. As a player he must strike teammates during scrimmages, and opposing players during games, fairly and within the rules, but with all the force he can muster. (Jeffrey, 2004)

It is therefore complicated to have males and females on certain types of playgrounds, participating as equals. If a male were playing against another male, he might use a number of aggressive tactics including: physical proximity, verbal taunting, feints, and actual aggression, among other things. It can be very difficult for a male to understand how much and to what degree he can use these kinds of behaviors when playing against a female opponent. In order to truly treat each other as equals, males and females have to willfully attempt to ignore years of cultural conditioning, which codifies inequality.

These difficulties can, however, be overcome if the concept of 'play' is correctly understood and applied. The philosophical premise of play is that whosoever steps onto the 'sacred space' (Huizinga, 1955) of the playing field sheds any discrimination/bias/advantage accrued to him or her outside of the playing field. Within that physical space and within the constraints of the rules of that game, contestants are measured purely by their ability to perform that particular action, in that particular place, at that particular time. The success of females at high

school wrestling, where females often compete on teams with and against males, for example, demonstrates that this can be accomplished even for contact sports.[4]

Consequences of Challenging Males

Despite the many changes in male–female relations over the past 50 years and the goals attained by women's rights movements in a variety of areas, play of almost all kinds remains rigidly gendered. From birth, children are given toys and encouraged to play in ways that reinforce cultural stereotypes of gender appropriateness (Martin and Ruble, 2004; Serbin et al., 2001). Toys "R" Us, Mattel, and other toy production and sales companies have separate product and sales teams for products aimed at separate gender markets. Studies on sex-role stereotypes demonstrate that in fact little has changed in the public's perception of what constitutes masculine and feminine traits (Broverman et al., 1972; Conway and Vartanian, 2000). Video game environments tend to emphasize the differences between gendered avatars rather than diminish them (Ray, 2004). Females often have enormous breasts, male avatars are muscular and heroic. Although this is often presented as a reason why females do not play video games, Waem et al. found that hyper-sexualized avatars are actually preferred by both male and female players (2005).

One result of Title IX legislation has been to encourage females to play more and to provide them with better equipment and better training (Dowling, 2000; Roberts, 2005). Enormous gains have been made in female sporting achievement as a result of this legislation. If anything though, these gains have further demarcated the 'separate but equal' approach to sports education in the USA. Play is fundamentally about power: who has the right to exercise it and how it is exercised (Bertozzi, 2003). Many kinds of play behavior reward aggression, competition and violence, within a system of checks and balances that control how these behaviors are expressed. Traditional male play behaviors often reward players for engaging in these behaviors appropriately. Males are taught that seeking power through socially sanctioned means is appropriate, and will result in deserved rewards. Interviews with CEOs and other successful businessmen often mention past or current participation in sporting events that helped them create a 'winning' work ethic. . . .

The tenacity of gender stereotypes becomes apparent when women attempt to cross the boundary lines and compete on the same terms as males (Roth, 2004). The fact that the female placekicker for the University of Colorado football team was subjected to constant hazing and then raped (CNN, 2004) is an example of how females can be overtly punished for putting themselves on a par with men. The response to events like these often suggests that the harm inflicted on the female in question was somehow deserved, because she put herself in a place where she did not belong:

> Only a few female kickers have played college football, but female high school players are more common. The National Federation of State High School Associations (NFHS), which represents state governing bodies for high school sports, says 1,477 girls participated on the tackle football teams last year at 306 U.S. high schools.
>
> That's a national disgrace. There is a connection between the increasing disrespect shown to women in our society and an ultra-feminist ideology that pushes teenage girls to play a brutal contact sport with teenage boys. (Jeffrey, 2004)

According to this columnist, girls are not freely choosing to participate in football. They are the unwitting pawns of feminist ideology, which places them in an arena in which they are certain to be hurt. This ignores the obvious point that the place-kicker in question was not hurt on the field, but in the locker rooms and other social settings, and that she was hurt by her own teammates, not by contact with the opposing team. When Annika Sorenson dared to challenge the men of the PGA, the media hubbub went on for weeks. Some of Sorenson's male colleagues made extremely unsportsmanlike comments regarding her ability despite her clear demonstration of competence.

> WOODRUFF: . . . fans of Annika Sorenson would like to believe that golfer Vijay Singh is eating a big plate of crow for dinner tonight. He's the man who said Sorenstam—quote—'doesn't belong here with the men of the PGA Tour.' And today, Sorenstam [sic] became the first woman since World War II to play at a PGA event, the Colonial in Fort Worth, Texas. And judging by her game and her game alone, she belonged there. (CNN, 2003)

Ambivalence towards players who represent themselves as females in digital games has been reported by many players. A player using a female avatar is very frequently subject to sexual innuendo and communication from other players that focuses on aspects of the female body, clothes she is wearing and so on. In her discussion of how she was treated differently while playing as male- and female-identified avatars in online poker environments, Slimmer points out that some males become extremely aggressive when beaten by a player using a female-identified avatar, and that her decision to play as a male-identified avatar resulted in part from real fear of retaliation from enraged male players (2007). This hostility towards women who dare to challenge gender norms in play is due to the fact that their presence on the playing field calls into question the very definition of masculinity.

Masculine Cultural Play Norms

Cultural norms are often reflected in banter, jokes, idiom and insults. Despite the media presence of many strong and athletically talented women, 'You play/throw/kick like a girl' remains a potent insult. When males play in groups, gendered terms such as 'sissy,' 'pussy' and 'fag,' are used as normal and acceptable putdowns. Some males have to differentiate themselves from females in order to prove their masculinity. In a culture where male traits are valued more highly than female, this process often involves devaluing and 'dissing' females and female traits (Messner, 2002). In fact, publicly devaluing females and feminine traits is considered by some researchers to be an integral part of the development of a culturally accepted 'male' gender persona (Butler, 1990; Connell, 1987; Nelson, 1994; Tolman et al., 2003). In digital gameplay, male conversational exchanges often emphasize the establishment of maleness through choice of language and the explicit enunciation of heterosexist norms (Herring, 2001). Other researchers have argued that in digital gameplay it is even more important for males to establish aggressive masculinity through language precisely because the male body is not present and can only be elicited through speech (Alix, 2007).

When a female steps onto the playing field as an equal, it is disruptive to deeply engrained cultural norms that males are different from females, males are better/stronger/more competent than females, and that males are more aggressive/competitive than females. In cultures where heterosexist cultural norms are especially powerful, in those very few sporting/play activities where males compete on the same level as females, the sport is branded as somehow 'gay' or appropriate only for homosexual men. In the USA these activities include competitive horseback riding events, such as dressage and hunter/jumper competitions, and dance of any kind.[5] The fact that calling someone or some activity 'gay' remains an insult, further underscores the tenacity of traditional binary gender roles in both analog and digital play activities.

The devaluation of the female in the culture at large creates a dilemma when males and females do compete. The stakes are particularly high for a male in this situation, especially if there are spectators. When a male is competing against a female, he is in a lose/lose situation. If he defeats his female opponent, it is not much of a victory, because the cultural expectation is that she is weak anyway. Beating an opponent that is known to be weaker can actually be seen as a kind of humiliation for the winner in this context. If he loses to the female, however, his defeat is compounded by the humiliation of having been defeated by 'a girl.' If this occurs in front of male spectators he is likely to hear about it for a long time afterward.

Female Unwillingness to Excel at Cross-Gender Play

Can we then assume that cross-gender competition is a win/win situation for females? If the female loses against the male, she is still admired for having dared to challenge someone 'superior' to her. If she wins, however, her victory has a different sort of taint to it. There are several terms in western culture for women who dominate men: 'shrew,' 'bitch' and 'ballbreaker' are examples. A man who is dominated by a woman can be called 'pussy-whipped' among other such terms.

Although a woman who defeats a man publicly at play does enjoy the extra status of beating a 'tough' opponent, she also risks being branded with one of these extremely negatively-valenced terms. If for a male, being beaten by a female is a form of emasculation, then the female who beats him is the agent. She, by winning, risks emasculating him. This is its own sort of catch-22. The female athlete, like any other athlete, simply wants to defeat anyone else in her class. She wants to compete against, and hopefully defeat the strongest contestants in her sport. In competing against a male, however, she has other stakes to consider. If she wins, she demonstrates her own superiority and at the same time is potentially responsible for inflicting a sort of societal harm upon her opponent.

Given the cultural norms that correlate femininity with passivity, females who dare to compete and win at the same level as males often find it necessary to emphasize the fact that they remain sexually 'female.' Florence Joyner, a world record holder in track and field, was notorious for her bright pink running suits and impossibly long nails. Female tennis, a sport long associated with powerful women and lesbianism (Nelson, 1994), now has female players who emphasize their femininity with the type of clothing they wear and their off-court behavior. A recent article in the *New York Times* on top-level female chess players pointed out that the top women players are ranked not only on how well they play the game, but also on their looks (Mclain, 2005). Such behavior suggests that women are not just focusing on success in the game, but are at the same time concerned with protecting their status as sexually viable females, because they feel that this status may be threatened by their successes in play. This may in part explain why hypersexualized avatars are often chosen as self-representations.

Another reason for choosing not to defeat males is that the act of doing so may make it more difficult for the female athlete to have sexual relationships with males. Given that male/female sexual relationships continue to reflect cultural stereotypes, a female who is known as someone capable of defeating males (thus potentially emasculating them) may encounter difficulties finding male sexual partners off the playing field. In my game design classes, I routinely ask the males in the class if they would date someone who is able to beat them at the games they consider themselves best at. They always say 'No,' except for the few that say 'It depends how hot she is.' Given the societal cost of defeating men, it is not a surprise that many women prefer to maintain their status as sexually attractive rather than choosing to be winners.

The 'it depends' comment just mentioned, however, does seem to indicate a change in attitudes. There has been a definite increase in the portrayal of strong, competitive athletic females as sexually attractive. Some female singers, such as Madonna, for example, include physically challenging routines in their performances that show off their sleekly muscled bodies. Advertisements for sportswear aimed at females are now often images of powerful-looking women making statements that suggest that they revel in their athletic abilities. 'Working out' is now a common activity among females both old and young, and many popular women's magazines promote a more physically powerful female self-image (*Fitness, Self,* and *Women's Health,* for example).

Some have argued, however, that the importance of fitness can be seen as just another way of pressuring women to obsess about and objectify their bodies, rather than in fact empowering women (Markula, 2001; Tiggemann and Williamson, 2000). Researchers and doctors who deal with anorexic patients have noted that there are pro-anorexia websites, where girls compete to see who can get by on the least amount of food per day and/or work out for the longest amount of time (Williams, 2006). Ryan's (1995) work on sports such as ice-skating and gymnastics found that these sports promote an ideal of fitness which is in fact damaging to a healthy adult female body, and which idealizes traditional norms of femininity:

The anachronistic lack of ambivalence about femininity in both sports is part of their attraction, hearkening back to a simpler time when girls were girls, when women were girls for that matter: coquettish, malleable, eager to please. In figure skating especially, we want our athletes thin, graceful, deferential and cover-girl pretty. (Ryan, 1995: 25)

These analyses suggest that play activities may provide women with physical, mental and emotional strength, and help them become more competent and capable in many areas of life, but that for some, the recent emphasis on fitness for women perpetuates an ethos in which females manipulate their bodies, sometimes in explicitly damaging ways, in order to be more attractive to males.

Women on Top

. . . Males tend to use play as a way of determining their rank and status within a group. Ranking in the group is achieved by ability/success at the game in question. Rank is mobile. A male can raise or lower his ranking by his play performance at any given time. One of the appealing things about play is that, unlike 'real life,' there is always the chance to play the game again. There is always the opportunity to make the attempt to prove yourself as better than you were the last time. DeBoer points out that although males are playing for the team, they are also always playing for themselves. Better individual performance (within limits) is better for the team overall. Males tend to want each other to excel, and respect each other for the levels of excellence achieved (DeBoer, 2004; Vincent, 2006). Competitiveness between males is overt, socially acceptable and rewarded by status.

Competitiveness between females is much more problematic. Generally it is not overt, and often it does not lead to positive outcomes. Recent books such as *Odd Girl Out* and the film *Mean Girls* (Mark Waters, UK, 2004) have documented the 'culture of hidden female aggression' (Simmons, 2002).

Overt female aggression and competitiveness have long been discouraged, but this does not signify that females are any less interested in achieving higher status and pursuing their own personal best interests. Evolutionary theory demonstrates that there is always competition for scarce resources and status within groups. Discouraged, and often punished by cultural norms, female aggression is often more subtle, nuanced and emotionally wounding. Unlike males who can publicly challenge one another to a contest, females tend to express aggression through social shunning and verbal harassment. It is much more difficult to confront this kind of aggression. It is also very complicated for an individual female to figure out how to improve her status.

Social status among young females continues to be determined by different criteria than it is among males. Rather than achieving status through physical strength, athletic skill, or intellectual achievement as is common among males, female rank is often determined by beauty, thinness, blondness, and attractiveness to males. Unfortunately, this does not appear to have changed significantly over the last 20 years. In 1984, Weisfeld et al., in a study on social dominance in adolescence, found that: 'Boys seem to strive for social success mainly through competence in athletics, and girls through cultivating an attractive appearance' (1984: 115). When Simmons asked young girls the traits of the 'ideal girl,' the top five characteristics were: 'Very thin, Pretty, Blond, Fake, Stupid' (Simmons, 2002: 124). She summarizes her results: 'The ideal girl is stupid, yet manipulative. She is dependent and helpless, yet she uses sex and romantic attachments to get power. She is popular, yet superficial. She is fit, but not athletic or strong' (Simmons, 2002: 126). In a 2003 study on the importance of facial attractiveness to social ranking, the authors found that attractiveness was a significant factor in social dominance, and particularly so among females (Gary et al., 2003).

Female status appears to be determined by factors that are difficult to change (prettiness, thinness). It is thus much more difficult for a female to raise her status in the group. If she overtly competes against other females the way males can, there are societal costs. This affects how females engage in gameplay. Not only is overt competition discouraged, but it can also be punished by social ostracism and shunning. Girls learn to be cautious about whether or not to seek improved status within a group and how to go about achieving it. They may also be reluctant to engage in any kind of activity that further diminishes their status in the female hierarchy (becoming very physically fit and/or more dominant, for example). In digital gameplay, however, these considerations disappear. Any player can choose to represent him/herself as thin, blond, pretty and stupid, and all avatars are fake by definition. Digital play offers female players the opportunity to represent themselves in a way that makes them look like a high ranking analog female, but it also makes the ranking moot given that anyone can achieve it and many players do. . . .

In her book, *Female Chauvinist Pigs*, Ariel Levy (2005) describes . . . women who have succeeded in male dominated fields as 'loophole women' who enjoy and exploit the fact that there are few women around them, because this increases their uniqueness and cachet. They are, in fact, invested in ensuring that other women do NOT succeed in order to maintain this status.

An interview with a senior *World of Warcraft* (WOW) player (Lehtonen, 2007), however, suggests that the situation, at least in *WOW*, is more complicated. She points out that women who have invested a great deal of time and energy in raising their ranking in Massively-Multiplayer Online Roleplaying Games have done so generally through diligence, practice and careful construction of social relationships with other players. Hostility towards new

female players does exist, but only if those females come into the game and attempt to circumvent the laborious process of earning status in the group through 'serious' gameplay. Some females come into the game and use heteronormative feminine wiles, such as flirting and sexual innuendo, to attempt to make progress in the game by bonding with higher ranked males. This kind of behavior is extremely irritating to experienced female players because it undercuts the idea that females can and should gain status by earning it, the same way males do (Lehtonen, 2007) . . . .

Changing the Paradigm

Claude Steele developed the term 'stereotype threat' to describe the experience of members of a minority group within the context of a majority group. His studies have demonstrated that dominant stereotypes about minorities will affect performance in certain group situations (Spencer et al., 1999). Elite female gamers playing a complex digital shooting game such as *Counter-Strike* against almost exclusively male opponents are clearly operating in a situation of stereotype threat. They are not just playing the game (as all the other participants are), but they are concurrently disproving a number of stereotypes about females and aggressivity, technology, and willingness to challenge males. Steele has suggested strategies of 'wise schooling' to counteract the effects of stereotype threat in academic environments (Steele, 1997). These strategies include changing attitudes and increasing numbers.

The ability of minority populations to succeed in an environment from which they were previously excluded appears to be related to percentages. Once a certain numeric threshold has been crossed, members of the minority population are less likely to feel the effects of stereotype threat. A study that sought to determine why there remain so few women at high levels of *Fortune* 500 companies found that once a critical mass of three women on the board of a company has been reached, other participants stop viewing gender as the reason underlying female recommendations (Kramer et al., 2006).

Policy Implications

. . . If game designers are aware of issues related to cross-gender play, these can be relatively easily addressed. Additionally, schools and other institutions hoping to attract women to technology might consider the following suggestions.

(1) *Normalize cross-gender play and competition by making it frequent, routine and pleasurable.* In game worlds, this can be accomplished by having many more female characters present in game narratives, and by having them engage with player avatars across a wide range of activities. Stereotype threat can be countered by increasing the number of the members of a minority population present in the majority population and by providing numerous examples of characters that counter stereotypes.

(2) *Create a broad range of non-playable female characters and female avatars who have attributes not stereotypically considered 'female.'* Certainly popular media will always include traditional, stereotypical representations of women. But by broadening the range of females depicted, female and male players alike can choose to represent themselves as a variety of types of female (muscled and timid, thin, blond and blood-thirsty, maternal and insanely competitive, and so on).

(3) *Reinforce emerging perceptions of physically strong, competitive, aggressive females as sexually desirable.* Cultural norms that penalize women for challenging men are a potent deterrent. Females (like males) want very much to be attractive to others and are unlikely to engage in behavior that they perceive as minimizing their attractiveness. By consciously creating representations of females who successfully defy existing gender norms, new norms will be developed. Given that both male and female players will play as female avatars, perceptions can be changed across genders.

(4) *Increase the number of female players and female avatars in digital games.* Games that have large numbers of female avatars and players, *Second Life* and *Sims* games, for example, are potential models for change. . . .

Notes

1. This is to differentiate digital games such as *Solitaire, Tetris,* or other games which do not require specialized equipment, software, or training, from games including *World of Warcraft, Counter-Strike, Civilization IV* and others, which are much more complicated to learn and play.

2. It is currently estimated that 16 percent of *WOW* players are female (Yee, 2006) while a surprising 46 percent of *SIMS* players are male (Microsoft, 2004).

3. See E. Castronova's article on gendered avatar pricing for an example of how these stereotypes are concretized economically (Castronova, 2003).

4. 'In 2004–5, there were 4334 girls competing in wrestling on the high school level. This total has increased every year since 1990. This actual number is much higher, as some states that have women competitors do not report them' (Abbott, 2006).

5. The film *Billy Elliot* (Stephen Daldry, UK, 2000) explored the gender issues of ballet.

References

AAUW (2000) *Tech Savvy.* Washington, DC: American Association of University Women Educational Foundation.

Abbott, G. (2006) 'Women's High School Wrestling Continues Growth with CIF Regional Tournaments,' *TheMat.com* (USA Wrestling), URL (accessed June 2008): http://www.themat.com/index.php?page=showarticle&ArticleID=13874

Alix, A. (2007) 'Online Game Talk and the Articulation of Maleness,' in *Flow TV 5* (special issue on video games). University of Texas at Austin. URL (accessed June 2008): http://flowtv.org/?p=53

Bertozzi, E. (2003) 'At Stake: Play, Pleasure and Power in Cyberspace,' PhD dissertation, European Graduate School, URL (accessed June 2008): http://www.egs.edu/resources/elena-bertozzi.html

Bertozzi, E. and Lee, S. (2007) 'Not Just Fun and Games: Digital Play, Gender and Attitudes Towards Technology,' *Women's Studies in Communication* 30(2): 179–204.

Broverman, I. K., Vogel, S. R., Broverman, D. M., Clarkson, F. E. and Rosenkrantz, P. S. (1972) 'Sex Role Stereo types: A Current Appraisal,' *Journal of Social Issues* 28(2): 59–78.

Butler, J. (1990) *Gender Trouble: Feminism and the Subversion of Identity.* New York: Routledge.

Cassell, J. and Jenkins, H. (1998) *From Barbie to Mortal Kombat: Gender and Computer Games.* Cambridge, MA: MIT Press.

Castronova, E. (2003) *The Price of 'Man' and 'Woman': A Hedonic Pricing Model of Avatar Attributes in a Synthetic World* (CESifo Working Paper Series No. 957). Munich: CESifo.

CNN (2003) CNN News night with Aaron Brown, 22 May, URL (accessed May 2003): http://transcripts.cnn.com/TRANSCRIPTS/0305/22/asb.00.html

CNN (2004) 'University Asks Police to Look Into Alleged Rape,' URL (accessed 5 December 2005): http://www.cnn.com/2004/US/Central/02/18/colorado.football/

Connell, R. W. (1987) *Gender and Power: Society, the Person and Sexual Politics.* Stanford, CA: Stanford University Press.

Conway, M. and Vartanian, L. R. (2000) 'A Status Account of Gender Stereotypes: Beyond Communality and Agency,' *Sex Roles* 43(3–4): 499–528.

DeBoer, K. J. (2004). *Gender and Competition: How Men and Women Approach Work and Play Differently.* Monterey, CA: Coaches Choice.

Dillon, B. (2006) E3 Panel: 'Analyzing World Markets,' *Gamasutra Industry News,* URL (accessed June 2008): http://www.gamasutra.com/php-bin/news_index.php?story=9298

Dowling, C. (2000) *The Frailty Myth.* New York: Random House.

Gary, L. A., Hinmon, S. and Ward, C. A. (2003) 'The Face as a Determining Factor for Social Manipulation: Relational Aggression, Sociometric Status, and Facial Appearance,' *Colgate University Journal of the Sciences,* pp. 93–114, URL (accessed June 2008): http://groups.colgate.edu/cjs/student_papers/2003/Garyetal.pdf

Hack, D. (2006) 'Dealing with the Wind is a Challenge in Hawaii,' *New York Times* Sports Section, Sunday 15 January: 2.

Hargreaves, J. A. (1990) 'Gender on the Sports Agenda,' *International Review for the Sociology of Sport* 25(4): 287–307.

Heintz-Knowles, D. K. (2001) *Fair Play? Violence, Gender and Race in Video Games.* Oakland, CA: Children Now.

Herring, S. (2001) 'Gender and Power in Online Communication,' CSI Working Paper no. WP-01–05, URL (accessed June 2008): http://rkcsi.indiana.edu/archive/CSI/WP/WP01–05B.html

Huizenga, J. (1955). *Homo Ludens: A Study of the Play-Element in Culture.* Boston, MA: Beacon Press.

Jeffrey, T. (2004) 'Ban Girls from Football,' *Townhall.com,* URL (accessed June 2008): http://www. townhall.com/columnists/Terence Jeffrey/2004/02/26/ban_girls_from_football

Kramer, V., Konrad, A. and Erkut, S. (2006) 'Critical Mass on Corporate Boards: Why Three or More Women Enhance Governance,' available from Wellesely Centers for Women's Publications, URL (accessed June 2008): http://www.wcwonline.org/

Lehtonen, E. (2007) In-person interview and email communication with author. (Lehtonen is a World of Warcraft Guild member; character: Jaspre, title: Ascent Position: 2nd Officer.)

Levy, A. (2005) *Female Chauvinist Pigs: Women and the Rise of Raunch Culture*. New York: Free Press.

Lucas, K. and Sherry, J. L. (2004) 'Sex Differences in Video Game Play: A Communication-Based Explanation,' *Communication Research* 31(5): 499–523.

Markula, P. (2001) 'Beyond the Perfect Body: Women's Body Image Distortion in Fitness Magazine Discourse,' *Journal of Sport and Social Issues* 25(2): 158–79.

Martin, C. L. and Ruble, D. (2004) 'Children's Search for Gender Cues: Cognitive Perspectives on Gender Development,' *Current Directions in Psychological Science* 13(2): 67–70.

Mclain, D. L. (2005) 'Sex and Chess. Is She a Queen or a Pawn?,' *New York Times* 27 November: 1.

Messner, M. (2002) *Taking the Field: Women, Men, and Sports*. Minneapolis: University of Minnesota Press.

Microsoft (2004) 'Women Get in the Game,' Microsoft, URL (accessed June 2008): http://www.microsoft.com/presspass/features/2004/jan04/01–08womengamers.mspx

Nelson, M. B. (1994) *The Stronger Women Get, the More Men Love Football: Sexism and the American Culture of Sports*. New York: Harcourt Brace.

Oxford, N. (2005) 'Venus or Mars: The Uneasy Relationship Between Gaming and Gender,' *1up,* URL (accessed June 2008): http://www.1up.com/do/feature?cId=3141723

Ray, S. G. (2004) *Gender Inclusive Game Design: Expanding the Market*. Boston, MA: Charles River Media.

Roberts, S. (2005) *A Necessary Spectacle: Billie Jean King, Bobby Riggs, and the Tennis Match that Leveled the Game*. New York: Crown Publishers.

Roth, A. (2004) 'Femininity, Sports, and Feminism,' *Journal of Sport and Social Issues* 28(3): 245–65.

Ryan, J. (1995) *Little Girls in Pretty Boxes: The Making and Breaking of Elite Gymnasts and Figure Skaters*. New York: Doubleday.

Schleiner, A.-M. (1998) 'Does Lara Croft Wear Fake Polygons?,' *Switch*, URL (accessed June 2008): http://switch.sjsu.edu/web/v4n1/annmarie.html

Serbin, L. A., Poulin-Dubois, D., Colburne, K. A., Sen, M. G. and Eichstedt, J. A. (2001) 'Gender Stereotyping in Infancy: Visual Preferences for and Knowledge of Gender-Stereotypical Toys in the Second Year,' *International Journal of Behavioral Development* 25(1): 7–15.

Simmons, R. (2002) *Odd Girl Out: the hidden culture of aggression in girls*. New York: Harcourt Inc.

Slimmer, J. (2007) 'Kings, Queens, and Jackasses: Playing with Gender in Online Poker,' *Flow TV 5* (special issue on video games). University of Texas at Austin, URL (accessed June 2008): http://flowtv.org/?p=52

Spencer, S. J., Steele, C. M. and Quinn, D. M. (1999) 'Stereotype Threat and Women's Math Performance,' *Journal of Experimental Social Psychology* 35(1): 4–28.

Steele, C. M. (1997) 'A Threat in the Air: How Stereotypes Shape Intellectual Identity and Performance,' *American Psychologist* 52(6): 613–29.

Taylor, T. L. (2006) *Play Between Worlds: Exploring Online Game Culture*. Cambridge, MA: MIT Press.

Tiggemann, M. and Williamson, S. (2000) 'The Effect of Exercise on Body Satisfaction and Self-Esteem as a Function of Gender and Age,' *Sex Roles* 43(1–2): 119–27.

Tolman, D. L., Spencer, R., Rosen-Reynoso, M. and Porche, M. V. (2003) 'Sowing the Seeds of Violence in Heterosexual Relationships: Early Adolescents Narrate Compulsory Heterosexuality,' *Journal of Social Issues* 59(1): 159–78.

Vincent, N. (2006) *Self-Made Man: One Woman's Journey into Manhood and Back Again*. New York: Viking.

Waem, A., Larsson, A. and Neren, C. (2005) 'Gender Aspects on Computer Game Avatars,' paper presented at the ACM SIGCHI International Conference on *Advances in Computer Entertainment Technology* at the Swedish Institute of Computer Science, Valencia Spain, URL (accessed June 2008): ftp://ftp.sics.se/pub/SICS-reports/Reports/SICS-T—2005–06—SE.pdf

Weisfeld, G. E., Bloch, S. A. and Ives, J. W. (1984) 'Possible Determinants of Social Dominance Among Adolescent Girls,' *Journal of Genetic Psychology* 144(1): 115–29.

Williams, A. (2006) 'Before Spring Break, the Anorexic Challenge,' *New York Times* Sunday Styles 2. April: 1.

Yalom, M. (2004) *Birth of the Chess Queen: A History.* New York: HarperCollins Publishers.

Yee, N. (2004) 'Avatar: Use/Conceptualization and Looking Glass Self': Terranova Blog, URL (accessed 17 May 2006): http://terranova.blogs.com/terra_nova/2004/01/the_avatar_and_.html

Yee, N. (2006) 'WoW Gender-Bending' Daedalus Project, URL (accessed 2 April 2006): http://www.nickyee.com/daedalus/archives/001369.php

PART VII

IS TV FOR REAL?

In this part, we focus on two forms of relatively unscripted TV programming: so-called reality TV and talk shows. In both genres, while audiences for the most part understand that the content is far from completely spontaneous, the appeal lies to a large extent in the voyeuristic expectation that we are going to catch glimpses of "real life." This makes it all the more important in a book that aims to cultivate greater media literacy that we look closely at such texts and learn how to see through and beyond their surface appearances and evaluate their claim to "reality."

At the outset, putting these individual television texts within the context of political economy helps ensure that we see how they work within and for the media industries globally. Chris Jordan's chapter (VII.50) on the wildly popular *Survivor* series explores "why reality television is a global staple of domestic and international prime time television" and concludes that such shows fit the needs of producers, networks, and advertisers in an age of global television. The formulas of a reality TV series lend themselves particularly well to international franchising. Jordan's study shows that

> *Survivor*'s relatively low cost and high ratings potential made the show imminently marketable worldwide. . . . Overseas broadcasters that have licensed the American format of *Survivor* and created their own versions include China's CCTV, the Middle East satellite

platform Gulf DTH, South Africa's SABC, Mexico's Televisa, and stations in Scandinavia, Eastern Europe, and throughout Asia. (p. 462)

The "relatively low cost" of such reality shows has been profitable for the owners of media companies, but it has had a detrimental effect on the employees who work to put such shows together. According to Andrew Ross (VII.51), because the producers and editors of reality shows were not deemed "writers" by employers, they were excluded from the recent partial victory won through the strike of creative employees by the Writers Guild of America (2008–2009).

As a result, the sector teems with substandard conditions—eighteen-hour work days, chronic job instability, no meal breaks, no health benefits, and employer coercion to turn in time cards early. Wage rates are generally *half* of what employees on scripted shows are paid, and most overtime goes unpaid. When employees of *America's Top Model* voted to join the WGA in summer of 2006, they were summarily fired. (p. 467)

Ross reminds us of the human costs of "the longstanding capitalist dream of stripping labor costs to the bone" in this rare critical look into the economic realities behind the scenes at reality TV program production.

Reality TV programming has come under fire in many critical quarters as a mindless form of entertainment, yet there are those who suggest that it has some progressive potential. For example, Debra C. Smith (VII.52) argues that (relatively) "unscripted 'reality' television has the capacity to present . . . Black family life in 'authentically' complex ways." She offers a cautiously positive reading of two reality shows featuring African American fatherhood and produced by African American male hip-hop celebrities Calvin Broadas (Snoop Dogg) and Joseph Simmons (Rev. Run of Run-DMC). Smith sees in these cable network reality

shows the possibility of counterhegemonic imagery in a post-*Cosby* era. She points also to the capacity of reality shows to display a welcome class diversity in the portrayals of Black family life from the perspectives of the new generation of African American producers. In her view,

The "safer" show, *Run's House*, demonstrates template-like similarities to Cosby, while *Father Hood* further drives behind the scenes to show the audience working-class realities consistent with Snoop's intentional opposition to Cosby's reality. (p. 478)

Drawing on viewer responses from the online websites of these shows, Smith analyzes the themes of father presence, fathers' disciplinary styles, and Black fathers as role models, concluding that these shows provide "much-needed visibility to alternative constructions of Black fatherhood/family."

Sharon Sharp's chapter (VII.53) on current media constructions of the housewife in what she calls "televisual discourse" takes a less sanguine view. Exploring the conventions of domestic reality television, such as Lifetime Television's *How Clean Is Your House?*, ABC's *Super Nanny,* and several wife swap shows, as well as the popular dramatic series *Desperate Housewives,* Sharp argues that domestic reality television

invites viewers inside the domestic sphere, where they discover that housewifery, motherhood and domesticity can be exhausting, empty and unfulfilling. Unlike the happy housewives idealised in sitcoms of the past, the housewives who are regularly swapped, scrutinised and shamed on domestic reality television are decidedly ambivalent, frustrated, overworked, neurotic and unhappy. (p. 482)

For Sharp, while the emphasis on the housewife's problems might seem to open space for a feminist critique of current family and gender arrangements, this promise is not fulfilled. Rather, "the new televisual discourse on the housewife blames individual women for problems of domesticity and invites viewers to feel superior" (p. 486). On balance, she finds that these shows "confirm dominant cultural beliefs about traditional gender roles as they ridicule housewives for their perfectionism and ambivalence about motherhood and domesticity" (p. 482).

Many critics of reality television place the genre within the context of the social and political context from the 1980s to the present, when Western industrial nations, including the United States, developed the "neoliberal" social policies that are based on the key belief that, according to the formulation of Laurie Ouellette (VII.54), the "free" market is "the best way to organize every dimension of social life." Ouellette's chapter invites us to see the long-running and popular courtroom reality show, *Judge Judy*, as a fusion of "television, neoliberalism, and self-help discourse" that "attempts to shape and guide the conduct and choices of lower-income women in particular" (pp. 488–489).

"Judge Judy," the former New York family court judge Judith Sheindlin, "plays judge, prosecutor, professional expert, and punctilious moral authority, handling an average of two cases per thirty-minute episode." Sheindlin is known for her no-nonsense treatment of the working-class people in financial and/or family trouble who appear in her simulated TV courtroom, having agreed to accept her decision as final. As Judge Judy, she offers "citizenship lessons" to those who are constructed as failing in their economic and familial responsibilities—especially couples who live together without marriage and people who must apply for public assistance. As Ouellette points out, in this show's version of "reality,"

> all women are presumed to be capable of supporting themselves and their children financially; accepting welfare is construed not as a reflection of gender or economic inequality but as a character flaw. (p. 493)

Janice Peck (VII.55) offers a similar critique of the neoliberal ideology embedded in Oprah Winfrey's media productions across a wide range of platforms, including *The Oprah Winfrey Show,* upon which Winfrey's immense cultural influence and fortune was built over the past quarter of a century. Using the "brand" of Oprah Winfrey as a cultural text, Peck points to the global impact that Oprah's key message of self-empowerment (especially for women) has had in an era of a widening gaps in resources between rich and poor, as well as shrinking government services to citizens. Against this backdrop, Peck examines Oprah's unifying theme of the "absolutely unlimited power within us." For Peck, this idea is part of "an ensemble of ideological practices that help legitimize a world of growing inequality and shrinking possibilities by promoting and embodying a configuration of self compatible with that world" (pp. 500–501).

While the concept of self-empowerment for women was first articulated within a liberal feminist discourse in the 1980s, it has since been repackaged for a "postfeminist" age, as several chapters in this part and elsewhere in the book point out. A particularly interesting example is what Sue Tait (VII.56) calls "the domestication of cosmetic surgery" in which television plays a significant role. Tait's study links the reality show *Extreme Makeover* with the edgy dramatic series *Nip/Tuck,* as manifestations and media vehicles of the "culture's surgical turn"—that is, the disappearance of prior negative associations with this radical approach to improving one's appearance. In contrast to surgical reality shows, Tait argues, "*Nip/Tuck*'s response to surgical culture provides moments of resistance." Yet these textual gestures in the direction of a critical perspective on the ideological underpinnings of cosmetic surgery are "frequently overwhelmed by the requirement to render the surgeon characters as redeemable, and by a sensationalism which prefers the dramatic over the political" (p. 516). In Tait's view, neither show challenges "a culture that is inevitably surgical," and she concludes critically,

> As these two shows illustrate, feminist responses to cosmetic surgery are overwhelmed by a post-feminism which asserts our right to shape ourselves. (p. 561)

Cosmetic surgery reality television is just one manifestation of the seemingly insatiable appetite in media audiences today for the "makeover" story, with bodily "self-improvement" front and center, especially for women. But for those celebrities who build successful media careers on the promise of empowerment through self-transformation, such as supermodel Tyra Banks, the host of *America's Next Top Model* and her own talk show, the slightest lapse in bodily self-discipline can lead to virulent media culture scrutiny and public humiliation, often with racialized gender implications.

According to Ralina Joseph's chapter (VII.57), when Banks gained some weight and was exposed by sensational tabloid reporting and other celebrity media as "fat," she was initially able to use her own talk show as a way to speak back defiantly to her accusers on behalf of herself and "other women who are built like me." Joseph sees this as a "rare moment" in popular culture when the hegemonic ideology of "postracism" and **"postfeminism"**

is "ruptured," whatever the subsequent retreat to "embracing the scale" in this case may have been.

In our final chapter in this Part, Candace Moore (VII.58) presents another example of a talk show in which forbidden truths about the celebrity host rupture the smooth surface of social harmony. Ellen DeGeneres, the stand-up comic who famously "came out" as a lesbian on her sitcom in 1997, has since adopted what is called "an everywoman approach" on her talk show, launched in 2003. According to Moore, DeGeneres "avoids the topic of her own homosexuality and actively closes down conversation in which the very word or concept comes up" (p. 531). However, by closely analyzing the persona and self-presentation of DeGeneres on this show, Moore is able to see a strategy more subtle than simply denying her lesbianism or returning to the closet, as some of her critics would have it. Moore argues that "she performs queerness through what implicitly 'exceeds' her stand-up jokes and sit-down talk, and, physically, through the ritual action of her daily dance sequence" (p. 532).

Through these methods, perhaps DeGeneres escapes being such a "convenient screen" for hate-mongers or bearing the responsibility of being a spokesperson for all of gay America, while she still maintains a *televisibility* of queer identity.

Marketing "Reality" to the World

Survivor, Post-Fordism, and Reality Television

Chris Jordan

. . . . This chapter analyzes the production, distribution, and consumption of *Survivor* in order to explain why reality television is a global staple of domestic and international prime time television.[1] It argues that intensifying concentration of ownership in the television industry, the worldwide proliferation of commercial television, the fragmentation of the global television audience, and the design of *Survivor,* as a thinly veiled advertisement, account for its success.

The centrifugal trends of media industry ownership concentration and global television audience fragmentation exemplify post-Fordism. . . . The Fordist system of manufacturing and marketing strove to maximize profits by making one commodity appeal to as many consumers as possible for as long as possible (Harvey 145). Under post-Fordism, capitalism responds to the global flow of labor and consumption markets within and between nation-states by transforming local and regional cultures into market segments and mobilizing citizens as consumers. By implementing a post-Fordist strategy of diversifying its products and their marketing in order to incorporate diverse locales, capitalism transforms a problem into an opportunity, as it markets products for both global markets and niche segments to take advantage of the countervailing flows of localism and globalism (Fiske, "Global" 58).

Stuart Hall contends that post-Fordism promotes democracy by globally circulating media products and other consumer goods (62). Reality television programs thus flow both ways between the United States and other nations. As John Fiske argues, globalization thus provokes localization, multiplying histories through migration and diaspora and eroding a sense of nationalism built around the interests of dominant groups ("Global"). . . .

From Jordan, C. (2006). Marketing "reality" to the world: *Survivor,* post-Fordism, and reality television. In D. Escoffery (Ed.), *How real is reality TV? Essays on representation and truth* (pp. 78–96). Jefferson, NC: McFarland & Co.

Production of Reality Television: The Medium Is the Advertiser's Message

. . . . Charlie Parsons and former rock band singer Bob Geldof developed the concept that became *Survivor* at their British TV production company, Planet 24. When Parsons and Geldof sold Planet 24 in 1999, they retained the rights to *Survive!*, which was being produced in Sweden by the duo's Castaway Productions, under the name *Expedition: Robinson*. The next year, Parsons and Geldof licensed the *Survive!* concept to Mark Burnett, for a U.S. version that ended up launching the reality TV craze in America.

As an independent producer, Burnett faced an uphill battle in gaining access to prime time, because the relaxation of government regulations in the 1990s made it possible for networks to produce many of their own shows. In 2000, all six broadcast networks either owned or co-owned more than half of their new shows, and three of them (ABC, CBS, and WB) owned or co-owned more than 75 percent of their new programs (Schneider and Adalian 70).

Survivor appealed to CBS because the co-production deal it struck with Burnett required no deficit financing, yet offered the network a program with the high quality production values that audiences expect of prime time television. Instead of paying Burnett a fee to license the show, CBS agreed to share the show's advertising revenue with him if he pre-sold sponsorship of the program. By pre-selling the show, Burnett raised the capital necessary to produce *Survivor*, provided CBS with essentially free prime time programming, and enjoyed a hefty share of the show's advertising revenue.

Advertisers readily sponsored *Survivor* because of its design as a virtual commercial for their products. Burnett acquired eight sponsors before the commencement of principal photography during the first season, selling not only 30-second spots, but also sponsorship space in the show itself. Anheuser-Busch, General Motors, Visa, Frito-Lay, Reebok, and Target paid approximately $4 million each for advertising time, product placement in the show, and a website link (McCarthy, "Sponsors" B1). Even though *Survivor* is one of the most expensive reality shows to date, with production costs escalating from $1 million an episode for the first season to $1.5 million an episode for subsequent editions, it is profitable. With presold sponsorships covering production costs, and 30-second spots commanding $445,000 during the 2001–2002 season, *Survivor* proved that lavishly produced reality television shows could be low-risk and lucrative (Raphael 122).

Burnett's success in pitching *Survivor* to advertisers enabled the producer to circumvent the role of the advertising agency as a liaison between program creator and sponsor, making it even more cost efficient for sponsors. Producers started working directly with products' brand managers, moving away from shows such as *Temptation Island*, with overt sexual innuendo, and towards shows such as *Survivor* (see Littleton). Praised by CBS President Les Moonves as a "great pitchman," Burnett steered away from sexual sensationalism and towards themes of competitive merit, by explaining to advertisers "how much sense it would make for someone on an island a million miles from home to crave a soft drink or something to eat from home" ("Burnett Likes Mad Ave" 3).

At one time, advertisers balked at the insertion of a bag of chips or a soda into a situation comedy or drama, because it might break the audience's suspension of disbelief. However, *Survivor* host Jeff Probst's act of rewarding winners of the show's challenges with Doritos and Mountain Dew integrated the products into a circumstance that abstracted the line between programming and advertising by associating them with adventure and heroism. During *Survivor: Africa*, for example, the word "avalanche" was the answer to a reward challenge.

Viewers then saw the winner driving a Chevrolet Avalanche across the African plain to deliver medical supplies to hospitals treating AIDS patients (McCarthy "Sponsors" B1). In 2001, Burnett received $14 million from marketers such as Mountain Dew and General Motors for the production of *Survivor: Africa* (McCarthy, "Also Starring" B1).

The design of *Survivor* as a virtual advertisement raises the issue of how television's goal of selling audiences to advertisers shapes the program. According to Sut Jhally, a television program must be able to attract large numbers of people. Second, it has to attract the "right" kinds of people. Not all parts of the audience are of equal value to advertisers. Television programs will also have to reflect this targeting, excluding demographic groups that lack the spending power to satisfy advertisers. Third, television must not only be able to deliver a large number of the correct people to advertisers, but must also deliver them in the right frame of mind. Programs should be designed to enhance the effectiveness of the ads in them (Jhally 76).

Survivor accomplishes all of these goals. Broadcast during prime time, it attracts a teen demographic sought by advertisers as well as a huge national audience composed of other age groups. According to *Variety*, *Survivor* delivered during its initial season more teens than *WWF Smackdown*, more young adults than *Friends*, more children than *Wonderful World of Disney*, and more 50-plus viewers than *60 Minutes* (Kissell 19). Rejecting the jittery hand-held camera style of public television documentaries of the 1970s, *Survivor* also boasts high quality production values that associate products woven into its text with adventure, heroism, and escape.

Survivor thus appeals to networks and advertisers because it combines high ratings with relatively low cost in comparison to comedies and dramas. The escalating cost of must-have sport and movie properties, and the success of special effects-driven docudramas such as BBC-Discovery's *Walking with Dinosaurs* during the 2000 television season, put drama budgets under scrutiny and encouraged U.S. producers to co-produce much more drama on the terms of European networks. Compounding the shift away from half-hour comedy shows and towards low-cost reality-entertainment hybrids was the lack of obvious successors to prime time smash hits such as *Seinfeld* [1989–1998] and *Friends* [1994–2004] (Fry M4). High quality production values and exotic locations became means through which *Survivor* targeted the prime time audience sought by advertisers, distinguished itself from cheaper crime-based reality shows, and blurred the line between prime time drama and reality shows ("TV's Peeper Producers Are Powerhouses" 1).

Reality television shows have thus proliferated on prime time television in recent years because they pose little financial risk for networks, yet offer prime-time-friendly production values and generate huge ratings. The use of Internet and cable television networks also attracts a young audience prized by advertisers. On this basis, *Survivor* became a valuable addition to Viacom's cradle-to-the-grave programming spectrum by enabling CBS, known for its primarily elderly audience, to capture a huge mass audience, as well as a slice of the highly coveted youth audience.

Distribution of *Survivor:* Creating a Global Franchise

. . . . While network television enables advertisers to target a huge audience, cable and the Internet can target specific viewer demographics and deliver them to advertisers at a lower cost. Viacom's cross-promotion of *Survivor* on CBS, its cable networks MTV and VH1, and its Internet websites CBS.com and MTV Networks Online enabled CBS to capture a young audience during the show's first episode and deliver it to advertisers along with a mass audience of 15.5 million. During its second week, the show attracted 18.1 million viewers, a 17 percent gain (Schneider and Adalian 70). According to *Variety, Survivor* "gave CBS and Viacom tangible proof that corporate synergy works," by being the first CBS program to get the full marketing treatment from Viacom's youthful properties, MTV and VH1 (Kissell and Schneider 19).

CBS's use of the Internet also promoted interactivity between viewers and *Survivor,* allowing the network to extend the program beyond the confines of the television set, by encouraging audiences to participate in its dramatic trajectory by using other media to stay in touch with the show. Viewers stayed in touch with the program through the official *Survivor* website. Prolific coverage from established news outlets also generated several unsanctioned online homages, as the websites *Survivor* Junkie and Megadice offered winner predictions, plot spoilers, conspiracy theories, and other information of varying quality (Bing and Oppelaar 5). Mobile media, such as cellular telephones, offer additional means of promoting this interactivity and provide valuable information about the audience that is impossible to gather from any other source. Text-based advertising campaigns have been conducted in various countries by major brands, including Coca-Cola, Nike, and McDonald's (McCartney C1).

The ability of Viacom to endlessly promote *Survivor* across multiple media improved CBS's ability to quickly capture a large audience, during an era in which the network practice of ordering shows in small batches makes it imperative to transform a new show into a smash hit as quickly as possible. Variety observed that "the numbers for *Survivor* all the more amazing given that *Survivor* had only 13 weeks to generate viewer interest and such a rabid following . . ." (Kissell and Schneider 19).

Survivor's relatively low cost and high ratings potential made the show imminently marketable worldwide, especially in the wake of CBS's purchase of television syndication giant, King World, in 1999. King World collaborates closely with international partners to produce shows carefully tailored to specific national markets, and creates customized promotional advertisements for international licensees (Compaine and Gomery 218). Overseas broadcasters that have licensed the American format of *Survivor* and created their own versions include China's CCTV, the Middle East satellite platform Gulf DTH, South Africa's SABC, Mexico's Televisa, and stations in Scandinavia, Eastern Europe, and throughout Asia (Guider 1).

The global popularity of *Survivor* is attributable, in part, to CBS's use of the economies of scale provided by the size of the U.S. television audience, to sell the program cheaply in developing countries. The proven commercial appeal of *Survivor*'s format, and the relatively low cost of reality television production, also encourage foreign broadcasters to create their own versions of the program. . . .

The formation of advertising agencies with global reach provides evidence of the role of advertising in propagating the overseas proliferation of reality television. . . . Global consolidation is encouraged because the larger an advertising agency, the more leverage it has getting favorable terms for its clients with global commercial media (McChesney 86). "More and more, what (advertisers) want is to distribute their global dollars into fewer agency baskets," the *Wall Street Journal* observed in 1998 (Beatty 1).

The rise of transnational advertising agencies also enables sponsors such as Proctor & Gamble to penetrate developing countries with the offer of "free" programming, through which advertisers underwrite programming of general appeal, and provide it free of charge to financially struggling broadcasters (Schiller 330). The top 10 global advertisers alone accounted for some 75 percent of the $36 billion spent by the 100 largest global marketers in 1997 (McChesney 84). Advertising sponsorship thus plays a pivotal role in determining the type of programming made and broadcast by foreign television producers in their native markets.

The competition for audiences and advertisers created by the proliferation of broadcast, cable, and satellite television overseas has led broadcasters in other countries to seek low-cost programming with immediate ratings potential attractive to advertisers. . . .

The consequence of an increasing number of channels in formerly public television markets competing for funding and audiences is that broadcasters must spend greater and greater sums on marketing to get their shows noticed, intensifying pressures on program funding. The pressures on overseas networks to control production costs has in turn led to the concentration of television production in the hands of companies most able to supply low-cost, high volume programming. . . .

The adaptability of reality television shows to local cultures and the convertibility of the format into a virtual infomercial for sponsors' products raises a concern about the role of reality television in propagating the culture of consumption, in both the United States and other nations targeted by transnational capitalism. . . .

Consumption of Reality Television: Transforming Citizens into Consumers

The global success of reality television is attributable to the practice of licensing the format of a show to overseas broadcasters for adaptation to specific markets. The strategy of formatting springs from the principal of product differentiation, through which network executives attempt to replicate a successful show by blatantly imitating it. Hits are so rare on network television that network executives think that a bald imitation stands a better chance of getting ratings

than a show that stands alone. This results in the repackaging of old forms in slightly different permutations (Gitlin 77–85). In the wake of *Survivor*'s success, television executives aggressively pursued imitations of it, as the number of reality television hours on broadcast television skyrocketed from four-and-a-half to 19 hours a week between Fall, 2002 and Fall, 2004 (McNary 21).

Paralleling this proliferation of reality television programming was the repetition of what the *New York Times* called a "hamsters-in-a-box" narrative design. The strategy of casting individuals on the basis of type, and forcing them to work and live together, became cross-pollinated with various genres, including game shows, gross-out contests, makeovers, dating programs, situation comedies, and satires (Nussbaum 2). The minimal difference between these many shows stems from the pressure of the marketplace to duplicate a financially successful show.

Financed by advertisers interested in cultivating new consumers abroad, the development of reality television as a format that flexibly incorporates national ideologies on a nation-by-nation basis further suggests that reality TV is first and foremost a commodity. In licensing the *Survivor* format from a British production company, CBS found a program that can be tailored on a market-by-market basis around the world, by integrating the game show and the adventure drama into a hybrid formula. Rather than democratizing global television programming, this trend organizes citizens into consumers by reifying capitalism as an ideology and a way of life. The design of *Survivor* as a game show/adventure/drama hybrid facilitates the placement of products in competitive circumstances that blend adventure and consumption.

In this way, the premise of the show—game show competitors seeking adventure in exotic locations that render global politics invisible—fuels demand for a lifestyle of conspicuous consumption around the world. The director marketing for Sony's

AXN Action TV Network, on which *Survivor* airs in East Asia, exclaimed that "the focus on action and adventure is something that's really picking up—it's a new lifestyle for the young in Asia, a fact borne out by the rise in sales of four-by-four vehicles, for example" (Osborne 32).

The design of *Survivor* also affirms consumption as a way of life, both by attracting advertising and by enabling its producers to develop lucrative licensing deals that extend its shelf life. By organizing leisure time around the consumption of both these programs and pricey ancillary merchandise, *Survivor* encourages viewers to participate in a commodified system of exchange. While merchandising tie-ins have been around since the advent of television, they are now far more commonplace. There are now 150 *Survivor*-themed products available, ranging from CDs to bug spray, to board games, and bandanas (Madger 150). Reality television's organization of the audience into consumers socializes the public into behaving like a market, and as consumers rather than citizens.

Conclusion

This chapter argues that the worldwide proliferation of reality television is a product of the increasing concentration of ownership in the television industry, the globalization of commercial TV, and the fragmentation of the worldwide audience. The dependence of the U.S. and other governments on capital investment has led to the implementation of policies that enable the largest media corporations to curtail access to prime time television through in-house production and co-production, and by favoring programs that offer the lowest risk and the highest potential for ratings. The privatization of formerly public overseas broadcasters has also led television programmers in developing nations to seek out inexpensive programming capable of attracting advertisers and viewers.

The first casualty of this trend is educational programming. Television producers, advertisers, and networks know that programs that are too long, too difficult to comprehend, or simply too boring will lead viewers to switch channels. In this way, reality television turns attention away from issues such as poverty in developing countries. The victory of a contestant from the African country of Zambia over a competitor from Tanzania on *Big Brother Africa* provided, according to *Variety*, "a welcome distraction from nationwide strikes in the impoverished country, where most people earn less than $1 a day" (De Jager 19). While some celebrate reality television's global popularity as a sign of the democratization of television production and distribution, a political economic study of reality television compels us to consider that economic determinism limits the possibilities of reality television's potential for democratic communication.

Note

1. Prime time refers to a twenty-two hour weekly period spanning 8PM to 11PM Monday through Saturday, with an extra hour on Sunday.

References

Beatty, Sally. "Survey Expects Pace of Mergers to Pick Up on Madison Avenue." *Wall Street Journal* 21 May 1998: 1.

———. "Who Owns Prime Time? Industrial and Institutional Conflict over Television Programming and Broadcast Rights." *Framing Friction: Media and Social Conflict.* Ed. Mary S. Mander. Urbana: University of Illinois Press, 1999. 125–160.

Bing, Jonathan and Justin Oppelaar. "'Rat' Race to Publish 1st Survivor Book Begins." *Variety* 28 August–3 September 2000: 4.

"Burnett Likes Mad Ave." *Advertising Age* 19 May 2003: 3.

Compaine, Benjamin and Douglas Gomery. *Who Owns the Media?: Competition and Concentration in the Mass Media*. Mahwah, N.J.: Lawrence Erlbaum Associates, 2000.

De Jager, Christelle "Big Bro' Gives Reality New Meaning." *Variety* 15–21 September 2003: 19.

Fiske, John. "Global, National, Local? Some Problems of Culture in a Postmodern World." *Velvet light Trap* 40 (1997): 58–66.

Fry, Andy. "Europe Secure as Leader of Reality Programming." *Variety* 25 September–1 October 2000: M4.

Gitlin, Todd. *Inside Prime Time*. New York: Pantheon Books, 1983.

Guider, Elizabeth. "Eye Floats Survivor Worldwide." *Variety* 18 January 2001: 1.

Harvey, David. *The Condition of Post modernity*. Boston: Blackwell, 1989.

Jhally, Sut. "The Political Economy of Culture." *Cultural Politics in Contemporary America*, Eds. Ian Angus and Sut Jhally. New York: Routledge, 1989. 65–81.

Kissell, Rick. "Survivor Fittest in All Demos." *Variety* 31 July–6 August 2000: 20.

Kissell, Rick and Schneider, M., "Summer Serves as Eye-Opener." *Variety* 28 August–3 September 2000: 19.

Littleton, Cynthia. "Dialogue: Mark Burnett." *Hollywood Reporter*. 26 May 2004. 18 Aug. 2004 <www.hollywoodreporter.com/thr/crafts/feature/display.jsp?vnu_content_id=10011523184>

Madger, Ted. "The End of TV 101: Reality Programs, Formats, and the New Business of Television." *Reality TV: Remaking Television Culture*. Eds. Laurie Oullette and Susan Murray. New York: New York University Press, 2004: 137–156.

McCarthy, Michael. "Also Starring (Your Product Name Here); Brands Increasingly Make Presence Known in TV Shows." *USA Today* 12 August 2004: B1.

———. "Sponsors Line Up Survivor Sequel." *USA Today* 9 October 2004: B1.

McCartney, Neil. "Can You Hear It Now?" *Variety* 29 March–4 April 2004: C1.

McChesney, Robert W. *Rich Media, Poor Democracy: Communication Polities in Dubious Times*. New York: The New Press, 1999.

McNarv, Dave. "Coming to Terms with Reality." Variety 4–10 October 2004: 21.

Nussbaum, Emily. "The Woman Who Gave Birth to Reality TV." *Variety* 22 February 2004: 2.

Osborne, Magz. "AXN Packs Reality Fare, Hopes Viewers Will Follow." *Variety* 5–11 February 2001: 32.

Raphael, Chad. "The Political Economic Origins of Reality TV." *Reality TV: Remaking Television Culture*. Eds. Laurie Oullette and Susan Murray. New York: New York University Press, 2004. 119–136.

Schiller, Herbert. "The Privatization of Culture." *Cultural Polities in Contemporary America*. Eds. Ian Angus and Sut Jhally. New York: Routledge, 1989. 317–332.

Schneider, Michael and Joseph Adalian. "Nets Get It Together." *Variety* 22–28 May 2000: 15.

"TV's Peeper Producers are Powerhouses." *Variety* 25 September–1 October 2000: 1.

The Political Economy of Amateurism

Andrew Ross

The WGA (Writers Guild of America) strike of 2008–09 will no doubt be remembered for the writers' struggle to claim a revenue share from online versions of content to which they had contributed. In the public mind, this was generally seen as a fair claim. Why? Because surely creators of intellectual property deserve to enjoy the fruits of their labor. But who will remember what was bargained away in return for recognition of this right? Since 2005, one of the WGA's top campaign goals has been to organize employees of TV reality shows, and while union leaders entered the strike vowing to achieve this goal, the media moguls' ultimate condition for reaching an agreement over new media residuals was that WGA take off the table its claim for jurisdiction over the reality (and animation) sector. The upshot? Concessions to those who feed the copyright milk cow at the expense of the rights of below-the-line employees.

This raw deal speaks volumes about the ongoing restructuring of the creative industries (or the copyright industries, as they are more bluntly termed in the United States). Since 2001, the space allotted to reality TV and "challenge" game shows has ballooned to more than 20 percent of primetime network programming. The production costs are a fraction of what producers pay for conventional, scripted drama, and the ratings and profits have been mercurial. If these numbers are sustained, it is highly unlikely there will ever be a post-reality TV era. From the outset, owners have insisted that producers and editors are not "writers" who pen scripts and dialogue, and so the WGA was shut out of reality programming. As a result, the sector teems with substandard conditions—eighteen-hour work days, chronic job instability, no meal breaks, no health benefits, and employer coercion to turn in time cards early. Wage rates are generally *half of* what employees on scripted shows are paid, and most overtime goes unpaid. When employees of *America's Top Model* voted to join the WGA in summer of 2006, they were summarily fired. Workers on other shows have been threatened with blacklisting if they sought to organize.

From Ross, A. (2009). The political economy of amateurism. *Television & New Media, 10*(1), 136–137. © 2009 Sage Publications.

Nor are the contestants any better off than the production employees. If they are paid, it is generally a minimal stipend, and the price for their shot at exposure is to endure conditions—sleep deprived and plied with hard alcohol—that are designed to spark tension, conflict, and confrontation onscreen. A growing number of lawsuits, in the United States, United Kingdom, and France, are aimed at establishing legal protections for talent, as well as for writers, editors, and production assistants. In the fall of 2007, New Mexico's Attorney General investigated allegations that the producers of CBS's *Kid Nation* had violated child labor laws by forcing the participants, ages 8 to 15, to haul wagons, cook meals, manage stores, and clean latrines as part of the reality show.

These violations of work standards occur in the sector of old media that is most clearly aligned with the neoliberal ethos of the jackpot economy—we are all participants in a game that rewards only a few, and the price of entry is modeled after the privations of the "struggling artist." Yet the infractions are only visible because they take place against the heavily unionized backdrop of the entertainment industries. In the world of new media, where unions have no foothold, the formula of overwork and underpayment is entirely normative. Weaned on the rebel diet of the New Economy, the promise of new media enterprise lay in its goal of circumventing the professional gatekeepers by bringing to maturity a more democratic, do-it-yourself media culture. All well and good. But the less appealing side of this amateurism is the cut-price labor economy it has established as the default mentality of the cyber-world, where sacrificial labor and self-exploitation are the order of the day. Forged in the trenches of pioneering web design

work, this mentality has become further institutionalized in the social networking frenzy of the Web 2.0 era, where users have unlimited access, but no rights over their content. In that world, all manner of active, volunteer content serves as the lucrative raw material for data mining, corporate market research, and entrepreneur hosts bent on getting bought out. Concomitant with the reality shows, the prize for users is to win attention, accumulate "friends," score a hit, and draw some bankable advantage from the exposure. But for the business entrepreneur, the outcome is a virtually wage-free proposition, in which users, or "prosumers," as industry strategists call them, create all the surplus value.

Those of us weaned on media studies' classic eulogies (Benjamin, Enzensberger, and McLuhan) of the concept of an active media audience might be forgiven for mouthing "watch what you wish for." Is it possible that all of the Web's rich sociality, unfiltered expression, and people-to-people communication could be little more than a free input for the latest model of capital accumulation? If so (and it looks as if some component of the answer is "yes"), then we need to start analyzing how it is that contemporary media, or the so-called creative industries, have emerged as an optimum field for realizing the longstanding capitalist dream of stripping labor costs to the bone. If, in addition, consumers are now willingly building the product and burnishing the brand, where does that leave the progressive dream of a cooperative media economy? Not deflated entirely, for sure, but with some of its fundamental assumptions sideswiped. Media studies itself may not be the best prepared discipline for undertaking analysis of how this happened, but it is certainly an appropriate one.

Critiquing Reality-Based Televisual Black Fatherhood

A Critical Analysis of *Run's House* and *Snoop Dogg's Father Hood*

Debra C. Smith

*T*he *Cosby Show* (*Cosby*), a network situational comedy, debuted September 20, 1984, to critical acclaim (Inniss & Feagin, 1995). From 1984 to 1992, Bill Cosby, producer and star of the show, unveiled a Black family who did not live in public housing or lament on how they would manage household expenses. In fact, scholars (Berman, 1987; Inniss & Feagin, 1995; Gray, 1995) declare that by design, the show was the first with an all-Black cast that managed to avoid racial stereotyping. Instead, the show focused on themes of family stability, heritage, and education, giving the NBC network a ratings winner, and instilling a sense of pride in Black people everywhere. Cosby himself said the show reflected his own philosophy that the Black community must take responsibility for its own fate ("The Cosby Show Legacy," 2005). Though *Cosby* was criticized as showcasing a Black family in White face that did not address racial and social issues, the show continued in the genre of happy endings, family values, and escapism, as it sauntered into the history books. The show was hailed as portraying Black men in a positive light; portraying Black families optimistically; showing Black Americans as being like other U.S. Americans; and modeling good examples for Black children (Inniss & Feagin, 1995). With its focus on parenting, values, and Black respectability, *Cosby* essentially normalized the nuclear family.

Two decades later, at least two Black families have emerged on reality television shows, both of which provide a platform from which to examine the televisual construction of Black fatherhood and family years after *Cosby*'s debut. *Run's House* and *Snoop Dogg's Father*

Hood (*Father Hood*), both shows based on "real" Black families, can be interpreted in comparison and contrast to Cosby's version of upper-middle class Black fatherhood to (a) investigate constructions of Black fatherhood in a variety of positive forms, while challenging limited images of Black fathers on television; and (b) revive debates from Jhally and Lewis' (1992) book *Enlightened Racism*, as the families in the reality sitcoms simultaneously shift away from issues of race and class while still attempting to foster a strong identification with viewers. Throughout this chapter, arguments [based on the texts] will be contextualized by comments from critics and fans of the shows.

According to Brooks and Jacobs (1996), attention must be given to the potential inherent in television's ability to promote anti-essentialist and nonstereotypical images of African Americans (see Orbe, 1998). That being the case, this focus on unscripted "reality" television has the capacity to present the whole of Black family life in "authentically" complex ways. Such possibilities appear more likely—outside of traditional networks—within the cutting edge programming found on cable networks (Brooks & Jacobs). MTV has certainly enjoyed success, while supporting this argument, with its own version of Black family life portrayed in the show *Run's House*, as has *Father Hood* on E! Channel, as the stars of both shows set out to construct their own version of the twenty-first century family.

Run's House

Multiple studies (Berry, 1980; Greenberg & Atkin, 1978; Greenberg & Neuendorf, 1980; Merritt & Stroman, 1993) have analyzed the imagery of Black families on television and considered the messages that are perpetuated by the media. Some of these messages include the Black family as female-headed, characterized by conflict, and having children in the home who experience little supervision and concern from their parents. But on Thursday,

October 13, 2005, MTV debuted a Black television family that appeared to be in direct contradiction to these "realities."

Run's House is, according to the main character and "father" of the household, Joseph Simmons (Rev. Run), of Run.DMC fame, what critics consider a "real life" version of *Cosby* and *Father Knows Best* (Collier, 2006). Presiding over discussions about education, empty nesting and child anger management, Simmons and his wife, Justine, put family life on display along with their children, Vanessa, Angela, JoJo, Daniel ("Diggy"), and Russell II ("Russy"). In constructing his version of the authentic Black family, Simmons says the show is less about dismantling longstanding Black stereotypes and more about toppling stereotypes about rap music artists: "I'm just trying to give another perspective and show what rap is all about, especially for someone who knows only the negative things. Me and my family are rap all grown up" (MTV Networks, 2008). . . .

Like *Cosby*, neither *Run's House* nor *Father Hood* deals in any strong way with racism, economic distress, or other societal barriers on their shows. Instead, like their predecessor show, both build their plots around family success, humor, and harmony. This is particularly curious, considering that Simmons and Snoop Dogg represent opposite sides of the unharmonious divide between East Coast and West Coast rap artists, respectively. From the 1990s to the present, rivalry through rap lyrics between East and West Coast rappers has stimulated record sales, to help situate rap music as a $1.6 billion industry (Leland, 2002). Yet the contentious nature of their art is never reflected in either of their shows. Instead, viewers continue in the ideal world of Black families as perpetuated for the most part by both of these reality shows.

Snoop Dogg's Father Hood

The rap artist Calvin Broadus (Snoop Dogg) leads the theme song to *Father Hood* by making a direct comparison of his show and parenting style to that portrayed in *Cosby*. The title of the show itself emphasizes that Snoop, a prominent West Coast rapper, is a father from the 'hood.

Snoop Dogg came to fame in the 1990s when his debut album, *Doggystyle*, became a platinum seller in its first week (Quinn, 1996). Now, as head of household in *Father Hood*, Snoop starts the show by rapping that "this ain't *The Cosby Show* . . . and I don't make my kids eat their vegetables . . .", establishing at the inception that the structured family life of the 1980s hit show will not be replicated in the Broadus household. In fact, notions of distinguished, high-brow and dignified Blackness (Gray, 1995) and controlled representation are overwhelmed by the Broadus family's antitypical representation of family (compared with the archetypical Huxtable and Simmons families).

The selection of Snoop and the Broadus family appears a likely choice for a new reality show, especially considering the liberties television takes in its 21st-century portrayals. Robinson and Skill (2001) contend that "it is clear that TV portrayals of family are becoming more complex and diverse," and "television portrayals of the family have become less conventional" (p. 160). Obscene language, references to illegal drugs, and memories of confrontations with the law all represent material explored in *Father Hood*. In this case, it is relevant to remember that the producers of *Father Hood* have labeled the show as "real" day-to-day activity, as opposed to material created for television. Consider that the "less conventional" Broadus family challenges stagnant impressions of family life, normal TV conventions for family, and anticipated roles for adults and children in families. . . .

Conceptual/Theoretical Framework

. . . . Enlightened racism is a concept that grew out of the audience analysis work of Jhally and Lewis (1992). . . . Jhally and Lewis' seminal work argued that hyper-visibility of the Huxtable family reinforced the notion of social mobility—in that they have achieved the upper echelons of the middle class. Their social mobility was made problematic in that no attention was given to the economic disadvantages and deep-rooted racial discrimination that prevent most African Americans from being socially mobile. As a result, the show contributed to a contemporary form of racism that is based on the idea that racism is no longer a problem in the United States, and that lack of African American success is caused by lack of effort and/or ability. The existence of the Cosbys—and other popular mass-mediated African American success stories, such as Oprah Winfrey, Michael Jordan, and Colin Powell—is taken as proof of this stance. The logic, then, is that "their success assures us that in the United States everyone, regardless of race or creed, can enjoy material success" (Jhally & Lewis, 1992, p. 73). If racism does exist, it is manifested within interpersonal interactions (and situated as a personal issue), with no connection to historical, institutionalized policies, procedures, and/or practices. Consequently, the media glamorization of these individuals reinforces belief in both the availability and desirability of the American Dream.

Similar to the Huxtable family, the Simmons family, from *Run's House*, can be critiqued as representing Black families "without struggle," who suggest "effortless" and "nice" Blackness (Jhally & Lewis, 1992, pp. 107, 47), further confirming the myth of easy access to the American Dream that *Cosby* started over 20 years earlier. Also, *Run's House* places emphasis on the tremendous wealth and comfortable lifestyles of the Simmonses, sustaining the fantastical "myth of social mobility" that Jhally and Lewis (1992) discuss in their work (p. 7). That is, they move, exertion-free, through their White-washed utopian lives, with little to no reference to struggle.

While *Run's House* tends to advance the notion of class trumping race, *Father Hood,* on the other hand, contends with this concept in a variety of ways. Simmons' "rap grown up" implies that he is beyond the reckless, gangster lifestyle that has, unfairly or not, characterized some rap artists. His retreat to family life in the New Jersey suburbs parallels the upper middle class existence of *Cosby.* Yet, though wealthy and famous, Snoop Dogg connects visibly on his show to working-class Black cultural "institutions," food, and environments. Snoop's reconnection to his old "hood," through frequent meals of fried chicken, and visits to soul-food chain Roscoe's House of Chicken 'n Waffles, identifies him with working- class Black people, in a way that was absent from *Cosby* and is also absent from *Run's House.* Further, Snoop's confrontations with the law are also realistic occurrences that are not addressed in the other two shows. . . .

Of *Cosby,* Jhally and Lewis said that viewers' class position, interestingly, did not diminish the vigor with which they identified with the Huxtables. In fact, they say "working class respondents were just as likely to relate the Huxtables' world to their own as middle or upper middle class respondents" (p. 24). Recognizing the world that the Huxtables lived in as one from which they could draw references to their own lives, with regard to culture, parenting styles, etc., was meaningful to audiences. Similarly, *Run's House* viewers indicated in their messages ["Run's House Official Blog," MTV website] that they too discovered a world they recognized and identified with in the wealthy Simmons'. Likewise, *Father Hood's* light treatment of real-life struggles and references to working-class culture prompted viewers to comment on *Father Hood* message boards that that Snoop "keeps it real" and, regardless of mobility and access, is inextricably linked to his "hood."

Thus I advance the argument that despite any issues of race and class, the perception that was overriding in *Enlightened Racism* works here as well: that the Simmonses from *Run's House* and the Broaduses from *Father Hood* are—to some extent—"just like a real family" (p. 24) to their viewers, who indicate a strong identification with the wealthy families.

Black Fathers' Disciplinary Styles

RUN'S HOUSE

In *Run's House,* the theme of Black father as disciplinarian is well demonstrated in the episode where Russy has issues of anger management ("Anger Management," Season 2, Episode 9). During the course of the show, Russy takes out his frustrations on expensive hand-held video games, which he destroys and expects to be replaced by his parents. Instead, they determine that professional consultation is necessary. Later, at the behest of the therapist—much like *Cosby's* light hand as disciplinarian—the strictest that Rev. Run gets is when he enrolls Russy in karate lessons to assist him in channeling his anger toward productivity and focus. Simmons' discipline style is considered to be positive [by a critic writing in *Jet* magazine]. Collier (2006) explains:

> Family discussions are a constant in the Simmons household. They can often be found all sitting around the sofa discussing such things as Russy's anger issues or how to resolve conflict. What fans see, in spite of some arguing and debating, is a very dose-knit and respectful family. (para. 10)

Such family discussions, where children and adults were provided equal time to articulate their ideas, were thematic of *Cosby.* Differently from *Cosby,* however, Rev. Run utilizes some time at the conclusion of each episode to provide the viewing audience with a covert important life lesson. For example, reflecting on Russy's problem with anger management, Rev. Run journals the following text on his Blackberry messaging device (while his voice-over verbalizes the message for the audience):

How do you channel your personal strength? In putting forth the effort that our daily life requires, energy plus optimism equals progress, while energy plus anger results only in frustration. Do the math and you'll soon add up the difference between what's work and what's whack. God is love.—Rev Run

Comments on *Run's House's* Official Blog indicate that viewers identify with the discipline displayed on the show and with the message that concludes the episodes. Without exception, the response was overwhelmingly positive. One person wrote: " . . . Rev. Run (is) never afraid to discipline and be a parent, but always loving and fun," while another said " . . . Love the way they all get along and seem to talk through issues as they come up." Still another person wrote, "This show should be required viewing for each and every family in this country. Ironically enough, a show on MTV that is promoting family values." Others lauded the reality show for featuring a Black family "with people that don't act up." In this regard, some viewers described the Simmons as an ideal family, like the person who shared: "I love this family so much . . . I hope I can have a family that's something like theirs. . . . The parents don't let their kids take anything for granted." Some viewers pointed to the positive nature of *Run's House,* despite not being a fan of the reality television genre as a whole: "I am not a fan of reality shows . . . but this is one . . . (that) shows the family in the 'FOR REAL' state . . . The greatest thing about this show is that each week, there is a learning lesson behind each episode." . . .

SNOOP DOGG'S FATHER HOOD

In the episode titled "Dogg Whisperer," Snoop complains that the family's more than 10 dogs have too much freedom in their home. In another episode he laments that the house is disheveled. Yet the first line of the show's theme song ("I don't make my kids eat their vegetables") provides the sense that Snoop is not a strict disciplinarian on any level. In fact, he frequently refers to his sons and others as "nigger," and uses profanity often as a matter of course. When Snoop complains that his home is untidy, the children do not react. Likewise, when their dogs run amok in the household, it is their father who hires a dog trainer to teach the dogs obedience. In comparing *Father Hood* to *Run's House,* one *Father Hood* viewer wrote: "They need to spend the day at Run's House. Please . . . drop this show. They can keep their business and nasty house to themselves . . . He needs to control his kids." Clearly this viewer sees a sense of order in the Simmons' household that is not visible in the Broadus'.

In another episode, Snoop's younger son, Cordell ("Rook"), rough-housing with friends, gets hit in the eye. Snoop, who had earlier cursed the kids and asked them to stop the rough activity, laughs and tells his son, "You got to be able to take a blow if you can give a blow, cuz." Despite resistance from his wife, who coddles her injured son and demands that her husband stop chiding the boy, Snoop continues to laugh and tease, rather than use the incident as a forum to display disciplinary action and teach a lesson to the children involved.

The E! Channel description of an episode featuring British soccer star David Beckham, says: "Snoop Dogg wants his kids to play soccer but they won't practice . . . , " reflecting that, at times, Snoop has failed as an authoritarian. In another incident, Snoop implores older son, Corde ("Spank"), to help him stop Rook from stealing money out of his pockets in his absence. On the other hand, the episode guides—and Snoop himself—brag about Rook's infatuation with money," sending a mixed message. Finally, Snoop's style of discipline is actually highlighted in advertisements for the show. The promotional photo advertising *Father Hood* features the Broadus family, at a dinner table loaded with fried chicken, corn bread, and waffles, even as three pet dogs stand atop the table.

Snoop's "honorary" son, Anthony, fares no better in the discipline arena, often behaving like a big kid himself. In one episode, where Snoop's sons were left alone in Anthony's care, they were cited by law enforcement, and had their car towed for illegal parking, prompting them to sell Snoop's $5,000 bedroom slippers for $500 to bribe their way out of the charge. In another episode, Anthony collaborates with the Broadus brothers to have a pizza party in their parents' absence. One *Father Hood* viewer wrote:

> I think "honorary son" . . . is a terrible adult to have around any children. I saw the episode where Snoop left "honorary son" in charge of his 2 boys. He covered for Snoop's son taking money . . . He participated in taking the Porsche without permission. The worst thing was lying to Snoop (in front of his sons) . . . He helped Snoop's sons to deceive their father. "Honorary Son" is nothing but a sorry oversized child. Snoop and his wife should never allow this man to ever be alone with their children.

Martel (2007) describes Snoop as "barely (rising) to the responsibility of fatherhood" (para. 1), and Johnson (2007) quotes the rapper as saying he "likes to be more of a friend than a father figure" (para. 6), both comments being oppositional to the order found in *Cosby* and *Run's House*.

In the same manner of the wives on *Cosby* and *Run's House*, Snoop's wife Shante is seen as the primary disciplinarian on the show. Even Snoop calls her "Boss Lady." Gamble (2007) says that while Snoop "may run things in his hip-hop career . . . at home, being the 'top dogg' is another story" (para. 1). He continues describing Shante as an authority in the Broadus household by saying: "his wife and high school sweetheart, Shante, a.k.a. Boss Lady, runs the show" (para. 2). Indeed she does, as in several episodes she not only disciplines the kids but

firmly regulates her husband as well. For instance, in the episode titled "The Doggs and the Bees," Shante tells Snoop to have a talk about sex and intimacy with his oldest son, which he does, but with little seriousness. This comes on the heels of Snoop's production of a video for his new sex-laden single, "Sensual Seduction." Yet what cannot be dismissed about this episode is that a real-life issue is being discussed by father and son. Issues of sex were not as prominent in either *Cosby* or *Run's House*.

Black Fathers as Positive Role Models

. . . . On *Cosby*, Cliff Huxtable's emphasis on education, and his own achievement as a medical doctor, place him in a position of influence, in what Jhally and Lewis (1992) call "demonstrating the opportunity for African Americans to be successful" (p. 94). Miller (as cited in Jhally & Lewis) describes Cosby, and his alter ego Dr. Huxtable, as verification of the access of the American Dream. Similar themes are evident in *Run's House* and *Father Hood*.

RUN'S HOUSE

The virtues of hard work and pulling one's self up by one's own bootstraps are rampant in *Run's House*. Joseph Simmons parlays humility and values to his children. Again, comparisons can be tied to *Cosby*. For example, as in *Cosby*, where the patriarch, a medical doctor, insisted that while he and his wife, an attorney, were "rich," his children had no wealth, Simmons implores his children to make their own living.

Further, Simmons' very real depiction of religious values closely aligns with those of "real" Black families. According to Pipes (1981), "preaching and churches have traditionally been a mainstay of Black families" (p. 54). As a Black father embracing religion, a key tenet of African American culture, Simmons shows the real existence of religion in a Black household in a way that *Cosby* did not. Simmons insists that religion and respect are staples of his household, whether the cameras are on or off (Collier, 2006). . . . As in *Cosby*, on the other hand, Simmons seeks the ear of his wife to recollect family issues, as the couple settles into bed for the night. Yet, a trip to a tattoo parlor with daughter Angela, a golf/spa outing with son JoJo, or a family vacation to Las Vegas so that the Simmons parents can renew their wedding vows—all simmer down to a ritual closing scene where the patriarch Simmons, amid a cozy bubble bath, emits lessons of the day via his electronic Blackberry. This "ownership" of the parental "lesson of the day," outside the influence of his wife, is the lasting impression at the close of each show.

As a Black father, then, Simmons seeks out his children to give judicious advice and coach them through obstacles they encounter. While Snoop Dogg may not achieve the same results in a fantasyland TV manner, he does make an attempt at being a role model for his children as well.

SNOOP DOGG'S FATHER HOOD

Perhaps the greatest commentary not only on Snoop Dogg's being a positive example for his children, but also on his relationship to Black working-class life, comes in the episode where he visits the Long Beach neighborhood where he grew up. This episode reflects an important point of distinction, in that such representations of social mobility are never explicit with *Cosby* or *Run's House*.

In the episode, which aired February 2008, Snoop takes his two young sons to the neighborhood where he was raised and socialized. During the episode he is pensive about his upbringing, admitting that his mother could not teach him what it meant to be a man. He talks about growing up without a father, and how that fact motivates him to have a presence in his own sons' lives.

Highlights of the boys' visit included a walk through Snoop's old high school and a conversation with his former teacher. The teacher implores them to get a good education, and Snoop laments that he wishes he had been more diligent as a student. One viewer said: "The episode that had any substance and positive influence was when Snoop took his children to Long Beach and left them alone with the principal [teacher]." Still another viewer stated that they enjoyed "the episode where Snoop speaks about how he came up without a father and how that pushes him to be a good father and how the public don't get to hear about these situations. [S]o from all us responsible fathers especially us single ones thanks."

During the episode, Snoop impressed upon his sons that they needed to understand where he came from to be able to better grasp where he is, admitting that his upbringing is not reflective of the current success he enjoys. While visiting Long Beach, the boys meet Snoop's uncle, a recovering crack cocaine addict, who advises them to stay away from drugs—but not before detailing the harsh realities of a drug addict's existence, including lying, stealing, and sexual acts to gain a fix. This lifestyle is certainly remote from the comfortable lifestyle the Broadus brothers enjoy as a result of their father's achievements in entertainment. And this conversation is like none ever seen on *Cosby* or *Run's House*. One viewer noted the show's value as an authentic representation of Black life— Black life in Long Beach, California, specifically—which was something valued by viewers, and commented on specifically on the *Father Hood* Message Board:

> This show is hilarious . . . he's definitely from "da LBC" . . . he even (has) a shack in the back like the (old) days . . . now if you don't know then you wouldn't understand . . . he's original and . . . and he definitely ain't front'n.

While Snoop's forays into his old neighborhood were meant as a lesson for his

476 PART VII IS TV FOR REAL?

sons, he still maintains his existence as a counter image to *Cosby*. For example, in contesting the image of the faultless Black father, during yoga class he daydreams that he's lying flat on his mat as a result of a police officer's mandate—reminiscent of his real-life brushes with the law. Later, he imagines that the mellow feeling he gets from yoga is really a result of being high. In another episode, Snoop ignores the complaints of his daughter, Cori ("Choc"), that she can't concentrate on her schoolwork because his music is playing too loudly.

Viewers have conflicting views on Snoop's ability to be a positive influence as a father. One person criticized the decision to provide a venue for highlighting his behavior:

> You have got to be kidding. Now they are giving a THUG like Snoop Dogg a TV show? . . . Now we have come down to watching absolute garbage on TV with watching self proclaimed thugs and gangsters like this idiot . . . Snoop Dogg is not a mainstream citizen and all the media are doing is helping a criminal . . . look legitimate and part of mainstream society . . . let's stop glorifying these criminals and remember just because they are famous does not mean they should be admired.

Other viewers were quick to take issue with this viewer's point of criticism. One questioned the problematic nature of the label "mainstream citizen," while another pointed out that "it's the MAINSTREAM WHITE media that has labeled Snoop as a gangster, thug and criminal." This issue was also addressed by others, such as the viewer who wrote:

> . . . when did Snoop ever state that he was a criminal or thug? . . . he professes to be . . . a father, husband, rapper, who hustles . . . and if you don't know what hustles means that is a slang word for he works hard to provide a LEGAL lifestyle for himself and family.

Other viewers make a comparison between Snoop's ability as a positive role model and that of Ozzy Osbourne, another famous father and musician, who also had his own family reality show on MTV, for three years, beginning in 2002:

> If someone like Ozzy Osbourne can have a show . . . why on earth can't Snoop Dogg? . . . I originally thought he was just a typical rapper jerk. But watching . . . Father Hood show has shown his "human" side . . . I may not agree with . . . his music, but I do commend him for how he cares and provides for his family.

Despite his laidback parenting style, most viewers have a positive reaction to *Father Hood*. Though Snoop raps in the opening song that he's a nonconventional father, some of the same lessons of humility and success through education, thematic of *Cosby* and *Run's House,* are also canons in the Broadus household.

Discussion: Reality TV and Enlightened Racism in the 21st Century

. . . . As the traditional roles and values of Black family life become increasingly dynamic, televisual constructions of Black fatherhood should reflect this reality. While Snoop's style is described as a "benign older brother," with gangster appeal (Martel, 2007, para. 8), Rev. Run is a more conventional father. This examination of Black fathers in reality television confirms, contradicts and challenges images of Black fathers that exist in our culture.

Orbe (1998) asserts that the lens through which we view Black life is skewed: "Many critics have posited that the vast majority of African American media images represent portrayals of Black life as European Americans see it" (p. 33). Both Simmons and

Snoop defy this view. *Run's House* is coproduced by Simmons, and Snoop's own Snoopadelic Films coproduces his show, on which he also serves as executive director. Therefore, both fathers have some degree of influence regarding their construction of Black fatherhood for reality TV. In other words, neither *Run's House* nor *Father Hood* are restricted to outsider perceptions about the Black father and family, and both make their intentions clear about what they hope to reveal through their snows. *Run's House* and *Father Hood* feature "real" daily-life activity that is actually constructed, just as *Cosby* was, to respond to a limiting view of Black fatherhood and family. Simmons' goal was to counter the negative stereotypes leveled at rappers, and though Snoop's goal was to deviate from *Cosby*, he rebuffs claims that he has "rebranded" himself as "family-friendly," instead insisting that he always was (Forrest, 2008): "I am. That's what I always been . . . People . . . always get information on me as far as when I go to jail and my criminal record . . . Negative things . . . They never hear about my football team, my wife, my kids, my standing in the community, the gang interventions that I do" (para. 26). . . .

Central to this analysis is the argument that *Run's House* and *Father Hood* work to extend the representation of successful Black fathers popularized through Cosby. The likelihood that these shows work to reinforce existing forms of enlightened racism is strong, given three points. First, all three shows display professional and material success in environments void of any race-based obstacles. Two, the two reality sitcoms, viewed as more "real" than traditional sitcoms, lend credence to belief of the [raceless] American Dream. Third, reality TV—like the Cosby Show—has proven its ability to attract diverse audiences, which increases opportunities for White exposure to Black fathers/families.[1] While such a stance is important to articulate, this discussion works to avoid critical analyses that utilize a dichotomous approach—where the media generally, and reality TV specifically, are described in

absolute terms. Instead, I advocate for more complex readings that interrogate the ways in which shows are both productive and unproductive, negative and positive, good and bad, and supportive yet resistant of enlightened racism. The remainder of this discussion is situated within this approach.

According to Jhally and Lewis (1992), the fact that White viewers of *The Cosby Show* thought of the Huxtables as unraced is not evidence that race was no longer an issue. On the contrary: their behaviors were seen as being able to transcend race as a means to be defined as "normal." In this context, viewers who described the family as "normal," "generic," and "average" were not using terms that were unraced; instead the terms were racially specific—the family was implicitly viewed as White. Jhally and Lewis found that *The Cosby Show* represented different things to its White and Black audiences. For most Whites, Bill Huxtable was a Black *father*; for most Blacks, he was a *Black* father (Jhally and Lewis). Whites saw a middle-class family that could transcend race; Blacks saw a middle-class Black family where positive images helped to counter negative media stereotypes.

Within the two reality TV shows analyzed here, interrogating the saliency of racial identity for Rev. Run and Snoop Dogg lends insight into the ways in which such upwardly mobile mass-mediated personalities can continue to centralize their presence as *Black fathers*. Both men represent "rap grown up" —albeit in diverse ways—an explicitly Black form of expression that situates their life experience in racialized ways. While this can assist in avoiding one of the building blocks of enlightened racism (i.e., race is no longer relevant), the fact that African American achievement of the American Dream is possible only through limited venues (e.g., rap music or sports) contributes to problematic existing stereotypes. . . .

One of the core elements of enlightened racism is acceptance of the desirability, and belief in the accessibility, of the American

Dream. While each of the Black fathers/ families analyzed within this chapter reflect "American success stories," how they live out their successes differs in significant ways. In *Father Hood,* for example, Snoop introduces how his past served as a challenge— but not a permanent barrier—for his success as a rap artist (he was cleared of a gang-related murder charge in 1993; his uncle continues to struggle with drug addiction). Interestingly, his race-, class-based struggle lends "street credibility" to his music, something that is also reflected in the ways in which he continues to live his life (e.g., "keepin' it real" by not losing his cultural edge). I would suggest that *Father Hood,* within this context, reinforces the *accessibility* of the American Dream, while simultaneously challenges its *desirability.*

. . . . Therefore, while the social mobility of both Rev. Run and Snoop Dogg is situated within their celebrity status as rap artists, their relationships to the "American Dream" are distinctly different. Snoop, as a successful *Black father,* refuses to leave behind his cultural upbringing, despite professional and material success. Rev. Run, in comparison, embraces his identity as a successful *Black father* and utilizes that success to facilitate the intergenerational transfer of wealth. (Within the multimillion dollar family of businesses instituted by Russell and Joseph Simmons, the next generation of entrepreneurs, the Simmons children, are seen getting specific instructions from their father and uncle on how to participate in, and subsequently influence, various business dealings, and working to establish themselves in music, publishing, fashion, footwear, and jewelry.) In this vein, both represent diverse ways of "rap all grown up" —which can serve the function of role model, albeit in different expressions of success.

This chapter looks to contribute to historical debates on race, class, and audience responses to Black television families. If *Cosby* is the quintessential Black family television show, what new observations and characteristics of Black fathers, Black mothers, and their families loom, post-*Cosby?* How are such constructions situated within shows that span the continuum of fictional and reality-based depictions of Black life? For starters, I would argue that *Run's House* and *Father Hood* succeed at providing a post-*Cosby* televisual look at Black fathers and families in U.S. society, while revealing further angles with which to discuss issues of race, class, and viewer identification with these shows.

The "safer" show, *Run's House,* demonstrates template-like similarities to *Cosby,* while *Father Hood* further drives behind the scenes to show the audience working-class realities consistent with Snoop's intentional opposition to *Cosby's* reality. *Run's House* and *Father Hood* are valuable in the movement against continual stereotypes about Black fathers and families, picking up the torch from *Cosby* and bringing much-needed visibility to alternative constructions of Black fatherhood/family. Jhally and Lewis (1992) suggest that "we learn to live in the dreams sold by network executives" (p. 133). Reality-based TV represents a genre that has opened the possibilities of diverse representations of Blackness—especially on cable networks that are more likely to assume the risk of less conventional programming. Within this expansion lies the potential to negotiate how diverse audiences embrace, negate, and adapt to living various forms of the American Dream.

Note

1. This point does not discount African Americans who also embrace enlightened racism. Such individuals were not explicitly evident within the work of Jhally and Lewis (1992); however, I would argue that they are increasingly prevalent in contemporary U.S. society. Ironically, Bill Cosby's recent criticism of African Americans participating in their own oppression, reflects

elements of an enlightened racist ideology ("Dr. Bill Cosby speaks at the 50th Anniversary Commemoration of Brown vs. Topeka Board of Education Supreme Court Decision," n.d.).

References

Berman, R. (1987). Sitcoms. *Journal of Aesthetic Education, 2*(1), 5–19.

Berry, G. L. (1980). Children, television, and social class roles: The medium as an unplanned educational curriculum. In E. L. Palmer & A. Dorr (Eds.), *Children and the faces of television* (pp. 71–81). New York: Academic.

Braxton, G. (2001, December 4). *My Wife and Kids* is no clone of *Cosby:* Damon Wayans goes domestic but keeps the attitude in his new sitcom on ABC. *The Charlotte (NC) Observer,* p. E-01.

Brooks, D. E., & Jacobs, W. R. (1996). Black men in the margins: Space Traders and the interpositional strategy against b(l)acklash. *Communication Studies, 47,* 289–302.

Budd, M., & Steinman, C. (1992, July). White racism and *The Cosby Show. Jump Cut: A Review of Contemporary Media, 37,* 5–12. [Online]. Retrieved February 17, 2008, from http://www.ejumpcut.org/archive/onlines says/JC37folder/Cosby.html

Collier, A. (2006, August 7). *Run's House:* TV's first family of hip hop shares values and leads by example on reality show. *Jet.* [Online]. Retrieved January 19, 2008, from http://findarticles.com/p/articles/mi_m1355/is_/ai_n16620295

Cornwell, N. C., & Orbe, M. (2002). "Keepin' it real" and/or "Sellin' out to the man": African American responses to Aaron McGruder's *The Boondocks.* In R. Means Coleman (Ed.), *Say-it loud!: African American audiences, media, and identity* (pp. 27–44). New York: Routledge.

Dates, J. L., & Stroman, C. (2001). Portrayals of families of color on television. In J. Bryant & J. Alison Bryant (Eds.), *Television and the American family* (pp. 207–228). Mahwah, NJ: Erlbaum.

"Dr. Bill Cosby speaks at the 50th Anniversary Commemoration of Brown vs. Topeka Board of Education Supreme Court Decision." (n.d.). Retrieved May 10, 2008, from www.eightcitiesmap.com/transcript_bc.htm

E-Channel Message Board for *Snoop Dogg's Father Hood.* Retrieved July 25, 2008, from boards.eonline.com

Fiske, J. (1994). Ethnosemiotics: Some personal and theoretical reflections. In H. Newcomb (Ed.), *Television: The critical view* (pp. 411–425). New York: Oxford University Press.

Forrest, E. (2008, April 3). At home with the Doggs: Rapper Snoop Dogg is reinventing himself as a family-friendly father on his own reality TV show. Is he serious? Retrieved April 15 from http://music.guardiaii.co.uk/urban/story/0,,2270399,00.html

Gamble, R. (2007, December 6). *Snoop Dogg gives fans access to his family life with 'Father Hood.'* [Online]. Retrieved February 28, 2008, from http://www.ballerstatus.com/article/news/2007/ 12/3678/

Gray, H. (1995). *Watching race: Television and the struggle for Blackness.* Minneapolis: University of Minnesota Press.

Greenberg, B. S., & Atkin, C. K. (1978, March). *Learning about minorities from television: The research agenda.* Paper presented at the conference on Television and the Socialization of the Minority Child, University of California, Los Angeles.

Greenberg, B. S., & Neuendorf, K. (1980). Black family interactions on TV. In B. S. Greenberg (Ed.), *Life on television: Content analysis of U S. TV drama* (pp. 173–181). Norwood, NJ: Ablex.

Herbert, B. (2007, October 16). Tough, sad and smart. *New York Times.* [Online]. Retrieved February 11, 2008, from http://www.nytimes.com/2007/10/16/opinion/16herbert./html?_r=18coref=slogin

Inniss, L. B., & Feagin, J. R. (1995). *The Cosby Show:* The view from the Black middle class. *Journal of Black Studies, 25*(6), 692–711.

Jhally, S., & Lewis, J. (1992). *Enlightened racism: The Cosby Show, audiences, and the myth of the American Dream.* Boulder, CO: Westview Press.

Johnson, C. A. (2007, December 4). Snoop gets real with kids. *The Showbuzz.* [Online]. Retrieved February 22, 2008, from http://www.showbuzz.cbsnews.com/stories/2007/12/04/tv/main 3573842.shtml

Leland, J. (2002, November 2). Feuding for profit: Rap's war of words; in rap industry, rivalries as marketing tool. *New York Times.* Retrieved February 22, 2008, from http://query.nytimes.corn/gst/fullpage,html?res=9C0CE2DE143EF930A35752C1A9649C8B63

Martel, N. (2007, December 29). Just chillin' with Snoop Dogg: A rapper's blend of offspring and entourage. *New York Times.*

Merritt, B., & Stroman, C A. (1993). Black family imagery and interactions on television. *Journal of Black Studies, 23,* 492–499.

MTV Networks. (2008). *Run's House (Season 1)* [Online]. Available: http://www.mtv.com/ontv/dyn/runs_house_season_01/series.jhtml

Orbe, M. P. (1998). Constructions of reality on MTV's "The Real World": An analysis of the restrictive coding of Black masculinity. *Southern Communication Journal, 64*(1), 32–45.

Pipes, W. H. (1981). 'Old-time religion': Benches can't say "Amen." In H. Pipes McAdoo (Ed.), *Black families* (pp. 54–76). Beverly Hills, CA: Sage.

Quinn, M. (1996). Never shoulda been let out of the penitentiary: Gangsta rap and the struggle over racial identity. *Cultural Critique, 34,* 65–89.

Robinson, J. D., & Skill, T. (2001). Five decades of families on television: From the 1950s through the 1990s. In J. Bryant & J. Alison Bryant (Eds.), *Television and the American family* (pp. 139–162). Mahwah, NJ: Erlbaum.

Run's House Official Blog. http://www.mtv.com

"The Cosby Show legacy." (2005, August 2). *USA Today,* p. D04.

Disciplining the Housewife in *Desperate Housewives* and Domestic Reality Television

Sharon Sharp

In an emblematic scene in ABC's prime-time breakout hit *Desperate Housewives*, Lynette Scavo, a stay-at-home mother who has been abusing her kids' ADD medication to keep up with the other Wisteria Lane mothers, has a physical and emotional breakdown and contemplates suicide to escape being trapped at home with her children (1: 8). Later, in a rare moment of sisterhood, Lynette's friends attempt to console her by relating their own moments of mommy trauma, and Lynette sobs: "Why didn't you ever tell me? We should tell each other this stuff." In an equally memorable moment about shame and secrets, Martha Stewart clone Bree Van de Kamp, who believes in the old-fashioned values of respect for God, the importance of family and love for country, removes freshly cleaned handcuffs, recently used to reluctantly dominate her husband in an S/M scenario, from the dishwasher (1: 14). These representations of the housewife are particularly notable in the way they offer a feminine perspective on the domestic sphere and the contradictions of lived female experience. But they are not limited to *Desperate Housewives*. . . . Domestic reality TV, a sub-genre of reality TV programming, has also trained its gaze on the housewife and home. Lifetime Television's *How Clean is Your House?* humiliates housewives and others with the exposure of bad housekeeping such as cat feces in the marital bed and mouldy food in the refrigerator. ABC's *Super Nanny* and Fox's clone *Nanny 911* feature stern British nannies who give exhausted mothers and distant fathers strict parenting rules for raising their unruly children. Fox and ABC also have offered up their versions of Britain's *Wife Swap*, which dramatise conflicted housewifery when two women from radically different social backgrounds swap households for two weeks. The housewife, relatively absent from prime-time programming since the departure of *Roseanne* in 1997, has returned with a vengeance.

From Sharp, S. (2006). Disciplining the housewife in *Desperate Housewives* and domestic reality television. In J. McCabe & K. Akass (Eds.), *Reading* Desperate Housewives: *Beyond the white picket fence* (pp. 119–128). New York: I. B. Tauris.

Like *Desperate Housewives,* domestic reality television, in which traditional concepts of gender are dramatised and debated, invites viewers inside the domestic sphere, where they discover that housewifery, motherhood and domesticity can be exhausting, empty and unfulfilling. Unlike the happy housewives idealised in sitcoms of the past, the housewives who are regularly swapped, scrutinised and shamed on domestic reality television are decidedly ambivalent, frustrated, overworked, neurotic and unhappy. The model of housewifery put forward by domestic reality television is a contradictory one: the ambivalence of the domestic reality television housewife subverts the ideology that women should find domesticity and motherhood fulfilling, yet she is ridiculed for breaking the TV rule that women should never express dissatisfaction with motherhood and domesticity. Similarly, when the domestic reality television housewife exhibits an over-investment in domesticity *a la* Martha Stewart, it is conceived of as a dysfunction that alienates her husband and children and she is punished with domestic discord.

This chapter explores how problems of housewifery and domesticity in *Desperate Housewives* resonate with the model of housewifery circulated in the current trend in domestic reality television. By examining the representation of housewifery in *Desperate Housewives,* as embodied in the characters Lynette and Bree, I focus on how these representations relate to cultural anxieties about the housewife and domesticity, and examine how they are indicative of the way the media currently construct the housewife. The key argument is that the cultural work being done in the televisual discourse of the housewife is both complex and contradictory. On the one hand, the emphasis on problems of the housewife in *Desperate Housewives,* like domestic reality television, seems to offer potential for feminist critique in their rebellion against what Susan Douglas and Meredith Michaels have described as the new "momismor," the insistence that no woman

is truly complete or fulfilled unless she has kids, that women remain the best primary caretakers of children, and that to be a remotely decent mother, a woman has to devote her entire physical, psychological, emotional being to her children 24/7" (2004: 4). On the other hand, *Desperate Housewives* and domestic reality television confirm dominant cultural beliefs about traditional gender roles as they ridicule housewives for their perfectionism and ambivalence about motherhood and domesticity.

The New Television Housewife

The idea for *Desperate Housewives* was born out of media coverage of a case of troubled domesticity that brought to the surface anxieties about social expectations of motherhood and housewifery. Show runner Marc Cherry's conceptualisation of the series originated in watching with his mother the news coverage of Andrea Yates, a mother convicted of systematically drowning each of her five children in the bathtub. As Cherry relates in his much-repeated origin story of the series, he turned to his mother and said:

> 'Can you imagine a woman being so desperate that she would hurt her own children?' And my mother took her cigarette out of her mouth and said, 'I've been there.' [. . .]Suddenly it occurred to me, 'Well gosh, if my mom had these moments, every woman has had a moment where she is close to losing it.' As I talked to her and found out these things, the genesis of this idea was born in that. (Genesis of Desperate Housewives, 2005:1)

The idea for *Desperate Housewives* thus begins with an ambivalent housewife and mother: a woman who had been discussed in the media (not always unsympathetically) in terms of her extreme deviation from normative conceptions of mother-hood and housewifery but also in terms of how she exemplified the difficulties women face living up to the new momism.

Cherry's 'comic soap opera' exploits a limited range of anxieties about housewives and domesticity through its five upper-middle-class female protagonists who live on the suburban cul-de-sac Wisteria Lane, each with her own mommy trauma (none of which approaches the trauma of Andrea Yates). Voiceover narrator Mary Alice Young's suicide, committed after performing her domestic routine and 'polishing her life until it gleamed with perfection,' opens the pilot episode and introduces the five main characters. Susan Mayer, a divorced single mother who works from home as children's book illustrator and seems incapable of mothering her child; Bree Van de Kamp, who has a Martha Stewart complex and alienates her husband and children on her quest for perfection; Lynette Scavo, a former corporate powerhouse who is stay-at-home mom to four unruly children (even though she was clearly more successful than her husband in the corporate world); Gabrielle Solis, a nouveau riche Latina gold-digger trophy wife who has an affair with her teenage gardener and contemplates aborting her unborn child of uncertain paternity; and last but not least, real estate agent Edie Britt, the neighbourhood slut, without the attachment of husband, family or friends and whose self-esteem is derived from male sexual attention, rounds out the cast.

Despite the women's movement's efforts to liberate women from the exile of the domestic sphere, *Desperate Housewives,* like domestic reality television, returns women to the home. As in the domestic reality tele-vision series in which housewives are taught traditional concepts of gender, and in which wives and not husbands are swapped, *Desperate Housewives* puts forward the assumption that domesticity is a female-oriented sphere. The series showcases a decidedly ambivalent take on 'retreatism,' which Diane Negra and Yvonne Tasker have identified as one of the most persistent

themes of post-feminist representation: 'In the retreatist scenario, a well-educated white female professional displays her "empower-ment" and caring nature by with-drawing from the workforce (and symbolically from the public sphere) to devote herself to husband and family' (2005: 108). While many post-feminist representations offer this choice as a form of empowerment and as the best option, *Desperate Housewives* obsesses over the anxiety of retreatism. As series creator and executive producer Marc Cherry describes the show:

> I call it a post-post feminist take. The women's movement said, 'Let's get the gals out working.' Next the women realised you can't have it all. Most of the time you have to make a choice. What I'm doing is having women make the choice to live in the suburbs but things aren't going well at all. The show is actu-ally a love letter to all the women out there who have issues and are trying their best to be stay at home moms. (Weinraub 2004: B7)

This 'love letter' to stay-at-home moms is most dramatically played out through the characters Lynette and Bree, who are, tech-nically, the only stay-at-home mothers in the first season, as they do not participate in any work outside of the home. Lynette most clearly articulates the ambivalent housewife model advanced in domestic reality television. As if to emphasise her ambivalence, a montage sequence featuring her washing dishes, feeding the baby and cleaning chocolate fingerprints off the win-dow is accompanied by Mary Alice's voiceover, sarcastically informing us that her friend used to 'see herself as a career woman and a hugely successful one at that, but she gave up her career to assume a new label—the incredibly satisfying one of full-time mother, but unfortunately this new label frequently falls short of what was advertised' (1: 4). Generally rumpled, exhausted and covered in baby spit, Lynette does not relish her role as housewife and mother and seems at times to hate her three unruly boys and young baby girl. Running into a former colleague, who tells her she would be running the firm by now if she had not left and asks Lynette how she likes domestic life, Lynette lies and tells her: 'It's the best job I've ever had,' (1: 1) expressing some of the contradictions of the ambivalent housewife: she is privileged enough to be able to retreat to home and family but once there finds it unfulfilling.

As domestic reality television's surveillance of the American home explores at length, the ambivalence of housewives almost always emanates from the wife's unequal shouldering of the domestic and childcare labour, and Lynette's ambivalence about being a stay-at-home mom has similar origins. Her husband, Tom Scavo, an advertising executive who spends much time away from home, is affably oblivious to Lynette's situation. Like the belligerent or distant patriarchs who make up most of domestic reality television's conflicts, Tom rarely helps with the childcare or domestic chores, and Lynette is often depicted pleading on the phone for him to come home, while her undisciplined children wreak havoc around her. In Lynette, *Desperate Housewives* comes closest to a feminist critique of patriarchy and the unequal division of labour. Without her husband's help, Lynette cannot keep up with the challenges of keeping house and keeping her unruly children under control, which leads her to abuse her children's Ritalin. When Lynette breaks down from her drug addiction (1: 8), she confesses to friends Bree and Susan that she feels humiliated and like a failure 'because the other moms make it look so easy.'

Lynette's confession demonstrates an extreme ambivalence towards the role of motherhood, and satirises the ways women internalise the social pressures of choosing to be stay-at-home mothers and living up to unrealistic standards of domestic perfection. Indeed, this scene has become a common referent in the popular media—from *Oprah* to *USA Today*—that is used to introduce problems related to the mommy mystique. This cathartic moment of rewriting the housewife is remarkable because it speaks to women's lived experience in a way that has been verboten or demonised in popular media. This housewife, to some degree, rejects the contemporary ideology of femininity that insists women should feel maternal and should find motherhood fulfilling. However, this critique is constrained by the series' emphasis on competition between women and the internalisation of cultural values that insist women should be in charge of domesticity and find it fulfilling.

While Lynette makes it clear that part of the problem is that her husband does not share the burden of childcare, this is addressed not through reconfiguring the burden of parenting, but by 'scoring some high-grade nanny.' As in domestic reality television, which rarely suggests more equal parenting or state-supported childcare as a solution to the overburdened housewife's plight, Lynette and her husband decide to hire a young, white, attractive woman as a nanny (1: 9). *Desperate Housewives* presents a solution to the mommy mystique problem that is decidedly upper-class: as much as this series articulates the ambivalence of being a housewife and mother, it is a distinctly upper-middle-class ambivalence. It is important to note that it is precisely the women, who have the choice to retreat into the home or stay in the corporate world, through whom this discourse is mobilised and to some extent ridiculed. Narratively, this discourse that rebels against the ideology of femininity is recuperated in the text, as the network of friendship between the suburban housewives is used more to judge and shame each other rather than as a network of support for sharing and debating problems of domesticity and motherhood. Lynette is constantly judged by her neighbours, even her friend Susan, who, while watching Lynette unsuccessfully corral her children, gives her a look that narrator Mary Alice tells us says: 'You should learn to control your kids, after all, they're your responsibility' (1: 10).

If *Desperate Housewives* is careful to police the housewife's ambivalence, as demonstrated by Lynette, it also goes to great lengths to ridicule the housewife's over-investment in domesticity. Like domestic reality television's control-freak housewives whose fervour for domestic order alienates their families, Bree's impeccable domestic comportment is characterised as an obsessive-compulsive disorder that causes her children and husband to loathe her. Bree's teenage son, Andrew, accuses her of 'running for mayor of Stepford' and her husband Rex wants a divorce because he is tired of 'living in a detergent commercial' with his 'plastic suburban housewife' (1: 1). Like the exploration of the verboten ambivalence towards housewifery and motherhood that *Desperate Housewives* circulates in the representation of Lynette, Bree's characterisation at first glance reads as a critique of the images of domesticity and femininity that are measured by the quality of housekeeping and cooking. *Desperate Housewives* derides Bree's belief that spending three hours to cooking osso bucco and basil puree for her family, zealously scrubbing toilets, and polishing the silver will lead to personal satisfaction and domestic bliss. And her retreat into the home and passion for domesticity demonstrate that home is not the site of love and fulfilment for many women but is, in fact, often based on repression of desires. In a session with her therapist Bree confesses that she would settle for a life of repression and denial with her philandering husband because it would allow her to continue to throw the dinner parties that she finds so 'elegant and civilised' (1: 14).

Much as Bree's investment in domesticity functions as a critique of social expectations about femininity and domesticity, it is also ridiculed as an investment in her upper-middle-class status. Her passion for domesticity is interwoven with her obsession with keeping up appearances and general upper-middle-class perfection. Rather than admit that her family has severe imperfections, Bree upholds a facade of perfection. When her son Andrew is involved in a hit-and-run accident,

she arranges for his car to be stolen and uses chemical solvent to clean the blood from the pavement (1: 8). Rather than confide in her friends that she and Rex are in marital counseling, she tells them they are taking tennis lessons at the country club (1: 3). While *Desperate Housewives* ridicules the housewife's ambivalence by constructing Lynette as an abject, jealous woman, the series mocks the housewife's over-investment in domesticity by constructing Bree as a cold and deeply dysfunctional woman. Her obsession with domesticity is not based on genuine affection for her family but is a product of her dysfunction. When Rex, convalescing from a heart attack, observes that the tray with freshly laundered napkins, flowers from the garden, and good china that Bree has prepared for him is proof of her affection, she coldly replies that he should not mistake her 'anal retentiveness for actual affection' (1: 13). Similarly, when Bree's argument with Rex causes him to suffer a second heart attack, she takes the time to neatly make the marital bed before driving him to the emergency room because she refuses to leave the house with an unmade bed (1: 22).

Like the Martha Stewart housewives in the domestic reality television series *Wife Swap* and *Trading Spouses* who are not welcomed home by their families upon their return from their swap, *Desperate Housewives* ridicules Bree's perfectionism as dysfunctional rather than validating her investment in domesticity and women's work at home in general. Further, even as *Desperate Housewives* ridicules the housewife's investment in domesticity, it also celebrates and glamorizes it through the language of domestic lifestyle television in the show's *mise en scène*. However dysfunctional Bree may be, she enjoys a life of leisure filled with commodities; domestic labour, when performed, is depicted as an obsessive yet pleasant hobby.

The disciplining of the housewife as embodied in Lynette and Bree is most apparent with regard to their sexuality. While domestic reality television goes to considerable lengths to keep out of the bedroom (aside from reminding house-wives that neither children nor cat feces belong in the marital bed, and despite the sexual implications of titles such as *Wife Swap* and *Trading Spouses*), in *Desperate Housewives* the bedroom is where house-wives are policed the most. Sex is another domestic duty that the housewives fail to perform without dysfunction and that pro-vides little personal satisfaction. Lynette's ambivalence is manifest in her abject appearance: unlike the other housewives, who wear lingerie and miniskirts, Lynette is often wearing baggy soccer mom garb and smelling of baby vomit. Her attempts at seduction are played for laughs: she falls asleep in a sexy French maid costume while waiting for Tom, only to be discovered later by him and the business associate he has brought home for the night (1: 21). When Lynette does get sex from her husband, it is because he is aroused by a glimpse of their young nanny in the nude (1: 11).

Similarly, Bree's obsessive-compulsive disorder interferes with her sex life. In another failed seduction played for laughs, Bree's attempts to win back her husband's affection, by seducing him in La Perla lin-gerie and a fur coat, is thwarted by her inability to look away from a sloppy bur-rito perched on the night table and dripping onto the carpet while they are having sex (1: 6). Later, after discovering that Rex vis-its another suburban housewife for his S/M pleasures, Bree decides to keep her marriage together by dominating her husband, an activity that she finds unpleasurable, 'sick' and 'dirty' (1: 14). If domestic reality television tells us that domestic bliss is the woman's job, *Desperate Housewives* tells us that having a pleasing sex life is the woman's responsibility too, only it will probably not be pleasurable for her. Pleasure is hard to come by for the housewife: it is clear that housewives are punished for their ambivalence or overinvestment in their roles as they are denied any pleasure in the domestic sphere.

While *Desperate Housewives* and domestic reality television that focuses on the housewife and home are certainly unique, they circulate similar cultural anxi-eties about the housewife. Surveying the American home, the new televisual dis-course on the housewife tells us that the choice to retreat into the home has resulted in ambivalence and dysfunction. The image of the conflicted housewife and troubled domestic sphere appears at a time when ideas about housewifery and family are being questioned and even transformed. We can read the trend to fixate on the housewife as an effort to contain and normalise these changes through the rhetoric of shame and ridicule. Although domestic reality televi-sion and *Desperate Housewives* belong to different genres, they operate within the same logic: they represent women judging other women for not living up to traditional norms of femininity and domesticity, and often shame the women they feature. Rather than sounding a critique of the social pres-sures that demand perfection and place an unequal burden on women, the new televi-sual discourse on the housewife blames indi-vidual women for problems of domesticity and invites viewers to feel superior. While we laughed at the antics and physical com-edy that ensued around the housewife of television's sitcom past, these new shows ask us to laugh at the housewife's predicament with a more malicious laughter.

References

Douglas, Susan and Meredith Michaels (2004). *The Mommy Myth*. NY: Free Press.

The Genesis of Desperate Housewives: Creator Marc Cherry Reveals the Surprising Truth. Dishmag.com/issue43/celebrity/3088/sex-in-the-suburbs-marcia-cross-marc-cherry.

Tasker, Yvonne and Diane Negra, ed. (2005). In Focus: Postfeminism and Contemporary Media Studies. *Cinema Journal* 44:2 (2005), 107–10.

Weinraub, Bernard. How Desperate Women Saved Desperate Writer. *N.Y. Times*, October 23, 2004.

"Take Responsibility for Yourself"

Judge Judy and the Neoliberal Citizen

Laurie Ouellette

A woman drags her ex-boyfriend to court over an overdue adult movie rental and unpaid loan. A woman is heartbroken when her best friend betrays her and ruins her credit. A smooth-talking ex-boyfriend claims money from his ex was a gift. Welcome to *Judge Judy,* queen of the courtroom program, where judges resolve "real-life" disputes between friends, neighbors, family members, roommates, and lovers on national television. For critics who equate television's role in democracy with serious news and public affairs, altercations over broken engagements, minor fender benders, carpet stains, unpaid personal loans, and the fate of jointly purchased household appliances may seem like crass entertainment or trivial distractions. But such dismissals overlook the "governmental" nature of courtroom programs like *Judge Judy,* which gained cultural presence—and a reputation for "zero tolerance when it comes to nonsense"—alongside the neoliberal policies and discourses of the 1990s.[1]

Judge Judy took the small claims–based court format from the fringes of commercial syndication to an authoritative place on daytime schedules when it debuted in 1996, the same year the U.S. Telecommunications Act was passed.[2] While the legislation has been critiqued for its deregulatory ethos as well as its affinity with the broader neoliberal forces behind welfare reform and the privatization of public institutions from the penal system to the post office, the cultural dimensions of these parallels remain less examined.[3] There is a tendency within policy studies to take the cultural impact of neoliberalism as self-evident—to presume that the laissez-faire principles codified by the Act will erode democracy in predictable ways that typically involve the decline of journalism, documentaries, and other "substantial" information formats found unprofitable by the culture industries. While such concerns have some validity, the metaphor of subversion needs to be jettisoned, for it reifies untenable cultural hierarchies, and neglects neoliberalism's productive imprint on contemporary

From Ouellette, L. (2004). "Take responsibility for yourself": *Judge Judy* and the neoliberal citizen. In S. Murray & L. Ouellette (Eds.), *Reality TV: Remaking television culture* (pp. 231–250). New York: New York University Press.

television culture and the "idealized" citizen subjectivities that it circulates.

Reality programming is one site where neoliberal approaches to citizenship have in fact materialized on television. From makeover programs (such as *What Not to Wear* and *Trading Spaces*) that enlist friends, neighbors, and experts in their quest to teach people how to make "better" decorating and fashion choices, to game-docs (like *Survivor* and *Big Brother*) that construct community relations in terms of individual competition and self-enterprising, neoliberal constructions of "good citizenship" cut across much popular reality television. The courtroom program is a particularly clear example of this broader trend because it draws from the symbolic authority of the state to promote both the outsourcing of its governmental functions and the subjective requirements of the transition to a neoliberal society. *Judge Judy* and programs like it do not subvert elusive democratic ideals, then, as much as they *construct* templates for citizenship that complement the privatization of public life, the collapse of the welfare state, and most important, the discourse of individual choice and personal responsibility.

This chapter situates *Judge Judy* as a neoliberal technology of everyday citizenship, and shows how it attempts to shape and guide the conduct and choices of lower-income women in particular. As we shall see, *Judge Judy* draws from and diffuses neoliberal currents by fusing an image of democracy (signified in the opening credits by a gently flapping U.S. flag, stately public courthouse, and gavel-wielding judge) with a privatized approach to conflict management and an intensified government of the self. *Judge Judy* and programs like it supplant institutions of the state (for instance, social work, law and order, and welfare offices), and using real people, caught in the drama of ordinary life as raw material, train TV viewers to function without state assistance or supervision as self-disciplining, self-sufficient, responsible, and risk-averting individuals. In this way, the courtroom

subgenre of reality TV exemplifies what James Hay has called a cultural apparatus for "neoliberal forms of governance."[4]

Neoliberalism and Television Culture

To understand *Judge Judy's* neoliberal alignments, a brief detour through the concept of neoliberalism is in order. My understanding of neoliberalism begins with political economy and the activism it inspires. From this vantage point, neoliberalism is generally understood as a troubling worldview that promotes the "free" market as the best way to organize every dimension of social life. According to activists Elizabeth Martinez and Arnoldo Garcia, this worldview has generated five trends that have accelerated globally since the 1980s: the "rule" of the market; spending cuts on public services; deregulation (including the deregulation of broadcasting); the privatization of state-owned institutions, "usually in the name of efficiency"; and "eliminating the concept of the public good or community and replacing it with individual responsibility."[5] For critics like Robert McChesney, the upshot of neoliberalism and the reforms it has spawned is that a "handful of private interests are permitted to control as much as possible of social life in order to maximize their personal profit."[6]

While I share these concerns, I have found Foucauldian approaches particularly useful for analyzing the subjective dimensions of neoliberalism that circulate on reality TV. Drawing from Michel Foucault, Nikolas Rose theorizes neoliberalism less as a simple opposition between the market (bad) and welfare state (good) than as a "changing network" of complex power relations. If neoliberal regimes have implemented an "array of measures" aimed at downsizing the welfare state and dismantling the "institutions within which welfare government had isolated and managed their social problems," they still rely on "strategies of government."[7] This manifests as various forms of "cultural training" that govern indirectly in the name of "lifestyle maximization," "free choice," and personal responsibility, says Rose. This diffused approach to the "regulation of conduct" escapes association with a clear or top-down agenda, and is instead presented as the individual's "own desire" to achieve optimum happiness and success. As Rose points out, the "enterprising" individual crafted by this discourse has much in common with the choice-making "customer" valorized by neoliberal economics. Both presume "free will," which means that those individuals who fail to thrive under neoliberal conditions can be readily cast as the "author of their own misfortunes."[8]

. . . . *Judge Judy* fuses television, neoliberalism, and self-help discourse in a governmental address to women living out what feminist philosopher Nancy Fraser has called the "postsocialist" condition.[9] The program presents the privatized space of the TV courtroom as the most "efficient" way to resolve microdisputes steeped in the unacknowledged politics of gender, class, and race, but it also classifies those individuals who "waste the court's time" as risky deviants and self-made victims who create their own misfortunes by making the "wrong" choices and failing to manage their lives properly. The imagined TV viewer is the implied beneficiary of this litany of mistakes, for one's classification as "normal" hinges on both recognizing the pathos of "others" and internalizing the rules of self-government spelled out on the program. The courtroom program has, for precisely this reason, been institutionally positioned as a moral and educational corrective to "permissive" entertainment, suggesting that the discourse of the "public interest" in broadcasting has not been squashed but rather reconfigured by neoliberal reforms. Indeed, it could be that television is increasingly pivotal to neoliberal approaches to government and the citizen subjectivities on which they depend.

"The Cases Are Real, the Rulings Are Final"

Judge Judy is not the first television program to resolve everyday microconflicts in simulated courtroom settings. The genre can be traced to 1950s programs like *People in Conflict* and *The Verdict Is Yours*. In the 1980s, retired California Superior Court judge Joseph Wapner presided over *The People's Court*, while *Divorce Court* used actors to dramatize "real" legal proceedings.[10] *Judge Judy* did, however, rework and revitalize the format, and the program's "no-nonsense" approach to family and small claims disputes generated notoriety and imitators (examples include *Judge Joe Brown*, *Judge Mathis*, *Judge Hatchet*, *Curtis Court*, a revitalized *People's Court*, and *Moral Court*). Well into the new millennium, courtroom programs abound on television, competing with talk shows, game shows, and soap operas for a predominantly female audience.

On *Judge Judy*, real-life litigants are offered travel costs and court fees to present their cases on national television. The price is to drop out of the public judicial process and submit to the private ruling of Judith (Judy) Sheindlin. A former New York family court judge, Sheindlin was recruited for the "tough-love" philosophy she first spelled out in an influential *60 Minutes* profile, and later expanded on in her best-selling book *Don't Pee on My Leg and Tell Me It's Raining*, which faulted the overcrowded court system as a lenient bureaucracy that reflects "how far we have strayed from personal responsibility and old-fashioned discipline."[11] Spotting ratings potential, Larry Lyttle, president of Big Ticket Television, a Viacom company, invited Sheindlin to preside over "real cases with real consequences in a courtroom on television." Called a "swift decision maker with no tolerance for excuses" by the program's publicity, Sheindlin claims to bring to her TV show the same message she advocated in the courts: "Take responsibility for yourself, your actions and the children you've brought into the world."[12] In interviews, she situates *Judge Judy* as a public service that can solve societal problems by instilling the right attitudes and choices in individuals:

> It's a much larger audience. Whatever message I spew—"Take responsibility for your life. If you're a victim, it's your fault. Stop being a victim. Get a grip! You're the one who's supposed to make a direction in your life." All those messages I tried in Family Court to instill in people—primarily women. [The TV show] sounded like something that would not only be fun, but worthwhile as well.[13]

Like other TV judges, Sheindlin now hears noncriminal disputes that rarely exceed several hundred dollars or the equivalent in personal property. While these conflicts often speak to broader social tensions and inequalities, the program's governmental logic frames the cases as "petty squabbles" brought about by the deficiencies of individuals. Sheindlin's courtroom is filled with feuding relations and typically devoid of people who wish to sue businesses, bosses, or least of all, big corporations. This focus makes perfect sense, for the program's impetus as a technology of citizenship is to scrutinize ordinary people who require state mediation of everyday affairs, a process that hinges more on the moral radar Sheindlin claims to have developed in the public court system than on time-consuming democratic processes (she has been known to snap, "I don't have time for beginnings" and "I don't read documents"). While TV viewers are situated outside Sheindlin's disciplinary address to litigants derided as losers, cheaters, liars, and "gumbos," their status as "good" citizens presumes the desire to adhere to the neoliberal templates for living she espouses.

While the opening credits promise "real people" involved in "real cases," a male narrator differentiates the program from the public court system with the reminder: "This is Judy's courtroom," where the "decisions are final." Onscreen, Sheindlin plays judge, prosecutor, professional expert, and punctilious moral authority, handling an average of two cases per thirty-minute episode and dispensing justice at "lightning speed," according to the program's publicity. Participants must abide by the program's rules, which include speaking only when spoken to, accepting the authority of the judge ("Just pay attention, I run the show" she tells litigants), and taking humiliating remarks and reprimands without rebuttal or comment ("Are you all nuts" and "I'm smarter than you" are typical examples). More important than the details of any particular case is Sheindlin's swift assessment of the choices and behaviors of the people involved in them. . . .

Sheindlin questions litigants about their employment history, marital and parental status, income, drug habits, sexual practices, incarceration record, and past or present "dependency" on public welfare.[14] Such information transcends the evaluation of evidence as the principal means whereby Sheindlin determines who is at fault in the citizenship lesson that accompanies every ruling. Sheindlin is also known to belittle the accents of non-English speakers, accuse litigants of lying and abusing the "system," and order individuals to spit out gum, stand up straight, and "control" bodily functions to her liking. In one episode, a male litigant who denied her accusations of pot smoking was ordered to take a live drug test. *Judge Judy* thus both duplicates and extends the surveillance of the poor and working class carried out by welfare offices, unemployment centers, and other social services.[15]

Judge Judy is part of the current wave of reality TV in that "real" people (not actors) involved in "authentic" disagreements are used as a selling point to differentiate the show from fictional entertainment. While scripts are not used, reality is, as John Fiske reminds us, "encoded" at every level.[16] The program scours small claims dockets for potentially "interesting" cases; would-be litigants must complete a questionnaire, and only those "actual" disputes that can be situated within the program's logic are presented on television. Offscreen narration, graphic titles, video replays, and teasers further frame the meaning of the cases by labeling the litigants, characterizing their purportedly real motivations to viewers and highlighting scenes from the program that reiterate Sheindlin's governmental authority. Due to increased competition for conflicts among the growing cadre of courtroom programs, viewers are now invited to bypass the courts altogether and submit their everyday disputes directly to *Judge Judy*. On-air solicitations like "Are You in a Family Dispute? Call Judy" promise an efficient, private alternative to public mediation of conflicts—and yet, individuals who accept the invitations are ultimately held responsible for their "mistakes" on cases like "The Making of a Family Tragedy."

Judge Judy's focus on everyday domestic conflicts has led some critics to denounce the courtroom program as a new twist on the sensational "low-brow" daytime talk show.[17] Yet Sheindlin insists that her program is a somber alternative to the participatory, carnivalesque atmosphere of the genre it now rivals in the ratings. Indeed, the court setting and overtly disciplinary address of the *Judge Judy* program "code" it in distinct ways that are easily distinguishable to TV viewers. Sheindlin's strict demeanor and authoritative place on the bench are accentuated by camerawork that magnifies her power by filming her from below. The silence of the studio audience, the drab, institutional-like setting of the simulated courtroom, and the presence of a uniformed bailiff also separate the court program from talk shows, a format that feminist scholars have characterized as a tentative space for oppressed groups (women, people of color, and the working classes) to discuss the politic of everyday life. . . .

On *Judge Judy*, the authority represented by the simulated courtroom setting is often enlisted to "force" . . . confessions. Sheindlin claims that her past experience as a frustrated state official has enabled her to "see through the bull" ("She can always tell if you're lying. All she has to do is make eye

contact," reported *USA Today*). Litigants who refuse to "confess" to suspected actions have been subjected to live background checks, but more often than not Sheindlin simply discounts "false" confessions and replaces the version of events offered by the litigant with an expert interpretation gleaned through biographical information as much as "evidence."

Court programs also magnify the disciplinary logic present on the talk show by disallowing audience participation, controlling the flow of personal revelations, and fusing the therapeutic ethos of the "clinic" with the surveillance of the welfare office and the authoritative signifiers of law and order. This distinction, as much as the absence of the carnivalesque, is what has allowed courtroom programs to be institutionally positioned as a cultural corrective to "tabloid" television. *Judge Judy* is the "antithesis of Jerry Springer," insists Sheindlin. "Jerry Springer encourages people to show off their filthiest laundry, to misbehave. I scrupulously avoid doing that. I cut them off."[18]

The television industry has also been quick to assert that courtroom television "educates" as well as entertains—a claim to public service that is rarely made of most popular reality formats. Big Ticket's Larry Lyttle maintains that courtroom programs function as a positive moral force because unlike on talk shows, where "conflicts are aired and tossed around" a court show like *Judge Judy* "ends with a decision that someone was right and someone was wrong."[19] WCHS-TV in Charleston, West Virginia, similarly praises the program's "unique ability to act as a true moral compass for people seeking guidance, insight and resolution."[20] Characterizing the courtroom genre as a technology of citizenship that can temper the "effects" of fictional television, one TV judge explained in an interview that

America's been looking at soap operas for going on 50 some years, and they legitimize the most back stabbing, low-down, slimeball behavior. That's gotten to be acceptable behavior. . . . We find ourselves confronted with a lot of soap-opera behavior in our courtrooms. And we resolve them and say, no, we know you may have seen this, but it's not right.[21]

Privatizing Justice, Stigmatizing "Dependency"

Judge Judy's claim to facilitate "justice at lightning speed" boldly implies that commercial television can resolve problems faster and more efficiently than the public sector. In this sense, the program affirms neoliberal rationales for "outsourcing" state-owned institutions and services. *Judge Judy* also complements neoliberal policies by conveying the impression that democracy (exemplified by the justice system) is overrun by individuals embroiled in petty conflicts and troubles of their own making. If the program feeds off of real-life microdisputes, Sheindlin chastises litigants for failing to govern their "selves" and their personal affairs. In addition to lecturing guests about their personal history, she often accuses participants of "wasting the court's time," conveying the idea that "normal" citizens do not depend on the supervision of the judiciary or any public institution for that matter. People who rely on professional judges (including TV judges) to mediate everyday problems are cast as inadequate individuals who lack the capacity or, worse, desire to function as self-reliant and personally responsible citizens.

On *Judge Judy*, citizenship lessons are often directed at people who reject marriage, the nuclear family, and traditional values; unmarried couples who live together are of particular concern. While Sheindlin (who is divorced) does not condemn such behavior as immoral conduct, she does present rules and procedures for navigating modern relationships, which include getting personal loans in writing, not "living together for more than one year without a wedding band," and not "purchasing homes, cars, boats or animals with romantic partners

outside of wedlock."[22] On *Judge Judy*, individuals are told that they must impose these rules on themselves—both for their own protection and because, as Sheindlin explains, there is "no court of people living together. It's up to you to be smart. Plan for the eventualities before you set up housekeeping." When former lovers dispute an unpaid car loan, Sheindlin takes the disagreement as an opportunity to explain the dos and don'ts of cohabitation without marriage. Sheindlin finds the couple incompatible and "irresponsible," and rules that it was an "error of judgment" for them to share an apartment together. This judgment is tied to a broader failure of appropriate citizenship when Sheindlin lectures the pair for then "asking the courts" to resolve a domestic property dispute. "You're not married—there is a different set of rules for people who choose to live together without marriage," she asserts, reiterating that people who stray from state-sanctioned conventions have a particular duty to monitor their own affairs.

If the idealized citizen-subject constructed by *Judge Judy* complements the choice-making neoliberal customer discussed by Rose, that individual is also a self-supporting worker. People who receive any form of public assistance are cast as deviants in particular need of citizenship lessons. The advice they receive evokes Nancy Fraser and Linda Gordon's observation that welfare has become cloaked in a stigmatizing discourse of "dependency" that presumes gender, class, and racial parity. As Fraser and Gordon point out, women (including single mothers) are now held accountable to the white, middle-class, male work ethic, even as they lack the advantages and resources to perform as traditionally male breadwinners. While this marks a shift away from the patronizing assumption that all women are helpless and therefore "naturally" dependent on men or, in their absence, the state, it conceals the structural inequalities that lower-income women in particular continue to face.[23]

On *Judge Judy* all women are presumed to be capable of supporting themselves and their children financially; accepting welfare is construed not as a reflection of gender or economic inequality but as a character flaw. Women are routinely asked to disclose their past or present reliance on government "handouts," and those who admit to receiving benefits are subsequently marked as irresponsible and lazy individuals who "choose" not to work for a living. Welfare recipients are also constructed as morally unsound citizens who cheat taxpayers, as was the case in an episode where Sheindlin demanded to know whether an unmarried woman with three children by the same father had "avoided" marriage merely to qualify for welfare benefits. In another episode, an unemployed twenty-something mother being sued by her baby's would-be adoptive parents was scolded for relying on public assistance to raise the child she had decided not to give up for adoption. While adoption law doesn't allow adoptive parents to reclaim monetary "gifts" to birth mothers, Sheindlin stressed the woman's "moral" obligation to repay them. Presuming that the mother had chosen poverty, Sheindlin also sternly advised her to get a job and "not have more babies she can't take care of." *Judge Judy's* disdain for so-called welfare dependency extends to charity and other forms of assistance. If individuals are told to take care of themselves and their families, empathy and social responsibility for others are discouraged. "No good deed goes unpunished," Sheindlin advised a family friend who took in a homeless woman who had spent some time in jail. At the societal and community level, the public good is cast in neoliberal terms, as a system of individual responsibilities and rewards. . . .

Since the litigants on *Judge Judy* are introduced by name and occupation this information also appears in onscreen titles—viewers know that individuals cast as risky are often working-class men who drive trucks, wait on tables, enter data, do construction, or perform low-paying forms of customer service. If female welfare recipients are cast as irresponsible nonworkers, men lacking middle-class occupations and salaries are routinely scorned for "choosing" a life of poverty, as

was the case when Sheindlin lectured a middle-aged male Wal-Mart cashier for failing to obtain more lucrative employment. In the adoption episode mentioned above, a similar evaluation of male employment was tied to a failure of citizenship. The infant's father, who had worked on and off as a gas station attendant but was currently unemployed, was characterized as a personal failure and societal menace, not just because he refused to admit "personal moral responsibility" to repay the money to the adoptive parents, but because he "refused" to enterprise himself in accordance with the middle-class work ethic.

Cases involving men who manipulate women out of money, gifts, rent, or property are a staple on *Judge Judy,* and in these cases, male unemployment and insolvency are closely tied to the detection and avoidance of romantic risk. In a case where a woman met a man on the Internet, loaned him money, and was dumped, Sheindlin fused a harsh judgment of the boyfriend's opportunism and dishonesty in his romantic relationship to an undeveloped work ethic. Demanding to know when he last "held a full-time job," she swiftly identified the man as a freeloader and "con artist," implying that men without economic means are especially dangerous and therefore not to be trusted when it comes to intimate relationships. Female litigants can also be categorized as identifiable romantic risks, as was the case in "Opportunity Knocks," where Sheindlin wanted an attractive young woman in court to resolve whether money from her ex-boyfriend was a gift or loan, accusing her of "using" the man financially with "no intention of marrying him." In most cases, though, it is lower-income men who play this role in a gender reversal of the gold digger stereotype. This complements the program's focus on solving the problem of female victimization through better self-management.

Women are typically cast as "self-created" victims in terms that articulate neoliberal currents to female self-help culture. Rejecting what she terms the "disease of victimization," or tendency to blame society for one's hardships, Sheindlin claims, in her books and on her TV program, that all women can achieve happiness and success with a little knowledge along with the right attitude. On *Judge Judy*, women's problems are blamed on their own failure to make good decisions, whether that means pulling one's self up from a life of poverty, "preparing" wisely for financial independence, or avoiding entanglement with unstable, manipulative, or abusive individuals. . . .

Women who claim to have been abused by men appear frequently on *Judge Judy*, where they, too, are lectured for creating their circumstances. Domestic abuse is never the basis of a legal case, but is typically revealed in the course of Sheindlin's interrogation of the participants involved. In a case involving cousins fighting over a family collection of knickknacks, Sheindlin determines that the man is a deranged and unstable individual, while the woman he bullied and harassed is an "adult" who has "chosen to let someone do this to her." When Sheindlin learns that an ex-boyfriend, in court over a minor car accident, has battered his former teenage girlfriend, she maintains that the girl made unwise "choices," sternly advising, "Never let a man put his hands on you." In a case involving former lovers disputing overdue phone and gas bills, the woman reveals that in refusing to pay household expenses, her former boyfriend was addicted to heroin and had spent time in jail for assaulting a minor. She also implies that he physically abused her. Typifying the program's neoliberal solution to the problem of domestic violence as well as the complexities of gender and class, Sheindlin faults the woman for failing to accept responsibility for her own conduct. Taking the troubled relationship as the raw material for a citizenship lesson aimed at women, Sheindlin determines that "being with him doesn't speak well of your judgment." As "young as you are, you allowed someone with a criminal history and no job to live with you . . . and you want the courts to fix that?"

Judge Judy seeks to instill in women a desire to avoid the "disease" of victimization along with the overreliance on state assistance and intervention it is said to have spawned. This message carries traces of liberal feminist discourse to the extent that it promotes female independence and agency. Presuming that barriers to social and gender equality have long been dismantled, the program places the onus to achieve these goals on individuals. Sheindlin, who considers herself a positive female role model, contends that all "women have the power to make decisions, to call it as they see it, to take no guff."[24] She claims that all women, however positioned by an unequal capitalist society, can reap the benefits of happiness and success so long as they exercise good judgment and cultivate self-esteem. Economic security and "feeling good about yourself" are thus closely bound in Sheindlin's blueprint for successful female citizenship. The responsibility for cultivating self-esteem is placed not on society but on individual women, whose job it is to train themselves and their daughters "to have a profession, have a career . . . so they will never be dependent on anybody."[25] On *Judge Judy*, female litigants are advised to avoid "depending" on boyfriends and husbands for financial assistance in particular. This message has less to do with dismantling dominant ideologies and institutions than it does with ensuring that women "take care of themselves" so that the state doesn't have to. *Judge Judy* conveys the idea that women can no longer "claim" a victim status rooted in bifurcated and hierarchical gender roles; nor, however, can they expect public solutions to the inequalities that structure women's lives.

Sheindlin presents "independence" as a responsibility that all women must strive to achieve, but she also promotes the hegemony of the nuclear family, reconstituted as a two-wage-earning unit. Family troubles underscore many of the cases heard on *Judge Judy*, where mothers suing daughters, children suing their parents, and parents suing each other are the norm. This steady stream of feuding relations paints a portrait of a troubled institution that clearly isn't working, yet Sheindlin uses her authority to promote the sacred importance of family bonds. The contradiction exists in perpetual tension, as illuminated by the treatment of family in two key episodes.

In the first, a male cashier is suing his unemployed ex-fiancée for bills paid when they lived together; she is countersuing for "mental distress." After Sheindlin interrogates the woman about why she wasn't working at the time, the woman replies that she quit her job to "build a home together." She also tells Sheindlin that her fiancé stalked her and threatened to come after her with a gun when they broke up. Although this scenario contains the material to cast the male as a deviant individual, Sheindlin rejects the woman's story as an "excuse" smacking of victimization, comparing her own success as a married working woman who didn't "quit her job to pick out furniture and dishes" to the failure of the "alleged victim of harassment," she orders the woman to pay the back rent. In this episode, the female litigant's embrace of traditional family values is denounced because it includes the desire for "dependency" on a male breadwinner, thereby violating the neoliberal mantra of self-sufficiency that *Judge Judy* espouses. In a dispute involving an estranged mother and daughter, though, the nuclear family is valorized against a woman's quest for independence. The mother, who divorced her husband when she came out as a lesbian, is implicitly cast as selfish and irresponsible for abandoning the heterosexual family unit to pursue her own personal fulfillment. While Sheindlin doesn't condemn the woman's homosexuality, she harshly criticizes her performance and "choices" as a mother, and recommends family counseling to repair the damage.

As these examples attest, *Judge Judy's* advice to women does not seek to expand women's choices, it merely guides them in particular directions. Operating as a technology of citizenship, the program steers women toward neoliberal reforms that are presented as their own responsibilities and in their own "best interests." In this sense, *Judge Judy* seeks to transform what Rose calls the "goals of authorities into the "choices and commitments of individuals."[26]

Judge Judy and the Normative Citizen

Judge Judy constitutes the normative citizen—the TV viewer at home—in opposition to both risky deviants and "self-made" victims. By scrutinizing the dos and don'ts of everyday life as it is presumed to be lived by "troubled" populations, it promotes neoliberal policies for conducting one's self in private. It scapegoats the uneducated and unprivileged as "others" who manufacture their hardships, and thus, require nothing more than personal responsibility and self-discipline in the wake of shrinking public services. Those who reject this logic are deemed abnormal and often unreformable: "I'm not going to get through to her. I have a sense that she's a lost cause at fourteen," Sheindlin once said of a female litigant.[27] TV viewers are encouraged to distance themselves from the "deficient" individuals who seep into Sheindlin's courtroom, therefore avoiding any recognition of the societal basis of women's problems and concerns. While Sheindlin's harshest derision is aimed at the socially "unrespectable," her governmental advice is intended for all women—particularly middle-class viewers—for according to the program's neoliberal logic, their happiness and success hinges on it. . . .

Notes

1. The popular press has emphasized the "no tolerance" ethos of the programs, contributing to the cultural context in which they are received. See, in particular, Melanie McFarland, "Tough Judges Show There's Justice in Watching Television," *Seattle Times,* 30 November 1998, http://archives.seattletimes.

2. See ibid.

3. For a critical analysis of the Telecommunications Act of 1996, see Patricia Aufderheide, *Communications Policy and the Public Interest* (New York: Guilford, 1999) and Robert McChesney, *Rich Media, Poor*

Democracy: Communication Politics in Dubious Times (New York: New Press, 2000).

4. James Hay, "Unaided Virtues: The (Neo)-Liberalization of the Domestic Sphere," *Television and New Media* 1, no. 1 (2000): 56.

5. Elizabeth Martinez and Arnoldo Garcia, "What Is Neoliberalism?" *Corpwatch,* 1 January 1997, www.corpwatch.org.

6. Robert McChesney, introduction to *Profit over People: Neoliberalism and Global Order,* by Noam Chomsky (New York: Seven Stories Press, 1999), 7, 11.

7. Nikolas Rose, "Governing 'Advanced' Liberal Democracies," in *Foucault and Political Reason: Liberalism, Neoliberalism, and Rationalities of Government,* ed. Andrew Barry, Thomas Osborne, and Nikolas Rose (Chicago: University of Chicago Press, 1996), 55, 58–59. For a Foucauldian approach to "governmentality," see also Graham Bruchell, Colin Cordon, and Peter Miller, eds., *The Foucault Effect: Studies in Governmentality* (Chicago: University of Chicago Press, 1991). I have also found Toby Miller's analysis of citizenship and subjectivity helpful for thinking through neoliberal modes of government. See his *The Well-Tempered Self: Citizenship, Culture, and the Postmodern Subject* (Baltimore, Md.: Johns Hopkins University Press, 1993).

8. Rose, "Governing 'Advanced' Liberal Democracies," 57–59.

9. Nancy Fraser, *Justice Interruptus: Critical Reflections on the "Postsocialist" Condition* (New York: Routledge, 1997).

10. Judge Wapner was brought back to resolve disputes between pet owners on the Animal Channel's *Animal Court.*

11. Luaine Lee, "Judge Judy Has Always Believed in the Motto 'Just Do It'," *Nando Media,* 28 November 1998, www.nandotimes .com; and Judy Sheindlin, *Don't Pee on My Leg and Tell Me It's Raining* (New York: Harper Perennial, 1997), 3.

12. Cited on www.judgejudy.com.

13. Cited in Lee, "Judge Judy."

14. Michel Foucault, "Complete and Austere Institutions," in *The Foucault Reader,* ed. Paul Rabinow (New York: Pantheon, 1984), 219–20. See also Michel Foucault,

Discipline and Punish (New York: Random House, 1995).

15. See Frances Fox Piven, *Regulating the Poor: The Functions of Public Welfare* (New York: Random House, 1971); and John Gillion, *Overseers of the Poor* (Chicago: University of Chicago Press, 2001).

16. John Fiske, *Television Culture* (New York: Routledge, 1987).

17. Michael M. Epstein, for example, argues that courtroom programs are an extension of the talk show to the extent that they use law and order to legitimate a sensationalist focus on personal conflict. Epstein also points out that the judge figure is construed as an "ultimate" moral authority less concerned with legal procedures than with the evaluation of personal behaviors. Presuming the "low" status of the genre and concentrating on its misrepresentation of the actual law, however, his critique overlooks the governmental nature and implications of this focus on everyday conduct and behavior. See Michael M. Epstein, "Judging Judy, Mablean, and Mills: How Courtroom Programs Use Law to Parade Private Lives to Mass Audiences," *Television Quarterly* (2001), http://www.emmyonline.org/tvq/articles/32–1–1.asp.

18. Cited in Barbara Lippert, "Punchin Judy," *New York Magazine,* 15 June 2001, www .newyorkmetro.com.

19. Cited in *Judge Judy* publicity, www .wchstv.com/synd_prog/judy.

20. Cited on www.wchstv.com/synd_prog/ judy.

21. Cited in McFarland, "Tough Judges Show There's Justice."

22. Judy Sheindlin, *Keep It Simple Stupid* (New York: Cliff Street Books, 2000), 2.

23. Nancy Fraser and Linda Gordon, "A Genealogy of 'Dependency': Tracing a Keyword of the U.S. Welfare State," in Fraser, *Justice Interruptus.*

24. Ibid., 105.

25. Sheindlin, cited in Lee, "Judge Judy."

26. Rose, "Governing 'Advanced' Liberal Democracies," 58.

27. The clip was replayed during an interview with Sheindlin on *Larry King Live,* CNN, 12 September 2000.

The Anxieties of the Enterprising Self and the Limits of Mind Cure in the Age of Oprah

Janice Peck

. . . . Oprah Winfrey rang in the 2007 new year from South Africa with the star-studded launch of the Oprah Winfrey Leadership Academy for Girls, a $40 million boarding school located an hour south of Johannesburg on "52 lush acres and spread over 28 buildings" (Samuels 2007). Outfitted in a pink taffeta ball gown, she presided over the opening ceremony alongside the academy's first class of 152 adolescent girls from "deprived backgrounds"—all personally selected because they possessed what she called the "it" quality ("Oprah Winfrey opens school" 2007; Gien 2007).[1] In addition to providing the girls with state-of the-art facilities and top-flight instructors, Winfrey plans to teach "leadership" classes by satellite from Chicago and occasionally in person. The most important lesson she hopes to instill in her charges: "that we are responsible for ourselves, that you create your own reality by the way you think and therefore act." As Winfrey stated in her magazine's feature story on the school, she wants the academy students to recognize "you cannot blame apartheid, your parents, your circumstances, because you are not your circumstances. You are your possibilities. If you know that, you can do anything" (Gien 2007, 160, 217).[2]

A month after the school's opening, Winfrey was back in Chicago sharing her excitement about *The Secret*—a DVD and book promising the key to attaining health, wealth, and happiness (*Oprah Winfrey Show*, Feb. 7, 2007). The brainchild of Australian reality TV producer Rhonda Byrne, *The Secret* had been gathering momentum since its March 2006 release, thanks to a "viral marketing" campaign targeting the Internet, New Age bookstores, and New Thought churches (Mastropolo 2006). By year's end it had been featured on *Larry King Live* and *The Ellen DeGeneres Show* and the DVD ranked in Amazon's Christmas week top five sellers (Ressner 2006). Given its compatibility with her own mind-cure leanings, it was only a

From Peck, J. (2008). The anxieties of the enterprising self and the limits of mind cure in the age of Oprah. In J. Peck, *The age of Oprah: Cultural icon for the neoliberal era* (pp. 211–239). Boulder, CO: Paradigm.

matter of time before *The Secret* caught Winfrey's attention; on February 7, she introduced Byrne and fellow "teachers of 'The Secret'" who, she told the audience, "say you can have it all. And, in fact, you already hold the power to make that happen."

In the opening segment, Byrne revealed "the secret" to be the "law of attraction," described as "the most powerful law in the universe," comparable to the law of gravity, which governs our existence because "we attract into our lives the things that we want . . . based on what we're thinking and feeling" (*Oprah Winfrey Show,* Feb. 7, 2007; Salkin 2007). Winfrey found this to be neither a secret nor a revelation, but merely confirmation of what she had long professed. "So what you're saying," she told Byrne, "is that we all . . . create our own circumstances by the choices that we make and the choices that we make are fueled by our thoughts. So our thoughts are the most powerful things that we have here on Earth." For Winfrey, the coincidence of nature's laws with her commitment to the power of mind was felicitous. "This is a happy, happy day for me," she beamed. "I've known 'The Secret'—I didn't call it 'The Secret'—for years. And for years on this show, this is what I've been trying to do, is to get people to see it." Just as the Leadership Academy students cannot blame society for their situation, those who embrace the law of attraction must also accept responsibility for their fate. As Winfrey told her audience, "It means that everything that happens to you, good and bad, you are attracting to yourself. It's something that I really have believed in for years, that the energy you put out into the world is always gonna be coming back to you. That's the basic principle" (*Oprah Winfrey Show,* Feb. 7, 2007).[3]

During the show, the various "teachers" counseled the audience to overcome "the tendency to believe in lack, limitation and scarcity" because it stands in the way of the "absolutely unlimited power within us." While a few directives were served

up—it is important to "be grateful," for example, to be "conscious" rather than "unconscious" and seek "alignment" of one's thoughts and actions—for the most part *The Secret* boiled down to "the primacy of simple 'wish fulfillment,'" or, as the DVD instructs, "Ask, believe, receive" (Starker 1988, 39; Salkin 2007). If the "law of attraction"—like the power of positive thinking of the 1950s and the nineteenth-century mind-cure cosmology that spawned them both—ultimately amounts to the "fulfilled wish and how to achieve it" (Starker 1988, 39), this did not appear to discourage Winfrey's followers. So great was the audience response to *The Secret* that it nearly overwhelmed the Oprah.com web site, which routinely receives 64 million hits per month, persuading Winfrey to add a second installment. In the follow-up show, she was heartened to find that the "law of attraction" had "sort of reached mass appeal" because

> It's what this show is all about, and has been about for 21 years, taking responsibility for your life, knowing that every choice that you've made has led you to where you are right now. Well, the good news is that everybody has the power, no matter where you are in your life, to start changing it today. (*Oprah Winfrey Show,* Feb. 16, 2007)

Uniting these seemingly disparate events—the opening of a school in Africa and the marketing of another "think and grow rich" scheme—is the heady concoction of makeover and magnanimity that defines Oprah Winfrey's technology of healing. Reviewing the premiere issue of *O, The Oprah Magazine,* Richard Roeper quotes a statement by Winfrey featured in an ad for her first Personal Growth Summit—"You only have to believe that you can succeed, that you can be whatever your heart desires, be willing to work for it, and you can have it"—to which he responds:

Only if you live in Tinkerbell's world. In the real world, of course, there are millions upon millions of people who have tried the believe-desire-work portion of that equation and yet will NEVER have what they want. They will experience an entire life are without escaping from poverty or despair, without ever finding love or happiness or wealth of material things and/or spirit. (Roeper 2000)

While Roeper is correct about the vast disparity between wish and reality for the large majority of human beings, this has in no way diminished the attraction of Winfrey's "ask, believe, receive" technology of healing or the configuration of self on which it depends. How, then, might we account for the appeal of the notion that the properly formulated wish can become reality?

Anthropologist Maurice Godelier says we should not seek explanations for the power of ideas within the ideas themselves, but look for them instead in "the social relations between humans beings and between human beings and nature" (Godelier 1986, 146). As he argues, "Ideas never contain in themselves all the reasons for their influence and their historical role. Thought alone can never produce those reasons, for this influence derives not simply from what they *are*, but from what they *do*, or better still, from what they *get done* in society" (ibid.). The dominance of an idea in any particular historical moment issues from its "capacity to explain the order or disorder reigning in society" and thereby "facilitate effective action upon the problems connected with the maintenance of this order or with the abolition of this disorder" (ibid.). Making sense of the appeal of mind cure—whether in the present or the past—therefore involves understanding what it gets done. What problems does this technology of healing purport to resolve, for whom is that promised resolution seductive, and why? Such questions lead us back to the historical conditions that have generated "thought as

power" (Satter 1999, 7) cosmologies and endowed them with explanatory power. . . .

In the late twentieth century the shift to a peacetime economy, international oil crisis, and worldwide recession brought to an end the post–World War II boom and launched a new period of stagnant growth, high inflation, deindustrialization, high taxes, rising unemployment, and decline of organized labor. These conditions eroded support for Great Society programs and exacerbated divisions and polarization between "haves" and "have nots," creating an opening for the "divide-and-conquer/unite-and-mobilize" strategies deployed by Reaganism (Reeves and Campbell 1994, 157). Bill Clinton's New Liberalism may have invoked the rhetoric of "empowerment" and "community," but its economic priorities and ideological strategies— rewarding those at the top; shrinking the state; exploiting racial divisions around issues of welfare, crime, and affirmative action to attract white voters; paying homage to "traditional values" —echoed those of its Republican predecessors.[4]

An outstanding feature of the neoliberal era has been the collapse of job security in the United States since the mid-1980s, as "the permanent separation of people from their jobs, abruptly and against their wishes, gradually became standard management practice" (Uchitelle 2006, ix). As Louis Uchitelle documents in *The Disposable American* (2006), between 1984 and 2004, "at least 30 million fulltime workers" were laid off—a figure that does not include "millions more who had been forced into early retirement or had suffered some other form of disguised layoff" (5).[5] By the late 1990s, mass layoffs had become "normal practice, ingrained behavior, just as job security had been twenty-five years earlier" (6). The institutionalization of "flexible" employment and "income volatility" has been central to the transfer of money upward and insecurity downward that has characterized the "new economy" (Hacker 2006; Henwood 2007). Economic uncertainty has been exacerbated by the steady deterioration of the minimum wage after the 1970s, an expanding low-wage workforce that exerts downward pressure on wages at all levels, and proliferating temporary work and low-paying, low-skill jobs (Uchitelle 2006, 143–144, 66–67).[6] Further, although the U.S. economy has grown by 60 percent since the end of the 1970s, that has not translated into a corresponding increase in "good jobs"—ones that pay a decent wage and offer health insurance and a pension plan. In fact, since 1980 "the economy has lost 25 to 30 percent of its capacity to generate good jobs," so that only a quarter of the workforce has such employment today (Schmitt 2005). A crucial consequence of these combined developments, Uchitelle argues, is "a massive shift from a shared, we're-in it-together way of thinking to a go-it-alone world of personal responsibility" (Uchitelle 2006, x). . . .

Corporate downsizing, the expansion of contingent labor, cutbacks in the public sector, and the outsourcing of jobs have had major ramifications for the college-educated middle class, which represents some 30 percent of the U.S. population and is a key target of the Oprah brand (Uchitelle 2006, 66). Whereas a high school education at one time sufficed for most jobs in the United States, by the late 1990s a college degree (or two) had become mandatory for those hoping to secure a spot on the higher rungs of the employment hierarchy. As layoffs spread across white-collar fields and invaded "once-sacrosanct occupations" (ibid., 151), the professional managerial class was simultaneously regaled with promises of the exciting high-tech workplace of the future and warned to beef up its human capital or risk becoming losers in the "new economy." Even as it became imperative to accrue the education and skills necessary to join the ranks of the "symbolic analysts" or "knowledge workers" (see Reich 1991), the downsizing of federal and state governments since the early 1980s had driven the cost of higher education beyond many Americans' reach. Significant numbers of the professional middle-class cadre were also discovering they

had more skills than their jobs demanded as the number of college graduates outpaced that of jobs requiring a degree (Uchitelle 2006, 66). At the same time, the professional managerial ranks were undergoing further stratification into an "haute expertoisie" (e.g., partners in major corporate law and accounting firms) at the top, followed by "small business people," the "lesser specialists in technical support, education and human services," and, at the bottom, an "apprentice class" of "graduate students, research assistants, interns and the like" (Brint 1994, 206).

From the 1980s on, then, as a limited subset of occupations and the education and credentials necessary to attain them were becoming the "key to prosperity in an increasingly polarized economy," competition for these scarce species of cultural capital grew increasingly fierce (P. Smith 1997, 245). In the face of this "intensified system of reward and punishment," economic anxiety marched "up the social ladder" (Henwood 2006, 1). Paeans to the "new economy" notwithstanding, real economic growth under neoliberalism has lagged well behind the growth or the rate of returns to capital, a disparity made possible through a "massive upward redistribution of income" (Baker 2007, 4; "Growth bypasses all but wealthiest" 2006). Having reduced government's function to facilitating this upward transfer of wealth, while thwarting its ability to provide infrastructural support for collective life, neoliberal restructuring has left us to stand alone before the rigid indifference of the market. Meanwhile, neoliberal ideology asserts the absolute determinism of natural economic laws while insisting we are also absolutely free to create our own destinies.

This is the context in which Oprah Winfrey has attained the status of inspirational phenomenon and ubiquitous soul brand. Her enterprise can be understood as an ensemble of ideological practices that help legitimize a world of growing inequality and shrinking possibilities by promoting and embodying a configuration of self compatible with that world. Proclaiming individuals' ability to become whatever their minds can conjure, Winfrey appeals to the upscale, middle-class "sweet spot" that is the prime real estate of her target market, by tapping into and flattering its petty bourgeois values. At the same time, by instructing the lower ranks of her following to adopt those values as their own, citing her own success as proof the prescription works, and scorning anyone who refuses it, her "personal responsibility" nostrum helps bind "broader social strata to the growing prosperity of the few, really or fictitiously" (Dumenil and Levy 2002, 45). That is, the ideological practice of Winfrey's enterprise prescribes and universalizes the values of the petty bourgeoisie—which is mind cure's original architect, strongest advocate, and principal beneficiary, the core target of the Oprah brand and the ideological home of Winfrey herself.[7]

That ideological labor was readily displayed in Winfrey's Leadership Academy project and in her promotion of *The Secret.* Although the launch of her namesake school won the international media attention such spectacles are designed to elicit, it was not entirely of the laudatory tenor Winfrey expected. Indeed, she quickly found herself having to justify spending $40 million on a sumptuous, exclusive[8] school for a few hundred girls in a country with one of the highest unemployment rates in the world (36–42 percent), where some 45 percent of the population lives on less than $2 a day, nearly 20 percent of those aged fifteen and older are infected with HIV/AIDS, and the average life expectancy is forty-seven years (Kingdon and Knight 2005; World Bank Group 2006; Population Reference Bureau 2006; United Nations Development Programme 2007).[9] The *Boston Globe* reported that the school was under attack from international aid groups in the United States and "leaders of grass-roots organizations" in Africa. Critics reproached Winfrey for spending "so much for so few," for failing

to ask local communities to identify their own development needs, and for fostering an "atmosphere of privilege" that divides the school's students from their communities (Donnelly 2007).

By way of contrast to Winfrey's multi-million-dollar investment, for $80,000 the Catholic AIDS Action program provided meals, school uniforms, and after-school programs for 1,500 orphans and vulnerable children in northeast South Africa in 2006; and the Rwanda Women Community Development Network, with an annual budget of $300,000, supported forty grassroots groups that care for 50,000 orphans (ibid.). The South African government, whose own adoption of neoliberal economic policies led to levying fees for school attendance that has put basic education beyond reach for millions of poor children (Hjort and Ramadiro 2004; see also Bond 2004; Ngonyama 2007), initially planned to partner with Winfrey in building the school but got cold feet amid mounting criticism of the facility's opulence. As a government school official told *Newsweek,* albeit anonymously to avoid offending Winfrey, "The country is obviously poor, and so few children have a chance at education. It is hard not to see that many feel that what Ms. Winfrey is doing is too much" (Samuels 2007).

Winfrey's response to the criticism was reminiscent of her reaction to condemnations of Change Your Life TV—a combination of dismissal and defensive explanation. At the school's January launch, where reporters questioned her about the project's "excesses" —among its amenities are a yoga studio, a beauty parlor, two theaters, "fireplaces in every building and white duvets for each bed" — Winfrey conceded that "many" in South Africa "feel that I'm going overboard," but added, "This is what I want to do" (Donnelly 2007). In a statement prepared for the *Boston Globe,* she described the school as "a symbol of leadership for all of Africa" and defended the price tag:

"I wanted these girls to have the best—the best campus, the best curriculum, and of course, the best opportunities" ("Statement" 2007). In fact, Winfrey oversaw every aspect of the school's design and construction, down to personally selecting the bedding, dishes, even the doorknobs. So too with the girls' clothing and shoes. As presented in her magazine and prime-time special, "Building a Dream," the school is akin to a grand makeover project that extends to the students themselves, who are to be transformed first into Winfrey's "dream girls" and then into South Africa's future "leaders" through her largesse. Or, more to the point, the girls are to become replications of their patron, who compared looking at their faces to "looking into the face of myself" and who decided to spare no expense in creating "everything in this school that I would have wanted for myself" (Gien 2007, 158, 156). Providing beautiful surroundings for the academy's students, Winfrey insisted to critics, would not only "bring out the beauty" of the fortunate few she would groom for leadership but also inspire "girls and boys all over Africa" ("Statement from Oprah Winfrey" 2007).

Interestingly, Winfrey's justification of her lavish investment in poor children in South Africa has been coupled with her critique of poor children in the United States. In a *Newsweek* interview, for example, Winfrey said she chose to build her school in South Africa rather than in impoverished U.S. communities because American youth fail to value the educational opportunities they have. She continued,

> I became so frustrated with visiting inner-city schools that I just stopped going. The sense that you need to learn just isn't there. If you ask the kids what they want or need they will say an iPod or some sneakers. In South Africa, they don't ask for money or toys. They ask for uniforms so they can go to school. (Samuels 2007)

She also portrayed the Leadership Academy as a corrective to previous mistaken efforts to help poor Americans. In her "What I Know For Sure" column in the January 2007 issue of *O, The Oprah Magazine,* Winfrey wrote of her decision to halt a "mentorship program for teenage girls living in the [Chicago] Cabrini-Green housing projects" because "I was able to work with them only once a week, which wasn't enough time to instill values in girls whose upbringing wasn't aligned with my teaching." Ditto for her "misguided idea of moving families out of the projects and into new homes." As Winfrey put it, "Trying to show people how to build successful lives was overwhelming—I had taken for granted that they understood what it means to go to work, be on time, and make sure their children go to school and do their homework. So I failed with that idea, but I learned something invaluable: In order to make meaningful changes, you have to transform the way people think" (Winfrey 2007, 218; also Edmonds 2006).

Winfrey displayed similar sentiments in April 2006, when she devoted two episodes of her show to "the disastrous consequences of America's failing high school education system" (two-part "Oprah's Special Report", 2006). Days later, in Baltimore to deliver the keynote address at a fundraiser for a private school, she called that city's public school system "an atrocity" and "a crime to the children" ("Oprah sounds off" 2006). Although many of said children also hailed from "deprived backgrounds," they did not warrant Winfrey's support. As she told a local broadcaster, who asked if she planned to give money to Baltimore public schools, "What I've learned from my philanthropic giving is that unless you can create sustainable change, then it's a waste, you might as well pee on it" (ibid.; also Rodricks 2006). The implication of this uncharacteristically crude response is that Baltimore's schools are beyond hope, a waste of good money. Unspoken, but also implied, is that the students themselves are incapable of "sustainable change"—and hence unworthy of resources—because the desire to learn "just isn't there."[10]

This reduction of material structural constraints to personal deficiencies also figured in her show's handling of *The Secret*. In the second installment, for example, Clarissa, a young single parent in the studio audience, described being summarily fired from her job and worrying about her toddler's future, to which Winfrey remarked, "Any time you get fired, you should say thank you," because "it obviously means you're not supposed to be there" (*Oprah Winfrey Show,* Feb. 16, 2007). Clarissa was featured because her story validated Winfrey's mind-cure message. Although she had initially been very angry with her boss, Clarissa explained that watching the previous week's "Secret" episode made her realize the problem "wasn't him, it was me. He was right. I was negative. It wasn't his fault." Winfrey affirmed this diagnosis and invited the young mother to read the letter she had since written her former boss, in which she thanked him for firing her and credited *The Oprah Winfrey Show* for supplying her with "key words" such as "forgiveness and gratitude." Significantly, Clarissa framed her loss of employment as freedom to go back to school, thus demonstrating her fitness for induction into the ranks of the educated middle class. Indeed, so well did her tale of personal responsibility illustrate the principles of *The Secret*— and of petty bourgeois values—that it was saved for the episode's closing segment.

As neoliberal restructuring has eroded public buffers against the vagaries of the market and undermined the "structure of solidarity" on which the welfare state was based, autonomous individuals like Clarissa must fend for themselves in a Hobbesian universe, armed only with their entrepreneurial spirit and positive thoughts (Van Der Pijl 2006, 28). In such a milieu of scarcity and competition, Kees Van Der Pijl argues, the "only aspiration meaningfully entertained is that of individual improvement, placing each and every citizen in the position where he or she must ask, 'How will I achieve this? What are my chances?'" (ibid., 30). Here we find the link between the "enchanted self" exalted by Winfrey and the "enterprising self" championed by neoliberalism. The former takes responsibility for her life and creates her own circumstances by thinking positive thoughts and making good choices. The latter "makes an enterprise of its life, seeks to maximize its own human capital, projects itself a future, and shapes itself in order to become what it wishes to be" (Rose 1998, 154).

The appeal of the enchanted/enterprising self—which simultaneously accounts for and naturalizes social inequality—is intimately bound up with the fortunes of Winfrey's upscale target audience faced with the demands of the neoliberal order. It reassures the "haves" (i.e., the "symbolic analysts" residing in the professional managerial sector of the middle class) that any benefits they have reaped from the "new economy" result from their positive attitudes and behavior, while absolving them of responsibility for the plight of their less affluent fellows. Conversely, as Nikolas Rose observes, the "have nots" can be "problematized in terms of their lack of enterprise, which epitomizes their weaknesses and their failings" (Rose 1998, 154). And because those weaknesses are posited as entirely self-induced, such irresponsible individuals deserve neither public assistance nor private empathy. Winfrey's brand of mind cure also acknowledges and tries to assuage the economic anxieties of her petty bourgeois followers in this "new gilded age" by promising to help them finesse the brute facticity of market logic so as to avert failure and secure abundance (Uchitelle 2007, 1).[11] Her multiple media outlets are filled with special techniques for harnessing the mind's natural powers, providing an edge to those struggling for a foothold in the professional/managerial ranks. Through this conflation of material and spiritual abundance, Winfrey's mind-cure mission not only supports, it helps sanctify the mutually reinforcing ideas of a self-ordering market and a self-interested human nature. Indeed, Kathryn Lofton writes that Winfrey's media products "serve as paradigmatic profiles in the spiritual practice of capitalism" (Lofton 2006, 599). . . .

Notes

1. In attendance were a roster of A list celebrities and members of what *Essence* magazine called "Black royalty," including Nelson Mandela, who had suggested to Winfrey that she donate money to support education in South Africa; his wife, Graca Machel; Winfrey's father, Vernon; Sidney Poitier; Cicely Tyson; Quincy Jones; Andrew Young; Spike Lee; Tina Turner; and Chris Rock (Taylor and Burns 2007).

2. Winfrey also plans to build a house for herself on the campus so as to be involved in the students' lives (Gien 2007, 217).

3. The effect of Winfrey's endorsement was predictable. As McGee notes, weekly sales of *The Secret* went "from 18,000 to 101,000 copies in the week after the first *Oprah* show endorsing the book and to a staggering 190,000 copies the week after the second program aired" (McGee 2007, 5). By late August the book had been atop the *New York Times* bestseller list for thirty-one weeks ("Advice, how-to" 2007).

4. The parallels between Reaganism and Clintonism are well documented. See Meeropol 1998; Klinkner 1999; Schell 1999; Miroff 2000; Diane Harvey 2000; Pollin 2000; Roediger 2002; and Perlstein 2005.

5. Taking into account both groups, a more realistic estimate would find 7 to 8 percent of full-time U.S. workers "had been laid off annually on average" from 1984 to 2004 (Uchitelle 2006, 5).

6. According to Uchitelle, 70 percent of the "ten occupations expected to grow the fastest" in 2002–2012 pay less than $13.25 an hour (Uchitelle 2006, 67).

7. In his study of Winfrey's genealogy, Henry Louis Gates, Jr., discovered that a decade after the end of slavery, her great-grandfather Constantine Winfrey had bartered cotton he picked on his own time for 80 acres of Mississippi farmland (Gates 2007a, 2007b). The impulse toward proprietorship was thus well established in her family's history. Although popular media accounts of Winfrey typically focus on her early childhood living in poverty in rural Mississippi under the care of her maternal grandmother, she spent a substantial portion of her youth—from age fourteen to twenty-two—living with her father and stepmother in a lower-middle-class area of Nashville. There she was schooled in traditional petty bourgeois values of self-discipline and hard work by her father, who owned a barber shop, and her stepmother, a strict churchgoing woman who made Winfrey read and report on ten books a month and dress and behave like "a lady." Mair writes that in Winfrey's "own assessment, if she hadn't moved back with her father and stepmother, today she would be a poor, unwed mother, just another failed statistic on the urban landscape" (Mair 1994/1998, 24). Both parents also insisted she earn top grades to be eligible for college (ibid., 27). Despite her vast wealth, Winfrey has retained a petty bourgeois orientation. Like her father, she started her own business to be her own boss. She runs Harpo with a high degree of personal involvement in every aspect of its extensive holdings and refuses to take the company public because it would mean relinquishing that control (Sellers 2002). Throughout its history, *The Oprah Winfrey Show* has regularly aired episodes featuring individuals who have realized their dreams and/or built their fortune by starting their own businesses. Winfrey's vision of herself as a self-made woman, her view of education and entrepreneurship as the chief gateways to success, and her insistence that upward mobility is available to anyone who puts her mind to it exemplify her core petty bourgeois values.

8. More than 3,000 girls applied for the 152 spots, a 4 percent acceptance rate, compared Harvard University (Samuels 2007).

9. According to the UN's human development index, South Africa ranks 121 of 176 countries, with an annual per capita income of $11,192; the United States ranks eighth, with a per capita income of $39,676 (United Nations Development Programme 2006).

10. For an analysis of Baltimore's public school system that considers the historical and political-economic forces that have made it one of the most racially and class-segregated in the nation, see Orr (1998), Kane (2004), and Dillon (2007).

11. One sign of the extent of that anxiety is the formation of United Professionals, a non-profit organization launched in 2007 by writer Barbara Ehrenreich to support "unemployed, under-employed and anxiously employed" Americans (Merritt 2007).

References

"Advice, how-to, and miscellaneous." 2007. *New York Times Book Review* (August 26): 24.

Baker, D. 2007. *The United States since 1980.* Cambridge, UK: Cambridge University Press.

Bond, P. 2004. "From racial to class apartheid, South Africa's frustrating decade of freedom." *Monthly Review* (March): 45–59.

Brint, S. 1994. *In an age of experts: the changing role of professionals in politics and public life.* Princeton, NJ: Princeton University Press.

Dillion, Naomi. 2005. "The loss of diversity." *American School Board Journal: December 2005 Special Report*, http://www.asbj.com/specialreports/1205SpecialReports/S2.html (accessed June 22, 2007).

Donnelly, J. 2007. "Outside Oprah's school, a growing frustration: critics in Africa urge wider impact." *Boston Globe* (January 20), http://www.boston.com/news/world/africa/articles/2007/01/20/outside_oprahs_school_a_growing_frustration?mode=PF/ (accessed January 30, 2007).

Dumenil, G. and D. Levy. 2002. "The nature and contradictions of neoliberalism." In *Socialist register 2002*, eds. L. Panitch and C. Leys, 43–71. London: Merlin Press.

Edmonds, P. 2006. "This time I won't fail." *USA Weekend* (December 15–17): 6–7.

Gates, H. L., Jr. 2007a. "Forty acres and a gap in wealth." *New York Times* (November 18): Sec. Week in Review, 14.

———. 2007b. *Finding Oprah's roots; finding your own.* New York Crown Publishers.

Gien, P. 2007. "Building a dream." *O, the Oprah Magazine* (January): 154–160, 217.

Godelier, M. 1986. *The mental and the material.* London: Verso.

"Growth bypasses all but wealthiest few." 2006. *The State of Working America*, http://www.stateofworkingamerica.org/new/SWApr-final.pdf (accessed August 31, 2007).

Hacker, J.S. 2006. *The great risk shift.* Oxford, UK: Oxford University Press.

Harvey, Diane H. 2000. "The public's view of Clinton." In *The postmodern presidency*, ed. S. Schier, 124–142. Pittsburgh: University of Pittsburgh Press.

Henwood, D. 2007. "LBO at 20." *Left Business Observer* (114) (January), http:www.leftbusinessobserver.com/LBOAt20.html (accessed August 24, 2007).

Herbert, B. 2005. "The mobility myth." New York Times (June 6): A19.

Hjort, L., and B. Ramadiro. 2004. "A long walk to nowhere—ten years of democracy in South Africa." AICD, Alternative Information and Development Centre, http:www:aidc.org.za/?q=node/view/585 (accessed July 2, 2007).

Kane, G. 2004. "50 years later, gaps separate the races in our schools." Baltimoresun.com (May 12), http:www.baltimoresun.com/news/local/bal-md.kane12may12,0,5312940.column (accessed June 22, 2007).

Kingdon, G., and J. Knight. 2005. "Unemployment, race, and poverty in South Africa." Global Poverty Research Group, http://www.gprg.org/themes/t2-inc-ineq-poor/unem/unem-pov.htm (accessed July 2, 2007).

Klinkner, P. A. 1999. "Bill Clinton and the politics of the new liberalism." In *Without justice for all*, ed. A. Reed, Jr., 11–28. Boulder, CO: Westview Press.

Lofton, K. 2006. "Practicing Oprah; or, the pre-scriptive compulsion of a spiritual capital-ism." *Journal of Popular Culture* 39 (4): 599–621.

Lowenstein, R. 2007. "The inequality conun-drum." *New York Times Magazine* (June 10): 11–12, 14.

Mair, G. 1994/1998. *Oprah Winfrey: the real story*. Secaucus, NJ: Carol Publishing.

Mastropolo, F. 2006. "'The secret' to success?" ABC News (November 26), http:www .chicagotribune.com/features/lifestyle/chi-1213oprahbacklashdec13,0,85399,story? page=1 (accessed December 13, 2007).

McGee, M. 2007. "*The Secret*'s success." *Nation* (June 4):4–6.

Meeropol, M. 1998. *Surrender: how the Clinton administration completed the Reagan revo-lution*. Ann Arbor: University of Michigan Press.

Merritt, J. 2007. "White-collar organizer: union workers have their locals. But in these scary times, who speaks for the anxious afflu-ent?" Cnnmoney.com (May 24), http:// money.cnn.com/magazines/moneymag/mo neymag_archive/2007/06/01/100033972/ index/htm (accessed August 15, 1007).

Miroff, B. 2000. "Courting the public: Bill Clinton's postmodern education." In *The postmodern presidency*, ed., S. Schier, 106–123. Pittsburgh: University of Pittsburgh Press.

Ngonyama, P. 2007. "Far from free education." Amandla, http://www.amandlapublishers .com/Site/Education.pdf (accessed July 2, 2007).

"Oprah sounds off on Baltimore's education cli-mate." 2006. wbaltv.com (April 11), http:// www.wbaltv.com/news/8627555/detail .html?subid=10100681 (accessed June 22, 2007).

"Oprah Winfrey opens school for girls in South Africa." 2007. CNN.com (January 2), http:// www.cnn.com/2007/WORLD/africa/01/ 02/oprah.school.ap/index.html/ (accessed January 30, 2007).

"Oprah's special report: American schools in crisis." 2006. http://www.oprah.com/about/

press/releases/200604/press_releases_2006 0404 (accessed May 29, 2007).

Orr, M. 1998. "Jobs or education: how racial politics in Baltimore thwarted education reform." http://www.children.smartlibrary .org/NewInterface/segment.cfm?segment= 2134 (accessed June 22, 2007).

Perlstein, R. 2005. "Party cannibals." *Nation* (February 7): 5–6.

Pollin, R. 2000. "Anatomy of Clintonomics." *New Left Review* (3) (May-June):17–46.

Population Reference Bureau. 2006. South Africa, statistics. http://www.prb.org/Countries/ SouthAfrica.aspx (accessed July 2, 2007).

Reeves, J, and R. Campbell. 1994. *Cracked cov-erage*. Durham, NC: Duke University Press.

Reich, R. 1991. *The work of nations*. New York: A. A. Knopf.

Ressner, J. 2006. "The secret of success." *Time* (December 28), http://www.time.com/time/ printout/0,8816,1573136,00.html/ (accessed February 19, 2007).

Rodricks, D. 2006. "Listen up, Oprah, there are other ways to help city kids." *Baltimore Sun* (April 13), http://find/galegroup.com/itx/ start.do?prodld=ITOF,Gale document number CJ144442614 (accessed February 12, 2007).

Roediger, D. 2002. *Colored whites*. Berkeley: University of California Press.

Roeper, R. 2000. "O, what an ego trip." *Chicago Sun-Times* (April 30): 11.

Rose, N. 1998. *Inventing our selves*. Cambridge, UK: Cambridge University Press.

Salkin, A. 2007. "Shaking riches out of the cos-mos." *New York Times* (February 25), http:// www.nytimes.com/2007/02/25/fashion/25 attration.html/ (accessed February 26, 2007).

Samuels, A. 2007. "Oprah Winfrey's lavish South African school." *Newsweek* (January 8), http://www.msnbc.msn.com/id/16396343/ site/newsweek/print/1/displaymode/1098/ (accessed January 30, 2007).

Satter, B. 1999. *Each mind a kingdom: American women, sexual purity, and the New Thought movement, 1875–1920*. Berkeley: University of California Press.

Schell, J. 1999. "Master of all he surveys." (Review.) *Nation* (June 21): 25.

Sellers, P. 2002. "The business of being Oprah." *Fortune* (April 1): 50–54, 58, 60–61, 64.

Sellers, P., A. Harrington and M. Shanley. 2003. "The fifty most powerful women in American business." *Fortune* (October 13): 103.

Smith, P. 1997. *Millennial dreams.* London: Verso.

Starker, S. 1998. *Oracle at the supermarket: The American preoccupation with self-help books.* New Brunswick, NJ: Transaction Publishers.

"Statement from Oprah Winfrey." 2007. *Boston Globe Online* (January 20), http://www.boston.com/news/world/africa/articles/2007/01/20/statement_from_oprah_winfrey?mode=PF (accessed January 30, 2007).

Taylor, S. L., and K. Burns. 2007. "Oprah opens school for girls in South Africa." *Essence* (January 2), http://www.essence.com/essence/print/0,14882,1573448,00.html/ (accessed February 20, 2007).

Tough, P. 2007. "The class-consciousness raiser." *New York Times Magazine* (June 10), 52–56.

Uchitelle, L. 2006. *The disposable American: layoffs and their consequences.* New York: Alfred A. Knopf.

United Nations Development Programme. 2006. "Beyond scarcity: power, poverty, and the global water crisis. South Africa." http://hdr.undp.org/hdr2006/statistics/countries/data_sheets/cty_ds_ZAF.html (accessed August 1, 2007).

Van Der Pijl, K. 2006. "A Lockean Europe?" *New Left Review* (January-February): 9–37.

Winfrey, O. 2007. "What I know for sure." *O, the Oprah Magazine* (January): 218.

Television and the Domestication of Cosmetic Surgery

Sue Tait

. . . . This chapter explores the discursive production of cosmetic surgery on *Extreme Makeover* (2002–2005), the most successful of television's surgical reality shows, and *Nip/Tuck* (2003–), the first drama series about cosmetic surgery. Both US produced shows are internationally syndicated and *Nip/Tuck* is available on DVD. My analysis attends to the ways in which particular meanings of cosmetic surgery are empowered within public culture through the way in which surgery and surgical patients are visualised and narrated on television. I argue that while *Extreme Makeover* at once spectacularises and domesticates the surgical body, *Nip/Tuck*'s rendering of surgical culture attempts to disrupt the prevailing cultural comfort with cosmetic appearance work. *Extreme Makeover* illustrates the manner in which the domestication of surgical culture relies on, and elaborates, a postfeminist cultural imaginary, whereby individual consumption rather than cultural transformation is posited as the means to empower the deviant gendered body. Feminist understandings of cosmetic surgery, as a cultural phenomenon which expresses gendered inequity, get left behind. . . .

As I shall elaborate, while *Nip/Tuck*'s critique of surgical culture is frequently curtailed by sensationalism and recourse to individualist explanatory frames, the show nevertheless remains a rare space through which a dystopic view of surgery is signalled within public culture. Identifying potentially resistive frames to the domestication of surgical culture, and the manner in which these are constrained by the conventions of television drama, illustrates the limited range of subject positions available to contemporary television viewers which may be marshalled when framing their own responses to cosmetic surgery. . . .

From Tait, S. (2007). Television and the domestication of cosmetic surgery. *Feminist Media Studies*, 7(2), 119–135.

Extreme Makeover: The Practice of Aesthetic Eugenics as Charity

Press statements released by both the American Society for Aesthetic Plastic Surgery (ASAPS) and the American Society of Plastic Surgeons (ASPS) in 2005 link the rise in the number of surgical procedures performed in 2004 to the trend in cosmetic surgery reality television. ASPS suggest that this increase is not "rampant," with the 9.2 million procedures performed in 2004, 5 per cent up on 2003 and 24 per cent up on 2000. Figures released by ASAPS differ markedly from ASPS's (which may be attributed to a different method of data collection), claiming that 11.9 million procedures were performed in 2004, a 44 per cent increase from 2003. The president of the organisation suggests this rise is connected to media coverage of plastic surgery: "[p]eople have had many more opportunities to see, first hand, what plastic surgery is like and what it can do for others. That can be a strong incentive for them to seek the same benefits by having cosmetic procedures themselves" (ASAPS 2005). The ideological labour *Extreme Makeover* performs in normalising cosmetic surgery was commented upon by a member of the "Extreme Team" on a follow-up special:

> I think the show has done a wonderful thing for plastic surgery and patients because it has brought it out of the closet. It's made it okay to have plastic surgery without hiding it, and that's an incredibly liberating thing for a lot of people for whom it makes a huge difference in their lives. (Life After *Extreme Makeover* 2004)

Extreme Makeover stages the surgical transformation of candidates in a manner which not only publicises cosmetic surgery, but makes it meaningful in ways which eschew perceptions of surgery as the practice of the vain or superficial. It contributes to a post-feminist surgical imaginary by

figuring surgery as the means to empower the suffering individual, a discursive production which domesticates practices of discrimination, along with their surgical solution. . . .

The opening sequence of *Extreme Makeover* introduces the candidates, who make a confession of ugliness and a confession of suffering which serve to legitimise their surgical candidacy. The candidate, friends and family, and the narrator testify to the suffering the appearance of the patient brings: David (improbably) claims his infant son finds him unattractive (season 1: episode 2); Lori and her children have been teased about Lori's "witch" nose (Lori's young daughter confesses "I feel sad that my mother can't go any places at school with me . . . because of her face and the stuff that's wrong with her") (season 3: episode 2); and James has been beaten and bullied (season 2: episode 19). Testimonies of suffering include accounts of loneliness, poor job prospects, social phobia, bullying, and the inability to find a mate. These confessions locate the physical appearance, rather than the cruelty of others, as the site which produces unhappiness, and posit surgical transformation as the most expedient cure. As Deery observes, *Extreme Makeover* may be regarded as a prime-time infomercial for cosmetic surgery which presents "individual stories which inspire empathy but short-circuit politicization" (2004, p. 212).

Viewers are often told that suffering and tragedy in the candidate's lives, or the work they do in the service of others, have taken a toll on their appearance. Kari (season 3: episode 12) has lost a son, Sandra spent 30 years caring for a disabled husband (season 1: episode 4), and Peggy claims her career in law enforcement has aged her (season 2: episode 2). These narratives are supplemented by testimony from loved ones as to the moral worthiness of the candidates, who are described as caring and self-sacrificing, kind and hardworking. This convention of the show performs important ideological labour in representing the bestowal of a make-over as an act of charity, awarded to a morally worthy recipient who has suffered unfairly. The implication is that the physical appearance of candidates does not reflect who they "truly" are, playing out the culturally produced belief that character is manifest in appearance (Sullivan 2001, p. 18). The show thus rewards a beautiful appearance to the moral individual, and in doing so makes things as they really "ought" to be. . . . This awarding of make-overs to the morally deserving contributes to post-feminist ideology by eliding feminist readings of surgical culture. Cosmetic surgery becomes about "justice"; it is framed a cure for suffering, eliding the feminist contention that "it is a significant contributory cause of women's suffering by continually upping the ante on what counts as an acceptable face and body" (Bordo 1997, p. 43).

The confession of ugliness which produces suffering is elaborated through sequences in each show where candidates describe and demonstrate their flaws before the camera. This stages the unruly and deviant body that may be redeemed through medical technologies. This is not so much a ritual in humiliation (Weber 2005); rather it is a visualising of proof central to the confession of suffering. These sequences function to recruit the viewing audience to share the candidate's assessing and disciplinary gaze and assent with the identification of the aberrant features of the displayed body. This ostensibly "proves" that surgical intervention is warranted, through implicit comparison to the bodies which are usually spectacularised within consumer and televisual culture: the hegemonic bodies which do not bear the traces of childbirth, aging or poverty. This demonstration of the pre-surgical body performs a pedagogy of defect (Bordo 1997, p. 37), inviting the viewing audience to compare themselves with the body on screen. The candidate's assessment of their body is subsequently confirmed by the surgeon, who names the aberrant features and prescribes surgical remedy. . . .

The boundary between the reconstructive and cosmetic procedure is further blurred on *Extreme Makeover* through the

inclusion of candidates with deformities, both congenital and resulting from illness. Several cleft palates have been treated, replacement breasts awarded to a breast cancer survivor, and state-of-the-art hearing aids fitted for a woman with a hearing impairment. These procedures, which restore function, intensify the charitable dimension of the show, and render all surgical intervention equivalent. A patient who receives an operation to restore function also receives multiple cosmetic operations. As Brenda Weber notes:

> [b]y pairing those with "legitimate" defects and those with "aesthetic" flaws, the show effectively collapses the difference between the two—if a cleft palate merits surgery, so does a weak chin. The subjects are not selected, then, according to their relative degree of "deformity," since all aesthetic anxieties signal crippling disabilities. (2005, p. 16)

The confession process continues in the surgeon's office, where the patient's defects are named and surgical solutions explained. These consultations with the surgeon function to extend the surgeon's gaze into the culture. Belling (1998) discusses the creation of "expert" patients via reality television depicting medical operations. Surgical make-over shows similarly offer a pedagogy which equips the viewer for the surgeon's office. This was illustrated in an episode of *Extreme Makeover* where, after listing the six facial operations she would like to receive, Kim's surgeon asked "Now, where did you learn about these procedures, from watching the show?" to which she replied, "Definitely!" (season 3: episode 9). The sharing of the surgeon's specialist language and aesthetic sensibility does not diminish his power—rather it multiplies it by enabling participation in surgical culture. Thus surgical television democratises knowledge of cosmetic surgery; its specialist discourse circulates beyond disciplinary confines and functions to authorise and extend its discursive field. Viewers may thus become experts, within a discourse which can identify a chin which "needs" an implant to "balance" a face, and this consent to the surgeon's expertise intensifies his authority.

As Sarah Banet-Weiser and Laura Portwood-Stacer observe, according to the post-feminist ideology of surgical television:

> The submission of one's body to a group of cosmetic surgeons to be reworked and redefined is never positioned as an issue about gender inequity or unattainable femininity—indeed, shows such as *The Swan* and *Extreme Makeover* provide "evidence" that *any* body is possible, if one simply has the desire. (2006, p. 269)

Of course, while any body may be possible, only particular kinds of body will do. Surgery for men is rendered as bestowing or restoring virility (indeed, one candidate received a reverse vasectomy), and descriptions of the effect procedures will have on the appearance often refer to gendered ideals: a chin implant will make a face more "masculine," a woman's nose may be rendered more "delicate" and "feminine," and the procedure most requested by female candidates is breast implants. During Mike's make-over, analogies were drawn between his surgeries and automotive body work (season 2: episode 20). Post-surgically, Dan exclaimed, "Oh my God, I look like an action hero" (season 2: episode 1), while the make-overs of female contestants are sometimes described as real-life "fairy tales."

Occasionally, people of colour are selected for a make-over. Angela's confession is an account of her experiences of racism: of being called "big nose," "big lips" and "monkey girl" (season 2: episode 12). It is reiterated again and again, by her surgeon (who is black) and the narrator, that Angela's surgery is not about race; that it is not an attempt to conceal her ethnic identity—rather it is about beauty and proportion. However, as Padmore instructs, "it is vital to interrogate the idea of cosmetic surgery as a movement towards 'better' looks.

The phrase implies there is a universal aesthetic paradigm; a series of features which 'everybody' knows are beautiful or ugly" (1998, p. 6). As Balsamo (1996) explains, this paradigm is shaped through particular raced, gendered and ageist sensibilities. The assertions that Angela's make-over is not about "race" are disingenuous on a fundamental level: Angela's experience of her body has been produced by a racism which codes her features as "too black." While Angela's make-over brings her happiness, at her reveal we see that her four children share their mother's original facial features. This highlights the impoverished form of power the individual's transformation consists of. It does nothing to unsettle, and may in fact reproduce, the cultural meanings of difference which "often offer a pedagogy directed at the reinforcement of feelings of inferiority, marginality, ugliness" (Bordo 1993, p. 262).

Extreme Makeover devotes scant screen time to the surgeries themselves. During these sequences the carnality of surgery is elided: incursions into the body are concealed as camera and editing coyly avoid shots of instruments or hands entering flesh, the presence of blood, or the opened body. Instead, up-beat narration accompanies close-ups of the surgeon's face and long shots, which signify surgical performance but mystify its specificities. This effacement of carnality, and, as the patients recover, pain, trivialise these aspects of the surgical process. Instead, narrative momentum builds towards the "reveal," the climax of each show where the transformed candidates are restored to friends and family. It is the "reveal" which demonstrates most graphically that cosmetic surgery "works" to heal the psyche. The candidates are invariably ecstatic, as they parade before assembled guests. Shame deriving from one's appearance has transformed into a desire to be looked at. Candidates testify to new, empowered subjectivities: Pam claims "I'm the person I always wanted to be on the outside, and that's completed me and made me whole" (season 2: episode 9).

The transformations performed on *Extreme Makeover* render the body "cultural plastic" (Bordo 1993; Brush 1998). As one patient expressed in relation to his presurgical body: "I'm just starting to understand that the limitations I thought I had, are not there" (season 2: episode 1). . . . Feminism, as a means to think beyond the body of the individual to the culture which produces the body's significance, becomes further displaced by a post-feminist logic of plasticity. By staging an ease and acceptability of cosmetic surgery, facial and bodily features which are culturally reviled become increasingly contingent: "ugliness" becomes our choice and responsibility.

Nip/Tuck: Melodrama and the Limits of Cultural Critique

Nip/Tuck is a melodrama about two philandering male plastic surgeons which has been condemned by both ASAPS and ASPS (Hopkins Tanne 2003). *Nip/Tuck* disrupts the culture's domestication of cosmetic surgery through the graphic realism of its depiction of surgery and through its ambivalent exploration of the impact of surgical culture on its gendered subjects. On *Extreme Makeover,* narrative drama is produced through the "before" and "after," and the attendant cultural assumption that the transformed appearance will transform the psyche. The boundary between reconstructive and cosmetic surgery is effaced and the carnality of surgery elided. *Nip/Tuck* eschews and inverts these conventions of the makeover: the surgery in between is the source of dramatic impact, the boundary between reconstructive and cosmetic surgery actively negotiated, and the latter is rendered as narcissistic; a practice through which "people externalise the hatred they feel about themselves" (season 1: episode 1). . . . *Nip/Tuck*'s surgical scenes display the intervention into healthy (though sometimes disfigured) bodies, and rather than

drawing the viewer towards a narrative outcome (the patient is saved), these scenes function as a display of the surgical as gruesome aesthetic. During these sequences, dialogue is replaced by a musical track which frequently functions as an ironic counterpoint to the surgery on screen. In the episode "Sean McNamara" (season 2: episode 1), the track "Eyes Without a Face" plays, while a large strip of flesh is sliced from the patient's leg in order to reconstruct the damage a gun shot has done to her face. This two minute sequence consists of quick edits cut in time to the music. The face is sliced above the brow and the flesh peeled down over the eye. A metal plate is screwed into the skull via the wound site. A scalpel slices through the flesh along the jawline and scissors are used to snip through the underlying layers of tissue to reveal a metal plate, which is removed. One of the surgeons peers through a large microscope, and our point of view follows his gaze upon his performance of a delicate microsurgery performed within a field of red. The lay viewer does not actually know the specifics of what is being performed here—rather, we are privy to a specialist, mystified, carnographic spectacle.

A facelift performed in the same episode is similarly graphic: skin is sliced and flesh loosened from the forehead, pulled, and stitched. These procedures, which are staged using elaborate prosthetic effects, are so realistic they prompted one reviewer to assume real life surgical footage was incorporated into the fictional text (Dumenco 2003). The realism here does not serve to facilitate communication between prospective patient and surgeon, as Belling (1998) argues may be the case for surgical reality television—rather, it draws a fascinated gaze upon the carnographic which is intended to reveal the mystification implicit in the term "cosmetic" surgery. As Ryan Murphy, creator of *Nip/Tuck* explains:

> When I was researching the show, one plastic surgeon told me that getting your

face done is basically the equivalent of going through a car window at 70 miles an hour and surviving. I wanted to do a show that really shows you: if you really want to have this done, there's a price to be paid on every single level. Surgeries are brutal. (Ryan Murphy cited in Mim Udovitch 2003, p. 22)

Murphy's agenda mirrors the agenda of feminist commentators who similarly underscore the violence of going under the knife. Murphy opens her critique of surgical culture with an illustration of surgical instruments: scalpels, knives, needles, and scissors, and directs the reader, "Now look at the needles and the knives. Look at them carefully. Look at them for a long time. *Imagine them cutting into your skin*" (1991, p. 26). Finkelstein (1991) provides detailed descriptions of surgical procedures, including face and eye lifts, rhinoplasty and chemabrasion, illustrating that rather than "cosmetic" procedures, a term which implies superficial ministrations, these are medical operations which rely on the slicing, pulling and grinding of flesh. In these feminist accounts, and on *Nip/Tuck*, graphic imagery works against the trivialization and domestication of cosmetic surgery within the culture. However, the feminist analyses are part of an explicit critique of the ideological, cultural and political implications of the pursuit of youth and beauty, while such an agenda on *Nip/Tuck* is sporadic. The graphic sequences, which are a signature of the show, are bracketed from the narrative, rarely advancing this resistive gesture into weightier critique. Through repetition, these scenes may even lose their shock value and instead train the viewer to look. Fascination may displace repulsion; awe at the skill of the *surgeons* may overwhelm the intended politics of the gruesome spectacle.

The spectacle of surgery on *Nip/Tuck* expresses a political posture, but this is rarely supported by sustained narratives which politicise surgical culture. Rather, while issues regarding the raced and gendered

politics of cosmetic surgery may be raised, the sensational is routinely favoured over coherent critique. For example, in the episode "Kurt Demsey" (season 1: episode 5), a white man wants his eyelids refashioned so that he can "pass" as Japanese and win the approval of a xenophobic prospective mother-in-law. Rather than tell a story of the "Westernisation" of the "Oriental" eye, thus politicising the manner in which race is in play within surgical culture (Balsamo 1996; Gilman 1999; Haiken 1997; Padmore 1998), the show opts to tell the story of an individual prepared to go to great lengths to prove his love. Nevertheless, Liz, the practice's anaesthesiologist, poses the procedure as an ethical, and political issue: "Does anyone here besides me think there is anything morally reprehensible about a white man trying to pass himself off as a victim of the American racial hierarchy?" Sean's response is that their job is to "alleviate pain," to which Liz replies "That's your answer? So why don't we turn everyone white and hetero?"

Liz acts as the show's moral compass. She routinely pops up, like a Shakespearian chorus, to espouse a feminist line on cosmetic surgery. The paradox that Liz works within an industry she so explicitly distains is never reconciled, and her complicity with the industry, coupled with the often caricature-like quality of her commentary, cast her criticism of surgical culture as ineffectual. Feminism is rendered as an opinion, rather than a means of intervening into the reproduction of surgical culture. As a patient lies on the table prior to the removal of her breast implants, Liz comments "every time I see what women do to themselves with these tit jobs, it makes me ashamed of what I do for a living" (season 1: episode 12). The audience is directed to concur as we watch an incision being made beneath a breast which slices the lower portion from the body. An instrument resembling a crow bar is used to prise the flesh from the chest, so that an entire hand can enter the body and pull the bloody implants from the breast cavity.

Nip/Tuck frequently explores the gendered cruelties of appearance work through the breast, rendering implants as dangerous and a site of exploitation. One storyline featured drug mules who trafficked heroin in breast implants in return for the promise of a modelling career in the U.S. (season 1: episode 12). A surgery depicting the removal of ruptured silicone implants showed the sticky silicone being pulled like taffy, slurping, from inside the breast (season 3: episode 1). Megan O'Hara's implants weakened her immune system and were cited as the reason for the return of her cancer (season 1: episode 10), and Julia McNamara's decision to have breast augmentation in a bid to win back her husband was met with derision (she subsequently had the implants removed). Responding to her mother's criticism of her new implants, Julia asks "You had a face lift, mother, what's the difference?" Her mother conjures the pornographic-ness of implants by responding "I did it for professional reasons. The only professional reason for that is to look better dancing on a pole" (season 2: episode 11). The unevenness of *Nip/Tuck*'s critique of cosmetic surgery is illustrated through this exchange: the pathologising of female aging is not addressed here, and the fact that Julia's mother is a psychiatrist adds weight to the arbitrary distinction she draws.

Kimber Henry is a recurrent character through whom a dystopian narrative of becoming surgical is presented. In the morning following their initial sexual encounter, Christian ranks Kimber's attractiveness as "an eight," promising that with surgery he can make her "a ten" (season 1: episode 1). Christian takes her red lipstick and marks her face and body with vivid gashes, which prefigure the blade that will follow. Thus Kimber's decision to become surgical is rendered as a product of shame and humiliation; a response to the violent misogyny of an unethical surgeon. Following her surgery, Kimber retains Christian's interest

only intermittently (at one point he trades her to a colleague for a sports car), her success as a model and mainstream actor is short lived, she becomes addicted to cocaine and ends up working in the porn industry.

Kimber's character is used to tell a cautionary tale about the excesses of surgical culture, but the show's preference for the prurient over the political limits this critique. In a second season episode, "Kimber Henry" (season 2: episode 10), Kimber asks the partners to make modifications to the vagina of a silicone sex doll made in her image. She explains: "The vagina looks too generic to me. I'd like it to be appealing and pretty. The folds are too fleshy." As Sean makes the mould of Kimber's vagina she asks him to "cheat" and "make the labia just a touch more delicate" than her own: "I'd like my vagina to be prettier." Rather than politicising the growing trend in cosmetic labia plasty, produced through women's subscription to increasingly pornographic beauty ideals (Braun 2005; Weil Davis 2002), women's literal embodiment of a pornographic aesthetic is displaced onto the doll.

Unlike *Extreme Makeover,* where the boundary between reconstructive and cosmetic surgery is elided, *Nip/Tuck* frequently asserts this boundary. However, the heroism through which reconstructive work is rendered at times deflects criticism from the practice of cosmetic surgery, rendering the individual's vanity as the appropriate target of critique. . . .

While *Nip/Tuck*'s critical sensibility is erratic in its target, there are rare moments at which it interrogates the logic behind the domestication of surgical culture. Mrs. Grubman, a polysurgical addict, blackmails the partners into performing her numerous surgeries. While on one level her vanity is punished—she suffers a stroke during a procedure and becomes partially paralysed—she is ultimately rendered sympathetically, and a broader cultural critique is levelled (season 2: episode 4). It emerges that Mrs. Grubman is clinically depressed because she is aging, and we are directed to consider both the way in which the culture pathologises female aging, and the folly in attempting to address a psychological problem with a surgical cure.

Conclusion

This chapter has examined what television offers publics to think about cosmetic surgery. *Extreme Makeover* domesticates cosmetic surgery by publicising its practice, and in so doing authorising synthetic beauty ideals. Surgery is rendered as an increasingly normative practice, and the post-feminist spectacle of transformation as a cure for suffering and a route to empowerment distances its practice from negative associations with vanity and gendered oppression. The imperative to conceal surgery as a mark of inauthenticity dissipates, as transformation is celebrated as self-actualisation. Surgical reality television provides viewers with tools for imagining themselves as clients of surgical services: a language for naming procedures, knowledge of the suitability of candidates, ways to imagine surgeons, and testimonials that surgical intervention "works" to cure suffering. *Extreme Makeover* further domesticates cosmetic surgery by eliding surgery's intervention into the body, and by constituting it as family entertainment. In conflating surgery and charity, the former is imbued with a moral dimension, rendering invisible concerns that may be raised about the commercialisation of medicine (Sullivan 2001), the risks people take for an altered appearance, and the cultural consequences of positing surgery as the means to remedy psychic distress. . . .

Nip/Tuck attempts to unsettle the domestication of cosmetic surgery by rendering its carnality and invoking its raced, gendered and ageist practices. The show represents the limited efficacy of feminist critique, within a culture which has embraced the post-feminist logic of the surgical cure.

Nip/Tuck's response to surgical culture provides moments of resistance, but these are frequently overwhelmed by the requirement to render the surgeon characters as redeemable, and by a sensationalism which prefers the dramatic over the political. . . .

Nip/Tuck's gestures towards a feminist sensibility serve to stage conflict between characters and, through the surgical scenes, render novel televisual spectacles which are rarely linked to sustained frameworks that coherently articulate the cultural consequences of the domestication of cosmetic surgery. Thus while *Nip/Tuck* conjures feminist critique, it is ultimately part of a post-feminist mediascape, where feminism is an occasional voice within a culture that is inevitably surgical. As these two shows illustrate, feminist responses to cosmetic surgery are overwhelmed by a post-feminism which asserts our right to shape ourselves. The individual's choice to transform their body is uncoupled from potential collective agendas to locate, and intervene on, a source of suffering outside of the individual's pre-surgical body.

References

American Society for Aesthetic Plastic Surgery (2005) '11.9 million cosmetic procedures in 2004', [Online] Available at http://www.surgery.org/pre/news-release.php?iid=395 (18 Oct. 2006).

American Society of Plastic Surgeons (2005) '9.2 million cosmetic plastic surgery procedures in 2004—up 5% growth paces US economy despite reality TV fad', [Online] Available at: http://www.plasticsurgery.org.news_room/Press_release/2004-Wverall-statistics (18 Oct. 2006).

Balsamo, Anne (1996) *Technologies of the Gendered Body: Reading Cyborg Women*, Duke University Press, Durham.

Banet-Weiser, Sarah & Portwood-Stacer, Laura (2006) "I just want to be me again!": beauty pageants, reality television, and post-feminism. *Feminist Theory*, vol. 7, no. 2, pp. 255–272.

Belling, Catherine (1998). `Reading The Operation: television, realism, and the possession of medical knowledge', *Literature and Medicine*, vol. 17, no. 1, pp. 1–23.

Bordo, Susan (1993) *Unbearable Weight Feminism, Western Culture, and the Body*, University of California Press, Berkeley.

Bordo, Susan (1997) *Twilight Zones: The Hidden Life of Cultural Images*, University of California Press, Berkeley.

Braun, Virginia (2005) 'In search of (better) sexual pleasure: female genital "cosmetic" surgery', *Sexualities*, vol. 8, no. 4, pp. 407–424.

Brush, Pippa (1998) 'Metaphors of inscription: discipline, plasticity and the rhetoric of choice', *Feminist Review*, vol. 58, no. 1, pp. 22–43.

Deery, June (2004) 'Trading faces: the makeover show as prime-time infomercial', *Feminist Media Studies*, vol. 4, no. 2, pp. 211–214.

Dumenco, Simon (2003) 'Their bodies, ourselves: why we like (not love) to watch plastic surgery on TV', *New York Magazine*, 6 Oct., [Online] Available at http://newyorkmetro .com/nymetro/health/bestdoctors/cosmetic surgery/2003/n_ 9285/ (18 Oct, 2006).

Extreme Makeover (television series) (2002–2005) Burbank, California, Lighthearted Entertainment.

Finkelstein, Joanne (1991) *The Fashioned Self*, Temple University Press, Philadelphia.

Gilman, Sander (1999). *Making the Body Beautiful: A Cultural History of Aesthetic Surgery*. Princeton University Press, Princeton.

Haiken, Elizabeth (1997) *Venus Envy: A History of Cosmetic Surgery*, The Johns Hopkins University Press, Baltimore.

Hopkins Tanne, Janice (2003) 'New US drama outrages plastic surgeons', *British Medical Journal*, vol. 327, 2 Aug, p. 295.

Life after Extreme Makeover (television series) (2004) Burbank, California, Lighthearted Entertainment.

Nip/Tuck (television series) (2003–) USA, Hands Down Entertainment.

Padmore, Catherine (1998) "Significant flesh: cosmetic surgery, physiognomy, and the erasure of visual difference(s)', *Lateral* no. 1, pp. 1–22, [Online] Available at http://pandora .nla.gov.au/nph-arch/1999/01999-Jul-2/ http;//www.latrobe.edu.au/www/english/ lateral/simple_cpl.htm (18 Oct. 2006).

Sullivan, Deborah A. (2001) *Cosmetic Surgery: The Cutting Edge of Commercial Medicine in America*, Rutgers University Press, New Brunswick.

The Swan (television series) (2004–5), USA, Galan Entertainment.

Udovitch, Mim (2003) 'The cutting edge of television: A bloody scape!', *The New York Times*, 3 Aug., p. 22.

Weber, Brenda (2005) 'Beauty, desire, and anxiety: the economy of sameness in ABC's *Extreme Makeover*', *Genders*, no. 41, [Online] Available at: http://www.gender.org/ g41/g41_weber.html (18 Oct. 2006).

Weil Davis, Simone (2002) 'Loose lips sink ships', *Feminist Studies*, vol. 28, no. 1, pp. 7–35.

"Tyra Banks Is Fat"

Reading (Post-) Racism and (Post-) Feminism in the New Millennium

Ralina L. Joseph

On January 3, 2007, celebrity tabloid websites exploded with gossip about African-American supermodel cum media mogul Tyra Banks's apparently precipitous weight gain. The headline on the first website to break the story (http://www.egotastic.com) read simply, "Tyra Banks is Fat." Subsequently, tabloid websites gleefully sniped in their titles:

'Tyra Banks gained some weight. And when I say some, I mean a lot.' 'Former model Tyra Banks reminds the world why she is now retired from the runway,' 'Dude, did Tyra gain like 50 pounds below the neck?,' 'Tyra pork chops,' and 'America's Next Top Waddle.' (*Good Morning America*, 2007)

The racialized and gendered nature of Banks's media coverage is evident in the headlines alone. Furthermore, in at least one of the headlines, a disciplining straight white male gaze is implicit, in the address of "dude." In a new-millennium, post-identity manner, Banks's race and gender appear through coded discussions of the black female body generally, and, more specifically, of black female breasts, thighs, and buttocks. The joking message from these headlines, nudgingly misogynistic and racist, and coded post-feminist and post-racial, is clear: Banks must be publicly upbraided for failing to maintain her black female body to impossible standards, for not sufficiently "disciplining" her physicality—a notion that feminist scholars like Sandra Bartky and Sarah Banet-Weiser have borrowed from Michel Foucault's notion that modern society exerts a painful and punishing control over women's

From Joseph, R. L. (2009). "Tyra Banks is fat": Reading (post-) racism and (post-) feminism in the new millennium. *Critical Studies in Media Communication*, 26(3), 237–254. Copyright © National Communication Association, reprinted by permission of Taylor & Francis Ltd. (http://www.tandf .co.uk/journals) on behalf of the National Communication Association.

bodies (Banet-Weiser, 1999; Bartky, 1990; Foucault, 1977). Banks becomes an object of derision because of her bodily failures.

The hyper-focus on her body is, of course, racialized as well as gendered. Banks is reprimanded for her pendulous breasts and behind, for the weight she has gained "below the neck."[1] Banks enters a new-millennium representational landscape that is overdetermined by race and gender, and at the same time in denial of its overdetermined nature. In the initial tabloid scoop on Banks's weight gain, two accompanying photographs provided visual proof that indeed Banks was belying her supermodel pedigree with the mere fact of an ostensible weight gain. This visual proof is clearly necessary here—we must see these images to believe them. This is particularly true in representations of women of color, as Evelynn Hammonds (1997) argues: "[I]n the US race has always been dependent upon the visual" (p. 108). In the revelatory photos, Banks wears an ill-fitting strapless swimsuit, long straight blonde hair extensions, and an expression of irritation.

The Banks "fat scandal" is emblematic of the manner in which women, and specifically women of color, are consumed and spat out in the popular sphere. Despite the racialized and gendered nature of all aspects of American life, including media coverage, twenty-first-century U.S. culture is replete with the idea that we are beyond, past, or "post" notions of race-, gender-, and sexuality-based discrimination. This thought stems partially from post-race and post-gender legislation (i.e., anti-affirmative action measures in the form of California's Proposition 209 and Washington's Initiative 200, to name just two), and partially from the wider variety of racialized and gendered representations in the media today. Indeed, even a cursory examination of popular culture reveals a fairly diverse universe where, for example, LGBT characters populate Oscar-nominated films, a Latino male, African-American male, and white female candidate vied for the Democratic presidential nomination, and black women are popular televisual subjects and media celebrities.

One such subject, supermodel-turned-media-mogul Tyra Banks, has made a career out of presenting herself, on the one hand, as a "post-identity" everywoman, who embodies a universal appeal because of her positioning as a liberal, democratic, colorblind subject, and on the other hand as an African-American supermodel, who embodies niche desirability because of her positioning as a racially specific, black female subject. This tricky balance ultimately showcases race and gender as malleable forces, deployed for strategic gain, and untouched by structures and institutions of racism and sexism. While this posturing has served her well in garnering commercial success, in this chapter I examine how Banks's attempts to go beyond race and gender, or what I read as performing a post-racial, post-feminist ideology, proved to be impossible in one telling incident, a tabloid-created "scandal" about Banks's apparent weight gain. . . . For women of color like Banks, while some "hegemonic instability" (Mukherjee, 2006) occurs in her response to the tabloids, post-modern identity play—or, in the language of Banks, shrugging "so what"—remains difficult, if not impossible, because of the structuring forces of race and gender. . . .

A wide array of scholars have interrogated the concept of "post-race," using a variety of related terms to denote a moment after race has ceased to be important—including "colorblindness," used by legal scholars like Lani Guinier and Gerald Torres (2002), "colorblind racism," utilized by sociologist Eduardo Bonilla-Silva (2003), "colormute," coined by anthropologist Mica Pollock (2005), "racial apathy," deployed by sociologists Tyrone Forman and Amanda Lewis (2006), and "post civil rights," applied by journalists, critics, and academics alike.[2] [Some write to critique the concept, and others write from within "post-race" thinking.] One of the more strident embraces of post-race comes from Paul Gilroy (2000), who challenges the "crisis of raciology," claiming that holding onto "race thinking," even, or perhaps especially, by anti-racist activists and critical race scholars, fosters "specious ontologies" and "lazy essentialisms" (p. 53). I favor using the term "post-race" to highlight the continued centrality of race within this ideology where race is ostensibly immaterial. I contend that in its very denial of the validity of uses of "race," post-raciality remains embroiled in precisely what it claims not to be. In other words, "post-race" is an ideology that cannot escape racialization, complete with controlling images or racialized stereotypes.

The assumption of post-racial ideology that inequality is at an end is also shared by the conjoined post- ideology of feminism, or post-feminism. . . . Media studies scholars including Angela McRobbie (2004, 2008), Sarah Banet-Weiser (1999, 2007), Susan Douglas and Meredith Michaels (2004), Charlotte Brunsdon (2005), and Yvonne Tasker and Diane Negra (2007) have produced critiques of post-feminism—which is also popularly known as girl-power feminism and anti-feminism. There has been less attention paid to women of color and fewer sustained critiques of post-race and post-feminism in tandem, outside of works by scholars like Banet-Weiser and Kimberly Springer (2002, 2007). I am attempting to build on Banet-Weiser's and Springer's works, as I scaffold a post-race and post-feminist critique. Such a critique is necessary because discourses of post-race are undeniably gendered, and discourses of post-feminism are undeniably raced. . . .

Bankable Commodity: Flexible Race, Sizable Profits, Tyra, and the Post-

As a result of her reality television show, *America's Next Top Model*, 34-year-old African-American supermodel-turned-media-mogul Tyra Banks has shot to multinational

stardom over a relatively short period of time. According to the narrative spun by Banks and her publicity team, she continuously transforms herself from (the post-feminized and post-racialized categories of) girl next door, to supermodel, to sex symbol, to media mogul: she is both any woman and a one-in-a-million star, someone destined for success because of her phenomenal looks, but truly excelling because of her "girl power" attitude.

Banks's slick official website (http://www.tyrabanks.com) is a treasure trove of Banks photographs; these images illustrate her production team's successful branding of her as all four of these marketable categories. Banks as the girl next door has a wide, friendly smile, a coy look, and long, carefully windswept hair. In three 1990s-era photographs, which I have identified as quintessentially "girl next door" pictures, Banks is positioned on the beach. She is a warm, sunny, inviting fantasy in which to engage, just like her backdrops. In Banks's supermodel poses and her *haute couture* persona she is not at all accessible or friendly, but desirable, in a punishing, inaccessible beauty. The sex symbol pictures include two of Banks's most profitable images, which form the basis of her brand identity. Both of these images mark historic moments in the modeling industry: Banks was the first black woman to be exclusively featured on the covers of both the *Sports Illustrated* swimsuit edition and the *Victoria's Secret* catalogue (Elber, 2006). The photographs of Banks as media mogul feature a coiffed, corporate hairstyle, business suit, and a self-confident half-smile, against the backdrop of news footage, and pictured with two unnamed, corporate-looking white men; both the news and the white men function as proof of her success.

On her website the pictures narrate a tale of success performed through various post-racial, post-feminist personae. At any given moment Banks moves recursively between each of these phases, cleverly matching fickle market desires. This is an important aspect of branding and brand culture, as activist-scholar Naomi Klein has illustrated (2000). It is also important to underscore the racially specific nature of Banks's photographs. As Jane Rhodes notes, building off the works of Stuart Hall, "[B]lackness is not a fixed racial category, but part of a rather fluid and malleable set of representations that change meaning depending on time, place, and context" (2007, p. 5). My analysis of Banks's carefully controlled, officially sanctioned website images illustrates the importance of Banks embodying characteristics that all young women can aspire towards and eventually, ostensibly, possess, while still fostering a uniqueness that makes her so "bankable." Although Banks's body is marked differently in each of these four personae—which is evident, for example, through signifiers of wardrobe, hair, posture, eye contact, and facial expression—her post-feminist, post-racial packaging remains constant, and this facilitates her movement through identities.

Just as a chameleonic identity play has proved to be profitable for Banks, a failure to change racialized and gendered personae has been grounds for Banks to upbraid contestants on her popular reality television show, *America's Next Top Model.* Indeed, Banks is notorious for disciplining women of color who are contestants on *ANTM* for non-fluid, non-post-racial, non-post-feminist behavior. This is a show where a brown-skinned African-American woman is maligned for the "ethnic" gap in her teeth and her working class, black southern accent. This is a show where a Latina contestant is told to "work it" as "Cha Cha," or risk elimination. This is a show where a mixed-race Asian-American contestant is eliminated because she fails to perform Asianness in a way the judging panel deems "authentic," and another Asian-American contestant is reprimanded because she reveals that she has not dated Asian-American men. This is the type of behavior that prompted the on-line cultural commentary magazine,

slate.com, to post an article, "Is Tyra Banks Racist?" where the columnist, J. E. Dahl, blasts Banks for "trying to eradicate ethnic idiosyncrasies in [*ANTM* contestants'] personality and appearance . . . [and for thinking] dark skin should be tougher than light" (Dahl, 2006). On *ANTM,* as in her website pictures, Banks performs a seemingly self-conscious decision to eschew explicit talk of race and gender while inserting codes for "appropriately" racialized and gendered behaviors.

Banks articulates a "post-" philosophy in the advice she gives aspiring models on *ANTM:* be racially specific enough to connote difference, desire, and exoticism, but enough of a colorblind, blank slate to acquire success in the commercial, white-desirous marketplace; be sexy enough to garner desire and media obsession, but be enough of a role model to earn a wide variety of corporate sponsorships. This post-philosophy has developed from *ANTM's* first airing in May 2003 through nine seasons to date. On this show young women are transformed by Banks and her fashion team, which largely consists of gay men and people of color, into models in the mold of Banks. They become "girl power" spokesmodels, women who understand the marketability and chameleonic nature of racial performance. The show boasts incredible popularity on the CW network (formed in 2006 as a union of two previous "urban" and "female" niche market stations, UPN and the WB). Across networks *Top Model* is frequently number one in its time slot with women 18–34, and it often shows up as the number one television show in its time slot in African-American households (Stack, 2007).

The success of *ANTM* led to Banks's eponymous talk show, *The Tyra Banks Show,* which had a five-year run [2005–2010]. Under the aegis of her production company, Bankable Productions, Banks has plans for a sitcom, a one-hour reality show featuring the former *ANTM* contestants back in their normal lives (an "all stars" show), and a live show (Sales, 2007). In Banks's own words to talk show host Larry King, "Bankable [Productions] mantra is things fantasy-based and also empowering to women as well as fantasy, too, and entertaining" (King, 2007). Brand Tyra, marked by the fantasies of post-race and post-feminism, sells big: her 2006 income was reportedly $18 million (Sales, 2007). Banks's production company owns 25% of the lucrative *ANTM* franchise, which has spawned 19 national versions across Europe and Asia, including shows in France, Israel, Malaysia, the Philippines, Slovakia, Sweden, Thailand, and Turkey.[3] The original *ANTM* enjoys syndication in 110 countries. On *ANTM* post-raciality and post-feminism amount to exceedingly savvy marketing techniques.

Banks's talk show *The Tyra Banks Show*, also on the CW network, began in the autumn of 2005, balancing race- and gender-themed shows with episodes emphasizing some aspect of Banks's physicality. For example, in the show's first episode, Banks had a doctor administer a sonogram on her breasts in front of the studio audience, in order to prove that they are not silicone-enhanced. Episodes celebrating Banks's exceptional physique play against "issue episodes" in which the show, often clunkily, examines various forms of prejudice (e.g., "Will Racial Stereotypes Hold the Next Generation Back?" and "Coming out as Transgender.") The end result of these issue episodes is ultimately Banks shrugging her shoulders and saying "So what?" as she upholds the power of individual choice, meritocracy, and the post-.

Banks's post- philosophy was particularly in effect during the premiere episode of her second season, airing on September 11, 2006, and entitled "Racial Injustice: Who's Got it Worst." During a first-person camera address that opens the episode, Banks gazes into the camera and earnestly explains that she intends for this episode to function as a commemoration for the devastation at the Twin Towers, five years earlier. The show, which Banks bills as a "social experiment," attempts to deal with racial prejudice faced by African-American, Muslim-American, Latino, Asian-American, and white women.[4] Inclusion of white women as a racially aggrieved group can be seen as an ultimate post-racial move, as it fends off allegations of "reverse racism," and also plays to sponsors and white audiences.

While most of the show features these women exploring their experiences of racism and racialized patriarchy, in emotional yet carefully controlled ways, when one of the audience members on the show explodes in frustration, Banks silences her and quells her fury by literally pulling the woman into her breasts and maternally patting and shushing her. (Banks's body, and more specifically her breasts, remain starring characters in her many media appearances. Banks is rarely without a low-cut, decolletage-emphasizing outfit, as her breasts are indeed a major signifier of the Tyra brand.) The episode ends with "race experts," a white male and black female professor from UCLA, leading the studio audience through a "unity" exercise which ends with all women holding hands and chanting. One of the final camera shots features a brown hand and white hand locked in embrace and thrust skyward in a triumphant, post-racial, post-feminist statement. This episode is emblematic of the way the *Tyra Banks Show* solves problems of racism, patriarchy, and discrimination: magically equalizing all, through multicultural celebrations of "women."

Nonetheless, some might read the ubiquitous visibility and success of Banks in the popular sphere as progress in and of itself. Indeed, not only is she an African-American woman in a position of incredible power, but on both of her television shows she highlights the stories of women of color, lesbian, gay, bisexual, and transgendered people, and working class and disabled women. In other words, while Banks's message is post-, many of her stories feature women struggling with the effect of structural inequalities. Banks herself met the effects of such inequalities during a media attack, when the fantasy space of television was unable to provide a shield from racism and misogyny. Thus, the post- that proves so profitable for much of Banks's career fell out during her tabloid weight-gain "scandal."

Calling Out Racism and Sexism: Banking Against the Post-

After the release of the "fat scandal" photographs on the internet, gossip magazines featured them also. This included tabloid *Star* magazines assessment of Banks as part of its "Weight Winners and Losers" of 2006 segment ("Weight," 2007). Shown as two halves of a picture, and therefore automatically posited as opposites, these two shots are markedly different in their *mise-en-scène*. In the posed "winner" shot, a publicity still from an episode on the *Tyra Banks Show* called "Panty Party," a celebration of women's undergarments, Banks's open-mouthed, smiling expression, open arms, and lingerie-clad body show her literal embrace of the viewer. In the opposition shot, "loser" Banks is shown turned away from the camera, refusing to connect with the viewer, not selling her image. These tabloid expose photos of the "real" Banks reveal the so-called "truth" of Banks, and posit that the smiling, friendly, post-feminist, post-racial version of Banks that audiences are privy to on television is a lie.

"Weight Winners and Losers" is part of a regular series that *Star* magazine puts out. Banks was one of seven people featured, including another black female star Banks has publicly idolized, fellow "loser" Oprah Winfrey. The numbers, glowing white against Banks's brown thighs, denote some claim to objectivity. So-called scientific, impartial numbers translate to a truth of "winning" or "losing" in beauty, gender, race, and commercial success. The fact that readers are given no clue as to how the magazine arrived at such numbers is simply ignored.

However, the media blitz did not end with talk about Banks. Instead, Banks and her publicity team sought to control the moment. She seized the opportunity to defend and uphold the beauty of her body, and created enough self-generated hype to ensure record-breaking numbers for the eighth-season premiere of *America's Next Top Model,* exactly eight weeks later on February 28, 2007. Banks told the press that instead of ignoring the unwanted weight-focused publicity, hiding out, and going on a crash diet, she wanted to use the opportunity to "speak back" to the world, defending her pictures and creating a "platform" for one of her "issues"—self-esteem. To "set the record straight," Banks appeared on the television talk show circuit, where she refocused the event as one of self-esteem, body love, empowerment, and embracing the scale. She used the opportunity to reframe herself as a positive role model for young women.

Moreover, in her response, Banks articulated an intersectional critique by linking issues of gender discrimination. As she said on the *Larry King Live* talk show:

> [I]n the modeling world they can tell you to your face, your skin does not look good with my clothes or I don't want black girls this season or I don't want you or I want to pay you less. They say those types of things . . . And it's not illegal. (King, 2007)

Banks's description of anti-black racism in the modeling industry is striking because her comments are indeed the very opposite of her pre-weight scandal post- and universal (all women, all races) response. So often Banks talks about expectations for all women, but here she spotlights the accepted racism against, in particular, black models in the industry. Banks places herself as part of a particularistic black female collectivity. In doing so she challenges post-feminism and post-racism in order to launch a race and gender critique.

Furthermore, the tenor of Banks's *Larry King Live* comment was duplicated on Banks's daytime talk show, when she devoted an episode to her response to the tabloids. On February 1, 2007, approximately one month after the release of the photos on the internet, the *Tyra Banks Show* aired an episode, "Tyra Confronts Her Fat Tabloid Photos," devoted to Banks's addressing the tabloid fury. Banks wears the same swimsuit as the tabloid expose photographs, but here looks far more svelte. In the climactic scene of the episode—which has been logged on her show's official website as stock footage—Banks stands next to a series of still images of the pictures that caused such an uproar. When Banks begins her first-person camera address, her voice cracks and her eyes tear up, but as she continues speaking, she gains more confidence in her delivery. Showing a self-reflexive understanding of her own corporate branding, she tells the camera that people are used to consuming a version of her body produced by careful poses that are the most flattering, "and everyone seems to be pretty ok with that." She continues, "For some reason people have a serious problem when I look like . . ."—and she proceeds to pose in unflattering ways, sticking out her stomach and patting her thighs and behind. This produces a comedic effect, as the audience laughs freely. Banks continues, and her tone shifts to a more serious one, to demonstrate that she is no longer trying to produce laughter:

> But luckily I'm strong enough and I have a good support system. I mean I love my mama. She has helped me to be a strong woman so I can overcome these kinds of attacks. But if I had lower self-esteem I would probably be starving myself right now. But that's exactly what is happening to other women all over this country. So I have something to say. To all of you who have something nasty to say to me or other women who are built like me. Women who sometimes or all the time

> look like this [at this point she sticks her stomach out and the audience does not laugh now]. Women whose names you know. Women whose names you don't. Women who've been picked on. Women whose husbands put them down. Women at work or girls at school. I have one thing to say to you: kiss my fat ass! (Banks, 2007a)

Banks punctuates this last part by slapping her behind and defiantly throwing her fist in the air. The crowd explodes, jumping to their feet, clapping, and cheering.

The content and tone of Banks's commentary mark a huge divergence from her typical public address. While Banks will discuss race and gender, such occasions, like the September 11 "Who's Got it Worst" episode, are highly mediated and appear to be overwhelmingly produced for a post-racial, post-feminist effect. Here she appears unguarded, vulnerable, and defiant. Although Banks does not name the racialized nature of the attack on her, she is not trying to be post-feminist-cute; she is not trying to woo the camera. She is a part of a collectivity, but, in contrast to post-feminism, there is no underlying competition. Banks is angry and she is looking out for her sisters. . . .

Interestingly, Banks's response illustrates the type of behavior she critiques *ANTM* contestants for: she is strong, defiant, and emotional—in sum, the image of an "angry black woman," for which she upbraids her contestants. On *ANTM*, Banks performs a seemingly self-conscious decision to eschew explicit talk of race and gender while inserting codes for "appropriately" racialized and gendered behaviors. This is the type of racial punishing/post-racial and self-sexualizing/post-feminist ideology I thought I would find with the weight gain scandal. Instead, Banks iterates an anti-racist and feminist message that is largely absent on commercial television. This is a rare moment in which the post- ideology is ruptured in popular culture, and Banks embraces what Sandoval (2000) designates an "oppositional consciousness," marking a moment of the "methodology of the oppressed."[5] More cynical readers of the event might dismiss Banks's comments as further branding. However, in the aftermath of the tabloid event, Banks explicitly analyzes the structural nature of race and gender, something usually absolutely taboo in the public sphere.

Returning to the Post-: The "So What" Movement

Nevertheless, Banks's fairly radical space of possibility was short-lived, as the post-ideologies overwhelmingly dominate popular culture. Soon after this show came a series of television spots and a *People* magazine cover story, where Banks regulated her formerly defiant self. Although not apologizing for her past declaration, Banks greatly mitigated her anti-racist and feminist statements, illustrating the hegemonic power of the post-.

In a series of interviews and talk show commentaries, Banks resituates her tabloid coverage onto a post-feminist, post-racial terrain, where one should simply assert "So what?" to racist, misogynistic attacks. On "Tyra's PEOPLE Magazine Cover Update," an episode of her talk show that aired three weeks after Banks's initial response, she dons not the same swimsuit, as she is clearly done with that, but instead a flattering red bodysuit, which all members of her studio audience also wear. She is shown with her audience, wearing the same outfit, but looking so much better, in an iteration of post-feminist competition. Onto all of the bodysuits are affixed white numbers, as all of the audience members are literally wearing their body weight on their chests. Unlike the feature in *Star*, where the magazine labeled Banks with their numbers, here Banks embraces her own chosen numbers. This is post-feminism at its finest—the guise

of sisterhood, a performance of homosocial camaraderie with underlying competition and choice.

This time, when Banks makes her first person camera address, she is positioned directly in front of the audience, instead of against a screen. Her words are positioned as representing not only herself, but also the women in the studio, and even "all women". In a smiling, breezy tone she tells the audience:

> Well, this is the movement where I'm giving you all, everybody here in the audience here and everybody watching at home, a self-esteem homework assignment that we can all do together. I want everyone to take a risk and to do something completely outside of your comfort zone and celebrate the fact that you did it. Whether it's running around your neighborhood in a bikini screaming 'So what?' Alright! Or it's walking through the supermarket and telling everyone in the frozen food section how much you weigh. Or stepping out of the dressing room and into the center of the lingerie department to say, 'I think my booty looks good in these panties!' Or allowing your man to take you to an all-you-can-eat buffet and allowing yourself to go back for seconds and maybe even thirds. . . . And I've got to let everybody know, my little call to action and my homework is being on the stage, is all ya'll seeing my cellulite. I've never done this. I have never done this. I know you guys are like, that's the dimples she's talking about! You're all getting a view of it! (Banks, 2007b)

Banks's statements are punctuated by clear statements of audience approval. The camera frequently pulls away from Banks for quick reaction shots of supportive laughter, whoops of agreement, or adoring looks from the audience members. In short, the audience's approval is shown to be full and frequent. . . . The tone, the message, and the breezy, cutesy attitude are markedly different from her earlier tabloid address. While Banks's terminology of a "call to action" sounds politically engaged, it ends up being a post-(per)version of the phrase.

It appears as though some forces have intervened in between these two episodes, to change Banks's response from intersectional to post-. Part of the way this happens is through re-framing the issue onto the safer post-racial, post-feminist topic of self-esteem, which is only coded as safer because it is presented as the effect of individual choice. Indeed, self-esteem remains a highly politicized, racialized notion.[6] By reinterpreting the attack as self-esteem-based instead of systemically race- and gender-hatred-based, Banks asserts that one can simply choose to rise above racism and misogyny.

The numbers on the bodysuits add to the post- performance. The weight numbers on Banks's chest are applied by one of Banks's assistants at her request. She chooses to place the numbers onto her body, and more specifically, onto her breasts. Later in the show Banks chooses to take off the numbers. Her legions of fans in the studio audience are shown following her lead, as they too remove their numbers. Absent from the discussion in the show is any admission of the real dieting to which Banks must have committed—despite assertions to the contrary, Banks is markedly smaller, from the scandal photos, to the "kiss my fat ass" address, and then to the "So what?' address. Also absent is a discussion of any possible airbrushing, on the ostensibly "real" *People* magazine cover. . . .

public sphere. Banks's feminist, anti-racist response cannot be taken back, despite her later regulation of her comments. . . .

This represents a space of possibility in commercial popular culture. While Banks may not be an anti-racist, feminist activist in most of her media representations, in a moment of attack, her intersectional response is significant. In addition, the strength of the post- ideology is highlighted in the aftermath of the attack, when Banks turns to a quintessentially post- response.

In the popular media, as in other expressions of U.S. race and gender ideologies, notions of post-race and post-feminism are entirely reliant upon each other, and are indeed operative because of the other. Whether perfectly posed and airbrushed on the cover of *People* magazine, "natural" on her talk show, semi-scripted on her nighttime program, or exposed in the tabloids, Banks attempts to look and speak the messages that people want to hear: both power and inequality associated with race and gender, if not the categories themselves, are largely inconsequential and ultimately changeable: "So what?" The message remains that race and gender are floating identities untouched by structure and therefore strategically deployed by individuals for gain. However, another message also arises out of Banks's "fat scandal" and her speaking-back moment. While race and gender might be popularly understood, through the post- discourses now prevalent in many arenas, from legislation to television, as personal, individual, and mutable traits, they also remain solidly structural, institutional, and historic forces.

Conclusion

In her response to the "fat scandal," Bank temporarily ruptured post- ideologies. Despite the fact that after her "kiss my fat ass" response she returned to a post- message, the rupturing words were released to the

Notes

1. This focus on black women "below the neck" can be traced through any number of figures, including Sarah Baartman, the eighteenth-century Khoisan woman better known as the "Hottentot Venus," whose naked body was displayed in an

animal cage when alive and whose genitalia were cast in wax for display after her death. Baartman was subjected to such debasement and violence because she was read as sexually dangerous and thus deserving of imprisonment and exhibition (Sharpley-Whiting, 1999). For hundreds of years black female bodies have been represented as not only sexually available but also complicit in their exploitation. In fact, in order to enjoy popular and commercial success, African-American women have sometimes been forced to take such exploitative roles. In an example of a contemporary representation, mixed-race African-American actress Halle Berry took a much lauded Academy Award-winning turn in 2001's *Monster's Ball* when she portrayed Leticia, a woman having an affair with a character played by Billy Bob Thornton, a white male prison guard and executioner of Leticia's African-American husband. In the film's climactic sex scene Berry repeatedly screams out to Thornton, who one could argue functions as the very agent of her oppression, "Make me feel good!" Berry's portrayal of Leticia follows a long line of chattel-slavery-based iterations of the "tragic mulatta" and "jezebel," controlling images documented by scholars like Deborah Gray White (1999). Berry was awarded the United States cinema industry's highest honor for this portrayal . . . .

2. In addition, historian David Hollinger (1995) uses the term "post-ethnic" in a prescriptive, celebratory manner. All of the scholars I have listed and a number of others also simultaneously use "post-civil rights" and the other terms, sometimes interchangeably.

3. Here is a complete list of countries with a national version of *Top Model*: Australia, Canada, Finland, France, Germany, Hungary, Israel, Malaysia, the Netherlands, Norway, the Philippines, Russia, Scandinavia (with contestants from Norway, Denmark, and Sweden), Slovakia, Spain, Sweden, Thailand, Turkey, and the UK (Sales, 2007).

4. I use the term "white" as opposed to "Anglo-American" or "European-American" to mark a linguistic difference between the groups of color and whites. I wish to underscore the fact that white is an expression of power and not merely an expression of ethnicity.

5. My goal to identify ideological rupture in the post- is inspired by Daphne Brooks's (2006) stated aim to name "the ruptures and blind spots where . . . performers defy the expectations and desires of the audience member/recorder" (p. 10).

6. The racialized and gendered concept of self-esteem has been operative in such important political moments as the black dolls/white dolls experiment used by psychologists Kenneth and Mamie Phipps Clark (1953). In the Supreme Court Case that ended *de jure* racial segregation, *Brown v. Board of Education of Topeka, Kansas* (1954), the Clarks' research was used to link internalized racism and the psychological harm to black children of segregated schools (Clark, 1953).

References

Banet-Weiser, S. (1999). *The most beautiful girl in the world*. Berkeley: University of California Press.

Banet-Weiser, S. (2007). *Kids rule!: Nickelodeon and consumer culture*. Durham, NC: Duke University Press.

Banks, T. (2007a, February 1). *Tyra confronts her fat tabloid photos*. Retrieved April 26, 2007, from http://tyrashouw.warnerbros.com/galler/video/index.html?=tyraclip0201

Banks, T. (2007b, February 26). *Tyra's PEOPLE magazine cover update*. Retrieved April 26, 2007, from http://tyrashow.warnerbros.com/gallery/video/index.html?=sowhattyraintro

Bartky, S. (1990). *Femininity and domination: Studies in the phenomenology of oppression*. New York: Routledge.

Bonilla-Silva, E. (2003). *Racism without racists: Color-blind racism and the persistence of racial inequality in the United States*. Lanham, MD: Rowman & Littlefield.

Brooks, D. (2006). *Bodies in dissent: Spectacular performances of race and freedom, 1850–1910*. Durham, NC: Duke University Press.

Brunsdon, C. (2005). Feminism, postfeminism, Martha, Martha, and Nigella. *Cinema Journal, 44*, 110–116.

Clark, K. (1953). The social scientist as an expert witness in civil rights legislation. *Social Problems, 1,* 5–10.

Dahl, J. E. (2006). Is Tyra Banks racist? The peculiar politics of *America's Next Top Model.* Retrieved October 9, 2007, from *Slate,* http://www.slate.com/id/2141972/

Douglas, S., & Michaels, M. (2004). *The mommy myth.* New York: Free Press.

Elber, L. (2006, March 1). Tyra takes on topics and takes off clothes. *Seattle Times,* p. F5.

Forman, T., & Lewis, A. (2006). Racial apathy and Hurricane Katrina: The social anatomy of prejudice in the post-civil rights era. *DuBois Review, 3,* 175–202.

Foucault, M. (1977). *Discipline and punish: The birth of the prison.* New York: Vintage Books.

Gilroy, P. (2000). *Against race: Imagining political culture beyond the color line.* Cambridge, MA: Belknap Press of Harvard University Press.

Good Morning America. (2007, January 31). Dangerously thin models; Too skinny for catwalk? Transcript retrieved via Lexis-Nexis search April 1, 2007.

Guinier, L., & Torres, G. (Eds.). (2002). *The miner's canary: Enlisting race, transforming power, creating democracy.* Cambridge, MA: Harvard University Press.

Hammonds, E. M. (1997). New technologies of race. In J. Terry & M. Calvert (Eds.), *Processed lives: Gender and technology in everyday life* (pp. 74–85). New York: Routledge.

Hollinger, D. (1995). *Postethnic America: Beyond multiculturalism.* New York: Basic Books.

King, L (2007). Tyra Banks speaks out. CNN Larry King Live. *Transcript retried via Lexis-Nexis search April1, 1,* 2007.

Klein, N. (2000). *No logo.* New York: Harper Collins.

McRobbie, A. (2004). Post feminism and popular culture. *Feminist Media Studies, 4,* 255–264.

McRobbie, A. (2008). *Displacement feminism: Gender, culture and social change.* Thousand Oaks, CA: Sage.

Mukherjee, R. (2006). *The racial order of things: Cultural imaginaries of the post-soul era.* Minneapolis: University of Minnesota Press.

Pollock, M. (2005). *Colormute: Race talk dilemmas in an American school.* Princeton, NJ: Princeton University Press.

Rhodes, J. (2007). *Framing the Black Panthers: The spectacular rise of a black power icon.* New York: New Press.

Sales, N. J. (2007, February). A model mogul. *Vanity Fair.*

Sandoval, C. (2000). *Methodology of the oppressed: Theory out of bounds.* Minneapolis: University of Minnesota Press.

Sharpley-Whiting, T. D. (1999). *Black Venus: Sexualized savages, primal fears, and primitive narratives in French.* Durham, NC: Duke University Press.

Springer, K. (2002). Third wave black feminism? *Signs: Journal of Women in Culture and Society, 27,* 1059–1082.

Springer, K. (2007). Divas, evil black bitches, and bitter black women: African American women in postfeminist and post-civil rights popular culture. In Y. Tasker & D. Negra (Eds.), *Interrogating postfeminism* (pp. 249–276). Durham, NC: Duke University Press.

Stack, T. (2007, April 27). The CW report card. *Entertainment Weekly,* p. 11.

Tasker, Y., & Negra, D. (2007). Introduction: Feminist politics and postfeminist culture. In Y. Tasker & D. Negra (Eds.), *Interrogating postfeminism* (pp. 1–25). Durham, NC: Duke University Press.

Weight winners and losers. (2007, January 15). *Star Magazine,* pp. 10–14.

White, D. G. (1999). *Aren't I a woman? Female slaves in the plantation South.* New York: W.W. Norton.

Resisting, Reiterating, and Dancing Through

The Swinging Closet Doors of Ellen DeGeneres's Televised Personalities

Candace Moore

Gushing to *The Advocate* about her new girlfriend, comedian Ellen DeGeneres, *Arrested Development* star Portia De Rossi says: "She was so courageous and loud in '97, and now she is doing something that is more subliminal. She's changing the world, she really is" (Kort, "Portia," 40). De Rossi subtly articulates a difference between Ellen's 1997 "coming out" and Ellen's current daily dance into America's living rooms as a beloved daytime talk show host who "happens to be" gay. LGBT activists and media critics slightly disagree, asserting that Ellen may be "softpedaling her lesbianism" on *Ellen: The Ellen DeGeneres Show* to find widespread acceptance (Lo, "The Incredible Story"; Heffernan, "The Perils" E5). As *New York Times* critic Virginia Heffernan puts it: "Ms. DeGeneres no longer wants to talk about being gay, so she discusses pleasant [topics]: décor, holidays and the fridge" (E5). Host of a mainstream variety show that has wowed NBC network executives by pulling in impressive numbers of its targeted demographic—women ages 25–54 (Deeken 30; Schnuer S1)—and hyped as an "everywoman approach" ("The Ellen DeGeneres Show"), DeGeneres avoids the topic of her own homosexuality and actively closes down conversation in which the very word or concept comes up.

. . . Not verbally addressing queer identity on her talk show is understandable from DeGeneres's personal perspective. Her career all but collapsed not long after the glow of her public coming-out party died down.

From Moore, C. (2008). Resisting, reiterating, and dancing through: The swinging closet doors of Ellen DeGeneres's televised personalities. In R. Beirne (Ed.), *Televising queer women: A reader* (pp. 17–31). New York: Palgrave Macmillan.

"To come out," according to [queer theorist David M.] Halperin,

> is precisely to expose oneself to a different set of dangers and constraints, to make oneself into a convenient screen onto which straight people can project all the fantasies they routinely entertain about gay people, and to suffer one's every gesture, statement, expression, and opinion to be totally and irrevocably marked by the overwhelming social significance of one's openly acknowledged homosexual identity. (30)

Following Ellen DeGeneres's self-outing, her private life (with ex-girlfriend Anne Heche) became unbearably public—their love affair's ups and downs became unending fodder for gossip columnists and paparazzi, who stalked the new couple. Ellen's groundbreaking sitcom was also summarily canceled the next year, due to advertiser pullouts, public attacks from the religious right, and, arguably, sabotage by the ABC network itself in imposing parental advisories because of the show's portrayals of same-sex romance. (Such advisories were not, of course, placed on programs that tackled more explicitly sexual subjects with heterosexual leads) (Gross 162). Throughout these trials, DeGeneres became an important icon of political courage for the LGBT community, even though she candidly expressed that she had neither intended her coming out as a political statement nor wished to become a poster-woman for the queer cause. . . .

Since its launch in 2003, Ellen has crafted herself a talk-show persona on *Ellen: The Ellen DeGeneres Show*, who linguistically sidesteps the word or concept of homosexuality. However, she performs queerness through what implicitly "exceeds" her stand-up jokes and sit-down talk, and, physically, through the ritual action of her daily dance sequence. Through these methods, perhaps DeGeneres escapes being such a "convenient screen" for hate-mongers or bearing the responsibility of being a spokesperson for all of gay America, while she still maintains a *televisibility*[1] of queer identity. Demonstrating how Ellen's coming out and her return to the closet become enacted again and again, ad infinitum, on television, my textual analysis involves queer ruptures on the primarily heterosexual text of Ellen's current Emmy-winning daytime talk show. Seeing "being in the closet" and "being out" as performances that are constantly negotiated socially— either actively resisted or reinscribed— rather than one-time denials or declarations of sexuality that hold, this chapter highlights ambiguous moments in DeGeneres's daily show. In specific instances that I explore, DeGeneres gestures rhetorically or symbolically to her sexual preference, absurdly omits or redirects possible discussions of homosexuality, or is subtly or not-so-subtly "called out" as gay by her celebrity guests. . . .

Repetition and reiteration is a central theme in Ellen's show, with her daily dances, recurring verbal noises and catch phrases. I ultimately argue that Ellen's many repetitious behaviors also serve as multiple self-outings. Anna McCarthy suggests that perhaps queer visibility on television is only permissible as spectacle; such televisibility becomes dangerous to heteronormativity when it presents queer lives and loves as "quotidian" ("Ellen: Making Queer Television History" 597). By repeatedly dancing to the same songs and expressing the same verbal ticks over and over again, Ellen seeks in the opening sequences of her talk show to present the out-of-the-ordinary repeatedly, until its very performance, occurring daily, becomes un-alarming and even infectiously celebratory.

During her ritual opening dance, Ellen looks into the camera, directly addressing the audience, and then follows by breaking the proscenium arch, dancing out into the pulsating, cheering, similarly dancing live studio audience. Her daily dances, set to a handful of uplifting disco, hip hop, and R&B songs, with their awkward, non-choreographed moves, together with her wide, toothy grin, seem to proclaim a message of self-acceptance: *This is me! I'm great just the way I am, and you can be great just the way you are too!* Her dance moves themselves evoke nostalgia for the gay-steeped, 1970s-era culture of disco. While Ellen does not remind her audience of her queerness over and over again verbally, Ellen does repeat acts that are both absurd and permissible, causing the most bizarre squawks and awkward dance moves to become a commonplace sight, and a site for pleasure.

Subliminal Rituals

While De Rossi's claim that Ellen is "changing the world" might represent the overstated rhetorical flourish of the lovestruck, De Rossi's use of the word "subliminal," meaning "below the threshold of conscious perception" (*Webster's II New Riverside University Dictionary* 1994: 1154), to describe what Ellen is "doing," does astutely point out the very *liminality* of Ellen's ritualistic daily performances.[2] To put it in other terms, De Rossi is here distinguishing between a media *event* and a repeated media *ritual*. A media *event* is a one-time, idiosyncratic phenomenon that acts as an exception to the usual rules of both television flow and content, and, if planned, is often surrounded by quite a bit of promotional hype (Hubert 31; McCarthy, "Ellen: Making Queer Television History" 593). A repeated media *ritual* also temporarily upends or stretches convention (only to reinstate it); however, it is less outwardly eventful; in fact, it gradually becomes perceived as a part of the normal flow, and signifies through repetition, over time, or through multiple broadcasts (Couldry 24). One punctuates the Nielsen's ratings, the other has the potential to slowly, rather than rapidly, shift consciousnesses through a

process of slow audience acclimation to, and reinforcement of, difference.

Encoding/Decoding the Dance

When asked why Ellen DeGeneres does not address her homosexuality on her talk show, lesbian actress and screenwriter Guinevere Turner (*Go Fish, The L Word*) declared emphatically "How could you dance like that and not be gay? That's a way of saying with every opening representation, I'm gay!" ("Personal Interview" 2005). Marusya Bociurkiw, in a recent critical essay published in *Canadian Woman Studies,* concurred with Turner's view that Ellen's lesbianism is palpable in her dancing: "As the music, usually hip hop, is played, Ellen's body is on display in a manner that is decidedly not heteronormative. Here DeGeneres displays the grace and confidence that her accessible, self-deprecating, 'kook' act disavows. DeGeneres looks like a butch lesbian dancing alone, in a club" (176).

However, these interpretations are just that, individualized readings of a polysemic text, and sometimes we see what we want to see. Furthermore, "what a dyke dancing looks like" is a nearly impossible thing to put one's finger on. Just as lesbians are a diverse, rather than homogeneous group, comprising women of varying ethnicities, cultural backgrounds, styles, classes, gender presentations, and so on, their dance moves likely vary enormously. So while a general consensus remains among these readings, that "something's queer" here, I try to show, through examining prior precedents of Ellen expressing herself physically—whether through physical humor or through dance—that not only does her opening "dance with herself" (and thus the viewer) represent a daily declaration of queer identity, but that she has previously coded it to mean exactly that.

Rather than revisit the coming-out media event of Ellen's "Puppy Episode"

(4.22 and 4.23, April 30, 1997), which has been explored in depth by Anna McCarthy, Susan J. Hubert, and Steven Capsuto, among others, I concentrate instead on two pre-coming-out episodes from the second season of *Ellen*—texts, which, like her talk show, operate "doubly." In "The Fix Up" (2.5, October 19, 1994), Ellen's dance moves are first foregrounded, and in "Thirty Kilo Man" part 1 and 2 (2.23, May 10, 1995; 2.24, May 17, 1995), her character has a heterosexual love affair that reads as unmistakably queer.

Elevator Music on Early *Ellen*

Early *Ellen* is best described as ABC's version of *Seinfeld*'s sitcom about nothing, since both half-hour shows center around known stand-up comedians and their witty banter about insignificant, repetitious, or everyday matters with friends. During the three seasons prior to Ellen DeGeneres's/Ellen Morgan's doubly momentous 1997 coming out, Ellen's character on the middling-rated sitcom was consistently stuck in a weekly cycle of dates-gone-wrong with guys, that, for an array of incidental and sometimes extravagantly bizarre reasons, just do not fit. In "The Gladiators" (2.19, March 1, 1995) for instance, Ellen's new beau, Nitro, a gladiator from the then-popular television show, *American Gladiators*,[3] is snapped away from her by an ultra-buff woman (Ice), leading the bookstore owner to jealously beat the pumped-up woman to a pulp with a padded lance.

The sitcom's season with the most overtly heterosexual storylines, the second, is also the season with the most queer subtext. Disney would not okay the idea of Ellen Morgan's coming out until more than a year later, when blatant hints began to be worked into the weekly scripts (Gross 157). Ellen's obsessive man-shopping in season two is painted by the writers and producers as

downright absurd, but what will serve as the alternative (asexuality, in most of season three, before facing her queer identity), is not quite clear yet. Journalist for *The San Francisco Examiner,* Joyce Millman, caught on early. In the spring of 1995, in a column entitled "The Sitcom that Dare Not Speak Its Name," the television critic prematurely outed Ellen Morgan: "As a gal sitcom, *Ellen* doesn't make any sense at all, until you view it through the looking glass, where the unspoken subtext becomes the main point. Then is Ellen is transformed into one of TV's savviest, funniest, slyest shows. Ellen Morgan is a closet lesbian" (B1).

In "The Fix Up" (2.5, October 19, 1994) of season two, the episode opens with Ellen inside an elevator—the enclosed space that arguably acts as the show's metaphorical stand-in for a closet. Ellen's adventures in (or waiting for) an elevator are a reoccurring trope on the show. Given the sitcom's frequent meta-references to sitcom history (see McCarthy, "Ellen: Making Queer Television History" 607–614), perhaps this trope, seen throughout the second season, is also a tip of the hat to the historically common "meat locker" sitcom scenario, wherein people with differences get stuck in a small space, often a meat locker or an elevator, and overcome differences (Sconce 104–105). In this case, the elevator's only other passenger exits, and finding herself alone, Ellen openly acknowledges the song playing over the loud speakers, Aretha Franklin's "Respect," by first tapping her feet, then swinging from side to side and lip-synching. As the song builds to crescendo, Ellen is observed flailing, rocking her head along to the words, and jumping into the air, landing with thumps. As audience members, we are in anticipation for the elevator doors to suddenly open and or Ellen to be "found out." Instead, Franklin's rousing tune halts abruptly and a male authoritarian voice comes over the loud speakers: "Excuse me, ma'am, this is security" the voice interrupts. "Please refrain from jumping in the elevator." The camera offers a shot from above, looking down at Ellen, as she immediately looks up to the speaker, with a petrified deer-in-the-headlights acknowledgment that she is being surveyed. She then cradles her head down in her hand, in embarrassment, before the camera cuts away.

This scene might be read divorced from any queer subtext, as mere silliness in an elevator, with Ellen as the 1990s Lucy Ricardo, always getting herself into a new kind of trouble. However, the larger text of the sitcom suggests the elevator as a contained closet, within which Ellen Morgan can finally release herself, be happy with who she is, until she is again reminded, reprimanded by a voice from outside, that others do not approve of her lifestyle. This is particularly suggested by the content of the dialogue between Ellen and her mother that immediately follows, and furthermore by the theme (failed heterosexual daring, what else?) of "The Fix Up."

In the scene that follows, Ellen's mother asks her a question over coffee that reoccurs, rephrased, throughout the series: "So, are you seeing anyone these days?" When Ellen's answer implies no, her mom continues in full fuss mode: "I just worry about you. You're not immortal . . . I just want you to be happy." Ellen retorts, "You know it's possible to be happy without a man." "Must you joke about everything?" her mom returns, and then promptly tries to fix Ellen up with someone she grew up with. Described by Ellen as the "weird" kid in the neighborhood who ate bugs, he has matured into an adult man who is not peculiar at all; in fact, Ellen seems to find him quite charming. In a plot reversal, he ends up finding Ellen entirely "weird," through the usual comedy of errors. "The Fix Up" is a stereotypical example of the pre-coming-out plotline, wherein events beyond Ellen's control, but generally propelled at least partially by her neurotic behavior, spiral, causing Ellen ultimately to be rejected by her possible heterosexual love interest, rather than force the thirty-something to own up to the fact that she is not truly interested in

the first place. There are also instances where Ellen rejects men; these generally involve Ellen's discovery that the man she thought was a dreamboat has an impossible-to-stand trait.

The "date that always goes wrong" plot is finally frustrated and complicated in the two-part season two finale, "Thirty Kilo Man" (2.23 and 2.24, May 10, 1995, and May 17, 1995). The first part of the finale opens in Ellen's apartment, with Ellen's mother asking her about her plans for the weekend. When Ellen makes a joke about getting a "Chia Date," so that she can sprinkle it and "watch it grow," Ellen's mom pulls out the claws: "You know what the problem with you is, Ellen? You're too picky. You always look for a man's faults. Greg was too nice, Roger watched too much TV, Carl was a drag." "Drag king, mother," Ellen corrects, "I know I nitpick . . ." As the episode continues, Dan, a man she was interested in during an earlier episode but rejected after discovering that he delivered pizza for a living, returns from Italy with a new, more prestigious job. The first ever return "beard" is also the one that actually ends up in bed with Ellen. A "next day" scenario finds Ellen strutting out from her bedroom in a robe, hair mussed, puffing on an imaginary cigarette. Dan emerges fully dressed and primped, and she kisses him, mumbling, "No fair, you brushed your teeth." "Sorry," he practically sings. They touch their way into the living-room, and in full soap-opera pitch, Dan gushes: "I never want this feeling to end. Ellen Morgan, I think I'm falling in love with you." In this scene, Ellen is scripted and choreographed into the position of the stereotypical man in a classic romance, who swaggers out of the bedroom, while Dan is the stereotypical woman, who rushes to say effusive things, to say "I love you" right away.

Later, when Dan comes back from work, Ellen backs him into the couch and gets on top, kissing him. His beeper starts to vibrate in his pants, she pauses to say, "What's that?" and then keeps kissing him, pressing into him, moaning "You are such a considerate man!" She grabs the cordless phone from the coffee table. "Okay, it stopped. What's your number?" This joke on his beeper as vibrator, a device implied as more pleasurable than perhaps his penis, again with the classic roles switched (her as the "horny" one), plays on the notion that, although he is a man, they are in a "lesbian" affair. This joke is toyed with even further in part two of the finale, when he figuratively "brings a U-Haul," moving in with her right away, and they spend all waking moments together. In their every dialogue and physical interaction, Ellen plays butch to Dan's femme, and the season uses the potential of their hetero-homo romance continuing as a cliff-hanger to the next season. Here the sitcom *Ellen* playfully *queers* heterosexual scenarios, since it cannot yet show a queer one. Ellen's otherness is continually the underlying gag.

In "Three strikes" (2.21, March 29, 1995), Ellen, forced under court order to live with her parents, is made, by her mother, to wear a dress. As she walks through work, the laugh track goes wild; Ellen in a flowery dress in which she looks awkward is a joke in and of itself. Ellen Morgan's (and, really, Ellen DeGeneres's) queerness is what always exceeds the text, both with her dates that do not work, and with the one, Dan, that does.

Heterosexual Talk

Ellen's closeted verbal discourse around the topic of her sexuality on *Ellen: The Ellen DeGeneres Show* functions similarly to the coded scripting of her pre-out counterpart, Ellen Morgan, on *Ellen*. . . .

Generally, when the topic of her own sexuality is broached, live, Ellen DeGeneres defers the question within a heterosexual paradigm, in which straight desire is always the point-of-reference, the norm. Like a pre–"Puppy Episode" Ellen Morgan, who

cannot seem to find the right man, Ellen DeGeneres never enunciates the nature of her desire on air, but always enunciates, rather, *what her desire is not*.

Two live tapings of *Ellen: The Ellen DeGeneres Show* demonstrate this point. In a November 10, 2005, interview with Jake Gyllenhaal, the young actor comes out on stage with 400 white roses for Ellen, to congratulate her on her 400th live talk show (3.49, November 10, 2005). When they sit down together, Ellen immediately declares Jake "cute" and gives him a publicity suggestion: "More shots with your shirt off," showing a clip of him naked from the waist up in *Jarhead*. Her studio audience, mostly women, cheer at the top of their lungs. "You should take it off right now," Ellen urges. "You don't have to . . . It's only going to help you." Gyllenhaal unbuttons his top button then closes it again. "It's my 400th show," begs Ellen. "Roses are sweet and everything . . . I'll give 'em back if you'll take your shirt off." Gyllenhaal becomes bright red and laughs, clearly bashful.

Ellen here mimics Rosie O'Donnell's "passing" as straight. Rosie O'Donnell, who came out as a lesbian *after* her popular television talk show wrapped, perfected "passing" by regularly harping on her ambiguously sexualized obsession with *Top Gun* star Tom Cruise. Gyllenhaal is verbally worshiped like Cruise; however, Ellen camps the faked crush even further, demonstrating her "passing" clearly as shtick. Acting similarly as a facilitator for straight women in their fantasies, DeGeneres's play act has a distinct difference from O'Donnell's: DeGeneres's homosexuality is a known secret—a secret the audience knows in an iconic way—and she trades on this knowledge to make her interaction funny.

"It's not for me," Ellen asserts, looking Gyllenhaal in the eye, smiling. He can barely talk; he refuses to budge, but good naturedly. "It's not for me!" she insists again, making it clear, as if he did not get it the first time, that she is not trying to sexually harass him; *besides, she's gay.* They share an understanding glance. "Are you single right now? I should ask that. Not for me, again, *I don't care,* but the women in the audience want to know." After the commercial break, Gyllenhaal loosens the collar of his shirt and exposes the top of his chest.

The sustained tease of Gyllenhaal's potential strip that never happens acts as a promotional para-text for the film *Jarhead.* Ellen even spells this out: "If you want to see what the rest of that looks like, you have to go see the movie *Jarhead."* Ellen focuses entirely on *Jarhead* and on her flirtation with Gyllenhaal about taking off his shirt. She gives his other about-to-release-film, *Brokeback Mountain,* an ever-so-quick mention at the end, but does not ask Gyllenhaal one question about this "film with Heath Ledger" (as she summarizes it), nor does she mention that the film deals with a homosexual romance between Gyllenhaal's and Ledger's characters. While implying that her own homosexuality gives her the social mobility to be so openly cheeky with him, without it constituting any kind of gender upheaval or sexual come-on, Ellen has, in this exchange, played butch to Gyllenhaal's femme, much like Ellen Morgan did with Dan, placing him in the position of the looked at, the desirable. . . . She insists, however, on her non-desire, and does not name why it is that she is not attracted to him— that is supposedly "understood," it goes without saying. Gyllenhaal gets visibly uncomfortable with his position as object, but becomes visibly more comfortable when Ellen finally asks whether he is single, since "the women in the audience want to know," because she is offering him the space of normal heterosexual identity by default. Therefore, she intelligently also skirts the question of *his* sexuality. Ellen comes out through negation, although a denial of a heterosexual desire for one person does not necessarily imply homosexuality. The way she addresses the subject matter is very crafty— to those that do not want to be reminded of the nature of her desires, she does not dare

speak its name; to those that do, she is, at least, honest.

In a special event edition of *Ellen: The Ellen DeGeneres Show* that aired on November 30, 2005, celebrating Ellen's twenty-fifth anniversary as a stand-up comedian, a similar incident takes place (3.63). Ellen's "anniversary" special revolves around clips shown from Ellen's career as a stand-up comedian, allowing her to poke fun at her many bad haircuts. Guest celebrities visit to reminisce about Ellen's start in "show biz." Jay Leno, for instance, discusses getting Ellen her first gig on the *Johnny Carson Show,* a show that obviously inspired her own. Her first Carson appearance was featured most prominently during the hour, and the fact that she was the first female comedian ever invited to be interviewed by Carson after her act was underscored. . . . Strangely, however, her sitcom was conspicuously missing from this retrospective. (Consider, for example, a retrospective on Jerry Seinfeld that fails to mention *Seinfeld* . . .) By focusing only on Ellen's stand-up career, not only was her sitcom and her "coming out" conveniently occluded from the history of Ellen that the talk show offers, but no clips with *any* gay content were shown. Ellen rehistoricizes herself as a stand-up comedian first and fore-most, and an asexual one at that.

David Spade joins Ellen on this episode, and we learn through their conversation that they met twenty years ago when the two traveled comedy circuits together, Spade opening for Ellen's headlining act. Spade admits a secret: "We used to do some of these gigs together . . . I had a big crush on her . . . then I got the news." Ellen becomes visibly embarrassed and just laughs for a long while, while Spade turns it into a joke: "What it was, was the fact that you had a Walkman . . . and a *sweet* mullet." "I thought you were adorable," Ellen finally responds, "No interest, other than the fact that you were adorable. Although I did . . . I had a crush on you and you know it." She goes right from this statement into a clip of David

Spade's vintage comedy. Those of us that are "in" on the joke, read David's crush on Ellen as real, and Ellen's crush on David as purely platonic. Again here Ellen discursively frames her queerness through expressing what she *does not desire,* and even that in a very mixed-up way, as is evident in the statement, "No interest, other than the fact that you were adorable." *What does that mean?* Ellen does not outright deny her homosexuality; when it comes up, she deflects mention of "gayness" with the double-speak and coded strategies of her pre-coming-out sitcom character. DeGeneres is comfortable expressing her nonheterosexuality (in a specific instance—so that it could be read as follows: she just does not like *him*) on air, but not her *homosexuality* directly.

John Limon points out that DeGeneres's strategy of "skirting" is not only admitted, but defined, in her book *My Point . . . and I Do Have One:*

> Someone recently wrote a letter . . . asking "Why does Ellen DeGeneres always wear pants and never skirts?" I'm guessing that the person who wrote that letter meant skirt, a noun signifying an article of clothing, and not skirt, a verb defined as, "to evade or elude (as a topic of conversation) by circumlocution." Because, if they mean the verb skirt, well, they're dead wrong. I'm always skirting. (DeGeneres 93; quoted in Limon 115)

Limon identifies DeGeneres's "skirting" as a form of "escapist art" that refuses "to put all kidding aside," and where "what is made visible . . . is evasion" (116–117). Her verbal skirts act as denials of reality that constantly rely on reality as their vanishing point. Rather than expressing information that can be pinned down or literally understood, she replaces objective "truths" with tangential flights of fancy, distractions, wordplay, while presenting the journey of the skirt itself as having *subjective* and transient values—of imagination, pleasure, possibility.

Limon lyrically asks of DeGeneres's skirting: "Is knowledge of the body repressed or unlearned? Is the body itself decoded or disclaimed?" (121). He dubs DeGeneres "an inverse Lenny Bruce, whose shame existed to be displayed as pride" (121). The notion that DeGeneres's *pride* (with all of the meanings attached to that word) exists to be *displayed* as shame, as the case may be, is a savvy way to view beneath her linguistic skirts. If skirting is DeGeneres's verbal strategy for, at least on the surface, distancing her comedy from the bodily, from *her body* and the material consequences of the world, while leaking other meanings, DeGeneres's physical displays, especially her dances, convey and rely on utter embodiment: the body engaged in ritual.

Interpretive Dance

. . . . Ellen's choice to deflect or redirect the question of her homosexuality in potentially heterosexual discursive terms on her talk show is one strategy to remove herself from the confessional paradigm, wherein an implied authority outside of herself (like the voice in Ellen Morgan's elevator), "the one who listens" (in the case of her show, the audience), is the implied judge or cheerleader of her private life. Instead, Ellen *performs* her daily dances—illustrating both her control over what is expressed and her pleasure in expressing it. Here Ellen presents her queerness, individuality, difference, otherness, in an expressive act that broadcasts her self-love, and as part of a daily ritual that is ultimately not all about her. Her daily dance also becomes a boundary-crossing ritual shared with all, where she encourages others (her studio audience and viewers at home) to join her—to get up and dance *themselves.* For Ellen, dancing with oneself becomes dancing with the watching world, fulfilling the wish of the final refrain of the 1980s Billy Idol tune, "Dancing With Myself": "If I had a chance,

I'd ask the world to dance." Dancing with oneself on television *presents* a dance *of oneself* to be received, shared, and potentially reciprocated.

Opening the stand-up special *Ellen DeGeneres: The Beginning,* which first aired on cable channel HBO on July 23, 2000, Ellen briefly addresses her coming-out saga before performing a dance about the very subject (set to disco music that devolves into chants of "nah nah, nah nah, nah"). A comedy special such as this one, on a pay cable network such as HBO, offers DeGeneres a markedly less censored venue in which to express herself than on network television, daytime or prime time. In her introduction, Ellen offers an extremely telling speech that I end this chapter with, because I believe it not only introduces Ellen's specific dance performance that night, but frames both her discursive closet and her soon-to-be-daily dance as "out." Speaking her mind about what should now be said, or not said, about her sexuality, Ellen successfully encodes the media ritual of dancing, later to appear on *Ellen: The Ellen DeGeneres Show,* as a performance of queerness that expresses meaning where words have been found to fail:

> Since I made the decision to come out three years ago, my life has been very interesting . . . I knew that people would want me to talk about it. Some people may not want me to talk about it. So I went back and forth, trying to decide should I talk about it, should I not talk about it, and ultimately I decided: No, I don't want to talk about it. It's been talked about enough, what can I say? I feel it would be best expressed through interpretive dance.

Notes

1. I use the word *televisibility* to refer to instances of visibility on television by queer subjects.

2. [Liminality refers to an in-between, or transitional, phase or state of consciousness. Ed.] . . .

3. *American Gladiators* (1989–1997, CBS) featured body builders competing against contestants on an obstacle course. Nitro was a regular gladiator and sometime co-host on the sensationalistic game show. Featuring *American Gladiators* on *Ellen* obviously served as an ABC-CBS cross-promotion.

References

Bociurkiw, Marusya. "It's Not About the Sex: Racialization and Queerness in Ellen and The Ellen DeGeneres Show." *Canadian Woman Studies* 24:2–3 (2005): 176–182.

Couldry, Nick. *Media Rituals: A Critical Approach.* London: Routledge, 2003.

Deeken, Aimee. "Syndies Score in February." *Mediaweek* March 14, 2005: 30.

DeGeneres, Ellen. *My Point . . . And I Do Have One.* New York: Bantam, 1996.

"The Ellen DeGeneres Show: About the Show." Warner Bros.com. December 31, 2006. http://ellen.warnerbros.com/showinfo/about .html.

Gross, Larry. *Up from Invisibility: Lesbians, Gay Men and the Media in America.* New York: Columbia University Press, 2001.

Halperin, David M. *Saint Foucault: Towards a Gay Hagiography.* New York: Oxford University Press, 1995.

Heffernan, Virginia. "The Perils of Pleasant, or Spacey, on Talk Shows." *New York Times,* September 16, 2003. E5

Hubert, Suan J. "What's Wrong with This Picture? The Politics of Ellen's Coming Out Party." *Journal of Popular Culture* 33:2 (1999): 31–37.

Kort, Michele. "Welcome Back to the L World." *The Advocate* February 1, 2005: 40–45.

———. "Portia Heart & Soul." *The Advocate,* September 13, 2005: 40–46.

Limon, John. *Stand-up Comedy in Theory, or, Abjection in America.* Durham and London: Duke University Press, 2000.

Lo, Malinda. "Does the L Word Represent? Viewer Reactions Vary on the Premiere Episode." *AfterEllen.com: Lesbian and Bisexual Women in Entertainment and the Media*. January 2004. May 3, 2006. http://www.afterellen.com/tv/thelword/reaction.html.

McCarthy, Anna. "Ellen: Making Queer Television History." *GLQ* 7:4 (2001): 593–620.

———. "Must-see Queer TV: History and Serial Form in Ellen." *Quality Popular Television: Cult TV, the Industry and Fans*. Ed. Mark Jancovich and James Lyons. London: BFI, 2003. 88–102.

Millman, Joyce. "The Sitcom that Dare Not Speak Its Name." *San Francisco Examiner* March 19, 1995: B1.

Schnuer, Jenna. "The Ellen DeGeneres Show: Upbeat Host Gains Fans, Feel-Good Marketers." *Advertising Age* May 16, 2005: S1.

Sconce, Jeffrey. "What If? Charting Television's New Textual Boundaries." *Television After TV: Essays on a Medium in Transition*. Eds. Lynn Spiegel and Jan Olsson. Durham: Duke University Press, 2004. 93–112.

Turner, Guinevere. "Lipstick Los Angeles." *OUT Traveler Magazine*. December 2004. September 7, 2006. http://www.thelwordonlin.com/lipstick_LA.html.

———. *Personal Interview with Candace Moore*. March 28, 2005.

Turner, Victor. *From Ritual to Theatre: The Human Seriousness of Play*. New York: PAJ Publications, 1982.

PART VIII

INTERACTIVITY, VIRTUAL COMMUNITY, AND FANDOM

As discussed elsewhere in this book, our commonsense view of the impact of media culture tends to highlight the all-powerful effects of ideology and the ways in which consumers internalize mediated messages into the way they make sense of the world. While research shows that there is much truth to this model of top-down media power, other media scholars, particularly those who study actual audiences, argue that the way consumers interact with texts is more complex and works on multiple levels. In recent years, students of media have increasingly emphasized not only the active audience but also in particular the fans, those consumers who are most highly engaged in making new meanings out of given cultural texts—sometimes producing not just readings but texts of their own. In this part, we focus on consumer productive activity and on activism—showing some of the many ways that people go beyond a passive relation to mass media culture.

We set these studies of audience activism, participation in production, and political lobbying to reshape mainstream media within the context of 21st-century media with the help of Henry Jenkins, a theorist of what is sometimes called "media convergence." According to Jenkins (VIII.59),

> Media convergence . . . involves the introduction of a much broader array of new media technologies that enable consumers to archive, annotate, transform, and recirculate media content . . . it alters the relationship among existing technologies, industries, markets, genres, and audiences. (p. 546)

In his view, we need to attend to the way in which two kinds of media **convergence** interact if we are to understand the dizzyingly unstable contemporary world of media production and consumption:

> *Corporate convergence*—the concentration of media ownership in the hands of a diminishing number of multinational conglomerates that thus have a vested interest in ensuring the flow of media content across different platforms and national borders.
> *Grassroots convergence*—the increasingly central roles that digitally empowered consumers play in shaping the production, distribution, and reception of media content. (p. 546)

Jenkins, a pioneer in the field of fandom studies (see his influential chapter on *Star Trek* fan fiction, included in Part I), questions the "media imperialism" argument, which holds that giant media corporations and cultural products based in the West completely dominate global media production and consumption. Applying the same principle by which audience and fandom studies complicated our understanding of the power dynamics between consumers and texts, he urges us to look carefully, through **ethnographic** study, at the ways in which regional and local audiences may actually read imported cultural texts like Disney goods "in radically different ways . . . against the back-

drop of more familiar genres and through the grid of familiar values" (p. 547). And beyond simply looking in more nuanced ways at how U.S. cultural texts are received in other nations, Jenkins points to the importance of understanding "grassroots convergence"—the digitally assisted ways in which U.S. media consumers, particularly the sophisticated group he calls "pop cosmopolitans," now embrace, **appropriate**, and help to circulate imported Asian cultural goods, such as Japanese anime and manga or Bollywood films.

We turn next to two studies of digitally enabled fan media productivity. In a direct line of descent from Janice Radway's well-known study of romance novel readers (her article title suggests a tip of the hat to Radway's book, *Reading the Romance*), Eve Ng (VIII.60) has explored how a small group of fans of the popular American daytime soap opera *All My Children* were able to create and circulate music videos that "rewrote the romance" of Bianca Montgomery and Lena Kundera, who shared a temporary lesbian relationship on the show. Lesbian fans may have particularly experienced disappointment with the way the soap writers had handled the relationship, which at that time (2003) was "the first and only lesbian romance on U.S. daytime television." According to Ng, "one reason was that physical and sexual intimacy between Bianca and Lena was depicted much less explicitly than is commonly seen between soap opera couples" (p. 556). In response, fans digitally edited together clips emphasizing the physical as well as emotional moments from the show "that would appeal to viewers looking for a text in which Bianca and Lena were the primary figures, with their love for each other apparent" (p. 557), and created the imagined possibility of a "happy ending" as an alternative to the unsatisfying narrative offered by the show's writers.

Fan alternative text production and distribution in **cyberspace** does often enable marginalized groups both to make themselves more visible to other cultural consumers and to push against the boundaries of mainstream representations, as this example shows. However, another study of fan productivity, this time in relation to *World of Warcraft,* the massively multiplayer online role-playing game (MMORPG), suggests that there are significant limits to the progressive potential of participatory media. Lisa Nakamura's essay (VIII.61) examines how the hostility that many players feel about the game's unintended subsidiary practice of "gold farming, or selling in-game currency to players for real money," has taken a visual and specifically racialized (anti-Chinese) form. Fan-produced *machinima* (homemade music videos using visuals appropriated from within the online world and distributed on the Internet outside the game) stereotype the "gold farmers" as faceless Chinese worker multitudes, a threat to the leisure players who cannot hope to compete with their relentless labor. She argues that in this case, participatory media, often seen by enthusiasts as able to extend the world of mainstream texts "in truly liberatory ways," can also be used by fans in destructive and divisive ways:

> If indeed machinima extend the world of gameplay, how are players co-creating this world? . . . A closer look at user produced content from Warcraftmovies .com reveals a contraction and retrenchment of concepts of gender, race and nation rather than their enlargement. (p. 566)

A similar critique of the impact of participatory media cultural production is offered by Brookey and Cannon (VIII.62), in their chapter on sexual representation within *Second Life,* another MMORPG. These researchers also question the **liberatory** potential many early proponents of cyberspace celebrated, in this case with respect to representations of gender and sexuality. In the virtual world created online by *Second Life* players, "users are able to build their own buildings, create their own clothing and accessories, and are usually at liberty to shape this virtual world in any way they see fit" (p. 571). Brookey and Cannon looked specifically at the ways in which players "are taking advantage of this liberty to refigure gender and sexuality"—or not. Focusing in particular on how players are enabled to construct their own *avatars* (the in-game embodiments or self-representations of the players themselves), the researchers looked at in-game stores selling clothing as well as sexual and fetish ware and found an emphasis on traditional femininity and female sexual submissiveness. While queer sexuality was not invisible in *Second Life,* they noted that in "queer spaces and 'islands,'" while sexual content was not restricted, many of the spaces were firmly gender segregated. Most restrictive was a voice verification system set up to make sure that players who patronize virtual "escorts" within *Second Life* are not inadvertently dating a transgender avatar. This study suggests how difficult it is even in cyberspace to reenvision gender and sexuality in ways that transcend the cultural norms and values of our real-life society.

As Lawrence McBride and S. Elizabeth Bird point (VIII.63) out in our next study of productive fandom, for backyard wrestling fans, the point is precisely not to challenge normative gender (in this case masculinity) but to create the most spectacular possible performance of it through careful mastery of its high-risk bodily moves. While a few lone critical voices (such as that of Jenkins, 1997) have argued that "pro wrestling can also be productively interpreted as melodrama, of a kind specially tailored to the male imagination," in general, "wrestling, and by extension, its fandom, is one of the most denigrated forms of popular culture." Some cultural studies scholars shudder at its apparent equation of manhood and extreme violence, and for most casual observers, "the 'meaning' of American wrestling is so often taken to lie at the surface, inscribed with a conventional, reactionary symbolism of racism, sexism, and jingoism, and thus meriting widespread condemnation" (p. 589). But McBride and Johnson offer a provocative interpretation of the risk-taking performative violence in the fan-generated spectacles of backyard wrestling, based on ethnographic research. They emphasize the productive role of the "smart fan"—the "would-be insider" who possesses vast information about the business and history of wrestling and the behind-the-scenes activities of the televised national World Wrestling Entertainment—in creating a special independent "aesthetic" for the new backyard style of wrestling.

Another way to become active as a fan of a particular media cultural product is to organize and lobby on behalf of its existence when threatened by economically driven decision making by its producers. Televised soap operas, another example of a cultural form heavily derided as "low culture" in the past, have played a major role in the imaginative lives of their predominantly female viewers for many years. In Melissa Scardaville's study (VIII.64) of activism around the 1999 cancellation of the 35-year-old daytime drama *Another World,* she shows how

> soaps may be seen as an apolitical medium, enjoyed only by complacent viewers, but in actuality, daytime television provides a powerful platform for activism. (p. 600)

While soap fan activism is not a new phenomenon, as Scardaville shows, a series of campaigns on behalf of this show were aided substantially by the Internet, which provided instant communication among potential fan activists as well as between fans and mainstream industry insiders (e.g., actors and executives). Although in this instance, the campaign to keep *Another World* on the air ultimately failed, Scardaville finds that "what is extremely meaningful about these movements . . . is not their success or failure, but the soap opera genre's ability to create these accidental activists" (p. 600). Most of the fans contacted by Scardaville were motivated to get involved in activism because of "their perception of the show as an extended family."

We end this chapter and the book with a nuanced study by Vincent Doyle (VIII.65) of a successful media activism campaign, which prevented the radio talk show host Laura Schlesinger from transplanting her highly socially conservative show to television. Schlesinger's defeat was to a large degree orchestrated by two stylistically and strategically distinct groups of activists: the long-established GLAAD (Gay and Lesbian Alliance Against Defemation) and the ad hoc group, StopDrLaura.com (SDL), that emerged specifically to wage a more assertive campaign against Dr. Laura. Although the two groups disagreed on tactics, the ultimate success of both groups' efforts provides us with a potentially inspiring example of what can be achieved when media activists organize for real-world change in media representation.

Reference

Jenkins, H. (1997). Never trust a snake! WWF wrestling as masculine melodrama. In A. Baker & T. Boyd (Eds.), *Out of bounds: Sports, media, and the politics of identity* (pp. 48–80). Bloomington: Indiana University Press.

Pop Cosmopolitanism

Mapping Cultural Flows in an Age of Media Convergence

Henry Jenkins III

If there is a global village, it speaks American. It wears jeans, drinks Coke, eats at the golden arches, walks on swooshed shoes, plays electric guitars, recognizes Mickey Mouse, James Dean, E.T., Bart Simpson, R2-D2, and Pamela Anderson.

Gitlin 2001

The twain of East and West have not only met—they've mingled, mated, and produced myriad offspring, inhabitants of one world, without borders or boundaries, but with plenty of style, hype, and attitude. In Beijing, they're wearing Levis and drinking Coke; in New York, they're sipping tea in Anna Sui. While Pizzicato Five is spinning heads in the U.S., Metallica is banging them in Japan.

Yang, Gan, Hong and the staff of A. Magazine, 1997

. . . . I have spent my career studying American popular culture, adopting an approach based on older notions of national specificity. In recent years, however, it has become increasingly difficult to study what's happening to American popular culture without understanding its global context. I mean this not simply in the predictable sense that American pop culture dominates (and is being shaped for) worldwide markets but also in the sense that a growing proportion of the popular culture that Americans consume comes from elsewhere, especially Asia. This chapter represents a first stab at explaining how and why Asian popular culture is shaping American entertainment.

From Jenkins, H. (2004). Pop cosmopolitanism: Mapping cultural flows in an age of media convergence. In M. M. Suarez-Orozco & D. B. Qin-Hilliard (Eds.), *Globalization: Culture & education in the new millennium*. Berkeley: University of California Press.

The analysis must start with the concept of media convergence. Most industry discourse about convergence begins and ends with what I call the black box fallacy: sooner or later all media are going to be flowing through a single black box in our living rooms, and all we have to do is figure out which black box it will be. Media convergence is not an end-point; rather, it is an ongoing process occurring at various intersections among media technologies, industries, content, and audiences. Thanks to the proliferation of channels and the increasingly ubiquitous nature of computing and telecommunications, we are entering an era when media will be everywhere and we will use all kinds of media in relation to each other. We will develop new skills for managing that information, new structures for transmitting information across channels, new creative genres that exploit the potentials of those emerging information structures, and new modes of education to help students understand their impact on their world. Media convergence is more than simply the digital revolution; it involves the introduction of a much broader array of new media technologies that enable consumers to archive, annotate, transform, and recirculate media content. Media convergence is more than simply a technological shift; it alters the relationship among existing technologies, industries, markets, genres, and audiences. This initial wave of media changes exerts a destabilizing influence, resulting in a series of lurches between exhilaration and panic. Yet media convergence is also sparking creative innovation in almost every sector of popular culture; our present media environment is marked by a proliferation of differences, by what Grant McCracken calls "plenitude" (see McCracken 2003). . . .

In this chapter I focus on the interplay between

Corporate convergence—the concentration of media ownership in the hands of a diminishing number of multinational conglomerates that thus have a vested interest in ensuring the flow of media content across different platforms and national borders

and

Grassroots convergence—the increasingly central roles that digitally empowered consumers play in shaping the production, distribution, and reception of media content.

These two forces—the top-down push of corporate convergence, the bottom-up pull of grassroots convergence—intersect to produce what might be called global convergence, the multidirectional flow of cultural goods around the world. Ulf Hannerz is describing global convergence when he writes: "[World culture] is marked by an organization of diversity rather than by a replication of uniformity. . . . The world has become one network of social relationships and between its different regions there is a flow of meanings as well as of people and goods" (Hannerz 1990, p. 237).

Global convergence is giving rise to a new pop cosmopolitanism.[1] Cosmopolitans embrace cultural difference, seeking to escape the gravitational pull of their local communities in order to enter a broader sphere of cultural experience. The first cosmopolitans thought beyond the borders of their village; the modern cosmopolitans think globally. We tend to apply the term to those who develop a taste for international food, dance, music, art, or literature—in short, those who have achieved distinction through their discriminating tastes for classical or high culture. Here, I will be using the term pop cosmopolitanism to refer to the ways that the transcultural flows of popular culture inspire new forms of global consciousness and cultural competency. Much as teens in the developing world use American popular culture to express generational differences or to articulate fantasies of social, political, and cultural transformation, younger Americans are distinguishing themselves from their parents' culture through their consumption of Japanese anime and manga, Bollywood films and bhangra, and Hong Kong action movies. This pop cosmopolitanism may not yet constitute a political consciousness of America's place in the world (and in its worse forms, may simply amount to a reformation of orientalism), but it opens consumers to alternative cultural perspectives and the possibility of feeling what Matt Hills calls "semiotic solidarity" with others worldwide who share their tastes and interests (Hills 2002). . . .

Pop cosmopolitanism cannot be reduced to either the technological utopianism embodied by Marshall McLuhan's "global village" (with its promises of media transcending the nation-state and democratizing cultural access) or the ideological anxieties expressed in the concept of media imperialism (with its threat of cultural homogenization and of "the West suppressing the Rest," as Ramaswami Harindranath describes it [see Harindranath 2003, p. 156]).

The media imperialism argument blurs the distinction between at least four forms of power—economic (the ability to produce and distribute cultural goods), cultural (the ability to produce and circulate forms and meanings), political (the ability to impose ideologies), and psychological (the ability to shape desire, fantasy, and identity). Within this formulation, Western economic dominance of global entertainment both expresses and extends America's status as a superpower; the flow of cultural goods shapes the beliefs and the fantasies of worldwide consumers, reshaping local cultures in accordance with American economic and political interests. The classic media imperialism argument ascribed almost no agency to the receiving culture and saw little reason to investigate actual cultural effects; the flow of goods was sufficient to demonstrate the destruction of cultures.[2] Ethnographers have found that the same media content may be read in radically different ways in different regional or national contexts, with consumers reading it against the backdrop of more familiar genres and through the

grid of familiar values. Even within the same context, specific populations (especially the young) may be particularly drawn toward foreign media content while others may express moral and political outrage. Most will negotiate with this imported culture in ways that reflect the local interests of media consumers rather than the global interests of media producers.

To be sure, there is probably no place on the planet where one can escape the shadow of Mickey Mouse. Entertainment is America's largest category of exports. The Global Disney Audiences Project, for example, deployed an international team of scholars to investigate the worldwide circulation of Disney goods. They found that in eleven of eighteen countries studied, 100 percent of all respondents had watched a Disney movie, and many of them had bought a broad range of other ancillary products (Wasko, Phillips, and Meehan 2001). But while still strong, the hold of American-produced television series on the global market has slipped in recent years (Foroohar 2002; Klein 2002). Local television production has rebounded, and domestic content dominates the prime evening viewing hours, with American content used as filler in the late-night or afternoon slots. Hollywood faces increased competition from other film-producing nations—including Japan, India, and China—that are playing ever more visible roles within regional, if not yet fully global, markets. Major media companies, such as Bertelsmann, Sony, and Universal Vivendi, contract talent worldwide, catering to the tastes of local markets rather than pursuing nationalistic interests; their economic structure encourages them not only to serve as intermediaries between different Asian markets but also to bring Asian content into Western countries. Many American children are more familiar with the characters of Pokemon than they are with those from the Brothers Grimm or Hans Christian Andersen, and a growing portion of American youth are dancing to Asian beats. With the rise of broadband communications, foreign media producers will distribute media content directly to American consumers without having to pass by U.S. gatekeepers or rely on multinational distributors. At the same time, grassroots intermediaries will play an increasingly central role in shaping the flow of cultural goods into local markets.

Adopting a position that if you can't beat them, merge with them, the American entertainment industry has become more aggressive in recruiting or collaborating with Asian talent. Sony, Disney, Fox, and Warner Brothers have all opened companies to produce films—aimed both at their domestic markets and at global export—in Chinese, German, Italian, Japanese, and other languages. American television and film increasingly remake successful products from other markets, ranging from *Survivor* and *Big Brother,* which are remakes of successful Dutch series, to *The Ring,* a remake of a Japanese cult horror movie, and *Vanilla Sky,* a remake of a Spanish science fiction film. Many of the cartoons shown on American television are actually made in Asia (increasingly in Korea), often with only limited supervision by Western companies.

Some have argued that Hollywood entertainment has always been global entertainment. Whereas many national cinemas respond to a relatively homogenous local market, Hollywood has had to factor in the tastes of a multicultural society. Richard Pells writes: "The United States has been a recipient as much as an exporter of global culture. . . . American culture has spread throughout the world because it has incorporated foreign styles and ideas. What Americans have done more brilliantly than their competitors overseas is repackage the cultural products we received from abroad and then retransmit them to the rest of the planet" (Pells 2002; also see Olson 1999). Pells sees this as an ongoing development that has shaped the evolution of American pop culture, not simply a cosmetic shift in response to recent economic trends or cultural developments.

These shifts complicate any simple mapping of the relationship among economic, political, and cultural power. We still must struggle with issues of domination and with the gap between media have and have-not nations, but we do so within a much more complicated landscape. . . . Arjun Appadurai writes, "Electronic mediation and mass migration . . . seem to impel (and sometimes compel) the work of the imagination. Together, they create specific irregularities because both viewers and images are in simultaneous circulation. Neither images nor viewers fit into circuits or audiences that are easily bound within local, national, or regional spaces" (Appadurai 1996, p. 4).

Strategies of Corporate Convergence

The flow of Asian goods into Western markets has been shaped through the interaction of three distinct kinds of economic interests: (1) national or regional media producers who see the global circulation of their products not simply as expanding their revenue stream but also as enhancing national pride; (2) multinational conglomerates that no longer define their production or distribution decisions in national terms but seek to identify potentially valuable content and push it into as many markets as possible; and (3) niche distributors who search for distinctive content as a means of attracting upscale consumers and differentiating themselves from stuff already on the market. For example, in the case of world music, international media companies, such as Sony, identify international artists and market them aggressively in their local or regional markets. As those artists are brought westward, the companies make a commercial decision whether they think the musicians will open mainstream, in which case the companies retain distribution rights within the United States, or niche, in which case they subcontract with a boutique label or third-party distributor (Levin 2002).

In a compelling analysis of the impact of Japanese transnationalism on popular culture, Koichi Iwabuchi draws a distinction between the circulation of cultural goods that are essentially "odorless," bearing few traces of their cultural origins, and those that are embraced for their culturally distinctive "fragrance" (Iwabuchi 2002). In some cases, mostly where these goods are targeting niche or cult audiences, these goods are strongly marked as coming from some exotic elsewhere; in other cases, especially where they are targeted to the mainstream, their national origins are masked and the content retrofitted to American tastes.

As Iwabuchi has documented, Japanese media industries sought ways to open Western markets to their "soft goods," or cultural imports, based on the overseas success of their hardware and consumer electronics. Seeking global distribution for locally produced content, Japanese corporations such as Sony, Sumitomo, Itochu, and Matsushita bought into the American entertainment industry. They saw children's media as sweet spots in Western societies. Much as Hollywood's ability to compete in international markets rests on its ability to recoup most of its production costs from domestic grosses, the success of Japanese-made comics and animation meant that these goods could enjoy competitive prices as they entered Western markets. In Japan, manga constituted 40 percent of all books and magazines published, and more than half of all movie tickets sold were to animated films (Ahn 2001). More than two hundred animation programs were aired each week on Japanese television, and about seventeen hundred animated films (short or feature length) were produced for theatrical distribution each year. Japanese media producers had created a complex set of tie-ins among comics, animated films and television series, and toys, which allowed them to capitalize quickly on successful content and bring it to the largest possible audience. They hoped to export this entire apparatus—the programs, the comics, and the toys—to the West. In the domestic market, anime and manga appealed to a broad cross-section of the public, but as they targeted the West, Japanese media companies targeted children as the primary consumers of their first imports. As this generation matured, the companies anticipated that they would embrace a broader range of Japanese-made media. . . .

Tactics of Grassroots Convergence

. . . . Grassroots convergence serves the needs of both cosmopolitan and local. A global communication network allows members of diasporic communities to maintain strong ties with their motherlands, ensuring access to materials and information important to their cultural traditions and preserving social connections with those they left behind (Punathambekar 2003). Cosmopolitans use networked communication to scan the planet in search of diversity and communicate with others of their kind around the world. . . .

The pop cosmopolitan walks a thin line between dilettantism and connoisseurship, between orientalist fantasies and a desire to honestly connect and understand an alien culture, between assertion of mastery and surrender to cultural difference.

These same paradoxes and contradictions surface when we turn our attention to American fans of Japanese anime, the otaku. Otaku is a Japanese term used to make fun of fans who have become such obsessive consumers of pop culture that they have lost all touch with the people in their immediate vicinity. American fans have embraced the shameful term, asserting what Matt Hills calls a "semiotic solidarity" with their Japanese counterparts (Hills 2002); constructing their identity as "otaku" allows them to signal their distance from American taste cultures and their mastery over foreign content. While a minority of otaku are Asian or Asian American, the majority have no direct ties to Japan. . . .

Initially, anime, like Bollywood videos, entered the United States through small distributors who targeted Asian immigrants. Fans would venture into ethnic neighborhoods in search of content; in New York and San Francisco they turned to a handful of Japanese bookstores for manga that had not yet been translated or distributed in North America.[3] The Web enabled fans to start their own small-scale (and sometimes pirate) operations to help import, translate, and distribute manga and anime. . . .

Ethnographers who have studied this subculture disagree about the degree to which otaku seek any actual connection with real-world Japan or simply enter into an imaginary world constructed via anime genres. As Susan Napier writes, "the fact that anime is a Japanese . . . product is certainly important but largely because this signifies that anime is a form of media entertainment outside the mainstream, something 'different'" (Napier 2000, p. 242; see also Newitz 1994; Tobin 1998). Napier suggests that fans are attracted to the strange balance of familiar and alien elements in Japanese animation, which openly appropriates and remakes Western genre conventions. Some anime fans do cultivate a more general knowledge of Japanese culture. They meet at sushi restaurants; clubs build partnerships via the Internet with sister organizations in Japan. Members often travel to Japan in search of new material or to experience the fan culture there more directly; some study the Japanese language in order to participate in various translation projects. As American fans go online and establish direct contact with their Japanese counterparts, they create an opening for other kinds of conversation. Discussion lists move fluidly from focus on anime- and manga-specific topics onto larger considerations of Japanese politics and culture. These different degrees of cultural engagement are consistent with what Hannerz has told us about cosmopolitanism more

generally: "[In one kind of cosmopolitanism], the individual picks from other cultures only those pieces which suit himself. . . . In another mode, however, the cosmopolitan does not make invidious distinctions among the particular elements of the alien culture in order to admit some of them into his repertoire and refuse others; he does not negotiate with the other culture but accepts it as a package deal" (Hannerz 1990, p. 240). What cosmopolitanism at its best offers us is an escape from parochialism and isolationism, the beginnings of a global perspective, and the awareness of alternative vantage points. . . .

Notes

1. For another take on what I am calling pop cosmopolitanism, see Roberts 2001.

2. For overviews of the debates on media imperialism, see Tomlinson 1991, Howe 1996, Liebes and Katz 1990, and Featherstone 1996.

3. On manga fandom, see Schodt 1996; Kinsella 2000; and Macias and Horn 1999.

References

Ahn, J. (2001). Animated subjects: On the circulation of Japanese animation as global cultural products. Paper presented at the Globalization, Identity and the Arts Conference, University of Manitoba, Winnipeg.

Appadurai, A. (1996). *Modernity at large: The cultural dimensions of globalization.* Minneapolis: University of Minnesota Press.

Featherstone, M. (1996). Localism, globalism and cultural identity. In *Global local: Cultural production and the transnational imaginary.* Rob Wilson and Wimal Dissanayake, eds. Durham: Duke University Press.

Foroohar, R. (2002). Hurray for Globowood: As motion-picture funding, talent and audiences go global, Hollywood is no longer a place, but a state of mind. *Newsweek International,* May 27.

Gitlin, T. (2001). *Media unlimited: How the torrent of images and sounds overwhelms our lives.* New York: Metropolitan.

Hannerz, U. (1990). Cosmopolitans and locals in world culture. In *Global culture: Nationalism, globalization, and modernity.* M. Featherstone, ed. London: Sage.

Harindranath, R. (2003). Reviving "cultural imperialism": International audiences, global capitalism and the transnational elite. In *Planet TV.* L. Parks and S. Kumar, eds. New York: New York University Press.

Hills, M. (2002). Transcultural Otaku: Japanese representations of fandom and representations of Japan in Anime/Manga fan cultures. Paper presented at Media-in-Transition 2: Globalization and Convergence Conference, Massachusetts Institute of Technology, Cambridge, MA.

Howe, D. (1996). Commodities and cultural borders. In *Cross-Cultural Consumption: Global Markets, Local Realities.* London: Routledge.

Iwabuchi, K. (2002). *Recentering globalization: Popular culture and Japanese transnationalism.* Durham: Duke University Press.

Kinsella, S. (2002). *Adult Manga: Culture and power in contemporary Japanese society.* Honolulu: University of Hawaii Press.

Klein, C. (2002). The globalization of Hollywood. Paper presented at the Modern Language Association conference, New York, NY.

Levin, M. (2002). Independent distributors and specialty labels move product in the U.S. by such international artists as Shakira. Copyright 2002 BPI Communications, Inc. Used with permission from Billboard, November 2.

Liebes, T., and E. Katz (1990). *The export of meaning: Cross-cultural readings of* Dallas. Oxford, UK: Oxford University Press.

Macias P., and C. G. Horn, eds. (1999). *Japan edge: The insider's guide to Japanese pop subculture.* San Francisco: Cadence Books.

McCracken, G. (2003). Plenitude. http://www.cultureby.com/books/plenit/cxc_trilogy_plenitude.html.

Napier, S. (2000). *Anime from Akira to Princess Mononoke: Experiencing Japanese animation.* New York: Palgrave.

Newitz, A. (1994). Anime Otaku: Japanese animation fans outside Japan. Bad Subjects 13. http://eserver.org/bs/13/Newitz.html.

Olson, S. R. (1999). *Hollywood planet.* New York: Lawrence Erlbaum.

Pells, R. (2002). American culture goes global, or does it? *Chronicle of Higher Education,* April. http://chronicle.com/free/v48/i31/31 boo701.htm.

Punathambekar, A. (2003). *Bollywood bytes: A story of how I found an Online Adda.*

Roberts, M. (2001). Notes on the Global Underground: Subcultural Elites, Conspicuous Cosmopolitanism. Paper presented at the Globalization, Identity and the Arts Conference, University of Manitoba, Winnipeg, http: //www.umanitoba.ca/faculties/arts/english/media/workshop/papers/roberts/roberts_papcr.pdf.

Schodt, F. (1996). *Dreamland Japan: Writings on modern Manga.* Berkeley, CA: Stone Bridge.

Tobin, J. (1998). An American Otaku or, a boy's virtual life on the Net. In *Digital diversions: Youth culture in the age of multimedia.* J. Sefton-Green, ed. London: University College of London Press.

Tomlinson, J. (1991). *Cultural imperialism.* Baltimore: Johns Hopkins University Press.

Wasko, J., M. Phillips, and E. R. Meehan, eds. (2001). *Dazzled by Disney? The global Disney audiences project.* London: Leicester University Press.

Yang, J., and D. Gan, T. Hong, and the staff of A. Magazine, eds. (1997). *Eastern Standard Time: A guide to Asian influence on American culture from Astro Boy to Zen Buddhism.* Boston: Houghton Mifflin.

Reading the Romance of Fan Cultural Production

Music Videos of a Television Lesbian Couple

Eve Ng

On April 23, 2003, viewers of ABC's *All My Children* (1970–present) saw Bianca Montgomery (Eden Riegel), daughter of cosmetics magnate Erica Kane, and Lena Kundera (Olga Sosnovska), a woman Bianca had first met as her mother's employee, close that day's episode with the first same-sex romantic kiss on an American daytime soap. Several years later, with their relationship having ended in November 2004, footage of this kiss, invariably among the favorite scenes of Bianca/Lena devotees, continues to circulate online, especially as incorporated with other clips into fan-made music videos focusing on Bianca and Lena's relationship. . . . This chapter argues that theories of fan cultural production and queer media representation are fruitfully extended by considering the characteristics and meanings of contemporary fan texts such as the Bianca/Lena videos, and how they are positioned in relation to dominant discourses, as they renegotiate the canon[*] in particular ways.

The sharing of fan videos online points to technology as one obvious dimension of difference characterizing the Bianca/Lena—or "Lianca"— fandom, compared to the first fan videos. These had used relatively expensive audiovisual equipment to physically splice together videotape clips and synchronize them with a soundtrack; duplicating the resulting music video required tape-to-tape copying, with distribution usually occurring in person at fan conventions. Digitization technology and the Internet now mean that fans can create their videos using readily available computer software, publicize these at online message boards, and share them via YouTube or various other Web sites. . . .

From Ng, E. (2008). Reading the romance of fan cultural production: Music videos of a television lesbian couple. *Popular Communication*, 6, 103–121. Reprinted by permission of Taylor & Francis Ltd.

[*]["The canon" and "canonical" refer throughout this chapter to the officially authorized texts of *All My Children* episodes, as broadcast by ABC, as opposed to unauthorized, fan-produced materials making use of those texts in new ways. Ed.]

Particularly pertinent to analyses of the Lianca fandom is another change in popular media: the increased regular or recurring presence of LGBT people on U.S. television, and not only as guest characters who often met untimely ends or who advance the dramatic trajectory for characters other than themselves (Gibson, 2006; Gross, 2002; Tropiano, 2002). Significant as this is, it also comprises and reflects the mainstreaming of gay culture that queer theorists such as Warner (1999) have argued seeks to assimilate a limited set of nonheterosexual identities and practices, while continuing to exclude others. . . . The Bianca/Lena romance on *All My Children* cannot be assumed to be unproblematically progressive. At the same time, the Lianca videos belong to a genre that has traditionally constructed narratives against the grain of the canon. Thus, a key question is what the implications of lesbian canonicity are for the versions of queer representation these texts offer as particular fan negotiations of mainstream media.

As scholars such as Russo (1987) and Doty (1993) have argued, even in periods when canonical depictions of same-sex romantic relationships were rare, popular cultural texts have hardly been devoid of queerness, with queer discourses constitutive of particular genres such as horror, and alternative readings of texts in general available to subtextual interpretations. Fan videos of the 1980s and early 1990s were often instances of *slash,* originally defined as involving two canonically heterosexual characters of the same sex who were paired romantically in fan narratives (Bacon-Smith, 1992; Jenkins, 1992; Penley, 1991; Russ, 1985). Initially most slash fiction circulating among fans featured two men and was usually written by straight women. From one queer analytical perspective, this sort of slash critically interrogates conventional understandings of gender and sexuality, with men's interactions typically depicted as more physically tender and emotionally open than dominant norms around masculinity would dictate, and the pairing of characters who have sexual

histories with women implying a more flexible view of sexuality than a strict heterosexual/homosexual divide (e.g., Cicione, 1998; Green, Jenkins, & Jenkins, 1998; Jung, 2004; Woledge, 2005), However, Scodari (2003) countered that the impulse to read or write slash does not necessarily stem from a politically progressive position with respect to gender, and Jenkins (1992) noted that even some fans found certain conventions of slash fiction problematic, including common disavowals of gay identity by the characters, lack of engagement with structural-level political issues, and "an often thinly veiled distaste for female sexuality and feminine bodies" (p. 219).

The counter-hegemonic dimensions of same-sex romance narratives based on canonical couples and produced by queer fans are also complex, though in different ways. First, the predominance of queer women in the Lianca creative fandom is part of an increase in the proportion of slash[1] authors who are not heterosexually-identified (Boyd, 2001; Russo, 2002; Wilder, 1998), a trend most fueled, at the outset, by a significant lesbian following for *Xena: Warrior Princess* (syndicated, 1995–2001). The ambiguity of the intensely devoted friendship between Xena and Gabrielle on the canonical show inspired a huge volume of fan fiction in which the relationship between the two was explicitly romantic. Many viewers also have been motivated to produce fan narratives for textually lesbian relationships on other television shows,[2] especially when the canon is found to be deficient in various ways.

As texts that generally end happily or hopefully, fan cultural forms such as the Lianca music videos constitute re-articulations that are what fans want in queer narratives, at least some of the time. In her groundbreaking ethnography, Radway (1984) argued that readers derived meaning from romance novels that helped them imagine women as strong, intelligent, and able to attain their goals; thus, their consumption of this denigrated genre was not simply an example of acquiescence to discourses of female inferiority and dependence on men.

A parallel can be drawn with the typical Lianca video, which refuses the narrative of sad, lonely queers, creating instead a text in which lesbians find the love that soap opera logic—and mainstream culture more generally—suggests is necessary for happiness. . . .

Fan texts, then, do not fully depart from conventional ideas and values about human relations, and compared to fan fiction, fan videos are particularly dependent on the canonical texts as source for their visual material. A fan fiction author can have characters engage in actions that have never been portrayed or described in the canon, as well as create new characters, settings, and situations. On the other hand, in most fan videos, "neither the sights nor the sounds . . . originate with the fan artists; the creator's primary contribution, in most cases, comes in the imaginative juxtaposition of someone else's words and images" (Jenkins, 1992, p. 225). . . .

It is certainly possible for fan videos to incorporate or produce various sorts of video outside of "official" sources, a common practice for some users of other media, such as creators of interactive Internet applications known as mashups[3] (Merrill, 2006), or video gamers who use commercially released software to create their own distinctive animations and narratives (Herman, Coombe, & Kay, 2006; Jones, 2006). Why the majority of television fan video makers do not do so probably has to do with audience expectation, with viewers of these videos generally looking for something that fits sufficiently within the confines of the visual and cultural world familiar to them from the show, even as narrative sequences are being reworked. As Stein (2006) argues, fan texts may be shaped not just by their canonical sources, but also by "shared understandings of generic codes and tropes" that "contribute story possibilities and yet also limit the ranges of types of stories told" (p. 248). The development of these generic codes warrants further investigation, but they surely draw not just on elements of fan cultures—the delight in slashing canonically straight men, for example, or the popularity

of the hurt-comfort dynamic[4]—but are also shaped by more mainstream norms, particularly those around relationships, sex, and gender. . . .

All My Children and the Bianca/Lena Relationship

Bianca and Lena's relationship played out onscreen on one of the longest-running soap operas of U.S. television, ABC's *All My Children*, set in the fictional town of Pine Valley, Pennsylvania. Bianca Montgomery was introduced in 1988 as the baby daughter of series matriarch Erica Kane, but was not written as lesbian until 2000 when, with a revised birth year of 1984, the character was aged to 16. At that time, Bianca became the first regular character on a U.S. daytime soap to come out (see Harrington, 2003a, b), and, like most lesbians on U.S. television, she fit dominant standards of female attractiveness: thin, long-haired, wearing make-up and feminine attire. Lena Kundera, also conventionally feminine, had first appeared on the show at the end of 2002 as a shadowy figure, and came to work at Erica Kane's cosmetics company, Enchantment, in January 2003. It became apparent a couple of months later that she was actually a spy for—and the lover of—Michael Cambias, a business rival of Erica's. In the course of Lena's espionage, she and Bianca met and fell in love, culminating in their first kiss in April 2003, and a couple of weeks later, a morning-after scene. The couple broke up and made up a couple of times in the next few weeks, primarily due to revelations about Lena's associations with Michael, and the fact that she was directed by him to seduce Bianca for strategic purposes. However, in early July, Bianca and Lena appeared headed toward a romantic vacation together—until Bianca was raped by Michael.

Bianca was, predictably, traumatized by her rape; she destroyed evidence of the attack and did not tell anyone about it for weeks. Various people close to her realized there was something wrong, but Bianca pushed them away, including Lena, with whom she ceased all intimacies and, indeed, meaningful conversation for months. Bianca's main storylines came to revolve around the pregnancy resulting from the rape; the murder of Michael Cambias, for which both Bianca and Lena were suspects; and the birth and then apparent death of her daughter Miranda (Miranda had actually been secretly given to another couple). Bianca and Lena appeared to have a mini-reconciliation around New Year's Eve, having slowly moved back to one another, and by March 2004 Lena noted that the two were "dating," but it was not clear that they ever resumed a sexual relationship. In April 2004, Lena was written out of the show, and the couple had a phone break-up in November, when Bianca, feeling an inexplicable tie to Pine Valley, refused to join Lena in Poland, where Lena was tending her ailing mother and in desperate need of Bianca's support.

Bianca has also been involved with Maggie Stone (Elizabeth Hendrickson), a young woman who first appeared on the show in early 2002. While Bianca's feelings for Maggie were mostly unreciprocated for the bulk of their time together in Pine Valley, they left for Paris in early 2005 as close friends open to a romantic relationship, and when Bianca showed up for a short stay around Christmas that year, viewers learned that the two had become lovers. Bianca returned to the show in October 2006 for a six-month stint, during which time she and Maggie broke up, due to Maggie's (off-screen) infidelity, and Bianca became attracted to Zarf/Zoe (Jeffrey Carlson), an MTF (male-to-female) transgender character. Support for a Bianca/Maggie pairing preceded Lena's arrival,[5] and throughout the Bianca/Lena relationship, there were still fans in favor of Bianca getting together with Maggie. Still, many switched their allegiance to Lianca, and die-hard Lianca fans have remained active at online message boards, if with varying degrees of disillusionment, through Bianca's other onscreen romantic attachments.

At the outset of Bianca and Lena's relationship, viewer reaction among a wide cross-section of viewers was, on the whole, positive, according to Eden Riegel, Olga Sosnovska, and the *All My Children* producers (Warn, 2003b). Bianca's long period of celibacy had been a source of discontent to many fans; at the time of Lena's arrival on the show in December 2002, it had been over two years since Bianca had come out, and she had consistently fallen in love with women who did not return her feelings (Maggie being, at the time, only one of several). Before Bianca and Lena's first kiss, *All My Children* head writer, Agnes Nixon, and the head of ABC daytime programming, Brian Frons, had made supportive public statements about the upcoming romance, so fans seemed to have good reason to be hopeful, protests from conservative groups such as Concerned Women for America notwithstanding (Kleder, 2003).

However, it is not hard to see why the portrayal of the relationship was ultimately found wanting by many fans. One reason was that physical and sexual intimacy between Bianca and Lena was depicted much less explicitly than is commonly seen between soap opera couples, and this was particularly galling when compared to the portrayal of Bianca's rape, where Michael was shown holding Bianca very closely for some time as well as touching her bare skin. Furthermore, for the months following the rape, Bianca, along with her relationship with Lena, were effectively desexualized, with only some scenes of prolonged eye contact, hand-holding, and hugging between the two before they shared a brief New Year's Eve kiss. Perhaps as disturbing to many fans was the loss of even emotional connection between Bianca and Lena. As others have noted, rape happens all too often to women onscreen, especially in soap operas, and these storylines frequently draw on and reinscribe problematic gender discourses (see Dutta, 1999; Projansky, 2001). However, the partners of straight characters who are raped aren't generally shut out of their recovery the way that Lena was; Bianca was shown opening up to her friend Maggie and to her mother Erica about the rape, but not to Lena.

Furthermore, the general characteristics of soap operas often frustrate fans of a particular character or couple. U.S. daytime soaps are generally ensemble shows, so screen time must be shared with other characters and storylines. Also, although *All My Children* is aired for an hour five days a week, the narrative proceeds slowly in typical soap opera fashion. Thus, although Bianca was a main character, she might appear on only three or four episodes a week without being the focus of all of those episodes, and Lena had even less screen time than Bianca.[6] Of course, viewers are often unhappy with how television shows depict relationships in which the fans are invested. However, the Bianca/Lena relationship was at the time the first and only lesbian romance on U.S. daytime television, and indeed was one of the few ongoing lesbian relationships on U.S. television at all. In other words, for many fans, it was not simply a matter of tuning off *All My Children* and moving onto programs with better depictions of lesbian characters. Although some posters at message boards did vow in disgust that they would never again watch *All My Children* after Bianca's rape, others continued seeing how the story unfolded on the canonical show, even as they expressed their criticism. A number of viewers also turned to existing fan genres, including music videos, for more satisfying narratives.

The Lianca Music Videos

The Lianca fandom, like others devoted to a series couple, has been a passionate one, but it was always relatively small, making the creative output of Lianca fans more easily surveyed than those produced by the huge followings for other shows, such as *Buffy, The X-Files,* or the *Star Trek* series. Bianca/Lena music videos have usually been publicized at either or both of the message boards associated with the Riegel Rebels and the Sosnovska Symposium Web sites,

(named for the actors playing Bianca and Lena, respectively).

. . . . Based on my observations at Bianca/Lena Web sites and online interviews with three video makers,[7] they, like the majority of Lianca fans, are mostly lesbian women.[8] A few of the Bianca/Lena *vidders* (as they are sometimes known in fan cultures) were also fairly frequent posters in discussion threads at the message boards, but others were most visible through their video productions. Vidders may be somewhat more computer/tech-literate than many other fans; one Lianca video maker was a computing major who later became a software engineer, while another was familiar with video editing techniques from her work. While vidders occasionally chose a song based on the requests of other fans, they were more often inspired when a certain song struck them as particularly appropriate for Bianca and Lena's relationship.[9] Feedback from video viewers was usually expressed on message board threads after the video had been publicized and distributed, and was invariably positive (nor did any of the video makers I interviewed recall receiving any negative feedback privately). Thus, the Lianca vidders had a good sense of what other fans wanted, and skillfully put together scenes and music that would appeal to viewers looking for a text in which Bianca and Lena were the primary figures, with their love for each other apparent.

Jenkins (1992) noted that a fan music video was almost always set to a contemporary popular song, and this is true of the Lianca videos.[10] In most of them, the songs are about love relationships and/or their associated difficulties, often falling into the "ballad" genre; thus, both the lyrics and the melody tend to conform to cultural understandings of emotionality. Crucially, with their compression and focus, music videos facilitate a unique intensity of media engagement: viewing a three-five minute video, where all or nearly all the images feature the characters and relationships in which a viewer is invested, is an experience that cannot be derived from watching the show. Also, as digital files on personal computers, music videos can easily be replayed. Fans sometimes comment that their consumption of fan texts is so much more pleasurable that they have replaced their viewing of the show with reading fan fiction or watching fan videos.

Unlike, for example, the Kirk/Spock music videos discussed by Jenkins and others, Lianca videos do not re-contextualize images to suggest a romantic relationship. Rather, the techniques of non-canonical sequencing and association of clips with a fan-selected song constitute a refusal of the loss of significant communication between Bianca and Lena that plagued them for months on *All My Children* after Bianca's rape; even when a video shows the women upset or angry, they are generally still interacting, or at least in the same frame together. In terms of clip selection, it obviously isn't possible to detail all of them here, but the following summary of some commonly used scenes should suffice to give the flavor. First and foremost are three kisses between Bianca and Lena: their first kiss, which occurs at the airport as Lena seemed about to leave Pine Valley, their second as they end a slow dance at midnight on New Year's Eve, and their last one in Lena's final onscreen appearance. Also popular are excerpts from Bianca and Lena's first (and only onscreen) date in March 2003, which involves touching hands, significant eye contact, and a long hug; a scene from a July 2003 episode when Bianca and Lena sit closely on a bench in a moonlit park, talking and touching each other tenderly; and clips from a November 2003 episode when Bianca is visiting Lena in jail, during which the two hold hands through the bars and look at each other intensely. Also, in an August 2003 episode, with Bianca having inexplicably pushed her away (after the rape), Lena has a daydream in which the two are dressed in faintly bride-like garb, with close-ups of their clasped hands showing both wearing the commitment rings that Lena had offered to Bianca a couple of

weeks prior (and which in reality, Bianca had declined).

Extracts from one of these scenes conclude 20 of the 29 Lianca videos I have, and another four videos end with a clip that suggests that Bianca and Lena are or will be together. This is a key narrative characteristic that distinguishes the videos from the Bianca/Lena relationship as it was depicted on the canonical show for much of the time. An upbeat final clip is frequently used, even in videos in which much of the visual narrative and the song's lyrics suggest a less heartening outlook on love and relationships. For example, one video set to 3 Doors Down's *Here Without You* (2002) mostly features clips of Lena being sad after Bianca had spurned her, yet it ends with Bianca lying in Lena's lap (a clip from a March 2004 episode); similarly, the second half of a video that uses *Why They Call it Falling* (2002) matches the disillusionment with love that Lee Ann Womack sings about, except for Bianca and Lena's New Year's Eve kiss in its final moments, a contrast to the song's more bittersweet tenor. Thus, a Lianca video with a generally downbeat tone that nevertheless closes with a moment of connection between the two women is one way that fans could assert the possibility, as well as the desirability, of this couple ending up together, even in the face of pain and other relationship difficulties. . . .

In the context of fan videos more generally, to some extent Lianca videos are like those centered on other canonical, and hence usually heterosexual, television pairings: creative efforts that allow fans to fashion narratives about their preferred couples that provide additional and often more rewarding viewing experiences than watching the show. On the other hand, the Bianca/Lena romance is one of several same-sex relationships on U.S. television that has disappointed viewers, and in that light, the Lianca video oeuvre has continuity with slash from an earlier generation of fan culture, in constructing more satisfying stories about queer relationships than those told by heterocentric and heterosexist television shows.

Still, analyses of male/male slash, as motivated, in part, by a theoretically interesting and politically significant impulse to re-imagine gender, do not apply to the Lianca videos as a whole. On *All My Children*, Bianca and Lena may have been in a lesbian relationship, but except for each woman's choice of another woman as a romantic partner, neither character departed from fairly conventional gender roles for female characters—Bianca the loving daughter, sister, and then mother; Lena starting out as a femme fatale, and then becoming the loyal would-be lover who seemed to have little of importance to do outside of her relationship with Bianca. Nor were Bianca and Lena's intimate interactions significantly different from what we are accustomed to seeing between other women onscreen—talking, touching, and hugging, with only a few kisses in the whole year of their relationship. . . .

Alternative modes of sexual expression— couplings motivated by sexual pleasure or multi-partner encounters, for example— remain backgrounded in much of popular fandom, as is true in the dominant culture. While popular media representation is only one domain in which normativity is constructed and contested, it is a significant one. With the fight for same-sex marriage occupying center-stage in the American gay rights movement, at the expense of a broader reconsideration of social strictures on sexual and gender expression, the Lianca music videos are also texts that reproduce and reinforce the dominant liberal defense of same-sex relationships—that they are (and should be) about love and long-term commitment. In writing about the formation of the gay commercial market in the United States, Sender (2004) notes that it was "constituted in part through the political marginalization of GLBT people" (p. 240) who did not fit the mould of ideal gay consumers. A comparable phenomenon of marginalization exists in lesbian fan culture,

in which dominant norms often remain uninterrogated. . . .

Notes

1. Although scholars have applied the term "slash" to narratives about both male-male and female-female relationships, authors of lesbian fan fiction often do not use the term. In the *Xena* fandom, for example, the categories Gen(eral) and Alt(ernative) emerged, with the first indicating heterosexual relationship and the second, same sex-relationships. Some writers use the term "femslash," while other consider stories about canonical relationships to not be slash at all. For convenience, I use "slash" to refer to narratives about both canonical and non-canonical same-sex pairings.

2. Post-*Xena*, besides Bianca and Lena on *All My Children,* these have included Willow and Tara on *Buffy the Vampire Slayer* (WB, 1997–2001; UPN, 2001–2003), Kerry and Kim on *ER* (NBC, 1994–present), Spencer and Ashley on *South of Nowhere* (The N, 2005–present), Paige and Alex on *Degrassi: The Next Generation* (CTV, 2001–present and The N, 2002–present), as well as couples on *Bad Girls* (first on Britain's ITV, 1999–2006; currently in North America on Logo, 2006–present), *The L Word* (Showtime, 2003–present), and other premium cable shows such as *Queer as Folk* (Showtime, 2000–2005) and *The Wire* (HBO, 2002–present).

3. "Mashup" also refers to audio products from musical blending, usually involving coupling the vocals from one song with the instruments from another (Cruger, 2003; Frere-Jones, 2005).

4. Hurt-comfort is a genre of fan fiction, although the basic elements are also often present in the narratives of source texts, particularly action-adventure shows. Generally, one character is physically and/or psychically injured, and another character cares for them, creating a context of greater intimacy and intensity of relating than usual.

5. Self-designated "BAMmers/bammers" (i.e., people in support of a Bianca und Maggie romantic relationship), these fans undertook a

campaign aimed at the *All My Children* writers and ABC daytime drama executives that, although not at the time successful in terms of having Bianca and Maggie get together, did alert ABC and *AMC* that there was interest in having Bianca depicted in a relationship with another woman, and helped pave the way for the introduction of Lena as Bianca's love interest (see Warn, 2003a).

6. Olga Sosnovska did not sign a contract as a regular with *All My Children* until May 2003; before that she had been a guest star.

7. This message board used to be officially associated with Olga Sosnovska, but at her request, this relationship was cordially terminated, and after some debate, the board moderators re-named it "The Symposium" in early 2006. Technical issues in 2007 resulted in the loss of many threads, including those which had publicized fan videos.

8. I recall a few posters at the message boards identifying themselves as male and/or straight in the context of pertinent discussions (e.g., threads about how broadly Lianca appealed to the *All My Children* audience), but most spoke of themselves as lesbians for whom much of the appeal of the Bianca/Lianca relationship was that it was a romance between two women.

9. For example, one Lianca vidder recalled that, for the sole Lianca music video she made, "I heard the Lianca story, from Lena's point of view, in Jonathan Brooke's song. It struck me that many of the lyrics could describe scenes shared by Lena and Bianca. It was just something that I saw in my head every time I heard the song, so I decided to create it for others to see." In a similar vein, another vidder, who made several Lianca videos, wrote that "I would just hear a song and start seeing clips. I would be driving down the road and it would just hit."

10. Twenty-six of the videos used a popular song released 1998 or later (i.e., within about five years of the time that most videos were made); eight used a song released 1990–1997 and one a song released in 1989; the other two were set to instrumental pieces. The songs included *Because I Told You So* (1997), sung by Jonathan Brooke; *Have You Ever Been in Love* (2002), sung by Celine Dion; *Mime* (1990), sung by Heart; *The Reason* (2003), sung by Hoobastank; *Loneliness* (2001),

sung by Annie Lennox; *When I Found You* (2001), sung by Britney Spears; and *Just Another* (2001), sung by Pete Yorn.

References

Bacon-Smith, C. (1992). *Enterprising women: Television fandom and the creation of popular myth*. Philadelphia: University of Pennsylvania Press.

Boyd, K. S. (2001). "One index finger on the mouse scroll bar and the other on my clit": Slash writers' views on pornography, censorship, feminism and risk. PhD dissertation, Simon Fraser University. Retrieved June 15, 2007, from http:www.collectionscanda.ca/obj/s4/f2/dsk3/ftp04/mQ61537.pdf

Cicione, M. (1998). Male pair-bonds and female desire in fan slash writing. In C. Harris & A. Alexander (Eds.), *Theorizing fandom; Fans, subculture and identity* (pp. 153–177). Cresskill, NJ: Hampton Press.

Cruger, R. (2003, August 9). The mash-up revolution. *Salon.com*. Retrieved June 15, 2007, from http://dir.salon.com/story/ent/music/feature/2003/08/09/mashups_cruger/index_np.html?pn=1

Doty, A. (1993). *Making things perfectly queer: Interpreting mass culture*. Minneapolis; University of Minnesota Press.

Dutta, M. B. (1999). Taming the victim: Rape in soap opera. *Journal of Popular Film and Television, 27*(1), 33–39.

Frere-Jones, S. (2005, January 10). 1 + I + 1 = 1: The new math of mashups. *New Yorker*. Retrieved June 15, 2007, from http.//www.newyorker.com/archive/2005/01/10/050110crmu_music

Gibson, R. (2006). From zero to 24-7: Images of sexual minorities on television. In L. Castaneda & S. Campbell (Eds.), *News and sexuality: Media portraits of diversity* (pp. 256–277). Thousand Oaks, CA: Sage.

Green, S., Jenkins, C., & Jenkins, H. (1998). "The normal female interest in men bonking": Selections from *The Terra Nostra Underground* and *Strange Bedfellows*. In C. Harris & A. Alexander (Eds.), *Theorizing fandom: Fans, subculture, and identity* (pp. 9–38). Cresskill, NY: Hampton Press.

Gross, L. (2002). *Up from invisibility: Lesbians, gay men, and the media in America.* New York: Columbia University Press.

Harrington, C. L. (2003a). Lesbian(s) on daytime television: The Bianca narrative on *All My Children. Feminist Media Studies, 3*(2), 211–232.

Harrington, C. L. (2003b). Homosexuality on *All My Children:* Transforming the daytime landscape. *Journal of Broadcasting & Electronic Media, 47,* 216–235.

Herman, A., Coombe, R., & Kaye, L. (2006). Your second life? Goodwill and the performativity of intellectual property in online digital gaming. *Cultural Studies, 20*(2–3), 184–210.

Jenkins, H. (1992). *Textual poachers: Television fans and participatory culture.* London: Routledge.

Jones, R. (2006). From shooting monsters to shooting movies: Machinima and the transformative play of video game fan culture. In K. Hellekson & K. Busse (Eds.), *Fan fiction and fan communities in the age of the Internet* (pp. 261–280). Jefferson, NC: McFarland & Company.

Jung, S. (2004). Queering popular culture: Female spectators and the appeal of writing slash fan fiction. *Gender Forum Gender Queeries, 8,* Retrieved June 15, 2007, from http://www.genderforum.uni-koeln.de/queer/jung.html

Kleder, M. (2003). Daytime goes pay time: *All My Children* features lesbian affair. Retrieved June 15, 2007, from http://www.cwa.org/articles/3814/CFI/cfreport/index.htm

Merrill, D. (2006, October 16). Mashups: The new breed of Web app. Retrieved June 15, 2007, from http://www.ibm.com/developerworks/xml/library/x-mashups.html

Penley, C. (1991). Brownian motion: Women, ladies, and technology. In C. Penley & A. Ross (Eds.), *Technoculture* (pp. 35–161). Minneapolis: University of Minnesota Press.

Projansky, S. (2001). *Watching rape: Film and television in postfeminist culture.* New York: New York University Press.

Radway, J. (1984). *Reading the romance: Women, patriarchy, and popular literature.* Chapel Hill, NC: University of North Carolina Press.

Russ, J. (1985). Pornography by women for women, with love. In J. Russ (Au.), *Magic mommas, trembling sisters, puritans & perverts: Feminist essays* (pp. 79–99). Trumansburg, NY: Crossing Press.

Russo, J. L. (2002). NEW VOY "cyborg sex" J/7 [NC-I7J 1/1: New methodologies, new fantasies]. Retrieved June 15, 2007, from http://j-1-r.org/asmic/fanfic/print/jlr-cyborgsex.pdf

Russo, V. (1987). *The celluloid closet: Homosexuality in the movies.* New York: Harper.

Scodari, C. (2003). Resistance reexamined: Gender, fan practices, and science fiction television. *Popular Communication, 1*(2), 111–130.

Sender, K. (2004). *Business, not politics: The making of the gay market.* New York: Columbia University Press.

Stein. L. (2006). "This dratted thing": Fannish storytelling through new media. In K. Hellekson & K. Busse (Eds.), *Fan fiction and fan communities in the age of the Internet* (pp. 245–260). Jefferson, NC: McFarland & Company.

Tropiano, S. (2002). *The prime tune closet: A history of guys and lesbians on TV.* New York: Applause Books.

Warn, S. (2003a). The battle for Bianca and Maggie on *All My Children.* Retrieved June 15, 2007, from http://www.afterellen.com/archive/TV/ame-bam.html

Warn, S. (2003b). *All My Children:* A lesbian kiss to build a dream on? Retrieved June 15, 2007, from http://www.afterellen.com/archive/ellenTv/amc-kiss.html

Warner, M. (1999). *The trouble with normal: Sex, politics, and the ethics of queer life.* Cambridge, MA: Harvard University Press.

Wilder, J. C. (1998, October) Romancing the fan: Romance and Xena fan fiction. *Whoosh, 25.* Retrieved June 15, 2007, from http://whoosh.org/issue25/wilder.html

Woledge, E. (2005). From slash to the mainstream: Female writers and gender blending men. *Extrapolation, 46*(1), 50–65.

"Don't Hate the Player, Hate the Game"

The Racialization of Labor in *World of Warcraft*

Lisa Nakamura

. . . Massively Multiplayer Online Role Playing Games (MMOs) such as *World of Warcraft* (*WoW*), *Lineage II,* and *Everquest* are immensely profitable, skillfully designed, immersive and beautifully detailed virtual worlds that enable both exciting gameplay and the creation of real time digitally embodied communities. This year, *World of Warcraft* surpassed 10 million users, confirming games economist Edward Castronova's (2005) predictions for exponential growth, and these players are intensely interested in and protective of their investments in the virtual world of Azeroth. This stands to reason: as Alexander Galloway (2006) writes, "virtual worlds are always in some basic way the expression of Utopian desire." One of their primary rallying points as a group has been to advocate strongly that Blizzard regulate cheating within the game more stringently; however, the definition of cheating is unclear, despite the game's End User License Agreement (EULA), since many players break these rules with impunity, a state of affairs which is actually the norm in MMO's.[1] As Mia Consalvo (2007) argues, it makes much less sense to see cheating within games as a weakness of game design or a problem with player behavior than to see it as an integral part of game culture, a feature that keeps players from getting "stuck" and quitting. "Cheating" thus benefits players and the game industry alike. However, cheating is as varied in its forms as is gameplay itself, and some varieties are viewed by players as socially undesirable, while others are not.

Though Consalvo (2007) stresses the extremely subjective ways that MMO players define cheating, asserting that "a debate exists around the definition of cheating and

From Nakamura, L. (2009). "Don't hate the player, hate the game": The racialization of labor in *World of Warcraft*. *Critical Studies in Media Communication, 26*(2), 128–144. Copyright © National Communication Association, reprinted by permission of Taylor & Francis Ltd. (http://www.tandf.co.uk/journals) on behalf of the National Communication Association.

whether it actually hurts other players [and] players themselves see little common ground in what constitutes cheating" (p. 150), real-money trading (RMT), or buying and selling in-game property for real money, is widely considered the worst, more morally reprehensible form of cheating. In particular, the practice of gold farming, or selling in-game currency to players for real money, usually through resellers such as IGE or EBay, is especially disliked. Leisure players have been joined by worker players from poorer nations such as China and Korea who are often subject to oppression as both a racio-linguistic minority, and as undesirable underclassed social bodies in the context of game play and game culture.[2] These "farmers," as other players dismissively dub them, produce and sell virtual goods such as weapons, garments, animals, and even their own leveled-up avatars or "virtual bodies" to other players for "real world" money. As Consalvo (2007) writes, the "gill-buying practice is viscerally despised by some players" (p. 164). . . .

Though as T. L. Taylor (2006) notes, MMOs are distinguished by their "enormous potential in a fairly divisive world," the "fact that people play with each other across regions and often countries" as often as not results in ethnic and racial chauvinism: "as a tag the conflation of Chinese with gold farmer has seemed to come all too easy and now transcends any particular game" (p. 321). Robert Brookey (2007) expands upon this claim; in his analysis of gaming blogs, he discovered "overt racist attitudes" towards Chinese farmers; most importantly, that "some players, who harbor negative feelings toward Chinese farmers, do not believe that these feelings denote racial discrimination." Thus, though it is the case that players cannot see each others' bodies while playing, specific forms of gamic labor, such as gold farming and selling, as well as specific styles of play have become racialized as Chinese, producing new forms of networked racism that are particularly easy for players to disavow.

Unlike the Internet itself, MMOs have *always* been a global medium, with many games originating in Asia.[3] Korea has been a major player in the industry from its beginning, but Asian players are numerous even in American-run MMOs such as Blizzard's *WoW;* in 2008, the number of simultaneous players on Chinese *WoW* servers exceeded 1 million, the most that have ever been recorded in Europe or the U.S. ("Blizzard," 2008). Thus, though gold farmers are typecast as Chinese, most Asian players are "leisure players," not player workers. . . .

Perhaps because most digital game scholars are players themselves, the economics of gold farming are usually discussed in the scholarly literature in terms of their negative impact upon the "world" of leisure players, who buy gold because they lack the time to earn virtual capital through "grinding" or performing the repetitive and tedious tasks that are the basis of most MMOs. However, as Toby Miller (2006) has advocated, digital games scholars need to attend to its medium's political economy, and to "follow the money" to its less glamorous, less "virtual" places, like games console and PC manufacturing plants, gold farmer sweatshops, and precious metals reclamation sites—in short, to China. Yet while many players are fairly unaware that their computer hardware is born and dies, or is *recycled,* in China, they are *exceptionally* aware of the national, racial, and linguistic identity of gold farmers. Gold farmers are reviled player-workers whose position in the gamic economy resembles that of other immigrant groups who cross national borders in order to work, but unlike other types of "migrant" workers, their labors are offshore, and thus invisible— they are "virtual migrants."[4] However, user generated content in and around MMOs actively visualizes this process. Machinima fan-produced video production racializes this reviled form of gameplay as "Oriental" in ways that hail earlier visual media such as music videos and minstrel shows. Gold farming, a burgeoning "grey market" labor practice in a disliked and semi-illegal industry that as Consalvo (2007) notes, may soon outstrip the primary games market as a source of revenue, has become racialized as Asian, specifically as Chinese. . . .

WoW and other virtual worlds have been touted for their democratic potential—as Castronova (2005) puts it:

> People entering a synthetic world can have, in principle, any body they desire. At a stroke, this feature of synthetic worlds removes from the social calculus all the unfortunate effects that derive from the body . . . all without bearing some of the burdens that adhere to the Earth bodies we were born with. (pp. 25–26)

The social calculus of race, nation, and class are burdens borne by Chinese gold farmers, Chinese leisure players, and ultimately, the gaming community as a whole. Hatred of Chinese gold farmers drives *WoW* users to produce visual and textual media that hews closely to earlier anti-Asian discourses, media that they broadcast to other users through forums, general chat in-game, and "homemade" videos.

World of Warcraft is a virtual world where significant numbers of people are conducting their psychic, financial, and social lives. This massively multiplayer online game continues to roll out content for its users in the form of expansion packs, frequent software updates, action figures and a feature film in development, and an extensive content-rich and frequently updated website for its community of users. Users are invited by Blizzard to get involved in some aspects of this world's production by contributing interesting screenshots, machinima, personal narratives, and advice on gameplay to their site, and even in cases when they are not, players actively produce in defiance of its wishes. Topics that the game industry may wish to avoid because they may seem divisive, or may reflect badly on the virtual

world, are confronted frequently in participatory media created by its users.

Machinima as User-Generated Racial Narrative: The Media Campaign Against Chinese Player-Workers in *WoW*

Machinima is a crucial site of struggle over the meaning of race in shared digital space, and it is a central part of the culture of MMOs such as *World of Warcraft*. Machinima has recently become the object of much academic interest because it exemplifies the notion of participatory media, an influential and useful formulation that is the basis for Jenkins' (2006) book *Convergence Culture*. In it, Jenkins describes how machinima are prime examples of users' seizing the right to contribute to media universes in defiance of industry wishes, standards, and control; their value lies in the ability to produce counternarratives whose impact lies in their active subversion of the narrow messages available in many dominant media texts. Machinima literally extend the storyspace of the games upon which they are based, and the most interesting of these actively work to reconfigure their original meanings in progressive, socially productive ways. Jenkins explains that transmediated storyspaces which exist across media platforms permit increased opportunities for engaged users like fans to insert their own content into these "synthetic worlds," to use Castronova's (2005) phrase—while game developers like Blizzard provide limited, licensed, and fairly tightly controlled virtual space for players to navigate, users extend this space by writing fan fiction, creating original artwork, and making their own movies or machinima using images, narratives, and tropes from the game.

While part of the pleasure of *World of Warcraft* consists in navigating its richly imaged, beautifully rendered spaces, users must rely upon the company to provide more of this valuable commodity in the form of expansion packs such as "The Burning Crusade" and "The Wrath of the Lich King," eagerly anticipated and extremely profitable products for which users are willing to stand in line for days at a time. Machinima permits users to expand this space for free; while navigable space is still tightly controlled by the company—unlike in *Second Life,* users are unable to build their own structures or objects to insert in the world—machinima allows users to extend its representational or narrative space, creating scenarios that are genuinely new because they depict activities or behaviors impossible in the space of the game. This is a fascinating area of study, and one that is a thriving and integral part of *WoW* in particular. The struggle for resources integral to the structure of MMOs can also be re-envisioned as the struggle to own or claim virtual space and to police national boundaries as well.[5] Player-produced machinima accessed from Warcraftmovies.com make arguments about race, labor, and the racialization of space in *World of Warcraft.*[6] These highly polemical texts employ the visual language of the game, one of the most recognizable and distinctive ever created for shared virtual play, to bring into sharp relief the contrast between the privileges of media production available to empowered players with the time and inclination to create machinima, and those who are shut out of this aspect of *WoW* by their status as worker players. Participatory media is a privilege of the leisure class; active fandom is too expensive a proposition for many digital workers, who as Dibbell explains poignantly, can't afford to *enjoy* the game that they have mastered, much less produce media to add to it.[7]

Unsurprisingly, there are two tiers of this type of user production—Blizzard frequently solicits screenshots, holds art contests, and showcases user-produced machinima that become part of the "official" canon of the game. However, there is extensive traffic in content that is not endorsed by the developer, but which is nonetheless part of the continuing rollout of the world. Racial discourse is a key part of this rollout. If the official *World of Warcraft* game is a gated community, one that users pay to enter, its covenants consist in its EULA [End-User License Agreement]. However, part of Jenkins' (2006) argument is that media technologies such as the Internet have made it impossible to "gate" media in the same way. The "underground" machinima I will discuss in this chapter build and expand the world of *WoW* in regards to representations of race in just as constitutive a way as its official content. As Lowood (2006) notes, *WoW* players have been creating visual moving image records as long as, or perhaps even longer than, they have been playing the game. Thus, machinima is anything but a derivative or ancillary form in relation to *WoW,* for its history runs exactly parallel, and in some sense, slightly in advance of the game itself—as Lowood notes, users were employing the beta version of *WoW* to make machinima before the game was available to the public. Lowood claims, "*WoW movies,* from game film to dance videos, have become an integral part of the culture shared by a player community" (p. 374).

If indeed machinima extend the world of gameplay, how are players co-creating this world? Anti-farmer machinima produces overtly racist narrative space to attach to a narrative that, while carefully avoiding overt references to racism or racial conflict in our world, is premised upon a racial war in an imaginary world—the World of Azeroth. While Jenkins (2006) celebrates the way that fans, particularly female fans, have extended the worlds of *Star Trek* in truly liberatory ways, inserting homosexual narratives between Captain Kirk and Spock that the franchise would never permit or endorse, a closer look at user produced content from Warcraftmovies.com reveals a contraction and retrenchment of concepts of gender, race, and nation rather than their enlargement.

Warcraftmovies.com, the most popular *World of Warcraft* machinima website, organizes its user generated content under several different categories. "Underground" machinima deals with topics such as "bug/exploit," "exploration," and "gold farming." "Ni Hao (A Gold Farmer's Story)" by "Nyhm" of "Madcow Studios" has earned a "4 x Platinum" rating, the highest available, from Warcraftmovies .com, and it is also available on YouTube, where it has been viewed 533,567 times, has been favorited 1,998 times, and has produced 981 comments from users ("Ni Hao"). This extremely popular, visually sophisticated machinima music video features new lyrics sung over the instrumental track of Akon's hit hip hop song "Smack That." This polemical anti-Asian machinima's chorus is:

> I see you farmin' primals in Shadow moon Valley, 10 cents an hour's good money when you are Chinese, I buy your auctions you sell my gold right back to me, feels like you're bendin' me over, you smile and say "ni hao" and farm some gold, "ni hao" it's getting old, ni hao, oh.

The claim that "10 cents an hour's good money when you are Chinese" displays awareness that the farmers' incentive for exploiting or "bending over" better-resourced players comes from economic need. Another part of the video shows a "farmer" shoveling gold into a vault, with the subtitled lyric "IGE's making bank now." The International Gaming Exchange is one of the largest re-sellers of gold, avatar level-ups, and other virtual property, and it is an American business, not an Asian one. Nonetheless, this commentary on the gold farming economic system resorts to the full gamut of racial stereotypes, including a Chinese flag as the background for a video scene of a sexy singing female Troll in a scanty outfit flanked by the human "farmers" wielding pickaxes and shovels.

Later in the video, a Chinese gold farmer is killed by another player, who comments as he kneels next to the corpse that "this China-man gets fired, that's one farmer they'll have to replace, not supposed to be here in the first place." . . . Clearly, Asian players, specifically those suspected of being "farmers" but as this image [suggests], all "China-men" have a diminished status on *WoW*: many American players fail to see them as "people." . . . The video depicts them as all owning exactly the same avatar, a male human wearing a red and gold outfit and wielding a pickaxe. This dehumanization of the Asian player—they "all look the same" because they all *are* the same—is evocative of earlier conceptions of Asian laborers as interchangeable and replaceable. . . .

Conclusion

The anti-Asian racial discourse in "Ni Hao," as well as that noted in Brookey's (2007), Steinkuehler's (2006), and Taylor's (2006) research are not necessarily representative of the *WoW* population as a whole (though it must be said that while YouTube and Warcraftmovies are full of machinima or trophy videos of farmer-killing replete with racist imagery, there are no pro-farmer user-produced machinima to be seen).[8] Machinima is a breakthrough medium because it differs from previous mass forms of media or performance; it is the product of individual users. However, like the minstrel shows that preceded it, it shapes the culture by disseminating arguments about the nature of race, labor, and assimilation. . . .

Similarly, it is certainly not the case that games must be entirely free of racist discourse in order to be culturally important or socially productive, in short, to be "good." No multiplayer social game could meet that criterion at all times. On the other hand, if we are to take games seriously as "synthetic worlds," we must be willing to take their racial discourses, media texts, and interpersonal conflicts seriously as well. As Dibbell (2006) claims, it is constraint and scarcity—the challenge of capital accumulation—that makes MMOs pleasurable, even addictive. Game economies based on cultures of scarcity engender Real Money Transfer, and as long as this form of player-work is socially debased and racialized, it will result in radically unequal social relations, labor types, and forms of representation along the axes of nation, language, and identity. Asian worker players are economically unable to accumulate avatarial capital and thus become "persons"; they are the dispossessed subjects of synthetic worlds. As long as Asian "farmers" are figured as unwanted guest workers within the culture of MMOs, user-produced extensions of MMO-space like machinima will most likely continue to depict Asian culture as threatening to the beauty and desirability of shared virtual space in the *World of Warcraft*.

Notes

1. Players of *WoW* regularly use an arsenal of "mods" and "add-ons" that are circulated on player boards online; though these are technically in violation of the End User License Agreement (EULA), many players consider the game unplayable without them, especially at the terminal or "end game" levels. Blizzard turns a blind eye to this, and in fact tacitly condones it by posting technical updates referring to the impact of add-ons on game performance.

2. See T. L. Taylor (2006), on in-game language chauvinism and the informal enforcement of "English only" chat in *WoW* even by players of non-Anglophone nationalities.

3. See Chan (2006), as well as the January 2008 special issue of *Games and Culture* on Asia, volume 3, number 1, in particular Hjorth's (2008) introductory essay "Games@Neo-Regionalism: Locating Gaming in the Asia-Pacific."

4. See (Aneesh, 2006).

5. As Brookey (2007) argues, national boundaries have been reproduced in cyberspace, and the location of the servers that generate these virtual environments are used to demarcate the borders. These respondents claim that if Chinese players experience discrimination on U.S. servers, it is because they have crossed the border into territory where they do not belong and are not welcome.

6. The phrase "player-produced machinima" is in some sense a redundant one, since machinima is from its inception an amateur form; however it is becoming an increasingly necessary distinction as professional media producers appropriate it. *South Park*'s "Make Love Not Warfare" was co-produced with Blizzard Entertainment, and Toyota has aired a 2007 commercial made in the same way. See http://www.machinima.com/film/view&id= 23588. In an example of media synergy, *South Park* capitalized on the success and popularity of the episode by bundling a *World of Warcraft* trial game card along with the DVD box set of its most recent season.

7. See Dibbell (2007) for an eloquent account of "Min," a highly skilled worker player who took great pride in being his raiding party's "tank," a "heavily armed warrior character who . . . is the linchpin of any raid" (p. 41). His raiding team would take "any customer" into a dangerous dungeon where a lower level player could never survive alone and let them pick up the valuable items dropped there, thus acting like virtual African shikaris or Nepalese porters. Min greatly enjoyed these raids but was eventually forced to quit them and take up farming again when they proved insufficiently profitable.

8. UC San Diego doctoral candidate Ge Jin's distributive filmmaking project on the lives of Chinese worker players in MMOs can be viewed at http://www.chinesegoldfarmers.com. His films, which can also be viewed on YouTube, contain documentary footage of Chinese worker players laboring in "gaming workshops" in Shanghai. His interviews with them make it clear that these worker players are well aware of how despised they are by American and

European players, and that they feel a sense of "inferiority" that is articulated to their racial and ethnic identity.

References

Aneesh, A. (2006). *Virtual migration: The programming of globalization.* Durham, NC: Duke University Press.

Blizzard Entertainment's World of Warcraft: The Burning Crusade surpasses one million peak concurrent player milestone in mainland China. (2008). *PR Newswire: United Business Media.* Retrieved May 28, 2008, from http://ww.pmewswiie.com/news/index mail.shtml?ACCT=104&STORY=/www/st ory/04–11–2008/000479086&EDATE=

Brookey, R. A. (2007, November). *Racism and nationalism in cyberspace: Comments on farming in MMORPGS.* Paper presented at the National Communication Association Annual Convention, Chicago.

Castronova, E. (2005). *Synthetic worlds: The business and culture of online games.* Chicago: University of Chicago Press.

Chan, D. (2006). Negotiating Intra-Asian games networks: On cultural proximity, East Asian games design, and Chinese farmers. *Fibreculture, 8.* Retrieved May 28, 2008, from http://journalfibreculture.org/issue8/issue8_chan.html

Consalvo, M. (2007). *Cheating: Gaining advantage in videogames.* Cambridge, MA: The MIT Press.

Dibbell, J. (2006). *Play Money.* New York: Basic Books.

Dibbell, J. (2007, June 17). The life of the Chinese gold farmer. *The New York Times Magazine,* 36–41.

Galloway, A. (2006). Warcraft and Utopia. *1000 days of theory.* Retrieved April 11, 2008, from ctheory.net/printer.aspx?id=507

Hjorth, L (2008). Games@Neo-regionalism: Locating gaming in the Asia-Pacific. *Games and Culture, 3*(1), 3–12.

Jenkins, H. (2006). *Convergence culture: Where old and new media collide.* New York: New York University Press.

Lowood, H. (2006). Storyline, dance/music, or PvP? Game movies and community players in *World of Warcraft. Games and Culture, 1*(4), 362–382.

Miller, T. (2006). Gaming for beginners. *Games and Culture, 1*(1), 5–12.

Ni Hao: A Gold Farmer's Story. Retrieved November 7, 2007, from http://youtube .com/watch? V=odllf5NEI00

Steinkuehler, C. (2006). The mangle of play. *Games and Culture, 1*(3), 199–213.

Taylor, T. L (2006). Does WoW change everything? How a PvP server, multinational player base, and surveillance mod scene cause me pause. *Games and Culture, 1*(4), 318–337.

Sex Lives in *Second Life*

Robert Alan Brookey and Kristopher L. Cannon

Second Life (SL) is a little hard to classify. It could be classified with other massive multiplayer online role-playing games (MMORPGs), because it shares several characteristics with these games. Multiple users from all over the world log onto SL and interact in a virtual environment. Users in SL also construct avatars, characters that function as in-game proxies, as do players in other MMORPGs. And like other MMORPGs, SL has an in-game economy that allows users to buy and sell various items and goods (Castronova, 2006). But when it comes to the actual "game" the comparison breaks down. First, there are no clearly defined role-play objectives in SL: no required missions, quests, or monsters to slay. Second, while the producers of many online commercial games discourage players from changing the elements of the game, users in SL are encouraged to manipulate the environment (Bartle, 2006). Although Linden Lab, the creative force behind SL, has established some rules and guidelines, users are able to build their own buildings, create their own clothing and accessories, and are usually at liberty to shape this virtual world in any way they see fit.

Consequently, SL has been used in a variety of ways, including educational and commercial applications, and as a means to interact with other people. Given the liberty available in SL, users have the opportunity to create new relationships, and create those relationships in new and different ways. Some SL users are taking advantage of this liberty to refigure gender and sexuality; when one of us first entered SL, we came upon a very large statue with prominent breasts and an erect penis; it was a shrine to "shemales," one that celebrated the sexual viability of transsexuals. Other SL users, however, reproduce traditional gender roles and sexual norms, and sometimes do so in disturbing ways.

We see SL as a valuable space in which to study gender and sexuality in cyberspace, because unlike traditional forms of print, film, or television media (hereafter, traditional media), SL users are primarily responsible for the content.[1] In other words, users have the agency to create the gender roles and the sexual experiences that they want. In many of the

From Brookey, R. A., & Cannon, K. L. (2009). Sex Lives in *Second Life*. *Critical Studies in Media Communication*, 26(2), 145–164. Copyright © National Communication Association, reprinted by permission of Taylor & Francis Ltd. (http://www.tandf.co.uk/journals) on behalf of the National Communication Association.

existing studies of gender and sexuality in cyberspace, this agency is theorized from a liberatory perspective that sees cyberspace as a unique social arena in which traditional gender roles and sexual norms are challenged and transgressed. Unfortunately, this theoretical perspective does not account for those who use their agency to reproduce the traditional roles and norms found in real life (RL).[2] . . .

Liberatory Perspective

The idea that cyberspace is a liberatory environment is certainly not new, and other scholars have challenged this idea (Gunkel, 2001). For our purposes, we are using the phrase "liberatory perspective" to refer to a critique of cyberspace that imagines it to be an arena in which subjects have greater agency to explore and refigure gender norms and sexual roles. When scholars first began studying relationships in cyberspace, there was a great deal of optimism about the potential for virtual environments to offer users opportunities to explore multiple identities. For example, Sherry Turkle (1995) looked at how users switched genders in online social environments, and how this gender switching allowed these users to assert new identities, and develop more empathy for the opposite gender. Allcurque're Rosanne Stone (1995) argued that online environments allowed for the exploration of fragmented identities, because subjects were able to operate independently of their bodies on which gender and sexual discipline has been exercised. She claims that successful gender switching online reveals both the instability of identity, and how new *media* "presaged radical changes in social conventions" (p. 81).[3]

. . . This liberatory perspective, however, teeters on the brink of technological determinism, and unfortunately cyberspace docs not always provide an escape. Lynne Roberts and Malcolm Parks (2001) have conducted one of the few social science studies about gender switching in cyberspace, and they found that the majority of people do not switch genders online. In addition, they found that some women switched genders in order to escape sexual harassment online. In these cases, gender switching may allow these women to escape, but this escape is merely a reaction to the reproduction of problematic RL sexual relations in cyberspace. This is not to suggest that cyberspace has not facilitated the potential for liberatory use. Indeed, scholars who have analyzed interactive online media contend that cyberspace has opened up opportunities for political resistance and community building, particularly for individuals with queer identities (Alexander, 2002; Bryson, 2004). . . .

In contrast to this liberatory perspective, queer scholars of traditional media have approached the representation of gender and sexuality with a healthy skepticism. For almost two decades, queer media scholars have examined how gender and sexual norms are reproduced, and how representation can function to exclude or contain sexual minorities (Battles & Hilton-Murrow, 2002; Brookey & Westerfelhaus, 2001; Dow, 2001; Shugart, 2003; Sloop, 2004). These studies focused on traditional forms of media, in which the agency of representation is in the hands of media producers. New media scholars, however, are often quick to point out that users have the agency of production where interactive media is concerned, and they maintain that this shift in agency is a significant difference.

Interactivity and the Docile Body

In the studies of interactive media generally, a great deal has been written about the agency of the user. Some have associated this agency with ideological resistance, suggesting that interactivity allows users to escape and challenge the influences associated with traditional media industries (Bryce & Rutter, 2002; Frasca, 2003). Other scholars question this agency (Brookey & Booth, 2006; Marshall, 2002), but where gender and sexuality are concerned, there are other influences that need to be considered. It is often the implicit assumption of queer scholars that traditional forms of media will cater to established norms in order to attract the broadest audience. Yet, these scholars acknowledge that these norms operate in larger social, cultural and political contexts, what Judith Butler (1990) would describe as a "heterosexual matrix," a grid of gender rules and sexual laws that favor and enforce procreative heterosexuality. While interactivity might create different relationships between users and media producers, interactivity does not categorically remove users from the influence of this social matrix. For example, users in SL create their own characters (avatars), give them primary and secondary sex characteristics, dress them and determine their sexual practices. Indeed, when it comes to the construction of gender and sexuality in SL, the users exercise a great deal of control. These users, however, represent subjects whose identities have been formed by the way gender and sexuality are "disciplined" in society.

In *The History of Sexuality*, Vol. 1, Michel Foucault (1978) outlines a program of discipline that explains how sexuality became a part of identity. He argues that with the rise of bourgeois society [historically, in the 19th century], there was thought to be a move to repress and censor the discussion of sex and sexuality ("the repressive hypothesis"), when in actuality a great deal of discourse emerged at this time articulating sexual norms, and delineating sexual perversity. In this discourse, sexual practice became an indicator of the psychological health of the individual, because sexuality was thought to reside in the psyche of the individual. Consequently, the individual was invested with the responsibility of maintaining proper sexual practices, and

seeking out help for perverse sexual behavior. In this way, the supposed social repression of sexuality resulted in a repression of sexuality within the psyche of the individual. Once sexuality was invested in the person, individuals aligned their sexual practices with established norms, and actively assumed the responsibility for their own sexual health. In other words, the sexual subject became a "docile body."

Foucault (1975) argues that the docile body is not passive, but rather the active embodiment of disciplinary practices, becoming a self-disciplined body. The concept of docility also informs Judith Butler's (1990) theory of gender performativity. She argues that individuals must constantly "perform" established gender norms, in order to escape the social discipline that is exercised against queer sexuality. In the repetition of the performance, the performativity of gender is forgotten, and the embodiment of gender norms is thought to be an expression of internal identity; in this way the gendered subject becomes a docile body.

Theorizing from Foucault and Butler, a fundamental problem with the liberatory perspective emerges. Although the disciplining of gender and sexuality may be exercised on the body, this discipline produces a sexual subject who imagines itself independent of the body. Liberating this subject from the body via cyberspace does not necessarily mean that this subject escapes the influential disciplinary practices that produced its identity. For example, Miroslaw Filiciak (2003, p. 100) posits that the creation of identities in cyberspace is not so much an escape from the "self" as it is "a longed-for chance of expressing ourselves beyond physical limitations." We would add, however, that these expressions might not move beyond the gender roles and sexual norms that created the "self."

Because docility is the underlying concept of performativity, we have chosen to use it in our analysis. Docility helps explain why individuals empowered with the agency to produce their own sexual world might choose to perpetuate the established norms of gender and sexuality. We have chosen SL as an environment in which to apply this critical concept, because SL is an interactive virtual world in which users are primarily responsible for creating the sexual content. Our purpose is specific: to offer an alternative to the liberatory perspective on gender and sexuality in cyberspace. Therefore our claims will also be specific; we do not offer our observations in order to generalize about the SL environment. In fact, a general analysis of SL would be beyond the scope of this chapter, because the environment is too large, and the content created by its users is too diverse. Instead, we focus on two types of sexual content created by SL users.

First, we analyze how certain users render women as sexual objects, designed to be sexually attractive, sexually available and sexually subordinate to men. Second, we show how gay, lesbian, transgender and "Furry"[4] users are marginalized in SL content, and in some instances participate in their own marginalization. To do so, we critically analyze advertisements and spaces in SL that we have found through our own exploration of SL.[5] We also analyze *The Second Life Herald,* a blog founded by University of Toronto philosophy professor Peter Ludlow, which publishes articles written by SL users and allows other SL users to comment on the articles published. We include *The Second Life Herald* in our analysis because it comprises the opinions of actual SL users, and it gives us an additional metatext to which we can compare the content we have found in SL.[6]

Virtual Objectification

The avatar is often considered the embodiment of identity in cyberspace, and SL provides various means with which to design avatars. As Linden Lab suggests:

Second Life is about personal expression and your avatar is the most personal expression of all. After all, an avatar is your persona in the virtual world . . . Despite offering almost infinite possibilities, the tool to personalize your avatar is very simple to use and allows you to change anything you like, from the tip of your nose to the tint of your skin. Don't worry if it's not perfect at first, you can change your look at any time. (Linden Research, 2006)

Clearly, Linden Lab has decided to highlight the agency that users can find in SL, and they suggest that users seem to have unlimited options available to them in the construction of their online identities. Users construct their avatars through the appearance editor in SL, which allows them to adjust their avatars' appearance including the body shape, the skin, the hair, and the eyes. Although Linden Lab may claim that there are almost infinite possibilities for the manipulation of an avatar, the ability to create an avatar is initially limited in an important way. The avatar's gender is the first trait that a user must designate before editing other aspects of the avatar body; a user must check one of two boxes: male or female. Granted, a user may switch between these two genders with relative ease (and, as we will discuss later, hermaphrodism is possible), but the default options available to users are limited to two choices. As Ann Fausto-Sterling (2000) observed, this bifurcation of gender is supported by the tendency to dichotomize biological sex, a dichotomy not supported by the biological record that includes a multiplicity of examples that defy easy categorization. In SL, this dichotomy is reproduced, and these default options introduce the user into SL in the same way that a gendered subject is introduced into a RL heterosexual world divided up into women and men.

The user can also choose "shapes" or "skins," which can cover the avatar's body.

A shape will reconstruct the form of the avatar body (e.g., adding a well sculpted build to the body), while a skin allows a user to replace an avatar's skin color and can contour a body shape (e.g., skin tones that are pigmented and can contour the musculature of a shape for more depth). A user can also replace default clothing with designed pieces (e.g., clothing or other costumes purchased in shops), and can add attachments, items that can be linked to a particular part of an avatar's body (e.g., jewelry). The user can personally create clothing, body parts and attachments by constructing these objects in the SL environment; however, many users choose to purchase these objects in SL stores. . . . All transactions within SL are conducted with an in-game currency called "Linden Dollars," and users can either earn these dollars by "working" in SL, or they can buy them outright with RL currency (Linden Research 2007). SL users can transfer U.S. currency into Lindens to purchase items in SL, and users who become merchants and sell content are able to transfer Lindens into U.S. currency.

Many of the stores in SL offer clothing, swimwear and lingerie which accentuate feminine sexual attractiveness. One store sells "Evening Starr Formals," gowns that accentuate the female form with tight bodices and plunging necklines. This store also offers more casual attire, including miniskirts and tight-fitting slacks. Another store, "Liberte Fashion," offers a similar selection of clothes that accentuate the female body. It also offers a selection of bridal gowns, for those who choose to reproduce the tradition of marriage in the SL environment. The critique of marriage as a power-laden institution is well established in feminist literature, and we will not revisit it here. We would note, however, that some work has gone into the design of these wedding gowns, and at $1,500 Lindens, SL users would have to work (either in SL or RL) in order to raise the money to purchase one. In other words,

a good deal of user agency is invested in the reproduction of the marriage tradition, in both the design and purchase of the dress.

Some of the clothing available for female avatars is modeled by the "Post 6 Grrls" in *The Second Life Herald*. The Post 6 Grrls are female avatars that are chosen to pose for "pictures" in which they are scantly dressed, posed provocatively, and often appear in the nude. The pictures are accompanied by short biographies, in which the Grrls discuss their likes and dislikes, as if they were the "Playmate of the Month." We should note that there are "Post 6" men, and robots as well, but the biographies of some of the Post 6 Grrls are as revealing as some of their pictures. For example, Kaylia Burgess (2007, ¶ 5), the Post 6 Grrl for March 9, 2007, lists the following interests: "I love fashion, makeovers, and just getting to know those I am close with (sic). And in SL, I can wear a bikini and lay on the beach all year round." Jabra Kostolany (2006, ¶ 4), the Post 6 Grrl for November 10, 2006, discusses what she would like to accomplish in SL: "One of the ideas is to make a woman's magazine like 'Cosmopolitan' for the Second Life woman. Woman (sic) need to know how to correct them and how to build and rebuild themselves (sic), where to buy, dresses, make-up and other accessories."[7] In addition to presenting their avatars as sexual objects, these Post 6 Grrls also seem to believe that women should be valued for their appearance, and indicate that their own agency is caught up in the purchase of clothes and accessories. . . .

This same value system is also apparent in the sexual and fetish ware stores in SL. Various bondage clothing, harnesses, and other types of sexual attachments are available for purchase, and the images and advertisements that appear in the stores often depict women as sexually submissive. For example, BDSM [bondage and discipline, sadism and masochism] toys and accoutrements include objects like a bullwhip, buggy whip, cattle prod, "Gorean" slave goad, spiked paddle, wooden paddle, cane, riding whip and hand crop. Any avatar can use these various toys, but female avatars are often depicted in the subordinate role in the advertisements. . . .

Actual sexual intercourse is available through various "pose balls" found in SL. Pose balls initiate directed animation, and are demarcated by colored balls that can be found in different areas of SL. When a user clicks on a pose ball, the avatar will move into the position and begin the animation that the pose ball directs. When pose balls are activated, the avatar will continue the movement, or sexual act, until the user directs the avatar to stop. Those pose balls that animate sexual positions are often color coded in ways that denote gender; for example, blue pose balls are usually for male participants, while red or pink balls are for female participants. Sexual pose ball colors also demarcate active and/or passive roles, and often the female role is the passive one. . . .

Several advertisements illustrate pose balls that include behaviors like "blowjobs" or "handjobs," and in these positions the female avatars service the male avatars. The sexual subjugation of women in SL is, however, perhaps best illustrated by the presence of advertisements for pose balls that allow avatars to engage in "roleplay rape." For example, a series of advertisements in the "M & P Shop" depicted two men who are engaged in the rape of a woman; one placed the woman on her hands and knees while she was orally and vaginally penetrated by two men, while another showed one man holding the woman by her shoulders while the other man held her legs in the air and penetrated her. On May 31, 2007 Linden Labs declared depictions of sexual violence, including rape, to be unacceptable, and the advertisements that once appeared in the M & P Shop were replaced with a posting that listed unacceptable content. Although they are not advertised, rape pose balls can still be found in other SL spaces. including the "Back Alley" area of "Bound &

Determined Fetish Club;" "Miss Lucie's Land of Fun and Fantasy" offers pose balls labeled "ravished" and "ravisher."

While the users with female avatars voluntarily participate in these rape scenes, just because the practice is volitional does not absolve it from critique. The fact that a user is complicit in the rape scene is very problematic, if we are to assume that a female user controls the female avatar. Such a scenario has implications more disturbing than the banal aspects of rape fantasy; it suggests that rape is just sexual play, in which the female is expected to say "no" even though she means "yes." Even more disturbing, however, is the possibility that the female avatar who "volunteers" for a rape scene or "ravishment" could be controlled by a man. The possible empathy generated by crossing genders withers in the light of this possibility: a man can create a female avatar with the purpose of having her submit to sexual violation and humiliation. In any case, it is important to note that users created these pose balls, and used their agency to construct a violent sexual experience.

In addition, there are the real world benefits available to SL users who have created this sexual content. Digital avatars and the content in SL become the intellectual property of their creators, and users can actually make RL money from creating and selling content in SL. . . .

Virtually Queer

When it comes to queer sexuality, it is not that such expressions are absent from SL. On the contrary, the visibility and presence of queer sexuality can be found in social spaces, sexual spaces, and market places. The "place" search function can be used to find queer spaces, just like other spaces in SL, and using this search function with the keywords "gay" or "lesbian" results in dozens of spaces and "islands." . . .

Islands in SL are similar to their RL equivalent, in that they are isolated from other areas in SL; many of these queer spaces exist on islands disconnected from other areas, and some are even further isolated within areas on islands. One example of such a space is the "Bad Boys Club" (a club for gay men on "Munford Island"), which does not allow avatars to freely move between the club and other locations on the island. This club restricts avatars from either entering or leaving the club through the conventional means of movement (walking and flying); thus this club cannot be entered unintentionally. Instead, a user must "teleport" into the club. (Teleporting occurs when a user jumps to a new location by entering spatial coordinates.) Some places in SL cannot be entered in any other way, and therefore a user must know the coordinate address to enter these spaces. When queer spaces restrict entry in this manner, it is reminiscent of early times in the gay community, when clubs, in order to protect the anonymity of their patrons, would only post the street address by the door, but offer no other signage. As then, to enter some queer spaces in SL, a user must know the exact address.

It is likely that many of these queer spaces are isolated because they rarely restrict sexual content. Sexual content permeates these queer spaces, whether they cater to males or females, and these spaces typically have sex clubs, or places for sexual activities, and contain shops that sell sexual paraphernalia. Sex clubs differ in style depending on each space and whether the content is for male or female avatars. The way that these sexual spaces are constructed is not always the same, but common elements appear. Many of the gay male spaces have a sex club within the vicinity of the dance floor, and lesbian sex spaces are often constructed similarly to gay male spaces. Many of these spaces, however, are segregated by gender; there are gay spaces that are designated for "men only," such as "Bad Boys Club" or "Devil Inside," and there are lesbian spaces that are labeled "women only," such as "Ruby Bayou Ladies Club" and "Pink Passions." The explicit segregation

of genders in SL is unique to queer spaces, and ensures that the sexual activity within these spaces does not include heterosexual behaviors. In this way, however, queers construct and congregate in spaces that ensure their isolation, and thereby reproduce their own marginalization.

Not every queer area or space includes sexual paraphernalia and/or sex clubs. "The L Word Island" is a reconstruction of a neighborhood from the Showtime cable television series *The L Word,* and this island does not offer any sexual content. The various shops on this island offer clothing (for both men and women), as well as skins and hair. This island is one of the few queer islands that seem to place an emphasis on relationships over sexual intercourse; the presence of a speed-dating lounge points to this emphasis. It is possible that Showtime, the owner of the island, wanted to restrict sexually explicit content, but this would suggest that the motive behind the construction of this queer space is different from other queer spaces in SL. This space has been developed to promote a television show, so restriction of sexual content may only serve the commercial interests of Showtime.

Therefore, we need to recognize that some queer sexuality in SL may not be designed for the interests of the sexual minorities represented. For example, in some of the sex clubs and dungeons that cater to heterosexuals, it is common to find pose balls for female-on-female sexual animations. While there is a prevalence of female-female and female-female-male pose balls in these spaces, male-male pose balls are not present. The absence of gay male sexual opportunities in these spaces might indicate that these particular instances of lesbian sexuality are being offered up for the pleasure of male heterosexuals. (Lesbian sex scenes are prevalent in the pornography marketed to heterosexual men, and it would seem that these lesbian pose balls are placed to create sexual acts primarily for the desires of heterosexual men, and not lesbians.) This is not to suggest that all lesbian sex in SL is served up for male heterosexual pleasure, because there are "women only" spaces where men cannot observe lesbian acts. Even in these contexts, however, we cannot assume that all of the female avatars signify female users; some may be cross-dressed male users enjoying lesbian experiences.

As we have mentioned, when a user begins SL, they can choose an avatar of the opposite sex, and use all of the clothing and attachments available in SL to construct the avatar. Not everyone, however, welcomes these transgender avatars in SL; for example, some men who patronize escorts in SL want to make certain the women they solicit have been created, and are played, by women in RL. In fact, a voice verification system has been set up so that female escorts in SL can be certified "GVF" (Gender-Verified Female) (Elliott, 2006). Therefore, voice becomes the ultimate gender signifier, separating the "real" women from the transgendered, and once again anchoring gender in biological sex.

Unfortunately for those who use SL to explore transgender experiences, voice has become an important issue. Integrated voice technology was recently made available to SL users; and this technology allows people to talk to one another, rather than using the text chat function. Some SL users who cross-dress saw this new technology as a threat to their existence in SL. For example, in *The Second Life Herald*, Prokofy Neva (2007, ¶ 15) writes about the harassment that transgender users already experience, and notes "Being forced to use a voice in a virtual world, something not of my choice, against my will . . . feels like the ultimate blow. It won't be—but you do get tired of this crap after awhile." In another *Second Life Herald* article, Aurel Miles mentions the ways that "shemales" can be identified in SL. A commenter to this article writes, "All of you are fussing over something that's going to be moot shortly anwyays (sic). As soon as Voice Chat is rolled out you'll see the number of gender benders suddenly dissolve" (realityfish,

2007, ¶ 62). As the comment reveals, this SL user looks to this technological change as a way of reasserting heterosexuality in SL. After all, the use of voice to identify the biological sex of users is a way to ensure that biological males will only interact sexually with biological females, and in this way, voice technology can be deployed to reduce the instances of queer sex.

The issue of voice in this controversy takes on a strange irony. Voice has often been equated with agency, and the act of speaking for oneself has been characterized as an act of visibility, and a sign of political viability (Morris, 2007). This is true of marginalized groups generally, and sexual minorities specifically; the slogan of AIDS activism, "Silence = Death", illustrates the point. The deployment of voice technology will allow the transgender users to be heard in SL, and will make them visible. Unfortunately, this visibility may be turned against transgender users, so the agency of voice becomes the material for marginalization. Therefore some of these transgender users do not want their voices to be heard, because they do not want to be recognized as transgender. In this way, silence becomes a means of survival in SL, and the political potential of queer voice and visibility is turned on its head. Still, while we are sympathetic to the plight of transgender users in SL, the decision to eschew voice chat accommodates a heteronormative demand that queers should be neither heard, nor seen. . . .

Same Old Game

At the beginning of this chapter, we discussed how it was difficult to classify SL as a game. Where the issues of gender and sexuality are considered, the question may be moot because the "play" in SL is quite serious. In *Bodies That Matter*, Butler (1993) explains that the performative nature of gender does not mean that the performance of gender does not matter. On the contrary, these performances constitute our identities, and locate us as sexual subjects in society. The gender and sexual play that we have observed in SL could also be regarded as part of a game, but we would argue that it is a game that matters. The users who perform these actions are identifying themselves as sexual subjects, and identifying others as sexual objects.

Given the agency to create their own sexual experiences, some users have chosen to create experiences that objectify women and marginalize queers. The possibility that heterosexual men would construct these experiences comes as no surprise; the possibility that both women and queers might assist in the construction is more surprising. Indeed, the enactment of self-subjugation and self-marginalization would seem to be the ultimate expression of docility. Women, who have chosen to construct identities in SL only to serve themselves up as objects of sexual desire, reassert an existing belief system that limits the value of women. Queers who have cloistered themselves on an isolated island, often segregated by gender, have complied with the heteronormative demand to keep their practices private.

Consequently, our analysis illustrates some problems with the liberatory perspective. To view cyberspace as liberatory rewrites RL as inherently repressive, and this is evident in some of the comments that we have discussed, where users refer to SL as a space where they are free to express themselves. Unfortunately, if cyberspace is liberatory, and SL specifically, then how do we challenge the politically retrograde content without inviting the charge of repression? After all, complaints about "political correctness" have been used to mock and undermine feminist and queer critiques of cultural representation in RL. Foucault argued that while it was possible to resist the sexual norms of society, it was not possible to move outside of the relations of power produced by the disciplining of sexuality. Consequently, he had his own suspicions about the liberatory promise of the sexual revolution of the sixties and

seventies, and he warned: "(w)e must not think that by saying yes to sex, one says no to power" (1978, p. 157). Arguing from Foucault, we suggest that cyberspace should not be regarded as an environment that moves the user outside of the political and social matrix of gender and sexuality. Cyberspace may allow us to rework those power relationships, but we cannot assume that liberation is obtained there, nor can we overlook the instances that clearly reproduce traditional gender roles and sexual norms, and willful sexual violence.

Applying Foucault's warning to SL, perhaps we should not think that by saying "yes" to cybersex, we are saying "no" to power. Indeed, we should not look to cyberspace as a universal panacea. Granted, technology can be quite attractive, and it would be nice to imagine that escape from oppression, and relief from violence is a mere keystroke away. The problems associated with gender and sexuality are RL social problems that predate the technology of SL, and therefore we should be mindful that the solutions to those problems might lie in RL as well. If our analysis reveals anything, it is that while SL may appear new and exciting, where gender and sexuality are concerned, too often it is the same old game.

Notes

1. We recognize that the term "traditional media" increasingly becomes a problematic term as various mediums begin to converge. Yet, we make this distinction to illustrate a difference between representations that are created within media by media producers versus representations that are created by users of an interactive medium.

2. Admittedly, the term "real life" is problematic, and we are aware of the debate about surrounding the distinctions draw between the real world and the virtual one. The players of SL, however, use this term, so we are merely reproducing a distinction that is made by these

players—the distinction of a virtual "second life" in contradistinction to the "first life" lived by flesh bodies.

3. Stone's observations are influenced by the work of Donna Haraway (1991), who has conceptualized the cyborg as a modern border/ed body (between animal, man, machine, and physicality) that has the potential to deconstruct hegemonic power. She specifically noted a possibility to imagine a world without gender or genesis. We do not feel, and will argue, that this rather Utopian possibility has come to fruition within SL.

4. The queerest of the queer in SL may be the "Furries." Furries are avatars that are anthropomorphic animals; they often have the body shape of humans, but the heads and fur of animals. Linden Lab has even made a furry avatar an option available to new users.

5. Both authors of this project have spent a considerable amount of time exploring the virtual SL environment. One has been a member of SL since December 9, 2006; the other has been a member since May 26, 2006. Each author has investigated various SL islands to obtain pertinent information for this article. Collectively we have spent approximately 140 hours in-world as active participants in SL. We should note that because the content in SL is user created, it is in constant flux, and we cannot be certain that the same content will be available in SL at the time of publication. Still, the content that we critique was created by users, and our argument is about the agency of creation.

6. James Gillett (2007) has demonstrated this integration of analyses of visual texts and blogs.

7. We are well aware of the fact that some of these female avatars are constructed and controlled by male players. Indeed, this possibility raises other concerns that we address later in the article.

References

Alexander, J. (2002). Homo-pages and Queer sites: Studying the construction and representation of Queer identities on the World Wide Web. *International Journal of Sexuality and Gender Studies, 7,* 85–106.

Bartle, R. (2006). Virtual worldliness. In J. Balkin & B. Novek (Eds.), *The state of play: Law, games, and virtual worlds.* New York: New York University Press.

Battles, K., & Hilton-Murrow, W. (2002). Gay characters in conventional spaces; 'Will and Grace' and the situation comedy genre. *Critical Studies in Media Communication, 19,* 87–105.

Brookey, R., & Booth, P. (2006). Restricted Play: Synergy and the limits of interactivity in "The Lord of the Rings/Return of the King" video game. *Games and Culture, 1,* 214–230.

Brookey, R., & Westerfelhaus, R. (2001). Pistols and petticoats, piety and purity: *To Wong Foo,* the queering of the American monomyth, and the marginalizing discourse of deification. *Critical Studies in Media Communication, 18,* 141–156.

Bryce, J., & Rutter, J. (2002). Spectacle of the deathmatch: Character and narrative in first-person shooters. In G. King & T. Krzywinska (Eds.), *Screenplay: Cinema/videogame/interfaces* (pp. 66–80). London: Wallflower Press.

Bryson, M. (2004). When Jill jacks in: Queer women on the Net. *Feminist Media Studies, 4,* 239–254.

Burgess, K. (2007, March 9). Kaylia Burgess-Post 6 Grrrl. *The Second Life Herald.* Retrieved on March 14, 2008, from http://www.secondlifeherald.com/ slh/2007/03/kaylia_burgess_.html

Butler, J. (1990). *Gender trouble: Feminism and subversion of identity.* New York: Routledge.

Butler, J. (1993). *Bodies that matter: On the discursive limits of "sex."* New York: Routledge.

Castronova, E. (2006). *Synthetic worlds: The business and culture of online games.* Chicago: University of Chicago Press.

Dow, B. J. (2001). Ellen, television and the politics of gay and lesbian visibility. *Critical Studies in Media Communication, 18*(2), 123–140.

Elliott, S. (2006, April 7). Escort Mission. Joystiq. Retrieved September 28, 2007, from www.1up.com/do/feature?cld=3149 323&did=4

Fausto-Sterling, A. (2000). *Sexing the body: Gender politics and the construction of sexuality.* New York: Basic Books.

Filiciak, M. (2003). Hyperidentities: Postmodern identity patterns in massively multiplayer online role-playing games. In M. Wolf & B. Perron (Eds.), *The videogame theory reader* (pp. 87–102). New York: Routledge.

Foucault, M. (1975). *Discipline and punish.* A. Sheridan, trans. New York: Vintage.

Foucault, M. (1978). *The history of sexuality, Vol. 1.* R. Hurley, trans. New York: Vintage.

Frasca, G. (2003). Simulation versus narrative: Introduction to Ludology. In M. Wolf & B. Perron (Eds.), *The video game theory reader* (pp. 221–235). London: Routledge.

Gillett, J. (2007). Web logs as cultural resistance: A study of the SARS arts project. *Journal of Communication Inquiry, 31,* 28–43.

Gunkel, D. (2001). *Hacking cyberspace.* Boulder, CO: Westview Press.

Haraway, D. (1991). A cyborg manifesto: Science, technology, and socialist-feminism in the late twentieth century. In *Simians, cyborgs, and women: The reinvention of nature* (pp. 149–181). New York: Routledge.

Kostolany, J. (2006, November 10). Jabra Kostolany-Post 6 Grrl. *The Second Life Herald.* Retrieved on March 14, 2008, from http://www.secondlifehearald.com/slh/2006/11/jabra_kostolany.html

Linden Research. (2007). Second life currency exchange. *SecondLife.com.* Retrieved May 01, 2007, from http://secondlife.com/whatis/currency.php

Marshall, P. (2002). The new intertextual commodity. In D. Harries (Ed.), *The new media book* (pp. 69–81). London: British Film Institute.

Morris, C. (2007). Introduction. In C. Morris III (Ed.), *Queering public address: Sexualities in historical discourse.* Columbia: University of South Carolina Press.

Neva, P. (2007, Feb. 27). Vox Lindeni. *The Second Life Herald.* Retrieved March 15, 2008, from http://foo.secondlifeherald.com/slh/2007/02/vox_lindeni.html#more

realityfish. (2007, April 22). Sex in SL: Dude looks like a lady. *The Second Life Herald.* Retrieved on March 15, 2007, from http://www.secondlifeherald.com/slh/2007/04/sex_in_sl_dude.html

Roberts, L., & Parks, M. (2001). The social geography of gender-switching in virtual environments on the Internet. In E. Green & A. Adam (Eds.), *Virtual Gender: Technology, consumption and identity.* New York: Routledge.

Shugart, H. (2003). Reinventing privilege: The new (gay) man in contemporary popular media. *Critical Studies in Media Communication, 20,* 67–91.

Sloop, J. (2004). *Disciplining gender: Rhetoric of sex identity in contemporary US culture.* Amherst: University of Massachusetts Press.

Stone, A. (1995). *The war of desire and technology at the close of the mechanical age.* Cambridge, MA: MIT Press.

Turkle, S. (1995). *Life on the screen: Identity in the age of the Internet.* New York: Touchstone.

From Smart
Fan to Backyard Wrestler

Performance, Context,
and Aesthetic Violence

Lawrence B. McBride and S. Elizabeth Bird

. . . . The backyard wrestling phenomenon illustrates the complexity of wrestling as a mass-mediated cultural phenomenon, operating on multiple levels of spectatorship and performance. This chapter draws from ethnographic research by McBride with two local wrestling promotions (such groups are called independent wrestling federations, or indy feds) that began as backyard groups: the Chicago area's Lunatic Wrestling Federation (LWF), and Fucked Up Wrestling (FUW), which operated in central Illinois. We show how fans, grounded in a media/audience spectator aesthetic, become active producers and performers themselves.

Wrestling as Ritual

Today's pro wrestling is the most recent manifestation of a century-old American tradition that has reconfigured itself often, adapting to the circus side-show, the saloon/vaudeville circuit, the first urban sports arenas, the earliest one-camera live television, then cable, then the Internet. Throughout, the show's core element has been a distinctive style of ritualized combat, taking place in a space resembling a boxing ring. The word "ritualized" is appropriate, in that the performers assume alien identities within the tight delimitations of the

From McBride, L. B., & Bird, S. E. (2007). From Smart Fan to backyard wrestler: Performance, context, and aesthetic violence. In J. Gray, C. Sandvoss, & C. L. Harrington (Eds.), *Fandom: Identities and communities in a mediated world* (pp. 165–176). New York: New York University Press.

wrestling show. These identities, called "gimmicks," are the morally significant agents in the plots of wrestling shows, which involve cheating villains ("heels") and honest heroes ("babyfaces"). But the spectators' performance of credulity in the face of the fantastic nature of the display is the primary element that qualifies the show as "ritual," distinguishing it from contemporary sports (Barthes 1972; Morton & O'Brien 1985). As Jenkins (1997) points out, pro wrestling can also be productively interpreted as melodrama, of a kind specially tailored to the male imagination. To point out that wrestling is fake is to miss the point; to suspend judgment and play along is to begin to enjoy it.

Nevertheless, wrestling, and by extension, its fandom, is one of the most denigrated forms of popular culture. Twitchell (1992) groups it with a few other genres as epitomizing the carnivalesque "trashing of taste" in American culture. Commentators decry the way televised wrestling validates the hegemony of class (Freedman 1983), gender and sexualities (Jhally 2003), or ethnicities (Lincoln 1989; Mondak 1989). Woo and Kim (2003:361) conclude that wrestling's "anti-social content" ("aggressive acts, rule violations, and glamorization of violence") may influence young people to become violent and antisocial.

Inherent in these critiques is the assumption that wrestling fans routinely take the staged contests at face value. It is not our intention to dispute the presence of violent, sexist, racist, and generally "antisocial" imagery in professional wrestling. However, wrestling is not monolithic; we argue that both scholars and social critics have missed many layers of meaning and experience, particularly those of backyard wrestlers, indy wrestlers, and Smart Fans (discussed below) where complex distinctions operate between spectators and performers, real and unreal. Backyard wrestling is an integration of productive practice and an aesthetic bound to a specific fandom context.

The Rise of Backyard Wrestling

To explain the structure of backyard wrestling federations, we invoke a participant's account, describing how a federation was formed, and revealing both the broader context of pro wrestling and the way specific fan behaviors such as backyard wrestling have meaning in that context.

In Spring 2000, McBride interviewed "Billy Whack," a young man who performed as the ring announcer and color commentator for the LWF, while observing a training session at "the Factory," LWF's rental space in a complex of small warehouses in Mokena, Illinois. One wall was a huge garage door, which was open. Most of the space was taken up by the ring, and in the deepest part of the room, behind the ring, a couch and some chairs were arranged around a TV and VCR. In the ring, young men performed drills, repeating the same moves over and over.

Whack described how LWF began. One summer in the early 1990s, he and some friends gathered at home to watch Wrestlemania, an annual Pay-Per-View wrestling show, staged by the WWF (later WWE). Afterwards, the fans went out to the yard, and "somebody stuck four sticks in the ground and put a crappy rope around, and we just jumped around like idiots. We're all winded and sore and tired, and we weren't even doin' any moves, just punchin' and kickin' and jumpin'." This odd diversion was captured on videotape. The next day, the young man who would become Billy Whack watched the tape with a friend:

> It was the worst, poorly lit, crappy [. . . .] And, I'm like "Wow [. . .] this is pretty cool. Pretty cool." And then me and him came to the idea that we should try to organize this, do it a little bit better, maybe write a little story line, come up with some characters[. . . .] Let's call it the Lunatic Wrestling Federation. So my

parents were going away for a weekend, so I ran out there and we put four poles in the ground, put these little clamp lights up and we jumped around like idiots and videotaped it, and we had the little bell and everything. We brought in more people; and that's what we did for the summer of 93.

The summer of 1994 saw more back-yard LWF shows, now featuring a plywood ring built by the wrestlers. Winters were spent planning and writing future shows and storylines. The year 1995 was a break-through one, with the opportunity to stage a show on a ten-acre property belonging to a friend's parents:

So we figured, let's try to promote this[. . . .] We handed out fliers at the high school. And we had like 350 people show up [. . .] we had lights and little cameras and everything. We were getting to be really good. Well, we were saving our money, let's just buy a wrestling ring. We spent everything we had, which was about four thousand five hundred bucks [. . . .] They delivered it, set it up. We jumped around like idiots. You see a recurring pattern. We said let's trademark everything: we have these names, we have these gimmicks. We had these ideas. And let's start putting on real shows. So we planned for a whole year and in October of '97, we had Bloodbath '97 at the Romeoville rec center. Like ten bucks a head, and we were makin' money and we couldn't believe it [. . . .] Then we found we had to get a promoter's license, and take out an insurance policy just for the night on the audience, rent the venue, and a DJ, for the music equipment. We were finding out it was pretty costly. It just gets cra-zier each day, like I never know what's going to happen next. I've met tons of wrestlers and the people I've met through this [gestures behind him to the students] we're running training camp

on Wednesdays, we're doing shows, we're about to get a TV deal. We have an actual TV camera crew come out and film it, edit the tape, we sell the tape, [and] we're about to start sellin' mer-chandise off our web site.

The FUW began in a similar way in Bloomington, Illinois, in 1999, when spon-taneous wrestling broke out as a few young fans were watching RAW on TV. Soon a committed group of about twenty 18–21-year-olds, most of them male, was devoting significant resources to FUW, practicing, buying costumes and props, and eventually paying dues to support the costs of promo-tion and insurance. When the group folded in 2003, it had performed in bars, the county fairgrounds, and the local National Guard Armory, charging anywhere from five dollars to fifteen dollars for admission. Neither the LWF nor the FUW turned a profit in the long term, despite their even-tual popularity.

Backyard wrestling federations are to World Wrestling Entertainment (WWE) what garage bands are to world-famous rock bands. Despite the staggering disparity in production values, all groups work in the same idiom: they write storylines and create original characters, who perform the same style of ritualized wrestling. Backyard wrestlers do not simply parody or role-play the WWE, but develop their own scenarios, even when they have no consistent fans of their own, using camcorders to record and then critique their performances.

Within wrestling culture, backyard wrestling emerged alongside and within the context of the "Smart Fan" phenomenon. When McBride first met FUW wrestlers, they stated immediately that the most important thing to know about wrestling was the difference between Marks and Smarts. Smarts are "Smart to the business," while Marks appear to believe in the authenticity of the competition—Smarts see them as the stereotypical "dupes" imagined by wrestling's critics. Smarts approach the genre of wrestling as would-be insiders, while Marks root unreflexively for the most popular faces. Smart Fans possess truly incredible amounts of knowledge about the history of wrestling, including wrestlers' real names and career histories, how various promotions began and folded, who won every Wrestlemania ever. Smart Fan informants defined a Mark specifically as someone who responds to wrestling in the way intended by the people who write the storylines (the bookers), describing Marks with statements such as "Kids are Marks" or "We were all Marks when we were kids." Smarts view Marks with scorn.

Interested in the behind-the-scenes action of WWE personnel decisions and the process of scripting the televised shows, Smart Fans parallel many other familiar fan cultures (Hills 2002), whose members are as much interested in movie studio politics and the strategic maneuvers of contract negotiations as in movies or TV shows themselves. Fully cognizant of the staged nature of wrestling, Smarts follow the WWE not just to see the shows, but to keep track of what "the Fed" is doing. Generally, backyard wrestlers considered themselves Smarts; however, their "readings" of the televised productions of the large promotions were not wholly ironic, in the self-conscious sense of some other consumers of "trash" media (see Bird 1992). Even though these fans' enjoyment of televised wrestling was occasionally preempted by their critical attitude, they respected the WWE as the elite level of the wrestling world, appreciating the artistry of the productions.

Smart fans also call themselves Internet fans. As noted by many scholars, the Internet has opened up a new world of communication for fan cultures (see Bird 2003; Hills 2002; McKee 2001), which also coincided with the appropriation of other communications technology, such as the video technology central to backyard wrestling, and the techniques of building rings and staging. Smarts voraciously consume information on insider websites, referred to as "dirt sheets," which also leak

results. When McBride met his FUW research participants, they would already know what was going to happen on Monday night televised wrestling, including match outcomes. Beyond reporting on the major wrestling promotions, dirt sheets also report on the indy feds, and the Internet provides an arena for Smart fans to meet and establish tape-trading relationships. Smarts and backyard wrestlers devote hours to watching tapes of independent wrestling federations from around the country, as well as Japanese and Mexican wrestling shows, old-school wrestling (from before cable TV), and the much-coveted shoot interviews, in which wrestlers would appear out of character and share humorous and harrowing stories about life in "the business."

Today's young people are often disapprovingly characterized as the "media generation." However, media saturation does not necessarily mean total subjection; media participation may produce rich intertextual productivity (Drotner 2000). For decades, fan cultures have translated smart spectatorship into shared storytelling through fan fiction, conventions, and dramatic recreations (Bacon-Smith 1992; Bird 2003; Jenkins 1992). The presence of a portable camcorder in a household hosting a large group of young fans watching WWE might be the decisive factor in the transition from play to production that we see in the LWF and FUW stories. The idea to "try to organize this, do it a little bit better" came to countless, isolated groups of young wrestling fans first watching themselves on tape—the recording, playing, critique, and exchange of tapes is as much part of the backyard wrestling phenomenon as the matches themselves. And the Internet was the medium that defined the further development of these groups. Online, the young fans could learn tricks of the business, such as "blading"—secretly cutting their own scalps during matches to create the illusion of having been "busted wide open." Using Abercrombie and Longhurst's (1998) fan typology, Smart fans could be defined as "enthusiasts," while backyard wrestlers have moved to become "producers," although generally emerging from and remaining in the Smart fan position.

Aesthetics and Contexts

By the time the Smart aesthetic in wrestling developed, the WWE had for years been distancing itself from the pretense of being a real sport, decreasing the physicality of its wrestling in favor of fantastic character development and storylines. Although the wrestling done at all three levels (national, indy, and backyard) fits within the same idiom, a qualitative difference among the shows is evident. The typical Monday night cable wrestling shows consisted of more talking and skits than actual wrestling, while indy shows are generally action packed, with more intense moves. There is a basic economic factor explaining this. When fully professional wrestlers are severely injured, they can suffer serious financial loss and carefully planned storylines can be disrupted. For indy wrestlers, however, paychecks are not as substantial; many view wrestling as a hobby, and almost all have day jobs. In that context, more risks are taken because, as at an "indy rock" show, it is the quality of the performers' and audiences' experience that is most important. In the backyard, many risks are taken, and the risks are compounded by lack of training. Yet FUW wrestlers argued that there is no excuse for being stupid and taking terrible risks, and certain moves, particularly the "pile driver," were banned in the FUW.

In backyard wrestling, some kids have taken such risks with their bodies that the phenomenon has been sensationalized by mainstream media as a horror story about deviant youth (e.g., Reilly 2001). However, risk is part of the idiom common to all three levels of wrestling. Wrestlers see wrestling moves as falling along a scale that runs from low-risk to high-risk. Low-risk spots include punches and kicks, and submission-style wrestling. Being thrown through a table is a high-risk spot. Ranged between the extremes are seemingly hundreds of variations of "hurricaneranas," "moonsaults" and "suplexes." Generally, low-risk spots have less potential for pain and injury.

When, in 1994, regional promotion Eastern Championship Wrestling changed its name to Extreme Championship Wrestling, it embraced what became known as the "hardcore" style. This meant that in some matches the face/heel distinction was deemphasized, and the action centered around extremes of violence, generous use of weapons, and copious amounts of (real) bleeding. The pick-you-up-and-slam-you-down moves were still there, but there might be thumbtacks or barbed wire spread around the ring. ECW crowds would chant "ta-ble! ta-ble! ta-ble!" as they waited for the inevitable slam-through-a-wooden-table move. Folding step ladders also became integrated into hardcore-technique ECW wrestling shows. Instead of jumping off the top rope to crush an opponent, wrestlers might reach under the ring and retrieve one of these ladders, to gain altitude for higher flight.

FUW wrestlers made it clear there was a limit to the acceptability of hardcore wrestling, beyond which was "garbage wrestling," seen as hardcore and bloody, but artless. They believed hardcore elements were best used sparingly, within the context of a good match. Good wrestling was supposed to look as if it hurt, but as far as possible, pain was to be controlled. The use of hardcore spots and weapons in the FUW reflected this. Getting hit on the head with a steel chair (a chair shot) looks brutal, makes a loud noise, but doesn't hurt too much, relative to the spot's effect on the audience.

Smart fans fueled the success of ECW and the indy wrestling scene, which in turn shaped the dominant aesthetic among Smarts and backyard wrestlers. This aesthetic was not centered on violence or bleeding; Smarts avidly sought out tapes of old American shows featuring what became known as "old school" wrestling, which mainly involves a seemingly infinite repertoire of ingenious submission holds. Japanese and Mexican wrestling, highly valued by Smarts, has evolved to include a much more intricate, stylized, and gymnastic set of high-flyer moves.

Among Smart fans and backyard wrestlers, high-risk moves are more valued, because they understand this behavior as a form of generosity. The generous wrestler will give his all in a performance to ensure a dual outcome: the match will be spectacular, benefiting the fans; and each wrestler will make his "opponent" look good, helping him "get over with the fans." Generosity in wrestling is a major theme in wrestler Mick Foley's (1999) memoir. Foley describes how selfish wrestlers, on the receiving end of a high-risk move, will be more concerned with avoiding injury than with making the wrestling look convincing. This prevents the wrestler on offense from looking powerful, and thus does his career little good. While the ideal in pro wrestling is a balance of concern for safety and willingness to absorb punishment, both are needed in a good match.

Smart fans, most of whom have read Foley's book, understand this ideal. Thus, unlike Marks, who are mostly content to go along for the ride, Smarts often form strong emotional attachments to those wrestlers who go to the greatest lengths to bear the burden of the performance. For instance, according to this aesthetic, the FUW research participants considered the famous Foley vs. Terry Funk "exploding ring match" of August 18, 1995, in Yokohama, Japan, to be "one of the greatest of all time" (see Foley 1999 for a full account). Foley and Funk were each badly burned in the match, for which the ring ropes had been replaced with barbed wire, and the ring rigged with firework-like explosives. At one point, Foley hit Funk in the head with a metal step ladder; Funk then pushed Foley off that ladder into the barbed wire ropes, as Foley was preparing to dive down onto Funk, leading with the elbow. Foley won the match:

While I celebrated, Terry was placed in an ambulance and rushed to the hospital. It was truly a touching scene as the adoring crowd reached out just to touch him, and chanted his name. Terry had done me a gigantic favor. Terry had only lost a couple of matches in the last decade in Japan, and a victory over the Funker was a huge milestone. Terry Funk [. . .] had just given me a hell of a gift. (Foley 1999: 337)

Thus, without the ideal of the generous wrestler, the hardcore aesthetic would indeed be meaningless violence. As to why Smart fans took the ideal to heart so completely as to begin wrestling in hardcore style in their backyards, we submit that the essence of wrestling must be experienced first-hand to be fully known. At a performance, the anticipation of the match, the crowd's noise, and the impact of the moves will trigger what wrestlers understand as an "adrenaline" or "fight or flight" response, which mitigates pain, and which arguably constitutes an altered state of consciousness. This response allows them to withstand a level of physical punishment (falls from high balconies, deep lacerations, serious burns, and so on) that shocks those not initiated into wrestling fandom. When wrestlers achieve this state, they can perform in seemingly superhuman ways, allowing wrestling to become truly spectacular; this altered state can become the motivation to continue (for an extended discussion, see McBride 2005).

Backyard wrestling, then, is a fan culture based on physical experience in a way rarely if ever described in the literature on fans, although perhaps closest to Grossberg's (1984) discussion of the physical experience of rock music fandom. The experience was described by FUW wrestler "Dre" following a match in which he had been "powerbombed" through a table, a spectacular move that shattered the table and caused a huge crowd reaction. "It just felt so good.

That table just exploded," commented Dre, adding later, "You know, when we're in the ring it's like a trance we go into." Another interviewee, South Florida indy wrestler Mark Zout, commented, "it just gets your blood pumping in a different way, and it's almost indescribable the rush you get" (McBride 2005: 69). . . .

Of course backyard wrestling is violent. Indeed, as we emphasize, the managed, performed pain is an integral and motivating part of the experience. We can see how the hardcore idiom within wrestling is the expression of the refinement of the physiological pathway to wrestling consciousness and peak wrestling experience. The realness of the spectacle runs away with the pageantry, as real weapons cause real injury, doubtless releasing the "adrenaline" that is repeatedly referenced by wrestlers as a goal. Nevertheless, the experience is not uncontrolled, mindless viciousness, as critics suggest.

Conclusion

The "meaning" of American wrestling is so often taken to lie at the surface, inscribed with a conventional, reactionary symbolism of racism, sexism, and jingoism, and thus meriting widespread condemnation [see Sut Jhally's critique, for example, in Souza 2002] . . . . This "cultural dupe" theory of the audience has been effectively dismantled when it comes to most media-reception situations, yet the idea of wrestling fans as critical readers seems hard for critics to grasp.

Smart wrestling fans indulge in elaborate criticism of wrestling (see Lipscomb 2005 for a discussion of websites), often showing a sophisticated grasp of nuance, and playing with the notions of reality and unreality: We would not deny that Vince McMahon's WWE glorifies images and themes that are disrespectful and harmful to women, gays, and minorities—but this in itself is often a subject of Smart discussion and ridicule. Moreover, the WWE is not the beginning and end of wrestling, and by contributing to this misperception, Jhally (2003) and other critics misunderstand the more creative and variable worlds of indy and backyard wrestling. Even Jenkins (1997), who has a more nuanced understanding of wrestling as melodrama, does not see the producerly potential in wrestling that he has identified among other fan groups.

Ethnographic studies of media audiences and fans reveal dimensions of experience that social criticism does not. A mass-mediated cultural phenomenon such as wrestling is sustained by the interaction of physical, productive practices within the context of a socially learned aesthetic. Audience ethnography can access the specific knowledge of the mediated phenomenon—the interaction of producer-fan practice and fan values.

In the case of the wrestling audience, the behavior patterns of wrestling shows in general, and backyard wrestling in particular, are meaningful in the specific contexts of Smart fandom versus Mark fandom. We argue that the backyard wrestling "ritual" was replicated so uniformly across the nation not solely because children were imitating what they saw on television, but also because a certain productivity was enabled by a particular configuration of material culture (video cameras and trampolines, cable TV and Internet service) that was available relatively uniformly. The wrestling experience offered something even more than active fandom, in that it allowed participants to explore the limits of physical sensation that goes far beyond the spectator role. Grossberg (1984) describes the yearning of young people to *feel* through music, in an alienating world of images: "I'd rather feel bad than feel nothing at all." Wrestling offers a similar rush of feeling—controlled, almost ecstatic pain that cuts through mundane and often alienating "reality."

References

Abercrombie, N & Longhurst, B 1998, *Audiences: a sociological theory of performance and imagination,* Sage, Thousand Oaks, CA.

Bacon-Smith, C 1992, *Enterprising women: television fandom and the creation of popular myth.* University of Pennsylvania Press, Philadelphia.

Barthes, R 1972, *Mythologies,* Hill & Wang, New York.

Bird, SE 1992, *For enquiring minds: a cultural study of supermarket tabloids.* University of Tennessee Press, Knoxville.

Bird, SE 2003, *The audience in everyday life: living in a media world,* Routledge, New York.

Drotner, K 2000, "Difference and diversity: trends in young Danes' media cultures," *Media, Culture, and Society* 22(2), 149–66.

Foley, M (1999), *Have a nice day: a tale of blood and sweatsocks,* HarperCollins, New York.

Freedman, J 1983, "Will the Sheik use his blinding fireball? The ideology of professional wrestling " in FE Manning (ed.), *The celebration of society: perspectives on cultural performance,* Popular Press, Bowling Green, OH.

Grossberg, L. 1984, "I'd rather feel bad than not feel anything at all: rock and roll, pleasure, and power," *Enclitic 8,* 94–111.

Hills, M 2002, *Fan cultures,* Routledge, New York.

Jenkins, H 1992, *Textual poachers: television fans and participatory culture,* Routledge, New York.

Jenkins, H 1997, "Never trust a snake! WWF Wrestling as masculine melodrama," in A Baker & T Boyd (eds.), *Out of bounds: sports, media, and the politics of identity,* Indiana University Press, Bloomington.

Jhally, S (dir.) 2003, *Wrestling with manhood: gender, race, and class in professional wrestling* Media Education Foundation, Northampton, MA.

Lincoln, B 1989, *Discourse and the construction of society: comparative studies of myth, ritual and classification,* Oxford University Press, New York.

Lipscomb, WP 2005, *The operational aesthetic in the performance of professional wrestling,* PhD dissertation, Louisiana State University.

McBride, LB 2005, *Professional wrestling, embodied morality, and altered states of consciousness.* MA dissertation, University of South Florida, Tampa.

McKee, A 2001, "Which is the best *Doctor Who* story? A case study in value judgments outside the academy," *Intensities* 1. Retrieved October 5, 2002, from http://www.cult-media .com/issuer/Amckec.htm.

Mondak, JJ 1989, "The politics of professional wrestling," *Journal of Popular Culture* 23(2), 139–49.

Morton, GW & O'Brien, GM 1985, *Wrestling to rasslin': ancient sport to American spectacle,* Popular Press, Bowling Green, OH.

Reilly, R 2001, "Kids are trying this at home!" *Sports Illustrated,* 12 February, 98.

Souza, A 2002, "Wrestling the WWE." Retrieved November 5, 2005, from http://www.new englandfilm.com/news/archives/02august/ wrestling.htm.

Twitchell, JB 1992, *Carnival culture: the trashing of taste in America,* Columbia University Press, New York.

Woo, HJ & Kim, Y 2003, "Modern gladiators: a content analysis of televised wrestling," *Mass Communication and Society* 6(4), 361–78.

Accidental Activists

Fan Activism in the Soap Opera Community

Melissa C. Scardaville

History of Organized Fandom

The origin of organized media fandom is considered by many scholars to be *Star Trek* fans mobilizing in the late 1960s to pressure NBC to keep and later return their show to the airways (Jenkins, 1992, p. 28). Although the *Star Trek* movement provided a model for future television advocacy campaigns (Jenkins, 1992), it is important to note that local pockets of soap fans had successfully lobbied against cancellation as early as 1941 (Cantor & Pingree, 1983).

In fact, soap fans have a long history of being active. During soaps' radio days (from the 1930s to the 1950s), many listeners would respond to certain events by sending cards and/or gifts to the characters, although the frequency with which this occurred is hard to determine because "in those days the severely embarrassed networks had a hush-hush policy about such identity-confusions on the audience fringe" (LaGuardia, 1974, p. 68). By the late 1950s, soap fans routinely contacted the network, most often when a character suddenly died. In 1958, outraged *Guiding Light* fans contacted CBS in droves when a wheelchair-bound character was killed after she was knocked into oncoming traffic (Schemering, 1986, p. 31). When a beloved *Edge of Night* heroine, Sara, was killed in 1961, CBS was hit with 8,000 telegrams and letters, 260 while the day's show was airing (LaGuardia, 1974, p. 119; Schemering, 1987, p. 90). The following year, the same network was bombarded by feedback from viewers protesting the death of a long-term *As the World Turns* character, Jeff,

From Scardaville, M. C. (2005). Accidental activists: Fan activism in the soap opera community. *American Behavioral Scientist*, 48(7), 881–901. Published by Sage, Inc.

so much so that "TV Guide called the uproar 'the automobile accident that shook the nation'" (Schemering, 1987, p. 31).

The main difference between science fiction activism and soap opera activity lies in their degree of organization (and, hence, why large-scale organized fandom sees its birth in science fiction, not soaps). Throughout much of soaps' history, there was no overarching structure that provided guidelines to the protestor and, perhaps even more important, a space where fans could gather. The first daytime fan clubs, most of which were not show- but actor-specific, were not established until the early 1970s. Large-scale gatherings occurred almost concurrently; the most common of which were when two or more actor-driven fan clubs joined forces to host a luncheon in New York City, the place where most soaps then taped. The main point of these clubs, and indeed their modern-day counterparts, was to operate as a publicity tool—as opposed to providing means for critical discourse (Bielby et al., 1999, p. 40). By the time *Star Trek* fans began to mobilize in the late 1960s, local, national, and global organizations dedicated to the science fiction fan had been in place for more than three decades, and these clubs had a long-established history of blending politics and activism into their activities (Lynch, 2001).

Soap fans may not have formed collective groups as early for one or two possible reasons. First, soap operas had the ability to address any fan outrage quickly, in part because they were broadcast live or taped very shortly in advance until 1975 (Cantor & Pingree, 1983, p. 61). In the case of *Edge of Night* character Sara, the producers, concerned that viewers were confusing reality and fiction, put the actress on television the day after her character was killed so she could inform the audience that it was her choice to leave (LaGuardia, 1974, pp. 119—20). When *Days of Our Lives* character Addie was diagnosed with cancer in 1973, letters poured in until the show's creator changed the direction of the story

and Addie lived, albeit temporarily (LaGuardia, 1983, p. 6). . . .

In addition, research done on the early soap audience reveals several key points: The majority were 18- to 49-year-old married women who stayed at home while their spouses worked, had no postsecondary education, were most likely to have been affected by the Great Depression, and lived in a rural area (Matelski, 1988, pp. 36–40). Resources—mainly time, space, and money—were not readily available to these women; any networking that did occur was limited. What soap fans needed was a space where they could gather to communicate about the show, a place that was eventually found on the Internet.

Online Communities and E-Activism

Soap communities exploded online in the 1990s, most specially, rec.arts.tv.soaps (r.a.t.s.), Usenet newsgroups dedicated to soap operas. During the early 1990s, out of almost 5,000 Usenet newsgroups, r.a.t.s. ranked in the top 15 of the highest traffic groups (Baym, 1995, p. 138).

Within this virtual space, fans bonded and could engage in faster and potentially more personal communication with executives and actors. For instance, when Brian Frons took over as head of ABC Daytime in 2002, he immediately began answering fan e-mails addressed to him. On personal Web pages, actors frequently began announcing storyline information before it was released to the press, posted messages to their fans, and established forums about their on- and off-screen lives. Actors not officially tied to a board still have chosen to post to a particular site. For those who preferred to remain anonymous, the Internet provided a relatively safe way to leak news soon after it occurred, particularly crucial now because soaps tape at least 3 weeks in advance. Whereas in the early days of soaps, a death would often take the audience by surprise, an active fan on the Internet could now be alerted to story points before they took place on air. The rapid-fire release and broad transmittal of that information virtually closed the gap between action and audience response. Moreover, because more behind-the-scenes happenings were revealed in another place (and arguably more often, and in more detail) than the soap press, often by those experiencing it firsthand, fans became more aware of what went into the decision-making process—such as an actor's likeability, who stormed off the set, and the data culled from a focus group. . . .

The Internet not only enabled fans to connect more easily with one another but also, according to Connie P. Hayman (personal communication, May 3, 2004), journalist and former opinion writer for *Soap Opera Weekly*, "[Fans] were emboldened by one another." Although Sloane believes that fan feedback is most likely to be incorporated when the show is struggling with ratings, or the fans' goals overlap with the course of action planned, she believes that "fans have much more power now, and it's because of the availability of the information. [For executives], it's like having a focus group right at your fingertips on the Internet" (S. Sloane, personal communication, May 14, 2004). . . .

Method

Ien Ang (1989) argued that any examination into television viewer activity would benefit from the author revealing how she or he is connected to the participants. To understand the genesis of this study, a brief look into my own history with soap fandom is warranted. In 1998, determined to save the show I had watched for 10 years, I joined the Save *Another World* campaign, after reading online rumors suggesting the show was in danger. After connecting with

other campaign members, I quickly learned that other fans had been engaged in an organized fight to keep the show on the air since 1993. In April 1999, NBC announced that they were indeed canceling the show; the final episode aired 2 months later. Shortly thereafter, I heard from a group of online fans that *Soap Opera Digest* online was holding an essay contest titled "What *Another World* Means to Me." I entered and won, and one of my prizes was a tour of the magazine's headquarters. While there, the editors suggested I send them a résumé. Two months later, I began working at the magazine as the show editor for another Procter & Gamble (P&G) soap opera.

After working at the magazine for several years—and encountering many of the same difficulties described by Bacon-Smith (1992) and Jenkins (1992) as when a science fiction fan/writer attempts to enter the world of professional authors—I desired to get a better understanding of the *AW* campaigns and their members. To that end, I designed a questionnaire with both closed and open questions to measure attitudes about soap opera activism. I sent the survey to fans I had known and who were willing to participate, including the various campaign leaders. They, in turn, put me in touch with other former members. . . .

Analysis

As for *AW* grassroots activism, the first of four distinct yet overlapping campaigns begin in 1993, when the Seattle affiliate pulled *AW*. This sparked a regional campaign to get it back on the air, and after that goal was realized, the group grew into a national organization, one that lobbied for a quality show and put pressure on NBC and P&G when the soap's contract was up for renewal. By 1998, the campaign had morphed into the version that existed through the actual end of the show.

Post-cancellation, the group continued to evolve, first focusing on bringing *AW* back to the air, and then lobbying for particular actors to find work on other soaps. Eventually it evolved into an advocacy group for all of daytime television, but by 2002, it had officially disbanded.

Each *AW* campaign had its own leaders, and although most members wore multiple hats, responsibilities were divided (such as designation of regional media contacts). Each group maintained a Web page that contained information about current activities, and usually had a listserver that distributed news updates and courses of action for the members. Other *AW*-orientated groups often would link their pages to the campaign's site. No monies were collected from members. Generally, only one *AW* campaign existed at a time, the new campaign usually arising when a leadership change occurred.

WHY A CAMPAIGN?

The reasons respondents gave for joining a campaign, as opposed to acting on their own, echoed the theme of Montgomery's (1989) work: They believed that speaking as a group amplified their voices. One respondent observed that

> it wasn't really important to be a "part" of anything. It was just important to me to make my own voice heard. I felt it might have a greater impact coming at the same time a lot of other people were making noise, too.

Being around like-minded individuals was also viewed as a relief. Said another respondent, "It was nice to know I wasn't the only person in the universe that was upset with the-powers-that-be at NBC daytime." Sympathetic insiders, usually actors, would pass information ranging from letter-writing strategies, to the status of a show's contract negotiations, to morale on set. These insider tips provided the same essential benefits as they had to the gay lobby with regard to primetime media, and allowed the *AW* campaigns to operate from an interesting gray area—they were fans who, at many times, possessed the knowledge and skills of insiders.

The tenuous identity of fan/insider also owes its formation to the extensive online networks the campaigns had created. Of those surveyed, all but one learned of the existing *AW* movements online, and the members communicated almost exclusively via the Internet. Moreover, the anonymity of the Web afforded interested *AW* cast and crew and NBC employees to contact the group to offer advice or advance warning. Use of Web pages, discussion forums, and real-time chat allowed more seasoned activist fans to quickly educate neophytes, exchange information on behind-the-scenes happenings, and develop strategies for protest, regardless of geography.

Although the Web was the site to gather and disperse information, most activist activities were carried out offline: petitions, wearing specific ribbons, placing calls to networks, talking to reporters, and boycotting or supporting particular P&G products. Non-virtual actions were selected so that those at NBC and P&G would take the group seriously, and not chalk up this movement to a small number of disgruntled Internet fans. In this way, group members themselves fought against the anonymity of the Web to put a face on fandom; power came from identifying who one was and that he or she was a fan. Centralization of information and leadership were similarly employed in primetime movements, yet not universally seen in Web-based movements. The interlocking identities of fan and activist in this case study are salient in the current cancellation-based primetime advocacy but definitely not present throughout the history of nighttime activism.

Before the Internet, soap fans typically gathered in one of two ways, which corresponded to the way people generally watched soaps—by show (such as the *AW*–fan club luncheon) or by network (such as NBC daytime stars' charity softball games). Both types of events were network and production-company sanctioned, where the focus was not on fan interaction but on the presence of actors. Ironically, this network division may have helped mobilized *AW* fans. Since *AW*'s debut in 1964, NBC had canceled more daytime soap operas than either ABC or CBS. Notably, 9 of the respondents had experienced the cancellation of at least one other NBC soap before. Just as soap watchers decode the fictional messages and devices used to tell these particular stories (Allen, 1985), and many media fans express interest in behind-the-scenes activities (Jenkins, 1992, p. 65), activist fans learn the codes of the network, the production company, the show executives, the ratings system, and the advertiser mentality—in effect, the soap behind the soap. Fans watched what, in retrospect, became precursors to cancellation—affiliates dropping the program, low ratings, storylines departing from themes traditionally associated with the show—occuring on NBC soaps such as *The Doctors*, *Search for Tomorrow*, and *Santa Barbara*. These viewers could now better recognize the red flags when they happened to *AW*—much like what happened with primetime *Arrested Development* fans. The survey suggests that going through these prior soap cancellations created an atmosphere of tension and distrust of the network that needed only a grassroots meeting place, where like minds could gather and find empowerment for community and action. . . .

WHY GET INVOLVED IN THE MOVEMENT—ANGER

> In my opinion, NBC's refusal to acknowledge the fans was basically telling all *AW* fans, "You don't matter to us anymore."
>
> —34-year-old male respondent

Perhaps more so than with any televised medium, soap opera fan feedback has played an essential role in shaping what is seen on-screen. Audiences' impact has

ranged from influencing content (for an *AW* example, see Scodari, 1995) to helping reinstate fired actors (Hayward, 1997, p. 165). In fact, show-initiated projects have long been designed to encourage, or at least support the illusion of, fan influence. The soap media also contribute to this participatory culture, as daytime television magazines have devoted more and more space to viewer feedback (Harrington & Bielby, 1995). How often and to what extent the shows listen to the fans is debatable (Harrington & Bielby, 1995, pp. 161–165), but the precedent that fans can and do have influence has been established.

The members of the *AW* campaign were first and foremost fans of the soap, and they acted precisely because they identified as fans. All survey respondents were regular viewers of *AW* and had watched an average of 22.7 years before they joined a campaign. From their point of view, this was their program and they needed to save it. The majority of respondents (15) had contacted the show prior to their campaign involvement, to express outrage at management decisions they feared would weaken *AW* and further depress ratings. In that sense, when one joined a campaign, his or her activity was a continuation and amplification of an established means of action. Given the climate of encouraged fan response, the respondents—whether they were campaign members at the time or not—became angry that the scope of their influence often appeared very limited. Then, for executives to say, on cancellation in 1999, that *AW* was a "lost cause" was seen by these fans as a slap in the face, because they had protested the very decisions that caused the show to decline. This declaration became an undercurrent for many fans that had not joined a campaign before cancellation to now do so.

Unlike their counterparts in the primetime sphere, according to those surveyed, the *AW* campaigns were not viewed as legitimate by broadcast or advertising executives, perhaps in part because the activism was so closely tied with their members' devalued status as soap fans (Harrington & Bielby 1995, p. 112). Their supporters within the industry were not in a position of power to affect larger, industry opinion of these groups, and the campaigns were not consulted on any P&G/NBC-sanctioned level. Said one member-respondent, "NBC hated what the campaigns were doing. NBC did its best to ignore, aggravate and dissipate AW's fan base any way it could. P&G refused to defend or support its show." AW-campaign members were more often seen as the antagonists, which, as shown below, affected their notions of success.

The executives' response also initiated anger of another kind that led to membership. The network explained that the show was cancelled simply for business reasons, meaning that it was not generating enough profit to justify NBC continuing its arrangement with P&G. Soap opera profit comes indirectly from the Nielsen Ratings, which provide data to advertisers. In the advertising world, some watchers—namely American women age 18 to 49—are more valuable than others. Of the survey participants, 32% indicated that the [industry subservience to] demographics—and the fact that they, the fans, were not members of the "desired demographic"—was a factor that drove them to join an AW campaign. They had begun watching the show while in the desired age range and now, because they had continued to be loyal viewers, had aged out of that demographic.

This presents an interesting conundrum, because soap opera itself was born out of advertising. When it debuted on radio, serial fiction was not targeted to a daytime audience (i.e., women) because it was thought that housewives would not be able to fulfill their duties if distracted (Simon, 1997, p. 15). Irna Phillips melded narrative and advertising and, thus, created soap operas—drama sponsored by and tied into corporate productions (Simon, 1997, p. 18). For instance, a piece of jewelry that the listener could acquire from the sponsor would be incorporated into the script as characters

described the lovely broach (LaGuardia, 1974, p. 72). In the late 1930s, production companies, rejoicing at the windfall profit that the soaps were generating, moved their headquarters from Chicago to New York, to be at the center of the entertainment and advertising world. Soap audiences quickly became well known for their steadfast loyalty to a program, even as it suffered the inevitable creative ups and downs—an advertiser's dream come true. The close relationship between the show and its advertisers may be another reason, in this case, why soap activists relied on numbers. The success of a program is tied to how many of what kind of people watch, therefore encouraging, as these campaigns did, those who represented the "right" demographics to indicate such on their correspondence to the executives, in an attempt to counter low ratings. In other words, the movement tried to say that the ratings system was broken, because they had proof that not only did many of the right people watch, but also there was an untapped audience of males and older female viewers who had discretionary income. . . .

WHY GET INVOLVED IN THE MOVEMENT—OWNERSHIP

It was not "my" *Another World* anymore.

—40-year-old female respondent

Soaps are designed to appear as if no one author creates the text (Allen, 1985), which leads to the phenomenon Harrington and Bielby (1995) called a "moral author," meaning that a viewer feels a claim to a program, even though he or she did not create it (pp. 155–161). Add to this the incredible longevity of soap operas—because a soap may survive for years, even decades, those who are with the show the longest are often the fans. Take, for instance, that during the years the AW campaign operated, the show had six different executive producers, and 11 head writing teams. Hence, once cancellation was announced, the desire for activism became even more salient—just whose show was it to cancel?

For an American soap opera, as opposed to other forms of serial media such as Latin telenovelas, reaching the end of its run violates its structure, because one of the basic tenets of this kind of daytime drama is its resistance to narrative closure (Allen, 1985). In primetime programming, broadcasting a show's 100th episode is a celebrated event. Yet eight out of the nine current soaps have been on the air 15 years or more; the oldest debuted in 1937, and each churns out 260 episodes a year. Therefore, the pay-off for viewing is not closure but, instead, the ability to watch the next episode with a deeper understanding of the events taking place (Brown, 1994; Hayward, 1997; Modleski, 1979). If there were nothing more to see, what value would one's dedication to, and knowledge of, the show now have?

What is tricky about that question is that, in theory, there was more to see. Like all soaps, *AW*'s stories were not designed to end, a concept best illustrated when looking at a soap's final episodes (Allen, 1985; Modleski, 1979). Most canceled soaps continue to pose new questions or introduce new elements, even in their final hour. In the case of *AW*, the reappearance of a presumed dead villain in the last episode created the possibility that he would once again stir up trouble in Bay City. In this sense, the fictional universe continues to exist, but viewers have lost access to it. The cancellation of *AW* seemed to say to fans that the network and sponsor had mishandled a fully functioning universe; access to Bay City could continue or be reinstated, if only the show were in more capable hands.

Because knowledge of a show's history is deeply valued by soap fans, for reasons herein explained (see also Harrington & Bielby, 1995), an *AW* fan's years of watching no longer held the same meaning after cancellation, or after the show had, in the fan's mind, veered so far off course that it rarely referred to or built from its own history. This cultural capital of *AW* knowledge

could neither be translated into symbolic capital—for example, becoming a soap writer or television executive—nor exist in its own right, because the universe that imbued it with meaning was now gone (Seiter, 2001, p. 26). So an undercurrent to many of the participants' responses was that the campaign became a means of validating their cumulative history as fans, and a way to reinvest meaning into something that had been devalued.

WHY GET INVOLVED IN THE MOVEMENT—EXTENDING THE FAMILY

> I felt protective of the actors that were on the show, as if it was almost like a family splitting up.
>
> —29-year-old female respondent

The most cited reason the respondents gave for their activism related to their perception of the show as an extended family. This motivating factor is a reason given by soap fans for why they continue to watch (Hayward, 1997, p. 164), so it is not surprising that this becomes a point of galvanization toward activism. This concept of family does not suggest an inability to separate reality from fantasy—a task at which soap fans excel (Harrington & Bielby, 1995)—rather, it demonstrates the distinct relationship that develops between a soap opera and its viewers.

For some respondents, they felt indebted to a group of actors or a show as a whole. "I felt I owed *AW* and some of the stars my life, and I wanted to do something to honor and thank them," explained one member-respondent. For others, they did not want to sever their connection to the show, either because it was a familiar constant or because its demise would trigger another loss—one's daily habit of watching *AW* was keeping something or someone else alive. Watching over the years gives one knowledge of the show's history; the act of watching creates a history of the self—the

6-year-old who watched with her mother, the 18-year-old who watched during college, the 45-year-old who watched on her lunch break. Being a fan becomes a through-line to one's life, and joining the campaign, especially after cancellation, enabled some to extend that *AW* meta-narrative, even though the show itself was gone. One respondent observed that *AW*

> represented a different time, kept alive my relationship with my grandmother and certainly was a topic of conversation with my mom over the years. . . . Letting go was hard because it was like letting go a piece of my family.

Another respondent said,

> When I was in junior high and high school, I didn't get home until 2:30 and my grandmother used to watch it for me (pre-VCR days) and tell me everything I missed. She died in 1998, and I felt like I was losing another connection to her.

The characters, too, became as close as family members to some viewers. "Victoria Wyndham [who played Rachel] seemed like a member of my family since I was so used to seeing her face on my TV screen," explained a member-respondent.

Other Activism Experiences

THE MOVEMENT'S RESULTS

. . . . Although fan activism may have prolonged *AW*'s life, ultimately it did not save it. Despite this, 13 of the 20 respondents deemed the campaign successful. Their answers about success were the most diverse. Perceptions ranged from those who rated the campaign as extremely successful to those who felt the exact opposite, as well as every combination in between. The variety in replies may be linked to the proliferation of diverse campaign goals.

Although almost everyone agreed that the initial objective was to keep *AW* on the air, especially after cancellation, people's goals splintered and transformed into a multitude of agendas. For some, the fight was over and they had lost. For others, they were intent on reviving *AW* on another network. Some wanted to punish NBC for its decision; others wanted to segue into a fan-based advocacy group for all of daytime television.

Within this diversity, however, a strong linkage did emerge: Those who considered the campaign successful also indicated that it had a major impact on their lives. "It gave me a voice and made me feel a bit more secure in myself and my opinions," said a member-respondent. Another shared, "I found myself speaking out and expressing my feelings to people I had never met before. I'm basically a shy person and the fact that the cancellation of a soap opera was bringing this part out actually surprised me." Stated one respondent, "The campaign gave me a sense of purpose and caused me to spend less time dwelling on myself. It came at a very low point in my life and . . . showed me that I had not lost my edge."

Their involvement helped them feel empowered and allowed them to discover dormant or previously unknown skills. In addition to personal impact, most of these individuals felt that their collective actions had changed the landscape of daytime television, even if it was only temporary. As one respondent stated, "I think fans, for many programs have become more radicalized [as a result] and see the public airwaves as owned by the consumer, not the broadcast company."

Conversely, 7 respondents felt that the campaigns were not successful and/or had no impact on soaps as a whole. "I doubt anyone even cared," remarked one respondent. The common threads uniting these participants were that they tended to focus on having *AW* exist only in the form they loved (e.g., no spin-off or reruns), that their involvement decreased with time, and that they shared the belief that they were rarely, if ever, heard by the network or P&G.

The level of success also correlated to whether friendships and the sense of belonging to a community had developed out of their involvement. Of the 7 respondents who did not feel their efforts were successful, 5 reported that they made no lasting friendships because of their participation, and did not become more involved in the daytime television community. Everyone else stated that new friendships and increased ties to the community were highly valued by-products. A sentiment echoed by many is summed up in the following answer by one respondent: "I had never participated in such an activity before, and it gave me such a feeling of kinship to other viewers." The desire to be part of a large network of fans motivated many individuals to join, not realizing that the connections that developed would give new meaning to their activity and mitigate the loss of their personal relationship to the show. . . .

As for other kinds of activism, 13 respondents indicated that their *AW*-campaign involvement increased their interest in other movements, but only 4 were somehow involved in any current efforts, and all but 1 of these respondents had been politically active before getting involved in the *AW* campaigns. Why have not more participants become active activists? For some, the reason stems from the fact that they are no longer daytime television viewers; 8 respondents stopped watching soaps after the cancellation of *AW*; none watched its replacement, *Passions*. For others, their involvement soured them on any future activism. Even if they deemed the campaign successful, they came to the conclusion that fan mobilization will never be taken seriously, and the emotional roller coaster that is campaigning would not be worth it. In fact, the reason given by those respondents who no longer watch soaps was that they did not want to be emotionally invested in any program again. The loss of *AW* hit

viewers on a very personal level, and without that attachment, many would not be inspired to act because of one of the two perceptions they took with them: "You can't fight city hall" or "You can fight city hall, but it's going to take everything out of you." Therefore, an issue would have to arise that invoked a personal response that superceded the perceived toll that one's involvement would take financially and especially, emotionally.

Conclusion

This case study offers another example of the manner in which many soap fans defy the popular cultural myths about them. In this sense, soap activism is not an evolutionary step on the fan activity ladder but instead, one of many tools employed by fans who want to take action. Under other circumstances, several of the survey participants would not have been propelled to mobilize, but their connection to AW inspired them to do so. Despite numerous obstacles, many of these viewers felt, at least for a time, empowered.

Although daytime activism and primetime activism certainly share similarities—most notably the way the groups form and the various methods of protest employed—they cannot be seen as interchangeable phenomena. The reasons why daytime television fans unite are tied directly to the genre itself, and the industry response to these soap activists is nowhere near as benign or accommodating as it has been to primetime television movements. As daytime television continues to lose ratings, placing more soaps in danger of cancellation, researchers may want to look to this arena, to investigate how viewers cope with the loss of their shows. The prior presumption in daytime television programming was that if a soap was cancelled, most people would simply watch the replacement. This case study provides evidence to the contrary and suggests that there may be a relationship between the rate at which shows are canceled and declining ratings for other programs.

Also, these results point to a possible new explanation for [industry investment in] primetime television's current reality show programming—programs where viewers' influence is either minimal or very carefully prescribed. The more activist media fans become, the less programming will be developed that can be subject to their input. Soaps may be seen as an apolitical medium, enjoyed only by complacent viewers, but in actuality, daytime television provides a powerful platform for activism. What is extremely meaningful about these movements, however, is not their success or failure, but the soap opera genre's ability to create these accidental activists.

References

Allen, R. C. (1985). *Speaking of soap operas.* Chapel Hill: University of North Carolina Press.

Ang, I. (1989). Wanted: Audiences. In E. Seiter, H. Borchers, G. Kreutzner, & E. Warth (Eds.), *Remote control* (pp. 96–115). New York: Routledge.

Bacon-Smith, C. (1992). *Enterprising women.* Philadelphia: University of Pennsylvania Press.

Baym, N. K. (1995). The emergence of community in computer-mediated communication. In S. G. Jones (Ed.), *Cyber society* (pp. 138–163). Thousand Oaks, CA: Sage.

Bielby, D. D., Harrington, C. L., & Bielby, W. T. (1999). "Whose stories are they?" Fans' engagement with soap opera narratives in three sites of fan activity. *Journal of Broadcasting & Electronic Media, 43*(1), 35–52.

Brown, M. E. (1994). *Soap opera and women's talk: The pleasure of resistance.* Thousand Oaks, CA: Sage.

Cantor, M. G., & Pingree, S. (1983). *The soap opera.* Beverly Hills, CA: Sage.

Harrington, C. L., & Bielby, D. D. (1995). *Soap fans: Pursuing pleasure and making meaning in everyday life.* Philadelphia: Temple University Press.

Hayward, J. (1997). *Consuming pleasures: Active audiences and serial fictions from Dickens to soap opera.* Lexington: University Press of Kentucky.

Jenkins, H. (1992). *Textual poachers: Television fans and participatory culture.* New York: Routledge.

LaGuardia, R. (1974). *The wonderful world of TV soap operas.* New York: Ballantine Books.

Lynch, R. (2001). *Fan history book of the 1960s.* Retrieved August 2, 2004, from http://www.jophan.org/1960s/

Matelski, M. (1988). *The soap opera evolution: America's enduring romance with daytime drama.* Jefferson, NC: McFarland & Company.

Modleski, T. (1979). The search for tomorrow in today's soap operas. *Film Quarterly, 33*(1), 12–21.

Montgomery, K. C. (1989). *Target: Primetime.* New York: Oxford University Press.

Schemering, C. (1987). *The soap opera encyclopedia.* New York: Ballantine.

Scodari, C. (1995, May). *He's May. She's September, but are they both from* Another World? *Mass media, soap opera and the older woman/younger man taboo.* Paper presented at the International Communication Association Conference, Albuquerque, NM.

Seiter, E. (2001). *Television and new media audiences.* Oxford, UK: Oxford University Press.

Simon, R. (1997). Serial seduction: Living in other worlds. In *Worlds without end: The art and history of soap opera* (pp. 11–39). New York: Museum of Television and Radio.

Insiders-Outsiders

Dr. Laura and the Contest for Cultural Authority in LGBT Media Activism

Vincent Doyle

I n April 1999, Paramount Domestic Television, a subsidiary of Viacom, signed the popular radio talk show host Laura Schlessinger, also known as Dr. Laura, to develop a new television talk show. The deal, reportedly worth $3 million to Schlessinger personally, represented a $76 million investment for Paramount, making it the most expensive new show in the studio's history. With 20 million weekly listeners and 3 million books in print, Schlessinger, known for haranguing her callers with moralistic invective, was riding a big wave of popularity. This made her extremely attractive to Paramount executives who hoped she would deliver a built-in audience for her show in the crowded afternoon television market. Within a few months of the announcement, without so much as a pilot or preview tape, Paramount had sold the new program to CBS and UPN local affiliates covering 90 percent of the U.S. television market.

The Gay and Lesbian Alliance Against Defamation (GLAAD), meanwhile, had been monitoring Schlessinger's radio program since 1997 as the result of complaints about her use of antigay rhetoric. GLAAD has a mandate to "promote and ensure fair, accurate and inclusive representation of individuals and events in all media as a means of eliminating homophobia and discrimination based on gender identity and sexual orientation" (GLAAD 2004). With an annual budget [in 2004] of about $6 million and a staff of about forty, GLAAD is one of the principal gay and lesbian movement organizations in the United States. . . .

This chapter begins from the claim by gay journalist and activist Michelangelo Signorile that the tactics GLAAD employed in its *Dr. Laura* campaign are evidence that the organization has overinvested in professionalization. GLAAD, he charged, has gone too far in the direction of Hollywood insider, lost touch with its gay and lesbian constituency, and

From Doyle, V. (2007). Insiders-outsiders: Dr. Laura and the contest for cultural authority in LGBT media activism. In K. G. Barnhurst (Ed.), *Media/queered: Visibility and its discontents* (pp. 107–126). New York: Lang.

compromised its ability to "apply pressure from the outside when needed" (Signorile 2000, 31). In contrast to his criticism of GLAAD, Signorile has championed an ad hoc group of gay and lesbian activists called StopDrLaura.com (SDL), which he called "one of the most impressive weapons in the American lesbian and gay activism arsenal" (29). More confrontational in its tactics, SDL made creative use of the internet to recruit and mobilize its constituency, to coordinate street protests and other forms of direct action, and to apply pressure on Schlessinger's corporate backers.

Based on ethnographic and archival fieldwork conducted in the New York and Los Angeles offices of GLAAD between January 2000 and June 2001, my account of the Schlessinger campaign supports many aspects of Signorile's critique of GLAAD but takes a wider view. The evidence argues against framing the success of the campaign too simply (and romantically) as the triumph of outsiders and their confrontational tactics over insiders and their polite politics. GLAAD and SDL are constituent parts of a common field of relations, and my aim is to describe the anti-Schlessinger campaign by incorporating some of the subtlety missing from Signorile's highly partisan reporting, and from the gay and lesbian press more generally. GLAAD leaders had complex motivations and faced difficult dilemmas in the struggle to reconcile their personal, professional, and institutional investments with their obligation to represent an LGBT constituency. This chapter asks what viewing the Schlessinger campaign as a competition for cultural authority among professionalized activists can reveal about the possibilities and limits of gay and lesbian media activism in the current cultural climate.

Insiders

From its grassroots beginnings in the mid-1980s, GLAAD has become a national organization controlled by a board of directors and staffed, in many cases, by skilled professionals who hail from corporate media and public relations. Before taking the top GLAAD job, Joan Garry was an executive at Showtime Networks, which is, like Paramount, part of the Viacom media empire. Before that, she was among the executives who launched MTV, also a Viacom subsidiary. Scott Seomin, the GLAAD director of entertainment media, had been a producer at *Entertainment Tonight,* a property of Paramount Domestic Television. Steve Spurgeon, the GLAAD director of communications at the time of the Schlessinger campaign, had been a vice president at one of the top public relations firms in the United States. Keven Bellows, Laura Schlessinger's head of public relations, had once been his boss.

In October 1999, Garry gave a speech to the gay and lesbian employee group at Bell Atlantic, in which she described herself as someone from a corporate background who, until she came to GLAAD, "did not consider myself political at all" (1999, n.p.). She said, "My activism was all about my family." As a partnered lesbian with kids living in the New Jersey suburbs, she told her audience, she brought a unique ability to put herself "in the other guys' shoes." She went on to describe her sense of how GLAAD evolved:

> Things have changed in fifteen years. We've made solid progress culturally. . . . And as a result of that progress, GLAAD's strategies have changed. Today I see our work is largely . . . about building relationships and much about education.

In a key section of the speech, Garry invited her audience of corporate managers and executives to "revisit the images we conjure up when we consider the word 'activist'" (1999, n.p.). Activism, she said, is no longer just the "direct action methods" that "helped create a picture for America of a gay rights activist." Referring to the early years at GLAAD, she said, "Back then, no one was paying any attention, and the only strategy that made any sense was of the 'in your face' variety," a mode of activism she compared to banging on the door. "Their job," she said, "was simply to be heard and to do what they could . . . to get that door open." The new professional activism, by contrast, is about building relationships and about education, Garry said. Her comments imply a shift in the ground of advocacy, away from the unruliness of the street and toward the businesslike efficiency of the boardroom. . . .

Although the new professional breed at GLAAD sometimes acknowledged their lack of prior involvement in the movement as a limitation, they pointed to their professional skills and connections as compensation. Steve Spurgeon, for example, told me in an interview that the movement now requires persons who have what he called a "sophisticated understanding of how the world works," a product of extensive corporate experience like his own. When he interviewed for the post of GLAAD director of communications, he said, someone with a long history of movement activism told him that they could not picture him "chained to the fence in front of the *New York Times*." He replied, "Why would I chain myself, when I can just call them up for meeting?" (2000, n.p.).

So it was that, when Schlessinger began spouting antigay rhetoric in 1997, referring to homosexuality in a syndicated column as a "biological faux pas," and to gay and lesbian parenting as a lesser form of child rearing ("Heterosexual Families Are Best for Kids," *Montreal Gazette,* 25 May 1997, D-6), Joan Garry called her up for a meeting. Schlessinger agreed, and discussions ensued. Afterward, GLAAD staff kept up their monitoring of the program. In August 1998, Schlessinger announced on air that she was officially changing her position on homosexuality, but not in the direction GLAAD leaders were hoping for; "I've always told people who opposed homosexuality that they were homophobic, bad, bigoted, and idiotic," she said. "I was wrong. It *is* destructive" (Premiere Radio Networks, n.p.).

In response, Garry asked for a second meeting, noting in a letter to Schlessinger that "your words about our community reaching 20 million people have become stronger and infinitely more damaging" (Garry 1998, n.p.). On March 10, 1999, Schlessinger and Garry met for a second time. Afterward, in a newsletter distributed to her fans, Schlessinger went out of her way to characterize the encounter as a "reasonable dialogue" between individuals who "respect each other personally" (1999, 2). Garry, she wrote,

is a thoughtful, intelligent woman with a good sense of humor (I love those!), and she is the first gay activist I've ever come across who actually takes the time to try and understand my positions. . . . As you might expect, we have a lot of differences. As you might not expect, we were also delighted to find some common ground. (2)

For Schlessinger, framing the dialogue in this way made it seem as though her perspectives on homosexuality are matters about which reasonable persons living in a pluralist society might expect to disagree. And, surprisingly, for the leader of a national gay and lesbian rights organization, Garry appeared eager to go along with this genteel framing of the encounter. According to a jointly produced transcript of the discussion, Garry told Schlessinger:

I think that we do need to engage people more in a conversation. . . . I think . . . that we are beyond the place in society where I stand on one side of the line and I shout and I scream and I wave my finger. I think I have to go across the line to the people who disagree and understand them. (GLAAD/Premiere Radio Networks 1999, n.p.)

Garry clearly hoped that this act of conciliation might lead Schlessinger to understand *her* and to realize that gays and lesbians are not so different or deviant after all. With tears welling up, she said, "I'm not here as an activist. I mean, I'm an activist because of my kids" (GLAAD/Premiere Radio Networks 1999, n.p.). Here, Schlessinger erupted, scoffing at the notion that the executive director of a national gay and lesbian organization was meeting her simply on behalf of her kids:

> Okay, if you're not here today as an activist, then let's go shopping and be friends. Because I don't need this crap. You're here as an activist and we're discussing my position. If you are here as my friend, let's go eat. I don't want to do this. I don't want to be sitting and having you cry.

Throughout the meeting, Garry tried to personalize the issues, downplay her role as an activist, and assert a common humanity with Schlessinger based on a shared sense of the importance of family. But the problem was neither Schlessinger's lack of personal acquaintance with gays and lesbians—she said during the encounter that she counts gay men among her colleagues and family—nor a disbelief that Garry could be a good parent to her children. The problem was the public position Schlessinger had taken on homosexuality. The position derived from a toxic and ideologically powerful mix of biological determinism (homosexuality as biologically disordered, a biological error or faux pas) and religious absolutism (acting on one's disordered impulses as immoral, because the Bible says so). To hold a polite meeting with a person holding such a position, let alone *two* meetings, lent Schlessinger legitimacy and may have contributed to her sense that she could not only get away with it but also likely profit from it.

Instead of toning down her rhetoric, Schlessinger followed the meeting with another public escalation. Emboldened by her deal with Paramount, signed in April, Schlessinger treated her listeners to this monologue on June 9, 1999:

Rights. Rights! Rights? For sexual deviant . . . sexual behavior there are now rights. That's what I'm worried about, with the pedophilia and the bestiality and the sadomasochism and the cross-dressing. Is this all going to be rights too, to deviant sexual behavior? It's deviant sexual behavior. (Premiere Radio Networks 1999a, n.p.)

Then, on June 22, 1999, Schlessinger said,

> If you folks don't start standing up for heterosexual marriage and heterosexuality pretty soon, that which you know as this country and family is going to be gone. . . . That men have to have sex with men is not something to celebrate. It's a sadness. It is a sadness, and there are therapies which have been successful in helping a reasonable number of people become heterosexual. (Premiere Radio Networks 1999b, n.p.)

The boldness of that rhetoric, combined with the prospect of having it reach a wider television audience, set off alarm bells. In the estimation of the GLAAD leaders, Schlessinger had become the most dangerous homophobe in the nation, and it was now time to mount a campaign to oppose her.

Introduced as the new GLAAD director of communications at a board meeting in September 1999, Steve Spurgeon presented a Schlessinger campaign plan defining its primary goal as to "stem the escalating influence of Dr. Laura Schlessinger's homophobic advocacy" (1999, n.p.). What he proposed was a public relations effort to counter Schlessinger's messages in the media. The ability of GLAAD to become visible with its opposing messages, he hoped, would persuade Paramount to regulate Schlessinger. The more high-profile media exposure GLAAD could get, the more influence it could hope to have with Paramount in private meetings. The only role imagined for the GLAAD membership was to monitor the local coverage of the campaign and respond with letters to the editor.

Shortly after Paramount announced its deal with Schlessinger, GLAAD staff requested to meet with top Paramount executives. They agreed to the meeting in principle but did not schedule it right away. In preparation for that eventual meeting, Steve Spurgeon and Scott Seomin of GLAAD held an informal lunch, in August 1999, with two Paramount media relations executives, one of them an openly gay man by the name of John Wentworth. In an interview I conducted with the entire GLAAD communications team, Seomin said the objective of the meeting was to get the message across to Paramount that they had bought themselves trouble by signing Schlessinger. The Paramount executives, however, did not react as Seomin and Spurgeon had hoped. As Seomin explained, "I believe he just felt that he did his job, so he could say, 'Well, I had lunch with the guys at GLAAD so I could hear them out'" (2000, n.p.). . . .

Seomin approached Brian Lowry, the *L.A. Times* television columnist, who published an article on January 11, 2000, describing GLAAD concerns about Schlessinger and the reactions of some gay employees at Paramount. Lowry quotes openly gay *Frasier* writer and Paramount employee Joe Keenan:

> What gay person working for Paramount could be happy about this? . . . We feel the way the Von Trapp children would feel if Dad decided to divorce Maria and marry Joan Crawford. She's not a happy addition to the family. ("Dr. Laura: All Is Fair in Syndication," F-1)

Interest in the campaign among the media exploded. GLAAD communications staffer Sean Lund told me that he sent out about 150 press kits in the two months following the publication of Lowry's article. And, ironically, many of the reporters requesting information were the same ones from the LGBT media who had little interest in the story when the GLAAD communications staff had approached them a few months earlier.

All the media attention had another desired effect: Paramount finally scheduled its top-level meeting with GLAAD. . . . The meeting, however, produced only *private* assurances from Paramount that Schlessinger's views on homosexuality would not go unopposed and that discussions of homosexuality would cite credible research. A joint public statement issued after the meeting characterized it as "a positive exchange of differing perspectives." Although it said that "the dialogue with Paramount executives is expected to continue," the statement gave no indication of when further discussions might take place. Schlessinger's program, it said in the vaguest of terms, would "vary from Dr. Laura's successful radio show" and offer "many points of view, derived from a variety of sources, guests, and a studio audience" (quoted in Joyce Howard Price, "Dr. Laura to Offer 'Many Points of View' on Homosexuals," *Washington Times,* 17 February 2000, A-9). Beyond this statement, the parties agreed not to discuss the specifics of the meeting in the media.

The statement, lukewarm as it was, created a stir in conservative circles. Responding to concerns that Schlessinger and Paramount might have caved into pressure from GLAAD, a spokeswoman for Schlessinger told the conservative *Washington Times,* "It's not true that Dr. Laura capitulated to anyone or anything . . . that's totally wrong" (Joyce Howard Price, "Dr. Laura to Offer 'Many Points of View' on Homosexuals," 17 February 2000, A-9). The article also quoted an unidentified spokesperson for Schlessinger, breaking the agreement not to discuss the meeting with the media, saying that she had retained total control over content. The statements by Schlessinger's public relations team left the GLAAD leadership in an embarrassing position, appearing as though its insider efforts were not bearing fruit. Its strategy compromised, the organization soon found itself under attack from within the gay and lesbian community.

Outsiders

A few days after the meeting with Paramount executives, gay journalist and activist Michelangelo Signorile interviewed Joan Garry on an internet radio show. Conceding the point that meeting with Schlessinger directly had not produced the desired toning down of rhetoric, Garry spent much of the interview defending the GLAAD strategy, which was still "to work with Paramount to make sure that they create a balanced show" (Garry 2000a, n.p.). Signorile, in his characteristically aggressive style, criticized this strategy as corporate because it consisted of meeting behind closed doors and asking only for balance, instead of calling for Paramount to cancel the show as a matter of principle. He questioned the motives behind the unwillingness at GLAAD to call on the community to put direct pressure on Paramount, implying that the strategy appeared designed to keep GLAAD in the good graces of Paramount. By repeatedly invoking the importance of holding on to what she called GLAAD's place at the table, Garry did little to dispel this impression. The organization had never before enjoyed such a level of access, Garry argued, and GLAAD still had an opportunity to use that access to persuade Paramount to control Schlessinger's speech.

A few days after the confrontational interview, an e-mail message from an unidentified source began circulating on the internet. It opened with three simple words and as many exclamation points: STOP DR. LAURA!!! It expressed its straightforward call to action in all capital letters, the internet equivalent of shouting: E-MAIL PARAMOUNT NOW AND DEMAND DR. LAURA BE DROPPED. Designed to

get gays and lesbians everywhere riled up, the message spread like wildfire.

On February 28, 2000, GLAAD leaders responded with "A Letter from GLAAD Executive Director Joan M. Garry." It began by acknowledging criticism within the community of how GLAAD had handled the campaign: "During the last two weeks, some of you have expressed concern about GLAAD's recent work concerning Dr. Laura Schlessinger and her move to television. Although some of this criticism has been hard to hear, we know how important it is to listen. And we've been listening" (Garry 2000b, n.p.).

At the end of the letter, Garry informed her readers that GLAAD had sent a letter to Paramount requesting a second meeting within seven days and a written assurance "that Paramount has a zero tolerance for defamation directed at the gay and lesbian community" (Garry 2000b, n.p.). Failing that, Garry wrote, GLAAD would "call on Paramount to pull the plug on Dr. Laura." And, for the first time since the campaign began, Garry called on the GLAAD membership to "put pressure on Paramount" by writing letters to its chairman.

The next day, GLAAD published full-page ads in two entertainment industry trade publications, *The Hollywood Reporter* (29 February 2000, 20) and *Daily Variety* (29 February 2000, 89). The top of the ad read, "Dr. Laura says: 'I have never made an anti-gay commentary,'" followed by the words, "Oh, really?" and four verbatim excerpts from Schlessinger's radio program. Meant for media professionals, the ad aimed to create pressure from the inside—from within Paramount and elsewhere in the media industry—and to embarrass Paramount executives.

For the ad hoc coalition of activists who had disseminated the Stop Dr. Laura e-mail message, the response from GLAAD leaders came as too little, too late. On March 1, 2000, they launched StopDrLaura.com, a web site that also gave the coalition its name. The SDL founders took the stand that calling for anything less than the cancellation of the program amounted to a capitulation to an unacceptable double standard. No television studio would give a platform to an avowedly racist or anti-Semitic host. So why give an unrepentant homophobe a national talk show? The response to this way of framing the issue was immediate and overwhelming: Within three days of going online, with the help of high-profile media coverage, the site logged more than a million hits.

The SDL home page, under the heading, "StopDrLaura: A Coalition Against Hate," featured a close-up photograph of Schlessinger, doctored to appear as if lit from a low angle, making her look like the caricature of an evil harridan. To the right of her face, the site designers added a scrolling list of some of her most infamous quotes about homosexuality. Designed as the hub of a grassroots mobilization effort, the SDL web site invited visitors to organize and attend demonstrations, as well as to flood Paramount and Viacom executives with telephone calls, faxes, and e-mail messages. Adopting aggressive tactics from the beginning, SDL listed the direct numbers and electronic addresses of key executives, with the goal of overwhelming their communication systems. Within a day of this information being posted on the web site, SDL reported, a senior Paramount executive had changed his number, and the studio had temporarily shut off all but the internal portion of its e-mail system. . . .

The Paramount response came in the form of two statements issued on March 10, 2000. The first, by Schlessinger, said, "I never intend to hurt anyone or contribute in any way to an atmosphere of hate or intolerance. Regrettably, some of the words I've used have hurt some people, and I am sorry for that" (Schlessinger 2000, n.p.). The second statement, by Paramount, affirmed "a commitment to present society's issues without creating or contributing to an environment of hurt, hate, or intolerance" (Paramount Television Group 2000, n.p.).

Was this akin to the statement of zero tolerance for which GLAAD had asked?

SDL leaders dismissed the statements as halfhearted and announced a major protest in front of the Paramount gates on March 21, 2000. The GLAAD leadership, by contrast, reacted with carefully worded optimism:

> GLAAD welcomes Schlessinger's new public commitment to conduct her self-proclaimed moral and ethical advocacy in an environment free from hate and intolerance. We will be listening to and watching her current and upcoming radio and television broadcasts to be sure she is true to her word. (GLAAD 2000a, n.p.)

It did not take long, however, for Schlessinger's apology, such as it was, to fall apart completely. On March 15, 2000, a column by conservative columnist Don Feder in the *Boston Herald* quoted her saying that her statement was a clarification, and not an apology. Feder wrote, "She will continue to recommend reparative therapy (for homosexuals who want to change), to oppose same-sex marriage and adoption, and [to] champion Judeo-Christian sexual ethics" ("Sham from GLAAD Won't Fly on Main St.," 33).

Sixteen days had passed since GLAAD had issued a seven-day ultimatum—and without a second meeting with Paramount executives. What was worse, the statements by Schlessinger and Paramount seemed little more than evasive rhetorical maneuvers now that Schlessinger had recanted her apology. Without much hope left for a continuing dialogue with Paramount, the GLAAD leadership issued this statement:

> GLAAD now has no assurance that Schlessinger will not publicly defame lesbians and gay men in her radio or upcoming television broadcasts. . . . GLAAD now calls upon Paramount to . . . [abandon] its plans to produce and

distribute any program featuring Laura Schlessinger. (GLAAD 2000b, n.p.)

With the announcement that GLAAD would join SDL in front of the Paramount gates, the Schlessinger campaign entered a new stage that had GLAAD engaging in public protest for the first time since 1995. The campaign would continue, but its tactics would shift to a wider set of targets: television critics, local UPN and CBS affiliates, and the advertisers planning to buy air time on the program. . . .

In the months that followed, SDL efforts, combined with those of a more assertive GLAAD, spelled disaster for Schlessinger's television debut. The turning point came with the early defection of household goods giant Procter & Gamble, which came under intense pressure from GLAAD and SDL the moment it announced its intention to sponsor the *Dr. Laura* program. The web sites of both organizations were quick to list contact information for the companies that remained, many of which dropped their advertising within a matter of days, after e-mail messages and phone calls overwhelmed them. Through its web site, SDL also coordinated protests of local CBS or UPN affiliates in thirty-four cities in the United States and Canada, while GLAAD helped local organizations obtain meetings with station managers and, through its web site, provided resources to local activists for monitoring and responding to local coverage of the controversy.

On the heels of the Procter & Gamble decision not to advertise on *Dr. Laura,* GLAAD launched an aggressive and high-profile advertising campaign. At a cost of $200,000, it bought full-page ads in the *New York Times* (24 May 2000, C-5) and the *Los Angeles Times* (24 May 2000, C-7) to appear on the Wednesday before Memorial Day weekend. Under the title, "Ad Time with *Dr. Laura* Is for Sale. Here's What You're Buying," the ad argued that

Laura Schlessinger has angry and hurtful things to say about all kinds of Americans. Many advertisers don't realize how alienating her program has become. Consumers judge brands by the company they keep. Aren't there better ways to reach women 18-49, or anyone else?

The last sentence, in bold, read, "*Dr. Laura.* We don't buy it." Targeted at media buyers (individuals who make decisions about where to place advertising), the ad ran a second time the following week in major trade publications (*Advertising Age* 29 May 2000, 91; *Adweek,* 29 May 2000, 83; and *Broadcasting and Cable,* 29 May 2000, 25; *Daily Variety,* 30 May 2000, 31), so that it would confront decision makers again upon their return from the long weekend.

The visibility of this ad campaign also helped the GLAAD communications team generate high-profile mainstream media exposure in the months that followed. The esteemed PBS *News Hour* featured a fifteen-minute debate (15 June 2000). Spurgeon and Garry secured a full-page opinion piece in *Time* magazine as a rebuttal to an interview they considered overly deferential toward Schlessinger (17 July 2000, 14). Spurgeon also worked with the producers of the NBC *Today* show on what became a seven-minute segment devoting exceptionally long coverage to the Schlessinger controversy (8 September 2000). All the media attention to the controversy, from the GLAAD perspective, amplified the message in the ad, that buying *Dr. Laura* was a bad business decision. . . .

It did not hurt the activists' cause that Schlessinger's program premiered to weak ratings and universally terrible reviews, almost all of which made some reference to the controversy over her views on homosexuality. Seomin, at GLAAD, helped plant the seeds for this critical drubbing when he attended the Television Critics Association conference the previous July, and distributed the GLAAD *Dr. Laura* media kit to more than fifty critics. In a widely syndicated September 15, 2000, review for the *Washington Post*, Tom Shales described the situation as "A Case of the Creeps: *Dr. Laura* on UPN Looks Better on Radio," (2000, C-l). The review made clear that Schlessinger's public image had taken a dramatic turn for the worse.

After just two weeks on the air, amid declining ratings and an unmistakable advertiser exodus, Paramount announced that it was stopping production of the show for retooling. Then, on October 4, 2000, four Canadian television stations announced that they were dropping the show. . . .

The death knell of the *Dr. Laura* program began resounding loudly during the November sweeps period, when affiliates in many large cities began shifting the program to time slots in the wee hours of the morning. Other affiliates soon followed suit, prompting Spurgeon to joke around the office that Schlessinger had expanded her audience to "breast-feeding mothers and insomniacs." Lowry reported, in the *Los Angeles Times* on December 6, 2000, that, since her move to late night in that market, Schlessinger had averaged a 0.6 share or a mere 30,000 viewers ("It Must Be the Neighbors Who Watch These Shows," F-l). By then, the only advertising left on the program was an odd assortment of supposedly exclusive television offers (for such gadgets as talking beer openers), Anne Murray CDs (which is ironic, given her lesbian following), psychic hot lines, and other so-called remainder ads that run only when no other advertisers will buy time at regular rates.

Reporter Melissa Grego wrote in a December issue of *Variety* that the *Dr. Laura* television show was a case study in "how to fail in syndicated television." She attributed the show's dismal showing to a "toxic mix of protesters' rancor, advertisers' anxiety, and Paramount's misguided spending." The most expensive new show in Paramount history had become its most disastrous failure, incurring "a loss said to be in the

seven-figure range" (Grego 2000, 1). Finally, on March 29, 2001, Schlessinger taped the last episode of her first television season. The next day, having fulfilled its contractual obligation to produce one full season of *Dr. Laura*, Paramount quietly announced it was canceling the program.

Any Number Can Play

Although the program had been on the air only a few weeks, it was already clear by the September 2000 GLAAD board meeting that *Dr. Laura* would not last beyond a first season. "When do we claim victory?" Spurgeon asked the board. "I would hate," he said, "for this whole thing to be summarized by . . . StopDrLaura.com." By the end of October 2000, John Aravosis of SDL would claim in the *New Republic* that no "matter when Schlessinger's TV show is finally canceled . . . StopDrLaura.com has already won" (2000, n.p.). Then, on January 17, 2001, he posted an article entitled, "We Stopped Dr. Laura," to a widely read internet newsgroup, announcing that the SDL site had shut down, even though, he said, "Dr. Laura's television show is still on the air in many U.S. markets, and Paramount has yet to announce that the show won't be coming hack next fall" (Aravosis 2001, n.p.).

The group that had called itself Stop Dr. Laura, and set itself up in opposition to the perceived willingness of GLAAD, in the words of SDL, to allow a known bigot to host a television show, was now claiming victory in terms reminiscent of the initial GLAAD campaign objective. SDL has already won, Aravosis wrote, because "we've gotten Schlessinger to tone down her anti-gay rhetoric" (2000, n.p.). The claim left GLAAD leaders with little choice but to occupy the space left by the abrupt departure of SDL, and to wait for the actual cancellation of Schlessinger's television program before it could declare *Dr. Laura* truly stopped. By then, exhausted GLAAD staffers had been feeling for months that, as Spurgeon told the GLAAD board of directors, StopDrLaura .com was actually StopGLAAD.com. . . .

In contrast to what they saw as the competitive SDL framing of the campaign, GLAAD leaders sought to affirm an "any number can play" view of movement politics (the phrase is Spurgeon's). In response to an internet newsgroup posting by Aravosis, for example, Garry wrote, "For our movement to have different dimensions, I don't believe we all should see and do things the same way. Working to combat Schlessinger has taught me that there is room here and a need for a variety of tactics and objectives" (2000c, n.p.).

Her statement of tactical pluralism might appear benign, but it betrays a limited picture of media activism as a level playing field, and of SDL as solely responsible for making the campaign competitive. Just as simplistic, or perhaps disingenuous, is the tendency in gay and lesbian press accounts to cast SDL as the outsiders who won the campaign on behalf of a grassroots constituency. Signorile suggested as much when he wrote on Gay.com that "the majority of thanks and congratulations need to go to the activists in StopDrLaura .com who weren't paid for their efforts, and who showed us all just how powerful we could be" (2001, n.p.). SDL efforts undeniably provided valuable opportunities for unaffiliated individuals to participate in the campaign, but the fact that SDL leaders did not get paid for their efforts does not, by itself, make them outsiders.

Whether directly or not, the leaders stood to benefit professionally from the Schlessinger campaign. SDL cofounder William Waybourn is a former GLAAD executive director who now owns Window Media, the largest group of gay and lesbian newspapers in the United States. (The LGBT press benefited from an ongoing story and rousing victory.) Another SDL founder, Alan Klein, is a public relations executive and a former GLAAD director of communications.

(The success of the campaign added to his resume.) Aravosis, the SDL web guru, is president of an internet consulting group that develops web-based strategies for non-profit organizations. (SDL gave him national prominence.) The other SDL founders were a television producer and public relations consultant, respectively. (SDL expanded their claim to professional expertise.)

Although SDL emphasized that most of its funding came from t-shirt sales, more than 25 percent of its $18,000 operating budget came from a grant by the Human Rights Campaign, the largest gay and lesbian rights organization in the United States—and arguably the most oriented to insiders. In sum, the outsiders in the Schlessinger campaign were not really outsiders at all but professionals, cut from the same cloth, who, using the internet in novel ways, stitched themselves into a competing banner (Henderson 2003).

Understanding the campaign as a contest for cultural authority among professionalized activists better recognizes the possibilities, limits, and power relations of gay and lesbian media activism as it exists today. Despite an indisputable room "for a variety of tactics and objectives" (2000c, n.p.) in media activism, as Garry pointed out in her response to Aravosis, the extent of network power to "disarm, contain, and control" advocacy groups constrains this tactical range (Montgomery 1989, 54), because the system is not of the activists' own making. It is the historical product of network strategies designed to channel grievances into manageable forms. In this system, as Thomas Streeter has argued, "not everyone is heard from, not all arguments are heard, and, even among those who do get a hearing, the power to influence the process is not evenly distributed" (2000, 80).

Getting heard at all requires the skills and connections that GLAAD and SDL possessed and ways of framing arguments that do not question the structural inequality at the heart of media activism—that large corporations can decide what to broadcast on the public airwaves, usually in the interest of profit. The system has, since the mid-1970s, offered limited opportunities for democratic participation, ranging from the cooperative to the moderately confrontational. It falls to those who possess the professional skills and connections necessary for functioning effectively within the system to select tactics from the available range, and to compete for the cultural authority to wield limited kinds of power and influence.

Confronted with the potential threat of being supplanted, GLAAD leaders took steps to secure their position. GLAAD became more like SDL in the process, even as SDL became more like GLAAD in declaring victory based on toning down Schlessinger's rhetoric. The two organizations appeared so similar in the end, because they were not so different to begin with, in large part because they held similar strategic objectives and possibilities for action. As significant as their victory was in defeating a homophobic media personality, it should not be mistaken for long-term structural change in the war to defeat media homophobia.

References

Aravosis, John. 2000. "StopDrLaura.Com." *New Republic*, 23 October. Available at http://www.wiredstrategies.com/tnr_sdl.htrn. Accessed 29 February 2004.

———. 2001. "We Stopped Dr. Laura." Soc.motss newsgroup, 17 January. Available at news:soc.motss. Accessed 17 January 2001.

Garry, Joan. 1998. Letter to Laura Schlessinger, 14 August.

———. 1999. Speech to Gay and Lesbian Bell Atlantic Employees (Globe), 15 October.

———. 2000a. Interview by Michelangelo Signorile. *The Signorile Show*, GAYBC Radio Network, 19 February.

———. 2000b. "A Letter From Glaad Executive Director Joan M. Garry on Glaad and Dr. Laura." E-mail posted on the Glaad listserv, 28 February. Accessed 28 February 2000.

———. 2000c. "Activism and Criticism." Posted on the soc.motss newsgroup, 13 September. Available at news:soc.motss. Accessed 13 September 2000.

Glaad. 2000a. "Statement by the Gay & Lesbian Alliance Against Defamation (Glaad) Regarding Laura Schlessinger." Glaad.org, 10 March. Available at http://www.glaad.org/publications/resource_doc_detail.php?id=2830&. Accessed 25 February 2004.

———. 2000b. "Glaad Calls on Paramount to Terminate Relationship with Laura Schlessinger; Move Comes after Schlessinger Recants Apology" Glaad.org, 15 March. Available at http://www.glaad.org/publications/resource_doc_detail.php?id=2830& Accessed 25 February 2004.

———. 2004 "About Glaad." Glaad.org. Available at http://www.glaad.org/about/index.php. Accessed 25 February 2004.

Glaad Communication Team. 2000. Interview with the author, Los Angeles, 6 November.

Glaad/Premiere Radio Networks. 1999. Transcript of meeting between Joan Garry and Laura Schlessinger, 10 March.

Grego, Melissa. 2000. *"TV's Gay Pride Parade."* *Variety*, 11-17 December, 1.

Henderson, Lisa. 2003. Personal correspondence with the author, 30 June.

Montgomery, Kathryn C. 1989. *Target, Prime Time: Advocacy Groups and the Struggle over Entertainment Television*. New York: Oxford University Press.

Paramount Television Group. 2000. "Following Is a Statement Released Today by the Paramount Television Group Regarding Dr. Laura Schlessinger." Glaad.org, 10 March. Available at http://www.glaad.org/publications/resource_doc_detail.php?id=2830& Accessed 25 February.

Premiere Radio Networks. 1998. *Dr. Laura*. Transcript, 13 August. Available at http://www.glaad.org/publications/resource_doc_detail.php?id=2856& Accessed 23 February 2004.

———. 1999a. *Dr. Laura*. Transcript, 9 June. Available at http://www.glaad.org/publications/

resource_doc_detail.php?id=2850&. Accessed 23 February 2004.

———. 1999b. *Dr. Laura*. Transcript, 22 June. Available at http://www.glaad.org/publications/resource_doc_detail.php?id=2847& Accessed 23 February 2004.

Schlessinger, Laura. 1999. "I'm Accused of Being Too Hostile and Too Soft!" *Dr. Laura Perspective*, August, 2.

———. 2000. "Statement by Dr. Laura Schlessinger." Glaad.org, 10 March. Available at http://www.glaad.org/publications/resource_doc_detail.php?id=2830& Accessed 25 February 2004.

Signorile, Michelangelo. 2000. "Takin' It to the Streets." *Advocate*, 9 May, 29–31.

———. 2001. "The Fall of *Dr. Laura* and the Rise of Internet Activism." Gay.com, 4 April. Available at www.gay.com Accessed 5 April 2001.

Spurgeon, Steve. 2000. Interview with the author, Los Angeles, 6 November.

Streeter, Thomas. 2000. "What Is an Advocacy Group, Anyway?" In *Advocacy Groups and the Entertainment Industry*, 77–84. Ed. Michael Suman, Gabriel Rossman & UCLA Center for Communication Policy. Westport, CT: Praeger.

ALTERNATIVE CONTENTS INDEX

Note: Identified by Part and Chapter Number.

A LIST OF RESOURCES AND MEDIA ACTIVIST ORGANIZATIONS

For fuller descriptions, see organizational websites.

ABOUT FACE

About Face equips women and girls with tools to understand and resist harmful media messages that affect their self-esteem and body image.

ACTION COALITION FOR MEDIA EDUCATION (ACME)

Free of any funding from Big Media, ACME is an emerging global coalition run by and for media educators, a network whose mission is teaching media education knowledge and skills, supporting media reform and democratizing our media system through education and activism.

ADBUSTERS MEDIA FOUNDATION & MAGAZINE

Adbusters is a global network of artists, activists, writers, pranksters, students, educators, and entrepreneurs who want to advance the new social activist movement of the information age.

Adbusters Media Foundation publishes *Adbusters* magazine, operates a website, and offers its creative services through PowerShift, its advocacy advertising agency.

ADIOS BARBIE! A BODY IMAGE SITE FOR EVERYONE

Their mission is to promote healthy body image and self-image for people of all cultures and sizes. Adios Barbie is dedicated to giving you

♦ 617

the tools and inspiration to love yourself through thick and thin.

ASSOCIATION FOR MEDIA LITERACY

The Association for Media Literacy (AML) is made up of teachers, librarians, consultants, parents, cultural workers, and media professionals concerned about the impact of the mass media on contemporary culture. AML is concerned with helping students develop an informed and critical understanding of the nature of the mass media, the techniques used by media industries, and the impact of these techniques. Media literacy also aims to provide students with the ability to create their own media products.

BLACK TALK MEDIA PROJECT

This organization was set up to teach students and adults in disadvantaged communities how to use the Internet and technology to their advantage. They have various "How to Articles" and "How to Videos" and are available to answer any questions you may have.

THE CENTER FOR MEDIA AND DEMOCRACY

This is an independent, nonprofit, nonpartisan, public interest organization that focuses on investigating and countering spin by corporations; informing and assisting grassroots action that promotes public health, economic justice, ecological sustainability, human rights, and democratic principles; advancing transparency and media literacy; and promoting "open-content" media that enable people from all walks of life to "be the media" and help write the history of these times.

THE CENTER FOR MEDIA LITERACY

The Center for Media Literacy (CML) is an educational organization that provides leadership, public education, professional development, and educational resources nationally. Dedicated to promoting and supporting media literacy education as a framework for accessing, analyzing, evaluating, creating, and participating with media content, CML works to help citizens, especially the young, develop critical thinking and media production skills needed to live fully in the 21st-century media culture.

CENTER FOR PUBLIC INTEGRITY

The Center for Public Integrity is a nonprofit organization dedicated to producing original, responsible investigative journalism on issues of public concern. The center is nonpartisan and nonadvocacy. It is committed to transparent and comprehensive reporting both in the United States and around the world.

COMMERCIAL ALERT

Commercial Alert's mission is to keep the commercial culture within its proper sphere and to prevent it from exploiting children and subverting the higher values of family, community, environmental integrity, and democracy.

FAIRNESS AND ACCURACY IN REPORTING (FAIR)

FAIR, the national media watch group, has been offering well-documented criticism of media bias and censorship since 1986. It works to invigorate the First Amendment by advocating for greater diversity in the press and by scrutinizing media practices that marginalize public interest, minority, and dissenting viewpoints. As an anticensorship organization, FAIR exposes neglected news stories and defends working journalists when they are muzzled. As a progressive group,

FAIR believes that structural reform is ultimately needed to break up the dominant media conglomerates, establish independent public broadcasting, and promote strong nonprofit sources of information.

FREE PRESS

Free Press is a national, nonpartisan, nonprofit organization working to reform the media. Through education, organizing, and advocacy, it promotes diverse and independent media ownership, strong public media, quality journalism, and universal access to communications.

GENDER ADS

Gender Ads.com provides gender studies educators and students with a resource for analyzing the advertising images that relate to gender. The website has more than 2,500 advertising images, and it is one of the largest collections of gender-related advertising materials on the Internet.

GLAAD

The Gay & Lesbian Alliance Against Defamation (GLAAD) is dedicated to promoting and ensuring fair, accurate, and inclusive representation of people and events in the media as a means of eliminating homophobia and discrimination based on gender identity and sexual orientation.

JUST THINK

Just Think teaches young people to lead healthy, responsible, independent lives in a culture highly affected by media. It develops and delivers cutting-edge curricula and innovative programs that build skills in critical thinking and creative media production.

MEDIA AWARENESS NETWORK

MNet focuses its efforts on equipping adults with information and tools to help young people understand how the media work, how the media may affect their lifestyle choices, and the extent to which they, as consumers and citizens, are being well informed.

MEDIA EDUCATION FOUNDATION

The Media Education Foundation produces and distributes documentary films and other educational resources to inspire critical reflection on the social, political, and cultural impact of American mass media.

MEDIA WATCH

Media Watch's goal is to challenge abusive stereotypes and other biased images commonly found in the media. Media Watch, which began in 1984, distributes educational videos, media literacy information, and newsletters to help create more informed consumers of the mass media.

STOP PORN CULTURE!

Stop Porn Culture! is dedicated to challenging the pornography industry and an increasingly pornographic pop culture. Its work toward ending industries of sexual exploitation is grounded in a feminist analysis of sexist, racist, and economic oppression.

TEEN VOICES

The mission of Teen Voices is to support and educate teen girls to amplify their voices and create social change through media. It helps girls achieve personal and community transformation first by providing them with the tools needed to articulate what they know, want, need, and deserve. Through the journalism mentorship program, girls learn writing and editing skills, develop critical thinking, and understand social justice.

Recommended Documentaries From the Media Education Foundation

Descriptions are taken from the websites and edited for brevity.

BEYOND GOOD & EVIL: CHILDREN, MEDIA & VIOLENT TIMES

This video examines how the "good and evil" rhetoric, in both the entertainment and the news media, has helped children to dehumanize the enemies, justify their killing, and treat the suffering of innocent civilians as necessary sacrifice.

CONSUMING KIDS: THE COMMERCIALIZATION OF CHILDHOOD

Consuming Kids throws light on the practices of a relentless multibillion dollar marketing machine that now sells kids and their parents everything from junk food and violent video games to bogus educational products and the family car.

DREAMWORLDS 3: DESIRE, SEX & POWER IN MUSIC VIDEO

Dreamworlds 3 examines the stories contemporary music videos tell about girls and women and encourages viewers to consider how these narratives shape individual and cultural attitudes about sexuality.

FURTHER OFF THE STRAIGHT & NARROW: NEW GAY VISIBILITY ON TELEVISION, 1998–2006

Against the backdrop of political and social issues affecting the gay, lesbian, bisexual, transgender (GLBT) community, such as gay marriage and AIDS, *Further Off the Straight & Narrow* takes a close look at sitcoms, reality shows, and premium cable programming as it explores how representations of GLBT characters have become more complex and varied in recent years.

HIP-HOP: BEYOND BEATS & RHYMES

Hip-Hop: Beyond Beats & Rhymes provides a riveting examination of manhood, sexism, and homophobia in hip-hop culture. Director Byron Hurt pays tribute to hip-hop while challenging the rap music industry to take responsibility for glamorizing destructive, deeply conservative stereotypes of manhood.

KILLING US SOFTLY 4: ADVERTISING'S IMAGE OF WOMEN

Jean Kilbourne looks at how advertising traffics in distorted and destructive ideals of femininity. The film marshals a range of new print and television advertisements to lay bare a stunning pattern of damaging gender stereotypes—images and messages that too often reinforce unrealistic and unhealthy perceptions of beauty, perfection, and sexuality.

THE MEAN WORLD SYNDROME: MEDIA VIOLENCE & THE CULTIVATION OF FEAR

The Mean World Syndrome, based on the groundbreaking work of media scholar

George Gerbner, urges us to think about media effects in more nuanced ways. Ranging from Hollywood movies and prime-time dramas to reality programming and the local news, the film examines how media violence forms a pervasive cultural environment that cultivates in heavy viewers, especially, a heightened state of insecurity, exaggerated perceptions of risk and danger, and a fear-driven propensity for hard-line political solutions to social problems.

MICKEY MOUSE MONOPOLY: DISNEY, CHILDHOOD & CORPORATE POWER

Mickey Mouse Monopoly takes a close and critical look at the world Disney films create and the stories they tell about race, gender, and class and reaches disturbing conclusions about the values propagated under the guise of innocence and fun.

OVERSPENT AMERICAN: WHY WE WANT WHAT WE DON'T NEED

Juliet Schor scrutinizes what she calls "the new consumerism"—a national phenomenon of upscale spending that is shaped and reinforced by a commercially driven media system. She argues that "keeping up with the Joneses" is no longer enough for middle- and upper-middle-class Americans, many of whom become burdened with debilitating debt as they seek to emulate materialistic TV lifestyles.

PRICE OF PLEASURE: PORNOGRAPHY, SEXUALITY & RELATIONSHIPS

This eye-opening and disturbing film places the voices of critics, producers, and performers alongside the observations of men and women as they candidly discuss the role pornography has played in shaping their sexual imaginations and relationships.

SHOP 'TIL YOU DROP: THE CRISIS OF CONSUMERISM

Shop 'Til You Drop moves beneath the seductive surfaces of the commercial world to show how the flip side of accumulation is depletion—the slow, steady erosion of both natural resources and basic human values.

TOUGH GUISE: VIOLENCE, MEDIA & THE CRISIS IN MASCULINITY

Tough Guise is the first educational video geared toward college and high school students to systematically examine the relationship between pop-cultural imagery and the social construction of masculine identities in the United States at the dawn of the 21st century.

To see the entire list of documentaries from the Media Education Foundation, go to http://www.mediaed.org/cgi-bin/commerce.cgi?display=home

Additional Recommended Documentaries

BLACK IS . . . BLACK AIN'T (CALIFORNIA NEWSREEL)

The final film by filmmaker Marlon Riggs jumps into the middle of explosive debates over Black identity. This documentary marshals a powerful critique of sexism, patriarchy, homophobia, colorism, and cultural nationalism in the Black family, church, and other Black institutions. This is Marlon Riggs's last film.

BLACKING UP: HIP-HOP'S REMIX OF RACE AND IDENTITY (CALIFORNIA NEWSREEL)

This documentary looks at the popularity of hip-hop among America's White youth. It asks whether White identification is rooted in admiration and a desire to transcend race or if it is merely a new chapter in the long continuum of stereotyping, mimicry, and cultural appropriation. Does it reflect a new face of racial understanding in White America, or does it reinforce an ugly history?

COVER GIRL CULTURE: AWAKENING THE MEDIA GENERATION (WOMEN MAKE MOVIES)

Cover Girl Culture pairs images of girls and women in television and print ads with footage from the catwalks and celebrity media. The filmmaker is given rare access to women editors from major magazines such as *Teen Vogue* and *ELLE* who provide a shocking defense of the fashion and advertising worlds. The film juxtaposes these interviews with revealing insights from models, parents, teachers, psychologists, body image experts, and, most important, the heartfelt expressions of girls themselves on how they feel about the media that surround them.

THE STRENGTH TO RESIST: THE MEDIA'S IMPACT ON WOMEN AND GIRLS (CAMBRIDGE DOCUMENTARY FILMS)

The documentary addresses strategies of resistance and the personal stories of girls and women working at the grass roots level and those working with issues of race.

WIRED FOR SEX, LIES AND POWER TRIPS: IT'S A TEEN'S WORLD (WOMEN MAKE MOVIES)

An inside look at the culture of sexual harassment and bullying widespread among many teens today, this documentary examines the price that adolescents, especially girls, pay to be cool, hip, and popular in our brave new wired world. Three different groups of culturally diverse teenagers share personal stories of navigating their hypersexualized, high-tech environment, where the online posting of racy photos, raunchy videos, and explicit gossip and lies is as commonplace as bombardment by provocative media messages that degrade and objectify.

GLOSSARY

Address, subject address. See **Subject position.**

Agency. See **Resistance.**

Appropriation. This term can refer, in a neutral sense, to how we make sense of the meanings encoded into cultural texts and incorporate these into our daily lives. It is frequently used by cultural critics to highlight power relations in an unequal society. Thus, "appropriation" can refer to the process whereby members of relatively privileged groups "raid" the culture of marginalized groups, abstracting cultural practices or artifacts from their historically specific contexts. Frequently this involves *co-optation*, by which a cultural item's resistant or counterhegemonic potential is lost through its translation into the dominant cultural context. Adding insult to injury, appropriation frequently means profit for the appropriator.

Binary. In critical race and gender studies, this refers to the "either-or" conceptualization of "race" as Black/White, or gender as masculinity/femininity, in contrast to a system allowing for multiple racial or gender identities.

Black feminist perspective. See **Feminism, Black feminism, feminist media studies.**

Capitalism. An economic system based on private (rather than public or collective) ownership of the means of production, the market exchange of goods and services, and wage labor. This book tends to adopt the Marxist critique of capitalism, which sees it as a system based on oppression and coercion, rather than consensus.

Class, social class. A much-debated term in both sociology and economics. It tends to be used by sociologists to refer to a social stratum whose members share certain social, economic, and cultural characteristics. However, critical sociologists use a modified version of the classic Marxist usage, which defined class as a group of people occupying a similar position within the social relations of economic production. Whereas Marx argued that there are only two major classes under capitalism, the bourgeoisie (owner class) and the proletariat (worker class), critical sociologists distinguish five: the ruling class, the professional/managerial class, small business owners, the working class, and the poor.

Codes, semiotic codes, media codes. A term used in *semiotics*-influenced media studies to refer to rules and conventions that structure representations on a number of levels—some specific to certain media such as narrative film or advertising photographs, while others are shared with other modes of communication. Audiences learn to "read" the conventional verbal, visual, and auditory features that make up the "languages" or "sign systems" of media and other cultural forms in much the same way children learn the complex, often arbitrary systems of meaning in natural languages. See **Semiotics, semiology and Encoding/decoding.**

Content analysis. A social scientific method of describing and analyzing the "content" of a range of media texts, either in qualitative or quantitative terms. Quantitative content analysis (counting the number of times certain types of material appear) is especially useful for describing the broad contours of a large quantity of texts, but it tends to miss the more subtle and complex ways in which texts construct meaning.

Convergence, media convergence. This term has been used, confusingly, to refer to many different processes in the current fast-changing media business environment. Henry Jenkins (2006) has usefully clarified the term this way: "the flow of content across multiple media platforms, the cooperation between multiple media industries, and the migratory behavior of media audiences who will go almost anywhere in search of the kinds of entertainment experiences they want" (p. 2).

Counterhegemonic, antihegemonic. See **Hegemony, hegemonic.**

Critical race theory. In contrast to older approaches to "race" that assumed "White" or Euro-American norms and focused on "non-White" identities as "the problem," critical race studies are based on the assumption that the proper object of study is the construction of hierarchical racial categories by which "White privilege" came to seem "natural." Critical race theorists are particularly concerned with challenging the Black/White *binary* that has dominated U.S. academic discourse on "race," rendering invisible anyone who cannot be made to exemplify one of these two artificially constructed categories. In general, critical race theorists view "race" as a purely historical construct in the service of political goals. See Omi and Winant (1993).

Critical theory, critical media theory, critical media pedagogy. Also see **Marxist, Marxism, Marxian.** An approach to the analysis of social and cultural phenomena that highlights the dominant role of a capitalist economic system and the resulting economic and social inequalities.

Cultural studies. An approach to the study of communications in society that is drawn from a number of sources, including Marxism, semiotics, literary and film analysis, psychoanalysis, feminism, and critical race and postcolonial theory. As used in this book, it locates the production, textual construction, and consumption of media texts in a society characterized by multiple systems of inequality. Of key importance is the study of the role media forms play in the production and reproduction of these systems of inequality. See Chapter 1 in this reader for an extended discussion of this approach.

Culture. A term with many different meanings, depending on the school of thought in which it occurs. In anthropology, it refers to everything created by humans, including artifacts or objects, ideas, institutions, and expressive practices. In traditional humanities fields such as art history and literature, "culture" has tended to be conceptualized as the highest status arts of the wealthy and socially dominant, such as oil paintings, opera, or poetry. *Cultural studies* rejects this view of culture as elitist, replacing it with the more anthropological usage. In particular, cultural studies takes as its area of study all of the expressive, meaningful, interactive aspects of everyday life in an industrial society.

Cyberspace. Cyberspace is a cover term referring to the *virtual* or disembodied world of Internet-facilitated communications, where social relationships and networks can be created and maintained without face-to-face contact among participants. Many social commentators and media critics have written both enthusiastically and warily about the potentially revolutionary impacts on society and individuals of Internet-facilitated communications and interactive media culture, including blogs, social networking sites, online games, fan-produced videos, and corporate appropriation of grassroots media productivity.

Decode. See **Encoding/decoding.**

Discourse(s), discourse analysis, discursive. An approach within cultural studies that emphasizes how power relations in societies are sustained by and reflected in a variety of specialized ways of speaking and writing, such as those of elite institutions and groups—like medical professionals, religious institutions, and academics—as influentially articulated in the work of the French historian/philosopher Michel Foucault, in *The History of Sexuality.*

Encoding/decoding. "Encoding/Decoding" is the title of an influential article by British cultural studies writer Stuart Hall (1980). It proposes that meaning does not simply reside in a *media text's codes* but is the result of a complex *negotiation* between specific audiences and texts. In contrast to former critical media theorists who assumed that audiences had very little control over meaning and were vulnerable to being "brainwashed" by the media, Hall proposed three possible audience responses to the dominant ideology contained in the media text's codes, or three distinct reading positions, corresponding to audiences' different social situations: *dominant reading* (accepting the *preferred meaning*), *negotiated reading* (accepting aspects of the preferred meaning but rejecting others), and *oppositional reading* (rejecting the preferred meaning).

Ethnography. This is a social research method first used by anthropologists and now adopted by some cultural studies scholars for understanding the role of media audiences in the production of meaning. In ethnographic media studies research, audience members are typically interviewed about their understandings of the media text, or they participate in guided discussions in focus groups. The study can also involve participant observation, which requires that the researcher becomes a part of the group studied for a specified period in order to understand directly the context in which the media text reception takes place. For an example of an ethnographic media study, see Chapter 6 in this reader.

Fans, fandom studies. Ethnographic media audience studies sometimes focus on specialized groups of audiences, the enthusiasts or fans, who seem to exemplify the "active audience" phenomenon in a particularly intensive way. As Henry Jenkins showed in his original study of *Star Trek* fans, excerpted in this volume (Chapter 7), a fan community can go beyond consumption of a media text to a more active relationship, in which new texts are created by fans who borrow ("poach") from and creatively rewrite aspects of commercial media texts, especially when the original texts are found lacking in some ways. Fans can bond with one another over their strong relationships with selected media texts, using passionate and interactive revision of such texts as one basis for community. Fandom studies tend to emphasize the potential of grassroots media culture productivity to undermine or challenge the dominance exercised by corporate producers over media culture.

Feminism, Black feminism, feminist media studies. A multidisciplinary approach to social analysis, rooted in the contemporary women's movement(s) and the gay/lesbian/bisexual/transgender (GLBT) liberation movement. Emphasizing gender as a major organizing feature of power relations in society, feminists argue that the role of the media is crucial in the construction and dissemination of gender ideology and thus in gender socialization. Feminists of color have critiqued the tendency in some feminist theory to privilege gender over other categories of experience; in particular, cultural analysts with a *Black feminist (sometimes called "womanist") perspective* have brought to the foreground the ways in which gender is "inflected" or modified by race and class factors. See Patricia Hill Collins (2000).

Feminist film theory. This strand of cultural studies, which was particularly influential in the 1980s, combines a feminist view of the centrality of gender in cultural analysis with a generally psychoanalytic orientation to the study of audience reception of film. Feminist film theorists working through textual analysis have explored such issues as *gendered spectatorship,* the ways in which the film text, through its formal codes, "addresses" or speaks directly to the hypothetical or ideal viewer as either male or female. An early formulation by Laura Mulvey (1975) asserted that any viewer of classic Hollywood narrative film was encouraged by both plot and camera work and editing to adopt a "masculine subject position" and share in the *male gaze* of both protagonist and camera at a female object of desire.

Gay and lesbian studies, gay/lesbian/bisexual/transgender studies (GLBT). See **Queer theory, queer studies.**

Gaze, male gaze. See **Feminist film theory.**

Gender, gendering, gendered. Whereas sex differences (anatomical and hormonal) between genetic males and genetic females are biological in nature, *gender* is a social concept, by which a society defines as "masculine" or "feminine" one particular set of characteristics and behaviors and then socializes children accordingly. Just which characteristics belong to which gender (and even how many gender categories there are) can vary tremendously over time and between cultures and even different social groups within cultures. Some contemporary scholars argue that both gender and sexuality (sexual identity, sexual preference, sexual object choice) are more accurately understood as continuums, rather than in binary (only two, either-or) categories. Gender is now commonly understood to be constructed in "intersectional" relationships with other aspects of social identity, such as race and class. Media theorists and critics generally try to locate their gender analysis within specific social contexts, distinguishing, for example, representations of Black middle-class masculinity of a particular time and place from other masculinities.

Globalizing media, globalization, global media. In this age of giant multinational media conglomerates and new digital and Internet technologies that allow for wide distribution of corporate-produced cultural products from the richer nations across the globe, the term *globalization* means different things for different media critics. Some, such as Robert McChesney (2008), warn of the dangers of cultural imperialism, which they see as threatening the integrity and autonomy of local cultures around the world, particularly those in the Global South that lack the wealth and industrial technology necessary to compete with the onslaught of Hollywood-produced imagery. Others, including Henry Jenkins (2006), argue against an entirely pessimistic view of the processes of cross-cultural "flow" and, while concerned with media business concentration, see the imperialistic model as too deterministic. Also see **Convergence.**

Hegemony, hegemonic. A term developed by Italian Marxist theorist Antonio Gramsci to refer to the process by which those in power secure the consent of the socially subordinated to the system that oppresses or subordinates them. Rather than requiring overt force (as represented by the military or police), the elite, through their control of religious, educational, and media institutions, attempt to persuade the populace that the hierarchical social and economic system is fixed and "natural" and therefore unchangeable. According to Gramsci, however, such consent is never secured once and for all but must continually be sought, and there is always some room for *resistance* through subversive (*counterhegemonic*) cultural work.

Heterocentrism, heteronormativity. These terms refer to the placing of heterosexual experience at the center of attention, or the routine assumption that heterosexuality is "normal" and any other expression of sexuality is "deviant."

Heterosexism. A term coined by analogy with *sexism.* The dictionary defines it as "discrimination or prejudice against gay or homosexual people by heterosexual people." As with *racism* and *sexism,* this book takes the view that it is structural or institutional forces that underpin social inequalities, rather than individual prejudiced attitudes. Thus, heterosexism would refer to the heterosexual ideology that is encoded into and characteristic of the major social, cultural, and economic institutions of our society. See **Race, racism and Sexism.**

Homophobia. A psychological concept, referring to deep-seated fear of homosexuality, in others or in oneself. Also see **Heterocentrism, heteronormativity and Heterosexism.**

Ideology. Traditionally used by Marxists to refer to ideas imposed on the proletariat (working class) by the bourgeoisie (owners of the means of production), in order to get the subservient classes to consent to their own oppression. Today, critical theorists tend to use a broader concept of ideology that emphasizes the way ideas embedded in all our social institutions (legal, educational, economic, military, etc.) create a dominant commonsense understanding of reality that supports the status quo. For a definition of ideology, see the essay by Stuart Hall in this reader (Chapter 10).

Intertextuality. John Fiske (1987) has explicated a theory of *intertextuality* to help explain the way audiences' experience a wide variety of media texts as interrelated, allowing their knowledge of one to influence their reading of another. For example, if a *primary media text* is a specific book, film, or television show, then *a secondary text* might be "studio publicity, journalistic features, or criticism" about the primary text, and *tertiary texts* might include viewers' letters, gossip, and conversation about the primary text (Fiske, 1987, pp. 108–109). Also see **Text.**

Image, media image. This term refers to any *representation* of social reality in media culture, as in "images of women in advertising." However, the word *image* as commonly used—as in "mirror image"—tends to suggest a more direct, uncomplicated, and less artificial or constructed relationship with "reality" than most scholars now propose for media representations. Image also refers, of course, to a specifically *visual representation.* See Sut Jhally, Chapter 22, in this volume.

Lesbigay, GLBTQ. See **Queer theory, queer studies.**

Liberatory. Like *emancipatory* or *progressive,* this term is used in critical cultural studies to indicate what the critic sees as a positive political impact, in which a socially subordinate group gains greater power or freedom (liberation or emancipation from oppression).

Marxist, Marxism, Marxian. A general theory of historical change originally developed by 19th-century German philosopher Karl Marx. Marx argued for the centrality of economics in social history and developed a critique of capitalism that has had a major influence on political theory and on social revolutions in the 19th and 20th centuries. In the realm of cultural studies, classic Marxism argued that the economic structure of society (the "base") shapes major cultural institutions (the "superstructure"), including the military, legal system, educational system, arts, and media. This is because, according to Marx, "the class which has the means of material production at its disposal has control over the means of mental production" (Marx & Engels, 1938). For a modification of classic Marxist ideas of this relationship, see **Hegemony, hegemonic.**

Masculinities. See **Gender, gendering, gendered.**

Media, mass media, mass communications media, mediated. The term *media* is originally the plural of *medium* (communications medium). It has become a shorthand way of referring to the whole range of technologically assisted means by which images and messages can be created and distributed by producers for later consumption by "the masses" (vast numbers of people). "The media" is sometimes a shorthand way of referring to news media in particular, but in the context of this book, we are referring primarily to entertainment media culture. To say that communication is "mediated" is to draw attention to its highly second-hand character (as opposed to real-time face-to-face traditional cultural forms such as storytelling, live theater, acoustic musical performances for live audiences, etc.).

Misogyny. Literally, this word means "hatred of women," and its use emphasizes the emotional or psychological basis for *sexism.* Feminist cultural critics analyze ways in which misogyny and sexism are embedded in culture, often in ways that make historically specific constructions social arrangements in which males are allocated social and cultural supremacy over females seem natural or inevitable.

Multicultural, multiculturalism. As used in this book, multiculturalism refers to a movement affecting curricula, teaching methods, and scholarship in a variety of fields, within universities and colleges in the United States. The broad objectives of activists in this educational movement include democratizing knowledge and education, by bringing to the foreground and validating the experiences and perspectives of all those groups formerly marginalized or culturally and socially dominated in our society.

Multidisciplinary, interdisciplinary. An approach that encourages students and teachers to cross the boundaries between traditional academic disciplines or areas of knowledge (such as history, sociology, philosophy, economics, or political science), in order to be able better to capture the complexity of the subject studied.

Negotiated reading. See **Encoding/decoding.**

Neoliberalism. This term refers to an economic ideology that has become widely influential in the economic policies of the wealthier nations and of international lender organizations such as the World Bank in the past several decades. Unlike the economic theories of John Maynard Keynes, which emphasized the role of government intervention in the economy when necessary to promote the well-being of citizens, this view greatly emphasizes (and some would say exaggerates) the beneficial workings of the unregulated private sector, through the magic of the workings of the free market. Embedded in this ideology is the idea that every individual is equally able to protect herself or himself from economic disaster—an idea that easily leads to "blaming the victim" when individuals do not achieve economic stability. In the context of cultural studies, critics argue that certain types of media texts, such as makeover reality TV, *Judge Judy,* or *The Oprah Winfrey Show,* encode and promote neoliberal ideas, teaching that the individual can and must empower herself without government support.

New media. This term generally refers to communications technologies that enable users or consumers to interact with one another and with the media texts, in contrast with traditional, older mass media technologies such as newspapers, radio and television broadcasts, films, and recorded music. New media would include blogs, social networking sites, online games, interactive websites such as YouTube, and many other examples that will be current by the time you read this book.

Oppositional reading. See **Encoding/ decoding.**

Patriarchal, patriarchy. Literally meaning "rule by the father" and referring to family (and clan) systems in which one older man had absolute power over all members of the group, including women, children, and younger male relatives and servants. As used by contemporary feminists, it is a concept developed to examine and critique continuing male domination of social institutions such as the family and the state, the educational system, and the media.

Political economy. In critical theory, a perspective that "sets out to show how different ways of financing and organizing cultural production have traceable consequences for the range of discourses and representations in the public domain, and for audiences' access to them" (Golding & Murdoch, 1991, p. 15). This often involves studying who owns the media industries and analyzing how ownership influences media content. (See, in particular, Chapter 13 in this reader.)

Polysemic text. One that is "open" to various readings or has multiple meanings. Cultural studies scholars currently disagree among themselves about how "open" texts are. See **Encoding/decoding.**

Postfeminism. This term has been used to describe and critique an apparent period of reaction against feminism that began in the 1980s, when some women sympathetic to the goals of feminism nevertheless refused to name themselves as feminists. As used by feminist media critics, however, it tends to refer to the idea embedded in some cultural texts that all the goals of the women's movement have already been achieved. In this way, it is parallel to *postracial discourse* (see **Race, racism**).

Postracial discourse. See **Race, racism.**

Pornography. Most broadly, this refers to sexually explicit graphic and/or written texts designed to produce sexual arousal in consumers. (Depending on one's political perspective and view of the social impact of the production and consumption of such materials, the same texts could be seen merely as *erotica*—a more neutral term—or as *pornography*—a term implying community disapproval.) The definition has been politicized and was strenuously contested during the 1980s, when feminists proposed city ordinances by which the production and distribution of certain classes of pornography could be prosecuted as civil rights violations, rather than under traditional anti-vice criminal law. Anti-pornography feminists argued that certain classes of pornography embodied and helped reproduce misogyny. See also **Misogyny.**

Preferred reading. A concept developed by Stuart Hall to circumscribe the degree of "openness" (*polysemy*) of media texts. According to Hall (1980), the structure of mainstream media texts always "prefers" or strongly suggests a single "correct" meaning that tends to promote the dominant ideology. Within cultural studies, there continues to be a lively debate over whether a preferred meaning can be said to be a property of the text; some would argue that the making of meaning ultimately resides with audiences. Also see **Encoding/decoding.**

Queer theory, queer studies. An interdisciplinary and politically radical approach to cultural studies that emphasizes the instability and fluidity of gender and sexuality categories, in contrast to the view that sexual identity is a fixed, permanent "essence." The term *queer* is adopted in order to reclaim it in a positive sense from derogatory usage, as well as to create a more inclusive vision of the areas of study.

Race, racism. Also see **Critical race theory.** Although the political importance of "race" as a social category is evident in today's world, most scholars agree that "race" is a convenient fiction with complex historical significance but no biological reality. In everyday usage, *racism* can be used to mean holding or displaying prejudiced or bigoted attitudes or indulging in discriminatory behavior toward someone else (usually people of color, but sometimes Whites as well), on the basis of that person's apparent race, ethnicity, or skin color. However, in critical theory, and in this book, we use the term to refer specifically to the White-supremacist ideology encoded into and characteristic of the major social, cultural, and economic institutions of this society. *Postracial discourse* is based on the view that in the post–civil rights era, race is no longer a major factor in determining one's access to resources and respect. This view is linked with the ideology of meritocracy, which assumes that individuals inevitably succeed in life and are rewarded in society as a result of hard work and motivation. Those who critique these concepts argue that such a view fails to see and acknowledge "structural inequalities" in our society, such as White privilege or class privilege, that provide hidden advantages to people from some groups from birth.

Representation, cultural representation, media representation. *Representations* is a current term used to include all kinds of media imagery (through words, pictures, or both) that, no matter how convincing their likeness to everyday social reality, are always to be recognized as illusions. More technically, media representations such as events seen on reality television shows or depictions of gangster life in the 'hood contained in hip-hop rap videos should be understood not as direct mirrorings of "real life." Rather, they are always the result of artistic and business judgments by their producers, "constructions taken from a specific social and physical viewpoint, selecting one activity or instant out of vast choices to represent, and materially made out of and formed by the technical processes of the medium and its conventions" (King, 1992, p. 131).

Resistance. In critical cultural studies, this can refer to the refusal of the reader, viewer, or audience to take up or accept the *preferred reading* and/or the *subject position* encoded into the media text and therefore to resist its power to reinforce hegemonic ideas. There is still debate among cultural studies scholars on how much opportunity to resist is offered by the text (how "open" or *polysemic* it is). Many scholars have criticized a tendency to "romanticize" the idea of interpretive community's resistance. Others question the notion that audience *resistance* is in and of itself positive, citing the resistance of those with conservative social ideologies to texts whose preferred meaning is politically "progressive." Finally, it has been asserted that "resistive readings" of specific texts do not necessarily translate into political resistance to cultural *hegemony*. (A related term, *agency*, refers to the degree to which a consumer of culture can be understood to be a free agent whose choices must be respected by the cultural critic, as opposed to merely being a passive victim of cultural brainwashing.)

Semiotics, semiology. Semiotics is a linguistics-based field of study that has had an important influence on the way cultural studies scholars discuss the "codes" in media texts. It is concerned with the study of "signification," or the ways in which both languages and nonlinguistic symbolic systems operate to associate meanings with arbitrary "signs" such as words, visual images, colors, or objects. Signs actually consist of two elements—that which is *signified* (the meaning) and that which signifies (the *signifier* or symbol itself). See **Encoding/decoding.**

Sexism. Coined by the women's movement in an analogy with *racism,* sexism is also used several ways. In common usage, it can refer to prejudicial or disrespectful attitudes or discriminatory behavior on the part of individuals toward others on the basis of gender. In this book, we use it to refer specifically to male-supremacist or patriarchal ideology encoded into and characteristic of the major social, cultural, and economic institutions of a society.

Signifier, signified. See **Semiotics, semiology.**

Spectatorship. See **Feminist film theory.**

Stereotype. This popular term was much used in 1970s media criticism and activism to describe and critique reductive, much-repeated social imagery (as in "Uncle Tom and Aunt Jemima are racist stereotypes"; "Aunt Jemima and the Playboy Bunny are sexist stereotypes").

Subject position. A concept developed within literary and film criticism, which claims that narrative texts themselves produce through their codes an ideal "viewing position" or subject position, from which the narrative is then experienced by any viewer/reader. A male viewer could be invited by a particular text to view it from a feminine subject position, for example, just as a heterosexual reader might temporarily occupy a queer subject position. A related term for this process is *interpellation*—which means that the text can be read as figuratively "hailing" or "calling out to" a particular ideal type of reader.

Text, media text. This term is used very broadly and can refer to any communicative or expressive media product, from a song lyric or magazine ad to a dramatic TV show or an online video game. *Textual*

analysis, or a close examination of how particular media texts generate meaning, is one of the key activities of contemporary cultural studies.

Textual analysis. *See* **Text.**

Transgressive. A term often used positively in cultural criticism to indicate the writer's approval of an act that challenges traditional (oppressive) rules or social or cultural hierarchies.

References

Collins, P. H. (2000). *Black feminist thought: Knowledge, consciousness, and the politics of empowerment* (2nd ed.). New York: Routledge.

Fiske, J. (1987). *Television culture.* London: Methuen.

Golding, P., & Murdoch, G. (1991). Culture, communication and political economy. In J. Curran & M. Gurrevitch (Eds.), *Mass media and society.* London: Edward Arnold.

Hall, S. (1980). Encoding/decoding. In S. Hall, D. Hobson, A. Lowe, & P. Willis (Eds.), *Culture, media and language.* London: Hutchinson.

Jenkins, H. (2006). *Convergence culture: Where old and new media collide.* New York: New York University Press.

King, C. (1992). On representation. In F. Bonner, L. Goodman, R. Allen, L. Janes, & C. King (Eds.), *Imagining women* (pp. 131–139). Cambridge, England: Open University Press.

Marx, K., & Engels, F. (1938). *German ideology* (R. Pascal, Trans.). London: Lawrence and Wishart.

McChesney, R. W. (2008). *Communication revolution: Critical junctures and the future of media.* New York: New Press.

Mulvey, L. (1975). Visual pleasure and narrative cinema. *Screen, 16*(3), 6–18.

Omi, M., & Winant, H. (1993). On the theoretical concept of race. In S. M. James & A. P. A. Busia (Eds.), *Theorizing Black feminisms: The visionary pragmatism of Black women.* New York: Routledge.

AUTHOR INDEX

SUBJECT INDEX

ABOUT THE EDITORS

Gail Dines is Professor of Sociology and Women's Studies at Wheelock College in Boston, where she is also chair of the American Studies Department. She has been researching and writing about the pornography industry for well over 20 years. She has written numerous articles on pornography, media images of women, and representations of race in pop culture. Her latest book is *PORNLAND: How Pornography Has Hijacked Our Sexuality*. She is a cofounder of the activist group Stop Porn Culture!

Jean M. Humez is Professor Emerita of Women's Studies at the University of Massachusetts, Boston, where she taught courses in both women's studies and American studies and chaired the Women's Studies Department. She designed and taught an undergraduate "Women and the Media" course early in her career and, through her interest in media text analysis, came to collaborate with Gail Dines on this book. She has also published books and articles on African American women's spiritual and secular autobiographies and on women and gender in Shaker religion. Her most recent book is *Harriet Tubman: The Life and the Life Stories*.

ABOUT THE CONTRIBUTORS

Lee Artz is an Associate Professor in the Department of Communication and Creative Arts at Purdue University Calumet. He has written numerous articles on cultural diversity and democratic communication for leading journals. His most recent books are *Public Media and the Public Interest* (2002, with Michael McCauley, Eric Petersen, and Dee Dee Halleck), *Communication and Democratic Society* (2001), and *Cultural Hegemony in the United States* (2000, with Bren Murphy).

Feona Attwood teaches Media and Communication Studies at Sheffield Hallam University, UK. Her research interests include new pornographies, online sex practices, and controversial images. She is the editor of *Mainstreaming Sex: The Sexualization of Western Culture* (2009) and *porn.com: Making Sense of Online Pornography* (2010), as well as the coeditor of journal special issues on "Controversial Images" (with Sharon Lockyer, *Popular Communication,* 2009) and "Researching and Teaching Sexually Explicit Media" (with I. Q. Hunter, *Sexualities,* 2009).

Marlo David Azikwe is a McKnight Doctoral Fellow in English at the University of Florida in Gainesville. Her research interests include conceptions of motherhood, African Diaspora literatures and cultural studies, African American vernacular expression, and issues of gender and sexuality.

Elena Bertozzi teaches game analysis, design, and development in the Media Arts & Game Development program at the University of Wisconsin, Whitewater. A book chapter, "Marking the Territory: Exploring Masculinities in Grand Theft Auto IV," is forthcoming in *Utopic Dreams and Apocalyptic Fantasies: Playing in Virtual Realms,* edited by Talmadge Wright (2010). She is the Director of the Engender Games Group lab, which is currently developing the Emergency Birth

Game aimed at teaching players how to safely deliver a baby in the absence of a physician.

S. Elizabeth Bird is a Professor and Chair of the Department of Anthropology at the University of Southern Florida. Her most recent book is *The Audience in Everyday Life: Living in a Media World* (2003). Author of many other publications, she is particularly interested in the role of news and journalism in framing cultural issues and the relationship of media texts and audience practices. Her most current research uses videotaped oral histories and survivor testimonies to document a little-known massacre of civilians that happened in 1967 during the Nigerian civil war.

danah boyd is a Social Media Researcher at Microsoft Research New England and a Fellow at Harvard University's Berkman Center for Internet and Society. She is author or coauthor of many papers examining social media, youth practices, tensions between public and private, social network sites, and other intersections between technology and society. She is also a coeditor of *Hanging Out, Messing Around, Geeking Out: Living and Learning With New Media* (2009).

Karen Boyle is a Senior Lecturer in Film & Television Studies at the University of Glasgow, UK. She is the author of *Media & Violence: Gendering the Debates* (2005) and editor of *Everyday Pornography* (2010). She has published widely on gendered violence, pornography, and feminist media studies. Her most recent work is on cinema audiences, parenting, and identity.

Robert Alan Brookey is an Associate Professor of Communication at Northern Illinois University. His research investigates the way traditional forms of entertainment media are responding to an emerging digital market, and his work has appeared in journals including *Games*

and Culture, Convergence, and *Critical Studies in Media Communication.* His most recent book is *Hollywood Gamers: Digital Convergence in the Film and Video Games Industries* (2010).

Richard Butsch is Professor of Sociology at Rider University. He is author of *The Making of American Audiences From Stage to Television, 1750 to 1990* and *The Citizen Audience: Crowds, Publics, and Individuals.* He is also editor of *Media and Public Spheres.* He is currently writing a history of screen culture and a book on the representation of manual labor and laborers in 20th-century America.

Kristopher L. Cannon is a PhD candidate in the moving image studies program, in the Department of Communication at Georgia State University. His research explores manifestations of bodies and queerness in new media and film. He has recently published "Cutting Race Otherwise: Considering Michael Jackson" in *Spectator* and is working on his dissertation, tentatively entitled "Oblique Optics: Illuminating the Queerness of Images in Mediation."

Jane Caputi is Professor of Women, Gender and Sexuality Studies and Communication and Mass Media at Florida Atlantic University. She is the author of several books, most recently *Goddesses and Monsters: Women, Myth, Power and Popular Culture* (2004). She also produced the educational documentary, *The Pornography of Everyday Life,* distributed by Berkeley Media (www.berkeley media.com).

Jay Clarkson is an Assistant Professor of Electronic Media at Indiana State University. He studies media representations of gender and sexuality and the proliferation of addiction narratives to explain media consumption patterns. He is author of several articles, including "Contesting Masculinity's Makeover: Queer Eye, Consumer Masculinity, and 'Straight-Acting' Gays" (2005).

Shelley Cobb is a teaching fellow at the University of Southampton, England. She has published several articles or book chapters on film adaptation and gender in contemporary cinema, including a chapter on the adaptation of *Bridget Jones's Diary* in *Authorship in Film Adaptation* from the University of Texas Press.

Lisa M. Cuklanz is Professor and Chair of the Communication Department at Boston College. She is author of *Rape on Trial: How the Mass Media Construct Legal Reform and Social Change* (1996) and *Rape on Prime Time: Television, Masculinity, and Sexual Violence* (2000), as well as numerous articles published in journals. Most recently, she coedited (2009, with Sujata Moorti) *Local Violence, Global Media: Feminist Analyses of Gendered Representations*.

Vincent Doyle is the author of the forthcoming book *Making Out in the Mainstream: Media Activism, Queer Autonomy and GLAAD*, as well as a forthcoming article in "Queer Futures," a special issue of *Radical History Review*. He is a fellow of the Sexuality Research Program of the Social Science Research Council.

Meenakshi Gigi Durham is an Associate Professor in the School of Journalism and Mass Communication at the University of Iowa and director of the Iowa Center for the Study of Communication. She is the author of *The Lolita Effect* (2008) and coeditor (with Douglas Kellner) of *Media and Cultural Studies: Key Works* (2001; rev. 2006). Her research engages feminist critical and cultural studies to interrogate media representations of women's and girls' sexuality. She has published extensively in leading scholarly journals in media studies.

Erika Engstrom is an Associate Professor of Communication at the University of Nevada, Las Vegas. Much of her research centers on love and romance as represented in reality television programming. She is the author of many articles, including "Buff Brides: Disciplining the Female Body" and "Creation of a New 'Empowered' Identity in WEtv's Bridezillas."

Jennifer Esposito is an Associate Professor in the College of Education at Georgia State University. Her research interests include analysis of popular culture texts representing traditionally marginalized groups, urban education, race, gender, class, and sexuality identity negotiation and qualitative methodology. In addition to various book chapters, she has published articles in journals such as *Gender & Education* and *Television & New Media*.

Thomas Fahy is the Director of the American Studies Program and a Professor of English at Long Island University. He has published nine books, including *Freak Shows and the Modern American Imagination* (2006), three novels, and several edited collections. Most recently, he is the editor of the forthcoming book, *The Philosophy of Horror*.

Kathleen P. Farrell is an Assistant Professor of Social Sciences and Education at Colby-Sawyer, New London, New Hampshire. Her primary research and teaching interests include gender and sexualities, with an emphasis on inequality studies. She is coeditor (with Nisha Gupta and Mary Queen) of *Interrupting Heteronormativity: Lesbian, Gay, Bisexual and Transgender Pedagogy and Responsible Teaching at Syracuse University* (2004).

Jane Gerhard is a Visiting Assistant Professor of History at Mount Holyoke College. Her interests are history of American feminism, particularly second-wave feminism and post-feminism; history of sexuality; and 20th-century cultural history. She is coauthor (with Mari Jo Buhle) and Terry Murphy of *Women and the Making of America* (2008). She has a new book on feminist artist Judy Chicago's *The Dinner Party*.

Rosalind Gill is Professor of Subjectivity and Cultural Analysis at the Open University.

Previously, she worked as a senior lecturer at the Gender Institute, London School of Economics. She is author of three books, including *Gender and the Media* (2006), and more than 60 scholarly articles and book chapters, and her work has been translated into several languages. She is known for her work on gender, media, and new technologies as well as for longstanding interests in discourse and narrative analysis.

Karen Goldman is an Associate Professor of Spanish and Cultural Studies and Chair of the Department of History, Policy, International and Cultural Studies at Chatham University, Pittsburgh, Pennsylvania. She is also a member of the Creative Writing faculty. She has published several journal articles and book chapters on gender themes in Spanish and Latin American film.

Stuart Hall is considered one of major founders of cultural studies and a leading figure of the British left. He is past director of the Centre for Contemporary Cultural Studies at Birmingham University and was a Professor of Sociology at the Open University from 1979–1997. Now Professor Emeritus, he is the author of many influential books and articles, including *Questions of Cultural Identity* (1996) and *Cultural Representations and Signifying Practices* (1997).

Chong-suk Han is an Assistant Professor of Sociology and Anthropology at Middlebury College in Vermont. His areas of expertise are race and sexuality, particularly the ways that categories of race and sexuality are socially constructed and the way multiple identities intersect. An award-winning journalist, he is the author of numerous articles.

Henry Jenkins III is the Provost's Professor of Communications, Journalism and Cinematic Art at University of Southern California and formerly the director of the Comparative Media Studies Program at the Massachusetts Institute of Technology. He is the author or editor of 13 books on

media and popular culture, including the recent *Convergence Culture: Where Old and New Media Collide* (2008). He blogs regularly at henryjenkins.org.

Sut Jhally is Professor of Communication at the University of Massachusetts at Amherst and Founder and Executive Director of the Media Education Foundation. He is the author of numerous books and articles on media, including *The Codes of Advertising* (1990) and *Enlightened Racism* (1992). He is also the producer and director of a number of media literacy films and videos for classroom use, including *Dreamworlds: Desire/Sex/Power in Music Video; Tough Guise: Media, Violence and the Crisis of Masculinity;* and *Hijacking Catastrophe: 9/11, Fear & the Selling of American Empire.*

Helen Johnson holds degrees from Monash University and lectured in anthropology at the University of Queensland, Australia. She is presently Principal Social Scientist for a major Australian consulting firm. Her articles have appeared in a range of national and international journals; she has contributed to significant publications, particularly those focusing on issues of gender and development; and she has written policy and reports for a number of governments and companies.

Chris Jordan is an Assistant Professor of Film Studies in the Department of Theatre, Film Studies, and Dance at St. Cloud State University. He is the author of *Movies and the Reagan Presidency: Success and Ethics* (2003) and essays and articles on film and television. His latest scholarly research is on the history of the Motion Picture Association of America.

Ralina L. Joseph is an Assistant Professor in the Department of Communication at the University of Washington. Her book in progress, *Transcending Blackness: From the New Millennium Mulatta to the Exceptional Multiracial,* critiques anti-Black racism in 1998–2008 era representations of multiracial African Americans.

With the support of the Ford and Woodrow Wilson/Mellon Foundations, she is working on her second book project, *Speaking Back: How Women of Color Resist Post-Identity Culture.*

Jackson Katz is an educator, author, and filmmaker. He is the cofounder of the Mentors in Violence Prevention (MVP) program, the leading gender violence prevention initiative in professional and college athletics. He is the director of the first worldwide domestic and sexual violence prevention program in the United States Marine Corps. Author of *The Macho Paradox: Why Some Men Hurt Women and How All Men Can Help* (2006), he is also the creator and co-creator of educational videos for college and high school students, including *Tough Guise: Violence, Media, and the Crisis in Masculinity; Wrestling With Manhood;* and *Spin the Bottle: Sex, Lies and Alcohol.*

Douglas Kellner is George Kneller Chair in the Philosophy of Education at UCLA and is the author of many books on social theory, politics, history, and culture. His works in cultural studies include *Media Culture and Media Spectacle,* a trilogy of books on postmodern theory with Steve Best; a trilogy of books on the media and the Bush administration; and *Media/Cultural Studies: Critical Approaches* (2009, coedited with Rhonda Hammer). His book *Guys and Guns Amok: Domestic Terrorism and School Shootings From the Oklahoma City Bombings to the Virginia Tech Massacre* (2008) won the 2008 AESA award as the best book on education. Forthcoming in 2010 is *Cinema Wars: Hollywood Film and Politics in the Bush/Cheney Era.* His website is at http://www.gseis.ucla.edu/faculty/kellner/kellner.html

Kathleen LeBesco is Professor and Chair of Communication Arts at Marymount Manhattan College. She is author of *Revolting Bodies? The Struggle to Redefine Fat Identity* (2006) and coeditor of *The Drag King Anthology, Edible Ideologies: Representing Food and Meaning* (2003, with Donna Jean and Jean Bobby) as well as *Bodies Out of Bounds: Fatness and Transgression* (2001, with Jana Evans Breziel). She is currently working on a new book about food and class politics.

Dafna Lemish is Professor of Communication and Chair of the Department of Radio-TV at Southern Illinois University, Carbondale, as well as founding editor of the *Journal of Children and Media.* She is author of numerous books and articles on children, media, and gender representations, including *Screening Gender on Children's Television: The Views of Producers Around the World* (2010) and *Children and Television: A Global Perspective* (2006).

George Lipsitz is a Professor of Black Studies at the University of California, Santa Barbara. His research interests include social movements, urban culture, and inequality. His books include *The Possessive Investment in Whiteness: How White People Benefit From Identity Politics* (1998; expanded 2006); *Dangerous Crossroads: Popular Music, Postmodernism and the Focus of Place* (1997); and *Footsteps in the Dark: The Hidden Histories of Popular Music* (2007). He serves as chairman of the board of directors of the African American Policy Forum and is a member of the board of directors of the National Fair Housing Alliance.

James Lull is Professor Emeritus of Communication Studies at San Jose State University, California, specializing in media and cultural studies. He is author or editor of a dozen books in English. His books include *Culture-on-Demand: Communication in a Crisis World* (2007), *Culture in the Communication Age* (2001), and *Media Scandals* (1997). He has appeared as a cultural commentator for a number of outlets that include Cable News Network (CNN), CNN Headline News, the British Broadcasting Company (BBC), and National Public Radio.

Lawrence B. McBride began carrying out ethnographic fieldwork with pro-wrestlers and wrestling fans in 2000. His M.A. thesis, "Professional Wrestling, Embodied Morality and Altered States of Consciousness," was written in 2005. He is currently a graduate student in the anthropology program at the University of North Carolina at Chapel Hill.

James McKay is the head of the School of Arts and Social Sciences at Southern Cross University, Australia. He is the author of five books, 30 book chapters, and many more refereed academic articles and keynote addresses.

Debra Merskin is Associate Professor in the School of Journalism & Communication at the University of Oregon. Her research focuses on representational ethics—who represents whom and how—in terms of race, gender, sexuality, and species. Her published book chapters and journal articles include "Truly Toffee and Raisin Hall: A Textual Analysis of Lipstick Names" (2007).

Candace Moore is an Assistant Professor in the Department of Screen Arts and Culture and the University of Michigan. Her research and teaching interests include film history, cultures of consumption, and feminist and queer media studies. She has published a number of articles on Showtime's *The L Word*.

Sujata Moorti is a Professor of Women's and Gender Studies at Middlebury College in Vermont. She is coeditor of *Global Bollywood: Travels of Hindi Song and Dance* (2008) and *Local Violence, Global Media: Feminist Analyses of Gendered Representations* (2009).

Kathryn C. Montgomery is cofounder and President of the Center for Media Education (CME), a D.C.-based nonprofit organization public interest group dedicated to ensuring that the electronic media serve the needs of children and families. Under her leadership, CME has helped frame the national public debate on a variety of critical media issues.

She is currently directing CME's research initiative on New Media and the Healthy Development of Children.

Barbara Mueller is a Professor of Advertising in the School of Journalism & Media Studies at San Diego State University. In addition to numerous articles in professional journals (both national and international), she is the author of *Communicating With the Multicultural Consumer: Theoretical and Practical Perspectives* (2007), *Dynamics of International Advertising: Theoretical and Practical Perspectives* (2004), and coauthor (with Katherine Toland Frith) of *Advertising and Societies: Global Issues* (2003). Her research interests focus on the role that culture plays in commercial communications.

Lisa Nakamura is the Director of the Asian American Studies Program, Professor in the Institute of Communication Research and Media Studies Program, and Professor of Asian American Studies at the University of Illinois, Urbana-Champaign. She is the author of *Digitizing Race: Visual Cultures of the Internet* (2007) and *Cybertypes: Race, Ethnicity, and Identity on the Internet* (2002) as well as many journal articles. She is also a coeditor of *Race in Cyberspace* (2000) and (with Peter Chow-white), *Race and New Media* (2010).

Eve Ng is a PhD candidate in the Department of Communication at the University of Massachusetts–Amherst. Her doctoral project considers how encounters of queer-friendly entertainment websites with media corporations figure in changes to the domain of the commercial and queerness in mainstream culture. Other areas of research interest include manifestations of taste and distinction in "progressive" contexts; the relationships between lesbian, gay, bisexual, transgender (LGBT) representations and identities; and consumer-producer dynamics in contemporary cultural production.

David Nylund has been a practicing therapist with over 25 years of clinical experience in a broad array of settings, including community mental health, non-profit agencies, managed care, and private practice. He is also an Associate Professor of Social Work at California State University, Sacramento. He is the author of several books, including *Beer, Babes, and Balls: Masculinity and Sports Talk Radio* (2007).

Laurie Ouellette is an Associate Professor in the Department of Communication Studies at the University of Minnesota, Twin Cities, where she teaches critical media studies and cultural theory. She is the author of *Viewers Like You? How Public TV Failed the People* (2002) and the coauthor of *Better Living Through Reality TV: Television and Post-Welfare Citizenship* (2008). She is coeditor (with Susan Murray) of *Reality TV: Remaking Television Culture* (2008). Most recently, she has edited *The Media Studies Reader* (2010).

Gilad Padva teaches in the Department of Film and Television at Tel Aviv University. He publishes extensively about cinema and television studies, gender and queer theory, media aesthetics, visual communications, camp subculture, and popular music. His articles have appeared in many journals, including *Cinema Journal, Feminist Media Studies, Sexualities, Journal of Communication Inquiry*, and *Women and Languages*.

Gareth Palmer teaches advertising and documentary at the School of Media, Music and Performance, University of Salford, UK. He is author of *Exposing Lifestyle Television* (2008), as well as *Discipline and Liberty: Television and Governance* (2003). He is also involved in practical media. Some of his audio advertising can be heard at life-fromelsewhere.com.

Janice Peck is an Associate Professor in the School of Journalism and Mass Communication at the University of Colorado at Boulder. She is author of *TV Talk Shows as Therapeutic Discourse* (1992), *The Gods of Televangelism* (1993), and *The Age of Oprah* (2008). Her current research projects include the cultural and political significance of celebrity philanthropy, social entrepreneurship, and "charity TV"; the future of journalism and news; and the centrality of historical knowledge for critical media research.

Marnie Pratt is an online instructor at Bowling Green State University. Her research interests include LGBTQ cultural histories and theories, popular culture (with an emphasis on film, television, and music), media/new media studies, celebrity, fandom, and consumer culture.

Janice Radway is a Professor of Literature and History at Duke University. She is the author of *Reading the Romance: Women, Patriarchy and Popular Literature* (1984, 1991) and *A Feeling for Books: The Book-of-the-Month Club, Literary Taste, and Middle Class Desire* (1999). Her current research interests are in the history of literacy and reading in the United States, particularly as they bear on the lives of women. Professor Radway is presently working on a book project titled *Girls, Zines, and Their Afterlives: Sex, Gender, Capitalism, and Everyday Life in the Nineties and Beyond.*

Mary F. Rogers, a longtime professor of sociology and anthropology at the University of West Florida and a pioneer in women's studies, died unexpectedly in 2009. She taught courses in feminist theory, social change and reform, social justice and inequality, and qualitative research. She was the author of *Barbie Culture* (1999, 2002), as well as *Contemporary Feminist Theory: A Text Reader* (1997). She was coauthor, with C. D. Garrett, of *Who's Afraid of Women's Studies: Feminisms in Everyday Life* (2002). With Susan E. Chase, she coedited *Mothers and Children: Feminist Analyses and Personal Narratives* (2001).

Tricia Rose is Professor and Chair of Africana Studies at Brown University. She specializes in 20th-century African American culture and politics, social history, popular culture, gender, and sexuality. Her scholarly interests include Black cultural production, the role of new technologies and ideologies about race in U.S. life, and the politics of intimacy and social justice. Her publications include *Black Noise: Rap Music and Black Culture in Contemporary America* (1994), *Longing to Tell: Black Women Talk About Sexuality and Intimacy* (2004), and *The Hip Hop Wars: What We Talk About When We Talk About Hip Hop and Why It Matters* (2008).

Andrew Ross is a Professor of Social and Cultural Analysis at New York University. His research interests are labor and work, urban and suburban studies, intellectual history, social and political theory, science, ecology and technology, and cultural studies. His published works include *Nice Work If You Can Get It: Life and Labor in Precarious Times* (2009) and *The Celebration Chronicles: Life, Liberty and the Pursuit of Property Values in Disney's New Town* (2000). He is coeditor of *The University Against Itself: The NYU Strike and the Future of the Academic Workplace* (2008).

John Sanbonmatsu is Associate Professor of Philosophy at Worcester Polytechnic Institute in Massachusetts. He is the author of *The Postmodern Prince: Critical Theory, Left Strategy, and the Making of a New Political Subject* (2003), and he is editor of the anthology *On the Animal Question: Essays in Critical Theory and Animal Liberation*.

Melissa C. Scardaville is a doctoral candidate in Sociology at Emory University, where she studies media, gender, and organizations. Formerly on the staff of *Soap Opera Digest*, she has also published an article about her soap opera research in the journal *Poetics*.

Juliet B. Schor is a Professor of Sociology at Boston College. Her research over the past 10 years has focused on issues pertaining to trends in work and leisure, consumerism, the relationship between work and family, women's issues, and economic justice. She is the author of numerous articles, and her books include *The Overspent American: Why We Want What We Don't Need* (2004) and *Born to Buy: The Commercialized Child and the New Consumer Culture* (2004). Her latest book is *Plenitude: The New Economics of True Wealth* (2010).

Kevin Schut is an Assistant Professor of Media Studies in the Department of Communications at Trinity Western University in British Columbia, Canada. He writes about the intersection of communication, culture, media, technology, and faith, primarily by talking about computer and video games. He has published articles or chapters on fantasy role-playing computer games and masculinity, on computer games and myth, on the presentation of history in computer games, and on evangelicals and games and is currently involved in guiding a student project to make and market a small indie-style computer game.

Sharon Sharp is an Assistant Professor of Communications at the California State University, Dominguez Hills. She specializes in the areas of film and television history and criticism and science fiction studies and has published articles in journals including *Women's Studies* and *Film Quarterly*. Her current book project examines how U.S. television circulates narratives about the nation's past and present through a framework of nostalgia that structures both televisual narratives and industry programming practices.

Debra C. Smith is an Associate Professor of Africana Studies at the University of North Carolina, Charlotte. Her research and teaching interests include e-Black studies, African Americans in communication and popular culture, minority images in the media, contemporary African American folklore, and developing teaching strategies that incorporate popular culture, language, and power. She is author of *The Words Unspoken: The Hidden Power of Language* (2008). Her website is www.debracsmith.com

Gloria Steinem is a well-known feminist activist, organizer, writer, and lecturer. Steinem was a founder in 1972 of *Ms. Magazine*, the first national women's magazine run by women, and she continues to serve as a consulting editor. She has been published in many magazines and newspapers here and in other countries and is also a frequent guest commentator on radio and television. Her books include *The Revolution From Within: A Book of Self-Esteem* (1992), *Outrageous Acts and Everyday Rebellions* (1983), *Moving Beyond Words* (1993), *Marilyn: Norma Jean* (1986), and, most recently, *Doing Sixty and Seventy* (2006). She is also an editor of *The Reader's Companion to U.S. Women's History* (1998).

Sue Tait is a lecturer in Media and Communication at the University of Canterbury, New Zealand. She is currently researching celebrity advocacy and practices of bearing witness through media. She has recently published on media representations of death in scholarly journals, including *Feminist Media Studies, Science as Culture,* and *Critical Studies in Media Communication.*

Jamie Warner is an Associate Professor at Marshall University in West Virginia, and she is also currently the Associate Dean for the College of Liberal Arts. Her research interests include the intersection of political theory and political communication, specifically how irony, parody, and humor work within a democratic system. She has published articles in both political science and communications journals, including *Polity, Popular Communication,* and *Politics & Gender.* She is currently at work on a book on political culture jamming.

Dwayne Winseck is an Associate Professor at the School of Journalism and Communication, Carleton University, Ottawa, Canada. His research focuses on the political economy of communication, new media, media history, media regulation, and theories of democracy and global communication. His latest book, *Communication and Empire: Media, Markets and Globalization, 1860–1930* (2007, coauthored with Robert M. Pike), won the Canadian Communication Association's G. G. Robinson Award for best book of the year in 2008.